INTERNATIONAL
BUSINESS

RAKESH MOHAN JOSHI

Indian Institute of Foreign Trade
New Delhi

OXFORD
UNIVERSITY PRESS

D1299367

OXFORD
UNIVERSITY PRESS

Oxford University Press is a department of the University of Oxford.
It furthers the University's objective of excellence in research, scholarship,
and education by publishing worldwide. Oxford is a registered trademark of
Oxford University Press in the UK and in certain other countries

Published in India by
Oxford University Press
YMCA Library Building, 1 Jai Singh Road, New Delhi 110001, India

© Oxford University Press 2009

The moral rights of the author have been asserted

First Edition published in 2009
Seventh impression 2012

ISBN-13: 978-0-19-568909-9
ISBN-10: 0-19-568909-7

Typeset in Baskerville
by Le Studio Graphique, Gurgaon 122001
Printed in India by Tan Prints (India) Pvt. Ltd. Jhajjar (Haryana)

To my
parents, Smt. Subhadra Sharma and Late Dr Chandra Mohan Sharma
wife, Dr Indu Joshi
and children, Vidhu and Chandrika
for
their deep emotional support and sacrifices for my academic achievements

Preface

Never before in the history of human civilization have the forces of globalization been so intense as to influence our daily lives. The breakthroughs in information, communication, and transportation technologies and the worldwide economic liberalization have led to the closer integration of countries, breaking down artificial barriers to the flow of goods, services, capital, knowledge, and even people across the borders.

The growth in international trade and investment was facilitated considerably by a number of multilateral organizations set up after World War II under the aegis of the United Nations, such as the World Bank, the International Monetary Fund (IMF), the General Agreement on Tariffs and Trade (GATT), and the World Trade Organization (WTO). The advent of the Internet led to the collapse of time and space barriers in human communications, transforming the world into a virtual 'global village'.

'Globalization' refers to the process of integration and convergence of economic, financial, cultural, and political systems across the world by adopting a holistic approach. From an economic or commercial perspective, so as to understand international business, 'globalization' may be defined as the increasing economic integration and interdependence of national economies across the world through a rapid rise in the cross-border movement of goods, services, technology, and capital. The rapid growth of integration and interdependence of economies may be attributed to the interconnectedness of the various dimensions of economic globalization such as the globalization of production, markets, competition, technology, corporations, and industries.

'International business' encompasses all those business activities that involve cross-border transactions of goods, services, and resources between two or more nations. The transactions of economic resources include capital, skills, people, etc. for the international production of physical goods and services such as finance, banking, insurance, and construction. An international transaction involves both international trade and international investments. In strict technical terms, 'global business' refers to the conduct of business activities in several countries, using a highly coordinated and single strategy worldwide. However, both these terms are generally used interchangeably, as the differences between the two are essentially semantic in nature. In view of its widespread use among practitioners and literature, the term 'international business' has been used in the book so as to denote virtually both 'global' and 'international' business.

As a subject of study, the scope of international business is highly comprehensive, involving a multi-disciplinary approach that draws significantly from diverse disciplines such as international economics, international trade, international marketing, international finance, international operations, global supply chain management, international human resource management, and, to some extent, anthropology and other social sciences.

In the earlier era of restricted trade and investment regimes with the much lower degree of interconnectedness among the countries, companies solely operating in their home countries were generally protected and isolated from the vagaries of upheavals in the international business environment. Globalization opens up new opportunities for business enterprises while offering numerous challenges. Therefore, developing a thorough conceptual understanding of international business has become crucial to success not only for the managers who operate internationally, but also for those who operate domestically.

About the Book

Although many books have been written on the subject, this book stands out in terms of its scope and content. It provides an easy access to the key theoretical concepts of international business and their applications, facilitating skill development in international business.

The book has been designed as an authoritative and comprehensive textbook with a global perspective so as to meet the requirements of management students and global managers. It brings out the principal concepts of international business in a very simple and lucid manner with numerous managerial examples, illustrations, flow diagrams, and diagrams, which make it interesting to read and easy to conceptualize and comprehend.

The book would find use as a textbook for the courses on international business such as global business environment, international management, and global business strategy and related courses such as export-import management, international trade operations and logistics, international economics, international marketing, international finance, global human resource management, trade policy, and business environment. Moreover, with its wealth of useful information, managerial focus, and integrated multi-disciplinary approach, the book would be equally useful for global managers.

Pedagogical Features

Authoritative, comprehensive, in-depth coverage The book presents an authentic text, dealing with the key areas of international business comprehensively, with exhaustive coverage and a wealth of information.

Global perspective   A global perspective is adopted in the book, rather than a country-specific orientation, making it suitable for use both in developed and developing countries alike.

Integrated multi-disciplinary approach   An integrated multi-disciplinary approach has been adopted to cover the principal areas of international business while maintaining a flawless flow across the chapters.

Remarkable blend of contemporary theory and practice   The book presents a befitting blend of the managerial applications of key theoretical concepts of international business so as to equip readers with the necessary skills of decision making and resolving problems, drawing on the sound theoretical foundations they learn here.

Critical and thought provoking   In order to stimulate the reader's thought process, a critical approach has been adopted to explain the key concepts rather than a mere presentation of facts.

Numerous vivid examples and illustrations   Each chapter presents plenty of examples, illustrations, figures, flow-diagrams, and diagrams in a vivid manner, which makes reading a rewarding experience and reinforces learning.

Lucid and user friendly   Each chapter has been written in a lucid and user-friendly manner, making it interesting to read and easy to comprehend. The book also provides chapter-end summary, key terms, concept review questions, and critical thinking exercises and suggests interesting classroom assignments and field projects so as to make it extremely user-friendly.

Application oriented with managerial focus   An application-oriented approach with managerial focus rather than a general environmental focus has been adopted in the book, making it highly useful for management students and practitioners alike and facilitating managerial decision making.

Contemporary realism with updated information   The book presents the contemporary concepts of international business such as e-business, ethics, and social responsibility, with the latest, updated information and analytical approach.

Coverage and Structure

Chapter 1 brings out the historical perspective of globalization of business and elucidates the concept of globalization and international business. It also explains the factors influencing globalization, the measuring techniques, its support and criticisms, and the response strategies for emerging market companies.

Chapter 2 explains the theories of international trade—historical and contemporary as well—such as mercantilism, theories of absolute and comparative advantage, factor endowment, country similarity, new trade, international product life cycle, and competitive advantage.

Chapter 3 provides an overview of international trade patterns and balance of payments and explores the gains from international trade.

Chapter 4 discusses the major international economic institutions and the institutional framework for promoting international trade.

Chapter 5 provides an overview of the World Trade Organization, its structure and agreements, dispute settlement process, ministerial conferences, and the emerging issues leading to conflict of interests between developed and developing countries.

Chapter 6 presents a theoretical framework of preferential trade agreements (PTAs) and forms of international economic integrations. It also discusses the major regional trade agreements (RTAs) such as the European Union, NAFTA, MERCOSUR, GCC, APEC, and ASEAN. Besides, India's participation in PTAs and RTAs vis-à-vis the multilateral trading system under WTO has also been examined.

Chapter 7 highlights the significance of culture in international business decisions, explicates the concept of culture, and carries out a comparison of the cross-cultural behaviour using Hofstede's, Trompenaars', and other classifications, cultural orientation in international business, the emic versus etic dilemma, and its operationalization.

Chapter 8 provides an overview of international political and legal environments and discusses the various types of risks and their measurement and management.

Chapter 9 explores the various trade policy options available and the instruments of trade policy and examines India's foreign trade policy and WTO's trade policy review mechanism.

Chapter 10 provides an overview of international business research, cross-country evaluation and selection, and discusses the various tools thereof.

Chapter 11 discusses the alternative modes of business expansion, strategic trade-offs, and their selection strategy.

Chapter 12 delineates foreign direct investment (FDI), types and theories of international investment, policy framework, and FDI patterns.

Chapter 13 elucidates the concept of MNCs, their types, and the impact on host economies, measuring the extent of their internationalization, and the emerging MNEs from rapidly developing economies.

Chapter 14 brings out the framework of international marketing and further elaborates market identification, segmentation and targeting, and entry mode decisions and international marketing mix decisions that include product, pricing, distribution, and communication.

Chapter 15 provides an overview of international monetary systems, contemporary exchange rate arrangements, the theoretical concepts of exchange rates determination, exchange rate quotation, and foreign exchange risks and exposures and their management. The modes of payment and international trade finance, credit risks insurance, and the WTO compatibility of various trade finance and insurance schemes have also been discussed in detail.

Chapter 16 delineates the globalization of operations, the strategic options for transnational operations, and the concept of global supply chain and its management.

It also discusses maritime transportation in international trade, including the various types of ocean cargo and commercial vessels, alternates for ocean shipment, charter shipping, liner shipping, and multi-modal transportation, organizations involved, and the institutional framework for maritime transport in India.

Chapter 17 explains the concept of international human resource management, international organizational structures, strategic orientations and managing international human resource activities such as staffing, managing expatriates, training and development, performance management, compensation, regulatory framework, and industrial relations.

Chapter 18 outlines export-import procedures, the terms of delivery, and documentation for international trade transactions with the help of self-explanatory flow diagrams.

Chapter 19 provides a conceptual framework of e-business technology and environment, e-business applications and models, and alternative e-business strategies. It also elaborates global e-marketing and e-services, electronic processing of international trade documents, and policy framework of e-business.

Chapter 20 explains the concept of ethics and explores unethical business practices such as corruption, bribe, smuggling, *hawala*, money laundering, tax havens, unethical marketing practices, grey marketing, counterfeiting and piracy, transfer pricing, dumping, and unethical marketing communications. The concept of corporate social responsibility and the related principals and international guidelines and frameworks have also been delineated.

Acknowledgments

Writing a quality book has always been an arduous task that requires enormous perseverance, endurance, and sustained commitment over a long period. It also involves incredible sacrifices of numerous other opportunities, social occasions, family leisure, and gatherings, and in my case, not only for me but also for the entire family, especially my wife—Dr Indu Joshi—and children—Vidhu and Chandrika—making it in real sense 'our' book rather than 'my' book.

I sincerely thank all my students and the participants of numerous management development programmes whom I taught in various parts of the world for their constructive criticism, comments, opinions, and suggestions that helped me in testing my ideas and hypotheses and that greatly added to my new insights. I also express sincere gratitude to all my faculty colleagues, at hundreds of institutions across the world, who have adopted my earlier book *International Marketing*, particularly those who sent their comments and suggestions, significantly contributing to my thought process. While writing the book, I was immensely benefited from the research work of several scholars, towards whom I remain highly indebted.

I am grateful to Shri K.T. Chacko, Director, Indian Institute of Foreign Trade, for providing generous support for my research and writings. I express my deep sense of gratitude to Prof. B. Bhattacharyya for his intellectual insights.

Special thanks are due to my research associate, Dr Shaily Verma, personal assistants—Lalita Gupta and Vijay Kumar—and other support staff for their unstinting help, sustained patience, and devoted assistance in preparing an excellent manuscript.

I owe the highest sense of appreciation for the talented editorial and production team of OUP and for the numerous other people who worked behind the scenes, for their hard work, forbearance, and inexorable quest for excellence in bringing out such an outstanding text.

I am deeply indebted to Ms Nirmala Dixit, Mr Rajesh Dixit, Dr Mamta Sharma, and Mr Mayank Mohan Joshi for their family support during the course of writing the book.

I eagerly look forward to receiving your valuable comments and suggestions for further improvements at drrmjoshi@yahoo.com, for which I would be highly grateful.

RAKESH MOHAN JOSHI
(website: www.rakeshmohanjoshi.com)

Contents

Abbreviations

3PL	Third Party Logistics	BA	Banker's Acceptance
AAI	Airport Authority of India	BAF	Bunker Adjustment Factor
ACI	Advance Commercial Information	BCI	Business Competitiveness Index
ACS	Association of Caribbean States	BERI	Business Environment Risk
ACU	Asian Currency Union		Intelligence
ADB	Asian Development Bank	BG	Bank Guarantee
ADP	Anti-Dumping Practices	BIMSTEC	Bay of Bengal Initiative for
ADS	Aligned Documentation System		Multi-sectoral Technical and
AEPC	Apparel Export Promotion Council		Economic Cooperation
AEZ	Agri-Export Zone	BIS	Bank for International Settlements
AMS	Aggregate Measurement of Support	BIS	Bureau of Indian Standards
AMS	Automated Manifest System	BOO	Build, Operate, and Own
ANDA	Abbreviated New Drug Application	BoP	Balance of Payment
APEC	Asia Pacific Economic Cooperation	BOT	Build, Operate, and Transfer
APEDA	Agricultural and Processed Food	BPLR	Benchmark Prime Lending Rate
	Products Export Development	BPO	Business Process Outsourcing
	Authority	BRIC	Brazil, Russia, India, China
APTA	Asia Pacific Trade Agreement	BSNL	Bharat Sanchar Nigam Limited
ARE	Application for Removal of Excisable	BT	Build and Transfer
	Goods	BTP	Bio-Technology Park
ASCI	Advertising Standards Council of	BTWC	Biological and Toxin Weapons
	India		Convention
ASEAN	Association of South East Asian	C&F	Clearing and Forwarding
	Nations	C2B	Consumers to Business (also known
ASIDE	Assistance to States for Development		as C-to-B)
	of Export Infrastructure and Other	C2C	Consumers to Consumers (also
	Allied Activities		known as C-to-C)
ASRS	Automated Storage and Retrieval	C2G	Citizens to Government (also known
	Systems		as C-to-G)
ATC	Agreement on Textiles and Clothing	CACM	Central American Common Market
ATRIC	Aggregated Trade-Related Index of	CAD	Computer-Aided Design
	Counterfeiting	CAF	Currency Adjustment Factor
AWB	Airway Bill	CAGR	Compound Annual Growth Rate
B/L	Bills of Lading	CAIR	Council for American-Islamic
B2B	Business to Business (also known as		Relations
	B-to-B)	CARICOM	Caribbean Community and Common
B2C	Business to Consumers (also known as		Market
	B-to-C)	CBD	Convention on Biological Diversity
B2G	Business to Government (also known	CBEC	Central Board of Excise and
	as B-to-G)		Customs

CBI	Centre for Promotion of Imports from developing countries
CCN	Cargo Community Network
CDMA	Code Division Multiple Access
CDSCO	Central Drugs Standard Control Organisation
CECA	Comprehensive Economic Cooperation Agreement
CENVAT	Central Value Added Tax
CFC	Common Fund for Commodities
CFR	Cost and Freight
CFS	Container Freight Station
CHA	Customs House Agent
CIB	Critical Infrastructure Balance
CIF	Cost, Insurance, and Freight
CII	Confederation of Indian Industry
CIM	Computer Integrated Manufacturing
CIP	Carriage and Insurance Paid to
CIS	Commonwealth of Independent States
CKD	Completely Knocked Down
CM	Common Market
CMC	Cash Management Centre
CMIE	Centre for Monitoring Indian Economy
CNC	Computer Numerical Control
COD	Cash on Documents
COLA	Cost of Living Allowance
COMESA	Common Market for Eastern and Southern Africa
CONCOR	Container Corporation of India
CoO	Country of Origin
CPT	Carriage Paid to
CRM	Customer Relationship Management
CSE	Centre for Science and Environment
CSR	Corporate Social Responsibility
CST	Central Sales Tax
CTD	Combined Transport Document
CTO	Combined Transport Operator
CU	Customs Union
CWC	Central Warehousing Corporation
CWC	Chemical Weapons Convention
D/A	Documents Against Acceptance
D/P	Documents Against Payment
DAF	Delivered at Frontier
DDA	Doha Development Agenda
DDP	Delivered Duty Paid
DDU	Delivered Duty Unpaid
DEPB	Duty Entitlement Pass Book
DEQ	Delivered Ex Quay
DES	Delivered Ex Ship
DFIA	Duty Free Import Authorization
DFRC	Duty-Free Replenishment Certificate
DGAD	Directorate General of Anti-Dumping

DGCI&S	Directorate General of Commercial Intelligence and Statistics
DGFT	Directorate General of Foreign Trade
DGRI	Directorate General of Revenue Intelligence
DIA	Direct Investment Abroad
DID	Densely Inhabited Districts
DMCs	Developing Member Countries
DoC	Department of Commerce
DTA	Domestic Tariff Area
DTAT	Double Tax Avoidance Treaty
DTRs	Daily Trade Returns
DWT	Dead Weight Tons
EAEC	East Asian Economic Caucus
EBR	Export Bills Abroad
ECA	Export Credit Agency
ECB	External Commercial Borrowing
ECGC	Export Credit Guarantee Corporation
ECOWAS	Economic Community of West African States
ECSC	European Coal and Steel Community
EDF	Export Development Fund
EDI	Electronic Data Interchange
EDIFACT	Electronic Data Interchange for Administration, Commerce and Transport
EEC	European Economic Community
EEFC	Exchange Earners' Foreign Currency
EFIC	Export Finance and Insurance Corporation
EFT	Electronic Funds Transfer
EHS	Early Harvest Scheme
EHTP	Electronic Hardware Technology Park
EIA	Export Inspection Agency
EIC	Export Inspection Council
EIU	Economist Intelligence Unit
EMR	Exclusive Marketing Rights
EOQ	Economic Order Quantity
EOU	Export Oriented Unit
EPA	Economic Partnership Agreement
EPC	Export Promotion Council
EPCG	Export Promotion Capital Goods
EPIP	Export Promotion Industrial Park
EPO	Education Process Outsourcing
EPS	Electronic Payment System
EPZ	Export Processing Zone
ERIA	Export Risk Insurance Agency
ESC	Eastern Shipping Corporation of India Ltd
ESCAP	Economic and Social Commission of Asia and the Pacific
ESP	Education Service Provider
ETA	Expected Time of Arrival
ETDS	Electronic Trade Documentation System

EU	Economic Union		G2B	Government to Business (also known as G-to-B)
EU	European Union			
EURATOM	European Atomic Energy Community		G2C	Government to Citizens (also known as G-to-C)
EURIBOR	Euro Interbank Offered Rates		GATS	General Agreement on Trade in Services
EURO LIBOR	London Interbank Offered Rates dominated in euros		GATT	General Agreement on Tariffs and Trade
EXIM	EXport-IMport			
Exim Bank	Export-Import Bank of India		GBC	Global Business Company
EXW	Ex Works		GCC	Gulf Cooperation Council
F&A	Finance and Accounting		GCI	Global Competitiveness Index
F.O.B.	Free on Board		GDP	Gross Domestic Product
FAC	As fast as the vessel can		GI	Geographical Indications
FAO	Food and Agriculture Organization		GNI	Gross National Income
FAS	Free Along Side		GPRI	Global Political Risk Index
FATF	Financial Action Task Force		GR	Guaranteed Remittance
FCA	Free Carrier		GRDI	Global Retail Development Index
FCL	Full Container Load		GRI	Global Reporting Initiative
FCPA	Foreign Corrupt Practices Act		GRT	Gross Registered Tonnage
FCS	Fully Consolidated System		GSLI	Global Services Location Index
FDI	Foreign Direct Investment		GSM	Global System for Mobile Communications
FE	Fisher Effect			
FEDAI	Foreign Exchange Dealers Association of India		GSP	Generalized System of Preferences
			GSTP	Global System of Trade Preferences
FEMA	Foreign Exchange Management Act		HACCP	Hazard Analysis Critical Control Programme
FER	Foreign Exchange Reserves			
FHEX	Fridays and Holidays Excluded		HCNs	Host Country Nationals
FHINC	Fridays and Holidays Included		HRM	Human Resource Management
FICCI	Federation of Indian Chambers of Commerce and Industry		HS (ITC) Codes	Harmonized System (International Trade Classification) Codes
FIEO	Federation of Indian Export Organisations		IATA	International Air Transport Association
FII	Foreign Institutional Investors		IBRD	International Bank for Reconstruction and Development
FIIA	Foreign Investment Implementation Authority			
			ICA	Indian Council of Arbitration
FILO	Free In Liner Out		ICAs	International Commodity Agreements
FIO	Free In and Out			
FIOST	Free In and Out, Stowed and Trimmed		ICB	International Competitive Bidding
			ICC	International Chamber of Commerce
FIPB	Foreign Investment Promotion Board		ICCT	Islamic Central Committee of Thailand
FIRC	Foreign Inward Remittance Certificate			
			ICD	Inland Container Depot
FMS	Flexible Manufacturing Systems		ICDS	Intelligent Content Delivery System
FMS	Focus Market Scheme		ICEGATE	Indian Customs and Excise Gateway
FOB	Free on Board		ICENET	Indian Customs and Central Excise Network
FPI	Foreign Portfolio Investment			
FPS	Focus Product Scheme		ICES	Indian Customs EDI system
FPS	Foot, Pound, and Second		ICS	Integrated Cargo System
FSA	Firm Specific Advantage		ICSID	International Centre for Settlement of Investment Disputes
FSAP	Financial Sector Assessment Programme			
			ICT	Information and Communication Technology
FTA	Free Trade Agreements			
FTO	Foreign Trade Organization		IDA	International Development Association
FTZ	Free Trade Zone			
G.N.I.E.	Government Not Included Elsewhere		IEC	Import-Export Code

IFC	International Finance Corporation	MAI	Market Access Initiative
IFE	International Fisher Effect	MARPOL	International Convention for the Prevention of Pollution from Ships
IFIA	International Federation of Inspection Agencies	MC	Management Company
IFT	Informal Funds Transfer	MC	Ministerial Conference
IHRM	International Human Resource Management	MDA	Market Development Assistance
		MDGs	Millennium Development Goals
II	Internationalization Index	MDP	Management Development Programme
IIFT	Indian Institute of Foreign Trade		
IIP	Indian Institute of Packaging	MDRI	Multilateral Debt Relief Initiative
ILFC	International Lease Finance Corporation	MEP	Minimum Export Price
		MERCOSUR	Southern Cone Common Market (*Mercado Comun del Sur*)
ILO	International Labour Organization		
IMF	International Monetary Fund	MES	Message Exchange Servers
IMO	International Maritime Organization	MFA	Master Franchisee Agreement
IMS	Integrated Multi-Modal Solution	MFA	Multi-Fibre Agreement
INCOTERMS	International Commercial Terms	MFN	Most Favoured Nation
IP	Intellectual Property	MIC	Methyl Isocyanate
IPLC	International Product Life Cycle	MIGA	Multilateral Investment Guarantee Agency
IPR	Intellectual Property Rights		
ISLFTA	India–Sri Lanka Free Trade Area	MKS	Meter, Kilogram and Second
ISO	International Organization for Standardization	MLC	Maritime Labour Convention
		MMTC	Minerals and Metals Trading Corporation
ISP	Internet Service Provider		
ISPS Code	International Ship and Port Facility Security Code	MNC	Multinational Company
		MNC	Multinational Corporation
ITC	International Trade Centre	MNE	Multinational Enterprise
ITeS	IT-enabled Services	MPEDA	Marine Products Export Development Authority
ITPO	India Trade Promotion Organization		
JIT	Just-in-Time	MSTC	Metal Scrap Trading Corporation
JWG	Joint Working Group	MTD	Multimodal Transport Document
KPO	Knowledge Process Outsourcing	MTO	Multimodal Transport Operator
KVIB	Khadi and Village Industries Board	MUI	Majelis Ulama Indonesia
KVIC	Khadi and Village Industries Commission	NAFED	National Agricultural Co-operative Marketing Federation of India Ltd
KYC	Know Your Customer	NAFTA	North American Free Trade Agreement
L/C	Letter of Credit		
LAC	Latin American Countries	NAMA	Non-Agriculture Market Access
LAIA	Latin American Integration Association	NCPs	National Contact Points
		NCTI	National Centre for Trade Information
LASH	Lighter Aboard Ship		
LCL	Less than Container Load	NELP	New Exploration Licensing Policy
LDCS	Least Developed Contracting States	NER	North Eastern Region
		NFE	Net Foreign Exchange
LDCs	Least Developed Countries	NIC	National Informatics Centre
LFTA	Latin American Free Trade Area	NIS	National Innovative System
LIBID	London Interbank Bid Rate	NLDCS	Non-Least Developed Contracting States
LIBOR	London Interbank Offered Rate		
LIFO	Liner In Free Out	NOR	Notice Of Readiness
LPG	Liquefied Petroleum Gas	NRI	Non-Resident Indian
LPI	Logistics Performance Index	NRT	Net Registered Tonnage
LUT	Legal Undertaking	NTMs	Non-Tariff Measures
LVC	Lifetime Value of Customer	NTP	Normal Transit Period
M&A	Mergers and Acquisitions	NVC	Non-Vessel Carrier

OECD	Organization for Economic Co-operation and Development
OEEC	Organization for European Economic Cooperation
OGL	Open General License
OHASAS	Occupational Health and Safety Standard
OMAs	Orderly Marketing Arrangements
ONGC	Oil and Natural Gas Corporation Ltd
OPEC	Organisation for Petroleum Exporting Countries
OPH	Original Patent Holder
OVL	ONGC Videsh Ltd
PAA	Pan Asia e-commerce Alliance
PAB	Project Approval Board
PCFC	Pre-shipment Credit in Foreign Currency
PCNs	Parent Country Nationals
PDA	Personal Digital Assistant
PEPFAR	President's Emergency Plan for AIDS Relief
PIC	Prior Informed Consent
PLA	Personal Ledger Account
PPP	Public-Private Partnership
PPP	Purchasing Power Parity
PTA	Preferential Trade Agreement
PU	Political Union
QS	Quality System
R&D	Research and Development
RA	Regional Authority
RBI	Reserve Bank of India
RCA	Revealed Comparative Advantage
RCMC	Registration-cum-Membership Certificate
RDEs	Rapidly Developing Economies
RES	Remote EDI System
RISC	Reduced Instruction Set Computing
RPA	Rupee Payment Area
RR	Railway Receipt
RTAs	Regional Trading Agreements
RTIA	Regional Trade and Investment Area
S&D	Special and Differential
SAARC	South Asian Association for Regional Co-operation
SACU	South African Customs Union
SAD	Special Additional Duty
SADC	Southern African Development Community
SAFE Framework	Framework of Standards to Secure and Facilitate Global Trade
SAFTA	South Asian Free Trade Agreement
SAP	Systems Applications and Products
SBUs	Strategic Business Units
SCI	Shipping Corporation of India Ltd

SCM	Subsidies and Countervailing Measures
SCOMET	Special Chemicals, Organisms, Materials, Equipments and Technologies
SDR	Special Drawing Right
SEI CMM	Software Engineering Institute Capability Maturing Model
SEZ	Special Economic Zone
SFIS	Served From India Scheme
SHEX	Sundays and Holidays Excluded
SHINC	Sundays and Holiday Included
SIA	Secretariat for Industrial Assistance
SION	Standard Input Output Norms
SKD	Semi-Knocked Down
SLEPC	State Level Export Promotion Committee
SME	Small and Medium Enterprise
SOE	State-Owned Enterprise
SOLAS	International Convention for the Safety of Life at Sea
SPS	Sanitary and Phytosanitary
SRC	Self-Reference Criteria
SSI	Small Scale Industry
STC	State Trading Corporation
STCW	Standards of Training, Certification, and Watch-keeping
STEOM	Senior Trade and Economic Officials Meeting
STP	Software Technology Park
SWIFT	Society for Worldwide Inter-bank Financial Telecommunication
TBT	Technical Barriers to Trade
TCNs	Third Country Nationals
TED	Turtle Excluder Device
TEE	Towns of Export Excellence
TEUs	Twenty-Feet Equivalent Units
TEXPROCIL	Cotton Textiles Export Promotion Council of India
THC	Terminal Handling Charge
TLP	Trade Liberalization Programme
TMB	Textiles Monitoring Body
TNC	Trade Negotiation Committee
TNC	Transnational Company
TNC	Transnational Corporation
TNI	Transnationality Index
ToR	Terms of Reference
TPR	Trade Policy Review
TPRM	Trade Policy Review Mechanism
TRAINS	Trade Analysis and Information System
TRIM	Trade Related Investment Measures
TRIPS	Trade Related Aspects of Intellectual Property Rights
TRQ	Tariff Rate Quota

TT	Telegraphic Transfer
UCPDC	Uniform Customs and Practices for Documentary Credit
ULCC	Ultra-Large Crude Carrier
UNCAC	United Nations Convention Against Corruption
UNCITRAL	United Nations Commission on International Trade Law
UNCTAD	United Nations Conference on Trade and Development
UNDP	United Nations Development Programme
UN-ESCAP	United Nations Economic and Social Commission for Asia and the Pacific
UNIDO	United Nations Industrial Development Organization
US FDA	US Food and Drug Administration
VA	Value Addition
VAN	Value Added Networks
VAT	Value Added Tax
VERs	Voluntary Export Restraints
VLCC	Very Large Crude Carriers
WB	World Bank
WCO	World Customs Organization
WHO GMP	WHO Good Manufacturing Practices
WHO	World Health Organization
WIPO	World Intellectual Property Organization
WSC	Western Shipping Corporation of India Ltd
WTO	World Trade Organization
WTPF	World Trade Point Federation
WWD	Weather Working Day

1

Globalization and International Business

LEARNING OBJECTIVES

> To outline the historical perspective of globalization of business
> To explain the concept of globalization
> To elucidate the factors influencing globalization
> To discuss the various techniques for measuring globalization
> To examine the reasons for support and criticism of globalization
> To discuss global business expansion strategy for emerging market companies
> To explicate the concept of international business
> To delineate the motives for international business expansion
> To expound the strategy for managing business in the globalization era

1.1 INTRODUCTION

The forces of globalization have hardly been as intense before as to be explicitly evident as influencing our daily lives. The advents in information and communication technology (ICT) and the rapid economic liberalization of trade and investment in most countries have accelerated the process of globalization. Markets are getting flooded with not only industrial goods but also with items of daily consumption. Each day, an average person makes use of goods and services of multiple origins—for instance, the Finnish mobile Nokia and the US toy-maker's Barbie doll made in China but used across the world; a software from the US-based Microsoft, developed by an Indian software engineer based in Singapore, used in Japan; the Thailand-manufactured US sports shoe Nike used by a Saudi consumer. The increased integration of markets—goods and financial—the mobility of people with transnational travels for jobs and vacations, and the global reach of satellite channels, the Internet, and the telephone all have virtually transformed the world into a 'global village'.

'Globalization', one of the most complex terms used in international business, has wide connotations. Interestingly, 'globalization' is a term not only used and heard frequently, but also as often misused and misinterpreted. Globalization is used to refer to the increasing influence exerted by economic, political, socio-cultural, and financial processes across the globe. Globalization not only offers numerous challenges to business enterprises but also opens up new opportunities. In the earlier era of restrictive trade and investment regimes with much lower degree of interconnectedness among countries, companies solely operating in their home markets were generally protected and isolated from the vagaries of upheavals in the international business environment. Therefore, developing a thorough conceptual understanding of international business has become inevitable not only for the managers who operate in international markets, but also for those who operate only domestically.

This chapter brings out the historical perspective of the globalization of business, which reveals that India and China were the world's two most dominant economies till the early nineteenth century whereas the US, the UK, and Japan emerged as strong economies only lately. Economic restrictions became pervasive around the world after World War I, leading to de-facto de-globalization. Besides, the import substitution strategies followed by most developing countries, which gained independence from colonial rule in the post-World War II era, considerably restricted international trade and investment.

A number of multilateral organizations set up after World War II under the aegis of the United Nations, such as the World Bank (WB), the International Monetary Fund (IMF), the General Agreement on Tariffs and Trade (GATT), and the World Trade Organization (WTO), facilitated international trade and investment.

Elucidating the conceptual framework of globalization, the chapter delineates a holistic approach to define the term, encompassing financial, cultural, and political aspects, besides the economic. Movers and restraining factors of globalization have also been examined at length. The arguments both for support and criticism of globalization have also been critically evaluated. Globalization offers challenges and opportunities for business enterprises and firms are required to adopt the most effective response strategy, which has been discussed with the specific perspective of emerging market companies.

The later part of the chapter also provides the conceptual framework of international business, elaborating various related terminologies. It examines the reasons for expanding business operations internationally. The distinguishing features of domestic versus international business have also been explicated. At the end, the chapter propounds strategy to manage businesses in the era of globalization.

1.2 GLOBALIZATION OF BUSINESS: A HISTORICAL PERSPECTIVE

Globalization is not a new phenomenon. In the initial years of human history, people remained confined to their communities, villages, or local regions. There were hardly any formal barriers, such as tariffs or non-tariff restrictions, for the movement of goods or visa requirements for people. The concept of globalization can be traced back to the phenomenon of a nation-state.

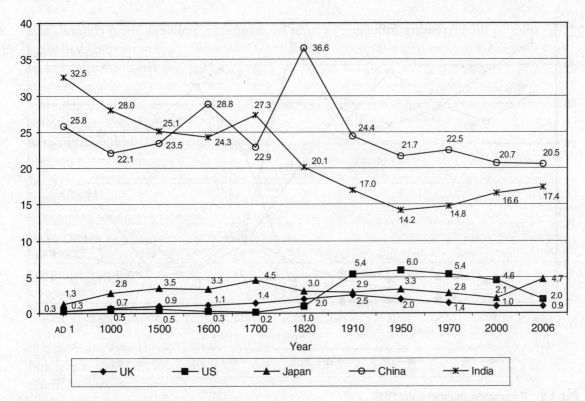

Fig. 1.1 Percentage share in world population

Source: The World Economy, Vol. 1: A Millennium Perspective, Vol. 2: Historical Statistics, Development Centre Studies, OECD, 2006, pp. 636–43; World Economic Outlook, Spillovers and Cycles in the Global Economy, IMF, April 2007, p. 204.

In the beginning of the Christian era, India was the most populated country with 75 million people constituting 32.5 per cent of the world population (Fig. 1.1), followed by China (25.8%) with 59.6 million, Italy (3%) with 7 million, France (2.2%) with 5 million, Spain (1.9%) with 4.5 million, Germany (1.3%) and Japan (1.3%) each with 3 million people, whereas the UK (0.34%) and the US (0.29%) inhabited merely 0.8 million and 0.7 million people, respectively, out of the total world population of 230 million.

Moreover, during this period, India was the world's largest economy with 32.9 per cent share of the world's GDP, followed by China (26.1%), the former USSR (1.5%), and Japan (1.2%). It was only after AD 1500 that some western economies, such as Italy, France, and Germany emerged with 4.7 per cent, 4.4 per cent, and 3.3 per cent share, respectively, in the world GDP whereas the UK and the US merely contributed 1.1 per cent and 0.3 per cent, respectively, of the world GDP (see Fig. 1.2). India and China continued to remain the two most dominant economies till the early nineteenth century.[1]

---

[1] *The World Economy*, Vol. 2: Historical Statistics, Development Centre Studies, OECD, Paris, 2006, pp. 636–38.

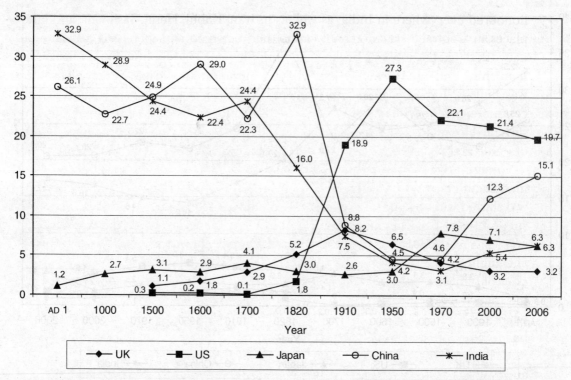

Fig. 1.2   Percentage share in world GDP

Source: The World Economy, Vol. 1: A Millennium Perspective, Vol. 2: Historical Statistics, Development Centre Studies, OECD, 2006, pp. 636–43; World Economic Outlook, Spillovers and Cycles in the Global Economy, IMF, April 2007, p. 204.

Venice played a key role from AD 1000 to AD 1500 in opening up trade within Europe and in the Mediterranean. It opened trade in Chinese products via caravan routes in the region around the Black Sea and in Indian and other Asian products via Syria and Alexandria. Trade was important in bringing high value spices and silks to Europe and also helped transfer technology from Asia, Egypt, and Byzantium. Portugal played the key role in opening up European trade, in navigation and settlement in the Atlantic islands, and in developing trade routes around Africa, into the Indian Ocean, and to China and Japan. Portugal became the major shipper of spices to Europe for the whole of the sixteenth century, usurping this role from Venice.

Right up to the eighteenth century, the 'Indian methods of production and of industrial and commercial organization could stand in comparison with those in vogue in any other part of the world' as written by Vera Anstey.[2] India was a highly developed manufacturing country and exported her manufactured products to Europe and other nations. Her banking system was efficient and well organized throughout the country, and the bills of exchange (*hundis*) issued by the great business or financial houses were

[2] Anstey, Vera, *Economic Development of India*, Longmans, Green and Co., 1929; Nehru, Jawahar Lal, *Discovery of India*, Penguin Books, New Delhi, 2004, pp. 308–09.

honoured everywhere in India, as well as in Iran, Kabul, Herat, Tashkent, and other places in Central Asia. Merchant capital had emerged and there was an elaborate network of agents, jobbers, brokers, and middlemen. The ship-building industry was flourishing and one of the flagships of an English admiral during the Napoleon wars was built in India by an Indian firm. India was, in fact, as advanced industrially, commercially, and financially as any country prior to the industrial revolution. No such development could have taken place unless the country had enjoyed long periods of stable and peaceful government and the highways been safe for traffic and trade.

Foreign adventurers originally came to India because of the excellence of her manufacturers, who had a big market in Europe. The British East India Company was started with the objective of carrying manufactured goods, textiles, etc., as well as spices and the like from the East to Europe, where there was a great demand for these articles. Such trading was highly profitable, yielding enormous dividends. So efficient and highly organized were the Indian methods of production, and such were the skills of India's artisans and craftsmen, that India could compete successfully even with the higher techniques of production that were being established in England. Even when the big machine age began in England, Indian goods continued to pour in and had to be stopped by very heavy duties and, in some cases, by outright prohibitions.[3]

By the middle of the eighteenth century, the main exports into Europe were textiles and raw silk from India and tea from China. The purchases of European products into India were financed mainly by the exports of bullion and raw cotton from Bengal, whereas the purchases into China were financed by the exports of opium. Until the eighteenth century, the British generally maintained peaceable relations with the Indian Mughal empire, whose authority and military power were too great to be challenged by the British.

It was only after the development of new industrial techniques that a new class of industrial capitalists emerged in Britain and under their influence, the British government began to take greater interest in the affairs of the East India Company. The British government now adopted the strategy to close the British market for Indian goods and get the Indian market opened for British manufacturers. To begin with, Indian goods were excluded by legislation in Britain. Since the East India Company had the monopoly in the Indian export business, the exclusion influenced other foreign markets as well.

During the pre-World War I period from 1870 to 1914, there took place a rapid integration of economies in terms of trade flows, movement of capital, and migration of people. The pre-World War I period witnessed the growth of globalization, mainly led by technological forces in the field of transport and communication.

However, between the first and second world wars, the pace of globalization decelerated. Various barriers were erected to restrict free movement of goods and services during the inter-war period. Under high protective walls, most economies

---

[3] Nehru, Jawahar Lal, *Discovery of India*, Penguin Books, New Delhi, 2004, pp. 308–09.

perceived higher growths. It was resolved by all leading countries after World War II that the earlier mistakes committed by them to isolate themselves should not be repeated. Although, after 1945, there was a drive to increased integration, it took a long time to reach pre-World War I levels. In terms of percentage of imports and exports to total output, the US could reach the pre-World War level of 11 per cent only around 1970. Most developing countries that gained independence from colonial rule in the immediate post-World War II period followed imports substitution strategies to promote local industrialization. The East European countries shielded themselves from the process of global economic integration.

Multilateral organizations, especially the World Bank, the IMF, and the GATT, set up in the post-war era contributed considerably to the economic integration of countries. Setting up of the WTO in 1995 provided an effective institutional mechanism for multilateral trade negotiations, integration of trade policies under the WTO framework, and even the settlement of trade disputes among the member countries.

During the recent decades, most developing countries made a strategic shift from their restrictive trade and investment policies to economic liberalization. The transformation of the Indian economy from one following the import substitution strategy with a highly complex system of licences and multiple procedures to an economy open to globalization is summarized in Exhibit 1.1.

The breakthroughs in information, communication, and transportation technologies and the growing economic liberalization have accelerated the process of global

---

Exhibit 1.1   India's journey from the licence *Raj* (era) to globalization

Phase I (1947–65)
- The focus was on government-led investments in manufacturing.
- Several large public sector units in steel, chemicals, and power were set up.
- Many of these companies exist even today and are among the largest companies in their sectors.

Phase II (1965–80)
- Government involvement in industry increased.
- Strong licensing laws were introduced with a sustained focus on import substitution.
- Public sector units and formation of several small-scale private sector manufacturing entities grew.

Phase III (1980–90)
- The government partially opened its economy to external trade and de-licensed some key

sectors for private participation, leading to strong growth in a few sectors.
- A key event was the formation of Maruti Suzuki as government's 50:50 joint venture with Japan's Suzuki motors.

Phase IV (since early 1990s)
- The industry was further liberalized.
- The scope of licensing was significantly reduced.
- Custom duties were slashed.
- FDI in various sectors was opened up.

Phase V (2000 onwards)
- Companies began to reap the rewards of the various phases of development learning.
- Many Indian business enterprises became quite competitive and looked at taking on global players.

Source: 'From Licence Raj to Globalization', *Hindustan Times*, New Delhi, 31 July 2006.

economic integration. The major concerns about present-day globalization are significantly higher than ever before because of the nature and speed of transformation. What is striking about the current globalization is not only its rapid pace but also the enormous impact of new information and communication technologies on market integration, efficiency, and industrial organization.[4]

1.3   CONCEPT OF GLOBALIZATION

'Globalization' has become the buzzword that has changed human lives around the world in a variety of ways. The growing integration of societies and national economies has been among the most fervently discussed topics during recent years. Globalization refers to the free cross-border movement of goods, services, capital, information, and people. It is the process of creating networks of connections among actors at multi-continental distances, mediated through a variety of flows including people, information and ideas, capital, and goods.[5]

The breakthroughs in the means of transport and communication technology in the last few decades have also made international communication, transport, and travel much cheaper, faster, and more frequent. Globalization is the closer integration of the countries and peoples of the world, brought about by the enormous reduction in the costs of transportation and communications and the breaking down of artificial barriers to the flow of goods and services, capital, knowledge, and (to a lesser extent) people across the borders. With the arrival of the Internet, the transaction costs of transferring ideas and information have declined enormously. 'Global village' is the term used to describe the collapse of space and time barriers in human communication,[6] especially by using the World Wide Web, enabling people to interact on a global scale.

Moreover, a number of interesting terms to signify the various aspects of globalization, such as Westernization, Americanization, Walmartization, McDonaldization, Disneyfication, Coca-Colanization, etc., have also emerged, as given in Exhibit 1.2.

Globalization tends to erode national boundaries and integrate national economies, cultures, technologies, and governance, leading to complex relations of mutual interdependence.

Globalization refers to the intensification of cross-national economic, political, cultural, social, and technological interactions that leads to the establishment of transnational structures and the integration of economic, political, and social processes on a global scale.[7]

[4] Rangarajan, C., 'Globalization and Its Impact' in *Indian Economy since Independence*, edited by Uma Kapila, 15th edn, Academic Foundation, New Delhi, 2003, pp. 728–33.

[5] Clark, William C., Robert O. Keohane, Joshep S. Nye, and Neal M. Rosendrof, in Joshep S. Nye and John D. Donahue (eds), *Governance in a Globalizing World*, Brooking Institution Press, Washington DC, 2000, pp. 1–44, 86–108, 109–34.

[6] McLuhan, Marshal, *The Gutenberg Galaxy: Making of Typographic Man*, University of Toronto Press, Toronto (1962); Wyndham, Lewis, *America and Cosmic Man*, Nicholson & Watson, London, 1948, pp. 1–19.

[7] Dreher, Axel, Noel Gaston, and Pim Marten, 'Measuring Globalization and Its Consequences', *Globalization and the Labour Market*, Department of Business Enterprise and Regulatory Reforms, 13 December 2007.

Exhibit 1.2   Globalization's neological terms

Westernization   The process of influence of the western culture on non-western society in terms of life style, value system, language, technology, etc. Westernization is sometimes equated, although inaccurately, with modernization.

Americanization   A term mostly used pejoratively for the influence of the US of America on other cultures that leads to a phenomenon of substituting indigenous cultures with the US culture.

Walmartization   Refers to business practices followed by the American retail chain Wal-Mart, which includes optimization concepts from logistics, purchasing, finance, and stores management, contributing to its maintaining 'Always low prices, Always'. Charles Fishman in his book *The Wal-Mart Effect* sheds light on the power of the retail giant to affect everyone's life. The economic effect of Wal-Mart include forcing smaller competitors to keep out of business and driving down wages, but helping to keep inflation low and productivity high.

Although Wal-Mart brings cheaper products to consumers in advanced countries, it epitomizes the conservative model that a company must cut costs to remain competitive, or a country must cut taxes and the welfare state to continue to be globally competitive.

McDonaldization   The term was used by sociologist George Ritzer in his book *The Mcdonaldization of Society* (1995) to describe the principles of the fast food restaurant likely to dominate more and more sectors of the American society as well as the rest of the world. According to Ritzer, the four dimensions of McDonaldization are

Efficiency   Refers to the optimal method for accomplishing a task, that is, the rational determination of the best mode of production with little scope for individuality.

Calculability   Objectives should be quantifiable (i.e., sales) rather than subjective (i.e., taste). Quantity gains significance over quality as McDonald's sells Big Mac, not the Quality or Superior Mac.

Predictability   Standardized and uniform services are guaranteed by the production process.

Control   Includes the substitution of more predictable non-human technologies for human-labour.

The McDonaldization of society has also been referred to as a system of the 'iron cage' in which all institutions come to be dominated by the same principles. The criticism of McDonaldization includes

Irrationality   Workers are expected to perform a single and highly rationalized task, which spawns irrationality and leads to workers' burnout.

Deskilling   Workers are supposed to perform simple and repetitive tasks with minimum level of complexity. This leads to quick and cheap training of workers, who can be easily replaced.

Consumer workers   McDonald's is criticized as being 'tricky' in making consumers its unpaid employees by carrying out the work usually performed by a service restaurant; for instance, serving food or a drive-through service.

Disneyfication   A term used to describe and denigrate a society that has an increasing similarity to the Disney theme parks. The term has been used by Sharon Zukin (1996) in *The Culture of the Cities* whereas the term 'Disneyization' was popularized by A. Bryman (2004) in *The Disneyization of Society*. 'Disneyfication' is used metaphorically to describe a society dedicated to themes, merchandising, huge consumption, and emotion-based labour. It also signifies a diluted or simplified version of an original form.

Contd

Exhibit 1.2 Contd

Coca-Colanization A portmanteau word derived from a combination of the words coca-cola and colonization to imply the invasion of Western, particularly American, cultural values considered as dangerous to indigenous cultures. The term Coca-Colanization was used by Arthur Koestler (1961) to refer to Americanization in his book *The Lotus and the Robot*.

Source: Charles, Fishman, *The Wal-Mart Effect: How the World's Most Powerful Company Really Works and How It's Transforming the American Economy*, Penguin Press, 2005, pp. 1–13; French Historical Studies, 17(1) Spring (1919), pp. 96–116; Ritzer, George, The McDonaldization of Society, Pine Forge Press, 2004, pp. 1–19; Koestler, Arthur, *The Lotus and the Robot*, Macmillan Company, New York (1961), pp. 1–34; Kuisel, Richard F., 'Coca Cola and the Cold War: The French Face Americanization', 1948–53.

Further, globalization is widely understood to imply economic globalization by way of free movement of factor inputs (both labour and capital) as well as output between countries. It is not only the economic integration of countries but also various other aspects such as financial, cultural, and political integration across the world, as depicted in Fig. 1.3.

Therefore, globalization may be defined as the process of integration and convergence of economic, financial, cultural, and political systems across the world.

1.3.1 Economic Globalization

The term 'globalization' is widely used in business circles and economics to describe the increasing internationalization of markets for goods and services, the financial system, corporations and industries, technology, and competition. In the globalized economy, distances and national boundaries have substantially diminished with the removal of obstacles to market access. Besides, there have been reductions in transaction costs and compression of time and distance in international transactions.

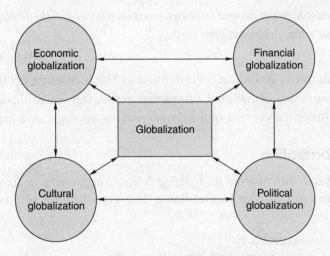

Fig. 1.3 Globalization: A holistic approach

The changes induced by the dynamics of trade, capital flows, and transfer of technology have made markets and production in different countries increasingly interdependent. The growing intensity of international competition has increased the need for cross-border strategic interactions, necessitating business enterprises to organize themselves into transnational networks. Globalization is characterized by the growing interdependence of various facets. For instance, foreign direct investment (FDI) is accompanied by transfer of technology and know-how, along with the movement of capital (equity, international loans, repatriation of profits, interest, royalties, etc.) generating exports of goods and services from the investor countries.

The growth in global economic integration is evident from the increase in the percentage share of world merchandise trade in the world GDP from 32.3 per cent in 1990 to 47.3 per cent in 2005, whereas trade in services grew from 7.8 per cent to 11 per cent during the same period. The gross private capital flows rapidly rose from 10.3 per cent of the world GDP in 1990 to 32.4 per cent in 2005. Here are some definitions of economic globalization.

The increasing integration of national economic systems through growth in international trade, investment and capital flows.

– *Dictionary of Trade Policy Terms*, WTO

A dynamic and multidimensional process of economic integration whereby national resources become more and more internationally mobile while national economies become increasingly interdependent.[8]

– OECD

Economic globalization constitutes integration of national economies into international economy through trade, direct foreign investment (by corporations and multinationals), short-term capital flows, international flows of workers and humanity generally, and flows of technology.[9]

– Jagdish Bhagwati

The activities of multinational enterprises engaged in foreign direct investment and the development of business networks to create value across national borders.[10]

– Alan Rugman

For the purposes of this book, globalization is defined as 'the increasing economic integration and interdependence of national economies across the world through a rapid increase in cross-border movement of goods, service, technology, and capital'.

1.3.2 Financial Globalization

The liberalization of capital movements and deregulations, especially of financial services, led to a spurt in cross-border capital flows. The globalization of financial

---

[8] *OECD Handbook on Economic Globalization Indicators*, 2005, p. 11.
[9] Bhagwati, Jagdish, *In Defence of Globalization*, Oxford University Press, New Delhi, pp. 1–17.
[10] Rugman, Alan, *The End of Globalization*, American Management Association, New York, 2001, p. 11.

markets has triggered a rapid growth in investment portfolio and a large movement of short-term capital borrowers and investors interacting through an increasingly unified market. The growing integration of financial markets has greatly influenced the conduct of business and even the performance of the industrial sector. This has significantly enhanced the vulnerability of stocks that were hitherto considered impervious. A liquidity crunch in the US makes stock markets across the world go berserk. Globalization of financial markets makes them inherently volatile with few options to control left with the national governments.

1.3.3 Cultural Globalization

The convergence of cultures across the world may be termed as cultural globalization. India's rich cultural heritage has a glorious history of globalization (Exhibit 1.3), which is evident even today by its profound impact on people and their lives. Globalization

---

Exhibit 1.3   India's cultural globalization

In the sixteenth century, at a time when the Northern part of India was reeling under the waves of conquests and cultural stagnation, people from South India were exporting Indianness to Southeast Asia. It was an anonymous task carried out not by warrior-heroes blazing across land bearing swords of conquest, but by individuals who had come in peace, to trade, to teach, and to persuade. Their impact was profound. Even to this day, the kings of Thailand are only crowned in the presence of Brahmin priests; Muslims in Java still sport Sanskrit names, despite their conversion to Islam, a faith whose adherents normally bear names originating in Arabia; Garuda is Indonesia's best-selling airline, and Ramayana its best-selling brand of clove cigars; and even the Philippines has produced a pop-dance ballet about Rama's quest for his kidnapped queen Sita. Right at the entrance of Thailand's Suwarnabhoomi International Airport in Bangkok is a fascinating sculpture depicting the Hindu mythological story of the 'Churning of the Oceans' (*samudra-manthan*) between the demons and the gods (Fig. 1.4).

Angkor Wat, perhaps the greatest Hindu temple ever built in the world, is in Cambodia, not in India. The exquisite sculptures in the temple recount tales from the great Indian epics—the Ramayana and the Mahabharata. At the site, Cambodian guides earnestly explain the significance of the symbols protecting the shrine—the *naga*, the *shimha*, and the *garuda*, corresponding to the present-day navy, army, and air force. The marvel of the epic scale of the Hindu temple, as impressive as the finest cathedral or mosque anywhere in the world, is also a marvel at the extraordinary reach of the Indian culture beyond its own shores.

Hinduism was brought to Cambodia by merchants and travellers more than a millennium ago, and has long since disappeared, supplanted by a Buddhism that was also an Indian export. But, at its peak, Hinduism influenced the culture, music, dance, and mythology of the Cambodian people.

The Indian culture can be characterized by its exceptional capability to imbibe align cultures, and this feature distinguishes it from the rest of the world. India's present-day civilization draws heavily from Islam and Christianity, consequent to Muslim invasions and British colonial rules. A Hindu bridegroom invariably puts on a *sherwani* during the wedding ceremony, a practice that did not exist before the Muslim invasion of India. The once-alien cricket is India's virtual national sport. In selecting the seven new wonders of the

Contd

Exhibit 1.3 Contd

Fig. 1.4 A grandiose sculpture at the entrance of Bangkok's Suwarnabhoomi International Airport, depicting the Hindu mythological story of the 'Churning of the Oceans' (*samudra-manthan*) between the demons and the gods, evidences India's deep-rooted cultural globalization.

world, Indians voted cynically for the Taj Mahal, constructed by the Mughal king Shah Jahan and not for Angkor Wat, the most magnificent architect of the Hindu religion, a fact that testifies to the uniqueness of the Indian culture.

Keeping its glorious cultural history in mind, India needs to invest more resources to gain from the globalization of its civilization by way of cultural diplomacy rather than merely focussing all its efforts on economic and political diplomacy.

Source: Based on Tharoor, Shashi, 'Let's Promote the Great Indic Civilisation', *Times of India*, New Delhi, 21 October 2007; http://www.airportsuvarnabhumi.com.

has led to the development of global pop culture. Coca-Cola is sold in more countries than the United Nations has as members. 'Coke' is claimed to be the second-most universally understood word after OK. McDonald's has more than 30,000 local restaurants serving 52 million people everyday in more than 100 countries. Levi's jeans are sold in more than 110 countries. Ronald McDonald is second only to Santa Claus in name recognition for most school children.

1.3.4 Political Globalization

The convergence of political systems and processes around the world is referred to as political globalization. International business is increasingly conducted across the juridical, socio-cultural, and physical borders of sovereign states. After World War II, there has been a proliferation of sovereign states. In 1914 there were 62 separate states, 74 in 1946, 149 in 1978, 193 in 1991,[11] and 209 in 2007.[12] The administrative set-ups and the decision-making processes in multilateral organizations and UN forums have considerably influenced the governance within sovereign states. Democratic processes of decision making and governance to a varying extent are increasingly receiving wider acceptance in most countries.

1.3.5 Dimensions of Economic Globalization

The rapid growth in integration and interdependence of economies can be explained by the interconnectedness of the various dimensions of economic globalization, as depicted in Fig. 1.5, such as the globalization of production, markets, competition, technology, and corporations and industries.

Globalization of production

The increased mobility of the factors of production, especially the movement of capital, has changed countries' traditional specialization roles significantly. Consequently, many firms in developing countries seek to strengthen their competitive advantage by

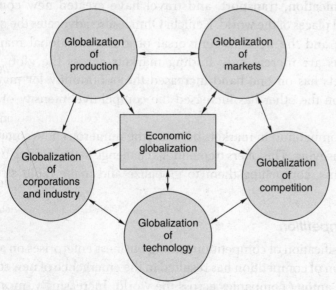

Fig. 1.5 Dimensions of economic globalization

[11] 'A Survey of the New Geopolitics', *The Economist*, 31 July 1999.
[12] 'World Development Indicators Databank', World Bank, July 2007.

specializing in differentiated products with an increasingly large technological content. Such specialization has given rise to intra-industry trade between developing countries. Abandoned activities are often acquired by other firms in the same industry to strengthen their positions. As a result, many firms, in all industries and different countries, establish co-operative agreements or adopt strategies of mergers and acquisitions and network organizations, which has contributed to a surge in FDI during recent decades. Moreover, the privatization of public enterprises across the world has also accelerated cross-border investments.

The globalization of production has led to multinational origin of product components, services, and capital as a result of transnational collaborations among business enterprises. Firms evaluate various locations world-wide for manufacturing activities so as to take advantage of local resources and optimize manufacturing competitiveness. Companies from the US, the EU, and Japan manufacture at overseas locations more than three times of their exports produced in the home country. Intra-firm export-import transactions constitute about one-third of their international trade.

Globalization of markets

Marketing gurus in the last two decades have extensively argued over customized marketing strategies in the globalization of markets. Theodore Levitt, in his path-breaking paper 'Globalization of Markets',[13] views the recent emergence of global markets on a previously unimagined scale of magnitude. Technology as the most powerful force has driven the world towards converging commonality. Technological strides in telecommunication, transport, and travel have created new consumer segments in the isolated places of the world. Kenichi Ohmae also advocates the concept of a borderless world and the need for universal products for global markets.[14] Standardized products are increasingly finding markets across the globe. Such globalization of markets has on one hand increased the opportunity for marketing internationally while on the other has increased the competitive intensity of global brands in the market.

The simultaneous competition in markets between the numerous new competitors across the world is intensifying. This offers tremendous challenge to the existing business competitiveness of firms, compelling them to globalize and make rapid structural changes.

Globalization of competition

This refers to the intensification of competition among business enterprises on a global scale. Such globalization of competition has resulted in the emergence of new strategic transnational alliances among companies across the world. Increasingly, more firms need to compete with new players from around the globe in their own markets as well

[13] Levitt, Theodore, 'Globalization of Markets', *Harvard Business Review*, May/June, 1983, pp. 92–102.
[14] Ohmae, Kenichi, 'Managing in the Borderless World', *Harvard Business Review*, vol. 53, May/June 1989, pp. 152–62.

as foreign ones. To cope with global competition, firms need to simultaneously harness their skills and generate synergy by a broad range of specialized skills, such as technological, financial, industrial, commercial, cultural, and administrative skills, located in different countries or even different continents.

Globalization of technology

The rapid pace of innovations with international networks and convergence of standards across countries has contributed to the globalization of technology. This rapid dissemination of technology internationally and the simultaneous shortening of the cycles of production has led to the globalization of technology.

Countries with advanced technologies are best placed to innovate further. Moreover, unlike in the past when inventions and innovations were considered breakthroughs, today they are a regular occurrence. This implies that the transformation process is continuous and thus has important consequences both for the overall organization of firms and for policy making. Global firms rely on technological innovations to enhance their capabilities. Thus, technology is both driven by and is a driver of globalization. Moreover, it has led to the emergence of new 'technologically driven character' of the global economy.[15]

Globalization of corporations and industries

The worldwide economic liberalization led to the rapid growth in FDIs and the relocation of business enterprises heavily driven by the various forms of international strategic alliances and mergers and acquisitions across the world. As a result, there has been widespread rise in the fragmentation of production processes, whereby different stages of production for a given product are carried out in different countries.

1.4 FACTORS INFLUENCING GLOBALIZATION

The process of globalization is characterized by the interplay of dynamic forces that act as movers and restraining factors, as shown in Fig. 1.6, which offers significant challenges to traditionally established ways of doing businesses. Since the driving forces of globalization are considerably stronger than the restraining factors, globalization of business assumes much higher significance.

1.4.1 Movers of Globalization

Economic liberalization

Economic liberalization, both in terms of regulations and tariff structure, has greatly contributed to the globalization of trade and investment. The emergence of the multilateral trade regime under the WTO has facilitated the reduction of tariffs and

---

[15] Asian Development Bank, 'Drivers of Change: Globalization, Technology and Competition', *Asian Development Outlook*, Oxford University Press, Hong Kong, 2003, p. 208.

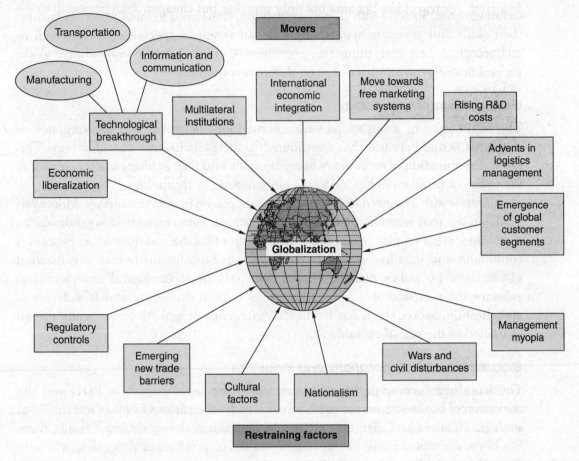

Fig. 1.6 Globalization: Movers vs restraining factors

non-tariff trade barriers. In the coming years, the tariffs are expected to decline considerably further.

Technological breakthroughs

The breakthroughs in science and technology have transformed the world virtually into a global village, especially manufacturing, transportation, and information and communication technologies, as discussed here.

Manufacturing technology Technological advancements transformed manufacturing processes and made mass production possible, which led to the industrial revolution. The production efficiency resulted in cost-effective production of uniform goods on a large scale. In order to achieve the scale economies to sustain large-scale production, markets beyond national boundaries need to be explored.

Transportation technology The advents in all means of transports by roads, railways, air, and sea have considerably increased the speed and brought down the costs incurred. Air travel has become not only speedier but cheaper. This has boosted the movement of people and goods across countries.

Information and communication technology   The advent of information and communication technology and the fast developments in the means of transport have considerably undermined the significance of distance in country selection for expanding business. There has been a considerable reduction in international telecommunication costs due to improved technology and increased competition. This has given rise to new business models, such as the off-shore delivery of services to global locations and electronic business transactions.

Multilateral institutions

A number of multilateral institutions under the UN framework, set up during the post-World War II era, have facilitated exchanges among countries and became prominent forces in present-day globalization. Multilateral organizations such as the GATT and WTO contributed to the process of globalization and the opening up of markets by consistently reducing tariffs and increasing market access through various rounds of multilateral trade negotiations. The evolving multilateral framework under the WTO regime, such as Trade-Related Investment Measures (TRIMS), Trade-Related Aspects of Intellectual Property Rights (TRIPS), General Agreement on Trade in Services (GATS), dispute settlement mechanism, anti-dumping measures, etc., has facilitated international trade and investment. Besides, the International Monetary Fund has contributed to ensuring the smooth functioning of the international monetary system.

International economic integrations

Consequent to World War II, a number of countries across the world collaborated to form economic groupings so as to promote trade and investment among the members. The Treaty of Rome in 1957 led to the creation of the European Economic Community (EEC) that graduated to the European Union (EU) so as to form a stronger Economic Union. The US, Canada, and Mexico collaborated to form the North American Free Trade Agreement (NAFTA) in 1994. The reduction of trade barriers among the member countries under the various economic integrations around the world has not only contributed to the accelerated growth in trade and investment but also affected the international trade patterns considerably.

Move towards free marketing systems

The demise of centrally planned economies in Eastern Europe, the former USSR, and China has also contributed to the process of globalization as these countries gradually integrated themselves with the world economy. The Commonwealth of Independent States (CIS) countries—all former Soviet Republics—and China have opened up and are moving towards market-driven economic systems at a fast pace.

However, the exceptions to free market systems are the autocratic countries, such as North Korea and Cuba.

Rising research and development costs

The rapid growth in market competition and the ever-increasing insatiable consumer demand for newer and increasingly sophisticated goods and services compel businesses to invest huge amounts on research and development (R&D). In order to recover the costs of massive investments in R&D and achieve economic viability, it becomes necessary to globalize the business operations. For instance, software companies such as Microsoft, Novel, and Oracle, commercial aircraft manufacturers like Boeing and Airbus, pharmaceutical giants such as Pfizer, Glaxo SmithKline, Johnson & Johnson, Merck, and Novartis, etc., can hardly be commercially viable unless global scale of operations are adopted.

Global expansion of business operations

Growing market access and movement of capital across countries have facilitated the rapid expansion of business operations globally. Since the comparative advantages of countries strongly influence the location strategies of multinational corporations, companies tend to expand their businesses overseas with the growing economic liberalization. As a result, multinational corporations constitute the main vectors of economic globalization.

Advents in logistics management

Besides these, the greater availability of speedier and increasingly cost-effective means of transport, breakthroughs in logistics management such as multimodal transport technology, and third-party logistics management contributed to the faster and efficient movement of goods internationally.

Emergence of the global customer segment

Customers around the world are fast exhibiting convergence of tastes and preferences in terms of their product likings and buying habits. Automobiles, fast-food outlets, music systems, and even fashion goods are becoming amazingly similar across countries. The proliferation of transnational satellite television and telecommunication has accelerated the process of cultural convergence. Traditionally, cultural values were transmitted through generations by parents or grandparents or other family members. However, with the emergence of unit families that have both parents working, television has become the prominent source of acculturation not only in Western countries but in oriental countries as well. Besides, advances in the modes of transport and increased international travel have greatly contributed to the growing similarity of customer preferences across countries. Thus, the process of globalization has encouraged firms to tap the global markets with increased product standardization. This has also given rise to rapid increase in global brands.

1.4.2   Factors Restraining Globalization

Regulatory controls

The restrictions imposed by national governments by way of regulatory measures in their trade, industrial, monetary, and fiscal policies restrain companies from global expansion. Restrictions on portfolio and foreign direct investment considerably influence monetary and capital flows across borders. The high incidence of import duties makes imported goods uncompetitive and deters them from entering domestic markets.

Emerging trade barriers

The integration of national economies under the WTO framework has restrained countries from increasing tariffs and imposing explicit non-tariff trade barriers. However, countries are consistently evolving innovative marketing barriers that are WTO compatible. Such barriers include quality and technical specifications, environmental issues, regulations related to human exploitation, such as child labour, etc. Innovative technical jargons and justifications are often evolved by developed countries to impose such restrictions over goods from developing countries, who find it very hard to defend against such measures.

Cultural factors

Cultural factors can restrain the benefits of globalization. For instance, France's collective nationalism favours home-grown agriculture and the US fear of terrorism has made foreign management of its ports difficult and restrained the entry of the Dubai Port World.

Nationalism

The feeling of nationalism often aroused by local trade and industry, trade unions, political parties, and other nationalistic interest groups exerts considerable pressure against globalization. The increased availability of quality goods at comparatively lower prices generally benefits the mass consumers in the importing country but hurts the interests of the domestic industry.

On one hand, consumers in general are hardly organized to exert any influence on policy making, while on the other, trade and industry have considerable clout through their associations and unions to use pressure tactics on national governments against economic liberalization.

War and civil disturbances

The inability to maintain conducive business environment with sufficient freedom of operations restricts foreign companies from investing. Companies often prefer to expand their business operations in countries that offer peace and security. Countries engaged in prolonged war and civil disturbances are generally avoided for international trade and investment.

Management myopia

A number of well-established business enterprises operating indigenously exhibit little interest in expanding their business overseas. Besides, several other factors such as resource availability, risks, and the attitude of top management play a significant role in the internationalization of business activities.

1.5 MEASURING GLOBALIZATION

Although quantifying globalization is difficult, a number of approaches have been used to measure globalization. As international managers are especially concerned about economic globalization that affects businesses the most, it can be measured based on the trade openness of a country, FDI inflows and outflows, capital account restrictions, trade barriers, etc.

1.5.1 Trade Openness

The trade openness of a country can be measured as the percentage share of total trade in the total GDP. The total trade is arrived by summing up exports and imports of goods and credit and debits of services. The cross-country comparison reveals (see Fig. 1.7) that Singapore is the most open economy with 474 per cent share of total trade to GDP in 2007, followed by Hong Kong (409%), Malaysia (210%), Netherlands (137%), Switzerland (115%), China (76%), Canada (68%), and South Africa (67%), whereas Brazil is the least open economy with the share of total trade to GDP as 26 per cent followed by the US (29%), Japan (35%), Australia (39%), India (45%), Russian Federation (51%), France (54%), and the UK (56%).

The percentage share of total trade in GDP increased only marginally for the US and the UK from 23.1 per cent and 54.3 per cent in 1998 to 29 per cent and 56 per cent, respectively, in 2007 whereas the percentage share of India and China increased remarkably from 25.7 per cent and 39.2 per cent in 1998 to 45 per cent and 76 per cent, respectively, in 2007. Countries with a higher degree of trade openness generally grew relatively faster compared to those with low trade openness. Switzerland is home to the largest number of the world's top global companies in relation to its population, followed by the US, Scandinavia, Britain, Belgium, Netherlands, and France.[16]

1.5.2 KOF Index of Globalization

A holistic approach to assess globalization is adopted under the KOF overall Index of Globalization based on three sub-indices, which are

Economic globalization This refers to the long distance flows of goods, capital, and services as well as information and perceptions that accompany market exchanges.

---

[16] 'Tomorrow the World', *The Economist*, 10 February 2007, pp. 5–6.

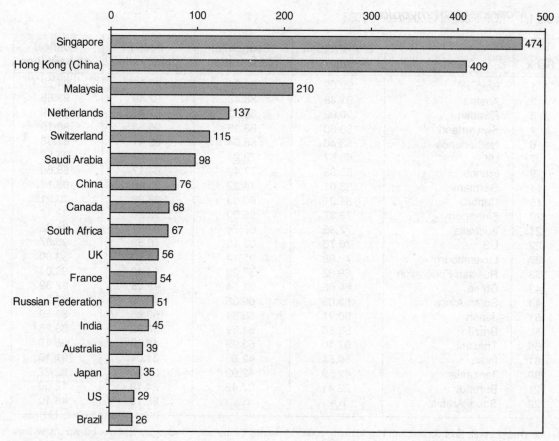

Fig. 1.7 Cross-country comparison of trade openness, 2007 (percentage share of total trade to total GDP)

Source: World Development Indicators, 2008, World Bank.

Social globalization This is characterized by the spread of ideas, information, images, and people.

Political globalization This is expressed as a diffusion of government policies.

Each of the above indices is allocated different weights: economic globalization (36%), social globalization (38%), and political globalization (25%). In constructing the indices of globalization, each of the variables introduced above is transformed to an index on a scale of one to hundred, where hundred is the maximum value for a specific variable over the period 1970 to 2005, and one is the minimum value. The higher values denote a higher degree of globalization. The availability of the indices for 122 countries consistently since 1970 enables the empirical comparison of global-ization trends during the period.

Belgium tops in overall globalization with a score of 92.09 under the KOF Index of Globalization, as shown in Table 1.1, followed by Austria (91.38), Sweden (90.02), and Switzerland (88.60), whereas the UK ranks seventh with a score of 86.67, the US

Table 1.1 KOF Index of Globalization, 2008

Rank	Country	Globalization index	Economic globalization	Social globalization	Political globalization
1	Belgium	92.09	91.94	90.82	94.22
2	Austria	91.38	88.48	92.49	93.86
3	Sweden	90.02	89.51	87.43	94.69
4	Switzerland	88.60	83.13	95.38	86.15
6	Netherlands	88.40	88.04	89.41	87.38
7	UK	86.67	79.24	87.87	95.52
9	France	85.38	77.42	84.17	98.68
11	Germany	83.01	74.22	83.30	95.17
15	Canada	81.21	80.83	86.85	73.21
20	Singapore	78.37	95.90	92.26	32.12
21	Australia	77.35	67.74	81.51	84.82
22	US	76.76	63.15	76.52	96.67
27	Luxembourg	72.88	95.14	78.10	33.00
33	Russian Federation	69.82	57.29	64.40	96.04
43	China	64.56	61.54	49.08	92.39
48	South Africa	63.03	69.38	43.99	82.20
51	Japan	60.91	53.84	52.66	83.59
52	Brazil	58.86	61.69	36.82	88.26
58	Thailand	57.10	63.99	43.10	68.45
81	India	50.54	42.89	31.04	91.10
99	Tanzania	42.59	42.92	29.34	62.22
121	Burundi	22.41	27.43	24.19	12.50
122	Saudi Arabia	n.a.	n.a.	68.18	48.10

Source: Dreher, Axel, Noel Gaston, and Pim Martens, 2008, 'Measuring Globalization—Gauging Its Consequence', New York, Springer.
n.a.: Data not available.

22nd (76.76), China 43rd (64.56), India 81st (50.54), and Burundi and Saudi Arabia rank the last.

1.5.3 A.T. Kearney/Foreign Policy Globalization Index

A.T. Kearney/Foreign Policy Globalization Index (2007) measures 72 countries that account for 97 per cent of the world's GDP and 88 per cent of population. A comprehensive framework to measure globalization is provided by the globalization index brought out by A.T. Kearney/Foreign Policy, based on 12 variables grouped into four 'baskets', as shown in Table 1.2, is discussed below.

Economic integration Trade, portfolio, and foreign direct investments

Personal integration International travel and tourism, international telephone calls, cross-boarder remittances, and personal fund transfers

Technological integration Number of Internet users, Internet hosts, and secured Internet servers

Table 1.2   A.T. Kearney/foreign policy globalization index rankings, 2007

	Overall ranking	Individual dimension's ranking			
		Economic	Personal	Technological	Political
Singapore	1	2	3	15	40
Hong Kong	2	1	1	17	71
Netherlands	3	4	16	6	8
Switzerland	4	11	2	7	28
Ireland	5	6	4	13	5
Denmark	6	5	13	5	7
US	7	71	40	1	51
Canada	8	34	11	2	13
Sweden	11	15	19	8	10
Britain	12	18	21	9	6
Australia	13	26	39	3	41
Belgium	15	7	7	22	16
New Zealand	16	57	23	4	34
Germany	22	45	34	16	19
France	25	31	29	24	3
Japan	28	70	65	12	15
Thailand	53	21	57	49	68
Russia	62	49	60	46	52
China	66	43	67	56	65
Brazil	67	69	71	39	42
India	71	66	59	63	69
Iran	72	65	72	54	70

Source: A.T. Kearney/Foreign Policy Globalization Index, 2007.

Political integration   Country memberships in international organizations, personal and financial contributions to UN peacekeeping missions, ratification of selected multilateral treaties, and amounts of government transfer payments and receipts

The A.T. Kearney Index ranks Singapore as the most globalized country in the world, followed by Hong Kong, Netherlands, Switzerland, Ireland, Denmark, the US, Canada, Jordan, and Estonia. Iran is the least globalized country in the index followed by India, Algeria, Indonesia, Venezuela, Brazil, China, Turkey, Bangladesh, and Pakistan.

It may be observed that most globalized countries are smaller in size. Eight of the index's top ten countries have land areas smaller than the US state of Indiana, and seven have fewer than 8 million citizens. Canada and the US are the only large countries that consistently rank in the top ten.

In fact, globalization is a matter of necessity when a country is a fly-weight. Reaching out beyond national borders is the only way to find new opportunities for tiny countries. Countries like Singapore and Netherlands lack natural resources. Small countries, such as Ireland and Denmark, can hardly rely upon their domestic markets to sustain large-scale production the way the US, India, and China can. Thus, these countries hardly have an option other than to open up their economies and attract trade and investment to be globally competitive.

1.6   GLOBALIZATION: REALITY OR MYTH

Rugman argues that globalization is a myth that never occurred anyway.[17] The riots in Seattle in December 1999 during the WTO ministerial and subsequent protests, sometimes violent, were interpreted as defeat of free trade and globalization.

It is also interesting to learn that 43 per cent (i.e., 107) of the world's top 250 retailers have not yet ventured beyond their own borders. An additional 35 companies operate in just two—typically contiguous—countries, such as the US and Canada, Spain and Portugal, or Australia and New Zealand. Foreign operations of the world's top 250 retail companies, on average, still account for only 14.4 per cent of their total retail sales. A country-wise analysis of the world's top 250 retailers reveals[18] the following astonishing facts:

- Over half of the US-based companies (i.e., 49 of 93 retailers) operate only in a single country.
- Japan remains the most insular as two-thirds of the top 250 Japanese retailers operate only in Japan.
- Asian, Latin American, and North American retailers are the least likely to have foreign operations, although globalization is slowly accelerating.
- European and African retailers dominate in terms of the degree to which they operate internationally.
- On an average, the top 250 European firms did business in 9.9 countries in 2005, generating 28.1 per cent of their sales from foreign operations.
- The five South African retailers in the top 250 list operated in an average of 8.8 countries, primarily throughout the African continent.
- French and German retailers are the most international in scope, primarily due to low consumer spending, fierce market competition, and the tough regulatory environment in home markets.

The sales analysis of the world's largest 500 firms astonishingly reveals that 70 per cent or more of their sales takes place in their home triad rather than global sales. It leads to infer that the world's largest companies hardly bother to be global; rather they act local (see Exhibit 1.4) to harness their core competencies.

1.7   SUPPORT OF GLOBALIZATION

Globalization means different things to different people and is considered to have both positive and negative impacts. Opinions vary widely on its influence on national economies. The major arguments in support of globalization include the following.

---

[17] Rugman, Alan, *The End of Globalization*, American Management Association, New York, 2001, pp. 1–18.
[18] '2007 Global Powers of Retailing', Deloitte, New York, 2007, pp. 9–12.

Exhibit 1.4   Forget global, think regional, act local

Major implications of global business require firms to work out regional strategies, rather than global ones. A global strategy of economic integration is viable only in a few sectors, such as consumer electronics. For most other manufacturing, such as automobiles and for services, regional strategies are required.

Therefore, the firms need to reconsider their strategies as discussed below:

- Analyse the regional sales data for the company as a whole and for each business unit.
- Find out if the company and/or business unit is global as defined. If it is, develop a global strategy and structure.
- If the company and/or business unit is actually home-region based (which is much more likely),

then design a regional strategy and structure, rather than a global one.

- Do not assume that a global strategy is either a necessary or significant condition for better performance; staying in the home region may be the optimal strategy.
- Look into the nature of the activities of leading competitors; if they operate regionally rather than globally, it sends a useful message to be regional too.
- Access and understand fully the business implications of regional trade organizations such as the EU and NAFTA; look into the WTO as it affects regional trade and investment, rather than global business.
- Think regional, act local, forget global.

Source: Adapted from Alan M. Rugman, 'The Regional Multinationals: MNEs and "Global" Strategic Management', Cambridge University Press, 2005.

1.7.1   Maximization of Economic Efficiencies

The global integration of economies has prompted a rapid rise in the movement of products, capital, and labour across the borders. It contributes to the maximization of economic efficiencies, including the efficient utilization and allocation of resources, such as natural resources, labour, and capital on a global scale, resulting in a sharp increase in global output and economic growth.

1.7.2   Enhanced Trade

Besides rapid trade growth, new patterns on international trade are fast evolving. The creation of foreign-based affiliates by national firms and of host-country affiliates by foreign parent companies has led to a rise in intra-firm trade.

1.7.3   Increased Cross-border Capital Movement

The economic liberalization across the world has paved way for FDIs even in a large number of developing countries that had a restrictive regulatory framework. This has opened up business opportunities for transnational corporations to expand their operations by way of ownership on one hand and benefited developing countries from increased flow of capital and other forms of finance on the other. Direct investment is increasingly becoming crucial to companies' international expansion strategies. This has led to the globalization of manufacturing and fragmentation of the production process into its sub-component parts in multiple countries.

1.7.4 Improved Efficiency of Local Firms

The heightened competition by multinationals compels local businesses to adopt measures to cut down costs and improve quality for survival. On one hand, competition makes the survival of inefficient businesses difficult; on the other, it encourages firms to evolve innovative methods to improve productivity. As a result, business enterprises become more competitive not only domestically but also internationally at times.

1.7.5 Increase in Consumer Welfare

Consumers benefit by increased access to products and services from manufactures across the world. Import restrictions in a large number of developing countries has deprived consumers of global brands and the quality thereof. Besides the intensification of market, competition has also compelled domestic producers to reduce prices. As all domestic and multinational companies compete with each other to woo the customer, the consumer became the ultimate gainer.

1.8 CRITICISM OF GLOBALIZATION

Globalization is often denounced by social organizations, NGOs, politicians, consumers, and even the general public on multiple grounds as the sole cause of all ills. It is often decried as just another term for Americanization and US global imperialism. There have been numerous protests against globalization in various parts of the world. Contrary to general belief, the support for globalization is the lowest in the US and even in certain other developed countries, including France, Britain, and Germany, whereas it is much higher in developing countries such as India and China (see Exhibit 1.5).

Exhibit 1.5 Globalization losing steam in the West

Developed countries seem to be losing their enthusiasm towards globalization, MNCs, and free markets, as revealed by a survey carried out by a Pew Global Attitudes Report covering 45,000 people across 47 countries. Countries like the US, Britain, France, and Italy are not so supportive of globalization any more, unlike their stand even five years ago, whereas people in China and India show much higher support for globalization. While supporting capitalism, people are wary of immigration that accompanies the opening up of the economy. People often feel threatened by this as it could endanger their culture and environment, which need to be protected.

The study reveals 64 per cent people in China and 73 per cent in India support foreign companies (see Table 1.3), while in the West, where economic growth has been relatively modest, the figure is as low as 45 per cent in the US.

Contd

Exhibit 1.5 Contd

Table 1.3 Support for globalization (in percentage)

Countries	Trade	MNCs	Free market
China	91	64	75
India	89	73	76
Germany	85	47	65
Britain	78	49	72
France	78	44	56
US	59	45	70

Source: The Pew Global Attitude Project Report, Washington DC, 4 October 2007.

Globalization is frequently criticised on several grounds as discussed below.

1.8.1 Developed versus Developing Countries: Unequal Players in Globalization

The dynamics of the globalization process reveals that developed and developing countries participate on unequal footings. Developed countries along with their mighty multinational corporations exert a very strong force globally while developing country governments and civil society organizations hold much less sway. Developed country governments often reserve and exercise the right to take unilateral and bilateral actions that have global scope and implications concurrently with their participation in debates and negotiations.

According to the neo-classical economic theories of equilibria, capital will flow towards areas of cheap labour but labour will flow towards the areas of expensive labour—thereby raising the cost of labour where it was once cheap by reducing the available numbers and bringing down the cost of labour where it was once expensive. Although there have to be some bottlenecks in the theoretical framework, it seems that the 'powerful' countries, the 'superpowers' themselves, use their power to create such bottlenecks. In the developed world, quotas, controls, and oppressive legislation curtailing the movement of people, derogatorily called 'economic refugees', are justified in the name of protecting 'national' principle but similar measures are seldom applied against the movement of capital.

Economic efficiency is often one of the strong reasons for advocating globalization in that allowing free movement of goods and capital across borders would lead to the lowest costs and thus the lowest prices. But this argument ignores the real social consequences of the search for economic efficiency. For instance, farmers in developing countries commit suicides as the commodity prices crash, workers are thrown out of jobs as factories close, unique and specialized businesses are driven out of the market because they do not have the advantage of economies of scale, etc.

Developing countries are continually preached about on the need to reduce tariffs by multilateral organizations. Ironically, the West and the European Union impose such rigid non-tariff barriers that firms from developing countries hardly have any chance to break into their markets. Global pharmaceutical companies often gang up against drug companies from developing countries.

For most Europeans and Americans, globalization only means two types of fear: fear of cheap Chinese goods and fear of Islamic immigrants. Business process outsourcing (BPO) still remains a big political issue in the US.[19] Getting 'Bangalored' is often used in a pejorative way in the US to refer to the loss of a job because it has been exported to India.

1.8.2 Widening Gap between the Rich and the Poor

The gains of globalization are not evenly distributed. Under globalization, those who possess capital and skills are better off, but the middle class is reported to get more and more squeezed. Noble laureate Joseph Stiglitz observes that globalization is creating rich countries with poor people. The benefits of globalization have failed to reach the poorest citizens of the world's wealthiest country and this was evident when Hurricane Katrina hit the US province of New Orleans. Globalization has applied intense downward pressure on the wages of the unskilled and the less skilled of the labour force even in advanced countries.

Globalization is often accused of contributing to the rise in poverty in developing countries, while in the developed world it is associated with growing economic inequality, unemployment, and fears about job security, which fuels demand for trade, protection, and more restrictive trade policies. Globalization, often characterized by connectedness among countries, has bypassed a huge swathe of territory from Africa, the Balkans, the Caucasus, Central and Southwest Asia to South Asia, parts of Southeast Asia, and parts of the Caribbean. Poorer countries' share in world trade has fallen over the past 20 years.

Income inequality as measured by the Gini coefficient has risen over the past decades in most regions, such as in developing Asia, emerging Europe, Latin America, and the newly industrialized economies of Asia as well as in advanced economies. In contrast, it has declined in sub-Saharan Africa and the Commonwealth of Independent States (CIS).[20]

The failure of the WTO's Doha round—because of the tenacity of both the US and Europe's persistent refusal to reduce trade-distorting subsidies and of the developing countries to open up their market access—was bad news for poor farmers in Africa, Asia, and Latin America. Rich countries spend US$300 billion a year on agriculture subsidies—more than six times the amount they give away as foreign aid. The subsidies

[19] Sanghvi, Vir, 'Liberalisation vs Globalization', *Hindustan Times*, New Delhi, 19 February 2006.

[20] Jaumotte, Florence, Subir Lall, Chris Papageorgiou, and Petia Tapalova, 'Technology Widening Rich-Poor Gap', *IMF Survey Magazine*, 10 October 2007.

depress world prices for such agricultural commodities as cotton, peanuts, and poultry, making it harder for farmers in developing nations to make a living.

Despite tall claims of welfare in the globalized era, more than a billion people in the world still live on less than a dollar a day. To the policy makers of rich countries, they are simply considered as forces of threats ranging from illegal immigration to drug smuggling to crime and as vectors of diseases.

Economic failure in countries in the 'non-integrating gap' has resulted in a global job crisis leading to migration problems. As the per capita GDP of the high-income countries grows at a rate of about 66 times that of the low-income countries, the lure of better-paid jobs has become stronger than ever. Tens of thousand of people from the hopeless economies of sub-Saharan Africa make desperate attempts to enter Europe. Unable to compete with cheaper imported grains, many Mexican farmers have abandoned their rural occupations for a hazardous journey to the US as illegal immigrants.[21]

Immigration laws in developed countries have been tightening against a rising tide of poor migrants, and the planned erection of a 700-mile long fence along the US–Mexican border has become a symbol of the anti-immigrant sentiment across the Western world. 'Globalization' has become a dirty word in Latin America, the continent described as 'the most inequitable' on the planet.

On an average, developed countries impose tariffs on developing countries four times higher than those on developed ones. Rich countries have cost poor countries three times more in trade restrictions than they give in development aid.[22]

1.8.3 Wipe-out of Domestic Industry

Opening up of countries for trade and investment for foreign corporations often leads to buying up of local industry by Western conglomerates. As a result, a few 'global brands' dominate the markets, no matter which country you are in.

The clusters of smaller firms in Italy and Germany that were once successful exporters have suffered as commoditized textiles, footwear, and toys from China have swamped the market. To cope up with the competition from cheap imports, companies keep the production of core parts of their output at their home base and send components for assembly in low-wage countries such as China.[23]

1.8.4 Unemployment and Mass Lay-offs

Globalization is reported to have pushed workers from the organized to the unorganized sector, where they enjoy much less job security and sometimes lower wages as well. This has aggravated the problems of unemployment, shifting labour from secured to casual or parttime jobs with little security and lower wages for tasks requiring lower

[21] Chanda, Nayan, 'Disruptive Events Can Derail Globalization', *Business World*, 16 July 2007, pp. 84–88.
[22] Stiglitz, Joseph, 'Globalization Is Creating Rich Countries with Rich People', *Business World*, 16 October 2006.
[23] 'In the Steps of Adidas', *The Economist*, 10 February 2007, p. 12.

skills. The process of cost-cutting has raised the share of capital in value addition. Higher business profits are often attributed to exploitative efficiency rather than increased opportunities.[24] The bargaining power of trade unions has considerably declined. In order to save the workers from job losses, trade unions are often forced to accept cuts in wages and salaries, freezing of numerous monetary and non-monetary benefits, increase in share of temporary workforce, and curbing of union activities and even lay-offs.

1.8.5 Balance of Payments Problems

The liberalization of foreign investment policies results in an increase in foreign capital inflows that leads to the appreciation of local currency. This adversely impacts the export competitiveness and in turn the export-intensive manufacturing industry in the country. Consequently, imports become relatively cheaper and the viability of indigenous industry even for the domestic market is adversely affected. This has led to mass lay-offs of the workforce besides exerting pressure on the country's balance of payments, especially in developing countries.

1.8.6 Increased Volatility of Markets

The global integration of economies has made markets highly vulnerable to external upheavals. For instance, the soaring popularity of the film *Titanic* in the US created a boom in the worldwide demand for the gem tanzanite whereas its subsequent association with a terrorist outfit drastically brought down its prices (see Exhibit 1.6).

Exhibit 1.6   Global reach of *Titanic* and Taliban affects tanzanite's glitter

The consequences of globalization have both desirable and undesirable influences on business activities. The globalization of markets with an emerging global customer segment leads to worldwide boom of market demand, whereas the global reach of terrorism is increasingly getting capable of creating tremors in business operations across the world.

The blue gem tanzanite swamped the West with the release of *Titanic* in 1997. The demand for tanzanite peaked in the global markets during this period as actress Kate Winslet hurls the gem into the sea in the film (Fig. 1.8). However, its sales came down drastically when the gemstone was regarded as a source of financial support for some terrorist outfits such as Al Qaeda. Tanzanite is mined at only one place on earth, a thirteen square kilometre catch of graphite rock in Mererani or Merelani hills in Tanzania. Tanzanite is known to be 1000 times rarer than diamond due to its rare occurrence. Although sapphire is a comparatively costlier blue stone than tanzanite, it is believed to carry Saturn effects with it whereas tanzanite is reported to be free from astrological impacts. Thus, tanzanite is known purely for its aesthetic value. Besides, it is available at prices ranging from US$2 per carat to US$500 per carat, making it affordable even to the developing country consumers.

Contd

---

[24] Datt, Ruddar and K.P.M. Sundharam, *Indian Economy*, S. Chand Publications, 56th edn, New Delhi, 2007, p. 255.

Exhibit 1.6 Contd

Fig. 1.8 Tanzanite swamped global markets with the release of *Titanic*, in which it was worn by Hollywood actress Kate Winslet.

The Indian city of Jaipur is the biggest processing hub of gem stones, claiming 95 per cent of the total exports of the finished gemstone. The other processing centres, Thailand and Germany, contribute a meagre 5 per cent of finished tanzanite. The US remains the largest market for tanzanite, which is second in popularity only to sapphire.

In 1997, when the popularity of tanzanite soared its crest, the US was selling US$380 million worth of tanzanite jewellery a year. This later nosedived to around US$200 after the 9/11 terrorist attack. Its sales hit rock bottom when the gem was rejected by the US market on the pretext of its Al-Qaeda links. As a result, Jaipur jewellers were left in tizzy as they imported roughs in large quantities from Tanzania. Jaipur was once exporting tanzanite worth Rs 2 billion, which came down to Rs 700 million by December 2007, out of the total Rs 10 billion coloured stone market.

The over-dependability on a particular market, that is, the US, which is highly sensitive to perceived threats of terrorism, led to the rapid fall of tanzanite, putting the tanzanite industry, which is largely export-based, into debacle. The industry now needs to explore new markets as one does not know when business blues will overpower the glitter of tanzanite blue.

Source: 'From Titanic to Taliban: The Saga of Tanzanite', *Economic Times*, 21 December 2007.

Use of lead to paint toys by Chinese manufacturers evokes serious concerns among consumers around the world, compelling children in several countries to abandon their favourite toys, including the Barbie doll. Stock markets have become highly interconnected to global happenings. Any plunge in the US stock market sends tremors to shareholders across the world.

1.8.7 Diminishing Power of Nation States

The global forces, the increasingly transnational character of capital, the erosion and sometimes the voluntary surrender of state sovereignty have all made countries less powerful, for instance the transnational alliances such as the European Union. As a result, less powerful countries find it difficult to control their own destinies and become victims of forces beyond their control. Diminishing sovereignty is reported to be the source of many of the ills of the contemporary world. Its citizens lose control of their day-to-day lives.

1.8.8 Loss of Cultural Identity

The proliferation of satellite channels, the Internet, and the means of transportation and communication have immensely affected the social and cultural values of masses across the world. Most people agree that globalization is changing our values and making lives too fast and impersonal.[25] The forces of globalization have led to cultural convergence across countries, and individuals tend to lose their country-specific cultural values and national identity.

1.8.9 Shift of Power to Multinationals

As a result of the globalization of markets and production, a number of transnational companies, such as Microsoft, General Electric, Unilever, Procter & Gamble, Sony, Ford, Toyota, etc., have emerged to operate across the globe. The total sales revenue of these MNCs is greater than the total national income of a large number of mid-sized and small countries. The global scale operations of multinationals empower them with enormous financial and political muscle to monopolize the markets and influence government decision making.

Nations often fear losing their sovereignty due to the shift of power to MNCs and supranational organizations. Multinationals are often accused of exploiting resources and abusing the environment. Consequent to economic liberalization, India's best-selling soft-drink brands, i.e., Parle's Thumps Up and Limca, were bought by the global giant Coke.

1.9 RESPONSE STRATEGIES TO GLOBALIZATION FORCES FOR EMERGING MARKET COMPANIES

Most books and business literature on the subject often discuss at length the global strategies of mammoth multinationals, such as Coke/Pepsi, Sony/LG, or Unilever/Nestle, but very little is known or written about local firms, especially from the emerging economies. Since local firms in the emerging markets can hardly match the resources, expertise, and experience of large multinationals, it becomes crucial to understand their strategic perspective to respond to the forces of globalization. Depending upon the industry pressure to globalize and the transferability of assets, the emerging market companies can adopt four strategic options[26] (Fig. 1.9) as follows.

1.9.1 Defender

In some industries, where the pressure to globalize is low and the local companies' primary competitive strength lies in their deep understanding of the markets or their

---

[25] Neilson, A.C., Global Consumer Opinion Survey, 2006; 'Global Villagers', *Hindustan Times*, 24 August 2006.

[26] Dawar, N. and T. Frost, 'Competing for Giants', *Harvard Business Review*, March–April 1999.

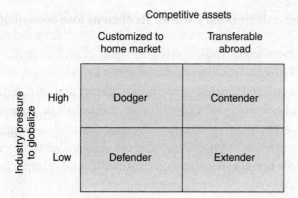

Fig. 1.9 Response strategies of emerging market companies to globalization forces

Source: Dawar, N. and T. Frost, 'Competing for Giants', *Harvard Business Review*, March–April 1999, 119–29.

competitive assets are customized to the local markets, companies should adopt a defensive strategy that focuses on leveraging local assets in market segments where multinationals are weak.

For instance, in order to successfully counter the multinational enterprise (MNE) competition from fully automatic washing machines in India, Videocon developed semi-automatic machines, targeting value-conscious Indian consumers by focusing on this segment. Similarly, when Western cosmetic multinationals entered China, the local cosmetic company Shanghai Jahwa did not compete with them head-on by targeting global range products; rather it responded by developing products to suit the local complexion and appeal to the local people. The Mexican food company Bimbo responded to global competition by defending their deep penetrating distribution system that reached far-off rural areas with 420,000 deliveries daily through 350,000 stores, thus creating a huge barrier to the entry of PepsiCo, whose reach was largely big supermarkets in urban areas. Thus, under the defender strategy, local firms concede some markets to multinationals while building strongholds on the other market segments.

1.9.2 Extender

When industry pressure to globalize is low and companies possess competitive skills and assets that can be transferred abroad, companies can focus on expanding to markets similar to the home base, using competencies developed at home.

Faced with intense competition from Western fast food chains, such as McDonald's and Pizza Hut in the Indian market, the Indian foodmaker Haldiram focussed on traditional Indian vegetarian food and expanded overseas primarily to cater to ethnic Indians. Similarly, Jolibee foods, a Philippines fast food chain, countered McDonald's by developing spicier products better suited to the Filipino palate. The company then followed the Filipino population across the world.

The Mexican media company Televisa globalized by marketing its Spanish language products to Spanish-speaking populations across the world. Asian Paints developed strong capability tailored to the unique Indian environment, characterized by the extensive network of thousands of small retailers and numerous low income customers whose primary requirement is confined to small quantities of paints that can be diluted to save money. The aggressive business model of multinational paint companies that largely focuses upon affluent customers in developed countries had a tough time cracking the markets with low-income customers, whereas Asian Paints leveraged such capabilities not only in India but also in other countries with similar requirements for low-end products, such as Asia, Pacific, and Africa.

1.9.3 Dodger

To compete in industries with high globalization pressures is a highly difficult situation for local companies. The situation becomes highly vulnerable when the competitive assets based on the superior understanding of local markets are neither adequate to face the competition from multinationals in the home country nor transferable overseas. Under such circumstances, local companies have no other option but to dodge the competition.

Such strategy may include cooperating through a joint venture with the MNE, selling off to the MNE, or become a supplier or service provider to the MNE. For instance, faced with MNC competition, Kwality, a dominant player in the Indian ice-cream market, sold its manufacturing assets and brand to Unilever. This paved way for Kwality Walls to become the market leader in the ice-cream market in India. Consequent to the changes in the economic policies in Russia after the iron curtain came down, Vist, the Russian manufacturer of personal computers, focussed itself on distribution rather than on competing with American and Japanese multinationals. As the distribution system in Russia was ridden with corruption and inefficiency, the foreign companies faced formidable difficulties. As a result, Vist is a vital link in supporting MNC distribution of personal computers in Russia. Skoda, the leading state-owned automaker in the Czech Republic, was sold by the government to Volkswagen much as the selling of government stake in Maruti-Suzuki to Suzuki by the Indian Government.

In situations, when local firms find it difficult to compete head-on with the multinationals, such co-operation becomes necessary. If you cannot beat them, join them.

1.9.4 Contender

Companies that have high pressure to globalize and competitive advantages that can be leveraged overseas can aggressively compete in the global market by focusing on upgrading their capabilities and resources in the niche segment to match multinationals globally. A large number of Indian companies have achieved global competitiveness in their niche segment. For instance, Bharat Forge, the second largest forging company in the world, is a global supplier of specialized engine and chassis components for trucks and passenger cars. One out of every two trucks in the US uses front axles made by Bharat Forge. Similarly, Sundram Fasteners competes in niche auto components, such as high tensile fasteners, radiator caps, precision forced differentiated gears, etc., and supplies to leading auto manufactures across the world. The company has also received a number of international quality recognitions, including the prestigious TPM Excellence and Consistency Award from the Japan Institute of Plant Maintenance. The Chinese company TCL not only rapidly caught up with global cellular phone companies such as Nokia and Motorola, but also emerged as a significant player in a number of consumer electronics.

Competition from multinationals in the home markets has driven a number of local firms in the emerging markets to become globally competitive. Some of the local firms, especially in India and China, have not only challenged supremacy of giant multinationals in their home markets, but leveraged their competitive advantage internationally. Indian companies' global expansion, such as Tata's buying Corus, Birla's buying Novelis, Ranbaxy acquiring Terapia, has not only affirmed their global competitiveness but also earned them global respect. This has convinced a number of Indian and Chinese companies of their global strengths in terms of quality, cutting-edge technology, cost competitiveness, and human capital. As a result, these companies are undoubtedly much better prepared and equipped to face competition in the global arena.

1.10   CONCEPT OF INTERNATIONAL BUSINESS

In simple terms, international business implies the conduct of business activities beyond the national boundaries. It is a much wider term comprising of all the commercial transactions taking place between two countries. These transactions, including sales, investment, and transportation, may take place by government or private companies with or without an objective to make profit.[27]

In order to facilitate understanding, some of the related terms widely used are explained below.

International trade

It refers to exports and imports of goods and services by a firm to a foreign-based buyer (importer) or from a seller (exporter).

International marketing

It focuses on the firm-level marketing practices across the border, including market identification and targeting, entry mode selection, and marketing mix and strategic decisions to compete in international markets.

---

[27] Daniel, John D., Lee H. Radebaugh, and Daniel P. Sullivan, *International Business: Environments and Operations*, Pearson Education (Singapore) Pvt. Ltd, New Delhi, 2004, pp. 1–27.

International investments

It implies cross-border transfer of resources to carry out business activities. It may either be portfolio investments with short-term objectives or capital investments with long-term objectives.

International management

It refers to application of management concepts and techniques in a cross-country environment and adaptation to different social-cultural, economic, legal, political, and technological environment.

International business

International business may be defined as all those business activities that involve cross-border transactions of goods, services, and resources between two or more nations. Transaction of economic resources include capital, skills, people, etc. for international production of physical goods and services such as finance, banking, insurance, construction, etc. An international transaction involves both international trade and international investments.

Global business

Global business refers to the conduct of business activities in several countries, using a highly co-ordinated and single strategy across the world.

As the differences in the terms 'international business' and 'global business' are more semantic in nature, both the terms are generally used interchangeably in business literature.

1.11 REASONS FOR INTERNATIONAL BUSINESS EXPANSION

The motives for expanding business operations overseas vary from company to company and depend upon a variety of factors. The basic motives for international expansion of businesses may be summarized under three heads: market seeking, economic, and strategic motives, as shown in Fig. 1.10.

1.11.1 Market-seeking Motives

Marketing opportunities due to life cycles

Businesses expand to foreign countries to seize marketing opportunities arising due to differences in stages of life cycle for different products, which varies considerably among different countries. When marketing opportunities for a product or service get saturated in a domestic or an international market, a firm can make use of such challenges and convert them into marketing opportunities either by expanding overseas or by shifting its operations from one country to another.

Uniqueness of product or service

Products with unique attributes are unlikely to meet any competition in the overseas markets. This offers enormous opportunities for marketing abroad. For instance,

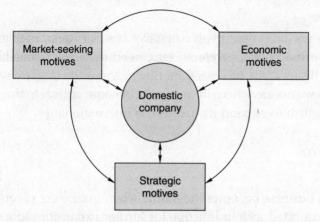

Fig. 1.10 Motives behind international business expansion

Himalayan herbs and medicinal plants from India and the value-added BPO services and software development at competitive prices provide Indian firms an edge for overseas expansion.

1.11.2 Economic Motives

Profitability

Higher profits from overseas business operations form a significant motive for international expansion. Such differences in profitability may be due to a variety of factors, including

- Price differentials among various country markets.
- Export incentives by home country government motivates firms to exports.
- Fiscal incentives by host country government makes foreign investments attractive.
- Low cost and abundant availability of factors of production, such as raw materials, human resources, capital, etc., in the host country leading to low costs of production compared to home country making businesses to invest abroad.
- Low intensity of competition in foreign markets.

High import tariffs discourage imports by making it less competitive in foreign markets while making direct investment a preferred choice for international expansion.

Achieving economies of scale

Large-size production capacities necessitate domestic firms to dispose off their goods in international markets, as the domestic markets become saturated. Businesses that require huge investments to build up production facilities with large production capacities have hardly any option to achieve scale economies unless they market internationally. Moreover, global business operations also contribute to business synergies and increased economies even in marketing, logistics, supply chain, and other functional areas.

Spreading R&D costs

Companies manufacturing products that involve massive costs of R&D, such as software, microprocessors, pharmaceutical products, etc., need to recover speedily the costs of such investments. Besides, the increased market size and the larger coverage of the profitable market segments anywhere in the world become critical to the firm's success. This necessitates a firm to expand its operations internationally.

1.11.3 Strategic Motives

Growth

International expansion of business becomes inevitable when marketing potential in the domestic market gets saturated with little scope for further expansion. Moreover, even for survival, companies from smaller countries such as Singapore, Hong Kong, Scandinavia, etc. are always required to expand their business internationally, given the small size of their home markets. For countries with a relatively larger market size, such as the US, China, and India, enormous marketing opportunities exist to sell domestically. Therefore, growth is hardly the motive for international expansion for most firms.

Risk spread

International expansion is also used as a risk mitigation strategy so as to offset the economic upheavals in the home market. Operating in several countries reduces dependence on any particular market and spreads the business risks.

1.12 DOMESTIC VERSUS INTERNATIONAL BUSINESS

The basic difference in domestic and international business arrives from the differences in environment of their operations. International managers have to deal with environmental challenges, which are beyond the firm's control and do vary significantly among countries. If a firm operates in multiple countries, the severity of business complexity increases multi-fold. Besides, the inter-country interaction among these environmental challenges influences the firm's international business strategy.

1.12.1 Economic Environment

International business decisions are greatly influenced by the economic environment, both of home and host countries. The domestic tariff structure and the various import duty exemption schemes offered by the home country government determine the cost of imported inputs, which contribute to the final cost of production and therefore affect the cost competitiveness. The exchange rates and the foreign exchange regulations of the country influence the cost of imported inputs and options available for making and receiving cross-country payments. The national policies on foreign direct investment determine the kind and magnitude of foreign investment in the country and the entry mode for foreign firms. With the process of gradual liberalization in FDI policy and exchange regulations, the business environment around the world, in general, has become friendlier to foreign investors. The economic conditions of a country, such as the state of foreign exchange reserves and inflationary conditions also affect the openness of a country's trade policies. In recent years, economic liberalization in developing countries, including India, has paved way for import and distribution of consumer goods. However, it has exerted considerable pressure on the domestic firms to compete with international brands.

The economic stability in the country of business operations facilitates an international manager's task. Economic uncertainties and hyper-inflation as experienced in the CIS countries, Brazil, Argentina, and Zimbabwe pose severe problems related to certainty of payment and call for specific strategies to manage delayed payments under inflationary conditions. However, the situation becomes graver in case the payment is to be received in the currency of the importing country. Besides, the soundness of the financial institutional system in the target country is also a pre-condition for the smooth flow of payments. In case of financial upheavals and instability, an international firm needs to adopt innovative ways to manage foreign exchange risks and exposures and payment modes.

1.12.2 Socio-cultural Environment

Cultural factors play an important role in operating business internationally. The countries that have cultural similarity to the target countries can generally be approached more easily as compared to the countries with cultural diversities. Traditional Indian products such as *sarees* and *salwar-kurta* and Indian ethnic foodstuffs are exported to the international markets that have sizeable Indian ethnic population. Similarly, Chinese foodstuffs, goods of worship, and Chinese traditional medicinal and herbal products find easy markets in the countries with sizeable population of ethnic Chinese, especially in East Asian countries. The culture of the target market affects the product modification, especially in consumer products such as garments and foodstuffs. The social environment also affects the motives to make a buying decision and communication strategies need to be customized as per the varied social traits for different countries. Social beliefs and aspirations also vary significantly among countries and the marketing mix has to be tailor-made to suit the social norms of the target market.

This socio-cultural environment of business has been discussed separately in Chapter 7. The international marketing strategy may vary from highly aggressive, as in case of the US, to extremely formal and polite, as in case of Japan. The French tend to be more formal, the Americans more result-oriented, while the Japanese emphasize more on building long-term relationship. A firm has to carefully study the socio-cultural traits of the countries of its operation while making international business decisions.

1.12.3 Legal Environment

The political forces within a country affect international business decisions. The changes in trade policies, fiscal policies, and other matters related to bilateral and multilateral trade are made in view of the political priorities of governments in power. Earlier, India had a ban on international trade transactions with South Africa and Fiji in protest to apartheid and violation of human rights. The change in government also affects the trade policy changes in a country. Besides, national governments have rights to impose restrictions on international trade transactions on the grounds of national security, integrity, and preservation of morale and cultural values.

A well-developed sound legal system in the target market facilitates the reduction of business risks and a firm can expect relatively unbiased and fair treatment. Countries with a higher stage of economic development and a democratic form of government generally provide a relatively independent and more just legal system. In countries that have switched over from planned economic systems to market-oriented economies, such as the CIS and China, various issues related to uniformity of interpretation of laws and clarity of legal procedures are also in transition phase and yet to stabilize.

1.12.4 Political Environment

Political stability and government policies greatly affect international business decisions. For instance, the passing of CIS countries through transitional phase makes the business environment very unpredictable for international business. Under such circumstances, a firm would like to adopt a risk avoidance strategy. It makes sound economic sense that would benefit the ultimate consumers in Pakistan to remove the trade barriers on import of goods from India and grant it the most-favoured nation (MFN) status. However, the political and strategic compulsions between the two countries prohibit the national governments from doing so.

1.12.5 Competition

A firm generally faces more severe competition in the international market as compared to its domestic market. The competition in international markets comprises of products imported from various parts of the world, those produced locally, and competitors from the exporter's own country. The products imported from other competing countries have significantly different business environment that affect its competitiveness. Besides, various trade barriers, both tariff and non-tariff, make business decisions much more complex for operating internationally compared to solely domestic operations.

1.12.6 Infrastructure

The development of physical, financial, human, and institutional infrastructure in a country has a positive impact in facilitating firms to operate. Places like Singapore, Hong Kong, and Dubai, which have got sound financial, institutional, and physical infrastructures, have become international trading hubs. Investors weigh various investment alternatives before deciding locations for export production, which has been dealt with in Chapter 11. The constraints faced by developing countries, including India, in terms of physical infrastructure, such as roads, telecommunication, and port-handling capacities, hinders international marketing efforts and adds to the cost of logistics for international trade.

1.12.7 Technology

There are vast variations in availability of technology between the developed and emerging economies. This opens up opportunities for developing countries like India and China to market their products at competitive prices in other developing and least-developed countries. India's indigenous technology is highly cost-effective and finds easy access to the developing and least-developed countries. India has carried out a number of turnkey projects and international management contracts in Africa, Middle East, and Latin America, primarily due to its cost effectiveness in their niche market segments.

1.13 MANAGING BUSINESS IN THE GLOBALIZATION ERA

Globalization is essentially a macroeconomic phenomenon driven by the strategies and behaviour of the firms that have responded to environmental changes. The high degree of economic integration among the countries has also posed considerable risks of contagion following economic and financial upheavals in foreign countries, even if a firm is not directly involved. Globalization offers both challenges and opportunities for business enterprises, including the following.

Challenges

- Opening up of domestic market to foreign companies increases competition even for the firms solely operating in domestic markets.
- Liberal investment regime facilitates international competitors in establishing business operations, giving rise to increased competition to firms that have been accustomed to operate in protected economies.

Opportunities

- Increased market access and reduced tariffs make foreign markets not only accessible, but increases competitiveness as well.
- Liberalization of regulatory framework for investment in target countries enables companies to invest and expand their business operations abroad.
- It offers opportunities for integration of business operations on a global scale.
- Provides increased opportunity to establish foreign collaborations and ownership.
- Facilitates consolidation of business operations in various countries and developing global capabilities.

Firms, whose output was previously significantly more limited by the size of the domestic market, now have the chance to reap greater advantages from economies of scale by 'being global'. Global companies are differentiated by their strong global position in terms of global assets, capabilities, brands, and their relative resilience to shocks and even to the business cycles.[28] The abilities to become globally competitive and leverage global opportunities are what make a firm global. Global companies can attract stronger talent, can enable cross-learning across markets, have greater opportunities to service and develop capabilities for global customers, and can invest more in R&D that can be spread over larger markets. Further, global companies can act in multiple markets to retaliate against increased competition from other large companies in any given market. The global strategies adopted by business enterprises may include

- Global conception of markets
- Multi-regional integration strategy
- Changes in external organization of multinational firms—Mergers and acquisitions, rather than greenfield operations, strategic alliances, international subcontracting, worldwide network structure, etc.
- Changes in internal organization—Just-in time inventories, global outsourcing, reduced emphasis on hierarchical relationships, need for greater transparency and for corporate governance regulations, etc.[29]

The book is conceptualized to facilitate both practitioners and beginners to develop a thorough understanding of international business for effective decision making. Although in precise theoretical terms, a company should follow a single business strategy for its operations in various countries in 'global business', the strategy adopted in 'international business' may vary to some extent. Since the differences in 'global' and 'international' business appear to be too semantic and obscure, the term 'international business' is used throughout this book. Explicating the concept of globalization, the book equips the readers to manage business in the globalization era.

SUMMARY

Globalization, one of the most widely-used terms in recent times, refers to free cross-border movement of goods, services, capital, information, and ideas. Movement of goods, capital, and people was much less restricted prior to World War I. Globalization has been defined as increasing economic interdependence of national economies across the world through a rapid increase in cross-border movement of goods, service, technology and capital.

Besides, a number of interesting terms such as Westernization, Americanization, Walmartization, McDonaldization, Disneyfication, Coca-Colanization, etc. have been coined to imply globalization. A holistic approach to globalization

---

[28] Tata, Ratan, 'Driving Global Strategy', *Tata Review*, vol. XXXIX, no. 1, January–March 2004, p. 8.

[29] *OECD Handbook on Economic Globalization Indicators*, 2005, pp. 16–20.

includes economic, financial, cultural, and political aspects. The various dimensions of economic globalization include globalization of production, markets, competition, technology, and corporations and industries.

Economic liberalization, rise in R&D costs, multilateral institutions, international economic integration, the move towards free marketing systems, breakthroughs in manufacturing, transportation, information and communication technologies, advents in logistics managements, and emerging global customers' segments have been the prime movers of globalization, whereas regulatory controls, emerging new trade barriers, cultural factors, nationalism, war and civil disturbances, and management myopia restrain globalization.

The empirical methods to measure globalization include trade openness, KOF index of globalization, and the A.T. Kearney/Foreign Policy globalization index.

Globalization is often supported on the grounds of maximization of economic efficiencies, enhancing trade, and increased cross-border capital movements. Developing and developed countries are unequal players in the process of globalization. Critics often accuse globalization for widening the gap between the rich and the poor, of wiping out domestic industry, leading to unemployment and mass lay-offs, bringing in balance-of-payments problems, increasing volatility of markets, diminishing power of nation states, leading to loss of cultural identity, and causing a shift of power to multinationals. Response strategies for globalization forces for emerging market companies include defender, extender, dodger, and contender.

International business refers to the conduct of business activities beyond national boundaries. Reasons for expanding business operations overseas include market-seeking, economic, and strategic motives. International business varies from operating domestic, primarily because of environmental differences such as economic, socio-cultural, legal, and political environment, besides competition, infrastructure, and technology.

KEY TERMS

Americanization A pejoratively used term for the influence of the US on other cultures that leads to a phenomenon of substituting indigenous cultures with the US culture.

Coca-colanization Implies invasion of Western, particularly American, cultural values considered as dangerous to indigenous culture.

Cultural globalization Convergence of cultures across the world may be termed as cultural globalization.

Disneyfication A term used to describe and denigrate a society that has an increasing similarity to the Disney theme parks.

Economic globalization Increasing economic interdependence of national economies across the world through a rapid increase in cross-border movement of goods, service, technology, and capital.

Financial globalization The liberalization of capital movements and deregulations, especially of financial services, led to a spurt in cross-border capital flows.

Global business Conduct of business activities in several countries, using a highly co-ordinated and single strategy across the world.

Globalization Free cross-border movement of goods, services, capital, information, and people.

International business All those business activities that involve cross-border transactions of goods, services, resources between two or more nations. Transaction of economic resources includes capital, skills, people, etc. for international production of physical goods and services, such as finance, banking, insurance, construction, etc.

International investments Cross-border transfer of resources to carry out business activities.

International management Application of management concepts and techniques in a cross-country environment and adaptation to different social-cultural, economic, legal, political, and technological environment.

International marketing Firm-level marketing practices across the border including market identification and targeting, entry mode selection, marketing mix, and strategic decisions to compete in international markets.

International trade Exports and imports of goods and services by a firm to a foreign-based buyer or from a seller.

McDonaldization The principles of the fast food restaurant likely to dominate more and more sectors of the American society as well as the rest of the world.

Walmartization Business practices followed by Wal-Mart, which include optimization concepts from logistics, purchasing, finance, and stores management.

Westernization Influence of western culture on non-western society in terms of life style, value system, language, technology, etc.

CONCEPT REVIEW QUESTIONS

1. Briefly describe the historical perspective of globalization of business.
2. Explain the concept of globalization, using the holistic approach.
3. Critically evaluate various dimensions of economic globalization and their impact on business enterprises.
4. Examine various factors influencing globalization.

5. Explaining the concept of international business, evaluate the distinguishing features vis-à-vis domestic business with suitable examples.
6. Write short notes on
   (a) Cultural globalization
   (b) Globalization of markets
   (c) Globalization of production
   (d) Trade openness

CRITICAL THINKING QUESTIONS

1. Carry out a comparison of trade openness of your country with the major economies of the world. Also examine its changes over the last two decades. Explore the reasons for the same.

2. Select any five firms that have been affected by the globalization forces. Identify the business strategies these firms adopted to respond. Evaluate the strategy used for their effectiveness with the help of the framework studied in the chapter.

PROJECT ASSIGNMENTS

1. Has globalization done more harm than led to benefits for your country? Put forward your arguments and discuss in class in the form of a debate.
2. Select a company that has expanded its business operations overseas. Find out the reasons

for its overseas expansion and compare with those of similar companies.

3. Visit a nearby company having operations in multiple countries. Explore the differences in its operations in various countries.

Theories of International Trade

LEARNING OBJECTIVES

> ➤ To discuss the implications of trade theories on international business
> ➤ To explain various theories of international trade and the underlying assumptions
> ➤ To examine gains from trade under various trade theories
> ➤ To explain the theoretical framework for shifting patterns of production and trade

2.1 INTRODUCTION

The exchange of goods across national borders is termed as international trade. Countries differ widely in terms of the products and services traded. Countries rarely follow the trade structure of other nations; rather they evolve their own product portfolios and trade patterns for exports and imports. Besides, nations have marked differences in their vulnerabilities to the upheavals in exogenous factors.

This chapter aims to discuss various theories of international trade in order to provide a conceptual understanding of the fundamental principles of international trade and the shifts in trade patterns. Trade is crucial for the very survival of countries that have limited resources, such as Singapore or Hong Kong (presently a province of China), or countries that have skewed resources, such as those located in the Caribbean and West Asian regions. However, for countries with diversified resources, such as India, the US, China, and the UK, engagement in trade necessitates a logical basis.

The trade patterns of a country are not a static phenomenon; rather these are dynamic in nature. Moreover, the product profile and trade partners of a country do change over a period of time. Till recently, the Belgian city of Antwerp, the undisputed leader in diamond polishing and trade, had witnessed a shift of diamond business to India and other Asian countries, as given in Exhibit 2.1. It is also imperative for international business managers to find answers to some basic issues, such as why do nations trade with each other? Is trading a zero-sum game or a mutually beneficial activity? Why do trade patterns among countries exhibit wide variations? Can

---

Exhibit 2.1 Antwerp diamonds may not be forever

Patience and precision may be a diamond worker's most important working tools but with increasing competition from low-cost Asian countries like India and China, Antwerp is discovering that diamonds may not be forever. The Antwerp tradition of cutting and trading the most precious of gems began about 560 years ago. After centuries of being the undisputed world leader in producing and marketing diamonds, the Belgian port city is facing new challenges of globalization that is threatening to take the shine off its traditional role.[a]

Antwerp's diamond industry contributes up to 8 per cent of Belgium's overall exports and has generated considerable job opportunities. However, its undisputed position as a leading diamond centre has been seriously challenged by upcoming commercial powers like tax-free Dubai and India. In recent times, India has emerged as the world's major diamond manufacturing hub. One reason for the diamond business shifting the bulk of manufacturing to low-wage countries like India and China is that in Asia, labour costs for polishing are about one-fifth lower than that in Antwerp. However, this is not the only cause behind the shift.

Jewish cutters and traders may have dominated Antwerp's diamond sector for centuries but with the arrival of Indian dealers in the 1970s, Jewish businesses in the city have been closing down and currently represent only 40 per cent of the city's diamond trade.[b] Indians initially sent their workers to Antwerp to learn and improve techniques. These workers, in turn, opened up their own businesses. Today, there is no denying that Indians are Antwerp's main diamond merchants. They handle two-thirds of the city's diamond trade, which recorded a total turnover of €30 billion in 2005.

The Indian diamond community in Antwerp has also gained control over the trade's main governing body, the Diamond High Council. Diamond traders from India won five out of the six seats on the board of the Hoge Raa Voor Diamant (HRD), the group that regulates and represents the diamond sector in the rough diamond capital of Antwerp. The HRD governs and represents Antwerp's diamond trade with the mandate of 13 different organizations, representing diverse elements of the diamond trade. This signifies a significant shift in the control of the world diamond business from other ethnic groups.[c]

Astonishingly, Indian factories process 92 per cent of the world's diamonds today. Indian firms have taken the majority of business away from the old master craftmen of Belgium, New York City, and Israel. Rapid growth in the diamond polishing industry has influenced the household economies of 10 million people in the state of Gujarat. It implies that a person or somebody in his/her family had a job polishing a diamond 12 hours a day at 10 cents a stone. It is the genius available in India that takes in the garbage of the diamond world, slaps 58 facets on it, sets it in gold, and sends it on. These tiny specks are now the fifth most valuable export of a nation that has not mined diamonds from its own soil for more than a century.[d]

Source:
[a] 'Antwerp Diamond Feels the Asian Heat', *The Economic Times*, 9 May 2006.
[b] 'Antwerp Diamonds', *Hindustan Times*, 8 May 2006.
[c] 'Indian Community in Antwerp Gains Control over HRD', *Professional Jewelers Magazine*, 15 May 2006.
[d] 'The Dark Core of a Diamond', *Global Business Time*, 26 June 2006, pp. 29–32.

government policies influence trade? Theories of international trade provide the *raison d'etre* for most of these queries.

Trade theories also offer an insight, both descriptive and prescriptive, into the potential product portfolio and trade patterns. They also facilitate in understanding the basic reasons behind the evolution of a country as a supply base or market for specific products. The principles of the regulatory frameworks of national governments and international organizations are also influenced to a varying extent by these basic economic theories.

2.2   THEORY OF MERCANTILISM

The theory of mercantilism attributes and measures the wealth of a nation by the size of its accumulated treasures. Accumulated wealth is traditionally measured in terms of gold, as earlier gold and silver were considered the currency of international trade. Nations should accumulate financial wealth in the form of gold by encouraging exports and discouraging imports. The theory of mercantilism[1] aims at creating trade surplus, which in turn contributes to the accumulation of a nation's wealth. Between the sixteenth and nineteenth centuries, European colonial powers actively pursued international trade to increase their treasury of goods, which were in turn invested to build a powerful army and infrastructure.

The colonial powers primarily engaged in international trade for the benefit of their respective mother countries, which treated their colonies as exploitable resources. The first ship of the East India Company arrived at the port of Surat in 1608 to carry out trade with India and take advantage of its rich resources of spices, cotton, finest muslin cloth, etc. Other European nations—such as Germany, France, Portugal, Spain, Italy—and the East Asian nation of Japan also actively set up colonies to exploit the natural and human resources.

Mercantilism was implemented by active government interventions, which focussed on maintaining trade surplus and expansion of colonization. National governments imposed restrictions on imports through tariffs and quotas and promoted exports by subsidizing production. The colonies served as cheap sources for primary commodities, such as raw cotton, grains, spices, herbs and medicinal plants, tea, coffee, and fruits, both for consumption and also as raw material for industries. Thus, the policy of mercantilism greatly assisted and benefited the colonial powers in accumulating wealth.

The limitations of the theory of mercantilism are as follows:

- Under this theory, accumulation of wealth takes place at the cost of another trading partner. Therefore, international trade is treated as a win–lose game resulting virtually in no contribution to the global wealth. Thus, international trade becomes a zero-sum game.
- A favourable balance of trade is possible only in the short run and would automatically be eliminated in the long run,[2] according to David Hume's Price-Specie-Flow doctrine. An influx of gold by way of more exports than imports by a

[1] Vaggi, Gianni, *A Concise History of Economic Thought from Mercantilism to Monetarism*, New York: Palgrave Macmillan, 2002.
[2] Hume, David, 'Of Money', *Essays*, Vol. 1, London: Green and Co., 1912, p. 319.

country raises the domestic prices, leading to increase in export prices. In turn, the county would lose its competitive edge in terms of price. On the other hand, the loss of gold by the importing countries would lead to a decrease in their domestic price levels, which would boost their exports.

- Presently, gold represents only a minor proportion of national foreign exchange reserves. Governments use these reserves to intervene in foreign exchange markets and to influence exchange rates.
- The mercantilist theory overlooks other factors in a country's wealth, such as its natural resources, manpower and its skill levels, capital, etc.
- If all countries follow restrictive policies that promote exports and restrict imports and create several trade barriers in the process, it would ultimately result in a highly restrictive environment for international trade.
- Mercantilist policies were used by colonial powers as a means of exploitation, whereby they charged higher prices from their colonial markets for their finished industrial goods and bought raw materials at much lower costs from their colonies. Colonial powers restricted developmental activities in their colonies to a minimum infrastructure base that would support international trade for their own interests. Thus, the colonies remained poor.

A number of national governments still seem to cling to the mercantilist theory, and exports rather than imports are actively promoted. This also explains the *raison d'etre* behind the 'import substitution strategy' adopted by a large number of countries prior to economic liberalization. This strategy was guided by their keenness to contain imports and promote domestic production even at the cost of efficiency and higher production costs. It has resulted in the creation of a large number of export promotion organizations that look after the promotion of exports from the country. However, import promotion agencies are not common in most nations.

Presently, the terminology used under this trade theory is *neo-mercantilism*, which aims at creating favourable trade balance and has been employed by a number of countries to create trade surplus. Japan is a fine example of a country that tried to equate political power with economic power and economic power with trade surplus.

2.3 THEORY OF ABSOLUTE ADVANTAGE

Economist Adam Smith critically evaluated mercantilist trade policies in his seminal book *An Inquiry into the Nature and Causes of the Wealth of Nations*, first published in 1776. Smith posited that the wealth of a nation does not lie in building huge stockpiles of gold and silver in its treasury, but the real wealth of a nation is measured by the level of improvement in the quality of living of its citizens, as reflected by the per capita income.

Smith emphasized productivity and advocated free trade as a means of increasing global efficiency. As per his formulation, a country's standards of living can be enhanced by international trade with other countries either by importing goods not produced by it or by producing large quantities of goods through specialization and exporting the surplus.

An absolute advantage refers to the ability of a country to produce a good more efficiently and cost-effectively than any other country. Smith elucidated the concept of 'absolute advantage' leading to gains from specialization with the help of day-to-day illustrations as follows:

> It is the maxim of every prudent master of a family, never to make at home what it will cost him more to make than to buy. The taylor does not attempt to make his own shoes, but buys them of the shoemaker. The shoemaker does not attempt to make his own clothes, but employs a taylor. The farmer attempts to make neither one nor the other, but employs those different artificers. All of them find it for their interest to employ their whole industry in a way which they have some advantage over their neighbours...
>
> What is prudence in the conduct of every private family can scarce be folly in that of great kingdom. If a foreign country can supply us with a commodity cheaper than we ourselves can make it, better buy it of them with some part of the produce of our own industry.[3]

Thus, instead of producing all products, each country should specialize in producing those goods that it can produce more efficiently. Such efficiency is gained through

- Repetitive production of a product, which increases the skills of the labour force
- Switching production from one produce to another to save labour time
- Long product runs to provide incentives to develop more effective work methods over a period of time

Therefore, a country should use increased production to export and acquire more goods by way of imports, which would in turn improve the living standards of its people. A country's advantage may be either natural or acquired.

2.3.1 Natural

Natural factors, such as a country's geographical and agro-climatic conditions, mineral or other natural resources, or specialized manpower contribute to a country's natural advantage in certain products. For instance, the agro-climatic condition in India is an important factor for sizeable export of agro-produce, such as spices, cotton, tea, and mangoes. The availability of relatively cheap labour contributes to India's edge in export of labour-intensive products. The production of wheat and maize in the US, petroleum in Saudi Arabia, citrus fruits in Israel, lumber in Canada, and aluminium ore in Jamaica are all illustrations of natural advantages.

2.3.2 Acquired Advantage

Today, international trade is shifting from traditional agro-products to industrial products and services, especially in developing countries like India. The acquired

---

[3] Smith, Adam, *An Inquiry into the Nature and Causes of the Wealth of Nations,* New York: Modern Library College Edition, Random House, 1985, p. 226.

advantage in either a product or its process technology plays an important role in creating such a shift. The ability to differentiate or produce a different product is termed as an advantage in product technology, while the ability to produce a homogeneous product more efficiently is termed as an advantage in process technology. Production of consumer electronics and automobiles in Japan, software in India, watches in Switzerland, and shipbuilding in South Korea may be attributed to acquired advantage. Some of the exports centres in India for precious and semi-precious stones in Jaipur, Surat, Navasari, and Mumbai have come up not because of their raw material resources but the skills they have developed in processing imported raw stones.

To illustrate the concept of absolute advantage, an example of two countries may be taken, such as the UK and India. Let us assume that both the countries have the same amount of resources, say 100 units, such as land, labour, capital, etc., which can be employed either to produce tea or rice. However, the production efficiency is assumed to vary between the countries because to produce a tonne of tea, UK requires 10 units of resources whereas India requires only 5 units of resources. On the other hand, for producing one tonne of rice, UK requires only 4 units of resources whereas India needs 10 units of resources (Table 2.1). Since India requires lower resources compared to UK for producing tea, it is relatively more efficient in tea production. On the other hand, since UK requires fewer resources compared to India for producing rice, it is relatively more efficient in producing rice.

Although each country is assumed to possess equal resources, the production possibilities for each country would vary, depending upon their production efficiency and utilization of available resources. All of the possible combinations of the two products that can be produced with a country's limited resources may be graphically depicted by a production possibilities curve (Fig. 2.1), assuming total resource availability of 100 units with each country. The slope of the curve reflects the 'trade-off' of producing one product over the other, representing opportunity cost. The value of a factor of production forgone for its alternate use is termed as opportunity cost. For instance, if the UK wishes to produce one tonne of tea, it has to forgo the production of 2.5 tonnes of rice. Whereas in order to produce one unit of rice, it has to relinquish the production of only 0.40 tonne of tea.

Suppose no foreign trade takes place between the two countries and each employs its resources equally (i.e., 50:50) for production of tea and rice. The UK would produce 5 tonnes of tea and 12.5 tonnes of rice at point B whereas India would produce 10 tonnes of tea and 5 tonnes of rice at point A as shown in Fig. 2.1. This would result in a total

Table 2.1   Absolute advantage: An illustration

	UK	India
Units required to produce one tonne of tea	10	5
Units required to produce one tonne of rice	4	10

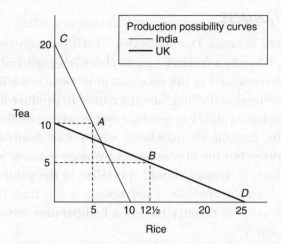

Fig. 2.1 Production possibilities under absolute advantage

output of 15 tonnes of tea and 17.5 tonnes of rice (Table 2.2). If both India and the UK employ their resources on production of only tea and rice, respectively, in which each of them has absolute advantage, the total output, as depicted in Fig. 2.1, of tea would increase from 15 tonnes to 20 tonnes (point C) whereas rice would increase from 17.5 tonnes to 25 tonnes (point D). Thus, both countries can mutually gain from trading, as the total output is enhanced (Table 2.2) as a result of specialization.

The theory of absolute advantage is based on Adam Smith's doctrine of laissez faire that means 'let make freely'. When specifically applied to international trade, it refers to 'freedom of enterprise' and 'freedom of commerce'. Therefore, the government should not intervene in the economic life of a nation or in its trade relations among nations, in the form of tariffs or other trade restrictions, which would be counterproductive. A market would reach to an efficient end by itself without any government intervention. Unlike as suggested by the mercantilist theory, trading is not a zero-sum game under the theory of absolute advantage, wherein a nation can gain only if a trading partner loses. Instead, the countries involved in free trade would mutually benefit as a result of efficient allocation of their resources.

Table 2.2 Gains of specialization and trade under absolute advantage

	Production without trade			Production with trade		
	UK	**India**	**Total**	**UK**	**India**	**Total**
Tea (tonnes)	5	10	15	0	20	20
Rice (tonnes)	12.5	5	17.5	25	0	25
			32.5			**45**

Note: Assuming 100 units of resources available with each country.

2.4 THEORY OF COMPARATIVE ADVANTAGE

In *Principles of Political Economy and Taxation*, David Ricardo (1817) promulgated the theory of comparative advantage, wherein a country benefits from international trade even if it is less efficient than other nations in the production of two commodities. Comparative advantage may be defined as the inability of a nation to produce a good more efficiently than other nations, but its ability to produce that good more efficiently compared to the other good. Thus, the country may be at an absolute disadvantage with respect to both the commodities but the absolute disadvantage is lower in one commodity than another. Therefore, a country should specialize in the production and export of a commodity in which the absolute disadvantage is less than that of another commodity or in other words, the country has got a comparative advantage in terms of more production efficiency.

To illustrate the concept, let us assume a situation where the UK requires 10 units of resources for producing one tonne of tea and 5 units for one tonne of rice whereas India requires 5 units of resources for producing one tonne of tea and 4 units for one tonne of rice (Table 2.3). In this case, India is more efficient in producing both tea and rice. Thus, India has absolute advantage in the production of both the products.

Although the UK does not have an absolute advantage in any of these commodities it has comparative advantage in the production of rice as it can produce rice more efficiently. Countries also gain from trade by employing their resources for the production of goods in which they are relatively more efficient.

Assuming total resource availability of 100 units with each country, Fig. 2.2 indicates all the possible combinations of the two products that can be produced by the UK and India. In case there is no foreign trade between India and the UK (Table 2.4) and both the countries are assumed to use equal (50:50) resources for production of each commodity, UK would produce 5 tonnes of tea and 10 tonnes of rice as shown at point A, whereas India would produce 10 tonnes of tea and 12.5 tonnes of rice at point B in Fig. 2.2. If the UK employs all its resources in the production of rice in which it is more efficient than the other, India can produce the same quantum of tea, i.e., 15 tonnes (Point C) by employing only 75 units of its resources. It can utilize the remaining 25 units of its additional resources for producing 6.25 units of rice, which would raise the total rice production from 22.5 tonnes without trade to 26.25 tonnes after trade (Table 2.4). Alternatively, the UK can employ its entire resources (i.e., 100 units) to produce 20 tonnes of rice and India can use only 10 units of its resources to produce 2.5 tonnes of rice so as to produce the same quantity of rice, i.e., 22.5 tonnes. The remaining 90 units of resources may be used by India for the production of tea,

Table 2.3 Comparative advantage: An illustration

	UK	India
Units required to produce one tonne of tea	10	5
Units required to produce one tonne of rice	5	4

Table 2.4   Gains of specialization and trade under comparative advantage

	Production without trade			Production with trade (increasing rice production)			Production with trade (increasing tea production)		
	UK	India	Total	UK	India	Total	UK	India	Total
Tea (tonnes)	5	10	15	0	15	15	0	18	18
Rice (tonnes)	10	12.5	22.5	20	6.25	26.25	20	2.5	22.5
			37.5			**41.25**			**40.5**

Note: Assuming 100 units of resources available with each country.

resulting in an increase in tea production from 15 tonnes without trade to 18 tonnes with trade as shown at Point E. Hence, it is obvious from the illustrations that countries gain from trade even if a country does not have an absolute advantage in any of its products as the total world output increases.

2.4.1 Measuring Comparative Advantage

The Balassa Index[4] is often used as a useful tool to measure revealed comparative advantage (RCA) that measures the relative trade performance of individual countries in particular commodities. It is assumed to 'reveal' the comparative advantage of trading countries, based on the assumption that the commodity patterns of trade reflects the inter-country differences in relative costs as the well as the non-price factors. The factors that contribute to the changes in the RCA of a country include economic factors, structural changes, improved world demand, and trade specialization.

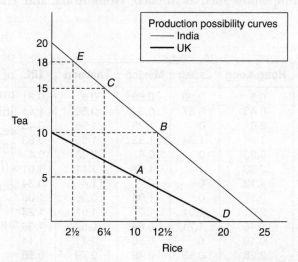

Fig. 2.2   Production possibilities under comparative advantage

[4] Balassa, B., 'Trade Liberalisation and "Revealed" Comparative Advantage', *The Manchester School of Economic and Social Studies*, vol. 33, 1965, pp. 99–123.

RCA is defined as a country's share of world exports of a commodity divided by its share in total exports. The index for commodity j from country i is computed as

$$RCA_{ij} = (X_{ij}/X_{wj})/(X_i/X_w)$$

where,

X_{ij} = ith country's export of commodity j
X_{wj} = world exports of commodity j
X_i = total export of country i
X_w = total world exports

If the value of the index of revealed comparative advantage (RCA_{ij}) is greater than unity (i.e., 1), the country has a RCA in that commodity. The RCA index considers the intrinsic advantage of a particular export commodity and is consistent with the changes in the economy's relative factor endowment and productivity. However, it cannot distinguish between the improvements in factor endowments and the impact of the country's trade policies.

As indicated in Table 2.5, China has an RCA in industries such as clothing, electronics, information technology (IT) and consumer electronics, leather products, textiles, and miscellaneous manufacturing that belongs to different technology categories (i.e., low, medium, and high) but not in resource-base manufacture. On the other hand, India has an RCA in resource-based and low-technological industries, such as fresh food, leather products, minerals, textiles, basic manufacture, chemicals, and clothing. It is also observed that the US, Japan, and the UK have an RCA in high- and medium-technology categories, such as IT, consumer electronics, electronics, manufacturing, etc., whereas China's main competitors such as Mexico, Hong Kong, and Thailand

Table 2.5   RCA index of specialization

Industry	China	India	Hong Kong	Japan	Mexico	Thailand	UK	US
Basic manufactures	0.96	1.36	0.5	0.99	0.69	0.6	0.81	0.63
Chemicals	0.42	1.06	0.43	0.87	0.34	0.65	1.41	1.18
Clothing	3.46	3.09	3.01	0	1.29	1.56	0.43	0.23
Electronics	1.04	0.23	1.94	1.64	1.53	1.55	0.63	1.33
Fresh food	0.68	2.23	0.23	0	0.8	2.33	0.4	1.52
IT/consumer elect.	2.43	0.1	2.33	1.2	1.75	2.11	1.01	0.92
Leather products	3.34	2.18	4.12	0	0	1.4	0.34	0
Minerals	0.28	2.03	0.17	0	1.06	0.36	1.08	0.35
Misc. manufactures	1.48	0.8	2.01	1.01	1.07	1.01	1.23	1.31
Non-elect. machinery	0.52	0.37	0.46	1.71	0.84	0.62	1.39	1.38
Processed food	0.47	0.76	0.19	0	0.56	1.71	1.14	0.75
Textiles	2.39	4.27	2.28	0.55	0.49	0.79	0.56	0.61
Transport equipment	0.27	0.23	0.08	2.03	1.34	0.37	1.07	1.22
Wood products	0.43	0.17	0.39	0.19	0.26	0.66	0.48	0.93

Source: Qureshi, Mahvash Saeed and Guanghua Wan, 'Trade Potential of China and India: Threat or Opportunity?' Annual Bank Conference on Development Economies, World Bank University, 29–30 May 2006.

have RCA in low-, medium-, and high-technology categories. This implies that countries specializing in medium- to high-technology products may explore opportunities of expanding bilateral trade with India and those in resource-based industries may stand to benefit substantially by an increase in demand of such products in China. For example, Latin American countries mainly produce and export various commodities. The major produce of Latin America is copper, oil, soy, and coffee, as the region produces about 47 per cent of the world soybean crop, 40 per cent of copper, and 9.3 per cent of oil. The rising demand for commodities in China and other countries presents opportunities to these countries for expanding their production and increasing foreign exchange revenues. Similarly, the rapid growth in economic activities in India and China opens up opportunity for oil exporting countries. Thus, revealed comparative advantage may be employed as a useful tool to explain international trade patterns.

2.4.2 Limitation of Theories of Specialization

Although the theories of specialization help in developing a conceptual understanding of why nations trade based on the differences in production efficiency, these have certain limitations too, as summarized below:

- Theories of absolute and comparative advantage lay emphasis on specialization with an assumption that countries are driven only by the impulse of maximization of production and consumption. However, the attainment of economic efficiency in a specialized field may not be the only goal of countries. For instance, the Middle East countries have spent enormous resources and pursued a sustained strategy in developing their agriculture and horticulture sector, in which these countries have very high absolute and comparative disadvantage, so as to become self-reliant.
- Specialization in one commodity or product may not necessarily result in efficiency gains. The production and export of more than one product often have a synergistic effect on developing the overall efficiency levels.
- These theories assume that production takes place under full employment conditions and labour is the only resource used in the production process, which is not a valid assumption.
- The division of gains is often unequal among the trading partners, which may alienate the partner perceiving or getting lower gains, who may forgo absolute gains to prevent relative losses.
- The original theories have been proposed on the basis of two countries–two commodities situation. However, the same logic applies even when the theories experimented with multiple-commodities and multiple-countries situations.
- The logistics cost is overlooked in these theories, which may defy the proposed advantage of international trading.
- The sizes of economy and production runs are not taken into consideration.

2.5 FACTOR ENDOWMENT (HECKSCHER–OHLIN) THEORY

The earlier theories of absolute and comparative advantage provided little insight into the *type* of products in which a country can have an advantage. Heckscher (1919) and Bertil Ohlin (1933) developed a theory to explain the reasons for differences in relative commodity prices and competitive advantage between two nations. According to this theory, a nation will export the commodity whose production requires intensive use of the nation's relatively abundant and cheap factors and import the commodity whose production requires intensive use of the nation's scarce and expensive factors. Thus, a country with an abundance of cheap labour would export labour-intensive products and import capital-intensive goods and vice versa. It suggests that the patterns of trade are determined by factor endowment rather than productivity. The theory suggests three types of relationships, which are discussed here.

Land–labour relationship

A country would specialize in production of labour intensive goods if the labour is in abundance (i.e., relatively cheaper) as compared to the cost of land (i.e., relatively costly). This is mainly due to the ability of a labour-abundant country to produce something more cost-efficiently as compared to a country where labour is scarcely available and therefore expensive.

Labour–capital relationship

In countries where the capital is abundantly available and labour is relatively scarce (therefore most costly), there would be a tendency to achieve competitiveness in the production of goods requiring large capital investments.

Technological complexities

As the same product can be produced by adopting various methods or technologies of production, its cost competitiveness would have great variations. In order to minimize the cost of production and achieve cost competitiveness, one has to examine the optimum way of production in view of technological capabilities and constraints of a country.

2.5.1 The Leontief Paradox

According to the factor endowment theory, a country with a relatively cheaper cost of labour would export labour-intensive products, while a country where the labour is scarce and capital is relatively abundant would export capital-intensive goods. Wassily Leontief carried out an empirical test of the Heckscher–Ohlin Model in 1951 to find out whether or not the US, which has abundant capital resources, exports capital-intensive goods and imports labour-intensive goods. He found that the US exported more labour-intensive commodities and imported more capital-intensive products, which was contrary to the results of Heckscher–Ohlin Model of factor endowment.[5]

2.6   COUNTRY SIMILARITY THEORY

As per the Heckscher–Ohlin theory of factor endowment, trade should take place among countries that have greater differences in their factor endowments. Therefore, developed countries having manufactured goods and developing countries producing primary products should be natural trade partners. A Swedish economist, Staffan B. Linder, studied international trade patterns in two different categories, i.e., primary products (natural resource products) and manufactures. It was found that in natural resource-based industries, the relative costs of production and factor endowments determined the trade. However, in the case of manufactured goods, costs were determined by the similarity in product demands across countries rather than by the relative production costs or factor endowments.[6]

It has been observed that the majority of trade occurs between nations that have similar characteristics. The major trading partners of most developed countries are other developed industrialized countries. The country similarity theory is based on the following principles:

- If two countries have similar demand patterns, then their consumers would demand the same goods with similar degrees of quality and sophistication. This phenomenon is also known as *preference similarity*. Such a similarity leads to enhanced trade between the two developed countries.
- The demand patterns in countries with a higher level of per capita income are similar to those of other countries with similar income levels, as their residents would demand more sophisticated, high quality, 'luxury' consumer goods, whereas those in countries with lower per capita income would demand low quality, cheaper consumer goods as a part of their 'necessity'. Since developed countries would have a comparative advantage in the manufacture of complex, technology-intensive luxury goods, they would find export markets in other high income countries.
- Since most products are developed on the demand patterns in the home market, other countries with similar demand patterns due to cultural or economic similarity would be their natural trade partners.
- Countries with the proximity of geographical locations would also have greater trade compared to the distant ones. This can also be explained by various types of similarities, such as cultural and economic, besides the cost of transportation.

[5] Leontief, Wassily, 'Domestic Production and Foreign Trade: The American Capital Position Re-examined', *Proceedings of the American Philosophical Society*, 97(4), September 1953, as reprinted in Leontief, Wassily, *Input-Output Economics*, New York: Oxford University Press, 1966, pp. 69–70.

[6] Linder, S.B., *An Essay on Trade and Transformation*, New York: Wiley, 1961.

The country similarity theory goes beyond cost comparisons. Therefore, it is also used in international marketing.

2.7   THE NEW TRADE THEORY

Countries do not necessarily trade only to benefit from their differences but they also trade so as to increase their returns, which in turn enable them to benefit from specialization. International trade enables a firm to increase its output due to its specialization by providing a much larger market that results in enhancing its efficiency. The theory helps explain the trade patterns when markets are not perfectly competitive or when the economies of scale are achieved by the production of specific products.[7] Decrease in the unit cost of a product resulting from large scale production is termed as economies of scale. Since fixed costs are shared over an increased output, the economies of scale enable a firm to reduce its per unit average cost of production and enhance its price competitiveness. The new trade theory emphasizes on the two types of economies of scale discussed here.

2.7.1   Internal Economies of Scale

Companies benefit by the economies of scale when the cost per unit of output depends upon their size. The larger the size, the higher are the economies of scale. Firms that enhance their internal economies of scale can decrease their price and monopolize the industry, creating imperfect market competition. This in turn results in the lowering of market prices due to the imperfect market competition. Internal economies of scale may lead a firm to specialize in a narrow product line to produce the volume necessary to achieve cost benefits from scale economies. Industries requiring massive investment in R&D and creating manufacturing facilities, such as branded software by Microsoft, microprocessors by Intel or AMD, and aircrafts by Boeing or Airbus, need to have a global market base so as to achieve internal economies of scale and compete effectively.

2.7.2   External Economies of Scale

If the cost per unit of output depends upon the size of the industry, not upon the size of an individual firm, it is referred to as external economies of scale. This enables the industry in a country to produce at a lower rate when the industry size is large compared to the same industry in another country with a relatively smaller industry size. The dominance of a particular country in the world market in a specific products sector with higher external economies of scale is attributed to the large size of a country's industry that has several small firms, which interact to create a large, competitive critical mass rather than a large-sized individual firm. However, external economies

[7] Krugman, P., 'Intra-industry Specialisation and the Gains from Trade', *Journal of Political Economy*, 1980, pp. 89, 959–73.

of scale do not necessarily lead to imperfect markets but may enable the country's industry to achieve global competitiveness. Although no single firm needs to be large, a number of small firms in a country may create a competitive industry that other countries may find difficult to compete with. The automotive component industry of India and the semiconductor industry in Malaysia are illustrations of external economies of scale. The development of sector-specific industrial clusters, such as brassware in Moradabad, hosiery in Tirupur, carpets in Bhadoi, semi-precious stones in Jaipur, and diamond polishing in Surat, may also be attributed to external economies of scale.

The new trade theory brings in the concept of economies of scale to explicate the Leontief paradox. Such economies of scale may not be necessarily linked to the differences in factor endowment between the trading partners. The higher economies of scale lead to increase in returns, enabling countries to specialize in the production of such goods and trade with countries with similar consumption patterns. Besides intra-industry trade, the theory also explains intra-firm trade between the MNEs and their subsidiaries, with a motive to take advantage of the scale economies and increase their returns.

2.8 INTERNATIONAL PRODUCT LIFE-CYCLE THEORY

International markets tend to follow a cyclical pattern[8] due to a variety of factors over a period of time, which explains the shifting of markets as well as the location of production. The level of innovation and technology, resources, size of market, and competitive structure influence trade patterns. In addition, the gap in technology and preference and the ability of the customers in international markets also determine the stage of international product life cycle (IPLC).

In case the innovating country has a large market size, as in case of the US, India, China, etc., it can support mass production for domestic sales. This mass market also facilitates the producers based in these countries to achieve cost-efficiency, which enables them to become internationally competitive. However, in case the market size of a country is too small to achieve economies of scale from the domestic market, the companies from these countries can alternatively achieve economies of scale by setting up their marketing and production facilities in other cost-effective countries. Thus, it is the economies of scope that assists in achieving the economies of scale by expanding into international markets.

The theory explains the variations and reasons for change in production and consumption patterns among various markets over a time period, as depicted in Fig. 2.3.

---

[8] Vernon, Raymond, 'International Investment and International Trade in Product Life Cycle', *Quarterly Journal of Economics*, May 1996, p. 199.

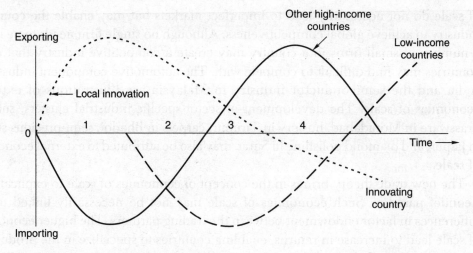

Fig. 2.3 International product life cycle

Source: Based on Sak, Onkvisit and John J. Shaw, 'Examination of International Production Life Cycle and Its Application within Marketing', *Columbia Journal of World Business*, Fall 1983, pp. 73–79.

The IPLC has four distinct (Exhibit 2.2) identifiable stages that influence demand structure, production, marketing strategy, and international competition as follows.

Stage 1: Introduction

Generally, it is in high-income or developed countries that the majority of new product inventions take place, as product inventions require substantial resources to be expended on R&D activities and need speedy recovery of the initial cost incurred by way of market-skimming pricing strategies. Since, in the initial stages, the price of a new product is relatively higher, buying the product is only within the means and capabilities of customers in high-income countries. Therefore, a firm finds a market for new products in other developed or high income countries in the initial stages.

Stage 2: Growth

The demand in the international markets exhibits an increasing trend and the innovating firm gets better opportunities for exports. Moreover, as the market begins to develop in other developed countries, the innovating firm faces increased international competition in the target market. In order to defend its position in international markets, the firm establishes its production locations in other developed or high income countries.

Stage 3: Maturity

As the technical know-how of the innovative process becomes widely known, the firm begins to establish its operations in middle- and low-income countries in order to take advantage of resources available at competitive prices.

	Exhibit 2.2 Stages of international product life cycle			
	IPLC stages			
	Introduction	**Growth**	**Maturity**	**Decline**
Demand structure	• Nature of demand not well understood • Consumers willing to pay premium price for a new product	• Price competition begins • Product standard emerging	• Competition based on price and product differentiation	• Mostly price competition
Production	• Short runs, rapidly changing techniques • Dependent on skilled labour	• Mass production	• Long runs with stable techniques • Capital intensive	• Long runs with stable techniques • Lowest cost of production needed either by capital intensive production or by massive use of inexpensive labour
Innovator company marketing strategy	• Sales mostly to home country (i.e., innovating country) consumers • Some exported to other high-income countries	• Increased exports to high-income countries	• Innovator company begins production in other high-income countries to protect its foreign market from local competition	• Innovator company may begin production in developing countries
International competition	• A few competitors at home (i.e., innovating country)	• Competitors in other high-income countries begin production for their domestic markets • They also begin exporting to the innovating country	• Companies from other high-income countries increase exports to the innovating country • They begin exporting to developing countries	• Competitors from other high-income countries may begin production in developing countries • Competitors from developing countries also begin exporting to the world

Source: Adapted from Wells, Louis T., Jr, 'International Trade the Product Life Cycle Approach', in Reed Moyer, ed., *International Business: Issues and Concepts,* New York: John Wiley, 1984.

Stage 4: Decline

The major thrust of marketing strategy at this stage shifts to price and cost competitiveness, as the technical know-how and skills become widely available.

Therefore, the emphasis of the firm is on most cost-effective locations rather than on producing themselves. Besides other middle-income or developing countries, the production also intensifies in low-income or least-developed countries (LDCs). As a result, it has been observed that the innovating country begins to import such goods from other developing countries rather than manufacturing itself.

The UK, which was once the largest manufacturer and exporter of bicycles, now imports this product in large volumes. The bicycle is at the declining stage of its life cycle in industrialized countries whereas it is still at a growth or maturity stage in a number of developing countries. The chemical and hazardous industries are also shifting from high-income countries to low-income countries as a part of their increasing concern about environmental issues, exhibiting a cyclical pattern in international markets.

Although the product life cycle explains the emerging pattern of international markets, it has got its own limitations in the present marketing era with the fast proliferation of market information, wherein products are launched more or less simultaneously in various markets.

2.9 THEORY OF COMPETITIVE ADVANTAGE

As propounded by Michael Porter in *The Competitive Advantage of Nations*, the theory of competitive advantage[9] concentrates on a firm's home country environment as the main source of competencies and innovations.[10] The model is often referred to as the diamond model, wherein four determinants, as indicated in Fig. 2.4, interact with each other.

Porter's diamond consists of the following attributes.

2.9.1 Factor (Input) Conditions

Factor conditions refer to how well-endowed a nation is as far as resources are concerned. These resources may be created or inherited, which include human resources, capital resources, physical infrastructure, administrative infrastructure, information infrastructure, scientific and technological infrastructure, and natural resources. The efficiency, quality, and specialization of underlying inputs that firms draw while competing in international markets are influenced by a country's factor conditions. The inherited factors in case of India, such as the abundance of arable land, water resources, large workforce, round-the-year sunlight, biodiversity, and a variety of agro-climatic conditions do not necessarily guarantee a firm's international competitiveness. Rather the factors created by meticulous planning and implementation, scientific and market knowledge, physical and capital resources and infrastructure, play a greater role in determining a firm's competitiveness.

[9] Porter, M.E., *The Competitive Advantage of Nations*, New York: The Free Press, 1990, p. 127.

[10] Porter, M.E., 'The Competitive Advantage of Nations', *Harvard Business Review*, vol. 90, no. 2, March–April 1990, p. 78.

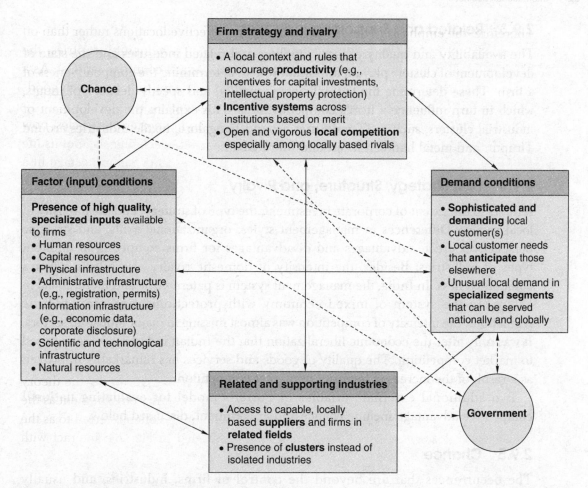

Fig. 2.4   Determinants of competitive advantage

Source: Porter, Michael E., 'Building the Micro-economic Foundations of Prosperity: Findings from the Business Competitiveness Index', The Global Competitiveness Report 2005–06, World Economic Forum, Geneva, 2005, p. 46 and Porter, Michael E., *The Competitive Advantage of Nations,* Free Press, New York, 1990, p. 127.

2.9.2   Demand Conditions

The sophistication of demand conditions in the domestic market and the pressure from domestic buyers is a critical determinant for a firm to upgrade its product and services. The major characteristics of domestic demand include the nature of demand, the size and growth patterns of domestic demand, and the way a nation's domestic preferences are transmitted to foreign markets. As the Indian market has long been a sellers' market, it exerted little pressure on Indian firms to strive for quality upgradation in the home market. However, as a result of India's economic liberalization, there has been a considerable shift in the demand conditions.

2.9.3 Related and Supporting Industries

The availability and quality of local suppliers and related industries and the state of development of clusters play an important role in determining the competitiveness of a firm. These determine the cost-efficiency, quality, and speedy delivery of inputs, which in turn influence a firm's competitiveness. This explains the development of industrial clusters, such as IT industries around Bangalore, textile industries around Tirupur, and metal handicrafts around Moradabad.

2.9.4 Firm Strategy, Structure, and Rivalry

It refers to the extent of corporate investment, the type of strategy, and the intensity of local rivalry. Differences in management styles, organizational skills, and strategic perspectives create advantages and disadvantages for firms competing in different types of industries. Besides, the intensity of domestic rivalry also affects a firm's competitiveness. In India, the management system is paternalistic and hierarchical in nature. In the system of mixed economy with protectionist and monopolistic regulations, the intensity of competition was almost missing in major industrial sectors. It was only after the economic liberalization that the Indian industries were exposed to market competition. The quality of goods and services has remarkably improved as a result of the increased intensity of market competition.

Two additional external variables of Porter's model for evaluating national competitive advantage include chance and government, discussed below.

2.9.5 Chance

The occurrences that are beyond the control of firms, industries, and usually governments have been termed as chance, which plays a critical role in determining competitiveness. It includes wars and their aftermath, major technological breakthroughs, innovations, exchange rates, shifts in factor or input costs (e.g., rise in petroleum prices), etc. Some of the major chance factors in the context of India include disintegration of the erstwhile USSR and the collapse of the communist system in Eastern Europe, opening up of the Chinese market, the Gulf War, etc.

2.9.6 Government

The government has an important role to play in influencing the determinants of a nation's competitiveness. The government's role in formulating policies related to trade, foreign exchange, infrastructure, labour, product standards, etc. influences the determinants in the Porter's diamond.

Assessing country competitiveness

In order to facilitate the quantifiable assessment of competitiveness, the World Economic Forum has developed the Global Competitiveness Index, which is discussed at length in Chapter 10. It presents a quantified framework aimed to measure the set of institutions, policies, and factors that set the sustainable current and medium-term levels of economic prosperity. The US was ranked as the most competitive economy in the world, followed by Switzerland, Denmark, Sweden, Singapore, Finland, and Germany whereas China and India were ranked at 30th and 50th positions, respectively.[11]

India has made remarkable progress in improving its global competitiveness during the recent years. The rapid rise in the share of the working age population for the last 20 years would add to favourable demographics to India's competitiveness. However, to benefit from this India will have to find ways to bring its masses of young people into the workforce, by spending on education and improving the quality of its educational institutions so as to enhance the productivity of its young. Moreover, the country still has to take effective measures (Exhibit 2.3) to deal with its bureaucratic red-tape, illiteracy, and infrastructure bottlenecks, especially road, rail, seaports and airports, and electricity, among others, so as to boost its global competitiveness.

Exhibit 2.3   Boosting India's global competitiveness

India's competitiveness has increased significantly in the recent years as it ranked to 50th place in 2008–09. Increasing trends in FDI inflows to the skill and technology-intensive sector over the past few years have led to an improvement in its position in the Technology Index. India's recent growth rates of over 7 per cent in the past few years reflect its economic success.

The significant increase in the degree of sophistication of India's private sector has markedly improved the business environment. Factors such as the sophistication in the production processes, levels of company's spending on R&D, the prevalence of foreign technology licensing, the sophistication of financial markets, greater openness in the economy, etc. have contributed to this improvement. Besides, the policy framework and institutional environment have also improved significantly and led to tangible progress over the past decade. However, India needs to address the following issues in order to maintain and improve its growth rates:

- High illiteracy rates and relatively low enrolment rates
- The extent of bureaucratic red tape and excessive regulations
- Significant improvement in infrastructure facilities, such as road, rail, airports, power generation, etc.
- Fiscal deficit problems

The Indian economy has the potential to become an engine of growth for the world. To realize its full potential, these challenges have to be jointly addressed by the government and the business community. India has to give special priority to boosting human capital endowment, improving physical infrastructure, reducing burden of needless over-regulation, and moving public finances onto a more sustainable path. If these challenges are met, there is no reason why India cannot join the ranks of the most competitive economies in the world.

Source: Claros, Augusto Lopex, Jennifer Blanke, Irene Mia, and Saadia Zahidi, 'Policies and Institutions Underpinning Economic Growth: Results from the Competitiveness Indexes', The Global Competitiveness Report 2005–06, 2006–07, and 2007–08, World Economic Forum, Geneva, 2008, pp. 18–19.

---

[11] The Global Competitiveness Report 2008–2009, *World Economic Forum*, Geneva, Switzerland, 2008, pp. 8–10.

2.10   IMPLICATIONS OF TRADE THEORIES

The trade theories provide a conceptual base for international trade and shifts in trade patterns. This chapter brings out the significance of developing a conceptual understanding of the trade theories as it deals with the fundamental issues, such as why international trade takes place, trade partners, shifts in trade patterns, and determinants of competitiveness. The initial theory of mercantilism was based on accumulating wealth in terms of goods by increasing exports and restricting imports. Trade was considered to be a zero-sum game under the mercantilism theory wherein one country gains at the cost of the other. However, a new form of mercantilism, known as *neo-mercantilism,* is followed by a number of countries so as to increase their trade surpluses. In 1776, Adam Smith advocated the concept of free trade as a means of increasing gains in world output from specialization. The theory of absolute advantage suggests that a country should produce and export those goods that it can produce more efficiently. David Ricardo's theory of comparative advantage was based on the international differences in labour productivity and advocates international trade even if a country does not have an absolute advantage in the production of any of its goods. Although it is possible for a country not to have an absolute advantage in production of any good, it is not possible for it not to have a comparative advantage in any of the goods it produces. In the later case, the country should specialize in the production and export of those goods that can be produced more efficiently as compared to others.

The factor endowment theory highlights the interplay between proportions in which the factors of production such as land, labour, and capital are available to different countries and the proportions in which they are required for producing particular goods. Trade between countries with similar characteristics such as economic, geographic, cultural, etc. is explained by the country similarity theory. The new trade theory explains the specialization by some countries in production and exports of particular products as international trade enables a firm to increase its output due to its specialization by providing much larger market that results into enhancing its efficacy. The shifting patterns of production location are elucidated by the theory of IPLC that influences demand structure, production, the innovator company's marketing strategy, and international competitiveness. The theory of competitive advantage comprehensively deals with the micro-economic business environment as the determinants of competitive advantage.

Earlier trade theories suggested the shift in comparative advantage in low-skilled production activities from advance economies to developing countries. The product life-cycle theory too heavily relied on such presumptions. However, in recent years, the rapid shift of high-value activities such as R&D, technology-intensive manufacturing, and white-collar jobs to India and other Asian countries have evoked considerable apprehension among intellectuals in the US and other advanced economies about whether free trade is still beneficial for their countries or not. This concern has been illustrated through Exhibit 2.4. It is likely to continue as a matter of serious debate

Exhibit 2.4   Mayhem over trade theories

The high cost of production in high-income countries, including the US, has led to the shift of manufacturing facilities to cheap labour countries such as India and China. Developing countries such as India and China can carry out labour-intensive production activities more efficiently, as they have got comparative advantage due to the abundance of less-educated workforce. In return, these countries would buy more of the high-value goods made by skilled labourers for which the US and other high-income countries have comparative advantage. The shift of production locations from high-income countries to lower-cost locations tend to result in job-cuts in high-income countries. But such lost jobs are more than offset when countries specialize, leading to more robust exports and lower prices on imported goods.

In recent years, the rapid shift of white-collar jobs to cheap-labour countries has caused deep concern in the US and other high-income countries. The rapid transfer of high-skilled jobs such as computer programming, engineering, project management, designing etc. to countries such as India and China seems to conflict head-on with the 200-year-old doctrine of comparative advantage. It is feared that the increased off-shoring of skilled activities could lower the US wages or slow the growth of the gross domestic product.

Ever since British economist David Ricardo spelled out the theory of comparative advantage in the early 1800s, most economists have believed that countries gain more than they lose when they trade with each other and specialize in what they do best. However, advances in information and communication technology have led to a new type of trade that does not fit neatly into this theory.[a] Since brainpower can be obtained anywhere from the world at low cost, a global labour market for skilled workers seems to be emerging for the first time, which has the potential to upset traditional notions of national specialization. It can disrupt the economies of high-income countries in the following ways.

If enough cheap, high-skilled workers become available around the world, competition may drive down US wages for a wide swathe of white-collar workers. It is for the first time that highly skilled workers in developed countries are going to be exposed to international competition.

The gains from trade that would flow to consumers in high-income countries needs to be assessed. So far the pain of globalization has been borne by less than a quarter of the workforce, mostly lower-skilled labours whose wage cuts outweighed the cheaper priced imported goods. But the majority of workers that constitute highly skilled jobs in developed countries were not affected by the foreign wage competition. If white- and blue-collared skilled workers alike are thrown to the global labour pool, it is feared that a majority of workers would end up losing more than they gain through lower prices. Then the benefits of increased trade would primarily go to the employers.

Even that would not completely derail the competitive advantage theory, which holds that higher profits from trade should more than offset the lower wages. But, for the first time economists have seen another factor at play. As the skill levels improve in cheap-labour countries, such as the growing scientific and engineering skills from India, the competition is confronting the very products, such as software, in which the US has a global advantage. If the new competition drives down prices considerably, US earnings would suffer and the US economy could end up worse off.

Prominent economists have viewed free trade to be beneficial for the US but the rising anxiety among high-skilled workers may erode the support for free trade and continued globalization.

[a] Bernstein, Aaran, 'Shaking Up Trade Theory', *Business Week*, 6 December 2004.

Sources: 'IT Job Losses: Don't Blame Off-shoring', *Business Week*, 6 March 2006 and 'White-Collar Outsourcing Pressure Builds', CNNMoney.com.

and the upcoming economic thought may witness a significant deviation in terms of the support to theories based on free trade and, in turn, globalization.

SUMMARY

This chapter discusses various theories of international trade so as to develop a conceptual understanding of the fundamental principles underlying international trade. Early trade was based on the theory of mercantilism that measured the wealth of a nation by the size of its accumulated treasures of gold and silver. In order to accumulate such financial wealth, the theory suggested a nation should encourage exports and discourage imports. Since one country's gain was dependent upon another's loss, trade was considered to be a zero-sum game. However, the later theories of specialization promulgated that trade enhances the overall global wealth by way of enhancing world production. The theory of absolute advantage emphasizes that a country should produce and export those goods that it can produce more efficiently than others. The theory of comparative advantage advocates that even if a country does not have an absolute advantage in the production of any goods, it should produce those goods that it can produce more efficiently than others.

As per the Heckscher–Ohlin factor endowment theory, a nation will export the commodity whose production requires an intensive use of the nation's relatively abundant and cheap factors and will import the commodity whose production requires the intensive use of the nation's scarce and expensive factors. However, the Leontief paradox does not support the factor endowment theory and finds that the US exports more labour-intensive commodities and imports more capital-intensive products. Leinder's country similarity theory brings out the relative cost of production and factor endowment as determinants of trade in a natural resource-based industry but postulates that in case of manufactured goods, trade is primarily determined by the similarity in product demands across the country. The new trade theory brings in the concept of economies of scale leading to increase in returns, enabling countries to specialize in the production of such goods. The shifting patterns of markets as well as manufacturing bases are aptly explained by the theory of international product life cycle. The theory of competitive advantage emphasizes upon environmental factors, such as factor conditions, demand conditions, related and supporting industries, firm strategy, structure, and rivalry as determinants of national competitiveness. The trade theories also provide guiding principles for the regulatory framework and trade promotion strategies to a varying extent to national governments and international organizations.

KEY TERMS

Absolute advantage The ability of a nation to produce the goods more efficiently and cost effectively than any other country.

Comparative advantage The inability of a nation to produce a good more efficiently than other nations, but the ability to produce that good more efficiently than it does any other good.

Competitive advantage Theory stating that a firm's home country environment is formed of determinants, such as factor conditions, demand conditions, related and supporting industries, firm strategy structure, and rivalry. These are the key determinants of competitive advantage.

Country similarity theory Theory stating that trade occurs between nations that have similar characteristics such as economic, geographic, cultural, etc.

External economies of scale The cost per unit of output depends upon the size of the industry, not on the size of the individual firm.

Factor endowment theory The theory that a nation will export the goods whose production requires intensive use of the nation's relatively abundant and cheap factors and import the goods whose production requires intensive use of its scarce and expensive factors.

Internal economies of scale Cost per unit of output depends upon the size of the firm. The larger the size, the higher the economies of scale.

International product life cycle The cyclical pattern followed by international markets due to a variety of factors over time. Explains the shifting of markets as well as locations of production.

International trade Exchange of goods and services across national borders.

New mercantilism Form of mercantilism presently followed by a number of countries aimed at creating a favourable trade balance.

New trade theory Theory that international trade enables a firm to increase its output due to specialization by providing larger markets, resulting in enhancing its efficiency.

Revealed comparative advantage A country's share of world exports of a commodity divided by its share of total exports.

Theory of mercantilism Theory that aims at accumulating financial wealth in terms of gold by encouraging exports and discouraging imports.

CONCEPT REVIEW QUESTIONS

1. Explaining the concept of mercantilist theory, evaluate its relevance in today's global economy.

2. On the basis of the theory of comparative advantage, illustrate how free trade is beneficial for each trading nation even if a country does not have absolute advantage in production of any single commodity.

3. Explain the concept of Leontief paradox and its present day implications on trade flows.

4. Critically evaluate the factors proportions theory and identify its strengths and weaknesses.

5. Which of the trade theories is most appropriate in explaining the high level of trade among high-income countries? Justify your answer with suitable arguments.

6. In view of the rapid strides in the field of information and communication technology and intensifying market competition, critically examine the relevance of the international product life cycle theory.

CRITICAL THINKING QUESTIONS

1. Shifting of knowledge-based tasks from their traditional strongholds, such as the US, the EU, and Japan to India and other Asian countries is likely to adversely impact the jobs in developed countries and influence their economies in more than one way. Do you still think that free trade is beneficial? Present your points in the form of a debate in class.

2. Critically evaluate the theory of international product life cycle for the following industries:
   (a) Bicycles
   (b) Textiles
   (c) Information technology (IT)

PROJECT ASSIGNMENTS

1. Compile data for the top 20 export products from your country and find out their major import destinations. Explain the trade patterns on the basis of the trade theories learned.

2. Find out the products in which India and China have comparative advantage.

CASE STUDY

Emergence of Chip Design Industry in Asia

The chip industry, one of the most dynamic industries in world trade, was among the earliest to globalize production. Chip design not only creates the greatest value in the Information and Communication Technology (ICT) industry while requiring highly complex knowledge, it also involves a generic technology that affects a large degree of user industries, including high-value services. Chip design has recently moved from centres of excellence in the US, Europe, and Japan to sites in some developing counties, notably in East Asia. From practically negligible value during the mid-1990s, this region's share of semiconductor design reached around 30 per cent in 2002. South-East and East Asia are now the fastest growing markets for electronic design automation tools, expanding by 36 per cent in the first quarter of 2004, compared to 5 per cent for North America (which has 60 per cent of the world market), 4 per cent for Europe, and 2 per cent for Japan. Developing Asia is not only undertaking more chip-related R&D, but also the levels of complexity are rising in terms of the line-width of process technology (measured in manometers), the use of analogue and mixed signal design (substantially more complex than digital design), the share and type of system-level design (e.g., system-on-chip), and the number of gates used in these designs.

Over recent years, the chip designing activity has been concentrated in a handful of clusters in India (Bangalore, Hyderabad, Noida/New Delhi), Singapore, Taiwan Province of China (Hsinchu and Taipei), China (Beijing, Shanghai, Hangzhou, Suzhou, and Shenzhen), Republic of Korea (Seoul), and Malaysia. The Asian chip design centres perform a diverse range of functions from routine (engineering support, adaptation, and listening posts for 'technology marketing') to highly strategic tasks (global development mandates for specific IT products, components, and services).

Factors responsible for moving of chip development industry to Asian countries[1] include the following.

Pull Factor

The cost of employing a chip design engineer in Asia is much lower than in the US, typically only 10–12 per cent of the cost in Silicon Valley, as shown in Table C.1.

But this is not only for the pull factor; demand factors are equally important. TNCs need to locate design near the rapidly growing Asian markets for communications, computing, and digital consumer equipment in order to interact with the lead users of new products. China is already the world's largest market for telecom equipment (wired and wireless) as well as a critical test bed for the third-(3G) and next-generation wireless communication systems. It is also among the most demanding markets for computing and digital consumer equipment. As most of the equipment is produced in China, the country has become the world's third largest market for semiconductors, generating substantial demand for chip design.

Table C.1 Annual cost of employing a chip design engineer, 2002

Location	Annual cost (in US$)
US (Silicon Valley)	300000
Canada	150000
Ireland	75000
Republic of Korea	<65000
Taiwan Province of China	<60000
India	30000
China (Shanghai)	28000
China (Suzhou)	24000

Source: Based on World Investment Report 2005: Transnational Corporations and the Internationalization of R&D, New York and Geneva: UNCTAD, United Nations, 2005, p. 174.

---

[1] Based on World Investment Report 2005: Transnational Corporations and the Internationalization of R&D, New York and Geneva: UNCTAD, United Nations, 2005, pp. 173–76.

Policy Factor

Policies cover a wide range of factors such as incentives, regulations, infrastructure, and education—all designed to attract R&D and other MNE innovative activities, including chip design, to particular locations.

Policies have played a powerful catalytic role in building the critical infrastructure, supporting industries, and design capabilities that allowed firms in Asian countries to invest in and upgrade chip design. The progress in chip design has owed much to concerted efforts by both governments and leading companies to establish new sources of innovation and global standards. In telecommunications, the four leading players in the Republic of Korea (Samsung, SK Telecom, KT, LG) are all trying to become major platforms and content developers for complex technology systems, especially in mobile communications. These efforts build on considerable capabilities accumulated in public research labs (like the Electronics and Telecommunications Research Institute), as well as in R&D labs of the Chaebol, to develop complex systems. China's attempt to develop an alternative 3G digital wireless standard has created a powerful incentive to expand the Asian electronic design activities. Thus, government procurement has been a powerful tool in driving innovation.

Push Factors

A number of factors in developed countries are also greatly contributing to pushing firms to expand chip design in Asia. Three such push factors can be distinguished, as below.

Changes in Design Methodology and Organization

Since the mid-1990s, growing pressures to improve design productivity, combined with increasingly demanding performance features of electronic systems, have produced turmoil in chip-design methodology. The so-called 'systems-on-chip design' combines 'modular design' and design automation to move design from the individual component on a printed circuit board closer to 'system-level integration' on a chip (Martin and Chang 2003). A key driver behind these changes has been a widening productivity gap between design and fabrication.

Chip design is also becoming increasingly complex.

- Progress in manufacturing technology ('miniaturization') has made it possible to fabricate million of transistors on a single chip. This increased complexity needs to be matched by a dramatic improvement in design productivity.

- The convergence of digital computing, communication, and consumer devices has raised the requirements for essential features of electronic systems—they need to become lighter, thinner, shorter, smaller, faster, and cheaper, as well as more multifunctional and less power-consuming. These features are expected to continue to improve.

- Companies are forced to speed-up time-to-market as product life cycles have been reduced to only a few months for some products. Time compression is, therefore, the key in designing chips for systems.

These changes in methodology have increased complexity at two levels of chip design, i.e., one on the chip ('silicon') and the other on the 'systems'. With growing design complexity, verifying at an early stage whether the design can be used to produce chips at acceptable yield and performance has become critical. Some 60–70 per cent of all system-on-chip hardware design time now goes into verification, leaving only 30–40 per cent for actual device development. This has inflated the cost of design. For instance, the overall development cost for complex system-on-chip design can be as high as US$100 million, a cost level few design companies and chip users can afford.

More Outsourcing and Multiple Design Interfaces

Until the mid-1980s, system companies and integrated device makers manufactured almost all their chip designs in-house. Since then system-on-chip design has fostered vertical specialization in project execution, enabling firms to disintegrate the design value chain and disperse it geographically. This has given rise to complex, multi-layered global design networks with variable configurations, depending on the needs of a specific project. Until the early 1990s, design networks retained a relatively simple structure. Over time, however, vertical specialization increased the number and variety of network participants, business models and design interfaces, bringing together design teams from companies that drastically differed in size, market power, location, and nationality.

A possible network might be comprised of the following players:

- A Chinese system company for the definition of the system architecture
- An electronic manufacturing supplier from the Taiwan Province of China
- A US integrated device manufacturer
- A European 'silicon intellectual property' firm
- Design houses from the US and Taiwan Province of China
- Foundries from Taiwan Province of China, Singapore, and China
- Chip packaging companies from China
- Tool vendors of design automation and testing from the US and India
- Design support service providers from various Asian locations

Vertical specialization within design networks has transformed the structure and the competitive dynamics of the global semiconductor industry. It has also increased the organizational complexity of the networks. A typical system-on-chip design team now needs to manage at least six types of design interfaces with system designers, silicon intellectual property providers, software developers, verification teams, electronic design automation tool vendors, and foundry services (fabrication). These design communities are rarely located in the same place, which makes coordination difficult. As design teams become larger and geographically dispersed, more formal interfaces are necessary for effective communication between them.

With product life cycles often as short as a few months, system design requirements keep changing rapidly. Communication problems between hardware and software designers are particularly serious. Hence, proximity and face-to-face contact become critical: global design networks increasingly need to locate in Asia those chip design stages that closely interface with local companies in mobile communications and digital consumer electronics. As most of the world's leading chip contract

manufacturers ('foundries') are in Asia, this creates powerful pressures to locate important stages of chip design in this region. New processes and changes in design methodology require closer interaction between designers and process engineers.

Changing Skills Requirements

Geographic proximity (in the established centres of excellence in the US or Europe) has sometimes been a disadvantage for design projects that require a large number of contributors with diverse knowledge sets and capabilities. For the MNEs involved in chip design, it has become costly to bring together a large group of diverse design communities in one location and keep them there. This is another reason for MNEs to offshore chip design to Asia.

Meanwhile, skill requirements and work organization are growing in importance as push factors. Some MNEs interviewed expressed concern that the supply of scientists and engineers in the US and Europe is inadequate. As noted above, some Asian governments have pursued policies that increase the availability of well-educated engineers, scientists, and managers. Engineers in some Asian countries are trained to use the latest tools and methodologies, and the main electronics exporting countries in Asia have also set up training institutions dedicated to chip design. These efforts are especially advanced in India and East Asia.

The expansion of chip design in Asia appears also to have been influenced by a perceived inflexibility on the part of design engineers in the US and Europe to adapt to a more structured ('automated') work organization (termed 'innovation factory'). MNEs have likewise sought to lower design costs by increasing the workloads and capping the design engineers' salaries, which rose rapidly during the boom of the 1990s. Cost considerations clearly favour design work in Asia.

Enabling Factors

Finally, new ICTs facilitate the internationalization of chip design. Coordinating specialized design networks in Asia vertically can involve high communication costs because of geographical distance combined with differences in levels of development and economic institutions (labour markets, education systems, corporate governance, legal and regulatory systems as well as IPR protection). New ICT-enhanced information management has helped reduce such costs, codify knowledge, enable remote control, and allow more knowledge to be shared via audio-visual media.

A second enabling factor is the spread of 'transnational knowledge communities', such as professional peer group networks, along with Asia's large diaspora of skilled migrants and 'IT mercenaries'. These networks help share complex design knowledge and provide experience and links with markets and financial institutions.

India: The Emerging Global R&D Hub

India's innovation basket is all set to swell, as it continues to be a hot R&D destination for companies large and small. The country is drawing 25 per cent of fresh global investments in R&D centres. Further, many of these centres set up by multinationals are among their largest R&D units outside the US or Europe. In the past few years, over 200 global companies across IT/telecom, biotechnology, chemicals, automobiles, consumer goods, and pharmaceuticals have set up their R&D hubs in India. In many cases, such as Oracle, Intel, Adobe, STMicroelectronics (STM), SAP and others, the India R&D centre is their largest facility outside the US or Europe.

Others, including IBM, Texas Instruments, Delphi, HP, Microsoft, GE, Philips, Motorola, Google, Cisco, Eli Lilly, Bayer, Siemens, and LG Electronics, have been tapping Indian talent for conducting cutting-edge research.

The value of R&D work done in India is also set to get a boost with new centres being set up in the country. The value of R&D work done in India is estimated to touch US$27.5 billion by 2010 (against US$8.5 billion in 2005), throwing up an additional manpower requirement of 2,94,000 researchers between 2006 and 2010 and another 3,00,000 professionals between 2011 and 2015.

Meanwhile, the companies that are already here are betting big on India. For instance, SAP Labs India is SAP's largest development facility outside Germany. Similarly, GE's R&D centre in Bangalore is its second largest centre. Philip's second campus in India is its largest research centre outside Eindhoven.

Adobe Systems has 900 people in its India R&D operations—the highest number outside the US. Chipmaker Intel has 3,000 staff in India, the majority in its R&D unit. Some of Intel India R&D's recent contributions include complete design of the Centrino mobile chip called Napa.

STM has built a state-of-the-art design campus in Greater Noida, near Delhi, which, when fully developed, will have 5,000 engineers. The company has earmarked US$30 million in investments over the next two years. India's contribution in the sphere of R&D to STM's worldwide operations is phenomenal and the success is reflected in the fact that ST India is today the company's largest advanced R&D design centre outside Europe. It is likely to get a boost in future as global majors are lining up major investments in India.[2]

Questions

1. Examine various factors critically that led to shift of chip designing industry from its traditional centres, such as the US, the UK, and Japan to Asian countries.

2. Critically evaluate the emergence of the chip design industry to India and other Asian countries on the basis of the following theories:

   (a) Theory of comparative advantage
   (b) Factor endowment theory
   (c) Country similarity theory
   (d) The new trade theory
   (e) International product life-cycle theory
   (f) Theory of competitive advantage

3. In your opinion, which of the trade theory/ theories is/are most appropriate to explain the shift of chip designing to India and other Asian countries? Give reasons to justify your answer.

[2] Pande, Bhanu, Shelley Singh, and Moumita Bakshi Chatterjee, 'Tech Hub India Draws 25% of Global R&D Funds', *The Economic Times*, 2 November 2006.

3

International Trade Patterns and Balance of Payments

LEARNING OBJECTIVES

> To explain the significance of international trade patterns
> To provide an overview of world trade
> To evaluate India's international trade
> To outline the concept of terms of trade
> To explicate balance of payments
> To highlight the key issues in India's foreign trade

3.1 INTRODUCTION

The patterns of international trade facilitate in developing an overview about the types of products traded and the countries involved in trade. The shifts in trade patterns and their causes provide insights into the upheavals in the economic environment and trade policies of nations. The macroeconomic factors in the trading countries as well as the overall world economic environment influence the international flow of goods and services. Thus, past international trade patterns reveal vital information about the macroeconomic environment and its changes. Besides, they provide a basic framework for country selection and evaluation for international business.

International trade in India is traceable to 3000 BC, since the Indus Valley period. Indian goods reached the markets of Mesopotamia, Egypt, Persia, and other parts of South East Asia (Exhibit 3.1). The Silk Road from Xian to Rome was connected to the eastern and western markets for regular trade and commerce. Over the years, trade grew multifold, became global in nature, and got much more complex than earlier. Strides in science and technology, especially in transport and communication, contributed to its rapid growth.

This chapter provides an overview of world trade and evaluates the trade patterns. About 30 economically advanced countries, consisting of only 15.3 per cent of the world's population, contribute to 52 per cent of world's GDP and account for 67.7 per cent of world's export of goods and services whereas 143 developing countries with 84.7 per cent of the world's population contribute to 48 per cent of world's GDP and account for 32.9 per cent of the world's export of goods and services.[1]

World trade grew at almost double the rate compared to world output during the last decade (1997–2007), as depicted in Fig. 3.1. Real merchandise exports were estimated to have grown by 5.5 per cent in 2007, almost three percentage points less than in 2006 but still close to the average rate of trade expansion over the last decade (1997–2007). The growth of real trade exceeded the real output growth by 2 percentage

---

Exhibit 3.1   The glorious history of India's international trade

India has a glorious history of international trade stretching as far back as 3000 BC during the Indus valley period. Manufactures from the Indus cities reached even the markets on the Tigris and Euphrates. Conversely, a few Sumerian devices in art, Mesopotamia toilet sets, and a cylinder seal were copied on the Indus. Trade was not confined to raw materials and luxury articles; fish, regularly imported from the Arabian Sea coasts, augmented the food supplies of Mohenjo Daro, as mentioned by Gordon Childe.[a] In the later centuries too, trade flourished not only in the country itself, but between India and foreign countries. About the fifth century BC, there was a colony of Indian merchants living at Memphis in Egypt, as revealed by the discovery of the modelled heads of Indians. Probably there was trade also between India and the islands of South East Asia. During the Buddhist period in India, exports from India included silks, muslins, the finer sorts of cloth, cutlery and armour, brocades, embroideries and rugs, perfumes and drugs, ivory and ivory work, and jewellery and gold (seldom silver).

Throughout the first millennium of the Christian era, India's trade was widespread and Indian merchants controlled many foreign markets. Indian trade was dominant in the eastern seas and it reached out also to the Mediterranean. Pepper and other spices went from India or via India to the West, often on Indian and Chinese boats; it is said that Alaric the Goth took away 3000 pounds of pepper to Rome. Roman writers bemoaned the fact that gold flowed from Rome to India and the east in exchange for various luxury articles.

This trade was largely, in India as elsewhere at the time, one of the give and take of materials found and developed locally. India was a fertile land and rich in some of the materials that other countries lacked, and the seas being open to her, she sent these materials abroad. It also obtained them from the eastern islands and profited as a merchant carrier. But India had further advantages. India had been manufacturing cloth from the earliest ages, long before other countries did so, and a textile industry had developed. Indian textiles went to far countries. Silk was also made from very early times though probably it was not nearly as good as Chinese silk, which began to be imported as early as the fourth century BC. The Indian silk industry may have developed subsequently. An important advance was made in the dyeing of cloth and special methods were discovered for the preparation of fast dyes. Among these was indigo, a word derived from India through Greece. It was probably this knowledge of dying that gave a great impetus to India's trade with foreign countries.

[a] Gordon Childe, *What Happened in History,* Pelican Books, New York, 1943, pp. 112.

Source: Adapted from Jawahar Lal Nehru, *The Discovery of India,* The Signet Press, Calcutta, 1946.

---

[1] *World Economic Outlook,* International Monetary Fund, Washington DC, October 2007, p. 209.

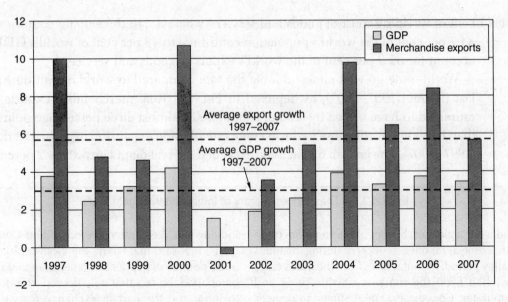

Fig. 3.1 Growth of world merchandise trade vis-à-vis GDP

Source: World Trade 2007: Prospects for 2008, press release, April 2008, World Trade Organization, Geneva, 2008, p. 6.

points. This reflects the increasing significance of international trade. This chapter examines the world trade patterns both for merchandise and commercial services.

India's exports grew remarkably in value terms from US$1.269 billion in 1950–51 to US$126.4 billion in 2006–07 but its share in the world exports declined considerably from 2.53 per cent in 1947 to 0.42 per cent in 1980. However, it rose gradually to 1 per cent by 2007.

As a proportion of GDP, on balance of payment (BoP) basis, India's exports consistently grew from 5.8 per cent in 1990–91 to 14 per cent in 2006–07, whereas the corresponding rise in imports was from 8.8 per cent in 1990–91 to 20.9 per cent in 2006–07 (Table 3.1). Trade deficits as a proportion of GDP, which had declined from 3 per cent in 1990–91 to 2.1 per cent in 2002–03, widened to 6.9 per cent in 2006–07. In 2004–05 and 2005–06, India's imports increased rapidly and the trade deficit widened sharply, primarily due to the higher outgo on the import of petroleum products and the steep increase in its international prices. It is estimated that an oil price increase of US$10 per barrel results in a deterioration of the trade balance of the oil importing developing countries by 1.2 per cent of GDP. India's import cover of foreign exchange reserves increased from 2.5 months in 1990–91 to 16.9 months in 2003–04 but subsequently declined to 12.5 months in 2006–07.

This chapter elucidates the patterns of India's international trade and evaluates the reasons for changes therein. The gains from international trade can be assessed by using the terms of trade, which have also been explained towards the later part of the chapter. BoP, which reflects the summary of all economic transactions of the country during the specified period, has also been dealt with.

Table 3.1   Selected indicators of India's external sector

	1990–91	2000–01	2001–02	2002–03	2003–04	2004–05	2005–06	2006–07	2007–08[a]
1. Growth of exports as a % of BoP	9.0	21.1	−1.6	20.3	23.3	28.5	23.4	21.8	19.9
2. Growth of imports as a % of BoP	14.4	4.6	−2.8	14.5	24.1	48.6	32.1	21.8	21.9
3. Exports/imports as a % of BoP	66.2	78.5	79.4	83.4	82.9	71.7	67.0	67.0	63.5
4. Import cover of FER (no. of months)	2.5	8.8	11.5	14.2	16.9	14.3	11.6	12.5	12.8
5. External assistance (net)/ TC (%)	26.2	4.8	13.4	−29.4	−16.5	6.7	6.8	3.8	1.4
6. ECB (net)/(TC) (%)	26.8	50.6	−19.0	−15.9	−16.9	18.1	10.1	34.8	20.6
7. NR deposits/TC (%)	18.3	27.2	33.0	28.0	21.0	−3.4	11.2	9.3	−0.2
As per cent of GDP at current market prices									
8. Exports	5.8	9.9	9.4	10.6	11.0	12.2	13.0	14.0	
9. Imports	8.8	12.6	11.8	12.7	13.3	17.1	19.4	20.9	
10. Trade balance	−3.0	−2.7	−2.4	−2.1	−2.3	−4.8	−6.4	−6.9	
11. Invisible balance	−0.1	2.1	3.1	3.4	4.6	4.5	5.2	5.8	
12. Current account balance	−3.1	−0.6	0.7	1.2	2.3	−0.4	−1.2	−1.1	
13. External debt	28.7	22.5	21.1	20.3	17.8	18.5	17.2	17.9	

[a] Data from April to September 2007.

Notes:
- TC—Total capital flows (net).
- ECB—External commercial borrowing.
- FER—Foreign exchange reserves, including gold, SDRs, and IMF reserve tranche.
- As total capital flows are netted after taking into account some capital outflows, the ratios against item nos. 5, 6, and 7 may, in some years, add up to more than hundred per cent.
- Rupee equivalents of BoP components are used to arrive at GDP ratios. All other percentages shown in the upper panel of the table are based on US dollar volumes.

Source: Economic Survey 2007–08, Ministry of Finance, Government of India, p. 112.

3.2   WORLD TRADE: AN OVERVIEW

World trade has grown considerably over the years. The world merchandise exports grew from US$59 billion in 1948 to US$13.57 trillion[2] in 2007, and imports grew from US$62 billion to US$13.94 trillion during the same period. The exports of services

---

[2] World Trade Report 2008, WTO, Geneva, p. 11.

grew more rapidly compared to merchandise exports from US$390.8 billion in 1980 to US$3.26 trillion in 2007 whereas during the same period, imports rose from US$431.8 billion in 1980 to US$3.06 trillion in 2007.

A cross-country comparison of the share of world merchandise exports (Table 3.2) reveals that the share of the US in the world merchandise exports significantly fell down from 21.7 per cent in 1948 to 8.6 per cent in 2007 whereas the share of the UK declined from 11.4 per cent in 1948 to 3.2 per cent in 2007 (Fig. 3.2). The share of Japan and China increased significantly from 0.4 per cent and 0.9 per cent in 1948 to 5.3 per cent and 9.0 per cent, respectively, in 2007. While the share of Asian countries

Table 3.2 Cross-country comparison of share in world merchandise exports (in percentage)

	1948	1953	1963	1973	1983	1993	2003	2006	2007
World	100.0	100.0	100.0	100.0	100.0	100.0	100.0	100.0	100.0
North America	28.3	24.9	19.9	17.3	16.8	18.0	15.8	14.2	13.6
US	21.7	18.8	14.9	12.3	11.2	12.6	9.8	8.8	8.5
Canada	5.5	5.2	4.1	4.3	4.2	4.0	3.7	3.3	3.1
Mexico	1.0	0.7	0.6	0.4	1.4	1.4	2.2	2.1	2.0
South and Central America	12.3	10.5	7.0	4.7	4.4	3.0	3.0	3.6	3.7
Brazil	2.0	1.8	0.9	1.1	1.2	1.0	1.0	1.2	1.2
Argentina	2.8	1.3	0.9	0.6	0.4	0.4	0.4	0.4	0.4
Europe	31.5	34.9	41.4	45.4	43.5	45.4	45.9	42.1	42.4
Germany[a]	1.4	5.3	9.8	12.5	9.2	10.3	10.2	9.4	9.7
France	3.5	4.8	5.1	6.1	5.2	6.0	5.3	4.2	4.1
UK	11.4	9.0	7.6	5.2	5.0	4.9	4.1	3.8	3.2
Italy	1.9	1.8	3.2	3.8	4.0	4.6	4.1	3.5	3.6
Commonwealth of Independent States (CIS)[b]	–	–	–	–	–	1.5	2.6	3.6	3.7
Africa	7.3	6.5	5.7	4.8	4.5	2.5	2.4	3.1	3.1
South Africa[c]	2.0	1.7	1.5	1.0	1.0	0.7	0.5	0.5	0.5
Middle East	2.0	2.7	3.2	4.1	6.8	3.5	4.1	5.5	5.6
Asia	13.6	13.1	12.4	14.9	19.1	26.1	26.2	27.8	27.9
China	0.9	1.2	1.3	1.0	1.2	2.5	5.9	8.2	8.9
Japan	0.4	1.5	3.5	6.4	8.0	9.9	6.4	5.5	5.2
India	2.2	1.3	1.0	0.5	0.5	0.6	0.8	1.0	1.1
Australia and New Zealand	3.7	3.2	2.4	2.1	1.4	1.5	1.2	1.2	1.2
Six East Asian traders	3.0	2.7	2.4	3.4	5.8	9.7	9.6	9.6	9.3

[a] Figures refer to the Fed. Rep. of Germany from 1948 through 1983.

[b] Figures are significantly affected by changes in the country composition of the region and major adjustment in trade conversion factors between 1983 between 1993.

[c] Beginning with 1998, figures refer to South Africa only and no longer to the Southern African Customs Union.

Note: Between 1973 and 1983 and between 1993 and 2003 export and import shares were significantly influenced by oil price developments.

Source: International Trade Statistics 2007, WTO, Geneva, p. 10.

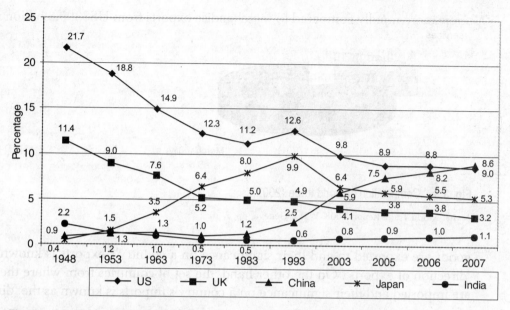

Fig. 3.2 Cross-country comparison of share in world merchandise exports

Source: Based on data from International Trade Statistics 2007, WTO, p. 10 and World Trade Report 2008, p. 11.

such as China and Japan grew remarkably in the world merchandise exports, India's share in world trade declined from 2.2 per cent in 1948 to 1 per cent by 1963 and further to 0.5 per cent in 1973. In 1980, the erosion was lowest at 0.42 per cent. However, it subsequently increased sluggishly to a 1.1 per cent share of world trade in 2007.

World merchandise exports in dollar terms rose by 11 per cent to US$11.76 trillion during 2000–06 whereas commercial services export during the same period rose by 10 per cent to US$2.71 trillion.[3] Inflation contributed to about 40 per cent of the value change in 2006 of the merchandise exports.

The commercial services with US$3.26 trillion accounted for 19.4 per cent whereas the merchandise exports with US$13.57 trillion in 2007 accounted for 80.6 per cent of world trade, as indicated in Fig. 3.3.

The review of world merchandise trade by leading exporters and importers reconfirms the importance of price developments and the outstanding trade performance of China and India. Since 2000, China has more than doubled its share in world merchandise exports.

3.2.1 Direction of World Trade

The direction of trade is often referred to describe the statistical analysis of the set of a country's trading partners and their significance in trade. The set of countries where the

---

[3] 'Risks lie ahead following stronger trade in 2006, WTO Reports', World Trade Reports, 2006 and 2007, WTO, Geneva, p. 6.

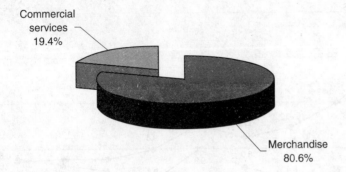

Commercial
services
19.4%

Merchandise
80.6%

Fig. 3.3 Composition of world trade (2007)

Source: World Trade Report 2008, WTO, Geneva, pp. 7–10.

goods are exported to and their significance on a country's exports is known as the 'direction of exports'. On the other hand, the set of countries from where the goods are imported and their significance on a country's imports is known as the 'direction of imports'.

There has been a considerable change in the direction of world merchandise exports over the years, as indicated in Fig. 3.4. The developed economies have traditionally dominated the world exports with 66.39 per cent share in 1980, which increased to 72.34 per cent in 1990 but subsequently declined gradually to 58.62 per cent by 2007 (Table 3.3). Developing economies that accounted for 29.41 per cent share in world

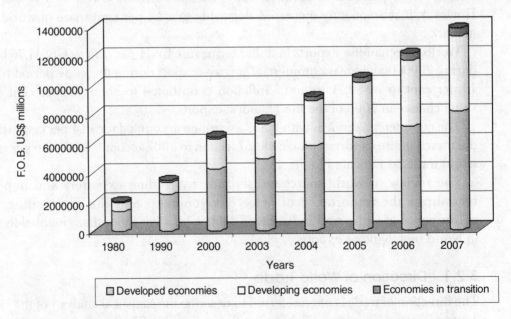

Fig. 3.4 Direction of world exports

Source: UNCTAD Handbook of Statistics 2008, United Nations, New York and Geneva, pp. 2–3.

Table 3.3   Direction of world exports

(F.O.B. US$ millions)

Year	Developed economies	Developing economies	Economies in transition	World
1980	1349154	597574	85426	2032154
1990	2516978	843904	118709	3479591
2000	4245074	2056407	154507	6455988
2003	4914115	2426752	206692	7547559
2004	5803521	3097429	282017	9182967
2005	6339799	3775908	359164	10474871
2006	7132590	4505697	449482	12087769
2007	8109330	5190026	533684	13833041

Source: *UNCTAD Handbook of Statistics 2008*, United Nations, New York and Geneva, pp. 2–3.

exports in 1980 declined to 24.25 per cent in 1990, grew to 31.85 per cent in 2000, and further increased to 37.52 per cent in 2007. The share of economies in transition in world exports fell from 4.20 per cent in 1980 to 3.41 per cent in 1990 and 2.39 per cent in 2000. However, it subsequently increased to 3.14 per cent in 2007.

The exports of developed economies increased by 86.56 per cent during 1980–90 whereas it increased by 41.22 per cent for developing economies during this period. However, exports from developing economies rose remarkably by 143.7 per cent during 1990–2000 and 152.38 per cent during 2000–07, compared to 68.66 per cent and 91.03 per cent, respectively, from developed economies. The exports from the economies in transition grew merely by 38.96 per cent during 1980–90, but declined to 30.16 per cent during 1990–2000. However, the economies in transition exhibited a further remarkable jump to 180.69 per cent during 2000–07, making it the region with the highest export growth.

A regionwise comparison indicates that the share of North America in world merchandise exports declined significantly from 28.3 per cent in 1948 to 14.2 per cent in 2006 whereas the share of South and Central America fell from 12.3 per cent in 1948 to 3.6 per cent in 2006 and the share of Africa dropped from 7.3 per cent in 1948 to 3.1 per cent in 2006 (Table 3.2). On the other hand, the share of Europe in world merchandise exports increased from 31.5 per cent in 1948 to 42.1 per cent in 2006, the share of the Middle East rose from 2 per cent to 5.5 per cent, and that of Asia grew from 13.6 per cent to 27.8 per cent during the same period.

Regions with the highest share of fuels and other mining products in their merchandise exports, such as the Middle East (70%), Africa (65%), the CIS (60%), and South/Central America (37%) recorded the highest increase in their exports in 2006. Out of the total world merchandise exports of US$13.57 trillions in 2007, Europe with US$5.76 trillion exports accounted for 42.5 per cent in 2007 followed by Asia with US$3.79 trillion (28.0%), North America with US$1.85 trillion (13.7%),

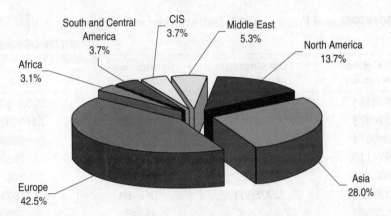

Fig. 3.5   Direction of world merchandise exports (2007)

Source: World Trade Report 2008, WTO, Geneva, p. 11.

Middle East with US$721 billion (5.3%), CIS with US$508 billion (3.7%), South and Central America with US$496 billion (3.7%), and Africa with US$422 billion (3.1%), as depicted in Fig. 3.5. In 2007, Europe with US$6.05 trillion accounted for 43.4 per cent of world merchandise imports worth US$13.94 trillion (Fig. 3.6), followed by Asia with US$3.52 trillion (25.3%), North America with US$2.70 trillion (19.4%), Middle East with US$462 billion (3.3%), South and Central America with US$455 billion (3.3%), CIS with US$377 billion (2.7%), and Africa with US$355 billion (2.6%).

Germany ranked as the leading exporter in 2007 with US$1.32 trillion accounting for 9.5 per cent share of world exports, followed by China (8.8%), the US (8.4%), Japan (5.1%), and France (4.0%), as given in Table 3.5.

The US remained the single largest importer with US$2.01 trillion, accounting for 14.2 per cent share of world imports, followed by Germany (7.5%), China (6.7%),

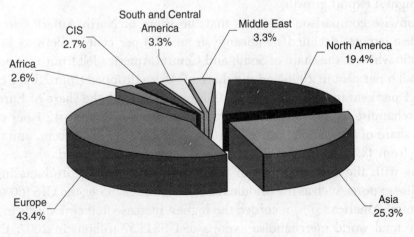

Fig. 3.6   Direction of world merchandise imports (2007)

Source: World Trade Report 2008, WTO, Geneva, p. 11.

Japan (4.4%), UK (4.3%), and France (4.3%). India ranked at 26th position with US$145 billion, accounting for 1.0 per cent share in exports of world merchandise trade whereas it ranked at 18th with US$217 billion with 1.5 per cent share in merchandise imports in 2007. The analysis provided in Exhibit 3.2 indicates that China and India are likely to dominate world trade in the future. Moderate and sluggish export value growth of less than 10 per cent was reported by Japan (9%), France (6%), Spain (7%), and Ireland (3%) during the period 2006. The merchandise imports (Table 3.5) of these countries also expanded far less rapidly than the world average. It is noteworthy that the ten leading exporters comprise the same countries as the group of the top ten leading importers, although the annual variation of trade differed markedly between the leading traders.

Exhibit 3.2 Chindia to dominate world trade

Since the early nineties, the economic performance of China and India, also referred to as Chindia, has been impressive. The average annual growth from 1990 to 2004 in real GDP and real GDP per capita was 9.31 per cent and 8.24 per cent for China and 5.71 per cent and 3.09 per cent for India. China's share in the world trade increased from a meagre 1 per cent in the early nineties to 8.2 per cent in 2006 whereas India's share grew from 0.5 per cent to about 1 per cent during the same period. Although the share of Chindia in global output and trade still lags behind their combined share of world population, this trend is expected to reverse in the future.

China's share in total imports to the top three markets of the world, i.e., the US, Japan, and Europe, has increased remarkably during the last two decades (Table 3.4). However, the share of imports from India declined in both Europe and Japan, although it increased slightly in the US. China's increasing presence in top markets has strengthened the fears of many developing countries that China's trade dominance is directly responsible for crowding out their exports and is at their expense. The various factors that contribute to the growth of Chinese exports include lower labour costs, infrastructure, flexible labour markets, and conducive government policies. Besides, the structure of China's trade is changing towards medium high technology and skill-intensive products and its reliance on labour-intensive products is gradually decreasing. The continuation of this trend has significant implications for developing countries, which currently face tough competition from China in third markets in labour-intensive products.

Table 3.4 Share of imports from China and India in total imports (per cent)

From	China			India		
To	US	Europe	Japan	US	Europe	Japan
1980–84	0.819	0.969	3.843	0.644	1.496	0.807
1985–89	1.756	2.119	4.998	0.674	1.714	0.973
1990–94	4.731	1.949	7.405	0.737	1.227	0.918
1995–99	7.294	1.537	12.330	0.856	0.539	0.793
2000–04	11.051	3.349	17.975	0.986	0.510	0.618

Source: World Economic Outlook, April 2006 and previous issues, Washington DC: International Monetary Fund.

Contd

Exhibit 3.2 Contd

The increase in the significance of the most populous countries' economies in the world has caused concerns about their growth and trade prospects and implications for other countries. The trade growth of China and India is likely to influence the world trade in the following ways.

Complimentarity effect—The growth of exports to Chindia from the rest of the world due to increased demand in Chindia

Competitiveness effect—Increased competition from Chindia for exports in third markets

Domestic competitive effect—Increased competition with Chindia in the domestic markets

Multiplier effect—Increased imports of Chindia that may have a multiplier effect and lead to growth in demand for imports in the economies exporting to Chindia

Spill-over effect—Benefit to neighbouring countries and trade partners of Chindia due to economic and technological spill-overs

Chinese exports have also led to crowd out exports of other Asian countries. This is especially true for consumer goods produced by less developed Asian countries but necessarily for capital goods produced by the more advanced Asian economies. Since China's income elasticity of import demand is the highest for capital goods, therefore, advanced Asian countries specializing in capital goods are likely to benefit from China's rapid economic boom.

China exports almost all types of manufactured products and has achieved impressive success in goods requiring high labour and high capital intensity. Whereas, India's leading sectors are of a high labour intensity and low capital intensity.

Source: World Economic Outlook, April 2006 and previous issues, International Monetary Fund, Washington DC; Qureshi, Mahvash Saeed and Guanghua Wan, 'Trade Expansion of China and India: Threat or Opportunity?' presented at Conference on Emergence of Large Developing Countries (BICS) and Implications for International Development, New Delhi, 28–29 June 2007; Wilson, Dominic and Roopa Purushothaman, 'Dreaming with BRICs: The Path to 2050', *Global Economics,* Paper No. 99, London: Goldman Sachs, 2003.

3.2.2 Composition of World Merchandise Trade

The statistical analysis of a country's product groups in its international trade is often referred to as the 'composition of trade'. This can be carried out for the trade with all the countries in the world collectively or individually, with a group of countries, or a particular country. Such analysis carried out for product groups exported is known as the 'composition of exports' whereas the analysis carried out for product groups imported is known as the 'composition of imports'.

There has been a significant shift in the composition of world merchandise exports over the last four decades, as shown in Fig. 3.7. Food exports that accounted for 18.2 per cent of the world merchandise exports in 1965 declined to 6.7 per cent in 2000 and 6.2 per cent in 2006 (Table 3.6). Agricultural raw material that constituted 7.8 per cent of world merchandise export in 1965 declined to 1.9 per cent by 2000 and 1.5 per cent in 2006. The share of ores, metals, and precious stones in world merchandise exports declined from 12 per cent in 1965 to 5.5 per cent in 2006, whereas the export of fuels

Table 3.5 Leading exporters and importers in world merchandise trade, 2007

Rank	Exporters	Value (billion dollars)	Share (percentage)	Rank	Importers	Value (billion dollars)	Share (percentage)
1	Germany	1327	9.5	1	US	2017	14.2
2	China	1218	8.8	2	Germany	1059	7.5
3	US	1163	8.4	3	China	956	6.7
4	Japan	713	5.1	4	Japan	621	4.4
5	France	552	4.0	5	UK	617	4.3
6	Netherlands	551	4.0	6	France	613	4.3
7	Italy	492	3.5	7	Italy	505	3.6
8	UK	436	3.1	8	Netherlands	491	3.5
9	Belgium	432	3.1	9	Belgium	416	2.9
10	Canada	418	3.0	10	Canada	390	2.7
11	Korea, Republic	372	2.7	11	Spain	374	2.6
12	Russia	355	2.6	12	Hong Kong, China	371	2.6
					retained imports[a]	96	0.7
13	Hong Kong (China)	350	2.5	13	Korea, Republic of	357	2.5
	domestic exports[a]	19	0.1				
	re-exports[a]	331	2.4				
14	Singapore	299	2.2	14	Mexico	297	2.1
	domestic exports	156	1.1				
	re-exports	143	1.0				
15	Mexico	272	2.0	15	Singapore	263	1.9
					retained imports[b]	120	1.1
16	Taipei, Chinese	246	1.8	16	Russia[c]	223	1.6
17	Spain	242	1.7	17	Taipei, Chinese	220	1.5
18	Saudi Arabia[a]	229	1.6	18	India	217	1.5
19	Malaysia	176	1.3	19	Turkey	170	1.2
20	Switzerland	172	1.2	20	Australia	165	1.2
21	Sweden	168	1.2	21	Austria	162	1.1
22	Austria	162	1.2	22	Poland	161	1.1
23	Brazil	161	1.2	23	Switzerland	161	1.1
24	United Arab Emirates[a]	154	1.1	24	Sweden	150	1.1
25	Thailand	152	1.1	25	Malaysia	147	1.0
26	India	145	1.0	26	Thailand	141	1.0
27	Australia	141	1.0	27	Brazil	127	0.9
28	Norway	139	1.0	28	United Arab Emirates[a]	121	0.9
29	Poland	138	1.0	29	Czech Republic	118	0.8
30	Czech Republic	122	0.9	30	Denmark	99	0.7
	Total of above[d]	**11497**	**82.7**		**Total of above[d]**	**11726**	**82.5**
	World[d]	**13900**	**100.0**		**World[d]**	**14200**	**100.0**

[a] Secretariat estimates.
[b] Singapore's retained imports are defined as imports less re-exports.
[c] Imports are valued f.o.b.
[d] Includes significant re-exports or imports for re-exports.

Source: World Trade 2007: Prospects for 2008, WTO press release, April 2008, p. 18.

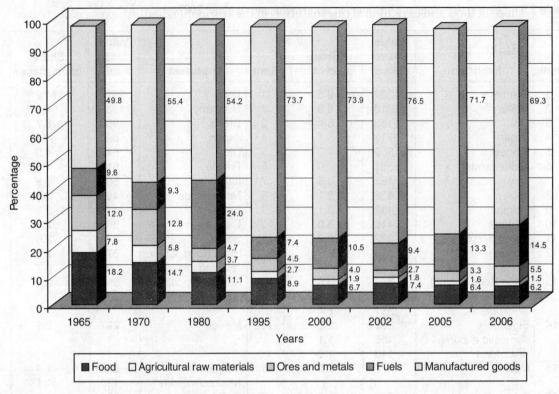

Fig. 3.7   Patterns of world merchandise exports

Source: UNCTAD Handbook of Statistics 2008, United Nations, New York and Geneva, p. 72 and previous editions.

grew from 9.6 per cent in 1965 to 24 per cent in 1980, but subsequently declined to 14.5 per cent by 2006. Manufactured goods have shown a gradual rise from 49.8 per cent in 1965 to 76.5 per cent in 2006.

During recent years, weak and stagnating prices of food, agricultural raw materials, and manufactured goods contrasted with a further steep rise in prices for metals and fuels. The share of fuels increased to 13.3 per cent in 2005. On the other hand, the

Table 3.6   Patterns of world merchandise exports

(percentage distribution)

	1965	1970	1980	1995	2000	2002	2005	2006
Food items	18.2	14.7	11.1	8.9	6.7	7.4	6.4	6.2
Agricultural raw materials	7.8	5.8	3.7	2.7	1.9	1.8	1.6	1.5
Ores, metals, and precious stones	12.0	12.8	4.7	4.5	4.0	2.7	3.3	5.5
Fuels	9.6	9.3	24.0	7.4	10.5	9.4	13.3	14.5
Manufactured goods	49.8	55.4	54.2	73.7	73.9	76.5	71.7	69.3

Source: UNCTAD Handbook of Statistics 2008, United Nations, New York and Geneva, p. 72 and previous editions.

share of food and agricultural raw materials in the world merchandise exports decreased to a historic record low of 8 per cent in 2005. Although recent oil price developments played a major role in the further relative decline of agricultural products in world merchandise exports, they only accentuated an existing long-term downward trend.[4] The share of agricultural products in the world merchandise exports has decreased steadily over the last six years from more than 40 per cent in the early 1950s to 10 per cent in the late 1990s, as both volume and price trends have been less favourable than for other merchandise products. Despite the decline in the share of agricultural products in world exports, the export value of agricultural products in world trade has increased thirty-folds between 1950 and 2005.

During the 1990s, the export value of electronic goods rose an average by 12 per cent or two times faster than all other manufactured goods. Among the manufactured goods, it is estimated that the largest value increases during recent years were for iron and steel products, as well as for chemicals. Although, there was a recovery in the global demand for computers and other electronic products, the growth rate of their trade value was less than that of manufactured goods.

Fuels with exports worth US$1.8 trillion, as given in Table 3.7, accounted for 17.2 per cent of world merchandise exports in 2006, followed by office and telecommunication equipments (14.1%), other machinery (14.0%), automotive products (9.8%), agricultural products (9.2%), other chemicals (9.1%), other semi manufactures (7.7%), iron and steel (3.6%), clothing (3.0%), pharmaceuticals (3.0%), scientific and control instruments (2.3%), textiles (2.1%), and ores and minerals (1.9%), as shown in Fig. 3.8.

Table 3.7   World merchandise exports by product group, 2006

Products	Value (US$ billions)
Fuels	1771
Ores & minerals	201
Iron & steel	374
Non-ferrous metals	306
Other chemicals	937
Scientific and controlling instruments	240
Office & telecom equipment	1451
Other semi manufactures	795
Pharmaceuticals	311
Other machinery	1448
Agricultural products	945
Automotive products	1015
Clothing	311
Textiles	219

Source: International Trade Statistics 2007, WTO, Geneva, p. 37.

---

[4] World Trade Report 2006, Geneva, WTO, p. 7.

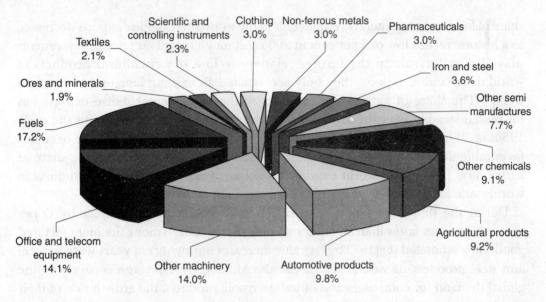

Fig. 3.8   Composition of world merchandise exports (2006)

Source: International Trade Statistics 2007, WTO, Geneva, p. 37.

The growth in share of manufactures in total exports has a significant impact on the overall export. The gradual shift towards manufacturing has led to rapid export growth where the share of manufactured exports was already large.

Developing countries derived 70 per cent of the merchandise export revenue from the sales of primary commodities—agriculture and energy—two decades ago, whereas presently 80 per cent of the revenue comes from the export of manufactured goods. Developing countries now rely less on the shipments of primary commodities than on manufactured goods. Even exports from sub-Saharan Africa are no longer resource based. The share of manufactures in African exports has risen from 25 per cent during the late 1970s to 67 per cent in 2006.

3.2.3 World Commercial Services Trade

The world commercial services exports rose by 21 per cent to US$3.26 trillion in 2007. Since the commercial services data are derived from BoP statistics, it does not include the sales of majority-owned foreign affiliates abroad. The expansion rate of global services trade has remained largely consistent during the last six years. 'Other commercial services', which includes software, education, health financial services, etc., has been the fastest growing category at 12 per cent growth in the world exports of commercial services trade. Asia's commercial services exports continued to expand faster than the global average for the third consecutive year in 2006 and also faster than the region's services imports, thereby reducing the region's deficit and service trade. India continues to excel in its services trade expansion.

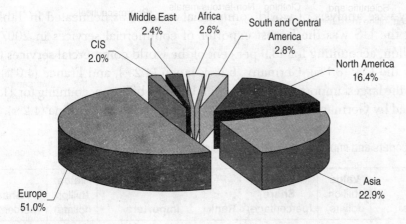

Fig. 3.9 Direction of world commercial services exports (2007)

Source: World Trade Report 2008, WTO, Geneva, p. 12.

3.2.4 Direction of World Commercial Services Trade

In 2007, Europe with US$1.66 trillion accounted for 51 per cent of total world commercial services exports (Fig. 3.9) worth US$3.26 trillion, followed by Asia with US$745 billion (22.9%), North America with US$533 billion (16.4%), South and Central America with US$91 billion (2.8%), Africa with US$84 billion (2.6%), Middle East with US$79 billion (2.4%), and CIS with US$64 billion (2.0%).

Europe also ranked as the highest importer of world commercial services with US$1.43 trillion (46.8%), followed by Asia with US$778 billion (25.4%), North America with US$440 billion (14.4%), Middle East with US$125 billion (4.1%), Africa and South Central America with US$97 billion (3.2%), and CIS with US$90 billion (2.9%) of the total import of world commercial services (Fig. 3.10) worth US$3.06 trillion in 2007.

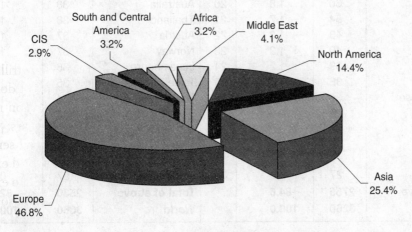

Fig. 3.10 Direction of world commercial services imports (2007)

Source: World Trade Report 2008, WTO, Geneva, p. 12.

A country-wise analysis of world commercial services as delineated in Table 3.8 reveals that the US was the largest exporter of commercial services in 2007 with US$454 billion, accounting for 13.9 per cent of the world commercial services trade, followed by the UK (8.1%), Germany (6.1%), Japan (4.2%), and France (4.0%). The US was also the largest importer of services with US$336 billion, accounting for 11.0 per cent, followed by Germany (8.0%), UK (6.3 %), Japan (5.1%), and China (4.2%). India

Table 3.8   Leading exporters and importers in world commercial services trade, 2007

Rank	Exporters	Value (billion dollars)	Share (percentage)	Rank	Importers	Value (billion dollars)	Share (percentage)
1	US	454	13.9	1	US	336	11.0
2	UK	263	8.1	2	Germany	245	8.0
3	Germany	197	6.1	3	UK	193	6.3
4	Japan	136	4.2	4	Japan	157	5.1
5	France	130	4.0	5	China	129	4.2
6	Spain	127	3.9	6	France	120	3.9
7	China	127	3.9	7	Italy	117	3.8
8	Italy	109	3.3	8	Spain	97	3.2
9	Netherlands	91	2.8	9	Ireland	93	3.0
10	Ireland	87	2.7	10	Netherlands	89	2.9
11	India	86	2.7	11	Korea, Republic of	85	2.8
12	Hong Kong (China)	82	2.5	12	Canada	80	2.6
13	Belgium	73	2.2	13	India	78	2.6
14	Singapore	66	2.0	14	Singapore	70	2.3
15	Korea, Republic of	64	2.0	15	Belgium	66	2.2
16	Sweden	63	1.9	16	Russia	57	1.9
17	Denmark	62	1.9	17	Denmark	56	1.8
18	Canada	61	1.9	18	Sweden	48	1.6
19	Switzerland	61	1.9	19	Hong Kong (China)	40	1.3
20	Luxembourg	60	1.8	20	Australia	38	1.2
21	Austria	54	1.7	21	Thailand	38	1.2
22	Greece	43	1.3	22	Austria	37	1.2
23	Australia	40	1.2	23	Norway	37	1.2
24	Norway	39	1.2	24	Luxembourg	36	1.2
25	Russia	38	1.2	25	Taipei, Chineese	35	1.2
26	Taipei, Chinese	30	0.9	26	Brazil	34	1.1
27	Thailand	28	0.9	27	Switzerland	33	1.1
28	Poland	28	0.9	28	Indonesia [a]	32	1.0
29	Malaysia	28	0.9	29	United Arab Emirates [a]	28	0.9
30	Turkey	27	0.8	30	Malaysia	27	0.9
	Total of above	**2755**	**84.6**		**Total of above**	**2530**	**82.7**
	World	**3260**	**100.0**		**World**	**3060**	**100.0**

[a] Secretariat estimates.

Source: World Trade 2007: Prospects for 2008, WTO press release, April 2008, p. 18.

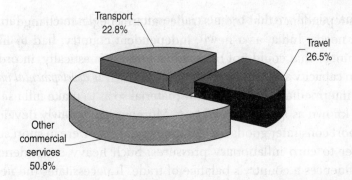

Fig. 3.11 Composition of world exports of commercial services (2007)

Source: World Trade Report 2008, WTO, Geneva, p. 9.

ranked at 11th position with US$86 billion, accounting for 2.7 per cent share in export of world commercial services whereas it ranked 13th with US$78 billion with 2.6 per cent share in services imports in 2007.

3.2.5 Composition of World Commercial Services Trade

The category-wise break-up of commercial services of exports in Fig. 3.11 indicates that travel accounted for US$862 billion (26.5%), transport for US$742 billion (22.8%), and other commercial services for US$1653 billion (50.8%). It is interesting to note that other commercial services are not only the largest category but also the fastest growing category. During 2000–06, the world trade of commercial services grew at the rate of 10 per cent, wherein transport increased by 10 per cent, travel by 7 per cent, and other commercial services rose by 12 per cent.

3.3 INDIA'S FOREIGN TRADE: AN OVERVIEW

India's foreign trade was largely determined by the strategic needs of the British colonial powers prior to its independence in 1947. Like other colonies, India too was a supplier of raw materials and agricultural commodities to Britain and other industrial countries and it used to import the manufactured goods from Britain. The dependence of colonial India on Britain for manufactured goods hindered the process of industrialization and obliterated the indigenous handicraft and cottage industries.

As a part of the British strategy, India had to export more than its imports prior to World War II, so as to meet the unilateral transfer of payments to Britain by way of the salaries and pensions of the British officers, both military and civil, dividends on British capital invested in India, and interest on sterling loans. This helped India to achieve a favourable trade balance. In April 1946, India was able to build a huge sterling balance of Rs 17.33 billion, even after paying of the sterling debt. However, the share of raw materials in India's exports declined from 45 per cent in 1938–39 to 31 per cent in 1947–48 whereas the share of manufactured goods increased from 30 per cent in 1938–39 to 49 per cent in 1947–48.

It was only after independence that India's trade patterns began to change in view of its developmental needs. India, as a newly independent country, had to import equipment and machinery that could not be manufactured domestically, in order to create new production capacity and build infrastructure, known as *developmental imports.* It also had to import intermediate goods and raw material so as to make full use of its production capacity, known as *maintenance imports.* Moreover, as a newly developing country, it had to import consumer goods such as food grains that were in short supply domestically, in order to curb inflationary pressures. Such heavy dependence on imports adversely influences a country's balance of trade. It necessitates the need to expand exports to finance its imports.

India's exports grew significantly from US$1.269 billion in 1950–51 to US$155.5 billion in 2007–08 whereas imports increased from US$1.273 billion to US$235.9 billion (Fig. 3.12) during the same period (Annexure I). Exports have shown an increase of about 20 per cent during the last four decades, in four phases, i.e., during 1972–77, 1987–90, 1993–96, and 2000–04. However, the exports increased remarkably at 30.8 per cent in 2004–05 and thereafter grew at around 23 per cent till 2007–08. A negative growth in exports was witnessed in the last three decades: in 2001–02, exports declined by 1.6 per cent, in 1998–99 by 5.1 per cent, in 1991–92 by 1.5 per cent, and in 1985–86 by 9.9 per cent. It is also interesting to note that the growth of India's exports has been much lower than that of some of the South East Asian economies whose share in international world trade rapidly increased.

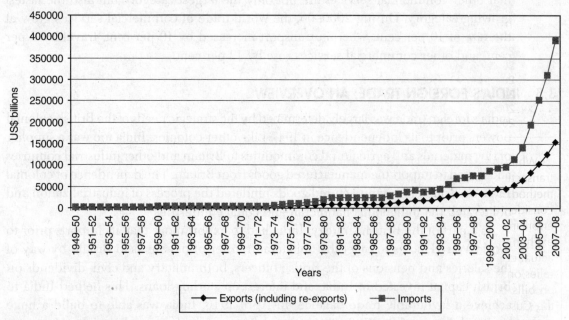

Fig. 3.12   India's foreign trade

Note: For the years 1956–57, 1957–58, 1958–59, and 1959–60, the data are as per the Fourteenth Report of the Estimates Committee (1971–72) of the erstwhile Ministry of Foreign Trade.

Source: Based on DGCI&S data.

Data from the Directorate General of Commercial Intelligence and Statistics (DGCI&S) has been used to carry out the analysis of India's trade patterns in this chapter. Trade data in India is also compiled by the country's central bank, the Reserve Bank of India (RBI). There exists wide divergence in the data compiled by the two government agencies, as explicated in Exhibit 3.3.

India's total external trade, including goods and services, grew to US$433 billion in 2006–07. The trade in services has been growing faster than the merchandise trade,

---

Exhibit 3.3 Divergence in India's trade statistics

Merchandise trade statistics in India is complied by two agencies, i.e., Directorate General of Commercial Intelligence and Statistics (DGCI&S), Kolkata, under the Ministry of Commerce, and the Reserve Bank of India, India's central bank. There is a considerable divergence in the data compiled by the two agencies, which is more pronounced in case of imports compared to exports, as indicated in Table 3.9. The divergence in data between the two agencies increased from US$3,840 million in 1990–91 to US$7,376 million in 2000–01. The gap narrowed down to US$1,853 million in 2003–04, subsequently increased to US$7,827 million in 2005—06, but declined to US$5,553 million in 2006–07.

Table 3.9 Divergence in India's import statistics

(in US$ millions)

Year	RBI data	DGCI&S data	Difference
1990–91	27915	24075	3840
1995–96	43670	36678	6992
2000–01	57912	50536	7376
2001–02	56277	51413	4864
2002–03	64464	61412	3052
2003–04	80003	78150	1853
2004–05	118908	111516	7390
2005–06	156993	149167	7827
2006–07	191300	185747	5553

While the two agencies are recording the same transactions, the scope, time period, definition, method, and coverage of items of trade differ considerably, besides inclusion and exclusion errors in trade items. While RBI relies on foreign exchange release/receipt returns, which are actual cash outgo and cover all flows, DGCI&S relies on customs data, which in turn are based on bills of entries (import document filed with the Customs), which might remain somewhat incomplete for a number of reasons in the short run. Defence imports are not reflected in the DGCI&S data. As such, for a particular time period at any specific date, given the leads and lags in reporting, the two sets of data would never match.

As per the present revision policy of the RBI, data on exports and imports are revised every quarter up to 24 months, while DGCI&S finalise their trade data after 8 months. However, the extent of this level of divergence in the current assumptions makes it difficult for calibrating the policy responses to external sector developments in the short run.

Source: Based on DGCI&S and RBI data; Economic Survey 2006–2007, Government of India, p. 112.

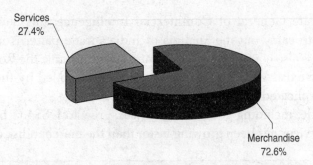

Fig. 3.13   Composition of India's external trade (2006–07)

Source: RBI Monthly Bulletin, Reserve Bank of India, April 2008, p. S 392.

and the share of services in the total external trade increased from 25.8 per cent in 2004–05 to 27.4 per cent in 2006–07 (Fig. 3.13). With a growth of 32 per cent in 2006–07, services trade reached to US$76.2 billion. Services exports constituted almost 60 per cent of merchandise exports in 2006–07.

The robust growth in exports and imports during 2006–07 is attributed mainly to the favourable global demand conditions, increasing competitiveness of India's manufactured products, firming up of commodity prices, and supportive domestic policy measures. In 2005, India was one of the fastest growing exporting countries in the world. Merchandise imports also registered a growth of 29 per cent in 2005–06 despite the previous year's robust growth of 43 per cent due to the sharp increase in oil imports in the wake of the rise in international crude oil prices.

India's goods markets reflected more openness as its merchandise trade as a per cent of GDP increased from about 21 per cent in 2001–02 to approximately 33 per cent in 2005–06. India's imports have grown at a much faster pace than its exports, leading to the widening of trade deficit. The strong growth of the manufacturing and services sector is reflected in its import bill—the share of telecommunications, equipment, office machines, and aircrafts have risen appreciably. Fuel imports remain a major import item accounting for 36.2 per cent of India's total imports in 2006–07.

3.3.1   Direction of India's Trade: Exports

Gradually, reliance of India's exports on the markets of a few countries has reduced considerably. India's over-dependence on the OECD countries, which accounted for 66.1 per cent of India's exports in 1960–61, declined to 41.2 per cent in 2006–07, as shown in Fig. 3.14. Exports to European Union declined from 25.1 per cent in 1987–88 to 20.4 per cent in 2006–07. In 1960–61, the UK was the largest destination for India's exports with 26.9 per cent share, which declined to 6.55 per cent by 1987–88, and further dropped to 4.39 per cent in 2006–07. The decline in US's share in India's exports was from 16 per cent in 1960–61 to 11.1 per cent in 1980–81, but the increase to 14.9 per cent made US the single largest destination for India's exports. India's exports to Japan have witnessed considerable fluctuations from 5.5 per cent in

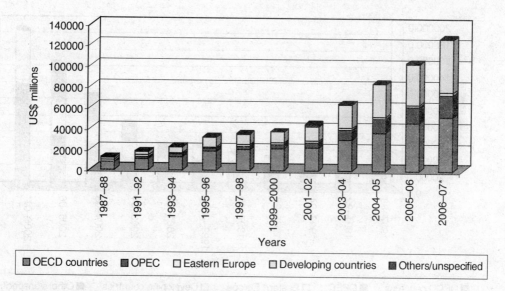

Fig. 3.14   Direction of India's trade: Exports

* Provisional.

Source: Based on DGCI&S data.

1960–61 to 13.3 per cent in 1970–71, which dropped down to 2.23 per cent in 2006–07. OPEC has emerged as an important export destination for India, from 1.4 per cent share in 1960–61 to 16.4 per cent share in 2006–07. India's share to Russia, which increased remarkably from 4.5 per cent in 1960–61 to 18.3 per cent in 1980–81, sharply declined from 16.1 per cent in 1990–91, following the break up of the USSR, to 3.3 per cent in 1995–96. This further reached the all-time low of 0.72 per cent in 2006–07. India's export share to developing countries remarkably increased from 14.2 per cent in 1987–88 to 40.1 per cent in 2006–07. India's exports to SAARC jumped from 2.6 per cent in 1987–88 to 4.98 per cent in 2006–07. Besides, its exports to China increased remarkably from a negligible 0.1 per cent in 1990–91 to 6.56 per cent in 2006–07. Moreover, India's exports to Africa also grew from 2 per cent in 1987–88 to 7.02 per cent in 2006–07 (Annexure II).

3.3.2   Direction of India's Trade: Imports

Over the years, there has also been a significant change in value terms in the direction of India's imports. India's dependence on OECD countries for imports substantially declined from 78 per cent in 1960–61 to 59.8 per cent in 1987–88, which further declined to 36.5 per cent in 2006–07 (Fig. 3.15). India's imports from European Union, which accounted for 33.3 per cent in 1987–88, declined to 17.5 per cent in 2006–07. In 1960–61, the UK accounted for 19.4 per cent of India's imports, which remarkably declined to 8.2 per cent by 1987–88 and came down to a meagre 2.19 per cent by 2006–07.

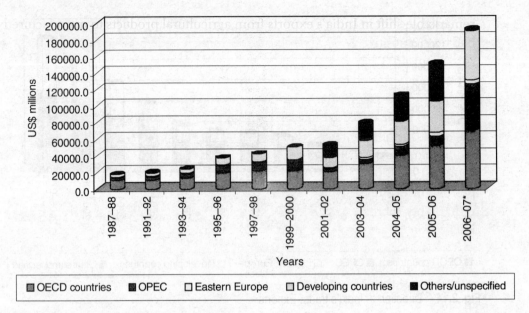

Fig. 3.15   Direction of India's trade: Imports

* Provisional.
Source: Based on DGCI&S data.

Moreover, the share of India's imports from North America also declined significantly from 31 per cent in 1960–61 to 10.3 per cent by 1987–88, which further reduced to 7.41 per cent in 2006–07, mainly because of a substantial decline in the share of imports from US from 29.2 per cent in 1960–61 to 6.61 per cent in 2006–07. The US still remains the single largest exporting country to India. The increase in the share of OPEC in India's imports jumped from 4.6 per cent in 1960–61 to its peak of 27.8 per cent in 1980–81 due to the rise in India's oil bill. However, this subsequently declined to 5.3 per cent in 2000–01 but remarkably grew later to 29.43 per cent in 2006–07, primarily due to the rise in oil prices. India's imports from developing countries grew remarkably from 17.3 per cent in 1987–88 to 31.27 per cent in 2006–07. The share of Asia in India's imports steeply rose from 12.1 per cent in 1987–88 to 24.78 per cent in 2006–07 mainly because of the increased imports from other Asian developing countries, especially China, whose share in India's imports jumped from 0.7 per cent in 1987–88 to 9.13 per cent in 2006–07. The share of India's imports from Africa also increased from 2.9 per cent in 1987–88 to 3.57 per cent in 2006–07. The share of other countries, which was almost negligible until 1999–2000, jumped to 31 per cent in 2001–02, which reveals increased diversification in India's imports (Annexure III). However, this share plummeted to 0.44 per cent in 2006–07.

3.3.3   Composition of India's Trade: Exports

Over the last five decades, the composition of India's exports has become more broad-based with visibly decreased dependency on any one product category. Moreover, a remarkable shift in India's exports from agricultural products to manufactured goods had been a positive move. The share of manufactured goods in India's exports steadily rose from 45.3 per cent in 1960–61 to 80.7 per cent in 1999–2000. However, it subsequently started declining steadily and reached to about 68.6 per cent in 2006–07 (Fig. 3.16). Among the manufactured goods, gems and jewellery, which accounted a meagre 0.1 per cent in 1960–61, increased remarkably to a 20.4 per cent in 1999–2000 but further declined to about 12.6 per cent in 2006–07. Besides, the share of readymade garments also grew remarkably from 0.1 per cent in 1960–61 to 12.9 per cent in 1999–00 but considerably declined to 7.0 per cent in 2006–07. Crude and petroleum products, which hardly had any exports of 0.1 per cent till 1999–2000, remarkably increased to about 15.0 per cent in 2006–07, mainly due to the higher international prices and the increased domestic refining capacity (Annexures IV and V).

The exports of agricultural and allied products that comprised a significant 44.2 per cent share in 1960–61 declined to 31.7 per cent in 1970–71. It further declined significantly to 15.2 per cent in 1999–2000 and subsequently to 10.3 per cent in 2006–07. The share of jute and jute products sharply dropped from 21 per cent in 1960–61 to 0.31 per cent in 2002–03 and thereafter became insignificant in India's export basket.

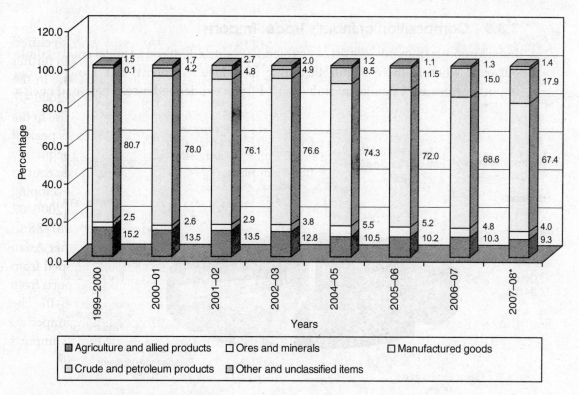

Fig. 3.16   Composition of India's trade export

* April–September 2007–08.

Source: Based on DGCI&S data.

The composition of exports of manufactured goods from India in 2006–07 consisted of gems and jewellery (18.4%), readymade garments (10.2%), machinery and instruments (7.7%), drugs, pharmaceuticals, and fine chemicals (6.9%), manufacturer of metals (5.8%), transport equipment (5.7%), primary and semi-finished iron and steel (5.1%), cotton yarn, fabrics, and made ups (4.8%), electronic goods (3.4%), dyes, intermediates, and coal tar chemicals (2.6%), leather and manufacturers (2.3%), handicrafts (1.6%), leather footwear (1.2%), and others (24.3%), as depicted in (Fig. 3.17). India's exports of agricultural and allied products include marine products (13.6%), raw cotton (10.7%), oil meals (9.7%), fruits and vegetables (7.8%), spices (5.8%), cashewnuts (3.9%), coffee and tea (2.9%), unmanufactured tobacco (1.9%), cereals (1.0%), and others (39.8%), as shown in Fig. 3.18.

An analysis of the share of major exports of India in world exports as given in Table 3.10 reveals that India has more than 10 per cent share of the world market in case of lac, gums, resins, etc., carpets and textiles, and floor coverings and silk. India's share in cotton declined from 6.6 per cent in 2000 to 5.4 per cent in 2006 whereas the share of coffee, tea, and spices declined from 5.8 per cent in 2000 to 3.7 per cent in 2005. India's share in world exports in ores, slag, and ash increased remarkably from 1.9 per cent in 2000 to 6.8 per cent in 2006.

3.3.5 Composition of India's Trade: Imports

India's imports primarily consist of petroleum products, fertilizers, capital goods, edible oils, etc., wherein there is little flexibility to reduce its imports bill. However, the imports witnessed a significant shift (Fig. 3.19) since independence. There had been a

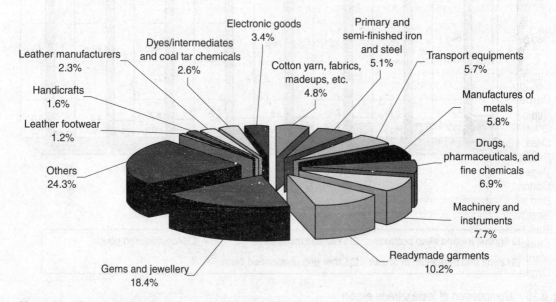

Fig. 3.17 Composition of India's exports of manufactured goods (2006–07)

Source: Based on DGCI&S data.

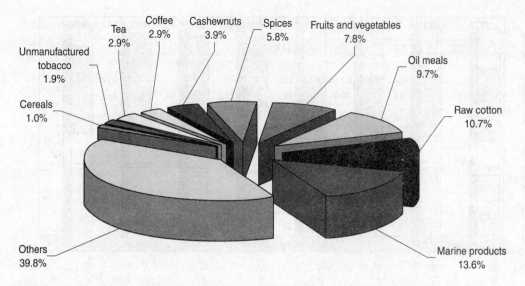

Fig. 3.18 Composition of India's exports of agricultural and allied products (2006–07)

Source: Based on DGCI&S data.

significant growth in India's import of petroleum products from 6.1 per cent in 1960–61 to about 30.8 per cent in 2006–07 due to the over all economic growth in the country, rise in petroleum prices, and limited indigenous exploration and refining (Annexure VI). The fertilizers accounted for 1.1 per cent of India's total imports in 1960–61, increased with India's green revolution to 5.2 per cent in 1970–71

Table 3.10 Share of India's major exports in world exports

Product	2002	2005	2006
Lac, gums, resins, vegetable saps, and extracts	10.0	11.4	11.3
Carpets and other textile floor coverings	7.3	9.6	11.1
Silk	12.9	12.3	10.2
Other textile articles, sets, worn clothing, etc.	6.1	7.1	6.8
Ores, slag, and ash	4.1	6.4	6.8
Pearls, precious stones, metals, coins, etc.	7.6	8.2	6.4
Vegetable plaiting materials, vegetable products	3.9	5.7	6.4
Cotton	5.9	6.3	5.4
Bird skin, feathers, artificial flowers, human hair	2.0	3.7	3.8
Residues, waste of food industry, animal fodder	1.4	3.8	3.0
Raw hides and skins (other than fur) and leather	2.2	2.4	2.8
Stone, plaster, cement, asbestos, mica, etc., articles	2.0	2.3	2.8
Manufactures of plaiting material, basketwork, etc.	0.3	0.1	2.0
Organic chemicals	1.3	1.8	1.9
Footwear, gaiters, and the like, parts thereof	1.3	1.6	1.8
Zinc and articles thereof	0.2	0.5	1.7

Source: Economic Survey 2007–08, Ministry of Finance, Government of India, New Delhi, p. 142.

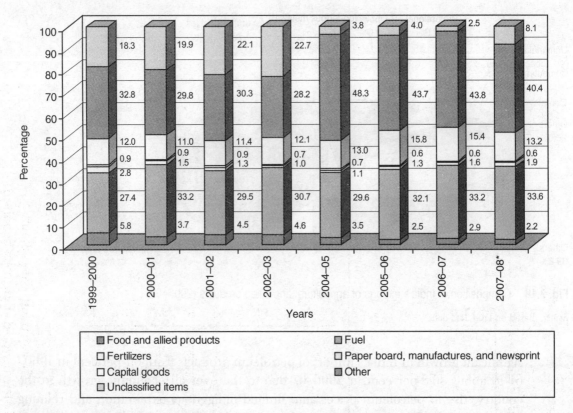

Fig. 3.19 Composition of India's imports

* April–September 2007–08.

Source: Based on DGCI&S data.

(Annexure VII) and remained around 5 per cent by 1989–90. However, its import came down to 1.6 per cent in 2006–07 as a result of India's remarkable progress in fertilizer production.

The share of cereal imports came down from 16.1 per cent in 1960–61 to 0.8 per cent in 1980–81. India became a net exporter of food grains, a fact that highlights the success story of the green revolution in India. However, the growing demands due to the rising population pressure and the vagaries of rain keep creating the need to import food grains from time to time. Due to the greater rise in the demand for edible oils as compared to production, India's dependency on edible oils increased remarkably as reflected by their import growth from 0.3 per cent in 1960–61 to 5.4 per cent in 1980–81. Subsequently, as a result of the comprehensive strategic measures taken to increase oilseed production, the import share declined to 0.6 per cent in 1989–90. However, it further increased to 3.7 per cent in 1999–2000, but declined later to 1.1 per cent in 2006–07 (Annexure VII). As India evolved its own capacity for manufacturing capital goods, its import share of capital goods declined substantially from 31.7 per cent in 1960–61 to 15.4 per cent in 2006–07.

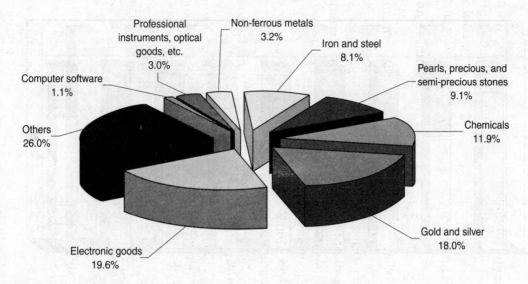

Fig. 3.20   Composition of India's imports: Other products (2006–07)

Source: Based on DGCI&S data.

The other product categories in India's imports, as depicted in Fig. 3.20, include electronic goods (19.6%), gold and silver (18.0%), chemicals (11.9%), pearls and precious and semi-precious stones (9.1%), iron and steel (8.0%), non-ferrous metals (3.2%), professional instruments, optical goods, etc. (3.0%), computer software (1.1%), and others (26.0%) in 2006–07.

3.3.6 India's Services Trade

The services sector in India has grown remarkably and accounts for over 55 per cent of India's GDP, making it the most significant component of the country's economy.[5] India's services exports[6] have significantly grown from a meagre US$295 million in 1970–71 to US$76.2 billion in 2006–07, with a growth of 32.1 per cent over the previous year.

India's services trade surplus as a percentage of GDP increased from 0.7 per cent in 2001–02 to 2.8 per cent in 2005–06 due to the surge in IT exports. There had been considerable growth in transport, travel, and other services, such as telecommunications, financial, construction, and legal. The exports of these services were matched by corresponding imports. Therefore, the software services were mainly responsible for the surplus in services trade.

Over the years, the composition of services exports from India has undergone considerable change. Transportation accounted for 49.7 per cent in 1970–71 of India's total services exports declined to 10.8 per cent in 2007–08 (Fig. 3.21 and Table 3.11).

[5] Monthly Economic Report, January 2008, Department of Economic Affairs, Ministry of Finance, 8(1)/Ec. Dn./2008, pp. 1–6.
[6] *RBI Monthly Bulletin,* April 2008, p. S 392.

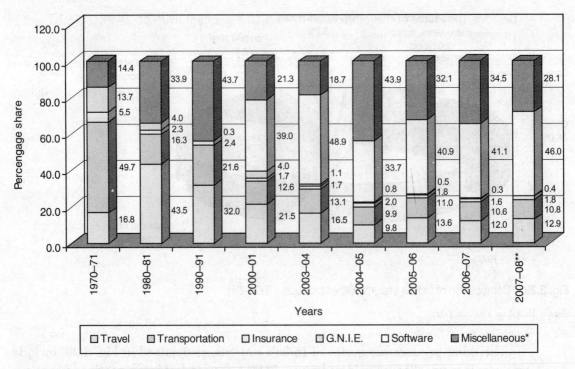

Fig. 3.21 Composition of India's services exports

* Excluding software services.

** Provisional.

Source: Economic Survey 2007–08, Government of India, New Delhi, p. 122.

Table 3.11 Composition of India's services exports

	Amount (US$ million)	Percentage share in total services exports					
		Travel	Transportation	Insurance	G.N.I.E.	Software	Miscellaneous[a]
1970–71	292	16.8	49.7	5.5	13.7	0.0	14.4
1980–81	2804	43.5	16.3	2.3	4.0	0.0	33.9
1990–91	4551	32.0	21.6	2.4	0.3	0.0	43.7
2000–01	16268	21.5	12.6	1.7	4.0	39.0	21.3
2003–04	24949	16.5	13.1	1.7	1.1	48.9	18.7
2004–05	51326	9.8	9.9	2.0	0.8	33.7	43.9
2005–06	57659	13.6	11.0	1.8	0.5	40.9	32.1
2006–07	76181	12.0	10.6	1.6	0.3	41.1	34.5
2007–08[b]	87687	12.9	10.8	1.8	0.4	46.0	28.1

[a] Excluding software services

G.N.I.E.: Government not included elsewhere.

[b] Provisional.

Source: Economic Survey 2007–08, Government of India, New Delhi, p. 122 and previous issues; *RBI Monthly Bulletin,* April 2008, p. S 392.

Besides, the share of travel increased from 16.8 per cent in 1970–71 to 43.5 per cent in 1980–81, but declined subsequently to 12.9 per cent in 2007–08. There were hardly any software exports from India till 1990–91, which rapidly became the largest constituent of India's services exports with 48.9 per cent share in 2003–04. However, this declined to 46.0 per cent in 2007–08. The exports of the miscellaneous services category, which comprises of business services, financial services, and commercial services, grew remarkably from 14.4 per cent in 1970–71 to 34.5 per cent in 2006–07, however declined to 28.1 per cent in 2007–08.

An in-depth analysis of services exports from India reveals that the largest services segment, software and IT-enabled services, has graduated to newer services, such as packaged software implementation, systems integration, network infrastructure management, and IT consulting. There remains a huge untapped potential for IT-enabled services.

Under the miscellaneous services segment, India's entertainment industry, with export earnings of about US$230 million annually, is likely to grow by 70–80 per cent over the next five to ten years. It covers film, music, broadcast, television, and live entertainment and is basically an intellectual-property-driven sector with small to large players spread across India. Education process outsourcing (EPO) includes imparting online education, training, and coaching, and other related services through the Internet and has emerged as a significant segment for services exports. India's cost competitiveness as an education service provider (ESP) is reflected by an average billing rate in India of about US$12 per hour compared to US$25 per hour in the US, which is expected to be the largest consumer of EPO. The travel and tourism sector has also shown significant growth in recent years.

3.4 GAINS FROM INTERNATIONAL TRADE

Trade indices are widely-used instruments to measure the benefits derived by a nation from international trade. Trade indices facilitate in assessing the impact of trade volume and/or unit value realization on a country's gains from trade. For instance, without any increase in the quantity of goods imported, the rise in the total value of imports implies only a financial burden for a country. In order to measure gains from international trade, net, gross, and income terms of trade are often used. The terms of trade is a measure of the relative changes in export and import prices of a nation. It reflects the quantity of imports that a given quantity of exports can buy.

The 'terms of trade' of a country are defined as the ratio of the price of its export commodity to the price of its import commodity. In case of a hypothetical assumption of a two-nation world, the export of a country equals its trade partner's imports wherein the terms of trade of a country are equal to the inverse of the terms of trade of its trade partner. Since, in the real world, numerous commodities are traded, the terms of trade of a nation are expressed by the ratio of price index of a country's exports to the price index of its imports. This ratio is usually multiplied by 100 in order to express the terms of trade in percentage. These terms of trade are often referred to as 'commodity' or 'net barter' terms of trade.

The terms of trade are mainly of the three types as given here.

1. *Net terms of trade*   It implies unit value index of exports expressed as a percentage of unit value index of imports.

$$\text{Net value terms of trade } (N) = \frac{\text{Unit value index of exports}}{\text{Unit value index of imports}} * 100$$

$$N = \left(\frac{Px}{Pm}\right) * 100$$

2. *Gross terms of trade*   It implies volume index of imports expressed as a percentage of volume index of exports

$$\text{Gross terms of trade } = \frac{\text{Volume index of imports}}{\text{Volume index of exports}} * 100$$

$$G = \left(\frac{Qm}{Qx}\right) * 100$$

3. *Income terms of trade*   It implies the product of net terms of trade and volume index of exports expressed as a percentage. It reflects a nation's capacity to import.

$$\text{Income terms of trade } = \text{Net terms of trade } * \text{Volume index of exports} * 100$$

$$I = \frac{Px}{Pm} * Qx * 100$$

In addition, single and double factorial terms of trade are also used to make adjustments for productivity changes, as follows.

Single factorial terms of trade   Net barter terms of trade adjusted for changes in productivity of exports

Double factorial terms of trade   Net barter terms of trade adjusted for changes both in productivity of exports and imports

Since developing countries considerably rely upon imported capital goods for their industrialization and development activities, the income terms of trade assume high significance.

3.4.1 Terms of Trade: Developed vs Developing Economies

The measures of trade volume are expressed by the volume indices of exports and imports. The volume indices of exports for developed economies increased by 276.4 per cent from 34 in 1980 to 128 in 2006, whereas it increased at a much higher rate by 579.1 per cent for developing economies from 24 in 1980 to 163 in 2006 (Table 3.12).

Table 3.12   Trade indices: Developed vs developing economies (base year 2000 = 100)

Year	Volume indices				Unit value indices				Terms of trade	
	Developed economies		Developing economies		Developed economies		Developing economies		Developed economies	Developing economies
	Export	Import	Export	Import	Export	Import	Export	Import		
1980	34	34	24	25	88	91	120	103	97	117
1990	52	52	40	41	114	111	103	102	103	101
1995	69	67	63	73	123	117	111	108	105	102
2001	99	100	98	98	98	97	95	97	101	98
2003	105	108	120	118	110	106	98	100	103	98
2005	119	125	149	152	124	122	123	117	102	105
2006	128	132	163	165	130	130	135	126	100	107

Source: UNCTAD Handbook of Statistics, United Nations, New York and Geneva, 2008, pp. 204–12.

Besides, the volume indices of imports also grew by 288.2 per cent from 34 in 1980 to 132 in 2006 for developed economies and by 560 per cent from 25 to 165 for developing economies during the same period.

The unit value indices, which measure the average price realization, indicate a significant improvement in unit value indices of exports for developed economies, rising by 39.8 per cent from 88 in 1980 to 123 in 1995 but significantly declining thereafter (–20.3) to 98 in 2001 whereas showing considerable deterioration (–20.8%) for developing economies from 120 in 1980 to 95 in 2001. However, by 2006, the indices improved by 32.6 per cent to 130 for developed economies and 42.1 per cent to 135 for developing economies. The unit value indices of imports grew considerably (42.8%) from 91 in 1980 to 130 in 2006 for developed economies whereas it increased only by 22.3 per cent from 103 in 1980 to 126 for developing economies[7] during the same period.

The terms of trade for developed economies improved by 3.1 per cent from 97 in 1980 to 100 in 2006, whereas it deteriorated during the same period by 8.55 per cent for developing economies from 117 in 1980 to 107, as shown in Fig. 3.22. This is because the exports basket of most developing countries comprises of agricultural products or raw materials wherein the price rise is much slower compared to that of manufactured goods. Besides, the growth in demand is also much slower compared to industrial goods. Moreover, developing countries generally market primary products as commodities whereas manufactured goods are marketed as branded products. The price realized from commodities in international markets is prone to heavy price fluctuations. In case of such products, any cost-cutting measure used by the producers is passed on to importers. Therefore, a country whose exports are mainly dependent on agricultural commodities and primary goods tends to require more volumes of

---

[7] *UNCTAD Handbook of Statistics 2008*, United Nations, New York and Geneva, pp. 204–12.

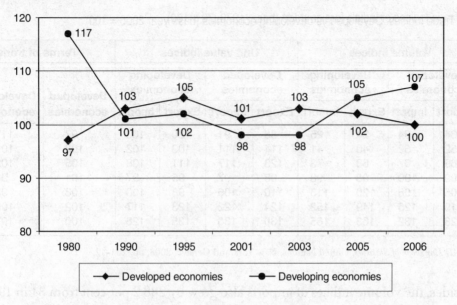

Fig. 3.22 Terms of trade: Developed vs developing economies (base year 2000 = 100)

Source: UNCTAD Handbook of Statistics, United Nations, New York and Geneva, 2008, pp. 204–12.

exports to buy the same amount of finished goods. This explains the inherent problem in lower gains by developing countries compared to developed countries.

The reasons for deterioration in terms of trade for developing countries may be summarized as follows:

- The international demand for export of manufactured goods by developed countries tends to increase at a much faster rate compared to the demand for agricultural commodities and primary goods as the income elasticity of manufactured goods is much higher than that of agricultural commodities and primary goods.
- Any productivity gain in manufactured goods by developed countries is generally passed on to its workers in the form of higher wages and income, whereas any such gains in productivity of agricultural commodities and primary products by developing countries are reflected in price decline. This leads to a consistent deterioration in the collective terms of trade of developing countries.

3.4.2 India's Terms of Trade

The unit value index for imports, as shown in Table 3.13, rose from 35.3 in 1970–71 to 608 in 2006–07 compared to corresponding rise in unit value index of exports from 45 to 863 during the period. It implies that the rise in the value of imports grew much more than the quantity of goods imported, which added to India's financial burden. A detailed analysis of unit value and volume indices reveals that the relative inelasticity of India's import demands for petroleum products, foodgrains, fertilizers, oilseeds, and capital goods constrained India in making any substantial cuts on imports.

Table 3.13 Trade indices of India's foreign trade (base: 1978–79 = 100)

Year	Unit value index		Volume index		Terms of trade		
	Exports	Imports	Exports	Imports	Gross	Net	Income
1970–71	45.0	35.3	59.0	67.2	113.9	127.4	75.2
1978–79	100.0	100.0	100.0	100.0	100.0	100.0	100.0
1980–81	108.5	134.2	108.1	137.9	127.6	80.8	87.3
1990–91	292.5	267.7	194.1	237.7	122.5	109.3	212.2
2000–01	624.3	487.5	571.4	697.7	122.1	128.1	732.0
2003–04	672.4	545.1	764.6	970.4	126.9	123.4	943.5
2004–05	732.0	663.0	899.0	1113.0	124.0	110.0	991.0
2005–06	798.0	592.0	1005.0	1649.0	164.0	135.0	1357.0
2006–07	863.0	608.0	1164.0	2047.0	176.0	142.0	1653.0

Source: DGCI&S, Kolkata; Economic Survey 2007–08, Ministry of Finance, Government of India, pp. A–104.

The volume index of India's exports grew from 59 in 1970–71 to 1164 in 2006–07 considering 1978–79 as the base year, whereas the volume index of imports increased from 67.2 in 1970–71 to 2047 in 2006–07. The gross term of trade improved significantly from 113.9 in 1970–71 to 176 in 2006–07.

Considering 1978–79 as the base year, India's net terms of trade deteriorated (–36.58%) from 127.4 in 1970–71 to 80.8 in 1980–81. This decline was primarily because of a quantum increase in petroleum imports from US$180 million in 1970–71 to US$6656 million in 1980–81. Besides, there has been a steep rise in the import prices of edible oils, fertilizers, and chemicals, but the net terms of trade declined over the subsequent years to 110 in 2004–05. However, it increased considerably to 142 in 2006–07, as shown in Fig. 3.23.

The income terms of trade that measures the import purchasing power of exports improved gradually from 75.2 in 1970–71 during the years, except for 1980–81, and reached to 1653 in 2006–07 on account of the strong growth of exports in volume terms. However, it was adversely affected during 2005–06 by the much higher rise in the unit value price of India's major importables, especially petroleum products, compared to its exportables.

3.5 BALANCE OF PAYMENTS

A country's balance of payments (BoP) is defined as the summary of all its economic transactions that have taken place between the country's residents and the residents of other countries during a specified time period. It is used as an indicator of a country's political and economic stability. A consistently positive BoP reflects more foreign investment and money coming into the country and not much of its currency being exported. On the other hand, adverse or negative BoP indicates more outflows of money compared to inflows. Thus, a surplus or positive BoP implies that a country has more funds from trade and investment coming in compared to what it pays out

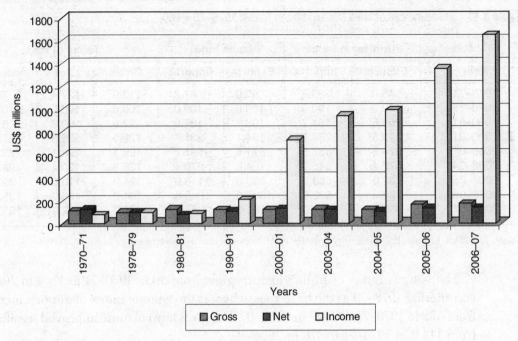

Fig. 3.23 India's terms of trade (base year 1978–79 = 100)

Source: DGCI&S, Kolkata; Economic Survey 2007–08, Ministry of Finance, Government of India, pp. A–104.

to other countries. It has a positive impact on a country's currency appreciation. Conversely, a deficit BoP implies an excess of imports over exports, a dependence on foreign investors, and an overvalued currency. BoP deficits needs to be made up by a country by exporting its hard currency foreign exchange reserves or gold.

The balance of payment is generally computed on a monthly, quarterly, or yearly basis. The balance of payments includes both visible and invisible transactions. The balance of payments reports the country's international performance in trading with other nations and the volume of capital flowing in and out of the country. Balance of payments accounting uses the system of double-entry bookkeeping, which means that every debit or credit in the account is also represented as a credit or debit somewhere else. In a balance-of-payment sheet, currency inflows are recorded as credits (plus sign), whereas outflows are recorded as debits (minus sign). The accounts used for computing balance of payments include the following:

Current account It includes import and export of goods and services and the unilateral transfer of goods and services.

Capital account It includes the transactions that lead to changes in financial assets and liabilities of the country.

Reserve account It includes only the 'reserve assets' of the country. These are the assets that the monetary authority of the country uses to settle the deficits and surpluses that arise when the two categories are taken together.

Since the crisis of 1991, India's BoP has strengthened in the post-reform period. India's current account balance witnessed surpluses from 2001–02 to 2003–04 and exhibited a reverse trend (Table 3.14) since 2004–05 of the current account deficit, along with a burgeoning trade deficit, primarily due to the steep rise in the prices of petroleum products. In spite of large re-payments of India Millennium Deposits (IMD) under external commercial borrowings, India has maintained a strong balance in the capital account even after financing the current account deficit. Foreign investments, both direct and portfolio, and inflow of non-resident deposits had been on the rise. The invisibles (net), comprising non-factor services (such as travel, transportation, software, and business services) for investment income, and transfers have traditionally compensated to a large extent the trade deficit. As a per cent of GDP, India's current account balance improved from a deficit of 3.1 per cent in 1990–91 to a surplus of 2.3 per cent in 2003–04 but declined subsequently to 1.1 per cent in 2005–06. India's invisibles (receipts) grew remarkably from 2.4 per cent of GDP in 1990–91 to 11.5 per cent of GDP in 2005–06.

The current and capital accounts both have witnessed surpluses over the recent years. Most economies in developing Asia, such as Indonesia, Malaysia, the Philippines, and Thailand, have also witnessed surpluses in their current accounts from the later part of the 1990s. The capital account has also continued to strengthen over the last few years. Earlier, the capital account surplus in India's balance of payments used to be partially offset by the current account deficits, leading to lower overall surpluses. However, since 2001–02, surpluses in both the current and capital accounts have resulted in larger overall surpluses, which has led to the accumulation of the foreign exchange reserves of the country.

The balance of payments profile also reveals some interesting trends at a micro level. In recent years, the deficits in the trade account have been more than made up by the large invisibles surpluses sustained by the large inflows of private transfers and non-factor services, resulting in positive current account balances. On the other hand, the growing strength of the capital account has arisen largely from the steady growth in non-debt creating foreign investment inflows. External commercial borrowings and external assistance have been showing net outflows in recent years. The trends indicate that the fast-growing invisibles and non-debt creating foreign investment inflows are the main factors behind the accumulation of foreign exchange reserves.

3.5.1 Balance of Trade

The difference between the value of exports and imports is termed as the balance of trade. India had negative balance of trade over the years except during two financial years, i.e., a positive trade balance of US$134 million in 1972–73 and US$77 million in 1996–97 (Fig. 3.24). Although India's trade deficit grew over the years from US$4 million in 1950–51, it significantly increased after 1995–96. There has been a steep rise in trade deficit from US$5.98 billion in 2000–01 to US$80.39 billion in 2007–08

Table 3.14 Summary of India's balance of payments

(in US$ millions)

	1990–91	2000–01	2001–02	2002–03	2003–04	2004–05	2005–06	2006–07[a]	2007–08[b]
1 Exports	18477	45452	44703	53774	66285	85206	105152	128083	73665
2 Imports	27915	57912	56277	64464	80003	118908	157056	191254	116066
3 Trade balance	–9438	–12460	–11574	–10690	–13718	–33702	–51904	–63171	–42401
4 Invisibles (net)	–242	9794	14974	17035	27801	31232	42002	53405	31688
Non-factor service	980	1692	3324	3643	10144	15426	23170	31180	14689
Income	–3752	–5004	–4206	–3446	–4505	–4979	–5855	–6573	–1444
Pvt. transfers	2069	12854	15398	16387	21608	20525	24493	27941	18420
5 Goods and services balance	–8458	–10768	–8250	–7047	–3574	–18276	–28734	–31361	–27712
6 Current account balance	–9680	–2666	3400	6345	14083	–2470	–9902	–9766	–10713
7 External assistance (net)	2204	410	1117	–3128	–2858	1923	1702	1767	729
8 Commercial borrowing (neta)c	2254	4303	–1585	–1692	–2925	5194	2508	16155	10557
9 Non-resident deposits (net)	1537	2316	2754	2978	3642	–964	2789	4321	–78
10 Foreign investment (net)	103	5862	6686	4161	13744	13000	15528	15541	22214
of which									
(i) FDI (net)	97	3272	4734	3217	2388	3713	3034	8479	3880
(ii) Portfolio	6	2590	1952	944	11356	9287	12494	7062	18334
11 Other flows (net)d	1090	–4356	–615	8321	5735	9476	–180	8967	17727
12 Capital account total (net)	7188	8535	8357	10640	17338	28629	24954	46372	51149
13 Reserve use (– increase)	1278	–5842	–11757	–16985	–31421	–26159	–15052	–36606	–40436

a Partially revised.

b Preliminary (April–September).

c Figures include receipts on account of India Development Bonds in 1991–92, Resurgent Indian Bonds in 1998–99, and India Millennium Deposits in 2000–01 and related repayments, if any, in the subsequent years.

d Include, among others, delayed export receipts and errors and omissions.

Source: Reserve Bank of India.

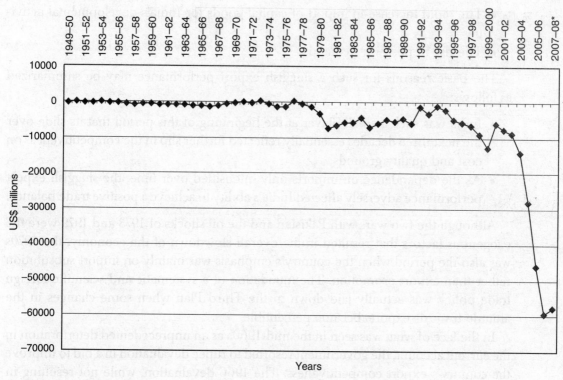

Fig. 3.24   India's trade balance

Source: Based on DGCI&S data.

mainly due to the steep rise in the unit value prices of India's import products, especially petroleum products and fertilizers, besides domestic demand.

3.6   INDIA'S SLUGGISH EXPORT PERFORMANCE: AN EVALUATION

Despite the significant growth in India's exports in value terms from US$1.27 billion in 1950–51 to US$126.3 billion in 2006–07, India's share in world exports declined from 2.2 per cent in 1948 to 0.5 per cent in 1973. Although, it gradually increased to 1 per cent in 2006, the growth achieved by other Asian countries such as China and Japan from 0.9 per cent and 0.4 per cent, respectively, in 1948 to 7.5 per cent and 5.9 per cent is highly impressive. India's export potential could hardly be harnessed optimally.

When India gained freedom in 1947, it accounted for 2.53 per cent of world exports and 2.33 per cent of world imports. As the British Government left to India's credit Rs 17.36 billions worth of sterling balance, the post-independence Government of India was anxious to utilize these balances as early as possible. After independence, the imports grew much rapidly compared to exports, primarily due to

- The scarcity of food grains and basic raw materials such as cotton and jute consequent to partition

- The rapid increase in import of capital goods for India's developmental activities
- The rise in post-war demands

The basic reasons for such a sluggish export performance may be summarized as follows:

- India was such a small player at the beginning of this period that its slide over the next three decades essentially reflected further slip in the competitiveness on cost and quality grounds.
- As the dependence on imports only intensified over time, the sluggish export performance adversely affected India's ability to achieve a positive trade balance.

Although the two wars with Pakistan and the oil shocks of 1973 and 1979 were the exogenous factors that resulted in the overall slowdown of the economy, the 1970s was also the period when the country's emphasis was mainly on import substitution rather than export promotion. The foundation of a systematic and scientific foreign trade policy was actually laid down in the Third Plan when some changes in the attitude towards exports became perceptible.

In the face of what was seen in the mid-1960s as an unprecedented deterioration in the current account, the government resorted to rupee devaluation in a bid to improve the country's export competitiveness. The 1966 devaluation, while not resulting in the expected improvement in trade deficit due to a combination of circumstances, brought out the problems stemming from an overvalued exchange rate. The export growth through the 1960s averaged just 4 per cent in value and volume. The Fourth Plan period stressed on the 'import more and export more' philosophy. The national commitment to exports manifested itself for the first time in the export policy resolution of the 1970s. The resolution aimed at expanding and reorienting export production. The export house scheme was also introduced in the Fourth Plan period. The international market also experienced boom conditions and the Indian export sector was able to take advantage by realizing higher unit values for a wide variety of export items. The emergence of Bangladesh and West Asian markets provided opportunities for trade diversification.

In 1980–81, recognizing the severe strains on the BoP front and the urgent need to expand exports, the government introduced a number of measures aimed at promoting exports. These included enabling the setting up of 100 per cent export-oriented units (EOUs) anywhere in India with facilities similar to those available in the free trade zones (FTZs), the setting up of Exim Bank to handle foreign trade finance, linking supplies of raw materials with export production to ensure timely deliveries, and paying attention on a priority basis to transport problems and bottlenecks inhibiting exports. These measures helped raise India's share in world exports to 0.45 per cent in 1985 and further to 0.53 per cent in 1989. Since 1985, the policy framework was systematically structured to improve the competitiveness of India's exports. India's share in world exports improved from 0.52 per cent in 1990 to 1 per cent in 2006.

3.6.1 Constraints in India's Exports Growth

There remain several bottlenecks that have hindered India's export growth, which are summarized here.

Adoption of import substitution rather than export promotion strategy   India's initial approach to foreign trade can hardly be termed as an 'export promotion' approach. Rather, it was an approach to substitute imports at all costs. Policies were designed so as to protect all those industrial activities that substituted imports resulting into savings in foreign exchange to the exchequer. This led to creeping inefficiency not only in industrial production but also in the implementing government agencies.

Overprotection to Indian industry from external competition   Indian economic policies were designed to encourage domestic production and imports were restrained. Special protection was available to the units in the small-scale sector. A large number of consumer goods could not be produced by the large-scale industrial units. Such over-protection to special segments not only caused production inefficiencies by way of low productivity but also deprived consumers of quality products.

High import barriers   The inward-looking trade policies with long lists of prohibited and restricted items restricted most consumer products from entering the Indian market. One could hardly get imported consumer goods in the open market. Only capital goods, that too generally for export-oriented industrial production, could be imported. Moreover, importers of such capital goods were required to make export commitments to the government. This restrained Indian manufacturing units in their quality upgradation.

High import tariff   The import tariffs in India have been among the highest in the world. Although imports in India were highly restricted till the nineties, even the products that could be imported became uncompetitive in the Indian market due to the high incidence of import tariffs. High import tariffs encouraged those who could manage to make imported goods available without paying customs duty. As a result, with the connivance of officials and politicians, smuggling took the magnitude of a full-fledged industry in India.

Inadequate infrastructure   Infrastructure has been a grey area that has considerably hindered India's economic growth. China's edge in the speedy development of infra-structure is one of the prime causes for its impressive export growth besides the over-all economic development. Infrastructure bottlenecks in India include not only sea ports and airports for cargo handling but also roads, railway, electricity, and telecom-munication. However, the infrastructure situation, especially in telecommunication, has improved remarkably in the last decade.

Complexity of trade procedures   India's trade procedures have been among the most complex in the world, resulting in much longer processing time and higher transaction costs. Prior to 1990, when the Aligned Documentation System was not yet implemented, there was hardly any synchronization among the documents required by the various government agencies. However, rationalization and the electronic processing of trade documents have facilitated international trade considerably.

International trade trends, as explained in this chapter, enable an international business manager at various stages of decision making to assess trade patterns and explore the reasons. This also provides an overview of the macroeconomic changes in the trade and business environment over the years. Gains from international trade can be assessed using trade indices. As brought out in this chapter, the terms of trade for developing countries have considerably deteriorated whereas it has improved for developed countries. The summary of all economic transactions of a country, termed as balance of payments, has strengthened for India in the post-reform period since 1991. India's sluggish performance in exports has been examined and constraints in India's exports growth have also been deliberated. Analysis of international trade trends can be used for country identification, evaluation, and selection. Besides, the trade composition patterns also facilitate decision making, regarding what to export and to which markets.

SUMMARY

The chapter highlights the significance of trade patterns in international business. The world merchandise exports have grown at almost double the rate compared to the world GDP. The shares of manufactured goods have significantly increased from 49.8 per cent in 1965 to 69.3 per cent in 2006, whereas the shares of food, agricultural raw materials, and ores and metals have considerably declined.

The commercial services with US$3.26 trillion accounted for 19.4 per cent whereas world merchandise exports with US$13.57 trillion accounted for 80.6 per cent of world trade in 2007. Transport and travel constitute the major commercial services in the world trade. Germany ranked as the leading exporter with 9.5 per cent share in world merchandise exports, followed by China (8.8%), the US (8.4%), Japan (5.1%), and France (4%) whereas the leading importers include the US (14.2%), Germany (7.5%), China (6.7%), Japan (4.4%), and the UK (4.3%). The US ranked as the leading exporter and importer of world commercial services with 13.9 per cent and 11 per cent share, respectively. Developed economies dominate the world exports with 58.62 per cent share whereas

developing economies account for 37.52 per cent share in 2007.

India's exports grew significantly in value terms but its export share in the world merchandise exports declined from 2.2 per cent in 1948 to 1 per cent in 2006. In contrast, the share of Japan and China increased significantly from 0.4 per cent and 0.9 per cent in 1948 to 5.9 per cent and 7.9 per cent, respectively, in 2006. Exports as a proportion of GDP grew from 5.8 per cent in 1991 to 14.1 per cent in 2006–07, whereas the corresponding rise in imports was from 8.8 per cent to 19.5 per cent. The remarkable reduction in the dependence of India's foreign trade on a few countries or a few products have been a positive development of India's trade patterns. The share of India's exports to OECD countries declined from 66.1 per cent in 1960–61 to 41.2 per cent in 2006–07 whereas India's share to developing countries remarkably increased from 14.2 per cent in 1987–88 to 40.1 per cent in 2006–07.

Moreover, the composition of India's exports has also become broad based. The share of manufactured goods steadily rose from 45.3 per cent in 1960–61 to 80.7 per cent in 1999–2000 but declined to 68.6 per cent in 2006–07. India's major export items include gems and jewellery, readymade garments, crude and petroleum products, machinery and instruments, drugs and pharmaceuticals, and agricultural products whereas its major imports include petroleum products, capital goods, and chemicals. Services exports from India have witnessed a significant growth during the last decade. Software is the largest sector of services exports, but other services such as education, health, and entertainment are also gaining momentum.

Terms of trade is a widely used instrument to measure the benefits a nation derives from exports. There has been deterioration in the terms of trade for developing economies, which reveals their disadvantageous position in gains from international trade. A country's balance of payment is the summary of all economic transactions of a country that have taken place between the country's residents and the residents of other countries during the specified period. The constraints in the growth of India's exports, as summarized in the chapter, include India's adoptation of the import substitution rather than export promotion strategy, overprotection to Indian industry from external competition, high import tariffs and other barriers, inadequate infrastructure, and complexity of trade procedures.

KEY TERMS

Balance of payment All economic transactions between the country's residents and residents of other countries during a specified time period.

Balance of trade Difference between the value of exports and imports of a country.

Capital account Transactions leading to changes in the financial assets and liabilities of a country.

Commercial service exports Total services exports minus exports of government services not included elsewhere.

Composition of exports Product profile of exports.

Composition of imports Product profile of imports.

Current account Includes imports and exports of goods and services and unilateral transfer of goods and services.

Direction of exports County's profile of export destinations.

Direction of imports Country's profile for sourcing imports.

Gross terms of trade Volume index of imports expressed as a percentage of volume index of exports.

Income terms of trade Product of net terms of trade and volume index of exports expressed as a percentage.

Merchandise exports f.o.b. (free on board) value of goods exported to the rest of the world.

Merchandise imports c.i.f. (cost, insurance, and freight) value of goods purchased from the rest of the world.

Net terms of trade Unit value index of exports expressed as a percentage of unit value index of imports.

Reserve account Includes only 'reserve assets' of the country.

CONCEPT REVIEW QUESTIONS

1. In view of the higher average growth of world merchandise exports compared to the average GDP growth, assess the significance of international trade.

2. Explain the terms 'composition' and 'direction' of trade. Critically evaluate the changes in the composition and direction of world exports.

3. Critically evaluate India's foreign trade since independence and identify constraints for its sluggish performance.

4. Explain the concept of terms of trade and its significance in assessing gains from international trade. Examine India's terms of trade since independence.

5. Briefly explain the concept of balance of payments. Examine India's balance of payments since its economic liberalization in 1991.

CRITICAL THINKING QUESTIONS

1. Compile export and import data for India from various sources. Data from sources such as Directorate General of Commercial Intelligence and Trade Statistics (DGCI&S), Reserve Bank of India (RBI), and Centre for Monitoring Indian Economy (CMIE) may be used. Find out the variation in the data compiled from the various sources and try to explore the reasons for such variation.

2. Compare India's terms of trade with any three other developing and developed nations each. Explore the reasons for the differences and discuss in class.

PROJECT ASSIGNMENTS

1. Collect data for trade between India and China. Critically evaluate the trade patterns for the direction and composition of trade.

2. India's agricultural trade has undergone considerable changes over the last three decades.

Compile the direction and composition of India's agricultural trade and find out the reasons for the shifts. Discuss your findings in class.

CASE STUDY

Developing Countries' Trade Dependence and Exports Growth Opportunities

Export opportunities for developing countries are strongly influenced by the economic upheavals of their trading partners. With the increase in global integration of trade across countries, this phenomenon has become more pronounced. Most developing countries rely upon a narrow range of countries as export destinations, as shown in Table C.1.

For a number of developing countries one single destination accounted for the vast majority of their exports during the period 2000–04. Most developing countries in geographical proximity of

the US ship a very large share of their exports to the US. For instance, about 90 per cent of the exports from Mexico are destined to the US.

The high level of import dependence of developing countries has hardly changed over the period. The average share throughout the three five-year sub-periods was 67.7 per cent (1990–94), 65.8 per cent (1995–99), and 67.2 per cent (2000–04). During the period 1990–2004, the average share of developing countries' five most important trading partners in their total exports was 66.9 per cent. It is also interesting to note that the five most

Table C.1   Developing countries with the highest concentration of exports to a single destination, 2000–2004

Exporter	Destination	Market share of destination (per cent)
Mexico	US	88.9
Dominican Republic	US	80.1
Trinidad and Tobago	US	67.7
Sudan	China	67.4
Nicaragua	US	66.8
El Salvador	US	65.9
Mozambique	Netherlands	64.6
Venezuela	US	63.8
Gabon	US	59.1
Cambodia	US	55.9

Source: UNCTAD secretariat calculations, based on IMF, *Direction of Trade Statistics,* October 2005; Trade and Development Report 2006, UNCTAD, p. 83.

important export destinations accounted for about 95 per cent of the total exports of a number of countries.

The trade patterns of developing countries reveal some interesting facts, as follows:

• Countries among the large economies, both developed and developing, top the list of the single most important destination for developing countries. All developing countries whose cumulated average exports accounted for

99.7 per cent of the total developing countries' exports during the period 2000–04 have been given in Table C.2. The table lists only those countries that were the main export destinations of at least two developing countries during these years. However, the significance of Japan and the large European developed economies declined over the past 10 years whereas the importance of the US and the rapidly growing developing countries such as China and India has grown significantly.

Table C.2   Main markets for developing country exports and number of developing countries for which they are the most important markets

1994		1999		2004	
US	33	US	40	US	40
Japan	11	Japan	9	China	9
France	7	France	5	Japan	8
Italy	5	Italy	5	France	3
Brazil	4	Brazil	3	India	3
Germany	4	China	3	Italy	3
UK	3	India	3	Netherlands	3
Australia	2	UK	3	Brazil	2
Belgium and Luxembourg	2	Australia	2	South Africa	2
China	2	China, Taiwan Province of	2	Thailand	2
Russian Federation	2	Germany	2		
Saudi Arabia	2	Saudi Arabia	2		
Spain	2	South Africa	2		
Thailand	2	Spain	2		

Source: UNCTAD Secretariat calculations, based on IMF, *Direction of Trade Statistics,* October 2005; Trade and Development Report 2006, UNCTAD, p. 84.

- The importance of the US, which had already been a major export destination for developing countries, has grown significantly past the mid-1990s. Since geographical proximity is the key determinant, the majority of developing countries for which the US is the most important export destination are in Central and South America. Besides, the US has also remained the most important destination of large African fuel-exporting countries, such as Angola, Gabon, and Nigeria, over the entire period 1990–2004. The US also temporarily gained importance for a number of Asian economies such as Cambodia, Iraq, Myanmar, and Nepal.

Several factors related to the trading partners' economic fortunes that influence the nature of impact on a country's export opportunity include the following:

'Good match' between the trading partners Various factors such as the geographical distance, which has a strong impact on the trading costs, the overlap between one country's export composition and the other country's import composition, and the export competitiveness of the country vis-à-vis competitors influence a good trading match.

Extent to which changes in a trading partners' economic performance influence a country's export opportunity Such influences are reflected in the trading partners' relative economic size, a change in their economic activity, the trading partners' import: GDP ratio, which measures the import propensity and import price elasticity of the trading partners.

Changes in export opportunities have been shown in Table C.3. The first variant measures the changes in each developing country's export opportunities as strongly influenced by the economic size of its main trading partners. The second variant measures improvement in export opportunities only on the basis of the export market shares and the aggregate income growth of its export partners. The economic size variable and the import propensity variable are excluded from the calculations while calculating the second variant. This

strongly increases the importance of developing countries as trading partners that provide the fastest increase in export opportunities.

China's rising importance as a destination of developing countries' exports is revealed in Table C.3. The table also reflects those developing countries identified as the main beneficiaries of improved export opportunities due to the changes in world import demand, as indicated in the second variant. However, the absolute value of exports is significantly higher for those countries identified on the basis of the first variant, i.e., the economic size of the main trading partner tends to experience significantly higher rates of growth.

This is probably due to the fact that the import composition of those economies that have experienced rapid growth over the past few years, especially China, significantly differs from that of very large economies, such as the US. Hence, the economic ascendance of the Asian drivers has come to be an important determinant of the developing countries' export opportunities.

Over the years, India's trade has diversified to a considerable extent. In 1960–61, the UK was India's largest trade partner, accounting for 26.9 per cent of India's exports and 19.4 per cent of its imports, which significantly dropped down to 4.39 per cent and 2.19 per cent, respectively, in 2006–07. India's imports from US declined substantially from 29.2 per cent in 1960–61 to 6.61 per cent in 2006–07. Although, the share of India's exports to the US declined considerably from 16 per cent in 1960–61 to 11.1 per cent in 1980–81, it substantially increased to 14.9 per cent in 2006–07, making the US the single largest destination for India's exports.[1]

Most countries for which the US is the main export destination tend to have highly concentrated destination patterns. As long as the main trading partners are large economies with a robust economic growth, such concentration of export destinations is beneficial. However, it strongly increases the risk of the adverse effect when the trading partners' economic fortune is on the decline. This is

---

[1] DGCI&S data; Economic Survey 2007–08, Government of India, pp. 106–07.

Table C.3   Increase in exports due to rising export opportunities from world import demand growth, 2000–04

| Exporting economy | Destination providing biggest improvement in export opportunities, 2004 | | Exports | | Purchasing power of exports, 2004 (Index number, 2000 = 100) |
	Destination	Market share	Average annual change 2000–2004 (per cent)	Total value 2004 ($ million)	
First variant[a]					
Mexico	US	88.4	3.0	189083	109
Dominican Republic	US	80.1	8.9	1299	121
Cambodia	US	55.9	14.5	2415	
El Salvador	US	65.9	2.4	1474	99
Venezuela	US	63.8	2.0	36200	92
Gabon	US	59.7	11.4	3970	151
China, Macao	US	49.9	−2.1	2160	
Guatemala	US	53.6	1.8	2938	98
Angola	US	38.0	16.6	13550	157
Trinidad and Tobago	US	67.7	5.6	5103	
Average		62.3	6.41	25819	118
Second variant[b]					
Mongolia	China	47.8	9.3	770	
Sudan	China	67.4	20.7	3778	194
Hong Kong (China)	China	44.1	6.9	259314	135
Yemen	Thailand	33.9	6.3	5109	112
Democratic Republic of the Congo	China, Taiwan Province of	27.8	7.3	3115	115
Oman	China	29.5	3.9	13342	125
Democratic People's Republic of Korea	China	41.8	8.9	1035	
Cuba	Netherlands	22.8	−0.8	1730	
Mali	China	32.7	18.2	1123	145
Myanmar	Thailand	41.4	12.6	2921	156
Average		38.9	9.3	29224	140
Average excluding Hong Kong (China)		38.3	9.6	3658	121

[a] Magnitude of improved export opportunities measured by export market share multiplied with export partner's composite index (economic size ∗ import propensity ∗ GDP growth).

[b] Magnitude of improved export opportunities measured by export market share multiplied with export partner's GDP growth.

Source: UNCTAD Secretariat calculations, based on IMF, *Direction of Trade Statistics*, October 2005; Trade and Development Report 2006, p. 87.

reflected in high level of sensitivity of Mexico's GDP to changes in import demand patterns of the US.

The evolution of import demand in developing countries' main trading partners also has had a significant impact on the developing countries' export opportunities. The structure of this demand growth has also strongly influenced the product-specific pattern of the developing countries' export dynamism since 1995. Demand growth in developing countries' main trading partners can significantly increase their export opportunities, but it also has a strong cyclical component and may, therefore, eventually prove to be unsustainable.[2] The challenge for developing countries is to translate these improvements in export opportunities into faster export growth. For this, it will be necessary to improve supply-side conditions, in particular through rapid productivity growth and technological upgrading.

Questions

1. In view of the export patterns of developing countries mentioned in the case, analyse the export patterns for your own country and identify the changes over the last three decades in its direction of exports.

2. Critically evaluate the implications of over-dependence of developing countries upon a narrow range of export destinations.

3. Select any two developing countries (including your own, if feasible) and assess the impact of economic changes of the main trade partners on its export opportunities.

---

[2] Trade and Development Report, UNCTAD, 2006, pp. 82–88.

India's Foreign Trade

(US$ millions)

	Exports (including re-exports)	Imports	Trade balance	Percentage change	
				Export	**Import**
1949–50	1016	1292	–276		
1950–51	1269	1273	–4	24.9	–1.5
1951–52	1490	1852	–362	17.4	45.5
1952–53	1212	1472	–260	–18.6	–20.5
1953–54	1114	1279	–165	–8.1	–13.1
1954–55	1233	1456	–223	10.7	13.8
1955–56	1275	1620	–345	3.3	11.3
1956–57	1259	1750	–491	–1.2	8.0
1957–58	1171	2160	–989	–7.0	23.4
1958–59	1219	1901	–682	4.2	–12.0
1959–60	1343	2016	–673	10.1	6.0
1960–61	1346	2353	–1007	0.3	16.7
1961–62	1381	2281	–900	2.6	–3.1
1962–63	1437	2372	–935	4.0	4.0
1963–64	1659	2558	–899	15.5	7.8
1964–65	1701	2813	–1112	2.6	10.0
1965–66	1693	2944	–1251	–0.5	4.7
1966–67	1628	2923	–1295	–3.9	–0.7
1967–68	1586	2656	–1070	–2.6	–9.1
1968–69	1788	2513	–725	12.7	–5.4
1969–70	1866	2089	–223	4.4	–16.9
1970–71	2031	2162	–131	8.8	3.5
1971–72	2153	2443	–290	6.0	13.0
1972–73	2550	2415	135	18.4	–1.1
1973–74	3209	3759	–550	25.9	55.6
1974–75	4174	5666	–1492	30.1	50.8
1975–76	4665	6084	–1419	11.7	7.4
1976–77	5753	5677	76	23.3	–6.7
1977–78	6316	7031	–715	9.8	23.9
1978–79	6978	8300	–1322	10.5	18.0
1979–80	7947	11321	–3374	13.9	36.4
1980–81	8486	15869	–7383	6.8	40.2
1981–82	8704	15174	–6470	2.6	–4.4
1982–83	9107	14787	–5680	4.6	–2.6
1983–84	9449	15311	–5862	3.8	3.5
1984–85	9878	14412	–4534	4.5	–5.9
1985–86	8904	16067	–7163	–9.9	11.5
1986–87	9745	15727	–5982	9.4	–2.1
1987–88	12089	17156	–5067	24.1	9.1
1988–89	13970	19497	–5527	15.6	13.6
1989–90	16612	21219	–4607	18.9	8.8
1990–91	18143	24075	–5932	9.2	13.5
1991–92	17865	19411	–1546	–1.5	–19.4
1992–93	18537	21882	–3345	3.8	12.7

Contd

Annexure I Contd

	Exports (including re-exports)	Imports	Trade balance	Percentage change	
				Export	Import
1993–94	22238	23306	−1068	20.0	6.5
1994–95	26330	28654	−2324	18.4	22.9
1995–96	31797	36678	−4881	20.8	28.0
1996–97	33470	39133	−5663	5.3	6.7
1997–98	35006	41484	−6478	4.6	6.0
1998–99	33218	42389	−9171	−5.1	2.2
1999–2000	36822	49671	−12849	10.8	17.2
2000–01	44560	50536	−5976	21.0	1.7
2001–02	43827	51413	−7586	−1.6	1.7
2002–03	52719	61412	−8693	20.3	19.4
2003–04	63843	78150	−14307	21.1	27.3
2004–05	83535	111516	−27981	30.8	42.7
2005–06	103092	149167	−46075	23.4	33.8
2006–07	126414	185735	−59321	22.6	24.5
2007–08	155512	235911	−80399	23.02	27.01

Note: For the years 1956–57, 1957–58, 1958–59, and 1959–60, the data are as per the Fourteenth Report of the Estimates Committee (1971–72) of the erstwhile Ministry of Foreign Trade.

Source: Directorate General of Commercial Intelligence and Statistics.

ANNEXURE II

Direction of India's Trade: Exports

(US$ millions)

Group/country	1987–88	1990–91	1991–92	1992–93	1993–94	1994–95	1995–96	1996–97	1997–98	1998–99	1999–00	2000–01	2001–02	2002–03	2003–04	2004–05	2005–06	2006–07*
I. OECD countries	7121.7	10248.8	10337.0	11209.8	12648.3	15443.8	17705.1	18601.4	19484.9	19264.0	21106.6	23473.6	21622.1	26382.6	29629.2	36494.8	45836.9	52058.7
A. EU	3034.1	4988.5	4826.9	5246.8	5796.9	7030.7	8708.3	8655.3	9144.6	8946.6	9382.4	10410.8	9845.9	11522.5	13890.0	17539.6	22385.0	25814.1
of which																		
1. Belgium	373.7	701.9	666.9	683.4	843.0	988.4	1120.4	1092.7	1215.5	1287.9	1367.7	1470.6	1390.6	1661.8	1805.7	2509.7	2871.2	3473.4
2. France	292.4	427.1	425.5	471.5	504.4	582.1	747.0	716.2	759.6	829.7	897.3	1020.0	945.0	1074.1	1280.9	1680.9	2079.6	2115.1
3. Germany	816.8	1420.5	1269.9	1427.0	1539.2	1747.7	1977.4	1893.1	1923.7	1851.9	1738.4	1907.6	1788.4	2106.7	2544.6	2826.2	3586.1	3987.5
4. Italy	384.4	558.1	580.0	622.1	604.1	857.9	1014.0	933.7	1115.2	1055.0	1119.8	1308.8	1206.5	1357.1	1729.4	2286.0	2519.0	3691.9
5. Netherlands	215.5	359.1	372.6	415.2	511.2	585.5	769.0	852.4	803.8	763.5	885.8	880.1	1047.9	1289.1	1604.9	2474.0	2668.9	5547.2
6. U.K.	783.1	1185.7	1138.1	1213.4	1379.1	1689.7	2010.8	2046.9	2140.8	1855.4	2034.8	2298.7	2160.9	2496.4	3023.2	3681.1	5059.3	5547.2
B. North America	2379.8	2829.6	3109.7	3707.1	4226.4	5287.5	5825.8	6908.4	7236.1	7672.6	8973.8	9961.6	9098.2	11594.0	12253.2	14632.6	18374.6	20026.0
1. Canada	127.7	156.4	188.6	191.1	227.8	266.8	305.4	353.0	433.2	473.0	578.3	656.5	584.8	698.3	763.2	866.8	1021.6	1154.0
2. U.S.A	2252.1	2673.2	2921.1	3515.9	3998.5	5020.7	5520.4	6555.4	6802.9	7199.6	8395.5	9305.1	8513.3	10895.8	11490.0	13765.7	17353.1	18872.0
C. Asia and Oceania	1402.7	1895.2	1878.2	1690.8	2020.0	2427.8	2651.9	2456.9	2408.7	2096.2	2153.0	2263.6	1990.7	2435.9	2379.6	2941.4	3444.4	4240.6
of which																		
1. Australia	138.7	179.0	202.5	223.2	245.3	346.4	375.7	385.4	438.3	387.4	403.3	405.9	418.0	504.2	584.3	720.2	821.2	924.6
2. Japan	1244.5	1693.7	1651.5	1436.5	1740.9	2026.6	2215.6	2005.9	1898.5	1652.0	1685.4	1794.5	1510.4	1864.0	1709.3	2127.9	2481.3	2812.8
D. Other OECD countries	305.1	535.6	522.2	565.1	605.1	697.7	519.1	580.7	695.5	548.6	597.4	837.6	687.3	830.2	1106.5	1381.3	1632.9	1978.0
of which																		
1. Switzerland	156.8	224.1	219.0	199.1	221.0	247.4	281.6	299.9	367.5	319.1	353.7	437.7	409.1	382.7	449.9	540.9	479.5	463.9
II. OPEC	741.9	1020.4	1561.8	1788.4	2382.2	2428.6	3079.0	3228.8	3527.4	3550.7	3895.8	4850.0	5224.5	6884.6	9544.4	13207.4	15242.2	20667.7
of which																		
1. Indonesia	20.7	109.4	146.7	138.5	234.9	277.7	662.4	591.8	437.3	185.3	325.6	399.8	533.7	826.1	1127.2	1332.6	1380.2	2027.3
2. Iran	107.4	78.5	122.5	114.4	159.7	156.8	155.0	195.0	171.7	159.1	152.1	227.0	253.0	654.7	918.1	1231.4	1188.3	1450.8
3. Iraq	13.5	24.2	0.0	5.9	3.9	0.2	0.6	2.2	11.2	36.3	49.4	84.0	206.8	214.9	75.2	131.2	155.9	203.5
4. Kuwait	81.8	41.1	52.3	108.3	106.0	133.9	135.5	154.7	185.9	164.7	154.3	199.1	206.2	250.6	319.1	421.4	513.7	611.2
5. Saudi Arabia	214.2	233.2	351.3	407.5	510.8	435.7	482.3	577.2	690.1	774.3	742.5	822.9	826.4	940.7	1123.3	1412.1	1809.8	2582.8
6. U.A.E.	238.8	438.9	738.5	814.3	1157.9	1265.9	1428.3	1476.0	1692.4	1867.6	2082.7	2597.5	2491.8	3327.5	5125.6	7347.9	8591.8	12014.7
III. Eastern Europe	2000.6	3243.2	1952.7	814.6	1001.4	1057.1	1340.0	1098.5	1283.3	1052.9	1292.9	1317.8	1254.8	1248.1	1555.4	1780.2	1980.4	2514.3
of which																		
1. Romania	47.3	53.2	12.5	7.8	22.4	16.2	29.9	17.8	15.3	17.6	12.6	12.2	11.4	27.4	47.8	106.0	84.4	169.2
2. Russia	1513.7	2928.6	1640.0	606.4	649.3	805.1	1045.0	811.2	953.0	709.4	947.9	889.0	798.2	704.0	713.8	631.3	733.1	908.2
IV. Developing countries	1718.8	3098.7	3587.1	4236.1	5797.6	6969.5	9198.4	10036.7	10312.1	9221.3	10460.0	13012.6	13535.5	17862.3	22784.3	31597.1	39736.4	50720.7
A. Asia	1443.2	2610.0	3016.4	3481.5	4892.0	5707.5	7307.8	8133.9	7972.4	6844.5	8205.5	10037.6	10332.7	13981.0	18426.7	24968.4	30981.2	37572.1
(a) SAARC	313.2	533.4	621.5	736.4	898.2	1215.0	1720.6	1701.6	1610.9	1679.2	1394.6	1928.5	2026.0	2724.1	4148.1	4440.7	5405.0	6289.7
1. Bangladesh	143.7	305.1	324.0	355.3	430.2	644.7	1049.1	869.0	786.5	995.6	636.3	935.0	1002.2	1176.0	1740.7	1631.1	1664.4	1628.6
2. Bhutan	0.0	2.2	2.2	2.2	9.9	11.1	17.2	22.0	13.3	9.6	7.6	1.1	7.6	39.0	89.5	84.6	99.2	58.7
3. Maldives	2.3	5.9	4.9	7.7	7.9	15.4	15.7	10.4	8.7	8.4	7.3	24.6	26.9	31.6	42.3	47.6	67.6	68.6
4. Nepal	72.7	48.3	77.1	72.5	98.1	120.1	160.0	165.7	170.0	122.4	151.2	140.8	214.5	350.4	669.4	743.1	860.0	931.4
5. Pakistan	14.7	14.7	40.1	50.8	64.1	57.2	76.8	157.2	143.2	106.1	92.9	186.8	144.0	206.2	286.2	521.1	689.2	1348.3
6. Sri Lanka	79.7	130.9	174.2	248.0	288.0	366.6	401.7	477.4	489.2	437.1	499.3	640.1	630.9	921.0	1319.2	1413.2	2024.7	2254.1

Contd

Annexure II Contd

Group/country	1987–88	1990–91	1991–92	1992–93	1993–94	1994–95	1995–96	1996–97	1997–98	1998–99	1999–00	2000–01	2001–02	2002–03	2003–04	2004–05	2005–06	2006–07*
(b) Other Asian developing countries	1130.0	2076.6	2394.9	2745.1	3993.7	4492.5	5587.2	6432.3	6361.5	5165.3	6810.9	8109.4	8306.6	11256.9	14278.6	20527.7	25576.2	31282.4
of which																		
1. China, People's Republic of	14.6	18.2	48.2	141.3	279.1	254.2	332.7	614.8	718.1	427.2	538.8	831.3	952.0	1975.5	2955.1	5615.9	6759.1	8290.7
2. Hong Kong	344.0	596.5	614.3	765.0	1249.6	1517.4	1821.4	1862.6	1932.0	1880.6	2510.9	2640.9	2366.4	2613.3	3261.8	3691.8	4471.3	4684.1
3. South Korea	112.4	182.7	238.7	174.9	206.4	332.4	448.3	518.5	467.6	307.9	476.6	450.8	471.4	644.9	764.9	1041.7	1827.2	2525.3
4. Malaysia	69.6	151.0	202.4	189.8	247.3	286.6	393.2	531.1	489.9	321.7	447.1	608.2	773.7	749.4	892.8	1084.1	1161.9	1304.8
5. Singapore	210.5	379.4	388.8	588.5	752.0	770.3	901.6	977.5	779.7	517.5	672.7	877.1	972.3	1421.6	2124.8	4000.6	5425.3	6021.1
6. Thailand	63.2	247.0	198.6	253.6	357.3	406.6	472.9	447.1	344.0	321.0	449.6	530.1	633.1	711.2	831.7	901.4	1075.3	1443.5
B. Africa	242.7	393.6	441.3	566.5	661.2	877.5	1512.7	1421.3	1637.8	1761.9	1554.6	1956.4	2260.9	2575.7	3094.4	4478.6	5699.0	8869.0
of which																		
1. Benin	9.1	13.1	10.6	8.5	8.6	7.1	11.3	16.6	20.7	27.1	28.4	45.1	55.4	64.4	52.7	47.1	96.6	151.5
2. Egypt, Arab Republic of	61.1	98.9	81.0	114.2	121.0	119.8	164.3	157.5	253.4	270.3	236.7	357.5	462.7	298.2	367.5	444.7	672.4	758.8
3. Kenya	27.4	36.0	41.7	57.7	70.8	122.7	245.1	168.5	123.9	145.2	116.7	140.9	156.0	203.6	229.5	426.6	576.5	1314.7
4. Sudan	16.5	21.5	15.8	14.2	14.6	16.4	30.6	26.9	44.6	55.0	71.5	97.8	122.2	105.2	107.4	317.4	294.6	403.1
5. Tanzania	16.8	29.6	48.0	70.0	63.7	65.8	81.4	67.6	68.9	85.4	82.0	102.0	90.8	115.5	175.8	173.9	243.5	288.6
6. Zambia	3.8	22.3	27.3	27.9	28.3	27.7	35.2	32.1	26.6	17.3	23.3	22.5	25.7	31.0	39.9	50.4	66.5	108.2
C. Latin American countries	33.0	95.2	129.5	188.1	244.4	384.5	377.9	481.4	701.9	614.8	699.8	1018.2	941.9	1305.6	1263.2	2150.1	3056.2	4279.6
V. Others/unspecified	505.5	534.1	426.8	488.3	408.8	431.5	472.4	504.3	398.7	129.8	67.1	1906.3	2189.8	341.8	329.3	456.5	294.7	369.5
Total trade	12088.5	18145.2	17865.4	18537.2	22238.3	26330.5	31794.9	33469.7	35006.4	33218.7	36822.4	44560.3	43826.7	52719.4	63842.6	83535.9	103090.5	126331.1

* Provisional.

Source: Directorate General of Commercial Intelligence and Statistics.

ANNEXURE III

Direction of India's Trade: Imports

(US$ millions)

Group/country	1987-88	1990-91	1991-92	1992-93	1993-94	1994-95	1995-96	1996-97	1997-98	1998-99	1999-00	2000-01	2001-02	2002-03	2003-04	2004-05	2005-06	2006-07*
I. OECD countries	10265.5	13773.0	10522.4	12269.3	13083.5	14731.7	19209.2	19456.6	21335.8	21859.7	21364.3	20157.0	20640.6	23301.1	29572.1	39989.9	51796.8	69527.3
A. EU	5707.5	7067.1	5665.5	6603.0	7002.0	7114.6	10303.2	10624.8	10680.6	10723.8	10967.8	10510.2	10436.5	12541.7	14717.0	18713.0	25151.3	33499.4
of which																		
1. Belgium	1057.1	1514.6	1388.0	1826.8	1874.8	1206.7	1701.9	2251.7	2668.1	2876.8	3681.3	2870.0	2763.0	3711.9	3975.9	4588.9	4725.1	4139.9
2. France	615.1	727.0	614.8	594.7	593.1	615.6	840.7	768.1	797.7	719.6	718.2	640.8	844.3	1094.2	1090.2	1894.1	4113.3	4155.7
3. Germany	1664.9	1935.6	1559.4	1656.9	1790.3	2187.0	3145.1	2831.1	2528.8	2140.7	1841.6	1759.6	2028.1	2404.5	2918.6	4015.3	6023.6	12666.5
4. Italy	395.4	608.2	448.1	524.3	537.5	741.0	1064.3	987.4	921.7	1088.3	734.6	723.6	704.8	812.0	1071.0	1373.1	1855.6	2681.1
5. Netherlands	341.2	442.1	279.3	381.7	384.3	385.9	570.2	494.0	445.2	464.2	470.9	437.5	466.5	385.7	535.6	791.5	1049.6	1156.5
6. U.K.	1410.2	1612.8	1201.9	1417.4	1536.1	1559.1	1917.1	2134.7	2443.6	2621.4	2706.8	3167.9	2563.2	2777.0	3234.3	3566.2	3930.3	4171.7
B. North America	1774.1	3234.7	2274.8	2552.6	2971.2	3171.2	4242.6	3999.3	4137.8	4025.8	3944.2	3412.1	3679.0	5009.9	5760.7	7777.1	10374.6	14118.9
1. Canada	230.4	311.7	280.1	405.2	234.6	265.5	381.2	313.4	420.9	385.6	380.5	397.1	529.4	566.3	725.9	775.7	919.9	1514.2
2. U.S.A	1543.8	2923.0	1994.7	2147.4	2736.7	2905.7	3861.4	3685.9	3716.9	3640.2	3563.7	3015.0	3149.6	4443.6	5034.8	7001.4	9454.7	12604.7
C. Asia and Oceania	2066.6	2689.5	2023.3	2326.8	2255.5	3031.0	3551.8	3584.1	3714.2	3999.1	3714.1	2984.3	3534.7	3249.5	5395.4	7187.6	9225.6	11692.5
of which																		
1. Australia	388.2	815.7	586.0	838.1	659.3	915.2	1021.9	1317.2	1485.6	1445.0	1081.8	1062.8	1306.1	1336.8	2649.2	3824.5	4947.9	6835.9
2. Japan	1639.8	1808.3	1369.3	1427.9	1522.1	2039.9	2467.6	2187.4	2144.9	2465.7	2535.8	1842.2	2146.4	1836.3	2667.7	3235.1	4061.1	4590.8
D. Other OECD countries	717.3	781.7	558.9	786.9	854.7	1414.9	1111.6	1248.4	2803.2	3111.0	2738.2	3251.3	2990.3	2500.0	3698.6	6312.2	7045.3	10216.5
of which																		
1. Switzerland	182.2	267.6	151.0	378.2	506.3	824.3	1020.5	1127.3	2640.7	2942.4	2597.7	3160.1	2870.7	2329.9	3312.7	5939.9	6555.8	9115.3
II. OPEC	2277.4	3924.0	3821.1	4776.7	5221.5	6050.1	7644.4	10142.6	9404.0	7765.4	12850.7	2688.8	2965.8	3479.4	5609.2	10022.5	11171.1	56084.6
of which																		
1. Indonesia	53.7	81.1	66.9	60.0	119.7	321.1	461.1	598.7	731.6	829.1	958.8	910.2	1036.8	1380.9	2122.1	2617.7	3008.1	4187.2
2. Iran	111.1	567.1	582.0	397.7	379.5	536.5	598.2	874.4	633.0	473.7	1251.3	211.2	283.8	258.3	266.8	410.2	702.5	7631.0
3. Iraq	471.5	276.2	2.5	7.7	0.0	0.0	0.0	0.0	185.4	151.2	199.7	6.9	0.0	0.0	0.0	1.1	2.1	5526.0
4. Kuwait	363.7	202.3	304.7	954.1	1126.2	1480.2	1970.1	2404.9	2299.5	1501.1	1912.2	112.7	73.7	179.5	142.5	305.9	461.9	5990.0
5. Saudi Arabia	590.4	1615.8	1442.5	1496.0	1541.7	1569.6	2024.7	2769.7	2508.3	1831.5	3016.5	621.1	464.0	504.7	737.8	1301.2	1632.3	13363.4
6. U.A.E.	588.4	1059.1	1247.5	1111.7	1003.1	1533.0	1606.6	1736.1	1780.0	1721.2	2334.2	659.0	915.1	957.0	2059.8	4641.1	4354.1	8639.0
III. Eastern Europe	1639.5	1882.2	991.6	554.4	563.1	967.6	1673.8	1102.7	1114.6	863.9	994.6	850.2	946.8	1139.9	1628.9	2514.2	3793.9	4562.1
of which																		
1. Romania	44.7	27.7	25.2	55.0	25.1	48.2	148.1	154.0	61.4	43.2	20.1	21.7	48.4	45.6	71.9	168.4	270.1	260.9
2. Russia	1240.0	1420.1	728.5	254.6	257.0	504.4	856.3	628.4	678.2	545.5	623.2	517.7	535.5	592.6	959.6	1322.7	2022.2	2114.1
IV. Developing countries	2967.2	4490.4	4074.0	4280.9	4435.4	6902.4	8145.0	8426.8	9626.1	11895.2	14524.0	11156.2	12776.4	15688.2	20567.2	28604.2	37890.5	59588.6
A. Asia	2076.1	3371.9	2872.4	3203.7	3573.9	5091.7	6426.0	6573.4	7258.9	8535.2	9942.2	8459.5	9264.7	11303.8	16269.8	22581.3	30450.6	47227.6
(a) SAARC	75.5	131.4	132.1	177.2	113.7	176.7	256.5	241.6	234.3	465.6	397.7	465.8	571.5	512.0	668.8	950.2	1354.9	1472.5
of which																		
1. Bangladesh	11.3	17.4	5.7	7.7	17.9	38.2	85.9	62.2	50.8	62.4	78.2	80.4	62.1	62.1	77.6	59.4	127.0	228.3
2. Bhutan	0.0	0.8	0.5	1.2	3.0	18.3	34.7	33.8	13.4	6.1	18.0	21.1	23.9	32.2	52.4	71.0	88.8	141.4
3. Maldives	0.0	0.0	0.0	0.1	0.1	0.2	0.2	0.2	0.2	0.1	0.4	0.2	0.4	0.3	0.4	0.6	2.0	3.1
4. Nepal	33.9	45.4	28.5	24.8	28.9	36.6	49.1	64.1	95.2	144.9	188.6	255.1	355.9	281.8	286.0	345.8	379.9	306.0
5. Pakistan	21.6	47.1	85.9	129.7	43.6	52.7	45.1	36.2	44.4	214.4	68.2	64.0	64.8	44.8	57.6	95.0	179.6	322.2
6. Sri Lanka	8.8	20.5	11.4	13.8	20.0	30.7	41.4	45.2	30.2	37.7	44.2	45.0	67.4	90.8	194.7	378.4	577.7	470.5

Contd

Annexure III Contd

Group/country	1987–88	1990–91	1991–92	1992–93	1993–94	1994–95	1995–96	1996–97	1997–98	1998–99	1999–00	2000–01	2001–02	2002–03	2003–04	2004–05	2005–06	2006–07*
(b) Other Asian developing countries	2001.2	3240.5	2740.2	3026.5	3460.2	4914.9	6169.4	6331.8	7024.6	8069.6	9544.5	7993.7	8693.2	10791.8	15601.0	21631.1	29095.7	45755.1
of which																		
1. China, People's Republic of	118.9	31.0	20.9	126.0	302.0	760.8	812.0	756.9	1119.3	1096.7	1286.7	1502.2	2036.4	2792.0	4053.2	7098.0	10868.0	17399.0
2. Hong Kong	92.6	165.6	106.2	170.4	188.7	287.0	388.0	319.1	316.3	449.3	817.9	852.1	728.9	972.6	1492.7	1730.1	2207.0	2481.7
3. South Korea	257.0	366.1	319.3	355.1	564.5	629.5	824.8	883.6	1001.8	1394.4	1273.3	893.8	1141.4	1522.0	2829.2	3508.8	4563.9	4778.7
4. Malaysia	648.3	554.8	394.3	405.9	249.9	490.1	902.7	1107.5	1178.9	1608.4	2024.0	1176.8	1133.5	1465.4	2046.6	2299.0	2415.6	5280.3
5. Singapore	323.4	795.7	694.7	632.1	626.9	899.7	1091.9	1063.3	1197.9	1384.2	1534.4	1463.9	1304.1	1434.8	2085.4	2651.4	3353.8	5470.2
6. Thailand	50.0	64.5	48.5	58.3	57.2	171.6	169.7	197.2	233.3	273.1	327.8	337.9	423.1	379.0	609.1	865.9	1211.6	1741.7
B. Africa	503.1	572.7	840.5	756.4	574.6	1038.6	1131.7	1293.7	1766.6	2635.5	3645.7	1996.1	2502.4	3348.2	3103.9	3930.4	4742.0	6797.2
of which																		
1. Benin	–	1.1	2.4	3.4	5.3	5.6	15.5	9.8	13.5	12.8	42.7	52.1	43.1	38.2	53.2	79.8	77.5	80.6
2. Egypt, Arab Republic of	75.9	43.9	66.7	88.2	68.5	228.3	72.6	65.2	192.6	192.4	443.9	38.8	99.9	226.6	98.2	152.6	220.4	1742.5
3. Kenya	5.2	21.8	9.2	9.8	12.3	13.8	15.0	19.6	20.9	36.2	21.0	19.0	31.9	33.5	41.9	46.7	48.5	55.4
4. Sudan	1.7	0.1	1.7	0.8	13.5	15.3	6.3	4.5	15.1	6.6	8.0	13.4	24.5	33.5	31.2	22.9	32.6	89.2
5. Tanzania	31.3	34.5	34.4	36.7	60.7	54.3	96.3	73.9	68.0	124.6	124.5	59.5	76.1	91.2	109.3	131.7	119.8	98.1
6. Zambia	108.8	86.0	49.1	69.6	50.5	54.7	59.9	104.1	97.2	39.1	26.0	11.6	13.5	14.4	18.6	23.0	40.6	86.2
C. Latin American countries	387.4	545.8	361.1	320.8	287.0	772.1	587.4	559.6	600.6	724.6	936.1	700.6	1009.3	1036.2	1193.6	2092.5	2697.9	5563.8
V. Others/unspecified	6.2	2.9	1.4	0.3	2.6	2.6	3.0	3.8	3.9	4.4	4.4	15683.4	14083.7	17803.5	20771.7	30386.7	44513.5	803.3
Total trade	17155.7	24072.5	19410.5	21881.6	23306.2	28654.4	36675.3	39132.4	41484.5	42388.7	49670.7	50536.5	51413.3	61412.1	78149.1	111517.4	149165.7	190566.0

* Provisional.

Source: Directorate General of Commercial Intelligence and Statistics.

ANNEXURE IV

Share and Percentage Change in India's Exports

Commodity group	Percentage change (US$)								Percentage share							
	1999–2000	2000–01	2001–02	2002–03	2004–05	2005–06	2006–07	2007–08*	1999–2000*	2000–01	2001–02	2002–03	2004–05	2005–06	2006–07	2007–08*
I. Agriculture & allied	-7.1	7.1	-1.7	14.1	11.7	19.8	23.5	15.1	15.2	13.5	13.5	12.8	10.5	10.2	10.3	9.3
of which																
1. Tea	-23.5	5.0	-16.7	-4.7	15.0	-12.4	21.3	-11.8	1.1	1.0	0.8	0.7	0.5	0.4	0.3	0.3
2. Coffee	-19.4	-21.7	-11.5	-10.5	0.7	64.3	11.3	-11.8	0.9	0.6	0.5	0.4	0.3	0.3	0.3	0.3
3. Cereals	-51.6	2.8	30.3	65.2	104.0	-42.0	29.1	17.6	2.0	1.7	2.2	3.0	0.2	0.1	0.1	0.1
4. Unmanufactured tobacco	37.8	-22.8	-15.7	25.0	20.0	10.2	19.9	17.6	0.5	0.3	0.3	0.3	0.3	0.2	0.2	0.2
5. Spices	5.1	-13.1	-11.4	9.2	24.7	14.0	46.0	64.7	1.1	0.8	0.7	0.7	0.5	0.5	0.6	0.7
6. Cashewnuts	46.6	-27.4	-8.8	13.1	49.3	5.8	-5.5	-11.8	1.5	0.9	0.9	0.8	0.7	0.6	0.4	0.3
7. Oil mels	-18.1	18.4	6.0	-34.9	-2.9	55.7	10.5	17.6	1.0	1.0	1.1	0.6	0.8	1.1	1.0	0.6
8. Fruits & vegetables	14.0	18.6	5.8	14.2	16.7	37.7	17.5	-2.0	0.6	0.6	0.6	0.6	0.8	0.6	1.0	0.6
9. Marine products	13.9	17.9	-11.3	15.8	8.3	10.4	11.3	-0.5	3.2	3.1	2.8	2.7	1.7	1.5	1.4	0.5
10. Raw cotton	-63.8	175.8	-81.8	16.5	-54.1	596.7	105.8	-41.2	Neg.	0.1	Neg.	Neg.	0.1	0.6	1.1	1.1
II. Ores and minerals, of which	2.5	26.5	8.9	58.7	136.5	17.4	12.6	20.6	2.5	2.6	2.9	3.8	5.5	5.2	4.8	4.0
11. Iron ore	-29.4	31.9	19.2	103.6	191.1	16.0	2.6	22.3	0.7	0.8	1.0	1.6	3.9	3.7	3.1	2.6
12. Processed minerals	9.5	36.2	-6.9	58.5	28.5	41.7	14.9	-14.5	0.8	0.8	0.8	1.1	1.0	1.1	1.0	0.8
13. Other ores and minerals	55.7	13.0	10.3	25.3	75.1	23.3	48.9	28.3	0.9	0.8	0.9	1.0	1.1	1.1	1.3	1.2
III. Manufactured goods, of which	15.2	16.9	-3.9	21.0	24.9	19.6	16.9	15.9	80.7	78.0	76.1	76.6	74.3	72.0	68.6	67.4
14. Leather & manufactures	-9.2	33.5	-3.2	-3.1	9.4	7.4	20.0	3.8	2.6	2.9	2.8	2.3	1.9	1.7	1.6	1.5
15. Leather footwear	16.3	1.6	3.1	7.1	17.2	18.1	-1.5	34.4	1.0	0.9	0.9	0.8	1.0	1.0	0.8	0.8
16. Gems & jewellery	26.4	-1.5	-1.1	23.9	30.2	12.8	2.9	20.4	20.4	16.6	16.7	17.2	16.5	15.1	12.6	13.0
17. Drugs, pharmaceuticals & fine chemicals	12.1	15.7	6.9	28.6	18.2	27.4	19.2	15.0	4.5	4.3	4.7	5.0	4.8	4.8	4.7	4.4
18. Dyes/intermediates & coat tar chemicals	25.4	5.5	-11.3	29.7	16.1	38.6	40.2	17.6	1.6	1.4	1.3	1.4	1.4	1.6	1.8	1.9
19. Manufactures of metals	17.8	31.3	-0.3	16.6	40.2	24.6	19.9	29.7	3.3	3.6	3.7	3.5	4.1	4.1	4.0	4.3
20. Machinery and instruments	2.4	37.7	6.5	16.1	34.0	30.6	38.4	28.7	3.2	3.7	4.0	3.8	4.5	4.7	5.3	5.8
21. Transport equipments	6.3	30.5	-3.4	31.0	44.7	52.8	14.5	32.7	2.2	2.4	2.3	2.5	3.4	4.2	3.9	4.4
22. Primary & semi-finished iron & steel	47.2	20.8	-17.1	116.7	63.4	-14.4	45.4	-12.6	2.0	2.0	1.7	3.0	4.2	2.9	3.5	2.6
23. Electronic goods	35.4	57.5	9.2	7.2	6.0	18.5	31.5	12.5	1.8	2.4	2.7	2.4	2.2	2.1	2.3	2.2
24. Cotton yarn, fabrics, madeups etc.	11.5	13.6	-12.4	9.6	1.6	14.3	7.0	0.8	8.4	7.9	7.0	6.4	4.1	3.8	3.3	3.0
25. Readymade garments	9.2	17.0	-10.2	14.6	5.3	30.6	3.7	-3.3	12.9	12.5	11.4	10.9	7.9	8.3	7.0	6.0
26. Handicrafts	6.6	2.2	-18.6	30.0	-7.0	30.2	4.1	-14.5	3.6	3.1	2.5	2.7	1.2	1.2	1.1	0.8
IV. Crude & petroleum products	-66.4	6212.8	12.0	22.0	91.2	66.2	59.3	27.6	0.1	4.2	4.8	4.9	8.5	11.5	15.0	17.9
V. Others & unclassified items	37.0	35.9	53.8	-11.8	60.8	12.0	49.0	2.9	1.5	1.7	2.7	2.0	1.2	1.1	1.3	1.4
Grand total	10.8	21.0	-1.6	20.3	30.8	23.4	22.6	17.6	100.0	100.0	100.0	100.0	100.0	100.0	100.0	100.0

Neg.—Negligible.

* Figures for April–September 2007.

Source: Directorate General of Commercial Intelligence and Statistics.

ANNEXURE V

Composition of India's Exports

Quantity: Thousand tonne
Value: Rupees crore and US$ millions

Item	1960–61			1970–71			1980–81			2000–01			2005–06			2006–07			2007–08**		
	Qty	Rs Cr	$ million	Qty	Rs Cr	$ million	Qty	Rs Cr	$ million	Qty	Rs Cr	$ million	Qty	Rs Cr	$ million	Qty	Rs Cr	$ million	Qty	Rs Cr	$ million
I. Agricultural and allied products	–	284	596	–	487	644	–	2057	2601	–	28582	6256	–	46703	10549	–	58959	13030	–	27349	6690
of which																					
I.1 Coffee	19.7	7	15	32.2	25	33	87.3	214	271	184.9	1185	259	162.9	1731	359	213.6	1969	435	87.8	851	208
I.2 Tea and mate	199.2	124	260	199.1	148	196	229.2	426	538	202.4	1976	433	177.7	1589	391	185.6	1970	435	82.1	893	218
I.3 Oil cakes	433.8	14	29	878.5	55	73	886.0	125	158	2417.8	2045	448	5976	4875	1101	6437	5504	1216	1973.9	1769	433
I.4 Tobacco	47.5	16	34	49.8	33	43	91.3	141	178	108.3	871	191	142.7	1330	300	158.2	1685	372	82.4	912	223
I.5 Cashew kernels	43.6	19	40	60.6	57	76	32.3	140	177	83.8	1883	412	131	2594	586	131	2506	554	60.6	1027	251
I.6 Spices	47.2	17	36	46.9	39	51	84.2	11	14	244.9	1619	354	400.2	2116	478	482.8	3158	698	307.4	1985	486
I.7 Sugar and molasses	99.6	30	60	473.0	29	39	97.0	40	50	769.0	511	112	394.1	598	135	1970.3	3260	720	2545.4	2514	615
I.8 Raw cotton	32.6	12	25	32.1	14	19	131.6	165	209	30.2	224	49	614.8	2904	656	1162.2	6108	1350	186.3	1000	245
I.9 Rice	–	–	–	32.8	5	7	726.7	224	283	1534.4	2943	644	4088.2	6221	1405	4747.9	7036	1555	3250.6	4641	1135
I.10 Fish and fish preparations	19.9	5	10	32.6	31	40	69.4	217	274	502.6	6367	1394	–	7036	1589	–	8001	1768	–	3088	755
I.11 Meat and meat preparations	–	1	2	–	3	4	–	56	70	–	1470	322	–	2750	621	–	3314	732	–	1885	461
I.12 Fruits, vegetables and pulses (excl. cashew kernels, processd fruits & juices)	–	6	13	–	12	16	–	80	101	–	1609	352	–	3649	824	–	4383	969	–	1825	446
I.13 Miscellaneous processed foods (incl. processed fruits and juices)	–	1	2	–	4	6	–	36	45	–	1094	239	–	1589	359	–	1836	406	–	1007	246
II. Ores and minerals (excl. coal)	–	52	109	–	164	217	–	414	523	–	4139	906	–	23733	5361	–	27311	6036	–	11995	2934
of which																					
II.1 Mica	28.4	–	36	26.7	16	21	16.7	18	22	63.2	64	14	–	77	17	–	76	17	–	39	10
II.2 Iron ore (million tonne)	3.2	17	36	21.2	117	155	22.4	303	384	20161.4	1634	358	–	16829	3801	–	17656	3902	–	7587	1856
III. Manufactured goods	–	291	610	–	772	1021	–	3747	4738	–	160723	35181	–	328507	74200	–	392447	86729	–	198029	48442
of which																					
III.1 Textile fabrics & manufactures (excl. carpets hand-made) of which:	–	73	153	–	145	192	–	933	1179	–	–	–	–	–	–	–	–	–	–	–	–
III.1.1 Cotton yarn, fabrics, made-ups, etc.	–	65	136	–	142	188	–	408	516	–	16030	3509	–	17456	3945	–	19089	4219	–	8774	2146
III.1.2 Readymade garments of all textile materials	–	1	2	–	29	39	–	550	696	–	25478	5577	–	37952	8572	–	40238	8892	–	17605	4307

	1960-61			1970-71			1980-81			2000-01			2005-06			2006-07			2007-08**		
	Qty	Rs Cr	$ million	Qty	Rs Cr	$ million	Qty	Rs Cr	$ million	Qty	Rs Cr	$ million	Qty	Rs Cr	$ million	Qty	Rs Cr	$ million	Qty	Rs Cr	$ million
III.2 Coir yarn and manufactures	–	6	13	–	13	17	–	17	22	–	221	48	–	590	133	–	660	146	–	310	76
III.3 Jute manufactures (incl. twist & yarn)	790.0	135	283	560.0	190	252	660.0	330	417	–	932	204	–	1318	298	–	1178	260	–	623	152
III.4 Leather & leather manufactures incl. leather footwear, leather travel goods & leather garments	–	28	59	–	80	106	–	390	493	–	8914	1951	–	11915	2691	–	13651	3017	–	6673	1632
III.5 Handicrafts (incl. carpets hand-made) of which:	–	11	23	–	73	96	–	952	1204	–	5097	1116	–	5683	1284	–	6049	1337	–	2352	575
III.5.1 Gems and jewellery	–	1	2	–	45	59	–	618	782	–	33734	7384	–	68752	15529	–	72295	15977	–	38311	9372
III.6 Chemicals and allied products@	–	7	15	–	29	39	–	225	284	–	22851	5002	–	52839	11935	–	64307	14211	–	30537	7470
III.7 Machinery, transport & metal manufactures including iron and steel*	–	22	46	–	198	261	–	827	1045	–	31870	6976	–	94369	21315	–	133166	29429	–	69071	16896
IV. Mineral fuels and lubricants (incl. coal)#	–	7	15	–	13	17	–	28	35	–	8822	1931	–	52538	11867	–	85542	18904	–	52579	12866
V. Others	–	8	16	–	100	132	–	466	589	–	1305	286									
VI. Total	–	642	1346	–	1535	2031	–	6711	8486	–	203571	44560	–	456418	103092	–	571779	126360	–	293964	71910

@ Chemicals and allied products figures relate to "Basic Chemicals" and "Plastic Linoleum Products".

* Also includes electronic goods and computer software.

During 1990–91, 1995–96, 1997–98, 1998–99, 1999–2000, 2000–01, 2001–02 and 2002–03 Crude oil exports amount to Rs Nil.

** Figures for April–September 2007.

Source: Directorate General of Commercial Intelligence and Statistics.

ANNEXURE VI

Share and Percentage Change in India's Imports

Commodity group	(Percentage share)								(Percentage change)*							
	1999–2000	2000–01	2001–02	2002–03	2004–05	2005–06	2006–07	2007–08*	1999–2000	2000–01	2001–02	2002–03	2004–05	2005–06	2006–07	2007–08*
I. Food and allied products	**5.8**	**3.7**	**4.5**	**4.6**	**3.5**	**2.5**	**2.9**	**2.2**	**–2.1**	**–35**	**23.5**	**22.2**	**16.7**	**–4.7**	**42.4**	**26.6**
of which																
1. Cereals	0.4	Neg.	Neg.	Neg.	0.0	0.0	0.7	0.1	–22.9	–91.3	–6.0	34.6	37.1	36.8	3589.6	–55.5
2. Pulses	0.2	0.2	1.3	0.9	0.4	0.4	0.5	0.5	–51.4	33.4	506.7	–14.6	–20.4	41.3	53.8	92.8
3. Cashewnuts	0.6	0.4	0.2	0.4	0.4	0.3	0.2	0.2	20.1	–23.8	–57.1	183.3	34.5	17.5	–14.7	–10.8
4. Edible oils	3.7	2.6	2.6	3	2.2	1.4	1.1	1.2	2.9	–28.2	1.6	33.8	–3.0	–17.9	4.2	32.9
II. Fuel	**27.4**	**33.2**	**29.5**	**30.7**	**29.6**	**32.1**	**33.2**	**33.6**	**84.6**	**23.0**	**–9.6**	**24.7**	**50.3**	**44.8**	**29.0**	**18.0**
of which																
5. Coal	2	2.2	2.2	2.0	2.9	2.6	2.5	2.6	2.9	9.7	3.4	8.4	126.8	21.0	18.3	32.2
6. POL	25.4	31	27.2	28.7	26.8	29.5	30.8	31	97.1	24.1	–10.5	26.0	45.1	47.3	30.0	16.9
III. Fertilizers	**2.8**	**1.5**	**1.3**	**1.0**	**1.1**	**1.3**	**1.6**	**1.9**	**30**	**–46.1**	**–9.9**	**–7.8**	**96.8**	**59.4**	**52.4**	**48.2**
IV. Paper board, manufactures & newsprint	**0.9**	**0.9**	**0.9**	**0.7**	**0.7**	**0.6**	**0.6**	**0.6**	**–3.8**	**1.1**	**–1.1**	**0.6**	**10.6**	**29.8**	**27.8**	**5.1**
V. Capital goods	**12.0**	**11.0**	**11.4**	**12.1**	**13.0**	**15.8**	**15.4**	**13.2**	**–22.2**	**–7.3**	**6.3**	**25.9**	**39.3**	**62.5**	**21.8**	**28.3**
of which																
7. Machinery except elec. & machine tools	5.5	5.4	5.8	5.8	6.7	7.4	7.5	8.2	–9.8	–0.9	9.2	20.0	42.9	49.0	24.9	28.3
8. Electrical machinery except electronic goods	0.9	1.0	1.2	1.1	1.1	1.0	1.1	1.1	4	11.3	21.9	11.7	37.1	25.9	30.3	28.6
9. Transport equipments	2.3	1.9	2.2	3.1	3.9	5.9	5.1	2.5	42.4	–16.2	20.6	65.1	34.1	104.2	6.8	51.2
10. Project goods	2.0	1.5	1.1	0.9	0.5	0.6	1.0	0.5	–63.3	–23.0	–25.1	–4.6	50.5	48.0	103.4	–31.5
VI. Others	**32.8**	**29.8**	**30.3**	**28.2**	**48.3**	**43.7**	**43.8**	**40.4**	**8.5**	**–7.7**	**3.7**	**10.8**	**31.0**	**21.1**	**24.6**	**36.4**
of which																
11. Chemicals	7.9	6.7	7.6	6.9	6.2	5.7	5.2	5.2	5.3	–14.7	16.4	8.7	48.6	23.2	14.1	19.8
12. Pearls, precious & semi-precious stones	10.9	9.6	9.0	9.9	8.4	6.1	4	4.2	44.6	–11.0	–4.4	31.2	32.2	–3.1	–18.0	30.6
13. Iron & steel	1.6	1.4	1.5	1.4	2.4	3.1	3.5	4.0	–20.1	–13.1	11.2	11.9	77.2	71.3	40.5	52.8
14. Non-ferrous metals	1.1	1.1	1.3	1.1	1.2	1.2	1.4	1.4	–8.5	–1.5	20.1	3.0	38.1	40.8	41.2	25.3
15. Professional instruments, optical goods etc.	1.7	1.7	2.0	1.8	1.4	1.3	1.3	1.3	3	4.1	18.4	8.8	24.4	28.9	18.7	24.4
16. Gold and silver	9.5	9.3	8.9	7.0	10.0	7.6	7.9	10.3	–7.2	Neg.	–2.7	–6.4	62.6	1.5	29.4	71.0
17. Electronic goods						8.9	8.6	8.9						32.5	20.6	26.2
18. Computer software						0.6	0.5	0.4						35.4	7.2	2.7
VII. Unclassified items	**18.3**	**19.9**	**22.1**	**22.7**	–	–	–	–	**15.6**	**11.7**	**12.1**	**22.8**				
Grand total	**100.0**	**100.0**	**100.0**	**100.0**	**100.0**	**100.0**	**100.0**	**100.0**	**17.2**	**1.7**	**1.7**	**19.4**	**42.7**	**33.8**	**24.5**	**27.7**

Neg.—Negligible.

* Figures for April to September 2007.

Source: Directorate General of Commercial Intelligence and Statistics.

ANNEXURE VII

Composition of India's Imports

Quantity: Thousand tonne
Value: Rupees crore and US$ millions

	1960–61			1970–71			1980–81			2000–01			2005–06			2006–07			2007–08[@]		
	Qty	Rs Cr	$ million	Qty	Rs Cr	$ million	Qty	Rs Cr	$ million	Qty	Rs Cr	$ million	Qty	Rs Cr	$ million	Qty	Rs Cr	$ million	Qty	Rs Cr	$ million
I. Food and live animals for food (excl. cashew raw) of which:	–	214	449	–	242	321	–	380	481	NA	NA	NA	NA	NA	NA	NA	NA	NA	NA	NA	NA
I.1 Cereals and cereal preparations	3747.7	181	380	3343.2	213	282	400.8	100	127	69.9	90	20	70.3	159	36	6125.9	5996.0	1325.1	161.1	23.0	5.6
II. Raw materials and intermediate manufactures	–	527	1105	–	889	1176	–	9760	12341	NA	NA	NA	NA	NA	NA	NA	NA	NA	NA	NA	NA
II.1 Cashewnuts (unprocessed)	NA	–	–	169.4	29	39	25	9	11	249.7	962	211	543.9	2089	472	586.5	1821.0	402.4	378.0	927.0	226.8
II.2 Crude rubber and reclaimed (including synthetic)	36.2	11	23	7.8	4	5	26.2	32	40	119.1	695	152	219.1	1833	414	316.8	2845.0	628.7	162.5	1464.0	358.1
II.3 Fibres of which:	–	101	212	–	127	168	–	164	208	NA	NA	NA	NA	NA	NA	NA	NA	NA	NA	NA	NA
II.3.1 Synthetic and regenerated fibres (man-made fibres)	0.2	–	–	15.8	9	12	68.8	97	122	42.6	275	60	37.9	345	78	44.1	439.0	97.0	22.2	223.0	54.6
II.3.2 Raw wool	1.9	1	2	19	15	20	18.8	43	55	53.7	458	100	90.2	903	204	99.6	1078.0	238.2	49.0	561.0	137.2
II.3.3 Raw cotton	237.1	82	172	139.1	99	131	NA	–	–	212.3	1185	259	98.8	704	159	81.5	663.0	146.5	76.4	498.0	121.8
II.3.4 Raw jute	100.4	8	17	0.7	0	0	8	–	1	67.3	84	18	61.3	93	21	83.1	115.0	25.4	68.4	74.0	18.1
II.4 Petroleum, oil and lubricants	800	69	145	12767	136	180	23537	5264	6656	–	71497	15650	–	194640	43963	–	258572.0	57143.0	–	141375.0	34583.2
II.5 Animal and vegetables oils and fats of which:	–	5	10	–	39	51	–	709	896	NA	NA	NA	NA	NA	NA	NA	NA	NA	NA	NA	NA
II.5.1 Edible oils	31.1	4	8	84.7	23	31	1633.3	677	857	4267.9	6093	1334	4288.1	8961	2024	4269.4	9540.0	2108.3	2629.0	5677.0	1388.7
II.6 Fertilizers and chemical products of which:	–	88	185	–	217	286	–	1490	1884	NA	NA	NA	NA	NA	NA	NA	NA	NA	NA	NA	NA
II.6.1 Fertilizers and fertilizer mfg	307	13	27	2392.7	86	113	5560.2	818	1034	7423.4	3034	664	11776.4	8815	1991	15618.9	13732.0	3034.7	8566.8	8771.0	2145.6
II.6.2 Chemical elements and compounds	–	39	82	–	68	90	–	358	453	–	1542	338	–	35582	8037	–	5980.0	1321.5	–	22437.0	5488.5
II.6.3 Dyeing, tanning and colouring material	–	1	2	–	9	12	–	21	26	–	874	191	–	2226	503	–	2695.0	595.6	–	1464.0	358.1
II.6.4 Medicinal and pharmaceutical products	–	10	21	–	24	32	–	85	107	–	1723	377	–	4551	1028	–	5866.0	1296.4	–	3359.0	821.7
II.6.5 Plastic material, regenerated cellulose and artificial resins	–	9	19	–	8	11	–	121	154	–	2551	558	–	10040	2268	–	11696.0	2584.8	–	7069.0	1729.2
II.7 Pulp and waste paper	80.3	7	15	71.7	12	16	36.9	18	23	1050.9	1290	282	2226.7	2537	573	2197.1	2893.0	639.3	1086.8	1484.0	363.0
II.8 paper, paper board and manufactures thereof	55.6	12	25	159	25	33	371.4	187	236	585.6	2005	439	1092.6	4180	944	1258.6	5461.0	1206.9	781.9	2793.0	683.2

Contd

Annexure VII Contd

	1960–61			1970–71			1980–81			2000–01			2005–06			2006–07			2007–08 [@]		
	Qty	Rs Cr	$ million	Qty	Rs Cr	$ million	Qty	Rs Cr	$ million	Qty	Rs Cr	$ million	Qty	Rs Cr	$ million	Qty	Rs Cr	$ million	Qty	Rs Cr	$ million
II.9 Non-metallic mineral manufactures of which:	–	6	13	–	33	44	–	555	702	–	797	174									
II.9.1 Pearls, precious and semi precious stones, unworked or worked	–	1	2	–	25	33	–	417	527	–	22101	4838	–	40441	9134	–	33881.0	7487.5	–	19255.0	4710.2
II.10 Iron and steel	1325.2	123	258	683.4	147	194	2031.1	852	1078	5778.5	3569	781	6748.2	20243	4572	4250.3	29071.0	6424.5	–	18167.0	4444.0
II.11 Non-ferrous metals	–	47	99	–	119	158	–	477	604	–	2462	539	–	58273	13162	–	78059.0	17250.6	–	53546.0	13098.4
III. Capital goods*	–	**356**	**747**	–	**404**	**534**	–	**1910**	**2416**	–	**25281**	**5534**	–	**104142**	**23522**	–	**129631.0**	**28647.7**	–	**60228.0**	**14733.0**
III.1 Manufactures of metals	–	23	48	–	9	12	–	90	113	–	1786	391	–	5362	1211	–	7256.0	1603.5	–	4053.0	991.4
III.2 Non-electrical machinery** appartus and appliances including machine tools	–	203	426	–	258	341	–	1089	1377	–	16915	3703	–	49081	11086	–	62672.0	13850.2	–	37190.0	9097.4
III.3 Electrical machinery, appartus and appliances**	–	57	120	–	70	93	–	260	328	–	2227	487	–	6660	1504	–	8868.0	1959.8	–	4995.0	1221.9
III.4 Transport equipment	–	72	151	–	67	88	–	472	597	–	4353	953	–	39131	8838	–	42709.0	9438.5	–	11597.0	2836.9
IV. Others (Unclassified)	–	**25**	**52**	–	**99**	**131**	–	**499**	**631**	NA	**NA**	**NA**									
V. Total		1122	2353		1634	2162		12549	15869		230873	50536		660409	149166		840506.0	185747.2		456103.0	111572.0

NA: Not available.

* From the year 1987–88 onwards, Capital Goods include project goods.

** From the year 1991–92 onwards, Items II.2 & II.3 exclude electronic goods.

[@] Figures for April to September 2007.

Source: Directorate General of Commercial Intelligence and Statistics.

4

Institutional Framework for International Business

LEARNING OBJECTIVES

➤ To understand the significance of institutional framework in international business
➤ To discuss the international economic institutions under the UN system
➤ To outline the international organizations in trade promotion
➤ To examine the institutional framework to facilitate international business

4.1 INTRODUCTION

Several international economic and trade organizations affect the environment of international business in a variety of ways, such as assessing the country's economic environment, extending credit facilities to national governments as well as individual organizations, undertaking equity investments, providing multilateral guarantees for trade and investment, settling disputes, keeping surveillance of international monetary systems, compiling and disseminating information, protecting intellectual property, providing technical assistance, and funding development projects. A thorough understanding of the institutional framework, both at the international and national level, thus becomes pertinent for international business managers for effective decision making.

The major international and multilateral institutions have come up under the aegis of the UN system, such as the World Trade Organization (WTO), the World Bank (WB), International Monetary Fund (IMF), United Nations Conference on Trade and Development (UNCTAD), and International Trade Centre (ITC). The WTO provides a rule-based multilateral framework for international trade and deals with a variety of issues, such as tariffs, non-tariff barriers, market access, intellectual property rights, subsidies, countervailing measures, rules of origin, policy framework, dumping, etc. Since it has been the most significant organization of the international economic institutions affecting international trade in the present context, it has been dealt with separately in Chapter 5.

Constituents of the World Bank group, such as the International Bank for Reconstruction and Development (IBRD), the International Development Association (IDA), the International Finance Corporation (IFC), the Multilateral Investment Guarantee Agency (MIGA), and the International Centre for Settlement on Investment Disputes (ICSID), represent the most significant framework of international economic institutions. The IMF came into existence in 1944, subsequent to the Bretton Woods conference, with an aim to maintain regular dialogue and policy advice to each of its member and providing exchange stability.

The UNCTAD helps create development-friendly integration of developing countries into the world economy, which has led to the launch of several useful agreements facilitating developing countries to promote trade. The World Intellectual Property Organization (WIPO) establishes an institutional framework for the protection of intellectual property internationally. In order to extend credit and technical assistance for improving the welfare of the people in Asia and the Pacific, the Asian Development Bank (ADB) undertakes projects in the region, aimed at pro-poor sustainable economic growth, social development, and good governance. Besides, some international organizations, such as the ITC, exclusively deal with the promotion of international trade. Most countries have their own independent organizations to promote international trade.

This chapter provides the broad framework of international and national institutions related to international trade. The institutional framework facilitating international business in India involves the Ministry of Commerce, advisory bodies, commodity organizations, and service organizations. Governmental trading organizations and trade promotion agencies at the state level have been separately examined in the later part of the chapter.

4.2 INTERNATIONAL ECONOMIC INSTITUTIONS

Economic development has been considered vital to improve the quality of life of millions of people across the world and to reduce poverty. A large number of organizations have been set up under the aegis of the UN to facilitate international trade and investment. This provides an institutional framework for multilateral trade, investment, and international economic growth.

4.2.1 World Bank Group

The World Bank Group consists of five closely associated institutions (Fig. 4.1), all owned by member countries that carry the ultimate decision-making power. Each institution plays a distinct role in the mission to fight poverty and improve living standards for people in the developing world. The term 'World Bank Group' encompasses all the five institutions, while the term 'World Bank' refers specifically to IBRD and IDA out of the five.

World Bank Group

| International Bank for Reconstruction and Development | International Development Association | International Finance Corporation | Multilateral Investment Guarantee Agency | International Centre for the Settlement of Investment Disputes |

Fig. 4.1   The World Bank Group

World Bank

The World Bank is a vital source of financial and technical assistance to developing countries around the world. As mentioned earlier, it is made up of two unique development institutions—the IBRD and the IDA, owned by 185 member countries. Each institution plays a different but supportive role in its mission of reducing global poverty and improving living standards. The IBRD focuses on middle-income and creditworthy poor countries, while IDA focuses on the poorest countries in the world. Together these institutions provide low-interest loans, interest-free credit, and grants to developing countries for education, health, infrastructure, communication, and many other purposes.

The World Bank is run like a co-operative, with member countries as its shareholders. The number of shares a country has is based roughly on the size of its economy. The US is the single largest shareholder with 16.41 per cent of votes, followed by Japan (7.87%), Germany (4.49%), the UK (4.31%), and France (4.31%). The rest of the share is divided among its other member countries.

The IBRD and IDA are run on the same lines. They share the same staff and headquarters, report to the same president, and evaluate projects with the same rigorous standards. But the IBRD and IDA draw on different resources for their lending. A country must be a member of the IBRD before it can join the IDA.

The International Bank for Reconstruction and Development

The International Bank for Reconstruction and Development (IBRD) is the oldest of the World Bank Group institutions established in 1944 to help Europe recover from the devastation of World War II. Subsequently, it shifted its attention to developing countries. It aims to reduce poverty in middle-income and creditworthy poor countries by promoting sustainable development through loans, guarantees, risk management products, and (non-lending) analytic and advisory services. The income that IBRD has generated over the years has allowed it to fund developmental activities and ensure its financial strength, enabling it to borrow in capital markets at low cost and offer good borrowing terms to clients. IBRD's 24-member board is made up of five appointed and 19 elected executive directors who represent the institution's 185 member countries.

IBRD helps clients gain access to capital and financial risk management tools in larger volumes, on better terms, at longer maturities, and in a more sustainable manner than they could receive from other sources. However, unlike commercial banks, IBRD is driven by development impact rather than profit maximization.

International Development Association

Established in 1960, the International Development Association (IDA) provides interest-free credits and grants to the poorest developing countries in order to boost their economic growth and improve people's living conditions. IDA funds help these countries deal with due complex challenges they face in striving to meet the Millennium Development Goals (MDGs), as given in Exhibit 4.1. It helps to reduce inequalities both across and within countries by allowing more people to participate in the

---

Exhibit 4.1   The Millennium Development Goals

Most of the world's nations committed themselves to working together to reduce poverty by half by 2015, signing the Millennium Declaration at a meeting at the United Nations in 2000, widely known as the Millennium Development Goals as summarized below:

Eradicate extreme poverty and hunger
Halve the proportion of people in extreme poverty, and the proportion of people who suffer from hunger by 2015.

Achieve universal primary education
Ensure by 2015 that all boys and girls complete a full course of primary schooling.

Promote gender equality and empower women
Eliminate gender disparity in primary and secondary education, preferably by 2005, and at all levels by 2015.

Reduce child mortality
Reduce by two-thirds the mortality rate among children under five by 2015

Improve maternal health
Reduce by three-quarters the maternal mortality ratio by 2015.

Combat HIV/AIDS, malaria, and other disease
Halt and begin to reverse the spread of HIV/AIDS, the incidence of malaria, and other major diseases by 2015.

Ensure environmental sustainability
Reverse the loss of environmental resources by 2015, reduce by half the proportion of people without sustainable access to safe drinking water, and by 2020, improve significantly the lives of at least 100 million slum dwellers.

Develop a global partnership for development
Develop further an open, rule-based, predictable, non-discriminatory trading and financial system, and address the special needs of the least developed countries, landlocked countries, and small island states; deal comprehensively with the debt problems of developing countries, develop and implement strategies for decent and productive work for youth; provide access to affordable essential drugs; and make available the benefits of new technologies.

Source: World Bank Group.

mainstream economy, reducing poverty, and promoting more equal access to the opportunities created by economic growth. IDA complements the World Bank's other lending arm, the IBRD. Presently it has 167 members.

The IDA depends on contributions from its wealthier member countries for most of its financial resources. The other important source is from repayment of outstanding credits, including by countries that received IDA assistance in the past but have since 'graduated' (reached the 'completion point') from the IDA. Since its inception, IDA credits and grants have directed the largest share, about 50 per cent to Africa.

At the July 2005 G8 Summit in Gleneagles, Scotland, G8 leaders agreed to write off completely the debt provided by IMF and World Bank to the world's 18 most indebted countries, 14 of which are located in Africa. Debt cancellation will be provided by IDA, the IMF, and the African Development Fund to countries that have graduated from the Enhanced Heavily Indebted Poor Countries (HIPC) Initiative. This effort, known as the Multilateral Debt Relief Initiative (MDRI), became effective on 1 July 2006, and is expected to provide about US$37 billion in debt relief over 40 years.

IDA provides highly concessional financing to the world's 81 poorest countries comprising about 2.5 billion people. IDA's resources help support country-led poverty reduction strategies in key policy areas, including raising productivity, providing accountable governance, building a healthy investment climate, and improving access to basic services, such as education and health care.

International Finance Corporation

The private sector arm of the World Bank Group, the International Finance Corporation (IFC), was founded in 1956. It promotes sustainable private sector investment in developing countries, helping to reduce poverty and improve people's lives. Corporate powers are vested in its board of governors, which meets annually and delegates many of its powers to a board of directors. Working at the headquarters, the board of directors reviews all investment projects and major policy decisions.

The IFC coordinates its activities with other institutions of the World Bank Group but is legally and financially independent. Its share-capital is provided by its member countries, who vote in proportion to the number of shares held. The IFC is owned by its 179 member countries with an authorized capital of US$2.45 billion.

The IFC promotes private businesses in developing countries by providing loans and making equity investments, helping companies mobilize financing in the international financial markets, and providing advice and technical assistance to businesses and governments. It charges market rates for its products and does not accept government guarantees. Financial products and services to client companies include

- Long-term loans in major currencies, at fixed or variable rates
- Equity investments
- Quasi-equity instruments (subordinated loans, preferred stock, income notes)
- Guarantees and standby financing

- Risk management tools
- Structured finance products

The IFC seeks to reach businesses in regions and countries that have limited access to capital. It also provides financing in markets deemed too risky by commercial investors in the absence of IFC participation and adds value to projects. It finances through its corporate governance and environmental and social expertise.

To be eligible for IFC financing, projects must be profitable for investors, benefit the economy of the host country, and comply with stringent social and environmental guidelines. IFC emphasizes five strategic priorities for maximizing its sustainable development impact:

- Strengthening its focus on frontier markets, particularly the SME sector
- Building long-term partnerships with emerging global players in developing countries
- Differentiating IFC from its competitors through sustainability
- Addressing constraints to private sector investment in infrastructure, health, and education
- Developing domestic financial markets through institution-building and the use of innovative financial products

The IFC's investments are funded out of its net worth, the total of paid-in capital and retained earnings. To ensure participation of investors and lenders from the private sector, IFC limits the finance provided of a project to 25 per cent of total estimated costs; it does not normally hold more than a 35 per cent stake or be the largest shareholder. For all new investments, the IFC articulates the expected impact on sustainable development, and, as the projects mature, the IFC assesses the quality of the development benefits realized.

The Multilateral Investment Guarantee Agency

The Multilateral Investment Guarantee Agency (MIGA) provides non-commercial guarantees (insurance) for foreign direct investment in developing countries (Fig. 4.2). It addresses concerns about investment environments and perceptions of risk, which often inhibit investment, by providing political risk insurance. It was established in 1988 and presently has 172 members. The MIGA's guarantees offer investors protection against non-commercial risks, such as expropriation, currency inconvertibility, breach of contract, war, and civil disturbance. MIGA also provides advisory services to help countries attract and retain foreign investment, mediates investment disputes to keep current investments intact and to remove possible obstacles to future investment, and disseminates information on investment opportunities to the international business community.

The MIGA provides private investors the confidence and comfort they need to make sustainable investments in developing countries. As part of the World Bank Group, and having shareholders of both host countries and investor countries, the

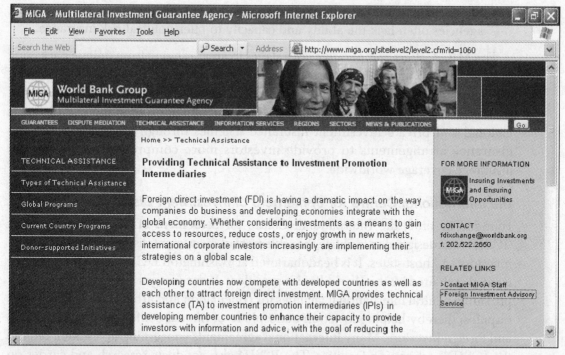

Fig. 4.2   MIGA offers a range of services for multilateral investment

MIGA brings security and credibility to an investment that is unmatched. The MIGA's presence in a potential investment can literally transform a 'no-go' into a 'go'. The MIGA acts as a potent deterrent against government actions that may adversely affect investments. And even if disputes do arise, leverage with host governments frequently enables resolving differences to the mutual satisfaction of all parties.

The MIGA's operational strategy, which plays to its foremost strength in the marketplace, attracting investors and private insurers into difficult operating environments, is as follows:

- Infrastructure development is an important priority to deal with rapidly growing urban centres and underserved rural populations in developing countries.
- Frontier markets—high-risk and low-income countries and markets—represent both a challenge and an opportunity. These markets typically have the most need and stand to benefit the most from foreign investment, but are not well served by the private market.
- Investment into conflict-affected countries is one of the operational priorities of MIGA. While these countries tend to attract considerable donor goodwill, once the conflict ends, aid flows eventually start to decline, making private investment critical for reconstruction and growth. With many investors wary of potential risks, political risk insurance becomes essential to additional investments.
- South–south investments (investment between developing countries) are contributing a greater proportion of FDI flows. But the private insurance market

in these countries is not always sufficiently developed and national export credit agencies often lack the ability and capacity to offer political risk insurance.

The MIGA offers comparative advantages in areas ranging from unique packaging of products and ability to restore the business community's confidence to ongoing collaboration with the public and private insurance market to increase the amount of insurance available to investors. The MIGA's guarantee programme complements national and private investment insurance schemes through co-insurance and re-insurance arrangements to provide investors more comprehensive investment insurance coverage worldwide.

The International Centre for Settlement of Investment Disputes

Founded in 1966, the International Centre for Settlement of Investment Disputes (ICSID) was designed to facilitate the settlement of investment disputes between foreign investors and host states. It is headquartered at Washington DC and its administrative council is chaired by the World Bank's president. It encourages foreign investment by providing neutral international facilities for conciliation and arbitration of investment disputes, thereby helping foster an atmosphere of mutual confidence between states and foreign investors. Many international agreements concerning investment refer to the ICSID's arbitration facilities. The ICSID also conducts research and carries on publishing activities in the areas of arbitration law and foreign investment law.

Recourse to ICSID conciliation and arbitration is entirely voluntary. However, once the parties have consented to arbitration under the ICSID convention, neither can unilaterally withdraw its consent. Moreover, all ICSID contracting states, whether or not parties to the dispute, are required by the convention to recognize and enforce ICSID arbitral awards.

Since 1978, for providing conciliation and arbitration, the centre has a set of additional facility rules authorizing the ICSID secretariat to administer certain types of proceedings between states and foreign nationals which fall outside the scope of convention. These include conciliation and arbitration proceedings where either the state party or the home state of the foreign national is not a member of the ICSID.

Arbitration under the auspices of the ICSID is one of the main mechanisms for the settlement of investment disputes under four recent multilateral trade and investment treaties, such as the North American Free Trade Agreement, the Energy Charter Treaty, the Cartagena Free Trade Agreement, and the Colonia Investment Protocol of Mercosur. During recent years, the caseload of the ICSID has increased considerably, mainly due to the proliferation of international investment treaties.

4.2.2 International Monetary Fund

The International Monetary Fund, also known as the IMF or simply the 'Fund', was conceived at a United Nations Conference convened in Bretton Woods, New Hampshire, US in July 1944. The 45 governments represented at the conference sought to build a framework for economic cooperation that would avoid a repetition of the disastrous economic policies that had contributed to the Great Depression of the 1930s.

The IMF offers regular dialogue and policy advice to each of its members. Generally, once a year, the Fund conducts in-depth appraisals of each member country's economic situation. It discusses with the country's authorities the policies that are most conducive to stable exchange rates and a growing and prosperous economy. In its overview of its members' economic policies, the IMF looks mainly at a country's macro-economic performance. This comprises total spending and its major components, such as consumer spending and business investment, output, employment, and inflation, as well as the country's balance of payments.

The main responsibilities of the IMF include

- Promoting international monetary cooperation
- Facilitating the expansion and balanced growth of international trade
- Promoting exchange stability
- Assisting in the establishment of a multilateral system of payments
- Making its resources available, under adequate safeguards to members experiencing balance of payments difficulties

The Fund seeks to promote economic stability and prevent crises; to help resolve crises when they do occur, and to promote growth and alleviate poverty. To meet these objectives, it employs three main functions, as discussed here.

Surveillance   A core responsibility of the IMF is to encourage a dialogue among its member countries about the national and international consequences of their economic and financial policies, to promote external stability. This process of monitoring and consultation, normally referred to as 'surveillance', has evolved rapidly as the world economy has changed. IMF surveillance has also become increasingly open and transparent in recent years.

The initiatives used to inform bilateral surveillance and aimed at promoting global economic stability are as follows:

- The IMF works to improve its ability to assess the member countries' vulnerabilities to crisis, identifying and promoting effective responses to risks to economic stability, including risks from payments imbalances, currency misalignment, and financial market disturbances.
- In collaboration with the World Bank, the IMF conducts in-depth assessments of countries' financial sectors under the Financial Sector Assessment Programme (FSAP). The Fund is further deepening financial and capital market surveillance, particularly in its analysis of emerging market members.
- The IMF has developed and actively promotes standards and codes of good practice in economic policy making. It is also involved in international efforts to combat money laundering and the financing of terrorism.

The importance of effective surveillance was underscored by the financial crises of the late 1990s. In response, the IMF has undertaken many initiatives to strengthen its capacity to detect vulnerabilities and risks at an early stage, to help member countries strengthen their policy frameworks and institutions, and to improve transparency and accountability.

Technical assistance The objective of IMF technical assistance is to contribute to the development of the productive resources of member countries by enhancing the effectiveness of economic policy and financial management. The IMF helps countries strengthen their capacity to design and implement sound economic policies. The IMF helps its member countries build their human and institutional capacity to design and implement effective macroeconomic and structural policies, put in place reforms that strengthen their financial sectors, and reduce vulnerability to crises.

The IMF generally provides technical assistance free of charge to any requesting member country within the IMF resource constraints. About three-quarters of the Fund's technical assistance go to low- and lower-middle income countries, particularly in sub-Saharan Africa and Asia, and post-conflict countries.

The IMF provides technical assistance in its areas of expertise: namely macroeconomic policy, tax policy and revenue administration, expenditure management, monetary policy, the exchange rate system, financial sector sustainability, and macroeconomic and financial statistics. Since the demand for technical assistance far exceeds supply, the IMF gives priority in providing assistance where it complements and enhances the IMF's other key forms of assistance, i.e., surveillance and lending.

Lending Even the best economic policies cannot eradicate instability or avert crises. In the event that a member country does experience financing difficulties, the IMF can provide financial assistance to support policy programmes that will correct underlying macroeconomic problems, limit disruptions to the domestic and global economies, and help restore confidence, stability, and growth. IMF financing instruments can also support crisis prevention.

The IMF is accountable to the governments of its member countries. At the apex of its organizational structure is its board of governors, which consists of one governor from each of the IMF's 185 member countries. All governors meet once a year at the IMF–World Bank Annual Meetings. The IMF's resources are provided by its member countries, primarily through payment of quotas, which broadly reflect each country's economic size. The annual expenses of running the Fund are met mainly by the difference between interest receipts on outstanding loans and interest payments on quota 'deposits'.

Special drawing right

The special drawing right (SDR) is an international reserve asset, created by the IMF to supplement the existing official reserves of member countries. SDRs, sometimes known as 'paper gold', although they have no physical form, have been allocated to member countries (as book-keeping entries) as a percentage of their IMF quotas. Its value is based on a basket of international currencies.

The SDR was introduced by the IMF in 1969 as an international reserve asset to support the Bretton Woods fixed exchange rate system. A country participating in this system needed official reserves, government or central bank holdings of gold, and widely accepted foreign currencies that could be used to purchase the domestic currency in world foreign exchange markets, as required to maintain its exchange rate. Since the supply of the two key reserve assets, i.e., gold and the US dollar, proved inadequate for supporting the expansion of world trade, the international community decided to create a new international reserve asset under the auspices of the IMF.

However, the Bretton Woods System collapsed barely two years later and the major currencies shifted to a floating exchange rate regime. Moreover, the growth in international capital markets facilitated borrowing by creditworthy governments. These developments lessened the need for SDRs. Presently, the SDR has only limited use as a reserve asset and its main function is to serve as the unit of account of IMF and some international organizations. Readers should note that the SDR is neither a currency, nor a claim on the IMF. Rather, it is a potential claim on the freely usable currencies of IMF members.

The value of the SDR was initially defined as equivalent to 0.888671 grams of fine gold, which at the time was also equivalent to one US dollar. After the collapse of the Bretton Woods System in 1973, the SDR was redefined as a basket of currencies. Presently, it comprises the Euro, Japanese Yen, Pound Sterling, and the US dollar. The basket composition is reviewed every five years to ensure that it reflects the relative importance of currencies in the world's trading and financial systems. The weights of currencies in the SDR basket were revised in the most recent review in November 2005, based on value of goods and services and the amount of reserves denominated in respective currencies, which were held by other members of the IMF. These changes became effective from 1 January 2006, and the next review is likely to take place in late 2010.

The distinguishing features of IMF and World Bank are shown in Exhibit 4.2.

4.2.3   The United Nations Conference on Trade and Development

In the early 1960s, growing concerns about the place of developing countries in international trade led many of these countries to call for the convening of a full-fledged conference specifically devoted to tackling these problems and identifying appropriate international actions. The first United Nations Conference on Trade and Development (UNCTAD) was held in Geneva in 1964. Given the magnitude of the problems at stake and the need to address them, the conference was institutionalized to meet every four years, with intergovernmental bodies meeting between sessions and a permanent secretariat providing the necessary substantive and logistical support.

Exhibit 4.2 IMF vs World Bank	
International Monetary Fund	**World Bank**
■ Oversees the international monetary system	■ Seeks to promote the economic development of the world's poorer countries
■ Promotes exchange stability and orderly exchange relations among its member countries	■ Assist developing countries through long-term financing of development projects and programmes
■ Assists all members—both industrial and developing countries that find themselves in temporary balance of payments difficulties—by providing short- to medium-term credits	■ Provides special financial assistance to the poorest developing countries whose per capita GNP is less than US$865 a year through the IDA
■ Supplements the currency reserves of its members through the allocation of SDRs in proportion to their quotas	■ Encourages private enterprises in developing countries through its affiliate, the International Finance Corporation (IFC)
■ Draws its financial resources principally from the quota subscriptions of its member countries	■ Acquires most of its financial resources by borrowing on the international bond market
■ Has at its disposal fully paid-in quotas totalling SDR 145 billion (about US$215 billion)	■ Has an authorized capital of US$184 billion, of which members pay in about 10 per cent
■ Has a staff of over 2600 drawn from 146 member countries	■ Has a staff of over 10,000 drawn from all its 185 member countries

Source: International Monetary Fund and World Bank Publications.

The UNCTAD aims at creating development-friendly integration of developing countries into the world economy. The basic functions of UNCTAD are

- To serve as the focal point within the UN for the integrated treatment of trade and development and interrelated issues in the areas of finance, technology, investment, and sustainable development
- To serve as a forum for intergovernmental discussions and deliberations, supported by discussions with experts and exchanges of experience, aimed at consensus building
- To undertake research, policy analysis, and data collection in order to provide substantive inputs for the discussions of experts and government representatives
- To facilitate cooperation with other organizations and donor countries providing technical assistance tailored to the needs of the developing countries, with special attention being paid to the needs of least developed countries, and countries with economy in transition

The UNCTAD secretariat works together with member governments and interacts with organizations of the UN system and regional commissions, as well as with governmental institutions, non-governmental organizations, and the private sector, including trade and industry associations, research institutes, and universities worldwide. The Ministerial Conference which meets every four years is the UNCTAD's highest decision-making body and sets priorities and guidelines for the organization and provides an opportunity to debate and evolve policy consensus on key economic and development issues.

The UNCTAD is the most visible symbol of the UN's assurance to promote the economic and social advancement of all people of the world and this remains equally relevant in the changing world economic order. The UNCTAD continues to be an important resource base for the South and it provides a forum to network and form issue-based coalitions with like-minded countries, especially the developing countries. The UNCTAD has played a valuable role in educative, early warning, and watch-dog capacities vis-à-vis developing countries' interests in the working of the WTO.

Over the years, the UNCTAD has focused its analytical research on the linkages between trade, investment, technology, and enterprise development. It has put forward a positive agenda for developing countries in international trade negotiations, designed to assist developing countries in better understanding the complexity of the multilateral trade negotiations and in formulating their positions. Moreover, it has expanded and diversified its technical assistance, which today covers a wide range of areas, including training trade negotiators, and addressing trade-related issues, debt management, investment policy reviews and the promotion of entrepreneurship, commodities, competition law, policy, trade, and environment.

Developing countries have found extremely useful UNCTAD's technical cooperation programmes (Fig. 4.3) in trade efficiency, Trade Points, harmonization of customs procedure, debt management programmes, database on trade information (TRAINS), etc.

UNCTAD XII

UNCTAD has continued to play a critical role in emphasizing the development dimension of issues in the fields of international trade and investment and related areas. In particular, UNCTAD has been addressing the imbalances of globalization and the need to overcome the supply constraints of developing countries, so as to ensure development gains and poverty reduction. The last UNCTAD XII held in Accra in Ghana during 20–25 April 2008, based on the theme of 'addressing the opportunities and challenges of globalization for development'. The sub-themes include

- Enhancing coherence at all levels for sustainable and poverty reduction in global economic policy making
- Taking up key trade and development issues and the new realities in world economy
- Enhancing an enabling environment at all levels to strengthen productive capacity, trade and investment
- Strengthening UNCTAD by enhancing its development role, impact, and institutional effectiveness

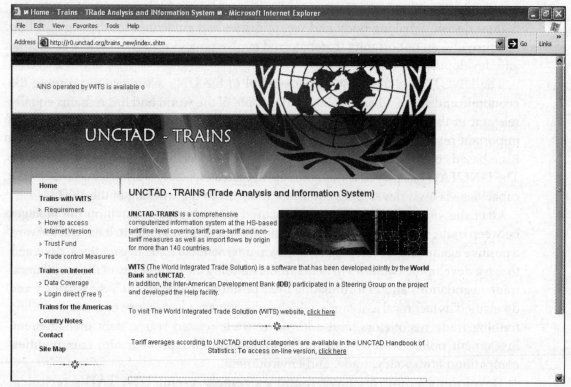

Fig. 4.3   UNCTAD's trade analysis and information services

The agreement reached at UNCTAD XII is called 'The Accra Accord and Declaration'. UNCTAD XII highlighted the challenges faced by many developing countries that strive to integrate successfully into the international economic and financial system. It sets out the agenda for economic and social development spanning areas ranging from commodities, trade and debt to investment and new technologies.

India wants UNCTAD to focus on certain aspects, such as enhanced and predictable market access for agriculture and better terms of trade, removal of market entry barriers to trade, financial support, volatility in the capital market, trade diversification and moving up the value chain into technology intensive manufactured exports, greater policy space to develop local industries, strengthening of technological capacity, and the need for a more benign and development sensitive international technology and Intellectual Property Rights (IPR) regime.

Generalized System of Preferences (GSP), International Commodities Agreements, Code of Conduct for Liner Conferences, Control of Restrictive Business Practices, Global System of Trade Preferences (GSTP) among developing countries are some of the major agreements launched under the UNCTAD.

Generalized System of Preferences

The Generalized System of Preferences (GSP) is a non-contractual instrument by which industrialized (developed) countries unilaterally, and on the basis of non-reciprocity, extend tariff concessions to developing countries. The GSP was formally accepted in 1968 by UN members at the second UNCTAD conference in New Delhi. The general underlying principles of the scheme are non-discrimination and non-reciprocity. The GSP offers developing countries tariff reductions, and in some cases, duty-free concessions for their manufactured exports and certain agricultural exports as well. The GSP is a tariff instrument, which is autonomous and complementary to GATT. Its aim is to grant developing countries tariff preferences over developed countries, thus allowing their exports easier access to the market.

Common Fund for Commodities

A Common Fund for Commodities (CFC) was established in 1989 with the following objectives:

- To serve as a key instrument in attaining the agreed objectives for the Integrated Programme for commodities adopted by the UNCTAD
- To facilitate the conclusion and functioning of International Commodity Agreements (ICAs), particularly concerning commodities of special interest to developing countries

In order to fulfil these objectives, the Fund has been authorized to exercise the following functions:

- To contribute, through its First Account to the financing of international buffer stocks and internationally coordinated national stocks, all within the framework of ICAs
- To finance, through its Second Account, measures in the field of commodities other than stocking
- To promote coordination and consultation through its Second Account with regard to measures in the field of commodities other than stocking, and their financing, with a view to provide commodity focus

Since the conception of the fund in 1970s, certain elements of commodity trade have changed dramatically, in particular the shift away from market regulating instruments to a liberalized system of market forces. Due to this, the Common Fund has not been able to put into operation the First Account capital, which was primarily meant for the financing of international buffer stocks and internationally coordinated national stocks within the framework of the ICAs.

The resources of the Common Fund are derived from subscription of shares of directly contributed capital paid in by member countries. The interest earned by the capital of the First Account is used to finance projects under the First Account Net Earning initiative and to cover the administrative expenses of the fund. Therefore, member countries do not need to pay annual membership fees. Commodity development measures of the Common Fund are financed by either loans or grants or a combination of both. The capital resources of the Second Account can only be used for loans whereas the voluntary contributions are available for grants and/or loans.

Global System of Trade Preference among developing countries

The agreement on the Global System of Trade Preferences (GSTP) among developing countries was established in 1988 as a framework for the exchange of trade preferences among developing countries in order to promote intra-developing-country trade. The idea received its first political expression at the 1976 ministerial meeting of the Group of 77 (G77) in Mexico City and was further promoted at G77 ministerial meeting in Arusha (1979) and Caracas (1981).

The GSTP lays down rules, principles, and procedures for the conduct of negotiations and for implementation of results of the negotiations. Coverage of the GSTP extends to arrangements in the area of tariffs, non-tariff measures, direct trade measures including medium and long-term contracts and sectoral agreements. One of the basic principles of the agreement is that it is to be negotiated step by step, and improved upon and extended in successive stages with periodic reviews. During the first session, India exchanged concessions with 14 countries. The number of tariff lines on which concessions were granted by India is 31 and India received tariff concessions in return on a wide range of products of its export interests from 14 countries. The major principles and features of the agreement are given here.

- The GSTP is reserved for the exclusive participation of members of the Group of 77 and China and the benefits accrue to those members that are also 'participants' in the agreement.
- The GSTP must be based and applied on the principle of mutuality of advantages in such a way as to benefit equitably all participants, taking into account their respective levels of economic development and trade needs. The agreement envisages preferential measures in favour of LDCs.
- To provide a stable basis for GSTP preferential trade, tariff preferences are bound and form part of the agreement.
- The GSTP must supplement and reinforce present and future sub-regional, regional, and inter-regional economic groupings of developing countries and must take into account their concerns and commitments.

The agreement in its present form is too modest; the concessions in scope and quality are few, limited, and insufficiently attractive to motivate greater trade among countries of the South. Additional efforts, additional instruments, additional participating countries, additional stimulus, and concessions are, therefore, required for the system to fully gain ground. Presently, 44 countries have acceded to the agreement; these include India, Pakistan, Bangladesh, Brazil, Indonesia, Malaysia, the Philippines, Singapore, Sri Lanka, Thailand, and Tanzania.

Participants may convene rounds of negotiations in order to broaden and deepen the scope of trade preferences. Three rounds of negotiations have so far been launched: the first in Brasilia (1986), the second in Tehran (1992), and the ongoing third round in Sao Paulo (2004). During UNCTAD XI, ministers of GSTP participants met at Sao

Paulo on 16 June 2004 to further negotiate tariff concessions and launch a new round of negotiations.

4.2.4 World Intellectual Property Organization

The World Intellectual Property Organization (WIPO) is a specialized agency of the United Nations headquartered at Geneva. The WIPO is dedicated to developing a balanced and accessible international intellectual property (IP) system, which rewards creativity, stimulates innovation, and contributes to economic development while safeguarding public interest. The WIPO was established by the WIPO convention in 1967 with a mandate from its member states to promote the worldwide protection of IP through cooperation among states and in collaboration with other international organizations.

The major functions of WIPO include providing

- Advice and expertise in the drafting and revision of national legislation which is particularly important for those WIPO member states with obligations under the TRIPS Agreement
- Comprehensive education and training programmes at national and regional levels for
  - o officials dealing with intellectual property, including those concerned with management of rights and enforcement; and
  - o traditional and new groups of users, on the value of intellectual property and how to create their own economic assets through better use of the intellectual property system
- Extensive computerization assistance to help developing countries acquire the information technology resources (both in human and material terms) to streamline administrative procedures for managing and administering their own intellectual property resources, and to participate in WIPO's *global information network*
- Financial assistance to facilitate participation in WIPO activities and meetings, especially those concerned with the progressive development of new international norms and practices

The WIPO treats IP as an important tool for the economic, social, and cultural development of all countries. This shapes its mission to promote the effective use and protection of IP worldwide. Strategic goals are set out in a four yearly medium-term plan and refined in the biennial programme and budget document. The five strategic goals defined by WIPO are

- To promote an IP culture
- To integrate IP into national development policies and programmes
- To develop international IP laws and standards

- To deliver quality services in global IP protection systems
- To increase the efficiency of WIPO's management and support processes

This international protection acts as a spur to human creativity, pushing forward the boundaries of science and technology and enriching the world of literature and arts. It also facilitates providing a stable environment to market intellectual property products internationally.

4.2.5 United Nations Industrial Development Organization

The United Nations Industrial Development Organization (UNIDO), set up in 1966, is headquartered in Geneva and became a specialized agency of the United Nations in 1985. It aims to promote industrialization in developing countries and in countries with economies in transition. UNIDO helps these countries in their fight against marginalization in today's globalized world. It mobilizes knowledge, skills, information, and technology to promote a productive employment, a competitive economy, and a sound environment.

UNIDO's assistance is delivered through two core functions, discussed below.

A global forum The UNIDO generates and disseminates knowledge related to industrial matters and provides a platform to various stakeholders to enhance cooperation, establish dialogue, and develop partnership.

A technical cooperation agency It designs and implements programmes to support the industrial development efforts of its clients. It also offers tailor-made specialized support for programme development.

These two core functions of the UNIDO are complementary and mutually supportive. On one hand, experience gained in the technical cooperation work of UNIDO can be shared with policy makers; on the other, the organization's analytical work shows where technical cooperation will have the greatest impact by helping define priorities.

4.2.6 Asian Development Bank

The Asian Development Bank (ADB) is a multilateral financial institution that aims to improve the welfare of people in Asia and the Pacific, particularly the 1.9 billion who live on less than US$2 per day. It is owned by 67 member countries, 48 from the region, and 19 from other parts of the globe. Japan and the US are coequally the largest shareholders, each with 12.8 per cent of total subscribed capital. The ADB has an important role to play in making the region free of poverty, as Asia and the Pacific region are home to two-thirds of the world's poor. The ADB's main instruments for providing help to its developing member countries include policy dialogue, loans, technical assistance, grants, guarantees, and equity investments.

The major functions of the bank are

- To extend loans and equity investments to its developing member countries (DMCs) for their economic and social development
- To provide technical assistance for planning and execution of development projects and programmes and for advisory services
- To promote and facilitate investment of public and private capital and development
- To respond to requests for assistance in co-ordinating development policies and plans of its developing member countries

The priorities of the ADB's projects and programmes include economic growth, human development, gender and development, good governance, environmental protection, private sector development, and regional co-operation. Pro-poor sustainable economic growth, inclusive social development, and good governance are the three pillars of ADB's poverty reduction strategy.

ADB lends to governments and to public and private enterprises in its developing member countries. Loans and technical assistance are its principal tools which are provided to governments for specific, high-priority development projects and programmes. ADB's lending both supports and promotes investment for development, based on a country's priorities.

4.2.7 United Nations Economic and Social Commission for Asia and the Pacific

The United Nations Economic and Social Commission for Asia and the Pacific (UN-ESCAP) is the most comprehensive of the UN's five regional commissions aimed at developing the Asia-Pacific region. It was established in 1947 with headquarters in Bangkok, Thailand. India is one of the founding members of the ESCAP. The main mandate of the ESCAP is to foster cooperation among its 53 members and nine associate members. ESCAP provides the strategic link between global and country level programmes and issues. It supports governments of the region in consolidating regional positions and advocates regional approaches to meet the region's unique socio-economic challenges in a globalizing world.

ESCAP's major activities include

- Regional economic cooperation
- Poverty alleviation through growth and social development
- Environment and sustainable development
- Development of transport communications, tourism, and infrastructure development in the region
- Enhancing capabilities of national statistical organizations

Trade and investment is one of eight sub-programmes of UN-ESCAP, which aims to benefit the region through the globalization process with the help of increased global and regional trade and investment flows. The trade and investment division assists countries to

- Understand trade and investment agreements, their implications, and economics
- Facilitate trade and investment flows, including trade finance and e-commerce
- Promote regional trade agreements in conformity with the multilateral trading system
- Understand the economics of trade policy
- Negotiate accession to the WTO, especially for least developed countries and economies in transition
- Formulate more effective policies and strategies for foreign direct investment promotion and facilitation
- Develop small and medium sized enterprises and promote entrepreneurship
- Access trade and investment related information

Trade facilitation, trade and investment information, regional trade agreements, Doha development agenda, investment promotion and facilitation, and enterprise development are its areas of focus.

4.3 ORGANIZATIONS FOR INTERNATIONAL TRADE PROMOTION

Most countries have set up their own independent organizations promoting international trade. Exhibit 4.3 lists major country-wise organizations promoting international trade. These organizations broadly aim at promoting the country's international trade and investment. The activities carried out by these organizations vary considerably. However, such organization usually carries out one or more of the following activities:

- Identifying trade and investment needs of local firms
- Keeping a watch on international business environment affecting the country's trade
- Gathering, compiling, and disseminating information
- Spotting opportunities for international trade and investment
- Matchmaking between buyers and sellers
- Organizing trade missions, trade delegations, buyer-seller meets, etc.
- Facilitating participation and organizing trade exhibitions
- Networking with foreign trade promoting organizations
- Carrying out generic market promotion and marketing services

4.3.1 International Trade Centre

The ITC is the focal point in the UN system for technical cooperation with developing countries in trade promotion. ITC was created by the General Agreement on Tariffs and Trade (GATT) in 1964 and since 1968 has been operated jointly by GATT (now

Exhibit 4.3   Country-wise organizations promoting international trade

Australia
Australian Trade Commission (AUSTRADE)
www.austrade.gov.au

Brazil
Agência de Promoção de Exportações do Brasil
www.apexbrasil.com.br

Canada
International Trade Canada
www.itcan-cican.gc.ca

China
China Council for the Promotion of
International Trade (CCPIT)
www.ccpit.org

France
The French Agency for International Business
Development (UBIFRANCE)
www.ubifrance.fr

**Hong Kong (Special Administrative Region of
China)**
Hong Kong Trade Development Council
www.tdctrade.com

India
India Trade Promotion Organization (ITPO)
www.indiatradepromotion.org

Indonesia
National Agency for Export Development
(NAFED)
www.nafed.go.id

Japan
Japan External Trade Organization (JETRO)
www.jetro.go.jp

Kenya
Export Promotion Council
www.cbik.or.ke

Korea, Republic of
Korea Trade-Investment Promotion Agency
(KOTRA)
www.kotra.or.kr/eng

Malaysia
Malaysia External Trade Development
Corporation (MATRADE)
www.matrade.gov.my

Oman
The Omani Centre for Investment Promotion
and Export Development (OCIPED)
www.ociped.com

Pakistan
Export Promotion Bureau (EPB)
www.epb.gov.pk

Singapore
International Enterprise Singapore (IE
Singapore)
www.iesingapore.gov.sg

Sri Lanka
Sri Lanka Export Development Board (EDB)
www.srilankabusiness.com

Sweden
Swedish Trade Council
EXPORTRADET
www.swedishtrade.se

Tanzania, United Republic of
Board of External Trade (BET)
www.bet.co.tz

United Arab Emirates
Dubai Chamber of Commerce and Industry
(DCCI)
www.dcci.ae

UK
UK Trade and Investment
www.uktradeinvest.gov.uk

United States of America
U.S. Department of Commerce's Commercial
Service
www.export.gov

by the WTO) and the UN, the latter acting through the UNCTAD. As an executing agency of the United Nations Development Programme (UNDP), the ITC is directly responsible for implementing UNDP-financed projects in developing countries and economies-in-transition related to trade promotion. ITC's activities aim to

- Facilitate the integration of its clients into the world trading systems
- Support national efforts to implement trade development strategies
- Strengthen key trade support services, both public and private
- Improve export performance in sectors of critical importance and opportunity
- Foster international competitiveness of SMEs

To achieve these goals, the ITC offers a range of global programmes, advisory and training services, information sources, tools, and products. Global programmes, based on proven ITC methodologies, and incorporating advisory services, tools, and products, respond to the needs of partners in all regions. Global programmes are replicable and adaptable, and have a perceptible time-proven impact. The ITC also participates in major trade-related multi-agency programmes. Advisory and training services are offered in key areas of international trade. Needs assessment, tailor-made advisory activities, and customized training are designed and delivered to build capacity in partner countries in close cooperation with trade support institutions. Information sources for international trade and business development are largely accessible through the Internet. Tools and products support, sustain, and improve the delivery of trade support services through partner institutions. They include practical guides which can be adapted to local requirements, methodologies and approaches for the development of review of trade support services, training materials, benchmarking, and assessment tools.

The ITC also supports developing and transition economies, particularly their business sector, in their efforts to realize their full potential for developing exports and improving import operations. ITC works in six areas:

- Product and market development
- Development of trade support services
- Trade information
- Human resource development
- International purchasing and supply management
- Assessment and programme design for trade promotion

ITC is headquartered at Geneva and is funded in equal parts by the UN and the WTO. It also finances general research and development on trade promotion and export development and information on international markets.

4.3.2 Import Promotion Organizations

Many countries are substantially dependent on imports due to limited availability of their resources. Besides, countries such as Japan import heavily due to heavy trade surpluses. These countries have set up institutional frameworks to promote imports so as to develop competitive supplier base for its importing firms. Such import promotion organizations also facilitate the foreign exporting firms to explore marketing opportunities and identify importers. Exhibit 4.4 indicates some major import promotion organizations.

Centre for Promotion of Imports from developing countries (CBI) established in 1971 (Fig. 4.4), facilitates imports into European countries. Major services offered by the CBI include

- Market information and matchmaking
- Export development of business
- Training
- Institutional development of business support opportunities

Its clients include companies willing to export to Europe, business support organizations in developing countries, and companies from Europe that wish to buy from developing countries.

Exhibit 4.4   Import promotion organizations

Australia
Pacific Islands Trade and Investment
Commission (PITIC)
www.pitic.org.au

Canada
Trade Facilitation Office Canada (TFOC)
www.tfoc.ca

Denmark
Danish Import Promotion Office for Products
from Developing Countries (DIPO)
www.dipo.dk

Germany
Deutsche Gesellschaft für Technische
Zusammenarbeit (GTZ) GmbH
www.gtz.de/english

Italy
Département de la coopération, des
investissements et des relations UE & OMC
Istituto Nazionale per il Commercio Estero
(ICE)
www.italtrade.com

Japan
Japan External Trade Organization (JETRO)
www.jetro.go.jp

Netherlands/EU
Centre for the Promotion of Imports from
Developing Countries (CBI)
www.cbi.nl

Sweden
Association of Swedish Chambers of
Commerce
www.cci.se

Switzerland
Swiss Import Promotion Programme (SIPPO)
www.sippo.ch

Norway
Norwegian Agency for Development
Cooperation (NORAD)
www.norad.no

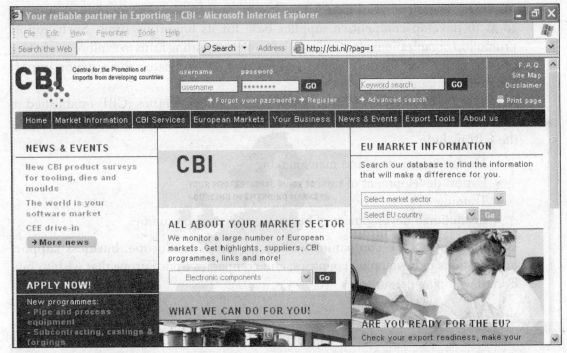

Fig. 4.4   Centre for Promotion of Imports from developing countries facilitates imports to European Union

4.4   INSTITUTIONAL FRAMEWORK FOR INTERNATIONAL TRADE IN INDIA

India has a comprehensive institutional set up to promote international trade. Exporting firms need to understand and appreciate the institutions involved and the functions carried out by them. The Department of Commerce is the prime agency of the country to promote international trade. It is supported by a massive institutional set up (Exhibit 4.5) at the union and state government levels, carrying out a range of trade facilitation activities.

	Exhibit 4.5 Institutional set-up for international trade promotion in India	
Tier level	**Bodies**	**Responsibilities**
Tier I	Department of Commerce	Framing of trade policy
Tier II	Advisory bodies	Coordinating discussion between industry and government for bringing in required changes
Tier III	Commodity organizations	Assist the export effort of specific product group
Tier IV	Service organizations	Facilitate and assist exporters to expand markets
Tier V	Government trading organizations	Handle export import of specific commodity
Tier VI	State export promotion agencies	Facilitate export promotion from the states

4.4.1 Department of Commerce

The Department of Commerce is the primary governmental agency responsible for developing and directing foreign trade policy and programmes, including commercial relations with other countries, state trading, various trade promotional measures and development, and regulation of certain export-oriented industries.

The principal functional divisions of the Department of Commerce engaged in export promotion activities are discussed as follows.

The *Economic Division* is engaged in export planning, formulating export strategies, periodic appraisal, and review of policies. The Economic Division also maintains coordination with and control over other divisions and various organizations set up by the Ministry of Commerce to facilitate export growth. Besides, the Economic Division monitors work relating to technical assistance, management services for exports, and overseas investment by Indian entrepreneurs.

The *Trade Policy Division* keeps track of development in international organizations, such as WTO, UNCTAD, Economic Commission of Europe, Africa, Latin America, and Asia and Far East (ESCAP). The Trade Policy Division is also responsible for India's relationship with regional trading agreements, such as EU, NAFTA, SAFTA, Commonwealth, etc. It also looks after GSP and non-tariff barriers.

The *Foreign Trade Territorial Division* looks after the development of trade with different countries and regions of the world. It also deals with state trading and barter trade, organization of trade fairs and exhibitions, commercial publicity abroad, etc. Further, it maintains contact with trade missions abroad and carries out related administrative work.

The *Export Product Division* looks after problems connected with production, generation of surplus, and development of products for exports. However, for products wherein the administrative responsibility remains with concerned ministries, the Export Product Division keeps in close touch with them to ensure that the production is sufficient to realize the full export potential besides ensuring the home consumption. The division is also responsible for the working of export organizations and corporations, which deal with commodities and products under their jurisdiction.

The *Exports Industries Division* is responsible for development and regulation of rubber, tobacco, and cardamom. It is also responsible for handling export promotion activities relating to textiles, woollens, handlooms, readymade garments, silk, and cellulosic fibres, jute and jute products, handicrafts, and coir and coir products.

The *Export Services Division* deals with the problems of export assistance, such as export credit, export house, market development assistance (MDA), transport subsidies, free trade zones, dry ports, quality control and pre-shipment inspection, assistance to import capital goods, etc.

The divisions mentioned here carry out their functions through export promotion councils, commodity boards, or other organizations, the details of which are given later in this chapter.

Subordinate offices

In addition to these divisions, attached and subordinate offices are also involved in the promotion of foreign trade. These are as follows.

Directorate General of Foreign Trade The directorate is responsible for execution of export-import policy announced by the Government of India. It is headed by Director General of Foreign Trade (DGFT). The directorate also looks after the work relating to issuing of licenses and monitoring of export obligations. Its headquarters are at New Delhi and subordinate offices are located at Ahmedabad, Amritsar, Bangalore, Baroda, Bhopal, Kolkata, Chandigarh, Chennai, Coimbatore, Cuttack, Ernakulam, Guwahati, Hyderabad, Jaipur, Kanpur, Ludhiana, Madurai, Moradabad, Mumbai, New Delhi, Panipat, Panaji, Patna, Pondicherry, Pune, Rajkot, Shillong, Srinagar (functioning at Jammu), Surat, Varanasi, and Visakhapatnam.

Directorate General of Commercial Intelligence and Statistics The Directorate General of Commercial Intelligence and Statistics (DGCI&S) was set up in 1962 and is headquartered at Kolkata. It is responsible for collection, compilation, and dissemination of trade statistics and commercial information. The DGCI&S also brings out a number of publications, mainly on inland and coastal trade statistics, revenue statistics, shipping and air cargo statistics, etc. Its main publications, such as *India Trade Journal* (weekly) and *Foreign Trade Statistics of India* (monthly) provide detailed information on export trade statistics. The DGCI&S uses mainly the Daily Trade Returns (DTRs), an authentic source, for compiling and generating export-import statistics.

Directorate General of Anti-Dumping and Allied Duties Constituted in April 1998, the Directorate General of Anti-Dumping (DGAD) is responsible for carrying out anti-dumping investigations and to recommend wherever required, the amount of anti-dumping/countervailing duty under the Customs Tariff Act, on identified articles which would be adequate to remove injury to the domestic industry.

4.4.2 Advisory Bodies

Advisory bodies provide an effective mechanism for continued interaction with trade and industry and increased coordination among various departments and ministries concerned with export promotion. The Government of India has set up the following advisory bodies for promoting international trade.

Board of Trade

In order to deploy an effective mechanism for maintaining continuous dialogue with trade and industry on issues related to international trade, the Board of Trade was set up under the chairmanship of the Union Minister of Commerce and Industry in May 1989. It was reconstituted on 1 April 2005 with an eminent representative from trade and industry as its Chairperson.

Secretaries of Commerce and Industry, Finance (Revenue), External Affairs (ER), Textile, Chairman of ITPO, Chairman/MD of ECGC, MD of Exim Bank, and Deputy Governor of Reserve Bank of India are official members of the Board. Representatives from FICCI, CII, FIEO and various trade and industries sector, media, and other important eminent personalities in the field of import and export trade are also board members.

The broad terms of reference (ToR) of the Board of Trade are given below:

- To advise the government on policy measures for preparation and implementation of both short- and long-term plans for increasing exports
- To review the export performance of various sectors, identify constraints, and suggest industry specific measures to optimize exports earnings
- To examine the existing institutional framework for exports and suggest practical measures for further streamlining to achieve the desired objectives
- To review the policy instrument, package of incentives, and procedures for exports and suggest steps to rationalize and channelize such schemes for optimal use
- To commence studies for promoting trade

Thus, the Board of Trade ensures a continuous dialogue with trade and industry in order to advise the government on policy measures, to review export performance of various sectors, identify constraints, and suggest industry specific measures to optimize export specific earnings. It meets at least once every quarter and has the power to set up sub-committees, co-opt experts, and make recommendations on specific sectors.

Export Promotion Board

In order to provide greater coordination among concerned ministries involved in exports, the Export Promotion Board works under the chairmanship of the Cabinet Secretary to provide policy and infrastructural support. The secretaries of all the ministries directly related to international trade are represented in this board, including secretaries of Departments of Commerce, Ministry of Finance, Department of Revenue, Department of Industrial Policy and Promotion, Ministry of Textiles, Department of Agriculture and Cooperation, Ministry of Civil Aviation, Ministry of Surface Transport, and others, according to the requirements of inter-ministerial coordination. The coordinated approach of the Export Promotion Board provides the required impetus to the export sector and resolves inter-ministerial issues in promoting exports.

4.4.3 Commodity Organizations

In order to focus on the commodity-/product-specific exports, there are various commodity organizations such as export promotion councils, commodity boards and autonomous bodies. These organizations look after sectors specific exports right from product development to export marketing.

Export Promotion Councils

Export promotion councils (EPCs) are non-profit organizations. They are supported by financial assistance from the central government. At present there are 21 EPCs, as given in Exhibit 4.6. The basic objective of the EPCs is to develop and promote the country's exports of specific products from India.

EPCs aim to project India's image abroad as a reliable supplier of high-quality goods and services. In particular, the EPCs encourage and monitor the observance of international standards and specifications by exporters. The EPCs also keep abreast of the trends and opportunities in international markets for goods and services and assist their members in taking advantage of such opportunities in order to expand and diversify exports. Each council is responsible for the promotion of a particular group of products, projects, and services.

The major functions of the export promotion councils are

- To provide commercially useful information and assistance to their members in developing and increasing their exports
- To offer professional advice to their members in areas, such as technology upgradation, quality and design improvement, standards and specifications, product development, innovation, etc.
- To organize visits of delegations of its members abroad to explore overseas market opportunities
- To organize participation in trade fairs, exhibitions, and buyer–seller meets in India and abroad
- To promote interaction between the exporting community and the government, both at the central and state levels
- To build a statistical database and disseminate information

The EPCs also issue registration-cum-membership certificates (RCMCs) to their members which are mandatory for getting export incentives.

Exhibit 4.6   Export promotion councils in India

- Engineering Export Promotion Council
- Project Export Promotion Council
- Pharmaceutical Export Promotion Council
- Basic Chemicals, Pharmaceuticals and Cosmetics Export Promotion Council
- Chemicals and Allied Products Export Promotion Council
- Council for Leather Exports
- Sports Goods Export Promotion Council
- Gem and Jewellery Export Promotion Council
- Shellac Export Promotion Council
- Cashew Export Promotion Council
- Plastics Export Promotion Council
- Apparel Export Promotion Council
- Export Promotion Council for EOUs and SEZ units
- Carpet Export Promotion Council
- Cotton Textile Export Promotion Council
- Export Promotion Council for Handicrafts
- Handloom Export Promotion Council
- The Indian Silk Export Promotion Council
- Synthetic and Rayon Textile Export Promotion Council
- Wool and Woollens Export Promotion Council
- Powerloom Development and Export Promotion Council

Commodity Boards

In order to look after the issues related to production, marketing and development of commodities, there are nine statutory commodity boards as under:

- The Tea Board
- The Coffee Board
- The Coir Board
- The Central Silk Board
- The All-India Handlooms and Handicraft Board
- The Rubber Board
- The Cardamom Board
- The Tobacco Board
- The Spice Board

The functions carried out by commodity boards are similar to those of export promotion councils. These boards broadly carry out the following functions:

- Provide an integrated approach for production development and marketing of the commodity under their purview.
- Act as a linkage between Indian exporters and importers abroad.
- Formulate and implement quality improvement systems, research and development programmes, education and training of farmers, producers, packers, and exporters on post-harvest management practices.
- Act as an interface between international agencies, such as the ITC, Geneva, Food and Agriculture Organization (FAO), and United Nations Industrial Development Organization (UNIDO), etc.
- Collect and disseminate information on production, processing, and marketing of the products under their purview.
- Export promotion activities, such as participation in international trade fairs, organizing buyer–seller meets, inviting foreign delegations, and taking Indian delegations abroad.

4.4.4   Autonomous Bodies

Agriculture and Processed Food Products Export Development Authority

Set up under an act of Parliament of 1986, the Agricultural and Processed Food Products Export Development Authority (APEDA) looks after the promotion of exports of agriculture and processed food products. It works as a linkage between Indian exporters and global markets. The products which fall under the purview of the APEDA, known as scheduled products, include fruits, vegetables and their products, meat and meat products, poultry and poultry products, dairy products, confectionary, biscuits and bakery products, honey, jaggery and sugar products, cocoa and its products, chocolates of all kinds, alcoholic and non-alcoholic beverages, cereal products, cashew nuts, groundnuts and papads, guar gum, floricultural products, and herbal and medical plants.

The basic functions of the APEDA are

- Development of database on products, markets, and services
- Publicity and information dissemination
- Inviting official and business delegations from abroad
- Organizing promotional campaigns abroad and visits of official and trade delegations abroad
- Participation in international trade fairs in India and abroad
- Organization of buyer–seller meets and other business interactions
- Distribution of annual APEDA awards
- Provides recommendatory, advisory, and other support services to trade and industry
- Resolving issues and problems of its members related to government agencies and organizations, RBI, customs, import–export procedures, problems with importers through Indian missions abroad

Like export promotion councils, the APEDA also registers its exporters and gives them RCMCs as a part of statutory requirement. The concept of agri-export zone (AEZ) to provide a focussed approach to agro-exports has been widely appreciated amongst producers and exporters that also call for active involvement of the state government. Recently, the APEDA has developed a system for grant of certification mark, i.e., 'Quality Produce of India' on the basis of compliance with hygiene standards, implementation of quality assurance system, such as ISO 9000, food safety systems, such as the Hazard Analysis Critical Control Programme (HACCP), backward linkage, residue testing of pesticides and contaminants, laboratory facilities, etc. Under the National Programme for Organic Agriculture, the APEDA is also an accredited inspection and certification agency for organically produced foods. It also provides financial support for export development under a number of schemes for development of infrastructure, market and quality, and R&D, and scheme for transport assistance.

Marine Products Export Development Authority

The Marine Products Export Development Authority (MPEDA), established in 1972, is an autonomous body under the Ministry of Commerce aimed at increasing export-oriented production, specifying standards, processing, and export marketing of all kinds of fisheries and its products. It offers a comprehensive range of services to exporters so as to develop exports of marine products from India including market promotion (Fig. 4.5).

The basic functions of MPEDA are

- Conservation and management of fishery resources and development of offshore fishing
- Registration of exporters and processing plants

Fig. 4.5   MPEDA's market services and market promotion

- Regulation of marine products export
- Laying down standards and specifications
- Helping the industry in relation to market intelligence, export promotion, and import of essential items
- Imparting training in different aspects of the marine products industry, such as quality control, processing, and marketing
- Promotion of commercial shrimp farming
- Promotion of joint ventures in aquaculture, production, processing, and marketing of value added seafood

Some of the major activities undertaken by the MPEDA include promotion of export-oriented aquaculture, production of scampi, crabs, lobsters, molluscs, and finned fishes and Integrated Development Programme for Sea Food Quality and Extension Services, training programme on implementation of HACCP, and various schemes to promote value addition and diversification of marine products to facilitate higher unit value realization.

4.4.5 Service Institutions

A number of institutions and organizations have been established to meet the requirements of industry and trade. The fields in which these institutions are engaged include development of export management personnel, market research, export credit insurance, export publicity, organization of trade fairs and exhibitions, collection and dissemination of export-related information, inspection and quality control, development in packaging, etc. A brief review of the activities and functions of some of these institutions is given below.

Indian Institute of Foreign Trade

The Indian Institute of Foreign Trade (IIFT) was set up in 1963 by the Government of India as an autonomous organization to induce professionalism in the country's foreign trade management. The institute has significantly contributed to India's foreign trade policies, rationalizing the framework of procedures and documentation, and developing the country's international trade strategy. The major objectives of the institute are

- To impart professional education in modern management techniques in the area of international business
- To enable participants to appreciate the interrelationship between the diverse and complex tasks of international business
- To develop capacities among business executives and government officials for improved understanding of various trade and economic issues
- To conduct high-quality research that addresses domestic as well as world trade and business issues

The institute conducts capacity building programmes and research apart from basic foundation programmes in international business (Fig. 4.6). The institute has achieved high standards of excellence and occupies the unique position today of being India's only premier institution that focuses on international business.

Export Inspection Council

The Export Inspection Council (EIC) is responsible for the enforcement of quality control and compulsory pre-shipment inspection of various commodities meant for exports, notified under the Export (Quality Control and Inspection) Act, 1963. Headquartered in New Delhi it functions through Export Inspection Agencies (EIAs) located at Chennai, Delhi, Kochi, Kolkata, and Mumbai besides a network of 38 sub-offices and laboratories.

Indian Council of Arbitration

The Indian Council of Arbitration (ICA) set up under the Societies Registration Act, promotes arbitration as a means of setting commercial disputes and popularizes the concept of arbitration among traders, particularly those engaged in international trade. The Council, a non-profit service organization, is a grantee institution of the Department of Commerce. The main objectives of the Council are to promote the knowledge and use of arbitration and provide arbitration facilities for amicable and quick settlement of commercial disputes with a view to maintain the smooth flow of trade, particularly, export trade on a sustained and enduring basis.

Fig. 4.6   Capacity building and research in international business constitute core activities of IIFT

India Trade Promotion Organization

The India Trade Promotion Organization (ITPO) is a premier trade promotion agency, which provides a broad spectrum of services to trade and industry so as to promote India's exports.

The major activities carried out by ITPO are

- Participating in overseas trade fairs and exhibitions
- Managing the extensive trade fair complex, Pragati Maidan in Delhi
- Establishing linkages between Indian suppliers and overseas buyers
- Organizing buyer–seller meets and other exclusive India shows in India and abroad
- Organizing India promotions with department stores and mail order houses abroad
- Arranging product displays for visiting overseas buyers
- Organizing seminars, conferences, and workshops on trade-related subjects
- Encouraging small and medium scale units in their export promotion efforts
- Conducting in-house and need-based research on trade and export promotion
- Trade information services through electronic accessibility at Business Information Centre

ITPO maintains India's largest trade fair complex—Pragati Maidan—spread over 149 acre of prime land in the heart of Delhi, having 62,000 sq. m. of covered exhibition space besides 10,000 sq. m. of open display area.

ITPO has its regional offices at Bangalore, Chennai, Kolkata, and Mumbai. Besides, ITPO also has overseas offices at New York, Frankfurt, Tokyo, Moscow, and Sao Paulo to promote India's international trade and investment.

National Centre for Trade Information

The National Centre for Trade Information (NCTI) has been set up as a registered company in March 1995 with a view to create an institutional mechanism for collection and dissemination of trade data and improving information services to the business community, especially small and medium enterprises. NCTI is a non-profit joint venture of ITPO and National Informatics Centre (NIC).

The major functions carried out by NCTI are

- To create databases and disseminate information on trade and commerce at national and international level
- To keep in constant communication with trade and commercial bodies throughout the world with a view to take appropriate measures for promoting exports and facilitating imports
- To advise or represent government, local authorities, and trade and commercial bodies on matters related to standardization, access, and dissemination of information on trade and commerce
- To create and maintain databases/trade statistics for the nodal ministry and to prepare region, country, and product-specific analytical and value added reports with a view of providing support for policy formulations and other strategic actions having bearing on the country's exports
- To keep abreast of emerging information technologies and standardizing formats for collection and dissemination of trade information in user-friendly formats

Under UNCTAD's trade efficiency programme, NCTI is certified as an operational trade point in India. It uploads the trade leads on the World Trade Point Federations (WTPF) as per UN/EDIFACT standard and provides value-added product, industry or country-specific information on international trade as per the request of the customer on payment of a fee.

Export Credit Guarantee Corporation

Operating in the international market is far more risky than operating in domestic markets. Due to little predictability on political and economic changes, such as an outbreak of war and civil war, a coup or an insurrection, economic difficulties or balance of payment problems, commercial risks of insolvency, and protracted default of buyers may result into delayed payments, restrictions on transfer of payments and non-payment. The Export Credit Guarantee Corporation (ECGC) provides credit insurance in order to protect exporters from consequences of payment risks, both political and commercial and to enable them to expand their overseas business without fear of loss. The type of insurance protection provided by ECGC may be grouped as follows:

- A range of credit risk insurance covers to exporters against loss in export of goods and services
- Guarantees to banks and financial institutions to enable exporters obtain better facilities from them
- Overseas investment insurance to Indian companies investing in joint ventures abroad in the form of equity or loan

In addition to insurance protection to exporters against payment risks, the ECGC facilitates the exporters by

- Providing guidance in export-related activities
- Making available information on different countries with its own credit ratings
- Providing information on the credit-worthiness of overseas buyers
- Making it easy to obtain export finance from banks/financial institutions
- Assisting exporters in recovering bad debts

Export-Import Bank of India

The Export-Import (Exim) Bank of India was setup by an act of parliament in September 1981. It aims to provide financial assistance to exporters and importers, and to function as the principal financial institution for coordinating the working of institutions engaged in financing export and import of goods and services with a view to promote India's international trade. It acts on business principles with due regard to public interest. The major programmes of Exim Bank are summarized in Fig. 4.7.

The major services extended by Exim Bank for promoting exports are

- It provides information and support services to Indian companies to help improve their prospects for securing business in multilateral agencies funded projects. These services include
  - Disseminating business opportunities in funded projects
  - Providing detailed information on projects of interest
  - Informing on procurement guidelines, policies, practices of multilateral agencies
  - Assisting with registration with multilateral agencies
  - Advising Indian companies on preparation of expression of Interest, capability profile, etc.
  - Intervening in bids
- In order to promote Indian consultancy, the Exim Bank has tie-ups with a number of international organizations, such as IFC, Eastern and Southern African Trade and Development Bank, etc.

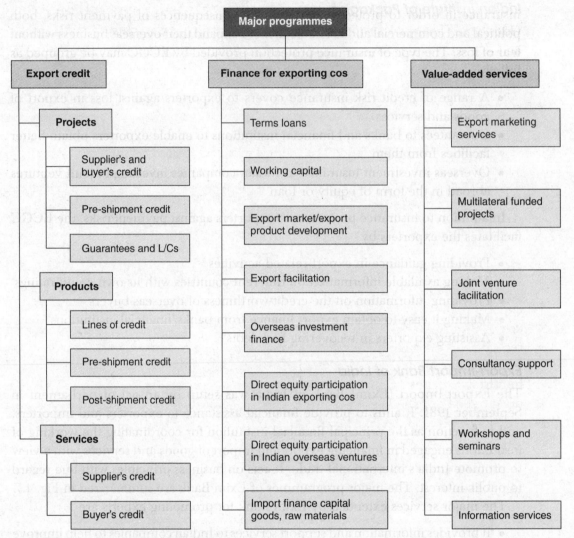

Fig. 4.7 Major programmes of Exim Bank

Source: Exim Bank.

- The bank also serves as a consultant to various developing countries for promoting exports and exports finance.
- The bank helps in knowledge-building by way of conducting seminars, workshops, and carrying out research studies on projects, sectors, countries, and macroeconomic issues relevant to international trade and investment. The bank has conducted sector-specific studies for identifying market potential for computer software, electric components, chemicals, floriculture, machine tools, pharmaceuticals, medicinal plants, sports goods, and financial services.
- The bank gathers and disseminates information on exporters/importers, industry/ market reports, trade regulations and laws, country reports, international quality standards, etc., so as to facilitate exporters.

Indian Institute of Packaging

Considering the existing deficiencies in the standards of packaging for eye-appeal and safe transit, the Government of India, in collaboration with the industry set up the Indian Institute of Packaging (IIP) in 1966.

The main objectives of the institute are

- To undertake research on raw materials for the packaging industry
- To keep India in step with international developments in the field of packaging
- To organize training programmes on packaging technology
- To stimulate consciousness of the need for good packaging
- To organize consultancy services for the industry

Its activities include effecting improvements in packaging standards and rendering testing facilities for packaging.

Federation of Indian Export Organizations

The Federation of Indian Export Organizations (FIEO) is the apex body of various export-promotion organizations and institutions in India. Set up in 1965, the FIEO acts as a primary servicing agency to provide integrated assistance to government-recognized export and trading houses. It also acts as the central coordinating agency for promoting exports of consultancy services from India. Representing more than hundreds of thousands exporters from India, FIEO is not a product-specific organization and the member exporters may be from any export sector.

The basic functions of the FIEO are

- Maintaining linkages with international agencies and export promotion organizations in other countries
- Organizing visits of multi-product delegations to prospective overseas markets and hosting foreign business delegations in India
- Organizing buyer–seller meets in India and abroad
- Providing advisory services to its members as well as foreign buyers in international markets
- Maintaining a comprehensive database on India's export sector
- Acting as a nodal agency for promoting exports of consultancy and other services
- Disbursing market development assistance to export and trading houses
- Keeping track of export-related policy changes and act as an interface between the government and the exporters so as to resolve the problems of its member exporters
- Interacting closely with the central bank, commercial banks, financial institutions and the ECGC and take up issues and problems of its member exporters

Indian government's trade representatives abroad

The institutional arrangements that have been developed and strengthened within the country are supplemented by the Indian trade representatives abroad. The trade representations in the Embassies and Consulates are continually being strengthened to enable them to effectively support trade efforts being made within the country. India's commercial representatives are expected to monitor the commercial events and developments of their accreditation, identify products with export potential and other trade opportunities, and study tariff and non-tariff barriers, government procedures, and shipping facilities. The representatives should also take initiative in cultivating specific trade contacts, undertake all publicity activities for image-building, organize participation in trade fairs and stores promotion, etc., effectively guide trade visitors and missions, maintain a flow of timely commercial intelligence, and deal with all problems of commercial complaints and bottlenecks. Further, they are expected to provide facilities to the Indian trade delegations and exporters visiting foreign countries, and help procure and forward samples of exportable goods imported from other countries.

4.4.6 Government Participation in Foreign Trade

For supplementing the efforts of the private sector in the field of foreign trade, the Government of India has set up a number of trading corporations, namely, the State Trading Corporation (STC), the Minerals and Metals Trading Corporation (MMTC), Spices Trading Corporation Limited, and Metal Scrap Trading Corporation (MSTC). The STC itself has a number of subsidiaries, namely the Handicrafts and Handlooms Export Corporation, the Projects and Equipment Corporation, the Tea Trading Corporation of India, and the Cashew Corporation of India. The Mica Trading Corporation is a subsidiary of the MMTC.

These corporations have provided the essential base for developing and strengthening efforts relating to specific commodities and products and diversifying the country's foreign trade. Briefly, their activities are

1. To arrange for exports where bulk handling and long-term contracts are advantageous
2. To facilitate exports of 'difficult to sell' items through various devices such as linking essential imports with additional exports under counter-trade
3. To organize production to meet export demands and to help production units overcome difficulties of raw materials and other essential requirements to meet export orders and develop lines of export by various methods
4. To undertake import of such commodities where bulk purchase is advantageous

The corporations handle actual transactions. They also maintain offices abroad and function like any commercial unit in the corporate sector.

However, the government is now reducing its direct participation in trade. Therefore, a number of items that were earlier canalized through government corporations have been removed from the canalized list. New governmental policies are expected to intensify competition for the government corporations from private sector companies. As a result, the government is moving towards privatization of these corporations.

4.4.7 States' Involvement in Promoting Exports

States being the prime centres for export production, need to be involved actively in export promotion. The central and state governments, therefore, have enacted a number of measures to promote exports; these measures are discussed under this section.

Inter-State Trade Council

The Inter-State Trade Council has been set up in order to ensure a continuous dialogue between the state governments and union territories. It advises the governments on measures for providing a healthy environment for international trade with a view to boost India's exports.

States' Cell in Ministry of Commerce

As an attempt to involve states in export promotion, the union government has created a State's Cell under the Ministry of Commerce with the following functions:

1. To act as a nodal agency for interacting with state governments/union territories on matters concerning imports and exports
2. To process all references of general nature emanating from state governments and state export corporations, which do not relate to any specific problem pending in a division in the Ministry
3. To monitor proposals submitted by the state governments to the Ministry of Commerce and coordinate with other divisions in the Ministry
4. To act as a bridge between state level corporations, associations of industries and commerce, and export organizations, such as ITPO, FIEO, EPZs, etc.
5. To disseminate information regarding export and import policy and export prospects to state governments and to other state level organizations
6. To provide guidance to state-level export organizations and assist in the formation of export plans for each state, in cases where export possibilities remain untapped

Further, the Ministry of Commerce has nominated nodal officers for maintaining liaison with the state governments in export promotion matters.

Institutional Infrastructure for Export Promotion by state governments

The State Level Export Promotion Committee (SLEPC) headed by the Chief Secretary is the apex body at state level promoting exports. It scrutinizes and approves projects and overseas implementation of union government's scheme on Assistance to States for Development of Export Infrastructure and other allied activities (ASIDE).

Most of the problems of exporters relating to infrastructure, availability of power, water, supply of raw material from within the state and inter-state movement of raw material, and remission of taxes by the state governments are dealt by separate departments within the state. In order to resolve the problems of exporters emanating from multiplicity of departments within the state, most state governments have nominated a senior officer as the nodal officer or *niryat bandhu* at the level of Commissioner or Secretary of Industries.

The Directorates of Industries in most states along with other industrial development organizations have shown interest in activities related to promoting exports of the goods produced in the state. There have been wide variations in the steps taken in this direction by various state governments.

Institutional framework at both international and national level influences international business environment. Although the foci of international economic organizations under the aegis of United Nations differ but complement each other, international economic growth is used as a strategic tool to reduce poverty and improve quality of life of millions of people, specially in the developing and the least developing countries as a part of its millennium development goals. Several international economic institutions have been established under the UN framework to perform a variety of functions such as technical assistance for development, information collection and dissemination, training, economic surveillance, extending loans, promoting multilateral trade and investment.

Individual countries do have independent trade promotion organization at national level. ITC headquartered at Geneva carries out a host of trade facilitation activities. Besides, most countries have got their own trade promotion organizations. Although the trade facilitation by national governments is primarily focussed on export promotion, some countries with considerable imports do facilitate imports by exclusive import promotion organizations. India has got a comprehensive set-up for trade promotion both at central and state levels.

SUMMARY

The chapter provides an overview of the institutional framework for international business. It discusses the World Bank Group constituents including IBRD, IDA, IFC, MIGA, and ICSID.

The IMF plays an important role in achieving the UN's vision to fight poverty and improve standard of living for people in the developing world by way of economic growth. The International Monetary Fund offers regular dialogue and policy advice to each of its members and promotes exchange stability. The special drawing rights (SDRs) created by IMF as an international reserve asset, supplement the existing official reserves of member countries. The UNCTAD provides an institutional framework for creating development friendly integration of developing countries into the world economy. The WIPO is a specialized agency of the UN aimed at developing the balanced and accessible international intellectual property system.

This chapter also discusses international trade promotion organizations. The Department of

Commerce is the main government agency responsible for development and monitoring international trade in India. The institutional framework for trade promotion in India includes advisory bodies, such as Board of Trade and the Export Promotion Board at the apex level. Besides, commodity organizations, such as export promotion councils, commodity boards and autonomous bodies, such as the APEDA and the MPEDA promote commodity or product specific exports. Indian Institute of Foreign Trade, Export Inspection Council, Indian Council of Arbitration, India Trade Promotion Organization, National Centre for Trade Information, Export Credit Guarantee Corporation, Export Import Bank of India, Indian Institute of Packaging, and Federation of Indian Exporting Organizations provide support services to promote India's foreign trade. Each of the Indian states has a State Level Export Promotion Committee (SLEPC) as an apex organization to promote exports from the state.

KEY TERMS

Fund   A name used for International Monetary Fund (IMF).

Generalized system of preferences (GSP)   A non-contractual instrument by which developed countries unilaterally and on the basis of non-reciprocity extend tariff concessions to developing countries.

Global System of Trade Preference (GSTP)   A framework for the exchange of trade preferences among developing countries in order to promote intra-developing-country trade.

Millennium Development Goals (MDGs) Goals to reduce world poverty by half by 2015 as signed under the Millennium Declaration at a Meeting at United Nations in 2000 by most of the world's nations.

Special drawing right   An international reserve asset created by the IMF to supplement the existing official reserves of member countries, also known as 'paper gold'.

World Bank Group   A group of five institutions, i.e., the International Bank for Reconstruction and Development (IBRD), International Development Association (IDA), International Finance Corporation (IFC), the Multilateral Investment Guarantee Agency (MIGA), and the International Centre for Settlement on Investment Disputes (ICSID).

CONCEPT REVIEW QUESTIONS

1. Explain the significance of economic and trade promotion institutions in international business.

2. Differentiate between International Monetary Fund and World Bank.

3. Describing the role of International Centre for Settlement on Investment Disputes (ICSID), critically evaluate its effectiveness under the present context.

4. Write short notes on
   (a) Special drawing rights (SDR)
   (b) Generalized system of preferences (GSP)
   (c) Global System of Trade Preference (GSTP)

5. Briefly explain the institutional set-up for promoting international trade from India.

6. Critically evaluate the role of state governments in promoting exports.

CRITICAL THINKING QUESTIONS

1. Explore the UNCTAD website (www.unctad .org) and list out the trade information provided by it. Find out its areas of use and limitations.

2. Visit the website of Korea Trade Investment Promotion Agency (KOTRA) (www.english. kotra.or.kr) and critically evaluate the services provided by it vis-à-vis the apex trade promotion organization in your country.

3. Find out the market development activities of the Tea Board. Critically evaluate its effectiveness in promotion of tea exports from India.

PROJECT ASSIGNMENTS

1. Contact a firm involved in international trade and find out the types of insurance covers taken by it from Export Credit and Guarantee Corporation (ECGC) or any other insurance agency. Compare the insurance schemes offered by it vis-à-vis other similar agencies.

2. Visit an export promotion organization in your vicinity. Explore its activities and find out limitations in promoting international business.

5

World Trade Organization

LEARNING OBJECTIVES

> To elucidate the significance of WTO and its genesis
> To briefly explain the functions and structure of WTO
> To describe the principles of multilateral trading system under WTO
> To provide an overview of WTO agreements
> To explicate the dispute settlement system under WTO
> To discuss the ministerial conferences and emerging issues
> To evaluate the WTO system in context of developing countries

5.1 INTRODUCTION

The World Trade Organization (WTO) is the only international organization that deals with global rules of trade between nations. It provides a framework for conduct of international trade in goods and services. It lays down the rights and obligations of governments in the set of multilateral agreements discussed later in this chapter. In addition to goods and services, it also covers a wide range of issues related to international trade, such as protection of intellectual property rights and dispute settlement, and prescribes disciplines for governments in formulation of rules, procedures, and practices in these areas. Moreover, it also imposes discipline at the firm level in certain areas, such as export pricing at unusually low prices.

The basic objective of the rule-based system of international trade under the WTO is to ensure that international markets remain open and their access is not disrupted by the sudden and arbitrary imposition of import restrictions. Under the Uruguay Round, the national governments of all the member countries have negotiated improved access to the markets of the member countries so as to enable business enterprises to convert trade concessions into new business opportunities. The emerging legal systems not only confer benefits on manufacturing industries and business enterprises but also create rights in their favour. The WTO also covers areas of interest to international business firms, such as customs valuation, pre-shipment inspection services, and import licensing procedures, wherein the emphasis has been laid on transparency of the procedures so as to restrain their use as non-tariff barriers. The agreements also stipulate rights of exporters and domestic procedures to initiate actions against dumping of foreign goods. An international business manager needs to develop a thorough understanding of the new opportunities and challenges of the multilateral trading system[1] under the WTO.

The WTO came into existence on 1 January 1995 as a successor to the General Agreements on Tariffs and Trade (GATT). Its genesis goes back to the post-Second-World-War period in the late 1940s when economies of most European countries and the US were greatly disrupted following the war and the great depression of the 1930s. Consequently a United Nations Conference on Trade and Employment was convened at Havana in November 1947. It led to an international agreement called Havana Charter to create an International Trade Organization (ITO), a specialized agency of the United Nations to handle the trade side of international economic cooperation. The draft ITO charter was ambitious and extended beyond world trade discipline to rules on employment, commodity agreements, restrictive business practices, international investment, and services. However, the attempt to create the ITO was aborted as the US did not ratify it and other countries found it difficult to make it operational without US support.

The combined package of trade rules and tariff concessions negotiated and agreed by 23 countries out of 50 participating countries became known as General Agreement on Tariffs and Trade (GATT): an effort to salvage from the aborted attempt to create the ITO. India was also a founder member of GATT, a multilateral treaty aimed at trade liberalization. GATT provided a multilateral forum during 1948–94 to discuss the trade problems and reduction of trade barriers. As shown in Exhibit 5.1, its membership increased from 23 countries in 1947 to 123 countries by 1994. GATT remained a provisional agreement and organization throughout these 47 years and facilitated considerably, tariff reduction. During its existence from 1948 to 1994, average tariffs on manufactured goods in developed countries declined from about 40 per cent to a mere 4 per cent. It was only during the Kennedy round of negotiations in 1964–67, that an anti-dumping agreement and a section of development under the GATT were introduced. The first major attempt to tackle non-tariff barriers was made during the Tokyo round. The eighth round of negotiations known as the Uruguay Round of 1986–94 was the most comprehensive of all and led to the creation of the WTO with a new set up of agreements.

5.1.1 WTO vs GATT

The distinguishing features of WTO vis-à-vis erstwhile GATT are as follows:

- GATT remained a 'provisional' agreement and organization throughout 47 years during 1948 to 1994, whereas WTO commitments are permanent.

---

[1] *Understanding WTO*, World Trade Organization, Geneva, 2007, pp. 9–74.

	Exhibit 5.1	Multilateral Trade Rounds under GATT/WTO	
Year	**Round name**	**Subjects covered**	**Countries**
1947	Geneva	Tariffs	23
1949	Annecy	Tariffs	13
1951	Torquay	Tariffs	38
1956	Geneva	Tariffs	26
1960–61	Dillon	Tariffs	26
1964–67	Kennedy	Tariffs and anti-dumping measures	62
1973–79	Tokyo	Tariffs, non-tariff measures, framework agreements	102
1986–94	Uruguay	Tariffs, non-tariff measures, rules, services, intellectual property, dispute settlement, textiles, agriculture, creation of WTO, etc.	123
2001–present	Doha	Tariffs on goods, Non-agriculture market access (NAMA), special and differential treatment, trade facilitation, etc.	150

Source: WTO.

- GATT rules mainly applied to trade in goods, whereas WTO covers other areas, such as services, intellectual property, etc.
- GATT had contracting parties, whereas WTO has members.
- GATT was essentially a set of rules of the multilateral treaty with no institutional foundation, whereas WTO is a permanent institution with its own Secretariat.
- A country could essentially follow domestic legislation even if it violated a provision of the GATT agreement which is not allowed by the WTO.
- In WTO, almost all the agreements are multilateral in nature involving commitment of the entire membership, whereas a number of GATT provisions by the 80s were plurilateral and therefore selective.
- The WTO also covers certain grey areas, such as agriculture, textiles and clothing, not covered under the GATT.
- The dispute settlement system under the WTO is much more efficient, speedy, and transparent unlike the GATT system which was highly susceptible to blockages.

5.1.2   Why Should a Country Join the WTO?

Despite the disciplinary framework for conduct of international trade under the WTO, countries across the world including the developing countries were in a rush to join the pack. The WTO has nearly 153 members, accounting for over 97 per cent of world trade. Presently, 34 governments hold observer status, out of which 31 are actively seeking accession, including large trading nations, such as Russia and Taiwan. The major reasons for a country to join the WTO are

- Since each country needs to export its goods and services to receive foreign exchange for essential imports, such as capital goods, technology, fuel, and sometimes even food, it requires access to foreign markets. But countries require permission for making their goods and services enter foreign countries. Thus countries need to have bilateral agreements with each other. By joining a multilateral framework like the WTO, the need to have individual bilateral agreements is obviated as the member countries are allowed to export and import goods and services among themselves.
- An individual country is unlikely to get a better deal in bilateral agreements than what it gets in a multilateral framework. It has been observed that developing countries had to commit to a greater degree to developed countries in bilateral agreements than what is required under the WTO.
- A country can learn from the experiences of other countries, being part of the community of countries and influence the decision-making process in the WTO.
- The WTO provides some protection against subjective actions of other countries by way of its dispute settlement system that works as an in-built mechanism for enforcement of rights and obligations of member countries.
- It would be odd to remain out of WTO framework for conducting international trade that has been in existence for about six decades and accounts for over 97 per cent of world trade. It may even be viewed as suspicious by others.

5.1.3 Functions of WTO

The major function of the WTO is to ensure the flow of international trade as smoothly, predictably, and freely as possible. This is a multilateral trade organization aimed at evolving a liberalized trade regime under a rule-based system. The basic functions of WTO are

- To facilitate the implementation, administration, and operation of trade agreements
- To provide a forum for further negotiations among member countries on matters covered by the agreements as well as on new issues falling within its mandate
- Settlement of differences and disputes among its member countries
- To carry out periodic reviews of the trade policies of its member countries
- To assist developing countries in trade policy issues, through technical assistance and training programmes
- To cooperate with other international organizations

5.1.4 Decision Making

WTO is a member-driven consensus-based organization. All major decisions in the WTO are made by its members as a whole, either by ministers who meet at least once every two years or by their ambassadors who meet regularly in Geneva. A majority vote is also possible but it has never been used in the WTO and was extremely rare in the WTO's predecessor, GATT. The WTO's agreements have been ratified in all members' parliaments. Unlike other international organizations, such as the World Bank and the IMF, in WTO, the power is not delegated to the board of directors or the organization's head.

In view of the complexities involved in multilateral negotiations among 150 member countries with diverse resource capabilities, areas of special interest, and geo-political powers, decision-making through consensus is highly challenging. Developed countries with much greater economic and political strengths often employ pressure tactics over developing and least developed countries in building up a consensus. This has led to considerable networking among the member countries and evolving of several country groups as shown in Exhibit 5.2.

When WTO rules impose disciplines on countries' policies, it is the outcome of negotiations among WTO members. The rules are enforced by the members themselves under agreed procedures that they negotiated, including the possibility of trade sanctions. The sanctions too are imposed by member countries, and authorized by the membership as a whole.

5.1.5 Organizational Structure of the WTO

The organizational structure of WTO as summarized[2] in Fig. 5.1, consists of the Ministerial Conference, General Council, council for each broad area, and subsidiary bodies.

First level: The Ministerial Conference

The Ministerial Conference is the topmost decision-making body of the WTO, which has to meet at least once every two years.

Second level: General Council

Day-to-day work in between the Ministerial Conferences is handled by the following three bodies:

- The General Council
- The Dispute Settlement Body
- The Trade Policy Review Body

In fact, all these three bodies consist of all WTO members and report to the Ministerial Conference, although they meet under different terms of reference.

[2] Annual Report 2006, World Trade Organization, Geneva, p. 93.

Exhibit 5.2   Country groups in WTO trade negotiations

African, Caribbean, and Pacific (ACP countries, also Lome Convention Countries)   Developing country group of former colonies of Europe which maintain strong ties to the EU.

Least Developed Countries (LDCs)   A group of countries identified by the UN and recognized by the WTO as 'least developed' in terms of their low GDP per capita, and their high degree of economic vulnerability.

Cairns Group   Grain exporters, i.e., Argentina, Australia, Brazil, Canada, Chile, Colombia, Fiji, Hungary, Indonesia, Malaysia, New Zealand, the Philippines, Thailand, and Uruguay.

Quad Group (also **'Old Quad'**)   Developed country trade leaders, i.e., the EU, the US, Japan, and Canada.

New Quad Group (also **Group of 4 or G4**)   Critical developed and developing market leaders, i.e., the US, the EU, Brazil, and India.

Five Interested Parties (FIPS, also Non-Group of 5 or NG5)   Nations that helped negotiate the 2004 Framework Agreement on Agriculture that now serves as the basis for the Doha round. Quad plus one, i.e., the US, the EU, Brazil, India, and Australia.

Friends of anti-dumping   A group of nations that seeks reforms of rules that would affect the US and European Union anti-dumping investigations. Members include Japan, South Korea, Chile, Colombia, Costa Rica, Hong Kong, Norway, Switzerland, Taiwan, and Thailand.

Friends of Mode 4   Mode 4 is the movement of natural persons in order to supply a service in another country. 12 member countries include India, Mexico, Indonesia, and Thailand.

Group of 10 (G10)   Net food importers and subsidizers, includes Switzerland, Japan, Norway.

Group of 20 (G20)   Primary developing nations united on agricultural negotiations, i.e., Argentina, Bolivia, Brazil, Chile, China, Egypt, Guatemala, India, Indonesia, Mexico, Nigeria, Pakistan, Paraguay, the Philippines, South Africa, Tanzania, Thailand, Uruguay, Venezuela, and Zimbabwe.

Group of 33 (G33)   Developing countries concerned with protecting agricultural markets of developing countries from low-priced import competition from industrialized countries and large agro-exporters.

Group of 90 (G90)   Poorest or least developed nations consisting of the African, Caribbean, and Pacific countries (ACP), the Least Developed Countries (LDCs), and the African Union (AU) countries.

Source: WTO.

Third level: Councils for each broad area of trade

There are three more councils, each handling a different broad area of trade, reporting to the General Council.

- The Council for Trade in Goods (Goods Council)
- The Council for Trade in Services (Services Council)
- The Council for Trade Related Aspects of Intellectual Property Rights (TRIPS Council)

Each of these councils consists of all WTO members and is responsible for the working of the WTO agreements dealing with their respective areas of trade. These three also have subsidiary bodies. Six other bodies, called committees, also report to

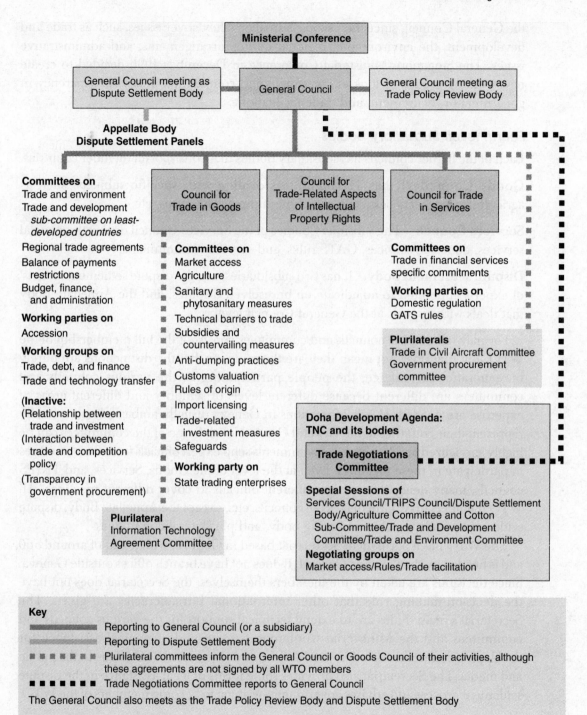

Key

▬▬▬▬ Reporting to General Council (or a subsidiary)

▬▬▬▬ Reporting to Dispute Settlement Body

■ ■ ■ ■ ■ ■ ■ Plurilateral committees inform the General Council or Goods Council of their activities, although these agreements are not signed by all WTO members

■■■■■■■ Trade Negotiations Committee reports to General Council

The General Council also meets as the Trade Policy Review Body and Dispute Settlement Body

Fig. 5.1   WTO structure

Source: WTO.

the General Council, since their scope is smaller. They cover issues, such as trade and development, the environment, regional trading arrangements, and administrative issues. The Singapore Ministerial Conference in December 1996 decided to create new working groups to look at investment and competition policy, transparency in government procurement, and trade facilitation.

Fourth level: Subsidiary bodies

Each of the higher councils has subsidiary bodies that consist of all member countries.

Goods Council   It has 11 committees dealing with specific subjects, such as agriculture, market access, subsidies, anti-dumping measures, etc.

Services Council   The subsidiary bodies of the Services Council deal with financial services, domestic services, GATS rules, and specific commitments.

Dispute settlement body   It has two subsidiaries, i.e., the dispute settlement 'panels' of experts appointed to adjudicate on unresolved disputes, and the Appellate Body that deals with appeals at the General Council level.

Formally all of these councils and committees consist of the full membership of the WTO. But that does not mean they are the same, or that the distinctions are purely bureaucratic. In practice, the people participating in the various councils and committees are different because different levels of seniority and different areas of expertise are needed. Heads of missions in Geneva (usually ambassadors) normally represent their countries at the General Council level. Some of the committees can be highly specialized and sometimes governments send expert officials from their countries to participate in these meetings. Even at the level of the Goods, Services, and TRIPS councils, many delegations assign different officials to cover different meetings. All WTO members may participate in all councils, etc., except the Appellate Body, dispute settlement panels, textile monitoring body, and plurilateral committees.

The WTO has a permanent Secretariat based in Geneva, with a staff of around 560 and is headed by the Director-General. It does not have branch offices outside Geneva. Since decisions are taken by the members themselves, the Secretariat does not have the decision-making role that other international bureaucracies are given. The Secretariat's main duties are to extend technical support for the various councils and committees and the Ministerial Conferences, to provide technical assistance for developing countries, to analyse world trade, and to explain WTO affairs to the public and media. The Secretariat also provides some forms of legal assistance in the dispute settlement process and advises governments wishing to become members of the WTO.

5.1.6   Principles of the Multilateral Trading System under the WTO

For an international business manager, it is difficult to go through the whole of the WTO agreements which are lengthy and complex being legal texts covering a wide range of activities. The agreements deal with a wide range of subjects related to international trade, such as agriculture, textiles and clothing, banking, telecommunications, government purchases, industrial standards and product safety, food sanitation regulations, and intellectual property. However, a manager dealing in international markets needs to have an understanding of the basic principles of WTO which form the foundation of the multilateral trading system. These principles are discussed below.

Trade without discrimination

Under the WTO principles, a country cannot discriminate between its trading partners and products and services of its own and foreign origin.

Most-favoured nation treatment   Under WTO agreements, countries cannot normally discriminate between their trading partners. In case a country grants someone a special favour (such as a lower rate of customs for one of their products), then it has to do the same for all other WTO members. The principle is known as Most-favoured nation (MFN) treatment. This clause is so important that it is the first article of the General Agreement on Tariffs and Trade (GATT), which governs trade in goods. MFN is also a priority in the General Agreement on Trade in Services (GATS, Article 2) and the Agreement on Trade-Related Aspects of Intellectual Property Rights (TRIPS, Article 4), although in each agreement, the principle is handled slightly differently. Together, these three agreements cover all three main areas of trade handled by the WTO.

Some exceptions to the MFN principle are allowed as under:

- Countries can set up a free trade agreement that applies only to goods traded within the group—discriminating against goods from outside.
- Countries can provide developing countries special access to their markets.
- A country can raise barriers against products that are considered to be traded unfairly from specific countries.
- In services, countries are allowed, in limited circumstances, to discriminate.

But the agreements only permit these exceptions under strict conditions. In general, MFN means that every time a country lowers a trade barrier or opens up a market, it has to do so for the same goods or services from all its trading partners—whether rich or poor, weak or strong.

National treatment   The WTO agreements stipulate that imported and locally-produced goods should be treated equally—at least after the foreign goods have entered the market. The same should apply to foreign and domestic services, and to foreign and local trademarks, copyrights and patents. This principle of 'national treatment' (giving others the same treatment as one's own nationals) is also found in all the three main WTO agreements, i.e., Article 3 of GATT, Article 17 of GATS, and Article 3 of TRIPS. However, the principle is handled slightly differently in each of these agreements. National treatment only applies once a product, service, or an item of intellectual property has entered the market. Therefore, charging customs duty on an import is not a violation of national treatment even if locally-produced products are not charged an equivalent tax.

Gradual move towards freer markets through negotiations

Lowering trade barriers is one of the most obvious means of encouraging international trade. Such barrier includes customs duties (or tariffs) and measures, such as import bans or quotas that restrict quantities selectively. Since GATT's creation in 1947–48, there have been eight rounds of trade negotiations. At first these focused on lowering tariffs (customs duties) on imported goods. As a result of the negotiations, by the mid-1990s industrial countries' tariff rates on industrial goods had fallen steadily to less than 4 per cent. But by the 1980s, the negotiations had expanded to cover non-tariff barriers on goods, and to new areas, such as services and intellectual property. The WTO agreements allow countries to introduce changes gradually through 'progressive liberalization'. Developing countries are usually given longer period to fulfil their obligations.

Increased predictability of international business environment

Sometimes, promising not to raise a trade barrier can be as important as lowering one, because the promise gives businesses a clearer view of their future market opportunities. With stability and predictability, investment is encouraged, jobs are created, and consumers can fully enjoy the benefits of competition—choice and lower prices. The multilateral trading system is an attempt by governments to make the business environment stable and predictable.

One of the achievements of the Uruguay Round of multilateral trade talks was to increase the amount of trade under binding commitments. In the WTO, when countries agree to open their markets for goods or services, they 'bind' their commitments. For goods, these bindings amount to ceiling on customs tariff rates. A country can change its bindings, but only after negotiating with its trading partners, which could mean compensating them for loss of trade. In agriculture, 100 per cent of products now have bound tariffs. The result of this is a substantially higher degree of market security for traders and investors.

The trading system under the WTO attempts to improve predictability and stability in other ways as well. One way is to discourage the use of quotas and other measures used to set limits on quantities of imports as administering quotas can lead to more red-tape and accusations of unfair play. Another is to make countries' trade rules as clear and public (transparent) as possible. Many WTO agreements require governments to disclose their policies and practices publicly within the country or by notifying the WTO. The regular surveillance of national trade policies through the Trade Policy Review Mechanism provides a further means of encouraging transparency both domestically and at the multilateral level.

Promoting fair competition

The WTO is sometimes described as a 'free trade' institution, but that is not entirely accurate. The system does allow tariffs and, in limited circumstances, other forms of protection. More accurately, it is a system of rules dedicated to open, fair, and undistorted competition.

The rules on non-discrimination—MFN and national treatment—are designed to secure fair conditions of trade. The WTO has also set rules on dumping and subsidies which adversely affect fair trade. The issues are complex, and the rules try to establish what is fair or unfair, and how governments can respond, in particular by charging additional import duties calculated to compensate for damage caused by unfair trade. Many of the other WTO agreements aim to support fair competition, such as in agriculture, intellectual property, and services. The agreement on government procurement (a 'plurilateral' agreement because it is signed by only a few WTO members) extends competition rules to purchases by thousands of government entities in many countries.

5.2 WTO AGREEMENTS: AN OVERVIEW

WTO agreements are often referred to as 'trade rules' and hence the WTO is described as a 'rule-based' system. These rules are actually agreements negotiated by the member countries' governments. The WTO agreements fall in a broad structure of six main parts as under:

- An umbrella agreement (the agreement establishing WTO)
- Agreements for each of the three broad areas of trade covered by WTO
  - ○ Goods
  - ○ Services
  - ○ Intellectual property
- Dispute settlement
- Reviews of governments' trade policies

The WTO agreements cover two basic areas—goods and services in addition to intellectual property. The agreements for goods under GATT deal with the following sector-specific issues, such as agriculture, health regulations for farm products (SPS), textiles and clothing, product standards, investment measures, anti-dumping measures, customs valuation methods, pre-shipment inspection, rules of origin, import licensing, subsidies and counter-measures, and safeguards. The specific issues covered by GATS include movement of natural persons, air transport, financial services, shipping, and telecommunications. Moreover, these agreements are dynamic rather than static in nature as they are negotiated from time to time. The new agreements can be added to the package. For instance, the Doha Development Agenda launched in the Doha Ministerial Conference is currently under negotiations. Major WTO agreements are briefly dealt with in this chapter.

5.2.1 General Agreement on Tariffs and Trade

The General Agreement on Tariffs and Trade (GATT) has significantly widened the access to international markets, besides providing legal and institutional framework. Under the WTO regime, countries can break the commitment (i.e., raise the tariff above the bound rate), but only with difficulty. To do so, a member country is required to negotiate with the countries most concerned and that could result in compensation for trading partners' loss of trade.

Opening up of the industrial sector

Market access schedules under GATT include commitments of member countries to reduce the tariffs and not to increase the tariffs above the listed rates, that means the rates are bound. For developed countries, bound rates are the rates generally charged. Most developing countries have bound the rates somewhat higher than actual rates charged, so the bound rates can serve as a ceiling.

Reduction in tariffs Individual member countries have listed their commitments to reduce the tariff rates in schedules annexed to the Marrakesh Protocol to the General Agreement on Tariffs and Trade, 1994, which is a legally binding agreement. Under these commitments, developed countries were to cut the average tariff levels on industrial products by 40 per cent in five equal instalments from 1 January 1995. However, the percentage of tariff reduction on some products of export interest to developing countries, such as textiles and clothing and leather and leather products is much lower than the average, as they are considered sensitive. A number of developing countries and economies-in-transition agreed to reduce their tariffs by nearly two-thirds of the percentage achieved by developed countries. As a result, the weighted average levels of tariffs applicable to industrial products were expected to fall in a period of five years from

- 6.3 per cent to 3.8 per cent in developed countries
- 15.3 per cent to 12.3 per cent in developing countries
- 8.6 per cent to 6 per cent in the transition economies

Additional commitments were made under the Information Technology Agreement in 1997 wherein 40 countries accounting for more than 92 per cent of trade in information technology products, agreed to eliminate import duties and other charges on most of these products by 2000 and on a handful of the products by 2005. As with other tariff commitments, each participating country is applying its commitments equally to exports from all WTO members, i.e. on a most-favoured nation basis, even from members that did not make the commitments.

Tariff bindings Besides the commitments to reduce tariffs, market access schedules represent commitments on the part of member countries not to increase the tariffs above the listed rates known as 'bound' rates. Binding of tariff lines has substantially increased the degree of market security for traders and investors. Developed countries increased the number of imports whose tariff rates are 'bound' (committed and difficult to increase) from 78 per cent of the product lines to 99 per cent. For developing countries, the increase was considerable, from 21 per cent to 73 per cent. Economies in transition from central planning increased their bindings from 73 per cent to 98 per cent.

5.2.2 Creating Fairer Markets in Agriculture Sector

Although earlier rules of GATT did apply to agriculture trade, they contained loopholes. Some developed countries protected their costly and inefficient production of temperate zone agricultural products (e.g., wheat and other grains, meat, and dairy products) by imposing quantitative restrictions and variable levies on imports in addition to the high import tariffs. This level of protection often resulted in increased domestic production which, because of high prices, could be disposed off in the international markets only under subsidy. Such subsidized sales depressed international market prices of such agro-products. Providing subsidies by developed countries also led to taking away of legitimated market share of competitive producers, mainly low income countries in the agro sector.

As a result, international trade in agriculture became highly 'distorted', especially with the use of export subsidies which would not normally have been allowed for industrial products. Trade is termed as 'distorted' if prices are higher or lower than normal, and if quantities produced, bought, and sold are also higher or lower than normal of the levels that usually exist in a competitive market.

The Uruguay Round produced the first multilateral agreement dedicated to the agriculture sector. The objective of the Agreement on Agriculture (AoA) was to reform trade in agriculture and to make policies more market oriented. This is likely to improve predictability and security for both importing and exporting countries. The salient features of the AoA (Exhibit 5.3) are discussed below.

Exhibit 5.3 Reduction of subsidies and protection under Agreement on Agriculture		
	Developed countries 6 years: 1995–2000	**Developing countries 10 years: 1995–2004**
Tariffs		
Average cut for all agricultural products	–36%	–24%
minimum cut per product	–15%	–10%
Domestic support		
Total AMS cuts for sector (base period: 1986–88)	–20%	–13%
Exports		
Value of subsidies	–36%	–24%
Subsidized quantities (base period: 1986–90)	–21%	14%

Note: Least-developed countries do not have to make commitments to reduce tariffs or subsidies.
Source: WTO.

Elimination of non-tariff measures through the 'tariffication' process
Subsequent to the Uruguay Round, quotas and other types of trade restrictive measures
were to be replaced by tariffs that provide more or less equivalent levels of protection.
This process of converting quotas and other types of non-tariff measures to tariffs that
represent about the same level of protection, is termed as 'tariffication'. Under the
Uruguay Round, member countries agreed that developed countries would cut the
tariffs by an average of 36 per cent in equal steps over six years while developing
countries would make 24 per cent cuts over 10 years. Several developing countries
also used the option of offering ceiling tariff rates in cases where duties were not
'bound' before the Uruguay Round. Least developed countries do not have to cut
their tariffs.

For products whose non-tariff restrictions have been converted to tariffs,
governments are allowed to take special emergency actions or 'special safeguards' in
order to prevent swiftly falling prices or surges in imports from hurting their farmers.

Binding against further increase of tariffs   In addition to elimination of all non-
tariff measures by *tariffication*, all countries have bound all their tariffs applicable to
agricultural products. In most cases, developing countries have given binding at rates
that are higher than their current applied or reduced rates.

Tariffs on all agricultural products are now bound. Almost all import restrictions
that did not take the form of tariffs, such as quotas, have been converted to tariffs.
This has resulted into substantial market predictability in agriculture. The tariffs have
also been reduced substantially. Besides, market-access commitments on agriculture
also eliminate previous import bans on certain products.

Domestic support   National policies that support domestic prices or subsidized
production often encourage over-production. This squeezes out imports or leads to
export subsidies and low-price dumping in international markets. Under the agreement
on agriculture, domestic policies that have a direct effect on production and trade
have to be cut back. The domestic support in the agriculture sector is categorized
under Green, Amber, and Blue boxes as shown in Exhibit 5.4.

Member countries quantified the support provided per year for the agriculture
sector which is termed as 'total aggregate measurement of support' (total AMS) in the
base years of 1986–88. Developed countries agreed to reduce total AMS by 20 per
cent over six years starting in 1995 while the developed countries agreed to make a
30 per cent cut over 10 years. Least developed countries were not required to make
any cut in AMS. The AMS is calculated on a product-by-product basis by using the
difference between the average external reference price for a product and its applied
administered price multiplied by the quantity of production. To arrive at AMS, non-
product-specific domestic subsidies are added to the total subsidies calculated on a
product-by-product basis.

Export subsidies   The agreement on agriculture prohibits export subsidies on
agricultural products unless the subsidies are specified in a member's lists of

---

Exhibit 5.4   Categories of domestic support in agriculture sector

Green Box All subsidies that have little or at most minimal trade distorting effects and that do not have the 'effect of providing price support to producers', are exempt from commitments towards reduction. The subsidies under the Green Box include

- Government expenditure on agricultural research, pest control, inspection and grading of particular products, marketing, and promotion services
- Financial participation by government in income insurance and income safety-net programmes
- Payments for natural disaster
- Structural adjustment assistance provided through
  - Producer retirement programmes designed to facilitate the retirement of persons engaged in marketable agricultural production
  - Resource retirement programmes designed to remove land and other resources, including livestock, from agricultural production

  - Investment aids designed to assist the financial or physical restructuring of a producer's operations.
- Payments under environmental programmes
- Payments under regional assistance programme

Amber Box This category of domestic support refers to the amber colour of traffic lights, which means 'slow down'. The agreement establishes a ceiling on the total domestic support that a government may provide to domestic producers.

Blue Box Certain categories of direct payment to farmers are also permitted where farmers are required to limit production. This also includes government assistance programmes to encourage agricultural and rural development in developing countries, and other support on a small scale when compared with the total value of the product or products supported (5 per cent or less in the case of developed countries and 10 per cent or less for developing countries).

Source: WTO.

---

commitments. Where they are listed, the agreement requires WTO members to cut both the amount of money they spend on export subsidies and the quantities of exports that receive subsidies. Taking averages for 1986–90 as the base level, developed countries agreed to cut the value of export subsidies by 36 per cent over six years starting in 1995 whereas developing countries by 24 per cent over 10 years. Developed countries also agreed to reduce the quantities of subsidised exports by 21 per cent over six years whereas developing countries by 4 per cent over 10 years. Least developed countries did not need to make any cuts. During the six-year implementation period, developing countries were allowed under certain conditions to use subsidies to reduce the costs of export marketing and transporting.

Developing countries' perspective of the Agreement on Agriculture

Contribution of agriculture to economies of developing countries is highly important in terms of sustaining livelihood of a significant proportion of the population, which includes a large number of low-income and resource-poor producers and landless agriculture labourers. This section of the population in developing countries, including India, lacks skills and is not covered under any safety net, which is essential for ensuring a minimal cross-sector labour mobility. Thus, the situation in developing countries is in sharp contrast to the reality of agriculture sector in developed countries. India and other developing countries have, therefore, been insisting that special and differential treatment for developing countries must be integral to all aspects, including the negotiated outcome on agriculture under the Doha Round in the WTO.

Mitigating the risks associated with price declines, price volatility, predatory competition, and other market imperfections that low-income, resource-poor, and subsistence farmers have to face, remains paramount. Key reasons for market imperfections include huge amounts of production and trade-distorting subsidies provided by some developed countries to their agricultural sector. Therefore, along with other developing countries, particularly its alliance partners in the G-20 and G-33, India has been emphasizing that the Doha agricultural outcome must include at its core

- Removal of distorting subsidies and protection by developed countries to the level playing field
- Appropriate provisions designed to safeguard food and livelihood security to meet the rural development needs in developing countries

Apart from insisting on appropriate policy and flexibilities to enable developing country governments to help low-income and vulnerable producers absorb or insure themselves against risks, India has also taken the stand that governments must be able to foster stable and remunerative prices for domestic producers to increase productivity and gradually move away from dependence on low-productivity agriculture. To these ends, meaningful and effective instruments such as Special Products and the Special Safeguard Mechanism are important for developing countries, such as India. At the Hong Kong Ministerial Conference, it has been agreed that Special Products and the Special Safeguard Mechanism shall be an integral part of the modalities and the outcome of negotiations in agriculture. Moreover, developing countries shall have the right to self designate an appropriate number of special products, guided by indicators based on the three fundamental criteria of food security, livelihood security, and rural development needs. These designated products will attract more flexible treatment. Developing country members will also have the right to recourse to a special safeguard mechanism based on import quantity and price triggers, with precise arrangements to be further defined.

5.2.3 Standards and Safety Measures

Article 20 of the GATT allows governments to act on trade in order to protect human, animal, or plant life or health, provided no discrimination is made and this is not used as disguised protectionism. In addition, there are two specific agreements dealing with food safety and animal and plant health and safety with product standards.

The Agreement on Sanitary and Phytosanitary (SPS) measures sets out the basic rules on food safety and plant health standards. This allows countries to set their own standards which have to be based on science and should be applied only to the extent necessary to protect human, animal, or plant life or health. These regulations should not arbitrarily or unjustifiably discriminate between countries where identical or similar conditions prevail. Member countries are encouraged to use or adhere to international standards, such as FAO/WHO Codex, Alimentarius Commission for food, International Animal Health Organization for animal health, etc. However, the agreement allows countries to set higher standards with consistency. The agreement includes provisions for control, inspection, and approval procedures. Member governments must provide advance notice of new or changed SPS regulations and establish a national enquiry point to provide information.

The Agreement on Technical Barriers to Trade (TBT) attempts to ensure that regulations, standards, testing, and certification procedures do not create unnecessary obstacles to trade. This agreement complements with the SPS measures. Firms engaged in international business and manufacturing products for international markets need to know about the latest standards in their prospective markets. All WTO member countries are required to maintain national enquiry points to make this information available.

5.2.4   Opening Up International Business Opportunities in Textiles

World trade in textiles and clothing had been subject to a large number of bilateral quota arrangements over the past four decades. The range of products covered by quotas expanded from cotton textiles under the short-term and long-term arrangements of the 1960s and early 1970s to an ever-increasing list of textile products made from natural and man-made fibres under five expansions of the multi-fibre agreement. From 1974 until the end of the Uruguay Round, the international trade in textiles was governed by the Multi-fibre Arrangement (MFA). This was a framework for bilateral agreements or unilateral actions that established quotas limiting imports into countries whose domestic industries were facing serious damage from rapidly increasing imports.

The quota system under MFA conflicted with GATT's general preference for customs tariffs instead of measures that restricted quantities. The quotas were also exceptions to the GATT principle of treating all trading partners equally because they specified how much the importing country was going to accept from individual exporting countries.

Since 1995, the WTO's Agreement on Textiles and Clothing (ATC) took over from the MFA and had been the WTO's significant agreement. The schedule of integration into GATT is shown in Table 5.1.

A Textiles Monitoring Body (TMB) supervised the implementation of the agreement. It monitored actions taken under the agreement to ensure that they are consistent, and reports to the Council on Trade in Goods and reviews the operation of the agreement. The TMB also dealt with disputes under the ATC. If they remain unresolved, the disputes could be brought to the WTO's regular Dispute Settlement Body.

Post-MFN textile and clothing scenario   On full integration into GATT and final elimination of quotas, the ATC ceased to exist on 1 January 2005. This has opened immense opportunities for developing countries as well as increasing challenges in international markets which are likely to be more competitive.

Table 5.1   Schedule of integration into GATT under ATC

Steps	Percentage of products to be brought under GATT (including removal of any quota)	Rate of opening up of quotas if 1994 rate was 6%
Step 1 1 Jan. 1995 (to 31 Dec. 1997)	16% (minimum, taking 1990 imports as base)	6.96% per year
Step 2 1 Jan. 1998 (to 31 Dec. 2001)	17%	8.7%
Step 3 1 Jan. 2002 (to 31 Dec. 2004)	18%	11.05% per year
Step 4 1 Jan. 2005	49% (maximum)	No quotas left

The elimination of quota restrictions on textiles and clothing at the beginning of 2005 did not appear to have a major impact so far on demand or domestic market conditions in the major importing markets—the US and the EU. What has perceptibly changed, however, is the composition of market shares among exporting countries. The per cent share[3] of China's import into the US and the EU increased by 43 per cent and 44 per cent respectively whereas India's share grew by 25 per cent in the US and 19 per cent in the EU in 2005. On the other hand, import share of countries from Sub-Saharan Africa and East Asia declined considerably during this period.

5.2.5   General Agreement on Trade in Services

The General Agreement on Trade in Services (GATS) is the first and only set of multilateral rules governing international trade in services. Negotiated in the Uruguay Round, it was developed in response to the strong growth of the services economy over the past three decades and the greater potential for marketing services internationally brought about by the communications revolution. The GATS has three elements:

1. The main text containing general obligations and disciplines
2. Annexes dealing with rules for specific sectors
3. Individual countries' specific commitments to provide access to their markets, including indications where countries are temporarily not applying the most-favoured nation principle of non-discrimination.

General obligations and disciplines   The agreement covers all internationally-traded services, e.g., banking, telecommunications, tourism, professional services, etc. It also defines four ways (or 'modes') of trading services internationally:

Mode 1   Services supplied from one country to another (e.g., international telephone calls), officially known as 'cross-border supply'

---

[3] *World Trade Report 2006*, World Trade Organization, Geneva, pp. 14–18.

Mode 2   Consumers or firms making use of a service in another country (e.g. tourism), officially 'consumption abroad'

Mode 3   A foreign company setting up subsidiaries or branches to provide services in another country (e.g., foreign banks setting up operations in a country), officially 'commercial presence'

Mode 4   Individuals travelling from their own country to supply services in another (e.g., fashion models or consultants), officially 'presence of natural persons'

Most-favoured-nation treatment   MFN also applies to the service sector, wherein a member country's trading partners are to be treated equally on the principle of non-discrimination. Under GATS, if a country allows foreign competition in a sector, equal opportunities in that sector should be given to service providers from all other WTO members. This applies even if the country has made no specific commitment to provide foreign companies access to its markets under the WTO. MFN applies to all services, but some special temporary exemptions have been allowed to countries that already have preferential agreements in services with their trading partners. Such exemptions are expected to last not more than 10 years.

Commitments on market access and national treatment   Individual countries' commitments to open markets in specific sectors and the extent of their openness has been the outcome of the Uruguay Round negotiations. The commitments appear in 'schedules' that list the sectors being opened, the extent of market access being given in those sectors (e.g., whether there are any restrictions on foreign ownership), and any limitation on national treatment (whether some rights granted to local companies will not be granted to foreign companies). For instance, if a government commits itself to allow foreign banks to operate in its domestic market, that is a market-access commitment. And if the government limits the number of licences it will issue, then that is a market-access limitation. If it also says foreign banks are only allowed one branch while domestic banks are allowed numerous branches, that is an exception to the national treatment principle.

These clearly defined commitments are 'bound'—like bound tariffs for trade in goods, and they can only be modified after negotiations with affected countries. Because 'unbinding' is difficult, the commitments are virtually guaranteed conditions for foreign exporters and importers of services and investors in the service sector.

Governmental services are explicitly carved out of the agreement and there is nothing in GATS that forces a government to privatize service industries. The carve-out is an explicit commitment by WTO governments to allow publicly funded services in core areas of their responsibility. Governmental services are defined in the agreements as those that are not supplied commercially and do not compete with other suppliers. These services are not subject to any GATS discipline, are not covered by the negotiations, and the commitments on market access and national treatment do not apply to them.

Transparency   GATS stipulates that governments must publish all relevant laws and regulations, as set-up enquiry points within their bureaucracies. Foreign companies and governments can then use these inquiry points to obtain information about regulations in any service sector. Further, the member countries' governments have to notify the WTO of any change in regulations that apply to the services that fall under specific commitments.

Objectivity and reasonability of regulations   Since domestic regulations are the most significant means of exercising influence or control over services trade, the agreement says governments should regulate services reasonably, objectively, and impartially. When a government makes an administrative decision that affects a service, it should also provide an impartial means for reviewing the decision (e.g., a tribunal). GATS does not require any service to be deregulated. Commitments to liberalize do not affect governments' right to set levels of quality, safety, or price, or to introduce regulations to pursue any other policy objective. A commitment to national treatment, e.g., would only mean that the same regulations would apply to foreign suppliers as to nationals. Governments naturally retain their right to set qualification requirements for doctors or lawyers, and to set standards to ensure consumer health and safety.

Recognition   When two or more governments have agreements recognizing each other's qualifications (e.g., the licensing or certification of service suppliers), GATS says other members must also be given a chance to negotiate comparable pacts. The recognition of other countries' qualifications must not be discriminatory, and it must not amount to protectionism in disguise. These recognition agreements have to be notified to the WTO.

International payments and transfers   Once a government has made a commitment to open a service sector to foreign competition, it must not normally restrict money being transferred out of the country as payment for services supplied (current transactions) in that sector. The only exception is when there are balance of payments difficulties, and even then the restrictions must be temporary and subject to other limits and conditions.

Progressive liberalization   As the Uruguay Round was only the beginning, GATS requires more negotiations, which began in early 2000 and formed part of the Doha Development Agenda. The goal is to take the liberalization process further by increasing the level of commitments in schedules.

Complexity of international trade in services

International trade in goods is a relatively simple idea to grasp—a product is transported from one country to another. Trade in services is much more diverse. Telephone companies, banks, airlines, and accountancy firms provide their services in ways quite different from each other. The GATS annexes cover some of the diversity as discussed here.

Movement of natural persons   This annex deals with negotiations on individuals' rights to stay temporarily in a country for the purpose of providing a service. It specifies that the agreement does not apply to people seeking permanent employment or to conditions for obtaining citizenship, permanent residence, or permanent employment.

Financial services   Instability in the banking system affects the whole economy. The financial services annex gives governments very wide latitude to take prudential measures, such as those for the protection of investors, depositors, and insurance policy holders, and to ensure the integrity and stability of the financial system. The annex also excludes from the agreement services provided when a government is exercising its authority over the financial system, e.g., central banks' services.

Telecommunications   The telecommunications sector has a dual role: it is a distinct sector of economic activity, and an underlying means of supplying other economic activities (such as, electronic money transfers). The annex says governments must ensure that foreign service suppliers are given access to the public telecommunications networks without discrimination.

Air transport services   Under this annex, traffic rights and directly related activities are excluded from GATS' coverage. They are handled by other bilateral agreements. However, the annex establishes that GATS will apply to aircraft repair and maintenance services, marketing of air transport services, and computer-reservation services.

The capabilities of services and areas of interests are vastly different in developed and developing countries. Developed countries have always been keen to use pressure tactics to access developing countries' markets in their areas of special interest, i.e., financial, and telecommunication services that received priority in the negotiation process. On the other hand, developed countries have been hesitant to open up their markets in the service sectors of interest to developing countries in Mode 4 and Mode 1.

India's efforts have been to secure binding commitments in Cross Border Supply of Services (Mode 1) and Movement of Natural Persons (Mode 4). Mode 4 objectives are driven by the competence of India's service professionals and Mode 1 objectives by its strong competitive edge in IT and IT enabled services (ITeS). India has been pushing for the elimination of the Economic Needs Test, clear prescription of the duration of stay, provisions for extension, etc. Some of these concerns have been addressed in the Hong-Kong Ministerial Declaration, which provides a direction for developing disciplines in domestic regulations.

5.2.6 Protection and Enforcement of Intellectual Property Rights

Knowledge and ideas are rapidly gaining increased significance in market offerings. Most of the value of technology-intensive products and medicines lie in the amount of invention, innovation, research, design, and testing involved. Films, music recordings, books, computer software, and on-line services are bought and sold because of the information and creativity they contain, not usually because of the plastic, metal, or paper used to make them. The objects of intellectual property are creation of human mind, the human intellect. Creators can be given the right to prevent others from using their inventions, designs, or other creations—and to use that right to negotiate payment in return for others using them. Such rights are known as 'intellectual property rights' which may take a number of forms. For example, books, paintings, and films fall under copyright; inventions can be patented; brand names and product logos can be registered as trademarks; and so on.

The extent of protection and enforcement of these rights varies widely around the world. Besides, tax or ineffective enforcement of such rights in a number of country markets may encourage trade in counterfeit and pirated goods, thereby damaging the legitimate commercial interests of manufacturers who hold or have acquired those rights.

Farmers and consumers in developing countries are highly apprehensive of misuse of patent laws by the developed countries. Patents in developed countries related to developing countries' traditional know-how, such as alternative uses of turmeric, *neem,* etc., and geographical indications such as Darjeeling tea and basmati rice have generated a lot of controversy in India and other South Asian countries.

Ineffective enforcement of protection to the intellectual property especially in the developing countries often leads to high incidence of piracy. This has been the key reason for knowledge-based firms such as Blockbuster Video, the world market leader in rented video to refrain from entering such markets despite large potentials. The WTO's agreement on Trade Related Aspects of Intellectual Property Rights (TRIPS), negotiated in the 1986–94 Uruguay Round, introduced intellectual property rules in the multilateral trading system for the first time. TRIPS lays down minimum standards for the protection of intellectual property rights as well as the procedures and remedies for their enforcement. It establishes a mechanism for consultations and surveillance at the international level to ensure compliance with these standards by member countries at the national level.

The WTO's TRIPS agreement attempts to narrow the gaps in the way these rights are protected around the world, and to bring them under common international rules. It establishes minimum levels of protection that each government has to give to the intellectual property of fellow WTO members. The trade disputes over intellectual property rights may also be dealt by WTO's dispute settlement system.

As in the other two agreements of GATT and GATS, the principles of non-discrimination, i.e., national treatment and MFN, features prominently in TRIPS agreement. Besides, the protection of intellectual property is expected to contribute to technical innovation and transfer of technology. This is especially significant while marketing technology intensive and knowledge-based products. The structure of the agreement is built on the existing international conventions dealing with IPRs, such as

- The Paris Convention for the Protection of Industrial Property (patents, industrial designs, etc.)

- The Berne Convention for the Protection of Literary and Artistic Works (copyright)

Its provisions apply to the intellectual property rights related to patents, copyright, and related rights, trademarks, industrial designs, layout designs of integrated circuits, undisclosed information and trade sectors, and geographical indications.

In order to ensure that the rights available to patent holders are not abused, TRIPS provides for compulsory licensing. The agreement also lays down procedures for consultations between governments when one party has reasons to believe that the licensing practices or conditions of an enterprise from another member country constitute an abuse of the agreement or have adverse effects on competition.

Once the WTO agreements took effect on 1 January 1995, developed countries were given one year to ensure that their laws and practices conform to the TRIPS agreement whereas developing countries and transition economies (under certain conditions) were given five years, until 2000. Least developed countries initially had 11 years, i.e., until 2006; the date was subsequently extended to 2016 for pharmaceutical patents.

TRIPS and developed–developing countries' divide

The amendment to the TRIPS agreement adopted by the General Council on 30 August 2003 was reaffirmed by the Hong Kong Ministerial Conference on 6 December 2005. The amendment aims to bring flexibility to address public health problems resulting from HIV/AIDS, tuberculosis, malaria, and other epidemics so as to enable manufacture and export of pharmaceutical products under compulsory licences to countries with limited or low manufacturing capabilities. The main issues presently being discussed in TRIPS council include

- TRIPS-CBD (Convention on Biological Diversity)
- Relationship and protection of additional knowledge
- Extension of additional protection to geographical indications other than wines and spirits
- Establishment of multilateral register for wines and spirits

India, along with a number of other developing countries rich in bio-diversity, has proposed that TRIPS agreements should be amended to provide for

- Disclosure of source and country of origin of biological resource and of the traditional knowledge used in the invention
- Disclosure of evidence of prior informed consent (PIC) under the relevant national regime
- Disclosure of evidence of benefit sharing under the relevant national regime

India favours extension of additional protection of Geographical Indications (GI) to obtain higher level of production for Indian geographical indications, such as basmati rice, Darjeeling tea, Nilgiri tea, and non-agriculture products as well, such as

Kanchipuram silk, Mysore agarbatti, etc. The multilateral register for wines and spirits too need to be opened to other geographical indications, for extending protection.

5.2.7 Curbing Unfair Marketing Practices

While making pricing decisions for international markets, a thorough understanding of 'unfair trade practices' under WTO agreements is required so as to assess their implications in the target markets. Subsidies may play an important role in developing countries and in the transformation of centrally-planned economies to market economies. The pricing strategy should be designed so as to deal with threats of anti-dumping and countervailing duties while using differential pricing strategies. International market competitions get distorted mainly by unfair trade practices, such as

- If the exported goods benefit from the subsidies
- If exported goods are dumped in overseas markets

The agreements on Anti-Dumping Practices (ADP) and on Subsidies and Countervailing Measures (SCM) authorize importing countries to levy compensatory duties on import of products.

Agreements on anti-dumping practices

The WTO agreement on anti-dumping allows governments to act against dumping where there is genuine (material) injury to the competing domestic industry. A product is considered to be dumped if

- The export price is less than the price charged for the same product in the exporting country, or
- It is sold for less than its cost of production

In order to do that, the government has to be able to show that dumping is taking place, calculate the extent of dumping (how much lower the export price is compared to the exporter's home market price), and show that dumping is causing injury or threatening to do so. Typically, anti-dumping action means charging extra import duty on the particular product from the particular exporting country in order to bring its price closer to the 'normal value' or to remove the injury to domestic industry in the importing country.

There are many ways of calculating whether a particular product is being dumped heavily or only lightly. The agreement narrows down the range of possible options. It provides three methods to calculate a product's 'normal value'. The main method is based on the price in the exporter's domestic market. When this cannot be used, two alternatives are available—the price charged by the exporter in another country, or a calculation based on the combination of the exporter's production costs, other expenses, and normal profit margins. And the agreement also specifies how a fair comparison can be made between the export price and what would be a normal price.

Anti-dumping measures can only be applied if dumping is hurting the industry in the importing country. Therefore, a detailed investigation has to be conducted according to specified rules first. The investigation must evaluate all relevant economic factors that have a bearing on the state of the industry in question. If the investigation shows dumping is taking place and domestic industry is being hurt, the exporting company can undertake to raise its price to an agreed level in order to avoid anti-dumping import duty.

Detailed procedures are set out on how anti-dumping cases are to be initiated, how the investigations are to be conducted, and on conditions for ensuring that all interested parties are given an opportunity to present evidence. Anti-dumping measures must expire five years after the date of imposition, unless an investigation shows that ending the measure would lead to injury.

Anti-dumping investigations are to end immediately in cases where the authorities determine that the margin of dumping is insignificantly small (defined as less than 2 per cent of the export price of the product.) Besides, the investigations also have to end if the volume of dumped imports is negligible, i.e., if the volume from one country is less than 3 per cent of total imports of that product, although investigations can proceed if several countries, each supplying less than 3 per cent of the imports, together account for 7 per cent or more of total imports.

Member countries are required to inform the committee on anti-dumping practices about all preliminary and final anti-dumping actions, promptly and in detail. When differences arise, members may consult each other and use the WTO's dispute settlement procedure.

India has been the leading user of anti-dumping measures[4] in the world (Fig. 5.2) followed by the US, the European Community, Argentina, South Africa, Australia, Canada, Brazil, China, and Turkey.

Circumvention   A situation where the exporters–importers manage to avoid anti-dumping duties is known as 'circumvention'. Exporters–importers may manage to avoid anti-dumping duties by

- Bringing products with minor modifications
- Importing parts and components with a view to carry out minor operations in the members' territory.
- Assembly in third countries for exports to the concerned importing member

Such a situation is opposed by most members, including India despite having faced circumvention in some cases.

The agreement on subsidies and countervailing measures

This agreement disciplines the use of subsidies. It also regulates the actions countries can take to counter the effects of subsidies by other countries. The importing country

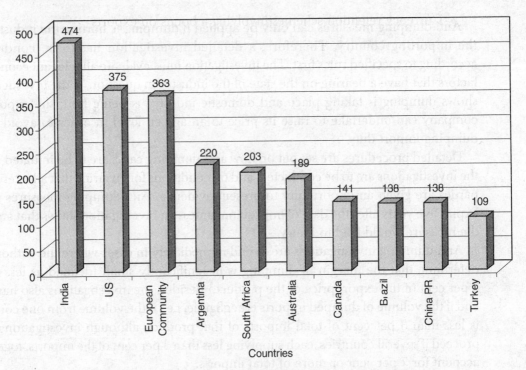

Fig. 5.2 Top 10 users of anti-dumping measures 1995–2007 (up to June 2007)

Source: Economic Survey 2007–08, Ministry of Commerce, Government of India, New Delhi, p. 148.

can use the WTO's dispute settlement procedure to seek the withdrawal of the subsidy or the removal of its adverse effects. It can launch its own investigation and ultimately charge extra duty (known as 'countervailing duty') on subsidized imports that are found to be hurting domestic producers. The agreement contains two categories of subsidies as under:

Prohibited subsidies Those subsidies that require recipients to meet certain export targets, or to use domestic goods instead of imported goods, are known as prohibited subsidies. They are prohibited because they are specifically designed to distort international trade, and are therefore, likely to hurt other countries' trade. They can be challenged in the WTO dispute settlement procedure where they are handled under an accelerated timetable. If the dispute settlement procedure confirms that the subsidy is prohibited, it must be withdrawn immediately. Otherwise, the complaining country can take counter-measures. If domestic producers are hurt by imports of subsidized products, countervailing duty can be imposed. The agreement's illustrative list of prohibited export subsidies[5] includes

- Direct subsidies based on export performance

[5] *Business Guide to Uruguay Round, International Trade Centre,* Geneva: UNCTAD/WTO, 1996, pp. 2–16; *Understanding WTO,* World Trade Organization, Geneva, 2007, pp. 45–46.

- Currency retention schemes involving a bonus on exports
- Provision of subsidized inputs for use in the production of exported goods
- Exemption from direct taxes (e.g., tax on profits related to exports)
- Exemption from, or remission of, indirect taxes (e.g., VAT) on exported products in excess of those borne by these products when sold for domestic consumption
- Remission of drawback of import charges (e.g., tariffs and other duties) in excess of those levied on inputs consumed in the production of exported goods
- Export guarantee programmes at premium rates inadequate to cover the long-term costs of the programme
- Export credits at rates below the government's cost of borrowing, where they are used to secure a material advantage in export credit items

Actionable subsidies   In this category the complaining country has to show that the subsidy has an adverse effect on its interest; otherwise the subsidy is permitted. The agreement defines three types of damage by such subsidies as under:

- One country's subsidies can hurt a domestic industry in an importing country.
- It can hurt rival exporters from another country when the two compete in a third market.
- The domestic subsidies in one country can hurt exporters trying to compete in the subsidizing country's domestic market.

If the Dispute Settlement Body rules that the subsidy does have an adverse effect, the subsidy must be withdrawn or its adverse effect must be removed. Again, if domestic producers are hurt by imports of subsidized products, countervailing duty can be imposed.

The agreement originally contained a third category, i.e., non-actionable subsidies. This category existed for five years, ending in December 1999, and was not extended. Some of the disciplines are similar to those of the anti-dumping agreement. Countervailing duty (the parallel of anti-dumping duty) can only be charged after the importing country has conducted a detailed investigation similar to that required for anti-dumping action. The exporter who has received subsidy can also agree to raise export prices as an alternative to exports being charged countervailing duty.

5.2.8   Emergency Protection from Imports

A WTO member may restrict import of a product temporarily (take 'safeguard' actions) if its domestic industry is seriously injured or threatened with injury caused by a surge in imports. Safeguard measures were always available under GATT (Article 19); however, they were infrequently used. A number of countries preferred to protect their domestic industries through 'grey area' measures—using bilateral negotiations outside GATT's auspices. They also persuaded exporting countries to restrain exports 'voluntarily' or to agree to other means of sharing markets. Agreements of this kind were reached at for a wide range of products among countries, e.g., automobiles, steel, and semiconductors.

The WTO agreements on safeguards prohibit 'grey-area' measures, and it set time limits (a sunset clause) on all safeguard actions. The agreement says members must not seek, take, or maintain any Voluntary Export Restraints (VERs), Orderly Marketing Arrangements (OMAs), or any other similar measure on the export or the import side. The bilateral measures that were not modified to conform with the agreement were phased out at the end of 1998. Countries were allowed to keep one of these measures an extra year (until the end of 1999), but only the European Union—for restrictions on imports of cars from Japan—made use of this provision.

Industries or companies may request safeguard action by their governments. The WTO agreement sets out requirements for safeguard investigations by national authorities. The emphasis is on transparency and on following established rules and practices, thus avoiding arbitrary methods. A safeguard measure should be applied only to the extent necessary to prevent or remedy serious injury and to help the industry concerned to adjust. Where quantitative restrictions (quotas) are imposed, they normally should not reduce the quantities of imports below the annual average for the last three representative years for which statistics are available, unless clear justification is given that a different level is necessary to prevent or remedy serious injury.

In principle, safeguard measures cannot be targeted at imports from a particular country. A safeguard measure should not last more than four years, although this can be extended up to eight years under special circumstances. When a country restricts imports in order to safeguard its domestic producers, in principle it must give something in return. To some extent developing countries' exports are shielded from safeguard actions. An importing country can only apply a safeguard measure to a product from a developing country if the developing country is supplying more than 3 per cent of the imports of that product, or if developing country members with less than 3 per cent import share collectively account for more than 9 per cent of total imports of the product concerned.

The WTO's Safeguards Committee oversees the operations of the agreement and is responsible for the surveillance of members' commitment. Member governments have to report each phase of a safeguard investigation and related decision making, and the committee review these reports.

5.2.9 Attempting to Reduce Non-tariff Barriers

In addition to import tariffs, an international firm faces a number of bureaucratic and legal issues in the target countries which hinders smooth flow of trade. Such barriers are generally employed to block market entry and often criticized as arbitrary as they lack transparency. Growing use of unconventional Non-Tariff Measures (NTMs), such as health and safety measures, technical regulations, environmental controls, customs valuation procedures, and labour laws by developed countries has become a major barrier to market access to exports from developing countries. Such trade barriers are considerably stiffer for products with lower value addition and technological content (agriculture products, textiles, leather products, etc.) products, which are of major interest to countries like India.

Import licensing procedures

Import licensing procedures are generally considered as complex and non-transparent with little predictability and had often been used to block market entry of foreign products. The agreement on Import Licensing Procedures attempts to simplify and bring transparency to import procedures. The agreement requires governments to publish sufficient information for international traders to know how and why licences are granted. It also describes how countries should notify the WTO when they introduce new import licensing procedures or change existing procedures. The agreement offers guidance on how governments should assess applications for licences. The agreement sets criteria for automatic issuance of some licences so that the procedures used do not restrict trade. Here, the agreement tries to minimize the importers' burden in applying for licences, so that the administrative work does not in itself restrict or distort imports. The agreement says agencies handling licensing should not normally take more than 30 days to deal with an application. However, 60 days are permitted when all applications are considered at the same time.

Customs valuation

For importers, the process of estimating the value of a product at customs presents problems that can be just as serious as the actual duty rate charged. The WTO agreement on customs valuation aims for a fair, uniform, and neutral system for the valuation of goods for customs purposes—a system that conforms to commercial realities, and which outlaws the use of arbitrary or fictitious customs values. The agreement provides a set of valuation rules, expanding and giving greater precision to the provisions on customs valuation in the original GATT.

The basic aim of the agreement is to protect the interests of firms engaged in international trade by requiring that customs should accept the price actually paid by the importer in the particular transaction for determining dutiable value. This applies to both arms-length and related-party transactions. The agreement recognizes that the prices obtained by different importers for the same product may vary. The mere fact that the price obtained by a particular importer is lower than that at which other importers have imported the product, cannot be used as a ground for rejecting the transaction value. Customs can reject the transaction value in such situations only if it has reasons to doubt the truth or accuracy of the declared price of the imported goods. Even in such cases it has to give importers an opportunity to justify their price and if this justification is not accepted, customs has to provide importers in writing the reasons for rejecting the transaction value and for determining the dutiable value by using other methods. Further, by providing importers the right to be consulted throughout all stages of the determination of value, the agreement ensures that the discretion available to customs for scrutinizing declared value is used objectively.

The agreement also requires national legislation on the valuation of goods to prove the following rights to importers:

- Right to withdraw imported goods from customs, when there is likely to be a delay in the determination of customs value, by providing sufficient quantities, in the form of surety or a deposit, covering the payment of customs duties for which goods may be liable
- Right to expect that any information of a confidential nature that is made available to customs shall be treated as confidential
- Right to appeal, without fear of penalty, to an independent body within the customs administration and to judicial authority against decisions taken by customs

Pre-shipment inspection

Pre-shipment inspection is the practice of employing specialized private companies (or 'independent entities') to check shipment details—essentially price, quantity, and quality—of goods ordered overseas. The basic purpose of pre-shipment inspection is to safeguard national financial interests (preventing capital flight, commercial fraud, and customs duty evasion, for instance) and to compensate for inadequacies in administrative infrastructures.

The Pre-shipment Inspection Agreement places obligations on governments which use pre-shipment inspection. Such obligations include non-discrimination, transparency, protection of confidential business information, avoiding unreasonable delay, the use of specific guidelines for conducting price verification, and avoiding conflicts of interest by the inspection agencies. The obligations of exporting members towards countries using pre-shipment inspection include non-discrimination in the application of domestic laws and regulations, prompt publication of those laws and regulations, and wherever requested, the provision of technical assistance.

The agreement establishes an independent review procedure administered jointly by the International Federation of Inspection Agencies (IFIA), representing inspection agencies, and the International Chamber of Commerce (ICC), representing exporters. Its purpose is to resolve disputes between an exporter and an inspection agency.

Rules of origin

'Rules of origin' are used as the criteria to define where a product was made. They are an essential part of trade rules because a number of policies, such as quotas, preferential tariffs, anti-dumping actions, countervailing duty (charged to counter export subsidies), etc., discriminate between exporting countries. Rules of origin are also used to compile trade statistics, and for 'made in...' labels that are attached to products. This is complicated by globalization and the way a product can be processed in several countries before it is ready for the market.

The Rules of Origin Agreement requires WTO members to ensure that their rules of origin are transparent; that they do not have restricting, distorting, or disruptive effects on international trade. The Rules are administered in a consistent, uniform, impartial, and reasonable manner. For the longer term, the agreement aims for common (harmonized) rules of origin among all WTO members, except in some kinds of preferential trade, e.g., countries setting up a free trade area are allowed to use different rules of origin for products traded under their free trade agreement.

5.2.10 Agreement on Trade Related Investment Measures

When investment is the mode of international business expansion, the host governments often impose conditions on foreign investors to encourage investments in accordance with certain national priorities. The Agreement on Trade Related Investment Measures (TRIMs) recognizes that certain measures can restrict and distort investment. It stipulates that no member shall apply any measure that discriminates against foreigners or foreign products (i.e., violates 'national treatment' principles in GATT). It also outlaws investment measures that lead to restrictions in quantities (violating another principle in GATT) and measures requiring particular levels of local procurement by an enterprise ('local content requirements'). It also discourages measures which limit a company's imports or set targets for the company to export ('trade balancing requirements').

However, countries are not prevented from imposing export performance requirements as a condition for investment. They are also not prohibited from insisting that a certain percentage of equity should be held by local investors or that a foreign investor must bring in the most up-to-date technology or must conduct a specific level or type of R&D locally. Under the agreement, countries must inform fellow-members through the WTO of all investment measures that do not conform to the agreement.

5.2.11 Plurilateral Agreements

All WTO agreements except four agreements, originally negotiated under the Tokyo Round became multilateral agreements. The four exceptions are known as plurilateral agreements as they had a limited number of signatories.

Fair trade in civil aircraft

The Agreement on Trade in Civil Aircraft entered into force on 1 January 1980 which presently has 30 signatories. The agreement eliminates import duties on all aircrafts other than military aircrafts, and their parts and components. The agreement also contains disciplines on government-directed procurement of civil aircraft and inducements to purchase, as well as on governmental financial support for the civil aircraft sector.

Opening up of competition in government procurement

In most countries, the government and its agencies together are the biggest purchasers of goods of all kinds, ranging from basic commodities to high-technology equipment.

At the same time, the political pressure to favour domestic suppliers over their foreign competitors can be very strong. It poses considerable barriers to international marketing firms in these countries.

An Agreement on Government Procurement was first negotiated during the Tokyo Round and entered into force on 1 January 1981 with a view to open up as much of this business as possible to international competition. The agreement was designed to make laws, regulations, procedures, and practices regarding government procurement more transparent and to ensure that they do not protect domestic products or suppliers, or discriminate against foreign products or suppliers. A large part of the general rules and obligations concern tendering procedures.

The Agreement on Government Procurement under the WTO became effective on 1 January 1996 and extends coverage to services (including construction services), procurement at the sub-central level (e.g., states, provinces, departments, and prefectures), and procurement by public utilities. It also reinforces rules guaranteeing fair and non-discriminatory conditions of international competition. For instance, governments are required to put in place domestic procedures by which aggrieved private bidders can challenge procurement decisions and obtain redress in the event such decisions were made inconsistently with the rules of the agreement. The agreement applies to contracts worth more than specified threshold values.

The International Dairy Agreement and International Bovine Meat Agreement, the two plurilateral agreements, were scrapped at the end of 1997. Countries that had signed the agreements decided that the sectors were better handled under the Agriculture and Sanitary and Phytosanitary agreements.

5.2.12 Ensuring Transparency in Trade Policy

An international marketing firm needs to know as much as possible the conditions of trade in the target market. The Trade Policy Review Mechanism (TPRM) aims to achieve transparency in regulations[6] in the following ways:

(a) Governments have to inform the WTO and fellow-members of specific measures, policies, or laws through regular 'notifications'.
(b) The WTO conducts regular reviews of individual countries' trade policies, i.e., trade policy reviews.

The objectives of trade policy review are

- To increase the transparency and understanding of countries' trade policies and practices, through regular monitoring
- To improve the quality of public and inter-governmental debate on the issues
- To enable a multilateral assessment of the effects of policies on the world trading system

---

6 *Trade Policy Review—India*, Geneva: World Trade Organization, 2002, 2007, pp. iii and vii–ix.

The reviews focus on members' own trade policies and practices. But they also take into account countries' wider economic and developmental needs, their policies and objectives, and the external economic environment that they face. These 'peer reviews' by other WTO members encourage governments to follow more closely the WTO rules and disciplines and to fulfil their commitments. These reviews enable outsiders to understand a country's policies and circumstances, and they provide feedback to the reviewed country on its performance in the system.

Over a period of time, all WTO members were to come under scrutiny. The frequency of the reviews depends on the country's size.

- The four biggest traders—the European Union, the US, Japan, and Canada (the 'Quad')—are examined approximately once every two years.
- The next 16 countries (in terms of their share of world trade) are reviewed every four years.
- The remaining countries are reviewed every six years, with the possibility of a longer interim period for the least developed countries.

For each review, two documents are prepared—a policy statement by the government under review, and a detailed report written independently by the WTO Secretariat. These two reports, together with the proceedings of the Trade Policy Review Body's meetings are published; these publications which may be consulted while making strategic business decisions.

5.2.13 Settlement of International Trade Disputes

Although trade disputes were handled by GATT as well, it had no power to enforce its decision. The process of dispute settlement often stretched on for years and the losing party was entitled to ignore its rulings. Due to its ineffectiveness in resolving trade disputes, GATT was often criticized as 'General Agreement to Talk and Talk'.

Dispute settlement is the WTO's unique contribution which provides effectiveness to the rule-based multilateral trading system. The WTO's procedure for settling disputes makes the trading system more secure and predictable. A classic case of dispute settlement under the WTO is given in Exhibit 5.5 regarding a dispute related to discrimination in enforcement of environmental legislation between member countries, wherein the US lost the case. The system is based on clearly-defined rules, with timetables for completing a case. First rulings are made by a panel and endorsed (or rejected) by the WTO's full membership.

The priority is to settle disputes, through consultations if possible. If the WTO members believe that fellow-members are violating trade rules, they can use the multilateral system of settling disputes instead of taking action unilaterally. Resorting to the dispute-settlement mechanism means abiding by agreed procedures and respecting judgements. A dispute arises when one country adopts a trade policy measure or takes some action that one or more fellow-WTO member considers to

---

Exhibit 5.5 Dispute settlement under WTO and India

- In early 1997, India, Malaysia, Pakistan, and Thailand brought a joint complaint against a ban imposed by the US on import of shrimp and shrimp products under section 609 of the US Public Law 101–102, enacted in 1989. It required the exporting countries to use 'turtle excluder devices' (TED) to protect sea turtles while harvesting shrimps. The US lost the case because it discriminated between the WTO members (i.e., between the countries of the western hemisphere, mainly those from the Caribbean, and the Asian countries) rather than seeking environment protection.

- Eleven WTO members led by the EU and Japan, together with India, Brazil, Chile, Indonesia, Korea, and Thailand, and later, Mexico jointly challenged the so called Byrd Amendment, a new anti-dumping legislation of the US incompatible with the WTO. The case was well coordinated.

- In 2007, a dispute settlement panel determined on the basis of a complaint filed by Ecuador with the Dispute Settlement Body in November last that the US has been inconsistent in imposing anti-dumping duties on frozen warm-water shrimp from countries, such as Ecuador, Brazil, China, India, Vietnam, and Thailand. India stands to benefit from this as it had enrolled itself a third party interest to the dispute. Such enrolments under the WTO rule help an affected country to reap the benefits of a ruling that goes in favour of the complainant.

Sources: 'US Shrimp Dumping Duty Faulty: WTO Panel', *Business Line*, 3 February 2007; Bhattacharyya, B., 'The Indian Shrimp Industry Organizes to Fight the Threat of Anti-Dumping Action', in *Managing the Challenges of WTO Participation: Case Study*, (ed.) Peter Gallagher, Patrick Low, and Andrew L. Stoler, Cambridge University Press, 2005.

---

breach WTO agreements, or fail to live up to obligations. A third group of countries can declare that they have an interest in the case and enjoy certain rights.

The Uruguay Round agreement introduced a more structured process with more clearly defined stages in the procedure. It introduced greater discipline for the length of time a case should take to be settled, with flexible deadlines set in various stages of the procedure. The agreement emphasizes that prompt settlement is essential if the WTO is to function effectively. It sets out the procedures in considerable detail and the timetable to be followed in resolving disputes.

The indicated time taken at each stage of dispute settlement is given below.

60 days	Consultations, mediation, etc.
45 days	Panel set up and panellists appointed
6 months	Final panel report to parties
3 weeks	Final panel report to WTO members
60 days	Dispute Settlement Body adopts report (if no appeal)
Total	*One year (without appeal)*
60–90 days	Appeal report
30 days	Dispute Settlement Body adopts appeals report
Total	*One year 3 months (with appeal)*

The target time schedules are flexible under the agreement. However, if a case runs its full course to a first ruling, it should not normally take more than about one year—15 months, if the case is appealed.

The Uruguay Round agreement also made it impossible for the country losing a case to block the adoption of the ruling. Under the previous GATT procedure, rulings could only be adopted by consensus, meaning that a single objection could block the ruling. Now, rulings are automatically adopted unless there is a consensus to reject a ruling; any country wanting to block a ruling has to persuade all other WTO members (including its adversary in the case) to share its view.

Dispute settlement process

Settling disputes is the responsibility of the Dispute Settlement Body (The General Council in another guise), which consists of all WTO members. The Dispute Settlement Body has the sole authority to establish 'panels' of experts to consider the case, and to accept or reject the panels' findings or the results of an appeal. It monitors the implementation of rulings and recommendations, and has the power to authorize retaliation when a country does not comply with a ruling. The dispute settlement mechanism is summarized in Fig. 5.3.

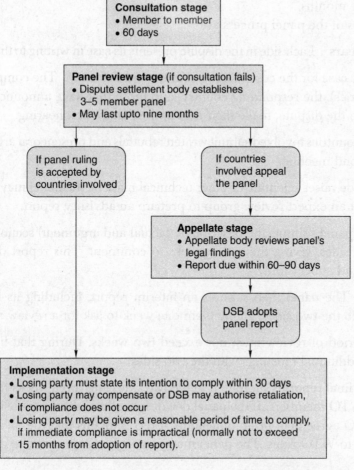

Fig. 5.3   Schematic diagram of the WTO's dispute settlement process

First stage—consultation (up to 60 days)   Before taking any other action, the countries in dispute have to talk to each other to see if they can settle their differences by themselves. If that fails, they can also ask the Director-General of WTO to mediate or try to help in any other way.

Second stage—the panel (up to 45 days for a panel to be appointed, plus 6 months for the panel to conclude)   If consultations fail, the complaining country can ask for a panel to be appointed. The country 'in the dock' can block the creation of a panel once, but when the Dispute Settlement Body meets for a second time the appointment can no longer be blocked (unless there is a consensus against appointing the panel).

Officially, the panel is helping the Dispute Settlement Body make a ruling for recommendations. But because the panel's report can only be rejected through a consensus in the Dispute Settlement Body, its conclusions are difficult to overturn. The panel's findings have to be based on the agreements cited. The panel's final report should normally be given to the parties to the dispute within six months. In cases of urgency, including those concerning perishable goods, the deadline is shortened to three months.

The main stages of the panel process are

Before the first hears   Each side in the dispute presents its case in writing to the panel.

First hearing (the case for the complaining country and defence)   The complaining country (or countries), the responding country, and those that have announced they have an interest in the dispute, make their case at the panel's first hearing.

Rebuttals   The countries involved submit written rebuttals and present oral arguments at the panel's second meeting.

Expert   If one side raises scientific or other technical matters, the panel may consult experts or appoint an expert review group to prepare an advisory report.

First draft   The panel submits the descriptive (factual and argument) sections of its report to the two sides, giving them two weeks to comment. This report does not include findings and conclusions.

Interim report   The panel then submits an interim report, including its findings and conclusions, to the two sides, giving them one week to ask for a review.

Review   The period of review must not exceed two weeks. During that time, the panel may hold additional meetings with the two sides.

Final report   A final report is submitted to the two sides and three weeks later, it is circulated to all WTO members. If the panel decides that the disputed trade measure does break a WTO agreement or an obligation, it recommends that the measure be made to conform to WTO rules. The panel may suggest how this could be done.

The report becomes a ruling The report becomes the Dispute Settlement Body's ruling or recommendations within 60 days unless a consensus rejects it. Both sides can appeal the report (and in some cases both sides do).

A panel's rulings can be appealed by either side or sometimes by both the sides. Appeals have to be based on points of law, such as legal interpretation. However, they cannot re-examine existing evidence or examine new issues.

Each appeal is heard by three members of a permanent seven-member Appellate Body set up by the Dispute Settlement Body and broadly representing the range of WTO membership. Members of the Appellate Body have four-year terms. They have to be individuals with recognized standing in the field of law and international trade, not affiliated with any government.

The appeal can uphold, modify or reverse the panel's legal findings and conclusions. Normally appeals should not last more than 60 days, with an absolute maximum of 90 days. The Dispute Settlement Body has to accept or reject the appeals report within 30 days; and rejection is only possible by consensus.

If a country has committed an error, it should swiftly correct its fault. If the country continues to flout an agreement, it should offer compensation or suffer a suitable penalty that has some bite. Even once the case has been decided, there is more to do before trade sanctions (the conventional form of penalty) are imposed. The priority at this stage is for the losing 'defendant' to bring its policy into line with the ruling or recommendations.

5.3 MINISTERIAL CONFERENCES AND EMERGING ISSUES

The highest decision-making body in the WTO is the Ministerial Conference (MC) that has to take place once in two years. Six ministerial conferences have taken place so far and have generated a lot of debate and controversies across the world, as discussed here.

5.3.1 Singapore Ministerial Conference

The first MC took place at Singapore during 9–13 December 1996 and reviewed the operations post-WTO. Major developed countries brought in proposals to start negotiations in some new areas, such as investment, competition policy, government procurement, trade facilitation, and labour standards. This evoked a lot of controversy. Significant pressure was built up by the developed countries for all members to accept their proposals; this was strongly opposed by developing nations. However, an agreement was finally reached to set up working groups to study the process of the relationship between investment and trade, competition and trade, and transparency in government procurement. These are generally termed as Singapore issues. The subject of trade facilitation was to be studied in the Council for Trade in Goods.

Conclusion of Information Technology Agreement was an important decision made during the Singapore Ministerial Conference based on the proposal brought by developed countries to have an agreement on zero duty on import of information technology goods.

5.3.2 Geneva Ministerial Conference

The second MC, held at Geneva (Switzerland) during 18–20 May 1998, discussed implementational concerns of developing and least developing countries that led to establishment of a mechanism for evaluation of implementation of individual agreements.

The US-sponsored proposals for zero duty on electronic commerce were discussed and an agreement was reached to maintain status-quo on the market access conditions for electronic commerce for 18 months. The agreement on status-quo actually meant that there would be zero duty on e-commerce since no country had been imposing duty on this mode of trade. A declaration on global electronic commerce was also adopted.

Electronic commerce was defined as the mode of commerce in which all operations of trade would be conducted through the electronic medium; these operations include placing the order, supplying the product, and making the payment. They also include sale and transfer of goods through electronic medium, such as music and cinematographic products, architectural and machine drawings and designs, etc. However, the sale in which goods are physically transferred to the buyer would not be considered e-commerce.

5.3.3 Seattle Ministerial Conference

The third MC, held in Seattle (US) from 30 November to 3 December 1999, witnessed dramatic changes in negotiations as the developing countries made intense preparations for the conference unlike in the previous MCs wherein issues brought in by the developed countries were chiefly discussed. In Seattle too developed countries tried to push forward new issues, such as investment, competition policy, government procurement, trade facilitation, and labour standards. However, developing countries insisted upon priority attention to their proposals as these were related to the working of the current agreement, before any new issue could be considered. No agreement on the issues could be arrived at, leading to a total collapse of the MC with a lot of confusion and without any decision.

5.3.4 Doha Ministerial Conference

The fourth MC held during 9–14 November 2001, at Doha in Qatar further built up the divide between the developed and the developing countries in the WTO. On the one hand, developed countries were keen on formally pushing forward a new round of multilateral trade negotiations, which would include the issues of investment, competition policy, transparency in government procurement, and trade facilitation. On the other hand, there was stiff resistance from developing countries to initiating a new round as they felt that they were still in the process of comprehending the implications of the last round, i.e., the Uruguay Round, of multilateral trade negotiations.

Finally a comprehensive work programme was adopted at the end of Doha MC. Although formally it was not called a new round of negotiations, the work programme had all the attributes of a fresh round of multilateral trade negotiations. Members decided to work out modalities for negotiations on the Singapore issues and then start negotiations on the basis of the modality to be agreed by explicit consensus. It was also agreed upon to make Special and Differential (S&D) treatment for developing countries more precise, effective, and operational.

The main commitments of the Doha Declaration were

- To continue the commitment for establishing a fair and market-oriented trading system through fundamental reform of support and protection of agricultural markets, specifically through
    - Substantial improvements in market access
    - Reductions of all forms of export subsidies, with a view of phasing them out
    - Substantial reductions in trade distorting domestic support
- To give developing countries Special and Differential Treatment in negotiations to enable them effectively to take into account their development needs
- To ensure negotiations on trade in services aimed at promoting the economic growth of all trading partners and the development of developing and least developed countries
- To reduce or eliminate tariffs and non-tariff barriers in non-agricultural markets, in particular on products of export interest to developing countries
- Doha Development Agenda (DDA) is a 'single undertaking' that means nothing is agreed until everything is agreed.

5.3.5 Cancun Ministerial Conference

The fifth MC was held in Cancun (Mexico) during 10–14 September 2003 under heightened strain between the major developed and developing countries. Developing countries believed that heavy subsidies on production and exports of agriculture in developed countries had been grievously harming their agriculture which is means of livelihood of their major population unlike in developed countries. There was hardly any significant action perceived on the part of the developed countries in the areas of implementation of issues and Special and Differential Treatment. On the other hand, developed countries insisted upon starting the negotiations on the Singapore issues. Under this atmosphere of complete apprehension, anger, and mistrust, no agreement could be reached and the MC terminated without any comprehensive declaration.

5.3.6 The Hong Kong Ministerial Conference

The sixth MC took place in Hong Kong during 13–18 December 2005. It called for conclusions in 2006 of negotiations launched at Doha in 2001 and establishment of targets and time frames in specific areas. The key outcomes of the Hong Kong Ministerial Conference included

- Amendment to TRIPS agreement reaffirmed to address public health concerns of developing countries.
- Duty free, quota free market access for all LDC products by all developed countries.
- Resolved complete Doha work programme and finalized negotiations in 2006.
- Elimination of export subsidies in cotton by developed countries in 2006; reduction of trade distorting domestic subsidies more ambitiously and over a shorter period.
- Elimination of export subsidies in agriculture by 2013 with substantial part in the first half of the implementation period. Developing countries, such as India will continue to have right to provide marketing and transport subsidies on agricultural exports for five years after the end date for elimination of all forms of export subsidies.
- The agreement that the three heaviest subsidizers, i.e., the European Union, the US, and Japan, were to attract the highest cut in their trade distortion domestic support. Developing countries like India with no Aggregate Measurement of Support (AMS) will be exempt from any cut on *de minimus* (entitlement to provide subsidies annually on product-specific as well as non-product specific basis each up to 10 per cent of the agricultural production value) as well as on overall levels of domestic trade distortion support (consists of the AMS, the Blue Box, and *de minimus*).
- Establishment of modalities in agriculture and Non-Agriculture Market Access (NAMA).
- The agreement that developing countries were to have flexibility to self-designate appropriate number of tariff lines as special products. In order to address situations of surge in imports and fall in international prices, both import quantity and price triggers have been agreed under the Special Safeguard Mechanism for developing countries.
- The agreement that in NAMA and Special and Differential Treatment (S&DT), elements such as flexibility and less-than-full reciprocity in reduction commitments for developing countries reassured.
- No sub-categorization of developing countries when addressing concerns of small, vulnerable economies.

Subsequently, at the General Council meeting held at Geneva on 31 July 2006, an agreement was reached on the framework in order to conduct the negotiations. Preliminary agreements were reached on broad approaches, especially in the areas of agriculture and industrial tariffs. It was decided to drop the three Singapore issues on investment, competition policy, and government procurement whereas negotiations on trade facilitation were to follow.

5.4 THE DEADLOCK IN WTO NEGOTIATIONS

Despite intensive negotiations, deadlines were missed and negotiations across all areas of the Doha work programme were suspended mainly due to lack of convergence on major issues in agriculture and NAMA in July 2006. Agriculture remains the most contentious issue in the recent Ministerial Conferences, widening the developed–developing country divide. Major developed countries continue to give high amount of subsidies to their farmers. Interestingly, developed countries have fulfilled their obligation of reduction in reducible subsidy in technical terms despite increasing the absolute amount of subsidy. Besides, the EU and the US continue to give export subsidies as well. Ironically, developed countries are pressurising developing countries to reduce their tariffs substantially. This poses a threat to the domestic farming sector of developing countries, which has got serious socio-economic and political implications. This makes negotiations in agriculture extremely complex. Developed countries, on the other hand, are keen on market access for their industrial products.

The issues leading to the deadlock of the Doha negotiations are shown in Fig. 5.4. In order to reach a settlement, the complexity of issues between the key players had to be addressed and a compromise reached. The US was looking for improved market access, with an average tariffs cut by around 66 per cent, while the G20 group of larger developed countries led by India and Brazil were looking for a cut of around 54 per cent. The EU had offered a 46 per cent average tariff cut. The G20 countries were looking for reduction in the US farm subsidies, greater than the cap offered by

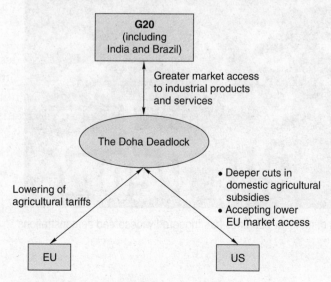

Fig. 5.4 Basic issues in the Doha deadlock

the US of around US$22.5 billion, as well as improved market access through lower tariffs.[7] The EU was looking for improved market access to larger developing country markets for industrial products with a maximum tariff of about 15 per cent, besides improved access to services trade. Any breakthrough in the negotiation process required further reduction of agricultural subsidies by the US, greater reduction in tariffs on agricultural goods by the European Union, and greater market access offered by larger developing countries such as India and Brazil to the industrial goods of other countries.

5.5   GATT/WTO SYSTEM AND DEVELOPING COUNTRIES

Over the years, the divide between the developed and developing countries in the WTO has widened, leading to deadlocks in the process of multilateral negotiations. It has also triggered widespread demonstrations (Fig. 5.5) across the world due to conflicting interests of member countries. Although developing countries form a much bigger group numerically under the WTO, decision making is significantly influenced by the developed countries.

The major issues of concern from the perspective of developing countries are summarized here:

- The basic objective of the WTO framework is to liberalize trade in goods and services and protection of intellectual property. Countries with supply capacity

Fig. 5.5   Conflicting interests of member countries has triggered widespread demonstrations around the world

---

[7] 'Doha Talks Suspended Indefinitely after G6 Talks Collapse', *ICTSD Bridges Weekly*, 26 July 2006.

directly benefit from expansion of exports whereas countries with intellectual property benefit from monopoly privileges, including high financial returns to owners of IPRs. As most developing countries neither have good supply base for goods and services nor much of IPRs, their direct gains form the WTO system is much lower compared to developed countries.

- Reciprocity is the basis for liberalization under the WTO system. Countries get more if they are able to give more; conversely, they also get less if they give less. Since member countries have vastly diverse levels of development, there is an in-built bias in the system for increasing disparity among countries. Although provisions such as differential and more favourable treatment have been incorporated in the WTO framework, these have several limitations and have hardly worked satisfactorily.

- Retaliation is the ultimate weapon for enforcement of rights of member countries. Since developing countries are weak partners and retaliation by them against any major developed country has both economic and political costs, they are at a considerably disadvantageous position in their capacity to enforce rights and obligations.

- The basic principals of the multilateral framework, such as national treatment, i.e., non-discrimination between imported and domestic goods, works against the process of development by discouraging domestic production by developing countries.

- Developed countries significantly influence the decision-making process as they possess enormous resources to make elaborate preparations for the negotiating process. As their views are put forth effectively and strongly, the issues of their interest take centre stage leading to frustration among developing countries.

- Substantial negotiations are carried out in small groups where developing countries are not present. Countries who have not participated are expected to agree when the results are brought forth in larger groups. It is difficult to stop decision-making at this stage as any such move by developing countries would mark them as obstructionists and have political repercussions.

- Developed countries often take advantage of escape routes and loopholes in the agreements. For instance, the Agreement on Textiles was back-loaded and left the choice of products to the importing countries. As developed countries were importers and had been imposing restraints, they chose only such products for liberalization that were not under import restraints without significantly liberalizing their textile imports until the end of 2004 when the agreement was automatically abolished. Similarly developed countries could fulfil their obligation of reduction of subsidies in agriculture despite actually increasing considerably the absolute quantum of subsidy.

- Developing countries view the WTO as an institutional framework to extract concessions from them, obstructing their goals of development and self-reliance.

Despite vast differences among the interests of member countries, the WTO remains the only international organization that provides a multilateral framework for international trade. Besides trade in goods, it covers a number of issues related to international trade, such as services, intellectual property rights, anti-dumping, safeguards, non-tariff barriers, dispute settlement, etc., making its approach highly comprehensive.

SUMMARY

The World Trade Organization (WTO) came into existence on 1 January 1995, as a successor to the General Agreement on Tariffs and Trade (GATT). Presently, nearly 153 WTO members account for over 97 per cent of world trade and about 30 others are negotiating its membership. The principles of multilateral trading system under WTO include trade without discrimination wherein a member country cannot discriminate between its trading partners and its own and foreign products and services. Further, the WTO attempts to reduce tariff and non-tariff trade barriers so as to facilitate freer trade among its members. Binding of commitments and transparency in trade rules under WTO contribute to increased predictability of the international business environment. WTO also helps promote fair competition in international markets.

The main agreement under the WTO includes an umbrella agreement for establishing WTO; agreements on goods, services, intellectual property, and dispute settlement; and reviews of governments' trade policies. The agreement for goods under GATT deals with sector-specific issues, such as agriculture, health regulations for farm products (SPS), textiles and clothing, product standards, investment measures, anti-dumping measures, customs valuation methods, pre-shipment inspection, rules of origin, import licensing, subsidies and counter-measures, and safeguards. WTO also attempts to create fairer markets in the agriculture sector by way of addressing issues related to trade distortions with extensive use of export and production subsidies, especially by developed countries. The international trade in textiles, which had been governed from 1974 to 1995 by the Multi-Fibre Agreement (MFA) was taken over on 1 January 1995 by WTO's Agreement on Textiles and Clothing and the quota system was phased out completely by 1 January 2005.

The agreement on services under GATS deals with specific issues including movement of natural persons, air transport, financial services, shipping, and telecommunications. The agreement on the Trade Related Aspect of Intellectual Property Rights (TRIPS) deals with protecting creators' rights for patents, copyright and related rights, trademarks, industrial designs, layout-designs of integrated circuits, undisclosed information and trade sectors, and geographical indications.

The WTO attempts to curb unfair trade practices by way of agreements on anti-dumping practices, subsidies, and countervailing measures which authorize importing countries to levy compensatory duties on import of goods. Customs valuation, pre-shipment inspection, rules of origin has also been dealt with. Agreement on Trade Related Investment Measures (TRIMs) imposes discipline on investment regulations that restrict international investment. Agreements having a limited number of signatories, known as plurilateral agreements, are exceptions to WTO's multilateral framework. Trade Policy Review Mechanism (TPRM) aims to achieve transparency in regulations. Dispute settlement mechanism is one of the most remarkable achievements of the WTO system.

The chapter also discusses various Ministerial Conferences, the highest decision-making body in the WTO. Further, issues related to the developing countries under the WTO system have also been examined.

KEY TERMS

Appellate body An independent seven-person body that, upon request by one or more parties to the dispute, reviews findings in panel reports.

Counterfeit Unauthorized representation of a registered trademark carried on goods identical or similar to goods for which the trademark is registered, with a view to deceiving the purchaser into believing that she/he is buying the original goods.

Countervailing measures Action taken by the importing country, usually in the form of increased duties to offset subsidies given to producers or exporters in the exporting country.

Distortion When prices and production are higher or lower than levels that would usually exist in a competitive market.

Dumping Dumping occurs when goods are exported at a price less than their normal value, generally meaning they are exported for less than they are sold in the domestic market or third–country markets, or a less than production cost.

GATT General Agreement on Tariffs and Trade, which has been superseded as an international organization by the WTO. An updated General Agreement is now one of the WTO's agreements.

Geographical indications Place name (or words associated with a place) used to identify products (e.g., 'Champagne', 'Tequila', or 'Roquefort') which have a particular quality, reputation, or other characteristic because they come from that place.

Intellectual property rights Ownership of ideas, including literary and artistic works (protected by copyright), inventions (protected by patents), signs for distinguishing goods of an enterprise (protected by trademarks) and other elements of intellectual property.

MFA Multi-Fibre Arrangement (1974–94) under which countries whose markets are disrupted by increased imports of textiles and clothing from another country were able to negotiate quota restrictions.

MFN Most-favoured nation treatment principle of not discriminating between one's trading partners.

National treatment The principle of giving others the same treatment as one's own nationals. GATT Article III requires that imports be treated no less favourably than the same or similar domestically produced goods once they have passed customs. GATS Article XVII and TRIPS Article 3 also deal with national treatment for services and intellectual property.

NTMs Non-tariff measures, such as quotas, import licensing systems, sanitary regulations, prohibitions, etc.

QRs (quantitative restrictions) Specific limits on the quantity or value of goods that can be imported (or exported) during a specific time period.

SPS regulations Sanitary and phytosanitary regulations—government standards to protect human, animal and plant life and health, to help ensure that food is safe for consumption.

Tariff binding Commitment not to increase the rate of import duty beyond an agreed level. Once a rate of duty is bound, it may not be raised without compensating the affected parties.

Tariffication Procedures relating to the agricultural market-access provision in which all non-tariff measures are converted into tariffs.

Tariffs Customs duties on merchandise imports. Levied either on an ad valorem basis (percentage of value) or on a specific basis (e.g., $5 per 100 kg.). Tariffs give price advantage to similar locally produced goods and raise revenues for the government.

Uruguay round Multilateral trade negotiations launched at Punta del Este, Uruguay in September 1986 and concluded in Geneva in December 1993, signed by Ministers in Marrakesh, Morocco, in April 1994.

CONCEPT REVIEW QUESTIONS

1. Briefly explain the genesis of the WTO. Identify the distinguishing features of WTO vis-à-vis GATT.

2. Briefly describe the key features of the General Agreement on Trade in Services (GATS). Identify the major issues leading to differences in opening up the services sector by the developed and developing countries.

3. Describe the dispute settlement process under WTO? Justify its effectiveness through examples.

4. Critically evaluate various issues leading to deadlocks in multilateral trade negotiations under the WTO.

5. Explain various reasons responsible for the widening gap between the developed and developing countries under the WTO system.

6. Write short notes on
   (a) WTO's organizational structure
   (b) MFN principle
   (c) Circumvention
   (d) Non-tariff barriers
   (e) TRIPS

CRITICAL THINKING QUESTIONS

1. The Agreement on Textiles and Clothing ceased to exist on 1 January 2005, following its full integration into GATT and the final elimination of quotas. Critically evaluate its impact on the textiles and clothing sector in your country.

2. Pick up a dispute settlement case in the WTO where your country was involved. Identify the key issues and explore the learning points for others.

PROJECT ASSIGNMENTS

1. Divide the class into three groups representing WTO members from each of the following countries:
   (a) The US
   (b) The EU
   (c) Developing countries

   Identify major issues of interest to each group and try to arrive at consensus in simulated multilateral trade negotiations in the class.

2. Visit a firm engaged in business process outsourcing (BPO) located near your place and find out its competitive strengths in international business. Identify the issues taken up in the WTO negotiations and critically evaluate its impact on a BPO industry from India.

6

International Economic
Integrations

LEARNING OBJECTIVES

> To provide an overview of international economic integration
> To elucidate the theoretical framework of preferential trading agreements
> To explicate the various forms of international economic integration
> To discuss the major international economic trade groups
> To briefly outline India's participation in preferential trade agreements
> To evaluate regional trading agreements under the WTO framework

6.1 INTRODUCTION

Economic integrations among countries significantly influence international business. The preferential treatment granted to the member countries of a trade group affects the competitiveness of goods in international markets. The elimination of import tariffs by the member countries of the trade group encourages the sourcing of goods from cost-efficient production locations. However, discriminatory tariff against non-members results in trade diversion to member countries, even at the cost of production efficiency. International business managers should develop a thorough insight into the concept and impact of international economic integrations, various forms of trade groups, major trade groups, and their legitimacy under the World Trade Organization's (WTO) multilateral trade regime.

Subsequent to World War II, economic integration among countries has been a widespread phenomenon that has greatly affected the patterns of international trade and investment. Along with growing multilateralism under the WTO framework, a large number of countries have entered into some sort of economic integration with other countries so as to facilitate intra-region trade. Regional economic integration was pushed in the post-world war era, and the Treaty of Rome in 1957 led to the creation of the European Economic Community. NAFTA, an acronym first coined for the North Atlantic Free Trade Area, rather than for the North American Free Trade Area, included the UK and was largely confined to the North American region.

The then NAFTA did not succeed in the 1960s. Moreover, the failure of the first wave of regionalism led to the slowdown of economic integration in Europe and other parts of the world. In the second half of the 1980s, the resurgence of preferential trading arrangements (PTAs) gave rise to the second wave of regionalism. This resulted in the emergence of strong PTAs in different parts of the world, led by the European Common Market and the European Union in 1992 and the North American Free Trade Agreement in 1994. This has effectively contributed to undermining multilateralism.

There has been a spurt in the growth of multilateral organizations since the 1980s. In the post-WTO era, the sluggish movement of trade negotiations at the WTO has led to frustration among its member countries to a varying extent and has contributed to the rapid proliferation of PTAs. It is estimated that about 60 per cent of the world trade is conducted on preferential basis rather than on most-favoured nation (MFN) basis.

Reasons for the attractiveness of regional agreements as compared to multilateral negotiations are

- These are much quicker to conclude compared to multilateral agreements. As the number of participating countries is less, preferential trade agreements can be wrapped up within a shorter duration. This makes preferential agreements more attractive to politicians and business communities who are looking for quick results.
- Because of similarities in interests and often more common values, bilateral trade agreements can go into new areas, such as investment, competition, technical standards, labour standards, or environment provisions, where there is no consensus among WTO members.
- Many of the recent PTAs contain political or geopolitical considerations. For developing countries negotiating with more powerful developed countries, there exist usually the expectations of exclusive preferential benefits, as well as expectations of development assistance and other non-trade rewards.
- Regional trade agreements are also useful for negotiators to learn how to negotiate, thus contributing to reinforce a country's trade institutions. PTAs are often used as instruments for domestic reform in areas where the multilateral system offers a weaker leverage.

If the major trading partners of a country are pursuing preferential regionalism, the conventional trade theories prescribing unilateral or multilateral trade liberalization as the most valid policy option hold no longer valid. This triggered off the formation of PTAs across the world such as Andean Pact and Mercado Comun del Sur (MERCOSUR) in South America, the Common Market for Eastern and Southern Africa (COMESA), South African Development Committee (SADC), and Southern African Customs Union (SACU) in Sub-Saharan Africa. The East Asian crisis in 1997 led to launch of various preferential trade initiatives in Asia too.

The coverage and depth of preferential treatment vary from one PTA to another. Present-day PTAs are not exclusively those linking the most-developed economies, rather they tend to go far beyond tariff-cutting exercises. They provide for increasingly complex regulations governing intra-trade (e.g., with respect to standards, safeguard provisions, customs administration) and often they also provide for a preferential regulatory framework for mutual services trade. The most sophisticated PTAs go beyond traditional trade policy mechanisms, to include regional rules on investment, competition, environment, and labour.

Such economic integrations have widely been referred to as 'regional economic integration'. However, in the present scenario, since a considerable number of these agreements for preferential trade are not necessarily on a contiguous-region basis, the term 'regional' in regional trading agreements (RTAs) has lost its connotation and the term 'preferential' is preferred over 'regional'. However, in the WTO terminology, the term RTA is used interchangeably for all types of economic groupings, such as PTA, FTA, and RTA.

This chapter provides an overview of international economic integration and its implications. Preferential treatment in trade to member countries under a PTA tends to influence the international trade patterns of the country. 'Trade creation' and 'trade diversion'—the two most significant aspects of PTAs have been explained in this chapter. Depending upon the level of economic integration, the major forms of trading arrangements include preferential trade agreement, free trade area, customs union, common market, and economic union culminating in a political union. The major regional trade blocks include the European Union, the North American Free Trade Area (NAFTA), MERCOSUR, Gulf Cooperation Council (GCC), Asia Pacific Economic Cooperation (APEC), and the Association of South East Asian Nations (ASEAN). India's participation in various PTAs has also been examined. Despite the fundamental conflict of PTAs with multilateralism, these are legally permitted as an exception under Article XXIV of WTO.

6.2 THEORETICAL FRAMEWORK OF PTAs

In his pioneering analysis of the impacts of RTAs, Jacob Viner, who introduced terms such as 'trade creation' and 'trade diversion', proved that customs unions (CUs) and free trade areas (FTAs) were not necessarily welfare improving,[1] either for member countries or for world welfare. Even though a CU represents a reduction of trade barriers among member countries, it may reduce economic welfare as it induces its members to import from high-cost rather than from low-cost sources.

Impact on consumers in country X as a result of the formation of FTA has been shown in Table 6.1. Three countries—X, Y, and Z—have been presumed hypothetically, which have domestic prices per unit of the goods at 100, 88, and 72, respectively, assuming supply to be indefinitely elastic.

---

[1] Viner, Jacob, *The Customs Union Issue*, New York: Carnegie Endowment for International Peace, 1950.

Table 6.1   Impact of creation of FTA

		Domestic prices in countries X, Y, and Z		Country of production			Impact on customer in country X
	Tariff by X			X	Y	Z	
				100	88	72	
Case I	50%	Price to consumer in country X	No FTA	100	132	108	Buys domestic product
			FTA with country Y	100	88	108	Buys produce imported from Y (so trade creation)
Case II	25%		No FTA	100	110	90	Buys produce imported from Z
			FTA with country Y	100	88	90	Buys produce imported from Y (so trade diversion)

Case I   Initially, when there is no FTA between the countries, country X imposes 50 per cent import tariff on MFN basis. Therefore, the unit costs to a consumer in country X would be 100, 132, and 108 for production carried out in countries X, Y, and Z, respectively. For the sake of simplicity, no additional cost such as transport has been assumed. So the consumer would buy, say, one unit out of domestic produce. It is assumed that, thereafter, countries X and Y formed an FTA. Therefore, the prices for consumers in country A become 100, 88, and 108 for production in countries X, Y, and Z, respectively. So the consumer in country A now buys produce imported from country Y. This creates one unit of trade due to formation of the FTA.

Case II   Country X originally imposes 25 per cent import tariff on MFN basis. Therefore, to a consumer in country X the unit price would be 100, 110, and 90 for production in countries X, Y, and Z, respectively. So the consumer buys produce imported from country Z.

However, on the formation of an FTA between countries X and Y, the price to consumers in country X becomes 100, 88, and 90 for production in countries X, Y, and Z, respectively. So now the consumer in country X buys the produce imported from country Y. This diverts one unit of trade from country Z to country Y, due to the formation of FTA.

6.2.1   Trade-creation Impact

Formation of PTA/FTA results in the expansion of consumption opportunities by making available low-cost goods. To illustrate, as depicted in Fig. 6.1, D_x is the demand curve of country X's consumers for the product and S_x is the supply curve of country X's home producers. The autarky price P_x prevailed in the home country X and quantity Q_1 was being produced. The price of the commodity is P_y and P_z in country Y and Z, respectively. Country X imposed a tariff t on the imports of the commodity—raising prices of imported goods higher than the prices of domestically produced goods. Under this situation, customers would tend to purchase domestic products.

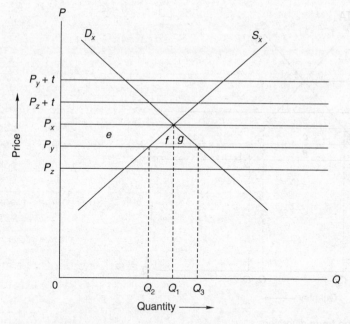

Fig. 6.1 Impact of FTA on trade creation

On the formation of FTA with country Y, the price of the goods imported in country X from country Y became cheaper than in domestically produced goods, as it no longer faced import tariff. This raises the demand for quantity consumed from Q_1 to Q_3, whereas the quantity produced at home falls from Q_1 to Q_2. The balance quantity (Q_3-Q_2) is imported from country Y.

The welfare gains in country X may be summarized as

Gains to consumer surplus (areas) $= e + f + g$
Loss to producer surplus $= (e)$
Government revenue $=$ remains zero

Therefore, net welfare gain of country X $= f + g$

Therefore, it is obvious that there is net welfare gain to country X, without any trade diversion from country Z on formation of an FTA.

6.2.2 Trade Diversion Impact

The formation of an FTA results in trade diversion to its members from non-members since the elimination of import tariffs among member countries makes sourcing of goods from member countries more attractive compared to the same from non-members, even at the cost of production efficiency. In this case, the autarky price P_x in country X is above the landed price of imports including tariff (Fig. 6.2); imports took place from country Z. Therefore, the quantity consumed in country X was Q_3, of which Q_2 was domestic production and the balance quantity Q_3-Q_2 was imported

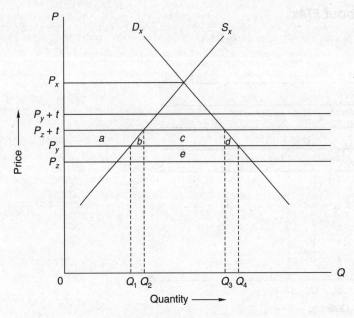

Fig. 6.2 Impact of FTA on trade diversion

from country Z at the landed price $P_z + t$, which was also the price charged by the domestic producers of country X.

Consequent to the formation of an FTA between country X and country Y, imports from Y takes place as it becomes cheaper, diverting trade from an efficiently producing country Z. Besides, the quantity consumed in country X increases to Q_4, of which Q_1 ($< Q_2$) is the reduced domestic production and the rest of $Q_4 - Q_1$ is imported at landed price P_y from country Y.

As a result of the formation of the FTA, the welfare changes in country X may be summarized as

Gain to consumer surplus (areas)	$= a + b + c + d$
Loss to producer surplus	$= a$
Revenue loss to government	$= c + e$
Therefore, net welfare gain of X	$= b + d - e$

As shown in Fig. 6.2, the net welfare gains to country X visually appear negative in this case. However, this position could reverse, if P_y was selected closer enough to P_z. Thus country Z, the non-member of the FTA, tends to lose in either case of trade diversion.

The net impact of an FTA on world welfare may either be positive or negative. However, trade diversion has a negative impact on the welfare of non-members even in the case of positive impact on world welfare.

Popular fallacies about FTAs

Contrary to popular opinion that equates FTAs with genuine free trade, FTAs are in fact preferential trading arrangements (PTAs). On the one hand, these offer free or preferential trade to members; on the other, implicit protection against non-members. The economics of PTAs is therefore far more complex than that of genuinely non-discriminatory free trade. Popular fallacies about PTAs include[2] that

- PTAs between natural trading partners are desirable. The naturalness is defined as large initial volume shares among member countries or relatively small distances between them.
- Regional PTAs where members share common borders or an ocean are necessarily beneficial.
- Simply because the PTAs formed under article XXIV of GATT are required to maintain the average external tariff against non-members, trade will not be diverted away from them to member countries.

6.3   FORMS OF INTERNATIONAL ECONOMIC INTEGRATION

There can be several types of economic integrations among member countries. The major forms of such arrangements, as depicted in Exhibit 6.1, include preferential trade agreement (PTA), free trade area (FTA), customs union (CU), common market (CM), and economic union (EU) culminating into a political union (PU).

	Exhibit 6.1	Forms of international economic integrations				
Integration type	Preferential tariffs on select products	No import tariff	Common external tariff	Freedom of cross-border investment, labour movement, and technology transfer	Uniform monetary/ fiscal policies and institutions	Political harmonization
PTA	✓	X	X	X	X	X
FTA	–	✓	X	X	X	X
Customs union	–	✓	✓	X	X	X
Common market	–	✓	✓	✓	X	X
Economic union	–	✓	✓	✓	✓	X
Political union	–	✓	✓	✓	✓	✓

---

[2] Bhagwati, Jagdish and Arvind Pangariya (eds), *Economics of Preferential Trade Agreements*, AEI Press, 1996.

As shown, the level of integration among countries increases as it moves from PTA to political union, which needs much greater commitment on the part of member countries. The basic attributes of such economic groupings are discussed here.

PTA   Member countries in a PTA lower the tariff barriers to the imports of identified products from one another. Examples of such associations include the Economic Community of West African States (ECOWAS), the Bangkok Agreement, the Global System of Trade Preferences (GSTP) among developing countries, and the Common Market for Eastern and Southern Africa (COMESA).

FTA   The FTA is the basic form of economic integration in which member countries seek to remove all tariffs and non-tariff barriers for cross-border trade of goods and services among themselves. Examples of FTAs include the NAFTA and the Latin American Free Trade Area (LFTA). However, the members are free to maintain their own tariffs and non-tariff barriers with non-member countries. Since in the case of an FTA, marketing firms from non-member countries may evolve ways to benefit from tariff differentials among member countries, this may result in parallel trade unless checked by effective legislation and implementation.

Customs union   In a customs union, countries not only eliminate tariff barriers among themselves but also apply common external import tariffs for non-members. Customs unions include the Caribbean Community and Common Market (CARICOM) and the Central American Common Market (CACM).

Common market   In addition to free trade among members and uniform tariff policy for non-members in a common market, such an arrangement ensures all restrictions on cross-border investments, movement of labour, technology transfer, management, and sharing of capital resources are eliminated. Common markets include the COMESA, MERCOSUR, etc.

Economic union   An economic union such as the European Union (EU) enjoys a much greater level of economic integration where free exchange of goods and services takes place. The member countries in an economic union maintain a fiscal discipline, stability in exchange, and interest rates by way of unified monetary and fiscal policies.

Political union   As a culmination of economic integration, the member countries strive to harmonize their security and foreign policies. A common parliament is created with the representatives of the member countries who work in synchronization with an individual country's legislature. At this stage, the member countries are willing to dilute their national identities to a considerable extent to become a part of the union.

6.4   GROWTH OF REGIONAL TRADING AGREEMENTS

There has been a sharp proliferation in RTAs in the last 50 years. WTO members, similar to earlier contracting parties of GATT, are bound to notify the RTAs in which they participate. During 1948–94, the GATT received 124 notifications of RTAs relating to trade in goods, while since the creation of WTO in 1995, over 240 additional agreements covering trade in goods and services have been notified. A total of over 380 RTAs had been notified by the WTO by July 2007. By 2010, around 400 of such agreements are expected to be active.

While the most common category is the FTA, which accounts for 70 per cent of all RTAs, the configuration of RTAs is diverse and is becoming more complex with overlapping RTAs and networks of RTAs spanning across continents.

There had been a sharp increase in intra-group trade among major RTAs (Table 6.2) over the last few decades. The intra-group trade increased from 62.3 per cent in 1980 to 67.6 per cent in 2006 within EU members, 43.4 per cent to 58.4 per cent within FTAA, 33.6 per cent to 53.8 per cent within NAFTA, 57.9 per cent to 69.4 per cent within APEC, 11.6 per cent to 13.5 per cent within MERCOSUR, 1.7 per cent to 10.7 per cent within APTA, 3.0 per cent to 4.8 per cent within GCC members, and 4.8 per cent in 1980 to 5.6 per cent in 2002 among SAARC countries during the same period.

6.5   MAJOR REGIONAL TRADE AGREEMENTS

RTAs are an important exception under Article XXIV of the GATT Agreement to the MFN (most-favoured nation) rule of the WTO agreements, under which tariff and other technical barriers to trade can be reduced on preferential basis by countries under the regional agreement. These are considered as initiatives to liberalize trade among a group of countries and used effectively as an instrument to market access among member countries. The major RTAs are shown in Exhibit 6.2.

6.5.1   European Union

Attempts for regional cooperation among countries in Europe were conceived after World War II in order to achieve some economic and political stability in the region. In 1948, the Organization for European Economic Cooperation (OEEC) was established, mainly to administer Marshall Plan Aid from the US that paved the way for deeper economic integrations in the future. Six European nations, i.e., West Germany, France, Italy, Belgium, the Netherlands, and Luxembourg, joined hands to establish the European Coal and Steel Community (ECSC), aimed at creating a common market in coal, steel, and iron ore.

The idea of the European Union was first proposed by the French Foreign Minister Robert Schumann in a speech on 9 May 1950, which is still celebrated as Europe Day. In the early years, much of the cooperation between EU countries was about trade and the economy, but now the EU also deals with many other subjects, such as citizens' rights, ensuring freedom, security, justice, job creation, regional development, environmental protection, and promoting globalization.

Table 6.2   Intra-trade of groups

(as percentage of total exports of each group)

Trade group	1980	1990	1995	2000	2005	2006
Europe						
EFTA	1.1	0.8	0.7	0.6	0.5	0.6
EU	62.3	67.6	66.8	67.7	67.3	67.6
Euro Zone	51.9	55.5	52.6	50.8	50.3	49.7
America						
ANCOM	4.1	4.0	8.6	7.7	9.0	8.4
CACM	24.4	15.3	21.8	19.1	18.9	16.8
CARICOM	5.4	8.0	12.1	14.6	11.6	11.3
FTAA	43.4	46.6	52.5	60.7	60.2	58.4
LAIA	13.9	11.6	17.3	13.2	13.6	14.3
MERCOSUR	11.6	8.9	20.3	20.0	12.9	13.5
NAFTA	33.6	41.4	46.2	55.7	55.8	53.8
OECS	9.0	8.5	14.5	13.7	15.1	11.2
Africa						
CEPGL	0.1	0.5	0.5	0.8	1.2	1.3
COMESA	1.8	4.7	6.1	4.6	4.5	4.2
ECCAS	1.4	1.4	1.5	1.1	0.6	0.6
ECOWAS	9.6	8.0	9.0	7.6	9.3	8.3
MRU	0.8	0.0	0.1	0.4	0.3	0.3
SADC	0.4	3.1	10.7	9.4	9.2	9.1
CEMAC (UDEAC)	1.6	2.3	2.1	1.0	0.9	0.9
UEMOA	9.6	13.0	10.3	13.1	13.4	13.1
UMA	0.3	2.9	3.8	2.3	2.0	2.0
Asia						
APTA	1.7	1.6	6.8	8.0	11.0	10.7
ASEAN	17.4	18.9	24.5	23.0	25.3	24.9
ECO	6.3	3.2	7.9	5.6	7.6	8.5
GCC	3.0	8.0	6.8	4.8	4.8	4.8
SAARC	4.8	3.2	4.4	4.2	5.6	5.6
Oceania						
MSG	0.7	0.3	0.4	0.6	0.8	0.8
Interregional Groupings						
ACP	4.0	6.3	11.1	10.4	11.0	10.9
APEC	57.9	68.3	71.7	73.1	70.8	69.4
BSEC	5.9	4.2	18.1	14.2	16.0	16.9
CIS	–	–	28.6	20.0	18.0	16.5

Sources: UNCTAD Secretariat computations based on International Monetary Fund, Direction of Trade Statistics, and UN/DESA/Statistics Division data; *UNCTAD Handbook of Statistics*, United Nations, Geneva, 2008, pp. 48–49.

The European Community (EC) was formed in 1967, as a result of a merger of ECSC, EEC, and the European Atomic Energy Community (EURATOM). Denmark, Ireland, and UK joined the European Union on 1 January 1973, thereby raising the number of member states to nine. Subsequently, Greece joined the EU in 1981, Spain and Portugal in 1986, and Austria, Finland, and Sweden in 1995.

Exhibit 6.2 Summary of major regional trade blocks	
Regional trade blocks	**Member countries**
High-income, low-income, and middle-income economies	
European Union	Austria, Belgium, Denmark, Finland, France, Germany, Greece, Ireland, Italy, Luxembourg, the Netherlands, Portugal, Spain, Sweden and the UK, Czech republic Cyprus, Estonia, Hungary, Poland, Slovenia, Slovakia, Latvia, Lithuania, Malta, Bulgaria, and Romania
North American Free Trade Area (NAFTA)	Canada, Mexico, and the US
Asia Pacific Economic Cooperation (APEC)	Australia, Brunei Darussalam, Canada, Chile, People's Republic of China, Hong Kong (China), Indonesia, Japan, Republic of Korea, Malaysia, Mexico, New Zealand, Papua New Guinea, Peru, the Republic of the Philippines, the Russian Federation, Singapore, Chinese Taipei, Thailand, US of America, and Vietnam
Latin America and the Caribbean	
Association of Caribbean States (ACS)	Antigua and Barbuda, the Bahamas, Barbados, Belize, Colombia, Costa Rica, Cuba, Dominica, the Dominican Republic, El Salvador, Grenada, Guatemala, Guyana, Haiti, Honduras, Jamaica, Mexico, Nicaragua, Panama, St. Kitts and Nevis, St. Lucia, St. Vincent and the Grenadines, Suriname, Trinidad and Tobago, and Venezuela
Andean Community	Bolivia, Colombia, Ecuador, Peru, and Republica Bolivariana de Venezuela
Group of Three	Colombia, Mexico, and Republica Bolivariana de Venezuela
Latin American Integration Association (LAIA) (formerly Latin American Free Trade Area)	Argentina, Bolivia, Brazil, Chile, Colombia, Ecuador, Mexico, Paraguay, Peru, Uruguay, and Republica Bolivariana de Venezuela
Southern Cone Common Market (MERCOSUR)	Argentina, Brazil, Paraguay, and Uruguay
Africa	
Common Market for Eastern and Southern Africa (COMESA)	Angola, Burundi, Comoros, the Democratic Republic of Congo, Djibouti, the Arab Republic of Egypt, Eritrea, Ethiopia, Kenya, Madagascar, Malawi, Mauritius, Namibia, Rwanda, Seychelles, Sudan, Swaziland, Uganda, Tanzania, Zambia, and Zimbabwe
Economic Community of West African States (ECOWAS)	Benin, Burkina Faso, Cape Verde, Cote d'Ivoire, the Gambia, Ghana, Guinea, Guinea-Bissau, Liberia, Mali, Mauritania, Niger, Nigeria, Senegal, Sierra Leone, and Togo

Contd

Exhibit 6.2 Contd

Regional trade blocks	Member countries
Southern African Development Community (SADC), formerly Southern African Development Coordination Conference	Angola, Botswana, the Democratic Republic of the Congo, Lesotho, Malawi, Mauritius, Mozambique, Namibia, Seychelles, South Africa, Swaziland, Tanzania, Zambia, and Zimbabwe
Middle East and Asia	
Association of South-East Asian Nations (ASEAN)	Brunei, Cambodia, Indonesia, the Lao People's Democratic Republic, Malaysia, Myanmar, the Philippines, Singapore, Thailand, and Vietnam
Asia Pacific Trade Agreement (APTA) (Bangkok Agreement)	Bangladesh, India, the Republic of Korea, the Lao People's Democratic Republic, the Philippines, Sri Lanka, and Thailand
Bay of Bengal Initiative for Multi-sectoral Technical and Economic Cooperation (BIMSTEC)	Bangladesh, India, Sri Lanka, Thailand, Myanmar, Nepal, and Bhutan
East Asian Economic Caucus (EAEC)	Brunei, People's Republic of China, Hong Kong (China), Indonesia, Japan, the Republic of Korea, Malaysia, the Philippines, Singapore, Taiwan (China), and Thailand
Gulf Cooperation Council (GCC)	Bahrain, Kuwait, Oman, Qatar, Saudi Arabia, and the United Arab Emirates
South Asian Free Trade Agreement (SAFTA)	Bangladesh, Bhutan, India, Maldives, Nepal, Pakistan, and Sri Lanka

Source: World Development Indicators, 2008, the World Bank.

The Single European Act, signed in 1987, paved the way to create the 'single market'. European countries came closer following the collapse of communism across central and eastern Europe. The single market was accomplished through the 'four freedom', i.e., freedom of movement of goods, services, people, and money. The Maastricht Treaty, signed in 1992 by all (then) the 12 member countries of the European Community (EC) resulted in the creation of the European Union, which became operational on 1 January 1994. Ten new countries, that is, the Czech Republic, Cyprus, Estonia, Hungary, Poland, Slovenia, Slovakia, Latvia, Lithuania, and Malta, joined the EU in 1994. Two more countries from eastern Europe—Bulgaria and Romania—joined the EU on 1 January 2007, bringing its membership to 27 states (see Fig. 6.3). Additionally, Croatia, the former Yugoslav Republic of Macedonia, and Turkey are also candidates for future membership.

Presently, the EU includes 497 million people and has 23 official languages. Each member country, when it joins the EU, has to stipulate the language or languages it

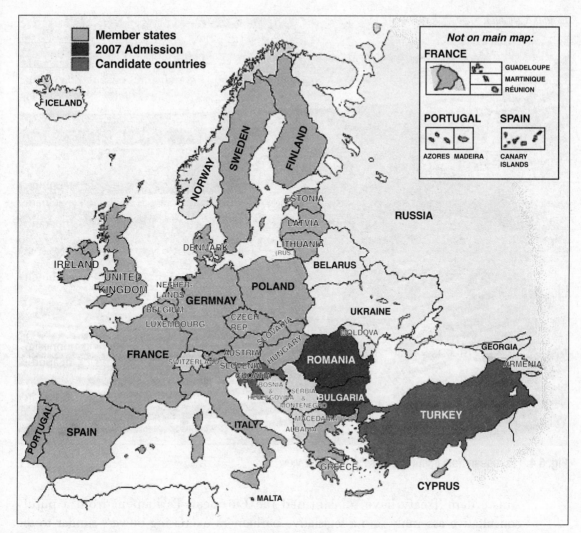

Fig. 6.3   The European Union

wants to have declared as the official language or languages of the EU. The major institutions of the European Union include

- European Parliament (elected by the people of the member states)
- Council of the European Union (representing the governments of the member states)
- Presidency (rotates every six months among member countries)
- European Commission (driving force and executive body)
- Court of Justice (ensuring compliance with the law)
- Court of Auditors (controlling and managing the EU budget)

The first direct elections of the European Parliament (see Fig. 6.4) were held in June 1979, 34 years after World War II. The 1992 Maastricht Treaty and 1997

Fig. 6.4 European Parliament in Brussels: An inside view

Amsterdam Treaty have transformed the European Parliament from a purely consultative assembly into a legislative parliament exercising powers similar to the national parliaments. The 785 members of the European Parliament represent the citizens of the member countries. The members are elected to the parliament once every five years by voters right across the 27 member states. All EU decisions and procedures are based on the treaties, which are agreed upon by all the EU countries.

The treaties are flanked by five other important bodies:

- The European Economic and Social Committee (expresses the opinions of organized civil society on economic and social issues)
- Committee of the Regions (expresses the opinions of regional and local authorities)
- European Central Bank (responsible for monetary policy and managing the euro)
- European Ombudsman (deals with citizens' complaints about maladministration by any EU institution or body)
- European Investment Bank (helps achieve EU objectives by financing investment projects)

6.5.2 North American Free Trade Area

The first ever reciprocal economic integration between two developed countries, that is, the US and Canada, and a developing country, Mexico, took effect on 1 January 1994. It created a market for 360 million people having a combined purchasing power of US$6.5 trillion. The agreement has facilitated the elimination of trade barriers related to industrial goods and services, besides separate agreements on agriculture, intellectual property rights, labour adjustment, and environmental protection. Under the NAFTA agreement, all three countries were required to remove all tariffs and barriers to trade over 15 years but each country would have its own tariff arrangements with non-member countries. Under the NAFTA country of origin rules, most products should have 50 per cent of North American content, while for most automobiles, the stipulated local content requirement is 62.5 per cent. This has resulted in the shift of US investment from Asian countries to Mexico. The benefits accrued to various member countries in the NAFTA have always been debated but this has significantly transformed the trade patterns in the region.

6.5.3 MERCOSUR

The Southern Common Market, or MERCOSUR, was created in March 1991 by Brazil, Argentina, Paraguay, and Uruguay with the signing of the Treaty of Asuncion. Common external tariffs were implemented by the MERCOSUR in 1995 and the tariffs on intra-group trade were abolished in 1996. Consequent to Chile and Bolivia joining in MERCOSUR in 1996, Latin America became the third largest business area of the world with 220 million people and a combined GDP of US$1 trillion. This common market is expected to allow free movement of goods, capital, labour, and services with a common uniform external tariff among member countries.

6.5.4 Gulf Cooperation Council

Aimed at promoting stability and economic cooperation among the Persian Gulf nations, the Gulf Cooperation Council (GCC) was established on 25 May 1981. It is officially known as Cooperation Council for the Arab States of the Gulf. Its members are Bahrain, Kuwait, Oman, Qatar, Saudi Arabia, and the United Arab Emirates. The principle objectives of GCC include

- Formulating similar regulations in various fields, such as economy, finance, trade, customs, tourism, legislation, and administration
- Fostering scientific and technical progress in industry, mining, agriculture, water, and animal resources
- Establishing scientific research centres
- Setting up joint ventures
- Encouraging cooperation of the private sector
- Strengthening ties between their people

An aid fund was also established to promote development in Arab states. It was used to help liberate Kuwait in 1991. GCC members agreed to establish a customs union in 2005 and a broader economic union (including a single market and currency) by 2010.

6.5.5 Asia-Pacific Economic Cooperation

The Asia-Pacific Economic Cooperation (APEC) was established in 1989 to enhance the economic growth and prosperity in the region and to strengthen the Asia-Pacific community. It is the only inter-governmental grouping in the world operating on the basis of non-binding commitments, open dialogue, and mutual respect. Unlike the WTO or other multilateral trade bodies, APEC has no treaty obligations required of its participants. Decisions made within APEC are reached by consensus and commitments are undertaken on a voluntary basis.

The APEC works in three broad areas to meet the broader goals of free and open trade and investment in the Asia-Pacific region by 2010 for developed economies and 2020 for developing economies, known as APEC's 'three pillars'. The key areas of focus are

- Trade and investment liberalization
- Business facilitation
- Economic and technical cooperation

APEC has 21 members, referred to as 'member economies', which account for about 40 per cent of the world's population, approximately 56 per cent of world GDP and about 48 per cent of world trade. Its member economies include Australia, Brunei Darussalam, Canada, Chile, People's Republic of China, Hong Kong (China), Indonesia, Japan, Republic of Korea, Malaysia, Mexico, New Zealand, Papua New Guinea, Peru, the Republic of the Philippines, the Russian Federation, Singapore, Chinese Taipei, Thailand, the US, and Vietnam. It represents the most economically dynamic region in the world, having generated nearly 70 per cent of global economic growth in its first 10 years.

6.5.6 Association of South East Asian Nations

The Association of South East Asian Nations (ASEAN) was established on 8 August 1967 in Bangkok by five original member countries, namely, Indonesia, Malaysia, the Philippines, Singapore, and Thailand. Subsequently, Brunei Darussalam joined on 8 January 1984, Vietnam on 28 July 1995, Laos and Myanmar on 23 July 1997, and Cambodia on 30 April 1999. The ASEAN region has a population of about 500 million, a total area of 4.5 million square kilometres, a combined GDP of about US$700 billion, and a total trade of US$850 billion. The major objectives of ASEAN are

- To accelerate economic growth, social progress, and cultural development in the region through joint endeavours

- To promote regional peace and stability through abiding respect for justice and the rule of law in the relationship among countries in the region and adherence to the principles of the United Nations Charter

Economic and functional cooperation

When ASEAN was established, trade among member countries was insignificant. Estimates between 1967 and the early 1970s showed that the share of intra-ASEAN trade from the total trade of the member countries was between 12 and 15 per cent. In order to promote inter-group trade, the Preferential Trading Arrangement, 1977, accorded tariff preferences for trade among ASEAN economies. The Framework Agreement on Enhancing Economic Cooperation was adopted at the fourth ASEAN summit in Singapore in 1992, which included the launching of a scheme toward an ASEAN Free Trade Area (AFTA). The strategic objective of AFTA is to increase the ASEAN region's competitive advantage as a single production unit. The fifth ASEAN summit held in Bangkok in 1995 adopted the Agenda for greater economic integration, which included the acceleration of the timetable for the realization of AFTA from the original 15 year timeframe to 10 years.

In addition to trade and investment liberalization, regional economic integration is being pursued through the development of the trans-ASEAN transportation network consisting of major inter-state highway and railway networks, principal ports and sea lanes for maritime traffic, inland waterway transport, and major civil aviation links. Building of trans-ASEAN energy networks, which consist of the ASEAN power grid and the trans-ASEAN gas pipeline projects, are also being developed. ASEAN cooperation has resulted in greater regional integration.

Institutional mechanism

The highest decision-making organ of the ASEAN is the meeting of the ASEAN heads of states and governments. The ASEAN summit is convened every year. The ASEAN ministerial meeting is also held on an annual basis. Also held are ministerial meetings on several other sectors, such as agriculture and forestry, economics, energy, environment, finance, information, investment, labour, law, regional haze, rural development and poverty alleviation, science and technology, social welfare, transnational crime, transportation, tourism, youth, and the AFTA Council. Supporting these ministerial bodies are 29 committees of senior officials and 122 technical working groups.

In January 2004, the Southeast Asian economic ministers agreed to 11 industry sectors, i.e., air travel, tourism, automotive, textile, electronics, agriculture, infotech, fisheries, health care, wood, and rubber. This is considered as an important catalyst in creating a single market[3] covering 530 million people by 2020.

---

[3] 'ASEAN vows for single market by 2020', *Times of India*, 21 January 2004.

6.6   INDIA'S PARTICIPATION IN PTAs

While these RTAs could serve to open up markets for India's exports, there could be scope for cost reduction through economies of scale, and sourcing materials and components from partner countries as well. Indian companies could also find it easier to set up projects in partner countries to cater to local and regional customers. Investments becoming more industry- or product-specific than country-specific in today's world, a lot of transnational FDI takes place across countries. It may promote FDI in India along with other member countries. Exhibit 6.3 provides a summary of PTAs in South Asia.

India has been a founder member of the SAARC, which was established in 1985. In April 1993, these countries signed a PTA named SAPTA, effective from 7 December 1995 that graduated into the South Asian Free Trade Area (SAFTA), which became operational from 1 January 2006. India has also been instrumental in forming BIMSTEC, the 'Bay of Bengal' initiative PTA. Besides, India's other PTAs include comprehensive economic partnership with ASEAN, a Comprehensive Economic Co-operation Agreement (CECA) with Singapore, and separate PTAs with Afghanistan and Thailand.

6.6.1   SAARC Preferential Trading Agreement

SAPTA has been notified under the enabling clause of the WTO, the participating countries being the developing countries of South Asia. In this case, trade liberalization has taken place on limited items and in the form of a preferential entry, not a zero-duty entry. Trade in goods has only been dealt with. However, non-tariff measures remain unaddressed. As a result, SAPTA has failed to produce the desired result. More importantly, India has not achieved the desired end from this regional trading arrangement.

India's comparative advantage in a range of products has resulted in asymmetric trade relations with her neighbours, hindering regional integration. Regional trade has also perhaps not taken off because until the late eighties, all the countries in the region had been pursuing, import substitution policies aimed at promoting domestic industries. Lastly, low growth and demand within the region itself, and historical trade links with developed countries, have resulted in extra-regional patterns of trade.

The agreement establishing the SAARC Preferential Trading Arrangement (SAPTA) was signed on 11 April 1993 at the seventh SAARC summit held in Dhaka. The agreement was signed by all seven SAARC countries namely, India, Pakistan, Nepal, Bhutan, Bangladesh, Sri Lanka, and the Maldives. It initially focussed on soft issues, such as social issues, culture, youth, and sports, while trade cooperation did not figure in its agenda. Creating a regional trading arrangement came up only in 1997, almost after 12 years of its formation.

SAPTA provides a framework for the exchange of tariff concessions with a view to promoting trade and economic cooperation among the SAARC member countries.

Exhibit 6.3	PTAs in South Asia	
Arrangements into force	**Signed/entered**	**Remarks**
BIMSTEC	2004	FTA-regional
SAFTA	2006	FTA-regional
SAPTA	1995	PTA-regional
ASEAN–India	2003	Framework Agreement
Bhutan–India	2006	Special Trade Agreement
Bangladesh–Sri Lanka	Proposed	FTA bilateral
Bangladesh–Pakistan	Proposed	FTA bilateral
India–Chile	2006	PTA
India–Gulf Cooperation Council (GCC)	2004	Framework Agreement
India–Nepal	1996	FTA–Unilateral non-reciprocal
India–South African Customs Union (SACU) Trade Agreement	Proposed	PTA
India–Singapore Comprehensive Economic Cooperation Agreement	2005	FTA-bilateral
India–Sri Lanka	1999	FTA bilateral
India–Afghanistan	2003	PTA-bilateral
India–Japan	–	Under negotiation
India–Korea Comprehensive Economic Partnership Agreement	2006/07	Under negotiation
India–MERCOSUR	2004	PTA
India–Thailand	2004	Framework Agreement-bilateral
India–Pakistan	Proposed	FTA-bilateral
Pakistan–China	2006	FTA-bilateral
Pakistan–Malaysia	2005	FTA-bilateral
Pakistan–Singapore	Proposed	FTA-bilateral
Pakistan–Sri Lanka	2002	FTA-bilateral
Pakistan–US Trade and Investment Framework Agreement	Proposed	Framework Agreement bilateral
Sri Lanka–Singapore Comprehensive Economic Partnership Agreement	Proposed	Framework Agreement–bilateral
Sri Lanka–Maldives	Proposed	FTA bilateral

Source: Chaturvedi, Sachin, 'Trade Facilitation Measures in South Asian FTAs: An Overview of Initiatives and Policy Approaches' *Research and Information System for Developing Countries,* February 2007, pp. 15; based on RIS database.

SAPTA extends to arrangements in the area of tariffs, non-tariff measures, and direct trade measures. Since the coming into force of the SAPTA agreement in December 1995, four rounds of negotiations have been concluded for exchanging tariff concessions among the member states. Up to the third round, India has provided concessions on a total of 2565 tariff lines.

It was only during the fourth special session of the SAARC standing committee held in Kathmandu between 9–10 July 2003 that bilateral negotiations between India and Pakistan were revived. These concluded in December 2003 at the SAARC Secretariat, Kathmandu. Pakistan agreed to the principle of free importability wherever concessions are granted to India under SAPTA. During this round, India granted concessions to Pakistan on a total of 262 tariff lines, ranging from 10 to 25 per cent while Pakistan has agreed to grant concessions on 223 tariff lines, ranging from 10 to 20 per cent.

SAPTA's constraints in promoting regional trade

Trade within the South Asian region has been limited by a host of economic and political factors. Although there is substantial informal trading, official trade among SAARC countries today accounts for only about 4.5 per cent of total trade volumes. The pace of regional cooperation among the SAARC countries has been slow owing to the poor state of physical and human infrastructure, the relatively underdeveloped states of economy of some member countries, and several policy-induced impediments. The existence of trade barriers and inadequate trade facilitation mechanism has further impeded the cooperation efforts. Besides, the region as a whole has a competitive rather than complementary nature of product mix.

SAARC member countries have not been a major player in world trade because of their long-standing policies of inward orientation. The inability of the region to diversify its export structure in favour of more modern products has resulted in slower export growth and lower value realization. There is an urgent need to diversify and sharpen the global competitiveness of exports of the region by value addition in traditional exports. As all member countries are import-dependent and exports from the region suffer low value addition, SAARC member countries should collectively try to tap the global market than out-compete each other.

South Asian Free Trade Agreement

During the twelfth SAARC summit at Islamabad, the historic agreement on South Asian Free Trade Area (SAFTA) was signed by all the SAARC members on 4 January 2004. SAFTA has come into force from 1 January 2006 and supersedes SAPTA. Under the agreement, India, Pakistan, and Sri Lanka are categorized as non-least developed contracting states (NLDCS) and Bangladesh, Bhutan, and Nepal as least developed contracting states (LDCS). SAFTA anticipates completion of the whole process of instituting free trade in 10 years. Measures for economic cooperation and integration of economies include removal of barriers to intra-SAARC investment, harmonization of customs classifications, transit facilities for efficient intra-SAARC trade, and simplification of procedures for business visas, customs procedures, import licensing, insurance, and competition rules.

The highlights of the agreement are given below.

(a) **Trade liberalization programme (TLP)** The agreement provides for trade liberalization as per this schedule.

Non-least developed country (non-LDC) members of SAARC (India, Pakistan, and Sri Lanka) Non-LDC countries would reduce their existing tariffs to 20 per cent within a time frame of two years from the date of coming into force of the agreement. If the actual tariff rates are below 20 per cent, then there shall be an annual reduction of 10 per cent on margin-of-preference basis for each of the two years. The subsequent tariff reductions from 20 per cent or below to 0–5 per cent shall be enacted within a period of five (for Sri Lanka, six) years, beginning from the third year from the date of coming into force of the agreement.

Least developed country (LDC) members of SAARC (Bangladesh, Bhutan, Maldives, and Nepal) The LDC member countries would reduce their existing tariffs to 30 per cent within a time frame of two years from the date of coming into force of the agreement. If actual tariff rates are below 30 per cent there will be an annual reduction of 5 per cent on margin-of-preference basis for each of the two years. The subsequent tariff reductions from 30 per cent, or below, to 0–5 per cent shall be achieved within a period of eight years beginning from the third year from the date of coming into force of the agreement. Besides, the non-LDC member states have agreed to reduce their tariffs to 0–5 per cent for the products of the LDC member states within a period of three years beginning from the date of coming into force of the agreement.

Sensitive list Tariff reduction shall be carried out on the basis of the negative list approach. Keeping in mind the interests of the domestic stakeholders, the agreement provides for a sensitive list to be maintained by each country (subject to a maximum ceiling), which will be finalized after negotiations among the contracting countries with provision that the LDC contracting states may seek derogation in respect of products of their export interest. The sensitive lists are subject to review after every four years or earlier with a view to reduce the number of items that are to be traded freely among the SAARC countries.

Non-tariff barriers The agreement also provides for elimination of non-tariff and para-tariff barriers with a view to facilitate trade among members.

(b) **Trade facilitation** Keeping in view the increasing importance of trade facilitation measures, the agreement provides for the harmonization of standards, reciprocal recognition of tests and accreditation of testing laboratories, simplification and harmonization of customs procedures, customs classification of HS coding system, import-licensing and registration procedures, simplification of banking procedures for import financing, transit facilities for efficient intra-SAARC trade, micro-economic consultations, development of communication systems transport, and infrastructure, and simplification of business visas.

(c) **Institutional mechanism** The agreement also provides for an institutional mechanism to facilitate the implementation of its provisions, which includes safeguard measures in case of a surge in the imports of products covered under the SAFTA concessions that threaten or cause a serious injury to the domestic industry and a dispute settlement mechanism for the interpretation and application of the provisions of this agreement or any instrument adopted within its framework concerning the rights and obligations of the contracting states.

(d) **Special provisions** The agreement provides for special provisions for LDCs, such as longer phase-out schedule, longer sensitive lists, and revenue compensation mechanism while considering the application of anti-dumping and/or countervailing measures. Maldives has been given special dispensation to retain the special provisions accorded to LDCs even after its graduation, and Sri Lanka has been given one year more for its TLP.

(e) **Implementation** The agreement on SAFTA came into force on 1 January 2006. The MFN-applied rate existing as on 1 January 2006 has been considered as the base rate for the purpose of tariff reduction.

Signed post-WTO accord, the SAFTA is designed to be compatible with WTO provisions in all its forms and contents. It leans heavily on WTO institutions and practices, which gets reflected in dispute settlement, safeguard measures, BOP exceptions, and special and differential treatment to LDC. Any member country will have the right to pull out of the treaty at any time by giving a six month notice in writing to the Secretary General of the SAARC.

In view of the different budget periods of the member states, the members decided to carry out phased liberalization from 1 July 2006 instead of 1 January 2006 (Nepal from 1 August 2006) with the condition that trade liberalization process for the first two years was to be completed by December 2007.

It was also decided that there would be a SAFTA ministerial council consisting of commerce or trade ministers of all the member countries and a committee of experts for the administration and implementation of the agreement. The dispute settlement mechanism is also modelled along the lines of WTO dispute settlement mechanism. The SAFTA agreement envisages amicable settlement of all disputes pertaining to interpretation and application of SAFTA provisions regarding rights and obligations of member states through bilateral consultations under the auspices of SAFTA forum.

The challenges before SAFTA that need to be addressed so as to make it successful and effective are discussed here:

• The momentum in improving India–Pakistan relations will have to be maintained.

- The economic insecurity-related concerns of the smaller nations will have to be addressed.
- There is a quick need to develop economic infrastructure. India and Pakistan have only one land crossing at Wagah. In this situation, it is only an ambitious aspiration to handle trade of such an anticipated huge magnitude.
- There are certain fears in specific sectors in each country that need to be allayed.

6.6.2 Comprehensive Economic Cooperation Agreement between India and Singapore

The India–Singapore Comprehensive Economic Cooperation Agreement (CECA) was signed on 29 June 2005 and came into force on 1 August 2005. It provides for phased reduction/elimination of duties on products other than those in the negative list by India by 1 April 2009 and an early harvest scheme (EHS) whereas Singapore has eliminated duties on all products originating from India from 1 August 2005. Besides trade in goods, the CECA also covers investment, services, mutual recognition agreements, and customs co-operations.

6.6.3 Framework Agreement on Comprehensive Economic Cooperation between the ASEAN and India

India has had close cultural and economic ties with Southeast Asian countries throughout history. ASEAN's political and strategic importance in the larger Asia-Pacific region and its potential to become a major partner of India in the area of trade and investment has encouraged India to seek closer linkages with these countries. India's engagement with ASEAN started with its 'look east policy' in 1991. India became a sectoral dialogue partner of ASEAN in 1992 and a full dialogue partner in 1996. The ASEAN-India relationship was upgraded to summit level in November 2001. The first ASEAN Economic Ministers (AEM)-India consultations were held in Brunei on 15 September 2002. An ASEAN-India economic linkages task force was set up to study and prepare a draft agreement for the next AEM-India consultations in 2003 through senior economic officials for further consideration and follow-up action.

The framework agreement on comprehensive Economic Cooperation[4] between ASEAN and India was signed on 8 October 2003 during the second ASEAN India Summit in Bali, Indonesia. It covers gradual tariff reductions leading to formation of FTA in goods, liberalization in services and investment, other areas of economic cooperation, such as trade facilitation measures, sectors of cooperations and trade, investment promotion measures and early harvest programmes covering areas of economic cooperation, and a common list of items for exchange of tariff concessions as a confidence building measure. The ASEAN-India trade negotiating committee

---

[4] Sen, Rahul, Mukul G. Asher, and Ramkishen S. Rajan, 'ASEAN-India Economic Relations: Current Status and Future Prospects', *Economic and Political Weekly*, July 17, 2004, pp. 3297–3307.

has also been set up to carry out the programme of negotiations of necessary agreements and other instruments thereof to establish the ASEAN-India Regional Trade and Investment Area (RTIA) in accordance with the provisions set out in the framework agreement.

The first meeting of the ASEAN-India Trade Negotiating Committee (TNC) was held on 7 March 2004 at the ASEAN Secretariat, Jakarta. During the first meeting of the ASEAN-India TNC, the terms of reference for the TNC were finalized. Due to difference in opinion, the early harvest programme, agreed under the agreement could not be implemented by early 2007 and the negotiations were targeted to be concluded by mid-2007. Negotiations in trade and services were likely to begin immediately after the agreement on trade in goods were concluded.

6.6.4 Bay of Bengal Initiative for Multi-sectoral Technical and Economic Co-operation

The initiative to explore economic cooperation on a sub-regional basis involving contiguous countries of Southeast and South Asia grouped around the Bay of Bengal was taken by Thailand in 1994. On 6 June 1997, the subgroup was renamed Bangladesh, India, Sri Lanka, and Thailand Economic Cooperation (BIST-EC). Myanmar was admitted in December 1997 as full member and the name of the group was changed to BIMST-EC. Subsequently, Nepal and Bhutan received full membership in 2003. During the summit in Bangkok on 31 July 2004, the name was again changed to Bay of Bengal Initiative for Multi-sectoral Technical and Economic Cooperation (BIMSTEC) (see Fig. 6.5).

BIMSTEC provides a unique link between South Asia and Southeast Asia, bringing together about 21 per cent of the world population having considerable amount of complementarities. During the first meeting of economic/trade ministers of BIMSTEC, which was held in Bangkok in August 1998, it was agreed that BIMSTEC should aim and strive to develop into an FTA and should focus on activities that facilitate trade, increase investment, and promote technical cooperation among member countries. It was further reiterated that BIMSTEC activities should be designed to form a bridge linking ASEAN and SAARC. Six areas were identified for cooperation, namely trade and investment, technology, transportation and communication, energy, tourism, and fisheries.

The text of the draft framework agreement on BIMSTEC FTA prepared by a group of experts was considered at the fourth Senior Trade and Economic Officials Meeting (STEOM) held in Bangkok during 14–15 January 2004. The framework agreement on the BIMSTEC FTA was signed on 8 February 2004 in Phuket, Thailand, by Bangladesh, India, Myanmar, Nepal, Sri Lanka, and Thailand. The framework agreement includes provisions for negotiations on FTA in goods, services, and investment. The major highlights of the framework agreement are as given here.

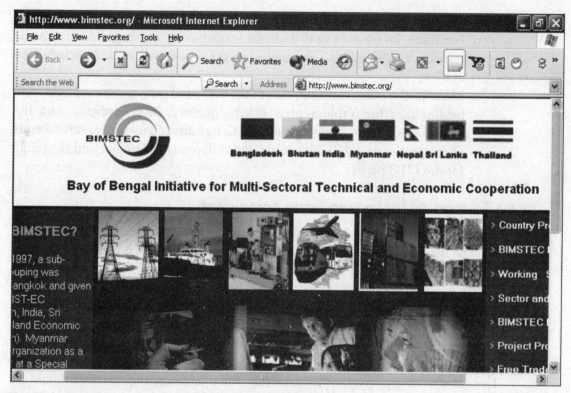

Fig. 6.5   BIMSTEC: A unique link between South Asia and Southeast Asia

- **FTA in goods**   The negotiations for tariff reduction/elimination for FTA in goods was to commence in July 2004 and conclude by December 2005.
  - *Fast track*   Products listed in the fast track by the party on its own accord shall have their respective applied MFN tariff rates gradually reduced/ eliminated in accordance with specified rates to be mutually agreed by the parties, within the following timeframe:

Countries	For developing country parties	For LDC parties
India, Sri Lanka, and Thailand	1 July 2006 to 30 June 2009	1 July 2006 to 30 June 2007
Bangladesh and Myanmar	1 July 2006 to 30 June 2011	1 July 2006 to 30 June 2009

  - *Normal track*   Products listed in the normal track by a party on its own accord shall have their respective applied MFN tariff rates gradually reduced/ eliminated in accordance with specified rates to be mutually agreed by the parties, within the following timeframe:

Countries	For developing country parties	For LDC parties
India, Sri Lanka, and Thailand	1 July 2007 to 30 June 2012	1 July 2007 to 30 June 2010
Bangladesh and Myanmar	1 July 2007 to 30 June 2017	1 July 2007 to 30 June 2015

- **FTA in services and investments**
  - For trade in services and trade in investments, the negotiations on the respective agreements commenced in 2005 and was to be concluded by 2007.
  - Identification, liberalization, etc., of the sectors of services/investments shall be finalized for implementation subsequently, in accordance with the timeframes to be mutually agreed; (a) taking into account the sensitive sectors of the parties and (b) with special and differential treatment and flexibility for the LDC parties.

6.6.5 Indo–Sri Lanka Free Trade Agreement

An FTA between India and Sri Lanka was signed on 28 December 1998 in New Delhi. The Indo–Sri Lanka Free Trade Agreement (ISLFTA) envisages phasing out of tariffs on all products except for a limited number of items in the negative list and tariff rate quota items over a period of time. The implementation of the agreement started in March 2000. As prescribed in the agreement, India has eliminated tariffs on all items other than those in the negative list or under Tariff Rate Quota (TRQ) with effect from 18 March 2003, and Sri Lanka is scheduled to phase out the tariffs by the year 2008, except for the items in the negative list.

The rules of origin specify that domestic value addition requirement should be 35 per cent for products to qualify for preferential treatment under the agreement. If the raw material/inputs are sourced from each others' country, the value addition requirement is reduced to 25 per cent within the overall limit of 35 per cent. The criterion of 'substantial transformation' has been provided in the rules. The goods must undergo transformation at 4-digit level of harmonized system.

The agreement provides for establishment of a joint committee at the ministerial level, which shall meet at least once a year to review the progress made in the implementation of the agreement and to ensure that the benefits of trade expansion emanating from this agreement accrue to both countries equitably. India and Sri Lanka have initiated negotiations to enter into a comprehensive economic partnership agreement (ECPA) and to deepen and widen the coverage by including trade in services, investment cooperation, etc.

6.6.6 Asia-Pacific Trade Agreement (Bangkok Agreement)

Under the auspices of Economic and Social Commission of Asia and Pacific (ESCAP), the first agreement on trade negotiations was signed in 1975 among developing member countries of ESCAP. India is a founder signatory to the Asia-Pacific Trade Agreement (APTA) along with Bangladesh, Laos, the Philippines, South Korea, Sri Lanka, and Thailand. It is essentially a PTA designed to liberalize and expand trade progressively in the ESCAP region through mutually agreed concessions by member countries. ESCAP functions as secretariat for the agreement. The Bangkok agreement was approved by the GATT council in March 1978. China acceded to this agreement in 2001. From 2 November 2005, this agreement is renamed the Asia Pacific Trade Agreement (APTA). The agreement is operational among five countries, namely Bangladesh, China, India, Republic of Korea, and Sri Lanka. Three rounds of negotiations have been concluded under this agreement and the third round has been implemented from 1 September 2006.

6.6.7 Global System of Trade Preferences

The agreement establishing the Global System of Trade Preferences (GSTP) among developing countries was signed in April 1988 at Belgrade. The GSTP establishes a framework for exchange of trade concessions among the members of the group of 77. It lays down the rules, principles, and procedures for conduct of negotiations and implementation of the decisions made. The fourth rounds of negotiations were launched during UNCTAD XII in April 2008 at Accra in Ghana.

6.6.8 Generalized System of Trade Preferences

The Generalized System of Trade Preferences (GSP) is a non-contractual instrument by which developed countries extend tariff concessions to developing countries unilaterally and on the basis of non-reciprocity. It was formally accepted in 1968 by the members of the UN at the second UNCTAD conference at New Delhi. Under the GSP, preferential tariff treatment is granted on a non-reciprocal and non-discriminatory basis by most developed countries to exports from developing countries, with most-favoured nation (MFN) treatment duties reduced or eliminated.

6.6.9 Framework Agreement for Establishing Free Trade between India and Thailand

In November 2001, a joint working group (JWG) was set up to undertake a feasibility study on a free trade agreement between India and Thailand. The JWG observed that the present policy regimes in both the countries are quite conducive to more intensive bilateral economic integration and an FTA could prove to be a building block for other sub-regional, regional, and global economic integration processes involving both countries. Having observed the rich potential of trade expansion, the study concluded that the proposed FTA between India and Thailand is feasible, desirable, and mutually beneficial. Accordingly, a joint negotiating group was set up to draft the framework agreement on the India–Thailand FTA.

The framework agreement for establishing an FTA between India and Thailand was signed on 9 October 2003 in Bangkok. The key elements of the framework agreement cover FTA in goods, services and investment, and areas of economic cooperation. The framework agreement also provides for an early harvest scheme (EHS) under which common items have been agreed for elimination of tariffs on a fast-track basis. The highlights of the various components of the framework agreement are given below.

- *FTA in goods*
  - ○ Negotiations to commence in January 2004 and conclude by March 2005
  - ○ Establishment of free trade area (zero-duty imports) by 2010
- *FTA in services*
  - ○ Negotiations to commence in January 2004 and conclude by January 2006
- *FTA in investments*
  - ○ Negotiations to commence in January 2004 and conclude by January 2006
- *Areas of economic cooperation*
  - ○ Areas of economic cooperation to include trade facilitation measures; sectors identified for cooperation and trade and investment promotion measures
- *Early harvest scheme*
  - ○ Both sides to agree to have a common list of 84 items (6-digit HS level) for exchange of tariff concessions
  - ○ Tariffs on these items to be phased out in a two-year timeframe, starting from 1 March 2004

The early harvest items covering 82 items for exchange of concessions between India and Thailand has been implemented with effect from 1 September 2004. Negotiations on FTA in goods are underway by the Trade Negotiating Committee (TNC).

6.6.10 Bilateral Preferential Trading Agreement with Afghanistan

The Preferential Trade Agreement between India and Afghanistan, signed on 6 March 2003, provide for establishing a preferential trading arrangement between the two countries to promote the harmonious development of the economic relations and the free movement of goods through reduction of tariffs. The objective is to provide for grant or concessions on a range of products of export interest to Afghanistan, as a part of India's endeavour to strengthen trade and economic relations between the two countries. The agreement is WTO-compatible.

Products covered under the agreement shall be eligible for preferential treatment,[5] provided they satisfy the rules of origin laid down under the agreement. India is granting Afghanistan 50–100 per cent tariff concession on 38 items of dry fruits, fresh fruits, seeds, medicinal herbs, and precious stones and in turn India is receiving duty-free access on eight tariff lines of its export interest, which include black tea, pharmaceutical products, Ayurvedic and Homeopathic medicines, refined sugar, cement, etc. The agreement would remain in force till either party gives notice to the other for termination of the agreement.

---

[5] *Annual Report 2003–04,* Ministry of Commerce, Government of India, New Delhi, pp. 103–22.

6.6.11   India–MERCOSUR PTA

A PTA was signed, aiming to expand and strengthen existing trade relations between India and MERCOSUR by granting reciprocal fixed trade preferences with the ultimate objective of creating an FTA. The PTA consists of five annexures, signed on 19 March 2005, including an offer list of India, rules of origin, safeguard measures, and dispute settlement procedure. In November 2006, preliminary discussions were held in New Delhi to work out modalities for future negotiations.

6.6.12   India–Chile Framework Agreement on Economic Cooperation

A framework agreement on economic cooperation was signed between India and Chile on 20 January 2005, which envisages a PTA between the two countries. The negotiations on the PTA were concluded and the agreement was signed on March 2006.

6.6.13   Indo–Gulf Cooperation Council FTA

A framework agreement between India and the Gulf Cooperation Council was signed on 25 August 2004. The first round of negotiations was held in Riyadh on March 2006, wherein the GCC side agreed to include services as well as investment and general economic cooperation along with goods in the proposed agreement.

6.7   LIMITATIONS OF REGIONAL ECONOMIC INTEGRATIONS

The regional trade agreements cannot replace the multilateral trade rules. Besides creating trade diversion and shifting imports from the most efficient global suppliers, the crucial limitations of RTAs include the following:

- The conclusion of preferential trade agreements can create an incentive for even further discrimination, which eventually will hurt all trading partners. Countries outside an agreement will try to conclude agreements with one of those that is inside to avoid exclusion. This has been called the 'domino' or 'bandwagon' effect and is the reason for much of the regional trade agreement activity seen in Asia recently. In other words, the consequence is that the preferences obtained through forming a preferential agreement against competitors tend to be short lived. The more agreements you have, the less meaningful the preferences would be.
- PTAs cannot solve systemic issues such as rules of origin, anti-dumping, agricultural, and fisheries subsidies. These issues simply cannot be handled at the bilateral or regional level. Take for instance negotiations to eliminate or reduce trade distorting agricultural subsidies or fisheries subsidies. There is no such thing as a 'bilateral' farmer, fisherman, or chicken and a 'multilateral' farmer, fisherman, or chicken. Subsidies are given to farmers for their poultry production. The same is true for rules on anti-dumping.

- The proliferation of RTA can greatly complicate the trading environment, creating a web of incoherent rules. Take the rules of origin: an increasing number of WTO members are party to ten or more RTAs, most of which are necessary to ensure that the preferences go to a partner country and not to others. This complicates the production processes of businesses that may be obliged to tailor their products for different preferential markets in order to satisfy the rules of origin. It also complicates life for customs officials who are obliged to assess the same product differently on the basis its origin, thus compromising the transparency of the trading regime. This leads to a real 'spaghetti bowl' of twisted rules of origin, as termed by Professor Jagdish Bhagwati. Figure 6.6 depicts the 'spaghetti bowl' or 'noodle bowl' effect of PTAs in Asia-Pacific.
- To many small and weak developing countries entering into a PTA with a powerful big country means less leverage and a weaker negotiating position as compared to that in the multilateral talks. It might not be the case for the US and the EU, but it is true for India and China. It will also be true for Mauritius, Sri Lanka, Cambodia, or Ghana.

6.8 REGIONAL TRADE AGREEMENTS VIS-À-VIS MULTILATERAL TRADING SYSTEM UNDER THE WTO

The PTAs do have a fundamental conflict with multilateralism, as these are built on the foundation of discrimination with the non-members while liberalizing trade. The multilateral initiative under the WTO rests on the principle of non-discrimination, the two main pillars being the MFN treatment and the national treatment. RTAs are an exceptional situation under the multilateral trading system enunciated within the WTO. Any RTA is bound to have certain trade distortion effects. This trade distortion arises because of the discriminatory treatment advanced to the non-members of the RTA vis-à-vis its members. This discriminatory treatment arises because of the increased market access granted to the members of the same regional block.

However, the GATT, and now the WTO, recognize the conditional right of members to form RTAs and, to the extent necessary, to set aside some WTO obligations. PTAs are legally permitted, subject to compliance of certain conditions, under Article XXIV of GATT 1994 as an integral part of the WTO agreement effective from 1995. These conditions stipulate that on the formation of a PTA, the customs duties shall not on the whole be higher or more restrictive than before. While liberalizing trade on MFN basis, member countries of the WTO are fast moving forward to form new PTAs and to strengthen the existing ones. The WTO imposes three types of substantive conditions for regional agreements to be WTO consistent:

- With respect to the overall impact of the RTAs vis-à-vis other members, there is the obligation not to raise barriers to trade with third parties. This is quantifiable in terms of tariffs, but less easy to measure in terms of other trade regulations such as standards or rules of origin.

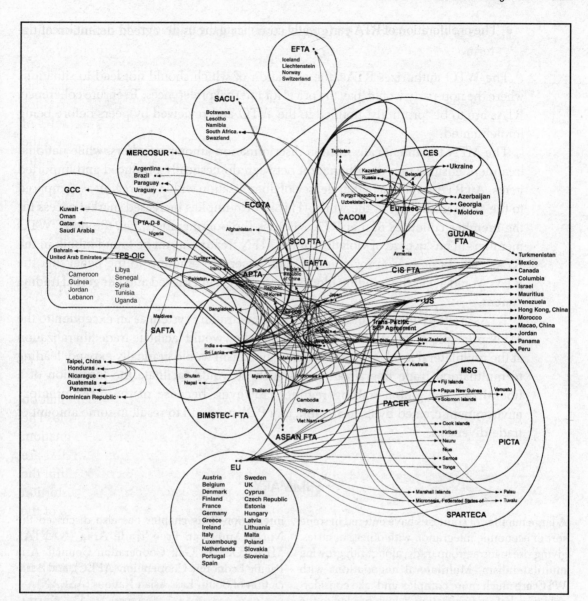

Fig 6.6   'Spaghetti-bowl effect' of PTAs in Asia-Pacific

Source: Regional Cooperation and Integration Strategy, Asian Development Bank, Manila, July 2006.

- With reference to the 'external requirement', an FTA cannot lead to higher import duties for its members while a customs union must harmonize the external trade policies of its members and compensate affected non-members accordingly.
- On the 'internal dimension' of regional trade agreements, tariffs and other restrictive regulations of commerce must be phased out substantially on all trade. Again the tariff component can be quantified, but it is harder to determine in the

case of their restrictive trade regulations, as there is no agreed definition of the term.

The WTO authorizes RTAs, the operation of which should not lead to situations where the non-party would 'pay the price' for internal preferences. To ensure coherence, RTAs are to be 'promptly' notified to the WTO and reviewed by peers before being implemented.

The MFN treatment calls for non-discrimination among members, while national treatment ensures non-discrimination between domestically produced and imported items. An RTA implies a higher degree of liberalization within the region as compared to the same in the rest of the world. This in turn implies increased market access for the member countries of that RTA, vis-à-vis the non-members, i.e., the other WTO members. Thus, a case of violation of the MFN treatment can be found inbuilt in the RTAs. The basic reason for granting such exception amounts to the belief that the RTAs would act as the building blocks for forming a liberalized and fair global trading system.

RTAs are thus allowed under the multilateral trading system as an exception to the MFN principle of the WTO in the belief that they would facilitate trade liberalization at the multilateral level. The idea is that regionalism would gradually expand, leading to multilateral trade liberalization. As such, it would facilitate the formation of a liberalized fair global trading regime. However, because of the discriminatory environment created by its formation, any PTA is bound to result in some amount of trade diversion.

SUMMARY

A large number of countries have entered in some sort of economic integration with other countries, giving rise to intra-group trade, along with growing multilateralism. Multilateral negotiations with WTO are much more complex and take considerable time before finalization, which has led to the growing attractiveness of regional agreements. Trade creation and trade diversion are the two significant impacts of formation of PTAs. The various forms of trade groups include preferential trading agreement, free trade area, customs union, common market, economic union, and political union, depending upon their level of economic integration.

The European Union with 67 per cent intra-group trade is the largest trade group in the world with considerably higher level of economic integration. This chapter has also discussed the North American Free Trade Area (NAFTA), MERCOSUR, Gulf Cooperation Council, Asia Pacific Economic Cooperation (APEC), and Association of South East Asian Nations (ASEAN).

India's participation in PTAs, such as SAFTA, ASEAN, BIMSTEC, India–Sri Lanka Free Trade Agreement, Asia Pacific Free Trade Agreement (APTA), Global System of Trade Preferences (GSTP), Comprehensive Economic Cooperation Agreement (CECA) between India and Singapore, etc., has also been examined.

Although PTAs do have a fundamental conflict with multilateralism being built in discrimination with non-members while liberalizing trade, they are legally permitted under Article XXIV of GATT 1994 of the WTO agreement.

KEY TERMS

Common market Removing all restrictions on cross-border investment and movement of factors of production besides free trade among members and uniform trade policy for non-members.

Customs union Having common external import tariffs for non-members, besides elimination of tariff barriers among the member countries.

Economic union Involves much greater level of economic integration with harmonization of monetary and fiscal policy.

Free trade area Removal of all tariff and non-tariff barriers among the member countries but members are free to maintain their own tariffs and non-tariff barriers with non-member countries.

Political union The highest level of integration with political and economic harmonization wherein the member countries are willing to dilute their national identities to a considerable extent.

Preferential trading agreement (PTA) Lowering tariff barriers among member countries to import identified products from one another.

Trade creation impact Expansion of consumption opportunity by making low cost goods available.

Trade diversion impact Shift of trade from non-member countries to member countries as a result of tariff elimination or preferential treatment.

CONCEPT REVIEW QUESTIONS

1. Along with growing multilateralism in the era of globalization, regional trading arrangements (RTAs) have also witnessed rapid increase during the recent years. Explain the reasons responsible for the growing attractiveness of regional agreements over multilateral negotiation.

2. Critically evaluate the impact of the formation of PTAs on members and non-member countries.

3. Explain the various types of economic integrations with suitable examples.

4. Briefly evaluate India's participation in PTAs.

5. Write short notes on
   (a) MERCOSUR
   (b) NAFTA
   (c) APEC
   (d) ASEAN

CRITICAL THINKING QUESTIONS

1. Carry out a comparative analysis of intra-group trade among member countries of major economic groups.

2. Under the 'most favoured nation' principle of the WTO framework, no member country can discriminate among its members whereas the PTAs are based on the principle of preferential treatments to its members and discriminatory treatment of non-members. This is against the fundamental of multilateralism under the WTO. How do you justify the legal status of PTAs under the WTO? Discuss your arguments in class in the form of a debate.

PROJECT ASSIGNMENTS

1. Visit the website of the European Union (http://europa.eu) and explore the measures taken for economic integration among the member countries. Compare these measures vis-à-vis SAFTA.

2. Carry out the trade analysis of your country and identify the major trading partners. Find out the impact of economic integration on the trade patterns and relate it with the concepts learnt in this chapter.

7

International Cultural Environment

LEARNING OBJECTIVES

> To understand the significance of culture in international business decisions
> To elucidate the concept of culture and its constituents
> To explain comparisons of cross-cultural behaviour
> To discuss cultural orientation in international business
> To appreciate *emic* versus *etic* dilemma and its operationalization

7.1 INTRODUCTION

A firm operating internationally comes across a wide range of diverse cultural environments, which significantly influence international business decisions. Managers operating across national borders need to appreciate the differences among the cultural behaviours of their business partners and consumers across various countries. As a matter of basic principle, an international manager visiting overseas is expected to follow local customs and a seller needs to adapt to the buyer's requirements.

This chapter brings out the significance of understanding culture in international business. When international managers are faced with a set of business situations overseas, they are prone to misjudge or erroneously react due to perceptual differences of cross-cultural nuances. Therefore, it becomes imperative for international managers to have a thorough conceptual understanding of cross-culture issues and its implications on international business decisions.

International managers need to develop cultural sensitivities in the countries of their operations and adapt their business strategies accordingly. The failure of Euro Disneyland is a classic example of the failure to understand a foreign culture and is often described as a 'Cultural Chernobyl'. Disney's insensitivity to French culture in terms of product designs, consumer habits, and local norms made the company enter into troubled waters in its French venture. For instance, alcoholic beverages are out of place in Disney's US 'family restaurants', whereas in most parts of Europe, alcoholic drinks form integral part of the meals.

Another example of cultural insensitivity was witnessed in May 2001 when a wave of anger erupted among vegetarian and Hindu consumers across the world, especially in India, within hours of receiving the news of McDonald's using beef extract for cooking its fries.[1] Over 80 per cent of India's one billion population is Hindu, for whom the cow is highly sacred and worshipped. Angry mobs in Mumbai vandalized McDonald's outlets. To combat public ire, McDonald's adopted a comprehensive approach integrating the use of public relations and media publicity and employing police security. McDonald's sent samples of the fries to leading Indian laboratories for testing on the same day the news broke in India, the results of which were published in leading dailies. Besides, McDonald's displayed prominent posters in its outlets stating '100 per cent Vegetarian French Fries in McDonald's India' and 'no flavours with animal products/extracts are used for preparing any vegetarian products in India'. Consequently, McDonald's emphasized on adapting a more vegetarian-friendly menu and became more sensitive to Indian culture.

The perception and behaviour of people varies widely across cultures (Exhibit 7.1). Several definitions have been discussed in this chapter to explain the concept of culture. Summarily, culture represents the collective or group behaviour of people that makes them different from others. The various constituents of culture such as value system, norms, aesthetics, customs and traditions, language, and religion have also been elaborated along with their implications in international business.

This chapter also elucidates the major types of cultural classifications so as to facilitate a comparison of cross-cultural behaviour. Major cultural orientations such as parochialism, simplification, and the ethnocentric, polycentric, regiocentric, and geocentric (EPRG) concept have also been explained. The chapter also brings out the *emic* vs *etic* dilemma in cross-cultural decisions and its operationalization.

Exhibit 7.1   Divergence of perceptions in cross-cultural survey

In a worldwide survey conducted by the UN, the only question asked was: 'would you please give your honest opinion about solutions to the food shortage in the rest of the world?' The survey was a huge failure, as

- In Africa, they didn't know what 'food' meant.
- In South Asia, they didn't know what 'honest' meant.
- In Europe, they didn't know what 'shortage' meant.
- In China, they didn't know what 'opinion' meant.
- In the Middle East, they didn't know what 'solution' meant.
- In South America, they didn't know what 'please' meant.
- In the US, they didn't know what 'the rest of the world' meant!

Source: Adapted from *The Economic Times*, 28 June 2006.

---

[1] Gupte, Sarika, 'McDonald's Avert a Crisis: Crisis Management Teams Reverse Damages to the Fast Food Giants in India', *Advertising Age Global*, 1 July 2000.

7.2 SELF-REFERENCE CRITERION AND ETHNOCENTRISM: MAJOR OBSTACLES IN INTERNATIONAL BUSINESS DECISIONS

The ability of an international manager to objectively evaluate environmental factors is severely affected by his/her own cultural conditioning in understanding the nuances of another culture. A self-reference criterion (SRC) is an unconscious reference to one's own cultural values, experiences, and knowledge as a basis for decision making. A person from one culture is often not aware that the reaction to any situation is influenced by one's own cultural background and is interpreted in different cultural situations in different perspectives. Market relativism is in fact a subtle and unintended result of cultural conditioning.

Ethnocentrism is a belief that considers one's culture as superior to others and contemplates that the business strategies that work in one's home country will work as well in foreign countries too. Most Indians find it difficult to understand how westerners eat the meat of the cow, which gives milk and is revered as the mother of mankind. Korea and other East Asian countries' love for foods such as bloodworm soup, snake, and dog meat is not easy for outsiders to rationalize. Sometimes, even consumers believe that buying foreign-made goods is wrong because it hurts domestic economy, causes loss of jobs, and, therefore, is unpatriotic. This phenomenon is known as *consumer ethnocentrism.*[2]

In order to arrive at an objective business decision, one has to isolate the influences of SRC while carrying out a cross-cultural analysis. James Lee has suggested a four-step approach to eliminate SRC:

Step 1: *Define the business problem or goal in home-country traits, habits, or norms.*

Step 2: *Define the business problem or goal in foreign country cultural traits, habits, or norms. Make no value judgments.*

Step 3: *Isolate the SRC influence in the problem and examine it carefully to see how it complicates the problem.*

Step 4: *Redefine the problem without the SRC influence and solve for the optimum business goal situation.*[3]

7.3 THE CONCEPT OF CULTURE

The word culture is derived from the Latin *cultura* which is related to cult or worship. Culture is the way of life of people, including their attitudes, values, beliefs, arts, sciences, modes of perception, and habits of thought and activity. The Oxford Encyclopaedic English Dictionary defines culture as 'the art and other manifestations of human intellectual achievements regarded collectively; the customs, civilization,

[2] Shimp, Terence A. and Subhash Sharma, 'Consumer Ethnocentrism: Construction and Validation of the CETSCALE', *Journal of Marketing Research,* August 1987, vol. 24, no. 3, pp. 280–89.

[3] Lee, James A. 'Cultural Analysis in Overseas Operations', *Harvard Business Reviews,* March–April 1966, pp 106–11.

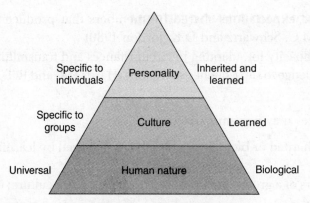

Fig. 7.1   Levels of human mental programming

and achievement of a particular time or people; the way of life of a particular society or group'.

Culture is the collective programming of the mind, which distinguishes the members of one group or category from those of another.[4] Hofstede's model indicates three level of uniqueness in human mental programming.[5] Culture lies between human nature on one side and individual personality on the other, as shown in Fig. 7.1. Each person has several layers of cultural 'programming' from basic values to practices at corporate level.

The Encyclopaedia Britannica defines culture as an integrated pattern of human knowledge, belief, and behaviour that is both a result of and integral to the human capacity for learning and transmitting knowledge to succeeding generations. Culture thus consists of language, ideas, beliefs, customs, taboos, codes, institutions, tools, techniques, works of art, rituals, ceremonies, and symbols.

The concept of culture may be explained by various definitions[6] as follows:

- Primarily a system for creating, sending, storing and processing information (E.T. Hall and M.R. Hall 1987)
- That complex whole which includes knowledge, beliefs, art, morals, laws, customs, and any other capabilities and habits acquired by man as a member of society (E. Taylor 1871)
- The man-made part of the human environment (M.J. Herskovits 1948)
- Transmitted patterns of value, ideas, and other symbolic systems that shape behaviour (A.L. Kroeber and C. Kluckhohn 1952)
- Set of common understandings expressed in language (Becker and Geer 1970)
- Values, beliefs and expectations that members come to share (J. Van Mannen and E.H. Schein 1979)

---

[4] Hofstede, Geert, 'National Cultures Revisited', *Asia Pacific Journal of Management*, September 1984, pp. 22–24.

[5] Hofstede, G., *Cultures and Organisations: Software of the Mind*, London: McGraw-Hill, 1991.

[6] Redding, Gordon, 'Managing Cultural Differences', in Stening, Bruce W. (ed.) *Cross-Cultural Management*, vol. II, Edward Elgar Publishing Limited, Cheltenham, UK, 2003, pp. 23–101.

- Pattern of beliefs and expectations shared by members that produce norms shaping behaviour (M.C. Schwartz and D.K. Jordon 1980)
- A distinctly human capacity for adapting to circumstances and transmitting this coping skill and knowledge to subsequent generations (Harris P.R. and R.T. Moran 1987)

Characteristics of culture[7] may be summarized as

Learned Culture is not inherited or biologically based; it is acquired by learning and experience.

Shared People as members of a group, organization, or society share culture; it is not specific to single individual.

Trans-generational Culture is cumulative, passed on from one generation to the next.

Symbolic Culture is based on the human capacity to symbolize or use one thing to represent another.

Patterned Culture has structure and is integrated; a change in one part will bring changes in another.

Adaptive Culture is based on the human capacity to change or adapt, as opposed to the genetically driven adaptive process of animals.

The process of adjusting and adapting to a new culture is known as *acculturation*, which is crucial to one's success in international business.

7.3.1 Constituents of Culture

As culture is an integrated sum of learned behaviour shared by a group of people that differentiates it from others, it becomes imperative to understand various constituents that contribute to the sum total of learned behaviour. Although a variety of learned traits that influence human behaviour can contribute to the culture of a social group, only the major constituents, such as value system, norms, aesthetics, customs and traditions, language, and religion, are discussed here.

Value system

Values are shared assumptions of a group regarding what is good or bad, right or wrong, and important or unimportant. Values are learnt by a person while being reared in a culture, which significantly influences one's behaviour. Business behaviour is considerably affected by a country's value systems. Value patterns vary among managers across countries, for instance, US managers are high-achievement and competition oriented and emphasize on profit maximization, organizational efficiency, and high productivity whereas Japanese managers lay strong emphasis on size and growth and high value for competence and achievement. Indian managers have moral orientation and a strong focus on organizational compliance and competence.

---

[7] Luthans, Fred, *Organization Behaviour*, 7th ed., New York: McGraw-Hill, 1995, pp. 33–55.

The Indian experience reveals that a consumer often attempts to emulate the behaviour of his/her peer group. The emotive side of the Indian consumer leads his/her to aspire to do better than his/her peers. But in China, the only recognized superiority is age. Moreover, there appears to be an extremely high level of contentment in the Chinese counterpart. So the 'competitive' aspect to life seems to be missing. Managers find this confounding. Most people in China are found to hardly even attempt to create or recognize a difference between themselves and others. In a cultural and social environment where it is deeply ingrained that only time will bring one prosperity, or betterment vis-à-vis another, that one cannot be prosperous before he/she reaches a certain age, and that one can be superior to one's neighbour only if one is elder, comparative advertising is completely irrelevant.

In such an environment, ad lines such as *Safedi aisi, ki nazar lag jaaye* (whiteness that creates envy) and 'Neighbour's envy, owner's pride' would mean cognitive dissonance. Privately one may feel good that her clothes look better, but socially such superiority is not acceptable. In a socially responsible environment, no marketer would want to exploit this overtly as it would be seen by the establishment, which is still in control, as defiance of the ethos they have protected for decades. So, straightaway comparative advertising is difficult to make in China.[8] Thus, one needs to be culturally sensitive while conducting business in alien countries.

In an advertisement used by Proctor & Gamble (P&G) for Camay soap, a man meeting a woman for the first time compares her skin to that of a fine porcelain doll. This worked well in Europe and South America, but failed miserably in Japan, where it was considered to be unsophisticated or rude to a Japanese woman. Another Camay ad that showed a man walking onto his bathing wife, who begins to tell him about her new beauty soap, worked well in Europe but not in Japan as it is considered bad manners for a husband to intrude upon his wife.

Cultural values tend to change over time. For instance, the Japanese business value system that lays high emphasis on life-time employment, group orientation, formal authority, seniority, and paternalism has witnessed considerable change over the years.

Norms

Norms are guidelines or social rules that prescribe appropriate behaviour in a given situation. For instance, in Japan, aggressive selling is not perceived in the positive spirit. Many companies, including Dell Computers, emphasize on the benefits in terms of lower price by direct selling instead of using aggressive selling tactics. Cultural norms affect consumption patterns and habits too. Indian and other South Asians generally use spoons of different sizes while eating. Chinese and Japanese use chopsticks as the meat is pre-cut to small pieces but Europeans and Americans use knives and forks to cut the meat on the dining table.

---

[8] Seth, Meera, 'When Old Strategies Don't Wash', *Business World*, 5 March 2001, pp. 37–40.

International managers should be able to differentiate between what is acceptable or unacceptable in a foreign culture and familiarize themselves with cultural tolerance to business customs that may be grouped as follows.

Cultural imperatives It refers to the norms that must be followed or must be avoided in a foreign country. Adherence to such business customs and expectations is crucial to one's success in foreign cultures. In relationship-oriented oriental cultures, one is expected to develop mutual trust and rapport as a precondition to successful business operations.

To operate effectively in cross-country business environments, international managers should develop a broad understanding of cultural imperatives that need to be followed in one culture and avoided in another. For instance, a prolonged eye contact is considered to be offensive in Japan and, therefore, needs to be avoided. On the other hand, unless you establish strong eye contact in Latin America and Gulf countries, you are likely to be perceived as untrustworthy and evasive. Therefore, one needs to establish a strong eye contact while negotiating with an Arab. It should be remembered at the same time that establishing eye contact with a woman in Islamic Middle East is frowned upon.

Cultural exclusives It refers to behaviour patterns or social customs that are appropriate for locals and in which foreigners are expected not to participate. For instance, foreign visitors should stay away from entering into any controversial discussions on the host country's internal politics, social customs, and practices.

Cultural adiaphora It refers to social customs or behaviour in which a foreigner may conform to or participate but it is not imperative to do so. Thus, it is the discretion of the international manager either to participate or avoid such social customs. For instance, the ritual of bowing among Japanese is a complex protocol and foreigners are not expected to follow the same. However, an attempt to follow a symbolic bowing by foreigners is taken positively and reflects sensitivity to Japanese culture. A foreigner has an option to refuse an offer to eat or drink on personal, health-related, or religious grounds.

Therefore, international managers need to appreciate the social norms either to be followed or excluded in foreign cultures so as to avert occasional cultural mistakes and operate effectively in cross-country business settings.

Aesthetics

Ideas and perceptions that a cultural group upholds in terms of beauty and good taste is referred to as aesthetics. It includes areas related to music, dance, painting, drama, architecture, etc.

Colours have different manifestation across cultures. For African consumers, bright colours are favourites, while in Japan pastels are considered to express softness and harmony and are preferred over bright colours. America's corporate colour blue is associated with evil in many African countries. In China, red is a lucky colour while it is associated with death and witchcraft in a number of African countries. Green is often associated with disease in countries that have dense, green jungles, but is associated with cosmetics by the French, Dutch, and Swedes. Various colours represent death. Black signifies death to Americans and many Europeans, while in Japan and many other Asian countries white represents death. Latin Americans generally associate purple with death, but dark red is the appropriate mourning colour in the Ivory Coast. And even though white is the colour representing death in some countries, it expresses joy to those living in Ghana.

Traditions and customs

The word tradition is derived from the Latin word *traditio*, which means 'to hand down' or 'to hand over'. Traditions are the elements of culture passed on from generation to generation. An established pattern of behaviour within a society is known as a custom. It is an accepted rule of behaviour that is regulated informally by the social group. Since customs and traditions in a social group are passed on from generation to generation over thousands of years, they become ingrained into the social system.

International managers are required to learn customs and traditions of the cultures being dealt with, appreciate them, and integrate the strategic response in the business strategy. Food habits exhibit a high level of cultural sensitivities across the world. For instance, Americans and Germans prefer blend chocolates, whereas the Dutch like white chocolates, and the French love the dark ones. The world's largest food company, Nescafe, manufactures over 200 varieties of coffee to suit local tastes. Britain, similar to most parts of India, takes coffee with milk whereas in the US 'regular' coffee means differently in different parts of the country. 'Regular' coffee in Chicago means 'black', in Boston it means 'with milk', in Rhode Island it means 'with milk and sugar'. Greeks prefer sweet and gritty coffee made with the grounds, Italians prefer a caramelized roast yielding a darker black colour, a strong taste, and a distinctive aftertaste whereas the French like French roast, a medium to medium dark colour and flavour. Coffee is sold in both hot and cold vending machines, as Japanese like canned coffee.

The concept of Indian vegetarianism is too complex for outsiders to comprehend, where even the interchange between utensils in which vegetarian and non-vegetarian food, respectively, is cooked and served, is frowned upon. Therefore, exclusive vegetarian food outlets, such as Haldiram and MTR thrive on a huge market segment. Kentucky Fried Chicken (KFC), synonymous with crispy chicken across the world, offers an exclusive vegetarian menu in India. Even McDonald's has adapted separate cooking facilities for vegetarian and non-vegetarian food and Pizza Hut has experimented with opening some exclusive vegetarian outlets in India.

In India and other South Asian countries, ghee (milk fat) is the most important constituent of milk and sells at premium price. Besides, ghee is used in preparation of a variety of Indian sweets and other cooking. On the other hand, in the majority of developed countries, defatted milk is preferred and costs higher than milk with fat.

Culture significantly influences the product modifications especially in consumer products such as garments and foodstuffs. Traditional Indian products, such as the saree, the salwar kurta, and Indian ethnic foodstuff are exported to the international markets that have sizeable Indian ethnic populations. Similarly, Chinese foodstuffs, goods of worship, and Chinese traditional medicinal and herbal products find easy market in countries with sizeable population of ethnic Chinese, especially in East Asian countries. Women's apparel designed for customers in the Middle East are likely to get little attention in European markets. Social environment also affects the motives behind a buying decision and communication strategies need to be customized as per the varied social traits for different markets. Social beliefs and aspiration also vary significantly among countries and the marketing mix has to be tailor-made to suit the social norms of the target market.

Language

Language can be described as a 'systematic means of communicating ideas or feelings by the use of conventionalized signs, gestures, marks, or especially articulate vocal sounds'.[9] Language is the most important element that sets human beings apart from the animals. Moreover, language is the most obvious difference among cultures. As languages evolve over considerable time, it also reveals several aspects about the nature and value of a culture. Sanskrit and Latin are the two major literary languages of the world from which a large number of languages have emanated over time. Besides, a number of modern languages are descendents of classical Chinese, ancient Greek, Persian, and Biblical Hebrew. The richness of vocabulary and grammar of a language reveals significant attributes of a culture. As depicted in Fig. 7.2, Mandarin is the most widely used language in the world, followed by English and Hindi.

Languages differ very widely among nations and even regions. Language reflects the nature and value system of a culture. There have been several incidences worldwide of resistance towards communicating in foreign languages, which is often viewed as cultural imperialism. It was the differences in languages and love of the natives' for their mother tongue—Bangla—that gave rise to a conflict leading to the separation of Bangladesh from Pakistan. The French majority in the Québec province of Canada forced upon a constitution amendment in 1992 to declare French as the official language, banning the use of foreign words in 1994. There is considerable resistance among Germans to learn French, which is perceived as cultural imperialism.

Ethnologue lists 6912 living languages[10] in the world. About 90 per cent of the world's languages are spoken by less than 1,00,000 speakers. Asia, with 61 per cent of total speakers in the world, accounts for 32.8 per cent of the total languages, whereas Europe with 26.8 per cent of speakers has merely 3.5 per cent of the world's total languages. Africa, with 11.8 per cent of speakers, has 30.3 per cent of the languages, America

9 *Webster's Dictionary.*
10 *Ethnologue: Languages of the World,* 15th edn, SIL International, US, 2005.

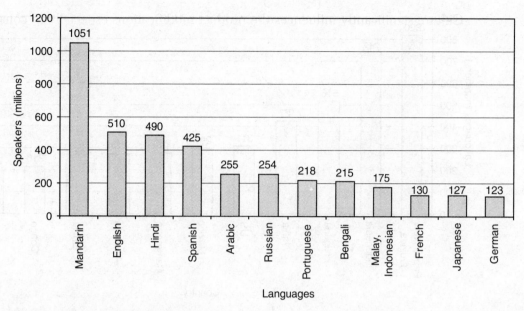

Fig. 7.2 World's most spoken languages

Source: KryssTal, 2006.

with 0.8 per cent of speakers has 14.5 per cent of languages, and the Pacific with 0.1 per cent speakers, 19 per cent of the languages.

The linguistic diversity as shown in Fig. 7.3 reveals that Papua New Guinea, a small country, has the highest number of 820 languages, followed by Indonesia (742 languages), Nigeria (516 languages), India (427 languages), and the US (311 languages). The ratio between the number of languages and the population of a country, known as the language diversity index, places Papua New Guinea, with 820 languages spoken by 5.4 million people, in the first place, followed by Vanuatu, where 115 languages are spoken by 1,20,000 people. Operating in linguistically diverse countries such as India makes business communication much more complex.

Contrary to China, where a large population can communicate in Mandarin, the variety of languages used in India poses considerable challenge. Even the Reserve Bank of India (RBI) uses 15 other languages, in addition to English and Hindi, in its currencies so as to communicate within the country. Therefore, while conducting field surveys, especially in rural areas, the local language has to be used in questionnaires or native field surveyors employed. For instance, Arunachal Pradesh, a state in the north-east India, with its population of about 1.1 billion has 26 major tribes and a number of sub-tribes with their own dialects, ethos, and cultural identities. The number of dialects and their distinction from each other in the state are so diverge that the people have adapted Hindi as the common language of the state to communicate with each other.

Despite linguistic differences, English has become *lingua franca* to communicate among non-English speaking people around the world. Conducting cross-country

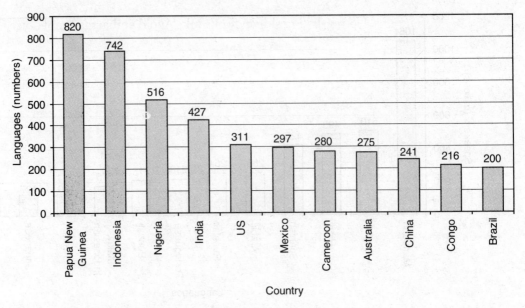

Fig. 7.3 Countries with highest number of languages

Source: Ethnologue: Languages of the World, 15th ed., SIL International, US, 2005.

business research in English often fails to provide non-verbal cues to the respondents. Besides, issues related to translation of questionnaires or the use of interpreters need to be addressed so as to ensure data compatibility. Therefore, the use of natives and communicating in local languages are of extreme importance in international business research across regions with linguistic diversity. The lack of understanding linguistic nuances has resulted in marketing blunders, as evident from the following instances.

- Coca Cola was named Ke-Kou-Ke-La, when it was first introduced in China. Later, the company found that the phrase translated in a Chinese dialect as 'bite the wax tadpole' or 'female horse stuffed with wax'. Subsequently, Coke found a close phonetic equivalent Ko-Kou-Ko-Le, which can roughly be translated as 'happiness in the mouth' after researching 40,000 Chinese characters.
- Chevrolet's highly popular US car Nova failed miserably in Latin America. Later, the company found that 'no va' means 'no go' in Spanish. It had to rename its car Caribe for the Spanish markets.
- The Swedish vacuum cleaner manufacturer Electrolux introduced the same print ad that had proved highly successful in Britain with its 'Nothing sucks like an Electrolux!' tagline in the US market. However, Electrolux found this to be a disaster in the US, as in American culture 'sucks' means 'really bad', i.e., Electrolux is a 'really bad vacuum cleaner'.
- Pepsi's slogan 'Come alive with the Pepsi generation' backfired in Taiwan and China, as it inadvertently translated to 'Pepsi will bring your ancestors back from the dead'.

- Parker pens' US marketing slogan for its ink, 'Avoid embarrassment—use Quink' boomeranged in Latin America as its Spanish version "Evite embarazos—use Quink' meant 'Avoid pregnancy—use Quink'.
- Parker's slogan for its ball point pen, 'It won't leak in your pocket and embarrass you' backfired in Latin America as its Spanish translation meant 'It won't leak and make you pregnant'. The company mistakenly translated 'embarrass' into 'embarazar' in Spanish.
- Much to its chagrin, Proctor and Gamble (P&G) learnt while introducing Vicks cough drops in Germany that *v* is pronounced as *f* in German, leading to a vulgar connotation for the word vicks. Consequently, P&G had to change the name to Wick in the German market (Fig. 7.4).

Coping with translation problems   In order to avoid such mistakes in international business communication, the matter needs to be written perfectly and reviewed by native(s) to the countries targeted. In order to minimize translation errors in international business, the major techniques[11] adopted include the following.

Back translation   The communiqué is translated from one language to another and then a second party translates it back into the original.[12] As a result, misinterpretations and misunderstandings are pinpointed beforehand.

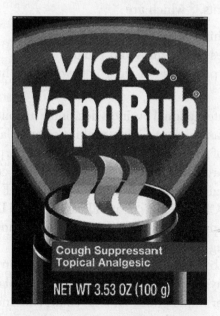 

Fig. 7.4   Pronounced Vicks, the brand name has a vulgar connotation in German, and P&G had to change it to Wick for the German markets.

---

[11] Cateora, Philip R. and John L. Graham, *International Marketing*, New Delhi: Tata McGraw Hill, 2002, p. 220.
[12] Iverson, Stephen P., 'The Art of Translation', *World Trade*, 2000, pp. 90–92.

Parallel translation   Due to commonly used idioms in both languages, back translations may not always ensure an accurate translation. In such cases, parallel translation is used wherein more than two translators are used for the back translation. Subsequently, the results are compared, differences discussed, and the most appropriate translation is selected.

Decentring   It is a hybrid of back translation wherein a successive process of translation and retranslation of a questionnaire is used each time by a different translator. For instance, an English version of the matter is translated into the foreign language (e.g. Japanese) and then translated back to English by a different translator. Then the two English versions are compared and where there are differences, the original English version of the second iteration is modified and the process repeated. The process is repeated until the Japanese version can be translated into English and back to Japanese by different translators without any perceptible difference. The wording of the original matter undergoes change in the process but the final version of the instrument has equally comprehensive and equivalent terminologies in both languages.

Religion

Religion is a vital constituent of culture that significantly influences people's behaviour. It is imperative to understand the 'meaning' and 'significance' of religion across cultures. Religion encompasses three distinct elements,[13] which are

Explanation   God seen as a 'first cause' behind the creation of the universe
A standard organization   Consisting of places of worships and rituals
Moral rules of good behaviour   Concerning principles of right and wrong in human behaviour

Religious beliefs considerably influence international business decisions. In Southeast Asia, *feng shui*, which means wind-water, an ancient Chinese philosophy, plays an important role in designing and placement of retail space and construction of corporate buildings. Designs conforming to *feng shui* are considered to allow free flow of cosmic energy and keep away evil spirits. Major religious festivals, such as Christmas in Europe and the US, Ramadan in Islamic countries, Chinese New Year in East Asia, and Diwali in India and Nepal, provide major business opportunities. Besides, the religious holidays also need to be considered while scheduling international business trips.

All advertisements need to be cleared by Islamic censoring authorities in Iran. Since Islam prohibits its followers from shaving, Gillette found it difficult to place an ad for its Gillette Blue II razor in Iran. After much effort, Gillette could convince the advertising manager of a local newspaper to this end by arguing that sometimes shaving becomes essential, for instance, in case of head injuries resulting from an accident.[14]

---

[13] Diamond, Jared, 'The Religious Success Story', *New York Review of Books*, 7 November 2002, pp. 30–31.
[14] 'Smooth Talk Wins Gillette Ad Space in Iran,' *Advertising Age International*, November 8 1993, p. I–21.

Christianity is the largest religion in the world with 2.1 billion adherents accounting for 33 per cent of the total population (Table 7.1) whereas Islam with 1.3 billion (21%) ranks second and Hinduism with 900 million (14%) ranks third.[15] About 1.1 billion people (16%) hardly follow any religion. Chinese traditional religion is followed by 394 million (6%), Buddhism by 376 million (6%), and Sikhism by 23 million (0.6%). Other religions followed include Judaism (14 million), Bahai (7 million), Jainism (4.2 million), and Shinto (4 million).

Table 7.1   Major religions of the world

	Christianity	Islam	Hinduism	Buddhism
Number of followers (percentage)	2.1 billion (33%)	1.3 billion (21%)	900 million (14%)	376 million (6%)
Founder	Jesus Christ	Muhammad	No founder	Gautam Buddha
Year and place of foundation	AD 30, Jerusalem	AD 570, Mecca (Saudi Arabia)	Dates to pre-historic times, oldest religion in the world, India	4th or 5th century BC, India
Number of gods	One	One	Numerous	None, but there are enlightened beings (Buddhas)
Holy book	Bible	Koran	No single holy book, the four Vedas are most ancient	Many including the Tripitaka, the Mahayana Sutras, Tantra and Zen texts
Types	Christians separated in 1054 into the Eastern Orthodox Church and the Roman Catholic Church. Major Protestant groups separated in 1500s. Subsequently, a variety of other groups also developed.	Sunnis (90%) and Shiites (10%). In 632, when Muhammad died, Shiites split from the Sunnis	No single belief system unites Hindus. A Hindu can believe in only one god, in many, or in none	Theravada (Way of the Elders) and Mahayana (Greater Vehicle)
Region	Spread to most parts of the world through missionary activity	Middle East Asia and the North of Africa	India (81%), Nepal (81%), Mauritius (48%), Fiji (38%), Guyana (35%), Suriname (27%), Bhutan* (25%)	East Asia

* Percentage population following the religion.

---

[15] Data for 2005, www.adherants.com assessed on 26 July 2007.

Islam is the fastest growing religion in the world with 1.84 per cent growth rate, followed by Bahai (1.70%), Sikhism (1.62%), Jainism (1.57%), Hinduism (1.52%), and Christianity (1.38%). Hinduism, followed by over 80 per cent of India's population, is the only surviving major ancient religion that has no founder. Hinduism had strong cultural influence on several other countries (Exhibit 7.2) too.

Exhibit 7.2 Global reach of Indian deities

Many Hindu and Buddhist deities worshipped in India are also revered in other countries. Ganesha, the destructor of all obstacles, is a true global Indian deity known as Sho-ten in Japan, Ho Tei in China, and Virakosha in Mexico. Ganesha (Sho-ten) in Japan symbolizes the joy of life that rises from the power rooted in the virtues of wisdom and compassion. Elderly people worship the deity to get prosperity and money whereas the young Japanese boys and girls worship him to achieve success in love. In Indonesia, the country with the world's largest Muslim population, Ganesha has been depicted even on currency notes and shares space along with the Indonesian President Kl Hadjar Dewantara.

The gobal Ganesha (Sho-ten) as a revered deity in Japan

Contd

Exhibit 7.2 Contd

Islamic Indonesia's currency with Hindu deity Ganesha

Three of the seven lucky gods worshipped in Japan, i.e., Daikoku-ten (Mahakala/ Maheshvara), Benten/ Benzai-ten (Saraswati), and Bishamon-ten (Kuber/ Kuvera) have an Indian origin from Hinduism. Besides, the 'seed mantra' used in many worships in Japan still continues to be from their original Sanskrit name. Some other Hindu gods and goddesses worshipped in Japan include the sea-god Varuna (Suiten), the king of gods Indra (Taishakuten), the goddess of fortune, Lakshmi (Kichijoten), and the divine architect Vishvakarma (Bishukatsuma). The four lokpalas (Shitenno) of Hindu mythology, i.e., Kuber (Bishamon), Yama (Zouchoten), Indra (Jikokuten), and Varuna (Koumokuten) also find place among Japanese deities. Some of the Hindu deities with multiple roles are split into multiple Japanese deities, each having a specific role. The Siddham Script used by Shingon Buddhists in Japan for Sanskrit mantras/sutras has its lineage from the Sanskrit script.

Saraswati is believed to be the goddess for learning and is also the name of a river in India. Saraswati is referred to as Benzaiten or Benten in Japan and is almost always associated with water. She is considered to be a beautiful goddess of fortune and is depicted holding a traditional Japanese musical instrument biwa (a Japanese counterpart of the Indian veena). Her shrines are built either on beautiful lakesides or seasides. Interestingly, the vahana (vehicle) of Indra, the elephant Airavata, has been reduced in size to a horse in Japanese mythology, perhaps due to the fact that the ancient Japanese people never had an opportunity to see a real living elephant.

Indra, Ganesha, Saraswati, Mahakala, Bodhisattva Manjusri, Bodhisattva Avalokitesvara or Lokesvara, Sakyamuni Buddha, and Amitabha Buddha are some of the examples that have widely attracted the worship of the Japanese people. The Hindu gods and goddesses worshipped in Japan today were originally introduced to Japan from China as an integral part of the Buddhist pantheon. These Vedic and Hindu deities had undergone certain transformations in terms of their appellations, characteristics, and even appearances in China in the course of acceptance, especially through the process of translating sutras and transliterating Buddhist terminology from Sanskrit to classical Chinese.

Source: 'Ganesha: A Global Indian', *Times of India*, 9 September 2006; Okabe, Takamichi, 'Nepalese Deities in Japan', Embassy of Japan, Nepal; Atjeh, Hidayat, 'Ancient Ganesha in Indonesia', Socio-Culture and Information Indonesian Consulate General in Mumbai.

Doing business in Islamic countries

Religions such as Christianity, Buddhism, and Hinduism largely remain in the private domain. On the other hand, in Islamic countries, business is considerably influenced by the religion. Nike introduced its 'Air' line of basketball shoes in 1996 with a stylized flame like logo of the word 'Air' on the shoe's backside and sole, as shown Fig. 7.5. A prominent Islamic organization, the Council for American-Islamic Relations (CAIR), declared that this logo could 'be interpreted' as the Arabic-script spelling of Allah. Nike initially protested its innocence.

But by June 1997, it had accepted multiple measures to ingratiate itself with the council. Nike did the following:

- Apologized to the Islamic community for any unintentional offence to their sensibilities
- Implemented a global recall of certain samples
- Diverted shipments of the commercial products in question from 'sensitive markets
- Discontinued all models with the offending logo
- Implemented organizational changes to their design department to tighten scrutiny of logo design
- Promised to work with CAIR 'to identify Muslim design resources for future reference'
- Took 'measures to raise their internal understanding of Islamic issues'
- Donated $50,000 for a playground at an Islamic school
- Recalled about 38,000 shoes and had the offending logo sanded off

Later, the company reported that 'CAIR is satisfied that no deliberate offence to the Islamic community was intended' by the logo.[16]

Islamic cultures greatly affect the behaviour of women consumers and emphasize upon separation of males and females in public places. Consequently, it is difficult to conduct field surveys or personal selling to women consumers by male researchers.

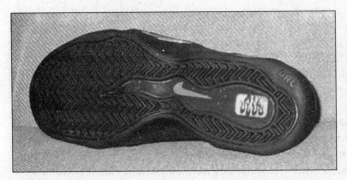

Fig. 7.5   Variation in interpretation of scripts across cultures may lead to business disasters.

---

16 Pipes, Daniel, 'How Terrorism Has Failed the Cause of Radical Islam,' *The Sun*, New York, 12 September 2006.

Therefore, it is better to engage women in business activities when interaction with women is needed in Islamic countries. In Arabian countries, the dolls Sara and Leila that compete with Barbie have 'brother dolls' and not 'boyfriend dolls' as the concept of having a boyfriend may not be acceptable to Islamic families. Implications of Islam on international marketing decisions are summarized in Exhibit 7.3.

Exhibit 7.3 Implications of Islam in international marketing decisions	
Elements	**Implications for marketing**
I. Fundamental Islamic concepts	
A. Unity (concept of centrality, oneness of God, harmony in life)	Product standardization, mass media techniques, central balance, unity in advertising copy and layout, strong brand loyalties, a smaller evoked size set, loyalty to company, opportunities for brand-extension strategies.
B. Legitimacy (fair dealings, reasonable level of profits)	Less formal product warranties, need for institutional advertising and/or advocacy advertising, especially by foreign firms, and a switch from profit maximizing to a profit satisfying strategy.
C. *Zakaat* (2.5 per cent per annum compulsory tax binding on all classified as 'not poor')	Use of 'excessive' profits, if any, for charitable acts: corporate donations for charity, institutional advertising.
D. Usury (cannot charge interest on loans; a general interpretation of this law defines 'excessive interest' charged on loans as not permissible)	Avoid direct use of credit as a marketing tool. Establish a consumer policy of paying cash for low-value products. For high-value products, offer discounts for cash payments and raise prices of products on an instalment basis. Sometimes it is possible to conduct interest transactions between local/foreign firm in other non-Islamic countries. Banks in some Islamic countries take equity in financing ventures, sharing resultant profits (and losses).
E. Supremacy of human life (compared to other forms of life, objects, human life of supreme importance)	Pet food and/or products are less important. Avoid use of statues and busts interpreted as forms of idolatry. Symbols in advertising and/or promotion should reflect high human values. Use floral designs and artwork in advertising as representation of aesthetic values.
F. Community (all Muslims should strive to achieve universal brotherhood, with allegiance to the 'one God'. One way of expressing community is the required pilgrimage to Mecca for all Muslims at least once in their lifetime, if able to do so)	Formation of an Islamic economic community; development of an 'Islamic consumer' served with Islamic-oriented products and services, for example, 'kosher' meat packages, gifts exchanged at Muslim festivals, and so forth; development of community services; need for marketing of non-profit organizations and skills.

Contd

Exhibit 7.3 Contd

Elements	Implications for marketing
G. Equality of peoples	Participative communication systems; roles and authority structures may be rigidly defined but accessibility at any level to be relatively easy.
H. Abstinence (consumption of alcohol and pork is forbidden; so is gambling. During the month of Ramadan, Muslims are required to fast without food or drink from the first streak of dawn to sunset—a reminder to those who are more fortunate to be kind to the less fortunate and as an exercise in self-control)	Products that are nutritious, cool, and digested easily to be formulated for Sehr and Iftar (beginning and end of the fast). Opportunities for developing non-alcoholic items and beverages (e.g., soft drinks, ice cream, milk shakes, fruit juices) and non-chance social games, such as Scrabble; food products to use vegetable or beef shortening.
I. Environmentalism (the universe created by God was pure. Consequently, land, air, and water should be held as sacred elements)	Anticipate environmental, anti-pollution acts; opportunities for companies involved in maintaining a clean environment; easier acceptance of pollution-control devices in the community.
J. Worship (five times a day; timing of prayers varied)	Need to take into account the variability and shift in prayer timings in planning sales calls, work schedules, business hours, customer traffic, and so forth.
II. Islamic culture	
A. Obligations to family and tribal traditions	Importance of respected members in the family or tribe as opinion leaders; word-of-mouth communication, customer referrals may be critical; social or clan allegiances, affiliations, and associations may be possible surrogates for reference groups; advertising home-oriented products stressing family roles may be highly effective, for example, that of electronic games.
B. Obligations toward parents are sacred	Image of functional products to be enhanced with advertisements that stress parental advice or approval; even with children's products, less emphasis on children as decision-makers.
C. Obligation to extend hospitality to both insiders and outsiders	Product designs that are symbols of hospitality outwardly open in expression; rate of new product acceptance may be accelerated and erased by appeals based on community.

Exhibit 7.3 Contd

Elements	Implications for marketing
D. Obligation to conform to codes of sexual conduct and social interaction. These may include 1. Modest dress for women in public 2. Separation of male and female audiences in some cases	More colourful clothing and accessories are worn by women at home, so promotion of products for use in private homes to be more intimate—such audiences to be reached effectively through women's magazines; avoid use of immodest exposure and sexual implications in public settings. Access to female consumers often gained only through women as selling agents, salespersons, catalogues, home demonstrations, and women's specialty shops.
E. Obligations to religious occasions. (two major religious observances, celebrated as Eid-ul-Fitr, Eid-Ul-Adha)	Purchase of new shoes, clothing, and sweets and preparation of food items for family reunions and Muslim gatherings; practice of giving money in place of gifts increasingly changing to more gift-giving; due to lunar calendar, festival dates not fixed.

Source: Mushtaq, Luqumain, Zahir A. Quraeshi, and Linda Delene, *Marketing in Islamic Countries: A Viewpoint*, MSU Business Topics Summer 1980, pp. 20–21.

All Muslims are expected to consume meat obtained through the *halal* (conforming to religious dietary laws) method of slaughter. Therefore, restaurants in Islamic countries highlight in their marketing communication that only halal meat is used for cooking food. Islamic countries also require from exporting countries a certificate along with the meat consignments, certifying that genuine halal process has been used in slaughtering the animals. India's second largest manufacturer of hard gelatine capsules, Medi-Caps Limited (MCL), an ISO 9002 certified company with an annual capacity of 3500 million capsules, has a turnover of over Rs 200 million. For Muslim consumers, availability of genuine halal products is a very sensitive issue in food and pharma products. Suppliers of genuine halal products are limited. In order to cater to Islamic markets, Medi-Caps manufactures Hala-Caps especially for Muslims[17] across the world. The Muslim community traditionally consumes only animals of bovine sources, slaughtered according to Islamic procedure (Shariah). Since gelatine is derived from animals, Muslims have to ensure that these are not just halal but also slaughtered accordingly. Medi-Caps manufactures Hala-Caps (Fig. 7.6) only from halal gelatine procured from Halagel, Malaysia. Moreover, Medi-Caps also get certifications of genuine halal process from the Islamic Development Department of Malaysia and halal certificates from Majelis Ulama Indonesia (MUI) and the Islamic Central Committee of Thailand (ICCT). Besides, the process of manufacturing the halal gelatine

---

[17] Basu, Sirshendu, Medi-Caps Ltd, http://content.icicidirect.com/PickofWeek.asp?id=223, accessed on 17 July 2007; 'Halal Gelatin Capsules' Product Brochure, Medi-Caps Ltd.

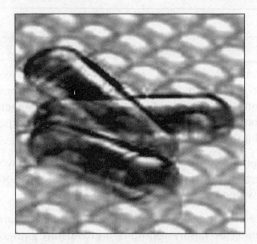

Fig. 7.6 Medi-Caps' halal capsules for Islamic markets

capsules has also been certified by the Jamiat Ulama-e-Maharashtra. The company has witnessed considerable success in marketing its halal products in Islamic countries, especially in the Middle East.

7.4 COMPARISON OF CROSS-CULTURAL BEHAVIOUR

Attempts have been made to carry out cross-country comparisons of cultural behaviour so as to develop better understanding among cultures. An appreciation of cultural differences facilitates international managers to conceptualize and implement business strategies in view of culture sensitivities in various countries. The major types of cross-cultural classifications are discussed here.

7.4.1 Hofstede's Cultural Classification

The most widely used tool to study cross-cultural behaviour is the Hofstede's classification, which identified cross-cultural differences based on a massive survey of 1,16,000 respondents from 70 countries working in IBM subsidiaries. Hofstede's classification involves the following.

Power distance

The degree of inequality among people that is viewed equitable is known as 'power distance'. It is the extent to which less powerful members of an institution accept that power is distributed unequally. As indicated in Fig. 7.7, power distance in Malaysia is the highest while it is the lowest in case of Austria. Power distance in India is on the higher side. In the UK and Scandinavian and Dutch countries, managers expect their decision-making to be challenged, while the French consider the authority to take decisions as their right. Germans feel more comfortable in formal hierarchies while the Dutch have a relaxed approach to their authorities.

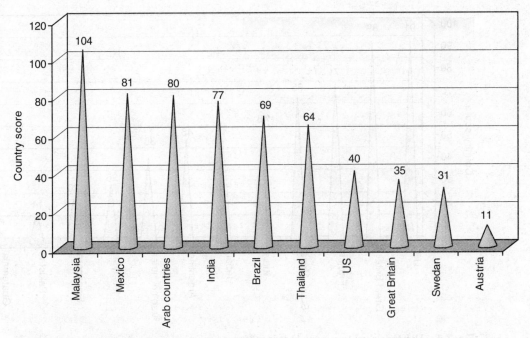

Fig. 7.7 Hofstede's value survey: Power distance

Source: Hofstede, Geert, *Culture's Consequences: International Differences in Work-related Values*, Beverly Hills, CA: Sage Publications, 1980.

In countries with large power distance, hierarchical organizational structures are based on inequality among superiors and subordinates and juniors blindly follow the orders of their superiors. Generally, high social inequalities are tolerated in cultures with wide differences in power and income distribution. Small power distance is characterized by egalitarian societies, in which superiors and subordinates consider each other equal. Organizations are relatively flatter and decision-making is decentralized.

Power distance greatly affects the international business decision-making process. In view of the power distance, an international manager has to assess the organizational dynamics, identify the key decision makers, and accordingly formulate their business strategy for different countries.

Individualism vs collectivisms

The tendency of people to look after themselves and only their immediate family is termed as 'individualism'. Societies with a high level of individualism tend to have strong work ethics, promotions based on merit, and involvement of employees in the organizations primarily calculative. Ability to be independent of others is considered to be the key criterion for success in individualistic societies. Collectivism is referred to the tendency of people to belong to groups and to look after each other in exchange for loyalty. The interests of group have precedence over individual interests.

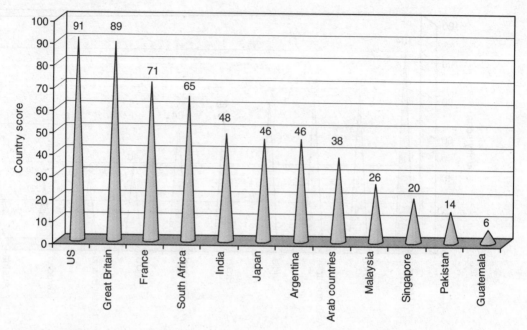

Fig. 7.8   Hofstede's value survey: Individualism

Source: Hofstede, Geert, *Culture's Consequences: International Differences in Work-related Values,* Beverly Hills, CA: Sage Publications, 1980.

As indicated in Fig. 7.8, the US, the UK, and France have highly individualistic societies while, Guatemala, Pakistan, Singapore, and Malaysia show a high level of collectivism. International business strategy is greatly influenced by individualism vs collectivism in terms of decision-making and market communication. For a product to be successful in collective societies, such as Guatemala, Ecuador, Panama, Venezuela, Malaysia, and Japan, it should have group acceptability unlike in the individualistic societies of the US, Australia, UK, and Canada.

Masculinity vs femininity

In masculine societies, the dominant values emphasize on work goals, such as earnings, advancement, success, and material belongings. On the other hand, the dominant values in a feminine society are achievement of personal goals, such as quality of life, caring for others, friendly atmosphere, getting along with boss and others. Summarily, in masculine societies, people 'live to work' while in feminine societies, people 'work to live'.

As indicated in Fig. 7.9, Scandinavian countries such as Sweden, Norway, and Denmark are highly feminine while, Japan is highly masculine. India falls in between, indicating a balanced emphasis on personal and work goals. In feminine societies, such as Sweden, Norway, the Netherlands, and Denmark, the gender equality is much greater as compared to the same in masculine societies such as Japan, Austria, Venezuela, Italy, and the US.

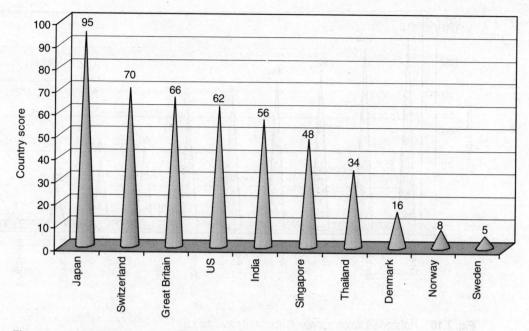

Fig. 7.9   Hofstede's value survey: Masculinity

Source: Hofstede, Geert, *Culture's Consequences: International Differences in Work-related Values,* Beverly Hills, CA: Sage Publications, 1980.

Uncertainty avoidance

Uncertainty avoidance refers to the lack of tolerance for ambiguity and the need for formal rules. It measures the extent to which people feel threatened by ambiguous situations. As indicated in Fig. 7.10, Greece, Portugal, and Japan are the most uncertainty avoidance societies, while Singapore, Denmark, and India are the least uncertainty avoidance societies. In high uncertainty avoidance societies, lifetime employment is more common, whereas in low uncertainty avoidance societies, job mobility is more common.[18]

7.4.2   Trompenaars' Cultural Classification

The Dutch researcher, Fons Trompenaars, conducted research over a ten-year period, administering questionnaires to over 15,000 managers from 28 countries and published the findings in 1994. Each of the cultural dimensions of Trompenaars' research is defined on the basis of the usable responses received from at least 500 managers in each country. The abbreviated terms for 23 countries, included in his report, are shown in Table 7.2.

---

[18] Adler, N.J. and S. Bartholomeu, 'Managing Globally Competent People', *Academy of Management Executive,* 1992, vol. 6, pp. 52–65.

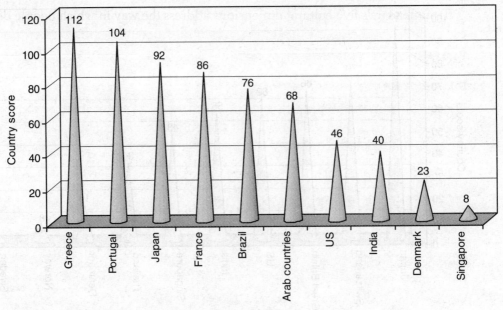

Fig. 7.10 Hofstede's value survey: Uncertainty avoidance

Source: Based on data from Hofstede, Geert, *Culture's Consequences: International Differences in Work-related Values*, 1980, Beverly Hills, CA: Sage Publications.

Table 7.2 Trompenaars' voluntary abbreviations

Abbreviation	Country
ARG	Argentina
AUS	Austria
BEL	Belgium
BRZ	Brazil
CHI	China
CIS	Former Soviet Union
CZH	Former Czechoslovakia
FRA	France
GER	Germany (excluding former East Germany)
HK	Hong Kong
IDO	Indonesia
ITA	Italy
JPN	Japan
MEX	Mexico
NL	Netherlands
SIN	Singapore
SPA	Spain
SWE	Sweden
SWI	Switzerland
THA	Thailand
UK	United Kingdom
USA	United States
VEN	Venezuela

Source: Trompenaars, F, *Riding the Waves of Culture,* London: The Economist Books, 1993.

Trompenaars's five cultural dimensions address the way in which people deal with each other. This helps in explaining the cultural differences and offers practical ways in which MNCs can do business in various countries.

Universalism vs particularism

Universalism is the belief that ideas and practices can be defined and applied everywhere without modification. On the contrary, particularism is the belief that unique circumstances and relationships, rather than abstract rules, are more important considerations that determine how ideas and practices should be applied.

In cultures with high universalism (Fig. 7.11), such as the US, Austria, Germany, Sweden, UK, etc., the focus is more on formal rules than on relationships, whereas in particularist cultures, such as Venezuela, CIS, Indonesia, China, Hong Kong, Thailand, etc., the focus is more on relationships than on rules. In high universalism cultures, business contracts are very closely adhered to and 'a deal is a deal' whereas in high particularism cultures, legal contracts may readily be modified, honouring the changing circumstances based on the reality of the situation.

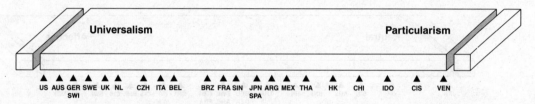

Fig. 7.11   Universalism vs prticularism

Individualism vs communitarianism

Trompenaars' communitarianism seems to be an analog of Hofstede's collectivism. Individualism refers to people regarding themselves as individuals whereas communitarianism refers to people regarding themselves as part of a group. Societies with high individualism make more frequent use of 'I' and 'me', decisions are typically made on the spot by a representative during business negotiations, and achievement and responsibility are also personal. On the contrary, in collectivist societies, 'we' is used more frequently than 'I', business decisions are typically referred back to the organization, achievement is considered to be a group achievement, and managers believe in joint responsibility. The US, Czechoslovakia, Argentina, the CIS, Mexico, and the UK rank high on individualism (Fig. 7.12) whereas Singapore, Thailand, Japan, and Indonesia rank high on communitarianism.

Neutral vs affective

All human beings have emotions but this dimension deals with the different contexts and ways in which emotions are expressed by various cultures. In affective cultures, emotions are expressed openly and are more 'natural' whereas in neutral cultures,

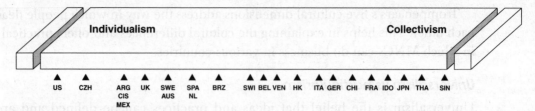

Fig. 7.12 Individualism vs collectivism

people tend to hold in check their emotions and try not to explicitly exhibit their feelings. Neutral cultures often consider anger, delight, or intensity in the workplace as 'unprofessional', whereas affective cultures regard holding back of emotions by colleagues to signify 'emotionally dead' or a 'mask of deceit'. In affective cultures, people often smile, laugh, talk loudly, and exhibit a great deal of enthusiasm in greeting each other. Managers from neutral cultures such as Japan, UK, Singapore, and Australia (Fig. 7.13) need to be open to the emotional behaviour displayed in affective cultures, such as Mexico, the Netherlands, Switzerland, China, Brazil, etc.

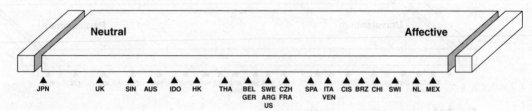

Fig. 7.13 Neutral vs affective

Specific vs diffuse

The degree of involvement, i.e., how comfortable individuals are in dealing with other people, varies across cultures. Individuals have various levels to their personality—from a more public or outer layer to a more private or inner level. The relative size of people's public and private 'spaces' and the degree to which individuals feel comfortable sharing it with others differ considerably among cultures. In specific cultures, individuals tend to have a large public space and a smaller private space. They readily share public space whereas the personal life is kept separate, closely guarded, and shared only with close friends and associates. On the contrary, in diffuse cultures, public and private spaces are more or less similar and public space is guarded more carefully because entry into public space gives more accessibility to individuals' private space.

Work and private lives are separate in specific cultures whereas these are closely linked in diffuse cultures. Countries like Australia, the UK, the US, and Switzerland (Fig. 7.14) are characterized by a small, intimate private layer that is well separated from more public outer layers. On the other hand, in Venezuela, China, and Spain, personality structures have large private areas separated from a relatively small public

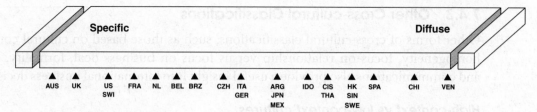

Fig. 7.14 Specific vs diffuse

layer. Doing business in cultures more diffused compared to one's own is considered highly time consuming. 'Work' is set apart from the rest of life in specific cultures whereas everything is connected to everything else in diffused cultures. Therefore, it is important to invest time and resources and build relationships for operating in countries with diffused cultures.

Achievement vs ascription

Cultures differ in the way status and power in a society are determined. Such social status and power may be attributed either to a person's own efforts and achievements or as a birthright. In achievement cultures, people are evaluated and accorded social status based on how well they perform their allocated functions. In ascription cultures, status is accorded to individuals who 'naturally' evoke admiration from others, such as the elderly, seniors in the organization, and highly qualified and skilled people. Status in ascription cultures is generally independent of a task or specific functions and society tends to show respect to such distinguished people who are not easily compared with others.

Austria, the US, Switzerland, the UK, Sweden, and Mexico (Fig. 7.15) possess high achievement cultures whereas Venezuela, Indonesia, China, the CIS, and Singapore have ascription cultures. Managers from ascription cultures doing business with achievement cultures need to emphasize upon facts and figures, data analysis, and sound technical strength. On the other hand, managers from achievement cultures doing business with ascription cultures need to be careful to show due respect to the elderly, seniors, and formal position holders.

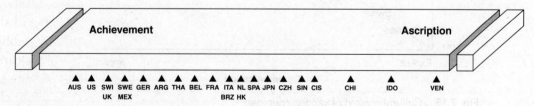

Fig. 7.15 Achievement vs ascription

7.4.3 Other Cross-cultural Classifications

Other forms of cross-cultural classifications, such as those based on cultural context, homogeneity, focus on relationship versus focus on business deal, formality, time, and communications also provide a useful insight into international business decisions.

High-context vs low-context cultures

The context of a culture has crucial implications[19] in communicating and interpreting verbal and non-verbal messages. Interpretation of verbal and non-verbal cues is different in different cultures.

In high-context cultures, implicit communications such as non-verbal and subtle situational cues are extremely important. On the other hand, in low-context cultures, communication is more explicit and relies heavily on words to convey the meaning. In high-context cultures the relationship is long lasting, while in low context cultures the relationship is shorter in duration. Verbal commitments are given high sanctity in high-context cultures, while commitments in low-context cultures are written. Fig. 7.16 indicates cultural context[20] for select cultures.

The cultural context influences international business decisions in several ways. International market promotion and advertising has to be subtle in high-context cultures, while it should focus on explicit display of information, facts, and figures in low-context cultures. Marketing firms rotate sales teams more frequently in low-context cultures. However, in high-context cultures, where building relationships with the

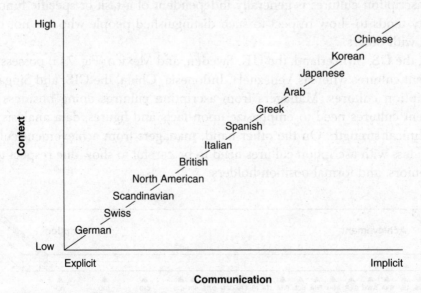

Fig. 7.16 Cultural context of various countries

[19] Hall, E.T., *Beyond Cultures,* New York: Anchor Press/Doubleday, 1976, pp. 1–16.
[20] Duleck, R.E., J.S. Fielden, and J.S Hall, 'International Communication: An Exclusive Premier', *Business Horizons,* January–February 1991.

clients is extremely important, the sales force tend to have longer duration of operation in assigned territories. Market research in high-context countries has to focus on subtle and non-verbal expressions of respondents, while in low-context countries, the focus is more on factual information.

Homophilous vs heterophilous cultures

On the basis of homogeneity, culture may be divided into the following sub-sets.

Homophilous cultures Cultures where people share the same beliefs, speak the same language, and practise the same religion are referred to as homophilous. Japan, Korea, and Scandinavian countries generally have homophilous cultures. Diffusion of new products takes much less time in homophilous cultures, in which relatively uniform marketing-mix decisions can be adopted.

Heterophilous cultures In countries with heterophilous cultures, there is a fair amount of differentiation in language, beliefs, and religions followed. India and China are countries with heterophilous cultures, wherein the variations in culture within states and provinces, are significant. Business communications need to be adapted from region to region.

Relationship-focussed vs deal-focussed cultures

Relationship-focussed cultures lay heavy emphasis on human relationship whereas deal-focussed cultures are task oriented. When managers from deal-focussed cultures do business with relationship-focussed cultures, conflicts often arise as relationship-focussed people find deal-focussed people aggressive, offensive, and even blunt, whereas deal-focussed managers find relationship-focussed people vague, slack, and enigmatic. The fundamental differences between relationship-focussed and deal-focussed cultures determine one's success in international business.

In China, *guanxi*, which means 'relationships', 'connections', or 'networks', is crucial to success. Establishing a guanxi makes a person feel obligated to help the other. Essence of guanxi lies in a strong emotional relationship that is often overlooked by outsiders. Building trust, understanding, and personal relationship is vital to developing economic relationship not only in China but also in other Asian countries. Guanxi can be established by having some commonalities, called *tong*, like being in the same industry, company, school or university, or coming from the same region. Sometimes, guanxi is also established through exchanging gifts or personal favours. In Egypt, *wastah*, an intermediary or personal contact, in Russia, *blat*, and in many Latin American countries, *palanca*, are used to express similar connotations. Although, it takes considerable time, patience, and commitment to establish personal relationships, such social contacts often help one in the time of need in relationship-focussed cultures.

Relationship-focussed cultures In relationship-focussed cultures, people have strong orientation towards building relationships and developing mutual trust. Relationship-focussed cultures include India, Bangladesh, Indonesia, Malaysia, Japan,

China, Vietnam, Thailand, the Philippines, South Korea, Singapore, Saudi Arabia, United Arab Emirates, Egypt, Brazil, Mexico, and Russia. The key features of relationship-focussed cultures include

- Reluctance to approach strangers for business; use of intermediaries, use of trade shows and exhibitions to meet prospects
- High emphasis on building relationship and establishing rapport
- Indirect, polite, and high-context communication
- Face-to-face negotiations and meetings
- Importance given to 'saving face', dignity, and respect
- Lawyers kept in the background during negotiations
- Verbal deals emphasized over written contracts

Therefore, it is important to establish personal rapport in relationship-focussed cultures, which are hesitant to conduct business with strangers. Business managers get things done in relationship-focussed cultures through intricate networks of personal contacts. Managers from relationship-focussed cultures prefer to deal with acquaintances, friends, and family members with greater trust. Thus, it is important to have a thorough understanding of prospective business partners in relationship-focussed cultures before entering into business deals with strangers, especially foreigners.

Deal-focussed culture Managers from deal-focussed cultures, such as the US and the Nordic countries, are open to discuss business prospects with strangers. Making appointments is easy and quick in deal-focussed cultures whereas in relationship-focussed cultures one has to establish indirect contacts through acquaintances or a third-party introduction. Trade missions and embassies are often considered in high esteem and are effective for getting initial contacts. Countries, such as France, Belgium, Italy, Spain, and Hungary form part of moderately deal-focussed cultures whereas Britain, the US, Germany, Denmark, Australia, Canada, Finland, the Netherlands, and the Czech Republic have deal-focussed cultures. Key features of deal-focussed cultures include

- Openness to talking business with strangers
- Directly approaching prospective clients
- Clarity of understanding given more importance than harmony
- Direct, frank, low-context communication
- Communication via telephone, e-mail, and faxes
- Little or no concept of 'saving face'
- Lawyers forming part of negotiations
- Reliance on written agreements and contracts

Formal vs informal cultures

When informal business managers from relatively egalitarian cultures interact with their formal counterparts from hierarchical cultures, there is a fear that their informality may offend status-conscious people from formal societies.

Formal cultures   Countries such as India, Bangladesh, Indonesia, Malaysia, Vietnam, Thailand, Philippines, Saudi Arabia, UAE, Egypt, Greece, Brazil, Russia, Poland, Romania, Japan, China, South Korea, Singapore, France, Belgium, Italy, Spain, Hungary, Britain, Germany, Denmark, Finland, the Netherlands, and the Czech Republic are classified as possessing formal cultures. In formal cultures

- Formality is used to show respect.
- Status differences are large and valued.
- Counterparts are addressed by title or family name.
- Protocol rituals are numerous and elaborate.

Informal cultures   The US, Canada, and Australia are among countries with an informal culture. In informal cultures

- Informal behaviour is not considered disrespectful.
- Status differences are not valued.
- Counterparts are addressed by first name.
- Protocol rituals are few and simple.

Polychronic (fluid time) vs monochronic (rigid time) cultures

Based on adherence to time schedules, cultures may be classified as polychronic or monochronic.

Polychronic (fluid time) cultures   In polychronic cultures, people have a relaxed approach to time schedules, punctuality, and meeting deadlines, which makes managers from rigid time cultures often frustrated. The word 'tip' is derived from the phrase 'to insure promptness' in such cultures. India, Bangladesh, Indonesia, Malaysia, Vietnam, Thailand, the Philippines, Saudi Arabia, UAE, Egypt, Greece, Brazil, Russia, Poland, and Romania may be classified under fluid time (polychronic) cultures. Key attributes of polychronic culture are that

- People and relationships are more important than punctuality and precise scheduling.
- Schedules and deadlines are flexible.
- Meetings are frequently interrupted.

In polychronic cultures, people often avert rigid deadlines. For instance, the Arabian term *Insha'Allah* frequently used in Middle East means 'god willing', i.e., things will happen if the Almighty wishes so. Thus, it is the God and not the man who is in-charge of what is going to happen. In oriental countries, such as India and Singapore, business meetings usually start within five to ten minutes of the schedule time whereas social functions, such as a dinner, a birthday, or a wedding party may begin even one to two hours late.

Therefore, international managers from polychronic cultures scheduling business meetings in monochronic cultures need to be extra punctual about time since any delay is considered to be rude. On the other hand, international managers from monochronic cultures when interacting with their counterparts from polychronic cultures need to have patience.

Monochronic (rigid time) cultures   France, Belgium, Italy, Spain, and Hungary form part of moderately monochronic cultures whereas Japan, China, South Korea, Britain, the US, Canada, Australia, Germany, Denmark, Finland, and the Netherlands have rigid time (monochronic) cultures. Salient features of monochronic culture include

- Primacy of punctuality and schedules
- Rigid schedules and deadlines
- Seldom interrupted meetings

Expressive vs reserved cultures

Communication patterns in expressive cultures are radically different from their non-reserved counterparts. This is true for all types of communications, such as non-verbal, para-verbal, and verbal. This can lead to major confusions and problems in international business activities.

Expressive cultures   Saudi Arabia, UAE, Egypt, Greece, Brazil, Mexico, France, Belgium, Italy, Spain, and Hungary possess expressive cultures whereas Russia, Poland, Romania, the US, Australia, and Canada may be said to have variably expressive cultures. The key characteristics of expressive cultures are that

- People speak louder, interrupt frequently, and are uncomfortable with silence.
- Interpersonal space is half-an-arm's length.
- There is considerable physical contact.
- There is direct eye contact.
- There are lively facial expressions and gesturing.

Reserved cultures   The cultures of India, Bangladesh, Indonesia, Malaysia, Vietnam, Thailand, the Philippines, Japan, China, South Korea, Singapore, Britain, Germany, Denmark, Finland, the Netherlands, and the Czech Republic may be said to be reserved. In reserved cultures

- People speak softly, interrupt less, and are comfortable with silence.
- Interpersonal space is arm's length.
- There is little physical contact.
- Eye contact is indirect.
- Facial expressions and gesturing are restrained.

7.5   CULTURAL ORIENTATION IN INTERNATIONAL BUSINESS

The orientation of its international managers affects the ability of a company to adapt any foreign business environment. The major types of cultural orientations include parochialism versus simplification and the EPRG (ethnocentric, polycentric, regiocentric, and geocentric) approach.

7.5.1   Parochialism vs Simplification

Parochialism

Parochialism is the belief that views the rest of the world from one's own cultural perspectives. This creates problems in international business situation. Such notion is found in all cultures of the world. The domestic business experiences of international managers often interfere in alien cultures. The tendency of one's culture to persuade thinking and behaviour without one being aware of it is generally known as 'cultural baggage'. Cultural baggage often becomes a liability when international managers encounter new cultures. The sheer gravity of one's memory of the domestic business experience pulls one down towards set thinking and set procedures. Therefore, an international manager needs to train his/her mind to operate from a zero base for which he/she virtually needs an eraser. One should go overseas for business with a clear mind and fill it with first-hand experience and feelings.

Simplification

Simplification is the process of exhibiting the same cultural orientation towards different cultural groups, for instance, a manager's behaving in the same manner while doing business with Swedish, Arabian, and Japanese managers, overlooking cultural differences.

As overseas markets are unique, people are different and so are their cultural responses. Although the fundamentals of human behaviour remain the same, the why people behave varies from country to country. Therefore, it is extremely important for international business managers to understand the cultural differences between countries and prepare themselves to meet business challenges.

7.5.2   EPRG Approach

The behavioural attributes of international managers may be portrayed through the EPRG[21] approach.

Ethnocentric orientation   The belief that considers one's own culture as superior to others is termed ethnocentric orientation. Many a times, a firm or its managers are obsessed with the belief that the business strategy that has worked in the home country would also be suitable in alien cultures. Thus, the ethnocentric approach ignores the cultural differences across countries.

[21] Adapted from Perlmutter, Howard, 'The Torturous Evolution of Multinational Corporation', *Columbia Journal of World Business*, January–February 1969, pp. 8–12 and Wind, Yoram, Susa P. Douglas, and Howard V. Perlmutter, 'Guidelines for Developing International Marketing Strategy', *Journal of Marketing*, April 1973, pp. 14–23.

These companies carry out either domestic business or export business as an extension of domestic business with minimum effort to adapt the business strategy to the needs of a foreign country. Generally, such companies attempt to sell their products in countries where either the demand is similar to that in the domestic market or where the indigenous products are acceptable. For instance, most Indian handicraft exporters who are primarily from the SME sector hardly appreciate the cultural differences and do not realize the need to adapt a business strategy in different countries. A number of Indian products sold abroad—garments like salwar-kurtas and sarees and food items such as dosa mix, idli mix, vada mix, sambhar mix, gulab jamun mix, papad, Indian sweets, etc.—primarily target the ethnic Indian population. Trade statistics also reveal that these products find major markets such as Dubai, Singapore, London, Canada, etc., which have sizable ethnic Indian or South Asian population. This marketing strategy can be used in South Asian markets as well where consumer tastes and preferences resemble to a large extent.

Polycentric orientation Contrary to ethnocentric, the polycentric approach recognizes cultural differences in the host countries and, therefore, is strongly market-oriented. It is based on the belief that substantial differences exist among various countries. Therefore, a single business strategy cannot be effective across the world and customized business strategies need to be adopted.

The HSBC Bank, with its network in six continents, total assets worth US$1,000 million, and serving over 100 million customers worldwide, advertises with the punch-line 'the world's local bank'. The bank focuses on the cultural differences between countries. HSBC's classic advertisement campaign as shown in Fig. 7.17 reveals that body tattoos are considered to be trendy in the East whereas colourful, glittery mehendi

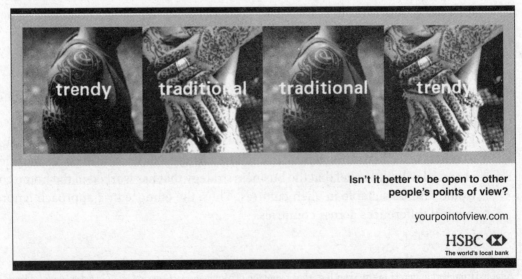

Fig. 7.17 HSBC's promotional campaign emphasizes cross-cultural differences among its world-wide customers.

is a popular tradition in India. On the other hand, Indian mehendi seems trendy to the Western world whereas body tattoos are considered traditional. Similarly, contrary perceptions do prevail among cultures about the medicinal effects of traditional herbs and modern allopathic drugs. Thus, HSBC emphasizes upon its adaptation of products offered and business strategies used across the countries.

Thus, under the polycentric approach, each country is considered unique in terms of business environment, which is made up of political, cultural, legal, and economic factors, consumer behaviour, market structure, etc. Business decisions in each country are made with the active involvement of local experts. The decentralization of business activities is the highest in polycentric orientation.

Regiocentric orientation   In the regiocentric orientation, the firm treats the region as a uniform cultural segment and adopts a similar business strategy within the region, but not across the region. Depending upon the convergence of the socio-cultural behaviour on the basis of geographical regions, a similar business strategy is used. McDonald's strategy not to serve pork and sell all meat preparations made out of halal process only in the Middle East or in countries dominated by Muslim consumers can be termed as regiocentric.

Geocentric orientation   The geocentric approach considers the whole world a single market and attempts to formulate integrated business strategies. A geocentric form attempts to identify cultural similarities across countries and formulates a uniform business strategy. Geocentric companies strive to analyse and manage the business strategy with an integrated global business programme. The Harry Potter series of books is a classic example of geocentric orientation (Exhibit 7.4), wherein the author J.K. Rowling has brought out a series of fictions that appeal to global readers and has marketed it globally using a highly integrated business strategy.

Exhibit 7.4   Harry Potter: Breaking cultural barriers

Cultural diversity makes it a formidable task to conceptualize and bring out market offerings that appeal to global consumers irrespective of their nationalities, ethnic groups, religion, and language. This becomes much more challenging in case of a book wherein the cultural experiences of readers vary widely in terms of inferences made across countries.

J.K. Rowling's Harry Potter series with its mass appeal among children across the world became an instantaneous success, breaking cultural barriers. The seven-book series is all set to sell four hundred million copies worldwide and has been translated in sixty-seven languages,[a] making Rowling the world's richest writer with an estimated net worth of US$1 billion. With universal themes—the struggle of Harry Potter against the dark forces of Voldemort and his Death Eaters cross-cut with magic rituals and the inadequacies of the establishment, i.e., the Ministry of Magic—every culture can relate to the plot of the series.

Contd

Exhibit 7.2 Contd

Australia

Africa

Germany

India

China

Japan

Rowling's seventh and the last book in the Harry Potter novel series

Rowling successfully brings people from all nationalities, colours, backgrounds, and religions under one roof, Hogwarts, their sole identity being that they are all a part of the wizarding community. For instance, Parvati and Padma Patil are twins of Indian origin. Lee Jordan is African, Cho Chang, Chinese, and Seamus Finnigan, Irish. This aspect of the story cuts across all boundaries of culture and nationalities and makes the story equally appealing to everyone around the world. Interestingly, fundamental Christians and Muslims alike protest Harry Potter as a de facto introduction into quasi-satanic rituals.[b]

Further, Joanne Rowling adopted a more gender-neutral pen name, J.K. Rowling (Joanne Kathleen Rowling), using her grandmother's name as her second name in order to appeal to male readers, feeling they would not be interested in reading a novel they knew to be written by a woman.

The books have also been made into highly successful motion pictures by Warner Brothers. A diverse range of merchandise, such as Harry Potter video games, calendar, metallic bookends, stickers, posters, buttons, chocolates, house crests, etc., based on Harry Potter characters are successfully marketed.

[a] 'Harry Potter Breaks 400 m in Sales', *Guardian*, 18 June 2008.
[b] Hutton, Will, 'Harry Potter and the Secret of Success', *The Observer*, 22 July 2007.
Source: J.K. Rowling, Harry Potter series.

7.6   EMIC VS ETIC DILEMMA: CULTURAL UNIQUNESS VS PAN-CULTURALISM

The two approaches of *emic* and *etic* represent the two different streams of thought at the polar extremes of cross-country business decision-making and research methodology. Emic emphasizes cultural uniqueness while etic, pan-culturalism.

The Emic approach   The *emic* school holds that attitudes, interests, and behaviour are unique to a culture and best understood in their own terms. It emphasizes studying the business research problem in each country's specific context and identifying and understanding its unique facets. Subsequently, cross-cultural differences and similarities are made in qualitative terms. As the motive to buy differs substantially across cultures, the multi-country research may call for an *emic* approach.

The Etic approach   The *etic* school emphasizes identifying and assessing universal attitudinal and behavioural concepts and developing 'pan-cultural' measures. Thus, *etic* is basically concerned with measuring universal behavioural and attitudinal traits. The assessment of such phenomenon needs unbiased measures. For instance, there appears to be convergence in preferences across cultures.

7.6.1   Operationalization of *Emic* and *Etic*

An international firm focuses on identifying similarities across national markets as it offers opportunities to transfer the products and services and integration of business strategies across the borders. Therefore, an international firm generally prefers *etic* strategy. While conducting cross-country research, emphasis is placed on identifying and developing constructs that are feasible across countries and cultures.[22]

An approach to resolve the *emic* versus *etic* dilemma was proposed by Berry,[23] as shown in Fig. 7.18. Under this approach, research is first conducted in one's own cultural context X and then the construct or instrument developed for cultural context is applied to another culture, i.e., of the host country; this is known as 'imposed *etic*'. Using an *emic* approach, the market behaviour is studied in the second culture from within. Then, the results of the *emic* and the 'imposed *etic*' approach are examined and compared. No comparison is possible if no commonality is identified between the two and the cultures are to be studied under the *emic* elements. In case some commonality is identified based on common aspects/features, a 'derived *etic*' comparison between the cultures is possible.

This chapter brings out the significance of the cultural environment in international business decisions. One has to develop cultural sensitivies to be effective in international business. Developing basic understanding about the nuances of a culture is fascinating and enables one to objectively evaluate and appreciate new cultures.

[22] Craig, C. Samual and Susan P. Douglas, *International Market Research*, 2nd ed., Singapore: John Wiley and Sons (Asia) Pvt. Ltd, 2003, pp. 153–57.

[23] Adopted from Berry, J.W., 'Imposed Etics–Emics-Derived Etics: The Operationalization of a Compelling Idea', *International Journal of Psychology*, vol. 24, 1989, pp. 721–35.

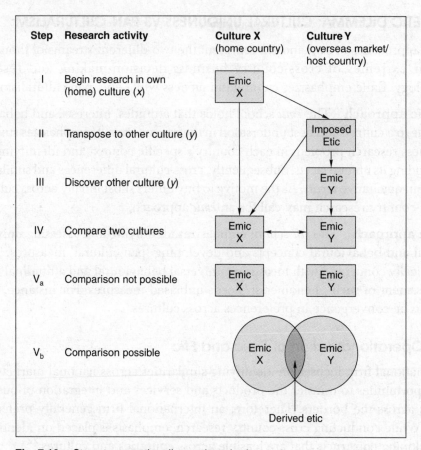

Fig. 7.18 Steps to operationalize *emic* and *etic*

One should understand that culture is not inherited and variations do not suggest what is right or wrong and good or bad, rather indicate mere cross-cultural differences. In order to effectively manage cross-cultural differences in international business, one has to

- Develop a conceptual understanding of one's own cultural biases and assumptions.
- Explore the reasons as to why the way of doing things in different cultures makes sense in view of their cultural assumptions.
- Treat ways of doing things and cultural assumptions as starting points that need to be integrated in developing culture-specific competitive solutions.

The conceptual understanding of the various constituents of culture, such as value systems, norms, aesthetics, customs and traditions, language and religion, and their implications help in increasing appreciation of culture and in formulating an effective business strategy. Cross-cultural classifications, as discussed in this chapter, facilitate international business managers to prepare challenges encountered in cross-cultural business situations. The etic-emic dilemma and its operationalization provides a practical tool to cope with cross-cultural divergence.

SUMMARY

International business decisions are considerably influenced by the socio-cultural environment of the country of its operation. Therefore, international managers need to develop a thorough conceptual understanding of the cross-cultural differences and sensitivities. Even the largest of international firms have committed blunders due to the lack of understanding and appreciation of foreign cultures. The ability of an international manager to objectively evaluate environmental factors is severely affected by his/her own cultural conditioning and limitations in understanding the nuances of another culture. In order to arrive at objective business decisions, international managers need to isolate the influences of their own cultural conditioning.

Culture is the way of life of a people, including their attitudes, values, beliefs, arts, sciences, modes of perception, and habits of thought and activity. It is the collective programming of the mind that distinguishes the members of one group or category from those of another. Culture is learned, shared, trans-generational, symbolic, and patterned; human beings have tremendous capacity for cultural adaptations. The various constituents of culture such as value systems, norms, aesthetics, customs and traditions, language, and religion considerably influence international business decisions.

Hofstede's and Trompenaars' cultural classifications are useful tools for carrying out comparison of cross-cultural behaviour. Besides, other cross-cultural classifications such as high versus low context, homophilous versus heterophilous, relationship versus deal focussed, formal versus informal, polychronic versus monochromic, and expressive versus reserved cultures provide useful insights into cross-cultural behaviours. Cultural orientation in international business may include parochialism versus simplication and the EPRG approach. In studying cross-cultural behavioural patterns, the emic approach emphasizes on cultural uniqueness, while the etic on pan-culturalism.

KEY TERMS

Achievement culture Culture in which status is accorded to high achievers and high performers.

Aesthetics Ideas and perceptions that a cultural group upholds in terms of duty and good taste.

Affective culture Culture where emotions are expressed openly.

Ascription culture Culture in which status is accorded to those who 'naturally' evoke admiration from others, such as the elderly, seniors, highly qualified, and skilled people.

Back translation Translating from one language to another and then a second party translating this back into the original.

Cultural adiaphora Social customs or behaviour in which a foreigner may participate, but the participation is not imperative.

Cultural exclusives Behaviour patterns or social customs that are appropriate for locals, and foreigners are not expected to participate.

Cultural imperatives Norms that must be followed or must be avoided in a foreign country.

Culture Derived from the Latin *cultura*, collective programming of mind that distinguishes members of one group or category from those of another.

Deal-focussed culture Task-oriented culture with openness to hold direct business talks with strangers.

Decentring A hybrid of back translation, wherein a successive process of translation and re-translation of a questionnaire is used each time by a different translator till there is no perceptible difference between the two versions.

Diffused culture Culture in which public and private space is more or less similar and public space is guarded more carefully.

Emic Concept that holds that attitudes, interests, and behaviour are unique to a culture and best understood in their own terms and that emphasizes studying the research problem in each country's specific context.

Ethnocentrism A belief that considers one's own culture superior to others and expects business strategies used in the home country to work overseas.

Etic Concept that emphasizes identifying and assessing universal attitudinal and behavioural concepts and developing 'pan-cultural' measures.

Feminine culture Culture in which the dominant social values are achievement of personal goals, such as quality of life, caring for others, and friendly atmosphere.

Geocentric orientation An approach that attempts to identify cultural similarities across the countries and formulates a uniform business strategy.

Heterophilous culture The culture in countries that have a fair amount of differentiation in languages, beliefs, and religions followed.

High-context culture Culture in which high significance is given to implicit communications, such as non-verbal and subtle situational cues.

Homophilous culture Culture where people share beliefs, speak the same language, and practise the same religion.

Individualism The tendency of people to look only after themselves and their immediate family.

Language Systematic means of communicating ideas or feelings by the use of conventionalized signs, gestures, marks, or especially articulate vocal sounds.

Low-context culture Culture in which communication is more explicit, with heavy reliance on words to convey the meanings.

Masculine culture Culture in which the dominant values emphasize work goals such as earnings, advancement, and success and material belongings.

Monochronic culture Culture with rigid time schedules and deadlines, with high emphasis on punctuality.

Neutral culture Culture in which people tend to hold back their emotions and try not to exhibit their feelings.

Norms Guidelines for social rules that prescribe appropriate behaviour in a given situation.

Parallel translation Translation technique in which more than two translators are used for the back translation and the results subsequently compared, differences discussed, and the most appropriate translation selected.

Parochialism Belief that views the rest of the world from one's own cultural perspective.

Particularism Belief that unique circumstances and relationships, rather than abstract rules, are more important considerations that determine how ideas and practices should be applied.

Polycentric orientation A strategic approach that recognizes considerable cultural differences among countries and formulates country-specific business strategies.

Polychronic culture Culture in which time schedules and deadlines are flexible and relationships take precedence.

Power distance The degree of inequality among people that is viewed as equitable.

Regiocentric orientation An approach that considers the region as a uniform cultural segment and adopts a similar business strategy within but not across the region.

Relationship-focussed culture Culture with strong orientation towards building relationships and developing mutual trust.

Self-reference criterion An unconscious reference to one's own cultural values, experiences, and knowledge as a basis for decision making.

Shariah Islamic canonical law based on the teachings of the Koran.

Simplification Exhibiting same cultural orientation towards different cultural groups.

Specific culture Culture in which individuals tend to have a large public space and a smaller private space, and the public space is readily shared.

Uncertainty avoidance The extent to which people feel threatened by ambiguous situations.

Universalism Belief that same ideas and practices can be defined and applied everywhere without modification.

Values Shared assumptions of a group on how things ought to be, or abstract ideas that a group believes to be good, desirable, or right.

CONCEPT REVIEW QUESTIONS

1. Explain the significance of culture in international business decisions.

2. How do self-reference criteria (SRC) become an obstacle in international business decisions? How would you minimize the influence of SRC? Substantiate your answer with suitable examples.

3. Critically evaluate the concept of culture.

4. Business firms across the world have committed blunders in translating from one language to another. As an international business manager, how would you cope with such mistakes?

5. Critically evaluate Hofstede's cross-cultural classification and its implications on international business decisions.

6. Differentiate between the following:
   (a) Homophilous vs heterophilous cultures
   (b) Universalism vs particularism
   (c) Individualism vs collectivism
   (d) Relationship-focussed vs deal-focussed cultures
   (e) Polychronic (fluid time) vs monochronic (right time) cultures
   (f) Emic vs etic

CRITICAL THINKING QUESTIONS

1. Explore the website of McDonald's and identify the cultural adaptations it has to make in different countries.

2. You are scheduled to visit Japan, Saudi Arabia, Sweden, and the US on a business trip. Based on the cross-cultural classification learnt in this chapter, prepare a checklist of cultural challenges you are going to face. Discuss your observations in the class.

PROJECT ASSIGNMENTS

1. Based on your foreign visits or interactions with foreigners in your own country, identify the differences in major cultural practices. Categorize such cultural norms under categories of cultural imperatives, exclusives, and adiaphora. Share your observations in class.

2. Identify a few mistakes made by foreign firms in India and Indian firms abroad due to lack of cultural understanding and appreciation. Discuss your findings in class.

3. Visit an internationally operating company based in your city/country and interact with its managers. Explore the cultural differences the company is facing in its international operations and identify the strategy to cope with these cultural issues.

CASE STUDY

Cross-cultural Misapprehensions over the Swastika in the West

Confusions leading to severe problems in international business often arise due to the lack of understanding of cross-cultural issues. The swastika is the most ancient surviving symbol, dating to prehistoric times. The word swastika is derived from the Sanskrit *svastika*: from the roots, *su* or good, *asti*, meaning 'to be', and *ka* as a suffix. *Svasti* connotes well-being and is a widely used religious symbol in Hinduism, Buddhism, and Jainism. The Thai greeting *sawasdee* is also derived from the same root and carries the same implication. Over the years, the swastika symbol became common in various cultures around the world, with some modifications. It was known as swastika and *hakenkreuz* in Germany, *svastika* in Denmark and Sweden, *svastica* in Italy, *wan* in China, *manji* in Japan, *fylfot* in England, *tetraskelion* and *gammadion* in Greece, and swastika in India.

Fig C.1 Swastika: An ancient symbol of well-being, love, and luck in Hinduism and other oriental cultures

The British author Rudyard Kipling was so strongly influenced by Indian culture that he had a swastika inscribed on all his books until the rise of Nazism made this inappropriate (see Fig. C.2). The swastika was also a symbol used by Scouts in Britain, although it was taken off Robert-Baden

Fig. C.2 The swastika engraved in Kipling's writings

Powel's 1922 Medal of Merit after complaints in the 1930s.

In the 1800s, countries around Germany were growing larger and forming empires; yet Germany was not a unified country until 1871. To counter the feeling of vulnerability and the angst of the youth, German nationalists in the mid-nineteenth century adopted the swastika for its ancient Aryan origins, to represent a long Germanic/Aryan history. By the end of the nineteenth century, the swastika could be found on nationalist German volkisch periodicals and was the official emblem of the German Gymnasts' League.

In the beginning of the twentieth century, the swastika was a common symbol of German nationalism and was placed in a multitude of places, such as the emblem for the Wandervogel, a German youth movement, on Joerg Lanz von Liebenfels' antisemitic periodical *Ostara*, on various Freikorps units, and as an emblem of the Thule Society.

On 7 August 1920, the swastika (*hakenkreuz*)[1] was formally adopted by the Nazi Party at the Salzburg Congress. This symbol became the official emblem of the Nazi Party and was used on the party's flag, badge, and armband. In *Mein Kempf*, Adolf Hitler described the Nazi's new flag as 'in red we see the social idea of the movement, in white the nationalistic idea, in the swastika, the mission of the struggle for the victory of the Aryan man, and, by the same token, the victory of the idea of creative work, which as such always has been and always will be anti-Semitic.'

Thus, from a symbol of well-being, love, and luck, the swastika was transformed by the Nazis into a symbol of hate, anti-Semitism, and death. The British documentary *Swastika,* directed by Philippe Mora and released in 1973, focussed on German history during the Nazi era. The post-world war criminal codes in Germany and Austria made the public showing of the swastika (*hakenkreuz*), except for scholarly purpose, illegal and punishable. However, the swastika on Hindu, Buddhist, and Jain temples are exempt as no religious symbol can be banned in Germany.

---

[1] 'Origins of the Swastika', *BBC News*, 18 January 2005.

Due to cross-cultural confusion over the swastika, Nintendo, the Japanese computer games giant, confessed that what is appropriate in one culture may not be so for another. It had to withdraw a Pokemon Trading Card (Fig. C.3) featuring *manji* (swastika) in 1999 from Western markets, following a complaint by the Anti-Defamation League (ADL).

Fig. C.3   Nintendo had to withdraw this Pokemon trading card from Western markets.

In December 2002, Christmas crackers imported from China by Walpert Industries in Canada were found to display the swastika on miniature panda bear (See Fig. C.4).[2] The swastika mark was placed on the toy pandas due to the lack of cross-cultural understanding by the Chinese manufacturer. Walpert personally called some of the people who received the bears with the swastika symbol and apologized. It also assured more stringent quality measures in the future.

Fig. C.4   Christmas crackers toy pandas imported from China with inadvertent swastika signs.

In December 2003, Microsoft faced a problem with its Bookshelf Symbol 7 as the font's array of graphic symbols resembled the swastika. Microsoft offered an apology for its 'unintentional oversight' that caused two swastikas to be included in a font in its new Office suite. Microsoft also released a utility that allowed its users removal of the offending fonts.

In January 2005, the photographs of British prince Harry in a costume with a swastika armband taken at a birthday party in Wiltshire created a furore and the prince had to issue a statement apologizing for the offence caused.[3] In 2006, a court in Stuttgart fined a 32-year-old man more than 7000 euros (8700 dollars) for selling anti-Nazi badges that showed a Swastika with a line through it.[4] The fashion firm Esprit was forced to recall 200,000 catalogues and came under investigation in Germany in October 2006 after accusations that British-made buttons appearing in their new collection had swastika designs.

[2] 'Toy Pandas Bearing Swastikas, a Cultural Mix-up', *CBC News*, 30 December 2002.
[3] 'Call for Europe-wide Swastika Ban', *BBC News*, 17 January 2005.
[4] 'Prosecutors Drop Probe into Swastika Buttons', *Expatica*, 19 October 2006.

Recent attempts to ban the swastika in the European Union have witnessed severe opposition from various socio-cultural groups, especially the Hindus, the Buddhists, the Jains, and other oriental religious groups.[5]

Questions

1. Carry out a cross-country comparison of the differences in perceptions and cultural implications of the swastika.

2. Critically evaluate how the use of swastika by the Nazis transformed its common perception to a symbol of hate rather than a symbol of well-being, love, and luck.

3. In your opinion, is the proposed ban on swastika on commercial products in the European Union justified? Discuss your views with your colleagues in class.

[5] 'Swastika Ban Left Out of EU's Racism Law', *Scotsman*, 30 January 2007.

8 Political and Legal Environment

LEARNING OBJECTIVES

- To explain the significance of the political and legal environment in international business
- To discuss the various forms of political systems
- To explicate the different types of legal systems
- To elaborate the principles of international law
- To elucidate the risks in international business
- To explain the methods of measuring and managing risks

8.1 INTRODUCTION

An international firm needs to operate in countries having diverse political and legal frameworks that at times conflict with those of its home country. International managers often make value judgments from the home country's perspective and tend to have an ethnocentric approach to the political and legal environments prevailing in other countries. Such value judgments made from the perspective of the home country considerably hinder objective decision making in the diverse international scenario. Therefore, international managers should develop a thorough conceptual understanding of the political and legal environments affecting international business operations.

The various players in international business have diverse and sometimes conflicting business interests that considerably influence their political agenda and constraints. For instance, foreign multinationals use diplomatic channels to get a favourable climate for foreign investments, whereas domestic firms often build up political pressure to oppose foreign investment to put off competition from foreign firms. Importers use political pressure to increase market access with little tariffs, whereas domestic manufacturers lobby to obstruct imports and to operate in a protected domestic environment. Meanwhile, exporters are concerned about the removal of all restrictions on exports and demand higher levels of export incentives so that exports remain attractive.

Political cataclysms, such as the attack by the US on Iraq in 2003, the Kosovo crisis in Yugoslavia in 1999, the Gulf War in the 1990s, the break-up of the USSR and the Iranian Revolution in the 1980s, and the Cuban crisis in the 1960s, have severely affected business operations of foreign multinationals in these countries. Political considerations in the 1970s significantly influenced international fruit trade in bananas that led to the famous 'Banana Wars'. The major cause behind this crisis was that most EU countries have been importing bananas with concessional market access to their former colonies in the Caribbean, Africa, and Asia, whereas bananas imported by the world's largest banana firm based in the US, Chiquita Brands International, were subjected to quotas and tariffs.

This chapter discusses the significance of political environment in international business. Political ideologies based on economic and political systems and governmental structures have been elaborated. Trade embargoes and sanctions are often used as instruments of foreign policy to achieve political rather than economic objectives. In the era of globalization, the impact of sectarian violence, terrorism, or erratic political decisions taken by any country is felt beyond national boundaries, affecting business operations.

Judicial independence and efficiency, which vary widely across countries, are crucial to fair treatment in foreign locations of business operations. International managers need to develop conceptual understanding of major types of prevailing legal systems, such as common law, civil law, and theocratic law and adapt their business strategies accordingly. Risks in international business, such as commercial, economic, and political risks need to be assessed and managed.

8.2 INTERNATIONAL POLITICAL ENVIRONMENT

The political environment of the country of operation becomes increasingly important for an internationalizing firm as it moves from exports to foreign direct investment (FDI) as the mode of international market entry. Exporting firms use political pressure tactics to have free exportability of the products in their home country regulations, hassle-free procedures, and legislative requirements and export incentives. Besides, diplomatic channels are utilized to get improved market access for imported goods in the target foreign country markets, reduced import tariffs, compatible quality regulations, etc. The dispute settlement mechanism, legal framework, and judicial independence are also critical to fair treatment expected in international business. Cordial political relations between the firm's home country and the host countries have a direct favourable impact on FDIs. As a firm expands internationally and begins to operate in multiple countries, the political and legal issues become increasingly complex.

Consequent to economic liberalization in the People's Republic of China, multi-level marketing firms, such as Amway, Avon, Tupperware, and Mary Kay Cosmetics grew rapidly. By 1997, Amway had approximately 80,000 sales representatives who generated $178 million in sales, whereas Avon had nearly 50,000 representatives who generated sales of $75 million. It was reported that some other companies using the so-called pyramid schemes were cheating consumers. Consequently, the Chinese government banned direct selling in April 1998. As a result, the direct marketing companies were prohibited to operate their business model in China.[1] It was only after diplomatic pressures and negotiations between the US and the Chinese governments that the policy was reversed.

Firm-level economic and political interests of the home and the host countries may differ widely. International managers need to understand the significance of political decision-making in the host country that may severely influence its overseas operations. International business relations between the firms are greatly affected by 'affinity' or 'animosity' among the countries based on historical or political reality. For instance, India's political affinity with Sri Lanka and Mauritius has led to high level of trade and investment whereas the reverse situation exists in case of Indo-Pak trade.

8.2.1 International Political Systems and Ideologies

International political and economic systems hardly function independently. The two are mutually inter-dependent. Political and diplomatic relations between two countries greatly influence their economic relations. The *political system* of a country comprise various stakeholders, such as the government, political parties with different ideologies, labour unions, religious organizations, environmental activists, and various NGOs. Each of these players in a political system has its own unique sets of beliefs and aspirations, and exerts its influence upon political decisions. The acquisition, development, securing, and use of power in relation to other entities, where power is viewed as the capacity of the social actors to overcome the resistance of the other actors is termed as *political behaviour*.[2] *Ideology* is a set of beliefs or ideas as to how the society or group should be organized, politically, economically, or morally. *Political ideology* is a set of ideas or beliefs that people hold about their political regime and its institutions about their position and role in it.[3] Ideologies of different groups or political parties are often conflicting and they keep on challenging each other. In democratic countries, such as India, the US, and the UK, the shift in the political parties and their ideologies puts pressure on business operations of foreign firms.

Power exerted by different pressure groups also varies from country to country. For instance, communist or socialist parties in countries, such as Russia and China hardly face any considerable challenge whereas such parties exert sizeable political pressure in countries like India, Sweden, Italy, and Greece. On the other hand, these parties hardly have any political viability in the US. Most religious organizations are apparently

[1] Normandy, Madden, 'China's Direct Sales Ban Stymies Marketers', *Advertising Age*, 18 May 1998, p. 56.

[2] Astley, W.G. and P.S. Sachdeva, *Structural Sources of Intra-Organisational Power: A Theoretical Synthesis*, Academy of Management Review 9(1), 1984, pp. 104–13.

[3] Macridis, Roy C., *Contemporary Political Ideologies*, 5th ed., New York: HarperCollins, 1992, p. 2.

politically neutral in India, whereas the Catholic Church played a crucial role in overthrowing Ferdinand Marcos in the Philippines and in the liberation of Poland from Soviet domination. Islamic religious leaders in Iran greatly influence political decision making.

Principal political ideologies may be categorized by way of economic systems, political systems, and governance structure as discussed below.

Types of government: Economic systems

Communism Based on Karl Marx's Theory of Social Change directed at the idea of a classless society, all the major factors of production in a country under communism are owned by the government and shared by all the people rather than profit-seeking enterprises, for the benefit of the society. Since the government controls all the productive resources and industrial enterprises, it exerts significant control on determining production quantity, price, employment, and practically everything else. The focus of communism is on human welfare rather than profit making.

Typically communism involves seizure of power by a political party, maintaining the power by suppression of any opposition and commitment to achieve the ultimate goal of a worldwide communist state. After the Bolshevik Revolution in 1917 in Russia, the government overtook all the private businesses and this was repeated after each communist take-over of a country.

Countries following the communist philosophy had non-market and weak economies and the governments had an active role in economic planning. These countries had rigid and bureaucratic, political, and economic systems and indulged in huge foreign debts. Countries such as China, the former Soviet Union, Eastern European countries, North Korea, and Vietnam are also referred to as 'centrally planned economies'. However, there exists marked difference between the communist countries too. Since there had been lack of incentive and motivation to workers and managers under communism to improve productivity, the system suffered from gross inefficiencies. For instance, the former Soviet Union and China follow the same basic communism ideology, but under the new type of communism Chinese citizens are allowed to work for themselves and keep the profit. Despite economic liberalization in China, the state's permission is needed for operation of 'free markets'.

Socialism In a socialist form of government, basic and heavy industries are operated by the government, whereas small businesses may be privately owned. Basic industries, such as mining, oil exploration, steel, ship building, railways, roads, airlines, etc., are kept under government control. The extent of government control under socialism is lower than communism. Countries following socialist system include Sweden, France, India, Poland, etc. However, the socialist countries too differ from each other in terms of the degrees of public and private ownership.

Capitalism In stark contrast to communism, capitalism is the economic system in which there is a complete freedom of private ownership of productive resources and industries. Thus, there is full freedom to both the business enterprises and the consumers that provides for a 'free market economy'. Under capitalism, individuals are allowed to produce goods and services under competitive conditions giving rise to a 'market-oriented system'. Market prices are determined by the forces of demand and supply. As individuals are motivated by private gains, it leads to product innovation, quality upgradation, increase in efficiency, and lower market prices. Capitalism too differs among countries. For instance, the US is highly capitalistic compared to Japan. Although business enterprises in Japan are privately owned, the Japanese Government does meticulously supervise their activities and, therefore, exerts indirect control.

The prevalence of the purest form of capitalism, *laissez-faire,* wherein the economic activity is left to the private sector with no government interference, is rare. Governments significantly influence a country's economic system. There is hardly any country that allows complete ownership either by the private sector or the government. Thus, the pure form of capitalism or communism hardly exists.

Types of government: Political systems

Democracy The word democracy is derived from *demokratia,* which means rule of the people or government by the people where citizens are directly involved in decision making. Over a period of time, there has been proliferation of population across the world and societies have become more complex. This has led to decision making by people's elected representatives in democratic countries. The most comprehensive definition[4] of democracy is the government 'of the people, for the people, and by the people'. India is the largest democratic country in the world.

Totalitarianism It is a dictatorial form of centralized government that regulates every aspect of public and private behaviour. Power is centralized in the hands of a dictator who operates through a mixture of cultivating devoted followers and terrorizing those who do not agree with its policies. Citizens in a totalitarian state are generally deprived of their basic rights of freedom of expression, organizing meetings, free media, tolerance, and elections, which are available under democracy. Major forms of totalitarianism include

Secular totalitarianism In secular totalitarianism, the government uses military power to rule.

Fascist totalitarianism Fascism is a right-wing nationalistic political ideology fundamentally opposed to democracy with a totalitarian and hierarchical structure. The term 'fascism' is derived from the Latin world *fasces* which refers to the bundle of rods bound around a projecting axe-head as a symbol of power and authority. In Italian, the word 'fascism' refers to radical political groups of many different and

---

[4] Basler, Roy P., ed., *The Collected Works of Abraham Lincoln,* vol. 7, 1953–55, p. 22.

sometimes opposing orientations. Fascist totalitarianism prevailed in Italy under Mussolini, Germany under Hitler, Spain under Franco, and Portugal under Salazar.

Authoritarian totalitarianism Authoritarianism aims to control both the minds and souls of people and to convert them to its own faith whereas totalitarianism aspires to just rule people. Chile under Pinochet and South Africa prior to apartheid are the examples of such authoritarian totalitarianism.

Communist totalitarianism This is the most widespread form of secular totalitarianism which advocates that socialism can be achieved only through totalitarian dictatorship. It is the left-wing totalitarianism that believes in equal distribution of wealth and complete government ownership and control on national resources. Since 1989, communist dictatorships in the former USSR and East European countries have collapsed and the former communist countries are moving gradually towards democratic governance. Moreover, countries, such as China, North Korea, Cuba, Vietnam, and Laos that follow communism also exhibit the signs of decline in the political monopoly enjoyed by communist power.

Theocratic totalitarianism Religious leaders also assume political leadership in theocratic totalitarianism, for instance, in the Islamic Republic of Iran.

Types of government: Structure

Parliamentary The government consults its citizens from time to time and the parliament has power to formulate and execute laws. The British parliamentary system is one of the oldest in the world whereas in the US, the congress passes the law and the executive branch of the government is independent. India follows a Westminster form of parliamentary democracy. Major forms of government are discussed below.

Parliamentary republics In parliamentary republics, the prime minister is the executive head of the government and also the leader of the legislature. The president is more of a titular head of the state with little executive power. India, Singapore, Finland, Italy, Germany, Austria, Greece, etc., represent parliamentary republics.

Semi-presidential system Under such systems, a president and a prime minister co-exist. The president has genuine executive authority, unlike in a parliamentary republic. But the prime minister is the head of the legislature and also heads the government. Systems followed in France, Russia, Pakistan, and the Republic of Korea fall under this category.

Fully presidential system The president is both head of the state and head of the government in fully presidential systems and there is no prime minister. This type of systems is followed in the US, Philippines, Mexico, Indonesia, Brazil, Tanzania, etc.

Commonwealth countries These countries represent constitutional monarchies that recognize the British monarch as head of the state over an independent government. A governor-general to each country other than the UK is appointed by the Queen as a representative. However, the active head of the executive branch of the government and also the leader of the legislature is the prime minister, such as in the UK, Australia, New Zealand, Canada, Jamaica, etc.

Monarchies

Constitutional monarchies A form of government in which a king or queen acts as head of state, while the ability to make and pass legislation resides with an elected parliament. Under such form of government, the monarch governs according to the constitution, i.e., according to rules rather than his/her own free will. The constitutional monarch cannot make or pass legislation, and must remain politically neutral. Countries that follow constitutional monarchies include Japan, Thailand, Spain, the Netherlands, Denmark, Sweden, Belgium, etc.

Absolute monarchies It includes countries that have monarchs as the executive heads of government, exercising all powers, such as in the UAE, Saudi Arabia, Oman, Qatar, Bhutan, Swaziland, etc.

Theocracy It is derived from the Greek word *theokratia*, which means the rule of god. The civil leader is believed to have a direct personal connection with god in a pure theocracy. For instance, the religious leadership in Iran exerts considerable political influence.

8.2.2 Trade Embargos and Sanctions

Trade embargos and sanctions are often used as hostile political measures rather than being based on economic considerations. Trade embargos prohibit trade completely with a country so as to economically isolate it and exert political pressure on its government. For instance, the UN imposed a trade embargo on Iraq, following its invasion on Kuwait in the 1990s. During the discriminatory apartheid regime, the UN also had an embargo on trade with South Africa.

Trade sanctions are used to impose selective coercive measures to restrict trade with a country. Under section 301 of the Trade Act of 1974, the US government exercises its authority to impose trade sanctions on foreign countries on the grounds of violation of trade or maintaining laws and practices that are either considered unjustifiable or restrict US trade. Use of trade sanctions as an instrument of foreign policy has always been debated in terms of achieving economic or political objectives. The imposition of trade sanctions has proliferated during recent years but their effectiveness has considerably declined. Since 1993, the US imposed more than 40 trade sanctions against about three dozen foreign countries. The US President's Export Council estimated that these sanctions did cost American exporters US$15 billion to US$19 billion in lost overseas sales. For instance, the sanctions under the Nuclear Proliferation Act failed to deter India and Pakistan from testing nuclear weapons in May 1994. Moreover, US sanctions have utterly failed to change the basic behaviour of governments in Cuba, Myanmar, Iran, Nigeria, Yugoslavia, and a number of other target countries.[5]

8.2.3 Bureaucracy

The term 'bureaucracy' refers to the form of administration based on hierarchical structure, governed by a set of written rules and established procedures. Since the officials in a bureaucratic system derive authority by virtue of their official position rather than their own personal traits or competence, it leads to an impersonal approach to administration and too much reliance on rules and routine regulations. In the present context, the term 'bureaucracy' is often used to describe inefficient and obstructive administrative process and red-tapism. The Indian bureaucracy has become apt at the art of shunning any direct responsibility in decision-making leading to avoidable delays, as given in Exhibit 8.1. An international firm often finds it difficult to deal with a foreign bureaucratic system.

For instance, local political interests in Japan overweigh those in the rest of the country. Therefore, Japanese bureaucracy is difficult to streamline as politicians are interested in the affairs of their own districts rather than the country as a whole.

8.2.4 Terrorism, Crime, and Violence

The term 'terrorism' refers to systematic use of violence to create fear among the general public with an objective to achieve a political goal or convey a political message.

Exhibit 8.1   Officialese ensures bureaucrats never take direct responsibility

Officialese is the refined art of speaking or writing, without actually committing to anything. Indian bureaucrats use this special skill to write wonderfully ambiguous file noting and make no mistake.

There is no place in the bureaucratic system that shows no aptitude for circumlocution. There seems to be an unwritten code that a bureaucrat must *never* say a direct 'approved' or *ever* take responsibility for a decision. Response and approval must always be couched in terms, such as 'approved if found in order', 'approved as proposed,' or 'there should be no objection to give approval'. A direct statement of the order of 'this can be done' goes completely against the grain. There may even be a ban on it hidden somewhere in the notes you find in the margins

of every file in proximity to a bureaucrat's desk. What would pass the mark would be 'there is no objection to doing this'.

Much like the bureaucrats themselves, the convoluted jargon of these file notes can be compared to the Indian sweet, *jalebis*. As a part of larger bureaucratic culture, there is a tendency to avoid decisions and hence use jargon that lets one get away from any sort of responsibility. An example is the often-used line, 'this issues with an approval of competent authority', which works without *ever* specifying the competent authority. Further, a senior is always addressed in the third person in an obsequious fashion, such as 'may *kindly* see', 'for *kind* perusal' or 'for *kind* approval', *kindness* being the prelude to any request.

---

[5] *Unilateral Sanctions*, Centre for Trade Policy and Research: Washington DC, 2007.

Thus, terrorism is a political tactic that uses threat or violence, usually against civilians, so as to frighten them and build political pressure on the government. International terrorist activities may range from mere threat or physical assault to vandalism, mass killing, kidnapping, hijacking, and bombing.

Although isolated acts of terror have been witnessed in the past too, these were generally confined to a country and region. Technological breakthroughs and emerging globalization have led to globalization of terrorism as well. Organized terrorist groups now conceptualize and accomplish worldwide acts of terror. During recent years, terrorism has become endemic and gained increased global attention consequent to 11 September 2001.

The global reach of mass media, transport, and telecommunication has made even the considerably immune western countries vulnerable to terrorist attacks. This has considerably influenced US business interests in a large number of countries where such terror groups are active. Following the US 'war on terror' and the attack on Afghanistan in October 2001, the perception of American companies operating in Islamic countries has suffered drastically; often franchises have come under assault with reported incidence of violence. In order to mitigate the negative perception, the US companies have had to proactively adapt to local sensitivities as shown in Exhibit 8.2.

Moreover, numerous terrorist outfits within a country or a region too, considerably influence international business decisions. A cross-country comparison of business costs of terrorism on a seven point scale is depicted in Fig. 8.1. At one extreme, 7 indicates that terrorism does not impose significant costs on business whereas 1 indicates most significant business costs due to terrorist activity. Finland (6.6), Brazil (6.2), South Africa (5.8), UAE (5.6), and Singapore (5.2) have much lower costs

---

Exhibit 8.2   McDonald's 'embraces' Islam in Indonesia: Surviving in troubled markets

After the US engaged in a war with Afghanistan, a number of US business organizations have been targeted around the world. The KFC outlet has been the target of a home-made bomb, while in central Java some protesters have plastered signs on McDonald's outlets, symbolically 'selling' them.

Step inside a Mcdonald's restaurant in Indonesia's capital, and the scene is still reminiscent of daily anti-American protests over US-led strikes on Afghanistan. The first thing one sees is not a Big-Mac but a large Islamic McDonald's crew with the women wearing elegant Muslim clothing and matching veils while men sport prayer caps. 'In the name of Allah, the merciful and the gracious, McDonald's Indonesia is owned by an indigenous Muslim in Indonesia', says the poster, painted the Islamic colour of green, which also dots other outlets in Jakarta.

Some of the posters are inscribed in Arabic, part of an apparent bid by franchise holder Bambang Rachmadi to project an image that the icon of American fast food is an Islamic-friendly business in a country where many US companies have been forced to lie low.

Source: Indian Express, 6 May 2002.

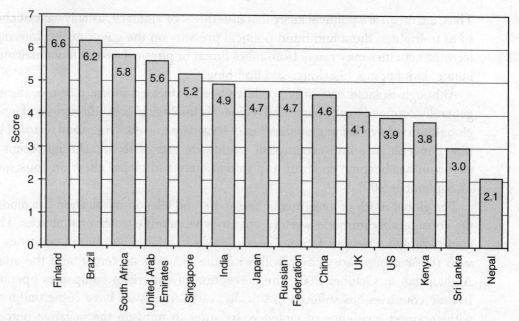

Fig. 8.1 Business costs of terrorism

Note: 1—most significant; 7—least significant (costs on business).
Source: The Global Competitiveness Report 2007–08, World Economic Forum, New York: Palgrave Macmillan, p. 386.

of terrorism on business activities against the global average of 5 whereas it is reported to be the highest[6] in Nepal (2.1), and above the global average in India (4.9), Japan and Russian Federation (4.7), China (4.6), the UK (4.1), the US (3.9), Kenya (3.8), and Sri Lanka (3.0).

Politically motivated use of computers and the Internet has led to the emergence of 'cyber-terrorism' that uses computers as weapons or as targets so as to create destructive or disruptive effects comparable to the physical form of terrorism. Since international business firms are highly integrated with the computer-networks, they become increasingly susceptible to 'cyber-terrorism' that impinges across national boundaries.

Incidence of crime and violence, such as street mugging, looting, etc., imposes considerable costs on international operations of a firm as well. The business cost of crime and violence (Fig. 8.2) is the lowest in Syria and Finland at 6.7 on a seven point scale whereas 6.4 in Germany, 6.3 in Singapore, 6.1 in UAE, 5.6 in Australia, 5.4 in Japan, and 5.2 in India against a global average of 4.3. On the other hand, it is the highest in El Salvador (2.0), also below global average in South Africa (2.3), Kenya (2.5), Brazil (2.8), and Russian Federation[7] (4.0).

There appears a negative co-relation between economic freedom and terrorism: The higher the level of economic freedom, the lesser is the prevalence of terrorism in

---

[6] The Global Competitiveness Report 2007–08, World Economic Forum, New York: Palgrave Macmillan, p. 386.
[7] The Global Competitiveness Report 2007–08, World Economic Forum, New York: Palgrave Macmillan, p. 387.

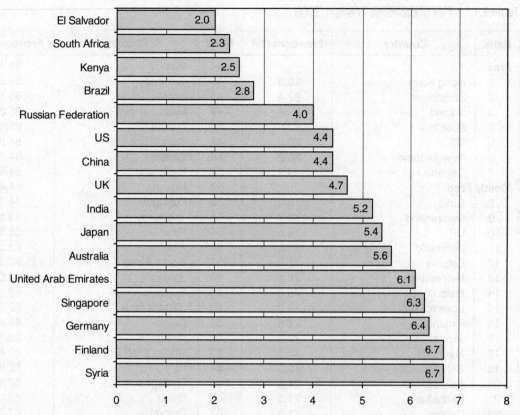

Fig. 8.2 Business costs of crime and violence

Note: 1—most significant; 7—least significant (costs on business).
Source: The Global Competitiveness Report 2007–08, World Economic Forum, New York: Palgrave Mcmillan, p. 387.

a country. Besides, countries with greater degree of economic freedom are also economically more developed with higher per capita income.

The Index of Economic Freedom measures and ranks 157 countries across 10 specific freedoms, such as business, trade, fiscal, government size, monetary, investment, financial, property rights, corruption, and labour freedoms. The overall scores given in Table 8.1 reveal Hong Kong, Singapore, Ireland, Australia, the US, New Zealand, and Canada are the countries with highest levels of economic freedom, whereas North Korea, Cuba, Zimbabwe, Libya, and Burma are the most economically repressed. The Indian economy is assessed to possess 54.2 per cent of economic freedom, whereas China has 52.8 per cent freedom. Thus India is the world's 115th freest economy whereas China at 126th rank have been classified under 'mostly unfree' category. India enjoys strong fiscal freedom (75.7%), freedom from government size (73.5%), and monetary freedom (70.3%). The top individual and corporate tax rates are moderate, and overall tax revenue is not excessive as a percentage of GDP but government price controls hinder market forces. Indian economy enjoys considerable

Table 8.1 Index of economic freedom, 2008

Rank	Country	Freedom (%)	Rank	Country	Freedom (%)
Free			44	Mexico	66.4
1	Hong Kong	90.3	45	Jamaica	66.2
2	Singapore	87.4	46	Israel	66.1
3	Ireland	82.4	47	Malta	66.0
4	Australia	82.0	48	France	65.4
5	US	80.6	49	Costa Rica	64.8
6	New Zealand	80.2	50	Panama	64.7
7	Canada	80.2	51	Malaysia	64.5
Mostly Free			52	Uganda	64.4
8	Chile	79.8	53	Portugal	64.3
9	Switzerland	79.7	54	Thailand	63.5
10	UK	79.5	55	Peru	63.5
11	Denmark	79.2	56	Albania	63.3
12	Estonia	77.8	57	South Africa	63.2
13	Netherlands	76.8	58	Jordan	63.0
14	Iceland	76.5	59	Bulgaria	62.9
15	Luxembourg	75.2	60	Saudi Arabia	62.8
16	Finland	74.8	61	Belize	62.8
17	Japan	72.5	62	Mongolia	62.8
18	Mauritius	72.3	63	United Arab Emirates	62.8
19	Bahrain	72.2	64	Italy	62.5
20	Belgium	71.5	65	Madagascar	62.4
21	Barbados	71.3	66	Qatar	62.2
22	Cyprus	71.3	67	Colombia	61.9
23	Germany	71.2	68	Romania	61.5
24	Bahamas	71.1	69	Fiji	61.5
25	Taiwan	71.0	70	Kyrgyz Republic, The	61.1
26	Lithuania	70.8	71	Macedonia	61.1
27	Sweden	70.4	72	Namibia	61.0
28	Armenia	70.3	73	Lebanon	60.9
29	Trinidad and Tobago	70.2	74	Turkey	60.8
30	Austria	70.0	75	Slovenia	60.6
Moderately Free			76	Kazakhstan	60.5
31	Spain	69.7	77	Paraguay	60.5
32	Georgia	69.2	78	Guatemala	60.5
33	El Salvador	69.2	79	Honduras	60.2
34	Norway	69.0	80	Greece	60.1
35	Slovak Republic, The	68.7	81	Nicaragua	60.0
36	Botswana	68.6	**Mostly Unfree**		
37	Czech Republic	68.5	82	Kenya	59.6
38	Latvia	68.3	83	Poland	59.5
39	Kuwait	68.3	84	Tunisia	59.3
40	Uruguay	68.1	85	Egypt	59.2
41	Korea, South	67.9	86	Swaziland	58.9
42	Oman	67.4	87	Dominican Republic	58.5
43	Hungary	67.2	88	Cape Verde	58.4

Contd

Table 8.1 Contd

Rank	Country	Freedom (%)	Rank	Country	Freedom (%)
89	Moldova	58.4	124	Ethiopia	53.2
90	Sri Lanka	58.3	125	Yemen	52.8
91	Senegal	58.2	126	China	52.8
92	Philippines, The	56.9	127	Guinea	52.8
93	Pakistan	56.8	128	Niger	52.7
94	Ghana	56.7	129	Equatorial Guinea	52.5
95	Gambia, The	56.6	130	Uzbekistan	52.3
96	Mozambique	56.6	131	Djibouti	52.3
97	Tanzania	56.4	132	Lesotho	51.9
98	Morocco	56.4	133	Ukraine	51.1
99	Zambia	56.4	**Repressed**		
100	Cambodia	56.2	134	Russia	49.9
101	Brazil	55.9	135	Vietnam	49.8
102	Algeria	55.7	136	Guyana	49.4
103	Burkina Faso	55.6	137	Laos	49.2
104	Mali	55.5	138	Haiti	48.9
105	Nigeria	55.5	139	Sierra Leone	48.9
106	Ecuador	55.4	140	Togo	48.8
107	Azerbaijan	55.3	141	Central African Republic	48.2
108	Argentina	55.1	142	Chad	47.7
109	Mauritania	55.0	143	Angola	47.1
110	Benin	55.0	144	Syria	46.6
111	Ivory Coast	54.9	145	Burundi	46.3
112	Nepal	54.7	146	Congo, Republic of	45.2
113	Croatia	54.6	147	Guinea Bissau	45.1
114	Tajikistan	54.5	148	Venezuela	45.0
115	India	54.2	149	Bangladesh	44.9
116	Rwanda	54.1	150	Belarus	44.7
117	Cameroon	54.0	151	Iran	44.0
118	Suriname	53.9	152	Turkmenistan	43.4
119	Indonesia	53.9	153	Burma	39.5
120	Malawi	53.8	154	Libya	38.7
121	Bosnia and Herzegovina	53.7	155	Zimbabwe	29.8
122	Gabon	53.6	156	Cuba	27.5
123	Bolivia	53.2	157	Korea, North	3.0

80–100 : Free
70–79.9 : Mostly free
60–69.9 : Moderately free
50–59.9 : Mostly unfree
0–49.9 : Repressed

Source: '2008 Index of Economic Freedom', Heritage Foundation, Washington and *Wall Street Journal,* New York, 2008.

labour freedom (68.6%), trade freedom (51%), business freedom (50%), freedom of property rights (50%), whereas investment freedom (40%), freedom from corruption (33%), and financial freedom (30%) are relatively low.

8.3   INTERNATIONAL LEGAL ENVIRONMENT

Firms operating internationally face major challenges in conforming to different laws, regulations, and legal systems in different countries. The legal framework to protect small and medium enterprises (SMEs), mainly to achieve social objectives, adversely influences the expansion of manufacturing capacities and achieving economies of scale in certain countries. International managers need to develop basic understanding of the types of legal systems followed in the countries of their operations before entering into legal contracts.

8.3.1   Judicial Independence and Efficiency

The independence of a country's judicial system from political influences of the members of governments, citizens, or firms is crucial for the fair treatment a firm receives in its overseas operations. A fair judicial system also reduces political risks in overseas markets. The level of judicial independence and efficiency differs widely among countries. Germany had the highest level of judicial independence[8] (Fig. 8.3) with a score of 6.5 on a 7 point scale whereas Netherlands and Australia had a score of 6.4, the UK (6.0), Singapore (5.6), Japan and South Africa (5.5), India (5.3), the US (5.1), and UAE (5.0). This was reported to be considerably lower in China (3.4), Brazil (3.1), Russian Federation (2.7) and the lowest in Venezuela (1.2).

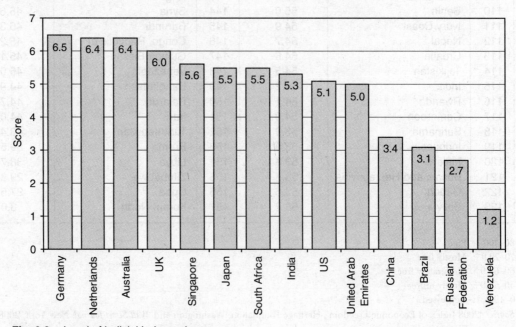

Fig. 8.3   Level of judicial independence

Note: 1—heavily influenced; 7—entirely independent.

Source: The Global Competitiveness Report 2007–08, World Economic Forum, New York: Palgrave Macmillan, p. 380.

---

[8] The Global Competitiveness Report 2007–08, World Economic Forum, New York: Palgrave Macmillan, p. 380.

The efficiency of legal framework for private businesses to settle dispute and challenge the legality of government actions or regulations also varies widely. A cross-country comparison on a 7.0 point scale as shown in Fig. 8.4 indicates that Denmark (6.5) had the highest level of efficiency of legal framework[9] followed by Germany (6.3) and Switzerland (6.1) whereas it was considerably efficient in Singapore (6.0), Australia (5.9), the UK (5.8), Japan (5.6), South Africa (5.4), the US (4.9), and India (4.8). The legal framework was the least efficient in Venezuela (1.5) and had relatively low level of efficiency in Russian Federation (2.8), Brazil (2.9), China (3.6), Tanzania (3.7), and Thailand (4.4).

The extent of separation of judicial powers between the judiciary and the public authorities varies considerably across nations. China, for instance, has generally followed 'rule by man and not by law', the tradition of which still remains despite the country developing a model legal system. The efficiency of enforcement of legal system is also lax in many low-income countries.

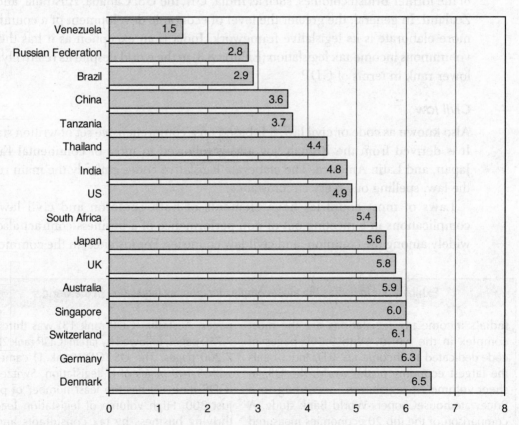

Fig. 8.4 Efficiency of legal framework

Note: 1—efficient; 7—inefficient.

Source: The Global Competitiveness Report 2007–08, World Economic Forum, New York: Palgrave Macmillan, p. 384.

---

[9] The Global Competitiveness Report 2007–08, World Economic Forum, New York: Palgrave Macmillan, p. 384.

In countries, such as Japan, the reliance on courts for conflict resolution is much lower compared to the US which is considered to be one of the most litigious societies in the world. On the other hand, Japan is considered to be a 'non-contractual' society where contracts signed represent general understanding and are subject to change depending upon the circumstance. There is heavy reliance on settling disputes through third party negotiations rather than courts.

8.3.2   International Legal Systems

The major types of legal systems are briefly mentioned here.

Common law

It is based on traditions, past practices, and legal precedents set by the courts through interpretation of statutes, legal legislations, and past rulings. It depends less on written statutes and codes. Common law originated from England and it is followed in most of the former British colonies, such as India, UK, the US, Canada, Australia, and New Zealand. In general, the greater the level of economic development of a country, the more elaborate is its legislative framework. India is an exception as it has the most voluminous income-tax legislation (Exhibit 8.3) in the world despite its relatively much lower rank in terms of GDP.

Civil law

Also known as code or civil law, it is based on a comprehensive set of written statutes. It is derived from the Roman law and is followed in most of continental Europe, Japan, and Latin America. The elaborate legislative codes embody the main rules of the law, spelling out every circumstance.

Laws of most countries have elements of both common and civil law. The complications in a meeting out of non-performance of a business contract also vary widely among the common- and civil-law countries. For instance, in the common-law

---

Exhibit 8.3   India has the most complex income tax legislation in the world

India's income tax legislations are the most complex in the world. With 9,000 pages of code dedicated to income tax (IT), India beats the largest economy of the world, the US, in sheer volume of legislation, according to a PricewaterhouseCoopers-World Bank study. A comparison of the top 20 economies measured by GDP to the volume of IT legislation, India (GDP rank 10) topped the list with 9,000 pages, followed by the UK (GDP rank 4) with 8,300 pages. Australia (GDP rank 13) was third with 7,750 pages, followed by Japan (GDP rank 2) with 7,200 pages. The US (GDP rank 1) came fifth with 5,100 pages of IT legislation. Switzerland (GDP rank 17) has the least number of pages, just 300. High volume of legislation leads to thriving business by tax consultants and the complicated procedures lead to tax evasion, often due to tax-payers' ignorance.

Source: 'India Has 9,000 Pages of Income Tax Laws', *Hindustan Times*, 13 November 2006.

countries, the non-performance of a contract due to an 'act of god' may include floods, earthquakes, lightening, or similar happenings whereas under the civil law, non-performance is not limited to 'acts of god', but also includes 'unavoidable interference with performance, whether resulting from forces of nature or unforeseeable human acts', including such factors as labour strikes and riots.

The distinction between the common law and civil law is more in theory rather than in practice. Many common law countries, including the US and India have adapted commercial codes to govern business.

The most significant difference in the common law and the civil law countries is in the protection of intellectual property. Ownership is established by use in common law countries whereas it requires registration in the civil law countries. It is extremely important for certain agreements in civil law countries to get registered, in order to be enforceable, whereas in common law countries, as long as the proof of the agreement can be established, an agreement is binding.

Although there is significant overlapping in practice under the two systems, laws are much more rigid in the countries with civil-law system compared to common-law systems. In 'civil law' countries, judges have to strictly follow the 'letter of the law', giving them low flexibility in judicial decisions whereas in common-law countries, greater reliance is placed on the previous rulings and interpretations by other judges in similar cases. Business contracts tend to be detailed and specific with all contingencies elaborated in civil-law countries whereas contracts tend to be shorter and less specific in common-law countries. The judiciary tend to be less adversarial in civil-law countries where little significance is accorded to legal precedence and traditions compared to common-law countries.

Socialistic law

This law is derived from the Marxist socialist system and continues to influence legal framework in former communist countries, such as the CIS, China, North Korea, Vietnam, and Cuba. Socialist law traditionally advocates ownership of most property by the state or state-owned public enterprises, prohibiting free entry to foreign firms.

Theocratic law

Theocratic law is the legal system based on religious doctrine, precepts, and beliefs. For instance, the Hebrew law and the Islamic law are derived from religious doctrines and their scholarly interpretations. Unlike the countries dominated by Christianity, Hinduism, and Buddhism where either common or civil law is followed, a large number of Islamic countries integrate their legal system based on the Sharia. The legal system in a number of Islamic countries, including Saudi Arabia, and Iran is integrated with Sharia.

In Arabic, 'Sharia' means the clear, well-trodden path to water. In Islam, Sharia is used to refer to the matters of religion that God has legislated for His Servants. Sharia is the canonical law derived from a combination of sources, such as the Koran, the holy book of Islam, the Sunna, teachings and practices of the prophet Mohammed, and the fatwas, the rulings of the Islamic scholars. The Sharia regulates all human actions and places them in five categories, i.e., obligatory, recommended, permitted, disliked, or forbidden. Classic Sharia manuals are divided in four parts: laws related to personal acts of worship, laws related to commercial dealings, laws related to marriage and divorce, and penal laws.

Major similarities between the Sharia and secular law are that in both

- All people are equal before the law.
- A person is innocent unless proved guilty.
- The burden of proof is on the plaintiff.
- Written contracts have a sanctity and legitimacy of their own.

The salient features of Islamic law concerned to business are that

- Contracts should be fair to all parties. Partnership is preferred over hierarchical claims.
- *Gharar,* the transaction involving fundamental uncertainty or speculation is prohibited. Gambling is not liked in Islamic countries, but futures and currency hedging also involves speculation. International managers need to be aware of such situations.
- Interest on money is prohibited but allows management fees and services. All business transactions must avoid *riba,* i.e., excessive profit, loosely defined as interest.
- Business involving forbidden products or activity, such as alcohol, pork, or gambling is prohibited.
- Normally award of damages are in line with practicality but not as inflated as is often the case in the West. In other words, the damages to property will be actual sums relating to repair and replacement of the property. The loss of opportunity for cost of money is not compensated under the Sharia.
- Compassion is required when a business is in trouble. In a country with Islamic legal structure, it is not considered appropriate to put pressure in the event of bankruptcy of one's business partner.

The major difference between Sharia law and the Western law is the idea of reference to a precedent. Under the Sharia, a ruling issued by a judge is not binding on other judges or on him in later cases. While doing business in Islamic countries, international managers need to appreciate the intertwining of religion and Islamic law and take care never to mention the Palestine-Israeli situation.

After independence from erstwhile colonial rulers, most Islamic countries have grappled with the problem of replacing colonial legal systems with the Sharia. The implications of Islamic law vary in terms of degree among the Islamic countries. In most countries, it is applied in conjunction with the common and the civil law.

Islamic finance   Under the Islamic law, western style finance is *haram,* or forbidden, to devout Muslims. The interest-bearing accounts and loans, which fall under the strict *riba* rules, most futures and options, which are considered speculative and *gharar,* and insurance, because the outcome of the contract can no way be determined beforehand[10], are all *haram.* In order to enable Islamic investors to benchmark their investment on a regional basis and give product providers the opportunity to develop structured products tailored to the Islamic market, Standard & Poor's (S&P), brings out Sharia Indices (Exhibit 8.4) that include only those stocks that comply with Sharia law. This provides investors with a comparable investable portfolio while adopting explicit investment criteria defined by the Sharia. All S&P indices constituents are

---

Exhibit 8.4   Sharia indices: A useful tool to assess compliance to Islamic law

Sharia indices developed by Standard & Poor's (S&P) provides a useful tool for investment into Sharia-compliant funds. For arriving at the Sharia Indices, a set of independent and objective guidelines are complied with. Sharia-compliance screening typically falls into two categories.

Sector-based: Certain businesses offer products and services that are considered unacceptable and non-compliant. Examples of these activities include gambling, banking, pornography, and alcohol.

Accounting-based: Certain financial ratios of businesses may violate the compliance measure. Three areas of focus are leverage, cash, and the share of revenues derived from non-compliant activities. All of these are evaluated on an ongoing basis.

While some of these restrictions are not absolute, the Sharia Supervisory Board makes these determinations on an index-by-index, stock-by-stock, or similar basis. For its daily maintenance, S&P has contracted with a Kuwait based consulting company specializing in solutions for the global Islamic investment market. Rating intelligence partners has a team of qualified Islamic researchers who work directly with the Sharia Supervisory Board, which

continually works with regional banks to create Sharia-compliant equity products and expands investment earnings. It screens stocks of each of the partner indices to implement Sharia Board rulings.

The number of stocks, for screening purposes, is limited to the top 15 from each country, having a market capitalization of at least US$1 billion. Each month, a universe of stocks conforming to these criteria, selected once a year on 31 March, is screened for Sharia compliance to form this index. Besides India, the countries eligible for inclusion in the index include China, Hong Kong, Malaysia, the Philippines, Singapore, South Korea, Taiwan, and Thailand.

Pan Asia, Sharia Index refers to 71 companies from nine Asian nations, 11 are from India.[a] This includes private sector petrochemicals major Reliance Industries, software leaders Tata Consultancy Services and Infosys, telecom major Bharti Airtel, and oil and gas sector major state-run Oil and Natural Gas Corporation. With the global crude oil prices more than double of their mid-2004 prices, a number of West Asian countries are now flush with funds. For the 11 Indian companies this could mean that Sharia-compliant funds to be benchmarked to the S&P index facilitate a pick up of these companies' stocks in Islamic countries.

[a] 'Eleven Indian Companies Make It to Shariah Index', *The Times of India,* 28 June 2007.

---

[10] 'Finance and Economics: West Meets East—Islamic Finance', *The Economist,* London, 25 October 2003.

monitored on a daily basis to ensure that the indices maintain strict Sharia compliance. A substantial amount of oil-money is invested in Sharia-compliant funds. As the index provides for benchmarking with Sharia, some of these funds may be invested as per the Sharia Indices.

8.3.3 Principles of International Law

International law is less coherent compared to domestic law since it embodies a multiplicity of treaties (bilateral, multilateral, or universal) and conventions (such as the Vienna Convention on Diplomatic Security, Geneva Convention on Human Rights, etc.) besides the laws of individual countries. International managers need to understand the basic principles that govern the conduct of international law. These are discussed here.

Principle of sovereignty

A 'sovereign' state is independent and free from all external control or enjoys complete legal equality with other states. It governs its own territory, has the right to select and implement its own political, economic, and social systems and has the power to enter into bilateral or multilateral agreements with other nations. Thus, a sovereign state exercises powers over its own members and in relation to other countries. This also implies that courts of a sovereign country cannot be used to rectify its injustices on other countries.

International jurisdiction

Under international law, there are three basic types of jurisdictional principles.

Nationality principle Every country has jurisdiction over its citizens, irrespective of their locations. For instance, an Indian citizen travelling abroad may be given a penalty by a court in India.

Territoriality principle Every country has the right of jurisdiction within its own legal territory. Therefore, a foreign firm involved in illegal business practices in India can be sued under Indian law.

Protective principle Every nation has jurisdiction over conduct that adversely affects its national security even if such behaviour occurs outside the country. For instance, an Italian firm that sells India's defence secrets can be booked under the Indian law.

Doctrine of comity

As a part of international customs and traditions, there must be mutual respect for the laws, institutions, and the government system of other countries in the matter of jurisdiction over their own citizens.

Act of state doctrine

Under this jurisdiction principle of international law, all acts of other governments are considered to be valid by a country's court, even if such acts are not appropriate in the country. For instance, foreign governments have right to impose restrictions related to financial repatriation to other countries.

Treatment and rights of aliens

Nations have the right to impose restriction upon foreign citizens on their rights to travel and stay, their conduct, or area of business operations. A country may also refuse entry to foreign citizens or restrict their travel. As a result of rise in terrorism during the last decade, the US and many European countries have imposed restrictions on foreigners.

Forum for hearing and settling disputes

Courts can dismiss cases at their discretion, brought before them by foreigners. However, courts are bound to examine issues, such as the place from where evidence must be collected, location of the property under restitution, and the plaintiff. For instance, after the disaster of Union Carbide's pesticide plant located at Bhopal in India, the New York Court of Appeals sent back the case to India for resolution.

8.3.4   United Nations Commission on International Trade Law

The United Nations Commission on International Trade Law (UNCITRAL) was established in 1966 by the UN General Assembly (Fig. 8.5) with the aim to reduce

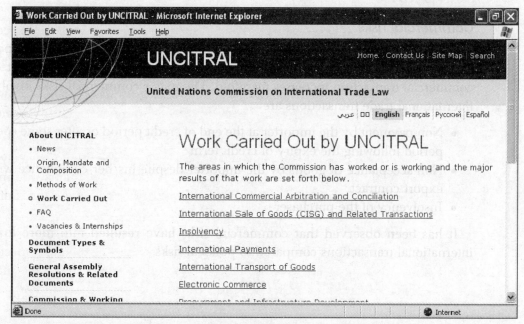

Fig. 8.5   UNCITRAL works towards 'harmonization' and 'unification' of international trade laws.

obstacles in international trade. Its general mandate is to harmonize and unify the laws of international trade. 'Harmonization' and 'unification' of the law of international trade refer to the process through which the law facilitating international trade is created and adopted.

The commission is composed of 60 member states elected by the General Assembly. Membership is structured so as to be representative of the world's various geographic regions and their principal economic and legal systems. Members of the commission are elected for terms of six years, the term of half-members expiring every three years. Presently, UNCITRAL has six working groups for areas, such as procurement, international arbitration and conciliation, transport law, electronic commerce, insolvency law, and security interests. It has prepared a wide range of conventions, model laws, and other instruments dealing with the substantive law that governs trade transactions or other aspects of business law influencing international trade.

8.4   RISKS IN INTERNATIONAL BUSINESS

An international business involves a number of risks that adversely affect a firm's smooth operation. Therefore, managers operating in international markets need to develop a thorough understanding of these risks and various options available to minimize them. Government regulations have been identified as the most critical risk factor in a firm's overseas operations.[11]

8.4.1 Types of Risks

The major types of risks in international business are summarized below.

Commercial risks

As a firm has to deal with an overseas buyer operating in a different legal and political environment in an international transaction, the risks to smooth conduct of the commercial transaction increases manifold. The major commercial risks involved in international trade transactions are

- Non-payment by the importer at the end of credit period or after some specified period following the expiry of credit term
- Non-acceptance of goods by the importer despite his/her compliance with the export contract
- Insolvency of the purchaser

It has been observed that commercial risks have resulted into more losses in international transactions compared to political risks.

---

[11] Kearney, A.T., 'FDI Confidence Index' Global Business Policy Council, vol. 7, October 2004, pp. 11–13.

Economic risks

Countries often impose restrictions on business activities on the grounds of national security, conserving human and natural resources, scarcity of foreign exchange, to curb unfair trade practices, and to provide protection to domestic industries. The Balance of Payment (BoP) position of a country greatly influences economic restrictions imposed on international business activities, therefore it has been discussed at length.

Principal economic risks in international markets are summarized here.

Import restrictions   In order to protect domestic industry, national governments often impose selective restrictions on import of goods. Such restrictions vary from total ban on imports to quota restrictions. Firms with operations in countries with import restrictions often have to source locally available inputs at higher costs, compromising on the product quality.

Local content requirements   Trade policies often make provisions for local content requirements for extending export incentives or putting a country-of-origin label. For instance, the European Economic Community (EEC) discouraged assemblers and termed them as 'screw-driver operations' imposing a local content requirement of 45 per cent. For all cars manufactured in member countries, NAFTA imposes 62 per cent as local content requirement.

Exchange controls   In view of the scarcity of foreign exchange, countries often adopt stringent exchange control measures. It adversely affects the repatriation of profits and sales proceeds to the home country. Certain countries do have multiple exchange rates for international transactions. For instance, Myanmar has three exchange rates for their currency Kyat (Kt), i.e., the official rate (Kt 6.4: US$1), the market rate[12] (Kt 1100–1400: US$1), and an import duty rate (Kt 450: US$1).

Political risks

The possibility of political decisions, events, or conditions in an overseas market or country that adversely affect international business is termed as political risk. Such risks occur due to discontinuities in the business environment that are difficult to anticipate resulting from political change.[13] Confiscation of goods by a foreign government is considered to be the most severe form of political risk and it varies from much lower level of risks arising due to a change in government regulations and controls directly affecting the performance of business activities. The major types of political risks are

Confiscation   It refers to the process of taking over a property without any compensation.

---

[12] *Washington Times*, Washington DC, 29 July 2008.

[13] Robock, Stefan, 'Political Risk: Identification and Assessment', *Columbia Journal of World Business*, July–August 1971, pp. 6–20.

Expropriation It refers to a foreign government's taking over of a company's goods, land, or other assets, by offering some kind of compensation. However, such compensation paid is generally much lower than the market value of the assets taken over.

Nationalization It refers to government's taking over the assets and property and operating the business taken over under its ownership.

Domestication It refers to a foreign company's relinquishing control and ownership to the nationals.

Over the recent years the political risks of explicitly unjustifiable measures, such as confiscation and expropriation have considerably reduced as countries are competing with each other for promoting foreign investments. However, countries often resort to *creeping expropriation* that refers to a set of actions whose cumulative effect is to deprive foreign investors of their fundamental rights in the investment. The economic impact is due to the fact that laws that affect corporate ownership, control, and profit and reinvestment can be enacted. Companies thus need to adopt adequate safeguards against these measures. Strategic alliance or joint ventures are often strategically used to mitigate the risks of confiscation or expropriation of a firm's assets in overseas locations.

8.4.2 Measuring International Business Risks

A number of risk analysis agencies provide specialized services for country risk ratings. The most significant and widely-used country risk ratings include Business Environment Risk Intelligence (BERI) Index, Economist Intelligence Unit (EIU) Indices, and PRS Group's International Country Risk Guide. These country risk ratings generally use different criteria to arrive at political, financial, economic, and overall risks. These ratings may be subscribed by international firms.

Business environment risk intelligence index

BERI provides risk forecasts for about 50 countries throughout the world and a broad assessment of the country's business climate. The index was developed by Frederich Haner of the University of Delaware in the US. It has since expanded into country-specific forecasts and country risk forecasts for international lenders, but its basic service is the Global subscription service. BERI's Global subscription service assesses about 48 countries, four times a year, on 15 economic, political, and financial factors on a scale from zero to four. As shown in Exhibit 8.5, zero indicates unacceptable conditions for investment in a country; one equates with poor conditions; two with acceptable or average conditions; three with above average conditions; and four with superior conditions. The key factors are individually weighted according to their assessed importance.

Exhibit 8.5	Criteria included in the overall BERI index		

Criteria	Weights	Multiplied with the score (rating) on a scale of 0–4[a]	Overall BERI index[b]
Political stability	3		
Economic growth	2.5		
Currency convertibility	2.5		
Labour cost/productivity	2		
Short-term credit	2		
Long-term loans/venture capital	2		
Attitude towards the foreign investors and profits	1.5		
Nationalization	1.5		
Monetary inflation	1.5		
Balance of payments	1.5		
Enforceability of contracts	1.5		
Bureaucratic delays	1		
Communications: Phone, Fax, Internet-access	1		
Local management and partner	1		
Professional services and contractors	0.5		
Total	25		
		× 4 (max.)	= max. 100

[a] 0 = unacceptable; 1 = poor; 2 = average conditions; 3 = above average conditions; 4 = superior conditions.

[b] *Total points:*

More than 80	: Favourable environment for investors, advanced economy
70–79	: Not so favourable, but still an advanced economy
55–69	: An immature economy with investment potential, probably an NIC
40–54	: A high-risk country, probably an LDC. Quality of management has to be superior to realize potential
Less than 40	: Very high risk, would only commit capital if there exists some extraordinary justification

EIU's risk indices

EIU brings out indices to monitor Business Environment Ranking so as to facilitate assessment of countries for doing business. It also monitors operational risks for 150 countries on a scale of 0 to 100, where 0 indicates the least risky and 100, the most risky place to operate. The overall score includes an aggregate of 10 categories of risks, such as security, political stability, government effectiveness, legal and regulatory, macroeconomic, foreign trade and payments, financial, tax policy, labour markets, and infrastructure. Switzerland (8), Denmark (9), Singapore (10), Sweden (10), and Finland (12) rank as the safest places, whereas Iraq (84), Guinea (80), Myanmar (79), Zimbabwe (77), and Uzbekistan/Turkmenistan (77) are the most risky countries to carry out business.[14]

---

[14] 'Risk Briefing', Economic Intelligence Unit, 6 May 2008.

Global Political Risk Index

The Global Political Risk Index (GPRI) developed by the Eurasia Group serves as a comparative index to monitor political risks in 24 emerging markets, including India, China, Brazil, Russia, and South Africa. It serves as an 'early warning' system to anticipate critical trends and provides a measure for the country's capacity to withstand political, economic, security-related, and social shocks. The index is based on 20 indicators in four equally weighted categories—government, society, security, and economy on a scale of 0 to 100. Pakistan is reported to have the highest level of political risks[15] in the emerging markets monitored, followed by Nigeria, Iran, Venezuela, the Philippines, Indonesia, and Saudi Arabia, whereas Poland is politically most stable followed by South Korea, Bulgaria, Mexico, Brazil, and China.

Failed states index

The Failed States Index, brought out by *Fund for Peace*, an independent organization and Foreign Policy magazine, is a useful tool to carry out the cross-country comparison of the world's weakest states. It uses 12 indicators covering social, economic, political, and military conditions and ranks on a scale of 0–120 (0 being the most stable and 120 the least stable) to assess about 177 states in order of their vulnerability to violent internal conflict and societal deterioration. These indicators cover a wide range of the elements of the risk of state failure, such as extensive corruption and criminal behaviour, inability to collect taxes or draw on citizen support, large-scale involuntary dislocation of the population, sharp economic decline, group-based inequality, institutionalized persecution or discrimination, severe demographic pressures, brain drain, and environmental decay. States can fail at varying rates through explosion, implosion, erosion, or invasion over different time periods.

Somalia tops the list of the world's failed states[16] (Fig. 8.6) with a score of 114.2, followed by Sudan (113), Zimbabwe (112.5), Chad (110.9), and Iraq (110.6). As indicated, India is surrounded by some of the world's highly unstable countries, such as Afghanistan (105.4), Pakistan (103.8), Bangladesh (100.3), Myanmar (100.3), Sri Lanka (95.6), and Nepal (94.2). This severely restrains India's international business opportunities with its neighbouring countries. Norway (16.8), Switzerland (20.3), Japan (29.7), the US (32.8), and the UK (32.9) rank among the most stable countries of the world.

Among the wide range of reasons that contribute to a state's failure are rampant corruption, severe ethnic or religious divisions, predatory elites who have long monopolized power, and an absence of rule of law. The world's weakest states are also the most religiously intolerant. The state's failure is contagious to neighbouring states mainly due to porous borders, cultural affinity, and widespread underdevelopment.

---

[15] livemint.com, *The Wall Street Journal*, 5 September 2008.
[16] 'The Failed States Index, 2008', *Foreign Policy*, July–August 2008.

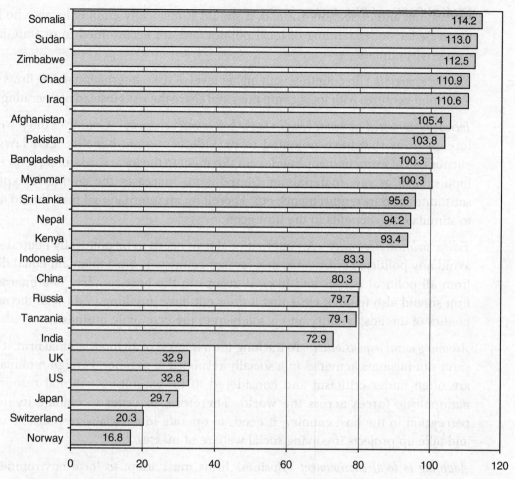

Fig. 8.6 Failed states index, 2008

Note: 0—most stable; 120—least stable.
Source: 'The Failed States Index, 2008', *Foreign Policy*, July–August 2008.

8.4.3 Managing Risks in International Business

Political risks in international business may be managed either through 'avoidance' or 'insurance'. 'Avoidance' means screening out the countries with higher political risks by carrying out a cross-country analysis. On the other hand, 'insurance' and 'guarantees' allow an international firm to shift the risks to a third party.

Strategic management of political risks

Political risks are beyond the control of a business firm, yet, in order to minimize them, certain measures can be employed.

Employing locals   An international firm should never make the costly mistake of underestimating the potential of locals in terms of their suitability of skills, competence, motivation, and education. Instead, it should strategically employ locals who have a much better understanding of local politics and are accustomed to operate in their own environments.

Sharing ownership   In countries with higher level of risks, internationalizing firms should form joint ventures with local companies and share the risks instead of operating alone.

Increasing perceived economic benefits to the host country economy   Countries often welcome foreign firms that have potential to provide economic benefits. FDI laws often encourage investment that provides employment to the local work-force, sources local inputs, such as raw materials or components, increases the country's exports or substitutes import requirements, etc. Therefore, an international firm should attempt to stimulate the benefits to the host economy.

Follow political neutrality   An international firm needs to be politically neutral so as to avoid any political controversy in a foreign country. It must maintain equal distance from all political parties and interest groups in the host country. The international firm should also make it clear that it does not have anything to do with the national politics of the host country and is solely in to the economic business.

Assuming social responsibility   In the long-term interest of an international firm, it should carry out business activities in a socially responsible manner. Foreign multinationals are often under criticism and considered to be exploiting national resources by nationalistic forces across the world. Therefore, in order to change its negative perception in the host country, it needs to operate in a socially responsible manner and take up projects involving social welfare of masses.

Adapting to local environment   Business firms must adapt to local environment and local character so as to be perceived as local rather than foreign entities. For instance, McDonald's hires local staff and bring out local products suiting to local tastes, such as McVeggie, McAloo Tikki, Veg McCurry Pan, and Chicken Maharaja Mac, in India.

Insurance and guarantees

The political and commercial risks involved in international business can be managed by way of insurance and guarantees. Exporters are subject to risk of receiving payments from overseas buyers. Due to the fast-emerging and far-reaching political and economic changes, the payment risks in international transactions have considerably increased. An outbreak of war or civil war may block or delay payment for goods exported. A coup or an insurrection may also bring about the same result. Economic difficulties or balance of payment problems may lead a country to impose restrictions on either import of certain goods or on transfer of payments for goods imported. In addition, exporters have to face commercial risks of insolvency or protracted default of buyers. The commercial risks of a foreign buyer going bankrupt or losing his capacity to pay are aggravated due to political and economic uncertainties. Most countries have central level Export Credit Agencies (ECA) to cover political and commercial risks, whereas the World Bank's subsidiary, Multilateral Investment Guarantee Agency (MIGA) guarantees against non-commercial risks (i.e., political) at the multilateral level.

Export Credit Guarantee Corporation   In India, the Export Credit Guarantee Corporation (ECGC) is the principal organization offering a variety of schemes for export credit and guarantee. The major types of insurance protection provided by the ECGC include a range of credit risk insurance covers to exporters against loss in export of goods and services and guarantees to banks and financial institutions to enable exporters to obtain better facilities from them. It also provides overseas investment insurance to Indian companies investing in joint ventures abroad in the form of equities or loans.

The basic objective of credit insurance is to provide protection to the exporters who sell their goods on credit terms. It covers both political and commercial risks. Credit insurance also facilitates exporters in getting export finances from commercial banks. The benefits provided by credit insurance to the exporters are that

- Exporters can offer competitive payment terms to their buyers.
- It protects exporters against the risk and financial costs of non-payment.
- Exporters also get covered against further losses from fluctuations in foreign exchange rates after non-payment.
- It provides exporters a freer access to working capital.
- The insurance cover reduces the exporter's need for tangible security while negotiating credit with their banks.
- Credit insurance provides exporters a second check on their buyers.
- Exporters get access to and benefits from the credit insurer's knowledge of potential payment risks in overseas markets, commercial intelligence including changes in their import regulations.

MIGA's guarantees against non-commercial (political) risks   MIGA, a World Bank Group subsidiary, helps foreign investors cover political risks by offering guarantees against the types of coverage discussed here.

Currency transfer restrictions   The coverage protects against losses arising from an investor's inability to convert local currency (for example, capital, interest, principal, profits, royalties, or other monetary benefits) into foreign exchange for transfering outside the host country. The coverage also insures against excessive delays in acquiring foreign exchange caused by the host government's actions or failure to act. However, it does not cover risks arising due to currency devaluation.

Expropriation   The coverage offers protection against loss of the insured investment as a result of acts by the host government that may reduce or eliminate ownership of, control over, or rights to the insured investment. This policy also covers partial losses, as well as the 'creeping' effect. However, bona fide, non-discriminatory measures taken by the host government in the exercise of its legitimate regulatory authority are not considered expropriatory.

War and civil disturbance The coverage protects against loss due to destruction, disappearance, or physical damage to tangible assets caused by politically motivated acts of war or civil disturbance, including revolution, insurrection, and coup d'etat. Terrorism and sabotage are also covered. It also extends to events that result in the total inability of the project enterprise to conduct operations essential to its overall financial viability.

Breach of contract Coverage protects against losses arising from host government's breach or repudiation of a contractual agreement with investor. In the event of such an alleged breach or repudiation, the investor must be able to invoke a dispute resolution mechanism (e.g., arbitration) under contract and obtain an award for damages. If the payment is not received even after a specified period of time, the investor may file for a claim.

MIGA's guarantee premiums are based on a calculation of both country and project risk ranging from 0.45 per cent to 1.75 per cent basis points per year for three coverages. Investors may choose from any combination of the four types of coverage discussed above. Equity investment can be covered up to 90 per cent and debt up to 95 per cent. MIGA may insure up to US$200 million.

This chapter shows that the government in power and the level of political opposition influences business viability in a country through changes in economic, industrial, and trade policies, regulations, and laws. A firm's economic interests can also vary widely with the economic interests of host countries. Political decisions often distort demand and supply in international markets and hamper free flow of goods and services. In the present era of globalization, the impact of sectarian violence, terrorism, or any erratic political decision in a country is felt beyond its national boundaries.

Political decisions often distort demand and supply in international markets and hamper free flow of goods and services. Political considerations often play an important role in determining the type and extent of concessions and protection granted to certain industries, labour, investment, and monitory policies. In addition, political stability in the host country also influences continuity of economic policies and a predicable business environment. Conceptual understanding of subtle differences in political and legal environment across the countries facilitate in formulating and implementing effective strategy for international business.

SUMMARY

International political and economic systems are mutually interdependent. As a firm expands internationally, it needs to operate in multiple countries with diverse politico-economic environments. Understanding the basic dynamics of international, political, and legal environments is crucial for effective decision-making in international business. The set of ideas or beliefs people hold about political regime and its institutions, known as political ideology, influences business environment considerably. Types of political ideologies may be categorized by way of economic systems (communism, socialism, and capitalism), political systems (democracy and totalitarianism), and structure (parliamentary, commonwealth, monarchies, and theocracy).

Trade embargos and sanctions are often used as hostile political measures rather than being based on economic considerations. The extent of bureaucracy, the inefficient and obstructive administrative process, and red-tapism adversely affect the smooth conduct of business operations. Technological breakthroughs in the means of transport and communication have led to globalization of terrorism, crime, and violence. The correlation between terrorism and degree of economic freedom between nations appears to be negative. Commercial, economic, and political risks adversely affect international business operations.

The extent of judicial independence and efficiency considerably mitigates political risks in international business that vary significantly across the countries. The principal legal systems followed include common law, civil law, socialist law, and theocratic law. Unlike the countries dominated by Christianity, Hinduism, and Buddhism where either common or civil law is followed, a large number of Islamic countries integrate their legal systems based on the Sharia, the Islamic law. The basic principles of international law include the principle of sovereignty, international jurisdiction, doctrine of comity, act of state doctrine, treatment and rights of aliens, forum for hearing and settling disputes. United Nations Commission on International Trade Law (UNCITRAL) aims to harmonize and unify the laws of international trade.

The major political risks include confiscation, expropriation, nationalization, and domestication. International firms may use various risk analysis indices, such as Business Environment Risk Intelligence (BERI) Index, EIU's Risk Indices, Eurasia Group's Political Risk Index, PRS Group's International Country Risk Indices, and Failed States Index. Political risks can strategically be managed by employment nationals, sharing ownership, increased perceived economic benefits to the host country economy, following political neutrality, assuming social responsibility and adapting to local environment. Political risks in international business can be managed either through 'avoidance' by screening out the countries with higher political risks or 'insurance' by national, such as ECGC, or multilateral agencies, such as the MIGA.

KEY TERMS

Act of state doctrine All acts of other governments are considered to be valid by a country's court, even if such acts are not appropriate in the country.

Bureaucracy Form of administration based on hierarchical structure governed by a set of written rules and established procedures. The term is often used to describe inefficient and obstructive administrative process and red-tapism.

Capitalism An economic system which provides complete freedom of private ownership of productive resources and industries.

Civil law Law based on a comprehensive set of written statutes, also known as code or civil law.

Commercial risks Risks, such as non-acceptance of goods, non-payment or insolvency of the importer.

Common law Law based on tradition, past practices, and legal precedents set by the courts through interpretation of statutes, legal legislations, and past rulings that depends less on written statutes and codes.

Commonwealth countries Countries representing constitutional monarchies which recognize Queen Elizabeth II as head of the state over an independent government.

Communism Theory based on the concept of a classless society, all the major factors of production being owned by the government and shared by all the people rather than profit-seeking enterprises, for the benefit of the society.

Creeping expropriation A set of actions whose cumulative effect is to deprive investors of their fundamental rights in the investment.

Democracy Government by the people where citizens are directly involved in decision making.

Doctrine of comity There must be mutual respect for the laws, institutions, and the government systems of other countries in the matter of jurisdiction over their own citizens.

Economic risks Restrictions imposed on business activities on the grounds of national security, conserving human and natural resources, scarcity of foreign exchange, to curb unfair trade practices and to provide protection to domestic industries.

Nationality principle Every country has jurisdiction over its citizens irrespective of their locations.

Parliamentary The government consults its citizens from time to time and the parliament has power to formulate and execute laws.

Political ideology A set of ideas or beliefs that people hold about their political regime and its institutions.

Political risks Possibility of political decisions, events, or conditions in an overseas market or country that adversely affect the international business that include confiscation, expropriation, nationalization, and domestication.

Political system A system that comprises various stakeholders, such as the government, political parties with different ideologies, labour unions, religious organizations, environmental activists, and various NGOs.

Principle of sovereignty A 'sovereign' state is independent and free from all external controls and enjoys complete legal equality with other states.

Protective principle Every nation has jurisdiction over conduct that adversely affects its national security even if such behaviour occurred outside the country.

Sharia law Canonical law based on combination of teachings, mainly from Islamic religious books such as the Koran and the Sunna.

Socialism A form of government where basic and heavy industries are operated by the government so as to ensure social welfare objectives whereas small business may be privately owned.

Territoriality principle Every country has the right of jurisdiction within its own legal territory.

Terrorism Systematic use of violence to create fear in general public with an objective to achieve a political goal or convey a political message.

Theocracy The rule of god where the civil leader is believed to have a direct personal connection with god.

Theocratic law Legal system based on religious doctrine, precepts, and beliefs.

Totalitarianism Dictatorial form of centralized government, usually in the hands of a dictator who regulates every aspect of the state.

Trade embargos Prohibiting trade completely with a country so as to economically isolate it and apply political pressure on its government.

Trade sanctions Imposing selective coercive measures to restrict trade from a country.

CONCEPT REVIEW QUESTIONS

1. Explain the significance of political environment in international business with suitable examples.

2. Describe various forms of government systems on the basis of economic systems and its impact on business decisions with suitable illustrations.

3. Distinguish between common law and civil law and overlaps in the two legal systems. What are the major implications of these legal systems on international business decisions?

4. Critically examine basic principles of international law.

5. Write short notes on
   (a) UNCITRAL
   (b) BERI Index
   (c) MIGA

CRITICAL THINKING QUESTIONS

1. Carry out an analysis of trade of your country with Iraq for the last 20 years and assess the impact of UN embargo imposed on Iraq in 1991 and of the US attack on Iraq in 2003 on the international business activities.

2. Visit website of a western bank operating in Saudi Arabia and identify the adaptations made to operate under the Sharia Law.

PROJECT ASSIGNMENTS

1. Visit a firm operating in a country with considerable influence of Islamic law. Discuss with its international managers and find out key difference in the legal framework that necessitated adaptation of business strategy in Islamic law countries vis-a-vis countries following common or civil law.

2. Contact a firm that operates in a country with high incidence of terrorism, crime, and violence. Explore the strategies adopted by the firm to operate in such countries and compare it with the strategic management of political risks learnt in the chapter. Discuss your findings in class.

9

Policy Framework for International Trade

LEARNING OBJECTIVES

> To explain the significance of foreign trade policy in international business
> To elucidate trade policy options for developing countries
> To discuss instruments of trade policy
> To provide an overview of India's foreign trade policy
> To explicate policy measures for trade promotion
> To explain policy initiatives and incentives by state governments
> To examine India's trade promotion measures in the context of the WTO

9.1 INTRODUCTION

International business operations at firm level are considerably influenced by various policy measures employed to regulate trade, both by home and host countries. Exportability and importability of a firm's goods are often determined by trade policies of the countries involved. Price-competitiveness of traded goods is affected by import and export tariffs. The host country's trade and FDI policies often influence entry decisions in international markets. Policy incentives help exporters increase their profitability through foreign sales. High import tariffs and other import restrictions distort free market forces guarding domestic industry against foreign competition and support indigenous manufacturing. Therefore, a thorough understanding of the country's trade policy and incentives are crucial to the development of a successful international business strategy.

Trade policy refers to the complete framework of laws, regulations, international agreements, and negotiating stances adopted by a government to achieve legally binding market access for domestic firms.[1] It also seeks to develop rules providing predictability and security for firms. To be effective, trade policy needs to be supported

---

[1] Goode, Walter, *Dictionary of Trade Policy Terms*, 4th ed., World Trade Organization, London: Cambridge University Press, 2003, p. 356.

by domestic policies to foster innovation and international competitiveness. Besides, the trade policy should have flexibility and pragmatism. This chapter examines the trade policy options for developing countries, explains various instruments of international trade, and provides a broad framework of India's foreign trade policy and major provisions, schemes, and incentives for trade promotion.

Trade in developing countries is characterized by heavy dependence on developed countries, dominance of primary products, over-dependence on few markets and few products, and worsening of terms of trade and global protectionism, all of which make formulation and implementations of trade policy critical to economic development. The strategic options for trade policy may either be inward or outward looking. As a result of liberalization and integration of national policies with WTO agreements, there has been a strategic shift in trade policies. Like other developing countries, India's trade policies have also made a gradual shift from highly restrictive policies with emphasis on import substitution to more liberal policies geared towards export promotion.

India's foreign trade policy is formulated under the Foreign Trade (Development and Regulation) Act, for a period of five years by the Ministry of Commerce, Government of India. The government is empowered to prohibit or restrict subject to conditions, export of certain goods for reasons of national security, public order, morality, prevention of smuggling, and safeguarding balance of payments. Policy measures to promote international trade, such as schemes and incentives for duty-free and concessional imports, augmenting export production, and other export promotion measures are discussed in-depth. Policy initiatives and incentives by the state governments have also been discussed. The multilateral trading system under the WTO trade regime significantly influences trade promotion measures and member countries need to integrate their trade policies with the WTO framework. The WTO trade policy review mechanism provides an institutional framework to review trade policies of member countries at regular intervals.

9.2 TRADE POLICY OPTIONS FOR DEVELOPING COUNTRIES

There exists a huge gap in per capita income between the developed and the developing countries. Most of the world's population lives in countries that are considerably poor. Efforts to bridge the income gap between developed and developing countries, to raise living standards by increasing income levels, and to cope with the uneven development in the domestic economy, remain the central concern of economic and trade policies of developing countries. With low production base and constraints in value addition, most developing countries remain marginal players in international trade. Key characteristics of developing countries' trade include the following.

Heavy dependence upon developed countries Developing countries' trade is often dependent upon developed countries which form export destinations for the majority of their goods. Moreover, developing countries also heavily depend on developed countries for their imports. Trade among developing countries is relatively meagre.

Dominance of primary products   Exports from developing countries traditionally comprised primary products, such as agricultural goods, raw materials and fuels or labour-intensive manufactured goods, such as textiles. However, over recent years, dependence on primary products has considerably decreased, especially for newly industrialized countries, such as South Korea and Hong Kong. India's dependence on agro exports has also declined considerably from 44.2 per cent in 1960–61 to about 10 per cent in 2006–07.

Over-dependence on a few markets and a few products   A large number of developing countries are dependent on just a few markets and products for their exports. For instance, Mexico is heavily dependent[2] on the US which is the destination for 89 per cent of its total exports whereas the Dominican Republic exports 80 per cent and Trinidad and Tobago 68 per cent of its goods to the US. In terms of product composition, petroleum accounts for 96 per cent of total exports from Nigeria, 86 per cent of total exports from Saudi Arabia, and 86 per cent of total exports from Venezuela. Over the years, India's basket of export products has widened remarkably with decreased dependence on any single product category.

Worsening terms of trade   Distribution of gains from trade has always been disproportionate and therefore, a controversial issue. Developing countries often complain of deterioration in their terms of trade, mainly due to high share of primary products in their exports.

Global protectionism   Developed countries often provide heavy subsidies to their farmers for agricultural production and shield them from competition from imported products, besides imposing tariffs. Moreover, a number of non-tariff barriers such as quality requirements, sanitary and phytosanitary measures, and environmental and social issues, such as child labour offers considerable obstacles to products emanating from developing countries.

9.2.1   Strategic Options for Trade Policy

'Economic dualism', where a high-wage capital-intensive industrial sector co-exists with a low-wage unorganized traditional sector, prevails in most developing countries. Promoting indigenous industrialization and employment generation become key concerns of their economic policies. A country may adopt any of the following strategic options for its trade policy.

---

[2] UNCTAD Secretariat calculations, based on IMF, Direction of Trade Statistics, October 2005; Trade and Development Report 2006, UNCTAD, p. 83.

Inward looking strategy (import substitution)

Emphasis is laid on extensive use of trade barriers to protect domestic industries from import competition under the import-substitution strategy. Domestic production is encouraged so as to achieve self-sufficiency and imports are discouraged. Import-substitution trade strategy is often justified by the 'infant industry argument', which advocates the need of a temporary period of protection for new industries from competition from well-established foreign competitors. Most developing countries, such as Brazil, India, Mexico, Argentina, etc., during the 1950s and 1960s employed an inward-looking trade strategy. The use of high tariff structure and quota restrictions along with reserving domestic industrial activities for local firms rather than foreign investors were the key features of this import substitution policy. The pros and cons of such strategy are given below.

Pros

- Protecting start-up industries so as to enable them to grow to a size where they can compete with the industries of developed nations
- Low risk in establishing domestic industry to replace imports especially when the size of domestic market is large enough to support such industries
- High import tariffs that discourage imports but provide foreign firms an inbuilt incentive to establish manufacturing facilities, leading to industrial development, growth in economic activities, and employment generation
- Relative ease for developing countries to protect their manufacturers against foreign competition compared to getting protectionist trade barriers reduced by developed countries, in which they have little negotiating power

Cons

- Overprotection of domestic industries against international competition tends to make them inefficient
- Protection primarily available to import substituting industries which discriminates against other industries
- Manufacturers based in countries with relatively small market size find it difficult to take advantage of economies of scale and therefore have to incur high per unit costs
- Industries that substitute imports become competitive because of government incentives and import prohibitions, leading to considerable investment. Any attempt to reduce incentives or liberalize trade restrictions face strong resistance
- Government subsidies and trade restrictions tend to breed corruption

Since independence, India's trade strategy had been largely inclined to import substitution rather than export promotion. Earning foreign exchange through exports and conservation thereof had always been a high-priority task for various governments, irrespective of their political ideologies. Till 1991, India followed a strong inward-oriented trade policy to conserve foreign exchange. In order to facilitate industrialization with the objective of import substitution, important instruments used by the government included outright ban on import of some commodities, quantitative restriction, prohibitive tariff structure, which was one of the highest in the world and administrative restrictions, such as import licensing, foreign exchange regulations, local content requirements, export obligations, etc. The policy makers of India had long believed that these policy measures would make India a leading exporter with comfortable balance of trade. In reality, these initiatives did not yield the desired results, rather gave rise to corruption, complex procedures, production inefficiency, poor product quality, delay in shipment, and, in turn, decline in India's share in world exports.

The protectionist measures of the inward-oriented economy increased the profitability of domestic industries, especially in the import substitution sector. The investment made to serve the domestic market was less risky due to proven demand potential by the existing level of imports. Formidable tariff structure and trade policy barriers discouraged the entry of foreign goods into the Indian market. There was little pressure on domestic firms to be internationally competitive.

Outward looking strategy (export-led growth)

Under the outward looking strategy, the domestic economy is linked to the world economy, promoting economic growth through exports. The strategy involves incentives to promote exports rather than restrictions to imports. Major benefits of an outward looking strategy include

- Industries wherein a country has comparative advantage are encouraged, for instance labour-intensive industries in developing countries
- Increase in competition in the domestic market leads to competitive pressure on the industry to increase its efficiency and upgrade quality
- Facilitating companies to benefit from economies of scale as large output can be sold in international markets

The economic liberalization during the last decade paved the way for access of foreign goods to Indian market, applying competitive pressure even on purely domestic companies. In order to make exports, the engine of growth, export promotion, gained major thrust in India's trade policies, especially in recent years. With the integration of national trade policies and export promotion incentives with the WTO, promotional measures to encourage international marketing efforts, rather than export subsidization, have gained increased significance. Accordingly, policies were aimed at creating a business-friendly environment by eliminating redundant procedures, increasing transparency by simplifying the processes involved in the export sector, and moving away from quantitative restrictions, thereby improving the competitiveness of Indian industry and reducing the anti-export bias. Steps were taken to promote exports through multilateral and bilateral initiatives. With the decline in restrictions on trade and investment, constraints related to infrastructure and regulatory bottlenecks became increasingly evident.

9.3   INSTRUMENTS OF TRADE POLICY

Various methods employed to regulate trade are known as instruments of trade policy, which include tariffs, non-tariff measures, and financial controls.

9.3.1   Tariffs

These are official constraints on import or export of certain goods and services and are levied in the form of customs duties or tax on products moving across borders. However, tariffs are more commonly imposed on imports rather than exports. The tariff instruments may be classified as below.

On the basis of direction of trade: import vs exports tariffs   Tariffs may be imposed on the basis of direction of product movement, i.e., either on exports or imports. Generally, import tariffs or customs duties are more common than tariffs on exports. However, countries sometimes resort to impose export tariffs to conserve their scarce resources. Such tariffs are generally imposed on raw materials or primary products rather than on manufactured or value-added goods.

On the basis of purpose: protective vs revenue tariffs   The tariffs imposed to protect the home industry, agriculture, and labour against foreign competitors is termed as protective tariffs which discourage foreign goods. Historically, India had very high tariffs so as to protect its domestic industry against foreign competition. A tariff rate of 200 to 300 per cent, especially on electronic and other consumer goods, created formidable barriers for foreign products to enter the Indian market.

The government may impose tariffs to generate tax revenues from imports which are generally nominal. For instance, the UAE imposes 3–4 per cent tariffs on its imports which may not be termed as protective tariffs.

On the basis of time length: tariff surcharge vs countervailing duty   On the basis of the duration of imposition, tariffs may be classified either as surcharge or countervailing duty. Any surcharge on tariffs represents a short term action by the importing country while countervailing duties are more or less permanent in nature. The *raison d'etre* for imposition of countervailing duties is to offset the subsidies provided by the governments of the exporting countries. Countervailing duties have already been discussed in detail in Chapter 5.

On the basis of tariff rates: specific, ad-valorem, and combined   Duties fixed as a specific amount per unit of weight or any other measure are known as specific duties. For instance, these duties are in terms of rupees or US dollars per kg weight or per meter or per litre of the product. The cost, insurance, and freight (c.i.f.) value, product cost, or prices are not taken into consideration while deciding specific duties. Specific duties are considered to be discriminatory but effective in protection of cheap-value products because of their lower unit value.

Duties levied 'on the basis of value' are termed as *ad-valorem* duties. Such duties are levied as a fixed percentage of the dutiable value of imported products. In contrast to specific duties, it is the percentage of duty that is fixed. Duty collection increases or decreases on the basis of value of the product. Ad-valorem duties help protect against any price increase or decrease for an import product.

A combination of specific and ad-valorem duties on a single product is known as combined or compound duty. Under this method, both specific as well as ad-valorem rates are applied to an import product.

On the basis of production and distribution points   These are as below.

Single stage sales tax   Tax collected only at one point in the manufacturing and distribution chain is known as single stage sales tax. Single stage sales tax is generally not collected unless products are purchased by the final consumer.

Value added tax   Value added tax (VAT) is a multi-stage non-cumulative tax on consumption levied at each stage of production, distribution system, and value addition. A tax has to be paid at each time the product passes from one hand to the other in the marketing channel. However, the tax collected at each stage is based on the value addition made during the stage and not on the total value of the product till that point. VAT is collected by the seller in the marketing channel from a buyer, deducted from the VAT amount already paid by the seller on purchase of the product and remitting the balance to the government. Since VAT applies to the products sold in domestic markets and imported goods, it is considered to be non-discriminatory. Besides, VAT also conforms to the WTO norms.

Cascade tax   Taxes levied on the total value of the product at each point in manufacturing and distribution channel, including taxes borne by the product at earlier stages, are known as cascade taxes. India had a long regime of cascade taxes wherein the taxes were levied at a later stage of marketing channel over the taxes already borne by the product. Such a taxation system adds to the cost of the product, making goods non-competitive in the market.

Excise tax   Excise tax is a one-time tax levied on the sale of a specific product. Alcoholic beverages and cigarettes in most countries tend to attract more excise duty.

Turnover tax   In order to compensate for similar taxes levied on domestic products, a turnover or equalization tax is imposed. Although the equalization or turnover tax hardly equalizes prices, its impact is uneven on domestic and imported products.

9.3.2 Non-tariff Measures

Contrary to tariffs, which are straightforward, non-tariff measures are non-transparent and obstruct trade on discriminatory basis. As the WTO regime calls for binding of tariffs wherein the member countries are not free to increase the tariffs at their will, non-tariff barriers in innovative forms are emerging as powerful tools to restrict imports on discriminatory basis. The major non-tariff policy instruments include

Government participation in trade State trading, governments' procurement policies, and providing consultations to foreign companies on a regular basis are often used as disguised protection of national interests and barrier to foreign firms. A subsidy is a financial contribution provided directly or indirectly by a government that confers a benefit. Various forms of subsides include cash payment, rebate in interest rates, value added tax, corporate income tax, sales tax, insurance, freight and infrastructure, etc. As subsidies are discriminatory in nature, direct subsidies are not permitted under the WTO trade regime.

Customs and entry procedure Custom classification, valuation, documentation, various types of permits, inspection requirements, and health and safety regulations are often used to hinder free flow of trade and discriminate among the exporting countries. These constitute an important non-tariff barrier. However, WTO legislation attempts to rationalize these barriers as discussed in Chapter 5.

Quotas Quotas are the quantitative restrictions on exports/imports intended at protecting local industries and conserving foreign exchange. The various types of quotas include

Absolute quota These quotas are the most restrictive, limiting in absolute terms, the quantity imported during the quota period. Once the quantity of the import quota is fulfilled, no further imports are allowed.

Tariff quotas They allow import of specified quantity of quota products at reduced rate of duty. However, excess quantities over the quota can be imported subject to a higher rate of import duty. Using such a combination of quotas and tariffs facilitates some import, but at the same time discourages through higher tariffs, excessive quantities of imports.

Voluntary quotas Voluntary quotas are unilaterally imposed in the form of a formal arrangement between countries or between a country and an industry. Such agreements generally specify the import limit in terms of product, country, and volume.

The multi-fibre agreement (MFA) had been the largest voluntary quota arrangement wherein developed countries forced an agreement on economically weaker countries so as to provide artificial protection to their domestic industry. However, with the integration of multi-fibre agreement with the WTO, the quota regime got scrapped by 1 January 2005. Summarily, all sorts of quotas have a restrictive effect on free flow of goods across countries.

Other trade restrictions Other trade restrictions include minimum export price (MEP), wherein the government may fix a minimum price for exports so as to safeguard the interests of domestic consumers. Presently, India's trade policy does not impose any restriction of minimum export price.

9.3.3 Financial Controls

Governments often impose a variety of financial restrictions to conserve the foreign currencies restricting their markets. Such restrictions include exchange control, multiple exchange rates, prior import deposit, credit restrictions, and restriction on repatriation of profits. India had long followed a stringent exchange control regime to conserve foreign currencies.

9.3.4 Demand vs Supply Side Policy Measures

Policy instruments for promoting exports may also operate on the supply and demand side. Initiatives for creating and expanding export production, developing transportation networks, port facilities, tax and investment systems form parts of supply side policies. The demand side initiatives for export promotion include programmes to alert companies to the opportunities present in international markets and to strengthen the commitment and skills of those already involved.

9.4 INDIA'S FOREIGN TRADE POLICY

The foreign trade policy in India is formulated and implemented mainly by the Ministry of Commerce and Industry, but also in consultation with other concerned ministries, such as Finance, Agriculture, and Textiles, and the Reserve Bank of India (RBI). The Directorate General of Foreign Trade (DGFT) under the Department of Commerce is responsible for the execution of the foreign trade policy. The Directorate General of Anti-Dumping and Allied Duties was constituted in April 1998 to carry out investigations and to recommend levels of anti-dumping duty. The responsibilities of the Ministry of Finance include setting import duties and other border and internal taxes, surveying the working of customs, assisting and advising on implementation of the WTO Customs Valuation Agreement, and undertaking investigations to impose safeguard measures. The Ministry of Agriculture designs the National Agriculture Policy, which is aimed at ensuring an adequate supply of essential food at 'reasonable' prices, securing a reasonable standard of living for farmers and agricultural workers, developing agriculture and rural infrastructure, and helping the sector face the challenges arising out of globalization in a WTO-compatible manner. The Ministry of Agriculture and the Ministry of Commerce formulate India's proposals for WTO negotiations on agriculture. The Ministry of Textiles is in charge of promoting exports of textiles, and of managing quotas maintained by importing countries. The RBI manages the exchange rate policy and also regulates interest rates, for instance, for pre- and post-shipment export credit.

The export-import (exim) policy was earlier formulated under Import and Export (Control) Act, 1947 which came into existence on 25 March 1947. Initially the Act was for a three-year duration but was extended till 31 March 1977 for varying periods. Thereafter, it was extended for an indefinite period. In 1992, the Import and Export (Control) Act, 1947 was replaced by the Foreign Trade (Development and Regulation)

Act, whereby the Chief Controller of Exports and Imports was designated as Director General of Foreign Trade.

Till 1985, the exim policy for each financial year used to be announced by means of public notice in the Gazette of India. In order to ensure continuity in operations and provide stability to the external sector the exim policy was first announced for a three-year duration during 1985–88. The objective of formulating long-term policy was to reduce unpredictability in the external trade regime with minimum changes of exceptional nature during the validity of the policy. However, the frequency of unabated changes has necessitated issuance of revised annual policies. The five year Exim Policy (2002–07) launched co-terminus with the tenth five year plan up to 31 March 2007, was terminated mid-length and replaced with the Foreign Trade Policy with effect from 1 April 2004 for a period of five years to remain in force up to 31 March 2009.

The foreign trade policy outlines a country's export promotion measures, policies, and procedures related to foreign trade. India's foreign trade policy is built around the following two objectives:

- To double India's share in global merchandise trade within the next five years
- To act as an effective instrument of economic growth by giving a thrust to employment generation

In order to achieve these objectives, the strategies adopted are

- Unshackling of controls and creating an atmosphere of trust and transparency to unleash the innate entrepreneurship of India's businessmen, industrialists, and traders.
- Simplifying procedures and bringing down transaction costs
- Neutralizing incidence of all levies and duties on inputs used in export products, based on the fundamental principle that duties and levies should not be exported
- Facilitating development of India as a global hub for manufacturing, trading, and services
- Identifying and nurturing special focus areas so as to generate additional employment opportunities
- Facilitating technological and infrastructural up gradation of Indian economy, especially through import of capital goods and equipment leading to increase in value addition, productivity, and quality
- Strengthening role of Indian embassies in export

The foreign trade policy is published in four volumes as given here.

1. *Foreign Trade Policy:* Contains provisions and schemes related to exports and imports
2. *Handbook of Procedures Volume I:* Contains export-import procedures to be followed by all concerned, such as an exporter or an importer, authorizing, or any competent authority

3. *Handbook of Procedures Volume II (Schedule of DEPB Rates):* Contains input-output norms used for working out the proportion of various inputs used / required in manufacture of resultant products so as to determine the advance authorization entitlement and Duty Entitlement Pass Book (DEPB) rates

4. *ITC (HS) Classification of Export and Import Items:* Serves as a comprehensive reference manual for finding out exportability or importability of products with reference to the current foreign trade policy

9.4.1 Export Prohibitions and Restrictions

Under the foreign trade policy, export prohibitions are maintained for environmental, food security, marketing, pricing and domestic supply reasons, and to comply with international treaties. Restrictions on exports on account of security concern through multilateral agreements are contained in the Special Chemicals, Organisms, Materials, and Equipments and Technologies (SCOMET) list. Export restrictions are GATT-compatible and permitted under Articles XIX and XX (Security Exceptions). Since the SCOMET list is a negative list, licensing procedure is based on the presumption of denial. The SCOMET list is an aggregated outcome of the country's commitments to international efforts towards non-proliferation and the combined elements of multilateral arrangements, such as the Chemical Weapons Conventions (CWC) and the Biological and Toxins Weapons Convention (BTWC) and unilateral controls that a country exercises on dual use of goods and technologies, including nuclear materials and technologies.

Exports from India are free except in case where these are regulated by the provisions of foreign trade policy or any other law in force. Under the current Foreign Trade policy, export of wild animals, exotic birds, tallow, wood products, beef and offal of cows, oxen and calves, undersized rock lobsters and sand lobsters, sandalwood products, certain species of sea shells, peacock tail feathers, including the handicrafts and other articles using them, manufactured articles and shavings from shed antlers of deer, human skeletons, certain endangered species of wild orchid and plants are prohibited. In addition to these export prohibitions, India also issues ad hoc prohibitions on exports of sensitive products, for example, export prohibitions have also been issued for wheat, pulses, and sugar.

Export of restricted items is permitted only after obtaining authorization from DGFT. The export licensing requirements have been reduced considerably and the remaining restrictions on exports are essentially maintained for food safety and security reasons. The list of items restricted for exports include cattle, horses, camel, seaweed, and chemical fertilizers.

Onions may be exported through designated state-trading enterprises, without quantitative ceiling, subject to conditions of quality laid out by the National Agricultural Co-operative Marketing Federation of India Ltd (NAFED) from time to time. In addition, quantitative ceilings are notified by the DGFT for sandalwood oil and sandalwood chips, recommended by the Ministry of Environment and Forests to conserve natural resources. All the quotas are allocated by the DGFT. Quotas for wheat and wheat products, grain and flour of barley, maize, bajra, ragi and jowar, butter, non-basmati rice and lentils, gram, and beans and flour made from them were removed in March 2002.

Trade with the Democratic People's Republic of Korea is prohibited. Additionally, export and import of arms and related material to and from Iraq is prohibited. Trade of all sorts of goods and technology related to nuclear facilities and its development to Iran is also prohibited. However, the earlier restrictions on exports to Libya, Fiji, and Iraq have now been lifted.

Export taxes

Presently there is no tax on exports from India with the exception of tanned and untanned hide, skins and leathers, except for manufacturers of leathers, ranging from 10 per cent to 20 per cent of freight on board (f.o.b.) value. However, in order to curb rapid price rise in the domestic markets and to discourage exports, an export duty of 15 per cent on semi-finished steel products, 5 per cent on galvanized sheets, and Rs 8,000 per ton on basmati rice was imposed[3] in April 2008. An export cess applied to various products including coffee, spices, tobacco and other agricultural commodities has been repealed by the Cess Laws (Repealing and Amending) Act, 2005, enacted in 2006.

9.4.2 Import Prohibitions and Restrictions

The Indian government is authorized to maintain import prohibitions and restrictions under section 11 of the Customs Act, 1962, which allows the central government to prohibit imports and exports of certain goods either absolutely or subject to conditions by notifications in the Official Gazette.[4] The DGFT may adopt and enforce any restrictive measure in the trade policy[5] through a notification necessary for

- Protection of public morals
- Protection of human, animal, or plant life or health
- Protection of patents, trademarks, and copyrights and the prevention of deceptive practices
- Prevention of use of prison labour
- Protection of national treasures of artistic, historic, or archaeological value
- Conservation of exhaustible natural resources
- Protection of trade of fissionable material or material from which they are derived
- Prevention of traffic in arms, ammunitions, and implements of war

---

[3] 'Government Imposes Export Duty on Basmati Rise', *Business Standard* and 'India to impose Export Duty on Steel, Rice', *Financial Express,* 29 April 2008, New Delhi.

[4] Under Section 11(2), Customs Act, 1962.

[5] Foreign Trade Policy (2004–09), Ministry of Commerce, Government of India, updated as on 1 April 2008, pp. 24–25.

Trade policies subsequent to 31 March 2001, provide free importability status of goods unless prohibited or restricted which can be freely imported by any person. This has been a reversal of the previous policies' 'Open General Licence (OGL)' status of the freely imported items which also needed permission from the licensing authorities who had discretion to modify, circumscribe, or deny permission on the grounds of regulating imports. Import prohibitions may be made for a number of reasons, such as national security, public order, morality, prevention of smuggling, conservation of foreign exchange, and safeguarding balance of payment. Presently, only a few items are prohibited for imports[6] as under:

- Tallow, fat and/or oils, rendered or unrendered of any animal origin
- Animal rennet
- Wild animals including their parts and products and Ivory
- Beef and products containing beef in any form
- Natural sponges
- Fish waste
- Domestic and wild birds, live pig; meat and meat products from avian species and pig; products from animal and bird origin intended for animal feed, agriculture, and industrial use
- Specified avian animal products from countries reporting the outbreak of highly pathogenic influenza

In view of integration of India's trade policy with the WTO, India was under obligation to remove import restrictions. However, India maintained import licensing measures under GATT article 18b for balance of payment reasons. As a result of consultation under WTO, India agreed and implemented the phasing out of remaining restrictions by 1 April 2001.

Presently, the import restrictions are maintained only on a limited number of products for reasons of health, security, and public morals. These include firearms and ammunitions, certain medicines and drugs, poppy seeds, some products for preservation of wild life and environment. Besides, India's sanitary and phyto-sanitary laws require authorization for import of seeds for sowing and for agriculture and processed food products. The policy also restricts import of second-hand motor vehicles more than three years old due to environmental reasons. The restricted items can only be imported subject to certain conditions stipulated in the foreign trade policy.

8.4.3   Policy Measures for Trade Promotion

A large number of measures taken to promote trade under the foreign trade policy include various schemes for duty-free and concessional imports for export production, schemes and incentives to augment export production, and other export promotion measures to facilitate marketing.

---

[6] Complied from Foreign Trade Policy 2004–09, Ministry of Commerce, Government of India, and related circulars.

Schemes for duty-free and concessional imports

In order to reduce or remove the anti-export bias inherent in the system of indirect taxation and to encourage exports, several schemes have been evolved allowing exporters to benefit from tariff exemptions, especially on imported inputs. Such schemes include drawbacks for customs duty paid and exemptions from payment of import duty. The government has estimated revenue forgone from these schemes at Rs 537.7 billion in 2006–07, up from provisional figures of Rs 375.9 billion for the previous year; the largest shares are accounted for the Advance Authorization Scheme (32.8%) and the EOU/EHTP/STP Scheme (25.4%). In order to facilitate readers' understanding, schemes for duty free and concessional imports have been summarized in Table 9.1.

Export promotion capital goods scheme   In order to strengthen the export production base, the Export Promotion Capital Goods Scheme (EPCG) was introduced in 1990 so as to enable import of capital goods at concessional rate of duty subject to an appropriate export obligation accepted by the exporter. The scheme aimed to reduce the incidence of high capital cost on export prices so as to make exports competitive in the international markets by way of reduced import duty on capital goods.

Initially, import of new capital goods up to a maximum c.i.f. value of Rs 100 million were permitted at concessional rate of customs duty of 25 per cent. The general rate of customs duty was very high when the scheme was introduced. As the customs duties on capital goods were reduced, the import duty under EPCG scheme also reduced gradually. In 1992, import duty on capital goods was lowered to 15 per cent with export obligation of four times to be fulfilled in five years which was further lowered to 10 per cent in 1997 and 5 per cent in 2000.

Under the foreign trade policy 2004–09, the EPCG scheme allows import of capital goods for pre-production, production, post-production, including semi-knocked down (SKD) or completely knocked down (CKD) conditions and computer software systems at 5 per cent customs duty subject to an export obligation equivalent to eight times the duty saved on capital goods imported under the scheme. However, the customs duty has further been reduced[7] to 3 per cent from 1 April 2008. The new foreign trade policy has dispensed with the block-wise fulfilment on export obligation, simplifying the scheme. The export obligation is to be fulfilled over a specified period of eight years from the date of issuance of the authorization. However, for EPCG authorizations for a duty-saved-value of Rs 1 billion or more, the same export obligation is to be fulfilled over a period of 12 years.

In case of agro units, and units in cottage or tiny sector, import of capital goods at 3 per cent custom duty shall be allowed subject to fulfilment of export obligation equivalent to six times the duty saved on capital goods imported in 12 years from authorization issue-date whereas the export obligation equivalent to six times of duty saved on capital goods in eight years is required for SSI units.

---

[7] Foreign Trade Policy (2004–09), Ministry of Commerce, Government of India, updated as on 1 April 2008.

Table 9.1 Schemes for duty-free and concessional imports

Scheme	Eligibility	Concessions	Performance requirements
Export Promotion Capital Goods (EPCG)	Manufacturer exporters with or without supporting manufacturers/vendors; merchant exporters tied to supporting manufacturers and service providers.	3% duty on imports of capital goods, spares, tools and consumables, existing plant and machinery imported/to be imported under the scheme.	Export obligation of eight times the duty saved on capital goods imported to be met over eight years (six times over 12 year for agri units, and six times over eight years for SSI units provided that, for SSIs, the c.i.f. value of the imported goods does not exceed Rs 2.5 million and the total investment in plants and machinery does not exceed the SSI limit.)[a]
Duty exemption schemes			
Advance authorization (previously advance licence)	Manufacturer exporter or merchant exporter tied up with the manufacturer subject to actual user condition even after fulfillment of export obligation.	Zero duty on imports of inputs for export production. Duty-free import of spare parts required for the manufacture of the finished products may also be permitted up to 10% of the c.i.f. value of authorization.	Export obligation of positive value addition (except for certain products such as gems and jewellery, tea, etc.) and export of goods within 24 months from the date of issuance of the authorization.
Duty-free import authorization	Manufacturer exporter or merchant exporter tied up with the manufacturer subject to actual user condition until export obligation is fulfilled.	Zero duty on imports of inputs including fuel, energy, etc. that are consumed or utilized in the course of exports production.	Export obligation with minimum value addition of 20% (except for certain items such as gems and jewellery, tea, etc.) and export of goods within 24 months from the date of the authorization.
Duty remission scheme			
Duty-Free Replenishment Certificate (DFRC)		Scheme phased out from 1 May 2006.	

Scheme	Eligibility	Concessions	Performance requirements
Duty Entitlement Passbook Scheme (DEPB)	Merchant exporter or manufacturer exporter entitled to duty-free import of inputs (basic customs duty component only) of inputs used in the manufacture of goods. This is a post-export scheme and the certificate is freely transferable.	Neutralization of the incidence of basic customs duty on the import content of the export product by way of grant of duty credit against the export product.	Duty reimbursed as a percentage of exports as notified separately for different products in the DEPB Schedule.
Deemed exports	Goods manufactured in India and supplied: against advance authorization/DFIA to EOUs, STPs, EHTPs or BTPs; EPCG licence holders; projects financed by multilateral or bilateral agencies; projects notified by the Ministry of Finance; power projects and refineries; projects funded by UN agencies; nuclear power projects through competitive bidding; and the supply of marinefreight container by 100% EOUs provided they are exported within six months or a period permitted by customs.	*Pre-export Duty Neutralization Schemes:* Duty Free import of inputs under Advance Authorization Scheme in addition, exemptions from excise duty by way of Central Excise exemption notification. *Post Export Duty Neutralization Schemes:* Customs/Excise duty neutralization by way of refund under deemed export drawback scheme, Terminal Excise Duty Refund Scheme etc.	Export obligation in terms of quantity and specified value added required. For post-export neutralization scheme, the duty component refunded is as per the actual exports and/or the notified rate schedule.

[a] 50% of the export obligation must be met within the first six years. If the duty saved is Rs 1 billion or more, the export obligation may be fulfilled over a 12-year period with the first 50% to be met within 10 years.

Source: *Foreign Trade Policy 2004–09,* and *Handbook of Procedures,* vol. 1, Department of Commerce, Government of India, New Delhi, as updated on 1 April 2008.

Besides, agro units in the Agri Export Zones and units under the rehabilitation package are eligible for a longer export obligation period of 12 years. The export obligation is over and above the average level of exports achieved by EPCG authorization holder in the preceding three licensing years for same or similar products. The export obligation must be fulfilled by the export of goods being manufactured or produced by the use of the capital goods imported under the scheme.

Manufacturing obligations under the scheme are, in addition to any other export obligation undertaken by the importer except the export obligation for the same product under advance authorization, DFRC, DEPB, or Drawback scheme.

Manufacturing exporters with or without supporting manufacturers or vendors, merchant exporters tied to supporting manufacturers, and service providers are eligible for import of capital goods under the scheme. Capital goods, including spares, jigs, fixtures, dies, and moulds can be imported under the scheme. Besides, components of such capital goods for assembly or manufacture of capital goods and spares of existing plant and machinery can also be imported under the scheme. Import of capital goods is subject to the actual user condition till the export obligation is fulfilled. For import of capital goods under the scheme for c.i.f. value upto Rs 500 million, authorization is granted by the Regional Authority (RA) while for c.i.f. value above Rs 500 million, application may be made directly to the DGFT headquarters with a copy endorsed to the concerned RA.

Benefits
- For firms with export markets, the scheme provides an opportunity to import capital goods at a concessional rate of import duty and substantial reduction in initial costs. Alternatively, a firm can opt for an export oriented unit (EOU) and import capital goods duty free.
- EPCG scheme is considered superior to EOUs as there are no liabilities for customs duties after fulfilment of export obligation whereas in case of EOUs, it is only deferment of import duties. However, customs duties are to be paid upon debonding at the depreciated value.
- Unlike EOUs, there are no restrictions on the quantum of domestic sales in case of imports under EPCG.

Limitations
- In case of failure to fulfil the export obligation, an exporter has to pay the customs duties saved in proportion of unfulfilled portion of export obligations along with interest as prescribed by the customs authority.

Duty exemption schemes   Duty exemption schemes enable duty-free import of inputs required for export production. Under the duty exemption scheme, an advance authorization is used as discussed below.

Advance authorization   An advance authorization is issued to allow duty-free import of physical inputs incorporated in export products after making normal allowance in wastage. In addition, consumables, such as fuel, oil, energy, catalysts, etc., are also allowed under the scheme. Advance authorization can be issued for

Physical exports (including exports to SEZs)   Advance authorization issued to manufacturer exporters or merchant exporters tied to supporting manufacturer(s) for import of inputs required for export production

Intermediate supplies   Advance authorization issued for intermediate supplies to a manufacturer exporter for the import of inputs required for the manufacture of goods for supply to the ultimate exporter/deemed exporter holding another advance authorization

Deemed exports   Advance authorization is also issued for deemed exports. The main contractor for import of inputs required in the manufacture of goods for supply to the categories specified in Chapter 8 of the foreign trade policy.

Advance authorization is issued for duty-free import of inputs, subject to actual user conditions and advance authorizations (other than advanced authorization for deemed exports) are exempted from payment of basic customs duty, additional customs duty, anti-dumping duty, and safeguard duty, if any. Advance authorization for deemed exports are exempted from only basic customs duty and additional customs duty. However, in case of supplies to EOUs/SEZs/EHTHs/STPs under advance authorizations, anti- dumping duty, and safeguard duty is also exempted.

Input output and value addition norms   Input output norms are description of inputs which are required for production of particular products. The compiled Standard Input Output Norms (SION) are published in volume II of the *Handbook of Procedures*. These SION are used for determination of proportion of various inputs which are physically used and consumed for export production and the packaging material.

The value addition is calculated as

$$VA = \frac{A - B}{B} \times 100$$

where,

VA   is value addition
A   is the f.o.b. (free on board) value of the exports realized/f.o.r. (free on rail) value of supply received.
B   is the c.i.f. (cost, insurance, and freight) value of the imported inputs covered by the authorization, plus any other imported materials used on which the benefit of duty drawback is being claimed.

In SION, a duty-free authorization is required to maintain minimum value addition of 33 per cent. However, minimum value addition condition is not applicable on authorizations issued under the Advance Authorisation Scheme as in such cases; the condition imposed is of positive value addition which means *any* positive value addition. Thus, even 1 per cent value addition is sufficient. Exports for which payments are not received in freely convertible currency are subject to value addition of 33 per cent or the percentage of value addition indicated in SION norms, whichever is higher. In case of advance authorization for deemed export, value addition to be maintained should be positive and not 33 per cent (Appendix 32 of *Handbook*) as which is applicable only for exports to Rupee Payment Area (RPA) and is in no way linked to deemed exports.

The period for fulfilment of export obligations under advance authorization commences from the date of issue of the authorization. The export obligation is to be fulfilled within a period of 24 months. In the case of supplies under advance authorization for deemed exports/advance authorization to the projects/turnkey projects in India or abroad where the export obligation must be fulfilled during the contracted duration of execution of the project.

Benefits and limitations of advance authorization   Since advance authorization provides duty free import of inputs and consumables for export production in advance, it is useful when large quantities of standard raw material are required for production.

As the import under advance authorization is allowed on actual-user condition, hence the authorization or materials imported against it are not transferable even after discharge of export obligation. Merchant exporters are not eligible for advance authorisation scheme but can avail benefits under Duty Free Import Authorization (DFIA), or Duty Entitlement Pass Book (DEPB), or Duty Drawback.

Duty Free Import Authorization Scheme   The scheme, launched on 1 May 2006 replaced the Duty Free Replenishment Certificate (DFRC) Scheme. Under the scheme, duty free import of inputs, including fuel, oil, energy sources, and catalysts is allowed for production of export products subject to manufacturer exporters or merchant exporters tied up with the manufacturer for the import of inputs used in the manufacture of exports. It offers exemptions in respect of custom duty, additional duty, education cess, and anti-dumping or safeguard duties in force for inputs used in exports. Duty-free imports of mandatory spares are also allowed up to a maximum of 10 per cent of import value, which must be exported with the manufactured product. The imported items or the authorization are subject to actual user conditions until the export obligation is fulfilled. The main difference between the DFIA and the Advance Authorization Scheme seems to be that the advance authorization scheme requires positive value added in exports and the DFIA requires minimum value added of 20 per cent.

Duty remission schemes

Duty remission schemes enable post-export replenishment of duty on inputs used for export production under various schemes, such as DEPB scheme, duty drawback, incentives for deemed exports, and the gems and jewellery sector.

Duty Entitlement Passbook Scheme   Under the DEPB, grant of customs duty credit against the export product is provided on its import content. The scheme was introduced in 1997 wherein actual imports going into the export products were calculated on a case-by-case basis under actual user conditions. Under the DEPB scheme, merchant or manufacturer exporters are entitled to duty-free import (basic customs duty component only) of inputs used in manufacture of goods, as a specified percentage of f.o.b. value of exports made in freely convertible currency. The scheme allows naturalization of the incidence of basic customs duty on inputs used for export production. The holder of DEPB also has an option to pay additional customs duty, if any, in cash. The DEPB is valid for a period of 12 months from the date of its issuance. It is also valid up to the last date of its month of expiry. The transfer of DEPB is subject to import at the specified port in DEPB or for the port from which exports have been made.

Benefits and limitations of DEPB   DEPB is a fully transferable instrument which can be availed by manufacturers as well as merchant exporters. The credit rates under DEPB are generally better than drawback since these rates are worked out to neutralize the incidence of customs duty by assuming the inputs as imported. Moreover, special additional duty (SAD) is not levied on the duty paid through DEPB, which has made it more attractive. The DEPB authorization as well as the goods imported against it are freely transferable.

DEPB rates are fixed only for those items for which standard input output norms exist, while export under DEPB is allowed only when DEPB rates for those items exist. Therefore, export of items for which DEPB rates are not declared cannot avail the benefit of DEPB. Further, DEPB is available against physical exports only and not against deemed exports. However, under the current foreign trade policy, DEPB has been made available on exports to Special Economic Zones (SEZs), which are treated as physical exports and not deemed exports.[8]

Promotional measures for deemed exports

Transactions in which goods supplied do not leave the country and payments for such supplies is received either in domestic currency (i.e. Indian rupees) or in free foreign exchange, are termed as deemed exports. Under the foreign trade policy, the following categories of supplies of goods manufactured in India, are considered 'deemed exports':

- Supply of goods against advance authorization/duty-free import authorization (DFIA)
- Supply of capital goods to holders of authorization under the EPCG Scheme
- Supply of goods to EOUs, STPs, EHTPs, or BTPs
- Supply of goods to projects financed by multilateral or bilateral agencies under specified conditions of the Ministry of Finance
- Supply to projects funded by UN agencies
- Supply of goods to nuclear power projects through competitive bidding

---

[8] Foreign Trade Policy (2004–09), Ministry of Commerce, Government of India, updated as on 1 April 2008.

- Supply of goods to power projects or refineries under specified conditions
- Supply of goods to any project or purpose where import of such goods at zero import duty is permitted by the Ministry of Finance
- Supply of 'stores' on board of foreign going vessels/aircrafts subject to conditions specified Standard Input-Output Norms (SION).

Manufacture and supply of goods qualifying as deemed exports are eligible for a number of benefits, including

- Supply of goods against advance authorization or DFIA
- Deemed export drawback
- Exemption from terminal excise duty where supplies are made against International Competitive Bidding (ICB). In other cases, refund of terminal excise duty is given.

Duty drawback

Duty drawback is admissible under Customs Act 1962 for re-exports of goods on which import duty has paid (section 7) and for imported material used in the manufacture of exports (section 75). Duty drawback is defined as the rebate of duty chargeable on any imported or excisable material used in the manufacture of goods exported from India. The drawback consists of two components:

- The 'customs allocation', which includes the basic customs duty rate and the special additional duty
- The 'central excise allocation', which includes the additional duty and the excise duty on locally produced inputs

Drawback rates are drawn up annually and released soon after the annual budget is introduced in Parliament. The rates are based on parameters, including the prevailing prices of inputs, standard input-output norms published by the DGFT, share of imports in total inputs, and the applied rates of duty; in most cases, the drawback is less than 100 per cent of the import duty paid. Although the rates are based on a mixed classification, they are fully aligned with the HS nomenclature at the HS 4-digit level. The rates are expressed as a percentage of the f.o.b. value of exports.

The drawback rates are fixed, either for any class of products manufactured, known as all industry rates, or for a product manufactured by a particular manufacturer, known as brand rates.

All industry rates These are published in the form of notification by the government every year and are normally valid for one year. All industry rates are calculated on the basis of broad averages of consumption of inputs, duties and taxes paid, quantity of wastages and f.o.b. prices of export products. The rates are either on quantity basis (e.g., per kg. or per tonne) or on *ad valorem* basis, for example, percentage of f.o.b. value. These rates are reviewed and revised periodically, taking into account variation in consumption pattern of inputs and duties offered thereon. It is estimated that all industry rates neutralize around 70–80 per cent of the total duty paid on the inputs for export production.

Brand rate/special brand rates   If all industry rates are unavailable or if it is felt that duty drawback provides inadequate compensation for import duty paid on inputs, the exporter may request for the establishment of 'special brand rates'. The special brand rates are envisaged to neutralise up to 90–95 per cent of total tax paid on inputs.

However, while the all-industry rates are based on average rates of consumption of inputs and rates of duty paid, the special brand rate scheme is product- and exporter-specific, requiring the detailed submission of proof of duty payments by the exporter.

Drawback is available on the following items.

- Materials and components used in the process of manufacture
- Irrecoverable wastage which arises in the manufacturing process
- Material used for packing the finished export products
- Finished products

Drawback is also allowed on good originally imported into India and exported within two years from payment of import duty under section 74 of Customs Act 1962. For goods exported without being used, 98 per cent of the import duty is refunded; for goods exported after use, the percentage of duty refunded varies depending on the period between import and export of the product. The rates range from 85 per cent of import duty for goods that remain in the country for up to six months, to 30 per cent for goods that remain in the country for between 30 and 36 months. Drawback under this provision is not allowed for apparel, tea chests, exposed cinematographic films passed by the Board of Film Censors in India, unexposed photographic films, paper and plates, and x-ray films, and for cars that have been used for over four years. Drawback is admissible, irrespective of the mode of exports.

The rate of drawback is notified by the Directorate of Drawback under the Ministry of Finance, generally three months after the budget is introduced in Parliament.

Duty drawback is an incentive widely used around the world with the objective to provide a level playing field to the country's exporters so as to exclude export production from the incidence of import duty and other indirect taxation. The duty drawback system has worked quite well in India, except for operational constraints faced by the exporters in getting drawback reimbursements.

Schemes for concessional imports for gems and jewellery

The gems and jewellery sector accounts for about 14 per cent of India's total exports. This sector is characterized by import of goods in rough or raw form of diamonds and semi-precious stones and gold and silver for value addition and conversion to finished products. Thus, this sector largely comprises export of services as a result of necessary skills and infrastructure available in India. The summary of sector-specific schemes for concessional imports in Table 9.2 indicates the government's concern to nurture and promote exports from the gems and jewellery sector.

Table 9.2   Schemes of concessional imports for gems and jewellery exports

Scheme	Eligibility	Concessions	Performance requirements
Replenishment authorization	Exporters of gems and jewellery	Post-export authorization for duty-free import of inputs such as precious stones, semi-precious and synthetic, and pearls and empty jewellery boxes up to 5% of the overall import value authorized.	Quantity of duty-free inputs allowed as per the entitlement and value addition notified in the Handbook.
Schemes for duty-free procurement of precious metal etc.	Manufacturers of jewellery for export; inputs are based on the actual user conditions	Duty-free purchase of precious metal inputs from nominated agencies (primarily banks) authorized by the Reserve Bank of India, MMTC Ltd., STC Ltd, Handicraft and Handloom Export Corporation, PEC. Certain Categories of exporters are also allowed to import directly.	Export obligation subject to minimum value added ranging from 2% to 6.5% depending on the products and the wastage norms as notified in the Handbook.
Advance authorization for import/ procurement for precious metal, mountings etc.	Manufacturers of jewellery for export; inputs are based on the actual user conditions	Duty-free import of gold of fineness of not less than 0.995 and mountings, sockets, frames, and findings of 8 carats and above; silver of fineness not less than 0.995 and mountings, sockets, frames, and findings containing over 50% silver by weight; and plaatinum of fineness not less than 0.900 and mountings, sockets, frames, and findings containing more than 50% platinum by weight.	All products using duty-free inputs to be exported subject to minimum value added ranging from 2% to 6.5%, depending on the products and the wastage norms as notified in the Handbook.
Diamond imprest authorization	Exporters of cut and polished diamonds who hold Status Certificate as stipulated in the Foreign Trade Policy	Duty-free import of cut and polished diamonds including semi-processed diamonds, cut and broken diamonds. The entitlement is 5% of the export performance of the preceding year of cut and polished diamonds.	The imported inputs must be exported within six months of import with minimum value added of 10%.

Source: Foreign Trade Policy 2004–09; Handbook of Procedures, vol. 1, Department of Commerce, Government of India, New Delhi as updated on 1 April 2008.

9.4.4 Schemes to Augment Export Production

Development of export-related infrastructure and enclaves providing an environment conducive for export production is crucial to sustain export growth. The government has always supported creation and strengthening of enclaves for export production so as to 'immunize' the firms engaged in export production from constraints, such as infrastructural and administrative, from the rest of the economy. Schemes to augment export production are summarized in Table 9.3. These schemes attempt to reduce the burden of import duty and indirect taxation on capital goods and consumables and reduce operational hassles.

Table 9.3 Schemes to augment export production

Scheme	Eligibility	Concessions	Performance requirements
Export-Oriented Units (EOUs), Electronic Hardware Technology Parks (EHTPs), Software Technology Parks (STPs) and Bio-Technology Parks (BTPs)	EOUs, or units set up in the EHTPs, STPs or BTPs that undertake to export their entire production of goods and services (except permissible sales in domestic tariff area (DTA)). Trading units are not covered.	Duty-free imports of all types of goods, including new and second-hand capital goods, provided these are not prohibited for import including from the DTA or bonded warehouses.	All products and services to be exported, with some exceptions.
Special Economic Zones (SEZs)	Units based in the special economic zones.	Duty-free imports of all types of goods. Imports from DTA treated as deemed exports. These units also benefit from tax holidays under the Income Tax Act.	Units based in SEZs have to be net foreign exchange earners, failing which punitive action can be taken. Performance is also evaluated on the basis of additional employment, investment, and infrastructure generation.
Free-Trade and Warehousing Zones		As above	As above
Agricultural Export Zones (AEZs)	Exporters of products in the agriculture and allied sectors that are based in the AEZs.	As for EPCG	

Source: Foreign Trade Policy 2004–09; Handbook of Procedures, vol. 1, Department of Commerce, Government of India, New Delhi, as updated on 1 April 2008.

Export oriented units, electronic hardware technology parks, software technology parks, and bio-technology parks

A number of schemes were introduced for units engaged in export production of goods and services such as Export Oriented Units (EOUs), Electronic Hardware Technology Parks (EHTPs), Software Technology Parks (STPs), and Bio-Technology Parks (BTPs). The schemes cover units engaged in manufacture of goods primarily for exports including repair, re-making, reconditioning, re-engineering, and rendering of services, but excludes trading units as discussed below.

Export Oriented Units The scheme was introduced under recommendations of Prakash Tondon Committee, in early 1981. It is complementary to EPZ scheme. As the FTZ/EPZ scheme introduced in early sixties had limitations of locational restrictions, a large number of exporters could not be attracted to set up their units. The Export Oriented Units (EOU) scheme adopts the same production regime but offers a wide option in locations with reference to factors like source of raw materials, ports of export, hinterland facilities, availability of technological skills, existence of an industrial peace, and the need for a larger area of land for the project.

The chemicals and pharmaceuticals sectors with exports worth US$2800.5 million accounted for 18.1 per cent of total exports from EOUs in 2006–07 followed by engineering goods with US$2422.7 million (15.7%), gems and jewellery with US$1979.44 million (12.8%), textiles and garments with US$1651.15 million (10.7%), computer software with US$993.67 million (6.4%), electronics hardware with US$767.31 million (5.0%), foods, agro and forest products with US$761.57 million (4.9%), plastics, rubber, and synthetics with US$411.63 million (2.7%), and leather & sports goods with US$320.93 million (2.1%) as shown in Fig. 9.1. The export from

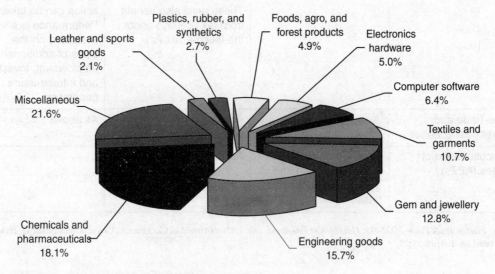

Fig. 9.1 Sectorwise exports of EOUs

Source: Based on data for 2006–07 from Export Promotion Council for EOUs and SEZ units.

EOUs increased significantly from US$748 million in 1992–93 to US$15,201 million in 2006–07 and thereafter rose rapidly to US$35194 million in 2007–08.

Software Technology Parks/Electronic Hardware Technology Parks In order to facilitate export-oriented production of computer software and hardware, units can be set up under the Software Technology Parks (STPs) and Electronic Hardware Technology Parks (EHTPs) schemes, respectively. Both these schemes are monitored by the Ministry of Information Technology. A software technology park may be set up by the central government, state government, public or private sector undertaking, or a combination thereof.

Under the STP scheme, a software development unit can be set up for the purpose of software development, data entry and conversion, data processing, data analysis and control data management, or call centre services for exports. The major STPs have been set up at Pune, Bangalore, Bhuvaneshwar, Hyderabad, Thiruvananthapuram, Gandhinagar, and Noida.

Under the EHTP scheme, a unit can be set up for the purpose of manufacture and development of electronic hardware and/or software in an integrated manner. For exports, the policy provisions for STP/EHTP are substantially the same as applicable to units under EOU scheme. However, in view of the sector-specific requirements, the following provisions have specifically been made.

- STP/EHTP units are allowed Domestic Tariff Area (DTA) sales through data communication/ telecommunication links.
- STP units are allowed telematic infrastructural equipment for creating a central facility for software exports without payment of duty.

Bio-Technology Parks In order to promote bio-technology exports, the DGFT notifies Bio-Technology Parks (BTPs) on the recommendation of the Department of Biotechnology. The approval for units in BTP and other necessary approvals are granted by the Department of Biotechnology.

Benefits The major benefits enjoyed by EOUs/STPs/EHTPs/BTPs are given below.

- The EOU scheme is complementary to the SEZ scheme, providing the choice of locating the unit anywhere in India unlike in case of the SEZ scheme.
- EOUs are required to be only net positive foreign exchange (NFE) earners[9] and the condition of export performance has been done away with effect from 1 April 2004. The positive NFE is to be achieved over a period of five years from the date of commencement of business or commercial production. The value of goods imported by EOUs is allowed to be amortized uniformly over 10 years. Earlier EOUs were allowed to sell in the domestic markets up to 50 per cent of

---

[9] Net foreign exchange (NFE) earnings is defined as the f.o.b. value of exports minus the c.i.f. value of all imported inputs, capital goods, and payments made in foreign exchange for royalties, fees, dividends, and interest on external borrowings during the first five-year period.

f.o.b. value of exports. Sales beyond this limit were made on payment of full duty. On the other hand, clearance from SEZ to DTA was allowed only at full rate of duty.

- Eligible for concession from payment of income tax for profit earners.
- Foreign direct investment in EOUs is allowed up to 100 per cent for manufacturing activities.
- Exempt from central excise duty in procurement of capital goods, raw materials, consumables, spares, etc.
- No authorizations are required for import or domestic procurement.
- Exemption of customs duty on import of capital goods, raw materials, consumables, spares, etc.
- Entitled for duty-free supply of furnace oil.
- Exempted even from anti-dumping duties.
- Reimbursement of Central Sales Tax (CST) paid on domestic purchases.
- Complete freedom to sub-contract part of the production and production process in the domestic area.
- Supplies can be made to other EOUs/SEZs/EHTPs/STPs/BTPs unit without payment of duty and such supplies are counted towards fulfilment of export performance.
- Supplies from domestic area to EOU are allowed deemed export benefits.
- Procurement of duty-free inputs for supply of manufactured goods to advance license holders is allowed.
- Exempted from industrial licensing for manufacture of items reserved for the small-scale industrial sector.

Limitations
- Duty drawback or DEPB credit is not allowed on exports affected by EOUs.
- Duty concession on import of capital goods is deferred only till the period for which the unit is working under the EOU scheme.
- With substantial liberalization and rationalization of the EPCG scheme and lesser quantum of export obligation, no liability with respect to duty exemption on capital goods after completion of export obligation and no restriction on sale in DTA, the attractiveness of the EOU scheme has declined. However, capital intensive units also targeting domestic markets, the EOU scheme still remains viable and attractive.

Assistance to states for developing export infrastructure and other allied activities

In order to involve states in export promotion efforts by providing assistance to state governments for creating infrastructure for development and growth of exports, the Assistance to States for Developing Export Infrastructure and Other Allied Activities (ASIDE) scheme was launched in April 2000 as a comprehensive scheme. Under the scheme, assistance is given for setting up new export promotion parks and zones and complementary infrastructure, such as road links to ports, container depots, and power supply. The scheme provides an outlay for development of export infrastructure which is distributed to the states according to pre-defined criteria. The earlier Export Promotion Industrial Parks (EPIP), Export Processing Zones (EPZ), and Critical Infrastructure Balance (CIB) schemes have been merged with this new scheme. The scheme for Export Development Fund (EDF) for the North East and Sikkim (implemented since 2000) has also been merged with this scheme. After this merger, ongoing projects under the earlier schemes are funded by the states from the resources provided under this scheme. Infrastructure-development activities can also be funded from the scheme, provided such activities have an overwhelming export content and their linkage with exports is fully established.

Allocation of funds in ASIDE   The outlay of the scheme has two components, as described here.

State component   On the basis of the approved criteria, 80 per cent of the funds have been earmarked for allocation to the states, as listed below.

- Creating new Export Promotion Industrial Parks (EPIPs)/Zones (including SEZs/ Agri-Export Zones (AEZs) and augmenting facilities in the existing ones
- Setting up of electronic and other related infrastructure in export enclaves
- Equity participation in infrastructure projects including the setting up of SEZs
- Meeting requirements of capital outlay of EPIPs/EPZs/SEZs
- Developing complementary infrastructure, such as roads connecting the production centres with the ports, setting up Inland Container Depots, and Container Freight Stations
- Stabilizing power supply through additional transformers
- Developing minor ports and jetties of a particular specification to serve export
- Assistance for setting up common effluent-treatment facilities
- Projects of national and regional importance
- Activities permitted as per Export Development Fund (EDF) in relation to North East and Sikkim

Central component   The balance 20 per cent, and amounts equivalent to the un-utilized portion of the funds allocated to the states in the past year(s), if any, are retained at the central level for meeting the requirements of inter-state projects, capital outlays of EPZs, and activities relating to promotion of exports from the north eastern region. It can also be used for any other activity considered important by the central government from the regional or the national perspective.

Modus operandi for ASIDE   The state component is allocated to states in two trenches of 50 per cent each. The inter-se allocation of the first trench of 50 per cent to the states is made on the basis of export performance. This is calculated on the basis of the share of the state in the total exports. The second trenche of the remaining 50 per cent is allocated inter-se on the basis of the share of the states in the average of the growth rate of exports over the previous year. The allocations are based on the exports of physical goods alone and the export of services is not to be taken into account.

A minimum of 10 per cent of the scheme outlay is reserved for expenditure in the North Eastern Region (NER) and Sikkim. The funding of EDF for NER and Sikkim is made out of this earmarked outlay and the balance amount is distributed inter-se among the states on the basis of the laid-down export performance criteria.

The export performance and growth of exports from states is assessed on the basis of the information available from the office of the Director General of Commercial Intelligence & Statistics (DGCI&S). The office of the DGCI&S compiles the state-wise data of exports from the shipping bills submitted by the exporter.

The states are required to set-up a State Level Export Promotion Committee (SLEPC) headed by the Chief Secretary of the state and consisting of the Secretaries of concerned departments at the state level, and a representative of the States Cell of the Department of Commerce (DoC), the Joint Director General of Foreign Trade posted in that state/region, and the Development Commissioners of the SEZs/EPZs in the state. SLEPC scrutinizes and approves specific projects and oversees the implementation of the scheme. The funds are disbursed directly to a nodal agency nominated by the state government where these are maintained under a separate head in the accounts of the nodal agency.

Critical infrastructure balance scheme During 1996–97, the Government of India launched the Critical Infrastructure Balance (CIB) scheme, with an objective of balancing capital investments for relieving bottlenecks in infrastructure for export production and conveyance. Under the scheme, the proposals from state governments are considered for removing bottlenecks related to infrastructure at ports, roads, airports, export centres, etc. In addition, the scheme also covers investments that are in the nature of exigency and emergency and which could not be foreseen as part of initial plan scheme proposals of the Ministry of Commerce. The scheme had conceptually been a good beginning for involving states in removing infrastructural bottlenecks in the states and a number of states have been benefited by improving the infrastructure. Presently, this scheme has also been merged with ASIDE.

Inland container depots and container freight stations A large part of India is land-locked and a number of states are at a disadvantageous position with no seaport. For these states, accessible transport to the seaports is one of the major concerns and multimodal transport is a very effective solution to these logistics bottlenecks. The first Inland Container Depot (ICD) in India was set up at Bangalore in August 1981. Initially, the Container Corporation of India had been involved in establishing and managing ICDs and Container Freight Stations (CFSs), mainly based on rail transport. Subsequently, ICDs and CFSs were established and managed by the Central Warehousing Corporation and some state corporations. There has been a major boost to containerized transportation of export cargo, with the enactment of the Multimodal

Transportation of Goods Act, 1993. An inter-ministerial committee functioning in the Ministry of Commerce provides Single Window Clearance to the proposal for setting up of ICDs/CFSs.

The central government has formulated a revised scheme for allowing the private sector to participate in setting up ICDs and CFSs across the country. The scheme of involving state governments in establishing and managing ICDs and CFSs has not only led to increased involvement of the state governments, but also helped them to generate some revenue along with infrastructure development. Presently, this scheme has also been merged with ASIDE.

Export promotion industrial park scheme With a view to involve the state governments in creation of infrastructural facilities for export oriented production, the central government introduced Export Promotion Industrial Park (EPIP) scheme in August 1995. The scheme was merged with ASIDE from 1 April 2002. The scheme provided that 75 per cent of the capital expenditure incurred towards creation of such facilities, ordinarily limited to Rs 100 million in each case, is met from a central grant to the state governments. In addition, a maintenance grant equivalent to 2 per cent of export turnover of each unit established therein is also given to state governments for a period of five years from the date of commercial production of that unit. The EPIPs are essentially industrial parks housing export-oriented units, which are expected to export at least 25 per cent of their total production.

The EPIP scheme has been one of its kind wherein the central government provides financial support to create infrastructure for export production. The basic infrastructure thus created could serve as a model for creating a planned export-oriented infrastructure in the states.

In most states, not much has been done under the scheme except for developing an infrastructure similar to any other industrial park. Exporters who have purchased land or put up their plants anxiously await the creation of additional facilities in these EPIPs as compared to other industrial areas. Therefore, it is crucial to provide superior infrastructure in the EPIPs with a focus on exports for achieving the objectives of the scheme. This scheme has also been merged with ASIDE.

Free trade zones and export processing zones

In order to develop infrastructure for export production at internationally competitive prices and environment, the concept of free trade zone (FTZ) was conceived. Subsequently, such zones were set-up in various parts of the country as export processing zones (EPZs). The FTZs or EPZs, set up as special enclaves, separated from the Domestic Tariff Areas (DTA) by fiscal barriers, are intended to provide an internationally competitive duty-free environment for export production, at low costs which enables the products of FTZs/EPZs to be competitive, both quality-wise and in terms of price, in the international market. The FTZs/EPZs aim at attracting foreign capital and technology to increase exports in particular and to contribute to economic development in general.

India's first FTZ was set up at Kandla (Gujarat) in 1965, followed by Santacruz (Mumbai) in 1973. Subsequently, EPZs were set up at Falta (West Bengal), Noida (UP), Cochin (Kerala), Chennai (Tamil Nadu), and Visakhapatnam (Andhra Pradesh). The Santacruz Electronics Export Processing Zone deals exclusively with export of electronics and gem and jewellery items whereas the other zones are multi-product zones. The incentives provided for investing in EPZs include income tax relief and tax holidays, exemption from customs duty for industrial inputs and export licenses, single window approval process, exemption from payment of excise duty, for inputs from domestic tariff area (DTA). The performance of EPZs in India has largely been very dismal. On the other hand, their performance in other Asian countries, such as South Korea, Malaysia, Taiwan, the Philippines, China, and Sri Lanka has been very impressive.

A thorough understanding should be developed of the various issues associated with the EPZs so as to effectively evaluate options for investment in these enclaves. The Kaul Committee set up by the government to evaluate the performance of the Kandla Free Trade Zone (KAFTZ), the Tandon Committee, and the Abid Hussain Committee have expressed their dissatisfaction over the poor performance of EPZs. The Kaul Committee felt that the KAFTZ had not been able to take off due to several handicaps and disadvantages. It observed that the facilities available to the entrepreneurs were far behind those obtainable in the more advanced regions of India. The need for more permissiveness and less procedural constraints, and a clear enunciation by the Government of India in its attitude to EPZs was recommended.

The Tandon Committee observed the problems of the KAFTZ and Santacruz Electronic Export Processing Zone as follows:

- Investors, especially the small ones, were hardly satisfied with the performance of the EPZs and often felt that EPZs did not offer the attraction they had initially perceived, or investors had undercapitalized the project, or had not carried out their groundwork.
- Foreign investors often compare the zone with those in other parts of the world and find that Indian zones do not offer enough attraction.
- Both Indian and foreign investors face administrative and procedural constraints and an absence of the freedom that is a *sine qua non* for a free zone.
- Administrative problems, such as lack of 'emotional' adjustment to the permissiveness that is demanded by a free zone, is missing from the planned and controlled environment under Indian bureaucratic system.

Realizing the plethora of procedures and multiplicity of systems which discouraged entrepreneurs in the FTZs, the Abid Hussain Committee observed that

(a) It is essential to create a fully empowered statutory authority for controlling all matters relating to all FTZs, which would, in effect, provide a single window clearance, without any reference to concurrence from other departments.

(b) The choice of industries to be located in FTZs should be a matter of careful consideration, because these zones should constitute a window to the world for acquisition of sophisticated technologies which are not readily available in the domestic tariff areas and also serve as a means to impart higher skills and expertise to workers and managers.

With the reduction of import tariffs during recent years in the post-WTO era, the significance and viability of these EPZs would mainly depend upon the quality of services and infrastructure provided in the EPZs as compared to units outside EPZs.

Private/joint sector EPZs The government has also permitted development of EPZs by the private, state, or joint sector since May 1994. These will work to the same regime as the EPZs, but can be developed and managed either privately, by the state governments or by private parties in collaboration with the state government or their agencies. The private investors could be Indian individuals, non resident Indians (NRIs), and Indian and foreign companies. The viability of such a scheme largely depends upon the initiatives taken and conducive environment provided by the state governments.

Special economic zones

With a view to provide an internationally competitive and hassle-free trade environment for export production, a scheme on special economic zone (SEZ) has been introduced in the Exim policy in April 2000. A SEZ is a designated duty-free enclave to be treated as foreign territory for trade operations and duties and tariffs. Units for manufacture of goods and rendering of services may be set up in SEZs. Besides, offshore banking units may also be set up in SEZs. All the import/export operations of the SEZ units are on self-certification basis. A unit in a SEZ should be a net foreign exchange earner but it is not subjected to any pre-determined value addition or minimum export performance requirements. However, sales made by SEZ units in the DTA are subjected to payment of full customs duty and import policy in force. As per the present foreign trade policy, SEZs may be set up in the public, private, or joint sector or by the state governments.

The distinguishing features of the SEZ policy are given below.

- The zones are to be setup by the private or public sector or by the state government in association with the private sector. The private sector can also develop infrastructure facilities in the existing SEZs.
- State governments have a lead role in the setting up of SEZs.
- An attempt is being made to develop a framework for creating special windows under existing rules and regulations of the central government and state governments for SEZ.

At the time of the conceptualization of the scheme, it was envisaged that the existing EPZs would be converted into SEZs. Subsequently, all the EPZs were converted into

SEZs. The role of the states in developing SEZs has significantly increased as this scheme has been merged with ASIDE.

The multi-product SEZs can be set up by the government or private entities over a minimum contiguous area of 1000 hectares or at least 200 hectares in select states. The SEZs are self-contained economic parks providing advance infrastructure. All units operating in the SEZs are offered simplified customs, other administrative procedures, and basic facilities, such as electricity, water, etc. Although SEZs are required to be net foreign exchange earners, there are no minimum export requirements in contrast to EPZs and EOUs. In addition to the tax incentives already provided to the EPZs and EOUs, investors in SEZs are eligible for other incentives, such as exemption from service tax and minimum alternate tax, up to 100 per cent FDI in most activities, and a relaxation of certain requirements, including environmental impact assessment, labour laws, and residence requirements for foreign managing directors of the companies.

Similar to the EPZs, each SEZ is governed by a Development Commissioner. For establishing a unit in an SEZ, an application has to be made to the Development Commissioner of the SEZ along with supporting documents. The decision to the applicant must be provided by the approval committee within 15 days of the receipt of the application whereas for applications requiring license, approval must be given within 45 days by the SEZ's Board of Approval in the Ministry of Commerce and Industry.

The exports from EPZs/SEZs grew significantly from US$474 million in 1992–93 to US$7629 million in 2006–07 and thereafter increased rapidly to US$16492 million in 2007–08, as shown in Fig. 9.2. All the seven SEZs under the central government are multi-product zones. Noida SEZ is the largest SEZ with physical exports worth Rs 168.43 billion, followed by SEEPZ (Rs 112.65 billion), Cochin (Rs 44.71 billion), MEPZ (Rs 30.46 billion), Kandla (Rs 18.82 billion), Falta (Rs 10.26 billion), and Visakhapatnam (Rs 7.41 billion) in 2007–08. Among the SEZs under the state governments/private sector, the Surat SEZ, which is a multi-product zone, had physical exports worth Rs 122.94 billion followed by Nokia, the electronic hardware zone (Rs 62.30 billion); Manikanchan, gems and jewellery (Rs 17.75 billion); Mahindra, IT and ITeS (Rs 7.63 billion); Mahindra, auto-ancillary (Rs 4.16 billion), Wipro, IT, and ITeS (Rs 3.66 billion); Indore, multiproduct (Rs 3.38 billion); Jaipur, gems and jewellery (Rs 2.96 billion); Manindra, textiles (Rs 2.68 billion), Jodhpur, handicrafts (Rs 300 million), and Surat Apparel Park (Rs 60 million) in 2007–08.

Conceptually, the scheme appears very sound for promoting export oriented production. The scheme has significantly reduced the shortcomings of the earlier EPZ/SEZ scheme and provides greater flexibility. However, the effectiveness of SEZs largely depends upon reducing operational hassles.

There has been a considerable debate over the effectiveness of SEZs in generating additional investment and employment. Besides, SEZs have also witnessed protests,

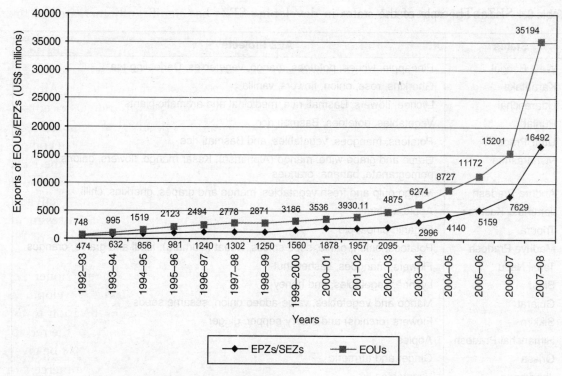

Fig. 9.2 Export performance of EOUs and EPZs/SEZs

Source: Based on data from the Export Promotion Council for EOUs and SEZs.

sometimes violent, from farmers over land-acquisition issues that have significant socio-economic implications.

Agri-export zones The concept of the Agri-Export Zones (AEZs) was floated with a view to promote agricultural exports from India and providing remunerative returns to the farming community in a sustained manner. State governments are required to identify AEZs and also evolve a comprehensive package of services provided by all state government agencies, state agriculture universities and all institutions and agencies of the union government for intensive delivery in these zones.

The emphasis in all the AEZs is on convergence. Thus, the objective is to utilize the ongoing schemes of various central and state government agencies in a coordinated manner to cover the entire value chain from farmer to consumer. The corporate sector with proven credentials are also encouraged to sponsor new AEZs or take over already notified AEZs or part of such zones for boosting agri-exports from the zones. Exporters under AEZs are also eligible for import of inputs, including fertilizers, pesticides, insecticides, and packaging material under advance authorization, DFIA, and DEPB schemes. Additionally, they may also avail the status of export houses or trading houses if the stipulated export performance is achieved.

Table 9.4 India's agri-export zones*

States	AEZ Projects
West Bengal	Pineapple, lychee, potatoes, mango, vegetables, Darjeeling tea
Karnataka	Gherkins, rose, onion, flowers, vanilla
Uttaranchal	Lychee, flowers, Basmati rice, medicinal and aromatic plants
Punjab	Vegetables, potatoes, Basmati rice
Uttar Pradesh	Potatoes, mangoes, vegetables, and Basmati rice
Maharashtra	Grape and grape-wine, mango (Alphonso), Kesar mango, flowers, onions, pomegranate, banana, oranges
Andhra Pradesh	Mango pulp and fresh vegetables, mango and grapes, gherkins, chilli
Jammu & Kashmir	Apple, walnuts
Tripura	Organic pineapple
Madhya Pradesh	Potatoes, onion, garlic, seed spices, wheat (Durham), lentil and grams, oranges
Tamil Nadu	Flowers, mangoes, cashew-nut
Bihar	Lychee, vegetables, and honey
Gujarat	Mango and vegetables, value-added onion, sesame seeds
Sikkim	Flowers (orchids) and cherry pepper, ginger
Himanchal Pradesh	Apples
Orissa	Ginger and turmeric
Jharkhand	Vegetables
Kerala	Horticulture products, medicinal plant
Assam	Fresh and processed ginger
Rajasthan	Coriander, cumin

* As on May 2007.

Source: Agricultural and Processed Food Products Export Development Authority (APEDA).

Services, which are expected to be managed and co-ordinated by state governments/ corporate sector and include provision of pre/post harvest treatment and operations, plant protection, processing, packaging, storage and related research and development, etc. The Agricultural and Processed Food Products Export Development Authority (APEDA), the nodal agency for promoting setting up of AEZs, is expected to supplement efforts of State Governments for facilitating such exports. A web-based monitoring system has also been evolved to pursue more than 120 activities in each agri-export zone.

The scheme has notified about 60 agri-export zones in 20 states for a wide range of agro products, as given in Table 9.4. However, the concept of AEZ could hardly take off as 54 out of 60 approved AEZs reportedly failed to meet the targeted level of exports or attracted envisaged investment.[10]

---

[10] 'Greenfield AEZs needed for Food Security and Exports', *Economic Times*, New Delhi, 8 August 2007.

9.4.5 Other Export Promotion Measures

In addition to the tariff concessions and exemptions, the trade policy provides a wide range of export promotion measures (Table 9.5), such as marketing assistance for export promotion, incentives to promote services exports, development of industrial

Table 9.5 Other export promotion measures

Scheme	Eligibility	Concessions	Performance requirements
Served from India scheme	All service providers listed in Appendix 10 of the *Handbook* with total foreign exchange earnings of at least Rs 1 million in the preceding financial year.	Duty-free imports of all goods including capital goods, office equipment, and consumables (except motor vehicles) up to 10% of the value of foreign exchange earnings of the previous financial year (up to 5% for hotels of one star and above).	
Focus market and focus product scheme	Exports to notified countries under the Focus Market scheme and notified products to all countries under the Focus Product scheme.	Duty-free imports of up to 2.5% of the f.o.b. value of exports for each licensing year, beginning 1 April 2006. For the Focus Product Scheme, only 50% of export turnover counted for benefits.	
Special agriculture and village industry scheme (*Vishesh Krishi and Gram Udyong Yojana*)	Exporters of fruits, vegetables, flowers, minor forest products, dairy, poultry and their value addd products and *Gram Udyog* Products.	Duty-free imports equivalent to 5% of the f.o.b. value of exports (3.5% if the exporter has benefited from duty-free imports of agriculture under any other concessional entry scheme).	Additional customs duty equivalent to excise duty to be adjusted as CENVAT credit or duty drawback according to Department of Revenue rules.
Export and trading houses	Merchant and manufacturer exporters, service providers, EOUs, units located in SEZs, AEZs, EHTPs, STPs and BTPs that meet certain prescribed export performance.	Authorization and Customs clearances for both imports and exports on self-declaration basis, fixation of Input-Output norms on priority within 60 days, exemption from compulsory negotiation of documents through banks, 100 percent retention of foreign exchange in EEFC account, enhancement in normal repatriation period from 180 days to 360 days and exemption from furnishing of BG in schemes under FTP.	Prescribed requirements for export performance ranging from Rs 200 million to Rs 100 billion during the current and previous three years.

Source: Foreign Trade Policy 2004–09; Handbook of Procedures, vol. 1, Department of Commerce, Government of India, New Delhi, as updated on 1 April 2008.

clusters for export potential, promoting export generating employment in rural and semi-urban areas, and giving recognition to established exporters.

Marketing assistance for export promotion

The market assistance schemes under the foreign trade policy facilitate market promotion activities. The Market Development Assistance (MDA) scheme supports efforts by the Export Promotion Councils (EPCs) in their export promotion activities whereas the Market Access Initiative (MAI) scheme provides assistance for research on potential export markets as well as incentives to improve quality, infrastructure, etc, related to agriculture through commodity boards and councils.

Market Development Assistance In order to facilitate exporters to explore the overseas markets and to promote their exports, the MDA scheme of the Department of Commerce provides assistance for participation in export promotion seminars, trade fairs, and buyer-seller meets in India and abroad. Assistance is available to exporters with annual export turnover up to Rs 150 million under specified conditions, as given below.

- To assist exporters for export promotion activities abroad
- To assist EPCs to undertake promotional activities
- To assist approved organization/trade bodies for carrying out non-recurring innovative activities for export promotion
- To assist focus export promotion programmes in specific regions abroad, such as Focus LAC (Latin American Countries), Focus Africa, Focus CIS, and Focus ASEAN programmes
- For other essential activities related with marketing promotion efforts abroad

Financial assistance with travel grant is available to exporters travelling to Latin America, Africa, CIS region, ASEAN countries, Australia, and New Zealand. In other areas, financial assistance without travel grant is available. The scheme is implemented by EPCs and other export-promotion bodies, Industry and Trade Associations (ITAs) on a regular basis every year.

Market Access Initiative In order to supplement the MDA scheme and facilitate promotional efforts on a sustained basis, MAI scheme was launched in 2001–02. The scheme is formulated on focus product–focus country approach to evolve specific strategy for specific market and specific product through market studies or survey.

Under the scheme, financial assistance is provided

- To identify the priorities of research relevant to the Department of Commerce and to sponsor research studies consistent with the priorities
- To carry out studies for evolving WTO compatible strategy
- To support EPCs/trade promotion organizations in undertaking market studies/ survey for evolving proper strategies

- To support marketing projects abroad based on focus product–focus country approach

  Under marketing projects, activities funded are

  o Market studies
  o Setting up of showrooms and warehouses
  o Sales promotion campaigns
  o International departmental stores
  o Publicity campaign
  o Participation in international trade fairs
  o Brand promotion
  o Registration charges for pharmaceuticals
  o Testing charges for engineering goods

Each of these export promotion activities can receive financial assistance from government ranging from 25 per cent to 100 per cent of total cost depending upon activity and implementing agency.

Under the scheme, financial assistance is provided to export/trade promotion organizations, national level institutions, research institutions, universities, laboratories and exporters for enhancement of exports through accessing new markets or through increasing the share in the existing markets. However, the assistance to individual exporters is available only for testing charges of engineering products abroad and registration charges of pharmaceuticals, bio-technology, and agro-chemicals. The proposals for assistance are examined by an empowered committee under the chairmanship of the Commerce Secretary for a particular product and a particular market.

The MAI scheme provides an excellent opportunity, especially for public and private sector export promotion organizations to finance their marketing activities for the thrust products in the pre-identified markets. The scheme could not make the anticipated headway, mainly due to limited initiatives by the state and central government organizations, which had been the targeted principal beneficiaries and also because of non-awareness among them due to poor marketing of the scheme.

Served from India scheme

In order to promote export of services from India, Served From India Scheme (SFIS) was introduced in 2004. All service providers are entitled to duty credit scrip equivalent to 10 per cent of free foreign exchange earned during the preceding year. However, hotels of one-star and above are entitled to duty credit scrip equivalent to 5 per cent. The scheme allows for import of any capital goods, including spares, office and professional equipment, office furniture and consumables; that are otherwise freely importable under the trade policy relating to any service-sector business of applicant. Import entitlement/goods imported under the scheme are non-transferable and subject to actual user condition. Further, all services rendered abroad and charged on exports from India also exempted from service tax from April 2007.

Towns of export excellence

The scheme aims at recognizing towns that have come up as industrial clusters with considerable exports so as to maximize their potential. The scheme notifies select towns producing worth Rs 10 billion as Towns of Export Excellence (TEE) whereas the threshold limit in the handloom, handicraft, agriculture, and fisheries sector is Rs 2.5 billion. The TEE notified include Tirupur for hosiery, Ludhiana for woollen knitwear, Panipat for woollen blanket, Kanoor, Karur, and Madurai for handlooms, AEKK (Aroor, Ezhupunna, Kodanthuruthu and Kuthiathodu) for seafood, Jodhpur for handicrafts, Kekhra for handlooms, Dewas for pharmaceuticals, Alleppey for coir products, and Kollam for cashew products.

Recognized associations of units in the town of export excellence are allowed to access funds under the MAI scheme for creating focused technological services. Common service providers in these areas are also entitled for EPCG scheme. However, such areas will receive priority for assistance under the ASIDE scheme.

Vishesh Krishi and Gram Udyog Yojana (special agriculture and village industry scheme)

In order to promote employment generation in rural and semi-urban areas (Exhibit 9.1), *Vishesh Krishi Upaj Yojana* (Special Agricultural Produce Scheme) was launched. Subsequently, the scheme was expanded and renamed as *Vishesh Krishi* and *Gram Udyog Yojana* (Special Agriculture and Village Industry Scheme). The scheme aims to promote the agricultural produce, minor forest produce, village industries' products, and forest-based products. Under the scheme, duty credit scrip equivalent to 5 per cent of f.o.b. value of exports is provided so as to compensate the high transport costs. However, duty credit scrip equivalent to 3.5 per cent of the f.o.b. value of exports is allowed if the exporter has benefited from duty-free imports of agriculture under any other concessional entry scheme.

Focus market scheme

In order to enhance India's export competitiveness to select strategic markets, the Focus Market Scheme (FMS) was introduced on 1 April 2006. This scheme aims to offset high freight cost and other externalities by allowing duty credit scrip equivalent to 2.5 per cent of f.o.b. value of exports to each licensing year to select countries. The scheme notifies 73 countries as focus markets as on 1 April 2007 from Latin America, Africa, and CIS. Ten additional countries have also been included[11] from 1 April 2008. Although the impact of the scheme remains to be evaluated, it appears to be too ambitious. By notifying a large number of countries as focus markets, there remains

---

[11] Foreign Trade Policy (2004–09), Ministry of Commerce, Government of India, updated as on 1 April 2008.

Exhibit 9.1   Employment generation through exports

International trade can be an effective instrument for generating employment. In the export sector, the total employment generation in 2004–05 was 16 million, 9 million direct, and 7 million indirect, against a total export of US$80 billion. India's exports are estimated to grow to US$165 billion in 2009–10 resulting in total employment of 37 million. In the export sector, the maximum employment was in agricultural products (6.2 million) followed by mineral products (1.7 million), textile and textile articles (1.7 million), and prepared foodstuff and beverages (1.6 million) in 2004–05. While export has recorded robust growth in recent years, the corresponding growth of export of labour-intensive goods has slowed down. Between 1995 and 2003, while labour-intensive exports (rice, tea, spices, horticulture and floriculture products, processed foods, textiles, gems and jewellery, handicrafts, sports goods) grew by 7.2 per cent per year, the growth of resource-intensive exports (iron ore), medium-technology-intensive exports (manufactures of metals, primary and semi-finished iron and steel, manmade yarns,

petroleum products) and knowledge-intensive exports (chemicals, drugs and pharma, plastics and linoleum, machinery, transport equipment and electronic goods) were of the order of 12 per cent, 19 per cent, and 14 per cent, respectively. India's relatively small share of global exports of labour-intensive goods relative to China reveals a huge potential for employment generation through exports.

Thus, certain industrial products, such as fish and leather products, stationery items, fireworks, sports goods, handloom, and handicraft items have potential to generate considerable employment per unit of investment compared to other products. Therefore, schemes aimed at promoting their exports are likely to give a thrust to their manufacturing leading to increased employment. In April 2006, the Focus Product Scheme was formulated to provide incentives for export of products that have high employment potential in rural and semi-urban areas. Besides, *Vishesh Krishi and Gram Udyog Yojana* also contribute to employment generation.

Source: Economic Survey, Government of India, 2006–07, pp. 106–35.

---

the concern of losing the very focus of the FMS. However, the scheme may help in broadening the destination profile of India's exports.

Focus product scheme

In order to provide incentives for export of select products that have high employment potential in rural and urban areas, the Focus Product Scheme (FPS) was introduced on 1 April 2006. The scheme notifies a number of products from product categories such as value added leather products and leather footwear, handicrafts items, handloom products, value added fish and coir products, and some additional focus products. It aims to offset the inherent infrastructure bottlenecks and other associated costs involved in marketing of such products. The scheme allows duty credit scrip equivalent to 1.25 per cent of f.o.b. value of exports of each licensing year for notified products.

The scrip and the items imported against both the FMSs and FPSs are freely transferable. The duty credit may also be used for import of inputs or goods, including capital goods, provided the same is freely importable. Exporters have the option to avail the benefits in respect of the same exported product/s under only one of the three schemes, i.e, FMS, FPS, or Special Agriculture and Village Industry Schemes.

High tech products export promotion scheme

In order to promote exports of high-tech products from India, the High Tech Products Export Promotion Scheme was launched on 1 April 2007. It provides duty credit scrip equivalent to 10 per cent of incremental growth in exports of notified products subject to a ceiling of Rs 150 million for each firm. From 1 April 2008, IT hardware sector has also been included[12] under this scheme.

Export/trading houses

The objective of the scheme of export and trading houses is to give recognition to the established exporters and large export houses to build up the marketing infrastructure and expertise required for export promotion. The registered exporters having a record of export performance over a number of years are granted the status of export/trading houses or Star Trading Houses subject to the fulfilment of minimum annual average export performance in terms of f.o.b. value or net foreign exchange earnings on physical exports or services prescribed in the foreign trade policy.

Category	Average FOB/FOR value* in Rupees
Export House** (EH)	200 million
Star Export House (SEH)	1 billion
Trading House (TH)	5 billion
Star Trading House (STH)	25 billion
Premier Trading House (PTH)	100 billion

* During current and preceding three licensing years.

** For export house, export performance in at least any two out of current and preceding three years is required.

Source: Foreign trade policy (2004–09), Ministry of Commerce, Government of India, updated as on 1 April 2008.

Besides, the following categories of exporters, both merchant as well as manufacturer, are eligible to get double weightage:

- Exporters in the small scale industry, tiny, and cottage sector
- Units registered with KVICs, KVIBs
- Units located in North Eastern States, Sikkim, and Jammu and Kashmir
- For exports of handloom, handicrafts, hand-knotted, or silk carpets
- For exports to Latin America, CIS, or Sub-Saharan Africa
- Units with ISO 9000 series, ISO 14000 series, WHO GMP, HACCP, SEI CMM Level-II and above status
- Exports of services and agro products

---

[12] Foreign Trade Policy (2004–09), Ministry of Commerce, Government of India, updated as on 1 April 2008.

The exporters who have been granted the status of export house/trading house are entitled to a number of benefits under the foreign trade policy, including

- Authorization and customs clearances for both import and export on self declaration basis
- Fixation of input/output norms on priority within 60 days
- Exemption from compulsory negotiation of documents through banks. The remittance, however, would continue to be received through banking channels.
- 100 per cent retention of foreign exchange in EEFC account
- Enhancement in normal repatriation period from 180 days to 360 days
- Exemption from furnishing bank guarantee in schemes under the foreign trade policy

The export and trading houses scheme allow registered exporters certain additional benefits available to them under the policy.

9.5 POLICY INITIATIVES AND INCENTIVES BY THE STATE GOVERNMENTS

State governments generally do not distinguish between production for domestic market and production for export market. Therefore, there had been few specific measures taken by state governments targeted at exporting units. Though, state governments have taken a number of policy measures so as to encourage industrial activity in the state which mainly relate to

- Capital investment subsidy or subsidy for preparation of feasibility reports, project reports, etc.
- Waiver or deferment of sales tax or providing loans for sales tax purposes
- Exemption from entry tax, octroi, etc.
- Waiver of electricity duty
- Power subsidy
- Exemption from taxes for certain captive power generation units
- Exemptions from stamp duties
- Provision of land at concessional rate

These concessions extended by state governments vary among policies of individual state governments and have broadly been based on the following criteria:

(a) Size of the unit proposed (cottage, small and medium industry)
(b) Backwardness of the districts or area
(c) Employment to weaker sections of society
(d) Significance of the sector, for example, software, agriculture
(e) Investment source, such as foreign direct investment (FDI) or investment by NRIs
(f) Health of the unit (sick), etc.

Therefore, it may be noted that most of the exemptions tend to encourage capital- or power-intensive units though some concessions are linked to turnover. Most of the concessions in the state industrial policies have been designed keeping in view the manufacturing industries. An analysis of industrial policies of various states indicates that most state governments do compete among themselves in extending such concessions.

On examination of export promotion initiatives by the state governments, it is difficult to find commonality among various states. However, some of the common measures taken by the state governments are

- Attempting to provide information on export opportunities
- Preference in land allotment for starting an EOU
- Planning for development of Export Promotion Industrial Parks
- Exemption from entry-tax on supplies to EOU/EPZ/SEZ units
- Exemption from sales tax or turnover tax for supplies to EOU/EPZ/SEZ units and inter-unit transfers between them

9.6 WTO AND INDIA'S EXPORT PROMOTION MEASURES

The emergence of the rule-based multilateral trading system under the WTO trade regime has affected India's trade policies and promotional efforts. It provides a rule based framework as to which subsidies are prohibited, which can face countervailing measures, and which are allowed. The details on the WTO agreement are discussed in Chapter 5. However, the impact of WTO agreements on trade policy and export promotion measures is examined here. The framework of the GATT is based on four basic rules:

1. *Protection to domestic industry through tariffs*
   Even though GATT stands for liberal trade, it recognizes that its member countries may have to protect domestic production against foreign competition. However, it requires countries to keep such protection at low levels and to provide it through tariffs. To ensure that this principle is followed in practice, the use of quantitative restrictions is prohibited, except in a limited number of situations.
2. *Binding of tariffs*
   Countries are urged to reduce and, where possible, eliminate protection to domestic production by reducing tariffs and removing other barriers to trade in multilateral trade negotiations. The tariffs so reduced are bound against further increase by being listed in each country's national schedule. The schedules are integral part of the GATT legal system.
3. *Most-favoured-nation treatment*
   This important rule of GATT lays down the principle of non-discrimination. The rule requires that tariffs and other regulations should be applied to imported

or exported goods without discrimination among countries. Thus it is not open to a country to levy customs duties on imports from one country, at a rate higher than it applies to imports from other countries. There are, however, some exceptions to the rule. Trade among members of regional trading arrangements, which are subject to preferential or duty-free rates, is one such exception. Another is provided by the Generalized System of Preferences; under this system, developed countries apply preferential or duty-free rates to imports from developing countries, but apply MFN rates to imports from other countries.

4. *National treatment rule*

While the MFN rule prohibits countries from discriminating among goods originating in different countries, the national treatment rule prohibits them from discriminating between imported products and equivalent domestically produced products, both in the matter of the levy of internal taxes and in the application of internal regulations. Thus it is not open to a country, after a product has entered its markets on payment of customs duties, to levy an internal tax (for example, sales tax or VAT) at rates higher than those payable on a product of national or domestic origin.

The four basic rules are complemented by rules of general application, governing goods entering the customs territory of an importing country. These include rules which countries must follow

- In determining the dutiable value of imported goods where customs duties are collected on an *ad-valorem* basis
- In applying mandatory product standards, and sanitary and phytosanitary regulations to imported products
- In issuing authorizations for imports

In addition to the rules of general application described above, the GATT multilateral system has rules governing

- The grant of subsidies by governments
- Measures which governments are ordinarily permitted to take if requested by industry
- Investment measures that could have adverse effects on trade

The rules further stipulate that certain types of measures which could have restrictive effects on imports can ordinarily be imposed by governments of importing countries only if the domestic industry which is affected by increased import petitions that such actions be taken. These include

- Safeguard actions
- Levy of anti-dumping and countervailing duties

Under safeguard action the importing country is allowed to restrict imports of a product for a temporary period by either increasing tariffs or imposing quantitative restrictions. However, the safeguard measures can only be taken after it is established through proper investigation that increased imports are causing serious injury to the domestic industry.

The anti-dumping duties can be imposed if the investigation establishes that the goods are 'dumped'. The agreement stipulates that a product should be treated as being 'dumped' where its export price is less than the price at which it is offered for sale in the domestic market of the exporting country, whereas the countervailing duties can be levied in cases where the foreign company has charged low export price because its product has been subsidized by the government.

9.6.1 The WTO's Trade Policy Review Mechanism

In order to enhance transparency of members' trade policies and facilitate smooth functioning of the multilateral trading system, the WTO members established the Trade Policy Review Mechanism (TPRM) to review trade policies of member countries at regular intervals. Under annexure 3 of the Marrakesh Agreement, the four members with largest shares of world trade (i.e., European communities, the US, Japan, and China) are to be reviewed every two years, the next sixteen to be reviewed every four years, and the others be reviewed every six years. For the least developed countries a longer period may be fixed.

Reviews are conducted by the Trade Policy Review (TPR) Body on the basis of a policy statement by the member under review and a report prepared by staff in the WTO Secretariat's TPR Division. Although the secretariat seeks cooperation of the members in preparing the report, it has the sole responsibility for the facts presented and the views expressed.

The TPR reports contain detailed chapters examining the trade policies and practices of the member and describing policy-making institutions and the macroeconomic situation. The member's subsidies contained in the TPR is of particular interest for the purpose of the report. Information on subsidies distinguished in the subsidies and countervailing measures (SCM) can be found in the following three parts of the TPR report:

- Measures directly affecting exports
- Trade policies and practices by sector
- Government incentives or subsidies that do not directly target imports and exports but nevertheless have an impact on trade flows

The contents of the report are mainly driven by the member's main policy changes and constraints rather than subsidy-related issues and problems. Besides, the coverage of the report is determined to a large extent by the availability of data. As a result, the amount of information contained in the reports varies from member to member. The TPR reports normally do not attempt to assess the effects of the subsidies on trade.

Due to limited availability of detailed information, in many cases, it is difficult to identify the extent to which a benefit is actually being conferred or the identity of the recipient of the subsidy.

Despite the shortcomings, especially with respect to cross-country comparability, the TPR report constitutes one of the few sources that systematically collects and compiles information on subsidies for a broad range of countries and economic activities.

This chapter brings out the significance of trade policy in international business decisions. Developing countries traditionally employed inward-looking trade strategy so as to protect their domestic industries from foreign competition. However, during the recent era of economic liberalization across the world, most countries gradually shifted their trade strategies to outward looking with greater integration with the world economy.

An overview of India's foreign trade policy, explaining various measures to promote international trade have been discussed. The impact of WTO agreements on trade policy and export promotion measures has also been examined. Readers should develop an insight into the trade policy and regulatory framework as it considerably influences the international business decisions.

SUMMARY

The trade policy and regulatory framework, both in home and host countries, significantly influence international business operations. Therefore, an appreciation of trade policies is crucial to development and implementation of successful strategies for international business. Most developing countries historically followed inward-looking trade strategies encouraging import substitution, gradually shifting towards outward-looking strategies involving greater integration with the world economy. Various methods employed to regulate trade, known as instruments of trade policy, include tariffs, non-tariff measures, and financial controls.

India's foreign trade policy is formulated under the Foreign Trade (Development and Regulation) Act, for a period of five years by the Ministry of Commerce, which outlines a country's export promotion measures, policies, and procedures related to foreign trade. It is published in four volumes: *Foreign Trade Policy, Handbook of Procedures Volume I, Handbook of Procedures Volume II (Schedule of DEPB Rates)*, and *ITC (HS) Classification of Export and Import Items*.

In order to reduce the anti-export bias, a number of duty exemption and remission schemes, such as Export Promotion Capital Goods (EPCG) Scheme, Advance Authorization, Duty-Free Import Authorization (DFIA) Scheme, Duty Entitlement Passbook (DEPB) Scheme, and Duty Drawback Schemes for concessional imports for gems and jewellery have been introduced. In order to augment export production, the trade policy provides for various schemes such as Export-Oriented Units (EOUs), Electronic Hardware Technology Parks (EHTPs), Software Technology Parks (STPs) and Bio-Technology Parks (BTPs), Assistance to States for Developing Export Infrastructure and Other Allied Activities (ASIDE), and Special Economic Zones (SEZs). Other promotional measures in the foreign trade policy include market assistance schemes, such as Market Development Assistance (MDA) and Market Access Initiative (MIA), Served From India Scheme (SFIS), Towns of Export Excellence (TEE), Special Agriculture and Village Industry Scheme (*Vishesh Krishi and Gram Udyog Yojana*), Focus Market Scheme (FMS), Focus

Product Scheme (FPS), and High Tech Products Export Promotion Scheme. Special incentives have been provided to trading houses. Policy initiatives and incentives provided by state governments have also been discussed.

The WTO agreements, especially Agreement on Subsidies and Countervailing Measures and on Agriculture, provide a framework for deciding the nature and scope of export promotion instruments. They also limit promotional efforts of member countries as to which subsidies are prohibited, which can face countervailing measures, and which are allowed. It also provides for integration of trade policies of member countries with the WTO's multilateral trading system and an institutional framework for periodical review.

KEY TERMS

Agri-export zones (AEZs)   A scheme involving comprehensive package of services in an identified zone by all related state and central government agencies, state agricultural universities, and related organizations so as to facilitate production and exports of agro products.

All industry rate   Average Industry Drawback Rates fixed by Ministry of Finance from time to time.

ASIDE   Scheme for providing Assistance to States for Developing Export Infrastructure and other allied activities by the Ministry of commerce on the basis of pre-defined criteria. It includes earlier schemes of EPIP, EPZ, CIB, and the Export Development Fund for the North East and Sikkim.

Brand rates   Drawback incentive for manufacture exporters determined on case-to-case basis for individual exporters on particular brands.

Critical infrastructure balance (CIB) scheme   Assistance to states to facilitate in balancing capital investments for relieving bottlenecks in infrastructure for export production and conveyance.

Deemed exports   Transactions in which goods supplied do not leave the country and payments for such supplies is received either in Indian rupees or in free foreign exchange.

Domestic tariff area (DTA)   Area where normal import tariffs and taxes are applicable for production and movement of goods.

Duty drawback   An export incentive to refund customs duty paid on imports of inputs used in manufacture of goods subsequently exported.

Duty entitlement pass book (DEPB) scheme   Grant of credit on post-export basis as specified percentage of f.o.b. value of exports made in freely convertible currency.

Duty exemption schemes (DES)   Allows duty-free import of inputs required for export production subject to certain export obligations as stipulated in foreign trade policy.

Duty free import authorization (DFIA) scheme   The scheme offers exemptions in respect of custom duty, additional duty, education cess, and anti-dumping or safeguard duties for inputs used in exports.

Export-oriented units (EOUs)   Complimentary to EPZ scheme for units located in DTA.

Export promotion capital goods (EPCG) scheme   The scheme allows for import of capital goods at concessional rate of duty subject to an appropriate export obligation accepted by the exporter.

Input output norms   Description on inputs required for production of particular products. The Standard Input Output Norms (SION) are published in *Handbook of Procedures*, Vol. II.

Instruments of trade policy   Various methods employed to regulate trade that include tariffs, non-tariff measures, and financial controls.

Inward-looking strategy (import substitution)   Systematic encouragement of domestic production of those goods and services which are otherwise imported. Emphasis is laid on extensive use of trade barriers to protect domestic industries from import competition.

Market access initiative (MAI) Scheme to support market promotion efforts of exporters and export promotion organisations based on focus product–focus country approach.

Market development assistance (MDA) Assistance given to exporters and export promotion organizations for market exploration and export promotion on cost-sharing basis.

Net foreign exchange earnings (NFE) Defined as the f.o.b. value of exports minus the c.i.f. value of all imported inputs, capital goods, and payments made in foreign exchange for royalties, fees, dividends, and interest on external borrowings during the first five-year period.

Outward-looking strategy (export-led growth) Aims at linking the domestic economy to the world economy, promoting economic growth, through exports involving incentives to promote exports rather than import restrictions.

Special economic zones (SEZ) Duty-free enclaves to be treated as foreign territory for trade operations so as to provide an internationally competitive and hassle-free environment for export production. It further reduces the operational hassles associated with earlier Export Processing Zones (EPZs) and Free Trade Zones (FTZs).

Value added tax (VAT) A multi-stage noncumulative tax on consumption levied at each stage of production and distribution system and each stage of value addition.

CONCEPT REVIEW QUESTIONS

1. In view of the problems associated with developing countries' trade, critically evaluate various trade policy options and their suitability to promote economic growth.
2. Evaluate various instruments of trade policy in context to your country's policy framework.
3. Briefly explain the prohibitions and restrictions on exports and imports in India's foreign trade policy currently in force.
4. Briefly describe various measures to promote trade under the foreign trade policy.
5. How does WTO affect a country's foreign trade policy and export incentives?
6. Write short notes on
   (a) Export Promotion Capital Goods (EPCG) Scheme
   (b) Advance Authorization Scheme
   (c) Duty Free Import Authorisation (DFIA) Scheme
   (d) Duty Entitlement Pass Book (DEPB) Scheme
   (e) ASIDE
7. Differentiate between
   (a) Tariff vs non-tariff measures
   (b) Specific, *ad-valorem*, and combined tariffs
   (c) Tariff surcharge vs countervailing duty
   (d) Absolute vs tariff quotas

CRITICAL THINKING QUESTIONS

1. Visit the WTO website at www.wto.org. Critically evaluate the WTO compatibility of export incentives under India's present foreign trade policy.
2. A well-established business firm in India had been catering to foreign markets infrequently. The management is serious about making a sustained presence in the international markets but has financial constraints. You have been hired to take charge of firm's expansion plan in international markets. Suggest suitable schemes for getting assistance for the market promotion campaigns.

PROJECT ASSIGNMENTS

1. Contact a trading house located in your city and find out the difficulties faced. Critically evaluate the effectiveness of the policy incentives received.

2. Visit a unit located in a Special Economic Zone. Find out incentives availed and constraints faced in its operation. Identify the key factors that have affected its operational viability.

CASE STUDY

Special Economic Zones under Fire

Introduction

Rising forces of globalization led to most developing countries shifting their development strategy from inward-oriented import substitution to outward-looking export promotion. Production for exports under world-class competitive conditions became increasingly important rather than import restrictions to protect domestic industry. In most developing countries, infrastructural bottlenecks had been the major obstacles to economic development and achieving global competitiveness in the world markets. Earmarking areas exclusively for export production, providing them world class infrastructure, relaxing statutory requirements applicable to domestic industry, and insulating them from incidence of import tariffs for inputs used became the new mantra in most developing countries, not only for export production but also for economic development.

Such enclaves were termed Free Trade Areas (FTAs), subsequently Export Pocessing Zones (EPZs), and presently Special Economic Zones (SEZs) with a much broader comprehensive approach. Set up as special enclaves separated from Domestic Tariff Area (DTA) by fiscal barriers, Export Processing Zones intended to provide an internationally competitive duty-free environment for export production at low cost, enabling the products from EPZ units to be competitive, both in terms of price and quality. SEZs are enclaves with streamlined procedures, tax breaks, and good infrastructure so as to lure investors to export-oriented industries.

Special Economic Zones in India

Asia's first Free Trade Zone (FTZ) was set up in 1965 at Kandla (Gujarat) in India. Subsequently Export Processing Zones were set up at Santacruz (Mumbai) in 1973, followed by Falta (West Bengal), Noida (UP), Cochin (Kerala), Chennai (Tamil Nadu), and Visakhapatnam (Andhra Pradesh). The performance of the SEZs had largely been dismal and most zones could not take off. A number of committees were set up from time to time, including the Kaul Committee, the Tandon Committee, and the Abid Hussain Committee, to find the problems and suggest measures to revitalize the zones.

The Special Economic Zone Act was passed by Parliament in May 2005, received presidential assent on 23 June 2005 and came into force on 10 February 2006. Major incentives provided to SEZs include

- Exemption from customs/excise duty for development of SEZs
- Income tax exemption for a block of 10 years in 15 years under Section 80-I AB of the Income Tax Act
- Exemption from minimum alternate tax under Section 115 JB of the Income Tax Act
- Exemption from dividend distribution tax under Section 115 O of the Income Tax Act
- Exemption from Central Sales Tax (CST)
- Exemption from Service Tax

Table C.1 The SEZ business model matrix

Types of SEZ	Minimum requirements*	Business model
Multi-product	1,000 hectares of land, net worth of Rs 2.50 billion, and investment of Rs 10 billion	■ Long gestation ■ High capital ■ High risk-high return
Sector-specific	10 hectares of land, net worth of Rs 50 million and investment of Rs 2.5 billion	■ Niche players with sectors skills ■ Moderate capex and gestation ■ Moderate returns
IT/IT Services	10 hectares of land, net worth of Rs 1 billion, and investment of Rs 2.5 billion	■ Short gestation ■ Easy to sell ■ Low capital ■ Project could be funded through client advances ■ Moderate to high returns
Captive SEZs	10 hectares of land, net worth of Rs 500 million, and investment of Rs 2.5 billion	■ Companies masquerade new export-oriented factories as SEZs ■ Fiscal incentives justify new investments

Source: 'The Business of SEZs', *Business World*, 13 November 2006, p. 36.

About 25 per cent of the area of SEZ must be used for export related industrial activities and the remaining 75 per cent of the area can be used for economic and social infrastructure whereas all the concessions and benefits may be availed for the whole zone. Social infrastructure, such as residential complexes, hospitals, recreational facilities, and educational institutes are allowed in the zone. The minimum area requirement stipulated for various categories for SEZs and Business Model needed is given in Table C.1.

The operational SEZs and their exports given in Table C.2 reveal that the SEZs under the central government and from state government/private sector accounted for 64 per cent and 36 per cent respectively of total physical exports from all SEZs during 2007–08.

Noida accounted for 27.41 per cent of total SEZ's exports in 2007–08 (Fig. C.1) followed by Surat (20.01%), SEEPZ (18.33%), Nokia (10.14%), Cochin (7.28%), MEPZ (4.96%), Kandla (3.06%), Manikanchan (2.89%), Falta (1.67%), Mahindra (1.35%), Visakhapatnam (1.21%), Wipro (0.60%), Indore (0.55%), Jaipur (0.48%), Surat Apparel (0.01%), and Jodhpur (0.05%).

Sector-wise analysis reveals that gems and jewellery accounted for 34.5 per cent of total exports from SEZs in 2007–08, followed by trading and service (31.3%), electronics hardware (16.7%), computer/electronic software (6.0%), engineering (2.5%), chemicals and pharmaceuticals (2.1%), textiles and garments (2.0%), food and agro industry (1.0%), plastic and rubber (1.0%), electronics (0.8%), and miscellaneous products (2.2%) (Fig. C.2).

SEZs in China vs India

The rapid economic growth of China fuelled by SEZs is often advocated as a reason to adopt similar approach of developing SEZs in India. Although China has achieved record economic development and export growth, this was not realized without problems and adverse ramifications. The income gulf between the rich and the poor in China widened rapidly. The Gini Index, a measure of income distribution, where 100 implies absolute inequality and 0 means absolute equality, revealed considerably higher level of income inequality[1] at 46.9 in China, compared to 36.8 in India and 40.8, in the US. Moreover, a staggering urban-rural divide has emerged as the annual income of

---

[1] *World Development Indicators*, World Bank, 2008, Washington DC, pp. 68–70.

Table C.2 Exports from SEZs by central government

(Rs in billions)

Name of the SEZ	Turnover and exports (2007–08)			
	Physical exports	Deemed exports (supplies counted for +ve NFE)	DTA sales (on full duty and not counted for +ve NFE)	Total turnover
Kandla	18.82	0.57	3.59	22.98
SEEPZ	112.64	0.03	0.61	113.28
Noida	168.43	0.31	2.44	171.18
MEPZ	30.46	1.22	1.12	32.81
Cochin	44.70	1.80	0.55	47.07
Falta	10.26	0.04	1.75	12.04
Visakhapatnam	7.41	0.60	4.33	12.34
Total	**392.75**	**4.56**	**14.40**	**411.70**

Table C.3 Exports from SEZs by state government

(Rs in billions)

Name of the SEZ	Turnover and exports (2007–08)			
	Physical exports	Deemed exports (supplies counted for +ve NFE)	DTA sales (on full duty and not counted for +ve NFE)	Total turnover
Indore	3.38	0.53	0.66	4.58
Jodhpur	0.30	Nil	Nil	0.30
Salt Lake Electronic City-Wipro-W. Bengal	3.66	Nil	Nil	3.66
Mahindra City (IT), T. Nadu	7.63	0	0	7.63
Mahindra City (Auto Ancillary), T. Nadu	0.41	0	0	0.41
Mahindra City (Textiles), T. Nadu	0.27	0	0	0.27
Nokia	62.30	59.04	11.19	132.54
Moradabad		Nil	Nil	0.11
Surat Apparel Park	0.06	0	0.002	0.06
Total	**221.67**	**60.87**	**12.06**	**291.76**

Source: Based on data from Export Promotion Council for EOUs and SEZ Units, Ministry of Commerce and Industry, Government of India.

Chinese city dwellers is around US$1000, which is more than three times their rural counterparts. Rural china witnessed peasants' protests against land acquisition, especially in the provinces of Guangdong, Sichuan, and Hebei. Guangdong has been the worst affected. Compared to China, dealing with mass protests is much more challenging in a democratic country like India. The United Nations' Environment Programme designated Shenzhen in China as the 'Global Environmental Hotspot' which means the region has suffered rapid environment destruction.

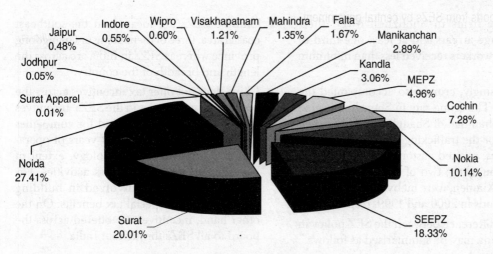

Fig. C.1   Zonewise physical exports of SEZs (2007–08)

Source: Based on data from Export Promotion Council for EOUs and SEZ Units, Ministry of Commerce and Industry, Government of India.

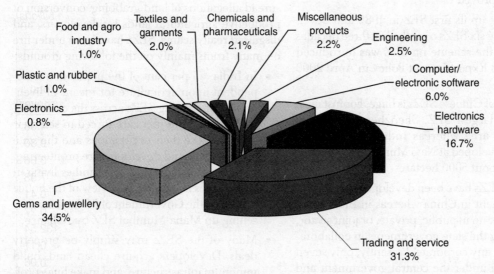

Fig. C.2   Sectorwise exports from SEZ (2007–08)

Source: Based on data from Export Promotion Council for EOUs and SEZ Units, Ministry of Commerce and Industry, Government of India.

In 1992, *The Economist* reported that the Hainan SEZ was the 'world's biggest speculative bubble'. In addition to real estate speculations, rampant abuse of labour is reported in Chinese SEZs in the avowedly communist regime.[2] Out of Shenzhen's total population of 12 million, almost seven million people are migrant workers with almost no legal or social protection.[3] In 2003, at

[2] 'Export Processing Zones: Symbols of Exploitation and a Development Dead-End', International Confederation of Free Trade Unions, ICFTU, Brussels, June, 2003.

[3] French, H., 'Chinese Success Story Chokes on Its Own Growth', *New York Times*, 19 December 2006.

384 International Business

least half the firms in Shenzhen owed their employees wage arrears and at least one-third of Chinese zone workers received less than minimum wage.[4]

Unsurprisingly, crime also accompanied the labour abuse. The crime rate in Shenzhen is nine times higher than that of Shanghai and Shenzhen is notorious for the trafficking of women and sex trade.[5] Besides, relaxed customs have also led to large-scale smuggling; two of the original zones, Shantou and Xiamen, were hit by massive tax and smuggling frauds in 2000 and 1999, respectively.[6]

The key difference between the SEZ policy in India and China may be summarised as follows.

- The number of SEZs in China is only six, i.e., Shenzhen, Zhuhai, Shantou, Xiamen, Hainan, and Pudong whereas in India 135 SEZs have already been notified, and 362 have been formally approved[7].

- China set up its first SEZ in 1980 and developed only six SEZs over the last three decades whereas the scheme on SEZ was introduced in India's Export Import Policy in April 2000 only.

- The size of Chinese SEZs is huge. For instance, China's largest SEZ, Shenzhen has 49,300 hectares area whereas India's largest SEZ being developed at Navi Mumbai by Reliance is only about 5000 hectares.

- All the SEZs have been developed only by the government in China whereas in India SEZs can be set up in public, private, or joint sector, including the state governments in collaboration with any corporate. Presently, only seven SEZs are under the central government and most SEZs are private initiatives in India.

- The primary driving force for SEZs in India is the fiscal sops being offered by the government whereas size, location, stable economic policies, and labour laws are primarily responsible for FDI inflows in Chinese SEZs.

- Chinese SEZs are located on the southeast coastal area, three of them being in Guangdong province whereas SEZs in India are across the length and breadth of the country.

- China does not offer tax incentives across the board to all companies in the SEZs. Incentives differ from zone to zone and for companies too, based on the number of years of operation, use of advanced technology, extent of exports, and type of business activities. For instance, companies involved in building infrastructure get special tax benefits. On the other hand, incentives are offered across the board to all SEZs throughout India.

Indian SEZs: Key Concerns

There has been a gold rush to set up SEZs among India's most famous companies. Rapid proliferation of SEZs across the country have led to widespread allegations of land-grabbing, conversion of productive agricultural lands by developers, and disguised realty scams. SEZs have been under fire on many fronts mainly on the following grounds:

- In India, 65 per cent of the population is dependent upon agriculture for means of livelihood. For creating SEZs across the country, it is alleged that farmers are forced to sell their land and lose their occupations and the state governments and developers are profiteering. For instance, about 150,000 families living in 100 villages fear eviction in view of the notice served by the Government of Maharashtra for setting up Maha-Mumbai SEZ by Reliance.

- Many of the SEZs may simply be property deals. Developers acquire cheap land, build minimum infrastructure, and make huge profits by selling it. Even the central bank, RBI, seems to have suspicion regarding this, classifying loans to SEZs as 'real estate' lending.

- Land acquisition for SEZs is carried out at prices determined by the government rather than at market prices. Therefore, SEZs are

[4] Jayanthakumaran, Kankesu, 'Benefit-Cost Appraisal of Export Processing Zones: A Survey of Literature', in *Development Policy Review*, Oxford: Blackwell Publishing, vol. 21, no. 1, pp. 51–65, 2003.

[5] Goswami, Bhaskar, 'Special Economic Zones: Lessons from China', *Motion Magazine*, New York: NPC Productions, 14 February 2007.

[6] 'Still in the Zone', *Business China, The Economic Intelligence Unit*, 22 May 2006.

[7] As on 31 July 2007.

Exhibit C.1   Rise and fall of SEZs: A hypothetical sketch

1947: India's share in world exports was 2.54 per cent at the time of independence. Agriclutral and primary products as major export items.

1960: India's share in world exports declines to 1.03 per cent.

1965: First Free Trade Zone of Asia set up at Kandla in Gujarat.

1980: China sets up its first SEZ at Shenzhen.

1980: India's share drops down to 0.4 per cent.

2000: SEZ scheme introduced in India's Export Import Policy.

2005: Indian Parliament passes Special Economic Zones Act, 2005 in May.

2006: SEZ Act, 2005 comes into force from 10 February 2006.

2006: Widespread farmers' protests witnessed over land acquisition.

June 2006: Farmers protest in Gurgaon district Haryana over land acquisition under compensation by Reliance Industries' SEZ.

July 2006: Protest in Pune district against auto-component maker Bharat Forge's proposed 5000 acre multi-product SEZ.

August 2006: The RBI annual report warns of revenue losses to the government from fiscal concessions extended to SEZs unless the projects ensure forward and backward linkages with the domestic economy.

Jan 2007: Protestors' clash results into six deaths in Nandigram, West Bengal over land acquisition for 18,000 acre multi-product SEZ to be developed by Indonesia's Salim Group.

March 2007: Farmers protest against the proposed 14,000-hectare Navi Mumbai SEZ of Reliance Group.

2010: Investors become averse to set up units in domestic tariff area and most new units set up in SEZs due to the too-attractive incentive, widening the gap in industrial development of the country. Relocation of units to SEZs also takes place.

2015: Confederation of SEZs of India (CSEZI) formed a few years back gains overwhelming strength in influencing political decisions.

2020: The social infrastructure and living conditions in SEZs radically improve. Even the common areas, such as walkways and parking lots become air-conditioned. Most super-rich relocate their residence to SEZs.

2024: The number of SEZs soar to 5000. The Zones become economically stronger and politically dominating with global clout. The economic gap between SEZs and rest of India deepens.

2025: SEZ's super-rich buy huge areas of land in the rest of India adding to their financial and economic clout. SEZs find the Indian laws irritants to their free environment and demand more political autonomy with the Indian government, negotiate agreements with the EU, the US, and Japan to form FTAs across the border.

2027: Due to mass political pressures in democratic India, the government attempts to contain SEZs.

2028: Difference between the Indian government and CSEZI deepens leading to conflict involving armed forces.

2029: Due to high-tech security systems of the SEZs, the attempts of the Indian armed forces fail and CSEZI declares political independence forming Federal Republic of Special Economic Zones of India (FRSEZI), one step ahead of the present day Regional Trading Agreements (RTAs) which are no longer confined to geographically contiguous areas.

2031: Conflicts between Indian government and the FRSEZI deepens and India prohibits entry of labour to FSEZI and severs all forms of physical connectivity.

2032: FRSEZI lose its competitive advantage and collapses to re-merge with India.

often accused of feeding the rich corporate houses and developers at the cost of poor farmers. In view of the forthcoming elections and rising public pressure, the Union Cabinet cleared new resettlement and rehabilitation policy under which the government can acquire 30 per cent of the land for SEZ only if the rest can be bought by the developer.[8] Besides, land can be acquired only after re-settlement of the displaced and payment of compensation. Payment is also to be made at commercial rates.

- Provision for construction of 25, 000 houses in multi-product SEZs implies that instead of focusing on export production, developers are looking at a goldmine in the form of escalation of realty prices.

- Extra-liberal incentives, such as exemption from import and excise duties and some licensing requirements, tax holiday on profit with the only performance rider being net foreign exchange earners make them attractive options to relocate for other units in the Domestic Tariff Area (DTA).

- Even the IMF expressed concern that the loss of huge tax revenue, estimated by the Finance Ministry as US$38.3 million (Rs1750 billion) by 2011, due to fiscal concessions to SEZs, can make things worse for India. National Institute of Public Policy and Finance estimate such revenue losses at Rs 970 billion during 2005–10.

- Exports by SEZ units was in the tune of Rs 177.3 billion in 2004–05 contributing to 4.9 per cent of India's total exports whereas the small sector exported worth Rs 1224 billion contributing to 34.4 per cent of country's total exports.

- Valuable resources are being spent in creating SEZs at the cost of building better infrastructure for the rest of the country, which may affect both the domestic industry as well as the agriculture.

The rush to SEZs in India is primarily to serve the huge domestic market rather than for export-related purposes as an SEZ unit is allowed to sell in DTA after payment of prevailing duties as long as it is the net foreign exchange earner for three years. The sops in SEZ would reduce the cost of capital whereas labour reforms would ensure trouble-free operations, enabling units based in SEZs to sell at highly competitive prices. The cheaper imports from SEZ based unit would adversely affect the existing industry in the DTA.

A purely hypothetical sketch of events of the rise and fall of SEZs is given in Exhibit C.1. Therefore, instead of replicating the Chinese model as a panacea to all problems related to economic development and export growth, countries should evolve their own models for economic growth. However, the debate over socio-economic implications of SEZs continues to concern Indian masses and socio-political groups.

Questions

1. Evaluate critically the salient features of India's SEZ policy.

2. Critically examine the key differences in the approach to develop SEZs in India vis-à-vis China. Find out the pros and cons of both the approaches.

3. 'SEZs are likely to cause more harm to India rather than benefit the society as a whole.' Explore your argument for and against the topic and discuss in the form of a debate in the class.

4. Explore the SEZ strategy used by any four developing countries and carry out a critical evaluation. Suggest a strategy for your own country to promote export production.

---

[8] 'New Policy Limits Government Role in Land Acquisition', *The Times of India*, 12 October 2007.

10 Country Evaluation and Selection

LEARNING OBJECTIVES

> To explain the basic approaches to country evaluation and selection
> To discuss the concept of international business research
> To elucidate different approaches for country evaluation
> To explain various tools for country evaluation and selection

10.1 INTRODUCTION

International expansion of a firm's activities requires identifying business opportunities across the borders, evaluating them, and selecting one or a few countries for the firm's operations. A business enterprise needs to employ its finite resources most gainfully in countries where it gets optimum returns to fulfil its goals and objectives. However large a business enterprise may be, it is always faced by the limitation of resources for expansion into new activities and geographical areas. Therefore, an internationalizing company should carefully evaluate the business environment and select the most appropriate location for its expansion—where it can operate and compete most effectively.

An internationalizing firm may adopt either a reactive or a proactive approach for identifying and evaluating business opportunities as discussed below.

Reactive approach Most firms, particularly small and medium enterprises (SMEs), internationalize as an unintended response to an international business opportunity in the form of unsolicited export orders. In doing so, the positive stimulus in terms of increased profitability, turnover, market share, or image leads to catering to overseas markets as a repeat activity. Over a period, the firm takes up overseas marketing on a regular basis. Consequently, carrying out business across the borders becomes an integral part of the firm's business strategy.

Systematic approach A systematic proactive approach is generally adopted by larger companies with relatively higher level of resources in country identification, evaluation, and selection. A firm has to carry out the preliminary screening of various countries before a refined analysis is carried out for country selection. Trade statistics available from secondary sources may be used for preliminary market scanning. One can use published data from multilateral organizations, such as UNCTAD, World Bank, International Monetary Fund, World Trade Organization and national organizations like India's Directorate General of Commercial Intelligence and Statistics (DGCI&S). Import promotion organizations, such as Centre for Promotion of Import (CBI) from developing countries, and import promotion offices from a number of high-income countries, such as the UK, Finland, Norway, and Japan also provide enormous information and services for investors. Besides, information provided by commercial banks, country's missions overseas and foreign missions in the home country, newspapers, magazines, and periodicals and research reports are also helpful for identifying and evaluating international business opportunities.

This chapter outlines the research process for international business and the issues related to equivalences in cross-country research. To identify the most suitable locations for business operations, countries can be evaluated by scanning the global economic environment, assessing market potential, evaluating country competitiveness, and assessing business environment. Further, various tools such as trade analysis and analogy methods, opportunity–risk analysis, products–country matrix strategy, growth–share matrix, and market attractiveness–company strength matrix may be used for country evaluation and selection.

10.2 INTERNATIONAL BUSINESS RESEARCH

A firm desirous of expanding internationally needs to carry out research so as to spot business opportunities, evaluate various countries, and select the most attractive locations for business. As the commitment of resources for international expansion is much larger than operating domestically, international business research is increasingly gaining significance.

The research conducted to assist decision making in more than one country is termed as international business research. It involves the systematic gathering, recording, and analysing of data in more than one country to resolve business problems. Since research is conducted across national borders, it involves respondents and researchers from different countries and cultures. It may be conducted simultaneously in multiple countries or sequentially over a period of time.

Key factors that hinder an objective evaluation and meaningful output while carrying out international business research include

- Overlooking cross-cultural behaviour
- Employing standardized research methodologies across international markets
- Using English as a standard language for market communication
- Inappropriate sample selection

- Misinterpretation of cross-country data
- Failure to use natives to conduct field surveys

10.2.1 International Business Research Process

The process of international business research involves problem identification, deciding research methodology, working out information requirements, identifying sources of information, preparing research designs, and collecting primary information and its analysis, evaluation, and interpretation. However, the process of business research should be developed taking into consideration the nature of the problem to be addressed.

Identifying sources of information

Secondary information plays an important role in cross-country research. Since carrying out overseas field surveys involves considerable cost and time, which may be saved by using secondary information. Besides, there may be situations when conducting field surveys is either difficult or unfeasible under the resource constraints of the firm. Often the secondary data related to a country's business environment, market estimation, regulatory framework, tariffs and taxation, etc., may be more reliable than what a firm can obtain through primary research. Specific data from secondary sources may also be obtained from outside agencies in lieu of payment.

Limitations of secondary data

Availability   The kind of secondary data needed for business decisions at times may not be available for all countries. Generally, availability of detailed secondary data is directly proportional to the state of economic development in a particular country. For instance, in countries like Japan, the US, Singapore, and in some European countries, comprehensive data are available on wholesalers, retailer, manufacturers, and traders, which are hardly available in many developing and least developed countries. However, the general data on demographic profile compiled by national governments and UN organizations are readily available.

Reliability   In order to make a business decision confidently, the information needs to be accurate and reliable. However, it is observed that the secondary data available from various agencies are influenced by various environmental and cultural factors in the country. For instance, the data collected by revenue and taxation authorities understate the sales and profitability figures due to fear of increased incidence of taxation. However, the data furnished by consumers in individual surveys by non-governmental agencies and even the data collected by government agencies are sometimes inflated as a manifestation of individual or national pride. It is reflected in the enormous size of parallel economies operating in several countries, especially in developing and least developed countries. It adversely affects the accuracy and reliability of data. Further, the secondary data available, at times, may not be updated, which requires additional collection of primary data.

Comparability Data collected from secondary sources by various agencies across nations may not be comparable, depending upon the methodology used in data collection. For instance, there is a wide variation in trade statistics collected by various agencies within a country as discussed in Chapter 3, such as by the DGCI&S and Reserve Bank of India (RBI) mainly due to the different methods used in data collection. Besides, differences in classification of various terminologies, such as consumer classifications also contribute to difficulties in comparison of cross-country research data.

Validity The secondary data collected from one source and the other should be consistent for assessing validity of the data which depends on a number of factors[1] including

- Who collected the data? Would there be any reason for purposely misrepresenting the facts?
- For what purposes were the data collected?
- How were the data collected? (methodology)
- Are the data internally consistent and logical in light of known data sources or market factors?

Generally, the availability and accuracy of secondary data increases with increase in level of the country's economic development. However, India is an exception which has accurate and relatively complete government collected data, despite its lower level of economic development than many other countries.

Preparing research design

Research design is the specification of methods and procedures for acquiring the information needed to structure or solve problems. It is the arrangement of conditions for collection and analysis of data in a manner that aims to combine relevance of research purpose with economy in procedures. Thus, research design is the conceptual structure within which research is conducted; it constitutes the blueprint for the collection, measurement, and analysis of data. It includes an outline of what the researcher will do—from writing the hypothesis and its operational implications to the final analysis of data.

Types of research designs

Exploratory research To gather preliminary information that will help better define problems and suggest hypothesis, exploratory research is conducted. It is used when one is seeking insight into the general nature of the problem, the possible research alternatives and relevant variables that need to be considered.

Descriptive research To describe business problems, situations, business environment or markets such as the market potential for a product or the demographics and attitudes

---

[1] Cateora, Philip R. and Graham John L., *International Marketing*, 11th ed., New Delhi: Tata McGraw Hill, 2002, p. 213.

of consumers, descriptive research is conducted. It is used to provide accurate snapshots of certain aspects of business environments.

Causative research   To test a hypothesis to establish cause-and-effect relationship, causative research is carried out. It is widely used to identify inter-relationship among various constituents of business strategy. Therefore, results under the causative research are unambiguous and often sought for.

Collecting primary information

The information collected by the researcher for the first time is termed primary information. Although it is comparatively costlier to collect primary data, such information is inevitable to get information specific to the research project. However, in view of the much higher costs and complexities involved in collecting primary data, the researcher should first collect secondary information as much as feasible and identify information gaps. Such information gaps may be filled-up by collecting primary information. Further, the cost-benefit analysis of collecting primary information should also be carried out. Firms operating internationally also collect primary information on a regular basis for monitoring their business strategy. Primary information may be collected by conducting field surveys, observations or conducting experiments. Various tools used to conduct field surveys include telephone interviews, mail surveys, electronic surveys, and personal surveys.

Analysis of information

Although the data analysis techniques in international business research remain similar to those used in domestic business research, these depend upon the nature of the problem and the type of data. Univariate techniques, such as cross-tabulation, t-test and multivariate techniques including analysis of variance, discriminant analysis, co-joint analysis, factor analysis, cluster analysis and multidimensional scaling can be used. However, the researcher needs to check the multi-country data for various equivalences as explained later in this chapter.

Evaluation and interpretation

Based on the data analysis, the results of the research need to be evaluated in view of the equivalences and constraints in obtaining cross-country information.

10.2.2   Equivalences in Cross-country Research

Equivalences in cross-country research (Fig. 10.1) refer to whether the particular concept being studied is understood and interpreted in the same manner by people in different cultures. As discussed earlier, it is the cultural background that determines the acceptability or unacceptability of family values. An ad copy that is considered sensual in the Middle East may fail to convey a similar message in Europe, as discussed in Chapter 7. Even the demographics which appear to have universal appeal may be

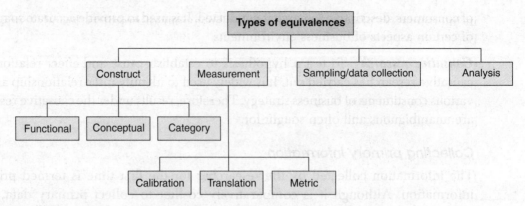

Fig. 10.1 Equivalences in cross-country research

very different. Thus, these concepts specific to culture have varied implications in international business.

Construct equivalence

Construct equivalence refers to whether the business/marketing constructs (i.e., product functionality, interpretation of marketing stimuli, and classification schemes) under the study have the same meaning across countries. The forms of construct equivalence are explained here.

Functional equivalence It refers to whether the function or purpose served or performed by a given concept or behaviour is the same across national boundaries. For instance, the sewing machine in developing countries with low per capita income is primarily a means of financial savings or adding to household income while in high-income countries, it is a means of recreation or a hobby. Similarly, the bicycle is a means of transport in low-income countries while it may be used as a means of recreation in high-income countries. Thus, the role or function served by the bicycle or the sewing machine vary in different countries. Possessing a car or air-conditioner is a necessity and no longer a status symbol in high-income countries, while it is considered to be a symbol of prestige or status in low-income countries. Therefore, for valid and meaningful comparison of the research data across nations, the functional differences in the use of a product or service need to be taken into consideration in the measuring instruments.

Conceptual equivalence The extent of variation in individual interpretation of objects, stimuli, or behaviour across cultures is termed as conceptual equivalence. This significantly affects interpretation of the marketing stimuli. The contextual background of cultures plays an important role in understanding such behaviour. In eastern societies, acceptance by group, unwillingness to express explicit disagreements, and giving each other the chance to save face are important cultural traits, which is hardly the case with Western cultures. Thus, the conceptual equivalence is important in interpretation of cross country market behaviour of products, brands, consumer behaviour and promotional campaigns.

Classification or category equivalence   Category equivalence refers to the category in which the relevant objects or other stimuli are placed. The definition of product class may vary from country to country. The demographic classifications also vary among nations. Such category-variation may be due to consumer perception or by official law-enforcing authorities. In a number of Mediterranean countries, beer is considered a soft drink, while it is an alcoholic beverage in most of the countries. Definition of 'urban' varies widely among nations. In Iceland, localities with more than 200 inhabitants are classified as urban, in Canada, places with more than 1000 inhabitants are treated as urban, whereas in Japan the term 'densely inhabited districts' (DID) is used for contiguous basic unit blocks with a population density of 4,000 inhabitants or more per square kilometre or for public, industrial, educational, and re-creational facilities whose total population is more than 5000 persons or more.[2] Therefore, while conducting cross-country marketing research, the researcher has to take into account such differences in demographic classifications.

Measurement equivalences

Measurement equivalences refer to establishing equivalence in terms of procedures used to measure concepts or attitudes.[3] There are significant differences in measuring methods or instruments as far as their applicability and effectiveness from one culture to another are concerned.

Calibration equivalence   The system of calibration include monitory units, measure of weight, distances, volume, and perceptual cues, such as colour, shape, and forms used to interpret visual stimuli. Units of weight and measure also differ across the countries. For instance, the US follows the FPS (foot, pound, and second) system where units such as ounces and pounds for weight; pint, quart, and gallon for volume; foot, yard, and mile for distance and Fahrenheit for temperature whereas most countries follow MKS (meter, kilogram, and second) system where units such as gram, kilogram, and ton for weight; litre for volume; centimetre, meter, and kilometre for distance and Centigrade for temperature are used. The differences in the perception of different colours in different countries should also be taken into account while conducting cross-country research. For instance, white colour is frequently used for wedding attire of the bride in the west while in the most oriental countries, it is the colour for mourning.

Translation equivalence   The translation of the instrument used should be such so that it can be understood by respondents in different countries and has equivalent meaning in each research context. Exact translation of the instrument is often difficult

---

[2] *World Urbanization Prospect*, 2007 revision, United Nations Department of Economics and Social Affairs, Population Division, 2008, New York, pp. 11–22.

[3] Crimp, Margaret and Len Tiu Wright, *The Marketing Research Process*, 4th ed., Herefordshire: Prentice Hall, 1995, p. 63.

as it may have different connotations in different country markets. In India a family can refer to parents, spouses, and children whereas in the US, a family refers to only a couple and its children. In India, Italy, and Pakistan, separate words are used for paternal and maternal uncles and aunts. Considerable differences exist even in the English used in various countries. Therefore, a questionnaire used for cross-country research needs to be written perfectly and reviewed by a native of the country.

Metric equivalence   Equivalence of scale or procedure to establish as measure and equivalences of responses of given measure in different countries are termed as metric equivalence. In different countries and cultures, the effectiveness of scales and scoring procedures varies widely. In English-speaking countries, a five- or seven-point-scale is common, whereas ten or twenty point scale is very common in many other countries.[4] There are also countries where the scale has 15–20 categories. Japanese generally avoid giving opinions; therefore a scale used in Japan does not have a neutral point. Further, the non-verbal response from across countries and cultures needs to be considered for comparability.

Sampling equivalence

Comparability of samples   The sampling methods among various countries need to be comparable for cross-country market research. For instance, the process of the purchase decision varies due to role variation among family members. In China and India, children have relatively much higher pester power to influence the buying decision as compared to their Western counterparts. In the US, the decision making for buying durables and major investments is collaborative whereas in the Middle East, womenfolk have little say in such decision making. It influences the sample selection for carrying out cross-country business surveys.

Sample's representativeness to the population   A sample should be representative of the population surveyed. Generally, availability and accuracy of customer database is proportional to the level of the country's development. For instance, the database in Japan, Singapore, and the US is far more detailed and precise compared to those available in developing and least developed countries. In a country, such as India, there are wide variations among the rural and urban population, therefore uniform sampling techniques within the country are hardly representative of the population surveyed.

Equivalence of data analysis

The country–culture bias needs to be taken into account while carrying out data analysis. The emphasis and expression of disagreement varies very widely among cultures. As the Japanese find it very difficult to say no and face-saving is an important

[4] Douglas, S.P. and P. Le Maire, 'Improving Quality and Efficiency of Life-Style in Research', in *The Challenges Facing Market Research: How Do We Meet Them?* XXV ESOMAR Congress, Hamburg, 1974.

cultural trait in Eastern cultures unlike the West, these factors need to be considered while applying uniform analytical techniques.

10.3 COUNTRY EVALUATION

Internationalizing firms need to evaluate business opportunities in countries so as to identify one or a select group of countries most suitable for operations. For identifying business opportunities, scanning the global economic environment provides useful insight. Countries may further be evaluated, based on their competitiveness, business environment and problems in carrying out business activities.

10.3.1 Scanning the Global Economic Environment

Carrying out a preliminary scanning of economic parameters such as population or income, an overall macroeconomic overview greatly facilitates country evaluation for international business decision.

Population

The population of a country broadly gives a rough estimation of availability of workforce and market potential, although it has to be used with some other indicators as discussed later in this chapter. It is not always true that the most populous countries are the largest markets in the world. However, for 'necessary goods' with low-unit value, such as food products, health care items, educational products, bicycles, etc., population provides a gross indicator of market size. The growth rate in population is an indicator of future market potential. However, for high-value products and luxuries, the size of population is often misleading.

China with 1.33 billion people is the most populated country in the world[5] in 2008, followed by India (1.15 billion), US (304 million), Indonesia (237 million), Brazil (196 million), Pakistan (173 million), Bangladesh (153 million), Nigeria (136 million) Russia (141 million) and Japan (127 million), as shown in Fig. 10.2. However, India is likely to take over China in terms of its population by 2026 to become the most populous country in the world whereas Japan slips to 13th place. By 2050, Congo is likely to be the tenth most populated country in the world whereas Russia and Japan slip to 15th and 17th places, respectively.

India is at an inflection point at which the increase in its share of the labour force is set to accelerate. The decline in India's population growth rate is mainly attributed to deceleration in the birth rate (per 1000) from 33.9 in 1981 to 29.5 in 1991 to around 25.2 in 2001 and 22 in 2008. This decline in birth rate has so far been reflected in a very gradual increase in the share of population of working age. Therefore, India is entering the second stage of demographic transition where the share of its working

---

[5] US Census Bureau, *International Database*, 2008.

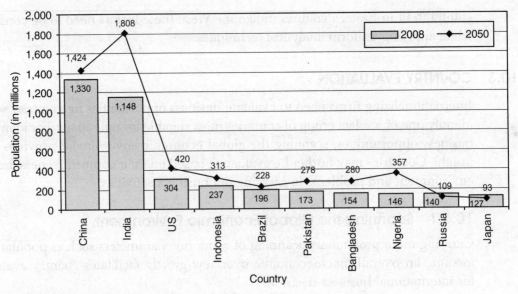

Fig. 10.2   World's most populated countries

Source: Based on US Census Bureau, International Database, 2008.

age population is expected to increase[6] over the next three decades. Most other Asian economies entered these demographic stage decades ago and some, especially Japan, have entered the next stage and are now aging rapidly. The share of workers in India will take over that of Japan around 2010 and that of China around 2030.

India is also likely to witness continued urbanization. The urban population is expected to rise from 28 per cent to 40 per cent of total population[7] by 2020. Future growth is likely to be concentrated in and around 60 to 70 large cities having a population of one million or more. This profile of concentrated urban population will facilitate greater customer access. India is likely to have a unique competitive advantage in terms of surplus workforce and its quality in terms of productivity, cost effectiveness, and English language skills.

Income

Consumption patterns in a country are significantly influenced by the level of income. The Gross Domestic Product (GDP) of a country provides a better estimate of the market size compared to its population. The US is the largest economy in the world[8] with total GDP of US$13,811 billion at purchasing power parity (PPP) followed by China (US$7,055 billion), Japan (US$4,283 billion), India (US$3,092 billion), Germany (US$2,751 billion), Russian Federation (US$2,088) and the UK (US$2,081, billion) as shown in Fig. 10.3. China with total GDP of US$29,590 billion, is likely to take over

[6] 'India's Changing Households', *Global Market Research,* Deutsche Bank, 18 November 2004, p. 3.

[7] Report of the Committee on India Vision 2020, Planning Commission, Government of India, New Delhi, December 2002.

[8] *World Development Indicators Database*, World Bank, 1 July 2008.

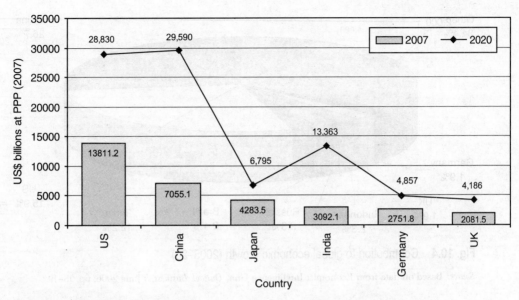

Fig. 10.3 World's largest economies

Source: Based on Economist intelligence Unit; *Outlook Business,* 5 June 2006, pp. 13–19; World Development Indicators Database, World Bank, 1 July 2008.

the US by 2020 to become the largest economy in the world followed by the US (US$28,830 billion), India (US$13,363 billion), Japan (US$6,795 billion), Germany (US$4,857 billion), and the UK[9] (US$4,186 billion).

India's rate of annual GDP growth, which was merely 0.9 per cent during 1900–1946, increased sharply by four times to 3.6 per cent during 1950/51–1980/81, compared to the British colonial rule. The growth of GDP further jumped to 5.9 per cent per year and the GDP per capita to an impressive 3.8 per cent during 1981/82–2005/06. Moreover, India's economic growth was reasonably sustained with no extended periods of decline. Besides, there were hardly any inflationary bouts of the kind that racked many countries in Latin America, the CIS, and even Southeast Asia. Nevertheless, the GDP growth was far below India's potential and much lower than the growth rate achieved by a number of countries in East Asia and Latin America. However, the sustained increase in India's economic growth and improvements in living standards gave rise to an increasing positive attitude among the policy-makers and investors alike of India's potential, unexplored hitherto.

The global economic growth during 2005–20 is likely to be driven by China[10] contributing to 26.7 per cent, followed by the US (15.9%), India (12.2%), Brazil (2.4%), Russia (2.3%), Indonesia (2.3%), the UK (1.9%), Germany (1.9%), and other countries (34.4%) as indicated in Fig. 10.4.

---

[9] Economist Intelligence Unit, *Outlook Business,* 5 June 2006, pp. 13–19.
[10] Economist Intelligence Unit, *Outlook Business,* 5 June 2006, pp. 13–19.

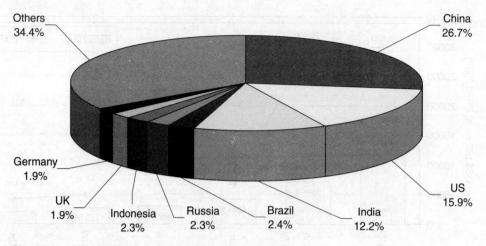

Fig. 10.4 Contribution to global economic growth (2005–20)

Source: Based on data from Economist Intelligence Unit, *Outlook Business,* 5 June 2006, pp. 13–19.

Per capita income provides a better indicator of the purchasing power of the residents of a country. The computation of per capita income is based on the assumption that the country's income is evenly distributed, which is seldom the case. India has a sizeable middle class but there are a number of countries that have a bimodal income distribution with no middle class. This indicates existence of different market segments within a country. The purchasing power of money varies significantly across countries which greatly influences the cost of living.

The growth rate per capita GNI as indicated in Fig. 10.5 facilitates in estimating market potential in future. Luxembourg has the highest GNI per capita[11] of US$64,400 at Purchasing Power Parity (PPP) compared to US$48, 520 in Singapore, the US (US$45,850), Switzerland (US$43,080), Canada (US$35,310), Japan (US$34,600), the UK (US$34,370), Germany (US$33,820), Australia (US$33,340), South Africa (US$9,560), Brazil (US$9,370), Thailand (US$7,800), China (US$5,370), India (US$2,740), Pakistan (US$2,570), and Liberia the lowest at US$290.

International firms need to identify some homogeneity in the countries of their operations and divide them into various segments using a pre-defined criterion known as country-segmentation. Countries can be segmented on the basis of income for operational and analytical purposes. The criteria used for classifying countries by the World Bank[12] on the basis of 2006 per capita gross national income (GNI) are as under:

- Low-income countries : US$935 or less
- Lower-middle-income countries : US$936–3,705
- Upper-middle-income countries : US$3,706–11,455
- High-income countries : US$11,456 or more

---

[11] *World Development Indicators Database,* World Bank, 1 July 2008.

[12] *World Development Indicators,* World Bank as on July 2008.

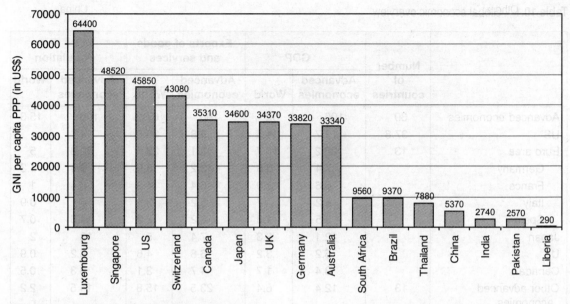

Fig. 10.5   GNI per capita PPP 2007 (in US$)

Source: Based on data from World Development Indicators Database, World Bank, 1 July 2008.

Lower-income and middle-income countries are sometimes referred to as developing economies. The country classification on the basis of per capita GNI facilitates preliminary screening of international markets and provides broad inferences on the consumption patterns.

Macroeconomic overview

Distribution of resources and wealth is highly skewed among the nations. 30 advanced countries in the world with only 15.3 per cent of world's total population account for about 52 per cent of the world's total GDP and 67.3 per cent of exports of goods and services. The US with merely 4.7 per cent of the world's population accounts for 19.7 per cent and 9.8 per cent of the world's GDP and exports, respectively. On the other hand, developing countries with 84.7 per cent of population account for only 48 per cent of the world's GDP and 32.7 per cent of world's exports. India and China with 17.4 and 20.5 per cent respectively of the world's population account for 6.3 and 15.1 per cent world GDP and 1.3 and 7.2 per cent of world's exports as given in Table 10.1.

10.3.2   Assessing Market Potential

Countries with high marketing potential are often preferred locations for business operations. Although market size and its estimated growth rates provide useful insights, the determination of overall market potential of a country is arrived at by eight dimensions and each of these dimensions is allocated weights to contribute to the overall market potential index as given in Exhibit 10.1.

Table 10.1 Global economic overview

	Number of countries	GDP		Exports of goods and services		Population	
		Advanced economies	World	Advanced economies	World	Advanced economies	World
Advanced economies	30	100	52	100	67.3	100	15.3
US	37.8	19.7	14.5	9.8	30.6	4.7	
Euro area	13	28.2	14.7	43.1	29	32.3	5
Germany		7.4	3.9	13.2	8.9	8.4	1.3
France		5.6	2.9	6.4	4.3	6.4	1
Italy		5.2	2.7	5.2	3.5	6	0.9
Spain		3.5	1.8	3.2	2.2	4.5	0.7
Japan		12.1	6.3	7.4	5	13	2
UK		6.2	3.2	6.8	4.6	6.2	0.9
Canada		3.4	1.7	4.7	3.1	3.3	0.5
Other advanced economies	13	12.4	6.4	23.5	15.8	14.5	2.2
Major advance economies	7	77.6	40.4	58.3	39.2	74	11.3
Newly industrialized Asian economies	4	6.5	3.4	13.7	9.2	8.4	1.3

	Number of Countries	Other emerging markets and developing economies	World	Other emerging markets and developing economies	World	Other emerging markets and developing economies	World
Other emerging market and developing economies	143	100	48	100	32.7	100	84.7
Regional groups							
Africa	48	7	3.4	7.7	2.5	15.3	12.9
Sub-Sahara	45	5.4	2.6	5.8	1.9	13.9	11.8
Excluding Nigeria and South Africa	43	2.9	1.4	2.8	0.9	10.2	8.7
Central and Eastern Europe	14	7.1	3.4	13.2	4.3	3.4	2.9
Commenwealth of independent states (CIS)	13	8	3.8	10.1	3.3	5.2	4.4
Russia		5.4	2.6	6.9	2.3	2.6	2.2
Developing Asia	23	56.3	27	38.6	12.6	61.7	52.3
China		31.4	15.1	21.9	7.2	24.3	20.5
India		13.1	6.3	4.1	1.3	20.6	17.4
Excluding China and India	21	11.7	5.6	12.6	4.1	16.9	14.3

Contd

Table 10.1 Contd

	Number of Countries	Other emerging markets and developing economies	World	Other emerging markets and developing economies	World	Other emerging markets and developing economies	World
Middle East	13	5.9	2.8	14.5	4.7	4.4	3.7
Western Hemisphere	32	15.7	7.6	15.9	5.2	10.1	8.5
Brazil		5.4	2.6	3.3	1.1	3.4	2.9
Mexico		3.7	1.8	5.5	1.8	1.9	1.6

Source: World Economic Outlook: Spillovers and Cycles in the Global Economy, IMF, April 2007, p. 204.

Emerging markets comprise more than half of the world's population, account for a large share of world output and have very high growth rates, which means enormous market potential. India is the second largest market after China among the emerging markets.[13] However, due to relatively lower ranking on other parameters that measure market potential, such as market-growth rate, market intensity, market consumption capacity, commercial infrastructure, economic freedom, market receptivity, country risk, India has been ranked as the world's ninth most attractive market while China is ranked as the fifth most attractive market, as shown in Table 10.2.

10.3.3 Evaluating country competitiveness

Competitiveness goes much beyond the classical and neo-classical trade theories as discussed in Chapter 2; it not only affects a country's economic growth and long-term prosperity but also significantly influences the business prospects for an international firm. Competitiveness of a nation is referred to a set of institutions, policies, and factors that determine the level of productivity of a country.[14] Therefore, a more competitive economy is one that makes better use of available factors and resources and is likely to grow faster in a medium to long-term perspective. The productivity level determines the rate of return obtained by investment in a country. Since the rates of return are the fundamental determinants of the growth rates of an economy, investments in a competitive economy are likely to grow faster.

Factors influencing country competitiveness

Global Competitiveness Index (GCI) brought out by the World Economic Forum provides a holistic overview of factors that are critical to driving productivity and competitiveness and groups them in 12 pillars as follows.

[13] 'Market Potential Indicators for Emerging Markets', *GlobalEDGE*, 2007.
[14] Sala-i-Martin, Xavier, Jennifer Blanke, Margareta Drzeniek Hanouz, Thierry Geiger, Irene Mia, and Fiona Paua, 'The Global Competitiveness Index: Measuring the Productive Potential of Nations', The Global Competitiveness Report 2007–08, Geneva, p. 3.

Dimension	Weight	Measures used
Market size	10/50	■ Urban population (million)—2005[a] ■ Electricity consumption (billion kwh)—2004[b]
Market growth rate	6/50	■ Average annual growth rate (%) of commercial energy use between years 1999–2003[a] ■ Real GDP growth rate (%)—2005[a]
Market intensity	7/50	■ GNI per capita estimates using PPP (US Dollars)—2005[a] ■ Private consumption as a percentage of GDP (%)—2005[a]
Market consumption capacity	5/50	■ Percentage share of middle-class in consumption/income (latest year available)[a]
Commercial infrastructure	7/50	■ Telephone mainlines (per 100 habitants)—2005[c] ■ Cellular mobile subscribers (per 100 habitants)—2005[c] ■ Number of PCs (per 100 habitants)—2005[c] ■ Paved road density (km per million people)—(latest year available)[a] ■ Internet hosts (per million people)—2005[c] ■ Population per retail outlet—2005[d] ■ Television sets (per 1000 persons)—(latest year available)[a]
Economic freedom	5/50	■ Economic freedom index—2006[e] ■ Political freedom index—2006[f]
Market receptivity	6/50	■ Per capita imports from US (US Dollars)—2005[g] ■ Trade as a percentage of GDP (%)—2005[a]
Country risk	4/50	■ Country risk rating—2006[h]

Exhibit 10.1   Computation of market potential indicators

Sources:
[a] World Bank, World Development Indicators, 2006.
[b] US Energy Information Administration, International Energy Annual, 2004.
[c] International Telecommunication Union, ICT Indicators, 2005.
[d] Euromonitor, European Marketing Data and Statistics, 2006.
[e] Heritage Foundation, The Index of Economic Freedom, 2005.
[f] Freedom House, Survey of Freedom in the World, 2006.
[g] US Census Bureau, Foreign Trade Division, Country Data, 2005.
[h] Euromoney, Country Risk Survey, 2006.

Institutions The institutional environment strongly influences a country's competitiveness and growth. It forms a framework within which private individuals, firms, and governments interact to generate wealth in the economy. It comprises both public and private institutions that include property rights and intellectual property protection, ethics and corruption, judiciary independence and favouritism in decision of government officials, government efficiency, security, and government accountability.

Table 10.2 Cross-country comparison of market potential indicators

Countries	Market size Rank	Market size Index	Market growth rate Rank	Market growth rate Index	Market intensity Rank	Market intensity Index	Market consumption Rank	Market consumption Index	Commercial infrastructure capacity Rank	Commercial infrastructure capacity Index	Economic freedom Rank	Economic freedom Index	Market receptivity Rank	Market receptivity Index	Country risk Rank	Country risk Index	Overall index Rank	Overall index Index
China	1	100	1	100	25	23	12	59	16	45	27	1	22	3	13	49	1	100
Hong Kong	24	1	20	23	1	100	13	54	2	97	6	79	2	75	2	90	2	96
Singapore	27	1	18	27	9	59	11	62	6	83	10	71	1	100	1	100	3	93
Taiwan	12	5	6	57	11	57	–	–	1	100	8	76	5	23	3	87	4	79
Israel	25	1	12	45	2	79	4	82	3	94	3	86	4	26	5	63	5	78
South Korea	7	12	16	30	5	63	2	99	5	90	7	78	10	13	4	65	6	75
Czech Rep.	23	2	9	48	13	55	3	97	4	91	2	93	9	15	6	63	7	73
Hungary	26	1	24	14	3	76	1	100	7	78	4	83	8	16	8	62	8	64
India	2	44	3	63	22	37	7	77	25	17	17	44	27	1	16	39	9	55
Poland	14	5	27	1	10	58	6	80	8	71	5	82	14	7	9	58	10	46
Turkey	9	8	7	55	12	57	10	67	12	51	16	45	18	5	20	27	11	37
Malaysia	20	3	2	70	26	19	19	42	10	53	20	39	3	30	11	53	12	35
Russia	3	34	15	38	23	30	16	53	9	54	25	5	19	4	17	35	13	35
Mexico	5	12	25	9	8	60	21	27	15	48	11	63	6	18	12	52	14	32
Thailand	17	4	11	46	18	44	14	54	20	38	15	49	7	18	15	43	15	31
Chile	21	2	19	25	17	44	23	13	13	51	1	100	12	10	10	57	16	26
Argentina	15	5	10	48	4	65	20	39	11	53	14	49	25	2	27	1	17	21
Saudi Arabia	13	5	4	59	27	1	–	–	14	48	22	15	11	11	7	62	18	18
Egypt	16	4	14	43	14	50	9	70	21	36	26	3	17	5	18	29	19	18
Pakistan	10	6	5	57	6	62	5	81	26	2	23	10	26	1	25	10	20	15
Indonesia	6	12	13	45	21	38	8	72	27	1	21	37	15	6	24	13	21	15
Philippines	11	5	21	22	7	60	18	47	22	29	19	42	13	10	23	17	22	14
Brazil	4	25	26	2	20	39	24	13	17	44	13	55	24	2	19	28	23	14
South Africa	8	8	17	28	15	49	25	1	24	22	9	75	20	4	14	44	24	10
Peru	22	2	22	20	16	46	15	53	23	23	12	62	23	3	22	19	25	9
Venezuela	18	4	8	51	24	27	17	52	19	39	24	5	16	6	26	4	26	3
Columbia	19	4	23	20	19	42	22	17	18	41	18	44	21	4	21	20	27	1

Source: Market Potential Indicators for Emerging Markets (2007), GlobalEDGE, http://globaledge.msu.edu/resourceDesk/MarketPotential.

Institutional framework considerably influences investment decision and organization of production.

Finland has the most efficient institutions in the world (Fig. 10.6) with the score of 6.16 on a seven point scale, followed by Denmark (6.14), Singapore (6.03) and Switzerland (5.90) whereas the UK (5.31) ranked at 15th position, Japan (5.06) at 24th, the US (4.76) at 33rd, India (4.32) at 48th, China (3.71) at 77th, Brazil (3.32) at 104th, and Russia (3.10) at 116th place. The institutions are least efficient in Venezuela (2.41).

Infrastructure   Availability of high quality of infrastructure is an important factor for efficient business operations. High-quality infrastructure reduces the effect of distance between regions, with the result of truly integrating the national market and connecting it to markets in other countries and regions. A well-developed transport and communication infrastructure network is a pre-requisite for the efficient functioning of markets and export growth. Effective means of transport for goods, quality of roads, railways and air, and people and services facilitate to get the goods to markets in a secure and timely manner and facilitate the movement of workers across the country to most suitable jobs. Ample supply of quality electricity without interruption is also essential for unimpeded manufacturing operations. Further, a strong telecommunication network facilitates a rapid and free flow of information contributing to growth.

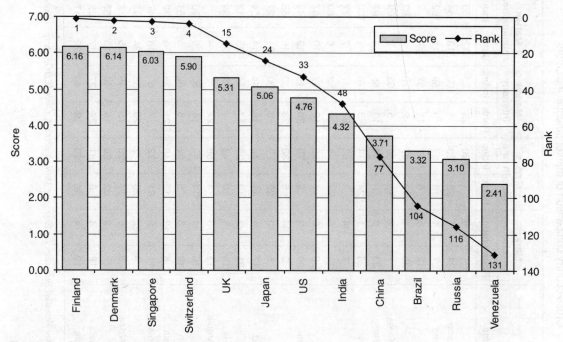

Fig. 10.6   Cross-country comparison of institutions

1—least efficient, 7—most efficient.

Source: Based on data from The Global Competitiveness Report 2007–08, World Economic Forum, Geneva, pp. 16–17.

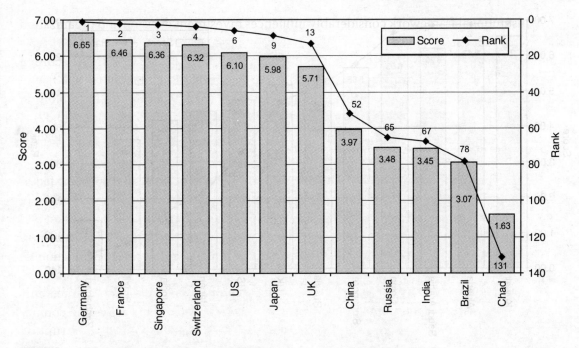

Fig. 10.7 Cross-country comparison of infrastructure

1—least developed, 7—as extensive and efficient as the world's best
Source: Based on data from The Global Competitiveness Report 2007–08, World Economic Forum, Geneva, pp. 16–17.

Germany ranked number one in terms of quality of infrastructure (Fig. 10.7) with a score of 6.65 on a seven point scale, followed by France (6.46), Singapore (6.36), and Switzerland (6.32) whereas the US (6.10) ranked at 6th, Japan (5.98) at 9th, UK (5.71) at 13th, China (3.97) at 52nd, Russia (3.48) at 65th, India (3.45) at 67th, Brazil (3.07) at 78th, and Chad (1.63) at 131st place.

Macro-economic stability The stability of macro-economic environment is important not only for business operations but also for overall competitiveness of a country. For instance, companies find it difficult to operate under the condition of hyper-inflation. Government surplus or deficit, savings, interest rates, and government debt too significantly influence a country's macro-economic stability.

Kuwait ranked at 1st position in macro-economic stability with the score of 6.56 on a seven point scale (Fig. 10.8), followed by Algeria (6.41) and Saudi Arabia (6.20) whereas China (6.03) ranks at 7th, Singapore (5.68) at 24th, Russia (5.35) at 37th, the UK (5.18) at 46th, the US (4.78) at 75th, Japan (4.45) at 97th, India (4.21) at 108th, Brazil (3.66) at 126th, and Zimbabwe (1.37) ranked last at the 131st place.

Health and primary education Availability of a healthy work-force is vital to a country's competitiveness and productivity. Poor health leads to significant cost to business, as sick workers are often absent or operate below the level of efficiency. Basic education increases the efficiency of workers. Therefore, lack of basic education

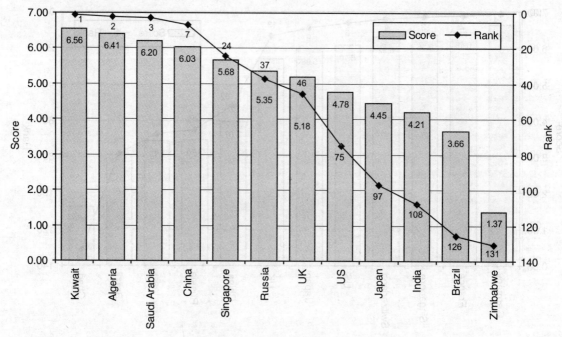

Fig. 10.8 Cross-country comparison of macro-economic stability

1—least stable, 7—most stable.

Source: Based on data from The Global Competitiveness Report 2007–08, World Economic Forum, Geneva, pp. 16–17.

becomes a constraint as a firm finds it difficult to move up the value chain by producing more sophisticated or value-intensive products.

Finland scores (6.58) the highest in Health and Primary Education on a seven point scale (Fig. 10.9), followed by Iceland (6.52) and Denmark (6.45), whereas Singapore (6.24) rank at 19th, the UK (6.16) at 21st, Japan (6.14) at 23rd, the US (6.00) at 34th, Russia (5.51) at 60th, China (5.49) at 61st, Brazil (5.23) at 84th, India (4.92) at 101st, and Mozambique (2.95), which is ranked last at the 131st place.

Higher education and training In order to move up the value chain beyond simple production processes and products, quality higher education and training is crucial. It also requires the pools of highly educated and trained workers capable of rapidly adapting to changing business environment Thus quantity of education, i.e., secondary and tertiary enrollment and educational expenditure, quality of educational system, maths and science education, and management schools and on the job training become imperative for business operations moving up the value chain.

Finland ranked the topmost in higher education and training (Fig. 10.10) with a score of 6.01 on a seven point scale, followed by Sweden (5.98) and Denmark (5.96) whereas the US (5.68) ranked at 5th, the UK (5.42) at 15th, Singapore (5.42) at 16th, Japan (5.21) at 22nd, Russia (4.33) at 45th, India (4.13) at 55th, Brazil (4.01) at 64th, China (3.77) at 78th, and Chad (2.00) ranked last at the 131st place.

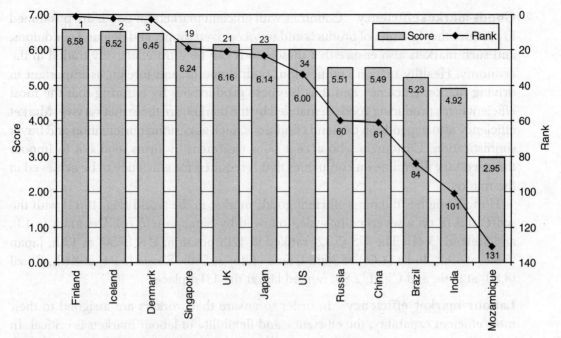

Fig. 10.9 Cross-country comparison of health and primary education

1—least, 7—highest (level of health and primary education).
Source: Based on data from The Global Competitiveness Report 2007–08, World Economic Forum, Geneva, pp. 16–17.

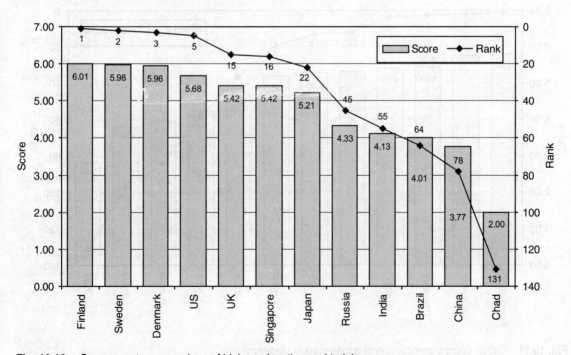

Fig. 10.10 Cross-country comparison of higher education and training

1—lowest, 7—highest (quality and quantity of higher education and training).
Source: Based on data from The Global Competitiveness Report 2007–08, World Economic Forum, Geneva, pp. 18–19.

Goods market efficiency Countries with efficient markets for goods are positioned to produce the right mix of products and services given supply and demand conditions, and such markets also ensure that these goods can be most effectively traded in the economy. Healthy market competition, both domestic and foreign, is important in driving market efficiency and thus business productivity by ensuring that the most efficient firms producing goods demanded by the market, are those that survive. Market efficiency also depends on demand conditions, such as customer orientation and buyer sophistication. Customers who accept poor treatment by firms tend not to impose the necessary discipline on companies that is required for efficiency to be achieved in the market.

Hong Kong has the most efficient goods market in the world (Fig. 10.11) with the score of 5.79 on a seven point scale, followed by Singapore (5.76), Denmark (5.43), and Ireland (5.41). The US (5.32) ranked at 12th position, UK (5.30) at 13th, Japan (5.22) at 19th, India (4.66) at 36th, China (4.26) at 58th, Russia (3.94) at 84th, Brazil (3.80) at 97th, and Chad (2.84) ranked last at the 131st place.

Labour market efficiency In order to ensure that workers are assigned to their most efficient capability, the efficiency and flexibility of labour markets is critical. In a productive economy, workers are allocated appropriately and provided with incentives that motivate them to put in their best effort in their jobs. In order to make

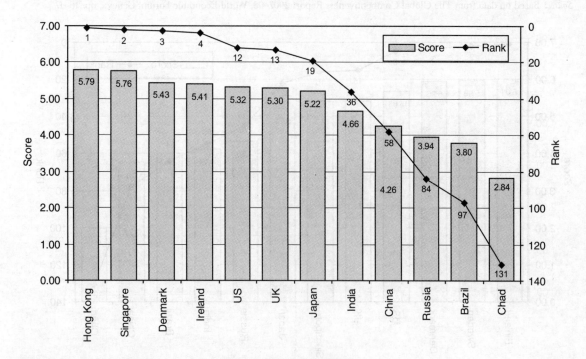

Fig. 10.11 Cross-country comparison of goods market efficiency

1—least efficient, 7—most efficient.

Source: Based on data from The Global Competitiveness Report 2007–08, World Economic Forum, Geneva, pp. 18–19.

the best use of their talents, a clear relationship between worker-incentives and their efforts, is required including gender equity in business.

Labour markets are the most efficient in the US with the score of 5.71 on a seven point scale, followed by Singapore (5.67), Switzerland (5.64), the UK (5.29), and Japan (5.11). Russia (4.70) ranked at 33rd position, China (4.40) at 55th, India (4.07) at 96th, France (4.06) at 98th, Brazil (3.96) at 104th, Italy (3.50) at 128th, and Libya (3.21) ranked last at the 131st place (Fig. 10.12).

Financial market sophistication An efficient financial sector is critical to canalize resources to the best investment projects or entrepreneurs rather than to those politically connected. Sophisticated financial markets that can make capital available for private sectors investment from sources, such as loans from a sound banking sector, well-regulated securities exchanges, and venture capital. A modern financial sector develops products and methods so that small innovators with good ideas can implement them. Providing risk capital and loans that are trustworthy and transparent is also critical for efficient financial markets.

Hong Kong has the most sophisticated financial markets (Fig. 10.13) in the world with the score of 6.23 on a seven point scale, followed by the UK (6.17), Singapore (6.02), and Ireland (5.91). The US (5.68) ranks at 11th, Japan (4.94) at 36th, India (4.93) at 37th, Brazil (4.14) at 73rd, Italy (3.96) at 86th, Russia (3.60) at 109th, China (3.35) at 118th, and Burundi (2.51) ranked last at 131st.

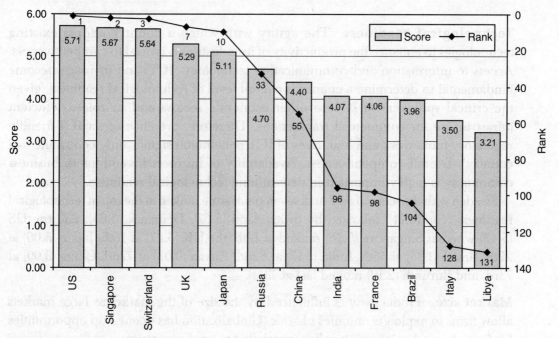

Fig. 10.12 Cross-country comparison of labour market efficiency

1—least efficient, 7—most efficient.

Source: Based on data from The Global Competitiveness Report 2007–08, World Economic Forum, Geneva, pp. 18–19.

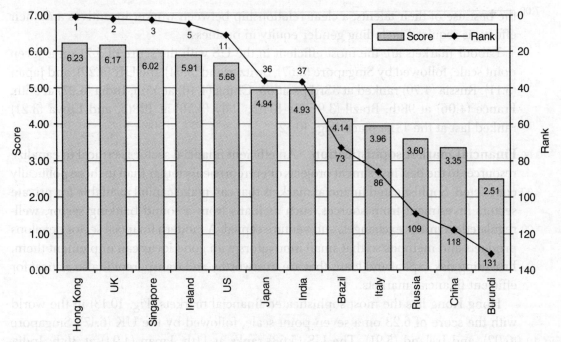

Fig. 10.13 Cross-country comparison of financial market sophistication

1—least sophisticated, 7—most sophisticated.

Source: Based on data from The Global Competitiveness Report 2007–08, World Economic Forum, Geneva, pp. 18–19.

Technological readiness The agility with which a country adopts existing technologies to enhance the productivity of its industries is crucial to competitiveness. Access to information and communication technology (ICT) and its usage become fundamental to determine a country's overall level of technological readiness, given the critical spillovers of ICT to other economic sectors and its role as efficient infrastructure for commercial transactions. Therefore, presence of an ICT-friendly regulatory framework and high rates of ICT penetration significantly contribute to a country's overall competitiveness. Availability of business inventions to business community is highly important in determining technological readiness.

Sweden with the score of 5.87 on a seven point scale ranked at the top in technological readiness (Fig. 10.14), followed by Switzerland (5.67), Denmark (5.64), and the US (5.43) whereas Singapore (5.36) ranked at 12th, the UK (5.27) at 16th, Japan (5.06) at 20th, Brazil (3.35) at 55th, India (3.17) at 62nd, Russia (3.03) at 72nd, China (3.00) at 73rd, and Burundi (2.10) ranked last at 131st.

Market size Productivity is influenced by the size of the market as large markets allow firms to exploit economies of scale. Globalization has opened up opportunities for firms to market internationally, especially for small countries.

The US was at first position with the score of 6.83 on a seven point scale in the market size (Fig. 10.15), followed by China (6.80), India (6.16), Japan (6.08), Germany (5.90),

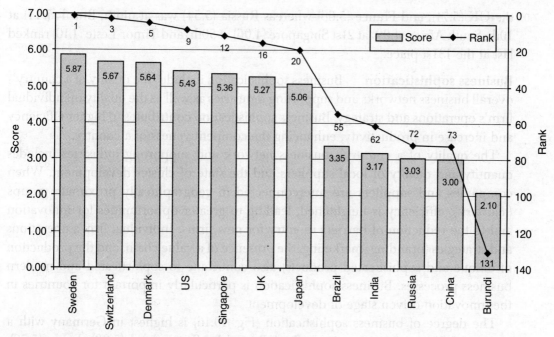

Fig. 10.14   Cross-country comparison of technological readiness

1—least, 7—highest (level of technological readiness).

Source: Based on data from The Global Competitiveness Report 2007–08, World Economic Forum, Geneva pp. 18–19.

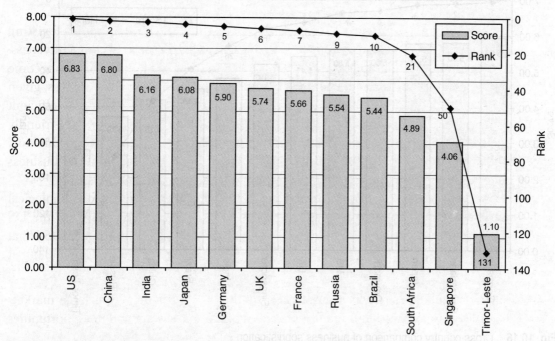

Fig. 10.15   Cross-country comparison of market size

1—small least, 7—largest (size of market).

Source: Based on data from The Global Competitiveness Report 2007–08, World Economic Forum, Geneva, pp. 18–19.

the UK (5.74), and France (5.66) whereas Russia (5.54) was at ninth, Brazil (5.44) at 10th, South Africa (4.89) at 21st Singapore (4.06) at 50th, and Timor-Leste (1.10) ranked last at the 131st place.

Business sophistication   Business sophistication includes the quality of a country's overall business networks and supporting industries as well as the quality of individual firm's operations and strategy. Business sophistication contributes to higher efficiency and increase in productivity, enhancing the competitiveness of a country.

The quality of a country's business network and supporting industries includes quantity and quality of local suppliers and the state of cluster development. When companies and suppliers are interconnected in geographically proximate groups ('clusters'), efficiency is heightened, leading to greater opportunities for innovation and to the reduction of barriers to entry for new firms. Individual firm's operations and strategies (branding, marketing, the presence of a value chain, and the production of unique and sophisticated products) also contribute to sophisticated and modern business processes. Business sophistication is particularly important for countries in the innovation-driven stage of development.

The degree of business sophistication (Fig. 10.16) is highest in Germany with a score of 5.93 on a seven point scale, followed by Switzerland (5.80), Japan (5.76), Denmark (5.60), and the US (5.60). The UK (5.41) ranked at the 13th place, Singapore

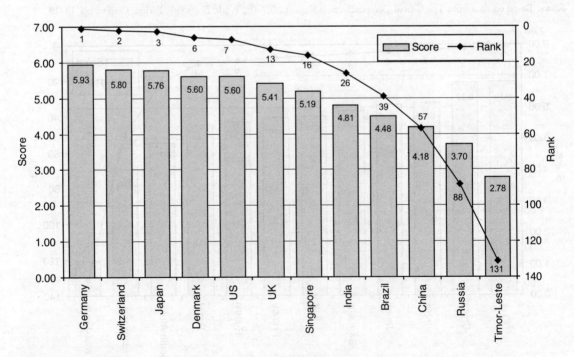

Fig. 10.16   Cross-country comparison of business sophistication

1—least, 7—highest (level of business sophistication).

Source: Based on data from The Global Competitiveness Report 2007–08, World Economic Forum, Geneva, p. 20.

(5.19) at 16th, India (4.81) at 26th, Brazil (4.48) at 39th, China (4.18) at 57th, Russia (3.70) at 88th, and Timor-Leste (2.78) last at the 131st place.

Innovation Improving institutions, building infrastructure, reducing macro-economic stability, improving the human capital or efficiency of the labour, financial, or goods market substantially contribute to a country's competitiveness. As these factors run into diminishing returns in the long run, a country's competitiveness can be enhanced by technological innovations.

Productivity can be improved by adopting existing technologies or making incremental improvements in other areas by the less-developed countries. However, this is no longer sufficient to increase productivity by the countries that have reached the innovation stage of development. In order to maintain a competitive edge, companies in these countries must design and develop cutting-edge products and processes. This requires an environment conducive to innovation activity by getting sufficient investments in research and development, especially by private, high-quality scientific research institutions, collaboration in research between universities and industry, and protection of intellectual property.

The US has the highest capacity for innovation (Fig. 10.17) with the score of 5.77 on a seven point scale, followed by Switzerland (5.74), Finland (5.67), and Japan (5.64). Singapore (5.08) ranked at 11th place, the UK (4.79) at 14th, India (3.90) at 28th,

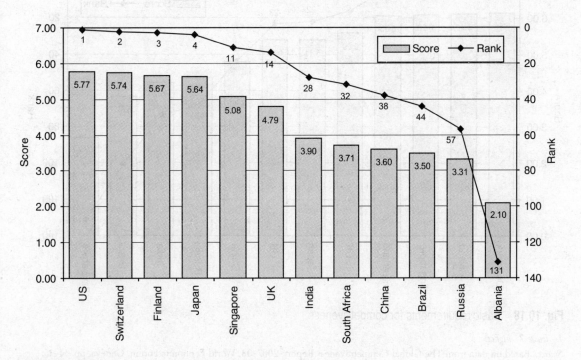

Fig. 10.17 Cross-country comparison of innovation

1—least, 7—highest (capacity to innovate).

Source: Based on data from The Global Competitiveness Report 2007–08, World Economic Forum, Geneva, p. 20.

South Africa (3.71) at 32nd, China (3.60) at 38th, Brazil (3.50) at 44th, Russia (3.31) at 57th, and Albania (2.10) ranked last at the 131st place.

All the above factors are not independent; rather they tend to reinforce each other to determine competitiveness.

Stages of development and country competitiveness

Although all the above factors contribute to a country's competitiveness, the importance of each depends on a country's particular stage of development[15] as follows.

Factor-driven economies Such countries principally compete based on their factor endowments, primarily unskilled labour, and natural resources. Companies from factor-driven economies compete on the basis of price and often sell basic products and commodities with their low productivity reflected in low wages. Maintaining competitiveness at this stage primarily hinges on the smooth functioning of public and private institutions, appropriate infrastructure, a stable macro-economic framework, and a healthy and literate workforce.

Denmark ranks at first position in the basic factors for competitiveness (Fig. 10.18) with the score of 6.14 on a seven point scale, followed by Finland (6.11), Singapore

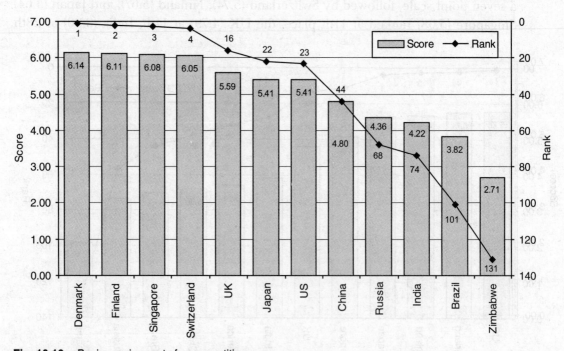

Fig. 10.18 Basic requirements for competitiveness

1—least, 7—highest.

Source: Based on data from The Global Competitiveness Report, 2007–08, World Economic Forum, Geneva, pp. 14–15.

---

[15] Porter, Michael, *The Competitive Advantage of Nations,* New York: The Free Press, 1990.

(6.08), and Switzerland (6.05), whereas the UK (5.59) is ranked at 16th place, Japan (5.41) at 22nd, the US (5.41) at 23rd, China (4.80) at 44th, Russia (4.36) at 68th, India (4.22) at 74th, Brazil (3.82) at 101st, and Zimbabwe (2.71) ranked last at the 131st place.

Efficiency-driven economies   Wages rise as a result of economic growth and countries are required to develop more efficient production processes, thereby moving into the efficiency-driven stage of development. Competitiveness is increasingly driven at this stage by higher education and training, efficient goods market, well-functioning labour markets, sophisticated financial markets, a large domestic and foreign market, and ability to harness the benefits of existing technologies.

The US is the most efficiency-driven economy (Fig. 10.19) with the score of 5.77 on a seven point scale, followed by UK (5.53), Hong Kong (5.45), Denmark (5.44), Canada (5.39), Singapore (5.38), Switzerland (5.35), and Sweden (5.34). Japan (5.27) ranked at 13th position, India (4.52) at 31st, China (4.26) at 45th, Russia (4.19) at 48th, Brazil (4.12) at 55th, and Burundi (2.59) last at the 131st place.

Innovation-driven economies   As the countries move to the innovation-driven stage, higher wages and associated standard of living can be sustained only if their businesses are able to compete with new and unique products. Companies must

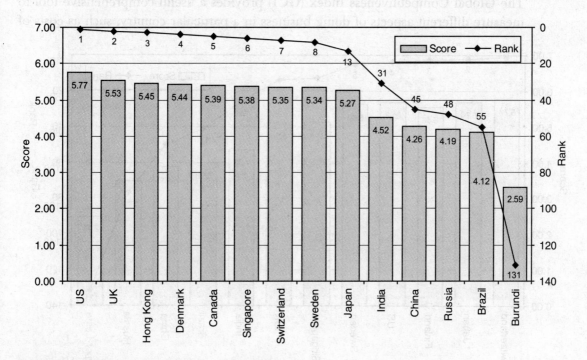

Fig. 10.19   Efficiency enhancers for competitiveness

1—least, 7—highest.

Source: Based on data from The Global Competitiveness Report, 2007–08, World Economic Forum, Geneva, pp. 14–15.

compete at this stage through innovation, producing new and different goods using the most sophisticated production processes.

Switzerland ranked at the first in innovation and sophistication (Fig. 10.20) with the score of 5.77 on a seven point scale, followed by Japan (5.70), Finland (5.56), the US (5.68), and Sweden (5.62). Singapore (5.14) ranked at 13th place, the UK (5.10) at 14th, India (4.36) at 26th, Brazil (3.99) at 41st, China (3.89) at 50th, Russia (3.50) at 77th, and Timor-Leste (2.47) last at the 131st place.

Countries are classified under various stages of development based on the level of GDP per capita at market exchange rates, which is a widely available measure used as proxy for wages and the extent to which countries are factor-driven. Share of exports of primary goods in total exports is used as a proxy and countries that export more than 70 per cent of primary products are, to a large extent, assumed to be factor-driven. Countries falling between the two stages are considered to be in transition, as indicated in Table 10.3.

The stages of development are integrated into the competitiveness index by assigning different weights to factors that are considered more relevant to a country's competitiveness.

Assessing overall country competitiveness

The Global Competitiveness Index (GCI) provides a useful comprehensive tool to measure different aspects of doing business in a particular country, such as costs of

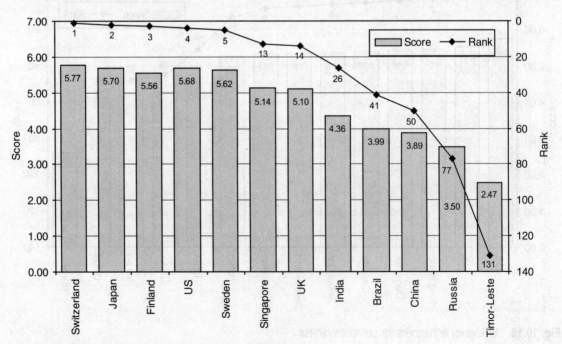

Fig. 10.20   Innovation and sophistication for competitiveness

1—least, 7—highest.

Source: Based on data from The Global Competitiveness Report, 2007–08, World Economic Forum, Geneva, pp. 14–15.

Table 10.3 Country classification based on stages of development

Contd

Stage 1	Transition from 1 to 2	Stage 2	Transition from 2 to 3	Stage 3
GDP p.c.<US$2,000	GDP p.c. US$2,000–US$3,000	GDP p.c.US$3,000–US$9,000	GDP p.c US$9,000–US$17,000	GDP p.c >US$17,000
Armenia	Albania	Algeria	Bahrain	Australia
Bangladesh	Azerbaijan	Argentina	Barbados	Austria
Benin	Bosnia and Herzegovina	Brazil	Croatia	Belgium
Bolivia	Botswana	Bulgaria	Czech Republic	Canada
Burkina Faso	China	Chile	Estonia	Cyprus
Burundi	Colombia	Costa Rica	Hungary	Denmark
Cambodia	Ecuador	Dominican Republic	Malta	Finland
Cameroon	El Salvador	Jamaica	Qatar	France
Chad	Guatemala	Latvia	Slovak Republic	Germany
Egypt	Jordan	Lithuania	Taiwan, China	Greece
Ethiopia	Kazakhstan	Macedonia, FYR	Trinidad and Tobago	Hong Kong SAR
Gambia, The	Kuwait	Malaysia		Iceland
Gerogia	Libya	Mauritius		Israel
Guyana	Oman	Mexico		Italy
Honduras	Saudi Arabia	Montenegro		Japan
India	Tunisia	Namibia		Korea
Indonesia	Ukraine	Panama		Luxembourg
Kenya	Venezuela	Peru		Netherlands
Kyrgyz Republic		Poland		New Zealand
Lesotho		Romania		Norway
Madagascar		Russia		Portugal
Mali		Serbia		Puerto Rico
Mauritania		South Africa		Singapore
Moldova		Suriname		Slovenia
Mongolia		Thailand		Spain

Table 10.3 Contd

Stage 1	Transition from 1 to 2	Stage 2	Transition from 2 to 3	Stage 3
Morocco		Turkey		Sweden
Mozambique		Uruguay		Switzerland
Nepal				United Arab Emirates
Nicaragua				UK
Nigeria				US
Pakistan				
Paraguay				
Philippines				
Senegal				
Sri Lanka				
Syria				
Tajikistan				
Tanzania				
Timor-Leste				
Uganda				
Uzbenkistan				
Vietnam				
Zambia				
Zimbabawe				

Source: The Global Competitiveness Report, 2007–08, World Economic Forum, Geneva, p. 9.

dealing with bureaucracy, costs of poor infrastructure, costs of an uneducated and unhealthy workforce, costs of dealing with violence, costs of hiring and firing workers, costs of not having access to an efficient financial sector, costs of not having suppliers or networks, costs of not being able to rely on universities, costs of not having the best available technology, etc.

The US is the most competitive economy in the world with the score of 5.67 on a seven- point scale, followed by Switzerland (5.62), Denmark (5.55), Sweden (5.54), Germany (5.51), Finland (5.49), Singapore (5.45), Japan (5.43), the UK (5.41), Australia (5.17), and Malaysia (5.10). China (4.57) ranked at 34th position, South Africa (4.42) at 44th, India (4.33) at 48th, Russia (4.19) at 58th, Brazil (3.99) at 72nd position, whereas Chad (2.78) is the least competitive (Fig. 10.21).

India's rank at 48th derives substantial competitive advantage from its market size, where it ranks third in domestic market size and fourth in foreign market size whereas China ranks second in domestic market size and first in foreign market size. This allows companies both in China and India to benefit from significant economies on scale. India also derives competitive advantage from sophistication of its business (ranked 26th) and its innovative potential (ranked 28th). It is also well assessed for the state of its business clusters and the availability of local suppliers, as well as its reliance

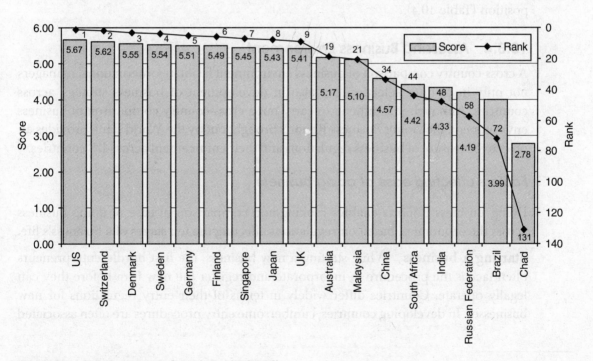

Fig. 10.21   Global competitiveness index (2007–08)

1—least competitive, 7—most competitive.

Source: Based on data from The Global Competitiveness Report 2007–08, World Economic Forum, Geneva, p. 10.

on professional management. India ranked impressively at fourth in the availability of scientists and engineers and 22nd in the quality of scientific research institutes.[16]

Evaluating business competitiveness across countries

Business Competitiveness Index (BCI), brought out by the World Economic Forum, provides a conceptual framework to rank business competitiveness across countries based on a rich set of measures drawn from over 11,000 responses to the World Economic Forum's Survey of senior business leaders[17] in 127 countries. The BCI is based on two sub-indices: company operation and strategy and national business environment. The two sub-indices in the overall BCI are determined from the coefficient of regression of GDP per capita (PPP adjusted) on the sub-index values.

The prosperity of a nation is determined by its competitiveness which is manifest in the productivity with which a nation utilizes its human, capital, and natural resources. Competitiveness is rooted primarily in a nation's macro-economic fundamentals, contained in the sophistication of company operations, the quality of the macro-economic business environment, and strength of clusters.

The US ranked at the top of the BCI, followed by Germany, Finland Sweden, Denmark, and Switzerland whereas Singapore ranks at ninth, Japan at 10th, the UK at 11th, India at 31st, China at 54th Brazil at 56th, Russia at 67th, and Chad at 127th position (Table 10.4).

10.3.4   Assessing Business Environment

A cross-country comparison of business environment facilitates international managers not only in country selection but also in development of business strategy across countries. Although it is difficult to carry out a cross-country comparison of business environment, the Doing Business Reports brought out by the World Bank provides an objective measure of business regulations and their enforcement across 178 countries.[18]

Factors affecting ease of doing business

Doing Business Reports enables ranking and comparison of ease of doing business across the economies, based on regulations affecting the ten stages of a business's life.

Starting a business   While starting a new business, the first hurdle entrepreneurs often face is the procedure to incorporate and register the new firm before they can legally operate. Countries differ widely in terms of their entry regulations for new businesses. In developing countries, cumbersome entry procedures are often associated

---

[16] Sala-I-Martin, Xavier et. al., 'The Global Competitiveness Index: Measuring The Productive Potential of Nations', The Global Competitiveness Report, 2007–08, World Economic Forum, Geneva, pp. 28–50.
[17] Porter, Michael E., Christian Ketels, Mercedes Delgado, 'The Microeconomic Foundations of Prosperity: Finding from the Business Competitiveness Index', The Global Competitiveness Report, 2007–08, World Economic Forum, Geneva pp. 51–75.
[18] Doing Business 2008, World Bank Group, Washington D.C., pp. 9–58.

Table 10.4 Business competitiveness index (2007)

Country	Ranking	Country	Ranking	Country	Ranking
US	1	Lithuania	38	Pakistan	75
Germany	2	Malta	39	Tanzania	76
Finland	3	Italy	40	Ukraine	77
Sweden	4	Bahrain	41	Gambia, The	78
Denmark	5	Slovak Republic	42	Bulgaria	79
Swiitzerland	6	Cyprus	43	Nigeria	80
Netherlands	7	Turkey	44	Namibia	81
Austria	8	Hungary	45	Honduras	82
Singapore	9	Jordan	46	Argentina	83
Japan	10	Kuwait	47	Dominican Republic	84
UK	11	Costa Rica	48	Benin	85
Hong Kong SAR	12	Sri Lanka	49	Mali	86
Norway	13	Greece	50	Macedonia, FYR	87
Canada	14	Latvia	51	Uganda	88
Belgium	15	Mauritius	52	Algeria	89
Iceland	16	Poland	53	Moldova	90
France	17	China	54	Georgia	91
Australia	18	Panama	55	Venezuela	92
Korea	19	Brazil	56	Madagascar	93
Israel	20	Croatia	57	Tajikistan	94
Malaysia	21	Jamaica	58	Zimbabwe	95
New Zealand	22	Kenya	59	Bosnia and Herzegovina	96
Taiwan (China)	23	Morocco	60	Armenia	97
Ireland	24	Mexico	61	Ecuador	98
Tunisia	25	Colombia	62	Mongolia	99
Estonia	26	Philippines	63	Nicaragua	100
Spain	27	Guatemala	64	Cambodia	101
United Arab Emirates	28	Urguay	65	Cameroon	102
Chile	29	El Salvador	66	Kyrgyz Republic	103
Portugal	30	Russia	67	Ethiopia	104
India	31	Kazakhstan	68	Bangladesh	105
Czech Republic	32	Romania	69	Guyana	106
Qatar	33	Trinidad and Tobago	70	Mozambique	107
South Africa	34	Botswana	71	Albania	108
Slovenia	35	Vietnam	72	Bolivia	109
Indonesia	36	Peru	73	Paraguay	110
Thailand	37	Azerbaijan	74	Chad	127

Source: The Global Competitiveness Report 2007–08, World Economic Forum, pp. 78–79.

with more corruption, with an opportunity to extract bribe at each point of contact. Burdensome entry procedures often constrain private investments, push more people into the informal economy, increase consumer prices, and fuel corruption.

To start a business is the easiest in Australia followed by Canada, New Zealand, the US, Ireland, and the UK that ranked at the top six places whereas the most difficult places to start business are Guinea Bissau (178th), Chad (177th), and Togo (176th). Singapore ranked at ninth place compared to Japan (44th), Russia (50th), India (111th), Brazil (122nd), and China (135th) in the ease of starting a business.

Dealing with licences   Once a business is registered, the companies have to comply with official procedures, such as licenses and safety regulations, including statutory inspections. These include procedures to complete utility connections for construction companies, such as electricity, water, telephone, sewage, etc. In low-income countries, complying with regulations is so burdensome that entrepreneurs often move their activity to informal economy.

St. Vincent and the Grenadines is the most friendly country to deal with licenses whereas New Zealand ranked at second place followed by Singapore (fifth), Denmark (sixth), the US (24th), Japan (32nd), the UK (54th), Brazil (107th), and India (134th). The countries with the most cumbersome licensing regime include Eritrea (178th), Russia (177th), and China (175th).

Employing workers   A complex system of laws and institutions has been established by most countries so as to protect workers and to guarantee a minimum standard of living for its people. Such a system encompasses four types of laws, such as employment, industrial relations, social security, and occupational health and safety laws. Most employment regulations are enacted in response to market failures. While employment regulations generally increase the tenure and wages of incumbent workers, rigid regulations have many undesirable effects, such as smaller company size, less job creation, less investment in research and development, and longer spell of employment leading to obsolescence of skills, hampering the productivity growth.

The system and regulations of employing workers are the easiest in Singapore and the US whereas Japan ranked at 17th followed by the UK (21st), India (85th), China (86th), Russia (101st), and Brazil (119th). Hiring workers is most cumbersome in Venezuela and Bolivia.

Registering property   Securing rights to the property strengthens incentives to invest and facilitate commerce. Entrepreneurs can obtain mortgages on their home or land and start business. A large share of the property in developing countries is not being registered, limiting financing opportunities for business. Efficient property registration reduces transaction costs and helps keep formal titles slipping into informal status. Simple procedures to register property reduce corruption and leads to greater perceived security of property rights. This greatly benefits small investors who have limited resources to invest in security measures to defend their property.

New Zealand is the friendliest place to register a property whereas the US ranked at 10th, Singapore at 13th, UK at 19th, China at 29th, Russia at 45th, Japan at 48th, Brazil at 110th, and India at 112th place. To register a property is most complex in **Timor-Leste**.

Getting credit   Easy access to credit is considered to be one of the most important pre-conditions of doing business. Credit constraints may be eased by effective regulation of secured lending through collateral and bankruptcy laws. By giving a lender the right to seize and sell a borrower's secured assets upon default, collateral limits the lender's potential losses and acts as a screening device for borrowers. More credits are extended in countries where good quality credit information is available and legal rights are strong.

Access to credit is easiest in the UK followed by Hong Kong, New Zealand Australia, Germany, Malaysia, Singapore, and the US whereas Japan ranked at 13th, India at 36th, China, Russia and Brazil at 84th place. To get credit is most difficult in Afghanistan and Cambodia.

Protecting investors   If the rights of investors are not protected, the entrepreneurship is suppressed, and fewer investment projects are undertaken. The investor protection is measured by using three sub-indices: extent of disclosure index, extent of director liability index, and ease of shareholders index. Where the use of corporate assets for personal gains is restrained, equity investment is higher and ownership concentration lower leading to deeper trust in the business. As a result, investors gain portfolio diversification and entrepreneurs gain access to cash.

Investor's protection is highest in New Zealand followed by Singapore, Hong Kong, Malaysia, and the US, whereas the UK ranked at ninth, Japan at 12th, India at 33rd, Brazil at 64th, China and Russia at 83rd places. Afghanistan provides the least protection to the investors.

Paying taxes   Each country levies taxes on business for funding developmental activities such as infrastructure development and welfare schemes, i.e., roads, water, hospitals, schools, waste collection, public utilities, etc., that facilitate businesses to be more productive. Investors are concerned about what they get for their taxes and contributions paid, such as quality of infrastructure and social services. Low-income countries tend to use businesses as collection points for taxes with a complex tax collection system whereas high-income countries tend to have lower taxes and less complex systems. Businesses face fewer hassles in countries where the tax rates are lower or moderate and the collection systems are simple and less complex. More burdensome tax regimes create an incentive to evade taxes.

Tax regime is most business-friendly in the Maldives followed by Singapore, Hong Kong, United Arab Emirates, and Oman whereas the UK ranks at 12th, the US at 76th, Russia at 130th, Brazil at 137th place. The tax regime is most cumbersome in Belarus (178th), Ukraine (177th), Congo Republic (176th), China (167th), and India (164th).

Trading across borders   Flow of goods across the borders often faces numerous hurdles leading to transaction costs. Countries that have efficient customs, good transport networks, and fewer document requirements make compliance with exim procedures faster and cheaper and are more competent globally. On the other hand, the need to file more documents is often associated with more corruption in customs. Many traders tend to smuggle goods across the border so as to avoid customs altogether due to the long delays and frequent demands for bribes. Thus, the very purpose of levying high taxes and ensuring high quality goods is defeated.

Singapore is the best place for trading across borders followed by Denmark, Hong Kong, Norway, Finland, and Sweden. The US ranks at 15th, Japan at 18th, the UK at 27th, China at 41st, India at 79th, Brazil at 93rd, and Russia at 155th places whereas Kazakhstan ranked at 178th, and thus the most difficult place to trade across borders.

Enforcing contracts Businesses are more likely to engage with new borrowers or customers where enforcement of contracts is efficient. The efficiency of the judicial system in resolving commercial disputes is important for the ease of business operations. The number of procedures, time, and costs incurred in courts contribute to the efficiency of commercial contract enforcement. Businesses that have little or no access to efficient courts need to rely on other mechanisms, both formal and informal, such as trade associations, social networks, credit bureaus, or private information channels, to decide whom to do business with and under what conditions. However, the informal justice system is vulnerable to subversion by the rich and powerful while too-heavy regulations of dispute resolution backfire. Alternatively, a conservative approach to business might be adopted, to carry out business dealings only with a small group of people linked through ethnic origin, kinship, or previous dealings and structuring transactions to forestall disputes. But again, the economic and social values may be lost in either case.

Enforcing contracts is the most efficient in Hong Kong, Luxembourg, Latvia, and Singapore respectively whereas the US ranked at eighth, Russia at 19th, China at 20th, Japan at 21st, the UK at 24th, and Brazil at 106th. Businesses find it most difficult to enforce contract in Timor-Leste (178th), India (177th), Angola (176th), and Bangladesh (175th).

Closing a business The economic crisis of the 1990s in the emerging markets from Russia to Mexico and East Asia to Latin America raised concerns about the design of bankruptcy systems and the ability of such systems to help recognize viable companies and close down unviable ones. In countries where bankruptcy systems are inefficient, unviable businesses linger for years, keeping assets and human capital from being reallocated to more productive uses. On the other hand, efficient bankruptcy laws encourage investors providing them freedom to fail through efficient processes and putting people and capital to their most efficient use. Measures used to assess closing business include the time to go through insolvency process, the costs involved, and the recovery rate, i.e., how much of the insolvency estate is recovered by stakeholders, taking into account the time, cost, depreciation of assets, and the outcome of the insolvency proceedings.

Closing a business is easiest in Japan, followed by Singapore, Norway, Canada, and Finland. The UK ranks at 10th, the US at 18th, China at 57th, Russia at 80th, Brazil at

131st, and India at 137th place. The most difficult countries to close a business include Central African Republic, Chad, Afghanistan, Madagascar, Cambodia, Sudan, and Iraq.

Assessing overall ease of doing business

The cross-country comparison reveals that Singapore is the friendliest place for doing business, followed by New Zealand, the US, Hong Kong, Denmark, the UK, and Canada whereas Japan ranks at 12th, China at 83rd, Russia at 106th, India at 120th, and Brazil at 122nd place (Table 10.5). Region-wise, OECD countries are most business friendly with an average rank of 22 followed by Eastern Europe and Central Asia (76), East Asia and Pacific (77), Latin America and Caribbean (87), Middle East and North Africa (96), South Asia (107), and Sub-Saharan Africa (136).

The environment of doing business monitored over the years provides some useful insights into the changing trends among countries. Top performers in 2006–07, determined by various indicators for overall ease of doing business, are

Starting a business	Saudi Arabia
Dealing with license	Georgia
Employing workers	Czech Republic
Registering property	Ghana
Getting credit	Croatia
Protecting investors	Georgia
Paying taxes	Bulgaria
Trading across borders	India
Enforcing contracts	Tonga
Closing a business	China

India has been the top performer in trading across borders in 2006–07. Traders can now submit a customs declaration and a custom fee online before the cargo arrives in port. In 2006, it took 27 days to meet all administrative requirements to export; this was reduced to 18 days in 2007. The time for document preparation was reduced from 11 days to nine days and customs and inspection reduced from four days to two days during the year. However, comparisons among cities within a country are even stronger drivers of reform. The time to obtain a business license in India ranges from 159 days in Bhubaneshwar to 522 days in Ranchi whereas the time to register property varies from 35 days in Hyderabad to 155 days in Kolkata.[19]

Limitations of doing business methodology

Since standard assumptions are used in data collection, comparisons and benchmarks are valid across countries. The data not only highlight the extent of obstacles to doing business, it identifies the sources of those obstacles, supporting policymakers in designing reforms and companies in developing strategies for international business.

---

[19] Doing Business 2008, World Bank Group, Washington D.C., pp. 1–8.

Table 10.5 Cross-country comparison of ease of doing business

		Singapore	US	UK	Japan	China	Russia	India	Brazil
Overall ease of doing business (rank)		**1**	**3**	**6**	**12**	**83**	**106**	**120**	**122**
Starting a business	Procedures (number)	5	6	6	8	13	8	13	18
	Duration (days)	5	6	13	23	35	29	33	152
	Cost (% GNI per Capita)	0.8	0.7	0.8	7.5	8.4	3.7	74.6	10.4
	Paid in Minimum Capital (% of GNI per capita)	0	0	0	0	190.2	3.2	0	0
Dealing with licences	Procedures (number)	11	19	19	15	37	54	20	18
	Duration (days)	102	40	144	177	336	704	224	411
	Cost (% of income per capita)	22.9	13.4	64.6	17.8	840.2	3788.4	519.4	59.4
Employing workers	Difficulty of hiring index	0	0	11	0	11	33	0	78
	Rigidity of hours index	0	0	0	20	20	60	20	60
	Difficulty of firing index	0	0	10	30	40	40	70	0
	Rigidity of employment index	0	0	7	17	24	44	30	46
	Nonwage labour cost (% of salary)	13	8	11	13	44	31	17	37
	Firing costs (weeks of wages)	4	0	22	4	91	17	56	37
Registering property	Procedures (number)	3	4	2	6	4	6	6	14
	Duration (days)	9	12	21	14	29	52	62	45
	Cost (% of property value)	2.8	0.5	4.1	5	3.6	0.3	7.7	2.8
Getting credit	Legal rights index	9	7	10	6	3	3	6	2
	Credit information index	4	6	6	6	4	4	4	5
	Public registry coverage (% adults)	0	0	0	0	49.2	0	0	17.1
	Private bureau coverage (% adults)	42.7	100	84.6	68.3	0	4.4	10.8	46.4
Protecting investors	Disclosure index	10	7	10	7	10	6	7	6
	Director liability index	9	9	7	6	1	2	4	7
	Shareholder suits index	9	9	7	8	4	7	7	3
	Investor protection index	9.3	8.3	8	7	5	5	6	5.3

		Singapore	US	UK	Japan	China	Russia	India	Brazil
Paying taxes	Payments (number)	5	10	8	13	35	22	60	11
	Time (hours)	49	325	105	350	872	448	271	2600
	Profit (%)	6.3	27.1	21.3	33.2	19.9	14	19.6	21.1
	Labour tax and contributions (%)	14.1	9.6	11.3	14.5	46	31.8	18.4	40.6
	Other taxes (%)	2.8	9.5	3.2	4.4	8	5.7	32.5	7.5
	Total tax rate (% Profit)	23.2	46.2	35.7	52	73.9	51.4	70.6	69.2
Trading across borders	Documents for exports (number)	4	4	4	4	7	8	8	8
	Time of export (days)	4	6	13	10	21	36	18	18
	Cost of export (US$ per container)	416	960	940	989	390	2050	820	1090
	Documents for import (number)	4	5	4	5	6	13	9	7
	Time for import (days)	3	5	13	11	24	36	21	22
	Cost to import (US$ per container)	367	1160	1267	1047	430	2050	910	1240
Enforcing contracts	Procedures (number)	22	32	30	30	35	37	46	45
	Duration (days)	120	300	404	316	406	281	1420	616
	Cost (% of Claim)	17.8	9.4	23.4	22.7	8.8	13.4	39.6	16.5
Closing a business	Cost (% of income per capita)	1	7	6	4	22	9	9	12
	Time (years)	0.8	1.5	1	0.6	1.7	3.8	10	4
	Recovery rate (cents on the dollar)	91.3	75.9	84.6	92.6	35.9	29	11.6	14.6

Source: Based on data from *Doing Business, 2008*, World Bank Group, Washington D.C., pp. 88–102.

Although the doing business methodology does not include some important areas of business operations, such as a country's proximity to large markets, the quality of its infrastructure services (other than those related to trading across borders), the security of property from theft and looting, the transparency of government procurement, macro-economic conditions or the underlying strength of institutions. Nevertheless, it serves as a useful tool to carry out cross-country comparisons objectively.

10.3.5 Country Assessment for Services Location

Advents of telecommunication and transport technology have paved way for global expansion of services. Moving operations to low-cost countries offers a variety of advantages from reduced wages for qualified workers to historically lower costs of businesses. In order to strategically choose global locations, the decisions should be based on maximising the long-term benefits of offshoring while offsetting rising wages and other developments. Rather than offshoring *per se*, companies often succeed in their offshore strategies by use of a holistic approach and focusing on global delivery models.

Key emerging markets in Southeast Asia, Latin America, and Eastern Europe are becoming more attractive in terms of talent, industry experience, quality certifications, and regulatory environment. As the relative cost advantage of leading offshore destinations has continually declined over the recent years, the key to maintain and enhance long-term competitiveness, for both developed and developing countries lies in skills-development, infrastructure, and investment and regulatory environment rather than in attempts to control wages. In the fast-moving remote services businesses, the failure to improve the skills of the workforce would lead to loss of competitiveness.

Top 50 locations worldwide that provide the most common remote functions, including IT services and support, contact centres, and back-office support have been analysed and ranked by A.T Kearney's Global Services Location Index (GSLI). Each country's score is composed of a weighted combination of relative scores on 43 measurements, which are grouped into three categories: financial attractiveness, people and skills availability, and business environment. The weight distribution for the three categories is 40:30:30. Financial attractiveness is rated on a scale of 0–4 and the categories for people and skill availability and business environment are on a scale of 0–3.

India is the most preferred country to locate services in the world as it offers an unbeatable mix of low costs, deep technical and language skills, mature vendors, and supportive government policies. After India, the other most preferred services locations include China, Malaysia, Thailand, Brazil, and Indonesia (Fig. 10.22). Although the double digit growth rate has fuelled wage inflation by around 30 per cent in China and 20 per cent in India, the cost escalation have been matched by corresponding increases in skills and quality. In terms of language skills and vendor maturity, India maintains a strong lead which makes a large number of Western companies increasingly outsource services. For instance in 2007, Citigroup Inc. announced to move as many

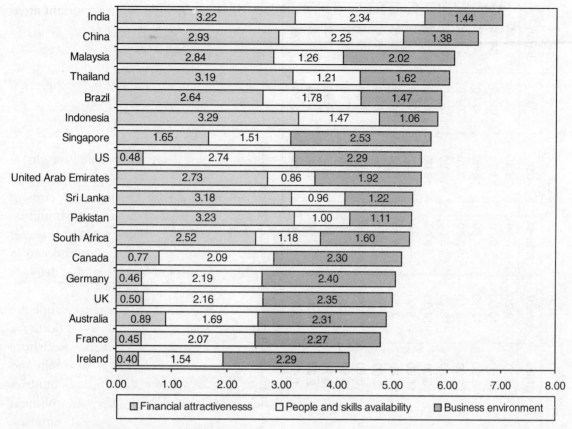

Fig. 10.22 Global services location index, (2007)

Source: Based on data from 'Off-shoring for Long-Term Advantage', A.T. Kearney Global Services Location Index, Chicago, 2007, pp. 1–15.

as 8000 positions to India, particularly in equity research, investment banking, and back-office transaction related activities, in addition to its 12,000 strong work-force in the BPO division. India's continued competitiveness can also be credited to in-country shifts of resources from expensive tier-one cities to tier-two and tier-three cities, with higher quality of life and lower costs. Developed nations rank poorly on the financial attractiveness of services; therefore they need to focus on moving up the value chain.

10.3.6 Assessing Problematic Factors for Doing Business

Companies often encounter a wide range of problems that vary from country to country, in carrying out business activities. Companies often face several constraints in their overseas business operations, such as inadequate supply of infrastructure, inefficient government bureaucracy, restrictive labour regulations, corruption, tax regulations, tax rates, policy instability, access to financing, poor work ethics in national labour force, inadequately educated workforce, inflation, foreign currency regulations, government instability, and crime and theft.

Table 10.6 Cross-country comparison of problematic factors for doing business

S.No.		India	China	Brazil	Russia	US	UK	Japan
1.	Inadequate supply of infrastructure	24.00	9.10	9.20	6.90	3.40	8.00	3.50
2.	Inefficient government bureaucracy	16.50	14.60	10.60	8.30	11.20	13.20	19.80
3.	Restrictive labour regulations	12.50	3.50	12.20	1.80	6.50	8.00	11.80
4.	Corruption	11.90	11.60	8.10	18.80	3.70	0.70	1.10
5.	Tax regulations	7.40	7.20	18.20	15.00	14.80	15.50	22.10
6.	Tax rates	4.90	5.30	16.00	10.00	15.00	16.20	18.60
7.	Policy instability	4.80	11.60	5.00	3.40	4.50	2.80	6.80
8.	Access to financing	4.10	14.80	7.80	8.20	5.30	4.90	4.60
9.	Poor work ethic in national labour force	3.70	5.60	1.20	3.40	7.60	8.10	3.40
10.	Inadequately educated workforce	3.10	6.60	3.30	5.90	9.60	15.10	4.40
11.	Inflation	3.00	2.50	1.30	7.00	9.70	3.70	0.70
12.	Foreign currency regulations	2.10	3.70	3.10	1.00	2.60	0.90	1.30
13.	Government instability/coups	1.30	2.30	1.10	2.00	2.00	0.50	1.20
14.	Crime and theft	0.70	1.60	3.00	8.40	4.00	2.50	0.80

Source: Based on The Global Competitiveness Report, 2007–08, World Economic Forum, Geneva, pp. 132, 150, 200, 212, 298, 348, and 350.

A cross-country comparison (Table 10.6) reveals that inadequate infrastructure, inefficient government bureaucracy, and restrictive labour regulations are the most problematic factors for doing business in India compared to financing, inefficient government bureaucracy, corruption, and political instability in China. Tax rates and regulations are the two most important problems in carrying out business both in the UK, the US, and Brazil whereas corruption is most problematic factor in Russian Federation and inadequately educated workforce in Singapore. An empirical approach to assess the problems across countries not only facilitates a firm in country evaluation and selection but also to take suitable proactive steps.

10.4   TOOLS FOR COUNTRY EVALUATION AND SELECTION

Analytical tools for country evaluation and selection facilitate firms to develop and adopt differentiated business strategies for different country segments. Widely used techniques, such as trade analysis and analogy methods, opportunity-risk analysis, products-country matrix strategy, growth-share matrix, market attractiveness-company strength matrix have been discussed below.

10.4.1   Trade Analysis and Analogy Methods

Trade analysis and country analogy methods are widely used for country evaluation by estimating their market size. In simple terms, the market size of a country may be determined by subtracting the exports of a product from the sum-total of its production and imports.

$$\text{Market size} = \text{Production} + \text{Imports} - \text{Exports}$$

One can arrive at market size by using data based on ITC(HS) code classifications up to eight digits for specific product categories. Published data on exports and imports can be obtained through international sources, such as the WTO, International Trade Centre, and the UNCTAD. National governments comply trade statistics through customs and central banks, for instance, in India, through DGCI&S and Reserve Bank of India (RBI). Production statistics are generally available through government organizations for broad product categories, such as agricultural commodities, textiles, steel, cement, minerals, etc. More product-specific statistics are compiled by commodity organizations and trade associations.

For new product categories, with little consumption and production in the past, various types of analogy methods are employed. In the analogy method, a country at similar stage of economic development and comparable consumer behaviour is selected whose market size is known. Besides, a surrogate measure is also identified, which has similar demand to the product for the international market. Alternatively, the analogy method for different time periods, which may be compared with similar demand patterns in two different countries, may also be used.

10.4.2 Opportunity–Risk Analysis

Carrying out a cross-country analysis of opportunities and risks provides a useful tool to compare and evaluate various investment locations based on a company's objectives and business environment. The internationalizing firm may choose variables both for opportunities (such as market size, growth, future potential, tax regime, costs, etc.) and risks (political, economic, legal, operational, etc.). Various types of risks and its assessment have already been discussed in detail in Chapter 8. Moreover, values and weights may be assigned to each of these variables depending upon their perceived significance by the firm. Thus, it provides an opportunity to a company to evaluate each country on the weighted indicators.

On the basis of business opportunities and risks, ranking of various countries may be made for investment. Countries with low-risks and high-returns are often preferred investment destinations. In addition, such grids may also be used for future projections. Although, such grids (Exhibit 10.2) serve as useful tools for cross-country comparison of opportunity versus risk, it hardly provides any insight into relationships among the investment destinations.

Countries for investment can also be plotted in form of a matrix, as shown in Fig. 10.23, to indicate opportunities and risks. Besides, the countries can be placed for

		Country			
Exhibit 10.2 Opportunity–risk grid for cross-country evaluation					
Variable	**Weight**	**A**	**B**	**C**	**D**
Opportunities					
▪ Market size					
▪ Growth					
▪ Competitive intensity					
▪ Operations costs					
▪ Marketing efficiency					
▪ Tax rates					
Total					
Risks					
▪ Political					
▪ Commercial					
▪ Economic					
▪ Operational					
Total					

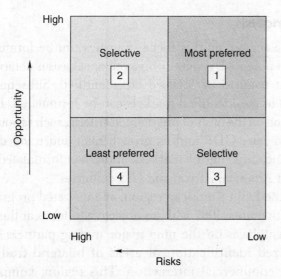

Fig. 10.23 Opportunity–risk matrix for country evaluation

a pre-defined future time, both for opportunities and risks. In addition to inter-country evaluation, the country placements and its benchmarking with the global average opportunities and risks may also be carried out.

10.4.3 Products–Country Matrix Strategy

With an objective to examine market diversification and commodity diversification, the product-country matrix strategy is employed. Under this approach, previous trade statistics are analyzed to identify the major markets and major products, based on which a suitable marketing strategy is developed. The matrix based on a predominantly supply side analysis reveals comparative advantages. In 1995, the Government of India carried out the analysis of trade data of the mid-nineties to prepare such a matrix. The analysis revealed the restricted commodity/country basket for India's exports. It was observed that 15 countries and 15 commodities accounted for around 75–80 per cent of India's exports. An attempt was made to involve trade and industry to set up trade facilitators for achieving increased exports in the 15 products and 15 markets. However, the exercise of the trade facilitation did not get enough support and response from various stakeholders.[20] The focus on the 15 × 15 matrix, based on past performance data was a useful exercise as it helped to focus on the importance of a few commodities and a few destinations in India's export performance.

There has been a market diversification for the top products though there has also been a product consolidation for the top markets. The analysis also reveals that the 15 × 15 matrix is dynamic and mature as it has undergone changes over the years and it requires modification of marketing strategy on a continuous basis.

---

[20] Medium Term Export Strategy (2002–2007), Ministry of Commerce, Government of India, pp. 1–90.

10.4.4 Market Focus Strategies

In view of market potential of a region, market focus strategies can be formulated. Under this technique, the market potential, generally on a regional basis is determined and major product groups that need to be focused are identified. Subsequently, strategies for increasing exports to the identified markets can be formulated. India's major markets have been identified on the basis of pre-defined criteria, such as country's share in imports and its growth rate, GDP and its growth rate, and trade deficits which facilitate segmentation and targeting of markets. India has formulated such market focus strategies for Latin America, Africa, and CIS countries.

Considering the potential of the Latin American region, an integrated programme 'Focus LAC' was launched in November 1997 with an objective to focus at the Latin American region, with added emphasis on the nine major trading partners of the region. The strategy emphasized identification of areas of bilateral trade and investments so as to promote commercial interaction. This region, comprising 43 countries, accounted for about 5 per cent of the world trade. But India is not a significant trading partner of this region. Under the programme, nine major product groups for enhancing India's exports to the Latin American region were identified. These included

- Textiles including ready-made garments, carpets, and handicrafts
- Engineering products and computer software
- Chemical products including drugs/pharmaceuticals.

On similar lines, Focus Africa was launched on 1 April 2002, which initially covered seven countries in the first phase of the programme to include Nigeria, South Africa, Mauritius, Kenya, Tanzania, and Ghana. Subsequently, it was extended to 11 other countries of the region, i.e., Angola, Botswana, Ivory Coast, Madagascar, Mozambique, Senegal, Seychelles, Uganda, Zambia, Namibia, and Zimbabwe along with the six countries of North Africa—Egypt, Libya, Tunisia Sudan, Morocco, and Algeria.

Focus CIS was launched on 1 April 2003, which include focused export promotion to 12 CIS (commonwealth of independent states) countries, i.e., Russian Federation, Ukraine, Moldova, Georgia, Armenia, Azerbaijan, Belarus, Kazakhstan, Uzbekistan, Kyrgyzstan, Turkmenistan, and Tajikistan—the Baltic states of Latvia, Lithuania, and Estonia. The programme was based on an integrated strategy to focus on major product groups, technology and services sectors for enhancing India's exports and bilateral trade and co-operation with countries of the CIS region. The strategy envisaged at making integrated efforts to promote exports by the Government of India and various related agencies, such as India Trade Promotion Organisation (ITPO), Export Promotion Councils (EPCs), Apex Chambers of Commerce and Industry, Indian missions abroad, and institutions such as Export Import Bank and Export Credit and Guarantee Corporation (ECGC). Such integrated and focused approaches are conceptually sound but their success depends upon effectiveness of implementation of the programmes.

On 1 April 2006, the Focus Market Scheme was launched in order to enhance the competitiveness in the select markets. The scheme notifies 83 countries form Latin America, Africa, and CIS.[21]

10.4.5 Growth–Share Matrix

The technique offers a useful tool to evaluate countries for different product categories based on their market share and growth rate. Products are classified under four categories on the lines of BCG matrix based on a model[22] developed by Boston Consulting Group for classification of strategic business units (SBUs) of an organization, as shown in Fig. 10.24.

Such a matrix can be prepared either for country's exports or firm's exports so as to facilitate segmentation of the products under the broad categories:

High-growth high-share (stars) products Such products offer high-growth potential but require lot of resources to maintain the share in high-growth markets.

Low-growth high-share (cash cows) products Products under this category bring higher profits, although have a slow market growth rate.

High-growth low-share (question marks) products These are the products under high risk category with an uncertain future, sometimes called *problem children.* A highly competitive strategic business decision is required to invest resources to bring it to the category of stars by achieving a higher market share.

Low-growth Low-share (dogs) products These products have low growth and low market share, therefore generally do not call for investing much resources.

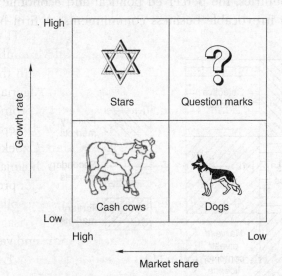

Fig. 10.24 Growth–share (BCG) matrix

[21] As on 1 April 2008, Ministry of Commerce, Government of India, New Delhi.

[22] 'The Experience Curve Reviewed: IV. The Growth Share Matrix of the Product Portfolio', Boston Consulting Group, Boston, 1973.

For each of the product groups under the growth share matrix, differentiated strategies need to be formulated and adopted. Similar matrix can also be prepared country-wise for formulating country-specific business strategies.

10.4.6 Country Attractiveness–Company Strength Matrix

An analysis may be carried out for country evaluation and strategy development based on business attractiveness of countries and the competitive strength of the company. Various factors, such as market size, market growth, customers' buying power, average trade margins, seasonality and fluctuations in the market, marketing barriers, competitive structures, government regulations, economic and political stability, infrastructure, and psychic distance may be taken into account to assess the country attractiveness. The competitive strength of a firm is often determined by its market share, familiarity and knowledge about the country, price, product-fit to the market, demands, image, contribution margin, technology position, product quality, financial resources, access to distribution channels, and their quality. An analysis can be carried out in the form of a matrix, assigning weight to each of these factors. Based on this analysis, a matrix may be drawn as in Fig. 10.25.

The countries depicted in the matrix may be segmented as

Primary markets These countries offer the highest marketing opportunities and call for a high level of business commitments. The firms often strive to establish permanent presence in these countries.

Secondary markets In these countries, the perceived political and economic risks are too high to make long-term irrevocable business commitments. A firm has to

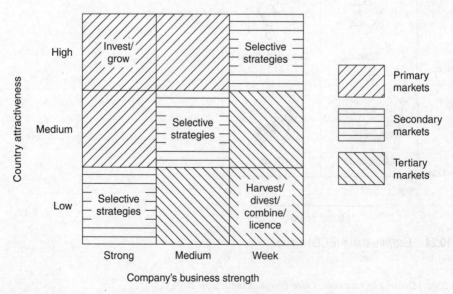

Fig. 10.25 Country attractiveness–company strength matrix

explore and identify the perceived risk factors or the firm's limitations in these countries and adopt individualised strategies, such as joint ventures so as to take care of the limitations of operating business.

Tertiary markets   These are countries with high perceived risks; therefore, allocation of firm's resources is minimal. Generally a firm does not have any long-term commitment in such countries and opportunistic business strategies such as licensing are often followed.

Based on the above analysis, a firm should focus its country selection and expansion strategies in countries at the top left of the matrix where the country attractiveness and the competitive strengths of the company are very high. On the other hand, the firm should focus on harvesting/divesting its resources from countries where the country attractiveness and company strength both are very low. However, a firm may use licensing as a mode of business operation with little resource commitment but continue to receive royalties. Countries at the extreme right top of the matrix signify higher country attractiveness but lower company strength. A firm should identify its competitive weaknesses in these countries and strive to gain the competitive strength. It may also enter into joint venture with other firms, which most of the time are local and have complementarities to gain competitive strength. In countries where a firm has medium competitive strength and country attractiveness needs to carefully study the market condition and adopt appropriate strategy. Ford tractors used the country attractiveness-company strength matrix and placed India under the extreme right top of the matrix wherein the country attractiveness was very high but the competitive strength of the company was low.

Decisions to expand business across national boundaries require much higher level of commitment of a company's resources as any business failure may have serious repercussions. By way of effective evaluation and selection of countries, the internationalizing firm avoids wastage of time and resources and it can focus its efforts on a few fruitful locations. This chapter has highlighted approaches to identification and evaluation of business opportunities and provides insight into the international business research. Various options available with the firm for country evaluation have also been discussed. This chapter also examines various tools for country evaluation and selection.

SUMMARY

A firm needs to spot international business opportunities, evaluate various countries, and select a few for business operation. Small and medium firms with limited resources often use a reactive approach for identifying opportunities whereas a systematic pro-active approach is adopted by larger companies. Cross-country research is employed for objective evaluation of business opportunities and country selection. Scanning the global macroeconomic environment often provides useful insights for evaluating countries.

Dimensions used to arrive at market potential of a country include market size, market growth rate, market intensity, market consumption capacity, commercial infrastructure, economic freedom, market receptivity, and country risk. Competitiveness of a country is referred to a set of institutions, policies, and factors that determine the level of productivity of a country. Global Competitiveness Index provides a useful tool to carry out cross-country comparison based on twelve pillars, i.e., institutions, infrastructure, macro-economic stability, health and primary education, higher education and training, goods market efficiency, labour market efficiency, financial market sophistication, technological readiness, market size, business sophistication and innovation. Country competitiveness depends on a country's stages of development which may be driven by factor, efficiency, or innovation. Business Competitiveness Index provides a conceptual framework to rank countries

based on two sub-indices: company operation and strategy and national business environment.

Ease of doing business across countries based on regulation is often affected by various stages of a business, i.e., starting a business, dealing with licences, employing workers, registering property, getting credit, protecting investors, paying taxes, trading across borders, enforcing contracts, and closing a business. Financial attractiveness, people and skill availability, and business environment are used to evaluate countries for locating services. Tools used for country evaluation and selection include trade analysis and analogy methods, opportunity-risk analysis, products-country matrix strategy, growth-share matrix, and market attractiveness-company strength matrix.

KEY TERMS

Calibration equivalence Whether the system of calibration such as monitory units, measure of weight, distances, volume are same across the countries.

Causative research Marketing research to test hypothesis to establish cause and effect relationship.

Classification or category equivalence Variation in the category or product class from country to country.

Conceptual equivalence The extent of variation in individual interpretation of objects, stimuli, or behaviour across the cultures.

Construct equivalence Whether the marketing constructs (product functionality, interpretation of marketing stimuli and classification schemes) under the study have same meaning across the countries.

Country competitiveness A set of institutions, policies, and factors that determine the level of productivity of a country.

Descriptive research Marketing research to better describe marketing problems, situations, or markets.

Efficiency-driven economies Such countries achieve competitiveness by bringing in efficiency

in production processes by way of higher education and training, efficient goods markets, well-functioning labour markets, sophisticated financial markets, a large domestic and foreign market, and ability to harness the benefits of existing technologies.

Equivalence of data analysis Taking into account the country-culture biases while carrying out data analysis.

Equivalences Whether particular concept being studied is understood and interpreted in the same manner by the people in various cultures.

Exploratory research Marketing research to gather preliminary information that will help better define problems and suggest hypothesis.

Factor-driven economies Countries that principally compete on the basis of their factor endowments, primarily unskilled labour, and natural resources.

Functional equivalence Whether the function or purpose served or performed by a given concept or behaviour is the same across the countries.

Innovation-driven economies Countries that compete through innovation, producing new and different goods using most sophisticated production processes.

International business research Business research which crosses national borders and involves respondents and researchers from different countries and cultures.

Measurement equivalence Equivalence in terms of procedures used to measure concepts or attitudes.

Metric equivalence Equivalence of scale or procedure to establish as measure and equivalences of responses of given measure in different countries.

Process of international business research The planned, systematic, and comprehensive approach to carry out international business research.

Research design The specification of methods and procedures for acquiring the information needed to structure or to solve problems.

Translation equivalence Equivalence in meaning while translation of the instrument across different languages.

CONCEPT REVIEW QUESTIONS

1. Explaining the significance of country selection in international business, discuss the major approaches used to identify and select countries for business operations.

2. Briefly examine the concept of equivalences in cross-country research.

3. Explaining the concept of competitiveness, examine various factors that influence country-competitiveness.

4. Elucidate the factors a company should evaluate to assess ease of doing business in a foreign country.

5. List the problematic factors for doing business and its significance in selecting business locations.

6. Write short notes on
   (a) Limitations of secondary data for international business research
   (b) Assessing market potential
   (c) Country classification based on stages of developments
   (d) Business Competitiveness Index
   (e) Country attractiveness-company strength matrix

PRACTICE EXERCISE

1. Visit a nearby library having information on international business and compile a detailed list of various sources of information that can be used for conducting international business research.

2. Explore the Internet sources that can be made use of for scanning business environment. Find out the limitations of each of these sources.

PROJECT ASSIGNMENTS

1. A US-based IT firm is looking at options to off-shore some of its services. Prepare a list of parameters you would use to evaluate various countries and suggest the most suitable location.

2. An Indian pharmaceutical company primarily engaged in manufacturing and marketing bulk

drugs domestically is looking at setting up manufacturing operations overseas. Select a few countries for its business expansion based on your evaluation, using risk-opportunity analysis. Discuss your findings in class.

11 Modes of International Business Expansion

LEARNING OBJECTIVES

> To explain the concept of expansion modes for international business
> To examine strategic trade-offs in selecting expansion modes
> To discuss trade-related expansion modes
> To evaluate contractual expansion modes
> To elucidate investment modes of expansion
> To explicate strategy for selecting the expansion modes
> To elaborate the decision-making process for selecting the expansion modes

11.1 INTRODUCTION

For expanding business in foreign countries, a firm has to choose an appropriate expansion mode from among available alternatives. Expansion modes are specific forms of entering a foreign country so as to have international presence and achieve the firm's strategic goals. The modes of expansion have also been referred to as entry modes in the international business literature. A thorough conceptual understanding of various expansion mode alternatives is imperative for making internationalization decisions.

The chapter explains various strategic trade-offs a firm is required to make in selecting the most appropriate expansion mode. A firm has to assess its ability and willingness to commit resources, its risk perception, anticipated returns, desired extent of control and internalization, and flexibility while evaluating such trade-offs. Right selection of modes of expansion has significant operational and strategic implications on the firm's success in internationalization. Alternative modes of international expansion have broadly been grouped as trade related, contractual, and investment. Marketing strategy and country segments also need to be contemplated while working out an expansion mode strategy. In order to facilitate the reader's conceptual understanding, a strategic decision tree is given at the end of the chapter.

Stage models of internationalization, such as Uppsala Model[1] (1975) and subsequent research identify five stages of internationalization as follows:

- Domestic operation and marketing activities
- Infrequent exports
- Exports through independent representatives or agents
- Establishment of sales subsidiaries
- Foreign production and manufacturing

Such models indicate that a firm's internationalization process follows a gradual pattern. A purely domestic firm, especially an small and medium enterprise (SME), expands its operations overseas by reluctantly fulfilling unsolicited export orders it gets through friends, acquaintances, or other business firms. Consequent to successfully completing such unsolicited export orders, positive stimuli, such as higher profitability, incremental revenue, or achievement of strategic goals make the firm further pursue its export plans. This transforms a purely domestic firm into a regular exporter. In order to consolidate its gains in the market, it further adopts contractual expansion modes that include various types of strategic alliances. Once the market potential and viability is assured, the firm invests overseas so as to gain complete ownership and control.

11.1.1 Strategic Trade-offs in Selecting International Business Expansion Modes

Given an ideal situation, hardly any firm would like to share the control and returns of its international operations and would prefer to internalize entire operating processes within the company. However, such an expansion mode would require high commitment of resources for foreign expansion associated with considerably high risk as depicted in Fig. 11.1. Moreover, high resource-commitment in a country by way of investment increases a firm's exit costs and provides much lower flexibility.

Selecting an expansion mode is an important decision for a firm since it involves long-term strategic implications and substantial commitment of resources. Besides, it involves considerable operational complexities and resources to switch over to another expansion mode from the existing one. A firm has to choose from a variety of expansion modes depending upon

- Ability and willingness to commit resources in the target country
- Magnitude of risk the firm is willing to take in its international expansion
- Types of return anticipated from overseas operations
- Extent of control to be exerted in the firm's foreign operations
- Level of externalization of the firm's resources including its intellectual property
- Desired flexibility of expansion modes

---

[1] Johanson, J. and P. Wiedersheim-Paul, 'The Internationalization of the Firm: Four Swedish Cases', *Journal of Management Studies*, 12(3), 1975, pp. 305–22.

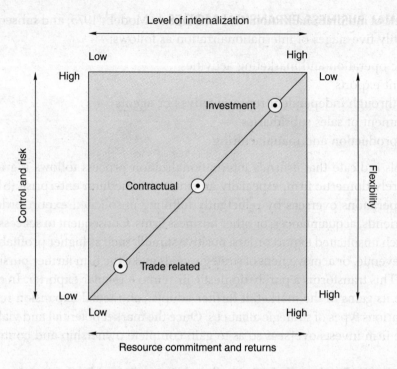

Fig. 11.1 Strategic trade-offs in selecting international business expansion modes

However large a firm may be, its resources are limited and need to be optimally employed so as to derive maximum returns. Therefore, when the market potential is not proven or the market size is not large enough to invest considerable resources, the firm has to make a trade-off between various benefits and costs as indicated in Fig. 11.1 and reconcile with expansion modes that share control and returns. SMEs generally adopt trade-related modes to enter international markets. Large companies also do adopt trade-related modes for expanding their business internationally to unfamiliar countries so as to get its first-hand experience.

By way of operating in a country over a period, a firm's uncertainty is gradually abridged and it becomes willing to commit more resources for expansion of existing activities. For example, as a part of international business expansion strategy, Heineken initially accesses a foreign market by way of exports. If Heineken finds a considerable market potential, it uses the contractual expansion mode by way of licensing to some local brewery in the identified target country. This provides flexibility to Heineken to exit the country if it is not found lucrative enough to operate. Operating into a foreign country through exports and later by licensing provides the firm enough insights into the country's business opportunities and its operational environment. Heineken eventually acquires its own licensee or some other brewer using investment expansion mode to have a long term strategic market commitment.

11.2 INTERNATIONAL BUSINESS EXPANSION MODES

Mode of international business expansion is an institutional mechanism by which a firm expands its operations overseas. Various modes for expanding a firm's business, summarized in Fig. 11.2, may be broadly classified as trade-related, contractual, and investment modes.

11.2.1 Trade-related Modes

Expansion modes that employ some form of trade to expand business in foreign countries are termed as trade-related modes. As financial requirements and resource commitment in trade-related modes are considerably less, these modes are often adopted in the initial phases of internationalization. Moreover, trade-related modes are

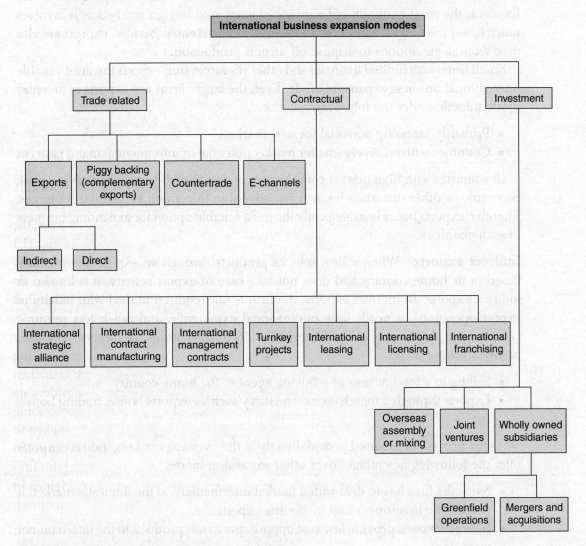

Fig. 11.2 Modes of international business expansion

low-risk expansion modes, highly suitable for simultaneous expansion in geographically diverse countries. The low exit-cost of trade-related modes adds to flexibility of winding up firm's business operations country or switching over to another expansion mode.

However, a firm has to substantially rely upon external agencies for its international expansion in trade-related modes. Further, trade-related modes maintain considerable distance between the internationalizing firm and the target country market. Major forms of trade-related modes, such as exports, piggybacking or complementary exports, countertrade, and e-channels are discussed below.

Exports

Exports may be defined as manufacturing the goods in the home country or a third country and shipping them for sales to a country other than the country of production. Export is the most common initial mode of entry into foreign markets as it involves much lower risks and is a low cost and simple mode of entry. Besides, exports are also used as strategic options to dispose off surplus production.

Small firms with limited financial and other resources find exports the most suitable international business expansion mode. Even the larger firms use exports as an entry mode suitable under the following situations:

- Primarily assessing potential for new markets
- Countries with relatively smaller market potential or infrequent demand patterns

In countries with high market complexities of operating business, such as political, economic or other uncertainties, it is not advisable to commit substantial resources. Thereby, exports become strategically the most suitable option for expanding business in such countries.

Indirect exports When a firm sells its products through an export intermediary based in its home country and does not take care of export activity, it is known as indirect exports. In indirect exports, the firm is not required to deal with hassles of export operations, it needs little international experience, and much less resource commitment. A firm may expand internationally through indirect exports using either of the following ways:

- Selling to a foreign firm or a buying agent in the home country
- Exports through a merchant intermediary such as exports house, trading house, etc.

As the firm is not required to deal directly in the overseas markets, indirect exports offer the following advantages over other expansion modes:

- Since the firm has to deal with a market intermediary in the domestic market, it needs little investment and marketing experience.
- Indirect exports provide low-cost opportunity to test products in the international markets.

However, indirect exports have certain limitations as well:

- As the firm has to heavily depend upon domestic market intermediary, its feedback from the ultimate customers is limited.
- The firm has to part with relatively higher share of its profit margins by way of commissions and other payments.
- The firm gets little insight into the markets served even after operating for several years.
- The firm does not develop its own contacts with the buyers in the overseas market.

As indirect exports offers a simple and low-cost expansion mode to foreign countries, this enables companies to test international markets before plunging into a more pro-active business expansion mode. Indirect exports can take place either through home-based agents or merchant intermediaries.

Agents   Agents do not take the title of the goods and operate on behalf of principal firms, rather than themselves on commission basis. Major types of export agents include

Importer's buying agents   A large number of international firms send their agents in overseas market to procure supplies. These agents work on commission basis for the overseas firms and procure samples and subsequent supplies from competing producers. The buying agents are highly useful, especially for small exporters as they come to exporters' doorsteps and assess the suitability of the products for exports to their principals in the importing country. Such importers' buying agents are common in the handicraft, handloom, and garment sectors.

Country-controlled buying agents   The country-controlled buying agents are appointed by an overseas government or a government organization. They identify countries and importers for supply of their requirements. Such agents make frequent visits to the suppliers' countries to establish their base there.

Buying offices   Overseas firms make their permanent presence in the suppliers' countries by way of establishing a permanent buying office. This indicates a long-term commitment on the part of the international firm to source supplies from such markets. For instance, a number of garment firms have established their buying offices in India.

Additionally, in view of India's strength as a low-cost manufacturing hub, global retail chains are sourcing a wide variety of products from India. These global retail chains not only provide a marketing outlet for Indian firms but also facilitate manufacturers of Indian goods to become globally competitive. Because of the renewed interest in sourcing from India, vendors are becoming more confident about investing in new product lines for Western consumers. Liberty Shoes, an Indian company, is in the process of developing a range of non-leather beachwear and sports footwear for American retail giant Wal-Mart.

Global retail chains, such as J.C. Penny and Target have set up their sourcing offices in India. Marks and Spencer, the UK based retailer with over 540 stores in 30 countries, is also in the process of setting up a sourcing centre in Bangalore. Bentonville based Wal-Mart now sources a total of US$1 billion worth of diamond, pens, shrimps, towels, and shoes from India through its procurement offices in Bangalore and Hong Kong. A few years ago, Wal-Mart sourced its merchandise through the Hong Kong-based Pacific Resource Export. Now, Wal-Mart is also sourcing directly from India.

Merchant intermediaries Exports intermediaries that buy and sell goods for a profit and take title of the goods and assume risks thereof are known as merchant intermediaries. Major types of merchant intermediaries include

Merchant exporter The merchant exporters collect produce from several manufacturers or producers and export directly in their own name. Generally, merchant exporters have longstanding relationships with their suppliers and work on profit margins. Home-based merchant exporters are easy to access and help in avoiding the hassles related to direct dealing with an overseas-based market intermediary.

International trading companies International trading companies are generally large companies that accumulate, transport, and distribute goods in various markets. Trading companies have been operating for centuries as pioneers of international trade. The British East India Company (1600), the Dutch East India Company (1602), and the French Compagine des Indes Orientales (1664) were supported by their governments and enjoyed not only trading rights but also military protection in exchange for tax and payments. The basic objective of these trading companies was to find markets for their industrial production and sell them at higher prices while sourcing raw materials and inputs for their manufacturing units.

As the international trading companies operate globally, they often have a presence in the exporting firm's home country and provide an easy access to international markets. Among the world's largest 10 global trading firms (Fig. 11.3) that include Mitsubishi, Mitsui, Marubeni, Sumitomo, Sinochem, Itochu, SHV Holdings, Samsung, COFCO, and SK Networks, of which five are of Japanese origin.

Earlier, large family-based businesses comprising financial and manufacturing capabilities in Japan were called *Zaibatsu,* which had been engaged in trading since 1700. After World War II, the large Japanese trading companies, *sogo shoshas,* came into existence as trading arms of large manufacturing firms called *keiretsus.* As the Japanese trading companies are very large, their presence is omnipresent within Japan. Therefore, for entering into Japanese distribution channels, these firms provide an easy and effective route.

Trading/export houses Home country-based firms involved in international trading activities, often known as trading/export houses, serve as important merchant intermediary for exports. As a part of export development strategies, most countries facilitate such trading/export houses. Certain incentives are available to these trading companies under the foreign trade policy[2] so as to assist them in their international

---

[2] Foreign Trade Policy (2004–09), Ministry of Commerce & Industry, Government of India, updated w.e.f. 1 April 2008.

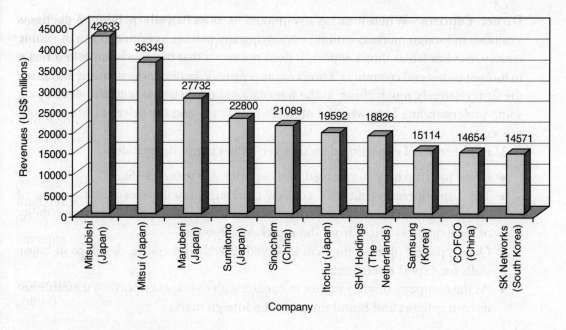

Fig. 11.3   Top 10 global trading companies

Source: Fortune Global 500, 25 July 2005.

marketing efforts. Merchant as well as manufacturer exporters, service providers, Export Oriented Units (EOUs) and units located in Special Economic Zones (SEZs), agri-export zones (AEZs), Electronic Hardware Technology Parks (EHTPs), Software Technology Parks (STPs), and Bio-Technology Parks (BTPs) are also eligible to get policy incentives available export/trading houses. Based on their exports performance, the Government of India recognizes these firms as export houses and allocates them various types of star status as dealt in detail in Chapter 9.

The State Trading Corporation (STC) and Metals and Minerals Trading Corporation (MMTC) are among India's largest trading houses. India's largest international business company, Tata International offers value-added services and international trading expertise and has stakes in a variety of businesses. Its trading operations are organized into five global business units (GBU), i.e., leather, steel, engineering, minerals, bulk commodities, and chemicals, each of which leverages the Tata Group's wide range of products and services and also sources from other non-Tata companies worldwide. Tata International trades with more that 110 countries and has a presence in 25 countries.

Since the export/trading houses are of the home country (i.e., Indian) origin, firms are familiar with the system and have a sense of security in transacting with them. Besides, the relations with export/trading houses are relatively on a long-term basis. The major bottleneck in exporting through export/trading houses is price realization and lack of knowledge about international markets.

Direct exports When a company makes its domestically produced products available in foreign markets without employing any market intermediary in the home county, it is known as direct export. It does not mean that the goods are sold directly to foreign-based end customers. Direct exports provide better understanding and bring the firm relatively much closer to the international markets that facilitate developing some understanding as to who the ultimate buyers are and the prices at which goods are sold.

Major benefits of exporting directly over indirect exports include

- As no intermediary is involved, the exporter gets more profit.
- The firm operating directly collects marketing intelligence about pricing of competing or substitute products in the markets, therefore, eliminating possibility of receiving less prices from the merchant exporter.
- Over a period of time, the firm involved directly in exports, develops in-house skills for export operations.
- As the company directly comes in contact with overseas importers, it establishes its own rapport and brand image in the foreign market.

Agents

Manufacturers' export agents or sales representatives The individual intermediaries who operate on a commission basis and travel frequently to overseas markets are known as export agents. These agents specialize in one or a few countries and offer their services to a number of manufacturers for non-competing products. These agents carry out business in the name of the firm rather than in their own name. In recent years, professionals with wide exposure and country specialization are increasingly working as export agents. Such export agents are generally employed by the small manufacturers who do not have their own distribution networks in overseas markets primarily due to

- Small size of operations
- Lack of experience in overseas markets
- Resources constraints
- Too small presence in target market to justify own sales force

As the export agent does not take ownership of the goods and operates on behalf of the principal firms, the producing firm retains the risk of any loss. Besides, they do not provide after-sales services, such as installations, complaint-handling, and repairs as these are passed on to the principal firm.

Overseas-based buying agents Some foreign companies have exclusive contract arrangements with some agents to perform their business. Generally, these agents are paid on the basis of a specific percentage of profit and the cost incurred. Such agents in China and in some Asian countries are also termed as 'compradors'. These agents have continuous relationship with buyers but not sellers. As these agents represent the buyer, they deal with all types of goods for their principals.

Merchant importers   A merchant importer is an overseas-based trader who imports products and further sells them to a wholesaler or a retailer for a profit. Generally, merchant importers are overseas-based trading firms that take possession and title of the goods, therefore assuming risks and responsibilities. These merchant importers serve as an effective marketing channel for bulk commodities to reach international markets, especially in agriculture and some industrial goods.

Distributors   The distributors in the target countries purchase the goods and subsequently sell them either to a market intermediary or to the ultimate customer. Thus, the distributors take the title of the goods and assume full risk and responsibility for them. The distributors have contractual agreements with the exporting manufacturers and deal with them on a long-term basis. Under the contract, distributors are authorized to represent the manufacturers and sell their goods in the assigned foreign territory. A distributor is generally appointed on exclusive basis for marketing the firm's products in the contracted overseas market territory. The distributor operates on margins. As the distributor has a long-standing relationship with the exporter, the level of control by the principal is relatively higher. The basic functions of distributors in international markets include

- To estimate market demand
- To conduct customers' need analysis and provide market feedback regularly
- To break bulk, meaning to buy goods in large quantity from the parent firm and break them up for market intermediaries
- To process orders and carry out proper documentation and billing
- To store goods and maintain inventories
- To provide low-cost storage and delivery
- To transport goods
- To undertake sales promotion and advertising
- To offer market credit and capital for financing inventory
- To handle complaints, guarantees, maintenance, after-sales service, repairs, and instructions for use on behalf of the supplier

A firm may select an overseas distributor based on several factors, such as firm size, its financial strength, type of the products dealt in markets covered, synergy with the firm's products, experience in dealing with similar products, physical infrastructure, such as transport, warehousing, etc., market goodwill, ability and willingness to carry the inventory, and public relations.

Piggybacking—complementary exports

A firm may expand its business in a foreign country by using the distribution network of another company, which is termed piggybacking or complementary exporting. SMEs that have limited resources may get access to a well-established distribution channel of a larger company in a foreign country. A company that is not willing to commit its own resources for creating its own distribution channel often prefers to piggyback. Under the piggybacking arrangement, the exporting firm is termed 'rider' whereas the other firm with established distribution channel in the target country is termed as the 'carrier'. Thus, the exporting firm 'rides' at the back of the 'carrier' through the later's well-established distribution channel and gets immediate access to the market with little investment. Piggybacking is generally used for related but non-competitive products of unrelated companies, which are complementary to the distributors' existing product lines.

To the carrier, piggybacking offers quick access to an outsider's product that fills gaps in its product line. This helps the carrier in widening its product range without investing in new product development and manufacturing. However, as the carrier has little control over continuity of supply and the quality and warranty of the products, it may adversely affect its brand name.

The exporting firm makes use of the experience of the carrier's marketing channels with little investment. If the country market is attractive enough to pump in more resources, the exporting firm may develop its own distribution channel. Since under the piggybacking arrangement, marketing of product is controlled by an outside agency, the exporting firm has little control over the carrier's marketing commitment and distribution efficiency.

In piggybacking exports, the branding and market promotion arrangements may differ. The carrier may buy the product outright and sell it under its own brand name. However, as a matter of common practice, the rider retains its brand name and the market promotion activity is carried out with mutual consent. There is an increasing trend in international markets of piggybacking taking various forms of strategic alliance.

In spite of considerable efforts to make a dent in the Indian market even after investing Rs 20 million in Indian operations, Fiat decided to use the extensive nationwide network of Tata Motors to market and service its passenger cars. Wrigley, the US based chewing-gum company entered India by piggybacking on the well-established distribution network of Indian confectionary firm Parry's Confectionary. It provided Wrigley's an instant access to over 250,000 retail outlets across India. Since Parry's product mix comprise hard-boiled sugar confectionary, Wrigley's chewing gums had a complementary effect on its product portfolios and marketing channels.

The European global IT supplier, Bull, operating in about 100 countries is using HCL's extensive distribution network of over 170 offices and 300 service centres spread across the country to market its enterprise class servers in India.[3] Since the products and technology offered by Bull are not in HCL's portfolio, Bull does not threaten HCL's existing products, rather complements it. Bull's servers provide HCL's customers the proven capability and mainframe class reliability of its traditional proprietary

---

[3] 'HCL Info in Pact with Bull', *Business Line*, Chennai, 25 October 2005.

reduced instruction set computing (RISC) platform used for central processing unit (CPU) design for computers.

Countertrade

Countertrade is a generic term that refers to various forms of trade arrangements wherein the payment is in form of reciprocal commitments for other goods or services rather than an exclusive cash transaction. Besides, trade financing and price setting are tied together in a single transaction. The modern forms of countertrade are sophisticated forms of the ancient practice of simple barter of goods and services to accommodate present-day business needs. Contrary to general belief, countertrade has grown over recent years. About 15 countries were believed to be involved in countertrade in 1972, which increased to 27 countries in 1979, and by the beginning of 1990s around 100 countries used countertrade.[4] It is estimated that about 20 to 30 per cent of the world trade takes in form of countertrade and is likely to increase in the future.

Although countertrade leads to market imperfections, it becomes inevitable in certain situations. Countertrade mainly takes place because of

- Scarcity of hard currency with the importing country
- Restrictive importing country's foreign exchange regulations to conserve hard currency
- Balance of trade problems of importing countries
- Trade opportunity with restrictive markets

Both exporters and importers find countertrade a useful tool in international transactions. Exporters favour it because countertrade

- Provides an opportunity to access the markets that do not have capability to pay in hard currency
- Facilitate higher capacity utilization
- Helps in finding alternate markets for their goods
- Establishes long-term relationship with international buyers
- Increases profits and market share

Since importers in low-income countries often face paucity of foreign exchange to finance their imports, countertrade is frequently used. Importers favour countertrade because of the following reasons:

- It is an effective source of finance for their purchase.
- It facilitates conservation of foreign exchange.
- It is used to cope with statutory requirements related to foreign currency.
- It helps them reduce their debt liability.

---

[4] Vertariu, P., 'Trends and Development in International Counter Trade', *Business America*, 2 November 1992, pp. 2–6.

- It serves as an effective instrument for industrial growth in countries with foreign exchange constraints.
- It helps them to establish a long-term relationship with suppliers.

Major forms of countertrade (Fig. 11.4) include the following.

Simple barter Barter is the most ancient and the simplest form of countertrade, which involves direct and simultaneous exchange of goods without use of money. Although barter, involves a simple exchange of goods but the goods to be exchanged

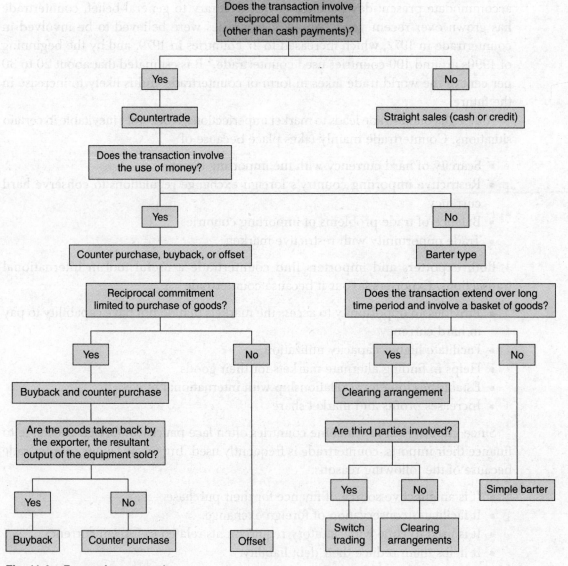

Fig. 11.4 Forms of countertrade

Source: Jean–Francois Hennart, 'Some Empirical Dimensions of Counter Trade', *Journal of International Business Studies*, Second Quarter, 1990, p. 245.

should be of some mutual value. This type of barter has been in practice for centuries right since the ancient civilizations of the Indus valley, Mesopotamia, Greek and Rome, wherein spices, grains, metals, olive oil, wine, and cosmetics were exchanged. Since it is not always possible to find a perfect match of mutual needs of the buyer and the seller, other forms of countertrade are also involved.

Clearing arrangement The transaction of goods and services extends over a long time under a clearing arrangement. Under such agreements, the governments of exporting and importing countries enter into an agreement to purchase the goods and services over an agreed period of time. India's rupee trade agreement with erstwhile USSR aimed at preserving hard currency and facilitated it through bilateral trade. Besides, the currency of transaction, such as Rupee or Rouble, was also agreed upon. The Soviet Union also had such clearing arrangements with Morocco.

Switch trading A third party, known as the switch trader, is involved in the transaction which facilitates buying of unwanted goods from the importer and making payment either by cash or barter to the exporter.

Counter purchase It involves two separate transactions payable in hard currency, each with its own cash value. Brazil has long been exporting vehicles, steel, and farm products to oil-producing countries, from which it buys oil in return.

Buyback (compensation) Firms supplying capital goods for technology often expand into international markets by using some sort of buyback arrangements wherein the output of the equipment and plants sold is taken back. This facilitates firms from low-income countries to arrange considerable finances for their projects. Thus, buyback is used as an effective marketing tool for equipment-manufacturing firms to expand into low-income countries.

Offset Under the offset arrangement, the importer makes partial payment in hard currency, besides promising to source inputs from the importing country and also makes investment to facilitate production of such goods.

In 2000, India and Iraq agreed on an 'oil for wheat and rice' barter deal, subject to UN approval under Article 50 of the UN Gulf War sanctions to facilitate 300,000 barrels of oil delivered daily to India at a price of US$6.85 a barrel while Iraq oil sales into Asia were valued at about US$22 a barrel. In 2001, India agreed to swap 1.5 million tonnes of Iraqi crude under the oil for food programme.[5]

Air India signed a countertrade agreement[6] with the European aircraft manufacturer Boeing in January 2006 for purchase of 68 aircrafts at an estimated cost of Rs 350 billion. As a part of the deal Boeing is committed to invest US$100 million in setting up an MRO (maintenance, repair, and overhauling) facility, US$75 million in a pilot

---

[5] 'India to Barter Wheat for Iraq's Crude Oil', *Indian Express*, Mumbai, 11 November 2000.
[6] 'AI Signs Deal for 68 Boeing Aircraft-Boeing to Invest US$185 million for Various Facilities', *Business Line*, 12 January 2006.

training institute, and US$10 million in other facilities. Besides, Boeing would also buy goods and services worth Rs 85 billion from Indian companies.

Despite several benefits, as discussed above, countertrade is not free of criticisms:

- Countertrade has a distorting effect on the free market competition as considerations other than currency payments are involved.
- As only a limited number of exporting firms are willing to enter countertrade, importers often have restricted choice and generally tend to pay higher than the free market price.
- Countertrade seldom improved the foreign exchange balance of importing countries that are generally low or medium-income countries.
- Large international firms often engage in dumping obsolete technology and plant and machinery in low- and middle-income countries through countertrade.

E-modes of business expansion

Use of information and communication technology has rapidly grown over the recent years for expanding business internationally. The advent of the Internet and its widespread applications have provided tremendous opportunities for rapid global expansion. The concept of e-business is discussed in detail in Chapter 19. Dell computer sells personal computers directly through the internet to its global customers on 'build to order' basis rather than 'build to forecast' basis. However, it has a very efficient supply chain management system so as to ship PCs on a local or regional basis.

HamaraCD.com, an Indian website, offers more than 25,000 of the most popular as well as truly rare songs from 100 years of music label Saregama's collection spread across various genres, such as songs in Assamese, Bengali, Hindi, Kannada, Malayalam, Marathi, Oriya, Punjabi, Tamil, and Telegu, ghazals, and Carnatic and Hindustani Classical. It ships CDs to all parts of the world, charging a shipping cost of US$10–15 for the first CD and for each additional CD US$1–2.

11.2.2 Contractual Modes

Contractual modes are often employed to make use of strategic strengths and resources of a foreign-based partner company for international business expansion. Such contractual arrangements are often complementary in nature and have mutually beneficial effect on a firm's overseas operations. In contractual expansion modes, the partner firms complement each other with one or more of their strategic strengths, such as superior technology, strong brand equity, manufacturing facilities, well-established distribution network, etc. However, the firm has to carefully choose its partners for such contractual arrangements. Factors influencing choice of foreign partners for contractual alliances include

- Strategic strength of partner that can be translated into some business value
- Commitment to cooperative goals

- Mutual trustworthiness
- Experience of operating in multi-cultural environment

Contractual modes are often preferred over other modes of international business expansion under the circumstances given below.

- Reluctance to invest considerable resources in a target country
- High level of perceived or actual risks due to unstable political and economic environment
- Differences in business environment where a local partner adds considerable value to firm's operations
- High tariffs on imported goods
- Socio-cultural differences
- Policy restrictions that prohibit use of other business expansion modes such as investment

Major forms of contractual expansion modes such as international strategic alliances, international contract manufacturing, international management contracts, turnkey projects, international leasing, international licensing, and international franchising are discussed below:

International strategic alliance

When a firm agrees to cooperate with one or more than one firm overseas, to carry out a business activity wherein each one contributes its different capabilities and strengths to the alliance, this is termed as an international strategic alliance. Such strategic alliances are long-term formal relationships for mutual benefit.

A firm has to be globally cooperative to be globally competitive. Rapid growth in global strategic alliance among large and small firms around the world highlights the significance of global strategic alliances. Perlmuter and Hennan[7] term such strategic alliance as Global Strategic Partnership (GSP) in which

- Two or more companies develop a common, long-term strategy aimed at world leadership as low-cost suppliers, differentiated marketers, or both, in an international arena.
- The relationship is reciprocal. The partners possess specific strengths that they are prepared to share with their colleagues.
- The partners' efforts are global, extending beyond a few developed countries to include nations of the newly industrialising, less developed, and socialist world.
- The relationship is organized along horizontal, not vertical, lines; technology exchanges, resource pooling and other 'soft' forms of combinations.
- The participating companies retain their national and ideological identities while competing in those markets excluded from the partnership.

[7] Perlmutter, H.V., and D.A. Heenan, 'Cooperate to Compete Globally', *Harvard Business Review*, March/April 1986, vol. 64, issue 2, pp. 136–52.

The Dutch electronic giant Philips has made a major strategic shift in its 100-years old corporate culture of self-sufficiency, heavily relying on multiple strategic alliances with external firms, as given in Exhibit 11.1.

Such global strategic alliances are aimed at blunting the forces of American, Japanese and more recently, Korean and Taiwanese competition in high-quality electronics and reducing the company's dependence on Europe, where one-half of its sales and almost two-thirds of its workforce and assets are located. Philips makes use of its global strategic alliance to have a balance of its business operations in major markets across the world.

Exhibit 11.1	Philip's global strategic alliances	
Industry	**Participating companies**	**Country of incorporation**
Advanced telephone systems	AT&T	US
Compact discs	Sony	Japan
Electronic credit cards	Compagnie des Machines Bull	France
Lighting and electronic components	Matsushita Electronic devices	Japan Hong Kong
Minicomputer software	Compagnie des Machines Bull ICL PLC Siemens Nixdarf Computer Olivetti	France Britain West Germany West Germany Italy
Mobile communications	CIT Alcatel Thomson Siemens	France France West Germany
Personal memory systems	Control Data Corona Data Systems Siemens	US US West Germany
Semiconductors and microchips	Intel Siemens Advanced Semiconductor Materials International	US West Germany Holland
Video recorders	Grundig Victor Company	West Germany Japan
Videotex software and systems	Enidata	Italy

Source: Perlmutter, H.V. and D.A. Heenan, 'Cooperate to Compete Globally', *Harvard Business Review*, March/April 1986, vol. 64, issue 2, p. 138.

The major advantages of international strategic alliances include the following:

- The investment cost is shared.
- The internationalizing firm gets access to tangible and intangible resources of the alliance partner.
- There is reduction in individual risks while operating overseas.
- The alliance partners often cooperate so as to make use of their specific individual strengths.
- Strategic alliances often promotes co-operation among competitors for mutual benefit.

However, the limitations of strategic alliance are that

- A firm has to share internal resources and information with its alliance partner
- Goal incompatibility with alliance partner leads to conflict
- Sharing resources may also nurture future competitors

Star Alliance (Fig. 11.5) launched on 14 May 1997, a strategic alliance in the airlines industry, is the largest in the world that runs about 18,100 daily flights to 975 airports in 162 countries, having a total fleet of 3,360 aircraft carrying abut 510 million passengers annually.[8] It includes major airlines, such as Air Canada, USA Airways, United Airlines, All Nippon Airways, Lufthansa, Air New Zealand, Asiana Airline,

Fig. 11.5   Star Alliance: The largest airline alliance in the world

---

[8] Based on information from www.star.alliance.com, accessed on 12 September 2008.

Austrian, BMI, South African Airways, Swiss International, Thai Airways, Singapore Airline, and Scandinavian Airlines.

The points of cooperation among the partner airlines in the Star Alliance are

- Frequent flyer programme integration allows airline miles to be earned and redeemed on all members of the alliance at the same level.
- Premium customers of the alliance have access to all members' airport lounges.
- Flight schedules are coordinated to permit almost seamless travel which may include several different carriers within the alliance, on a single ticket.
- Special fares for round-the-world and similar travel using alliance members offer discounts over booking individual itineraries.
- Customer service processes are harmonized in an effort to promote a consistent experience.
- There is cooperation in development of a common information technology platform.

The alliance developed the 'regional' concept in 2004 which helps it penetrate individual markets through regional carriers, which requires sponsorship from existing members. Star Alliance was voted the best airline alliance in the 2005 World Airline Award for the second time in three years.

Due to high level of R&D intensity and resources involved, worldwide strategic alliances are common in IT and other high-tech industries. Exhibit 11.2 illustrates Infosys' global strategic alliance with leading IT firms around the world.

India's largest pharmaceutical company Ranbaxy entered into a strategic alliance in 2005 with Nippon Chemiphar Ltd for joint-marketing their products[9] in Japan.

Exhibit 11.2   Infosys' international strategic alliances

India's leading IT company, Infosys, works with alliance partners with the best in class technologies in specific industries to develop business solutions for its clients. Infosys Alliances can be characterised either as

- A marketing alliance for jointly developing, selling and delivering business solutions that leverage Infosys' industry, functional, and technical expertise, Global Delivery Model, and the alliance partner's technology and services, or
- A technology alliance in which Infosys works with an alliance partner in order to build business

and technical competence in the alliance partner's technology through training, engagement with the alliance partner's technical support and development teams, and the development of tools and methodologies

The Infosys' alliance partners include FileNet, IBM, Informatica, Intel, Mantas, MatrixOne, Microsoft, Netegrity Inc., Oracle, Pinnacle, SAP, Siebel, Sun Microsystems, SupplyChainge, TIBCO Software Inc, Wavecom, and Yantra.

Source: Compiled from various Infosys' reports and publications.

---

9 'Ranbaxy Launches Clarithromycin Terbinefine Tablets in Japan', *Economic Times*, 18 July 2006.

Shilla Hotels and Resorts of Korea forged a marketing alliance with India's Taj Hotels to develop cross-promotional opportunities for both companies to harness each other's strengths in their respective markets of dominance. Taj Hotels also entered a marketing alliance in 2004 with Raffles Hotel in Singapore.

International contract manufacturing

In order to take advantage of lower costs of production, a firm may sub-contract manufacturing in a foreign country. International sub-contracting arrangements may involve supply of inputs, such as raw materials, semi-finished goods, components and technical know-how to a local manufacturer in a foreign country. The contract manufacturer limits itself to production activities whereas marketing is taken care of by the internationalizing firm. A processing fee is paid to a foreign-based manufacturer who is primarily responsible for processing or assembly. Overseas-based contract manufacturers are often expected to supply the goods directly to the firm's clients and invoice for processing fee to the internationalizing firm, as elucidated in Fig. 11.6. The firm in turn directly raises invoice for finished goods to its customer.

Globalization of business technology and increasing pressure on international firms to be globally competitive in their costs, product offerings, speed in bringing new products into the market, quality, and customer service have been the primary driving forces of international contract manufacturing. A number of global companies outsource their manufacturing activities to low-cost locations. A substantial part of manufactured exports comes from such activities. Contract manufacturing has also been used as a strategic tool for economic development in a number of countries, such as Korea, Mexico, Thailand, China, etc. For instance, Taiwan is a world leader in semi-conductor manufacturing. China produces 30 per cent of air conditioners, 24 per cent of washing machines, and 16 per cent of refrigerators sold in the US.

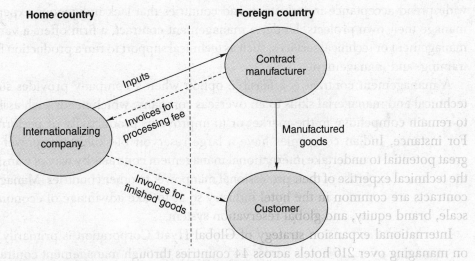

Fig. 11.6 International contract manufacturing

Nike, the leading international shoe brand, does not own a single production facility and gets its manufacturing done through contract manufacturing throughout the world. It provides raw materials and manufacturing know-how to contract manufacturers for manufacturing shoes in Asian countries, such as China, Vietnam, Indonesia, Thailand, and Bangladesh for payment of processing fees. However, Nike maintains its proprietary rights over materials and products, and exerts stringent control over production processes and product quality.

Indian pharmaceutical companies find contract manufacturing an effective tool for maintaining a high growth rate in view of limited resources for research and development. Ranbaxy and Lupin Laboratories were among the first Indian companies to get manufacturing contracts from multinational companies, Eli Lilly and Cynamid. When Ranbaxy developed an alternative process for manufacturing Eli Lilly's patented drug Cefaclor, the American company became concerned that the low-cost drug manufactured by the Indian company would take away its market share in countries which do not recognize product patents. Subsequently, Wockhardt India, Cadila Health Care, Sun Pharma, and Dr. Reddy's Laboratories Ltd have also entered into contract manufacturing with several overseas firms.

Contract manufacturing provides an excellent opportunity to firms located in developing countries, including India, to take advantage of their strategic strength of low labour cost and ample availability of skilled and semi-skilled human resources to make their product available in international markets. This opens up new avenues, especially for firms with strong production bases but limited resources and skills to market the products internationally.

International management contracts

A firm that possesses technical skills or management know-how can expand overseas by providing its managerial and technical expertise on contractual basis. It has widespread acceptance in industries and countries that lack indigenous expertise to manage their own projects. Under a management contract, a firm offers a variety of management or technical services, such as technical support to run a production facility, training, and management.

A management contract is a feasible option when a company provides superior technical and managerial skills to an overseas company, which needs such assistance to remain competitive in the market or to improve its productivity or performance. For instance, Indian companies have a large reservoir of skilled manpower and a great potential to undertake international management contracts by way of transferring the technical expertise of their professional manpower to other countries. Management contracts are common in the hotel industry so as to take advantage of economies of scale, brand equity, and global reservation system.

International expansion strategy of Global Hyatt Corporation is primarily based on managing over 216 hotels across 44 countries through management contracts. In order to prevent dilution of quality and hence brand erosion, it ensures that all the properties under its management contract follow and maintain rules, regulations, benchmark practices, and standards as per its corporate policy. Similarly, India's Taj Hotels have also employed management contracts (Exhibit 11.3) for international expansion.

Engineers India Ltd (EIL) got a project management contract for providing project consultancy[10] for the revamp and up-gradation of the Skikda Refinery in Algeria in February 2005 and for up-gradation of tank farm area in Abu Dhabi in August 2005.

Turnkey projects

A company may expand internationally by making use of its core competencies in designing and executing infrastructure, plants, or manufacturing facilities overseas. Conceptually, 'turnkey' means handing over a project to the client, when it is complete in all respect and is 'ready to use' on 'turning the key'. International turnkey projects include conceptualizing, designing, constructing, installing, and carrying out preliminary testing of manufacturing facilities or engineering projects at overseas locations for a client organization. It often includes providing training to the client's personnel to operate the plant.

Exhibit 11.3   Taj Hotels' international expansion through management contracts

The Indian Hotel Company and its subsidiaries, collectively known as Taj Hotels, Resorts and Palaces are recognized as one of Asia's largest and finest hotel companies. Taj Hotels, Resorts and Palaces comprises 57 hotels in 40 locations across India with an additional 18 international hotels in the Maldives, Mauritius, Malaysia, Seychelles, the UK, the US, Bhutan, Sri Lanka, Africa, the Middle East, and Australia.

Although Taj Hotels expands internationally by way of equity participations and international acquisitions, management contract remains the preferred mode of international expansion. Taj Hotels has secured management contracts at Palm Island, Jumeirah in Dubai, Langkawi in Malaysia, and Thimpu in Bhutan.

The Indian Hotels Company Ltd (IHCL) entered into a 10-year management contract in April 2005 with Dubai-based property developer, ETA Star, to develop and manage the Taj Exotica Resort and Spa, a luxury resort at the Palm Island Jumeriah Cresent in Dubai. ETA Star would develop the US$330 million project, which would comprise a luxury hotel and 200 luxury residential apartments for sale and lease. IHCL's luxury brand Taj Hotels operates and manages the Taj Exotica Resort and Spa and the Grandeur Residences located at the Palm Jumeirah Crescent in Dubai.

In June 2005, Indian hotels entered into a 30-year management contract to operate and manage Piere, a luxurious hotel in New York, which was earlier managed by Four Seasons. The average management fee is likely to be about 12 per cent to 15 per cent of the total average revenue subject to occupancy and average room rents.

Management contracts facilitated rapid international expansion of Taj Hotels without any equity commitment.

Source: 'Taj to Run Spa in Dubai', *Asian Age*, 7 April 2005; 'Taj Hotels Turns Globetrotter for More Revenues', *The Telegraph*, Kolkata, 6 April 2006; www.tajhotel.com.

---

[10] 'EIL Secures PMC Contract from Algeria', *The Hindu Business*, 25 February 2005.

The major types of turnkey project include the following.

Build and transfer (BT)   The firm conceptualizes, designs, builds, carries out primary testing, and transfers the project to the owner. Important issues negotiated with the overseas firm include design specifications, price, make and source of equipment, man specifications, performance schedules, payment terms, and buyer's support system.

Build, operate, and transfer (BOT)   The internationalizing firm not only builds the project but also manages it for a contracted period before transferring it to the foreign owner. During the operational period, the functional viability of the project is established and the technical and managerial staff of the buyer may be trained during this period. However, the exporting company needs additional resources and competence to run such a project.

Build, operate, own (BOO)   The internationalizing firm is expected to buy the project once it has been built, which results in foreign direct investment after a certain time period. For executing projects on BOO basis, the exporting company has to be highly integrated, providing technical and management services, besides having experience in owning and controlling infrastructure projects.

The global market leader in telecommunications, Nokia, used enterprise solution providing and networking to key players in emerging markets as strategic business expansion strategy. It focussed upon providing turnkey solutions to India's state-owned telecom giant, Bharat Sanchar Nigam Limited (BSNL). In 2004, Nokia was awarded a US$284 million deal with BSNL for network expansion project in North India to tap about two million additional subscribers. Besides, Nokia is likely to provide turnkey solution to Idea cellular to launch Nokia's Intelligent Content Delivery System (ICDS) on all Idea mobile networks across India.

Construction and engineering projects are often highly capital-intensive, involving extremely in-depth engineering, and are usually cross-country in nature of execution. Therefore, such projects are carried out at turnkey basis. Besides, these projects also involve strategic alliances, international process/engineering licensees (in case of patented process), sub-contracting, management contracts, etc.

One of the world's premier engineering, construction, and project management companies, Bechtel, with a fleet of 40,000 employees and 40 offices around the world has completed more than 22,000 projects on turnkey and contractual basis in more than 140 countries. Overseas Construction Council of India is the nodal Indian export promotion agency for project exports. A number of engineering firms, such as Engineers India Ltd (EIL), Voltas, Larsen & Toubro (Fig. 11.7), Ircon International Ltd, and Balmer Lawrie & Company, have carried out several overseas projects on turnkey basis.

International leasing

In low-income countries, manufacturers often do not possess enough financial resources or necessary foreign currency to pay for equipment and machinery. A firm can expand

Fig. 11.7 L&T's turnkey project in Saudi Arabia: 120 TPD formaldehyde plant for Saudi Formaldehyde Chemical Co. Ltd, Al Jubail

its business by leasing out new and used equipment to a manufacturing firm in such countries. The ownership of the property retains with the leasing firm (i.e., lessor) throughout the lease period during which the foreign-based user (i.e., lessee) pays leasing fee. Leasing provides international business opportunities by rapid market access using idle and obsolete equipment in an efficient manner. It also benefits low-income country-based manufacturers to reduce cost of getting machinery and equipment from overseas and reduces investment and operational risks.

International Lease Finance Corporation (ILFC), headquartered in Los Angles, is the largest aircraft lessor by value that had an inventory of about 1000 aircrafts by 2008. It leases Airbus and Boeing aircraft to airlines worldwide, such as Emirates, Lufthansa, Air France, KLM, American Airlines, Continental, Vietnam Airlines, etc.

International licensing

In licensing, a firm makes its intangible assets, such as patents, trademarks and copyrights, technical know-how and skills (technical guidance, feasibility and product studies, manuals, engineering, designs, etc.) available to a foreign company for a fee termed as royalty. The home-based firm transferring the intellectual property is known as the licensor whereas the foreign based firm is known as licensee. The licensee makes use of these intangible assets in production processes. International licensing is common in pharmaceuticals, toys, machine tools, publishing, etc.

Licensing serves as a powerful tool for international expansion with little financial commitment. A firm's limited financial resources to invest in several countries and lack of foreign market knowledge influences a company to expand business overseas by way of licensing. Besides, licensing is often adopted in view of environmental factors, such as country entry barriers, to curb product piracy and counterfeiting, and for expanding into countries where the market size is not large enough to justify higher investments.

Arrow, 'America's shirt maker since 1851' follows the licensing strategy to expand worldwide. Presently, it has licensees in more than 90 countries, with a wholesale value approaching US$300 million. It entered India in 1993 through licensing to Arvind Clothing,[11] a wholly owned subsidiary of Arvind Mills Ltd. Arrow became the market leader in India in the premium man's shirt category. Phillips Van Heusen was the licensee for Arrow shirts and sportswear in the US market and generated sales of up to US$170 million through licences.

Licensing may involve either process or trade-mark licensing agreement, as discussed here.

Process licensing The licensee gets the right to manufacture, produce, and market the product in the defined market area.

Trade-mark licensing The licensee also gets the rights to use trade-marks/trade-names, besides using the process know-how. Trade-mark licensing is used as an effective strategy to control counterfeit products in the market. However, over-licensing may damage the firm's interest in the long-run. For instance, the brand equity of Pierre Cardin was considerable affected adversely consequent to its licensing about 800 brands.

The licensee makes a payment of royalties to the licensor in exchange for intellectual property by any one or a combination of following methods:

- A lump-sum payment is made in the beginning after initial transfer of intangible assets, such as know-how, drawings and designs, blueprints, spare parts, machinery, etc., not related to the output of production processes
- A minimum annual royalty guaranteed to the licensor
- Continued royalty computed as a percentage of sales revenue or amount per unit of output

While expanding to countries with unstable business environment by way of high political and economic risks, higher initial payment and shorter duration of agreement

---

[11] Sachitanand, N.N., 'Arrow and the Apparel Industry', *The Hindu Business*, 12 October 2003.

is preferred. International licensors need to adopt a competitive strategy to gain market share in relatively low-risk countries with sizeable markets. Licensing arrangements from CIS countries do involve other forms of payments, such as technical and management fee, conversion of royalties into equity, etc.

International licensing facilitates foreign-based firms to access established products, processes, and brand names with little investment in in-house R&D. It also enables them to access the know-how and technology that is otherwise not available due to government restrictions on inward foreign investment. The US firm Qualcomm owns the bulk of the intellectual property behind the Code Division Multiple Access (CDMA) standards and thus earns substantial profits from royalty when companies like Nokia make CDMA products.

The Indian pharmaceutical company Dr Reddy's licenses its anti-diabetic molecules, DRF 2593 (Balaglitazone) and DRF 2725 (Ragaglitazar) to Novo Nordisk, a Danish firm that is the world leader in diabetes care. Asian Paints adopted technology and brand licensing for its international expansion (Exhibit 11.4).

Exhibit 11.4   Asian Paints' technology and brand-licensing

Berger International, the Singapore-based subsidiary of Asian Paints entered into a technology and brand-licensing deal with PT Abadi Coatings Solusi of Indonesia in 2003. The Indonesian company will use the trademark and technology of Berger International for products in the protective and marine coating fields. Asian Paints will provide production technology and also oversee supply chain management. The deal will be valid till 2010. The main reasons for adopting the licensing strategy for the Indonesian market are summarized here.

- As a part of their revised business strategy, Asian Paints decided to exit the markets, which do not fit in with its strategy. In its new business strategy, it has decided to generate additional revenues by licensing out its brands and technology. This was a major shift from its earlier strategy of growing through acquisitions. In 2002, Asian Paints sold its Malta plant to a local company called Vangeebee Ltd and also licensed out the brand name and technological know-how to Vangeebee. The market entry to Indonesia through licensing is also in line with Asian Paints' revised business strategy.

- PT Abadi Coatings, which supplies coatings to oil and gas companies, chemical and petrochemical plants, and shipping companies, caters to a very specialized kind of market. But the market size of about 20,000 tonnes in Indonesia is quite reasonable and PT Abadi is one of the largest paint manufacturers of Indonesia. For Asian Paints it is 'another direction' (deviation) to expand its international reach. Asian Paints is likely to opt for a low-risk strategy of licensing to venture, especially when it has been able to tie up with the market leader.

- Berger brand is not available in Indonesia but it is one of the major brands in the neighbouring Malaysian, Singapore, Thai, Myanmar, and Chinese markets. Asian Paints wanted to leverage the popularity of Berger brand name by licensing it out in Indonesia.

Besides, Asian Paints also entered into a licensing agreement as an exit strategy from Malta so as to generate some revenue by way of royalty with minimum cost.

Source: Sabarinath, M., 'Berger Licences Tech, Brand to Indonesian Co.', *The Economic Times,* 10 July 2003 and company literature.

The limitations of international licensing include problems related to maintaining product quality by the licensee, leading to sullying the brand image of the licensor. Licensing may also restrict the licensor's future activities in the country. Besides transferring know-how and technology outside the firm may nurture a future competitor, thus having an adverse impact on the firm's long term interests.

Cross-licensing   It is a form of licensing involving mutual exchange of intangible assets that may not involve a cash payment. In cross-licensing, companies swap their intellectual property for mutual benefit. Thus, cross-licensing is the mutual sharing of patents between two companies without exchange of licensing fee. It is used extensively by software companies to pile up more licenses.

International franchising

Franchising is a special form of licensing in which an internationalizing firm (known as franchisor) provides intangible assets, such as trademarks, process know-how, etc., and methods of doing business in a prescribed manner in return for a franchising fee. The term 'franchising' is derived from the French word *francorum rex* which means 'freedom from servitude'. In franchising, the franchisor grants the franchisee the right to carry out business in a prescribed manner in a specified place for a pre-decided period of time.

Franchising is a low-risk low-cost business expansion mode enabling a firm to simultaneously expand in multiple countries with little financial commitments. It actively involves small independent investors who have adequate working capital but little or no prior business experience.

In legal terms, franchising as a business expansion mode has four distinct characteristics:[12]

- A contractual relationship in which the franchisor licenses the franchisee to carry out business under a name owned by or associated with the franchisor and in accordance with a business format established by the franchisor
- Control by the franchisor over the way in which the franchisee carries on the business
- Provision of assistance to the franchisee by the franchisor in running the business both prior to commencement and throughout the period of contract
- The franchisee owns his/her business, which is a separate entity from that of the franchisor; the franchisee provides the capital and assumes risks in the venture

International franchising is beneficial as it

- Facilitates rapid country entry with low risk
- Requires low investment and overheads

---

[12] Adams, J. and M. Mendelsohn, 'Recent Development in Franchising', *Journal of Business Law*, 1986, pp. 206–19.

- Avoids day-to-day hassles of business operations
- Makes use of local entrepreneurs as business partners and their skills

Apart from benefiting the franchisor, franchising is also advantageous to the franchisee because

- It facilitates speedy transfer of technology and business skills
- It provides access to well-established products and brand names
- It makes available standardized and tried and tested processes
- It benefits from shared responsibility
- International market promotions by the franchisor help in marketing
- It involves legal independence

The internationalizing firm exerts much higher control over its franchisee so as to ensure quality standards across countries. Besides, transfer of business know-how is also an ongoing process. Franchising is widely used in international business expansion of fast food chains and the hotel industry. Franchising offers greater control over international business operations, involves longer commitment, and ongoing transfer of intellectual property and know-how. The top global franchisors include[13] Subway, Quiznos Sub, Curves, SPS Stone, the Pizza Hut Inc, WSI Internet, and KFC Corp.

Franchising is widely used in the service sector wherein transfer of intangible assets and other assistance is required for an extended period. Thus, a firm has a greater degree of control over its franchising operation compared to licensing.

However, franchising also has its own limitations for the internationalizing firm:

- Restrictive host country regulations
- Problems in identifying and selecting right franchisees
- Franchisor gets 'franchising fee' rather than sharing the profits
- Lack of direct control over franchisee operations
- It adversely affects the brand equity if quality is lowered by the franchisee
- There are uncertainties and conflicts in receiving franchising fee
- Franchisor does not gain market knowledge even after firm's overseas presence for a considerable time

OSIM International Limited, the Singapore-based manufacturer of lifestyle products primarily expands internationally through franchising. OSIM has entered into a Master Franchisee Agreement (MFA) with an Indian manufacturer of surgical products, Paramount Surgimed Limited, to import and trade OSIM products in India and Nepal.

11.2.3   Investment Modes

If a country is found to be attractive enough to justify a firm's long-term commitment, investment modes of expansion are often adopted. Foreign Direct Investment (FDI)

---

[13] http//:www.entrepreneur.com/franzone/listings/topglobal.

is discussed in detail separately in Chapter 12. A firm shifts its manufacturing operations in foreign countries

- To effectively respond to market competition
- To take advantage of host country incentives
- To gain access to host country resources to be used as inputs
- To shift manufacturing operations overseas to a relatively cost effective location
- To have manufacturing base in market proximity
- To circumvent host country regulations such as trade restrictions and prohibitive import duties
- To minimize logistics cost, which offers considerable cost disadvantage especially for geographically distant countries or low unit value products.

Major forms of investment modes, such as overseas assembly or expansion, joint ventures, and wholly owned subsidiary are discussed below.

Overseas assembly or mixing

In order to respond to import restrictions, high tariff and freight charges, assembling operations overseas is often adopted to expand business. In international assembly, a manufacturer exports components, parts or machinery in Completely Knocked Down (CKD) conditions and assembles these parts at a site in a foreign country. Supplies from other suppliers are often sourced at the foreign assembly site. In the food and pharmaceutical industry, the equivalent of assembly is known as mixing wherein imported ingredients are used at the firm's overseas facilities.

Assembling is often used to overcome the import restrictions in target countries. Japanese automobile manufacturers had to begin assembling in Europe mainly to deal with import barriers. As the local content in these assembly operations was negligible, these were also termed as 'screwdriving operations'.

Joint ventures

International joint ventures offer equity investment opportunities in foreign countries with sharing resources and risks with partner firms. It serves as an effective strategy to expand in countries with investment restrictions. A firm shares equity and other resources with other partner firms to form a new company in the target country. In addition to capital, joint ventures give access to other resources and strengths of the partner, such as market know-how, technology, skills, local operating knowledge, etc. The partner firms may be either one or more local companies in the target country or firms either from third country or home country. Based on the equity stake joint ventures may be of the following three types:

- Majority with more than 50 per cent ownership
- A 50–50 equity with equal ownership
- Minority with less than 50 per cent ownership

During the 1990s, India and other emerging markets had much greater level of investment restrictions. In order to overcome these restrictions, Suzuki entered India, forming a joint venture with the Indian government. Subsequently, a large number of automobile manufacturers, such as Honda Motors, Kawasaki, etc., too formed joint ventures with other Indian companies. A few years later when investment norms were liberalized, these foreign firms established their own wholly owned subsidiaries.

The major benefits of international joint ventures are that

- They provide access to countries where complete ownership is restricted
- Equity sharing also provides access to complementary strengths of the partner firm besides capital
- They require less investment compared to complete ownership
- There are higher returns compared to trade related and contractual expansion modes
- There is greater degree of control vis-à-vis contractual modes
- They reduce operating and political risks
- They effectively overcome tariff and non-tariff barriers of the host country

The limitations of joint ventures include

- Shared control over overseas operations
- Risk of equity partner becoming a future competitor
- Management problems due to cultural differences
- Difference in goals and objectives of partner firms lead to conflicts
- Trade secrets, processes, and know-how are often shared
- Selection of right partner having compatible goals is a difficult task
- Lack of flexibility as partnering firms have long-term investments

Japanese consumer electronics company Sony Corporation and Swedish telecommunication firm Ericsson merged to establish a 50-50 joint venture headquartered in London in 2001 so as to combine Ericsson's technological leadership in telecommunication and Sony's global marketing strengths to make mobile phones. Both companies have stopped making their own mobile phones in 1995. Sony Ericsson also introduced Walkman branded w-services music phones. In the first quarter of 2006, Sony Ericsson was the fourth largest manufacturer of mobile phones in the world with 7 per cent global market share after Samsung, Motorola, and Nokia. Similarly, in June 2006, Nokia's Network Business Group and Siemens AG's communication division also announced its merger by way of a 50-50 joint venture to form a new company, Nokia Siemens Networks. The new JV entity would have a synergistic effect to make it the largest telecommunication company of the world.

In the oil and gas industry, international joint venture is common phenomenon where one or more international firms often cooperate with a local firm.

Wholly owned subsidiaries

A firm expands internationally to have complete control over its overseas operations by way of 100 per cent ownership in the new entity, known as wholly owned subsidiary. Besides ownership and control, wholly owned subsidiaries help the internationalizing firm protect its technology and skills from external sharing. Major benefits of wholly owned subsidiaries are

- The firm exerts complete control over its foreign operations
- The trade secrets, proprietary technology, and other firm specific advantages (FSAs) retains within the company

However, the limitations of wholly owned subsidiaries are

- They require commitment of large financial and other operational resources
- There is high investment, if also associated with high risk exposure
- Considerable international experience and exposure is required to establish a wholly owned subsidiary abroad

Wholly owned subsidiaries often face numerous prejudices in host countries which may be summarized here.

- Completely owned operations are generally not allowed in vital and sensitive industrial sectors such as defence, nuclear energy, media, select infrastructure, etc.
- Since virtually there is little control over wholly owned foreign subsidiaries, the host country's governments generally set stricter scrutiny and operational norms, such as pollution control, foreign exchange administration, technology level, etc.
- There exist high vulnerability to criticism by various social activists, NGOs, political parties, and other interest groups in the host country

Therefore, for successful operation of a wholly owned subsidiary, one has to take care to

- Actively involve indigenous people at all levels of managerial and operational decision making
- Ensure extensive use of local marketing and supply channels, to the extent possible

As discussed earlier, firms invest overseas either by way of greenfield operations or mergers and acquisitions (M&As). The choice of FDI mode is largely influenced by industry-specific factors, as greenfield investment is the preferred mode of expansion in technology-intensive industries. The choice may also be influenced by institutional, cultural, and transaction cost factors, in particular the attitude towards takeovers, conditions in capital markets, liberalization policies, privatization, regional integration, currency risks, and the role played by intermediaries (for example, investment bankers) actively seeking acquisition opportunities and taking initiatives in making deals.

Greenfield operations   Creating production and marketing facilities on a firm's own from scratch is termed as greenfield operations. Greenfield operations are preferred over M&A under the following situations:

- In least developed and some developing countries where right targets for acquisition are barely available
- When smaller firms do not possess required finances for acquisition
- When attractive incentives are offered by the host country to encourage foreign investment leading to increased financial viability.
- When expanding in countries with regulatory barriers to international acquisition

Mergers and acquisitions   Transfer of existing assets of a domestic firm to a foreign firm lead to mergers and acquisitions. In cross-border mergers, a new legal entity emerges by way of merging assets and operations of firms from more than one country. Cross-border acquisitions involves transferring management control of assets and operations of a domestic company to a foreign firm. As a result, the local firm becomes an affiliate of the foreign company. Generally mergers occur in friendly settings wherein two firms come together to build a synergy. On the other hand, acquisitions can be hostile takeovers by purchasing the majority of shares of a firm from the open market.

M&As are preferred over greenfield investments due to the following reasons:

- They provide a rapid expansion of the firm's business in foreign countries. Therefore, M&A become crucial when the speed of business expansion is important.
- The acquiring firm gets ready access to tangible and intangible assets of the target firm overseas. In addition to acquisition of manufacturing and other physical facilities, the target firm's brand equity, marketing channels, skilled manpower, patents and trademarks do have strategic significance for business expansion.
- The investing firm also acquires technical know-how, process, and management skills that add to its operational efficiency overseas.

Acquisitions can be of the following three types:

Minority   When a foreign firm acquires 10 per cent to 49 per cent interest in a firm's voting stock

Majority   When a foreign firm acquires 50 per cent to 99 per cent voting interest

Full outright stake   When a foreign firm acquires 100 per cent of voting stock

Certain industries, such as telecommunications, energy distribution, pharmaceuticals, and financial services have exhibited a high level of cross border M&A activity

The US telecommunications firm Lucent Technologies announced in April 2006 its merger with its French competitor Alcatel, which is 1.5 time the size of Lucent. The combined entity is likely to generate revenues of approximately US\$25 billion from Lucent's existing revenues of US\$9.50 in 2005. Expansion or re-investment in existing foreign affiliates or sites is also referred as Brownfield investment.

Procter and Gamble (P&G) acquired Gillette in October 2005 and became the world's largest consumer company, displacing the Anglo Dutch Unilever to second place from 1 June 2006. The company's area of operations include P&G beauty and health; household care and global Gillette. Hewlett Packard merged with Compaq in 2002 with a strategic objective to acquire the leadership position in personal computing.

World's top 10 cross-border M&A deals are shown in Table 11.1. Cross-border M&A increased by 23 per cent to US$880 billion and in 2006, the number of transactions increased by 14 per cent to 6,974, reflecting strong global M&A activity. The recent M&As were largely driven by favourable financing conditions worldwide, reflecting low debt-financing costs and an abundant supply of credit as a result of high corporate profits.

In contrast to the M&A boom of the late 1990s and early 2000s, which was largely driven by takeovers in the Information and Communication Technology (ICT) industries, the current M&As were in the consumer goods and service industries (including financial services) and in energy supply and basic materials. Besides, in the previous M&A boom, transactions were to a large extent financed by the exchange of shares. Recent cross-border M&A transactions have been carried out primarily through cash and debt financing.[14] For instance, in large deals, including many in mining and oil industries, cash is now the standard payment method. Emerging economies awash with petrodollars (West Asia) and foreign exchange (China) have become very active in cash based cross-border acquisitions. The increasing role of debt financing in cross-border acquisitions may be explained by the fact that the cost of equity capital remains significantly higher than the cost of debt financing. This reflects a corporate strategy of not holding excessive equity capital and instead using borrowings and internal funds in investment to attain high managerial efficiency.

M&As by Indian firms

Setting up a subsidiary and attempting to grow organically could take years. Moreover, major costs are to be incurred in building up marketing channels and brands. In high-cost economies, such as Europe with stringent labour and environment regulations, the synergy of a local distribution network and low-cost manufacturing in India makes strategic sense. As companies grow, have surplus funds, and want to expand their markets, they find the virtues of foreign acquisition.

India's deepening integration into the global economy led to corporate restructuring and significant growth in mergers and acquisitions, especially in high-tech, energy, and core industries. Grant Thornton, a global consulting firm estimates that the value of cross-border deals, both inbound and outbound, by Indian firms tripled from US$15.31 billion in 2006 to US$48.26 billion in 2007 but declined to US$25.63 billion[15]

---

[14] World Investment Report, Transnational Corporations, Extractive Industries and Development, United Nations, New York and Geneva, 2007, pp. 3–16.
[15] 'M&A Deals Lack Lustre on Slowdown Blues', *Business Line*, Chennai, 25 December 2008.

Table 11.1 World's top 10 cross-border M&A deals*

Rank	Value ($ billions)	Target company	Target nation	Target industry	Acquiring company	Acquiring nation	Acquiring industry
1	32.7	Arcelor SA	Luxembourg	Steel works, blast furnaces, and rolling mills	Mittal Steel Co Nv	Netherlands	Steel works, blast furnaces, and rolling mills
2	31.7	O2 PLC	UK	Radiotelephone communications	Telefonica SA	Spain	Telephone communications, except radiotelephone
3	21.8	BAA PLC	UK	Airports and airport terminal services	Airport Development	Spain	Special purpose finance company
4	17.4	Falconbridge Ltd	Canada	Ferroalloy ores, except vanadium	Xstrata PLC	Switzerland	Bituminous coal underground mining
5	17.2	Inco Ltd	Canada	Ferroalloy ores, except vanadium	Cia Vale do Rio Doce SA	Brazil	Iron ores
6	14.1	BOC Group PLC	UK	Industrial gases	Linde AG	Germany	General industrial machinery and equipment
7	13.6	Lucent Technologies Inc	US	Telephone and telegraph apparatus	Alcatel SA	France	Communications equipment nec
8	10.6	TDC A/S	Denmark	Telephone communications, except radiotelephone	Nordic Telephone Co ApS	US	Telephone communications, except radiotelephone
9	10.0	Winterthur Schweizerische	Switzerland	Life insurance	AXA SA	France	Life insurance
10	9.6	VNU NV	Netherlands	Periodicals: publishing, or publishing and printing	Valcon Acquisition BV	US	Special purpose finance company

* Completed in 2006.
Source: World Investment Report: Transnational Corporations, Extractive Industries and Development, New York and Geneva, 2007, pp. 212–15.

in 2008. During the recent years, there had been significant M&As in commodities, such as steel, aluminium, metals and ores, telecom, power and energy, etc. The ability of many Indian companies to raise money at lower rates due to prevailing market conditions in India seems to be an enabling factor driving overseas acquisitions. The factors that enabled Indian companies to go on an acquisition spree include

- Major Indian companies had surplus cash reserves that were to be better invested in the production facilities.
- The financial reform process simplified the process of overseas acquisitions by removing the cap of US$100 million on foreign investment in 2001.
- The rupee grew strong in international markets that made better sense to invest outside.
- Balance of payments surplus ensured that the dollar became available easily.
- Exposure to the international competitive environment underlined the need to incorporate professional work environment available in the developed countries.

Reasons for international acquisitions by Indian firms Opening up of the domestic market to foreign companies has the potential to obliterate the difference between the domestic and the international markets. Domestic players with substantial market share have been forced to increase their standards to international levels to survive even in the domestic market in the long-run. Such internationalization can best be brought about by taking the M&A route to rope in foreign firms. The major objectives of the acquisitions abroad are

- To increase productivity levels to internationally accepted standards
- To raise the profitability by achieving scale economies in logistics, transportation, etc.
- To improve their competitiveness in the global market by strategic location of the manufacturing facilities closer to the user markets
- To get better access to foreign markets especially when there are strong entry barriers in the shape of Sanitary and Phytosanitary (SPS) restrictions and environmental constraints

The main motives for Indian companies to undertake cross-border M&As were to gain access to new technologies and competencies, and to build stronger positions in global markets. The acquisition by the Mittal Steel group, a company of Indian origin headquartered in the Netherlands, of the European Steel company Arcelor for $32 billion, was the world's largest cross-border M&A transaction in 2006, and the largest deal ever made by a company with origins in a developing country. In the same year, the Indian Tata Group acquired the Corus Group (UK/Netherlands), also in the steel industry, for $9.5 billion. Broadly, the acquisition strategy followed by Indian firms was to

- Acquire companies in the developed countries that were facing mounting costs and falling profit levels

- Turn them around through a synergy of a local distribution network and low-cost manufacturing based in India, so as to make the companies financially viable and competitive
- Develop the developed country markets through a barrier free entry riding on the brands of the foreign 'acquired' firms
- Protect the developing country markets by sustaining the existing distribution network and by introducing premier products of the 'acquired' firm

11.3   STRATEGY FOR SELECTING INTERNATIONAL BUSINESS EXPANSION MODE

A firm has to decide upon the modes of business expansion in foreign countries so as to achieve its internationalization objectives. The basic decision rules for selecting business expansion modes may be covered by the following fundamental rules.[16]

Naive rule   The management uses same expansion mode for all foreign markets ignoring the heterogeneity of different foreign markets and expansion conditions. The inflexibility of the naive rule prevents the firm from exploiting foreign market opportunities to the full extent.

Pragmatic rule   The firm enters a new market initially with a low-risk entry mode. It looks for a workable entry mode, only if the initial entry mode is not feasible or profitable. Following pragmatic rule minimizes the risk of spending resources on investigating alternate entry modes and using wrong types of entry modes as unworkable ones are already rejected. Since, all potential entry mode alternatives are investigated, the workable mode may not be the 'best mode'.

Strategy rule   All alternative expansion modes need to be systematically compared and evaluated before a decision is made. As a firm has multiple objectives for its international business expansion, it would require a trade off between various objectives for making an expansion mode choice. The Strategy Rule helps maximize the profit contribution over the strategic planning period subject to availability of resources, risks, and non-profit objectives.

11.3.1   Marketing Strategy and Expansion Modes

A firm's marketing strategy also acts as a key determinant for expansion mode decision. When a firm focuses itself on a select few countries, it adopts a market penetration strategy whereas when a firm either simultaneously or in quick succession enters a large number of countries, it adopts a market-skimming strategy. Figure 11.8 depicts the strategic options available for expanding business internationally in view of complexities of a country's business environment and a firm's marketing strategy.

---

[16] Ranklin, R. Root, *Entry Strategies of International Markets*, New York: Lexington, 1994, pp. 4–16.

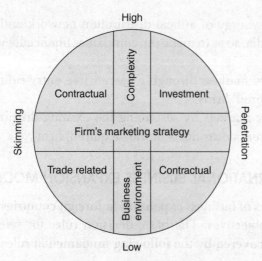

Fig. 11.8 Strategic options for international business expansion modes

- A firm expanding its business in a large number of countries simultaneously using market-skimming strategy with relatively low complexity of business environment, generally prefers trade-related expansion modes due to low resource commitment, low risk, and low exit costs. On the other hand if the business environment is highly complex and the firm is adopting a market-skimming strategy, contractual expansion modes are preferred.
- Expanding business into a select few countries calls for deep market penetration. An internationalizing firm generally prefers the contractual expansion mode in case the complexity of business environment is less whereas investment mode of expansion is preferred if the level of business complexity is high.

11.3.2 Sequential Adoption of Business Expansion Modes

A firm may expand its operations internationally in a sequential manner based on country market segments, as depicted in Fig. 11.9. To illustrate, based on distinct market attributes, the Asia Pacific region may be divided into the following five segments:

Platform countries The firm can use countries, such as Singapore and Hong Kong as initial bases to gather intelligence and initiate first contacts. These countries later may serve as coordination centres for the region.

Emerging countries Firms build up their initial presence in countries, such as Vietnam, Myanmar, Laos, and Cambodia by way of a representative office or a local distributor who may in turn lead to establishment of a local operation either through a local subsidiary or a joint venture.

Growth countries In order to capitalize on future market opportunities, companies often build a significant presence in countries, such as China, India, Thailand, Indonesia, Malaysia, and the Philippines so as to take first mover advantage.

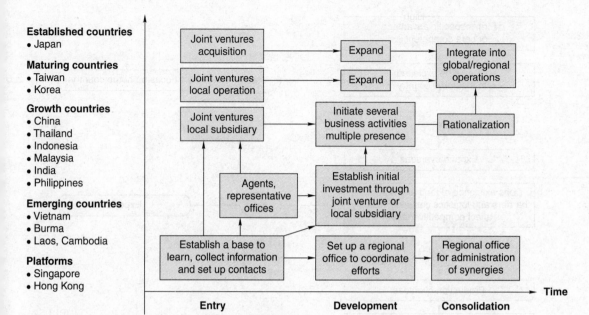

Fig. 11.9 Sequential adoption of business expansion modes

Source: Lasserre, Philippe, 'Corporate Strategies for the Asia Pacific Region', *Long Range Planning*, 1995, 28(1), p. 21.

Maturing countries The prospects offered by maturing countries, such as Korea and Taiwan are much lower as they have significant economic infrastructure and well-established local and international competitors. The prime task here is to look for ways to further develop the market via strategic alliances, major investments, or acquisitions of local or smaller foreign players.

Established countries Similar to maturing countries, the growth prospects are much higher in established countries, such as Japan compared to other countries. An international firm often enters these markets by way of joint ventures or acquisitions and integrates into regional or global operations as a part of its consolidation strategy.

Although this framework of sequential expansion using various expansion modes is given in context with Southeast Asia Pacific, it can also be used for expanding in other parts of the world.

11.3.3 Decision-making Process for Selecting Modes of International Business Expansion

The expansion mode strategy should aim at achieving a firm's strategic goals. It should take into consideration the firm's long-term goals so as to establish its international presence. A company is believed to possess some core competencies or advantages that are specific to the firm and hardly available to its competitors. As depicted in Fig. 11.10, the firm may exploit its existing core competencies in the domestic market or focus its resources to develop new competitive advantages for home country. In

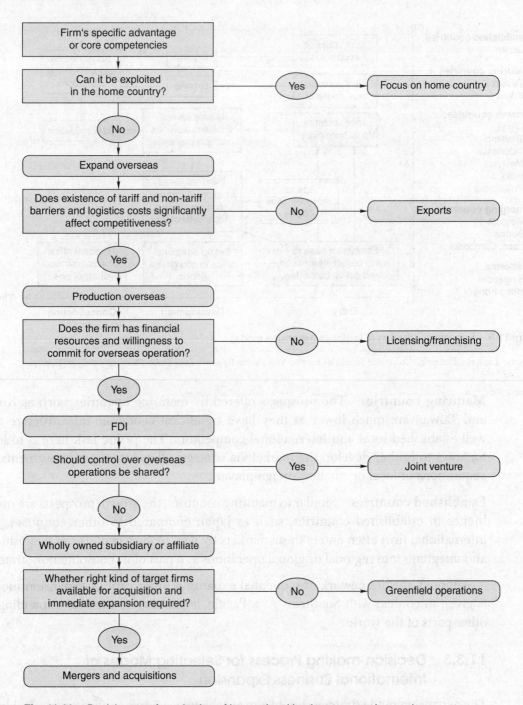

Fig. 11.10 Decision-tree for selection of international business expansion modes

case the opportunities to exploit such competencies in the home country are limited, the firm expands overseas. Firms often decide to pursue international business expansion as a strategic goal in addition to exploiting home country market.

Cost of logistics, depending upon geographical distances and unit value realization of goods, forms a significant constituent of price competitiveness in the target country. Besides, various trade restrictions and import tariffs of host country governments considerably affect a firm's competitiveness. Expanding through exports is suitable for countries having low transportation cost and lower import tariffs and other import restrictions.

The firm needs to begin overseas production, if expanding through exports adversely affects its competitiveness either due to prohibitive costs of logistics or imports restrictions, including tariffs and non-tariff barriers. Choice of expansion mode may be made, depending upon the availability and willingness to commit financial and other resources. For rapid expansion into multiple markets with little financial commitments, licensing or franchising serve as effective expansion tools so as to exploit a firm's core competence internationally. Although, licensing is a low-cost expansion mode, it requires the firm to share its intangible assets, such as technology, processes, skills, know-how, etc. with its business partner. A firm's strategy to have control over its intellectual property serves as key determinant in licensing.

If the intangible assets are not amenable to licensing and the firm wants to commit sizeable resources overseas and exert control, it expands through foreign direct investment. It is the extent of control desired, likely risks, ability, and willingness to commit resources, besides the long-term business prospects of the host country that determine the extent of investment. In case the firm is not willing to share control and ready to assume complete risk, it opts for a wholly owned subsidiary. If the right kind of target firm with goal compatibility is available in the target country, mergers and acquisition is a preferred strategy that also facilitates speedy expansion. Otherwise greenfield investment is adopted.

Selecting an appropriate mode of business expansion is an important decision, having both short-term and long-term operational and strategic ramifications on a firm's success in its internationalization process. Although it is difficult to make a readymade prescription about the most appropriate expansion mode, a firm has to critically evaluate various internal and external factors before deciding upon an entry mode.

Trade-related modes generally need much lower level of resource commitment and provide greater flexibility to switch over to other entry modes. Therefore, these are highly suitable for smaller firms with limited resources and even for larger firms for preliminary assessment of new markets. However, trade-related modes generally involve much lower profit and control.

A firm may enter into a contractual agreement with another firm for serving a target market. Depending upon a firm's business goals and strategy, it may choose from one or more contractual expansion modes, such as international strategic alliances, contract manufacturing, management contracts, turnkey projects, international leasing, international licensing, and international franchising. Markets with considerable size and growth potential require long-term commitment and firms strategically cater to such markets by way of foreign direct investments.

SUMMARY

A firm has to choose from various alternative options to expand its business in foreign countries. The institutional mechanism by which a firm expands its business overseas is termed as expansion mode. International business managers need to develop a thorough understanding of various modes of expansion and their selection strategies.

Various expansion modes differ from each other in terms of resource commitment, risk, and control, returns, flexibility, and level of internalization. There is no readymade prescription as to which expansion mode a firm should adopt, and a trade-off needs to be arrived at considering its strategic implications. A firm may expand internationally either by adopting trade-related, contractual, or investment modes.

Major trade-related modes include exports, piggybacking, countertrade, and e-channels. Exports are considered to be low-cost, low-risk entry mode with minimum financial commitment. SMEs with limited resources often internationalize by way of indirect exports using a home-based export intermediary. Once the firm gains some understanding of foreign sales, it may sell directly in a foreign market without any intermediary. Such direct exports provide a firm much greater exposure to foreign markets and associated risk and benefits. Alternatively a firm may piggyback on a well-established distribution channel of another firm which has a non-competing but complementary product portfolio. Countertrade is often the preferred mode of business expansion in countries with scarcity of hard currency and restrictive foreign exchange regulations. Trade financing and price-setting are tied together in a single transaction under countertrade. Major forms of countertrade include simple barter, clearing arrangement, switch

trading, counter purchase, buyback (compensation), and offset. Due to the proliferation of the Internet and advances in information and communication technologies, e-channels have gained popularity as an effective expansion mode over the recent years.

Depending upon the core competencies and business needs, a firm may also adopt contractual modes for international business expansion. International strategic alliances, contract manufacturing, management contracts, turnkey projects, international leasing, international licensing, and international franchising are major forms of contractual expansion modes. Although the contractual expansion mode relies to a great extent on resources and strengths of foreign partners, the internationalizing firm has to share its know-how and trade secrets. Direct investment abroad is preferred as a strategic option to have a long-term commitment in the host country that requires considerable financial and other resources. Besides, wholly owned subsidiaries provide complete control over its operation and facilitates in keeping the know-how within the company.

A firm may use naive, pragmatic, or strategy rules for selecting an expansion mode. The impact of marketing strategy, such as skimming or penetration on expansion modes has also been discussed in this chapter. Based on market segments, such as platform, emerging, growth, maturing, or established countries, a firm may sequentially adopt business expansion modes. A self-explanatory decision tree given at the end of the chapter serves as a useful tool for selecting an appropriate international business expansion mode.

KEY TERMS

Brownfield investment Expansion or re-investment in existing foreign affiliates or sites.

Buyback Often used as a marketing tool to sell plant and equipment wherein the payment is

recovered by way of output from plant and equipment sold.

Clearing arrangement Transaction of goods and services extends over an agreed period of time.

Contract manufacturing A contractual arrangement under which a firm's manufacturing operations are carried out in foreign countries.

Counter purchase A deal involving two separate transactions payable in hard currency, each with its own cash value.

Countertrade Various forms of trade arrangements wherein the payment is in the form of reciprocal commitments for other goods and services rather than an exclusive cash transaction.

Direct exports Selling domestic products directly in foreign markets without employing any market intermediary in the home country.

Exports Manufacturing the goods in home market or a third country and shipping them to a country other than the country of production.

Greenfield operations The establishment of production and marketing facilities by a firm on its own from scratch.

Indirect exports Selling goods through an export intermediary in the firm's home country.

International assembly Exports of components, parts, or machinery in CKD condition and assembling these parts at a site in a foreign country.

International franchising A special form of licensing in which intangible assets are transferred to a foreign firm along with methods of doing business in a prescribed manner and other assistance over an extended period of time in return for a franchising fee.

International leasing Making available new and used equipment through a foreign-based firm for use, in return of a fee called leasing fee.

International licensing Making available intangible assets to a foreign company, such as patents, trademarks and copyrights, technical know-how and skills (technical guidance, feasibility and product studies, manuals) engineering, designs, etc., for a fee termed as royalty.

Joint venture Equity participation of two or more firms resulting in formation of a new entity.

Management contract Providing managerial and technical expertise to an overseas firm on contractual basis.

Mode of international business expansion An institutional mechanism by which a firm expands its operations overseas.

Naive rule Using same expansion mode for all foreign markets ignoring the heterogeneity of different foreign markets and entry conditions.

Offset Partial payment is made by the importer in hard currency, besides promising to source inputs from the importing country and also make investment to facilitate production of such goods.

Piggybacking (complementary exporting) Business expansion in a foreign country using the distribution network of another company.

Pragmatic rules Using a low-risk expansion mode for initial market entry followed by a workable entry mode if the initial entry mode is not feasible or profitable.

Simple barter Direct and simultaneous exchange of goods without use of money.

Strategic alliance Cooperation between two firms to carry out the business activity wherein each one contributes their different capabilities and strengths to the alliance.

Strategy rule Systematically comparing and evaluating all alternative expansion modes before a decision is made.

Switch trading Trading involving a third party, known as switch trader in the transaction to facilitate buying of unwanted goods from the importer and making payment by cash or barter to the exporter.

Turnkey project Conceptualizing, designing, constructing, installing, and carrying out preliminary testing of manufacturing facilities or engineering projects at overseas locations for a client organization.

CONCEPT REVIEW QUESTIONS

1. Critically evaluate various strategic trade-offs a firm is required to make in selecting modes of international business expansion.

2. A family-run handmade manufacturing unit located in Sanganer near Jaipur is desirous of international expansion. The entrepreneur has little knowledge about international markets and ways to enter. In your opinion, which mode of entry should be adopted? Give reasons to justify your answer.

3. Differentiate between management contracts and contract manufacturing for international business expansion.

4. Why should a firm make direct investments abroad when low investment modes of business expansion such as licensing are available?

5. Critically examine use of country segments in sequencing business expansion modes.

6. Write short notes on
   (a) International franchising
   (b) International licensing
   (c) Piggybacking
   (d) Greenfield operations

CRITICAL THINKING QUESTIONS

1. Select an Indian company that has made international acquisitions. Critically evaluate the reasons for such acquisitions and their business implications.

2. Critically evaluate entry mode strategy of an identified company using the decision tree approach.

PROJECT ASSIGNMENTS

1. Identify an international trading company located near your place and contact it. Make a list of its activities and countries of operations. Critically evaluate the pros and cons of indirect exports through a trading company vis-à-vis direct exports.

2. Visit a franchisee of a multinational fast food company located in your city, such as Pizza Hut, McDonald's KFC, etc., and find out the benefits and problems being faced.

3. Form groups in class and each group should identify one firm from your country operating overseas and one foreign firm operating in your country adopting one of the following expansion modes:

   - Overseas turnkey projects
   - International management contracts
   - International strategic alliance
   - International contract manufacturing

   Critically examine the business expansion strategy used by a firm, including the following parameters:

   - Brief about the firm
   - Reasons for using the expansion strategy
   - Effectiveness of business expansion strategy

   Make a group presentation of your findings and discuss in class.

CASE STUDY

International Business Expansion Strategy of ONGC

The Oil and Natural Gas Corporation Ltd (ONGC) is a premier business organization involved in the exploration and production of hydrocarbons in India and abroad, besides refining and selling of crude oil. It has a net worth of Rs 535.93 billion as of 2005–06 and a market share of about 80 per cent in India's crude oil and natural gas exploration and production.

The ONGC is the leader in the upstream petroleum sector and a leading *navratna* (the nine jewels) Public Sector Undertaking (PSU) with 74 per cent Government of India ownership. Its

operations span almost all the sedimentary basins of India. ONGC Videsh Ltd (OVL) was set up in 1996 as a wholly owned subsidiary to function as the ONGC's overseas arm for foreign ventures in the field of exploration and production of hydrocarbons. The OVL operates 35 overseas projects in 17 countries (Fig. C.1).

In the late 1990s, the ONGC was earning handsome profits under the government's restrictive policies for other oil companies to enter the domestic upstream exploration and production (E&P) business, but it realized that this rosy

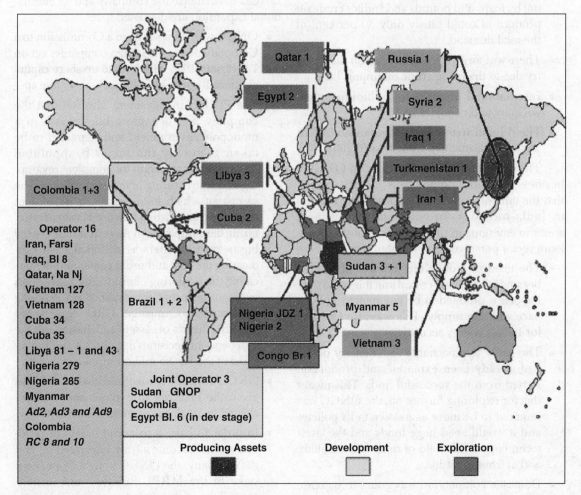

Fig. C.1 ONGC's global operations

Qatar 1

Russia 1

Egypt 2

Syria 2

Iraq 1

Turkmenistan 1

Libya 3

Iran 1

Colombia 1+3

Cuba 2

Operator 16
Iran, Farsi
Iraq, Bl 8
Qatar, Na Nj
Vietnam 127
Vietnam 128
Cuba 34
Cuba 35
Libya 81 – 1 and 43
Nigeria 279
Nigeria 285
Myanmar
Ad2, Ad3 and Ad9
Colombia
RC 8 and 10

Brazil 1 + 2

Sudan 3 + 1

Nigeria JDZ 1
Nigeria 2

Myanmar 5

Vietnam 3

Congo Br 1

Joint Operator 3
Sudan GNOP
Colombia
Egypt Bl. 6 (in dev stage)

Producing Assets

Development

Exploration

picture was not going to last forever. The major factors that influenced ONGC's business operations in domestic oil and gas industry during the late 90s include

- The new New Exploration Licensing Policy (NELP) came into force wherein it was stipulated that the oil and gas sector would no longer be restricted to public sector players and private firms could also participate in the award of license for exploration acreages and production sharing contracts.
- Domestic oil and gas production had stagnated in the range of 25–27 MMT (million metric tonnes) per annum and there were no significant discoveries of reserves.
- On the other hand, the demand was increasing by leaps and bounds and India's crude oil production could satisfy only 30 per cent of the total demand.
- There was an increasing burden on the country due to the rising crude oil import bill.
- International prices were exhibiting great volatility and rising trend.
- The Administrative Price Mechanism (APM) was to be dismantled from 1 April 2002.

The impact of the above factors on ONGC's business operations domestically made it explicit that the time of exploring and producing easy oil in India was over. In addition, the business scenario emerging in the late 1990s for the petroleum sector perceived is elucidated here:

- The need to reduce the import bill burden became increasingly critical and this could only happen if production be augmented to keep pace with the supply. This was also essential for India's energy security.
- The easily approachable sedimentary basins had already been explored and production started from the successful finds. This meant that for exploring further oil, the ONGC was required to be more aggressive in its policies and it would need huge funds and the latest technology in the field of deep-water drilling and in frontier basins.
- Domestic competition was going to increase with the entry of firms, such as Essar and Reliance.

- The ONGC's bottom-line was solely dependent on crude oil prices and these prices were very volatile; the organization could suffer on account of this. This made it imperative for the ONGC to diversify or enter the downstream industry to even out its basket of products offered.

Consequently, the ONGC was compelled to expand internationally. However, a sleeping giant could not suddenly be catapulted into the highly competitive world of international business. It required drastic incremental and fundamental changes and restructuring to become competitive. Hard strategic decisions had to be taken to achieve these objectives and gain foothold in the international arena. Major strategic decisions taken by ONGC to revitalize the company and its international expansion are discussed here:

- ONGC was changed from a Commission to a Company under the Indian companies act on 1 February 1994 with its paid up share capital of about Rupees 1.4 billion.
- The ONGC management also felt that the company had become a bit sluggish in a monopoly environment and steps had to be taken to rectify the same. It appointed Mckinsey as consultant for complete revamping and restructuring of the organization. The campaign which followed was a movement away from an existing functional way of organizing the company. An Asset-and Basin-based business goal model was identified, clearly indicating the cost and profit center and demarcating the exploring of producing zones. This restructuring programme named as Corporate Rejuvenation Campaign (CRC) empowered the SBU heads of Assets and Basins to take independent decisions upto Rs 250 million instead of the Rs 2.5 million stipulated earlier.
- ONGC's wholly owned subsidiary OVL was given the mandate to explore opportunities abroad in an all out aggressive manner.
- In order to have a balanced basket of products and to become a truly integrated oil and gas company, the ONGC bought 71 per cent stake in the MRPL Refinery and turned-around the company in one year.

- Having carried out all of the above, the ONGC decided to acquire equity oil abroad through the endeavours of the OVL as brought out in its strategic goal.

- In order to develop its human resource base for international expansions, the ONGC deputed 20 middle-level executives for advance study of international business in India's premier business school, the Indian Institute of Foreign Trade (IIFT).

The strategic objectives of ONGC were

- Doubling reserves to 6 billion tonnes by 2020; out of this 4 billion tonnes are targeted from the deep-waters

- Improving average recovery from 28 per cent to 40 per cent

- Tying up 20 MMT per annum of equity of hydrocarbon from abroad

- Monetizing the assets as well as assetizing the money

While identifying countries for international expansion, the ONGC found that it was a late starter in its internationalization drive and all the better fields and countries with political peace, good infrastructure, and proximity of processing industries had already been taken by the giant multinational companies, such as Exxon-Mobil, Shell, etc.

ONGC accepted the challenge to take up any feasible internationalization opportunities that came its way, even under adverse climatic and socio-economic conditions. It operates in Sakhalin (Russia) with minus 30 degree centigrade temperatures (Fig. C.2) and also the plus 55 degree centigrade of Africa in Sudan. Many advised ONGC against venturing into Sudan, which was facing an ongoing ethnic conflict. But the ONGC reasoned that if Chinese and Malaysian Oil companies (Petronas) could work there, so could ONGC. The decision taken paid rich dividends and the Sudanese Government, pleased with the organization's work, also allotted other related jobs to ONGC.

Fig. C.2   ONGC's Orlan Platform, Sakhalin I, in Russia

The internationalization strategy adopted by ONGC after much groundwork may be summarized as follows:

- It carried out in-house studies of various moderate and semi-major, and major offshore and onshore fields all over the world and came up with about 400 Oil and Gas blocks that deserved closer scrutiny, keeping in mind ONGC's comparative advantage.

- It evaluated these fields with the available data and came up with a priority list for foreign foray, should the opportunity present itself. This list was under the constant scanner of the study group and the top management and was updated with data and facts and figures as soon as they came to light.

- The management decided to enter foreign market for oil and gas exploration and production through its overseas arm, the OVL, adopting any or a combination of the market entry strategies of

  - Joint venture with equity participation in producing oil/gas fields

  - Joint venture with equity participation for exploration and development blocks

  - Consortium approach, pooling other Indian oil companies, such as IOC Ltd, GAIL, etc. to acquire attractive oil and gas exploration and development blocks

  - Operator ship contracts (management contracts)

  - Turnkey engineering contracts related to the oil industry, like laying of oil/gas pipelines

OVL has producing assets located in Russia, Syria, Sudan, Columbia, and Vietnam (Fig. C.3), assets with discoveries and exploration in Qatar, Egypt, Brazil, and Myanmar (Fig. C.4), and assets under exploration in Iran, Iraq, Syria, Libya, Cuba, Colombia, Nigeria, Sudan, Congo, Myanmar, Vietnam, and Turkmenistan (Fig. C.5).

The expansion mode strategy adapted by ONGC in its major overseas operations can be briefly described as follows:

- Production sharing contract in Vietnam for a gas field having reserves of 2.04 TCF, with 45 per cent stake in partnership with British Petroleum and Petro Vietnam. Production commenced from January 2003.

- 20 per cent holding in the Sakhalin I production sharing agreement. The US$2.77 billion investment in Sakhalin offshore field is the single largest foreign investment by India in any overseas venture and the single largest foreign investment in Russia.

- 25 per cent equity in the Greater Nile Oil Project in Sudan, the first producing oil property. ONGC Nile Ganga BV, a wholly owned subsidiary, has been set up in the Netherlands to mange this property. OVL has over 3 million tonnes of operational production of crude oil from this project. This is the first time that part of the equity crude of a group of companies is being imported into India for refining by the group.

- Participating interest of 20 per cent in the 'Shwe' gas field in block A1 in Myanmar, which has estimated recoverable reserves of 4–6 trillion cubic feet of gas.

- Acquired around 24 per cent in Blocks 5A and 5B in Sudan.

- Bagged a pipeline contract in Sudan, which is the first ever engineering project of the ONGC Group abroad and is helping in improving the bottom-line of the Sudan Project. This will be another area of specialization to market in the global business arena in the future for the ONGC.

The OVL's sales revenue jumped from Rs 77.9 billion in 2006 to Rs 167.4 billion in 2008 whereas its net profits increased remarkably from Rs 9.01 billion in 2006 to Rs 23.97 billion in 2008 as shown in Table C.1.

Strategic partnerships and joint ventures were used as the preferred mode of expansion for rapid country penetration. This also helped ONGC in sharing risks and capital, besides taping local market knowledge and networking and getting technical support and expertise from established multinationals.

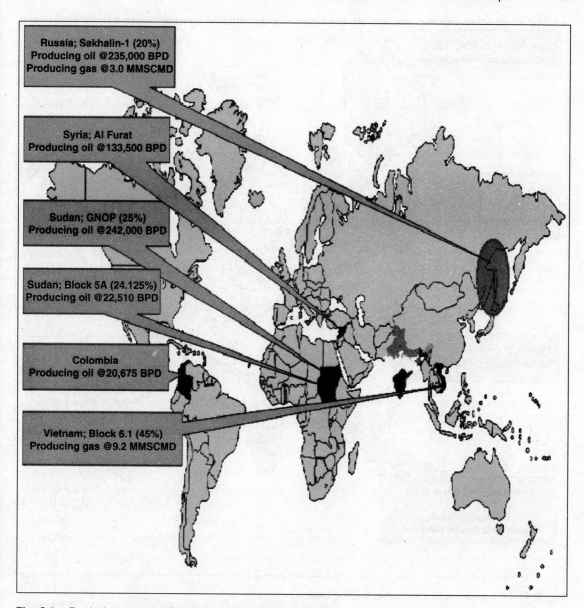

Fig. C.3   Producing assets of OVL (as on 31 December 2007)

Source: ONGC.

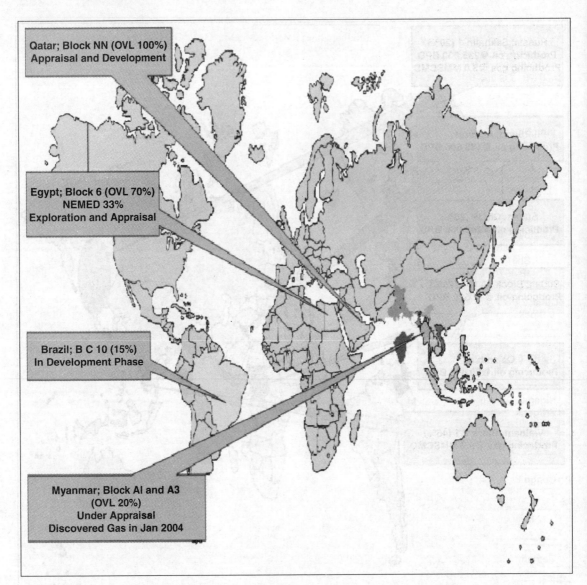

Qatar; Block NN (OVL 100%)
Appraisal and Development

Egypt; Block 6 (OVL 70%)
NEMED 33%
Exploration and Appraisal

Brazil; B C 10 (15%)
In Development Phase

Myanmar; Block Al and A3
(OVL 20%)
Under Appraisal
Discovered Gas in Jan 2004

Fig. C.4 OVL assets with discoveries and exploration

Source: ONGC.

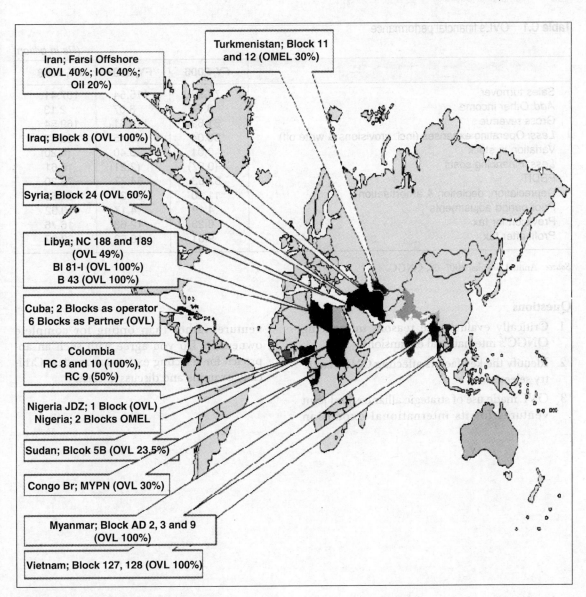

Fig. C.5   OVL assets under exploration

Source: ONGC.

Table C.1 OVL's financial performance

(Rs in billion)

	FY, 2006	FY, 2007	FY, 2008
Sales turnover	77.92	115.54	167.41
Add: Other income	3.77	3.07	2.13
Gross revenue	81.69	118.61	169.54
Less: Operating expenses (incl. provisions & write off)	50.04	66.45	80.43
Variation in stock	0.01	0.40	(0.20)
Less: Financing costs	(0.97)	(2.21)	10.61
PBDIT	32.63	54.77	78.30
Depreciation, depletion & amortisation	11.20	21.34	36.65
Prior period adjustments	4.19	4.17	0.92
Provision for tax	8.23	12.63	16.76
Profit after tax	9.01	16.63	23.97

Source: Annual Results, 2007–08, ONGC.

Questions

1. Critically evaluate the reasons influencing ONGC's international expansion.

2. Identify the key factors affecting OVL's country selection.

3. OVL made use of strategic alliances and joint ventures for its international expansion ventures rather than opting for complete ownership. Do you agree with such an approach for selecting expansion modes? Critically examine and discuss in class.

12 Foreign Direct Investment

LEARNING OBJECTIVES

> To explain the concept of foreign direct investment
> To discuss the various types of foreign direct investment
> To develop a conceptual understanding of the theories of international investment
> To understand policy framework to promote foreign direct investment
> To discuss the patterns of foreign direct investment

12.1 INTRODUCTION

International trade and foreign direct investment (FDI) are the two most important international economic activities integrating the world economy. With the increase in the mobility of factors of production across countries, FDI has become an integral part of a firm's strategy to expand international business. FDI is the largest source of external finance for developing countries. At present, inward stock of FDI amounts to about one-third of the developing countries' gross domestic product (GDP), compared to merely 10 per cent in 1980.

FDI plays a crucial role in the development process of host economies. It also has a significant role in enhancing exports of the host country. It is estimated that the sales from foreign-owned facilities are about double the value of world trade. FDI not only serves as a source of capital inflow into host economies, but also helps to enhance the competitiveness of the domestic economy through transfering technology, strengthening infrastructure, raising productivity, and generating new employment opportunities.

FDI has often been viewed as a threat by host countries due to the capacity of transnational investing firms to influence economic and political affairs. Many developing countries often fear FDI as a modern form of economic colonialism and exploitation, similar to their previous unpleasant experiences with colonial powers.

Yet, FDI flows are generally preferred to other forms of external finance because these are non-debt creating, non-volatile, and the returns depend on the performance of the project financed by the investors.

FDI is considered superior to other types of capital flows due to various reasons:

- Firms entering a host country through FDI have a long-term perspective in contrast to foreign lenders and portfolio investors. Therefore, FDI flows are less volatile and easier to sustain at the time of economic crisis.
- Debt inflows may finance consumption whereas FDI is more likely to be used to improve productivity.
- Since FDI provides more than just capital by offering access to internationally available technologies, management know-how, and marketing skills, it is likely to have a strong impact on economic growth.

A firm has to evaluate various options to cater to foreign markets and select the most appropriate mode of international business expansion. This chapter aims at explaining the concept of FDI and examines the theoretical basis as to why a firm invests abroad when it can opt for low-risk entry alternatives, such as exporting and licensing. Geographical distances of markets or resources, especially for low-value products, make it more attractive to get into manufacturing operations overseas. In addition, the firm has to carry out a risk benefit analysis of licensing vis-à-vis ownership for its international operations.

As FDI is considered to be a key component of most countries' development strategies, various investment promotion measures to attract FDI have been discussed in this chapter. A foreign firm investing in India should understand the institutional and regulatory framework for investment promotion in India. This chapter brings out the policy framework and various agencies involved in clearances and approvals of foreign investments in India. As developing an understanding of trends in FDI flows is also very important for international business managers, these are also examined at the end of this chapter.

12.1.1 Concept of FDI

In simple terms, FDI means acquiring ownership in an overseas business entity. It is the movement of capital across national frontiers, which gives the investor control over the assets acquired. FDI occurs when an investor based in one country (the home country) acquires an asset in another country (the host country) with the intent to manage it. It is the management dimension that distinguishes FDI from portfolio investment in foreign stocks and other financial instruments. Conceptually, a firm becomes a multinational corporation (MNC) by way of FDI as its operations extend to multiple countries.

FDI is defined as an investment involving a long-term relationship and reflecting a lasting interest and control by a resident enterprise (foreign direct investor or parent enterprise) in one economy in an enterprise (FDI enterprise or affiliate enterprise or foreign affiliate) resident in an economy other than that of the foreign direct investor.[1]

---

[1] Based on *Detailed Benchmark Definition of Foreign Direct Investment*, 3rd edn, OECD, 1996; 4th edn, OECD, 2008.

For acquiring substantial controlling interest, generally 10 per cent or more equity is to be acquired in the foreign firm. The 'lasting interest' implies the existence of a long-term relationship between the direct investor and the enterprise wherein a significant degree of influence is exerted by the investor in the management of the direct investment enterprise.

Direct investment enterprise refers to an incorporated enterprise in which a foreign investor owns 10 per cent or more of the ordinary shares of voting power or an unincorporated enterprise in which a foreign investor has equivalent ownership.[2] Ownership of 10 per cent of the ordinary shares or voting stock is the criterion for determining the existence of a direct investment relationship. These are either directly or indirectly owned by the direct investor. The definition of direct investment enterprise extends to the branches and subsidiaries of the direct investor.

FDI is characterized by decreased sensitivity to fluctuations in foreign exchange rates. Since FDI is the result of a long-term perspective by the investor, it is much less volatile than foreign portfolio investment. It has been reported that most FDI (i.e., more than 90%) leads to intra-corporate trade at international level. The returns of FDI are generally in form of profit, i.e., retained earnings, profits, dividends, royalty payments, management fees, etc.

12.1.2 Foreign Portfolio Investment

Foreign portfolio investment (FPI) is defined as an investment by individuals, firms, or a public body in foreign financial instruments, such as foreign stocks, government bonds, etc. In FPI, the equity stake in the foreign business entity is not significant enough to exert any management control. Thus, FPI is the passive holding of securities and other financial assets by a foreign firm, which does not entail management control of the issuing firm. High rate of returns and mitigation of risks due to geographical diversification positively influence FPI. Thus, FPI is passive whereas FDI is active. The returns in the case of FPI are generally in the form of non-voting dividends or interest payments. Portfolio investment, like FDI, is part of the capital account of balance of payment (BoP) statistics.

12.1.3 *Raison d'etre* for FDI

It is important to understand why a firm takes a decision to invest in foreign countries when low-risk alternatives to cater to foreign markets, such as exporting and licensing, are already available. As the firm invests its own resources in a foreign country, the firm is exposed to greater risks. Major factors that influence a firm's decision to invest in foreign markets are discussed below.

---

[2] International Monetary Fund, *Balance of Payments Manual*, 5th edn, IMF, 1993.

Cost of transportation

Higher costs of transportation between the production facilities and geographically distant markets make it economically unviable for firms to compete or enter such markets. Substantial costs of transportation have to be incurred for marketing products in countries located at larger geographical distances. For a product with low unit value, i.e., value to weight ratio, such as steel, fast food, cement, etc., the cost of transportation has much larger impact on its competitiveness in foreign markets compared to a high-unit value product, such as watches, jewellery, computer processors, hard-disks, etc. Therefore, for low-unit value products, it becomes more attractive to manufacture the products in the foreign country itself either by way of licensing or FDI.

Liability of foreignness

A firm's unfamiliarity with the host country and lack of adaptation of business practices in a foreign country often result in a competitive disadvantage vis-à-vis indigenous firms. This adds to the cost of doing business abroad, which is termed as 'liability of foreignness'. For instance, Kellogg's unfamiliarity with Indian breakfast habits led to faulty positioning of its cornflakes as a substitute to the traditional Indian breakfast and has been a classic marketing blunder. It took several years for Kellogg's to understand the centrality of its traditional food in India's lifestyle before repositioning its cornflakes as a complementary rather than a substitute to the Indian breakfast. In another instance, Disneyland failed miserably in its French venture primarily due to lack of product adaptation in view of significant differences in customers' preferences in Europe vis-à-vis the US market.

A firm has to decide on the mode of international business expansion, as discussed in Chapter 11, either through trade or investment. It has to arrive at a trade-off between scale benefits from concentrating production at a single location and exporting or benefits of FDI, such as proximity of production locations, higher level of control, and gaining better access to the market.

12.1.4 Benefits of FDI

Potential benefits of FDI to host countries include the following:

Access to superior technology Foreign firms bring superior technology to the host countries while investing. The extent of benefits depends upon the technology spillover to other firms based in the host country.

Increased competition The investing foreign firm increases industry output, resulting in overall reduction in domestic prices, improved product or services quality, and greater availability. This intensifies competition in host economies, resulting in net improvement in consumer welfare.

Increase in domestic investment It is found that capital inflows in the form of FDI increase domestic investment so as to survive and effectively respond to the increased competition.

Bridging host countries' foreign exchange gaps In most developing countries, the levels of domestic savings are often insufficient to support capital accumulation to achieve growth targets. Besides, the level of foreign exchange may be insufficient to purchase imported inputs. Under such situations, the FDI helps in making available foreign exchange for imports.

12.1.5 Negative impact of FDI

In most countries, public opinion towards foreign enterprises is not very favourable and FDI is feared due to its impact on domestic firms, the economy, and culture. The major concerns about the negative aspects of FDI are as follows:

Market monopoly Multinational enterprises (MNEs) are far more advanced than domestic companies, owing to their large size and financial power. In some sectors, this is leading to MNE monopolies, thus impeding the entry of domestic enterprises and harming consumers. MNEs' ability to operate at a large scale and invest heavily in marketing and advertising and R&D activities differentiate their products and makes entry of new firms far more difficult as they are unable to make similar investments in R&D and marketing strategies.

Crowding-out and unemployment effects FDI tends to discourage entry and stimulates exit of domestic entrepreneurs, often termed as the crowding-out effect. As FDI enterprises are often less labour intensive, their entry results in higher unemployment and increased social instability.

Technology dependence MNEs often function in a way that doesn't result in technology-sharing or technology-transfer, thereby making local firms technologically dependent or technologically less self-reliant.

Profit outflow Foreign investors import their inputs and use the host country as a processing base, with little value-added earnings in the host country. A large proportion of their profits may be repatriated.

Corruption Large foreign investors often bribe government officials and distort market forces.

National security With MNEs holding a dominant position in sensitive industries, such as telecommunications, and the supply of core equipment and software for the information technology (IT) industry, there is a danger that the strategic interests of the host country may be compromised.

12.1.6 Selection of FDI Destinations

A firm has to evaluate various countries as investment destinations and select the most appropriate one for investment. The identification and selection of a country as an investment destination has been covered separately in Chapter 10. Briefly, the factors influencing net profit of an MNE's operations in a host country include the following:

Cost of capital input Cost includes interest rate and financial capital employed for setting up of plant or the rent.

Wage rate Wage rate is highly significant for the manufacture of labour-intensive products.

Taxation regime The prevailing taxation rates of the host country are of prime importance while making an investment decision. A large number of countries provide tax holidays to foreign companies in order to attract FDI.

Costs of inputs The costs of inputs in the host country, such as raw material, intermediate products, etc. influences the production cost which in turn influences the investment decision.

Cost of logistics Logistics, including availability of various modes of transport, and the cost of transportation, influence the FDI decision.

Market demand Demand of a product in the host country market, including consumer preferences and their income levels, significantly affects the investment decisions.

In terms of 'most attractive' global FDI locations,[3] four of the top five countries, as ranked by trans-national corporations TNCs are surprisingly, countries from developing economies. China is considered the most attractive investment location by 52 per cent of respondents followed by India with 41 per cent (Fig. 12.1). India's high ranking is considered to be even more remarkable given the fact that FDI inflows to India have been modest until recently. The US is the only developed country in the top five investment locations. Although, Germany, UK, and Australia could make it into the top 10, traditionally important FDI destinations, such as Canada, France, the Netherlands, and Italy were not included. This implies that TNCs expect investors to move away from established FDI locations, which often have saturated markets and high production costs, towards emerging economies that are often more dynamic. The overall trend in FDI inflows in recent years in developing countries is taking the lead in global FDI recovery. As indicated in Exhibit 12.1, India has emerged as a hot investment destination. Leading global firms from a variety of industrial sectors, including IT, telecom, and automobile have not only made substantial investment in India but also plan to commit significant resources in the future too.

12.2 TYPES OF FDI

Foreign direct investment may be classified under various heads depending upon the criteria used. Major types of FDI are discussed here.

---

[3] World Investment Report 2007: Transnational Corporations, Extractive Industries and Development, UNCTAD, Geneva, 2007, pp. 28–30.

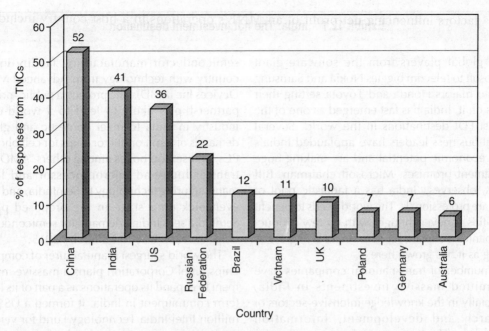

Fig. 12.1   Most attractive global FDI locations, 2007–09 (per cent of responses)

Source: World Investment Report 2007: Transnational Corporations, Extractive Industries and Development, UNCTAD, Geneva, 2007, pp. 28–30.

12.2.1   On the Basis of Direction of Investment

Inward FDI

Foreign firms taking control over domestic assets is termed as inward FDI. From an Indian perspective, direct investments made by foreign firms, such as Suzuki, Honda, LG, Samsung, General Motors, Electrolux, etc., in India are examples of inward FDI.

Outward FDI

Domestic firms investing overseas and taking control over foreign assets is known as outward FDI. Such outward FDI is also known as Direct Investment Abroad (DIA). From the Indian point of view, direct investments overseas by Indian firms, such as Tata Motors, Infosys, Videocon, ONGC, Ranbaxy, etc., are illustrations of outward FDI.

12.2.2   On the Basis of Types of Activity

Horizontal FDI

When a firm invests in a foreign country in similar production activity as carried out in home country, it is termed as horizontal FDI. Thus, horizontal FDI occurs when the multinational undertakes the same production activities in multiple countries. Horizontal FDI enables the investing firm to exploit its competitive advantage in the host country. Multinational firms from both developed and developing countries use

---

Exhibit 12.1   India: The hot investment destination

With global players from the software giant Microsoft to telecom biggies Nokia and Samsung to auto majors Honda and Toyota setting their sights on it, India has fast emerged as one of the hottest FDI destinations in the world. Several global business leaders have applauded India's great economic potential and are making huge investment promises. Microsoft chairman, Bill Gates, observes, 'India has a fantastic pool of software professionals. The world needs to benefit from this. I never thought with so few product companies, software services sector will grow as strong as it has grown here.'

A number of trans-national companies have committed massive investments in India, especially in the knowledge intensive-sectors of research and development, information technology (IT), telecom, and services. Besides hiring thousands of professionals, Microsoft Corporation plans to invest billions of dollars to make India a major hub of Microsoft's research, product and application development, services, and technical support for both global and domestic companies.

SemIndia, a consortium of overseas Indians, plans considerable investment in an advanced semiconductor manufacturing facility in the country with technology from Advanced Micro Devices Inc (AMD). The project, a public–private partnership is likely to lead to a world-class industry in India to meet domestic and global demands of semiconductor chips for cell phones, PCs, and set-top boxes among others. AMD will transfer high-end microprocessor and logic manufacturing technology to SemIndia, and may even pick up a stake in the proposed plant. SemIndia sees Indian demand for semiconductor chips to reach US$30 billion by 2015.

The world's largest manufacturer of computer chips, Intel Corporation plans a massive investment to expand its operations as a part of its long-term commitment in India. It formed a US$250 million Intel India Technology Fund for venture capital investment in technology start-ups in India. Networking major Cisco's chalked out a sizable investment package for India to set-up a manufacturing base, a new R&D campus in Bangalore besides significantly increasing its existing head count. Leading telecom and consumer electronics companies, such as Nokia, Motorola, LG, and Samsung are all in the process of substantially investing in India.

Source: 'India, the Hottest Investment Destination', *Rediff Business Desk*, Mumbai, 27 December 2005; 'India Calling', *Times of India*, 9 December 2005.

---

horizontal FDI to establish their competitive advantage abroad. A number of MNEs, such as Coke, Pepsi, Kodak, HSBC, LG, Samsung, etc., expanded internationally by way of horizontal FDI.

Vertical FDI

Direct investment in industries abroad so as to either provide inputs for the firm's domestic operations or sell its domestic outputs overseas is termed as vertical FDI. Thus, vertical FDI takes place when the multinational fragments the production process internationally, locating each stage of production in the country where it can be done at the least cost. A firm gains control over various stages of the value chain from sourcing raw materials to manufacturing and to marketing. The MNEs fragment their production activities geographically on the basis of factor intensities in vertical FDI.

Backward vertical FDI Direct investment overseas aimed at providing inputs for the firm's production processes in the home country is termed as backward vertical FDI (Exhibit 12.2). Such FDI is historically common in extractive industries, such as mining (gold, copper, tin, bauxite mining, petroleum extraction). Companies like British Petroleum and Shell have expanded their international business by backward vertical FDI.

Forward vertical FDI Direct investment in a foreign country aimed to sell the output of the firm's domestic production processes is referred to as forward vertical FDI. Setting up a marketing network, assembly, or mixing operations overseas are illustrations of forward vertical FDI.

Conglomerate FDI

Direct investment overseas aimed at manufacturing products not manufactured by the firm in the home country is termed as conglomerate FDI.

Exhibit 12.2 Hindalco's backward vertical FDI in Australia

Hindalco Industries Ltd, a flagship company of the Aditya Birla Group, is in the business of copper smelting with a capacity of 500,000 tonnes per annum (TPA). Hindalco boasts of the world's largest smelter at a single location, in the coastal town of Dahej in the Bharuch district of Gujarat. The company did not have its own copper mines, instead it sources the main raw material, i.e., copper concentrate from all over the world, smelts, and refines it to produce copper cathode, the final output traded on the London Metal Exchange. Since India has limited proven copper reserves, mainly concentrated in Khetri, in Rajasthan, Hindalco acquired two captive copper mines in Australia, i.e., Straits (Nifty) Pty Ltd and Mt Gordon Pty Ltd, in 2003. The quality of copper offered by these two mines is of high grade, i.e., approximately 2.8 per cent copper, making them among the richest copper mines worldwide.

The Asian region accounted for around 40 per cent of the world's copper consumption in 2005 and the figure is likely to grow in the coming years. Copper mines are largely found in Africa and South American countries, such as Chile and Argentina. But these regions have high political risks and costs for foreign investors. Law and order are prime requisites for successful conduct of business; therefore Hindalco preferred acquiring mines in Australia. As mining contributes significantly to the Australian economy, adequate availability of trained manpower in various disciplines becomes an added advantage. Nifty Mines, which had proven reserves but were largely undeveloped, and Mt Gordon Mines with larger resources to be explored were both running huge losses in the hands of their former owners. Hindalco acquired the mines in 2003 when copper prices were very low which forced high-cost miners out of the market, thus creating a significant deficit. Low copper prices benefited the acquiring firm by way of lower mine valuation. Backward vertical integration was likely to provide Hindalco with secure raw material supply.

Source: 'Aditya Birla Group Acquire Mount Gordon Copper Mine in Australia', *Australia-India Focus,* issue 26, September–October 2003, p. 2; 'Aditya Birla Minerals Makes Strong Debut Down Under', *Business Line,* 13 May 2006.

12.2.3 On the Basis of Investment Objectives

Resource-seeking FDI

In order to gain privileged access to resources vis-à-vis competitors, MNEs invest in countries with availability of natural resources. This ensures the MNE of stability of raw material supply at right prices. The major economic determinants for resource seeking FDI include

- Availability of raw material
- Complementary factors of production
- Physical infrastructure

When resource-abundant countries lack capital and necessary technical skills for resource extractions, such FDI is favoured. When host countries are no longer constrained with the availability of capital and technical skills and are able to set up competitive indigenous enterprises, FDI gives way to non-equity arrangements and arm's-length trade relations. Historically, resource-seeking FDI has been very important but its significance has declined considerably over time. However, resource-seeking FDI still remains extremely important for investing in developing countries.

Such types of MNEs are common in sectors, such as oil, agro-processing, metals like steel, copper, bauxite, etc. Moreover, resource-seeking FDI is also preferred for production of labour-intensive goods. For instance, naturally occurring soda ash in Kenya reduces the cost of production by half for chemical industries. Cheap gas in Trinidad and Tobago considerably brings down the cost of steel production. Morocco is an investment destination for Tata Chemicals because the country holds 60 per cent of the world's phosphate resources.

Market-seeking FDI

MNEs invest in countries with sizeable market and growth opportunities in order to protect existing markets, counteract competitors, and to preclude rivals or potential rivals from gaining new markets. Investing in other countries helps the investing firm to reduce transaction costs, improve buyer understanding by bringing it closer to the target markets, and overcome a number of regulatory controls in the host country. The major economic determinants of market-seeking FDI include

- Market size
- Market growth
- Regional integration

Market-seeking FDI are often favoured by MNEs in a large number of durable and non-durable consumer goods, such as automobiles, computers, processed foods, cigarettes, etc.

Efficiency-seeking FDI

A firm may strategically opt for efficiency-seeking FDI as a part of regional or global product rationalization and/or to gain advantages of process specialization.

Efficiency-seeking FDI provides the investing firm not only access to markets but also economies of scope, geographical diversification, and international sourcing of inputs. The major economic determinants of efficiency seeking FDI include

- Productivity adjusted labour costs
- Availability of skilled labour
- Availability of business related services
- Trade policy

Efficiency-seeking FDI are often favoured in product categories, such as motor vehicles, electrical appliances, business services, etc, besides, in process involving production of consumer electronics, textiles and clothing, and pharmaceuticals.

12.2.4   On the Basis of Entry Modes

Modes of international business expansion have been discussed in detail in Chapter 11. On the basis of entry modes, foreign direct investment may be of the following two types.

Greenfield investments

Investing in creation of new facilities or expansion of existing facilities is termed as greenfield investment. Firms often enter international markets by way of greenfield investments in industries where technological skills and production technology are the key. Further, the selection of FDI mode is influenced by

- Institutional factors
- Cultural factors
- Transactional cost factors

Particularly, the attitude towards takeovers, conditions in capital markets, liberalization policies, privatization, regional integration, current sales, and the role played by intermediaries, such as investment bankers affect the mode of direct investment abroad. Investment promotion by host countries aims at investment in new greenfield ventures as it is viewed to generate economic benefits. In developing countries where the right types of companies are not available for acquisition, greenfield operations are the preferred mode of FDI.

Mergers and acquisitions

For establishing overseas production facilities, mergers and acquisitions (M&As) are crucial tools for a firm's internationalization strategy. M&As have become an increasingly popular mode of investment among firms worldwide in order to enhance their competitiveness so as to consolidate, protect, and advance their position by acquiring companies internationally. It is estimated that about 70–80 per cent of FDI are in the form of M&As.

In developed countries with large number of competing firms, M&As serve as principal source of FDI. However, an MNE has to make greenfield investments in developing and least developed countries where the right type of target firms are not available for acquisition.

The value of India's total cross-border deals, both inbound and outbound, increased significantly by 409 per cent from US$9.5 billion in 2005 to US$48 billion in 2007 but declined to US$25.63 billion in 2008. The value of inbound deals increased by 200 per cent from US$5.1 billion in 2005 to US$15.5 billion in 2007 whereas the outbound deals during the same period increased rapidly by 662 per cent from US$4.3 billion to US$32.8 billion. However, both inbound and outbound deals declined[4] to US$12.48 billion and US$13.15 billion, respectively in 2008.

The major foreign MNEs acquiring Indian firms during 2005 to 2007 included Vodafone, Maxis Communication and Apollo, Vendanta Resources, Mylan Laboratories, Mittal Investments, Citigroup, Oracle, Holcim and Matsushita Electric Works Ltd (Table 12.1) whereas major overseas acquisitions by Indian firms included

Table 12.1   India's top inbound cross-border deals*

Acquirer	Target	Sector	Acquisition price US$ million	Deal type	Year
Vodafone	Hutchison Essar	Telecom	10830.00	Majority stake	2007
Maxis Communications Bhd and Apollo Hospitals	Aircel Ltd	Telecom	1080.00	Acquisition	2005
Vendanta Resources	Sesa Goa	Metals and Ores	981.00	Majority stake	2007
Mylan Laboratories Inc	Matrix Laboratories	Pharma and Healthcare	736.00	Majority stake	2006
Mittal Investments	Guru Gobind Singh Refineries Ltd	Oil and Gas	711.00	Strategic stake	2007
Citigroup	HDFC	Banking and Financial Services	671.11	Strategic Stake	2006
Oracle	i-flex Solutions	IT and ITeS	593.00	Ownership stake	2005
Holcim	Gujarat Ambuja Cements	Cement	470.00	Strategic Stake	2006
Matsushita Electric Works Ltd	Anchor Electricals	Electricals and Electronics	420.00	Majority stake	2007

* Based on data from January 2006 to February 2008.

Source: Dealtracker, Grant Thornton, annual issues, 2005, 2006, 2007, and vol. I, 2008.

---

[4] 'M&A Deals Lachs Lustre on Slowdown Blues', *Business Line*, Chennai, 25 December 2008.

that of Tata Steel, Hindalco, Suzlon, Essar Steel Holdings, Great Offshore, United Spirits, Tata Power, Tata Chemicals, JSW Steel Limited, Wipro Technologies, Dr. Reddy's Laboratories, and Suzlon Energy (Table 12.2).

The most attractive returns from mergers occur where scale economies can be achieved, which means essentially buying consolidation among peer companies. India is likely to witness a relatively large volume of horizontal combinations[5] where companies buy their peers.

Table 12.2 India's top outbound cross-border deals*

Acquirer	Target	Sector	Acquisition price US$ million	Deal type	Year
Tata Steel	Corus	Steel	12201.60	Acquisition	2007
Hindalco Industries	Novelis Inc	Aluminium	6000.00	Acquisition	2007
Suzlon Energy Ltd	RE Power	Power and Energy	1700.93	Controlling stake	2007
Essar Steel Holdings Ltd	Algoma Steel Inc	Steel	1580.00	Acquisition	2007
Great Offshore	SeaDragon Offshore	Shipping and Ports	1400.00	Acquisition	2008
United Spirits	Whyte and Mackay	Breweries and Distilleries	1112.99	Acquisition	2007
Tata Power	PT Kaltim Prima Coal and PT Arutmin Indonesia	Power and Energy	1100.00	Significant stake	2007
Tata Chemicals Ltd	General Chemical Industrial Products Inc. (GCIP)	Plastic and Chemicals	1005.00	Acquisition	2008
JSW Steel Limited	Jindal United Steel Corpn., Saw Pipes, Jindal Ent. LLC	Steel	900.00	Majority stake	2007
Wipro Technologies	Infocrossing Inc and Subsidiaries	IT and ITeS	600.00	Acquisition	2007
Dr Reddy's Laboratories	Betapharm Arzneimittel GmbH	Pharma and Healtcare	597.33	Acquisition	2006
Suzlon Energy	Hansen Transmissions International NV	Manufacturing	558.00	Acquisition	2006

* January 2006 to February 2008.
Source: Dealtracker, Grant Thornton, annual issues, 2005, 2006, 2007, and vol. I, 2008.

---

[5] Makhijani, Vishnu, 'Globalization to Encourage M&As in India', *Economic Times*, New Delhi, 22 December 2005.

An acquisition may be termed as a 'hostile takeover' when it is resisted by the target firm's management and board of directors. Such takeover attempts are strongly resisted by the target firm. In order to prevent the acquiring firm from such takeovers the target firm often resort to use of 'poison pills' by increasing the cost of negative items as a strategic option, as discussed in Exhibit 12.3. However, the acquiring firm may raise the attractiveness of its offer, through a 'sweetener' to effectively counter the target firm's resistance.

Exhibit 12.3   Poison pill and sweetener: Strategic options for hostile takeovers

Originally, the term 'poison pill' was used for literal poison pills used by spies in ancient times. In business strategy, the term 'poison pill' refers to any strategy which attempts to avoid a negative outcome by increasing the costs of the negative outcome to the acquiring firm. 'Poison pills' are often used to avoid a hostile takeover bid by a potential acquirer to obtain management control.

The basic types of 'poison pills' used by target firms in international business are discussed here.

- A 'shareholders rights plan' is designed to make it expensive for an acquirer to make a hostile bid for a company through an issue of convertible preferred stock distributed as a dividend to existing shareholders. The preferred stock is convertible into common shares equal to or greater than the number of outstanding shares. The rights offer is automatically triggered when any hostile investor acquires or offers to acquire 10 per cent or more of a target company's shares or when an existing shareholder raises his/her stake by 5 per cent. Once triggered, the company's shareholders, barring the acquirer, can exercise rights or warrants to buy additional equity in their company at a discount.

  This makes it much more expensive for the acquiring firm to get management control. The attempted takeover becomes its own poison because it vastly increases the number of shares that will have to be acquired to get management control and thereby raises the cost of the hostile takeover.

- The target firm takes on huge debts so as to make the debt load too high to be attractive as the acquiring firm would be required to pay heavy debts.

- The company buys a number of smaller firms using stock swap, thereby diluting the value of its stock.

- Stock options are given to its employees by the target firm so as to create an incentive to continue working with the target company instead of looking for a new job, at least till the merger is completed. Many discontented employees may leave the company after cashing in their stock options consequent to release of stock options to them. It creates an exodus of bright employees leaving a few talented employees for the acquiring firm.

Poison pills, which can hinder hostile bids by granting existing shareholders the right to buy more shares at a lower price, have become a hot topic in Japan after some recent high-profile bids that shook the traditional, behind-the-scenes consensus approach to deal-making. The new poison pill law will permit Japanese companies to use their poison pill defences in a wide variety of classified shares, including shares with repurchase rights, which give boards the option to forcibly buy share back from specific shareholders in case of a hostile takeover threat. A large number of Japanese companies, including top steel maker Nippon Steel, leading retailer Aeon, and the drug maker Eisai have plans to adopt poison pill defences.

In a classic defence to hostile takeover bid by Mittal Steel, Arcelor promised its shareholders annual earnings before interest, tax, depreciation, and amortization of €7 billion a year compared

Exhibit 12.3 Contd

with 2005's €5.6 billion, and annual free cash flow of €4.4 billion in 2006. The improvements were expected to accrue from a scaling back of capital spending, a reduction in working capital, and contributions from acquisitions, notably the Canadian steel company Dofasco. Arcelor's stainless steel arm could also be sold. The extra cash generated was likely to be used to bump up dividends to 30 per cent of disposable funds, and all cash from disposals was promised to be given to shareholders 'as soon as possible'. Besides, Arcelor management also promised to re-work executive pay packages to bring them in like with shareholders' interest.

In order to raise the attractiveness of its acquisition offer, the acquiring firm extended increased benefits by raising the bid as a part of its takeover strategy. This is termed as 'sweetening' the bid. In order to effectively counter the 'poison pills' used by Arcelor, Mittal Steel raised its bid to Euro 26 billion (US$33 billion) in cash and stock. This made Arcelor's resistance crumble in the face of a shareholder's revolt, leading to yielding of Arcelor's Board to merge with Mittal Steel.

Source: Reuters, 21 April 2006: 'Arcelor Chief Throws Up a Ring of Steel', *The Sunday Times,* 5 March 2006.

12.2.5   On the Basis of Sector

Industrial FDI

Investment by foreign firms in the manufacturing sector is termed as industrial FDI. Major objectives of FDI in the manufacturing sector include

- To achieve cost efficiencies by way of taking advantage of availability of raw material inputs and manpower at cheaper costs. Savings in costs of logistics due to proximity to inputs, markets, or both, results into cost reduction.
- To bypass trade barriers such as high import tariffs and other import restrictions.
- To be closer to the markets and serve them more efficiently.
- To have physical presence due to strategic reasons.

Non-industrial FDI

Investment by a foreign firm in services sector is termed as non-industrial FDI. The major reasons for non-industrial FDI are

- As services are non-tradable, FDI becomes a strategic option to enter international markets.
- To overcome regulatory obstacles.
- To create regular contact with the customer.

12.2.6   On the Basis of Strategic Modes

Export replacement

In response to trade barriers of the host country, such as import restrictions and prohibitive tariff structure, FDI is made a substitute for exports. It is aimed to serve the target market and its surroundings effectively. Entry mode for such types of FDI is typically through M&As. Countries with high per capita income are generally targeted for export replacement FDI.

Export platforms

In order to minimize a firm's cost of production and distribution, FDI is made so as to utilize the target country to serve the global markets. The competitive advantage and the incentives offered by the host country plays a crucial role in attracting such FDI. Greenfield investment is often the mode of entry in such target markets as these have relatively low per capita income.

Domestic substitution

Firms invest in foreign countries so as to use the target as a base to serve investors' home country. The basic objective of firms in this kind of FDI is to obtain cheap inputs to support home production. Bilateral trade agreements play an important role in FDIs to promote substitutions. Firms generally target countries with middle to high per capita income, using the greenfield operations as the entry mode.

12.3 THEORIES OF INTERNATIONAL INVESTMENT

Various trade theories explaining the conceptual basis of international trade and trade patterns have been discussed in detail in Chapters 2 and 3, respectively. However, most trade theories fail to explain why a firm invests in foreign countries in unfamiliar environments, making its operations much more complex, difficult to manage and, therefore, running additional risks. An FDI theory should help one conceptualize answers to typical 'W' and 'H' questions such as

Who is the investor? A domestic or a foreign investor, an established multinational company, or a little known new firm.

What kind of investment is to be made? Whether it is greenfield or merger or acquisition? Whether the investment is first-time or sequential?

Why should the firm go abroad? Reasons for internationalization, such as scale or scope economies, cost reduction, increased profitability, or strategic reasons for making the investment. The firm has to carry out analysis of socio-cultural, political, and economic factors before deciding upon the selection of host country for investment.

When to invest? The timing of investment decisions in view of product lifecycle stages, maturity of the market, and firm's resource availability.

How to internationalize? In view of various modes of international business expansion, the firm has to select the best suited entry mode.

Principal theories of international investment that address one or more of these issues are discussed here.

12.3.1   Capital Arbitrage Theory

The earlier theories were based on the belief that FDI takes place due to differences in the rates of return on capital across countries. Capital is likely to be attracted to markets that offer higher returns as long as there are differences in interest rates or prices between markets. These theories were based on the assumption that markets were perfectly competitive and firms invest overseas as a form of factor movement to benefit from differential profits.

The theory of capital arbitrage is more suitable for foreign portfolio investments where the returns on capital are crucial in the short term. As discussed earlier, a firm has long-term interest in FDI, a variety of multiple factors influence the investment decision, besides higher rate of return. Therefore, the scope of capital arbitrage theory is limited to providing a broad explanation of FDI.

12.3.2   Market Imperfection Theory

Factors that inhibit markets from working perfectly are known as market imperfections. Government policies, including import restrictions and quotas, incentives on exports and FDI, tax regimes, restrictions on FDI, and government's participation in trade are some of the examples of government intervention that create market imperfections. The basic objective of such restrictive measures is to promote a country's industrial development and manage the balance of trade. Most developing countries often practise the import substitution strategy by restricting imports and promoting domestic production of less competitive indigenous firms. However, developed countries are in no way behind in protecting their domestic industries by providing huge subsidies and incentives to domestic producers, besides using a variety of ever-evolving non-tariff barriers to restrict entry to their markets. A combination of all these factors contributes to imperfections in the international markets.

Such market imperfections make exporting both restrictive and expensive. In order to access restrictive markets with market imperfections,[6] FDI is often employed as a strategic tool for international business expansion. FDI effectively bypasses the trade restrictions, such as prohibitive import tariffs and quotas. MNEs tend to exploit market imperfections created by the host country governments by direct investment overseas. Such protectionist measures decreased profitability of exporting automobiles from Japan to Europe and increased profitability of FDI to cater to the market. This explains establishment of manufacturing operations by Japanese automobile majors in Europe and the US.

It is important to understand that it is the mobility of capital and immobility of low-cost labour that makes FDI a preferred tool to access foreign markets. Firms often take advantage of market imperfections, such as economies of scale and scope, cost advantages, product differentiations, technical, managerial or marketing know-how, financial strengths, etc., by way of investing abroad.

---

[6] Hymer, S.H., *The International Operations of National Firms: A Study of Direct Foreign Investment*, MA: MIT Press, Cambridge, 1976.

12.3.3 Internalization Theory

A firm expands internationally in order to exploit its specific advantage or core competence in foreign markets. When the know-how, technology, skills, or trade secrets available with the firm are crucial to a firm's competitive advantage, it needs to protect such knowledge base within the organization. Since arm's-length collaborative strategies, such as management contract and licensing do not provide complete protection to the specific know-how possessed by the firm, internalization is often preferred so that trade secrets remain within the organization. Therefore, a firm expands into international markets by way of investing in a foreign country in order to have control over its overseas operations.

12.3.4 Monopolistic Advantage Theory

An MNE is believed to possess monopolistic advantage, which enables it to operate overseas more profitably and compete with local firms. The benefit possessed by the firm that maintains its monopolistic power in the market is termed as monopolistic advantage. For a firm to invest in physical resources overseas, the following conditions are required:

- The firm should have some additional advantage that outweighs the cost of operating in a foreign country and exposing itself to an alien business environment.
- The firm can exploit such specific advantage only through control of foreign operations by ownership rather than other low-risk means of market access requiring less commitment of resources such as exporting and licensing.

Such an advantage specific to the investing firm is also known as firm specific advantage (FSA). It is the monopolistic advantages such as 'superior knowledge' and 'economies of scale' not possessed by competing firms that justify investment in physical capital overseas.

12.3.5 International Product Life Cycle Theory

The international product life cycle (IPLC) theory developed by Raymond Vernon provides an explanation as to why production locations are shifted across countries.[7] Although the theory was developed in the American context, it can be extended to other countries too. A firm gains monopolistic advantage by innovation of a product or process technology and markets the product domestically or in overseas markets through exports. The product is initially manufactured in the country of innovation even though the cost of production in other countries may be lower. Subsequently, in the growth phase of the product life cycle, when the product becomes standardized,

---

[7] Vernon, Raymond, 'International Investment and International Trade in Product Life Cycle', *Quarterly Journal of Economics*, May 1996, p. 199.

the innovating firm takes advantage of lower cost of manufacturing abroad, and starts investing in other countries to create its own manufacturing facilities.

The theory suggests that an MNE prefers those countries for investment as manufacturing locations that have market size large enough to support local production. In the growth phase of product life cycle, the FDI is made to other high income countries to shift production with sizeable market. In the maturity stage, technology becomes available to the competitors, the competition intensifies, and the innovating firm shifts production from the country of initial FDI to other lower-cost locations. As a result, the products manufactured in overseas locations become more cost-competitive vis-à-vis those manufactured in the home country and the foreign-based subsidiaries become not only more competitive to serve overseas markets but their production is also imported into the innovating country even to serve its domestic market.

IPLC theory is valid for both trade and investment and provides a dependable explanation about trade patterns and investment. The theory explains why firms undertake FDI in countries with low production costs and considerable demand to support local production. However, the IPLC theory does not touch upon the reasons for undertaking international investment rather than exporting or licensing, which are low cost alternatives for international business expansion. The theory applies mainly to industrial FDI in manufacturing sector. It is generally relevant to large firms with innovating capabilities. The IPLC theory ignores revenue as it is too cost-oriented. Further, it does not discuss opportunities when FDI is more profitable.

12.3.6   Eclectic Theory

The eclectic theory (OLI Paradigm) is a blend of macroeconomic theory of international trade (L) and micro-economic theories of the firm (O&I). As suggested by the eclectic theory,[8] the extent and pattern of FDI are determined by a combination of three factors as discussed here.

The ownership (O) factor

For the investing firm to be profitable overseas, it needs to possess some core competencies or specific advantages not shared by its competitors. Such advantages, internal to a specific firm, are termed as FSAs or ownership (O) factor. Such advantages should enable the firm either to have a lower marginal cost or higher marginal returns vis-à-vis its competitors so as to enable it to reap more profits from overseas investment.

An MNE possesses firm-specific advantages, such as

- *Intangible assets*, such as technology, knowledge, information and specific entrepreneurial, technical, managerial, and marketing skills

[8] Dunning, J.H., 1980, 'Toward an Eclectic Theory of International Production: Some Empirical Tests,' *Journal of International Business Studies*, 11(1), 1980, pp. 9–31.

- *Tangible assets*, such as natural resources, capital, and manpower
- *Size economy* Due to large size of MNEs they often enjoy economies of scale and scope, access to finance within the MNE, benefits emanating from diversification of assets and risks spread
- *Monopolistic advantage* An MNE may benefit from its monopolistic ownership of scarce natural endowments, privileged access to raw materials, ownership of patent rights, and other inputs.

Since an MNE is required to have its operations in foreign countries, it has to incur additional costs due to

- Psychic distance because of differences in socio-cultural environment of the host country
- Unfamiliarity with the host country's market conditions
- Differences in legal, political, economic environment, and institutional framework
- Increased expenses of operation and communication in a foreign country due to geographical difference

As the indigenous firm in the host country is not required to incur the above costs, the 'costs of foreignness' are specific to foreign firms. Therefore, in order to operate profitably and to remain in a foreign market, an MNE has to posses firm-specific advantages that either lower its operational costs or earn higher revenue.

The location factor

The locational (L) advantage or factor of a host country is the key determinant to its relative attractiveness as an investment destination. The major country-specific advantages can be as follows:

Economic Availability of factor endowments, availability of raw materials and other inputs, productivity and costs of inputs, market size and its growth, cost of logistics, efficacy, and cost of communication channels

Socio-cultural Familiarity of operational environment, socio-cultural similarity, language, low psychic distance between the firm's home country and the host country

Political The host country government's attitudes and policies towards foreign firms and investment, incentives to promote FDI, continuity of economic policies, and the stability of the government

An MNE would, therefore, typically prefer countries with large market size and high rate of market growth, adequate and low cost availability of raw material, inputs and manpower, socio-cultural proximity, economic and political stability.

The internalization factor

The internalization (I) factor explains the entry mode used by an MNE to access international markets. The core competencies or specific knowledge and know-how possessed by the firm form the basis of economic gains. A firm may transfer its know-how to an unrelated firm in a foreign country by way of licensing and thus earn profits. A firm attempts to internalize its operations

- To protect its proprietary knowledge from competitors
- To create and maintain monopolistic or oligopolistic power in the market by placing entry barriers to its competitors, forming cartels, predatory pricing, cross-subsidizing among its international operations, etc.
- To protect itself against market uncertainties

Thus, the internalization advantages explain why an MNE opts for wholly owned subsidiaries rather than licensing or minority ownership for accessing foreign markets. Internalization helps a firm lessen the incidences of market failure.

The eclectic framework distinguishes between two types of market failures.

Endemic market failure   Such market failure occurs due to natural market imperfections, such as unfamiliarity with markets or lack of market knowledge, the incidence of transaction costs in external markets, interdependence on demand and supply, uncertainty and risks, etc.

Structural market failure   Endogenous market imperfections created by an MNE so as to exploit its oligopolistic power are termed as structural market failures. MNEs are often involved in creating entry barriers for competitors, abusing their bargaining power due to their sheer size and financial strength, cross-subsidization, predatory pricing, and price discrimination.

Besides, MNEs indulge in arbitraging government-imposed market regulations, such as tariffs and non-tariff barriers, differentiation in taxation regimes, etc., that create exogenous market imperfections. MNEs are often criticized for adopting unfair practices, such as transfer pricing and under-invoicing, through their affiliates for their own advantage so as to bypass high tariffs and the taxation differences among various countries. Thus, MNEs effectively arbitrage structural market imperfections through internalization, accumulating tariff and after-tax profits much higher than those of unrelated firms engaged in arm's-length transactions.

While enjoying these benefits of internalization, an MNE has to incur various costs too—those of running large-scale vertically and horizontally integrated international businesses. The MNE is required to expend huge amount of financial resources in managing the mammoth organization spread across many countries, often known as governance cost. Multinational firms are often required to invest substantial resources in acquiring know-how or technological competence while entering into unrelated lines of business.

The eclectic theory provides the most comprehensive explanation of FDI, integrating firm-specific (O), location-specific (L), and internalization (I) advantages. It logically examines the reasons for investing overseas, the selection of country location for investment, and the cost-benefit analysis for selecting the mode of international expansion in a holistic manner.

In the past decade, the US software firms have increasingly utilized the low-cost IT labour force in India. Companies wishing to capture the benefits of outsourcing can engage in contracting (hiring an Indian contracting company to perform the service) or foreign direct investment (opening an Indian subsidiary and hiring Indian employees). Modern FDI theories predict that Indian software outsourcing should occur primarily in the form of FDI.

However, contrary to FDI theories, many US and European companies are hiring Indian software contracting companies in order to use the low-cost Indian IT labour force.[9] Hybrid model suggests that contracting companies provide their clients with a combination of the advantages of both FDI and contracting.

12.4   PATTERNS OF FDI

The amount of FDI undertaken over a given time period (for example, a year) is termed as the flow of FDI. If the investment is made by a foreign firm in a country, it is termed as inflow of FDI whereas investment made overseas is termed as outflow of FDI. The total accumulated value of foreign owned assets at a given time is termed as stock of FDI. FDI comprises equity capital and re-invested earnings as per IMF norms. Besides, capacity expansion financed by firms of foreign origin as well as short-term or long-term loans that form part of original packages are also treated as FDI.

There has been significant growth in FDI over the years. Globally, FDI inflows increased[10] from US$742143 million in 2004 to US$1305852 million in 2006 whereas FDI outflows rose from US$877301 million in 2004 to US$1215789 million in 2006. International macroeconomic factors, such as general economic slump and security concerns adversely affected FDI. This growth reflected increased flows to developing countries as well as to South East Europe and the Commonwealth of Independent States (CIS) which more than offset the decline in flows to developed countries. Between 2006 and 2007, FDI inflow[11] to Netherlands exhibited the highest growth by 2285 per cent from US$4.4 billion in 2006 to US$104.2 in 2007 followed by the US (30.3%), Czech Republic (27.3%), and the UK (22.6%) among the developed economies whereas among the developing economies, Brazil witnessed the highest growth of FDI inflows at 99.3 per cent, followed by Mexico (92.9%), Chile (92.2%), and Singapore (52.6%) (Table 12.3). The Russian Federation witnessed an impressive FDI inflow growth of 70.3 per cent whereas FDI declined by 9.4 per cent for India and 3.1 per cent for China.

---

[9] Meehan, Michael J., 'Outsourcing Information Technology to India: Explaining Patterns of Foreign Direct Investment and Contracting in the Software Industry', *International Law and Management Review*, vol. 2, spring 2006.

[10] World Investment Report 2007: Transnational Corporations, Extractive Industries and Development, UNCTAD, Geneva, 2007, pp. 251–53.

[11] UNCTAD Investment Brief, no. 1, Geneva, 2007 and 2008.

Table 12.3   FDI inflows, by host region and selected host economy, 2003–07

(Billions of dollars)

Host region/economy	2003	2004	2005	2006	2007*	Growth rate (%)
World	**637.8**	**710.8**	**916.3**	**1305.9**	**1537.9**	**17.8**
Developed economies	**441.7**	**396.1**	**542.3**	**857.5**	**1001.9**	**16.8**
Europe	358.9	217.7	433.6	566.4	651.0	14.9
European Union (25)	340.1	213.7	421.9	531.0	610.0	14.9
EU-15	327.6	185.2	387.9	492.1	572.0	16.2
UK	27.4	56.2	164.5	139.5	171.1	22.6
New 10 EU member states	12.5	28.5	34.0	38.9	38.0	−2.3
Czech Republic	2.1	5.0	11.0	6.0	7.6	27.3
US	56.8	122.4	99.4	175.4	192.9	30.3
Japan	6.3	7.8	2.8	-6.5	28.8	10.0
Developing economies	**172.1**	**275.0**	**334.3**	**379.1**	**438.4**	**15.7**
Africa	17.2	17.2	30.7	35.5	35.6	0.1
Latin America and the Caribbean	48.0	100.5	103.7	83.8	125.8	50.2
Brazil	10.1	18.1	15.1	18.8	37.4	99.3
Chile	4.4	7.2	6.7	8.0	15.3	92.2
Mexico	12.8	18.7	18.1	19.0	36.7	92.9
Asia and Oceania	106.9	157.3	200.0	259.8	277.0	6.6
West Asia	11.9	18.6	34.5	59.9	52.8	−11.9
South, East and Southeast Asia	94.7	138.0	165.1	199.5	224.0	12.3
China	53.5	60.6	72.4	69.5	67.3	−3.1
Hong Kong, China	13.6	34.0	35.9	42.9	54.4	26.9
India	4.3	5.5	6.6	16.9	15.3	−9.4
Singapore	9.3	14.8	20.1	24.2	36.9	52.6
Transition economies	**24.0**	**39.6**	**39.7**	**69.3**	**97.6**	**40.8**
Russian Federation	8.0	15.4	14.6	28.7	48.9	70.3

* Preliminary estimates.

Source: UNCTAD Investment Brief, no. 1, Geneva, 2006, 2007, and 2008.

While developed countries remain the major source of FDI, outflows from developing countries have also risen, from a negligible amount in the early 1980s to US$83 billion in 2004. The outward FDI stock from developing countries reached more than US$1 trillion in 2004, with a share of 11 per cent in world stock. Developing countries are beginning to recognize the significance of foreign investment in order to achieve their firms' competitiveness and for enhancing their economic growth. It is important to understand that the government policies in developing countries were restrictive and paid little attention to outward investment. Moreover, the ratio of FDI outflows to gross capital formation was 25 per cent for Singapore in 2002–04 compared to 8 per cent for the US. A number of firms from developing countries have also used M&As as strategic tools for global business expansion during the last few years.

The global FDI increased faster than world trade and world output. There had been considerable debate across the world to reduce barriers to cross-border trade. Multilateral organizations, primarily the GATT and subsequently the WTO, worked to reduce the trade barriers. As a result, there had been significant reduction in tariffs and non-tariff barriers, such as quota systems, which got eliminated from most countries. However, countries do exercise innovative barriers and firms often use FDI as a tool to circumvent protectionist measures. FDI by Japanese automobile companies in Europe, the US, and some other countries was primarily aimed to circumvent their trade protectionist measures. Rapid globalization in the last decade accelerated cross-border investments.

12.4.1   Modes of FDI Entry

Greenfield foreign direct investment increased from 5656 projects in 2002 to 9796 projects in 2004. Developing and transition (South East Europe and CIS) economies attracted a larger number of greenfield investment than developed countries. Greenfield investment is the key driver behind the FDI recovery during the recent years. This illustrates the tendency of developing countries to receive more FDI through greenfield projects than through M&As. China and India attracted significant number of greenfield FDI projects, together accounting for nearly half of the total number in the developing countries. Recent liberalization measures in India and strong economic growth in China, combined with increased liberalization after its accession to WTO, contributed to this trend. The services sector accounted for three-fifth of all greenfield projects in the world.

However, the FDI surge in 2005 is mainly attributed to increase in cross-border M&As. Global M&As increased by 40 per cent to US$2.9 trillion whereas greenfield projects marginally dropped in 2005. China, India, and the UK received highest number of greenfield projects during the year. It has been observed that

- The increase in share of M&As in the total FDI is adversely affecting greenfield FDI
- The growing trend of M&As is leading to creation of oligopolistic world, especially in case of strategic industries
- M&As severely affects survival of indigenous firms and industries from developing countries and they need to be more watchful

12.4.2   Components of FDI Flows

FDI is mainly financed by MNEs through

Equity capital   The foreign direct investor's purchase of share of an enterprise in a country other than its own

Intra-company loans   Short- or long-term borrowings and lending of funds between direct investors, i.e., parent enterprises and affiliate enterprises

Reinvested earnings   The direct investor's share (in proportion to direct equity participation) of earnings not distributed as dividends by affiliates, or earnings not remitted to the direct investor. Such retained profits by affiliates are reinvested.

Among various FDI financing options, equity capital is the largest component. Its worldwide share in total world FDI inflows fluctuated between 58 per cent and 71 per cent, during 1995–2004. The intra-company loans accounted for 23 per cent and re-invested earnings for 12 per cent of the world FDI inflows during the same period. The later two components are also much less stable. In 2001, the share of reinvested earnings in FDI financing reached a low of 2 per cent of worldwide FDI whereas the equity capital registered a higher share. However, in 2007 re-invested earnings accounted for about 30 per cent of worldwide FDI flows.[12]

12.4.3 FDI Performance Indices

For carrying out cross-country comparison of FDI performance and FDI potential, the UNCTAD's FDI performance and potential indices serve as useful tools.

Inward FDI performance index

It is a measure of the extent to which a host economy receives inward FDI compared to the relative size of its economy. It is calculated as the ratio of a country's share in global FDI inflows to its share in global GDP.

$$\text{IND}_i = \frac{\text{FDI}_i/\text{FDI}_w}{\text{GDP}_i/\text{GDP}_w}$$

where,

IND_i = The inward FDI performance index of the ith country
FDI_i = The FDI inflows in the ith country
FDI_w = World FDI inflows
GDP_i = GDP in the ith country
GDP_w = World GDP

A value greater than 'one' indicates that the country receives more FDI compared to its relative economic size, a value below one that it receives less, a negative value means that foreign investors disinvest in that period.

Thus, the index captures the influence of FDI on factors other than market size, assuming that, other things being equal, size is the 'baseline' for attracting investments. These other factors can be diverse, ranging from the business climate, economic, and political stability, the presence of natural resources, infrastructure, skills, and technologies, to opportunities for participating in privatization or the effectiveness of FDI promotion.

The countries with top inward FDI Performance Index[13] in 2006 included Luxembourg, Hong Kong, China, Suriname, Iceland, Singapore Malta, Bulgaria,

---

[12] World Investment Report 2008: Transnational Corporations and the Infrastructure Challenge, UNCTAD, Geneva, 2008, p. 4.
[13] World Investment Report 2007: Transnational Corporations, Extractive Industries and Development, UNCTAD, Geneva, 2007, p. 14.

Jordan, Estonia, and Belgium. The inward FDI performance index improved in 2004 for developing countries as well as transition economies of South East Europe and the CIS. The improvement had been remarkable in South, East, and Southeast Asia. However, it worsened in developed countries compared to 2003. For instance, the US where the FDI inflows rose by 69 per cent in 2004 had a lower performance index and ranked 114th out of 140 countries of the world due to its lower FDI flows in 2002–03. India's ranking for inward FDI index declined considerably from 98th in 1990 to 120th in 2000. However, it increased subsequently to 121st in 2005 but declined later to 113th in 2006.

Outward FDI performance index

Performance in FDI outflows relating to the size of economies is measured by outward FDI performance index. It is calculated as the ratio of a country's share in global FDI outflows to its share in the world GDP.

$$OND_i = \frac{FDI_i / FDI_w}{GDP_i / GDP_w}$$

where,

OND_i = The outward FDI performance index of the ith country
FDI_i = The FDI outflows in the ith country
FDI_w = World FDI outflows
GDP_i = GDP in the ith country
GDP_w = World GDP

The differences in the index values among countries reflect differences in these two sets of factors determining outward FDI by Trans-national Companies (TNCs) headquartered in different countries:

- 'Ownership advantages', or firm-specific competitive strengths of TNCs (such as innovation, brand names, managerial and organizational skills, access to information, financial or natural resources, and size and network advantages) that they are exploiting abroad or wish to augment through foreign expansion
- 'Location factors', which reflect primarily economic factors conducive to the production of different goods and services in home and host economies, such as relative market size, production or transport costs, skills, supply chains, infrastructure, and technology supply.

Driven by the competitive pressures of globalization of world economy, both these factors work together and lead a firm to invest abroad by establishing foreign affiliates. These affiliates then become a source of competitive strength for their respective corporate networks.

The leading investor economies, in term of outward FDI performance index include Iceland, Hong Kong, China, Luxembourg, Switzerland, Belgium, Netherlands, Panama, Ireland, Azerbaijan, and Bahrain. India's ranking in outward FDI performance index improved[14] considerably from 94th in 2000 to 65th in 2005 but declined later to 56th in 2006.

Inward FDI potential index

The inward FDI potential index reflects the stability of structure variables comprising the index. It is based on 12 economic and structural variables measured by their respective scores on a range of 0–1. It is the unweighted average of scores based on

- GDP per capita
- The rate of growth of GDP
- The share of exports in GDP
- Telecom infrastructure
- Commercial energy use per capita
- The share of R&D expenditures in gross national income
- The share of tertiary students in the population
- Country risk
- Exports of natural resources as a percentage of the world total
- Imports of parts and components of electronics and automobiles as a percentage of the world total
- Exports in services as a percentage of the world total
- Inward FDI stock as a percentage of the world total

The top economies by inward FDI potential index in 2006 include[15] the US, Singapore, the UK, Canada, Luxembourg, Germany, Qatar, Sweden, Norway, and Hong Kong (China).

Cross-country comparison of FDI performance vs potential indices

A comparison of rankings by the FDI potential index with those of FDI performance index gives an indication of how each country performs against its potential. Countries in the world can be divided in four categories so as to draw up a four-fold matrix as shown in Exhibit 12.4.

Front-runners: countries with high FDI potential and performance
Above potential: countries with low FDI potential but strong FDI performance
Below potential: countries with high FDI potential but low FDI performance
Under performers: countries with both low FDI potential and performance

---

[14] World Investment Report 2007: Transnational Corporations, Extractive Industries and Development, UNCTAD, Geneva, 2007.
[15] World Investment Report 2008: Transnational Corporations and the Infrastructure Challenge, UNCTAD, Geneva, 2008, pp. 214–15.

Exhibit 12.4 Matrix of inward FDI performance and potential, 2005		
	High FDI performance	**Low FDI performance**
	Front-runners	**Below potential**
High FDI potential	Azerbaijan, Bahamas, Bahrain, Belgium, Botswana, Brunei Darussalam, Bulgaria, Chile, China, Croatia, Cyprus, Czech Republic, Dominican Republic, Estonia, Hong Kong (China), Hungary, Iceland, Israel, Jordan, Kazakhstan, Latvia, Lithuania, Luxembourg, Malaysia, Malta, Netherlands, Panama, Poland, Portugal, Qatar, Singapore, Slovakia, Thailand, Trinidad and Tobago, Ukraine, United Arab Emirates, and the UK.	Algeria, Argentina, Australia, Austria, Belarus, Brazil, Canada, Denmark, Finland, France, Germany, Greece, Ireland, Islamic Republic of Iran, Italy, Japan, Kuwait, Libyan Arab Jamahiriya, Mexico, New Zealand, Norway, Oman, Republic of Korea, Russian Federation, Saudi Arabia, Slovenia, Spain, Sweden, Switzerland, Taiwan Province of China, Tunisia, Turkey, the US, and Venezuela.
	Above potential	**Under-performers**
Low FDI potential	Albania, Angola, Armenia, Colombia, Congo, Costa Rica, Ecuador, Egypt, Ethiopia, Gabon, Gambia, Georgia, Guyana, Honduras, Jamaica, Kyrgyzstan, Lebanon, Mali, Mongolia, Morocco, Mozambique, Namibia, Nicaragua, Republic of Moldova, Romania, Sierra Leone, Sudan, Suriname, Tajikistan, Uganda, United Republic of Tanzania, Uruguay, Vietnam, and Zambia	Bangladesh, Benin, Bolivia, Burkina Faso, Cameroon, Democratic Republic of Congo, Cote d'Ivoire, El Salvador, Ghana, Guatemala, Guinea, Haiti, India, Indonesia, Kenya, TFY Rep. of Macedonia, Madagascar, Malawi, Myanmar, Nepal, Niger, Nigeria, Pakistan, Papua New Guinea, Paraguay, Peru, Philippines, Rwanda, Senegal, South Africa, Sri Lanka, Syrian Arab Republic, Togo, Uzbekistan, Yemen, and Zimbabwe.

Source: World Investment Report 2007, Transnational Corporations, Extractive Industries and Development, UNCTAD, Geneva, 2007 p. 14.

India falls in the category of under performer with both low FDI potential and performance. Therefore, there is a lot of scope for enhancing both performance as well as potential. The concern for below potential countries is how they could raise their FDI performance to match their potential whereas the above potential countries need to continuously strive so as to sustain their FDI performance at levels comparable with those of past while addressing their structural problems.

12.5   POLICY FRAMEWORK TO PROMOTE FOREIGN DIRECT INVESTMENT

Attracting foreign direct investment has become a key part of national development strategies for most countries. Such investments are often viewed to augment domestic capital, employment, and productivity, leading to economic growth. Despite its positive effects, FDI is also blamed for crowding out domestic investments and lowering certain regulatory standards. The impact of FDI depends on many conditions. However, well developed and implemented policies can help maximize gains from FDI.

12.5.1   Investment Promotion

Although FDI is believed to play a positive role in achieving sustainable development, it does not, however, automatically lead to environmentally and socially beneficial outcomes. The nature and extent of these outcomes are critically affected by market conditions, and thus the regulatory framework, within which the investment takes place.[16] Investment promotion by host countries is broadly made through three different 'generation' policies, which are discussed as follows.

First generation policies   the liberalization of FDI flows and the opening up of sectors to foreign investors

Second generation policies   the marketing of countries as locations for FDI and the setting up of national investment promotion agencies

Third generation policies   the targeting of foreign investors at the level of industries and clusters, and the marketing of regions and clusters with the aim of matching the locational advantages of countries with the needs of foreign investors.

Major regulatory and incentives measures[17] for FDI may be summarized as

- *Screening, admission, and establishment*
  - Closure of certain sectors, industries, or activities to FDI
  - Minimum capital requirements
  - Restrictions on modes of entry
  - Eligibility for bidding on privatization
  - Establishment of special zones (such as EPZs/SEZs) for FDI with legislation distinct from that governing the rest of the country
- *Fiscal incentives*
  - Reduction in standard corporate income tax rates
  - Tax holidays
  - Reductions in social security contributions
  - Accelerated depreciation allowances
  - Duty exemptions and drawbacks
  - Export tax exemptions
  - Reduced taxes for expatriates
- *Financial incentives*
  - Investment grants
  - Subsidized credits
  - Credit guarantees

---

[16] 'Investment and the WTO–Busting the Myths', *World Development Movement*, London, June 2003.
[17] 'Investment and Development: Where Do We Stand', JBICI Research Paper No. 15, JBICI, Tokyo, June 2002.

- *Other incentives*
  - Subsidized service fees (electricity, water, telecommunications, transportation, etc.)
  - Subsidized designated infrastructure such as, commercial buildings
  - Preferential access to government contracts
  - Closure of the market to further entry or granting of monopoly rights
- *Performance requirements*
  - Protection from import competition
  - Local content requirements (value added)
  - Minimum export shares
  - Trade balancing
  - Technology transfer
  - Local equity participation
  - Employment targets
  - R&D requirements

More generally, countries typically have a mix of both resource-seeking and efficiency-seeking FDI, reflecting partial reform of their trade regimes, and the political economy of dispensing patronage. Consequently, most countries follow dual policy regimes. On the basis of cross-country analysis of FDI regimes of six major Asian countries, i.e., India, People's Republic of China (PRC), Republic of Korea, Malaysia, Thailand, and Vietnam, the following observations[18] may be made:

- FDI policy may differ between regions. Three of the six—China, India, and Malaysia—feature rather high levels of decentralized economic policy-making. Thailand has been pursuing a policy of 'industrial decentralization' for some time. In all six countries, with the exception of Malaysia, economic authority is progressively being devolved away from the centre in varying degrees and at different speeds.
- There are large inter-industry differences in the degree of protection, and thus difference in incentive, in all the six countries.
- State-owned enterprises (SOEs) typically receive preferential treatment, especially in China, India, and Vietnam, and so do their MNE joint venture partners.
- Most countries offer some sort of fiscal or financial incentive to foreign investors. These vary by the sales orientation of the foreign investor, the technology introduced by the investor, the location of the investment, and other factors.
- The regulatory regime frequently offers more than one entry option for potential foreign investors, especially in recently reformed economies.

---

[18] Hill, Hall, 'Six Asian Economies: Issues and Lessons', in Douglas H. Brooks and Hal Hill ed., *Managing FDI in Globalizing Economy Asian Experiences*, New York: Palgrave Macmillan, 2004, p. 40.

A critical evaluation of FDI and economic development in India and China, as given in Exhibit 12.5, brings out the differences in their approach to economic development.

Exhibit 12.5   FDI and economic development: India vs China

Economists and analysts have constantly derided India's inability to attract FDI. This single-minded obsession with FDI is as strange as it is harmful. Academic studies have not produced convincing evidence that FDI is the best path to economic development when compared with responsible economic policies, investments in education, and sound legal and financial institutions. In fact, one can easily think of counter-examples. Brazil was a darling of foreign investors in the 1960s but ultimately let them down. Japan, Korea, and Taiwan received little FDI in the 1960s and 1970s but emerged among the world's most successful economies.

The litmus test for a country's economy is not its ability to attract a lot of FDI but whether it has a business environment that nurtures entrepreneurship, supports healthy competition, and is relatively free of heavy-handed political intervention. In this regard, India has done a better job than China. A group of world-class companies have emerged from India ranging from Infosys in the field of software, Ranbaxy in pharmaceuticals, Bajaj Auto in automobile components, and Mahindra and Mahindra in car assembly. This did not happen by accident.

Although it has many flaws, India's financial system did not discriminate against small private companies the way the Chinese financial system did. Many companies, such as Infosys benefited from this system. Infosys was founded by seven entrepreneurs with few political connections who, nevertheless, managed without significant hard assets, to obtain capital from Indian banks and the stock market in the early 1990s. It is unimaginable that a Chinese bank would lend to a Chinese equivalent of an Infosys.

With few exceptions, the world-class manufacturing facilities for which China is famous are results of FDI and not investment from indigenous Chinese companies. Though, 'Made in China' labels are still more ubiquitous than their 'Made in India' counterparts; but what is 'Made in China' is not necessarily 'Made by China'. Soon, 'Made in India' will be synonymous with 'Made by India' and an Indian will not just get the wage benefits of globalization but will also keep its profits—unlike so many cases in China.

Pessimism about India has often been proved wrong. For example, the view that India lacks the level of infrastructure that China has and, therefore, cannot compete with China. This is another 'China myth'—that the country grew, thanks largely to its heavy investment in infrastructure. This is a fundamentally flawed reading of China's growth story. In the 1980s, China had poor infrastructure but turned in a superb economic performance. China built its infrastructure after—rather than before—many years of economic growth and accumulation of financial resources. The 'China miracle' happened not because China had glittering skyscrapers and modern highways but because bold economic liberalization and institutional reforms—especially agricultural reforms in the early 1980s—created competition and nurtured private entrepreneurship.

For both China and India, there is a hidden downside in the obsession with building world-class infrastructure. As developing countries, if they invest more in infrastructure, they invest less in other areas. Typically, basic education, especially in rural areas, falls victim to massive investment projects, which produce tangible and immediate results. China made a costly mistake in the 1990s when it created many world-class facilities, but badly under-invested in education. Research from China revealed that during the country's economic rise, a staggering percentage of rural children could not finish secondary education. India, meanwhile, has quietly but

Contd

Exhibit 12.5 Contd

persistently improved its provision for education, especially in the rural areas. For sustainable economic development, the quality and quantity of human capital will matter more than physical capital. India seems to have the right policy priorities and if China does not invest in rural education soon, it may lose its true competitive edge over India—a well-educated and skilled workforce that drives manufacturing success. China was several light years ahead of India in economic liberalization in the 1980s. Today it lags behind in critical aspects, such as reforms that would permit more foreign investment and domestic private entry in the financial sector.

Unless China embarks on bold institutional reforms, India may very well outperform it in the next 20 years. But, hopefully, the biggest beneficiary of the rise of India will be China itself. It will be forced to examine the imperfections of its own economic model and to abandon its sense of complacency acquired in the 1990s.

Source: Huang, Yasheng, 'China Can Learn from India's Slow and Quiet Rise', *The Financial Times*, 27 January 2006.

12.5.2 Promotion of Foreign Direct Investment in India

Institutional framework

The Department of Industrial Policy and Promotion is responsible for facilitating and promoting FDI inflows into the country. It plays an active role in investment promotion through dissemination of information on investment climate and opportunities in India. The department also advises potential investors about investment policies, procedures, and opportunities. It also helps resolve problems faced by foreign investors in the implementation of their projects through the Foreign Investment Implementation Authority (FIIA) which interacts directly with the investors.

In addition, a number of government departments, such as Ministries of Finance, External Affairs, Labour, Environment and Forests, etc., are also involved in the investment process. Exhibit 12.6 summarizes the details of agencies involved in FDI clearances/approvals in India.

Policy framework

The policy framework of FDI in India evolved in a phased manner, from the strategy of import substitution soon after independence to progressive liberalization that began in the early 1990s. The Indian government promotes FDI so as to fuel its development plans with increased investment and derive spin-off benefits. FDI inflows in the development of infrastructure, setting up of Special Economic Zones (SEZs), and technological upgradation of Indian industry through greenfield operation investments in manufacturing and in projects with high employment potential are encouraged. The FDI policy in India[19] may be summarized as

---

[19] Foreign Direct Investment Policy 2006, Department of Industrial Policy and Promotion, Ministry of Commerce and Industry, Government of India, New Delhi, 2006, and subsequent amendments, updated till April 2008.

Exhibit 12.6	Selected agencies involved with FDI clearances/approvals in India
Subject matter	**Government agency**
Industrial entrepreneur Memorandum for de-licensed industries	Department of Industrial Policy and Promotion, SIA (Secretariat for Industrial Assistance)
Approval for industrial license/carry-on-business license	Department of Industrial Policy and Promotion, SIA
Approval for technology transfer (i) Automatic route (ii) Government approval: Project Approval Board (PAB)	Reserve Bank of India Department of Industrial Policy and Promotion, SIA
Approval for financial collaboration: (i) Automatic route (ii) Government approval: Foreign Investment Promotion Board (FIPB)	Reserve Bank of India Department of Economic Affairs
Approval for industrial park (i) Automatic route (ii) Non-automatic route (Empowered Committee)	Department of Industrial Policy and Promotion, SIA
Registration as a company and certificate of commencement of business	Department of Company Affairs (Registrar of Companies)
Matters relating to FDI policy	Department of Industrial Policy & Promotion, SIA
Matters relating to foreign exchange	Reserve Bank of India
Matters relating to taxation	Department of Revenue
Matters relating to direct taxation	Central Board of Direct Taxes
Matters relating to Excise and Customs	Central Board of Excise and Customs
Import of goods	Directorate General of Foreign Trade
Environmental clearance	Ministry of Environment and Forests
Overseas investment by Indians	Overseas Investment Division, RBI

Source: Foreign Direct Investment Policy 2006, Department of Industrial Policy and Promotion, Ministry of Commerce and Industry, Government of India, New Delhi, 2006, and subsequent amendments, updated till September 2008.

FDI prohibited

- Retail trading (except single brand product retailing)
- Atomic energy
- Lottery business
- Gambling and betting sector
- Business of chit fund and *nidhi* company
- Plantation except tea
- Trading in Transferable Development Rights (TDR)
- Activity/sector not opened to private sector investment

FDI up to 24 per cent allowed

- Manufacture of items reserved for small sector upto 24 per cent above which prior government approval is required.

FDI up to 26 per cent allowed

- *FM broadcasting:* FDI and FII investment upto 20 per cent with prior government approval
- Up-linking a news and current affairs TV channels with prior government approval
- *Defence production:* with prior government approval
- *Insurance:* FDI and FII under the automatic route
- *Publishing of news papers and periodicals:* with prior government approval

FDI up to 49 per cent allowed

- Broadcasting
  - *Setting up hardware facilities,* FDI and FII equity with prior government approval
  - *Cable network:* FDI and FII with prior government approval
  - *Direct to Home (DTH):* FDI and FII with prior government approval. FDI cannot exceed 20 per cent
- Scheduled air transport services under the automatic route
- Commodity exchanges with prior government approval
- Credit information companies with prior government approval
- Refining in case of PSUs with prior government approval
- Asset reconstruction companies with prior government approval

FDI up to 51 per cent allowed

- Single brand product retailing subject to prior approval

FDI up to 74 per cent allowed

- *ISP with gateways, radio-paging, and end-to-end bandwidth:* 49 per cent under automatic route and beyond 49 per cent with prior government approval
- *Establishment and operation of satellites:* with prior government approval
- *Private sector banking:* FDI and FII under the automatic route
- *Telecommunications services:* Basic, cellular, unified access services, global mobile personal communication services, and other value added telecom services with 49 per cent under the automatic route and beyond 49 per cent with prior government approval
- Non-scheduled air transport services, ground handling services under the automatic route

Foreign direct investment up to 100 per cent allowed with prior government approval subject to conditions:

- *Trading:*
  - Items from small scale sector
  - Test marketing of items approved for manufacture

- *Courier services*
- *Tea sector, including tea plantation:* subject to divestment of 26 per cent equity in favour of Indian partner/public within five years
- ISP without gateway, infrastructure provider, electronic mail, and voice mail: FDI up to 49 per cent under the automatic route and beyond 49 per cent with prior government approval
- Mining and mineral separation of titanium bearing minerals and ores, its value addition and integrated activities
- Cigars and cigarettes manufacture
- Airports-existing projects with prior government approval beyond 74 per cent
- Up-linking of a non-news and current affairs TV channel
- Investing companies in infrastructure/ services sector (except telecom sector)
- Publishing of scientific magazines, speciality journals and periodicals

Foreign direct investment allowed up to 100 per cent under automatic route
- Agriculture sector
  - Floriculture
  - Horticulture
  - Development of seeds
  - Animal husbandry
  - Pisciculture
  - Acquaculture
  - Services related to agro and allied sectors
- Industrial sectors
  - Mining
    - (a) Covering exploration and mining of diamonds and precious stones, gold, silver, and minerals
    - (b) Coal and lignite for captive consumption
  - Manufacturing activities
    - (a) Alcohol distillation and brewing
    - (b) Coffee and rubber processing and warehousing
    - (c) Hazardous chemicals
    - (d) Industrial explosive—manufacture
    - (e) Drugs and pharmaceuticals
    - (f) Manufacture of telecom equipment
  - Petroleum sector
    - (a) Petroleum sector other than refining including market study and formulation; investment/financing; setting-up infrastructure for marketing.
    - (b) Petroleum refining for private companies
  - Power
    - (a) generation (except atomic energy), transmission, distribution, and power trading

> o Special Economic Zones and Free Trade Warehousing Zones
> o Industrial Parks
> o Construction development projects
> o Services
>> (a) Civil aviation
>>> o Airports: Greenfield projects
>>> o Helicopter/seaplane services
>>> o Maintenance and repair organizations, flying and technical training institutes
>>> o Air transport services for NRI investment
>>> o Ground handling services for NRI investment
>> (b) Non-banking finance companies
>> (c) Trading
>>> o Wholesale/cash & carry trading
>>> o Trading for exports
> o In sectors/activities not listed above, FDI is permitted upto 100 per cent through automatic route subject to prevailing rules and regulations applicable.

12.6 FDI TRENDS IN INDIA

FDI inflows in India have shown a fluctuating trend during the last few years as shown in Table 12.4 and Fig. 12.2. It increased from US$4029 million in 2000–01 to US$6130 million in 2001–02. However, the FDI inflows declined to US$4322 million in 2003–04 but subsequently exhibited a rising trend to US$8,961 million in 2005–06 and thereafter jumped to US$22,079 million 2006–07 and US$29,893 million[20] in 2007–08.

The equity capital accounted for 74.8 per cent, whereas re-invested earnings were 21.8 per cent, and other capital for 3.4 per cent of the total FDI inflows in India, as shown in Fig. 12.3 during April 2000 to May 2008.

Sector-wise composition of FDI inflows as shown in Fig. 12.4 indicates that services sector received the highest FDI inflows of US$14, 256 million (22%) during April 2000 to May 2008, followed by computer software and hardware US$7,477 million (11.5%), construction activities US$4325 million (6.7%), telecommunications US$4074 million (6.3%), housing and real estate US$3745 million (5.8%), power US$2643 million (4.1%), automobile industry US$2582 million (4.0%), metallurgical industries US$2377 million (3.7%), petroleum and natural gas US$2007 (3.1%), chemicals US$1519 million (2.3%), and others US$19800.3 million (30.6%).

Mauritius has been the top investor in India with US$28493 million (40.6%) as shown in Fig. 12.5. followed by the US with US$5327 million (7.6%), Singapore with US$4973 million (7.1%), the UK with US$4579 million (6.5%), Netherlands with

---

[20] Factsheet on Foreign Direct Investment from August 1991 to May 2008, Department of Industrial Policy and Promotion, Government of India, September 2008.

Table 12.4   FDI inflows in India

(in US$ millions)

Financial year (April-March)	Equity		Re-invested earnings	Other capital[b]	Total FDI inflows
	FIPB route/ RBI's automatic route/ acquitization route	Equity capital of unicorporated bodies[a]			
August 1991–March 2000	15483	–	–	–	15483
2000–01	2339	61	1350	279	4029
2001–02	3904	191	1645	390	6130
2002–03	2574	190	1833	438	5035
2003–04	2197	32	1460	633	4322
2004–05	3250	528	1904	369	6051
2005–06	5540	435	2760	226	8961
2006–07(P)[c]	15585	897	5091	506	22079
2007–08(P)[b]	24574	500	4476	343	29893
2008–09 (April to May)	7681	–	–	–	7681
Total (April 2000 to May 2008)	**67644**	**2834**	**20519**	**3184**	**96181**
Cumulative Total (August 1991 to May 2008)	**83127**	**2834**	**20519**	**3184**	**109664**

[a] Figures for equity capital unincorporated bodies for 2006–07 and 2007–08 are estimates.
[b] Data in respect of 'Re-invested earnings' and 'Others capital' for the year 2005–06 & 2006–07are estimated as average of previous two years.
[c] Include swap of share US$3.1 billion.
P denotes provisional figures.
Source: Department of Industrial Policy and Promotion, Government of India, New Delhi.

US$2791 million (4.0%), Japan with US$2151million (3.1%), Germany with US$1637 million (2.3%), Cyprus with US$1162 million (1.7%), France with US$997 million (1.4%), UAE with US$802 million (1.1%), and others with US$17279 million (24.6%) during April 2000 to May 2008.

12.6.1   Foreign Direct Investment in Retail Sector

India is the second largest market in the world after China and it fascinates global retailers to invest. Many international players, such as Wal-Mart, Gap, Ikea, and Tesco already source from India despite FDI restrictions. Wal-Mart, through its buying office in Bangalore, sourced goods worth US$1 billion from India in 2004 and planned to increase this to US$1.5 billion in 2005. The major pros and cons of opening up FDI in the retail sector are discussed here.

Pros

- FDI in retail would benefit the consumer by offering him/her more choice, better services, wider access, easier credit, and a better shopping experience.

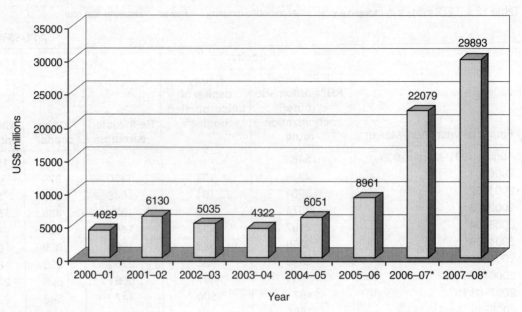

Fig. 12.2 FDI inflows in India

* Provisional figures.

Source: Department of Industrial Policy and Promotion, Government of India, New Delhi, September 2008.

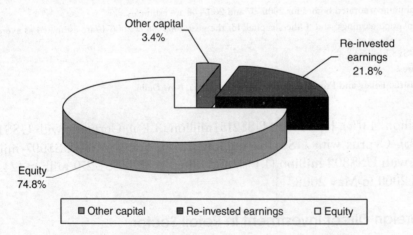

Fig. 12.3 Composition of FDI inflows in India*

* Figures for April 2000 to May 2008.

Source: Department of Industrial Policy and Promotion, Government of India, New Delhi, 2008.

- Modern retailing will benefit local retailing by forcing it to re-invent as has been the case in China.
- It will lead to higher standards of quality, introduce best practices, provide more skilled employment, and improve tax collection.

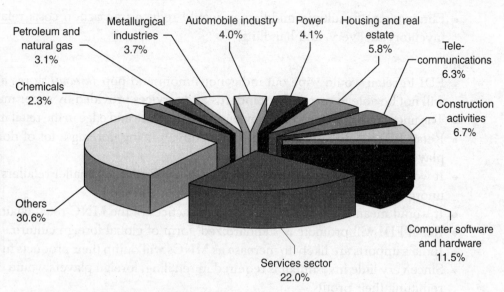

Fig. 12.4   Sector-wise composition of FDI inflows

* Figures for April 2000 to May 2008.

Source: Factsheet on FDI, Department of Industrial Policy and Promotion, Government of India, New Delhi, 2008.

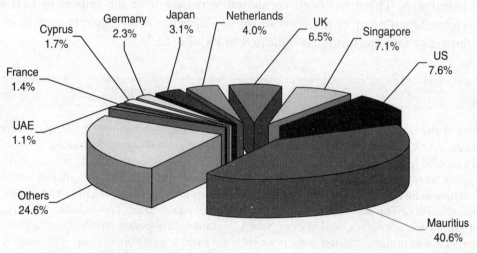

Fig. 12.5   Country-wise composition of FDI inflows

* Figures for April 2000 to May 2008.

Source: Factsheet on FDI, Department of Industrial Policy and Promotion, Government of India, New Delhi, 2008.

- Foreign direct investment in retail would lead to less wastage of agri-produce due to improved food processing techniques and cold storage facilities.
- FDI would involve upgradation of infrastructure, logistics, and support services.
- It would help Indian products get global recognition.
- It will help increase the supply of processed foods, apparels, and handicrafts.

- Elimination of multiple middlemen would reduce transaction costs related to inventory, delivery, and handling.

Cons

- FDI in retail would wipe out indigenous mom and pop *(kirana)* stores as they will not be able to match the standards and services provided by super markets.
- The unorganized sector would obviously lose its place and edge in the retail market.
- Retail FDI would also introduce competitive pricing, forcing a lot of domestic players out of the game.
- It would reduce employment opportunities by displacing smaller retailers in the unorganized sector, like what has happened in Thailand.
- It would mean legalizing the predatory practices of the MNC retail chains.
- Retail-FDI will promote a 'standardized' form of global foreign culture.
- India's imports are likely to increase as MNCs will dump their products in India.
- Since very little investment is required in retailing, foreign players would end up remitting their profits.

Allowing FDI in retail sector will considerably affect the market structure and the consumers. The government of India opened up FDI upto 51 per cent in retail trade to 'single brand products' with effect from 10 February 2006, with prior government permission. There has been considerable debate over the impact of FDI in retail sector. Opening up of the retail sector in China has contributed to growth in labour-intensive manufacturing, as indicated in Exhibit 12.7.

Exhibit 12.7   Opening up FDI in retail sector

Retailing is the world's largest private industry with sales over US$6 trillion. India remains the world's second largest market after China and is set to grow from the present US$394 billion to US$608 billion by 2009, according to economic intelligence unit of *The Economist*.

In 1992, China opened its market in a phased manner. FDI was initially capped at 49 per cent and was restricted to limited areas. Most restrictions have now ended and a major part of China's US$22 billion retail FDI has gone into labour-intensive manufacturing. A robust GDP growth rate has created more jobs than redundancies. Most other developing countries have gained in employment as the reforms have accelerated their growth rates.

The Chinese example is significant for India. Having started over a decade earlier, the impact of Chinese reforms can dispel some of India's worst apprehensions. Organized sector retail stands at 20 per cent in China and 40 per cent in Brazil against 3 per cent in India. In China, global retailers buy goods worth about US$60 billion for exports every year. China is the largest source for 5,300 stores of Wal-Mart, the world's biggest retail chain.

India can also learn from many other countries where FDI was initially allowed with conditions for minimum capital, product sourcing, or export commitment.

Source: 'Status Quo May Prove Costly', *Hindustan Times,* New Delhi, 12 December 2005; 'FDI in Retail Sector Will Not Be Allowed', *The Hindu,* Chennai, 30 April 2008.

This chapter explains the concept of foreign direct investment wherein long-term interests to control and manage overseas operations are key considerations of the investing firm. It also brings out the benefits and negative impacts of FDI to the host countries. Factors influencing a firm's profitability in selecting international investment destinations have also been dealt with. India features as the second most attractive global FDI location[21] after China for 2007–09. Various types of FDI on the basis of direction of investment, types of activity, investment objective, entry modes, sector, and strategic modes have also been explained.

The theoretical framework, as explained in this chapter, helps develop a conceptual understanding of why the firms decide to invest in foreign countries when alternate entry modes, such as exporting and licensing, which involve much lower risks, are available. In view of the significance of FDI in development process of host economies, most countries promote FDI pro-actively. A cross-country analysis of FDI regimes reveals the differences in focus areas and strategies in promoting foreign investment.

This chapter provides a comprehensive account of institutional and regulatory framework for foreign firms looking at India as an investment destination. An overview of FDI trends given at the end gives an insight into patterns of FDI so as to facilitate the readers in making foreign investment decisions.

SUMMARY

FDI is considered a crucial component of development strategies of host economies. As FDI flows are non-debt creating and non-volatile, preserving the long-term interest of the investor, these are preferred over other forms of external debts. FDI means investment by a firm with the intent to control and manage a business entity in a foreign country. Foreign direct investment takes the long-term perspective of gaining control in a foreign business entity whereas foreign portfolio investment has got a short-term perspective of earning profits.

Access to superior technology, increasing competition, increase in domestic investment, bridging host countries' foreign exchange gaps are few of the benefits of FDI to host countries whereas its negative impacts include market monopoly, crowding out and unemployment effects, technology dependence, profit outflow, corruption, and threat to national security. Profitability of a firm's foreign operations is influenced by cost of capital and other inputs, wage rate, taxation regime, cost of inputs, cost of logistics, and market demand.

FDI may be of various types, such as inward or outward; horizontal, vertical or conglomerate; backward or forward vertical; resource-, market-, or efficiency-seeking; industrial or non-industrial; export replacement, export platforms, or domestic substitution. Major theories of FDI explaining the rationale behind international investment, i.e., portfolio approach, market imperfection theory, internalization theory, monopolistic advantage theory, international product life cycle theory, and eclectic theory, have been discussed.

Most countries actively promote foreign direct investment by providing favourable regulatory environment and incentives. India promotes FDI inflows by providing several incentives, especially for development of infrastructure, setting up of Special Economic Zones (SEZs), technological upgradation of Indian industry through greenfield

[21] World Investment Report 2007: Transnational Corporations, Extractive Industries and Development, UNCTAD, Geneva, 2007, pp. 28–30.

investments, and projects with high employment potential.

FDI has shown a much higher growth compared to world trade and world output. The flow of FDI is measured through equity capital, intra-company loans, and re-invested earnings. Equity capital is the largest component among various FDI financing options. UNCTAD's FDI performance and potential indices facilitate cross-country comparisons. India has made remarkable progress in FDI inflows, especially in electrical equipment, computer software and electronics, transportation industry, services, telecommunication, etc. Major investors in India include Mauritius, US, Japan, Netherlands, UK, Germany, and Singapore.

KEY TERMS

Backward vertical FDI Direct investment aimed at providing inputs for a firm's production processes.

Conglomerate FDI Direct investment overseas aimed at manufacturing products not manufactured by the firm in the home country.

Cross-border acquisition Taking over management control of assets and operations in a foreign country.

Efficiency-seeking FDI Direct investment overseas so as to improve efficiency and/or seek advantages of process specialization or product rationalization.

Firm-specific advantage Core competencies or specific advantages possessed by a firm, not shared by competitors.

Flow of FDI The amount of FDI undertaken over a given time period.

Foreign direct investment (FDI) Investment overseas so as to acquire controlling interest in a foreign business entity.

Foreign portfolio investment (FPI) Investment in foreign financial instruments such as foreign stock, government bonds, etc., aimed at earning profit.

Forward vertical FDI Direct investment overseas aimed to sell the output of a firm's domestic production processes.

Greenfield investment Overseas investment to create new facilities or expansion of existing facilities.

Horizontal FDI Overseas investment in a similar activity as carried out in the home country.

Inward FDI Foreign firms taking control over domestic assets.

Inward FDI performance index Measure of the extent to which a host economy receives inward FDI relative to its economy size.

Market imperfection Factors that inhibit markets from working perfectly, such as import restrictions and quotas, incentives on exports and FDI, taxation, restrictions of FDI, government participation in trade, etc.

Market-seeking FDI Direct investment overseas with sizeable market and growth in order to protect existing markets, counteract competitors, and to preclude rivals from gaining new markets.

Outward FDI Domestic firms investing overseas and taking control over foreign assets.

Outward FDI performance index The ratio of a country's share in global FDI outflows to its share in the world GDP.

Poison pill Strategy to avoid a hostile takeover bid to obtain management control by a potential acquirer.

Resource-seeking FDI Direct investment overseas so as to gain privileged access to resources vis-à-vis competitor.

Stock of FDI Total accumulated value of foreign owned assets at a given time.

Vertical FDI Overseas investment so as either to provide inputs for the firm's domestic operations or sell its domestic outputs abroad.

CONCEPT REVIEW QUESTIONS

1. Explain the concept of FDI. How does it differ from FPI?
2. Write down the pros and cons of foreign direct investment for the host country.
3. Differentiate between the following with suitable examples:
   (a) Horizontal vs vertical FDI
   (b) Resource seeking vs market seeking FDI
   (c) Greenfield investment vs acquisition
   (d) Industrial vs non-industrial FDI
4. Briefly explain the market imperfection theory of FDI. Illustrate your answer with suitable examples.

CRITICAL THINKING QUESTIONS

1. A Bangalore based firm has developed a personal computer costing less than US$120. The key element in the success of the PC in the market is its technology. The newly developed computer has a lot of demand in Southeast Asia. As the head of the international business division of the company, critically examine various options available with the firm to expand its operations overseas, such as exporting, licensing, or direct investment, and suggest the most suitable one.

2. 'One of India's major attractiveness as an investment destination is its vast pool of skilled and professional workforce. However, India is yet to catch the eye of foreign investors as an export platform or a manufacturing base.' Do you agree with this statement? Justify your answer with suitable illustrations.

3. Compare the trends in foreign direct investment in India, China, and Japan. Find out the reasons for differences in the investment patterns.

PROJECT ASSIGNMENTS

1. Visit the office of an investment promotion agency near your place and meet the officer involved in investment promotion. List out the activities carried out by the organization to promote foreign direct investment.

2. Select a foreign firm that has direct investment in your country. Meet a senior official and find out the problems being faced by it in operating at a foreign location. Identify the measures being taken to cope with the problems arising due to 'the foreignness of the firm'.

CASE STUDY

FDI in Automobile Sector in India

Introduction

Auto-making in India has a long history, longer than in many emerging economy competitors. The first motor car was brought to India in 1898. However, until 1928, cars were not assembled in India. An assembly plant was established in Mumbai in 1928 by General Motors that imported Completely Knocked Down (CKD) kits from the US to assemble cars and trucks. Subsequently, assembly plants were established by Ford Motor Company in 1930 in Madras (now Chennai) and in 1931 in Calcutta (now Kolkata). The Indian major, Birla

Group established Hindustan Motors Ltd in Kolkata in 1942. A few years later, Premier Automobile Ltd was set up by the Walchand Group in 1944 in Mumbai. Standard Motor Product Ltd began to manufacture automobiles in 1948 in Madras.

A panel of automobiles and tractors was appointed by the Government of British India in 1947 to examine the feasibility of establishing auto-manufacturing facilities in India. It strongly recommended the promotion of a transport vehicle industry in India for faster economic development. At that time passenger cars were considered a luxury by the Indian government and development of automobile industry was not a matter of high priority. However, the Government of India did encourage private investment for local manufacturers of passenger cars. A regulation was passed by the Indian government in 1953 that the assemblers would be required to wind up their operations in India within three years in case they did not have plans for phased manufacture of cars in the country. As a result, major automobile assemblers, such as General Motors and Ford Motors had to close down their operations from India.

Subsequently, the Indian passenger car market became a duopoly of Hindustan Motors with its ambassador brand and Premium Automobiles with its brand Fiat. These cars were expensive, considerably large, and gave poor mileage. Therefore, use of passenger cars was confined to the rich and government officials and was out of the reach and affordability of the masses as a means of personal transport. Besides restrictive policies, the volume of cars sold in India was miserably low, and there was hardly any incentive to invest in the automobile sector.

Investment Framework in Automobile Sector

The investment regime in the automobile sector may be classified into three phases as discussed below:

Import Substitution Phase (1947–81)

After independence, the Government of India emphasized the development of infrastructure and heavy industry. The automobile sector was not a priority industry for the government. Besides, there was a lot of emphasis on conserving foreign exchange and promoting those industrial sectors that contributed to import substitution. The degree of government control was high, to the extent that the government decided how much a firm should produce and where. Besides, companies needed licences to operate and the government restricted capacity in all product lines. Indeed government restrictions were used in granting licenses to promote heavier vehicles over passenger cars, which were considered a luxury for the majority of the Indian population. For instance, the government restricted production of passenger cars to less than 25,000 cars in a year and emphasized production of utilitarian vehicles, such as buses, trucks, tractors, jeeps, and heavy vehicles through its licensing policies.

This era was characterized by small volumes, sluggish growth, and slow technological changes. There was little competition in the automobile market, mainly due to governmental policy restricting new players, leading to very slow growth in volumes. Besides, there was hardly any pressure on the existing players to continually reduce the costs, introduce new models, and upgrade products and designs. Most technology used was licensed as in the case of Fiat, Premium Auto, Standard Auto, and even the Ambassador–Morris; additionally, there were high degrees of vertical integration in production technology. Industrial relations between the employer and its employees were broadly confrontational in nature whereas the arm's-length approach was followed between the suppliers and the manufacturers. The big manufactures used the forced 'exit' strategy of supplier development and encouraged the development of a large number of suppliers to bid down prices as low as possible. There was a strong focus on the automobile sector in the domestic market. High tariff barriers and import restrictions led to minimal exports.

Despite government controls and restrictions, a base was created during this period that paved way for future development of automobile industry by way of

- Large skill base and technical workforce, which developed in and around the centres of automotive industries

- The development of an indigenous auto component industry which was largely unlicensed.
- With the passage of time, the auto component industry spawning its own machinery base.

The Maruti Suzuki Era (1981 to 1991)

The Suzuki Motor Company of Japan established a 50:50 joint venture, the Maruti Udyog Ltd, with the Government of India in 1982. This triggered a revolutionary phase in the Indian auto industry. It was for the first time that economies of scale in production were generated and the company was allowed to grow in size to reach closer to minimum efficient scale than previous producers. Maruti is also credited to transform supply chain management in auto industries by introducing Japanese style of supplier manufacturers' relations in India. Besides, Maruti Udyog Limited brought about massive transfer of technology and continuous technical assistance to its suppliers.

It is pertinent to note that Maruti had high profile backing from the then political establishment and the company's profitability was crucial to validate the government's foray into auto production. Besides, the protection from competition was the key to Suzuki's decision to expand its production substantially during this period. As it came in under tariff protection, with tight restrictions against imports of fully assembled old or new cars that characterised the Indian Customs policy, Suzuki was able to expand its market share under little threat from other foreign competitors. As a result, Maruti dominated the Indian passenger car market with 75 per cent of market share in 1991.

The Post-liberalization Era (1991 onwards)

The economic liberalization that began in 1991 paved way for FDI in the automobile sector. This led to a multi-fold rise in market competition, compelling the automobile and component manufacturers to reduce production costs and improve efficiency.

The turning point for the industry came in 2002, when the Indian government lifted all equity caps for foreign investors in the automobile sector. The automotive sector was identified as a key focus area for improving India's global competitiveness and achieving high economic growth. The Government of India formulated the Auto Policy for India with a vision to establish a globally competitive industry in India and to double its contribution to the economy by 2010. It intended to promote R&D in the automotive industry by strengthening the efforts of industry in this direction through the provision of suitable fiscal and financial incentives. Policy initiatives include

- Automatic approval for foreign equity investment up to 100 per cent of manufacture of automobiles and component is permitted.
- The customs duty on inputs and raw materials was reduced from 20 per cent to 15 per cent. The peak rate of customs duty on parts and components of battery operated vehicles was reduced from 20 per cent to 10 per cent. Apart from this, custom duty was also reduced from 105 per cent to 100 per cent on second-hand cars and motorcycles.
- National Automotive Fuel Policy was announced, which envisaged a phased programme for introducing Euro emission and fuel regulations by 2010.
- Tractors of engine capacity more than 1800 cc for semi-trailers would attract excise duty at the rate of 16 per cent.
- Excise duty was reduced on tyres, tubes, and flaps from 24 per cent to 16 per cent. Customs duty on lead is 5 per cent.
- A package of fiscal incentives, including benefits of double taxation treaty was made available.

As a result of progressive liberalization in automobile sector

- 100 per cent foreign direct investment was allowed in auto sector
- Manufacturing and imports were made free from licensing and approvals
- No local content regulation in auto industry

FDI in Automobile Sector

Automobile industry accounted for 3.7 per cent of FDI inflows in India during April 2000 to December, 2007. Progressive reduction in import tariffs on auto components from 30 per cent in 2001–02 to 7.5–10 per cent in 2007–08 (Fig. C.1) has significantly contributed to enhance the competitiveness of the industry.

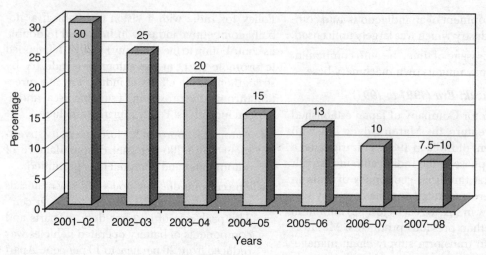

Fig. C.1 Import tariff on auto components in India

Source: Automotive Components Manufacturers Association of India.

The auto industry in India is maturing. Most foreign investors are very upbeat about India. It has not only been growing but also likely to grow fast in the future as well. India's competitive advantage in the automobile sector may be summarized under the following heads:

- Availability of skilled manpower with engineering and design capabilities
- Huge domestic market with high growth potential
- Rising income levels of target customers
- Increase demand in new segments due to rapidly changing life styles
- Strong base of supporting industries such as auto components
- Presence of strong industry associations

Foreign Auto Companies in India

Suzuki Motor Company was the first entrant into the Indian automobile sector with its joint venture with Maruti Udyog Ltd in 1982. However, foreign manufacturers began to take India seriously in the 1990s, and many now operate as wholly owned subsidiaries which started as joint ventures. Maruti Udyog, the biggest manufacturer of passenger cars by market share, is now wholly controlled by the former JV partner Suzuki of Japan.

Consequent to liberal policy framework for foreign direct investment in automobiles, foreign companies accounted for 58 per cent of production of four-wheelers during 2005–06 in India. As Suzuki was the first entrant in the Indian market, it's wholly owned subsidiary Maruti Udyog Ltd accounted for 33.24 per cent share in total four wheeler production during the period. Japanese companies accounted for 39 per cent of total production of four wheelers during 2005–06, followed by Korean (15%), American (3%), and European (1%) companies as shown in Fig. C.2. On the other hand, in 2005–06, Japanese companies account for 51 per cent and Indian companies for 49 per cent of the two wheeler production in India (Fig. C.3).

Indian Automobile Market

Two-wheelers accounted for 75.13 per cent of the market share of automobiles in India in 2007–08, followed by passenger vehicles 16.04 per cent, commercial vehicles 5.05 per cent, and three-wheelers 3.78 per cent (Fig. C.4).

Major domestic players in the Indian automobile industry include Tata Motors Ltd, Mahindra and Mahindra Ltd, Hindustan Motors, Ashok Leyland, TVS Motor, Bajaj Auto, and LML (Exhibit C.1) whereas the foreign players include

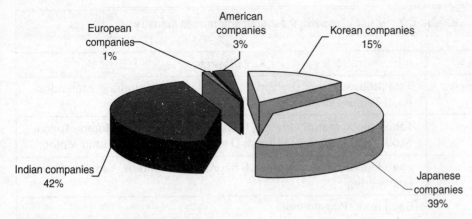

Fig. C.2   Production of four-wheelers in India*

* Based on data for 2005–06.

Source: Automotive Components Manufacturers Association of India.

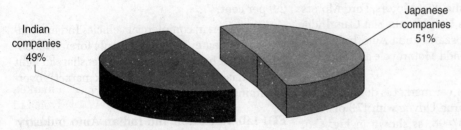

Fig. C.3   Production of two-wheelers in India*

* Based on data for 2005–06.

Source: Automotive Components Manufacturers Association of India.

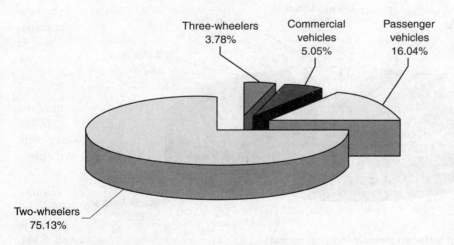

Fig. C.4   Market share of automobiles in India (2007–08)

Source: Society of Indian Automobile Manufactures.

Exhibit C.1	**Major players in the Indian automobile industry**

Segment	Key players
Commercial vehicles	Tata Motors, Ashok Leyland, Swaraj Mazda, Mahindra & Mahindra, Bajaj Tempo, Eicher Motors
Passenger vehicles	Tata Motors, Maruti Udyog, Honda Motors, Hyundai Motors, Toyota, Skoda, Mahindra & Mahindra, Daimler Chrysler, Hindustan Motors
Two wheelers	Hero Honda, Honda Motors, Bajaj Auto, TVS Motos, Yamaha, Kinetic Engineering
Three wheelers	Bajaj Auto, Piaggio India

Source: 'Automotive', *India Brand Equity Foundation,* 21 February 2006.

Maruti Udyog Ltd, Hyundai Motors India Ltd, Daimler Chrysler India, Fiat Motors, Ford Motors Ltd, General Motors Ltd, Honda Siel Cars India (HSCI), Toyota Kirloskar, Skoda Auto India, and Hero Honda and Honda Motorcycle and Scooters India Pvt. Ltd.

India's passenger car market is dominated by the Japanese firm Maruti Udyog with 47.3 per cent market share in 2007–08, as shown in Fig. C.5, followed by Hyundai Motors 25.5 per cent, Tata Motors 12.7 per cent, Honda Siel 4.2 per cent, General Motors 3.2 per cent, Ford India 2.4 per cent, Mahindra Renault 1.8 per cent, and others 2.9 per cent.

However, in commercial vehicles Indian companies dominate: Toyota is the only foreign manufacturer that has a significant market share in light commercial vehicles, while the truck market is overwhelmingly dominated by India's Tata.

FDI Liberalization and Indian Auto Industry

The Indian auto industry witnessed a rapid transformation over the last decade. The production volume and capacity grew rapidly after the end of

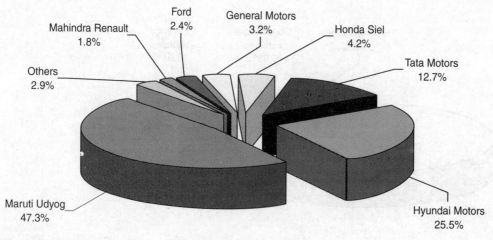

Fig. C.5 Market share of auto companies in India car market*

* Based on data for 2007–08.

Source: Automotive Components Manufacturers Association of India.

licensing in 1993. The automobile sector employs about 0.45 million people directly and around 10 million people indirectly. Automobile production in India has remarkably increased[1] from 5,005,375 vehicles in 2000–01 to 11,325,671 vehicles in 2006–07 (Table C.1). The Light Commercial Vehicles (LCVs) witnessed the highest overall Combined Average Growth Rate (CAGR) at 18.84 per cent during 2000–01 to 2007–08, followed by busses and trucks (16.10%), motor-cycles (14.62%), cars (13.40%), and three-wheelers (11.93%).

Production of passenger cars in India witnessed the highest growth of 30 per cent among the top 12 countries in 2005 against 17 per cent growth in Brazil, 15 per cent in China, 13 per cent in Korea, 10 per cent in Russia, whereas the US and the UK had negative growth of 6 per cent and 1 per cent, respectively. Besides, India was the fourth largest producer of heavy trucks with 202, 435 units in 2004, with an impressive growth rate of 32 per cent.

India is now the world's fastest-growing large market for passenger cars, albeit from a low base. Disposable income is rising fast and Indian consumers are more strongly predisposed than other Asian consumers to commit rising incomes to buying vehicles. India currently has one of the world's lowest per capita passenger car ownership rates, with less than six cars per 1,000 people in 2004. The next 10 years are likely to witness the market grow dramatically as consumers upgrade rapidly from motorcycles and three-wheeled vehicles: light vehicle sales passed the one million mark in 2005.

The Indian passenger car market has a high potential for growth as the per capita passenger car penetration per 1000 persons is merely seven against 10 in China, 90 in Brazil, 147 in Malaysia, 180 in Korea, 414 in Japan, 480 in the UK and the US each, and 500 in Germany.

India is not only emerging as one of the most attractive automotive markets in the world, but is also poised to become a key sourcing base for auto components. The industry's capabilities in design, engineering, and manufacturing have been recognized the world over, and most automotive majors are looking to increasingly source auto components from India.

There had been a substantial upgradation in the capability of Indian automobile component suppliers, such as

- Increased proficiency in understanding, global automotive standards and technical designs
- Increased automation leading to cost economies in production
- Flexibility in small batch production
- Growing IT capability for design, development, and simulation

India has developed excellent IT skills with automotive domain knowledge. India is among the few countries in the world that have the indigenous capability to design an automobile. Some of the world class automobiles designed in India are depicted in Fig. C.6. As a result, major MNCs, including General Motors, Mercedes Benz, Ford, Caterpillar, Honda, Suzuki, Cummins, etc., are shifting their automobile manufacturing to India. Exhibit C.2 summarizes production details of major automobile companies in India. Further, India is also an excellent base for prototyping, testing, validating and production of auto components.

Auto components are increasingly exported from India by manufacturers. DaimlerChrysler do not export cars but it does export components back to Europe and the company has about 15 per cent cost advantage over components sourced from Europe.

The auto sector is one of the most significant attractors of FDI in India, and competition is making it among the most fiercely contested markets. The Indian automobile market is also becoming increasingly competitive. The biggest maker of passenger cars, Maruti, has seen its share eroded quite sharply in recent years by newer entrants. Indian competitors are offering a strong challenge to foreign manufacturers. Tata, for example, has developed the Nano, a small car priced at Rs 100,000 (US$2100), less than half the cost of the lowest priced passenger car now on the market. Indian companies are

- Investing substantially in increasing production capacities

[1] Based on data from Automotive Components Manufacturers Association of India.

Table C.1 Automobile production in India

(Number of vehicles)

Category	2000–01	2001–02	2002–03	2003–04	2004–05	2005–06	2006–07	2007–08
Cars	517,907	564,052	608,851	843,235	1,027,858	1,112,542	1,238,021	1,416,480
Multi utility vehicles	125,938	105,667	114,479	146,325	182,018	196,371	222,495	244,648
LCVs	63,869	65,756	83,195	108,917	138,896	171,781	225,724	254,062
Buses and trucks	88,185	96,752	120,502	166,123	214,807	219,297	294,258	291,114
Scooters	879,759	937,506	848,434	935,279	987,498	1,020,013	943,944	1,074,933
Motor cycles	2,183,430	2,906,323	3,876,175	4,355,168	5,193,894	6,201,214	7,112,281	6,503,532
Mopeds	694,974	427,498	351,612	332,294	348,437	379,574	379,987	430,827
Three wheelers	203,234	212,748	276,719	356,223	374,445	434,424	556,126	500,592
Tractors	248,079	207,324	166,889	191,633	249,077	296,080	352,835	n.a.
Grand Total	**5,005,375**	**5,523,626**	**6,446,856**	**7,435,197**	**8,716,930**	**10,031,296**	**11,325,671**	**10,716,188***

n.a.—Figures not available.

* Grand total for 2007–08 does not include tractor production.

Source: Based on data from Automotive Components Manufacturers Association of India.

Fig. C.6 World class automobiles designed and manufactured in India

Exhibit C.2 Major automobiles companies in India				
Name of the company	**Parent company**	**Output**	**Models**	**Plants**
I. Domestic players				
Tata Motors Ltd	Largest commercial vehicle players in the country and one of the largest in the passenger vehicles segment	Capacity: 160,000 unit pa Volumes: 171,870 units in 2004 Operating income US$3.8 billion in 2005	Sierra, Sumo, Safari, Indica, Indigo	Pune (Maharashtra)
Mahindra and Mahindra Ltd	Flagship company of the Mahindra Group; largest player in the tractor segment in India	Capacity: 125,000 units pa Volumes: 69,737 Units in 2004 Operating income US$1.47 billion in 2005	Armada, Bolero, Commander, Marshall, Maxx, Voyager, Scorpio	Mumbai, Nashik (Maharashtra)

Contd

Exhibit C.2 Contd

Name of the company	Parent company	Output	Models	Plants
Hindustan Motors	A C.K. Birla group flagship and one of the oldest auto companies in India	Capacity: 64,000 units p.a. Volumes: 15,782 units Operating income US$159.7 million in 2004	Lancer, Ambassador, Contessa, Trekker, RTV, Pushpak, Pajero	Uttarpara (West Bengal), Pithampur (Madhya Pradesh), Trivellore (Tamil Nadu)
Ashok Leyland	Hinduja group	Operating income US$952.9 million in 2005	Multiaxle vehicles, tractor, ecomet, engines, Viking BS-1, Viking BS-II, Vestibule Bus, 222 CNG bus etc.	Ennore, Two plants at Hosur, the assembly plants at Alwar, Bhandara, castings plant at Hyderabad
TVS Motor	TVS Group	Operating income US$641.9 million in 2005	Mopeds- Excel, Champ, TVS 50 Scooterettes- Scooty Motorcycles— Max 100, Victor, Centra, Fiero	Hosur, Mysore
Bajaj Auto	Bajaj Group	Capacity: 2.52 million units p.a. Operating income US$1.3 billion in 2005	Motorcycles— Boxer, CT 100, Discover, Wind, Caliber, Pulsar, Eliminator Scooters—Spirit, Saffire, Wave	3 Plants at Akurdi, Waluj, Chakan
LML	Lohia Group		Freedom, Graptor	Kanpur
II. Foreign Players				
Maruti Udyog Ltd	Suzuki of Japan, holds a 54.2 per cent stake in the company	Capacity: 500,000 units pa Volumes: 472,122 units including exports in 2004 Operating income US$2.4 billion in 2005	800, Omni, Alto, WagonR, Zen, Baleno, Esteem, Gypsy, Vitara, Versa	Gurgaon (Haryana)

Contd

Exhibit C.2 Contd

Name of the company	Parent company	Output	Models	Plants
Hyundai Motors India Ltd	Wholly owned subsidiary of a Hyundai Motors Company, S. Korea	Capacity: 150,000 units pa Volumes: 171,905 units	Santro, Accent, Sonata, Terracan	Irrungattukottai (Tamil Nadu)
Daimler Chrysler India	100 per cent subsidiary of Daimler Chrysler group	Capacity: 10,000 units pa Volumes: 1,640 units	E class, S class, C Class	Pune (Maharashtra)
Fiat Motors	Subsidiary of Fiat Auto SpA	Capacity: 50,000 units pa Volumes: 10,428 units	Uno, Siena, Palio, Palio Adventure	Mumbai (Maharashtra)
Ford Motors Ltd	Ford Motr Company, the world's second largest automaker	Capacity: 100,000 units pa Volumes: 45,723 units	Ikon, Mondeo	Chengaipattu (Tamil Nadu)
General Motors Ltd	Collaboration between General Motors Corporation and C.K. Birla Group of companies	Capacity: 25,000 units pa Volumes: 17,986 units	Astra, Corsa, Swing, Forrester, Vectra, Sail, Optra, Chevrolet Optra	Halol (Gujarat)
Honda Siel Cars India (HSCI)	Established in 1995, with Honda Motor Company (Japan) and Siel Ltd (India) being the key promoters	Capacity: 30,000 units pa Volumes: 20,550 units	City, Accord, CR-V	Noida (UP)
Toyota Kirloskar	Joint Venture between Kirloskar Group and Toyota Motor Corp.	Capacity: 50,000 units pa Volumes: 42549 units	Qualis, Camry, Corolla	Bidadi (Karnataka)
Skoda Auto India	Skoda Auto, based in Czech Republic, is a part of Volkswagen group	Capacity: 10,000 units pa Volumes: 3,712 units	Octavia, Laura	Aurangabad (Maharashtra)

Contd

Exhibit C.2 Contd

Name of the company	Parent company	Output	Models	Plants
Hero Honda	Joint venture between Hero group, the world's largest bicycle manufacturers and the Honda Motor company of Japan	Capacity: 2.8 million units pa Operating income US$1.66 billion in 2005	Motorcycles— CD Dawn, CD Deluxe, Splendour, Passion, Gurgaon Karizma, CBZ, AmbitionStep Through-Street	2 plants at Daruhera and Gurgaon
Honda Motorcycle and Scooters India Pvt. Ltd (HMSI)	Whooly owned subsidiary of Honda Motor Company Ltd, Japan	Capacity: 200,000 vehicles pa	Scooters—Activa, Dio, Eterno, Motorcycle— Unicom	1 plant at Manesar

Source: 'Automotive', India Brand Equity Foundation, 21 February 2006.

- Committing substantial resources in indigenous R&D
- Forging strategic alliances in India and abroad so as to enhance their competitiveness
- Investing overseas by way of acquisitions as well as establishing greenfield manufacturing facilities

Increased competition in the domestic market has not only boosted competitiveness of Indian automobile firms in the domestic market but also a number of Indian firms have moved forward to invest overseas, as given below.

Overseas Investments by Indian Auto Companies

Tata Motors	Daewoo Commercial vehicles Plant, Korea
Mahindra & Mahindra	Jiangling Motor Company, China Sar Auto Products Ltd
Bharat Forge Ltd	Carl Dan Peddinghaus, Germany CDP Aluminiumtechnik Germany Federal Forge, US Imatra Kilsta AB, Sweden Scottish Stampings Ltd, Scotland
Motherson Sumi	WOCO Group, Germany G&S Kunststofftechnik
Amtek Auto	GWK, UK New Smith Jones Inc of US Zelter, Germany

UCAL Fuel Systems	AMTEC Precision Products Inc, US
Sundram Fasteners Ltd.	Blesisthal Produktions Gmbh, Precision Forging unit of Dana Spicer (UK) Cramlington Forge, UK Greenfield Plant in Zhejiang, China CDP GMBH
EI Forge Ltd.	Shakespeare Forging, UK
TVS Logistics Services	CJ Components, Ltd, UK
TVS Autolec Ltd	RBI Autoparts SND BHD, Malaysia
Sona Koyao	Fuji Autotech, France

Besides, TVS and Bajaj Groups are investing in Indonesia to manufacture two wheelers.

The increasing competitive intensity has also contributed considerably to quality upgradation of Indian auto component industry. It is reported that 456 auto component companies have acquired ISO 9000, 248 TS 16949, 136 QS 9000, 129 ISO 14001, and 32 OHASAS 18001 certification. Besides, a number of international awards, such as the Deming Prize, the JIPM Award, and Japan Quality Medal have been conferred to a number of Indian firms.

Questions

1. Critically evaluate impact of protectionist measures restricting foreign direct investments in India's automobile sector.
2. Find out the strengths and weaknesses of Indian automobile industry under different frameworks of investment policy regimes.
3. Identify and discuss the reasons that a foreign firm should invest in India for manufacturing automobiles or its components.
4. How did FDI liberalization contribute to Indian firms' enhancing their competitiveness?

13 Multinational Enterprises

LEARNING OBJECTIVES

➢ To explain the concept of an MNE
➢ To discuss the various types of MNEs
➢ To examine the impact of MNEs on host economies
➢ To explore the various techniques to measure MNEs' internationalization
➢ To assess emerging MNEs from rapidly developing economies

13.1 INTRODUCTION

Multinational enterprises (MNEs) are considered powerful drivers of globalization. It is estimated that MNEs account for two-thirds of world trade, and about one-third of the total world trade is intra-firm trade. The universe of MNEs is considered to be large, diverse, and expanding. The role of multinationals in the world economy has continued to grow as reflected by the expansion of foreign direct investment (FDI) stocks and operations of foreign affiliates. This makes the study of multinationals imperative for business students.

Certain aspects of modern multinationals have a long history and date back to the period of ancient human civilization. Around 2500 BC, Sumerian merchants found that they needed men stationed abroad to receive, store, and sell goods for their foreign commerce.[1] Thirteenth century Italian bankers have been considered among the first multinationals by some authors. The East India Company of England and the Dutch East India Company of the seventeenth century are widely believed to qualify as multinationals since they had large corporations that spread across national borders (Exhibit 13.1) with sizeable international business.

---

[1] Wilkins, Mira, The *Emergence of Multinational Enterprise: American Business Abroad from the Colonial Era to 1914*, Cambridge, MA: Harvard University Press, 1970; 'The History of Multinational Enterprise', in *The Oxford Handbook of International Business*, (eds) Rugman, A.M. and T.L. Brewer, 2001, pp. 5–12.

Exhibit 13.1   East India Companies: The first multinationals

In 1600, the British East India Company, considered to be the first multinational enterprise of modern times, was formed in London. The purpose of the East India Company was to unite the English merchants doing business in Southeast Asia. There was cut-throat competition for trade in this region, which had first been controlled by the Spaniards and the Portuguese. In the seventeenth century, the contest for the lucrative trade with the East was between the Dutch, the English, and the French. The Netherlands followed England and set up a Dutch East India Company in 1602, with its headquarters in Amsterdam and also in Batavia (Jakarta) on the island of Java. The French formed their version of the East India Company later, in 1664.

These organizations became immensely powerful. Trading was just one of their activities— they also exercised political influence. They armed their ships to fight at sea and maintained private armies. The East India Companies set up military as well as trading bases and made treaties with local rulers in the neighbourhood. They waged war on neighbouring nations and on each other. In many ways they behaved like independent states.

The English lost the contest to control the spice trade in the East Indies to the Dutch—India then became the centre of their activities. By 1700, England had sole trading rights in India, with a number of key ports, notably Calcutta (now Kolkata), Madras (now Chennai), and Bombay (now Mumbai). The Dutch had ports on the Cape in South Africa, in Persia, Ceylon, Malaya, and Japan, and also dominated the Spice Islands (now Indonesia). The French were less successful in their attempt to dominate India. Besides the East India Companies, some traders made homes in Asia, founding European centres in India, Southeast Asia, and China.

Source: The Concise History Encyclopaedia, Kingfisher Publications Plc., London, 2001, p. 17.

There has been a rapid growth in MNEs after the Second World War. The United Nations Conference on Trade and Development (UNCTAD) estimates that there were about 37,000 transnational corporations (TNCs) in the world by the early 1990s, of which 33,500 were parent corporations based in developed countries. The number of TNCs had grown to 78,000 parent companies by 2006 with at least 780,000 foreign affiliates. Of these, about 58,000 parent TNCs are based in developed countries and about 18,500 in developing countries and 1650 in transition economies. The number of TNCs from developing and transition economies has increased more than those from developed countries over the past 15 years. In 2006 there were 260,000 foreign affiliates located in developed countries, 407,000 in developing countries, and 111,000 in the transition economies. China is home to 3429 parent companies, compared to 587 from India; China also hosts the largest number of 280,000 foreign affiliates in the world compared to only 1796 in India. Thus, China hosts one-third of the TNCs worldwide foreign affiliates.[2]

The world's largest MNEs have home base in the Triad countries—the US, Europe, and Japan—which account for about 91 per cent of MNCs, as indicated in Fig. 13.1.

---

[2] World Investment Report 2007, *Transnational Corporations, Extractive Industries and Development,* New York and Geneva: United Nations, 2007, pp. 11–13.

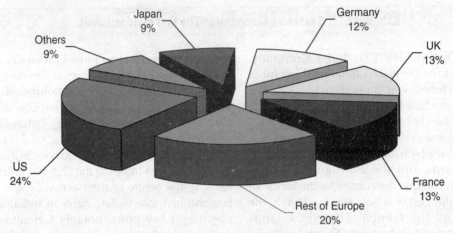

Fig. 13.1 Home country composition of top 100 MNCs (figures for 2005)

Source: World Investment Report 2007, *Transnational Corporations, Extrative Industries and Development,* New York and Geneva: United Nations, 2007, pp. 229–31.

A country-wise break up of the world's largest 100 non-financial transnational corporations (TNCs) suggests that the US accounted for 24 per cent of MNEs in 2005, followed by France (13%), the UK (13%), Germany (12%), and Japan (9%) whereas the rest of Europe (excluding UK, France, and Germany) accounted for 20 per cent and other countries 9 per cent.

An industry-wise analysis of the world's top 100 MNEs indicates that 11 per cent of the MNEs are in the motor vehicles sector in 2005, followed by 10 per cent in electrical and electronic equipments; 10 per cent in petroleum exploration, refinery, and distribution; 9 per cent in telecommunications; 8 per cent in pharmaceuticals; 6 per cent in electricity, gas, and water; and 5 per cent in retail besides 41 per cent in others (Fig. 13.2).

For managers engaged in international business, it is important to develop a conceptual understanding of multinational firms and strategic options for their operations across the world. This chapter examines the concept of 'multinationals' and brings out the subtle differences among 'international', 'multinational', 'transnational', and 'global' firms. It also reveals that firms across the world increasingly attempt to globalize their corporate strategies so as to integrate and consolidate their resources as a part of their internationalization efforts. A comprehensive classification of MNEs on the basis of investment, operations, and management orientation has also been given so as to enable the readers to appreciate various types of MNEs. The impact of multinationals on the host economies is often debated and is considered to have both positive and negative effects, as discussed later in this chapter.

Various criteria used to measure the extent of internationalization of an MNE, such as, size, structure, performance, and management orientation, have also been explained. The transnationality index and internationalization index developed by UNCTAD serve as highly useful and effective tools to measure and compare the

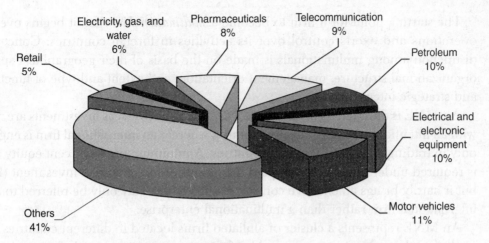

Fig. 13.2   Industry composition of world's top 100 MNCs (figures for 2005)

Source: World Investment Report 2007, *Transnational Corporations, Extractive Industries and Development,* New York and Geneva: United Nations, 2007, pp. 229–31; UNCTAD/Erasmus University database.

extent of internationalization of MNEs. A large number of companies from rapidly developing economies (RDEs) are set to become the multinationals of the future, posing considerable challenge to well-established MNEs of the developed world. In India too, consequent to economic liberalization in 1991, a number of Indian firms are rapidly marching ahead to expand internationally and become multinationals.

13.2 CONCEPT OF A MULTINATIONAL ENTERPRISE

In simple terms, a *multinational enterprise* means a firm that operates in more than one country, i.e., in multiple countries. International business literature mentions various definitions of multinational firms. Readers often come across terms like *international, multinational, transnational,* and *global,* occurring before the words, *corporation* and *enterprise.* Although conceptual distinctions may be made among these terms, in practice, these are often used interchangeably. In order to understand what precisely constitutes a multinational firm, one must know what constitutes a non-multinational firm. The key attributes of a non-multinational firm are

- It produces and markets goods and services in one country
- It is headquartered in one country
- It faces low international risk exposure

Further, firms headquartered and producing their goods in a single country but marketing their output overseas by way of exports, cannot be termed multinationals even though the risk exposure of exporting firms would be much greater than purely domestic firms due to market and foreign exchange fluctuations. A firm which exports the majority of its output may be termed as an *export-oriented, internationally-oriented,* or *international* firm.

The starting point for a firm to become a *multinational* is when it begins overseas operations and exerts control over its activities in foreign countries. Conceptual distinction among multinationals is made on the basis of their geographical spread, organizational structure, management orientation, and extent and type of functional and strategic integration.

An MNE is different from an *international firm* as its overseas investments are made with an intention to acquire effective control, whereas an international firm is engaged only in trading activities in several countries. A minimum of 10 per cent equity stake is required under the widely accepted definitions of foreign direct investment (FDI), but it hardly brings an effective control, so such a firm may only be referred to as an international firm rather than a multinational enterprise.

An MNE represents a cluster of affiliated firms located in different countries[3] that are linked through common ownership, draw upon a common pool of resources, and respond to a common strategy. An MNE does not merely export to unaffiliated firms overseas, but internalizes its core competencies by way of FDI that provides it effective control on overseas operations.

A firm is termed as *multi-domestic* when the structural configuration and strategic integration among its affiliates and the headquarters is low and decision-making is highly decentralized. On the other hand, a *global firm* has high levels of coordination and integrated strategic approach among its subsidiaries and the headquarters. *Transnational firms* have complex organizational structures wherein the subsidiaries do have local flexibility in performing their functions but these are integrated globally.

Often the United Nations refer to the term *transnational corporation* or TNC as an economic entity operating in more than one country or a cluster of economic entities operating in two or more countries, whatever their legal form, whether in their home country or country of activity, and whether taken individually or collectively.

A large number of contemporary authors prefer the term multinational *enterprise* (MNE) over multinational *corporation* (MNC). It is believed that the term 'multinational enterprise' is more general in nature and has broader application as every multinational firm is not a corporation. The term 'enterprise' is much less restrictive in scope and is preferred over 'corporation'.

Numerous definitions are available in the international business literature for multinational firms. Various authors have attempted to distinguish among various types of international firms using several attributes. For a firm to be an MNE, the following criteria need to be fulfilled:

- The firm should own or control operations in multiple countries, typically across the world.
- It should generate a substantial portion of its revenues by its operations from foreign countries.

---

[3] Wells, L.T. Jr., *Manager in the International Economy*, Englewood Cliffs: Prentice-Hall, 1986.

- It should employ workforce from multiple countries, including employees at senior levels.
- It should have a strategic management perspective and a vision of multinational operations.

However, multinationals do vary in

- Their capability to expand their international operations
- Intra-firm transnational trading among subsidiaries
- Exploitation of the firm's specific advantage
- Exploitation of host country resources
- Transnational organization and management for corporate gains

In this book, an MNE is defined as a business entity that operates in multiple (i.e., more than one) countries with effective control over its operations by way of FDI. Under this definition, a firm producing in the home country and exporting a substantial part or even whole of its production would not fall under the category of multinational, but may be termed an internationally-oriented or international firm. Thus, an Indian firm having a 10 per cent equity stake in a foreign firm with no control over its operations and management would not qualify as a multinational and would fall under the category of international firms.

13.2.1   From Multinational to Global Enterprises

Ensuing international economic integration, more and more firms across the world, in their drive to internationalize, are rapidly marching towards becoming 'global' in terms of their vision, strategy, and operations. Therefore, it becomes pertinent to develop a thorough understanding of what a global company is and what distinguishes it from other types of internationalizing firms.

A global company is characterized by a strong global positioning in terms of global assets, capabilities, brands, and its relative resilience to shocks and even to the business cycle.[4] A company does not become global by merely operating in a certain number of geographical markets. It is its ability to become globally competitive, leverage global opportunities, and acquire the required global capabilities that makes it global. The globalization strategy itself could be asset-based, capability-based, or opportunity-based. Globalization also includes global employment, i.e., the firm employs the best available people without any national barriers. A firm's financial strength is crucial to sustain entry into new foreign markets, especially when large investment is required in acquiring and building global brands. Management capability often helps in lowering the cost of succeeding in new markets and is yet another important factor that facilitates a firm to become global.

Global companies can attract stronger talent, enable cross-learning across markets, have greater opportunities to service and develop capabilities for global customers,

---

[4] Tata, Ratan, 'Driving Global Strategy', *Tata Review*, vol. XXXIX, no. 1, Jan–March 2004.

and can invest more in research and development (R&D) that can be spread over larger markets. Further, global companies can act in multiple markets to retaliate against increased competition from other large companies in any given market.

A global enterprise must have a seamless movement of people, processes, and technology across all the locations of its operations. The decision-making in the enterprise is not influenced by geographical or national boundaries. Each part of a global enterprise must have access to all other units across the globe. There must be a feeling of belongingness to the greater whole. The major advantages of a truly global enterprise are as follows:

- Ability to move its products, finances, and skilled people quickly and efficiently to those areas where they are most required at a given time.
- Leveraging its financial strength across geographical boundaries. The availability of appropriate finances at the right location and time is a tremendous advantage for multinationals and crucial in making a corporation globally successful. Investments in one region might require a considerable outlay of money and if that region cannot provide it, the global corporation has the advantage of leveraging its financial strength from other areas of the world where it has already built up reserves.
- A global company can also emerge relatively unscathed in times of political upheavals. It has the advantage of being able to relocate its finances and products to other regions during such times. Later, when political and social conditions become stable, it can return to the area it had temporarily vacated. Coca-Cola and IBM withdrew from India in the 1970s, when it was not conducive for them to carry on business here, only to return to the subcontinent two decades later when the business environment improved.

Despite rapidly growing globalization, as indicated in Exhibit 13.2, surprisingly, a majority of the world's largest companies are not global; rather, they operate regionally.

Exhibit 13.2   The myth of global enterprises

Contrary to the generally understood concept of global corporations, empirical evidence indicates that a large majority of the world's largest firms are hardly global. Far from operating in a single global market, most business activities by large firms take place within the 'triad', consisting of the three major regional blocks of the European Union (EU), North America, and Japan. Professor Rugman (2003) observes that the world's largest 500 firms have 70 per cent or more sales in their home triad. Interestingly, about 100 of the world's largest firms are actually domestic, with almost zero sales in foreign markets, about which no data was available. Among the 380 firms for which the data analysis was carried out, it is revealed that 320 firms (84.2%) were home-triad based (Table 13.1) with at least 50 per cent of sales in the home-region; 25 firms (6.6%) were bi-regional with less than 50 per cent sales in the home region and over 20 per cent sales in each of the home and the other regions, whereas 11 firms (2.9%) were host-region oriented with over

Contd

Exhibit 13.2 Contd

Table 13.1   Classification of the top 500 MNEs

Type of MNE	Number of MNEs	% of 500	% of 380	Average of % intra-regional sales
Global	9	2.0	2.6	38.2
Bi-regional	25	5.0	6.6	42.0
Host-region oriented	11	2.2	2.9	30.9
Home-region oriented	320	64.0	84.2	80.3
Insufficient data	15	2.8	3.7	40.9
No data	120	24.0		NA
Total	**500**	**100.0**	**100.0**	

Source: Based on data for 2001 from *Fortune Global 500*, 2002.

50 per cent of sales in a region other than home. Thus, only 9 firms (2.6%) qualify as truly global in their operations with 20 per cent or more sales in each of the triad regions of North America, Europe, and Asia Pacific.

Therefore, while most of the world's largest 500 companies are multinational enterprises (i.e., they produce/distribute products/services across national borders), very few are global firms with a global strategy, defined as the ability to sell the same product/services all around the world. Instead, the data indicates that most MNEs are regionally based in their home-triad market. An apparent paradox is that an MNE can be internationally active in its home-triad region but not be global.

For instance, Wal-Mart became the world's largest company in terms of sales revenues in 2001 and continued to top the list of *Fortune Global 500* in 2008. Wal-Mart's success can be attributed to a scale strategy based on reduction of costs to steadily generate its 'always low prices' formula and physical growth or market coverage. Wal-Mart's international expansion began in 1992 when it entered into a joint venture with Cifra S.A., a successful Mexican retailer. In 1998, Wal-Mart acquired a controlling interest in Cifra and officially changed the company's name to Wal-Mart of Mexico. Since 1992, Wal-Mart has also expanded into eight other international markets—Argentina, Brazil, Canada, China, Germany, South Korea, Puerto Rico, and the UK.

A more careful analysis reveals that 'international' expansion does not necessarily mean global expansion. For example, Wal-Mart is a regional company, and not a global one, as it has only about 10 per cent of its stores outside North America. At the beginning of 2008, Wal-Mart had a total of 7262 stores. It reported that 3121 of its stores were international and the remaining 4141 were in the domestic US market. Of these 3121 'international' stores, 1023 were in Mexico and another 305 were in Canada. Thus, a total of 5469 of its stores were in the North American Free Trade Agreement (NAFTA) region. Only 1793 stores are truly international, i.e., outside Wal-Mart's home-triad. In other words, Wal-Mart is still a North American business. The locus of its business model strategy and structure is regional and triad-based.

In addition, although Wal-Mart's international sales are estimated to be 16.3 per cent of total sales, extra-regional sales represent just 5.9 per cent of total sales and the NAFTA market stands at an estimated 94.1 per cent of its total sales. Further, it only has 4.8 per cent of total sales in Europe and 0.4 per cent in Asia. This means that the home-triad is still Wal-Mart's locus for strategy. Thus, the retail giant still has a long way to go before it becomes a real global retailer.

Another paradox is that an MNE can have a global strategy within its home region. This occurs if the MNE sells the same product and/or service in the same manner within the home-triad region.

Contd

Exhibit 13.2 Contd

This allows the MNE to gain all the potential economies of scale and scope and/or differentiation advantages within its home-triad market. There are no additional scale, scope, or differentiation advantages to be gained by going global or even venturing into the other parts of the triad.

If MNEs have exhausted their growth in the home-triad and still go into other regions, they then face a barrier of 'foreignness' and other risks. In other words, all of the advantages of homogeneity can be achieved within the home-triad, especially if the governments of the home-triad pursue policies of an internal market such as social, cultural, and political harmonization (as in the EU) or economic integration (as in NAFTA and ASEAN).

Source: Rugman, A.M. and Verbeke, 'A Perspective on Regional and Global Strategies of Multinational Enterprises', *Journal of International Business Studies*, 35(1), 2004, pp. 3–18; Rugman, Alan M., 'Think Regional, Act Local, Forget Global?', Rugman, Alan M. and C. Brain, 'Multinational Enterprises Are Regional, Not Global', *The Multinational Business Review*, vol. 11, no. 11, Spring 2003, pp. 3–12; Wal-Mart Annual Report, 2008, p. 51.

13.3 TYPES OF MULTINATIONALS

Multinationals can be classified under various heads depending upon criteria used, such as investment, operations, management orientation, etc.

13.3.1 On the Basis of Investment

Direct investment enterprise comprises those entities that are

Associates An enterprise in which a non-resident investor owns between 10 and 50 per cent

Subsidiaries An enterprise in which a non-resident investor owns more than 50 per cent

Branches Unincorporated enterprises wholly or jointly owned by a non-resident investor

To illustrate this classification, ownership and control of a hypothetical MNE operating in countries X, Y, and Z is depicted in Fig. 13.3.

The per cent of ownership of parent P located in country X depending on the investment made is as follows:

	Per cent of ownership by P
Country X	
A is a subsidiary of parent company P, 100% controlled by P	100%
B is a subsidiary of A, which owns 60% of B	60%
C is an associate of B, which owns 12% of C	7.2%

	Per cent of ownership by P

Country Y

D is a subsidiary of parent company P, which owns 70% of D	70%
E is a subsidiary of D, which owns 65% of E	45.5%
G is a subsidiary of E, which owns 60% of G	27.3%
F is an associate of E, which owns 25% of F, and F is an associate of G, which owns 30% of F	19.6%

Country Z

H is a subsidiary of P, which owns 80% of H and an associate of I, which owns 20% of H	80%
I is a subsidiary of H, which owns 55% of I	44%
J is an associate of I, which owns 15% of J	6.6%
K is a subsidiary of J, which owns 80% of K, and K is an associate of I, which owns 30% of K	18.5%

International standards developed by IMF/OECD recommend the use of a 'fully consolidated systems' (FCS) to identify an indirectly owned direct investment

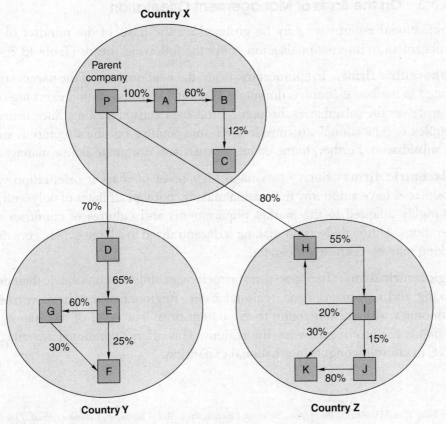

Fig. 13 3   MNE structure: Ownership and control

relationship. It applies not to the concept of ownership but to that of direct or indirect control in the MNE's structure. In Fig. 13.3, the parent company P exerts direct or indirect control over A and B in country X; D, E, F, and G in country Y; H, I and K in country Z. Therefore, these firms belong to the MNE whereas firm C in country X and firm J in country Z are controlled by some other group and these do not belong to the group or MNE.

13.3.2 On the Basis of Operations

- *Horizontally integrated multinationals* have manufacturing operations located in different countries to produce same or similar products. They have multi-plant firms replicating roughly the same activities in many locations.
- *Vertically integrated multinationals* have manufacturing operations in certain country/countries to manufacture products that serve as inputs to their production establishments in other country/countries. Such firms fragment production geographically into stages in multiple countries on the basis of factor intensities.
- *Diversified multinationals* have manufacturing operations located in different countries that are either horizontally or vertically integrated.

13.3.3 On the Basis of Management Orientation

Multinational enterprises may be grouped on the basis of the mindset of the top management to internationalization under the following[5] heads (Table 13.2).

Ethnocentric firms   In ethnocentric firms, the headquarters of the parent company, located in the home country, dominate the strategic decisions and exert high level of control over the subsidiaries through centralized decision making. Such firms have a complex organizational structure in the home country but the structure is simple in the subsidiaries. Further, home country expatriates dominate senior management.

Polycentric firms   Such firms have high level of market orientation wherein subsidiaries have autonomy in decision making. Foreign affiliates of polycentric firms are highly adapted to the market requirements and cultures of countries of their operations. Although decision-making is decentralized to a large extent, core decision-making may be centrally integrated.

Regiocentric firms   In regiocentric firms, foreign affiliates consolidate their decision-making and organization on regional basis. Regional offices have considerable autonomies with accountability to the parent firm. The level of integration is high *within* the regions but *not across* the regions. This offers operational advantage to an MNE in consolidating its international expansion.

---

[5] Chakravarthy, Balaji S. and Howard V. Perlmutter, 'Strategic Planning for a Global Business', *Columbia Journal of World Business*, 20(2), 1985, p. 5.

Table 13.2   Orientation of an international enterprise

Orientation		Ethnocentric	Polycentric	Regiocentric	Geocentric
1.	Mission	Profitability (viability)	Public acceptance (legitimacy)	Both profitability and public acceptance (viability and legitimacy)	
2.	Governance ■ Direction of goal setting	Top down	Bottom up (each subsidiary decides upon local objectives)	Mutually negotiated between region and its subsidiaries	Mutually negotiated at all levels of the corporation
	■ Communication	Hierarchical with headquarters giving high volume of orders, commands and advice	Little communication to and from headquarters and between subsidiaries	Both vertical and lateral communication within region	Both vertical and lateral communication within company
	■ Allocation of resources	Investment opportunities decided at headquarters	Self-supporting subsidiaries, no cross-subsidies	Regions allocate resources under guidelines from headquarters	Worldwide projects, allocation influenced by local and headquarters' managers
3.	Strategy	Global integrative	National responsiveness	Regional integrative and national responsiveness	Global integrative and national responsiveness
4.	Structure	Hierarchical product divisions	Hierarchical area divisions, with autonomous national units	Product and regional organizations tied through a matrix	A network of organizations, (including some stakeholders and competitor organizations)
5.	Culture	Home country	Host country	Regional	Global

Sources: Perlmutter, H.V., 'Building the Symbiotic Societal Enterprise: A Social Architecture for the Future', in *World Futures* (3/4), 1984, pp. 271–84; Heenan, D.A. and H.V. Perlmutter, *Multinational Organisational Development: A Social Architecture Perspective*, Reading, MA: Addison-Wesley, 1979.

Geocentric firms   Organization of geocentric firms is relatively more complex and inter-dependent than that of the other types. The firm follows a collaborative approach to decision-making between headquarters and subsidiaries. Such firms use universal standards for evaluation and control. The best workforce is employed for key positions from across the world. Most geocentric firms develop global products while taking into account sensitivities of local and regional cultures and their peculiar market needs.

13.4   IMPACT OF MNEs ON HOST ECONOMIES

Views on the impact of MNEs on host economies are polarized. Multinational corporations are considered to spread wealth, transfer technologies, and improve skill base, promote research and development, and benefit customers by raising their standard of living. On the other hand, MNEs are often blamed for influencing the host country's politicians and institutions to further their own interests, as also for transfer of inappropriate technology, dumping of obsolete technology, cultural imperialism, ruthless exploitation of resources, and promoting hostile mergers and acquisitions and unhealthy market competition.

13.4.1   Positive Effects of MNEs

Some positive effects of MNEs are discussed in this section.

Bring in FDI   Multinational enterprises bring in foreign direct investment (FDI) to the host countries, leading to their industrial and economic development.

Transfer of technology   Multinationals serve as agents for transfer of technical know-how, managerial skills, and marketing strategies to the host countries. This has a favourable impact on overall industrial growth.

Promote competition   The operations of MNEs increase competitive intensities in the host countries which compel domestic firms to improve their efficiency in terms of costs, product attributes, and marketing. Post-liberalization, the opening up of the Indian market to foreign MNEs has increased the level of competition in the Indian market, leading to improvements in overall product quality and marketing efficiency.

Promote research and development   Multinationals have a positive impact in promoting research and development in host countries, as depicted in Fig. 13.4.
Potential benefits from internationalization of research and development[6] by MNEs include

- Improved structure and performance of national innovative systems (NIS)
- Contribution to human resource development, such as R&D, employment, training, support to higher education, reverse brain drain effect
- Knowledge spillovers
- Contribution to industrial upgrading

However, such internationalization efforts by MNEs may result in the downsizing of existing local R&D or loss of technology, unfair compensation for locally developed intellectual property, technology leakage, and race to the bottom and unethical behaviour in the host countries.

[6] UNCTAD, World Investment Report 2005, *Transnational Corporations and the Internationalization of R&D*, p. 181; Liang, Guoyong, 'New Competition: Foreign Direct Investment and Industrial Development in China', *Research in Management*, ERIM Ph.D. Series, 47, 2004, p. 171.

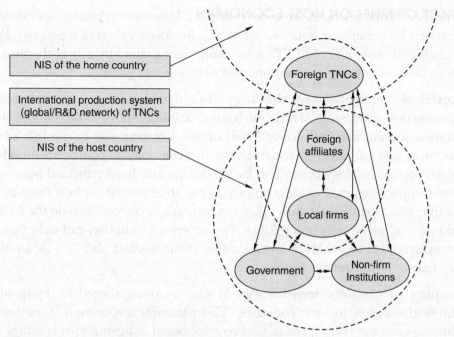

Fig. 13.4 Impact of MNEs on national innovative systems

Source: UNCTAD, World Investment Report 2005, *Transnational Corporations and the Internationalization of R&D*, p. 181; Liang, Guoyong, 'New Competition: Foreign Direct Investment and Industrial Development in China', *Research in Management*, ERIM Ph.D. Series, 47, 2004, p. 171.

Benefit customers Prior to liberalization, India was a sellers' market with few choices available to its customers. It was not uncommon for customers in India to wait for years to get the delivery of several household goods and services, such as a telephone connection, liquefied petroleum gas (LPG), a car or a scooter. The arrival of MNEs in India not only improved the product quality but also brought in the concept of 'efficient services to the customers' and made products available without any waiting period.

Promote exports in the host economies Manufacturing operations of MNEs reduce the need for imports, resulting in import substitution in host economies. Also, their operations add capacities to promote exports. Multinational enterprises in low-cost developing countries strategically use these countries as their bases to manufacture and export to high-cost developed country markets.

13.4.2 Negative Effects of MNEs

Influencing host-country government decisions MNEs are often mammoth corporations. The total turnover of a number of MNEs, such as Wal-Mart, British Petroleum, Exxon Mobil, Royal Dutch, etc., is much higher than the total GDP of a number of small countries. Thus, MNEs do possess massive financial strength besides state-of-art technology, extensive networking, and large workforce. Due to enormous financial and networking strengths, MNEs exert their influence and power on the political decision-making in the host economies. Low-income countries especially get influenced by conditions imposed by MNEs for foreign direct investment. Further, the goals and objectives of MNEs principally cater to the interests of the firm rather than to the host country's aspirations and development goals.

Transfer of inappropriate technology In order to maintain a technological edge in production processes, MNEs do transfer capital-intensive technology to host countries. In countries with lower levels of development, due to the lack of skilled manpower and supporting industries, such technology becomes unsuitable. The sophisticated technology brought in by MNEs has also been criticized because of its adverse impact on job creation, contrary to the objectives of the host country. MNE operations also increase the host country's technology-dependence on the MNE and lead to a decline in indigenous R&D. The superior technology not only provides a competitive edge to an MNE over existing industries but also acts as an effective entry barrier to indigenous firms.

Dumping of obsolete technology MNEs are often alleged to dump obsolete technologies in low-income countries. This phenomenon is more common when technology transfer takes place to host country-based indigenous firms rather than to the MNE's own subsidiaries.

Cultural imperialism In order to retain its global identity, MNEs often adopt their global business strategies across subsidiaries in host countries across the world. Marketing systems, work culture, and management philosophies are perceived as cultural invasion in many host countries. Popularly known as its 'cultural chernobyl', Walt Disney's failure in its French theme park Euro Disney is a classic case of French resistance to 'American cultural imperialism'. McDonald's international expansion has had a significant effect over eating habits in many countries. McDonald's meticulous supply chain management and use of franchising as a business model has also influenced the service industry in several countries. The influence has been so significant that MNEs are often seen to wield the effect of 'McDonaldization', a symbol of American cultural imperialism.

Exploitation of host country resources MNEs are often accused of indiscriminate exploitation of natural resources, such as mineral wealth, forests, water, land, and manpower of host countries with the sole objective of meeting their global economic targets. The high returns earned are also denied to the host economies as these are expatriated to the MNEs' home countries.

Perceived as agents of neo-colonialism It is a well-known fact that several East India Companies from Europe came to India in late seventeenth century mainly for trade and subsequently became instrumental in the colonial rule that lasted for more than two centuries. In India, and many other erstwhile colonial countries, multinationals are often perceived as a threat to the country's sovereignty, perpetrating a new form of colonialism.

Promotes unhealthy market competition   The tendency of MNE affiliates to opt for non-price models of rivalry has important implications for market structure and competition in the host developing countries. MNE affiliates' preference to operate at a larger scale, depend more heavily on marketing and advertising, and invest in R&D activities so as to differentiate their products and raise barriers to entry of new firms. These 'contrived barriers' to entry explain the continued domination by MNE affiliates of several brand-sensitive consumer goods industries despite the host country's government policies seeking to curb monopolies. Additionally, MNEs discourage competition among their subsidiaries as a part of their global integration strategy through globally integrated financial policies, transfer pricing, etc. This adversely affects the local industry.

Promotes hostile mergers and acquisitions   As a part of business entry strategy, MNEs often engage in hostile mergers and acquisitions (M&As), resulting in stifling of domestic enterprises. Coke's ugly takeover of Parle is one such classic example in India's business history. Coke's takeover led to the virtual annihilation of Indian soft-drink firms from the market, leading to market duopoly in the soft-drink industry.

Crowding out domestic entrepreneurship   The financial muscle, extensive networking, superior technology, and skills base of MNEs make it difficult for domestic firms to withstand competition. It leads to crowding out of domestic firms and indigenous entrepreneurship.

Limited benefits to host countries   MNEs seeking markets produce and sell their output in the host economies, but this hardly has any positive impact on the host economies' balance of payments. Supporting industries and suppliers may not benefit if MNEs have vertical integration and produce most of their requirement themselves.

Circumventing host countries' regulatory framework   MNEs often circumvent rules and regulations of host countries. Global integration among MNE affiliates is used for achieving MNE's corporate objectives. For instance, transfer pricing is widely used as a tool to abuse the host country regulations by way of exhibiting higher profits in low-tax countries or tax heavens so as to evade host country's taxes and maximize their own profits.

13.5   MEASURING THE EXTENT OF MNE'S INTERNATIONALIZATION

A variety of criteria can be used for assessing how multinational a multinational is. It may include one or more aspects of the following.

13.5.1   Size

A multinational is perceived to have a mammoth size. Major criteria used for determining the size of a firm include sales revenue, profits, market value, return of equity, etc. It is generally believed that firm size has a positive influence on its internationalization, though not accepted universally. A number of multilateral organizations do ignore small and medium enterprises while compiling information on MNCs.

13.5.2 Structure

Structure implies the number of countries an MNE operates in and the citizenship of its top managers and corporate owners influence the level of internationalization of an MNE.

13.5.3 Performance

The extent of commitment of the firm's resources to foreign operations and the reward from these commitments may be used to determine an MNE's performance. Various performance based parameters, such as foreign sales, profits, assets, etc., may be used to gauge the extent of a firm's internationalization.

About 99 per cent sales revenue of Nokia came from foreign sales in 2005 whereas Nokia gets merely 1 per cent sales from its home market. Besides, multinationals with highest foreign sales (Fig. 13.5) include Novartis (98.86%), Roche Group (98.59%), Nestle SA (98.38%), Liberty Global Inc (97.38%), Thomson Corporation (96.55%), Philips Electronics (96.51%), Volvo (93.63%), CRH Plc (91.94%), and GlaxoSmithkline (91.89%).

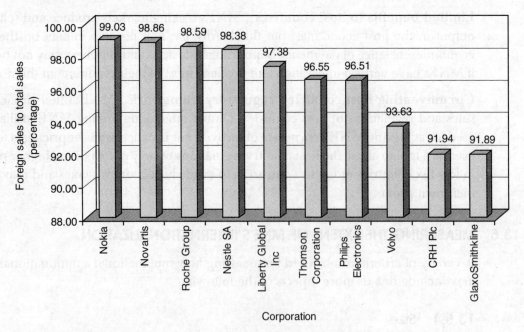

Fig. 13.5 World's top 10 companies with highest share of foreign sales*

* Figures for 2005.

Source: World Investment Report 2007, *Transnational Corporations, Extractive Industries and Development*, New York and Geneva: United Nations, 2007, pp. 229–31.

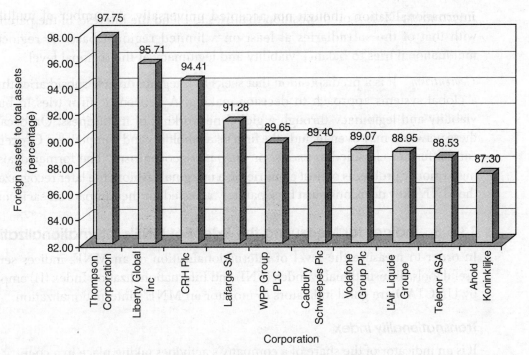

Fig.13.6 World's top 10 companies with highest share of foreign assets*

* Figures for 2005.

Source: World Investment Report 2007, *Transnational Corporation, Extractive Industries and Development,* United Nations, New York and Geneva, 2007, pp. 229–31.

Thompson Corporation has got 97.75 per cent of its assets overseas in 2005 as depicted in Fig. 13.6, followed by Liberty Global Inc 95.71 per cent, CRH Plc 94.41 per cent, Lafarge SA 91.28 per cent, WPP Group PLC 89.65 per cent, Cadbury Schweepes Plc 89.40 per cent, Vodafone Group Plc 89.07 per cent, L'Air Liquide Groupe 88.95 per cent, Telenor ASA 88.53 per cent, and Ahold Koninklijke 87.30 per cent.

13.5.4 Management Orientation

Attitude and behaviour of top management towards internationalization, though abstract, are crucial factors in determining the extent of a firm's internationalization. Management orientation of a multinational may vary from home country (ethnocentric) orientation to global (geocentric) orientation, also known as EPRG concept:

Ethnocentrism It is a predisposition where all strategic decisions are guided by the values and interests of the parent firm. Such a firm is predominantly concerned with its viability worldwide and legitimacy only in its home country.

Polycentrism It is a predisposition where strategic decisions are tailored to suit the cultures of various countries in which the MNE competes. A polycentric multinational is primarily concerned with legitimacy in every country that it operates in, even if that means some loss of profits.

Regiocentrism   It is a predisposition that tries to blend the interests of the parent firm with that of the subsidiaries at least on a limited regional basis. A regiocentric multinational tries to balance viability and legitimacy at the regional level.

Geocentrism   It is a predisposition that seeks to integrate diverse subsidiaries through a global systems approach to decision-making. A geocentric firm tries to balance viability and legitimacy through a global networking of its business. On occasions, these networks may even include the firm's stakeholders and competitors. Geocentrism can be further classified as *enclave* or *integrative* geocentrism. The former deals with high-priority problems of host countries in a marginal fashion; the later recognizes that the MNE's key decisions must be separately assessed for their impact on each country.

13.5.5   Indices for Measuring the Extent of MNE's Internationalization

In order to measure the level of internationalization of an MNE, indices serve as useful tools. Transnationality index (TNI) and Internationalization Index (II) employed by UNCTAD are good indicators to monitor an MNE's internationalization.

Transnationality index

It is an indicator of the share of a company's activities taking place in a country other than its own. It is calculated as the average of the following three ratios:

- Foreign assets to total assets
- Foreign sales to total sales
- Foreign employment to total employment

Thomson Corporation, Canada has been ranked[7] as an MNE with the highest TNI (97.2%) in 2005 (Fig. 13.7), followed by Liberty Global Inc, US (96.5%), Roche Group, Switzerland (90.5%), WPP Group PLC, UK (87.8%), Philips Electronics, Netherlands (87.4%), Nestle SA, Switzerland (86.8%), Cadbury Schweepes PLC, UK (86.7%), Vodafone Group Plc, UK (82.4%), Lafarge SA, France (81.9%), and Sabmiller Plc, UK (81.1%).

Internationalization index

It is calculated as the number of foreign affiliates divided by the number of all affiliates. Only majority owned affiliates are taken into consideration while computing the internationalization index (II).

Firms with the highest II among the top 100 non-financial MNCs in 2005, as depicted in Fig. 13.8 include[8] InBev SA, Belgium (98.3%), Mittal Steel Company

[7] World Investment Report 2007, *Transnational Corporations, Extractive Industries and Development*, New York and Geneva: United Nations, 2007, pp. 229–31.

[8] World Investment Report 2007, *Transnational Corporations, Extractive Industries and Development*, New York and Geneva: United Nations, 2007, pp. 229–31.

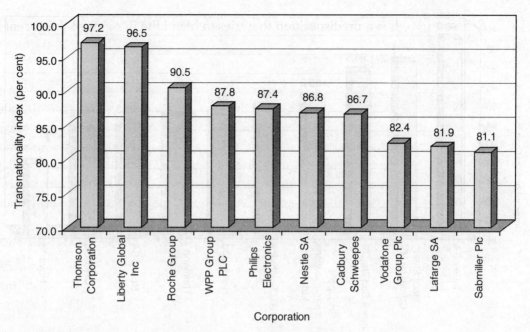

Fig. 13.7 World's top 10 companies with highest transnationality*

* Figures for 2005.

Source: World Investment Report 2007, *Transnational Corporations, Extractive Industries and Development,* New York and Geneva: United Nations, 2007, pp. 229–31.

NV, Netherlands (97.1%), Comex Sab De CV, Mexico (96.6%), Singapore Telecommunications Ltd, Singapore (95.2%), GlaxoSmithkline, UK (94.7%), Holcim Ltd, Switzerland (94.3%), Thomson Corporation, Canada (94.2%), Nestle SA, Switzerland (93.8%), CRH Plc, Ireland (93.6%) and Novartis, Switzerland (91.7%).

13.6 EMERGING MNEs FROM RAPIDLY DEVELOPING ECONOMIES

Companies from rapidly developing economies (RDEs) are on the fast track to become major twenty-first century multinationals and would play an important role in the radical transformation of industries and market access worldwide. These firms are fast gaining global market share, making worldwide acquisitions and emerging as important customers, business partners, and competitors for the world's largest companies.

These emerging multinationals from RDEs with low production costs, leadership, appealing products and services, state-of-art facilities and systems with their overseas expansion are likely to radically transform industries and markets around the world. These emerging multinationals are likely to offer challenges to the established companies in quest for innovation, in competition for supplies, in search for talents, in worldwide acquisitions, and in capturing markets.

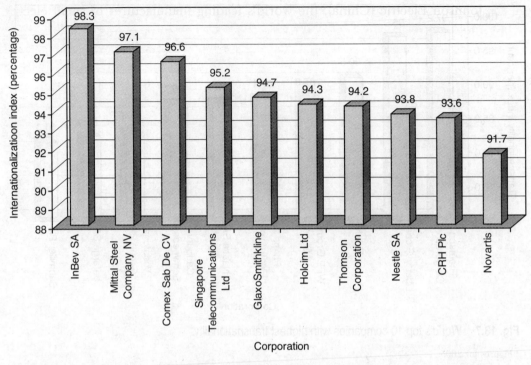

Fig. 13.8 World's top 10 companies with highest level of internationalization*

* Figures for 2005.

Source: World Investment Report 2007, *Transnational Corporations, Extractive Industries and Development,* New York and Geneva: United Nations, 2007, pp. 229–31.

The Boston Consulting Group has identified 100 leading RDE-based companies[9] that already have combined annual revenue of US$715 billion and are growing at an annual average rate of 24 per cent. Forces of globalization, such as access to international markets by way of world-wide economic liberalization, multilateral trading systems under the World Trade Organisation (WTO), access to the Internet and low-cost communication technologies, and improvement in the means of transport have boosted their internationalization drive. Some of the prominent emerging MNEs from RDEs are

- Bharat Forge (India), now the world's second largest forging company
- Ranbaxy Pharmaceuticals (India), among the top 10 generic pharmaceutical players in the world
- Wipro (India), the world's largest third-party engineering services company
- BYD Company (China), the world's largest manufacturer of nickel-cadmium batteries with a 23 per cent share of the market for mobile-hand-set batteries

---

[9] 'The New Global Challengers', The Boston Consulting Group, May 2006, pp. 5–26.

- Johnson Electric (China), the world's leading manufacturer of small electric motors
- Pearl River Piano Group (China), the global volume leader in piano manufacturing
- China International Marine Container Group Company (China), with a 50 per cent share of the marine container market, supplying the top 10 shipping companies globally
- Chunlan Group Corporation (China) with a 25 per cent share of the Italian air-conditioner market
- Galanz Group Company (China), commanding a 45 per cent share of the microwave market in Europe and a 25 per cent share in the US
- Hisense (China), the number one seller of flatpanel TVs in France
- Techtronic Industries Company (China), now the number one supplier of power tools to Home Depot in the US
- Cemex (Mexico), which has developed into one of the world's largest cement producers
- Embraer (Brazil), which has surpassed Bombardier as the market leader in regional jets
- Nemak (Mexico), one of the world's premier suppliers of cylinder head and block castings for the automotive industry.

13.6.1 Advent of Indian Multinationals

Consequent to economic liberalization in India, which began in 1991, the licensing system was dismantled to facilitate setting up industries and liberalization of norms for foreign direct investment. At the time, it was feared that the Indian industry would be swamped by multinational companies. However, economic liberalization opened up India's industrial sector for multinational enterprises, paving way for entry of several MNEs into India.

The liberalization experience reveals that not only have Indian companies fought off the MNC challenge, but also they have taken the commercial battle overseas by acquiring scores of companies abroad. Indian businesses are fast expanding globally and this brings them closer to becoming multinationals. *Fortune* included seven Indian companies, i.e., Indian Oil, Reliance Industries, Bharat Petroleum, Hindustan Petroleum, Tata Steel, Oil & Natural Gas Corporation (ONGC), and State Bank of India in its Global 500 list for the year 2008 (Table 13.3). Also, as of 2008, the rankings of Indian companies had considerably improved over the previous years.

All these firms are primarily from the petroleum sector. However, a large number of Indian firms from diverse sectors, such as automobiles, pharmaceuticals, engineering, IT services, non-ferrous metal, steel, food and beverages, telecom services, financial services, and consumer electronics are in the process of becoming multinationals, as projected by the Boston Consulting Group (Table 13.4).

Indian companies have become global, with their presence not only in the major markets of the US, the UK, China, Germany, Japan, Switzerland, Australia, Korea,

Table 13.3 Indian companies in fortune global 500

Country rank	Company	Global 500 rank				Revenues 2008 ($ millions)	City
		2008	2007	2006	2005		
1	Indian Oil	116	135	153	170	57,427	New Delhi
2	Reliance Industries	206	269	342	417	35,915	Mumbai
3	Bharat Petroleum	287	325	368	429	27,873	Mumbai
4	Hindustan Petroleum	290	336	378	436	27,718	Mumbai
5	Tata Steel	315				25,707	Mumbai
6	Oil and Natural Gas Corporation	335	369	402	454	24,032	Dehradun
7	State Bank of India	380	495	498	nil	22,402	Mumbai

Source: Fortune Global 500, 21 July 2008, 2007, 2006, and 2005.

Table 13.4 Indian multinationals of the future

Company	Sector	Turnover (in US$)
Bajaj Auto	Two wheelers	1.81 billion
Bharat Forge	Auto components	685 million
Cipla	Pharmaceuticals	690 million
Crompton Greaves	Engineering equipment	567 million
Dr. Reddy's Lab	Pharmaceuticals	539.26 million
Hindalco Industries	Non-ferrous metals	2.58 billion
Infosys Technologies	IT services	2152 million
Larsen & Toubro	Heavy engineering	3.29 billion
Mahindra & Mahindra	Automobiles	1.85 billion
ONGC	Oil exploration	8.6 billion
Ranbaxy	Pharmaceuticals	1.178 billion
Reliance Group	Diverse business	19.97 billion
Satyam Computer	IT services	1.06 billion
Tata Motors	Automobiles	4.57 billion
TCS	IT services	2.94 billion
Tata Steel	Steel	4.94 billion
Tata Tea	Food and beverages	683 million
TVS Motor Company	Two wheelers	740 million
Videocon Industries	Consumer electronics	1.27 billion
VSNL	Telecom services	757 million
Wipro	IT services	2.30 billion

Source: 'The Giants Ahead', *Hindustan Times*, 8 June 2006.

and Singapore, but also in countries, such as France, Sweden, Brazil, Malaysia, Thailand, Iran, Russia, Ukraine, Romania, Spain, etc. A snapshot of major Indian MNCs is given below:

- Indian pharmaceutical firm Ranbaxy Laboratory Ltd is ranked among the top 10 generic companies worldwide. It has manufacturing operations in eleven countries with a ground presence in 49 countries and its products are available in over 125 countries. Its overseas markets account for 80 per cent of its global sales.

- Aditya Birla Group, with a market capitalization of US$28 million, gets 50 per cent of its revenues from overseas operations. It operates in 25 countries across four continents with a strong workforce of about 100,000 of over 25 nationalities.
- The Indian IT giant Infosys operates in over 22 global locations employing over 103,000 persons. It receives 98 per cent of its total revenue of US$4 billion from overseas markets.
- Indian IT services firm Tata Consultancy Services (TCS) received 87.5 per cent of its total revenue of US$5.7 billion from overseas markets, operating in over 42 countries, and employing 120,000 IT professionals.
- ONGC, through its overseas arms, ONGC Videsh Ltd operates 35 overseas projects in 17 foreign countries, and is ranked as Asia's best oil and gas company in a survey conducted by *Global Finance,* a US Magazine.
- Asian Paints ranks among top 10 paint companies of the world with an annual turnover of US$1.1 billion, having 29 paint manufacturing operations in 22 countries and catering to consumers in 65 countries.

Describing the historical background, the chapter brings out the concept of multinational enterprises. The chapter classifies the MNEs on the basis of investment, operations, and management orientations. Frequently debated positive and negative effects of MNEs have also been examined. Imperial criteria used to measure the extent of internationalization of MNEs have also been explicated. During the recent years, there has been remarkable growth of multinationals from rapidly developing economies including India.

SUMMARY

In simple terms, a firm operating in more than one country may be termed as a multinational. We refer to an MNE as a business entity that operates in multiple (i.e., more than one) countries with effective control over its operations by way of foreign direct investment (FDI).

Multinationals are prominent drivers of globalization. The rapid growth of multinationals in the post-war period had greatly affected the business norms across the world with growing emphasis from international to global business strategies. It has been observed that two-third of the world trade is carried out by MNEs and one-third of the total world trade is intra-firm trade, making it imperative that business managers understand MNEs well.

Theoretical differences between various terms, such as, 'international', 'multi-domestic', 'transnational', and 'global', have been explained on the basis of the firm's extent of internationalization and control and integration of its international operations. Consequent to globalization, a number of firms are moving towards global strategies, but a majority of the world's largest firms are surprisingly not global. A foreign enterprise is known as an *associate* wherein a non-resident investor owns between 10–50 per cent equity, a *subsidiary* if a non-resident investor owns more than 50 per cent, and a *branch* if the unincorporated enterprise is jointly or wholly owned by a non-resident investor. An MNE may either be horizontally or vertically integrated or diversified in its operations. On the basis of the mindset of its top management to internationalization, an MNE may be ethnocentric, polycentric, geocentric, or regiocentric in nature. An indicator of the share of a company's activities taking place in a country other than its own is known as transnationality index, whereas the ratio of the number of foreign affiliates to the total number of affiliates in the firm is termed as its internationalization index. Although more than 90 per cent of world's largest MNEs have a home base in the triad countries, i.e., the US, the Europe, and Japan, a number of companies from rapidly developing economies, including India, are fast emerging as multinationals.

Multinationals can be classified under various heads on the basis of investment, operations, and management orientation.

Multinationals have a mix of positive and negative impacts on host economies. The advantages of MNEs are that they bring in foreign direct investment, effect transfer of technology, promote competition, benefit customers, promote exports in the host economies, and promote research and development. At the same time, MNEs can adversely affect host economies by influencing host country government decisions, transferring inappropriate technology, dumping obsolete technology, being instrumental in cultural imperialism, exploiting the host country's resources, being seen as agents of neo-colonialism, promoting unhealthy market competition, promoting hostile mergers and acquisitions, crowding out domestic entrepreneurship, allowing limited benefits to host countries, and circumventing host countries' regulatory frameworks.

Criteria used for measuring the extent of internationalization of MNEs include size, structure, performance, and management orientation. Transnationality index and internationalization index developed by UNCTAD are the most accepted and widely used methods for measuring the internationalization of an MNE. The chapter has highlighted the significance of emerging multinationals from rapidly developing economies, a phenomenon more in play due to globalization. The advent of Indian multinationals has also been discussed.

KEY TERMS

Associate   An enterprise in which a non-resident investor owns between 10 and 50 per cent equity.

Branches   Unincorporated enterprises wholly or jointly owned by a non-resident investor.

Ethnocentrism   A predisposition where all strategic decisions are guided by the values and interests of the parent firm.

Geocentrism   A predisposition that seeks to integrate diverse subsidiaries through a global systems approach to decision-making.

Internationalization index (II)   The ratio of the number of foreign affiliates to the total number of affiliates in the firm.

Multinational firm   A business entity that operates in multiple (i.e., more than one) countries

with effective control over its operations by way of foreign direct investment.

Polycentrism   A predisposition where strategic decisions are made to suit the countries of the firm's operations.

Regiocentrism   A predisposition that tries to blend the interest of the parent firm with that of subsidiaries on a regional basis.

Subsidiary   An enterprise in which a non-resident investor owns more than 50 per cent equity.

Transnationality index (TNI)   The average of the ratios of foreign assets to total assets; foreign sales to total sales; foreign employment to total employment.

CONCEPT REVIEW QUESTIONS

1. Critically evaluate and explain the concept of a multinational enterprise.

2. 'In spite of rapid globalization, most MNCs focus on their home markets, belying the concept of global corporations.' Critically examine with suitable examples.

3. Differentiate between associates, subsidiaries, and branches of an MNE.

4. Critically examine the impact of MNEs on host economies.

5. Evaluate the major reasons for the increase in the number of multinationals from rapidly developing economies.

6. Write short notes on
   (a) Geocentrism
   (b) Polycentrism
   (c) Transnationality index
   (d) Internationalization index

CRITICAL THINKING QUESTIONS

1. Select a few firms having considerable revenue and find out the extent of their internationalization using transnationality index and internationalization index. Compare your results for these firms with firms having the highest level of internationalization.

2. Identify a firm with international presence and prepare a detailed structure of its ownership and control.

PROJECT ASSIGNMENTS

1. Visit a multinational firm in your vicinity and find out its management orientation. Use your assessment to classify it under the EPRG framework explained in the chapter. Discuss your observations in class.

2. Based on interactions with various stakeholders, critically evaluate the costs and benefits of MNEs operating in your country.

3. Meet the senior officials of an Indian MNE or an MNE from a rapidly developing economy and identify the problems in its expansion in global markets.

CASE STUDY

Ranbaxy: No more an Indian multinational

Background

Ranbaxy's journey to become a multinational is an interesting story of how it transformed from a petty distributor of foreign medicines to India's largest pharmaceutical company. Presently Ranbaxy has manufacturing facilities in 11 countries: the US, Romania, Malaysia, Ireland, India, China, Vietnam, Nigeria, South Africa, Japan, and Brazil. The company has ground operations in 49 countries (Fig. C.1) and serving its customers in over 125 countries employing 12,000 personnel from 50 nationalities. The company's international business

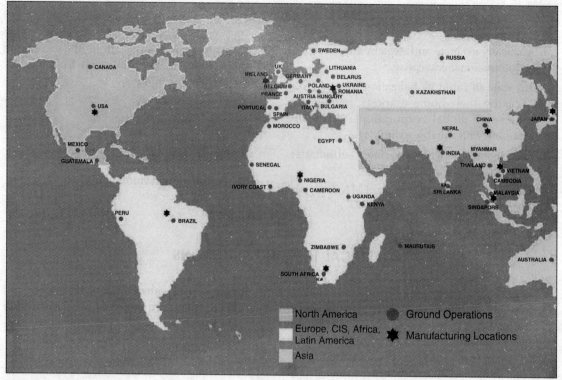

North America
Europe, CIS, Africa, Latin America
Asia
● Ground Operations
✦ Manufacturing Locations

Fig. C.1 Ranbaxy's global presence

comprises about 80 per cent of its total sales.[1] Besides, Ranbaxy is among the top ten generic companies of the world. In February 2004, Ranbaxy joined the elite club of billion dollar companies achieving global sales of US$1 billion. Its revenue has shown an impressive annual compound growth rate of 19 per cent over the last five years. Moreover, it aspires to achieve a revenue target of US$5 billion by 2012 and become amongst the top five generic companies of the world.

The genesis of Ranbaxy dates back to 1937 when cousins Ranjit Singh and Gurbax Singh, formed a company at Amritsar and named it Ranbaxy & Co. The company's primary aim was to distribute locally the medicines of foreign pharmaceutical companies. Initially, it got sole distributorship of a Japanese pharmaceutical company, Shiniogi that manufactured anti-tuberculosis medicines and vitamins. In 1951, when Gurbax Singh was experiencing financial crisis, the company was

bought by Bhai Mohan Singh who hardly had any experience of dealing in pharma products. In order to conserve foreign exchange and enhance indigenous manufacturing capability, the Government of India promulgated a new rule in 1956 restricting import of finished pharmaceutical products and requiring packaging of imported bulk drugs in India. This compelled Indian firms engaged in pharma business to establish their own packaging facilities. Consequently, Ranbaxy established its first plant at Okhla in New Delhi in 1960, aimed at creating packing facility for imported bulk drugs.

In June 1961, Ranbaxy was incorporated as Ranbaxy Laboratories and the company became public in 1973. The company launched its own blockbuster formulation of diazepam under the brand name 'Calmpose' in 1968, which became India's first pharmaceutical superbrand.

---

[1] Annual Report 2007, Ranbaxy Laboratories Limited.

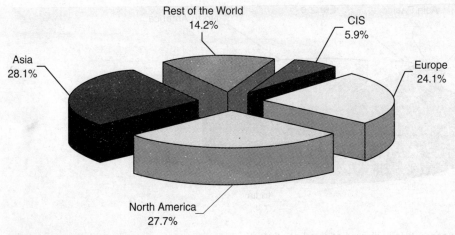

Fig. C.2   Ranbaxy's revenue composition*

* 2007 figures.

Source: Annual report 2007, Ranbaxy laboratories limited.

Ranbaxy may be regarded as truly international as it generated only 28.1 per cent of its total revenue[2] from Asia including India in 2007, as depicted in Fig. C.2, whereas North America contributed 27.7 per cent, Europe 24.1 per cent, CIS 5.9 per cent, and the rest of the world 14.2 per cent. Developed countries accounted for 40 per cent of Ranbaxy's global sales of about US$1.6 billion in 2007 whereas emerging markets for 54 per cent, and others 6 per cent. Interestingly, the company received the highest contribution of 62 per cent in its growth from the rest of the world, followed by 37 per cent from Europe, including CIS and 7 per cent from North America compared to 16 per cent from Asia.

Ranbaxy's fixed assets are geographically diversified too. India accounts for 74 per cent of its total investment of Rs 17,325 million on property, plant, and equipment followed by North America 20 per cent, Europe 3 per cent, Asia Pacific 2 per cent, and the rest of the world 1 per cent as depicted in Fig. C.3.

The unprecedented success of Ranbaxy is not just because of its competitive advantage, comprising of elements, such as low cost, global generic opportunities, worldwide demand for low-healthcare cost, and quality manufacturing, which was also available to all the other major Indian pharma companies but in its internationalization strategy that helped the company to effectively leverage its strengths globally.

The Internationalization Process

In the 1980s, the Indian pharmaceutical market was highly regulated, with the government controlling drug prices. Like most other contemporary Indian companies, Ranbaxy too was hardly serious about exports and its sole objective was to get export incentives from the government. However, Ranbaxy soon realized that the company had to internationalize if it was to grow. Profit margins overseas were substantially higher compared to the domestic market. In the early eighties, when the size of the company was considerably small, its internationalization process began through exports with the hiring of an export manager in January 1969. Ranbaxy received its first export order from Mauritius in 1970. Although it was a low-volume export order, it had high profitability vis-à-vis domestic sales that gave Ranbaxy its first exposure to a foreign market.

Independent India inherited the product patent regime from the British under the Patent Act, 1930. As the Product Patent legislation favoured

2 Annual Report 2007, Ranbaxy Laboratories Limited.

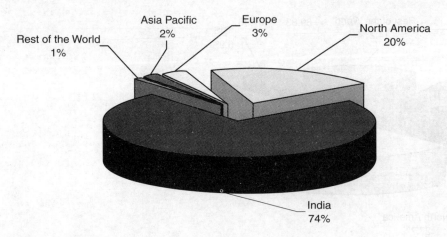

Asia Pacific
2%

Europe
3%

North America
20%

Rest of the World
1%

India
74%

Fig. C.3   Ranbaxy's geographically diversified fixed assets*

* 2005 figures.

Source: Annual Report 2005, Ranbaxy Laboratories Limited.

multinationals, Indian companies could only make those drugs that got off-patent. The prices of medicines in India were among the highest in the world. Besides, the Patent Act severely hampered the development of indigenous capability to manufacture pharmaceuticals. Despite tremendous pressure from multinationals, the Indian government took a bold decision to introduce the new Patent Act, 1970, replacing product patent with process patent with an objective to conserve foreign exchange and facilitate Indian pharma industry to develop indigenous manufacturing capability. This enabled Indian firms to sell drugs at a fraction of cost compared to multinationals not only in India but also in overseas markets.

Ranbaxy was among the first few Indian companies to take advantage of the change in the patent regime. Ranbaxy made use of reverse engineering to develop alternate processes for manufacturing drugs. It identified other developing countries for exports that, like India, did not recognize product patents. In the initial years of exports, Ranbaxy faced several legal conflicts from established multinationals, such as ICI, Roche, Glaxo, etc., in its overseas markets, but it very aptly overcame the problems. Ranbaxy's exports have rapidly grown from Rs 7324 millions in 1999 to Rs 26,411 millions in 2007. Its ratio of exports to total sales changing (Fig. C.4) from 47 per cent in 1999 to 63 per cent in 2007 reveals its rapid internationalization.

Ranbaxy was among the pioneering Indian pharmaceutical companies that set up their manufacturing operations overseas. The company set up its first joint venture in 1977 in Lagos in Nigeria with 10 per cent stake. This gave Ranbaxy access to high-priced African markets with hefty profits. Subsequently, the company set up joint ventures in Malaysia in 1982 and Indonesia in 1984. Ranbaxy's international operations at Nigeria, Malaysia, and Indonesia served as experimental laboratories for the company. Ranbaxy entered into an agreement with Eli Lilly & Co. of US in 1992 for setting up a joint venture in India to market select Eli Lilly products. It established regional headquarters in London (UK) and Raleigh (US) in 1994. Presently Ranbaxy has wholly owned subsidiaries in 48 countries (Exhibit C.1) besides an overseas joint venture.

Similar to other Indian pharmaceutical firms, Ranbaxy too had to struggle hard to improve its perception and image. Its Tongsa plant in Punjab, which commenced production in 1987, got US Food and Drug Administration (US FDA) approval in 1988. The company was granted a US patent for Doxycyline in 1990 and Cephalosporins in 1991. It received India's first approval from US FDA for an Anti Retroviral (ARV) drug under the the US President's Emergency Plan for AIDS Relief (PEPFAR).

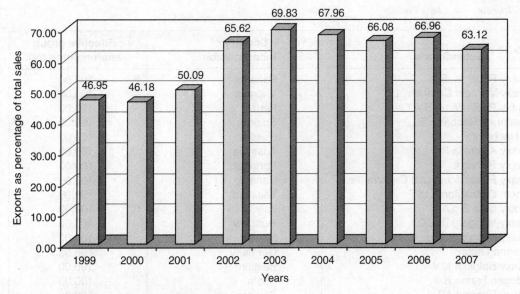

Fig. C.4   Ranbaxy progressive international focus

Source: Based on data from Ranbaxy Annual Report 2007, p. 46.

Exhibit C.1 Ranbaxy's overseas subsidiaries and joint ventures		
Subsidiaries	**Country of incorporation**	**Effective group shareholding (%)**
Ranbaxy (Netherlands) B.V. ('RNBV')	The Netherlands	100.00
Ranbaxy N.A.N.V.	Antilles, Netherlands	100.00
Ranbaxy (S.A.) (Proprietary) Ltd	South Africa	68.40
Sonke Pharmaceuticals (Pty) Ltd	South Africa	100.00
Ranbaxy Inc.	US	100.00
Ranbaxy Pharmaceuticals, Inc.	US	100.00
Ranbaxy US, Inc.	US	100.00
Ohm Laboratories Inc.	US	100.00
Ranbaxy Laboratories Inc.,	US	100.00
Ranbaxy Holdings (U.K.) Ltd	UK	100.00
Ranbaxy (U.K.) Ltd	UK	100.00
Ranbaxy Pharmacie Generiques SAS	France	100.00
Office Pharmaceutique Industriel Et Hospitalier SARL	France	100.00
Ranbaxy Ireland Ltd	Ireland	100.00
Ranbaxy (Hong Kong) Ltd	Hong Kong	100.00
Ranbaxy Egypt (L.L.C)	Egypt	100.00
Ranbaxy Poland S.P.Z.o.o.	Poland	100.00
Ranbaxy Pharmaceuticals BV	The Netherlands	100.00
Ranbaxy Europe Ltd	UK	100.00
Basics GmbH	Germany	100.00
Ranbaxy Do Brazil Ltda	Brazil	100.00

Contd

Exhibit C.1 Contd

Subsidiaries	Country of incorporation	Effective group shareholding (%)
Ranbaxy Panama, S.A.	Panama	100.00
Ranbaxy Vietnam Company Ltd	Vietnam	100.00
Ranbaxy-PRP (Perul) S.A.C.	Peru	100.00
Laboratories Ranbaxy, S.L.	Spain	100.00
ZAO Ranbaxy	Russia	100.00
Ranbaxy Australia Pty. Ltd	Australia	100.00
Ranbaxy Portugal	Portugal	100.00
Ranbaxy Pharmaceuticals Canada Inc.	Canada	100.00
Unichem Distributors Ltd*	Thailand	99.96
Ranbaxy Italia S.p.A	Italy	100.00
Ranbaxy Hungary (L.L.C.)	Hungary	100.00
Ranbaxy Mexico S.A. de C.V.	Mexico	100.00
Lapharma Gmbh	Germany	100.00
Ranbaxy Belgium N.V.	Belgium	100.00
Mundogen Farma S.A.	Spain	100.00
Ranbaxy Pharma AB	Sweden	100.00
Bounty Holdings Co. Ltd*	Thailand	99.30
Unichem Pharmaceuticals Ltd*	Thailand	98.50
Gufic Pharma Limited	India	98.00
Terapia S.A.	Romania	96.70
Ranbaxy Unichem Company Ltd	Thailand	88.56
Ranbaxy Nigeria Ltd	Nigeria	84.89
Ranbaxy (Guangzhou China) Limited	Republic of China	83.00
Ranbaxy Farmaceutica Ltda.	Brazil	93.67
Ranbaxy Signature L.L.C.	US	67.50
Ranbaxy Malaysia Sdn. Bhd.	Malaysia	68.05
Joint Ventures		
Nihon Pharmaceutical Industry Co., Ltd	Japan	50.00

* Under liquidation during 2006.
Source: Annual Report 2006, Ranbaxy Laboratories Ltd.

Ranbaxy realized that internationalization involved much more than merely fulfilling export commitments. Even in 1993, Ranbaxy was still a company more like a global trader of pharmaceutical goods with an export mindset. In 1994, Ranbaxy formulated 'Vision 2004' to evolve from about a US$100 million company to a billion dollar enterprise in 10 years time by 2004. It brought out a corporate mission to become a 'research-based international pharmaceutical company'. The key strategic elements of Ranbaxy's mission involved

• Its focus on pharmaceuticals signified that the company would not look at diversification into unrelated or even related areas and it would stick to its core area.

• The mission stated Ranbaxy's intent to be an international company. This implied a focussed and rapid expansion in foreign countries.

• The mission clarified that Ranbaxy would be a research-based company, which meant that it would discover its own proprietary innovative drugs. It would be a generic company to expand, but eventually its mission was to become a research-based company which meant in practical terms, investment in innovative research.

This was the point when Ranbaxy made many basic changes in direction and started becoming a truly international company. The basic plans for infrastructure and investment were implemented during 1994 to 1998 by way of investing in multiple subsidiaries, affiliates, joint ventures, and acquisitions. Drawing commitment for the company's mission, values, and vision from each employee was the biggest challenge. Every employee was communicated the internationalization and R&D message. The main hurdle in the period of transition was to overcome traditional mindsets. The company took great pains to take its vision and mission 1994 to every single employee at Ranbaxy, including the workers on the shop-floor. A series of presentations were made and a basic discipline was followed that at least one of the management committee members would personally attend such sessions.

A lot of doubts were raised within and outside the company about the success of its internationalization efforts. The company encountered every sort of cynicism: pharmaceuticals is a tough industry, the Indian image is poor, the Indian quality is average, the 'made in India' label is unattractive, it is only the West which can discover and make high-quality pharmaceuticals, one cannot sell Indian pharmaceutical products in the US and even

in some of the under-developed countries, and so on. However, Ranbaxy was committed to its mission and went ahead with its internationalization process.

In the early 1990s, most of Ranbaxy's major decisions, i.e., product selection, business development policy, research, and investment decisions were guided by the needs of the Indian market as India was its strongest market. Presently, as the US market is the key driver of the international pharmaceutical business, most of the core decisions of Ranbaxy, such as generic product selection, the cost structure, and the quality are driven by the US. All of Ranbaxy's manufacturing units have to be US FDA compliant. Ranbaxy operates as an integrated international pharmaceutical company with business encompassing the entire value chain in production, marketing, and distribution.

Emerging Opportunities and Challenges

Ranbaxy's key strength is in generics that makes it among the world's top 10 generic companies. The world market for generic prescription drugs was presumed to increase from US$44.4 billion in 2005 to US$83.9 billion in 2010 (Fig. C.5). The growth rate of 13 per cent in the generic industry was estimated to be much higher than for branded pharmaceuticals. Moreover, nine of the top 10 fastest

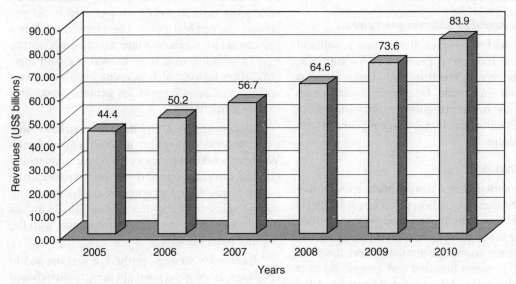

Fig. C.5 Estimated world generic revenue growth

Source: Visiongain, 2005.

growing pharma companies are generic. The world generic market is characterized by a low-price high-volume system. Global generic companies have a low mark-up on their products but make profits through high-volume sales.

The major drivers in the generics markets include

Patent Expiration

The most important growth factor for the generics market is the expiration of branded patents that allows marketing of a generic alternative. After the expiry of a patent, generic companies immediately launch the products and consequently, there is a sharp fall in prices. A generic company with 180 days exclusivity can make over 1000 per cent returns on investment with no authorized generic in the market. However, this drops by half with the authorized generic present in the market. An authorized generic is where the pharmaceutical company that markets the original patented drug will, when the drug goes off-patent, market the original drugs' generic alternative.

There are 35 major drugs expected to come off-patent by 2009 (Exhibit C.2), losing the branded industry an estimated US$40 billion. A proportion of this very high revenue amount is then available to the generic industry which will account for much of the industry's growth to 2010.

Cost containment by national governments

The markets for generics grow when a national government focuses on generics as a solution to control the respective drug bill. However, this depends on the means by which governments persuade doctors to prescribe generics and on the price differential existing between generics and branded drugs.

Price differentials

Unlike branded drugs whose main competitive factor is through drug efficacy and low side effects profile, the overwhelming principal competitive advantage in the generics market is through price. Generics have enormous markets where the price difference between branded and generic drugs is high. If the price difference between branded and generic drugs is small, then there is a little incentive to prescribe them. Not only the price

difference between competing generic drugs, but the price differential between the branded drugs and their generic equivalents matters significantly.

Price differential between branded and generic drugs varies widely from 80 per cent in the UK to 30 per cent in Germany and France, 25 per cent in Italy and Spain. In a market where branded drugs are very expensive, viz. the US, the UK, and Germany, generics flourish the best. However, in countries where branded drugs are less expensive, such as in Italy, Spain, and Japan, the generics market is relatively much smaller.

The US is the largest generic market in the world with 45 per cent share of worldwide generic revenues worth US$39.6 billion (Fig. C.6). Interestingly, Germany has a higher generic market share than Japan, 14 per cent compared to 11 per cent, but with a substantially smaller population at 82.4m compared to 127.4m. Further, the market of generics in the US is 50 per cent in terms of volume, as depicted in Fig. C.7 whereas it is 49.3 per cent in the UK, 41.1 per cent in Germany, 12 per cent in France, 9.1 per cent in Spain, and 4 per cent in Italy. The market for generics is much less pronounced in Japan than in Germany because branded drug prices are much lower, making the price difference between generics and branded drugs less attractive. The gains are immense for the company making the generic version, as by selling the drug at nearly 40 per cent to 50 per cent of the original price. Therefore, the US is a key market for Ranbaxy's internationalization strategy. In addition to a large market size and margins, other factors, such as rising health care cost and the congress support for generics make this market attractive.

Moreover, the US is the only market where exists a legal protection in the form of Hatch Waxman's Act that provides the opportunity to any company to challenge and win the nearly expiring patent of any drug, by giving the challenging company Exclusive Marketing Rights (EMR) for six months to market the product in parallel with the original patent holder.

Ranbaxy's strategy in the US market was to challenge the original patent in the US courts based on its own strength, and that too the primary patent (patent in ingredients used in the drug) rather than

	Exhibit C.2	Patent expirations: 2007–2009	
Brand	**Generic**	**Manufacturer**	**Patent expiration**
Lortel	Amlodipine and Benazepril	Novartis	31 January 2007
Norvasc	Amlodipine and Benazepril	Pfizer	31 January 2008
Actiq	Fentanyl transmucosal	Cephalon	5 February 2007
Aceon	Perindopril	Solvay	21 February 2007
Alocril	Nedocromil	Allergan	2 April 2007
Imitrex	Sumatriptan	GlaxosmithKline	28 June 2007
Geodon	Ziprasidone	Pfizer	2 September 2007
Coreg	Carvedilol	GlaxosmithKline	5 September 2007
Meridia	Sibutramine	Abbot Laboratories	11 December 2007
Mavik	Trandolapril	Abbot Laboratories	12 December 2007
Tequin	Gatifloxacin	GlaxosmithKline	25 December 2007
Zyrtec	Cetirizine	Pfizer	25 December 2008
Clarinex	Desloratadine	Schering-Plough	2007 (Generics expected 2008)
Fosamax	Alendronate	Merck	6 February 2008
Camptosar	Irinotecan	Pfizer	20 February 2008
Effexor/XR	Venlafaxine	Wyeth	13 June 2008
Zymar	Gatifloxacin	Allergan	25 June 2008
Dovonex	Calcipotriene	Bristol-Myers Squibb	29 June 2008
Kytril	Granisetron	Roche	29 June 2008
Risperdal	Risperidone	Janssen	29 June 2008
Depakote	Divalproex sodium	Abbot Laboratories	29 July 2008
Advair	Fluticasone and Salmeterol	GlaxosmithKline	12 August 2008
Servent	Salmeterol	GlaxosmithKline	12 August 2008
Casodex	Bicalutamide	Bristol-Myers Squibb	1 October 2008
Trusopt	Dorzolamide	Merck	28 October 2008
Zerit	Stavudine	Bristol-Myers Squibb	24 December 2008
Lamictal	Lamotrigine	GlaxosmithKline	22 January 2009
Vexol	Rimexolone	Alcon Labs	22 January 2009
Avandia	Rosiglitazone	GlaxosmithKline	28 February 2009
Topamax	Topiramate	Johnson & Johnson	26 March 2009
Glyset	Miglitol	Pfizer	27 July 2009
Acular	Ketorolac tromethamine	Allergan	5 November 2009
Xenical	Orlistat	Roche	18 December 2009
Valtrex	Valacyclovir	GlaxosmithKline	23 December 2009
Avelox	Moxifloxacin	Bayer	30 December 2009

Source: Express Scripts and Generic Pharmaceutical Association.

the secondary (challenging the manufacturing process), which most of the generics manufactures do, and win over the exclusive marketing rights. It employed the same strategy for many drugs to enter the US market as it did for Ceftin (Cerfuroxime Axetil). Ceftin, with a market size of US$400 million, was a blockbuster of original patent-holder Glaxo SmithKline (GSK), won by Ranbaxy. It boosted the company's turnover in 2002 to US$290 million from US$116 million in 2001 (increase of about 150%). As a result, Ranbaxy could wipe off its heavy legal cost of Rs 1 billion within a year of its US launch, i.e., in 2002 itself.

Ranbaxy also successfully invalidated Pfizer's Lipitor US patent besides obtaining US FDA approval for Simvastain 80 mg tablets with 180 day exclusivity. Pfizer, the world's biggest drug-maker

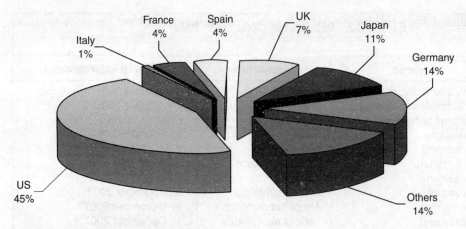

Fig. C.6   World generic market share*

* 2004 figures.
Source: Visiongain, 2005.

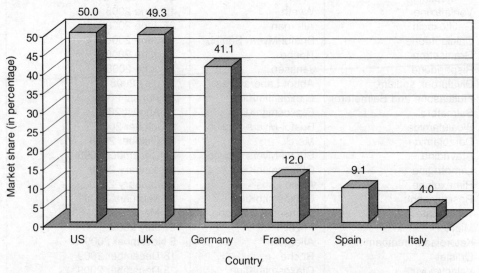

Fig. C.7   Cross-country comparison of generic market share* (by volume)

* 2004 figures.
Source: Visiongain, 2005.

has patent protection until March 2010 on its global top-selling brand of the cholesterol-cutting drug Lipitor with sales of US$12.2 billion[3] in 2005. Ranbaxy filed an application with the US Food and Drug Administration to produce a generic version of Lipitor over which a patent infringement suit was filed by Pfizer. The US Federal Court invalidated Pfizer's second patent on Lipitor which could have protected the drug until June 2011.

However, there is a flip side to the success of the strategy of focused differentiation as it is highly risk prone and legal failure can see not only the erosion of margins accrued elsewhere in form of high legal cost but also lead to a compensation

---

[3] 'Pfizer May Lose Billons in Lipitor Sales', *CNN*, 2 August 2006.

claim by the Original Patent Holder (OPH) as happened in case of Dr Reddy's Laboratories failure to challenge the patent of Omeperazole with OPH Astra Zenca. However, Ranbaxy uses the revenues so generated from sale of blockbuster generics to fund their R&D effort.

However, Ranbaxy did not follow the same route to expand its business to other countries. Acquisition is the preferred mode of international expansion for most countries. For instance, the expansion strategy into generics followed in the French market was quite different from what was followed in the US. The route here was acquisition rather than fighting legal battles in exporting. The strategy was dependent on the nature of the market as the French market is the fifth largest market for generics and the French Perfect Generic Manufacturers Act works as an entry barrier for new entrants; thus, the chief expansion route available is acquisition or joint venture. Ranbaxy preferred the first approach, based on the criteria of experience, risk, and control. The acquisition of RPG Aventis took Ranbaxy to the fifth position among the perfect generics manufacturers in the French market.

Although the generics market is valuable with significant clinical and commercial unmet needs, the challenge for Ranbaxy remains to maintain its leadership position. The company's present strategy includes the generic approval process, also

known as Abbreviated New Drug Application (ANDA). Ranbaxy's future strategy needs to aim at increasing significance of research-based formulations. The company has to focus intensely on innovation to compete with the best in quality yet to maintain low costs. Besides, to keep itself abreast with the pulse of the market is still more important when it goes into innovative research where the gestation period is between eight and 10 years. In order to sustain its competitiveness in the long term, the company may be required to move rapidly from generic dosage to branded formulations.

Ranbaxy Becomes an Acquisition Target of Japanese Company

Ranbaxy had long presented India's national technological capabilities, built brand equities of India Inc. and had been among the national champions that exploited opportunities emanated from India's economic liberalization and globalization forces to emerge as an Indian multinational in true sense. In June 2008, a Japanese pharmaceutical firm Daiichi Sankyo announced to acquire the majority equity stake[4] in Ranbaxy. Although there had been a lot of apprehensions about the regulatory hurdles for the deal, the Indian government approved the deal[5] in August 2008. The deal was completed in November 2008 with Daiichi Sankyo buying 63 per cent stake in Ranbaxy[6] for US$4.2 billion. As a result, Ranbaxy ceased to remain an Indian multinational.

Questions

1. Identify the reasons that led Ranbaxy to internationalize rather than focussing on the home market.

2. Explore the challenges a company from a developing country has to face for its international expansion.

3. Critically evaluate the factors contributing to Ranbaxy's success in its international expansion.

4. What lessons can one learn from Ranbaxy's transformation from a small firm to become a

global conglomerate? Discuss your observations in the class.

5. The leading Indian multinational Ranbaxy became an acquisition target of a Japanese firm Daiichi Sankyo in 2008 which reveals vulnerability of rising multinationals from emerging economies. Critically assess the pros and cons of such acquisitions and their desirability with reference to various stakeholders.

---

[4] Press release, Ranbaxy Laboratories Limited, 11 June 2008.

[5] 'Government Approves Daiichi's Takeover of Ranbaxy', *Business Standard*, 6 August 2008.

[6] 'Japan's Daiichi in Ranbaxy Deal', *BBC News*, 7 November 2008.

14

International Marketing

LEARNING OBJECTIVES

> To explain the concept and framework of international marketing
> To discuss market identification, segmentation, and targeting
> To elucidate international marketing mix decisions
> To examine the framework for international product promotion strategy

14.1 INTRODUCTION

Consequent to the global economic integration, a firm operating in the domestic market can no longer rely upon its home market because the home market is now an export market for everybody else. Earlier, it was believed that in order to compete in international markets, a firm needed to be competitive in the domestic market. But in view of the liberal economic policies, a business enterprise needs to compete with international firms in the domestic market too. Thus, in order to even remain domestically competitive, a firm needs to be internationally competitive. As a strategic response to the globalization of markets, business enterprises need to adopt a proactive approach and learn to transform emerging marketing threats and challenges into viable business opportunities. Thus, the significance of developing a thorough understanding of international marketing has become inevitable for managers not only for operating in international markets, but also as a pre-condition for success in operating domestically.

In the mid-1950s, the orientation towards markets shifted from selling to marketing. Earlier, under the concept of selling, the focus was on aggressive selling and sales promotion of products so as to achieve sales maximization, which in turn was expected to maximize a firm's profit earnings. Conversely, under the marketing concept, the target market is the starting point in the marketing approach with the focus on customer needs. Profit maximization under marketing is achieved through customer satisfaction by way of integrated marketing efforts. Marketing scholar Theodore Levitt explains this distinction thus: selling focuses on the needs of the seller while marketing on the needs of the buyer. Selling is pre-occupied with the seller's need to convert his/her product into cash whereas marketing with the idea of satisfying the needs of the customer by means of the product and the entire cluster of issues associated with creating, delivering, and finally consuming it.[1] However, as per the legendary management guru Peter Drucker, there would always be the need for some selling. But the aim of marketing is to make selling superfluous by developing a thorough understanding about the customer so that the product or service fits him/her and sells itself.

Marketing guru Philip Kotler defines marketing as 'the human activity directed at satisfying needs and wants through exchange processes'. Achieving customer-satisfaction has been given the utmost significance in the concept of marketing because procuring a new customer costs far more (estimated to be five times) than retaining the existing.[2] It is likely to cost 16 times as much to bring the new customer to the same level of profitability as the lost customer. Emphasizing on exchange processes, the American Marketing Association defines Marketing as 'the process of planning and executing the conception, pricing, promotion, and distribution of ideas, goods, and services to create exchanges that satisfy individual and organizational goals'. With manifold increase in competitive intensity in the present marketing era, the focus is shifting fast to marketing orientation.

In simple terms, international marketing is defined as marketing carried out across national boundaries. International marketing may also be defined as 'the performance of business activities, designed to plan, price, promote, and direct the flow of a company's goods and services to consumer or users in more than one nation for a profit'.[3] International marketing takes place when marketing is carried out 'across the border' or between 'more than one nation'. Global marketing is the process of focussing resources and objectives of an organization on global marketing opportunities and needs.[4] The thrust of international marketing consists of locating and satisfying global customer needs in a manner more efficient than competitors, both domestic and international, and co-ordinating marketing activities within the constraints of the global environment.[5] Thus, international marketing would involve

- Identifying needs and wants of customers in international markets
- Taking marketing mix decisions related to product, pricing, distribution, and communication, keeping in view the diverse consumer and market behaviour across different countries on one hand, firms' goals towards globalization on the other

[1] Levitt, Theodore, 'Marketing Myopia', *Harvard Business Review*, September–October 1975, pp. 26–48.
[2] Sellers, Patricia, 'Getting Customers to Love You', *Fortune*, 13 March 1989, pp. 38–49.
[3] Cateora, Philip R. and John L. Graham, *International Marketing*, 11th ed., Tata McGraw-Hill, 2002, pp. 7–8.
[4] Keegan, Warren J., *Global Marketing Management*, New Delhi: Pearson Education (Singapore) Pvt. Ltd, 2002, pp. 5–8.
[5] Terpestra, Vern and Ravi Sarthy, *International Marketing*, New Delhi: Harcourt Asia Pvt. Ltd, 2000, pp. 4–5.

- Penetrating into international markets using various modes of entry
- Taking decisions in view of dynamic international marketing environment

14.2 FRAMEWORK OF INTERNATIONAL MARKETING

This chapter provides an overview of the concepts, processes, and strategic aspects of international marketing. In order to facilitate readers' understanding of the concepts and processes involved in international marketing, the schematic framework is presented in Fig. 14.1. Once a firm decides to enter international markets, it needs to set objectives as to what it intends to achieve out of its international marketing operations. The next important challenge is to identify marketing opportunities, evaluate and select the most appropriate one so as to meet its objectives. 'How to enter international markets?' is the next big challenge, in view of the resource constraints, risks, and marketing opportunities.

In view of the external environmental factors, the key decisions related to the marketing mix, i.e., product, pricing, distribution, and marketing communications,

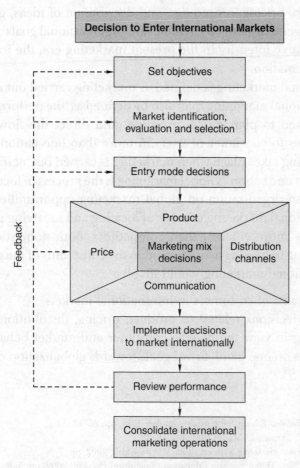

Fig. 14.1   International marketing framework

have to be made. Taking such decisions is much more complex in the international context owing to greater complexity of external factors which are beyond the control of the business enterprise. Once these decisions are implemented and the firm begins international marketing operations, the performance, primarily in terms of sales, profits, or market share needs to be reviewed and remedial measures taken, if required. The firm further consolidates its international marketing operations from a long-term perspective and becomes an established player in global markets.

14.3 SETTING MARKETING OBJECTIVES

Once a firm decides to enter international markets, it needs to set objectives, as to what it aspires to achieve, both in the short as well as the long term. The objectives vary widely from one business enterprise to another and even for a company from one market to another. The objectives to be achieved from international marketing operations may include

- Increase in total sales turnover
- Percentage of revenue earned from international markets to company's domestic sales
- Market share in the target markets
- Profitability
- Utilization of production capacity
- Geographical spread of the company's marketing operations
- Brand promotion in target markets
- Any other strategic objectives

An empirical evaluation of the above is to be carried out so as to decide upon one or a combination of objectives to be achieved from international marketing operations.

14.4 MARKET IDENTIFICATION, SEGMENTATION, AND TARGETING

A firm has to identify countries, which offer relatively higher opportunities to market its products. As discussed in Chapter 10, a company may either use a reactive or a pro-active approach to identify markets. International trade statistics from various secondary data sources published by international organizations, such as the WTO, UNCTAD, World Bank, ITC, etc., or national sources, such as a country's central banks, ministries of trade and commerce or finance may be utilized. In India, the Directorate General of Commercial Intelligence and Statistics (DGCI&S) under the Ministry of Commerce and the Reserve Bank of India compiles and publishes trade statistics.

The direction and composition of trade statistics as discussed in Chapter 3 may be used to find out markets for the products of interest for a business enterprise using HS (ITC) code up to eight digit levels. Besides, the data may also be used to identify competing countries and products thereof. One can also compute market share for the entire world trade, region, or a specific country. A cross-country comparison of unit-value realization is also possible that provides a gross estimate of prevailing price realization in different countries.

The size of a market is crucial to a firm's decision to target a country. A cross-country comparison of market size and its growth rate are the key indicators that determine market potential for targeting the market. Market size of a country can be estimated as follows:

$$\text{Market Size} = \text{Gross Domestic Product (production)} + \text{Value of imports of goods and services} - \text{Value of exports of goods and services.}$$

By normalizing the domestic market size on a scale of 1–7, the US has the largest domestic market (7.0) (Fig. 14.2), followed by China (6.7), India (6.2), Japan (6.2), Germany (5.8), the UK (5.7), Brazil (5.5), Russian Federation (5.5), Australia (4.9), South Africa (4.9), Thailand (4.8), Singapore (3.5), Tanzania (2.9), and Timor-Leste[6] (1.0).

Values of exports of goods and services imply the foreign market size of a country. Normalised on 1–7 scale, China (7.0) has the highest foreign market size (Fig. 14.3), followed by the US (6.3), Germany (6.2), India (6.0), Japan (5.8), the UK (5.8), Russian

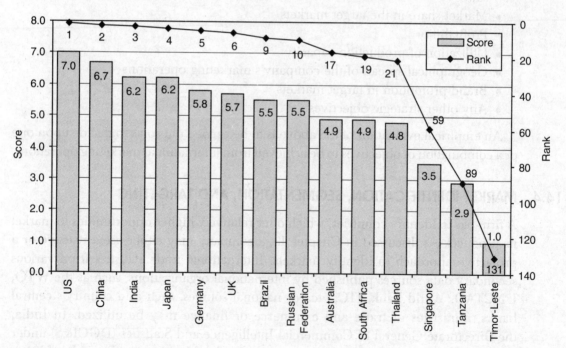

Fig. 14.2 Domestic market size index

1—smallest, 7—largest

Source: Based on data from The Global Competitiveness Report 2007–08, World Economic Forum, Geneva, 2008, p. 488.

---

[6] The Global Competitiveness Report, 2007–08, World Economic Forum, Geneva, 2008, p. 488.

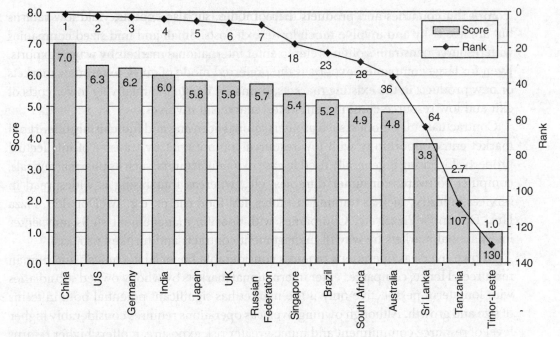

Fig. 14.3   Foreign market size index

1—smallest, 7—largest

Source: Based on data from The Global Competitiveness Report 2007–08, World Economic Forum, Geneva, 2008, p. 489.

Federation (5.7), Singapore (5.4), Brazil (5.2), South Africa (4.9), Australia (4.8), Sri Lanka (3.8), Tanzania (2.7), and Timor-Leste (1.0).

Dividing the markets into homogenous sub-groups is referred to as market segmentation. Since there exist considerable differences among markets in terms of their response to a given marketing strategy; market segmentation often helps concentrate a firm's resources to a specific market segment so that the firm may compete more effectively. For a market segment to be effective, it must be measurable, substantial, accessible, differentiable, and actionable. International markets may be segmented on the basis of geography; demographical factors, such as income, age, gender, etc.; psychographic profiles; marketing opportunity; market attractiveness; etc.

Preliminary screening of international markets may be carried out on the basis of market size, accessibility in terms of both tariff and non-tariff barriers, and profitability of the market. Besides, specific tools and techniques, as discussed in Chapter 10, may also be used for empirical evaluation and market selection.

14.5   ENTRY MODE DECISIONS

An entry mode is the institutional mechanism to make the company's products and services available in international markets. The entry mode may vary from simple indirect exports through a merchant intermediary to owning overseas operations. Various types of entry modes have been discussed in depth in Chapter 11.

As a thumb rule, low-investment entry modes, such as exports, yield low returns but are less risky and involve much lower exit costs. Small and mid-sized companies with resource constraints often prefer to enter international markets by way of exports. Even for large companies, exports is the preferred mode of entry to test new markets or new products in the existing markets, primarily due to the relatively lower costs of exit and low resource-commitment in test markets it involves.

Contractual entry modes, such as international licensing and franchising, offer rapid market entry opportunity with low-resource commitment by transfer of intellectual property. Licensing is generally used in case of manufacturers, such as pharmaceuticals, computer software, consumer durables, etc., whereas franchising is widespread in services industry, such as training institutes, fast food chains, e.g., McDonald's, Pizza Hut, Domino's Pizza, etc. Companies with specific management skills may enter international markets by way of management contracts and turnkey projects.

To own overseas operations requires considerable financial, technical, and human resources. Hence, companies enter international markets by wholly owned subsidiaries with long-term perspective only if the market has significant potential both in terms of size and growth. Although owning overseas operations requires considerably higher level of resource commitment and much greater risk exposure, it offers higher returns and operational control.

The company may decide upon the entry mode depending on resource availability and willingness to invest in international marketing operations. Besides, the risk it is willing to take and the control to exert, also play an important role in determining the entry mode.

14.6 INTERNATIONAL MARKETING MIX DECISIONS

The set of marketing tools a firm uses to pursue its marketing objectives in a target market is termed as 'marketing mix'.[7] Various tools used in marketing may be classified into the four Ps of marketing: product, price, place, and promotion, widely known as marketing mix.[8] As a company can modify the four Ps in response to the environmental variables, these are often referred to as controllable factors. A business enterprise has to operate under the constraints of a number of external environmental factors, such as social, economic, political, legal, technological, cultural, etc. These environmental factors are known as uncontrollable elements over which a marketer hardly has any influence, but the marketing challenge is to adapt the controllable elements of the marketing mix, i.e., product, price, distribution, and promotion so as to ensure marketing success. Although the fundamentals of marketing remain the same and are universally applicable, the flexibility of marketing decisions is limited by a variety of uncontrollable factors in international markets. This makes decisions for international markets much more complex compared to domestic markets.

---

[7] Borden, Neil H., 'The Concept of Marketing Mix' *Journal of Advertising Research*, 4 June 1964, pp. 2–7.
[8] McCarthy, E. Jerome, *Basic Marketing: A Managerial Approach*, 12th ed., Homewood, IL: Irwin, 1996.

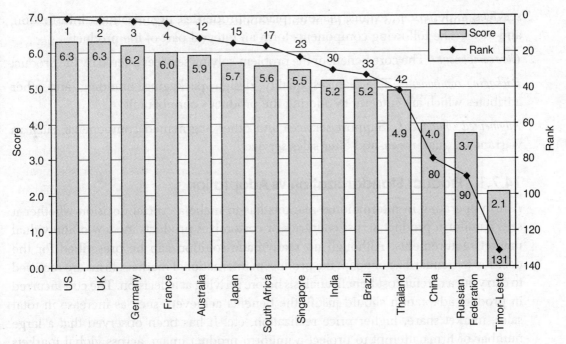

Fig. 14.4   Extent of employing sophisticated marketing tools and techniques

1—limited and primitive, 7—extensively employed
Source: Based on data from The Global Competitiveness Report 2007–08, World Economic Forum, Geneva, 2008, p. 501.

The extent of employing sophisticated marketing tools and techniques varies across countries. The world's most sophisticated tools and techniques are employed in the US with a score of 6.3 on a 7 point scale[9] (Fig. 14.4) followed by the UK (6.3), Germany (6.2), France (6.0), Australia (5.9), Japan (5.7), South Africa (5.6), Singapore (5.5), India (5.2), Brazil (5.2), Thailand (4.9), China (4.0), the Russian Federation (3.7), and Timor Leste (2.1). International firms have to take crucial decisions either to make use of a standard marketing strategy across countries or adapt it to suit the needs of different country markets.

14.7   PRODUCT DECISIONS

As the basic purpose of any marketing activity is to satisfy the customers' needs in a superior manner vis-à-vis its competitors, product-decisions become vital for success in international markets. Perceptions and expectations about the products differ to a varied extent across countries which makes decision-making about products much more complex for international markets. A product is anything that can be offered to a market[10] to satisfy a want or need. Products that are marketed include physical goods,

[9] The Global Competitiveness Report 2007–08, World Economic Forum, Geneva, 2008, p. 501.
[10] Kotler, Philip, *Marketing Management*, 11th ed., New Delhi: Prentice Hall, 2002, p. 407.

services, experiences, events, persons, places, properties, organizations, information, and ideas. The following components form an integral part of the product.

Core component   The core benefit or the problem-solving services offered by the product

Packaging component   The features, quality, design, packaging, branding, and other attributes which are integral to offering the product's core benefit

Augmented component   Support services and other augmented components, such as warrantees, guarantees, and after sales service

14.7.1   Product Standardization vs Adaptation

A firm operating in international markets has to make a crucial decision whether it sells a uniform product across countries or customizes products in view of individual market requirements. Although no readymade solution can be prescribed for the decision to standardize or adapt the product in international markets, firms are required to carry out a careful cost-benefit analysis before arriving at a decision. The cost incurred in product adaptation should justify the benefits achieved, such as increase in total sales, market share, higher price realization, etc. It has been observed that a large number of firms attempt to project a uniform product image across global markets but often customize the perceived value of the product to suit the target market customers. While retaining its core product component and even the brand name as common, firms attempt to customize the augmented product components, such as features, packaging, and labelling. Support service components, including warrantees, guarantees, delivery schedule, installation, and payment terms are most often adapted to suit the needs of the target market.

Generally, industrial products and services are insensitive to cross-country preferences and may be marketed as standardized products, whereas foods, fads, fashions, and styles are highly sensitive and customer preferences for these items vary widely across markets. Such products often require a much higher level of customization.

Product standardization

Product standardization refers to marketing a product in the overseas markets with little change except for some cosmetic changes such as modifying packaging and labelling. Generally, products with high technological intensity such as heavy equipments, plants and machinery, microprocessors, hard disks, projectors etc. are marketed as standardized products across the world. Some of the consumer products with global appeal, viz. Big Mac, Coke, Budweiser, Heineken, etc., are also marketed as globally standardized products. The benefits associated with using standardized products in international markets include

- Projecting a global product image
- Catering to the global customers moving across countries

- Cost savings in terms of economies of scale in production
- Economy in designing and monitoring various components of the marketing mix
- Facilitates in developing the product as a global brand

Major factors favouring product standardization

High level of technology-intensity   Products with high-technology content are marketed as standardized products so as to maintain uniform international standards and reduce confusion across international markets. Besides, using standard specifications facilitates product compatibility internationally. For instance, computer servers, micro- and macro-processors, Value Added Networks (VAN), etc., are marketed worldwide as standard products.

Formidable adaptation costs   Nature of product and market size determines the cost of adaptation that may be too high to recover. A number of foreign books and motion pictures are primarily sold as standardized products worldwide. Only a few books written in the foreign context are adapted or even translated due to prohibitive adaptation costs that are difficult to recover.

Convergence of customer needs worldwide   Customers in diverse country markets increasingly exhibit convergence of their needs and preferences, resulting into growing psychographic market segments across the borders. It has resulted in an increase in demand for similar goods across the world. Products, such as Levi's jeans, MTV, and McDonald's have become increasingly popular among international consumers as a result of growing convergence worldwide (Fig. 14.5). Besides, the rapid growth of

Fig. 14.5   Convergence of customer tastes and preferences has facilitated product globalization

transport and telecommunications has resulted in increase in trans-national travel among people who exhibit similar tastes and preferences across the markets.

Country-of-origin impact The customers' perception of the products often differ on the basis of the country of its origin. For instance, consumer electronics durables from Japan, fashion designs from Italy, fragrances from France, instruments from Germany, computer software from India, and herbal products from China and India are perceived to be superior in quality and fetch a premium price in international markets. The international firms attempt to retain their country-of-origin (CoO) image and market, at least the packaging product component, with little customization.

Product adaptation

Making changes in the product in response to the needs of the target market is termed as product adaptation or customization. In view of local consumption requirements, the product for international market is often customized. Adaptation of a product may vary from major modifications in the product itself to minor alterations in its packaging, logo, or brand name. A thorough market research needs to be conducted so as to identify the customers' requirements in the target market. Customizing products for international markets offers a number of benefits such as

- It makes it possible to tap markets, which are otherwise not assessable due to mandatory requirements
- It competitively fulfils the customers' needs and expectations in varied cultures and environments
- It facilitates gaining market share
- Increased sale leads to scale economies

The secret of the success of Japanese goods in the international markets lies in the capacity of Japanese manufacturers to develop a thorough understanding of customer demand in its target market and customizing products accordingly. In recent years, China has fast emerged as the global hub to manufacture goods to suit diverse needs and preferences of the customers in different countries (Exhibit 14.1).

Mandatory factors influencing product adaptation Product adaptation includes mandatory product modifications that a firm has to carry out in international markets, not as a matter of choice but compulsion. The major factors influencing product adaptation are

Government regulations A firm needs to adapt its products to various markets in order to comply with government regulations. The differing quality specifications also require marketers to follow the quality norms, such as approval by the Food and Drug Administration (FDA) for marketing a product in the US or following codex standards for European Union. The ban on the use of azo-dyes in Europe requires use of natural dyes in all products. Maps are a sensitive issue all over the world and the exporting company needs to follow the regulations of the importing country.

Exhibit 14.1   Chinese firms: The masters in product adaptation

Consumer durables made in China of the value of over Rupees one million are sold everyday in India. Goods made in China have established a vast retail network all over India down to the remotest villages without the help of media hype or publicity campaigns.

The product adaptation by Chinese manufacturers and marketers is exemplary. 'Made in China' idols of Hindu gods and goddesses in all shapes, colours, and sizes, even with fitted electronic gadgets and pre-recorded devotional music in most Indian languages apart from Hindi and Sanskrit, swamp the Indian markets during festive seasons. China-made idols of god Ganesha during the Ganpati festival in Maharashtra, goddess Durga during the Puja festival in West Bengal, and goddess Lakshmi and a host of other Indian deities during Diwali are a common sight. Moreover, these are far more attractive and cost-effective than their traditional counterparts.

The modus-operandi of Chinese manufactures is to send to the target market a team of experts who pick up the locally-made items which are in high demand, either during festival season or otherwise. The Chinese visiting team takes back a variety of samples of locally manufactured popular products. Extensive innovations are made by the Chinese manufacturers and similar products are manufactured in bulk and sold in foreign markets at much lower rates than the domestically manufactured products. To illustrate, a few years back, a team of Chinese experts visited Mumbai to pick up specimens of clay Ganesha idols. Back in China, the team manufactured idols in different materials, such as paper-mashie, plastic, fibre, and glass and innovated them with the latest electronic technology. The Chinese idols looked far more attractive and full of life, and at the same time were cheaper too (Fig. 14.6).

Concerns about quality and adverse impact on indigenous manufacturing industry hardly deterred Indian consumers and the market intermediaries from falling in love with Chinese goods. The customer was delighted to get western-style goods at much lower costs. Besides, such goods are available in wide ranges and the compromise in quality hardly impacts the customer.

On the other hand, the rapid influx of low-cost Chinese goods has created considerable concern among the Indian manufacturers. Low-cost Chinese goods have severely affected the competitiveness of various industrial clusters mainly dominated by SMEs, for instance, the lock industry in Aligarh, glassware industry in

Fig. 14.6   'Made in China' idols of Hindu gods and goddesses flood Indian markets

Contd

Exhibit 14.1 Contd

Firozabad, and firecrackers in Shivakashi. The cheap imports of Chinese goods are reported to have forced many small industrial units to shutter down, leading to the growing threat of loss of the jobs by unskilled to skilled workers.

Sources: 'Made in China, Sold in India', *Business Economics*, 1–15 October 2006, pp. 27–31; 'Guru Nanak Looks Chinese in China-made Idols' *Times of India*, 13 August 2007.

Chinese-made toy-globes that depicted the northern territory of Kashmir in a different colour to the rest of India were found offensive by an Indian court and their imports were banned.[11]

Standards for electric current The electrical current standards also vary from country to country. In India, the standard electric current supply is 220 volts with a frequency of 50 Hz while these values in these US are 110–120 volts with 60 Hz. Electrical equipment need to be modified for use in the target countries, depending upon the prevailing electrical standards.

Operating systems Differences in operating systems influence the product designs that need to be adapted to suit the target market. In India, China, the UK, Singapore, Pakistan, UAE, and Tanzania, televisions operate on PAL (*Phase Alternation Lines*) while in the US, Japan, Philippines, and South Korea they work on NTSC (*National Television Systems Committee*) standards. Televisions operate on SECAM (*System Electrique Pour Couleur Avec Mémoire*) in France, Vietnam, Russia, and Mauritius. Therefore, a television operating on PAL System in India is unsuitable in countries that have different operating systems, such as the US, Japan, and France. Thus, in order to market televisions in countries with incompatible operating systems, suitable adaptations are mandatory.

Measurement systems Product design is influenced by the measurement systems followed in a country. India follows the metric system with kilograms, metre, or litre as measurement units whereas the US follows the imperial system of measurement using pound, feet, and gallons. Therefore, the packaging size, weights, and measures of the product need to be modified, depending upon the measurement system followed in the target market.

Packaging and labelling regulations Regulations for packaging and labelling vary across the countries, which need to be followed for selling a product. Most countries in the Middle East emphasize the use of Arabian language while similar linguistic regulations are also required in a number of European countries. In India, food products generally bear the duration for use of a product whereas in most developed countries

[11] 'India Court Bans Kashmir Globes', *BBC News*, 11 November 2004.

the date of expiry is mentioned explicitly. Even regulations requiring magazines to display the date after which it should not be put on the book-stand are not uncommon in a number of high-income countries. Keeping in mind vegetarian sensibilities, regulations in India require food packages to exhibit a mark either in green or red colour indicating vegetarian or non-vegetarian ingredients used, so as to explicitly inform the consumers about its contents.

Voluntary factors influencing product adaptation Products modifications that are not compulsory but are based on the international marketer's own discretion to meet the marketing challenges competitively are known as voluntary factors. Major factors influencing product adaptation by marketer's own choices in the international market are as under:

Consumer demographics Product modifications are required to suit the physical attributes of the target consumers. Chinese and most East Asian people are shorter in size while Europeans and Germans are generally taller. Consumer products, such as readymade garments, undergarments, beds, and bed-sheets differ significantly among these markets and the products need to be adapted depending upon the consumer demographics. Consumers also look for images matching their own demographic attributes in the products. For instance, Mattel markets a variety of Barbie dolls to match customer demographics in different markets.

Culture Cultural factors, such as local tastes, traditions, religious beliefs, etc., considerably affect the products-decisions for international markets, as discussed in detail in Chapter 7. However, the sensitivity to culture varies with product categories. Food items and clothing are generally more sensitive to culture whereas products with high technical intensity, such as software, electronic goods, plant, and machinery are hardly sensitive. It takes a long time to change the food and clothing habits of consumers and market the standardized products. Western food items, such as burgers, pizzas, ice creams, soft drinks, etc., have gained global acceptance. Increased contact with alien cultures primarily due to augmented movement of people across the countries has made even Chinese and Indian foods popular in the West (Exhibit 14.2).

The largest global fast food marketer, McDonald's, faces the biggest challenge of adapting its menu to local tastes without compromising on its strong universal appeal of an American icon. The majority of Hindus in India are ardent vegetarians. Although McDonald's serves its famous Big Mac, the beef burger, across the Globe, it promises an authentic vegetarian burger in India (Fig. 14.8). Moreover, the concept of vegetarianism in India is the most complex in the world wherein even the slightest interchange of 'veg' and 'non-veg' cooking and serving utensils is shunned. Hence, India is the only country where McDonald's has got separate utensils and areas in the kitchen for making vegetarian and non-vegetarian food. Consumption of beef is not only unacceptable but also an extremely sensitive social issue, besides being faced with statutory provisions to prohibit cow slaughter in most Indian states. India is also home to the second-largest Muslim population in the world, which considers pork as

---

Exhibit 14.2   Ethnic Indian food for global customers' palate

Although food habits are peculiar to a culture, some foods have become global in nature. Changing global taste buds is not easy, but Chinese hakka noodles, pizzas and hamburgers are on the world menu. This does not happen just by chance or design. For most Americans and Europeans, the first taste of Asia is Chinese food. This is not a recent phenomenon, but has evolved over several years as Chinatowns and Chinese emigrants have influenced Western eating habits.

Overseas markets are now experiencing an Indian culture curry, not only because of crossover films and ethnic wear, but also because of something a little more literal and overriding—pre-cooked packaged foods and the rising awareness of India. Companies, such as MTR and ITC Hotels have made it possible to package Indian dishes. This means that one can buy Indian chole-masala, Kashmiri rajma, and chicken Patiala off the shelf and heat it in the microwave to have authentic Indian food.

Culinary tastes are highly influenced by culture. Like Chinatowns, a number of smaller towns in the UK, such as Norwich, which has a population of approximately 1,75,000 people, has streets devoted to Indian cuisine only. Deewan Street in Chicago, which has a lane dedicated to Indian and Middle Eastern Cuisine and fast food, sees huge traffic during peak hours all through the week. The focus on Indian food can also be seen in the Aishwarya Rai starrer *Mistress of Spices*. While the movie may have

Fig. 14.7   Growing popularity of Indian cuisine and spices in the West

not done well in India, it did re-introduce the Western world to Indian culinary and spices (Fig. 14.7).

Manufacturers of packaged foods are tapping into this segment of non-Indians trying out Indian food across the world. Indian restaurants are the first to lay the stepping-stone and inculcate Indian tastes in overseas communities, which brings about a desire in non-ethnic customers to try out Indian cuisine at home and to buy ready-to-eat Indian curries. In turn, people try and cook at home also and hence buy curry pastes, which add Indian flavours. There is always a need for unique cuisine in European markets. With packaged foods being increasingly available in the West, there is a huge potential for ready-to-eat and frozen Indian foods to click with the non-Indian consumer.

Source: 'India Ready to Spice Up Global Taste Buds', *Economic Times*, 5 May 2006.

---

impious and the religion prohibits its consumption. As a result, McDonald's does not serve either beef or pork in the Indian market. Even among the non-vegetarian Indian consumers, red meat is not preferred, which made it necessary for McDonald's to serve chicken burger. In response to the Indian consumer's preference for spicy food, McDonald's not only serves spicier preparations but it also serves sauces, such as McMasala and McImli, customized for the palate of the Indian consumer. Moreover, in order to compete with popular Indian preparations, McDonalds has also introduced McMaharaja and Chicken Tikka Burger in the Indian market.

Fig. 14.8 McDonalds' serves Big Mac across the globe, and promises to offer an authentic vegetarian burger in India.

As Jewish law forbids cooking, serving, or eating meat and milk products together, in Jerusalem, McDonald's has both kosher and non-kosher restaurants. McDonald's kosher restaurants do not have milkshakes, ice creams, and cheeseburgers. McDonald's even serves beer and wine in some countries, such as France, the UK, Germany, Brazil, etc. The McDonald's' in Brazil has a 'happy hours' with a salsa band playing. It offers soup and fried rice to cater to Japanese eating habits as well.

In another instance, camera sales in Saudi Arabia were historically low. Sales boomed with the advent of Polaroid instant photography as this allowed Arab men to photograph their wives and daughters in the privacy of their homes without the need of strangers handling the film in a processing lab.

Conditions of use Products have to be adapted depending upon the conditions of use in the international markets. These include climatic conditions, such as cold and hot weather, humid and dry conditions, and the local dusty conditions of use. Nokia introduced its brand 'Nokia 1100' emphasizing its 'Made for India' features, such as anti-slip grip, built-in torchlight, dust resistance cover, and of course at a lower price. The condition of product use is a significant reason for operational problems of highly sophisticated electronic gadgets in low-income countries that have robust conditions of use. This opens up tremendous marketing opportunities for products manufactured in India which can withstand robust operating conditions in other developing and least developed countries.

Price Low-income countries are highly sensitive to price, which constitutes the most significant determinant of a purchase decision. The level of sophistication of buyers in adopting new products and processes also varies among countries. Therefore, core product benefits become the key to lower costs in developing and least developed countries where the augmented product component, such as packaging, product sophistication, and additional features are emphasized in developed countries where the buyer has the capacity to pay considerably higher prices.

Trade-off strategy between product standardization and adaptation

A firm operating in international markets has to carefully carry out the cost-benefit analysis of the decision to market the standardized product across countries or customize it, depending upon the market requirements. Selling standardized products in international markets leads to economies of scale in production and other components of the marketing mix. However, the purpose of a business organization is not to save the cost but to maximize the market share and profitability. Therefore, firms need to carry out product adaptation tailored to specific marketing needs. If a firm sells standardized products across world markets, this results in a decline in its market share and consequently benefits the competitors. On the other hand, customization of products for different markets involves substantial commitment of financial resources and adversely affects scale economies. Therefore, a trade-off has to be evolved to assess the extent of product adaptation in international markets.

14.7.2   Product Launch for International Markets

Ever-growing market competition compels firms to innovate so as to maintain their market share. The pressure to bring out new products is much more intense on firms operating in international markets. The global market leader in safety razors, Gillette, positions its products on functional superiority by adding more number of blades to its razors (Exhibit 14.3).

New product launch

Depending upon the market and the product attributes, a firm may adapt one of the following strategies (Fig. 14.10) for launching its products in international markets.

'Waterfall' approach   Under the 'waterfall approach' products trickle down in the international markets in a cascade manner and are launched sequentially. In the 'waterfall approach', generally longer duration is available for a product to customize in a foreign market before it is launched in another market. The waterfall approach is generally more suitable for firms that have limited resources and find it difficult to manage multiple markets simultaneously. In case the size of the target market and its growth potential is not sufficient to commit considerable resources, product launch may be carried out in a phased manner.

This strategy had long been followed in international marketing. It took a long time for a number of firms, which are now global, to launch their products in international markets. For instance, it took almost 22 years for McDonald's to market outside the US whereas Coca Cola took about 20 years and Marlboro about 35 years to market overseas.

Exhibit 14.3   The cutting-edge innovation

After King Gillette invented the safety razor, it took a leisurely 70 years for someone to come up with the idea that twin blades might be more effective or at least sell better. Since then, the pace of change has accelerated, as blade after blade has been added to razors in an attempt to tech-up the 'shaving experience'.

For the most cynical shavers, this evolution is mere marketing. The concept of twin blades seemed plausible. Three were a bit unlikely. Four, ridiculous. And five seems beyond the pale. Few people, though, seem willing to bet that Gillette's five-bladed Fusion is the end of the road for razor-blade escalation. More blades may seem impossible for the moment though strictly speaking the Fusion has six, because it has a single blade on its flip-side for tricky areas, but anyone of a gambling persuasion might want to examine the relationship between how many blades a razor has, and the date each new design was introduced.

This relationship suggests shavers are going to get more blades whether they need them or not. However, just like Moore's law—the observation that computer chips double in power every 18 months or so—it seems that technology as well as marketing determines the rates at which new blades are introduced.

It is simply not possible to add a new blade whenever the marketing department wants one. Since every additional blade adds weight and size

Source: The Economist, London, 18 March 2006.

to a razor, firms must, therefore, find ways of making both razor and blades lighter, which means thinner blades, more closely spaced, made of special materials, with new coatings.

So what does the future hold? With only five data-points, it is hard to be sure exactly which mathematical curve is being followed. If it follows a power law, then the 14-bladed razor should arrive in 2100. The spate of recent innovation, however, suggests it may be a hyperbola. In that case, blade hyperdrive will be reached in the next few years and those who choose not to sport beards might be advised to start exercising their shaving arms now (Fig. 14.9).

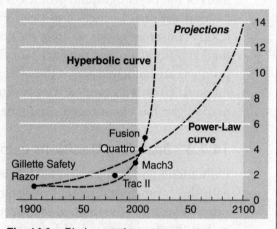

Fig. 14.9   Blade growth per razor system

Source: The Economist, 18 March 2006.

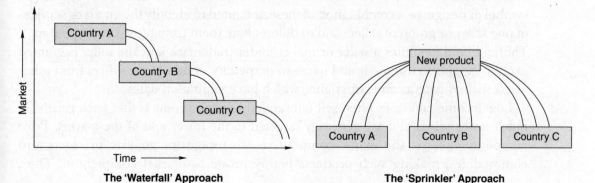

The 'Waterfall' Approach   The 'Sprinkler' Approach

Fig. 14.10   Product launch approaches for international markets

'Sprinkler' approach Under this approach, the product is simultaneously launched in various countries. The sprinkler approach of simultaneous market entry is preferred over 'waterfall' approach under the following circumstances:

- The competitive intensity of the market is very high with strong and fierce competitors
- The life cycle of the product is relatively short
- The markets have high potential such as
  - Large market size
  - Rapid growth
  - Cost of entry is relatively less
- The firm has large resources to manage simultaneous product launch in multiple markets

Firms catering to international markets are increasingly segmenting markets on the basis of the psychographic profiles of their customers. Such market segments extend beyond national borders and need to be approached at the same time. In case of luxury consumer goods wherein the fashion trends rapidly change across international markets, simultaneous product launch is preferred. IT software, such as Microsoft products are launched across the world simultaneously as there is no time lag between markets. Growing competitive pressure in international markets and the decreasing market gap has encouraged simultaneous product launch.

14.7.3 Branding Decisions in International Markets

Unbranded goods are marketed just as products wherein the scope of differentiation with the competitors' market offerings is limited and difficult to sustain in the long run, whereas it is the intangible aspect of the brand that wraps around a product and makes the brand special. When consumers think of a product or service, they only compare the basic attributes and features and compare it with those of competitors whereas branding adds an emotional dimension to the product-consumer relationship and creates a bond between them.

A brand is defined by the American Marketing Association as a name, term, sign, symbol or design, or a combination of these, intended to identify the goods or services of one seller or group of sellers and to differentiate them from those of competitors.[12] Thus, a brand identifies a seller or maker under trademark law; the seller is granted exclusive rights to use the brand name in perpetuity. Brand name differs from other assets such as patents and copyrights, which have expiration dates.

Low-income countries often sell unbranded generic products that fetch relatively much lower prices and are generally targeted to the lower end of the market. Price competitiveness is the major competitive advantage for generic products and commodities, making such products highly prone to market competition. Thus,

---

[12] American Marketing Association.

branding creates differentiation between the firm's and competitors' products, and provides marketing edge to the brands to price them relatively higher than competitors' and fetch better margins. Besides, brands facilitate coping with market competition and increasing the life of the product. In present times when the mobility of the consumers, including trans-national travel, is rapidly growing, brands serve as an effective tool in international marketing since the image of the brand crosses national boundaries. Brands contribute to forge an emotional relationship with the consumers and facilitate their buying decisions by enhancing their confidence while purchasing their favourite brand. With the increased competitive intensity in the markets, even basic commodities, such as rice, tea, edible oils, salt, and petroleum are branded widely.

Strategy for building global brands

A global brand should have a minimum level of geographical spread and turnover in various markets worldwide. However, in the fields of information and communication technology, a lot of leapfrogging has taken place; for instance, a number of Indian IT companies with little domestic presence aim at global markets. Quelch identifies six traits[13] for a brand to be global:

- Dominates the domestic market, which generates cash flow to enter new markets
- Meets a universal consumer need
- Demonstrates balanced country-market coverage
- Reflects consistent positioning worldwide
- Benefits from positive country-of-origin effect
- Focus is on the product category

Developing a global brand requires enormous resources and enduring commitment. Therefore, most brands that have global reach emanate from high-income countries. Among the top hundred global brands, the US is home to the highest at 52 brands, followed by 10 from Germany, nine from France, eight from Japan, six from the UK, four from Switzerland, three from South Korea, two from Italy, and one each from Sweden, Spain, Finland, and Bermuda. Interestingly, no brand either from India or China falls in the top 100.[14]

Coca-cola is the world's top brand in terms of brand value, followed by Microsoft, IBM, GE, Nokia, Toyota, Intel, McDonald's, Disney, and Mercedes-Benz, as shown in Fig. 14.11. Seven of the top 10 brands are from the US, except Nokia of Finland, Japan's Toyota, and Mercedes Benz of Germany.

14.8 INTERNATIONAL PRICING DECISIONS

Pricing is the only component of the marketing-mix decisions, which is often adopted in international markets with the least commitment of the firm's resources. The price

---

[13] Quelch, J., 'Global Brands: Taking Stock', *Business Strategy Review*, vol. 10, no. 1, 1999, pp. 1–14.
[14] Based on Interbrand data, *Business Week*, 6 August 2007.

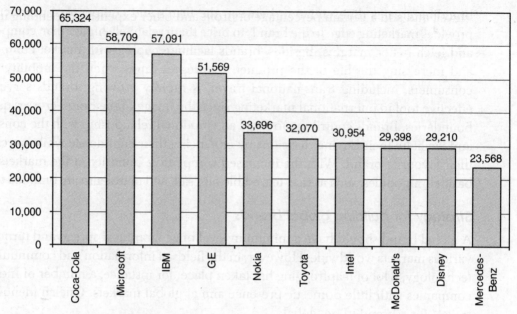

Fig. 14.11   Top 10 global brands

Source: Based on Interbrand data, *Business Week*, 6 August 2007.

is the sum of values exchanged from the customer for the product or service. Price is generally referred to in terms of amount of money but it may also include other tangible and intangible items of utility.

Pricing decisions in international markets are extremely significant for developing and least developed countries mainly due to the following reasons:

- The lower production and technology base often results in higher cost of production.
- As the market share of developing countries is relatively lower and these countries are marginal suppliers in most product categories; therefore, they have little bargaining power to negotiate. This compels them to often sell their products in international markets at prices below the total cost of production.
- Since the majority of products from developing and least developed countries are sold in the international markets as commodities with marginal value addition, there is limited scope for realizing optimal prices.
- In view of the fiercely competitive markets and complex pricing strategies adopted by multinational marketers, formulation of appropriate pricing strategies with innovation becomes a pre-condition for success in international markets.

14.8.1   Pricing Approaches for International Markets

Cost-based pricing

Costs are widely used by firms to determine prices in international markets, especially in the initial stages. New exporters often determine export prices on 'ex-works' price level, and add a certain percentage of profit and other expenses, depending upon the term of delivery used. However, such cost-based pricing methods are not optimal because

- The price quoted by the exporter on the basis of cost calculations may either be too low vis-à-vis competitors that allow importers to earn huge margins
- The price quoted by the exporters may be too high to make their goods uncompetitive resulting in the outright rejection of the offer

Full cost pricing   It is the most common pricing approach used by exporters in the initial stages of their internationalization. It includes adding a mark-up on the total cost to determine price. The major benefits of the full cost pricing approach are as follows:

- Widely used by exporters in the initial phases of international marketing
- Speedy recovery of investment
- Useful for firms that are mainly dependent upon international markets and have very low or negligible sales in domestic markets
- Ease of operations and implementation

Nevertheless, certain bottlenecks are also associated with full cost pricing approach:

- It often overlooks the prevailing price structure in international markets, which may either make the product uncompetitive or deprive the firm from charging higher prices.
- As competitors often use price-cutting strategies to penetrate or gain share in international markets, the full cost pricing approach fails to withstand the price competition.

Marginal cost pricing   In view of the huge size of international markets compared to domestic market, exports are considered to be outlets to dispose off surplus production that a firm finds difficult to sell in the domestic market. As the intensity of competition in international markets is much higher than the domestic market, competitive pricing becomes a pre-condition for success. Therefore, a large number of firms adopt the marginal costing approach for pricing decisions in international markets.

Marginal cost is the cost of producing and selling one more unit. It sets the lower limit to which a firm can reduce its price without affecting its overall profitability. Under the marginal cost approach, the firm realizes its fixed cost from domestic markets and uses variable costing approach for international markets (Fig. 14.12). The major reasons for adopting pricing based on marginal cost are

- In cases where foreign markets are used to dispose off the surplus production, marginal cost-based pricing provides an alternate marketing outlet.
- As products from developing countries seldom compete on brand image or unique value, marginal costing is used as a tool to penetrate into international markets.

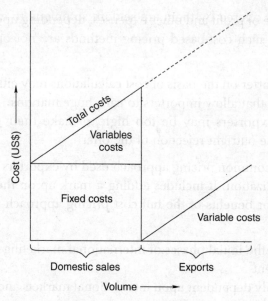

Fig. 14.12 Marginal vs full cost pricing

Source: Joshi, Rakesh Mohan, *International Marketing,* New Delhi: Oxford University Press, 2005, p. 368.

- Selling on marginal cost-based pricing provides some contribution that the firm would forego in case it decides not to export at marginal cost-based price.

Nevertheless, major limitations associated with marginal cost-based pricing approach are

- In case the firm is selling most of its output in international markets, it cannot use marginal cost-based pricing as the fixed cost is also to be recovered
- Pricing based on marginal cost may be charged as dumping in overseas markets and is liable to anti-dumping action subject to the investigations
- Such pricing tends to trigger price wars in overseas markets and lead to price undercutting among the suppliers
- Use of marginal cost-based price with little information on prevailing market prices leads to unrealistic low-price quotations

Market based pricing

It is a popular myth that costs alone determine the price. In fact, it is the interaction of a variety of factors, such as costs, competitive intensity, demand structure, consumer behaviour, etc., that contribute to price determination in international markets. However, costs serve as useful indicators of the profitability of a firm. Therefore, a market-based pricing approach is generally preferred to a cost-based pricing.

As developing countries are marginal suppliers of goods in most markets, they hardly have market shares large enough to influence prices in international markets. Hence, the exporters in developing countries are generally price followers rather than price setters. Besides, the products offered by them are seldom so unique to enable them to dictate prices. Under such market situations, the pricing decisions by price followers from developing countries involve assessment of prevailing prices in international markets and working out prices based on top down calculations.[15]

14.8.2 Factors Influencing Pricing Decisions

Cost

A large number of exporters in the initial stages of their business use cost-based pricing which is hardly the best way to determine price in international markets. However, the cost is often the key determinant of the profitability of a firm in selling the product. Firms located in different countries do have significant variations in their costs of production and marketing but the price in international markets is determined by market forces. Therefore, the profitability among international firms varies widely, depending upon their costing. In general, the ex-works cost is only about 20 per cent to 30 per cent of the price the consumer pays for the product; any savings in cost of production is likely to have a multiplier effect on the final price paid by the consumer. Since cost incurred on logistics forms a substantial part of the final consumer price, the efficiency and cost-cutting on logistics considerably influence a firm's price competitiveness in international markets.

Competition

Competition is much higher in international markets compared to the domestic market. Besides, the competitive intensity and its nature vary widely across countries. In a large number of markets, the competition is from international firms while the local firms or local subsidiaries of multinationals offer major competition in some markets. Competition in local markets is the most intense in Germany[16] with a score of 6.3 on a 7 point scale (Fig. 14.13), followed by Japan (6.0), the UK (6.0), the US (5.9), India (5.9), Australia (5.7), Singapore (5.5), UAE (5.4), China (5.3), Brazil (5.3), South Africa (5.1), Russian Federation (4.5), Pakistan (4.2), and Timor Leste (3.1).

Purchasing power

Purchasing power of customers varies very widely among countries. Gross domestic product (GDP) per capita, as discussed in Chapter 10, serves as a broad indicator for purchasing power. A firm operating in international markets should take into consideration the ability of buyers to pay while making pricing decisions. A company has leverage to provide additional product features and charge relatively higher prices in countries with high purchasing power.

---

[15] Johan F. Laman Trip, *CBI Export Planner—A Comprehensive Guide for Prospective Exporters in Developing Countries*, 3rd ed., CBI Rotterdam, The Netherlands, 1997, pp. 1–6.

[16] The Global Competitiveness Report 2007–08, World Economic Forum, Geneva, 2008, p. 436.

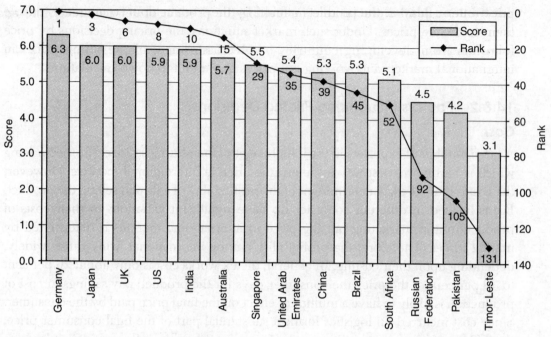

Fig. 14.13   Intensity of local competition

1—least intense, 7—most intense

Source: Based on data from The Global Competitiveness Report 2007–08, World Economic Forum, Geneva, 2008, p. 436.

Buyers' behaviour

The rise in purchasing power of customers leads to increased demand for additional product features. Buyers from countries with high income are more demanding and knowledgeable and the buying decision is primarily based on superior performance attributes whereas the buyers from low-income countries have been reported to make choices based on the lowest price.

Foreign exchange fluctuations

A firm operating in international markets has to keep a constant vigil on fluctuations of exchange rates while making pricing decisions. The currency of price quotation has to be decided by watching its movements over a period. As a general rule, firms prefer to quote prices in strong currencies for exports and weaker currencies for imports.

14.9   INTERNATIONAL DISTRIBUTION CHANNELS

Ensuring smooth flow of goods from the place of the manufacturer to the ultimate customer is critical to success in international markets. For making the goods available from the producer or manufacturer in one country to an overseas customer, a number of market intermediaries are involved for physical transfer of goods. Besides, the firm receives the payments through a channel of such intermediaries. Channels of distribution play a crucial role in making the product or services reach the end consumer.

Channels of international distribution may be defined as 'a set of interdependent organizations networked together to make the product or services available to the end consumer in international markets'. The major functions performed by distribution channels include

- Physical flow of goods from the producer or manufacturer to the ultimate customer
- Transfer of ownership to the ultimate customer
- Realizing payment that flows from the ultimate customer through market intermediaries to the producer or manufacturer
- Regular flow of information from the ultimate customer and within the channel intermediaries
- Promotion flow from the manufacturer to the end customer and receiving feedbacks

Managing distribution channels in international markets is much more complex than domestic market due to a number of factors:

- The distribution system in international markets varies significantly from one country to another. Therefore international managers have to develop a thorough understanding of the distribution channels in target markets. For instance, prior to Perestroika, the marketing channels in the erstwhile USSR were controlled by the government. The Foreign Trade Organization (FTO), the enormous government body, was involved in bulk imports and distribution through a government-controlled distribution network. However, after the disintegration of USSR, it was found that private distribution channels were largely non-existent in CIS markets and the international firms were required to create their own distribution networks.
- Firms are more familiar with the system of marketing channels in their home market; therefore, selection of distribution channels in overseas markets often is a complex decision.
- Collecting information about distribution channels in overseas markets requires greater resources, both managerial and financial.
- In addition to the considerable physical distance in managing the overseas distribution channels, the marketing systems' distance is also much higher.
- Since a firm commits substantial resources for its overseas marketing operations, the long-term commitment of channel members is an important but difficult-to-assess aspect in channel design.

14.9.1 Types of International Distribution Channels

International distribution channels may broadly be divided into two categories: direct and indirect channels. In indirect channels, a firm deals with only a home-based

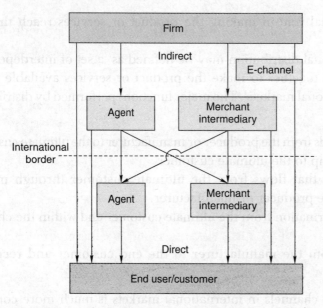

Fig. 14.14 Channels of international distribution

Source: Joshi, Rakesh Mohan, *International Marketing,* New Delhi: Oxford University Press, 2005, p. 415.

intermediary and does not come in direct contact with the overseas-based market intermediary as shown in Fig. 14.14. The home-based market intermediary may include agents, such as broker/commission agent, importer's buying agents, country-controlled buying agents, and buying offices of overseas firms or merchant intermediaries, such as merchant exporters, international trading companies, and export/trading houses. In case of direct channels, the firm comes in direct contact with foreign based market intermediaries that include agents, such as overseas-based commission agent/broker, manufacturers' export agents or sales representatives, overseas-based buying agents, or merchant intermediaries, such as merchant importer, distributor, wholesaler, and retailer.

Various channel intermediaries have been discussed in detail in Chapter 11 while explaining modes of international business expansion. Over recent years, the advent of e-channels have revolutionized international marketing channels, overcoming the barriers of distance, speed, and transportation cost, thereby opening up enormous marketing opportunities, especially in the service sectors, even for developing countries, such as India. A firm now has the option to make its products available in the international market through either of the e-channels or a combination thereof.

14.9.2 International Retailing

The retailer buys the goods from wholesalers or distributors and sells it to the ultimate customers in the international markets. The retailers serve the important function of carrying inventories, displaying products at sales outlets, providing points of purchase (PoP) promotions, and extending credits. Retailers do provide market feedback to the firm that is highly significant in reviewing its marketing decisions. The retailing system varies widely among various countries.

Organized retailing is gaining significance across the world and has therefore emerged as a powerful marketing channel. The global trend indicates a decline in the number of retail outlets but an increase in their average size with the increase in per capita income of a country. As the size of retail outlets increases, the emphasis shifts to market expansion and efficient management of international logistics. The large retailers expand their operations in international markets and evolve supply chain systems in an internationally integrated manner so as to achieve efficiency. The legal frameworks also varies significantly across countries. In countries such as Japan, France, Italy, and Belgium the legal framework serves as deterrent to the establishment of new large-scale retailers.

Sales for top 10 retailers reached US$978 billion, which represents 30.1 per cent of sales of the total sales by top 250 retailers. Wal-Mart is the world's largest retailer with retail sales of US$344,992 billion in 2006 followed by Carrefour SA (France), Home Depot (US), Tesco (UK), Metro (Germany), Kroger (US), Target (US), Costco (US), Sears (US), and Schwarz (Germany), as shown in Fig. 14.15. Interestingly, out of the top 10 retailers, six are from the US and four from Europe. Kroger and Target Corp., which rank as the sixth and seventh largest retailers globally, do not have any operations outside the US.

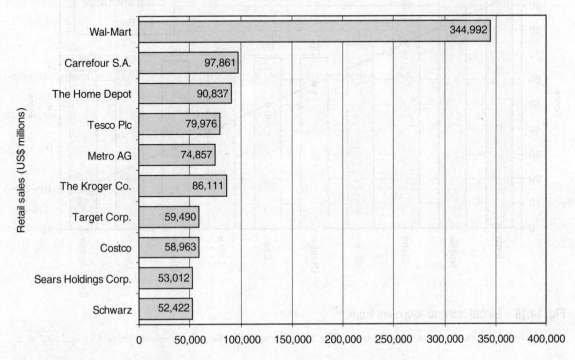

Fig. 14.15   Top 10 global retailers

Source: 2008 Global Powers of Retailing Stores, Deloitte, Czech Republic, 2008, p. 26.

The Global Retail Development Index (GRDI) developed by A.T. Kearney facilitates international retailers to identify the most promising markets for strategic investments. The GRDI is computed based on the weighted average of country risk, market attractiveness, market saturation, and time pressure. India remains the hottest investment destination for global retailers as it ranks at the top of the index followed by Russia, China, and Vietnam, as indicated in Fig. 14.16. Wal-Mart, Carrefour, and Tesco established a presence in India. Modern retail, accounting for 2 to 3 per cent of the Indian market, is expected to grow at a compound annual growth rate (CAGR) of 40 per cent, from $8 billion to $22 billion, by 2010. Overall, India's retail sector is expected to grow[17] from its current $350 billion to $427 billion by 2010 and $635 billion by 2015.

Under India's present law, relaxed in 2006, single-brand retailers are allowed to own a 51 per cent majority stake in a joint venture with a local partner. However, this does not extend to multi-brand retailers, such as Wal-Mart, Tesco, and Carrefour, forcing these major companies to operate through a franchise or cash-and-carry wholesale model. This made Wal-Mart join hands with Indian telecom giant Bharti Enterprises that will own retail shops under the Wal-Mart franchise, and Wal-Mart will operate the logistics, procurement, and storage activities. Carrefour is engaged in

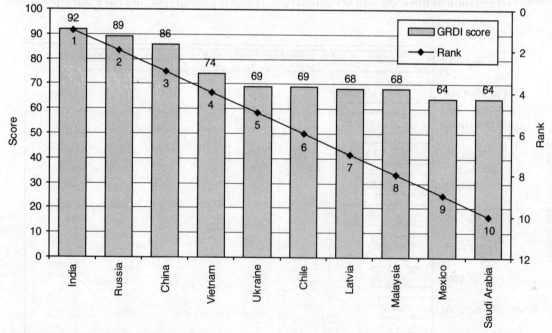

Fig. 14.16   Global retail development index

Source: 'Growth Opportunities for Global Retailers', The A.T. Kearney Global Retail Development Index, Chicago, 2007, p. 2.

---

[17] 'Growth Opportunities for Global Retailers', The A.T. Kearney Global Retail Development Index, Chicago, 2007, p. 9.

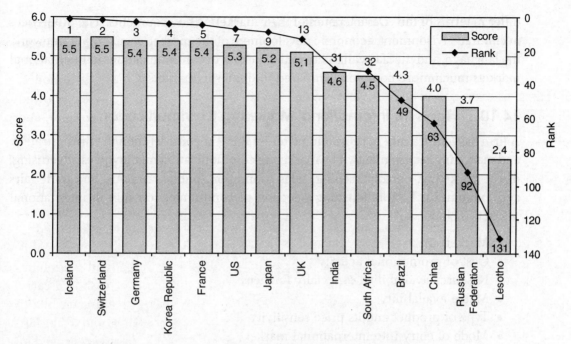

Fig. 14.17 Local companies' control over international distribution and marketing

1—Complete control by foreign companies; 7—Complete ownership and control by local companies
Source: Based on data from The Global Competitiveness Report 2007–08, World Economic Forum, Geneva, 2008, p. 499.

talks with the India-based Wadia group and Britannia to negotiate an agreement that would establish its presence in the market. Indian hypermarket retailers, such as Pantaloon Retail, RPG Group, Tata Group's Trent, K. Raheja Corp., and Reliance Industries are also making their moves before foreign direct investment in retail is further opened up.

The control of local companies over international distribution and marketing is the highest in Iceland and Switzerland with a score of 5.5 (Fig. 14.17) on a 7 point scale where 7 indicates complete ownership and control by local companies whereas 1 implies complete control by foreign companies, followed by Germany (5.4), Korea Republic (5.4), France (5.4), the US (5.3), Japan (5.2), the UK (5.1), India (4.6), South Africa (4.5), Brazil (4.3), China (4.0), Russian Federation (3.7), and Lesotho (2.4).

14.10 COMMUNICATION DECISIONS FOR INTERNATIONAL MARKETS

Communication is crucial to a firm's success in international markets. This has also been referred to as promotion, the fourth P of the marketing mix. Firms attempt to convey a set of messages to the target customers through some channel in order to create a favourable response for their market offerings and regularly receive market feedback. While marketing across countries, a firm has to communicate to the customers and the channel intermediaries located in overseas markets that considerably differ in terms of the characteristics of their marketing environments. The differences in cultural environment, economic development of the market, regulatory framework, the language, and media availability make the task of communications in international markets much more complex compared to domestic markets.

14.10.1 Tools for International Marketing Communication

A firm has to use a mix of promotional tools taking in consideration the firm's strategy and marketing requirements. The marketing communication mix involves advertising, direct marketing, personal selling, sales promotion, public relations, and trade fairs and exhibitions. Factors affecting selection of communication mix in international markets include

- Market size
- Cost of promotional activity
- Resource availability, especially finances
- Media availability
- Type of product and its price sensitivity
- Mode of entry into international market
- Market characteristics

Advertising is a paid form of mass communication through newspapers, magazines, radio, television, or any other mass media by an identified sponsor. Besides, advertising is a non-personal form of communication. Sales promotion comprises short-term marketing measures so as to stimulate quick buyers' action or immediate sale of the product. It includes rebates and price discounts, catalogues and brochures, samples, coupons, and gifts. As a part of the image-building exercise, a firm invests in building public relations. It may include sponsorship of sports and cultural events, press releases, and even lobbying at government levels. Direct marketing is also an effective marketing communication tool wherein the firm has direct interaction with customers. Personal selling involves direct selling by firm's sales force and is considered to be a two-way method of marketing communication, facilitating a stronger relationship with the customers. As the firms from low-income countries have limited financial and other resources to invest in marketing communication, participation in international trade fairs and other modes of two-way communications are often considered more cost effective and feasible for most firms.

Advertising

Any paid form of non-personal communication by an identified sponsor is termed as advertising. It can be for a product, service, an idea, or organization. Non-personal communication uses a mass media, such as newspapers, magazines, TV, or radio to transmit the message to a large number of individuals, often at the same time. Advertising is the most widely used form of promotion, especially for mass marketing.

Advertising: Standardization vs adaptation   An international marketing firm may either use a standardized advertising strategy or customize it, depending upon the needs of the target markets. Firms have to carefully scrutinize the decision to use standardized ads as these may face socio-legal implications when used in the context of another country. The adaptation of advertising may be either due to mandatory reasons or voluntarily due to competitive market response.

Advertising standardization   Using the same advertising strategy across countries is termed as standardization. Adopting a standardized advertising strategy is gaining wider acceptance due to a large number of factors:

- The preferences and lifestyles of consumers are increasingly becoming homogeneous, enabling psychographic segmentation of markets that can be targeted through a uniform message.
- Consumer behaviour is becoming increasingly similar in urban centres across the world. City-dwellers exhibit increasing similarity in their working patterns, shopping, travelling, and lifestyles across the countries.
- Sharp increase in international travel among customers favours standardized advertising strategy.
- International reach of media, such as television programmes, magazines, and certain newspapers have also encouraged standardized advertisements. For instance, programmes on channels, such as BBC, CNN, ESPN, Discovery, Zee TV, Star Plus, etc., are telecast and watched across the globe.
- The standardized advertising approach facilitates creation of a uniform corporate image.
- Economies of scale are achieved while using standardized advertising.

However, the extent of standardization varies under the following broad categories:

Ad with no change   The same advertisement is used with no change in theme, copy, or illustration except for translation. Benetton Group Spa, the Italy-based global clothing retailer uses global advertising campaigns with the same theme 'The United Colours of Benetton'. However, Benetton's ads use shocking photos to attract public attention on global issues related to environment, terrorism, racism, and HIV. Many of Benetton's ad campaigns have been under criticism and attack in a number of countries. But in so far as an ad creates and sustains customers' interest, Benetton is moving ahead with its standardized shock advertising campaigns worldwide.

Ad with changes in illustration   Ads using local models worldwide maintaining the ad copy and the theme are also considered standardized advertisement.

The major benefits of standardized advertising include economies of scale and projection of uniform image in international markets. Such an approach may be adopted in the following marketing situations:

- The target market is segmented on the basis of psychographic profile of the customers, such as their lifestyles, behaviour, and attitudes

- Cultural proximity among the customers
- Technology-intensive or industrial products
- Similarity in marketing environment such as political, legal, and social

Advertising adaptation Modification in the message, copy, or content of an advertisement is termed as adaptation or customization. However, the emphasis in communication varies among markets. Communication adaptation is often needed in international markets due to

- Difference in cultural values among countries
- Difficulties in language translation
- Variations in level of education of the target groups
- Media availability
- Social attitudes towards advertising
- Regulatory framework of the target market

As customer behaviour is greatly influenced by cultural factors in the target market, it is difficult for a standardized communication strategy to be effective across markets. Therefore, to convey a similar concept across various cultures, a firm has to adapt advertising in different markets. For instance, especially in products with image-based positioning, such as Pepsi, an ad in Western countries may depict scantily clad women on a beach or at a bar, which is not feasible to adapt in Islamic countries, both due to the statutory framework and cultural environment.

However, global brands have a challenging task to build a global image while remaining sensitive to cultural nuances in different countries in their advertising strategy. The world's most popular male grooming brand, Axe, launched by Unilever in 1983 in France, is one of the rarest global brands that replicates its marketing mix across geographical boundaries. Although targeted at males aged 16–25, it really aims at 'naughty guys of all ages' and those 'young at heart'. The brand has an excellent track record of advertising honours, with several international advertising and marketing awards. Despite a globally uniform central theme, which revolves around seduction by the girls, the Axe ad campaigns are adapted aptly to suit local cultures. In Western liberal societies, explicit ads are used to portray such scenarios whereas brilliantly subtle ads are used to convey the theme in highly conservative societies, such as Saudi Arabia, as shown in Fig. 14.18. Such adaptations become crucial to marketing success for global brands in diverse cultural contexts.

Direct marketing

Selling products and services to customers, without using any market intermediary is termed as direct marketing. It deals with customers on a one-to-one basis directly, unlike conventional mass marketing that deals indirectly. Direct marketing has little dependence on mass promotion or advertising whereas conventional marketing relies heavily on mass promotion. Technological advances, such as proliferation of telecommunication and information technology have facilitated direct marketing across

Japan

Portugal

Brazil

Saudi Arabia

India

Fig. 14.18   Cross-cultural adaptation of Axe ads to communicate globally the uniform core theme

the world. The fast growth of credit cards has facilitated international sales transactions by enabling buyers to make payments over the Internet.

Direct mailing   It involves sending letters, brochures or catalogues, e-mails, faxes, or even product samples directly to the customers who may in turn purchase by mail.

Door-to-door marketing Receptivity of door-to-door marketing varies considerably among cultures. In Japan, even motorcars and stocks are sold door to door. Amway, Avon, and Tupperware are some of the largest firms relying on door-to-door marketing worldwide.

Multi-level marketing It involves a revolutionary distribution system with little spending on advertising and infrastructure. In multi-level marketing, a core group of distributors are recruited who generally pay the company a registration fee and often have to be introduced to the company by a sponsor. Each of these distributors picks up products worth a certain sum, for instance US$50 or Rs 1,000, with a mandate to sell them directly to the customer. The mark-up is generally pegged at 25–30 per cent. However, the distributor can charge a lower price, reducing the seller's commission. These core distributors appoint further distributors and get additional commission from the sales made by them also. The major global firms involved in multi-level marketing include Amway, Avon, Oriflame, Marykay Cosmetics, etc. The major benefits of multi-level marketing involve a rapid, continuous, and automatic growth of distribution networks. Besides, it is a quick and cost-effective marketing method. As the marketing system depends upon the continuity of the network, any snap in its linkage creates major setbacks for the entire distribution-cum-sales system. Since direct sellers repeatedly approach prospects, this is often a perceived irritant by prospects. The high-pressure tactics used to push the product many a times adversely affect the brand image. The firm has limited control over the sales force in terms of prices offered.

Personal selling

It involves a firm's representatives personally meeting with customers. Personal selling is widely used for selling plants and machinery, heavy equipment, or high-value products to institutional buyers. As languages, customs, and the business culture differ across countries, personal selling becomes much more complex. Generally, firms employ local salespersons for personal selling in international markets. Personal selling is generally employed effectively in markets where

- Wages are low compared to advertising expenses. Thus, personal selling is highly cost-effective in low-income countries.
- Customers are multi-linguistic, such as in India, where communication in single language is hardly effective
- Literacy level is low
- The sellers' one-to-one contact with the customers pays, as in oriental cultures, as it facilitates establishing relationships

The international firm should also provide periodic inputs to the distributors' sales force, such as periodic trainings, sales literatures, and direct mailing; through such means the firm facilitates distributors' tasks and improves efficiency.

Sales promotion

Sales promotion refers to use of various tools as short-term incentives in order to induce a purchase decision. Due to increased competitive intensity in the market, firms often make use of sale promotion aimed at immediate results. Besides, buyers also expect some purchase incentives in view of competitors' market offerings. It is estimated that the manufacturers as a group spend about twice as much on trade promotion as they do on advertising and an amount about equal to their expenditures on consumer promotions.[18] The promotional offers have a local focus and generally varies from country to country. The basic objectives of consumer promotion programmes are

- To solicit product enquiries
- To generate trials for new or related products
- To generate additional sales
- To motivate customers for repeat purchase

Sales promotion may be categorized as

Trade promotions   These are the promotional tools aimed at market intermediaries.
Consumer promotions   These are the promotional tools directed at the ultimate consumers.

Various tools used for consumer promotion include discounts, free samples, contests, gifts, gift coupons, festival sales, special price offers for bulk purchase, etc.

Public relations

In overseas markets, for a firm to be perceived as an 'insider' is increasingly becoming important. Public relations aim at building a corporate image and influencing media and other target groups to garner favourable publicity. Various methods used for public relations may be

- Sponsorship of sports, cultural events, etc.
- Press releases
- Contribution to awards and prices for sports and other events
- Publicity of firm's promotional campaign
- Lobbying at government level

Public relations may aim at internal as well as external communication directed at employees, shareholders, suppliers of inputs and components, customers, and the general public. The firm attempts to create links with the media, politicians, bureaucrats, and other influential groups and persons in the target markets so as to gain positive publicity. In high-income countries, professional firms offer specialized public relations

[18] Hume, Scot, 'Trade Promos Devour Half of All Marketing $', *Advertising Age*, 13 April 1992, p. 3.

services, whereas in low-income countries the 'word of mouth' has high significance for spreading the message.

International trade fairs and exhibitions

Trade fairs and exhibitions are the oldest and most effective tools to explore marketing opportunities. Trade fairs are organized gatherings wherein the buyers and sellers come into contact with each other and establish communication. A trade fair may be international, regional, national, or provincial in terms of its scope and participants. Trade fairs provide opportunities for buyer-seller interface. The international trade fairs

- Serve as a meeting place for potential importers, agents, and distributors in the international markets.
- Provide publicity and generate goodwill
- Provide opportunity to meet existing clients in the market and assess their performance vis-à-vis competitors
- Provide an opportunity to get information on the competing products, their attributes, prices, etc. in the market
- Help assess customer's response to the firm's products

A firm needs to consider while selecting an international trade fair

- Compatibility with firm's product profile and marketing objectives
- Location of the fair
- Visitors' and participants' profile
- Performance of the fair in terms of the sales concluded, exhibitors participated, and the number of visitors during previous years
- Experience of previous business exhibitors
- Cost of participation vis-à-vis other promotional alternatives

14.10.2 Factors Influencing International Communication Decisions

As the marketing environment across countries varies considerably, various factors influencing international marketing communication include

Culture

Culture influences customers' behaviour across countries as discussed in Chapter 7. Besides, customers are highly sensitive about the cultural nuances in marketing communications. Advertising in the US and a number of Western countries often reflects the direct approach, assertiveness, and competitiveness, whereas advertising themes in most oriental countries imbibe social acceptance, mutual dependence, respect for elders and traditions, harmony with nature, use of seasons, innovation and novelty, distinctive use celebrities, changing family role, are often effective.[19]

---

[19] Ricks, David A., *Blunders in International Business,* Cambridge, MA: Blackwell Publishers, 1993.

India's leading pharmaceutical company, Ranbaxy Laboratory's Revital, which is a balanced combination of vitamins, minerals, and ginseng, is promoted differently in different countries, primarily due to varying cultural sensitivities of customers. In India, Revital is promoted as a daily health-supplement diet defining the target customer as a 'regular man (urban-office goer) who is able to do more in life and that with a smile, after using Revital'. In Malaysia, it is targeted to young people and active sportsmen as a health supplement. Revital is marketed as a multi-vitamin supplement for expecting mothers in Nigeria. In countries like Russia, Thailand, and South Africa, Revital is targeted at couples as a product promoting 'health and love', aimed at enhancing vitality and romance. In Southeast Asia and China, where ginseng is a highly desirable herb with numerous health benefits, the product packaging depicts a picture of the herb and prominently mentions in the local language, 'A combination of Korean Panax Ginseng extract with minerals and vitamins'. On the other hand, as ginseng is less known in India and South Africa, the picture of ginseng is not shown on the packaging.

Indians are highly fond of sweets and astonishing varieties of locally made sweets are available across the country. No celebration in India is complete without offering and consuming sweets. In response to the enormous customer demands for sweets, Nestle promotes its chocolates as sweets in the Indian markets. As a result, the ad campaign with the punch line, '*Pappu pass ho gaya*' (Pappu got passed), implying celebrating Pappu's success with Cadbury chocolates instead of sweets, became highly popular.

Language

Translation from one language to another is crucial in international communications. Literal translation may fail to convey the desired message across countries due to cultural factors. For instance the word 'yes' is understood differently across countries. In low-context societies, such as the US and the Europe, 'yes' means 'yes' but in high-context societies, such as Japan, 'yes' means 'I am listening, what you are saying' and not necessarily just a 'yes'. In Thailand 'yes' means 'OK'. Such vast differences in inferring the meaning of 'yes' is due to the fact that in high-context cultures, the other person is given an opportunity to save his/her face and direct refusals are hardly appreciated by society.

In 2001, Honda introduced its new car 'Fitta' in Nordic countries; subsequently it was found that 'Fitta' was an old vulgar word in Norwegian, Swedish, and Danish. Honda had to rename it as 'Honda Jazz'. Colgate's popular toothpaste in the US, 'Cue' miserably failed in France, as 'Cue' is the name of a French pornographic magazine.

The problems related to translation may be overcome by using a variety of techniques, such as back translation, parallel translation, and decentring, as discussed in detail in Chapter 7. Therefore, communication decisions in international markets have to take into consideration not only the literal translation in the foreign language, but also subtle nuances.

Education

The level of literacy plays an important role in deciding communication tools and the message in international markets. Market segments with lower level of adult literacy need to be addressed by way of more audio-visual content rather than a written message. It should be ensured that the visuals, rather than the text, convey the desired message.

Media infrastructure

Availability of media that varies widely across the countries often influences advertisers' options for using a medium. Outdoor ads are cost-effective and widely used, especially in low-income countries due to constraints related to media penetration. Movies, posters, puppet shows, mime, etc., are frequently used methods of communication in low-income countries that have lower levels of literacy. These methods are extremely popular in social marketing, such as anti-HIV campaigns, contraceptives, and family welfare and preventive health.

Government regulations

The regulatory framework of a country influences the communications strategy in international markets. The government regulations in various countries relates to

- Advertising in foreign language
- Use of pornography and sensuality
- Comparative advertising referring to competing products from rival firms
- Advertisements related to alcohol and tobacco
- Use of children as models
- Advertisements related to health food and pharmaceuticals

Some of the advertising regulations in various countries[20] are summed up here:

- In Malaysia, the Ministry of Information's Advertising Code states that women should not be the principal objects of an advertisement or intend to attract sales unless the advertised product is relevant to women.
- The Ministry of Information in Saudi Arabia prevents any advertising depicting unveiled women.
- Portuguese law prohibits sex discrimination or the subordination or objectification of women in advertising.
- The use of foreign words and expressions, when French equivalents can be found in the dictionary, are prohibited in France.
- Norway requires that advertising not portray men or women in an offensive manner or imply any derogatory judgment of either sex.
- Most Arab countries prohibit explicit depiction of sensuality.

---

[20] Boddewyn, Jean J., 'Controlling Sex and Decency in Advertising around the World', *Journal of Advertising*, 20 December 1991, pp. 25–36.

14.11 FRAMEWORK FOR INTERNATIONAL PRODUCT PROMOTION STRATEGIES

The need satisfied or the product function considerably influences product adaptation and promotion strategies. Depending upon the product function or need satisfied, the condition of product use and customers' ability to buy, the Keegan's framework for international product promotion strategies[21] (Exhibit 14.4) provides a good insight.

Under the first four marketing situations, potential customers have the ability to purchase the product while in case of the fifth option, customers do not have the ability to buy. The framework offers certain alternative strategies for products as well as promotion.

Straight adaptation

In cases, when the need satisfied and the conditions of product use is the same, the product as well as the marketing communication is extended across markets. Global brands, such as Pepsi, Coke, Gillette, Benetton, Heineken, and BMW often use a global product and global communication strategies. The straight adaptation of product and promotion strategies for global markets results in enormous cost savings for the firms on R&D for product development, market research, and marketing

Strategy	Product function or need satisfied	Conditions of product use	Ability to buy product	Recommended product strategy	Recommended communications strategy	Rank order from least to most expensive	Product examples
			Exhibit 14.4 International product promotion strategies				
1	Same	Same	Yes	Extension	Extension	1	Soft drinks
2	Different	Same	Yes	Extension	Adaptation	2	Bicycles, motor-cycles, scooters
3	Same	Different	Yes	Adaptation	Extension	3	Detergents
4	Different	Different	Yes	Adaptation	Adaptation	4	Clothing, greeting cards
5	Same	-	No	Invention	Develop new communications	5	Washing machines

Source: Keegan, Warren J., 'Multinational Product Planning: Strategic Alternatives' *Journal of Marketing*, vol. 33, January 1969, American Marketing Association, pp. 58–62.

---

[21] Keegan, Warren J., 'Multinational Product Planning: Strategic Alternatives', *Journal of Marketing*, January 1969, pp. 58–62.

communication. Additionally, a universal approach also helps create global awareness of the brands and customer base.

Product extension–promotion adaptation

When the condition of product use remains the same whereas the needs satisfied or the product function is different, the product is extended as such but the promotion strategy is adapted. The use of bicycles vary among low-income and high-income countries: the bicycle is used as a means of cost-effective transport in low-income countries, whereas it is a tool for recreation in high-income countries. Thus, its promotional campaigns are customized across countries.

Chewing gum is viewed primarily as a children's product in India whereas it is considered a substitute to smoking in the US. It is supposed to provide dental benefits in Europe while considered beneficial for facial fitness in Far Eastern countries. Under such situations, no changes are made in the product but the promotional strategy is customized so as to address the customers' needs. To tap the Indian customers' quest for traditional styles and imagery, Reid and Taylor features the Bollywood icon Amitabh Bachhan in its promotional campaign, clad in a typical Jodhpuri ethnic costume.

Product adaptation–promotion extension

In markets where the condition of product use is different but the product performs the same function or satisfies the same needs, the strategy of product adaptation–promotion extension is employed. Detergent is primarily used around the world for washing and cleaning clothes. Nevertheless, the washing habits of people vary widely in various markets. Indians use lukewarm water whereas French wash their clothes in scalding hot water and Australians, in cold water. Indians and French generally use top loading washing machines while most Europeans use front loading washing machines. The differences in electrical voltage require product modifications in electrical appliances being marketed from India to the US. Due to difference in TV operating systems, Japanese consumer electronics firms customize their products for marketing in countries which do not use NTSC systems, viz. India, Pakistan, UK, UAE, and Russia. Under such situations the promotional strategy remains the same but the product modification is made depending upon the customers' needs in different markets.

Dual adaptation

In countries where the functions of the product and the need satisfied are different and the conditions for the product use is also different, a firm has to customize both the product and the promotional strategies. Clothing in low-income countries serves the basic purpose of physical protection whereas in high-income countries or even in urban centres of medium and low-income countries it symbolizes the personality and status of the user. Therefore, a firm has to customize both the product and promotion.

Developing new product

In markets where the product function and need satisfied remain the same, but the conditions of product use differ and also the consumers do not necessarily possess the ability to pay for the product, it requires product invention and developing new marketing communication. For instance, in countries with very low income, specifically in rural areas in Africa, Asia, and Latin America, the buying power of the people is limited. Therefore, firms have to develop technologies suitable to the target markets. This condition necessitated firms to develop hand-powered washing machines for African markets. Philips India introduced a hand-wound radio in 2003 that can be powered by hand wounding, primarily to address the needs of rural India, where the electrical supply is erratic and constant use of batteries makes the radio expensive. The product has fared exceedingly well in rural markets.[22]

This framework of product promotion strategies serves as a useful tool in developing broad understanding about the adaptation–standardization decisions related to product and promotion in international markets. However, firms need to further evaluate marketing conditions before formulating their specific strategies.

14.12 REVIEWING PERFORMANCE AND CONSOLIDATING INTERNATIONAL MARKETING OPERATIONS

Once a business enterprise implements international marketing decisions, as discussed above, it needs to periodically review the performance for whether the desired marketing objectives are met. The gaps in terms of its total revenue from overseas markets and its percentage share in the total revenue, both in absolute terms and growth, need to be identified. One may also look into market share and its growth in overseas markets besides profitability achieved.

The reasons for the gaps in performance need to be identified and remedial actions initiated. Appropriate modifications may be made in various components of marketing mix, i.e., product, price, distribution channels, and communication. If need be, the target markets may be reviewed, which may also lead to taking up new markets and reducing efforts or even dropping existing markets. Even if the pre-determined goals are not met, the company may modify its marketing objectives.

The forces of globalization have opened up marketing opportunities for firms across borders, increasing competitive pressures. Innovative marketing tactics, such as cross-subsidization of production, neo-marketing barriers, and marketing strategies to circumvent these barriers, and locating global market segments have become the order of the day. The breakthroughs in information and communication technology and means of transport have contributed to increased convergence in tastes and preferences of consumers across the globe, giving rise to the global consumer segment. Income growth triggered consumers' desire for more and newer varieties of goods,

---

[22] Sadagopan, S., 'Enter, Made for India Product', *Economic Times*, 1 April 2004.

creating marketing opportunities for foreign products. Apart from global consumers, global competitors with competitive marketing strategies in various markets have also emerged.

The distinction between international and domestic marketing mainly arises due to the differences in the challenges a firm has to face in the marketing environments, which are invariably much higher than what a firm faces while operating exclusively in domestic markets. Since the environmental challenges are beyond the control of marketer, the key to success in international markets lies in responding competitively by way of adopting an effective marketing strategy.

SUMMARY

Marketing carried out across national borders is termed as international marketing. The basic principles of marketing, especially its technical aspects, remain the same both in domestic and international marketing. It is the environmental factors, such as social, economic, political, legal, and technological, that varies across countries and significantly influences international marketing decisions.

Market size and growth potential are crucial to a firm's decision to select a target market. In addition, entry barriers, both tariff and non-tariff, and profitability need to be evaluated. This chapter also discusses the marketing-mix decisions in the international perspective. A product is anything offered to the market to satisfy a need or a want. Selling a standardized product across countries or customizing it for different markets is the key product decision international managers are required to take. Factors favouring product standardization include high level of technological intensity, formidable adaptation costs, convergence of customer needs worldwide, and country-of-origin impact. The product may be adapted for international markets due to mandatory factors, such as government regulations, electric current standards, operating or measurement systems, and packaging regulations. Additionally, a number of voluntary factors, such as consumer demographics, culture, local customs and traditions, conditions of use and price also influence product adaptations. There is no single readymade recipe whether one should sell standardized products across the markets or adapt it differently to suit market requirements. In fact, a

cost-benefit analysis has to be carried out so as to arrive at a trade-off for product adaptation. A brand is defined as a name, term, sign, symbol, or design, or a combination thereof, intended to identify the goods or services of one seller or a group of sellers and to differentiate them from competitors. For a brand to be global, it should have a worldwide geographical spread.

Price is the sum of values exchanged from the customer for a product or service. Since competition is much higher in international markets, marginal cost pricing is preferred over full-cost pricing in situations where fixed costs are recovered from the domestic markets and there is enough surplus production capacity. Pricing decisions in international markets are often influenced by cost, competition, purchasing power, buyers' behaviour, and foreign exchange fluctuations.

Channels of international distribution may be defined as the set of interdependent organizations networked together to make a product or service available to end customers in the international markets. A firm may use either an indirect, where it does not come in direct contact with a market intermediary, or a direct, where it directly deals with an overseas-based market intermediary, channel of distribution.

The marketing communication mix involves advertising, sales promotion, public relations, personal selling, and direct and interactive marketing. A firm is required to use a judicial mix of these marketing communication tools. The environmental factors, such as culture, government regulations, language, and media availability in multi-country marketing environments make international marketing communication decisions much more complex compared to domestic marketing. Based on the product function or needs satisfied, the condition of product use and the customers' ability to buy, the framework discussed in this chapter provides a good insight into product promotion adaptation or extension decisions in international markets.

KEY TERMS

Advertising Any paid form of non-personal communication by an identified sponsor.

Agent A market intermediary that does not take title of the goods and represent the principal firm and work on commission basis.

Augmented product components It includes the support services and other augmented components, such as warrantees, guarantees, and after-sales services.

Brand A name, term, sign, symbol or design, or a combination thereof, intended to identify the goods or services of one seller or group of sellers to differentiate them from those of competitors.

Core product components Refers to the core benefit or the problem solving services offered by the products.

Direct mailing Sending letters, brochures, catalogues, e-mails, or faxes directly to the customers.

Direct marketing Selling products and services to customers without using any market intermediary.

International distribution channel A set of interdependent organizations networked together to make the product or services available to the end consumer in international markets.

Marginal cost Cost of producing and selling one additional unit.

Marketing communication mix Involves advertising, sales promotion, public relations, personal selling, and direct marketing.

Merchant intermediary A channel member that buys the goods, takes its title and sells it on his own account working on margins.

Multi-level marketing A distribution system recruiting a core group of distributors who in-turn recruit sub-distributors and thus the distribution chain is continued.

Packaging product component The features, quality, design, packaging, branding, and other attributes, which are integral to products offering core benefit.

Price Sum of values exchanged from the customer for the product or service.

Product A product is anything that can be offered to a market to satisfy a want or need. It may include physical goods, services, experiences, events, persons, places, properties, organizations, information, and ideas.

Product adaptation Modification of products for international markets.

Sales promotion Various tools used as short-term incentives in order to induce a purchase decision.

Sprinkler approach Simultaneous product launch in international markets.

Trade fairs Organized gatherings wherein the buyers and sellers come into each others' contacts and establish communication.

Waterfall approach Launching of a new product in international markets in a phased manner.

CONCEPT REVIEW QUESTIONS

1. 'Operating in international markets is much more complex than marketing domestically'. Critically evaluate this statement with suitable examples.

2. 'An international marketer has to find out a trade-off between a standardized and customized product as it is difficult to evolve a global product.' Do you agree with this statement? Justify your answer with suitable illustrations.

3. Explain the concept of marginal-cost pricing. Give reasons for its implications in international marketing vis-à-vis domestic marketing.

4. Briefly describing the channels of international distribution, identify the factors that make managing distribution channels in international markets much more complex compared to domestic markets.

5. Examine the factors influencing the communication decisions in international markets.

6. Explain Keegan's framework for product-promotion strategies in international markets with suitable examples.

CRITICAL THINKING QUESTIONS

1. Consult your library and explore the Internet to find out packaging and labelling regulations for cigarettes in Canada, France, Japan, and Singapore. Compare it with the prevailing regulations in your country. Identify the similarities and differences and discuss your findings in class.

2. Explore the Internet and identify an ad used globally for a brand of your choice. Also find out a brand that uses different ads for different markets. Critically examine the reasons for use of such an advertising strategy. Collect such ads and share your findings with your colleagues.

PROJECT ASSIGNMENTS

1. Visit a few toy shops in your city and find out the toys manufactured in China. Estimate the percentage of Chinese toys sold in your city and the country as whole. Explore the reasons for customers' preference for Chinese products over indigenous toys.

2. Contact a local firm operating in international markets and find out its pricing strategy in different markets. Compare and discuss your results with your colleagues who have visited other firms.

CASE STUDY

Barbie Faces Islamic Dolls

Barbie, so named by businesswoman-inventor Ruth Handler after daughter Barbara's nickname, became the world's most popular fashion doll. Handler found that young girls enjoyed playing out their dreams in adult roles when she saw her daughter Barbara playing with a paper doll and imagining it as a grown up. Most children's dolls available at that time represented infants. This gave rise to an idea of a teenage doll, Barbie. Handler co-founded Mattel, a Southern California toy company with her husband Elliot Handler, and

spearheaded the introduction of the doll. Barbie's physical appearance was modelled on the German *Bild Lilli* doll, a risqué gag gift for a man, based upon the cartoon character featured in the West German newspaper *Bild Zeitung*. Barbie made its debut in the American International Toy Fair in New York on 9 March 1959. This date is also considered to be Barbie's official birthday.

Barbie sells over £1 billion annually across 150 countries. It is estimated that three Barbie dolls are sold every second.[1] Although Barbie was

---

[1] 'Vintage Barbie Struts Her Stuff', *BBC News*, 22 September 2006.

positioned as the ultimate American girl, it was never manufactured in the US, primarily to avoid higher production costs. The first Barbie dolls were manufactured in Japan with their clothes hand-stitched by Japanese home-workers. In the first year of production, around 350,000 Barbie dolls were sold. The Mattel-owned four factories, two in China and one each in Malaysia and Indonesia,[2] produce over 100 million Barbie dolls a year. However, a number of other companies produced Barbie-licensed products.

The process of Barbie production is very complex, which includes shipping the dolls from one country to another for different processes. To illustrate, the US ships the cardboard packaging, paint pigments, and moulds to manufacturing facilities in China that provides the factory space, labour, electricity, and cotton cloth for Barbie dresses. Taiwan refines the oil into ethylene for plastic pellets for Barbie's body whereas Japan attaches the nylon hair. International shipping operations are carried out by Hong Kong-based managers.

Barbie is a plastic vinyl doll with the figure of an adult woman whose full name is Barbie Millicent Robert. Initially, Barbie was marketed as a glamorous, physically developed teenage fashion model with a range of fashion accessories. With her hair in a ponytail, and dressed in a black and white stripped bathing suit and sunglasses, Barbie proved an instant and phenomenal marketing success among young girls. Barbie has had over 40 pets, including 21 dogs, 14 horses, 6 cats, parrot, chimpanzee, panda, lion cub, giraffe, and a zebra. In response to consumer demand, in 1961, Mattel brought out Barbie's ultimate 'accessory'—her boyfriend, the fashion conscious Ken (Fig. C.1). Unlike other baby-like dolls, Barbie did not teach nurturing. Barbie has no parents or offspring.

Over the years Barbie has become very popular among young girls. She has been the subject of numerous books and controversies, besides, being the star in her own movies. Young girls love Barbie because she continually evolves as girls change. Barbie remains paramount in the hearts and minds

Fig. C.1   Barbie with her boyfriend Ken

of girls and moms alike because she reflects the interests, activities, and aspirations of present-day girls. Barbie offers a way for girls to play out their dreams and fantasies in a way that is relevant to today's girls. She is also credited to have provided many young girls an alternative to restrictive fifties' gender roles. She demonstrates girls that they can be anything they want to be—a princess, a teacher, an Olympic athlete, a doctor, a pilot, or even an astronaut. The doll became a role model for financial self-sufficiency, outfitted with career paraphernalia.

Barbie's marketing strategy involved meticulous product customization to suit diverse cultures across the world. The dolls are customized to represent varied cultures, regions, and occasions (Fig. C.2). It is estimated that since 1959, over a billion Barbie dolls representing over 45 nationalities and 80 occupations have been sold worldwide.

The Chinese Barbie evokes the exotic Far East with a costume inspired by those of the Qing Dynasty. The Egyptian Barbie wears a serpent ornament with a stunning golden crown inspired by the royalty of ancient Egypt. The Moja Barbie perfectly reflects the grandeur of the African continent. Mattel has customized the Barbie doll for

[2] Ritz, Ashish, 'Introducing: Slave Barbie', available at http://ihscslnews.org/view_article.php?id=187, December, 2006; 'The Creation of a Barbie', available at http://www.lclark.edu/~soan221/97/Barbie5.html.

Irish

Indian

Japanese African German Chinese

Fig. C.2 Barbie's customization across world markets

India as well by cladding her in the conventional sari and traditional jewellery especially designed to appeal to Indian masses.

Barbie dolls have also been designed to symbolize various festivals across the world. Indian Barbie symbolizes Diwali; Kwanzaa Barbie, the

African-American celebrations kwanza, meaning the first fruit of the harvest; Carnival Barbie, the week-long joyous Brazilian celebrations of music, dance, sequins, and feathers at Rio de Janeiro; Chinese New-year Barbie, the ancient festival of Chinese New year beginning with the new moon on the first day of the year that ends the evening of the full moon on the 15th day, called the Lantern festival, etc.

Barbie is also known as the 'most collectible doll in the world'. Through the years, she has developed from a teenage fashion model to a trendsetter and fashion adventurer. The four major types of Barbie collectors include pink, silver, gold, and platinum label Barbies. Packaged in pink-trimmed boxes, Pink Label Barbies are widely available and not limited to production numbers. Silver Label Barbies, packaged in silver-trimmed boxes are only available at select retailers and can be produced at only 50,000 per edition. Gold Label barbies are even more difficult to find as only 25,000 of each edition can be produced worldwide.

Despite Barbie's diverse product portfolio, considerable competition has evolved from new dolls like the funky Bratz, the long-term UK rival Sindy, and the Islamic dolls

Barbie's Criticism and the Islamic Markets

In many countries, Barbie's curvaceous body and revealing garments are perceived to promote sexuality and promiscuity. The standard size of the Barbie doll, 11.5 inches, corresponds to a real height of 5 feet 9 inches at 1/6 scale. Barbie's vital statistics have been estimated at 36 inches (chest), 18 inches (waist), and 33 inches (hips). Barbie has been criticized for unrealistic body proportions and for promoting materialism associated with amassing cars, houses, and clothes. Girls tend to develop an inferiority complex, as they grow up, if they can't look exactly like Barbie. The desire to attain the physical appearance and lifestyle similar to Barbie has been termed as 'Barbie syndrome'. Although pre-teen and adolescent females are more prone to the Barbie syndrome, it is applicable to any age group.

Barbie came under fire in Russia and was banned in 2002 because the doll was thought to awaken sexual impulses in the very young, and encourage consumerism among Russian children.[3] The Commission for the Propagation of Virtue and Prevention of Vice, known as moral police or *mutaween* in Saudi Arabia, declared Barbie dolls a threat to morality and offensive to Islam.[4] Barbie was banned in Saudi Arabia[5] in 2003 as Saudi Arabia's religious police found the Jewish Barbie dolls with their revealing clothes and shameful postures, accessories, and tools, as a symbol of the decadence of the West.

Dolls for the Islamic World

Product adaptation to cultural sensitivities is crucial to success in international markets. Mattel markets a Moroccan Barbie and collectors' doll Leyla that represent Muslim women. Leyla's elaborate costume and the backstory of being enslaved in the court of a Turkish sultan were intended to convey the tribulations of a popular Muslim character from the 1720s. However, Mattel's portrayal of the Middle Eastern Barbie as the stereotype of a belly dancer or a concubine hardly appealed to present-day Muslim customers.

A number of dolls have been launched for Islamic markets (Fig. C.3) not only to fill the marketing void but also to offer Muslim girls someone they can relate to. Therefore, most Muslim buyers identify more closely with Islamic dolls as one of them rather than with the stranger Barbie. Islamic dolls generally show young girls that the *hijab* (veil) is a normal part of a woman's life. If the girls put scarves on their dolls when they are young, the parents believe it might be easier to do so for themselves in real life, when their time comes. Sometimes, it is difficult for girls to put on the hijab. They feel it is the end of their childhood. Muslim parents often prefer to buy Islamic dolls over Barbie as it expresses their way of life. Islamic dolls are conceptualized to be the role model for children

---

[3] 'Barbie Is Banned from Russia, Without Love', *The Observer*, 24 November 2002.

[4] 'Barbie Deemed Threat to Saudi Morality', *US Today*, 10 September 2003.

[5] 'Saudi Bans Female Doll Imports', *Guardian*, 18 December 2003.

Razanne (In–Out)   Fulla

Fig. C.3   Dolls for the Islamic markets

in Islamic cultures, representing how most Muslim buyer like their daughters to dress and behave.

Islamic dolls launched in the market, include Sara from Iran, Fulla form Syria, Razanne by a Michigan-based US Company, Saghira from Morocco, and Salma from Indonesia.

Fulla

Conceptualized by a Damascus-based Syrian toy manufacturer, New Boy Toys, Fulla was aimed at children in Islamic markets across the world. The concept to bring out an Islamic doll evolved around 1999 and was carefully honed. Fulla's creators have gone to great length to make her modest and conservative. It took 50 animators, artists, and psychologists 18 months to design her face. Like any Western ad agency with a product or politician to sell, Fulla's creators turned to focus groups to test their progress. The product development team considered 10 different faces before settling on the Fulla look: large brown eyes and long, coal-black hair streaked with auburn.

Fulla, an alternative to Barbie for children in the Islamic countries, hit stores in late 2003. Within a couple of years of its launch, Fulla became the dream of every Arab girl and the hottest-selling

doll in the Middle East. Over the years, the product profile of Fulla and her accessories have grown manifold. Now there is a 'Singing Fulla' and a 'Talking Fulla' pushing a luggage cart with suitcases to hold the dozens of seasonal outfits that crowd their closets. The product catalogue runs to almost 80 pages and includes 150 Fulla-licensed items, ranging from cameras to CD players to inflatable chairs and swimming pools. Girls from Beirut to Bahrain carry Fulla umbrellas, wear Fulla watches, ride Fulla bicycles, and eat Fulla corn-flakes.

The name Fulla is derived from a fragrant jasmine flower found only in the Middle East. Like Barbie, she is 11½ inch tall, but unlike Mattel's products, she is visibly less bosomy. There is no such thing as a single Arab look, but broader features and heavier figures are more the norm among Arab women. However, Fulla's button nose, bow mouth, and svelte figure testify to the internationalization of Western standards of beauty, superceding indigenous ideas of beauty. Fulla's complexion is olive compared to Barbie's peaches-and-cream skin-tone, her hair is much thicker than Barbie's blonde mane and her face is fuller than[6] that of the typical American, but otherwise she is much the same.

---

[6] 'Fulla—The Arab World's Barbie', *Khaleej Times*, 25 November 2006.

To make her more acceptable in Saudi Arabia, one of the richest and most conservative Islamic countries, she was initially dressed in a black abaya and headscarf, but without the veil most Saudi women wear. The manufacturer did not go to the extremes of covering the face of the little girl. Although, Fulla was dressed in a black abaya and headscarf for the Saudi market, it had no veil in other markets. For relatively liberal Islamic countries, such as Syria and Lebanon, Fulla has a white scarf and pastel coat making her outdoor clothes more colourful. Since Muslim women do not show much skin unlike their Western counterparts, Fulla's shoulders are always covered and the skirt always falls below her knees. The carefully drawn marketing strategy could maintain the brand identity of a conservative girl rather than being just another doll trying to reflect Barbie.

The toy capitalizes on the Islamization of cultural life in the Arab world as evidenced in a heightened focus on dress and rituals. Like most Muslims in the Arab world, Fulla has two sets of clothes. Form-fitting, revealing outfits are sported at home, while items that cover the arms, legs, neck, and often the hair are donned in public (Fig. C.3). This concept of two wardrobes and especially that of the conservative 'outdoor' outfits is what mainly distinguishes the Arab dolls from their Western counterparts. Fulla's clothes include cloaks and prayer outfits that conceal her long dark-brown hair. She also has her own prayer mat,[7] in pink felt.

With her two wardrobes, Fulla taps into the Arab Muslim market by combining religious identity with femininity. The skirts in Fulla's 'home' wardrobe may not rise north of the knee, but many of her tops are close fitting and brightly coloured. Nowadays, many Arab women sport these 'home' outfits outdoors, topped with a scarf.

The brand personality of Fulla is designed to be 'loving, caring, honest, and respectful to her parents'. She is honest and does not lie. Fulla has two friends, Yasmeen and Nada, as well a little brother and sister. Fulla has an older protective brother too. Fulla would never have a boyfriend unlike her Western counterpart, Barbie, as this is frowned upon in Islam.

Even the commercials for dolls in the Middle East are designed to represent Islamic values. For instance, in Saudi Arabia, Barbie is shown to offer her prayers as the sun rises, bake a cake to surprise her friend, or read a book at bedtime. Fulla is also depicted to be family-oriented promoting modest outfits. Commercials even promote, 'when you take your Fulla out of the house, don't forget her new spring abaya'.

Barbie vs Fulla

Barbie and Fulla offer contrasting role models (Fig. C.4) to customers. Although both Barbie and Fulla have a wide range of costumes, jewellery, furniture, and other accessories, the outdoor clothes

Fig. C.4   Barbie and Fulla: Contrasting role models

---

[7] 'Barbie Hasn't a Prayer against Devout Islamic Doll,' *The Sunday Times*, 22 January 2006.

of Fulla do not include swimwear or anything revealing. Besides, Fulla has a smaller chest, is skinnier compared to Barbie's curves, large breasts and shapely legs. An average Barbie is designed to have blond hair, blue eyes, and fair skin whereas Fulla has dark hair, brown eyes, and olive skin. New Boy also introduced dolls with lighter hair and eyes, assuming they would be popular in Mediterranean regions where blue-eyed blonds are not unknown. However, both the dolls have been criticized for presenting the same unrealistic idea of beauty, a certain image for women to conform to.

Fulla is differentiated from Barbie in terms of her lifestyle and appearance. Shopping, spending time with her friends, cooking, reading, and praying are Fulla's favourite activities whereas Barbie has a wide range of hobbies and careers. Unlike Barbie, a perennial job-hopper for about last half a century, who has been everything from an astronaut to the US president, Fulla remains a traditional Arab woman, whose life revolves around the family, serving as a role model for Muslim girls. Fulla has also been designed to be a doctor and a teacher, the two most respected careers in the Islamic world.

A large number of Fulla items are manufactured in the same Chinese factories that turn out Barbie and her related products. That's partly because the items are identical and partly because these factories meet the safety standards set by the United Arab Emirates, through which the Fulla line is distributed.

Other Dolls for the Islamic Markets

Dolls aimed at the Islamic markets also include Sara, Razanne, Saghira, and Salma. The Iranian doll Sara was introduced as an alternative to Barbie in 2002 by the Institute for the Intellectual Development of Children and Young Adults, a government agency affiliated with the Ministry of Education. She has a brother doll Dara unlike Barbie's boyfriend, Ken (Fig. C.5). The dolls have a distinct 'eastern look' complete with Iranian clothes. The siblings help each other to solve problems and turn to their loving parents for guidance.

The children are supposed to be eight years old, young enough under the Islamic law for Sara to appear in public without a headscarf. But each model of Sara comes with a white scarf to cover her brown or black hair. In the first round of production, 100,000 dolls were made by a manufacturer in China.

Razanne was created as an alternative to Barbie for American Muslim girls by Ammar and Sherrie Saadeh at their toy company NoorArt based in Livonia, Michigan, outside of Detroit. Razanne has long-sleeved dresses, a head scarf, and a not-so-buxom bustline. Unlike Barbie, Razanne, with her modest dress and a removable hijab, exemplifies the virtues of a proper, young Muslim woman, such as modesty, piety, and humility. Moreover, the doll is more than a toy. It is a tool for young Muslim girls to learn the value of things like education and religious piety instead of focusing on their bodies as the most significant aspect of their lives. Razanne has the body of a pre-teen. The doll comes in various types: fair-skinned blonde, olive-skinned with black hair, or black skin and black hair. Her aspirations represent a modern Muslim woman. Praying Razanne, who comes complete with a long *hijab* and a modest prayer gown, is aimed to attract Saudi Arabia and other Islamic markets. There's In-Out Razanne (Fig. C.3), whose wardrobe also includes a short, flowery dress she can wear at home, in view of the men in her family only.[8]

Fig. C.5   Instead of a beau, Iranian doll Sara has a brother doll Dara.

---

[8] 'Muslim Doll Offers Modest Alternative to Barbie', *CNN*, 8 October 2003.

Saghira was created by a Moroccan manufacturer in 2005–06 and launched in January 2007 in the Morocco market. She has a mix of both authentic traditional and Western attire, but her accessories, even if Western versions, are based on the articles usually found in Arabic and Muslim households. The dolls come both in veiled and unveiled models, the later representing Saghira within her home or in a family environment. Each model has a different Arabic girl's name: Amira (princess), Doaa (Prayer), Aya, Abir, Ahd, Shada, Nada, Dahab, Najma, Nour, Lina, etc.

Little Farah is designed to recite some most commonly used Islamic phrases (Fig. C.3) in Arabic and English. For instance: 'Welcome, *Assalamu*'; '*Alaikum* peace be upon you'; 'Lets begin, *Bismillah* in the name of Allah'; 'I promise, *Inshallah* if Allah wills'. An Indonesian businesswoman, Sukmawati Suryaman, created Salma,[9] which means 'peace' in Arabic, targeted at young Muslim girls. The toy is marketed as the 'Muslim Barbie Doll' on the net.

The world's bestselling doll, Barbie, which enchanted little girls across the globe, is being elbowed off the toy shelves in the Middle East markets by Islamic playmates. The new dolls aimed at Islamic markets strive to create a character that parents and teachers want children to relate to. These represent that Muslim girls too have options, goals, and dreams and also the ability to realize them unlike the stereotype Barbie aimed at Muslim consumers. Moreover, the surge in sales of Muslim girls' toys, including the veiled dolls, comes amid new enthusiasm among Muslim women for wearing the veil.[10]

Questions

1. Explore the secret of Barbie's success that made it the dream-toy for girls across the world.

2. Sensitivity to culture is crucial to success in international markets. Evaluate Barbie's product adaptation for different markets.

3. Barbie has been criticized for its curvaceous, unrealistic body and materialism, leading to controversies and its ban in some countries, such as Saudi Arabia and Russia. On the other hand, Islamic dolls are criticized for promoting gender stereotypes and restrictive roles. In your opinion, to what extent are such criticism and bans justified?

4. Despite adaptation to represent vast ethnic groups, nationalities, and occasions, Barbie dolls have been jostled out from the Islamic markets. Identify the key reasons.

5. In view of the fast-growing popularity of Islamic dolls among Muslim customers across the world, suggest a marketing plan for Barbie to address the specific needs of the Islamic markets. Also evaluate the impact of suggested plan on the brand image of Barbie in other markets.

---

9 'Barbie Inspires Modest, Muslim Alternative', Reuters, UK, 10 October 2007.
10 'Barbie Looses Out to Veiled Rival', *BBC News*, 12 January 2006.

15 International Finance

LEARNING OBJECTIVES

> - To elucidate the concept of international monetary systems
> - To discuss contemporary exchange rate arrangements
> - To evaluate various theories of exchange rate determination
> - To discuss foreign exchange market and exchange rate quotations
> - To explain foreign exchange risks and exposure
> - To examine various modes of payment
> - To elaborate various techniques of financing international trade

15.1 INTRODUCTION

The complexity of managing finances on a global scale increases as a firm expands its business in several countries and graduates its entry mode from exporting to equity investment, establishing its own foreign subsidiaries. A large number of firms, such as Coke, Unilever, HSBC, Nestle, Nike, Colgate Palmolive, etc., have expanded internationally and possess considerable assets in foreign countries, often generating larger revenues from their overseas operations. Thus, developing a thorough conceptual understanding of international financial management has become crucial to the success of international managers. Moreover, globalization has made understanding international finance pertinent even to business enterprises solely operating domestically in order to assess the impact of movements in exchange rates, foreign interest rates, labour costs, and inflation on the costs and prices of their foreign competitors.

This chapter provides a broad overview of managing international finance. Historical background of international monetary systems helps in developing a conceptual understanding of the evolution of the present-day exchange rate systems. Further, it is important to know the contemporary exchange rate arrangements, which vary across countries and range from market-determined independently floating exchange rates systems to arrangements using foreign currency with no separate legal tender of their own. The theoretical framework for exchange rate determination that mainly comprises purchasing power parity (PPP) theory and interest rate theory has been examined in this chapter.

Developing a basic knowledge of the foreign exchange market, its participants, and the various types of exchange rate quotations is highly significant for international managers. This chapter also covers the different types of foreign exchange risks, exposures, and their management.

International managers need to develop a conceptual understanding of the various alternatives as to *how* and *when* money is transferred from a buyer to the seller in an international trade transaction—in other words, the modes of payment. As international markets are becoming increasingly competitive, overseas buyers often demand credits from exporters. Therefore, the ability of exporters to extend attractive and competitive credit terms to their buyers is crucial to their being internationally competitive. Commercial banks extend pre-shipment and post-shipment credits to exporters, often at concessional rates in most countries, as a part of the export promotion strategy. This chapter also examines the various instruments used for financing international trade. Most banks insist upon credit risk insurance for financing export transactions in order to get assured of the borrower's ability to repay the loan. This too has been discussed.

15.2 INTERNATIONAL MONETARY SYSTEMS

Money includes anything that is generally accepted in exchange as payment for goods and services. Although, the key function of money is to act as a medium of exchange, it also serves as a store of value, unit of account, and standard of deferred payment. The development of currencies in various parts of the world involved great innovations. The international monetary system refers to a set of rules, regulations, policies, practices, instruments, institutions, and mechanisms that determine exchange rates between currencies. Evolution of monetary systems is explained here to help readers in developing a conceptual understanding of contemporary monetary arrangements.

15.2.1 Gold Standard

Gold has historically been used as a medium of exchange primarily due to its scarce availability and desirable properties. Besides its durability, portability, and ease of standardization, the high production costs of the yellow metal make it costly for governments to manipulate short-run changes in its stock. As gold is a commodity money, it tends to promote price stability in the long run. Thus, the purchase power of an ounce of gold will tend toward equality with its long-run cost of production.[1] The various versions of gold standards used were

---

[1] Shapiro, Alan C., 'Defining and Analyzing the International Monetary System', in *Multinational Financial Management*, 8th edn, John Wiley & Sons, New Delhi, 2006, p. 93.

Gold specie standard The actual currency in circulation consists of gold coins with fixed gold content

Gold bullion standard The currency in circulation consists of paper notes but a fixed weight of gold remains the basis of money. Any amount of paper currency can be converted into gold and vice versa by the country's monitory authority at a fixed conversion ratio.

Gold exchange standard Paper currency can be converted at a fixed rate into the paper currency of the other country, if it is operating a gold specie or gold bullion standard. Such an exchange regime was followed in the post-Bretton Woods era.

Exchange rates from 1876 to 1913 were generally dictated by gold standards. Each country backed up its currency with gold, and currencies were convertible into gold at specified rates. Relative convertibility rates of the currencies per ounce of gold determined the exchange rates between the two currencies.

Gold standard was suspended following World War I in 1914 and governments financed massive military expenditure by printing money. This led to a sharp rise both in the supply of money and market prices. Hyperinflation in Germany presents a classic example[2] where the price index rapidly shot form 262 in 1919 to 12,61,60,00,00,00,000 (a factor of 481.5 billion) in December 1923. The US and some other countries returned to gold standards so as to achieve financial stability, but following the Great Depression in 1930, gold standards were finally abandoned. Some countries attempted to peg their currencies to the US dollar or British pound in the 1930s but there were frequent revisions. This followed severe restrictions on international transactions and instability in the foreign exchange market, leading to a decline in the volume of international trade during this period.

15.2.2 Fixed Exchange Rates

In July 1944, representatives of 44 allied nations agreed to a fixed rate monetary system and setting up of the International Monetary Fund in a conference held in Bretton Woods, New Hampshire. Each member country pledged to maintain a fixed or pegged exchange rate for its currency vis-à-vis gold or the US dollar. Since the price of each currency was fixed in terms of gold, their values with respect to each other were also fixed. For instance, price of one ounce of gold was fixed equal to US$35. This exchange regime, following the Bretton Woods Conference, was characterized as the Gold Exchange Standard.

In the Bretton Woods era, which lasted from 1944 to 1971, fixed exchange rates were maintained by government intervention in the foreign exchange markets so that the exchange rates did not drift beyond 1 per cent of their initially established levels.

---

[2] Krugman, Paul R. and Maurice Obstfeld, 'The International Monetary System, 1870–1973', *International Economics Theory and Policy*, 6th edn, Pearson Education, Boston, 2003, p. 543.

Under the Bretton Woods system, the US dollar effectively became the international currency. Other countries accumulated and held US dollars for making international payments whereas the US could pay internationally in its own currency.

By 1971, the foreign demand for the US dollar was substantially less than the supply and it appeared to be overvalued. On 15 August 1971 the US government abandoned its commitment to convert the US dollar into gold at the fixed price of US$35 per ounce and the major currencies went on a float. In an attempt to revamp the monetary system, consequent to a conference of various countries' representatives, the Smithsonian Agreement was concluded in December 1971, which called for a devaluation of US dollar by 8 per cent against other currencies and pegging the official price of gold to US$38 per ounce. Besides, 2.25 per cent fluctuations in either direction was also allowed in the newly set exchange rates.

Pros and cons of fixed exchange rate system   Under the fixed exchange rate system, international managers can operate their international trade and business activities without worrying about future rates. However, companies do face repercussions of currency devaluation both by their home and the host countries. Further, the currency of each country becomes more vulnerable to economic upheavals in other countries.

15.2.3 Floating Exchange Rate System

Even after the Smithsonian Agreement, governments still faced difficulty in maintaining their exchange rates within the newly established exchange rates regime. By March 1973, the fixed exchange rate system was abandoned and the world officially moved to a system of floating exchange rates. Under the freely floating exchange rate system, currency prices are determined by market demand and supply conditions without the intervention of the governments.

Pros and cons of floating exchange rates   A country under the floating exchange rate system is more insulated from inflation, unemployment, and economic upheavals prevalent in other countries. Thus, the problems faced in one country need not be contagious to another. The adjustment of exchange rates serves as a form of protection against exporting economic problems to other countries. Besides, the central bank of a country is not required to constantly maintain the exchange rates within the specified limits and to make frequent interventions.

Although other countries are reasonably insulated from the problems faced by one country under the freely floating exchange rates, the exchange rates themselves can further aggravate the economic woes of a country plagued by economic problems and unemployment. This possibility makes it essential for international managers to devote substantial resources to measure and manage the exposure to exchange rate fluctuations.

15.3 CONTEMPORARY EXCHANGE RATE ARRANGEMENTS

The IMF groups exchange rate arrangements, based on members' actual arrangements as identified by its staff, that may differ from the arrangements officially announced by the countries. Exchange rate arrangements are classified on the basis of the degree of the variability of the observed exchange rate and the past official actions affecting the exchange rate over the time period.

15.3.1 Floating Exchange Rate System

Floating exchange rates are neither characterized by par values, nor by official exchange rates. This allows complete flexibility of exchange rates unlike the rigidity of currency movements under the fixed rate system.

Independently floating

Under the 'independent' or 'free' float, the exchange rates are market-determined and central banks intervene only to moderate the speed of change or to prevent excessive fluctuations without any attempt to maintain it or drive it to a particular level. About 35 countries, including the US, the UK, Japan, Switzerland, Germany, France, New Zealand, Mexico, Australia, Canada, and Brazil have adopted independently floating exchange rate regimes.

Managed float with no pre-determined path for the exchange rate

Although currencies are allowed to fluctuate on a daily basis with no official boundaries, national governments may and sometimes do intervene so as to prevent their currencies from moving too far in a certain direction. Such a system is known as 'managed' or 'dirty' float contrary to 'free' or 'clean' float wherein currencies are allowed to move freely without government intervention. Such exchange rate arrangements prevail in about 48 countries, including India, Singapore, the Russian Federation, Malaysia, Kenya, Thailand, Indonesia, Tanzania, Bangladesh, and Mauritius.

The managed float system is criticized on the ground that it allows governments to manipulate exchange rates for the benefit of their countries at the expense of others. For instance, a government may weaken its currency to attract foreign demand with an objective to stimulate its stagnant economy.

15.3.2 Pegged Exchange Rate System

Pegging value of home currency to a foreign currency or a basket of currencies is known as pegged exchange rate system. Although the home currency value is fixed in terms of a foreign currency or unit of account to which it is pegged, it is allowed to move in line with that currency against other currencies. IMF classifies pegging exchange rate system as soft and hard pegs.

Soft pegs

Conventional fixed peg   The currency fluctuates for at least three months within a band of less than 2 per cent or ±1 per cent against another currency or a basket of currencies. The basket of currencies is formed from the geographical distribution of trade, services, or capital flows. The monetary authority stands ready to maintain the fixed parity through direct intervention (i.e., via sales or purchase of foreign exchange in the market) or indirect intervention (i.e., via aggressive use of interest rate policy, imposition of foreign exchange regulations, exercise of moral suasion that constrains foreign exchange activity, or through intervention by other public institutions). About 70 countries follow the conventional fixed peg arrangements, out of which 63 countries are pegged against a single currency whereas seven countries are pegged against other currency composites. The United Arab Emirates, Saudi Arabia, Qatar, Argentina, Egypt, Ethiopia, Kuwait, Oman, Syria, Venezuela, Vietnam, and Zimbabwe are among the 40 countries that peg their currencies to the US dollar. The currencies of 19 countries, including Senegal, Niger, Gabon, Cameroon, and Malta, are pegged to the euro. Nepal and Bhutan peg their currencies to the Indian rupee, whereas the currencies of Swaziland, Namibia, and Lesotho are pegged to the South African Rand. Fiji, Iran, Morocco, Samoa, Seychelles, and Vanuatu peg their currencies against other currency composites.

Intermediate pegs

Pegs within horizontal bands   Currencies are generally not allowed to fluctuate beyond ±1 per cent of the central parity. Denmark, Slovak Republic, and Cyprus follow such an exchange rate system within a cooperative arrangement, whereas Hungary and Tonga adopt other band arrangements.

Crawling peg   Under the crawling peg system, a currency is pegged to a single currency or a basket of currencies, but the peg is periodically adjusted with a range of less than 2 per cent in response to changes in selective micro-economic indicators, such as inflation differentials vis-à-vis major trading partners. Maintaining a crawling peg imposes constraints on the monetary policy in a manner similar to a fixed peg system. China is among the six countries following such an exchange rate system, apart from Botswana, Azerbaijan, Iraq, Nicaragua, and Sierra Leone.

Crawling bands   The currency is adjusted periodically at a fixed rate or in response to changes in selective quantitative macroeconomic indicators, with a range of fluctuation of 2 per cent or more. The degree of exchange rate flexibility is a function of the bandwidth. The commitment to maintain the exchange rate within the band imposes constraints on monetary policy making, with the degree of policy independence being a function of the bandwidth. Costa Rica is the only country following the crawling bands exchange rate system.

Hard pegs

Currency board arrangements Currency board arrangements refer to a monetary regime based on an explicit legislative commitment to exchange domestic currency for a specified foreign currency at a fixed exchange rate. It combines restrictions on the issuing authority to ensure the fulfilment of its legal obligations. The board must maintain foreign currency reserves for all the currency that it has printed. A currency board facilitates the stabilization of a country's currency and maintains the confidence of foreign investors. About 13 countries have such arrangements. For instance, Hong Kong SAR, Djibouti, and Dominica have such an arrangement with the US dollar. The currency board of a country maintains a reserve of the US dollar for every unit of home currency circulated. Bulgaria, Estonia, Lithuania, and Bosnia have such arrangements with euro, and Brunei Darussalam with Singapore dollars. Since 1983, Hong Kong has tied the value of the Hong Kong dollar with the US dollar (HK$7.80 = US$1.00).

Arrangements with no separate legal tender Replacement of a country's local currency with US dollars is termed as 'dollarization'. It may be formal or informal. Under this regime, the currency of another country circulates as the sole legal tender (formal dollarization) or the member belongs to a monetary or currency union in which the same legal tender is shared by the members of the union. Adopting such an exchange rate regime implies the complete surrender of the monetary authority's independent control over domestic policies. Ecuador, El Salvador, Marshall Islands, Micronesia, Palau, Panama, and Timor-Leste do not have their own separate legal tender, and instead use the US dollars, whereas the euro is used in Montenegro and San Marino, and the Australian dollar in Kiribati.

Consequent to the sharp depreciation of about 97 per cent in the sucre, Ecuador's currency, against the US dollar from 1990 to 2000, due to unstable trade conditions, high inflation, and volatile interest rates, Ecuador decided to replace its currency with the US dollar. As a result, dollarization showed positive effects as the economic growth increased and the inflation declined by November 2000.

15.4 PREVAILING CURRENCIES AND MARKETS

Foreign exchange includes any type of financial instrument that is used to make payments between countries. Examples of foreign exchange assets include foreign currency notes, deposits held in foreign banks, debt obligations of foreign governments and foreign banks, monetary gold, and special drawing rights (SDRs). The US dollar is the most widely traded currency in the world as it comprises at least one aspect (i.e., buy or sell) of the 86.3 per cent of total foreign currency transactions[3] in the world,

---

[3] 'Triennial Central Bank Survey: Foreign Exchange and Derivatives Market Activity in 2007', Bank for International Settlements, pp. 6–7.

followed by euro (37%), yen (16.5%), pound sterling (15.0%), Swiss franc (6.8%), and the Australian dollar (6.7%), whereas the Indian rupee comprises merely 0.7 per cent and the Chinese renminbi 0.5 per cent. Thus, the US dollar is the most significant and widely circulated currency in the world primarily because it is

- Used as a reserve currency by several central banks
- Used as a currency for intervention by central banks in foreign exchange markets
- Used widely as a currency for invoicing in international trade contracts
- Used as a currency for investment in many capital markets
- Used as a currency of transaction in the international commodity market

Eurocurrency

A currency deposited in a bank outside the country of its origin is known as euro currency. It is used as a generic term rather than being confined to the geographical boundary of Europe. Thus, dollars deposited in banks outside Europe are known as eurodollars. Similarly, sterling pounds deposited in a bank outside the UK are called euro sterling, detusche mark deposited outside Germany as euro mark, and yen outside Japan as euro yen.

Euro markets have grown considerably over the years primarily due to

- The rapid growth of transnational operations of business enterprises leading to enhanced requirement to deal in and maintain a number of currencies across the world
- The increasing stringencies of banking regulations in the US worked as a strong stimulus for US banks to explode growth opportunities beyond national boundaries
- The liberalization of exchange rate regimes and growing free convertibility of currencies

Banks trading in markets for eurocurrencies are known as *eurobanks* and international bonds sold in countries other than the country of the currency dominating the bond are known as *eurobonds*.

The eurocurrency market is the set of banks that accepts deposits and makes loans in Eurocurrencies. Its name is often a misnomer as considerable eurocurrency trading occurs in non-European financial centres such as Hong Kong and Singapore. Markets in Asia, mainly in Singapore and Hong Kong, in which banks collect deposits and extend loans in US dollars, are known as Asian currency or Asian dollar markets.

15.5   DETERMINATION OF EXCHANGE RATES

15.5.1   Purchasing Power Parity Theory

Assuming non-existence of tariffs and other trade barriers and zero cost of transport, the *law of one price*, the simplest concept of purchasing power parity (PPP), states that identical goods should cost the same in all nations. Therefore, prices of goods sold in different countries, converted to a common currency, should be identical. The equilibrium price rate between two currencies, according to the purchase power parity theory, would be equal to the ratio of price levels in two countries, as indicated below:

$$S_e = \frac{P_x}{P_y}$$

where, S_e indicates spot exchange rate, and P_x and P_y indicate the price level in two different countries x and y.

However, prices can be distorted by a range of factors, such as taxes, transport costs, labour laws, and trade barriers like tariffs.

Based on PPP, the cross-country comparison of the exchange rates of currencies may be carried out using the Big Mac Index and CommSec iPod index.

The Big Mac index

McDonald's prices its products in international markets depending upon the country's purchasing power as indicated in Exhibit 15.1. Hamburger prices vary from US$1.70 in Malaysia and US$6.37 in Sweden. The Big Mac Index was invented in September 1986 as a light-hearted guide for cross-country comparison of currencies based on prices of McDonald's Big Mac produced locally and simultaneously in almost 120 countries. Big Mac is considered a global product that involves similar inputs and processes in its preparation across the world. The purchasing power parity is calculated by dividing the price of Big Mac in a country with the price in the US.

$$\text{PPP} = \frac{\text{Big Mac prices in local currency}}{\text{Big Mac prices in the US}}$$

For instance, the PPP of dollar works out to 3.50 (12.5/3.57) of the Chinese yuan, which is its 'theoretical' exchange rate. The over or under-valuation of currency may be arrived at as follows:

$$\frac{\text{Over (+) valuation of currency}}{\text{Under (−) valuation of currency}} = \frac{\left\{ 1 - \left(\dfrac{\text{Implied PPP of the US dollar}}{\text{Actual dollar exchange rate}} \right) \right\}}{100}$$

As the actual dollar exchange rate was 6.83 yuan in mid-2008, it may be inferred that Chinese yuan was undervalued by 49 per cent [{1 − (3.50/6.83)} * 100]. Using a similar formula, it is found that the currencies of Hong Kong and Malaysia (52%), Thailand (48%), Sri Lanka, Pakistan, and the Philippines (45%), and Indonesia (43%) were among the most undervalued. On the other hand, currencies on the rich fringe of the European Union, i.e., Norway (121%), Sweden (79%), Switzerland (78%), and Denmark and Iceland (each 67%) were the most overvalued.[4]

---

[4] 'The Big Mac Index', McDonald's, *The Economist*, London, 24 July 2008.

Exhibit 15.1   The Big Mac Index

	Big Mac price		Implied PPP[a] of the dollar	Actual exchange rate	Under (−)/ over (+) valuation against the dollar
	in local currency	in dollars[f]			
US[b]	$3.57	3.57	−	−	
Argentina	Peso 11.0	3.64	3.08	3.02	2
Australia	A$3.45	3.36	0.97	1.03	−6
Brazil	Real 7.50	4.73	2.1	1.58	33
Britain	£2.29	4.57	1.56[e]	2.00	28
Canada	C$4.09	4.08	1.15	1.00	14
Chile	Peso1550	3.13	434	494	−12
China	Yuan 12.5	1.83	3.50	6.83	−49
Czech Republic	Koruna 66.1	4.56	18.5	14.5	28
Denmark	Dk 28.0	5.95	7.84	4.70	67
Egypt	Pound 13.0	2.45	3.64	5.31	−31
Euro area[c]	€3.37	5.34	1.06[d]	1.59	50
Hong Kong	HK$13.3	1.71	3.73	7.80	−52
Hungary	Forint 670	4.64	187.7	144.3	30
Indonesia	Rupiah 18,700	2.04	5,238	9,152	−43
Japan	Yen 280	2.62	78.4	106.8	−27
Malaysia	Ringgit 5.50	1.70	1.54	3.2	−52
Mexico	Peso 32.0	3.15	8.96	10.2	−12
New Zealand	NZ$4.90	3.72	1.37	1.32	4
Norway	Kroner 40.0	7.88	11.2	5.08	121
Poland	Zloty 7.00	3.45	1.96	2.03	−3
Russia	Rouble 59.0	2.54	16.5	23.2	−29
Saudi Arabia	Riyal 10.0	2.67	2.80	3.75	−25
Singapore	S$3.95	2.92	1.11	1.35	−18
South Africa	Rand 16.9	2.24	4.75	7.56	−37
South Korea	Won 3,200	3.14	896	1,018	−12
Sweden	SKr 38.0	6.37	10.6	5.96	79
Switzerland	SFr 6.50	6.36	1.82	1.02	78
Taiwan	NT$75.0	2.47	21.0	30.4	−31
Thailand	Baht 62.0	1.86	17.4	33.4	−48
Turkey	Lire 5.15	4.32	1.44	1.19	21
UAE	Dirhams 10.00	2.72	2.80	3.67	−24
Iceland	Kronur 469.00	5.97	131.37	78.57	67
Pakistan	Rupee 140.00	1.97	39.22	70.90	−45
Philippines	Peso 87.00	1.96	24.37	44.49	−45
Sri Lanka	Rupee 210.00	1.95	58.82	107.55	−45

[a] Purchasing power parity; local price divided by price in the US;

[b] Average of New York, Chicago, Atlanta, and San Francisco.

[c] Weighted average of prices in euro area.

[d] Dollars per euro.

[e] Dollars per pound.

[f] At current exchange rates.

Source: 'The Big Mac Index', McDonald's, *The Economist*, London, 24 July 2008.

Despite certain limitations, such as variations in taxation and tariffs and in profit margins due to competitive intensity and the lack of using a basket of commodities, the Big Mac Index serves as a useful tool for cross-country comparison of the exchange rates of currencies.

CommSec iPod Index

Launched in January 2007, the Commsec iPod Index presents a modern-day variant of the Big Mac Index. Both the indices work on the theory of 'same goods, same price'. That is, the same goods should trade at broadly the same price across the globe if exchange rates are adjusted properly.

This index too represents a light-hearted approach to assessing the pricing of a standard product sold worldwide. The index is based on the price variation of 4 gigabytes Apple iPod across countries. Hong Kong is the cheapest place to buy a 4 gigabyte iPod nano at just US$147.47 whereas Brazil is the costliest place to buy at US$403.14. The cross-country price comparison suggests that the iPod nano can be bought at US$149 in the US, US$159.42 in India, US$168.26 in Japan, US$174.77 in Singapore, US$181.50 in Australia, US$196.54 in China, US$197.37 in the UK, US$202.78 in South Africa, US$222.34 in Russia, US$241.06 in Bulgaria, US$279.65 in Turkey, US$302.64 in Iceland, and US$330.58 in Argentina (Fig. 15.1).

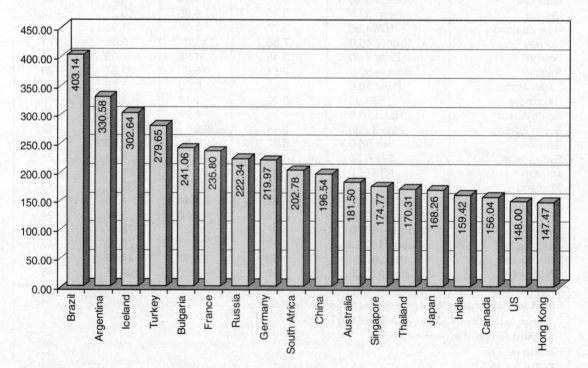

Fig. 15.1   CommSec iPod nano Index (4 gigabytes, July 2008)

Source: Based on James Craig, 'Commsec iPod Index: Australia Loses Ground—Global Comparison and Currency Changes', *Economic Insights*, Commonwealth Bank of Australia, July 2008, pp. 1–3.

The key difference between the iPod and Big Mac approaches is that Big Macs are made in a host of countries across the globe whereas iPods are predominately made in China. There remain several limitations in both these indices as a variety of factors, such as transportation costs, labour laws, tariffs, and taxes, have distorting effects.

15.5.2 Interest Rate Theories

Interest rate theories use the inflation rates in determining the exchange rates, unlike the price levels used under the PPP theory.

Fisher Effect theory

Establishing a relationship between the inflation and interest rates, the Fisher Effect (FE) theory states that the nominal interest rate 'r' in a country is determined by the real interest rate 'R' and the expected inflation rate 'i' as follows:

$$(1 + \text{Nominal interest rate}) = (1 + \text{Real interest rate})$$
$$(1 + \text{Expected inflation rate})$$
$$(1 + r) = (1 + R)\,(1 + i)$$

or $r = R + i + Ri$

Since, Ri is of negligible value, the preceding equation is generally approximated as

$$r = R + i$$

Nominal interest rate = Real interest rate + Expected inflation rate

Real interest rate is used to assess exchange rate movements as it includes interest and inflation rates, both of which affect exchange rates. Given all other parameters constant, there is a high co-relation between differentials in real interest rate and the exchange rate of a currency.

International Fisher Effect theory

The International Fisher Effect (IFE) combines the PPP and the FE to determine the impact of relative changes in nominal interest rates among countries on their foreign exchange values. According to the PPP theory, the exchange rates will move to offset changes in inflation rate differentials. Thus, a rise in a country's inflation rate relative to other countries will be associated with a fall in its currency's exchange value. It would also be associated with a rise in the country's interest rate relative to foreign interest rates. A combination of these two conditions is known as the IFE, which states that the exchange rate movements are caused by interest rate differentials. If real interest rates are the same across the country, any difference in nominal interest rates could be attributed to differences in expected inflation. Foreign currencies with relatively high interest rates will depreciate because the high nominal interest rates reflect expected inflation. The IFE explains that the interest rate differential between any two countries is an unbiased predictor of the future changes in the spot rate of exchange.

15.5.3 Other Determinants of Exchange Rates

In addition to inflation, real income, and interest rates, other market fundamentals that influence the exchange rates include bilateral trade relationships, customer tastes, investment profitability, product availability, productivity changes, and trade policies.[5]

15.6 FOREIGN EXCHANGE MARKET

In order to facilitate international trade transactions, the foreign exchange market allows currencies to be exchanged. The foreign exchange market refers to the organizational settings within which individuals, businesses, government, and banks buy and sell foreign currencies and other debt instruments. It is an over-the-counter market, which means there is no single physical or electronic marketplace or an organized exchange, unlike a stock exchange with a central clearing mechanism, where traders meet and exchange currency. The market consists of a global network of inter-bank traders, primarily the banks, connected by telecommunication facilities.

The foreign exchange market has grown considerably over the years from US$880 billion in 1992 to US$3210 billion in 2007 (Fig. 15.2) mainly due to the deregulation of international capital flows, gains in technology, transaction cost-efficiency, and the increased volatility of international financial markets. The foreign exchange market is the largest and the most liquid market in the world, with estimated worldwide foreign

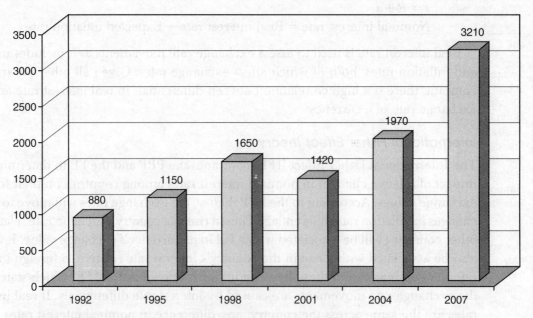

Fig. 15.2 Global foreign exchange market turnover (US$ in billions)

Source: 'Triennial Central Bank Survey, December 2007', Bank for International Settlements, Basel, Switzerland, 2007, p. 4.

---

[5] Carbaugh, Robert J., *International Economics*, 9th ed., Thomson South-Western, 2004, pp. 401–09.

exchange transactions of about US$3.21 trillion a day. It is estimated that quoted prices change as often as 20 times in a minute and the world's most active foreign exchange rate can change in a single day up to 18,000 times.

The foreign exchange market turnover volume (Table 15.1) is the highest in the UK with a 34.1 per cent share, followed by the US 16.6 per cent, Switzerland 6.1 per cent, Japan 6.0 per cent, Singapore 5.8 per cent, Hong Kong SAR 4.4 per cent, Australia 4.3 per cent, France 3.0 per cent, and Germany 2.5 per cent in 2007. India's share in the geographical distribution of forex market turnover has risen from 0.3 per cent in 2004 to 0.9 per cent in 2007 while the amount traded on an average per day has risen around five times from US$7 billion in 2004 to US$34 billion in 2007. China had the highest growth of 800 per cent to an average daily turnover of US$9 billion during this period.[6]

International trade in goods and services accounts for less than 5 per cent of the world's foreign exchange trading, whereas international capital flows, i.e., cross-border purchase and sales of assets account for 95 per cent of the foreign exchange trading. The majority of the world's foreign exchange trading takes place in large financial

Table 15.1   Geographical distribution of foreign exchange market turnover[a]

(daily averages in April)

	1998		2001		2004		2007	
	Amount	% share	Amount	% share	Amount	% share	Amount	% share
UK	637	32.5	504	31.2	753	31	1359	34.1
US	351	17.9	254	15.7	461	19.2	664	16.6
Switzerland	82	4.2	71	4.4	79	3.3	242	6.1
Japan	136	6.9	147	9.1	199	8.2	238	6.0
Singapore	139	7.1	101	6.2	125	5.2	231	5.8
Hong Kong SAR	79	4	67	4.1	102	4.2	175	4.4
Australia	47	2.4	52	3.2	102	4.2	170	4.3
France	72	3.7	48	3	64	2.6	120	3
Germany	94	4.8	88	5.5	118	4.8	99	2.5
Denmark	27	1.4	23	1.4	41	1.7	86	2.2
Canada	37	1.9	42	2.6	54	2.2	60	1.5
Russia	7	0.4	10	0.6	30	1.2	50	1.3
Belgium	27	1.4	10	0.6	20	0.8	48	1.2
Sweden	15	0.8	24	1.5	31	1.3	42	1.1
Luxembourg	22	1.1	13	0.8	14	0.6	43	1.1
Italy	28	1.4	17	1	20	0.8	36	0.9
India	2	0.1	3	0.2	7	0.3	34	0.9
China	0	0	0	0	1	0	9	0.2
Brazil	5	0.3	5	0.3	3	0.1	5	0.1

[a] Adjusted for local double-counting ('net-gross')

Source: 'Triennial Central Bank Survey, December 2007', Bank for International Settlements, Basel, Switzerland, 2007, pp. 6–7.

---

[6] Based on 'Triennial Central Bank Survey, December 2007', Bank for International Settlements, Basel, Switzerland, 2007, pp. 6–7.

centres, such as New York, London, and Tokyo. Volumes of foreign exchange traded are generally very high during the morning hours, decline in the afternoon, and wind down to a miniscule amount during the evening hours.

The 'foreign exchange market' is not confined to a specific building or location where traders exchange currencies. Currencies are generally exchanged for one another by business firms over a telecommunication network. Trading in the foreign exchange market has historically taken place by telephone, telex, or the Society for Worldwide Inter-bank Financial Telecommunication (SWIFT) system. The SWIFT supplies secure messaging services and interface software to wholesale financial entities. It has a customer base in 208 countries, serving 8,332 live users with an average daily traffic of 13,976,699 messages.[7] In November 2007, SWIFT opened its first office in India at Mumbai.

Commercial banks of a country operate as 'clearing houses' for the foreign exchange demanded and supplied for foreign transactions by the country's residents. In the process, banks of a country will have over-supply of some of the foreign currencies whereas they would have shortage of others. This imbalance in demand and supply of foreign currencies would be overcome by the commercial banks by selling and buying from each other through the intermediary of foreign exchange brokers. Bank for International Settlements (BIS) is the principal financial institution that acts as the prime counterparty for central banks in their financial transactions and serves as the bank for central banks (Exhibit 15.2).

Exhibit 15.2   Bank for international settlement

Established on 17 May 1930, the Bank for International Settlement (BIS) is the world's oldest financial organization that fosters international monetary and financial co-operation and serves as a bank for central banks. It acts as

- A forum to promote discussion and policy analysis among central banks and within the international financial community
- A centre for economic and monetary research
- A prime counterparty for central banks in their financial transactions
- An agent or trustee in connection with international financial operations.

The BIS is headquartered in Basel, Switzerland, and there are two representative offices in the Hong Kong SAR and Mexico City. The members of BIS are central banks or monetary authorities of 55 countries, including the US, the UK, Japan, Switzerland, Australia, Singapore, China, Brazil, India, Russia, Saudi Arabia, Malaysia, Thailand, and the European Central Bank.

As its customers are central banks and international organizations, the BIS does not accept deposits from, or provide financial services to, private individuals or corporate entities. The BIS strongly advises caution against fraudulent schemes.

Source: Bank for International Settlements, Basel, Switzerland.

---

[7] 'Swift in Figures', *SWIFT*, 23 January 2008.

15.6.1   Types of Foreign Exchange Markets

Inter-bank or wholesale market

A bank can purchase a foreign currency from other banks if there is a shortage. Such trading between banks is termed as the 'inter-bank market' wherein banks can obtain quotes, or they can contact brokers who sometimes act as intermediaries, matching a bank desiring to sell a given currency with another desiring to buy that currency. Thus, the inter-bank is the wholesale foreign exchange market in which major banks trade currencies with each other. Large proportion inter-banks transaction volumes are handled by about 10 major foreign exchange firms.

Retail market

Transaction size of retail foreign exchange market is very small whereas the spread between buying and selling prices is large. It consists of travellers and tourists who exchange one currency to another in the form of travellers cheques or currency notes.

15.6.2   Participants in the Foreign Exchange Market

Traders use forward contract to eliminate or cover the risk of loss on export or import orders that are denominated in foreign currencies. More generally a forward-covering transaction is related to a specific payment or receipt expected at a specified point in time.

Hedgers are mostly multinational firms engaged in forward contracts to protect the home currency value of various foreign currency-denominated assets and liabilities on their balance sheets, which are not to be realized over the life of the contracts.

Arbitrageurs seek to earn risk-free profits by taking advantage of differences in interest rates among countries. They use forward contracts to eliminate the exchange risk involved in transferring their funds from one nation to another.

15.6.3   Exchange Rate Quotations

The value of one currency in the units of another is known as exchange rate. The demand and supply of currencies lead to fluctuations in the exchange rates of currencies. Factors influencing exchange rate of a currency vis-à-vis another foreign currency include change in differential between the home country and foreign country inflation rates, interest rates, income levels, and changes in government controls and future exchange rates.[8]

Spot vs forward quote

The amount agreed for foreign exchange transaction may be delivered either immediately (*spot*) or at a later date (*forward*).

---

[8] Madura, Jeff, *International Corporate Finance*, New Delhi: Thompson South Western, 2006, pp. 102–03.

Spot rate Spot rate is the price agreed for purchase or sale of foreign currency with delivery and payment to take place not more than two business days after the day the transaction has been concluded. The two-day period is known as 'immediate delivery'. The settlement date, by convention, is the second business day after the date on which the transaction is agreed upon between the two traders. The two-day period provides ample time for the two parties to conform to the agreement and arrange the clearing and necessary debiting and crediting of bank accounts in various international locations.[9]

Transactions with value dates up to and including seven business days from the date of trading are also considered as spot transactions. However, in such cases, a special agreement on the value date is necessary at the time of dealing, since the extending delivery and payment dates are reflected in the exchange rate quoted. The markets where spot transactions occur are known as spot markets.

Transactions that call for settlement before the spot date are known as *short date transactions*. 'Cash' transactions are to be settled on the same day, while some deals require settlement on the next day, i.e., one business day ahead when a spot deal would be settled within two business days.

Forward rate Forward rate is the price at which the foreign exchange rate is quoted for delivery at a specified later date. The date of maturity of a forward contract is more than two business days in future whereas the exchange rate is fixed at the time of entering the contract. No money necessarily changes hands at the time of entering the forward contract, until the transaction actually takes place, although dealers may require some customers to provide collateral in advance.

Direct vs indirect quotes

Direct quotes Under direct quotes, units of the home currency per unit of a foreign currency are quoted. For instance, Indian Rs 39.5075 per US$ is a direct quote in India whereas yen ¥ 106.5050 per US$ is a direct quote in Japan. In the US context, exchange rate quotation in US$ per unit of foreign currency is also termed as *American* or direct term.

$$\text{Direct quote} = \frac{1}{\text{Indirect quote}}$$

Indirect quote Indirect quote is also known as reciprocal or inverse quote to indicate units of foreign currency per unit of home currency. For instance, US$0.0253 per Indian rupee is an indirect quote in India. It may be arrived at by inversing the direct quote as follows:

$$\text{Indirect quote} = \frac{1}{\text{Direct quote}}$$

---

[9] Carbaugh, Robert J., 'Foreign Exchange', in *International Economics*, 9th ed., Thomson Learning, 2004, p. 359.

$$\frac{1}{39.5075 * 100} = \text{US\$0.0253 per Indian rupee}$$

The exchange rate quotations in a number of foreign currency units per US\$ is referred to as '*European terms*' or indirect terms. For instance, US\$2.067 per pound and US\$1.442 per euro are quotes in European terms.

Cross-exchange rate

Quoting exchange rates of two currencies without using the US dollar as the reference currency is termed as cross-exchange rate.

$$\text{Value of Indian rupees in British pounds} = \frac{\text{Value of an Indian rupee in US\$}}{\text{Value of a British £ in US\$}}$$

$$= 39.5075/0.5106$$
$$= \text{Rs } 77.3746 \text{ per British £}$$

Thus, exchange rate for 1 British £ equals Rs 77.3746. Similarly cross-currency rates are available for other currencies as well.

Bid vs ask quotations

The price that a bank is willing to pay for a foreign currency is termed as 'bid' rate whereas the price at which a bank is willing to sell the currency is known as 'ask' or offer rate. Bid and ask rates are influenced by the volume, competition, currency risks, order, and inventory costs. The offer rate of a currency is always higher than the bid rate at any given point of time. The spread is aimed to cover the bank's costs of implementing the exchanges of currencies. The difference between the bid and the offer rate is known as the spread of the currency.

$$\text{Bid/ask spread} = \frac{(\text{ask rate} - \text{bid rate})}{\text{ask rate}}$$

15.7 FOREIGN EXCHANGE RISKS AND EXPOSURE

The transnational operations of a company require it to deal with multiple exchange rate regimes and cash-flow across countries, making it vulnerable to foreign exchange fluctuations. The impact of foreign exchange fluctuations not only depends on how a firm reacts but also on how the firm's competitors, customers, and suppliers react.[10] In an international transaction, exporters and importers both are exposed to foreign exchange risks as the payment of the specific amount already agreed upon under the contract is to be received or made in foreign currency at a future date. While managing

---

international finances, one should develop a clear conceptual understanding of the two distinct concepts discussed below.

15.7.1 Foreign Exchange Risk

Foreign exchange risk refers to the variance of domestic currency value of assets, liabilities, or operating income attributable to unanticipated changes in exchange rates. Thus, it refers not to the unpredictability of foreign exchange rates but to the uncertainty of the values of a firm's assets, liabilities, and operating income due to the unanticipated changes in exchange rates. Therefore, exchange risks arise only if the changes in exchange rates translate into volatility in the domestic currency value of assets, liabilities, and operating income. Unless 'exposed' to foreign exchange fluctuations, a firm may not face foreign exchange risk. Thus, foreign exchange risk becomes dependent on foreign exchange exposure.

15.7.2 Foreign Exchange Exposure

This refers to the sensitivity of the real value of assets, liabilities, and operating income to unanticipated changes in exchange rates expressed in its functional currency. The exposure includes 'real' value, which means the value has been adjusted by a country's inflation. The functional currency is the primary currency of a firm in which its financial statements are published. The domestic currency of firm's home country is often the functional currency for most companies.

Thus, foreign exchange risk is a function of variance both in unanticipated changes in exchange rates and foreign exchange exposures. Unanticipated changes in exchange rates do not imply foreign exchange risk for items that are not exposed. Similarly, if exchange rates are precisely predictable with accuracy, exposure on its own does not mean foreign exchange risk. Although it is difficult to forecast the exchange rates with precision, an international company can at least measure its exposure to exchange rate fluctuations and use available tools and techniques. Exchange rate fluctuations can lead to three types of exposures as discussed below.

Transaction exposure

This is the effect of exchange rate fluctuations on the value of anticipated cash-flows, denominated in home or functional currency terms, relating to transactions already entered into in foreign currency terms. Transaction exposure may arise due to conversion of currency in order to

- Make or receive payments for imports or exports of goods and services
- Repay a loan
- Make interest payment or to pay dividends

Transaction exposure arises due to various transactions denominated in foreign currency, including foreign currency denominated assets (export receivables or bank deposits), liabilities (account payable or loans), revenues (expected future sales), expenses (expected purchase of goods), or income (dividends). An exporting firm has a transaction exposure from the time it accepts an export order till the time the payment is received and converted into domestic or functional currency. Thus, a company makes 'exchange gain' if a currency has appreciated between the receivables booked and the payments received and 'exchange loss' if the currency has depreciated.

Strategies used to manage the transaction exposure include hedging with financial instruments forward, futures or options markets, and hedging with contract invoicing such as home currency and mix currency invoicing or using the price escalation clause.

Economic exposure

The effect of exchange rate fluctuations on a firm's future operating cash flows, i.e., its future costs and revenues, is termed as operating exposure. Any business enterprise whose revenue and costs are affected by currency fluctuations has operating exposure even if it solely operates domestically and has all its cash flows denominated in the home currency.

In technical terms, both the operating and transaction exposures equal a firm's economic exposure. Economic exposure assesses the effect of exchange rate changes on future revenue costs, cash-flows, and profits of the firm.

The economic exposure refers to the effect of the present value of future cash-flows influenced by unanticipated changes in exchange rates and macroeconomic factors such as unexpected changes in inflation rates and interest rates. Economic exposure of a firm is determined by the localization of production inputs and export-orientation, flexibility in pricing, and the firm's ability to shift production and sourcing of inputs among countries.

Strategies used to manage economic exposure include financial initiatives, such as leads and lags, netting, matching, and intra-company re-invoicing, apart from production initiatives, such as input outsourcing in the same currency as the one used for exports and adjusting production quantity and location. 'Lead' refers to making payments early by using soft currency to pay the hard currency debts before the soft currency drops in value. Conversely, 'lag' refers to paying late when a firm holds a hard currency with debts denominated in a soft currency which decelerates by paying late. It reduces the transaction exposure too. 'Netting' refers to the settlement of inter-subsidiary debts for the net amount within affiliates of an MNE, as discussed later in this chapter. The mechanism of matching a firm's foreign currency inflows with its foreign currency outflows in respect of the amount of currency unit and timing is termed as 'matching'.

Translation exposure

Also known as accounting exposure, translation exposure arises due to the conversion or translation of the financial statements of foreign subsidiaries and affiliates denominated in foreign currencies into consolidated financial statements of an MNE in its functional or home currency. The fluctuations in exchange rates affect the earnings of subsidiaries and affiliates and get translated into consolidated income statement. The translation exposure depends upon the share of a firm's business from overseas operations, location of foreign subsidiaries, and accounting methods used.

15.7.3 Managing Foreign Exchange Risks

A company operating internationally has to deal in multiple currencies and exchange rate regimes, which makes it vulnerable to foreign exchange risks and exposures. Some of the important techniques used for managing foreign exchange risks are explained here.

Hedging is a common terminology in foreign exchange management and refers to the avoidance of foreign exchange risk and covering an open position. In international operations, firms often receive payments in a foreign currency at a future date, which is a cause for concern due to the changes in the spot rate that may cause them to make higher payment or receive less than expected in terms of their domestic currency. This may significantly affect the anticipated profits. Among the various hedging techniques available, the principal techniques include forward contracts, options, and swaps.

Forward contracts

A forward contract is a commitment to buy or sell a specific amount of foreign currency at a later date or within a specific time period and at an exchange rate stipulated when the transaction is struck. The delivery or receipt of the currency takes place on the agreed forward value date. A forward transaction cannot be cancelled but can be *closed* out at any time by the repurchase or sale of the foreign currency amount on the value date originally agreed upon. Any resultant gains or losses are realized on this date.

Generally, there is variation in the *forward* price and *spot* price of a currency. In case the forward price is higher than the spot price, a forward premium is used whereas if the forward price is lower, a forward discount is used. To compute annual percentage premium or discount, the following formula may be used:

$$\text{Forward premium or discount} = \frac{(\text{Forward rate} - \text{Spot rate})}{\text{Spot rate}} \times \frac{360}{\text{Number of days under the forward contract}}$$

In this formula, the exchange rate is expressed in terms of domestic currency units per unit of foreign currency. To illustrate, if the spot price of 1 US dollar is Indian rupees 39.3750 on a given date and its 180-day forward price quoted is Rs 39.8350, the annualized forward premium works out to 0.92, as under:

$$\text{Forward premium or discount} = \frac{(39.8350 - 39.3750) * 360}{180}$$

$$= 0.92$$

The forward differential is known as swap rate. By adding the premium (in points) to or subtracting the discounts (in points) from the spot rate, the swap rate can be converted into an outright rate.

These forward premiums and discounts reflect the interest rate differentials between the respective currencies in the inter-bank market. If a currency with higher interest rates is sold forward, sellers enjoy the advantage of holding on to the higher earning currency during the period between agreeing upon the transaction and its maturity. Buyers are at a disadvantage since they must wait until they can obtain the higher earning currency. The interest rate disadvantage is offset by the forward discount. In the forward market, currencies are bought and sold for future delivery, usually a month, three months, six months, or even more from the date of transaction.

Future contracts

Commonly used by MNEs as hedging instruments, future contracts are standardized contracts that trade on organized futures markets for a specific delivery date only. The major difference in forward and future markets is summarized as follows:

- The forward contract does not have lot size and is tailored to the need of the exporter, whereas the futures have standardized round lots.
- The date of delivery in forward contracts is negotiable, whereas future contracts are for particular delivery dates only.
- The contract cost in future contracts is based on the bid/offer spread, whereas brokerage fee is charged for futures trading.
- The settlement of forward contracts is carried out only on expiration date, whereas profits or losses are paid daily in case of futures at the close of trading.
- Forward contracts are issued by commercial banks, whereas international monetary markets (for example, the Chicago Mercantile Exchange) or foreign exchanges issue futures contracts.

Options

Foreign currency options provide the holder the right to buy or sell a fixed amount of foreign currency at a pre-arranged price, within a given time. An option is an agreement between a holder (buyer) and a writer (seller) that gives the holder the right, but not the obligation, to buy or sell financial instruments at a time through a specified date. Thus, under an option, although the buyer is under no obligation to buy or sell the currency, the seller is obliged to fulfil the obligation. This provides the flexibility to the holder of a foreign currency option not to buy or sell the foreign currency at the pre-determined price, unlike in a forward contract, if it is not profitable. Price at which the option is exercised, i.e., at which a foreign currency is bought or sold, is known as strike price. Both currency call and put options can be purchased on an exchange. There are two types of foreign currency options:

Call option gives the holder the right to buy foreign currency at a pre-determined price. It is used to hedge future payables.

Put option gives the holder the right to sell foreign currency at a pre-determined price. It is used to hedge future receivables.

Foreign currency options are used as effective hedging instruments against exchange-rate risks as they offer more flexibility than forward or future contracts because no obligation is required on the part of the buyer under the currency options.

Swap

In order to hedge long-term transactions to currency rate fluctuations, currency swaps are used. Agreement to exchange one currency for another at a specified exchange rate and date is termed as currency swap. Currency swaps between two parties are often intermediated by banks or large investment firms. Foreign exchange swap accounts for about 55.6 per cent of the average daily foreign exchange turnover of the world, whereas spot deals account for 32.6 per cent and outright forward for 11.7 per cent.

Buying a currency at a lower rate in one market for immediate resale at higher rate in another with an objective to make profit from divergence in exchange rates in different money markets is known as 'currency arbitrage'. To capitalize on discrepancy in quoted prices, arbitrage is often used to make riskless profits.

15.7.4   Business Strategy to Manage Foreign Exchange Fluctuations

When the currency of a country appreciates, its goods become more expensive in foreign markets whereas imported goods become cheaper. Change in value of a foreign currency may cause a currency to appreciate or depreciate. A currency is said to appreciate when its value increases whereas depreciates when its value decreases with reference to the foreign currency. An increase in the domestic price of the foreign currency is referred to as depreciation, whereas the decline in the domestic price of foreign currency is termed as appreciation. For example, an increase in the price of one US\$ from Rs 43 to Rs 46 would be depreciation of Indian rupee whereas its decrease to Rs 40 would be appreciation of Indian rupee. A depreciation of domestic currency means appreciation of foreign currency and vice-versa.

$$\text{Per cent change in value of a foreign currency} = \frac{S - S_t - 1}{S_t - 1}.$$

Where, S denotes the most recent spot rate and $S_t - 1$ as the spot rate at a previous date.

Under the currency fluctuations, a firm is required to adopt different strategies.[11] When the domestic currency is weak, the firm should

- Stress price benefits
- Expand product line and add more costly features

---

[11] Cavusgil, S. Tamer, 'Unravelling the Mystique of Export Pricing', reprinted from *Business Horizons,* May–June 1988.

- Shift sourcing and manufacturing to the domestic market
- Exploit export opportunities in all markets
- Conduct conventional cash-for-goods trade
- Use full-costing approach, but use marginal-cost pricing to penetrate new or competitive markets
- Speed repatriation of foreign-earned income and collections
- Minimize expenditures in local, host country currency
- Buy needed services (advertising, insurance, transportation, etc.) in domestic market
- Minimize local borrowings
- Bill foreign customers in domestic currency

When the domestic currency is strong, the firm should

- Engage in non-price competition by improving quality, delivery, and after-sales service.
- Improve productivity and engage in vigorous cost reduction.
- Shift sourcing and manufacturing overseas.
- Give priority to exports to relatively strong-currency countries.
- Deal in counter trade with weak-currency countries.
- Cut profit margins and use marginal-cost pricing.
- Keep the foreign-earned income in host country, slow collections.
- Maximize expenditures in local, host-country currency.
- Buy needed services abroad and pay for them in local currencies.
- Borrow money needed for expansion in local market.
- Bill foreign customers in their own currency.

15.8 GLOBAL CASH MANAGEMENT

Global expansion of business operations involves transnational interchange of raw materials, equipment, spare parts, and finished goods among various subsidiaries of a multi-national enterprise. Such transactions involve buying and selling within the company, and intra-company transfer of funds. Large volumes of fund transfers within the company leads to substantial transaction costs, such as the cost of purchasing foreign exchange (the foreign exchange spread), the opportunity cost of float (time in transit), and other costs. Such transaction costs are estimated between 0.25 per cent and 1.5 per cent of the volume of funds transferred. To illustrate, Fig. 15.3 indicates the amount due to and from each of the affiliated companies. A large number of currency conversions and transactions would be involved with substantial transaction costs if all cash flows are executed on a bilateral basis.

Using a centralized system, a cash management centre (CMC) may be established that nets out receivables against payables and only the net cash flows are settled among different units of the MNE. The receivables against the payables of each subsidiary

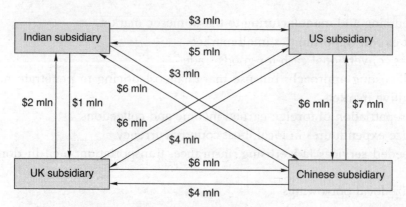

Fig. 15.3 Cash flows before multilateral netting

are net out by the CMC as given in Table 15.2. The CMC acquires the necessary currencies at the spot rate ruling at that time (two days before the settlement date). Any exchange gains or losses are attributed to the individual units.

Based on the net positions of each of the subsidiaries, intra-firm payments may be made through the CMC. Multilateral netting considerably reduces the total number of currency conversions from 12 to 4 as shown in Fig. 15.4, and results in significant savings due on transaction costs.

15.9 MODES OF PAYMENT IN INTERNATIONAL TRADE

A firm has to decide the terms of payment while executing an export order. The terms or mode of payment describes how and when the money is transferred from the buyer to the seller. The mode of payment differs widely, depending upon the nature of market competition, type of products dealt in, credit worthiness of buyers, and exporters' relationship and experience with the importer. The problem faced in realizing the payment varies from case to case. Various factors affecting the terms of payment include the risks associated, speed, security, cost, and the market competition. Various modes of payments in international trade include advance payment,

Table 15.2 Intra-firm payments matrix

(in million US dollars)

Receiving subsidiaries	Paying subsidiaries				Total receipts	Net receipts/ payments
	India	US	China	UK		
India	0	5	6	2	13	13 − 7 = 6
US	3	–	7	6	16	16 − 15 = 1
China	3	6	–	6	15	15 − 17 = − 2
UK	1	4	4	–	9	9 − 14 = − 5
Total payments	**7**	**15**	**17**	**14**		

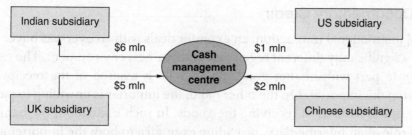

Fig. 15.4 Cash flows after multilateral netting

documentary credit with letter of credit (L/C), sight and time drafts, consignment sales, and open account.

The costs incurred to the importer and the risks associated to the exporter vary widely among different payment modes. As a matter of thumb rule, the lower the risk to the exporter, the higher is the cost to the importer, as shown in Fig. 15.5. While agreeing to the payment mode, both the exporter and the importer have to carry out a trade-off between the risks to the exporter and the costs to the importer.

15.9.1 Advance Payment

Under this, the payment is remitted by the buyer in advance, either by a draft mail or telegraphic transfer (TT). Generally, such payments are made on the basis of a sample receipt and its approval by the buyer. The clean remittance is made after accepting the order but before the shipment, through banking channels.

It is the simplest and the least risky form of payment from the exporter's point of view. Besides, no post-shipment finance is required if the payment is received in advance. There is no payment of interest on the funds and no commission is required to be paid as in other modes of payment, which makes it the cheapest mode of receiving payment. As it involves the highest level of risk for the buyer, advance payment is used only in cases where the exporter is in a position to dictate his/her terms. For instance, advance payment is often used if the product supplied is unique or has some sort of monopolistic power. However, such forms of payment is common mainly in case of overseas affiliates of the exporting firm.

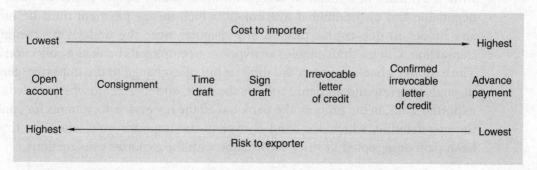

Fig. 15.5 Risk-cost trade-off for international payment modes

15.9.2 Documentary Credit

In a typical international transaction, an exporter deals with an overseas buyer who is situated in a significantly different regulatory and business environment. The exporter is unwilling to part with his/her goods unless s/he is assured of the receipt of the payment from the importer. On the other hand, the importer is unwilling to part with the money unless assured of receiving the goods. In such a situation, the bank plays the crucial role of an intermediary, providing assurance to both the importer and the exporter in an international transaction.

The payment collection mechanism that allows exporters to retain ownership of the goods or reasonably ensures their receiving payments is known as documentary collection. The bank acts as the exporter's agent in a documentary collection and regulates the timing and the sequence of the exchange of goods for value by holding the title of the documents until the importer fulfils his/her obligation as given in the Uniform Customs and Practices of Documentary Credits (UCPDC), brought out by the International Chamber of Commerce (ICC) in its publication no. 600, widely known as UCPDC 600, implemented on 1 July 2007.

The two principal documents used in documentary collection are the bills of lading (B/L) issued by the shipping company and the draft (bill of exchange) drawn by the exporter. B/L are issued by the shipping company to the shipper for accepting the merchandise for the carriage. As the document of title, it has a unique significance in shipping that only its legitimate holder is entitled to claim ownership of the goods covered therein. The importer simply cannot take possession of the goods unless the B/L is surrendered in original to the shipping company at destination. The procedure and the process involved in documentary credit employing banking channels assures both the exporter and the importer that the former gets the payment and the later receives the goods.

The draft, commonly known as bill of exchange, is used as an instrument to effect payment in international commerce. It is an unconditional order in writing, signed by the seller (exporter), also known as drawer, addressed to the buyer (importer) or importer's agent, known as drawee, ordering the importer to pay on demand or at a fixed or determinable future date, the amount specified on its face. The draft provides written evidence of a financial obligation in clear and simple terms. Besides, it is a negotiable and unconditional instrument, which means payment must be made to any holder in due course despite any disputes over the underlying commercial transaction. Using a draft enables an exporter to employ its bank as a collection agent. The exporter's bank forwards the draft or bill of exchange to the importer, generally through a correspondent bank, collects the draft, and then remits the proceeds to the exporter. Thus, in the process, the bank has all the necessary documents for control of the merchandise, which are handed over to the importer only when the draft has been paid or accepted in strict accordance with the exporter's instructions.

Documentary credit with letter of credit

A documentary credit represents a commitment of a bank to pay the seller of goods or services a certain amount, provided s/he presents stipulated documents evidencing the shipment of goods or performance of services within a specified period. The modus operandi of an L/C is depicted in the form of a self-explanatory diagram in Fig. 15.6. The exporter gets in touch with the importer and based on mutual communications, either by telephone, fax, or electronic messaging, and mutually agrees on terms of sale and enters into a sales contract (1) the importer, also known as applicant, applies to the issuing bank located in his/her country (2) for opening an L/C in accordance with the terms already agreed upon between the buyer and the seller in the sales contract. The issuing bank opens the L/C and delivers it (3) to the corresponding bank located in the exporter's country, which in turn advises (4) it to the exporter,

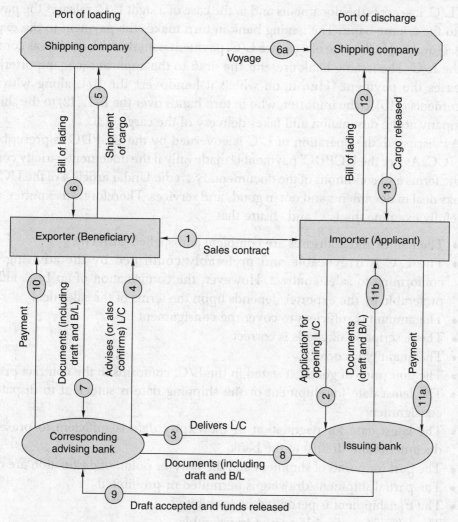

Fig. 15.6   Operation of letter of credit: A schematic diagram

also known as beneficiary. The exporter carefully scrutinizes the L/C and ensures that all the terms and conditions agreed upon in the sales contract are mentioned. In case there is any variation or discrepancy, it is brought to the notice of the applicant (i.e., importer) and got rectified.

Once the exporter gets satisfied of the terms and conditions contained in the L/C, s/he makes shipment (5). Soon after delivering goods to the shipping company, the B/L are obtained, (6) which serve as the cargo receipt, contract of carriage, and the document for the title of the goods. The shipment procedure requires a number of documents, both commercial and regulatory, to be prepared, which are dealt in detail in Chapter 18. The exporter submits the complete set of documents as mentioned in the L/C, including the B/L along with the draft drawn by the exporter (7) to the advising bank, which in turn sends it to the issuing bank (8). The issuing bank scrutinizes the documents and if found in accordance with the terms and conditions contained in the L/C, it accepts the documents and in the case of a sight L/C, releases the payment (9) to the issuing bank. The issuing bank in turn makes the payment to the exporter (10). However, in the case of a usance L/C, payment is made at a later date as contained in the L/C. The issuing bank presents the draft to the applicant (i.e., importer), who releases the payment (11a), upon which it handovers the B/L along with other documents (11b) to the importer, who in turn hands over the B/L (12) to the shipping company at the destination and takes delivery of the cargo (13).

As discussed, the operation of L/C is governed by the UCPDC as prescribed by the ICC. As per the UCPDC, payment is made only if the documents strictly conform to the terms and conditions of the documentary credit. Under article 4 of the UCPDC, banks deal in documents and not in goods and services. Therefore, an exporter should carefully examine the L/C and ensure that

- The names and addresses are complete and spelled correctly
- The L/C is irrevocable and preferably confirmed by the advising bank, conforming to sales contract. However, the confirmation of an L/C, although preferable by the exporter depends upon the terms of the sales deal
- The amount is sufficient to cover the consignment
- The description of goods is correct
- The quantity is correct
- The unit price of goods, if stated in the L/C, conforms to the contract price
- The latest date for shipment or the shipping date is sufficient to dispatch the consignment
- The latest date for negotiation or the expiry date is sufficient to present the documents and draft(s) to the bank
- The port (or point) of shipment and the port (or point) of destination are correct
- The partial shipment/drawing is permitted or prohibited
- The transhipment is permitted or prohibited
- The L/C is transferable or non-transferable

- The type of risk and the amount of insurance coverage, if required
- The documents required are obtainable
- The following words, or similar, are present in the L/C:
'Unless otherwise expressly stated, this credit is subject to the Uniform Customs and Practice for Documentary Credits, International Chamber of Commerce Publication No. 600'

Under a documentary credit, a debt relationship exists between the issuing bank and the beneficiary. Therefore, it is advisable to assess the issuing bank's standing, besides the sovereign and transfer risk of the importing country.

The issuing bank authorizes a corresponding bank in the beneficiary's country to honour the documents in its place. Under the UCPDC, unless the credit stipulates that it is available only with the issuing bank, all credits should nominate the bank (the 'nominated bank'), which is authorized to pay (to incur a deferred payment undertaking to accept drafts) or negotiate. However, in a freely negotiable credit any bank is treated as a nominated bank.

Types of letters of credit

According to methods of payments, the letters of credit may be of following types:

Irrevocable   The issuing bank irrevocably commits itself to make payment if the credit terms as given in the L/C are satisfied under article 9A of UCPDC. A unilateral amendment or cancellation of an irrevocable L/C is not possible.

Revocable   A revocable L/C is highly risky for the exporters as it can be revoked any time without consent of or notice to the beneficiary. For an L/C to be revocable, it should explicitly indicate as 'revocable', otherwise under article 6C of UCPDC, in absence of any explicit indication that the credit is revocable, it is deemed as irrevocable. Nowadays, revocable letters of credit are rare, although these were not uncommon in the 1970s and earlier, especially when dealing with less developed countries.

Confirmed   The confirming bank (generally a local bank in the exporter's country) commits itself to irrevocably make payment on presentation of documents under a confirmed L/C. The issuing bank asks the corresponding bank to confirm the L/C. Consequently, the corresponding bank confirms the L/C by adding a clause, 'The above credit is confirmed by us and we hereby undertake to honour the drafts drawn under this credit on presentation provided that all terms and conditions of the credit are duly satisfied.' A confirmed L/C provides additional protection to the exporter by localizing the risk of payment. Thus, the exporter enjoys two independent recognitions: one by the issuing bank and the other by the confirming bank. However, the confirming banks require the following criteria to be fulfilled:

- The L/C should be irrevocable.

- The credit should clearly instruct or authorize the corresponding bank to add its confirmation.
- The credit should be available at the confirming bank.
- The contents of credits should be unambiguous and free of 'stop' clauses (that allows buyer to prevent the terms of credit being fulfilled).

Unconfirmed   Under such credit, the issuing bank asks the corresponding bank to advise about the L/C without any confirmation on its part. It mentions, 'The credit is irrevocable on the part of the issuing bank but is not being confirmed by us.'

Sight   The beneficiary receives payment upon presentation and examination of documents in a sight L/C. However, the bank is given a reasonable time (generally not more than seven banking days) to examine the documents after its receipt.

Term credits   Term credits are used as financing instruments for the importer. During the deferred time period, the importer can often sell the goods and pay the due amount with the sales proceeds.

Acceptance credit   The exporter draws a time draft, either on the issuing or confirming bank or the buyer or on another bank depending upon the terms of credit. When the documents are presented, the draft is accepted instead of payment being made. For instance, the payment date may be 60 or 90 days after the invoice date or the date of transport documents.

Deferred payment credit   Such credits differ from the time draft in terms of lack of acceptance of a draft. The bank issues a written promise to make the payment on due date upon presentation of the documents. The due date is calculated on the basis of the terms of the credit. The deferred payment credit is generally more economical from the point of view of commission than the credit with time draft. However, an advance payment of credit amount may normally be obtained only from the issuing or confirming bank whereas there are various possibilities for discounting a draft.

Revolving   Under 'revolving letters of credit' the amount involved is reinstated when utilized, i.e., the amount becomes available again without issuing another L/C and usually under the same terms and conditions.

Back to back   Such back-to-back letters of credit are used when exporter uses them as a cover for opening a credit in favour of the local suppliers. As the credits are intended to cover same goods, it should be ensured that the terms are identical except that the price is lower and validity earlier.

Documentary credit without letter of credit

Documents are routed through banking channels that also act as the seller's agent along with the bill of exchange. The major documents should include a full set of B/L, commercial invoice, marine insurance policy, and other stipulated documents. The major types of bills of exchange can either be sight or usance, as discussed here.

Sight draft (documents against payment)   Similar to L/C, as discussed above, the exporter and the importer enter into a sales contract (1) on mutually agreed terms. Upon finalization of contract, the exporter (drawer) ships (2) the goods and submits the documents along with the bill of exchange through his/her bank, also known as the remitting bank (3), to the corresponding bank, also known as collecting bank (4), in the importer's country. The corresponding bank presents the draft to the importer (drawee) who makes payment at sight (5a) and thereafter the documents (5b) are handed over. The collecting bank transfers the payment (6) to the remitting bank in exporter's country, which in turn makes payment (7) to the exporter (Fig. 15.7).

Thus, under 'documents against payment', the importer can take physical possession of the goods only when s/he has made the payment before getting the documents from the bank. Sight drafts are generally considered safer as the exporter has possession and title of the goods till the time payment is made.

Usance or time draft (documents against acceptance)   Once a sales contract (1) is signed between the exporter and the importer, the exporter (drawer) ships the goods (2) and submits the draft along with documents and the collection order (3) to the bank located in his/her country, known as the remitting bank, which in turn sends (4) the draft along with documents to a corresponding bank, also known as the collecting bank, in the importer's country. The collecting bank presents the draft to the importer (drawee), who indicates his/her acceptance of the payment obligations (5a) by signing the draft, upon which the B/L along with other documents is handed over to the importer (5b) for taking delivery of the goods.

The payment under time draft is usually to be made at a later date, after 30, 60, 90 or more days. However, the bill of exchange already accepted by the drawee (i.e., importer) is again presented to the buyer (6a) on the due date, who in turn releases

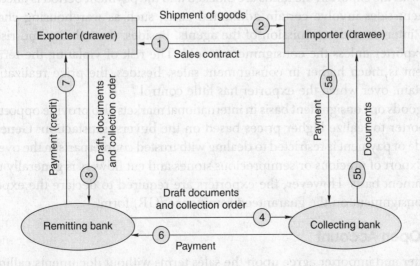

Fig. 15.7   Operation of sight draft (documents against payment): A schematic diagram

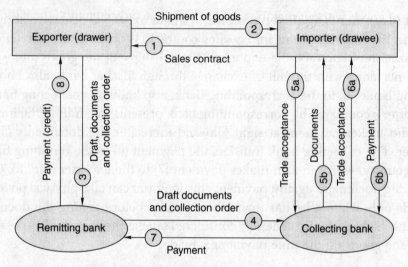

Fig. 15.8 Operation of usance or time draft (documents against acceptance): A schematic diagram

the payment (6b). The collecting bank transfers the funds to the remitting bank (7) for onward payment to the exporter (8) (Fig. 15.8).

This mode of payment poses a much greater risk as the documents are delivered to the importer, who subsequently takes title of the goods before the payment is released. In case the importer fails to make payment, the recovery of the sales proceeds is difficult and involves a cumbersome process.

15.9.3 Consignment Sales

Under the consignment sales, the shipment of goods is made to the overseas consignee and the title of goods is retained with the exporter until it is finally sold. As the title of goods lies with the exporter, the funds are blocked and the payment period is uncertain. Consignment sales involve certain additional costs, such as warehousing charges, insurance, interest, and commission of the agents. Besides, the liability and risks lie with the exporter unless the consignment is sold. The risk of violating the terms of consignment is much higher in consignment sales. Besides, the price realization is also uncertain, over which the exporter has little control.

Selling goods on consignment basis in international markets also provide opportunity to the exporter to realize higher prices based on the buyers' satisfaction. Generally, such a mode of payment is restricted to dealing with trusted counterparts in the overseas markets. Export of precious or semiprecious stones and cut flowers is generally made on consignment basis. However, the exporters are required to declare the expected value of consignment on the guaranteed remittance (GR) form.

15.9.4 Open Account

The exporter and importer agree upon the sales terms without documents calling for payments. However, the invoice is prepared by the exporter, and the importer can take delivery of goods without making the payment first. Subsequently, the exporting and importing firms settle their accounts through periodic remittances.

As the payment is to be released later, it serves as an instrument to finance the importer for the transaction and the importer saves the cost of getting bank finances. It requires sufficient financial strength on the part of the exporter. The operation of open account is hassle free and simple. The major drawback of an open account is the lack of safeguard measures against non-payment by the importer. Therefore, the open account is generally restricted to firms with longstanding dealing and business relationship and intra-company transactions among subsidiaries and affiliates. The statutory provisions related to foreign exchange often restrict using open account for receiving payments in international transactions. Generally, the central banks in most countries permit open accounts to foreign firms operating in their country and restrict it for domestic firms.

15.10   INTERNATIONAL TRADE FINANCE

Access to adequate finance at competitive rates is crucial to successful completion of an export transaction. Finances are required to complete an export trade cycle right from receiving the export order till the realization of final payment from the importer as indicated in Fig. 15.9. A firm has to procure raw materials, inputs, spares, or capital equipment for export production. Many a times the exporting firm is required to import the inputs or spares required for export production, and finances are needed much in advance. Export credit is extended both at pre-shipment and post-shipment stages.

International managers need to understand various alternatives available for trade finance as discussed in this chapter. However, the choice of trade finance strategy depends upon several factors:

- Financing alternatives available
- Nature of goods sold, as capital goods require long-term financing whereas perishables or consumer goods require short-term financing
- Intensity of market competition; exporters are expected to offer long-term credit to importer in buyers' market, whereas the reverse is the case in sellers' market
- Relationship between the exporter and the importer

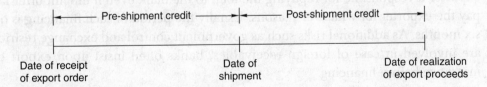

Fig. 15.9   Pre-shipment vs post-shipment credit

Source: Joshi, Rakesh Mohan, *International Marketing,* New Delhi: Oxford University Press, 2005, p. 554.

Various types of international financing alternatives available include banker's acceptance, discounting, accounts receivables financing, factoring, forfeiting, L/C, and counter trade. Besides commercial banks also extend export finance at subsidized rates under the guidelines of country's central bank.

15.10.1 Banker's Acceptance

Since centuries, banker's acceptance (BA) has been widely used in financing international trade. BA is the time draft or bill of exchange drawn on and accepted by a bank. By 'accepting' the draft, the bank makes an unconditional promise to pay the holder of the draft the specified amount of money on maturity. Thus, the bank effectively substitutes its own credit with that of a borrower. BA is a negotiable instrument that can be freely traded. The bank buys (discounts) the BA and pays the drawer (exporter) a sum less than the face value of the draft followed by selling (rediscounting) to an investor in the money market. The discount reflects the time value of money. The bank makes full payment at maturity to the investor who presents it. Banker's drafts by definition are time drafts with varying maturity of 30, 60, 90, or 180 days. The fee charged by the accepting bank varies, depending upon the maturity period and the creditworthiness of the borrower.

15.10.2 Discounting

Exporters can convert their credit sales into cash by way of 'discounting' the draft even if it is not accepted by the bank. The draft is discounted by the bank on its face value minus interest and commissions. The discounting may be 'with' or 'without' recourse. If the importer fails to pay, the bank can collect from the exporter in case of 'with recourse' discounting, whereas the collection risk is borne by the bank in case of 'without recourse' discounting. Usually the discounting rates are lower in many countries including India than other means of financing, such as loans, overdraft, etc., mainly due to government's export promotion schemes and subsidies.

15.10.3 Accounts Receivable Financing

In an open account shipment or time draft, goods are shipped to the importer without assurance of payment from a bank. Banks often provide loans to the exporter based on its creditworthiness secured by an assignment of the accounts receivables. The exporter is responsible for repaying the loan to the bank even if the importer fails to pay the exporter for whatever reasons. Usually the period of such financing is one to six months. As additional risks such as government control and exchange restrictions are involved in case of foreign receivables, banks often insist upon export credit insurance before financing.

15.10.4 Factoring

Factoring is widely used in short-term transactions as a continuous arrangement. It involves purchase of export receivables by the factor at a discounted price, i.e., generally 2 per cent to 4 per cent less than the full value. However, the discount depends upon a number of other factors such as the type of product, terms of the contract, etc. Generally, factors advance up to 85 per cent of the value of outstanding invoices. The factoring service may be undertaken by the factor *with recourse* to the seller, wherein the exporter remains exposed to the risk of non-payment by the importer. Besides, the factoring may be *without recourse*, wherein the factor assumes the credit and non-payment risks.

The operation of export factoring is depicted in Fig. 15.10, which involves the following steps:

- The importer and exporter enter into a sales contract and agree on the terms of sale (i.e., open account) (1).
- The exporter ships the goods to the importer (2).
- The exporter submits the invoice to the export factor (3).
- The export factor pays cash in advance to the exporter against receivables until the payment is received from the importer (4).
- However, the exporter pays interest to the factor on the money received or the factor deducts commission charges before making payment to the exporter.
- The export factor transfers the invoice to the import factor who in turn assumes the credit risks and undertakes administration and collection of receivables (5).
- The import factor presents the invoice to the importer on the due date for payment (6).

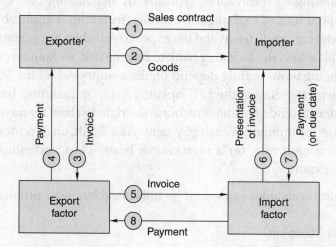

Fig. 15.10   Operational mechanism of factoring

Source: Joshi, Rakesh Mohan, *International Marketing*, New Delhi: Oxford University Press, New Delhi, 2005, p. 561.

- The importer makes payment to the import factor (7).
- The import factor in turn pays to the export factor (8).

Benefits to exporters   The benefits of using a factoring service for the exporter are

- It facilitates expanding sales in international markets by offering prospective customers the same terms and conditions as local competitors.
- It facilitates immediate payment against receivables and increases working capital.
- Tasks related to credit investigations, collecting account receivables from the importer, and providing other book-keeping services are carried out by the factors.
- In the event of buyer's default or refusal to pay, factors assume credit risk.
- Factoring often serves as a good substitute for the bank credit especially when the bank credit is either uneconomical too restrictive.

Besides, factoring is also beneficial for the importers as it

- Increases their purchasing power without drawing on bank credit lines
- Facilitates procurement of goods with little hassles

15.10.5 Forfeiting

The term 'forfeiting' is derived from the French word *forfait*, which means to relinquish or surrender the rights. Thus, forfeiting refers to the exporter relinquishing his/her rights to a receivable due at a future date in exchange for immediate cash payment at an agreed discount, passing all risks and the responsibility for collecting the debt to the forfeiter. Forfeiting is particularly used for medium-term credit sales (1 to 3 years) and involves the issue of a bill of exchange by the exporter or promissory notes by the buyer on which a bank and the buyer's country guarantee payment.

Forfeiting is the discounting of receivables, typically by negotiating bills drawn under an L/C or co-accepted bills of exchange. Generally, forfeiting is applicable in cases where export of goods is on credit terms and the export receivables are guaranteed by the importer's bank. This allows the forfeiting bank to buy the risk 'without recourse' to the exporter. The financing terms mainly depend on the country risk of the buyer, size of the contract, financial standing of the L/C opening bank or guarantor bank.

By forfeiting, the exporter surrenders without recourse the right to claim for payment of goods exported in return for immediate cash payment. As a result, an exporter can convert a credit sale into a cash sale, on a no-recourse basis. Thus, forfeiting is a mechanism for financing exports

- By discounting export receivables evidenced by bills of exchange or promissory notes
- On a fixed rate basis (discount)
- Without recourse to the exporter
- Carrying medium-to long-term maturities (usually over 120 days)
- Up to 100 per cent of the contract value

Avalization (co-acceptances) Avalization or co-acceptance is a means of non-fund based import finance whereby a bill of exchange drawn by an exporter on the importer is co-accepted by a bank. By co-accepting the bill of exchange, the bank undertakes to make payment to the exporter even if the importer fails to make payment on due date.

Operation of a forfeiting transaction

Receivables under a deferred payment contract for export of goods, evidenced by bills of exchange or promissory notes (pro notes), can be forfeited. Bills of exchange or promissory notes backed by avalization (co-acceptance) of the importer's bank are endorsed by the exporter, without recourse, in favour of the forfeiter in exchange for discounted cash proceeds. Some transactions are taken without such a guarantee or co-acceptance, provided the importer is of an acceptable standing to the forfeiter. The operation of a forfeiting transaction is briefly discussed below.

Step 1: Pre-shipment stage

- As the exporter is in the process of negotiating a contract with the overseas buyer, s/he provides the bank the following details to enable it to give an 'indicative quote':
  - Name and full address of the foreign buyer
  - Details of goods (quantity, base price, etc.)
  - Amount of the contract
  - Number and expected dates/period of shipments
  - Security-banker's name (under L/C or bills of exchange avalized by bank)
  - Repayment schedule
  - Country to which exports are to be made
- Based on the details provided, the bank contacts the forfeiting agencies/exim bank, who are given an indicative quote with details of discounting cost, commitment fees, etc.
- After confirming that the terms are acceptable, the exporter informs the bank, who accordingly calls for the final quote.
- After confirming acceptance of the forfeiting terms to the bank, the exporter signs off the commercial contract with her/his buyer. The contract must provide for the buyer to furnish avalized bills of exchange. Simultaneously, a forfeiting contract is entered into with the forfeiting agency through the bank.
- Once the forfeiting contact is duly signed, the bank issues the following certificates:
  - A certificate giving permission to the exporter to remit commitment fees.
  - A certificate showing the discount payable by the exporter to the forfeiting agency to enable them to declare the same on the GR form. Otherwise, the customs clearance of the goods would be held up.

Step II: Post-shipment stage

- On shipment of goods, the exporter presents the documents to the bank who in turn forwards them to the buyer or buyer's bank. The set of documents being forwarded must contain the bills of exchange for the total amount (inclusive of the forfeiting cost, drawn on the importer or importer's bank).

- The importer's bank would accept, co-accept, or avalize the bill of exchange and send it back to the exporter's bank.
- The exporter's bank would ensure that the bill of exchange is endorsed 'without recourse' in favour of the forfeiting agency.
- After checking the documents, the forfeiter would deposit the forfeited proceeds in the specified account.
- The bank after checking the proceeds would issue an foreign inward remittance certificate (FIRC) and the GR form.

Costs involved in a forfeiting transaction

A forfeiting transaction generally has three cost elements.

Commitment fee   The commitment fee is payable by the exporter to the forfeiter for his/her commitment to execute a specific forfeiting transaction at a discount. Generally, the commitment fee ranges from 0.5 per cent to 1.5 per cent per annum of the utilized amount to be forfeited. Besides, the commitment fee is payable regardless of whether or not the export contract is ultimately executed.

Discount fee   It is the interest payable by the exporter for the entire period of credit involved and is deducted by the forfeiter from the amount paid to the exporter against the availized promissory notes or bills of exchange. The discount fee is based on the market interest rates as determined by the prevailing London Inter-Bank Offered Rate (LIBOR) for the credit period and the currency involved plus a premium for the risk assumed by the forfeiter. The discount rate is agreed upon at the time of executing the contract for forfeiting.

Documentation fee   Generally, no documentation fee is incurred in a straight forfeit transaction. However, a documentation fee may be levied in case extensive documentation and legal work is required.

Benefits to the exporter

The major advantages of forfeiting to exporters are summarized below:

- In India, post-shipment finance extended by bankers is limited to 180 days at subsidized rates. The exporter converts a deferred payment export into a cash transaction, improving liquidity and freeing the balance sheet of debt, thus also improving leverage.
- Forfeiting frees the exporter from cross-border political risks and commercial risks associated with export receivables. There is no contingent liability in the balance sheet of the exporter.
- As forfeiting offers 'without recourse' finance, it does not impact the exporter's borrowing limits. It represents an additional source of finance, outside working capital limits, providing a convenient option if funded limits are not sufficient.

- Since it is fixed rate finance, it hedges against interest and exchange risks arising out of deferred export payments.
- The exporter saves on insurance costs as forfeiting obviates the need for export credit insurance.
- Forfeiting is transaction-specific as the exporter need not have a long-term relationship with the forfeiting agency abroad.
- There is simplicity of documentation as the documents being submitted are readily available with the exporter.
- Forfeiting is not bound by any retention percentages. It offers 100 per cent financing and there is no restriction on the type, condition, or age of the products.

15.10.6 Letters of Credit

One of the oldest forms of international finance is still used in international transactions. As discussed in detail earlier in this chapter, in an L/C, the issuing bank undertakes a written guarantee to make the payment to the beneficiary, i.e., the exporter, subject to the fulfilment of its specified conditions. In the process, a debt relationship exists between the issuing bank and beneficiary. Terms credit is often used as financing instrument for the importer who gets delivery of the goods without making payment to the exporter.

15.10.7 Counter-Trade

Counter-trade is used to combine trade financing and price setting in one transaction. It involves various forms of reciprocal transactions such as barter, clearing arrangements, switch trading, counter purchase, buy-back, and off-set, as already discussed in Chapter 11. Counter-trade finances imports in form of reciprocal commitments from countries that have payment problems, especially in hard currencies.

15.11 EXPORT FINANCE

In order to be competitive in markets, exporters are often expected to offer attractive credit terms to their overseas buyers. Extending such credits to foreign buyers put considerable strain on the liquidity of the exporting firms. Therefore, it is extremely important to make adequate trade finances available to the exporters from external sources at competitive terms during the post-shipment stage. Unless competitive trade finance is available to the exporters, they often resort to quote lower prices to compensate their inability to offer competitive credit terms. As a part of export promotion strategy, national governments around the world offer export credit, often at concessional rates to facilitate exports.

15.11.1 Export Credit in India

In India, export credit is available both in Indian rupees and foreign currency as discussed here.

Export credit in Indian rupees

The Reserve Bank of India (RBI) prescribes a ceiling rate for the rupee export credit linked to Benchmark Prime Lending Rates (BPLRs) of individual banks available to their domestic borrowers. However, the banks have the freedom to decide the actual rates to be charged with specified ceilings. Generally, the interest rates do not exceed BPLR minus 2.5 percentage points per annum for the specified categories of exports[12] as under:

1. Pre-shipment credit (from the date of advance)
   (a) Up to 180 days
   (b) Against incentives receivable from the government covered by Export Credit and Guarantee Corporation (ECGC) guarantee up to 90 days
2. Post-shipment credit (from the date of advance)
   (a) On demand bills for transit period, as specified by FEDAI (Foreign Exchange Dealers Association of India)
   (b) Usance bills (for total period comprising usance period of export bills, transit period as specified by FEDAI, and grace period, wherever applicable)
      (i) Up to 90 days
      (ii) Up to 365 days for exporters under the Gold Card Scheme
   (c) Against incentives receivable from government (covered by ECGC Guarantee) up to 90 days
   (d) Against undrawn balances (up to 90 days)
   (e) Against retention money (for supplies portion only) payable within one year from the date of shipment (up to 90 days)

Pre-shipment credit   Pre-shipment credit means any loan or advance granted by a bank to an exporter for financing the purchase, processing, manufacturing, or packing of goods prior to shipment. It is also known as packing credit. As the ultimate payment is made by the importer, his/her creditworthiness is important to the bank. Banks often insist upon the L/C or a confirmed order before granting export credit. The banks reduce the risk of non-payment by the importer by collateral or supporting guarantee.

Period of advance   The period of packing credit given by the bank varies on a case to case basis, depending upon the exporter's requirement for procurement, processing,

---

[12] Rupee/Foreign Currency Export Credit and Customer Service to Exporters, Master Circular, RBI/2008–09/66, 1 July 2008.

or manufacturing and shipping of goods. Primarily, individual banks decide the period of packing credit for exports. However, the RBI provides refinance to the banks only for a period not exceeding 180 days. If pre-shipment advances are not adjusted by submission of export documents within a period of 360 days from the date of advance, the advance cease to qualify for concessive rate of interest *ab initio*. Banks may release the packing credit in one lump sum or in stages, depending upon the requirement of the export order or L/C.

Liquidation of packing credit   The pre-shipment credit granted to an exporter is liquidated out of the proceeds of the bills drawn for the exported commodities on its purchases, discount, etc., thereby converting pre-shipment credit to post-shipment credit. The packing credit may also be repaid or prepaid out of the balances in Exchange Earners' Foreign Currency (EEFC) Account. Moreover, banks are free to decide the rate of interest from the date of advance.

Running account facility   Generally, pre-shipment credit is provided to exporters on lodgement of L/Cs or firm export orders. It has also been observed that in some cases the availability of raw material is seasonal whereas the time taken for manufacture and shipment of goods is more than the delivery schedule as per the export contracts in others. Besides, often the exporters have to procure raw material, manufacture the export products, and keep the same ready for shipment, in anticipation of the receipt of firm export orders or L/Cs from overseas buyers. In view of these difficulties faced by the exporters in availing the pre-shipment credit in such cases, banks are authorized to extend pre-shipment credit 'running account facility'. Such running account facility is extended in respect of any commodity without insisting upon prior lodgement of a firm export order or an L/C depending upon the bank's judgment.

Post-shipment credit   Post-shipment credit means any loan or advance granted or any other credit provided by a bank to an exporter of goods from the date of extending credit after shipment of goods to the date of realization of export proceeds. It includes any loan or advance granted to an exporter, in consideration of any duty drawback allowed by the government from time to time. Thus, the post-shipment advance can mainly take the form of

- Export bills purchased, discounted, or negotiated
- Advances against bills for collection
- Advances against duty drawback receivable from government

Post-shipment finance can be categorized as

- Advances against undrawn balances on export bills
- Advances against retention money
- Exports on consignment basis
- Exports of goods for exhibition and sale
- Post-shipment credit on deferred payment terms

Post-shipment credit is to be liquidated by the proceeds of export bills received from abroad in respect of goods exported.

Period of post-shipment credit In the case of demand bills, the period of advance is the normal transit period (NTP) as specified by the FEDAI. Normal transit period means the average period normally involved from the date of negotiation, purchase, or discount till the receipt of bill proceeds in the Nostro account of the bank concerned, as prescribed by the FEDAI from time to time. It is not to be confused with the time taken for the arrival of goods at overseas destination.

The demand bill is not paid before the expiry of the normal transit period whereas the usance bill is paid after the due date and is also termed as an overdue bill. In case of usance bills, credit can be granted for a maximum duration of 365 days from date of shipment inclusive of NTP and grace period, if any. However, banks closely monitor the need for extending post-shipment credit up to the permissible period of 365 days and they also influence the exporters to realize the export proceeds within a shorter period.

Export credit in foreign currency

In order to make credit available to the exporters at internationally competitive rates, banks (authorized dealers) also extend credit in foreign currency[13] (Exhibit 15.3) at LIBOR (London Interbank Offered Rates), EURO LIBOR (London Interbank Offered Rates dominated in Euro), or EURIBOR (Euro Interbank Offered Rates). LIBOR is a daily reference rate based on the interest rates at which banks offer to lend unsecured funds to other banks in the London wholesale (or 'interbank') money market. The rate paid by one bank to another for a deposit is known as London Interbank Bid Rate (LIBID).

Pre-shipment credit in foreign currency To enable the exporters to have operational flexibility, banks extend pre-shipment credit in foreign currency (PCFC) in any one of the convertible currencies, such as US dollars, pound sterling, Japanese yen, euro, etc, in respect to an export order invoiced in another convertible currency. For instance, an exporter can avail of PCFC in US dollars against an export order invoiced in euro. However, the risk and cost of cross-currency transaction are that of the exporter. Under this scheme, the exporters have the following options to avail export finance:

- To avail of pre-shipment credit in rupees and then the post-shipment credit either in rupees or discounting/re-discounting of export bills under Export Bills Abroad (EBR) scheme
- To avail of pre-shipment credit in foreign currency and discount/rediscounting of the export bills in foreign currency under EBR scheme

---

[13] Rupee/Foreign Currency Export Credit and Customer Service to Exporters, Master Circular, RBI/2007–08/30.

	Type of credit	**Interest rate** (percent per annum)
(i)	**Pre-shipment credit**	
(a)	Up to 180 days	Not exceeding 1% over LIBOR/EURO LIBOR/ EURIBOR
(b)	Beyond 180 days and up to 360 days	Rate for initial period of 180 days prevailing at the time of extension plus 2 percentage points (i) (a) above + 2%
(ii)	**Post-shipment credit**	
(a)	On demand bills for transit period (as specified by FEDAI)	Not exceeding 1% over LIBOR/EURO LIBOR/ EURIBOR
(b)	Against usance bills (credit for total period comprising usance period of export bills, transit period as specified by FEDAI and grace period wherever applicable)	
	Up to 6 months from the date of shipment	Not exceeding 1% over LIBOR/ EURO LIBOR/ EURIBOR
(c)	Export bills (demand or usance) realised after due date but up to date of crystallization	Rate applicable up to the due date plus 2 percentage points

Exhibit 15.3   Export credit in foreign currency

Source: Rupee/Foreign Currency Export Credit and Customer Service to Exporters, Master Circular, RBI/2008–09/66, 1 July 2008.

- To avail of pre-shipment credit in rupees and then convert at the discretion of the bank

Banks are also permitted to extend PCFC for exports to Asian Currency Union (ACU) countries. The applicable benefit to the exporters accrues only after the realization of the export bills or when the resultant export bills are rediscounted on 'without recourse' basis. The lending rate to the exporter should not exceed 1.0 percent over LIBOR, EURO LIBOR, or EURIBOR, excluding withholding tax.

Post-shipment credit in foreign currency   The exporters also have options to avail post-shipment export credit either in foreign currency or domestic currency. However, the post-shipment credit has also to be in foreign currency if the pre-shipment credit has already been availed in foreign currency so as to liquidate the pre-shipment credit. Normally, the scheme covers bills with usance period up to 180 days from the date of shipment. However, RBI approval needs to be obtained for longer periods. Similar to the PCFC scheme, post-shipment credit can also be obtained in any convertible currency. However, most Indian banks provide credit in US dollars.

Under the rediscounting of Export Bills Abroad Scheme (EBR), banks are allowed to rediscount export bills abroad at rates linked to international interest rates at post-shipment stage. Banks may also arrange a Banker's Acceptance Factor (BAF) for rediscounting the export bills without any margin and duly covered by collateralized documents. Banks may also have their own BAF limits fixed with an overseas bank, a rediscounting agency or factoring agency on 'without recourse' basis.

Exporters also have the option to arrange for themselves a line of credit on their own with an overseas bank or any other agency, including a factoring agency for rediscounting their export bills directly.

15.11.2 Financing to Overseas Importers

Generally, commercial banks extend exports credit, often at concessional rates, to finance export transactions to the exporters as a part of their export promotion measures. In addition, credit is also available to overseas buyers so as to facilitate import of goods from India, mainly under two forms:

Buyer's credit

It is a credit extended by a bank in exporter's country to an overseas buyer, enabling the buyer to pay for machinery and equipment that s/he may be importing for a specific project.

Line of credit

It is a credit extended by a bank in exporting country (for example, India) to an overseas bank, institution, or government for the purpose of facilitating the import of a variety of listed goods from the exporting country (India) into the overseas country. A number of importers in the foreign country may be importing the goods under one line of credit.

Commercial banks carry out the task of export financing under the guidelines of the central bank (for example, Reserve Bank of India). The export financing regulations are modified from time to time. Most countries have an apex bank coordinating the country's efforts of financing international trade. For instance, the Export-Import Bank of India is the principal financial institution coordinating the working of institutions engaged in export import finance in India, whereas the US too has the Export-Import Bank of the US for carrying out similar activities.

15.11.3 Credit Risk Insurance

Easy and hassle-free access to export finance significantly enhances firms' abilities to compete in international markets. Prior to agreeing to finance a firm's export transactions, banks need to be assured of the ability of the borrowers to repay the loan. Generally, banks insist on pleading adequate collateral before sanctioning export finance. In an international transaction, as a firm has to deal with an overseas buyer operating in a different legal and political environments, the risks increases manifolds on the smooth conduct of the commercial transaction. The major commercial risks in international trade transactions are as follows:

- Non-payment by the importer at the end of the credit period or after some specified period after the expiry of credit term
- Non-acceptance of goods by the importer despite of its compliance with the export contract
- Insolvency of the purchaser

It has been observed that commercial risks have resulted in more losses in international transactions compared to political risks.

Credit risk insurance provides protection to exporters who sell their goods on credit terms. It covers both political and commercial risks. Credit insurance also facilitates exporters in getting export finances from commercial banks. The benefits provided by credit insurance to the exporters are

- Exporters can offer competitive payment terms to their buyers.
- It protects the exporters against the risk and financial costs of non-payment.
- Exporters also get covered against further losses from fluctuations in foreign exchange rates after the non-payment.
- It provides exporters a freer access to working capital.
- The insurance cover reduces exporters' need for tangible security while negotiating credit with their banks.
- Credit insurance provides exporters a second check on their buyers.
- Exporters get access to and benefit from the credit insurer's knowledge of potential payment risks in overseas markets and their commercial intelligence, including changes in their import regulations.

Insurance policies and guarantees extended by export credit agencies such as ECGC can be used as collateral for trade financing. Once the perceived risks of default are reduced, banks are often willing to grant favourable terms of credit to the exporters. Thus, in addition to funding for exports, export finances also limit the firm's risk of international transactions.

Most countries have central-level export credit agencies (ECAs) to cover credit risks offering a number of schemes to suit varied needs of the exporters for export credit and guarantee. Examples include Export Credit and Guarantee Corporation (ECGC) in India, Export Credit Guarantee Department (ECGD) in the UK, Export Risk Insurance Agency (ERIA) in Switzerland, and Export Finance and Insurance Corporation (EFIC) in Australia.

Export Credit Guarantee Corporation   Export Credit Guarantee Corporation (ECGC) of India, established in 1957 by the Government of India is the principal organization for promoting exports by covering the risks of exporting on credit. It functions under the administrative control of the Ministry of Commerce. ECGC is the world's fifth largest credit insurer in terms of coverage of national exports. The ECGC mainly

- Provides a range of credit risk insurance covers to exporters against loss in export of goods and services
- Offers guarantees to banks and financial institutions to enable exporters obtain better facilities from them
- Provides overseas investment insurance to Indian companies investing in joint ventures abroad in the form of equity or loan

15.11.4 WTO Compatibility of Trade Finance and Insurance Schemes

The multilateral trade regime under the WTO sets the framework for the types of subsidies that can be provided by a country for export promotion. As discussed in Chapter 5, the agreement on Subsidies and Countervailing Measures (SCM) prohibits national governments from providing subsidies that are contingent upon export performance or upon the use of domestic goods over the imported ones. Among the prohibited subsidies in the first category are direct subsidies to a firm or industry contingent on export performance, such as

- Currency retention schemes giving a bonus to the exporters
- Internal transport and freight charges on export shipments on more favourable terms than for domestic shipment
- The provision of subsidized inputs for the production of goods for exports
- Remission or exemptions from direct taxes and charges for export products

The SCM agreement also constrains government intervention in the area of export financing and insurance. In particular, it prohibits the provision of export credits at conditions more favourable than those set in international capital markets and the extension of export credit insurance and guarantee programmes at subsidized premium rates.

This chapter facilitates readers to develop a conceptual understanding of basic issues of international finance. Evolution of international monetary systems, prevailing exchange rate arrangements, and exchange rate quotations used in foreign exchange markets help international managers in making foreign exchange decisions. Besides, this chapter also brings out the conceptual framework of foreign exchange risks and exposures and techniques for its management.

Alternative modes of payment used in international trade have been elucidated so as to make readers appreciate, evaluate, and select the most suitable option, depending upon the speed, security, cost, market competition, and risks associated. Access to adequate finance is crucial to successful completion of an export transaction. Various instruments used for financing international trade have also been examined. Further, the chapter elaborates various export credit and insurance schemes.

SUMMARY

This chapter provides an overview of international finance. Exchange rates refer to the price of one currency in terms of another, which is determined by the international monetary system. Historically, prevailing gold standards moved to fixed exchange rate system and later on to floating exchange rate system where currency prices are determined by market demand and supply conditions. The contemporary exchange rate arrangements classified by IMF include floating and pegged exchange rate systems that comprise of soft and hard pegs. Economic theories use purchasing power parity and interest rate differentials to determine exchange rates.

The foreign exchange market, which refers to the organizational setting within which individuals, businesses, governments, and banks buy and sell foreign currencies and other debt instruments, is the largest and the most liquid market in the world. Traders, hedgers, and arbitragers are the major participants in the foreign exchange market. Foreign exchange quotations may be spot or forward, direct or indirect, and bid or ask quotations. An international company has to deal with multiple exchange rate regimes and cash flows across the countries, making it vulnerable to foreign exchange fluctuations. Sensitivity of the real value of assets, liabilities, and operating income to unanticipated changes in exchange rates expressed in its functional currency is known as foreign exchange exposure. Transaction, economic, and translation are the three major types of exposures caused by exchange rate fluctuations. Various hedging techniques used to manage foreign exchange risks involve forward transactions, options, and swaps. Multilateral netting is often employed as an effective technique for global cash management.

The mode of payment describes how money is transferred from buyer to the seller. Advance payment, documentary credit with L/C or without L/C using sight or time draft, consignment sales, and open account are the major types of payment modes in international trade. Banker's acceptance, discounting, accounts receivables financing, factoring, forfeiting, L/C, and counter trade are the major forms of international trade finance. Most countries, including India, provide export credit at concessional rates. Credit risk insurance provides protection to the exporters who sell their goods on credit terms and also facilitates them in getting financing from commercial banks.

KEY TERMS

Bid rate Price that a bank is willing to pay for a currency.

Call option Gives the holder the right to buy foreign currency at a pre-determined price.

Co-acceptance Non-fund based import finance whereby a bill of exchange drawn by an exporter on the importer is co-accepted.

Cross exchange rate Exchange rates of two currencies without using the US dollar as the reference currency.

Currency appreciation Decline in domestic price of foreign currency.

Currency arbitrage Buying a currency at a lower rate in one market for immediate resale at a higher rate in another with an objective to make profit.

Currency board arrangement A monetary regime based on an explicit legislative commitment to exchange domestic currency for a specified foreign currency at a fixed exchange rate.

Currency depreciation An increase in domestic price of the foreign currency.

Currency spread The difference between the bid and the offer rates.

Direct quotes Units of the home currency per unit of a foreign currency.

Discount The margin charged by the forfeiter as the base interest for discounting.

Dollarization   Replacement of a country's local currency with US dollars.

Economic exposure   The effect of exchange rate fluctuations on a firm's future operating cash-flows.

Eurocurrency   A currency deposited in a bank outside the country of its origin.

Eurocurrency market   The set of banks that accept, deposit, and make loans in euro currencies.

Factoring   Purchase of receivables by the factor at a discounted price.

Fisher effect theory   The nominal interest rate in a country is determined by the real interest rate and the expected inflation rate.

Fixed rate   A firm rate of discount quoted that protects the exporter from interest rate fluctuations caused by movements in LIBOR.

Floating exchange rate system   A monetary system where currency prices are determined by market demand and supply conditions.

Foreign currency option   Providing the holder the right to buy or sell a fixed amount of foreign currency at a pre-arranged price, within a given time.

Foreign exchange   Any type of financial instrument that is used to make payments between countries such as foreign currency notes, monetary gold, special drawing rights (SDRs), etc.

Foreign exchange exposures   The sensitivity of the real value of assets, liabilities, and operating income to unanticipated changes in exchange rates expressed in its functional currency.

Foreign exchange market   The organizational setting within which individuals, businesses, governments, and banks buy and sell foreign currencies and other debt instruments.

Foreign exchange risk   The variance of domestic currency value of assets, liabilities, or operating income attributable to unanticipated changes in exchange rates.

Forfeiting   Discounting of the receivables, typically by negotiating bills drawn under a letter of credit or co-accepted bills of exchange.

Forward rate   The price at which the foreign exchange rate is quoted for delivery at a specified date after two business days.

Forward transaction   A commitment to buy or sell a specific amount of foreign currency at a later date and at an exchange rate stipulated when the transaction is struck.

Gold bullion standard   The currency in circulation consists of paper notes but a fixed weight of gold remains the basis of money.

Gold exchange standard   Paper currency can be converted at a fixed rate into the paper currency of the other country that is operating a gold specie or gold bullion standard.

Gold specie standard   The actual currency in circulation consists of gold coins with fixed gold content.

Hedging   The avoidance of foreign exchange risk and covering an open position.

'Independent' or 'Free' float   Exchange rates are market determined, the central banks intervene only to moderate the speed of change or to prevent excessive fluctuations.

Indirect quote   Units of a foreign currency per unit of home currency.

International fisher effect (IFE) theory   The interest rate differential between any two countries serves as an unbiased predictor of future changes in the spot exchange rate.

International monetary system   Set of rules, regulations, policies, practices, instruments, institutions, and mechanisms that determine exchange rates between currencies.

LIBOR   London Inter-Bank Offer Rate serves as the base cost of funds for the prime banks.

'Managed' or 'Dirty' float   Currencies are allowed to fluctuate on a daily basis with no official boundaries with government intervention so as to prevent their currencies from moving too far in a certain direction.

Normal transit period (NTP)   The average period from the date of negotiation, purchase or discount till the receipt of bill proceeds in the Nostro account of the bank.

Offer rate   Price at which a bank is willing to sell the currency.

Pegged exchange rate system   Pegging value of home currency to a foreign currency or a basket of currencies.

Post-shipment credit Any loan or advance granted to an exporter from the date of shipment till the realization of export proceeds.

Pre-shipment credit Any loan or advance granted to the exporter for financing the purchase of inputs, raw materials, etc., for processing, manufacturing, or packaging of goods prior to shipment.

Purchasing power parity (PPP) theory If prices of goods sold in different countries, converted to a common currency, it should be identical.

Put option Gives the holder the right to sell foreign currency at a pre-determined price.

Short date transaction Transaction that call for settlement before the spot date.

Spot rate Price agreed for purchase or sale of foreign currency with delivery and payment to take place not more than two business days after the day the transaction has been concluded.

Transaction exposure The effect of exchange rate fluctuations, on the value of anticipated cash-flows, denominated in home or functional currency terms, relating to transactions already entered into in foreign currency terms.

CONCEPT REVIEW QUESTIONS

1. Briefly explain evolution of international monetary systems.
2. Critically examine various theories for determination of exchange rates.
3. Elucidate the concept of multilateral netting in managing cash flows for a multinational enterprise.
4. Explain with help of a suitable diagram the modus operandi of an L/C.
5. Distinguish between the sight and time drafts and its implications on international trade.
6. Explaining the operational mechanism of forfeiting, enumerate its benefits for exporters.
7. Write short notes on
   (a) Bank for International Settlements (BIS)
   (b) Foreign exchange exposure
   (c) Banker's acceptance
8. Distinguish between
   (a) Gold Specie and Gold Bullion Standards
   (b) Independent and managed floats
   (c) Soft and hard pegs
   (d) Direct and indirect quotes
   (e) Bid and ask quotes

PROJECT ASSIGNMENTS

1. Explore the exchange rate fluctuations in the last five years in the currency of your country vis-à-vis any three major currencies, which may include the US$, British £, Japanese ¥, or the Euro € and assess its impact on international business strategy of local companies.

2. Explore the Internet to find out export credit schemes at subsidized rates offered in your country and compare with those of other countries. Identify the significant differences and assess its implications on exports.

FIELD ASSIGNMENTS

1. Visit a company having global operations and explore the techniques used by it in managing foreign exchange risks and exposure.
2. Contact a local bank dealing in international transactions and find out various types of payment modes used in export transactions through the banking channels. Discuss the pros and cons of each of the payment mode used.

16 Global Operations and Supply Chain Management

LEARNING OBJECTIVES

> To explain the significance of managing global operations and supply chain
> To elucidate the concept of global operations management
> To explicate global supply chain management
> To discuss key concepts and issues of maritime transportation in international trade
> To elaborate containerization and multi-modal transportation
> To examine international organizations associated with international maritime transportation
> To discuss institutional framework for maritime transport in India

16.1 INTRODUCTION

In order to create value to its customers, a firm needs to manage logistics, operations, marketing, and services in an integrated manner. The ability of a firm to procure the raw materials and inputs and make its finished products available to the ultimate customer in the most cost-effective and efficient manner is crucial to a firm's competitive advantage in international business.

Operations management has become an integral part of business strategy. It is one of the four primary functional areas of managing business, the others being marketing, finance, and human resources. Historically, 'production' or 'manufacturing' has been regarded as the core functional area of management, interacting with other activities to produce goods for delivering to the customers. The chapter makes use of the term 'operations' management, which is more comprehensive and implies both physical goods, services, and a combination thereof. Rapid rise in global competition, improved means of travel and transport, and cost differentials among the countries have greatly contributed to expansion of companies' operations at a global scale. This makes it pertinent to understand the various strategic options available for transnational operations and select the most appropriate.

The ability of firms to move the goods from one place to another beyond national boundaries, not only in a cost-effective manner but also rapidly and reliably, has become increasingly significant in a world of just-in-time production sharing on global basis. The intensification of global competition, shortening of production cycles, and global scale of business operations make global supply chain management the strategic source of competitive advantage. Therefore, international managers need to develop a thorough conceptual knowledge of supply chain management to achieve global competitiveness.

This chapter brings out in detail the concept of global supply chain management and international logistics. Since maritime transport constitutes 90 per cent of the world trade, it has been separately dealt in, covering key aspects of international shipping. Various types of ocean cargo, types of commercial vessels, alternatives for ocean shipment, such as charter vs liner shipping have been elucidated at length. 'Multi-modal' or 'inter-modal' transport which provides an efficient and cost-effective alternative through more than one means of transport has also been explicated. Besides, international organizations regulating international maritime transport and institutional framework in India have also been briefly discussed.

16.2 GLOBAL OPERATIONS MANAGEMENT

16.2.1 Concept of Operations Management

Traditionally 'production' or 'manufacturing' management has been used to imply production of physical goods, which are tangible in nature, such as automobiles, computers, televisions, camera, furniture, equipment, etc. During recent decades, 'services' that are 'intangible' in nature but also satisfy needs of a customer have grown rapidly. Service providers like educational institutes, banks, insurance companies, amusement parks, etc., form a part of services. A combination of goods and services may also form a product. For instance, meals served in a restaurant comprise both the tangible physical core product and intangible services aspects, such as cleanliness, ambience, delivery, etc. Therefore, in this chapter, the term 'operations' is used which is much more comprehensive.

Operations management refers to planning, organizing, and controlling all resources and activities to provide goods and services, which applies equally to manufacturing and services in the private and public sectors and even governments.

Operations management refers to the process which transforms inputs such as materials, machines, labour, capital and management, into outputs (i.e., goods and services), as shown in Fig. 16.1 The transformation process in 'operations' can have different forms, such as

Physical	:	As in manufacturing operations
Locational	:	As in transportation or warehouse operations
Exchange	:	As in retail operations
Psychological	:	As in entertainment
Physiological	:	As in health care
Informational	:	As in communication

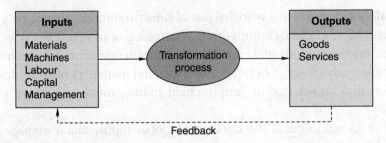

Fig. 16.1   The operations model

The objective of any operation is to use available resources productively. High productivity translates into lower costs and higher profits for a given price. Thus, operations is a function or system that transforms inputs into outputs of greater value. The ratio of the value of the output achieved to the inputs used is also used to express productivity, which is a measure of how efficiently the resources are used.

$$\text{Productivity} = \frac{\text{Output}}{\text{Input}}$$

Therefore in any operation, the economic value of output should be greater than the economic value of input. Resources used in an operation may include land or storage space, materials, labour, water, energy, and financial resources. To illustrate, a finished automobile has a higher value than raw steel or a graduating management student should have higher economic value than a fresher.

16.2.2 Globalization of Operations

The forces of globalization, such as reduction in trade barriers, cheaper and easier means of international transportation and communication, wage differential, and market saturation in the home markets on one hand and rapidly growing marketing opportunities overseas, especially in emerging economies on the other, have led to expansion of operations on a global scale. Globalization of operations include

- Global sourcing of inputs
- Global production of goods and services
- Global transportation of products
- Global management of entire supply chain

An MNE headquartered in New York, New Delhi, or London may have production operations in a few countries and warehousing and marketing across the world. For instance, Exxon Mobil, the world's largest integrated oil company has its upstream drilling activities in about 50 countries; Siemens, the leading manufacturer of high technology industrial and consumer equipment, operates in over 190 countries with about 500,000 employees, and Boeing, the world's largest manufacturer of commercial aircraft has operations in 26 countries with customers in over 100 countries.

16.2.3 Off-shoring

Relocation of business processes to a low-cost location by shifting the task overseas is termed as 'off-shoring'. Capital assets may be shifted to a new production location by relocating the business processes to a new country within the company or by being sold to others. Such assets include business processes, such as production, manufacturing, or services from high-cost locations (for example, the US or Europe) to low-cost locations, such as India, China, or Latin America. With digitization, the Internet, and high-speed data networks as the driving forces, all kinds of knowledge related work can now be performed almost anywhere in the world. Activities which are particularly suitable for off-shore sourcing are discussed as follows:

- Products at the maturity stage of their product life cycle where technology has become standardized and widespread, requiring long-production runs making labour costs crucial to achieve competitiveness, are suited for off-shoring.
- In case of technology- and capital-intensive industries, such as electronics, telecommunication, and software, certain parts of the production process are labour-intensive and need to be off-shored to low-cost locations.

Relocating the business processes for quality reasons at higher costs to another country are not considered off-shoring, for instance, shifting a costume-design centre from an East European or a South Asian country to Italy or France.

China and India, besides other developing countries, have become the most sought after off-shoring locations. Exhibit 16.1 illustrates the emergence of China as a global manufacturing hub, primarily due to low-cost large-scale production facilities whereas India, as a result of abundance of highly-skilled and knowledge-intensive manpower, has become the virtual service centre for the world.

Types of off-shoring

Captive off-shoring   Relocating business processes to a low-cost location and delivering from a shared service centre owned by the company itself is known as captive off-shoring.

Third party off-shoring   Also known as *outsourcing*, third party off-shoring involves relocation of business process from within the client country to an outside vendor operating at low-cost location. For the client company, the 'outsourced' services are performed by the outside vendor.

Near-shoring

Relocation of a business process to a country within the same geographical region is referred to as near-shoring. For instance, shifting business processes from the US to Mexico or from Western to Eastern Europe.

Exhibit 16.1   Off-shoring operations: China vs India

China: The global manufacturing hub

China has emerged as the world's largest manufacturer. It has been the preferred location for the manufacture of low-technology intensive products, such as garments, toys, components, furniture, etc. In the initial stages of its industrialization, China gained prominence as a strategic location in which almost every industry would like to have a manufacturing base.

For Western investors, China is considered a source of cheap labour and it is perceived that for every factory that closes in the US and Europe, a new factory opens in China. During recent years, China has focused on acquiring the technological skills needed to keep up its competence with international standards. While the wealthiest nations over the last decade have reduced their share in the global manufacturing output, China has doubled its share.

Manufacturing operations in China are highly concentrated in a small number of cities. Five cities, i.e., Shanghai, Beijing, Shenzhen, Guangzhou, and Hong-Kong contribute to more than two-third of Chinese operations. During recent years, the major manufacturing locations in China have been reported to become too expensive relative to other countries, including India.

India: The service centre of the world

If China can be termed the 'factory' of the world, India can be termed the world's 'service centre'. Global outsourcing from India began with the basic back-office work in call centres that mainly comprised handling customer queries, computer programming, claim processing, accounting, etc. Over a period, India graduated to offer a number of value-added diverse range of outsourcing activities, such as financial analysis and management, engineering designs, medical diagnosis, architectural design, distance education, etc.

The rapid development of IT, Business Process Operations (BPO), and telecom has significantly contributed to the growth of the service industry in India, which has become the country's biggest industry, contributing the highest percentage to the National GDP. India is not only the low-cost offshore location where global companies are setting up their operations, but it is also emerging as a fast-growing consumer market. Although, presently manufacturing is the least off-shored activity to India, it has considerable potential to become the topmost activity to be off-shored to India in the near future. The anticipated growth in manufacturing activities in India is likely to make it a global manufacturing hub too, besides it being an IT and BPO powerhouse.

Source: 'Offshoring Evolution: Changing Trends in India and China across Industries', Capgemini, New York (2007), pp. 3–6; 'India to Challenge China's Forte as Manufacturing Hub, *The Times of India*, New Delhi, 14 October 2007.

16.2.4   Strategic Options for Transnational Operations

Various alternatives for transnational operations available to a firm may be categorized into four major types,[1] discussed as follows:

Globally concentrated operations

In the simplest form, the business enterprise concentrates all its production at a single location and exports its products to the world market. Such a strategy is often adopted by small and medium enterprises (SMEs) with limited resources for international expansion (Fig. 16.2).

---

[1] Based on Dicken, P., *Global Shift—Transforming the World Economy*, London: Paul Chapman, 1998.

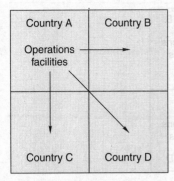

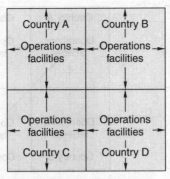

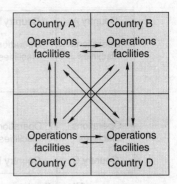

Fig. 16.2 Globally concentrated operations

Fig. 16.3 Host market operations

Fig. 16.4 Product specialization for a global or regional market

Host market operations

Under this strategy, each production unit produces a range of products to serve the host country markets (Fig. 16.3). Since no sales across national boundaries are carried out, individual plant size is limited by the size of the host country market. This strategy has become popular among large global business enterprises to establish their stronghold in foreign markets.

Product specialization for a global or regional market

This strategy is becoming increasingly popular in large integrated markets, such as the European Union. The strategy is based on the specialization of production in a few plants supplying a multi-country market as a part of product or process rationalization strategy (Fig. 16.4). Under this approach, each production unit produces only one product for sale throughout a regional market comprising of several countries. Due to scale economies offered by large regional markets, individual plant size under such a strategy is generally very large.

Transnational vertical integration

The strategy consists of specialization by semi-finished products or processes (Fig. 16.5) rather than by final products as discussed above in product specialization strategy. Each operations facility located in different countries either perform a separate part of operations in a 'chain like' sequence (alternative I) or performs a separate operation in the production process and ships its outputs to the final assembly plant in another country (alternative II). This calls for extensive coordination among subsidiaries. Rapid increase in off-shore processing has made vertically integrated global production networks a strategic tool to consolidate global operations.

Selection of global operations strategy A transnational company has to strike a balance between the extra costs of moving products between the plants or from plants to markets against the economies of scale to be achieved through plant specialization. Besides, other factors that need to be evaluated include risks associated with plant

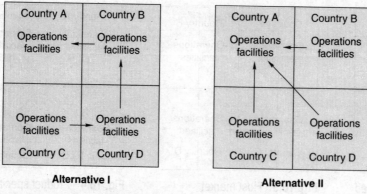

Fig. 16.5 Transnational vertical integration

specialization, need for product adaptation in different markets, import regulations, and investment policies, including incentives or disincentives of the host governments. Moreover, the rapid changes in the external business environment and the company's own internal pressures may require rationalization and reorganization of internal production networks of a transnational firm.

16.2.5 Global Integration vs Local Responsiveness

An international firm operating across countries needs to strike a balance[2] between Global Integration (I) and the Local Responsiveness (R) known as I-R balance, not only for its growth globally but also for survival.

Global integration   The coordination of activities across the countries so as to build an efficient operations network and take optimal advantage of internalized synergy at similarities across operational locations is termed as 'global integration'.

Local responsiveness   It refers to a firm's attempt to respond to specific needs within various host countries. The diverse socio-political, cultural, economic, and market conditions in different countries of a firm's operation requires it to respond to country-specific local conditions.

Based on a variety of factors, a firm may adopt a globally integrated, locally responsive, or multi-focal business strategy which simultaneously responds to and balances the forces of global integration and local responsiveness.

16.3 GLOBAL SUPPLY CHAIN MANAGEMENT

16.3.1 The Value Chain Concept

The objective of any business firm is to create value by way of performing a set of activities, such as to conceptualize, design, manufacture, market, and service its

[2] Shenkar, Oded and Luo Yadong, 'Organizing and Structuring Global Operations', *International Business*, Singapore: John Wiley & Sons (Asia) Pte. Ltd, 2004, pp. 291–93.

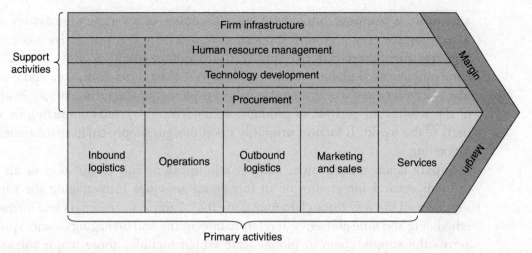

Fig. 16.6 The concept of value chain

Source: Porter, Michael, *The Competitive Advantage of Nations*, New York: The Free Press, 1991, pp. 40–45.

offerings. This set of interrelated activities is termed as the value chain. To gain competitive advantage over its rivals, a firm must provide comparable buyer value by performing activities more efficiently (at lower cost) than its competitors or perform activities in a unique way that creates greater buyer value and commands a premium price (differentiation) or accomplish both. Figure 16.6 provides the basic framework of Michael Porter's concept of value chain to carry out these interrelated activities. The primary activities include inbound logistics, operations (manufacturing), outbound logistics, marketing and sales, and after-sales services whereas the support activities include firm infrastructure (finance, planning, etc.), human resource management, technology development, and procurement.

This model suggests that two of the primary activities relates to supply chain, i.e., procuring inputs, components, raw materials, parts, and related services (inbound logistics), and operations and transfer of finished products to the end customer (outbound logistics). Therefore, the competitive advantage of a firm is dependent upon a firm's organizing and performing discrete activities. Firms create value for their buyers through performing these activities in a competitive manner. The ultimate value created by a firm is measured by the amount buyers are willing to pay for its products and services. If the value of performing the required activities exceeds the collective costs, the firm becomes profitable. Thus, achieving competitive advantage in managing supply chains at global scale becomes crucial to the success of a business enterprise.

16.3.2 Concept of Global Supply Chain Management

Supply chain management is considered a function crucial to a large number of industries to achieve and maintain its global competitiveness. For instance, in the airlines industry, logistics is not only the scheduling of flights and passengers but also a meticulous planning, implementing, and control of a variety of activities, such as scheduling for crews, ground support, airport scheduling, preventive maintenance, luggage, meals, etc. Global supply chain management is most crucial to the competitiveness of global retailers, such as Wal-Mart, Carrefour, etc., and e-retailers like Amazon.com. Nike does not own a complete manufacturing facility in any part of the world, but gets all its products manufactured by sub-contracting in various parts of the world. It focuses primarily upon design, supply chain management, and marketing.

Supply chain management aims at minimization and elimination of all wastes through vertical integration of all functional activities in managing the suppliers' suppliers all the way through to managing the customers' customers and focussing on scheduling and time efficiency. It refers to integrating and managing business processes across the supply chain at global scale which includes three major sub-systems: suppliers/sub contractors, transformation/manufacturing, and distribution, as depicted in Fig. 16.7. In order to optimize the supply chain system, suppliers, manufacturers, and distributors should work in close harmony and achieve the lowest possible lead-time with lowest cost and maintaining quality. The integrated supply chain refers to a material flow stream from purchase to transformation to distribution. It also includes financial and information flows, as shown in Fig. 16.7, from the clients to the suppliers.

The concept of supply chain management

- Evolves around the primary objective to serve its customers through improved cost economies and efficiencies
- Includes all functional activities in products and materials flow from procurement, through operations to delivery to the final customer
- Identifies complete process of sourcing inputs to providing goods and services to the final consumer

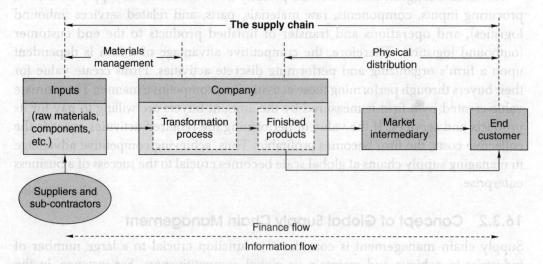

Fig. 16.7   Concept of supply chain

- Integrates all the participants and operations from suppliers to the end users
- Extends beyond organizational boundaries
- Is co-ordinated through an information system assessable to all its participants
- Ensures performance of the supply chain as a whole is crucial to achieve objectives of individual supply chain members

Global supply chain management focuses on managing flow of information, products, and services across the network of customers, enterprises, and suppliers on a global scale. Thus, global supply chain refers to global integration and management of business processes across the three major sub-systems of the supply chain as explained above. With the rapid growth of outsourcing of even the transformation process, the supply chain management also includes ensuring timeliness, quality, and legalities of suppliers' operations.

16.3.3   International Logistics

The word logistics is derived from the French word *loger* that means art of transport, supply, and quartering of troops. Thus, logistics was conceptually designed for use in military so as to ensure meticulous planning and implementation of supply of weapons, food, medicines, and troops in the battlefield. However, over the years logistics has become an integral part of present-day business.

Conceptualization, design, and implementation of a system to direct flow of goods and services across national borders is termed as international logistics. Thus, logistics consists of planning and implementing the strategy for procurement of inputs for the production process to make goods and services available to the end customers.

The ability of firms to move goods across borders rapidly, reliably, and at lower costs is crucial to success in integrating global supply chains. The Logistics Performance Index (LPI) (Exhibit 16.2) developed by the World Bank is a bench-marking tool to measure performance along the logistics supply chain among countries.[3] International managers have to comprehensively assess and evaluate logistics facilities available in various countries before designing strategy for global supply chain management.

Logistics has two distinct components, i.e., materials management and physical distribution as elucidated below.

Materials management

Materials management is the upstream part of the supply chain, which involves procurement of inputs, such as raw materials and components for processing or value addition by the firm. This is also known as inbound logistics. Procurement of inputs is no longer limited to national boundaries or neighbouring countries for international companies. Instead, globally integrated sourcing of inputs, through most cost-effective and efficient sources, known as global sourcing has become crucial to achieving global business competitiveness.

---

[3] Connecting to Compete: Trade Logistics in the Global Economy, World Bank, Washington DC, 2007, pp. 1–38.

Exhibit 16.2 Logistics performance index (LPI)

The Logistics Performance Index (LPI) developed by the World Bank serves as a useful tool to enable international managers to carry out an empirical assessment of logistics gaps and constraints and allow comparisons across 150 countries. The index comprises several areas of supply chain performance elaborated, such as customs procedures, logistics costs, quality of

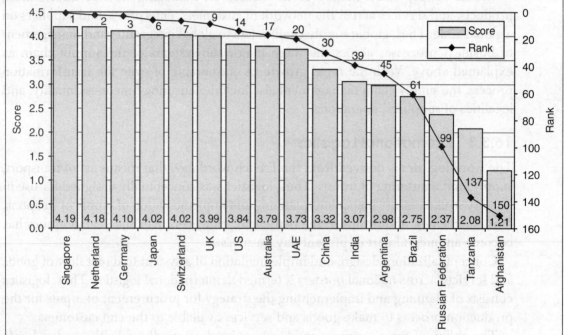

Fig. 16.8 Logistics performance index (2007)

Note: 1—lowest; 5—highest.

Source: Based on data from *Connecting to Compete: Trade Logistics in the Global Economy*, World Bank, Washington DC, 2007, pp. 1–38.

infrastructure, the ability to track and trace shipments, timeliness in reaching destination, and the competence of the domestic logistics industry. The LPI is built upon a web-based questionnaire completed by more than 800 professionals worldwide and more than 5,000 country evaluations, based on seven areas of performance as follows:

- Efficiency of the clearance process by customs and other border agencies
- Quality of transport and information technology infrastructure for logistics

- Ease and affordability of arranging international shipments
- Competence of the local logistics industry
- Ability to track and trace international shipments
- Domestic logistics costs
- Timelines of shipments in reaching destination

A cross-country comparison of LPI (Fig. 16.8) reveals that Singapore ranks at the top with a score of 4.19 on a five point scale, being the major global transport and logistics hub, followed by Netherlands (4.18), Germany (4.10), Japan (4.02), and Switzerland (4.02) whereas Afghanistan (1.21) ranks at the last.

Source: Based on *Connecting to Compete: Trade Logistics in the Global Economy*, World Bank, Washington DC, 2007, pp. 1–38.

Global sourcing   As the firm expands its business operations internationally, market forces increasingly compel the firm to evolve ways to reduce costs and improve quality to remain competitive. Instead of manufacturing a product or delivering a service itself, the international company often resorts to outsourcing and procures its inputs from the most cost-effective diverse sources across the globe. Global sourcing refers to procurement of inputs for production of goods and delivery of services globally from the most optimal sources. The major reasons for global outsourcing include:

- Price differentials leading to lower prices form foreign sources
- Need for foreign products not available domestically
- Global strategy and operations of the company
- Need for technology- and R&D-intensive foreign products
- Requirement for superior quality overseas products

A business enterprise may use a number of global sourcing arrangements, as already discussed in Chapter 11 on modes of international business expansion. These include

- Import from a foreign manufacturer
- Overseas contract manufacturing
- International joint venture
- Wholly owned subsidiaries

Physical distribution management

It is the downstream portion of the supply chain which involves all the activities, such as transportation, warehousing, and inventory, carried out to make the product available to the end customers. This is also known as outbound logistics. Physical distribution has already been discussed in detail in Chapter 14.

16.3.4 Managing Global Supply Chain

Managing a supply chain globally is far more complex due to physical distances, differences in logistics systems and their compatibility, different legal systems, and numerous intermediaries involved. However, the principal objective of any supply chain systems remains that the goods reach the final customer

- In correct quantity
- At desired location
- At right time
- In usable condition
- In the most cost-efficient manner

All these logistics objectives are interrelated to each other and may be achieved by a firm's integrated logistics management strategy. The integrated system comprising inbound and outbound logistics, is nowadays also referred to as supply chain management. If the unit value of the product is low, the cost of transportation of inputs and final product has proportionately greater impact on the final cost of the product.

A seamless and efficient global supply chain consists of major constituents, such as transportation, warehousing, inventory management, packaging and unitization, and information and communication technology, as discussed below. Since ocean transportation is the most significant and distinct aspect of global logistics, it is dealt in detail separately later in the chapter.

Warehousing

A firm is required to store the goods so as to bridge the time gap between the production and meeting the customer demand. The major functions of warehousing are

Storage of goods   The basic function of warehouses is to store inventories in safe and orderly conditions till the time of export shipment. Besides, the storage facilities at overseas locations facilitate holding inventories that are released as and when demanded by the market.

Consolidation   Storage is used to consolidate cargo from various locations or shippers before it is loaded on board the vessel. Besides, warehouses are also used to consolidate the Less than Container Load (LCL) cargo for stuffing in the container before despatching the container to the port of shipment or destination.

Breaking bulk   In the overseas markets, the import cargo received either in container load or bulk is divided into several small parts in the warehouse before despatching it to wholesalers or distributors.

Mixing or assembly   A shipper may procure the goods from various suppliers and mix them before shipment. Similarly, an importer may import the goods from a number of exporters located in different countries and mix them before despatching them to wholesalers and distributors. Assembly is an equivalent term used for mixing in case of industrial or semi-manufactured goods in Completely Knocked Down (CKD) or Semi-Knocked Down (SKD) condition.

Various types of warehouses include commodity bulk storage, refrigerated, or general merchandise warehouse. In India, Central Warehousing Corporation (CWC) provides custom-bonded warehouses at ports and air cargo complexes. A firm has an option to use its own warehouse or a leased private warehouse or may use a public warehouse depending upon its requirements and availability. Various factors affecting selection of warehouse include the inventory level to be maintained by the firm, location of the warehouse, the level of customer service provided, and the warehousing costs.

Inventory management

Maintaining inventories is an integral part of supply chain management. The principal reasons for holding inventories are

To maintain uninterrupted supply   In order to meet the demand fluctuations in the markets, a firm has to maintain inventories so that its supply to market remains uninterrupted.

To optimize buying costs   A firm has to hold certain level of inventory so as to optimize the administrative costs associated with procuring the goods. A widely used classical technique for inventory decisions is Economic Order Quantity (EOQ) for cost optimization.

To economize production costs   Inventories facilitate continued production runs that help in keeping production costs lower due to optimum utilization of fixed costs.

To take advantage of quantity discounts   Firms usually get quantity discounts for buying products in bulks.

To cope up with seasonal fluctuations   Demand and supply patterns for most products in the markets are cyclical in nature. In order to maintain continued production and cope up with seasonal demand variations in the market, a firm is required to carry inventory.

Packing and unitization

Packaging of export cargo is an important logistics activity as it facilitates safe and smooth shipment of goods. Besides, packaging facilitates unitization of export cargo that further facilitates cargo-handling during transit. Standardized practices for cargo unitization are used so as to increase its acceptability internationally. Sling loads and pallets are widely accepted unitized cargo in air transport while containers with 20 or 40 ft length, 8ft height, and 8ft width are widely used for ocean transport. A container is an article of transport equipment, strong enough for repeated use, to facilitate handling and carriage of goods by one or more modes of transport. Containerization increases the size of unit load and facilitates handling and transportation of cargo.

Transporting the cargo by containers offers the following benefits to shippers:

- Facilitates door-to-door delivery
- Reduces cost of packing as the container acts as a strong protective cover
- Reduces documentation work
- Lowers warehousing and inventory costs
- Prevents pilferage and theft
- Reduces susceptibility to cargo damage

Transportation

Transportation is an important part of international logistics. Various modes of transport used are as follows:

Air transportation   Transportation of goods by air accounts for only 1 per cent in terms of volume but about 20 to 30 per cent in terms of value of the total world trade. Thus, it is the most preferred mode of transport for high-value goods. Besides, due to the increase in market competition and increasing availability of air cargo services, air transportation is rapidly gaining popularity in international trade. The major benefits of transporting cargo by air are

- Speedier delivery
- Highly suitable for perishable goods, such as foods, fresh fruits and vegetables, flowers, meat, etc.
- Does not require robust packaging as in case of ocean transport
- Low risk of pilferage or cargo damage with competitive rate of insurance
- The system of documentation for air transport is simple and, therefore, cost effective.
- Low inventory and storage cost
- Reliability of service

However, the limitations associated with air transport are

- As air freight is more expensive compared to ocean transport, the value of the cargo or the significance of speed of delivery should justify the cost incurred
- Limited capacity with air freighters
- The packaging needs to be small so as to fit in the air carrier
- Air services are vulnerable to disruption by weather

Road transportation Transport by road provides flexibility to the exporter. However, this can be used only with the bordering countries. The major advantages of road transport are

- Facilitates door-to-door delivery with little intermediate handling
- Flexibility of operation
- Competitive for small distances compared to air freight in respect of transit time and freight
- Economy on packaging cost compared to conventional ocean shipping
- Lower risk of cargo damage during transit

A firm has the option to use its own private carriers, contract carriers (with formal agreement to transport, such as oil or milk tankers), or public carriers (that can be used by anyone). Road transportation is common for cross-country trade in land-locked nations and countries with strong economic groupings, such as European Union, NAFTA, etc. In India, the major Land Customs Stations notified for cross-border trade include Attari in Punjab at the Indo-Pak border, Petrapole in West Bengal, Dwaki in Meghalaya at the Indo-Bangladesh border, and Moreh in Manipur at the Indo-Myanmar border.

Rail transportation India has the distinction of having a highly developed rail transport system in the world, but it can be used to transport goods to bordering countries only. The major benefits of using rail for cargo transport are

- Economic vis-à-vis road transport
- Bulk cargoes can be handled in higher volumes

The major limitations in transporting the cargo by rail include limited availability of the railway network and the trade relations between India and its neighbouring countries. The major railway networks for international trade in India are Attari in Punjab at Indo-Pak border and Petrapole in West Bengal that links Benapole in Bangladesh. However, the transport of cargo through railway is widely used in European Union, NAFTA, i.e., Canada, the US, and Mexico, and CIS countries that not only have good railway network but also much liberalized trade relations.

Ocean transportation Transportation of cargo by sea is the largest means of transportation in international trade. Operation of merchant ships is estimated to generate over US$500 billion in freight rates, representing about 5 per cent of the total global economy. The shipping industry presents healthy competition among over 10,000 individual shipping companies involved in international trade operating over 50,000 ships. The deep sea trade is served by over 3000 ports and the cargo carried by the shipping industry consists of many millions of separate consignments, of different sizes, and with different physical characteristics. In view of high significance of ocean transport in international trade, it has been discussed at length later in the chapter.

Information and communication technology

Developments in information and communication technology (ICT) have revolutionized the entire concept of logistics management. It has evolved new areas of logistics management, such as Just-in-Time (JIT) management wherein the emphasis is on continued and reliable supply with much lower level of inventories holdings. Firms have to develop an integrated logistics management system with meticulous conceptualization, planning, co-ordination, and implementation so as to create competitive advantage in the marketplace.

16.4 THIRD PARTY LOGISTICS

Since the advent of modern trade several centuries ago, the international movement of goods has been primarily organized by freight forwarders, typically large networks of companies with worldwide coverage, capable of handling and coordinating diverse actions required to move goods across long distances and international borders. The rapid rise of express carriers and third party logistics providers has expanded the scope of services available to traders.

Third party logistics (3PL) provider refers to a company that provides multiple logistics services for its clients and customers. Thus, outsourcing of more sophisticated logistics and supply chain services, especially on a global scale may be defined as 3PL. In recent years, many freight forwarders have developed their operations to introduce value-added services at both ends of the supply chain to become globally integrated service providers. Europe is the largest market for freight forwarding and logistics services[4] with a share of just over a third followed by Asia Pacific (29%) and North America (27%). The global logistics and freight forwarding market is in the process of rationalization and consolidation with a handful of major players that have global coverage. DHL Global Forwarding, with 9 per cent share, is the largest logistics provider, followed by Kuehne and Nagel (7%), Schenker (6%), Panalpina (4%), and others.

16.5   MARITIME TRANSPORTATION IN INTERNATIONAL TRADE

Since ocean transport is responsible for carriage of 90 per cent of world trade, making it the largest means of transport in international trade, it is elucidated separately. The bulk transport of raw material for import and export of affordable food and manufactured goods would not have been possible without shipping. It is the low-cost availability and efficiency of maritime transport that has made it possible to shift industrial production to low-cost countries. Costs of ocean transport are very competitive due to continuous improvements in technology and efficiency. To illustrate, the typical cost of transporting a 20 feet container from Asia to Europe, carrying over 20 tons of cargo is about the same as the economy journey for a single passenger on the same journey. Table 16.1 reveals that the typical international shipping costs from Asia to the US or Europe are minuscule compared to products' shelf-price. Moreover, over the last 50 years, bulk shipping costs have increased only by 70 per cent, whereas the retail prices have grown by more than 800 per cent.

Since ocean transport is the oldest mode of international business, a large number of shipping practices are derived by the customs of trade. An international sales agreement and arrangement of transport goes hand in hand. Basic concepts of international shipping practices have been discussed in this chapter.

Table 16.1   An overview of typical ocean freight costs

(Asia–US or US–Asia)

Product	Unit	Typical shelf price (US$)	Shipping costs (US$)
TV set	per unit	700	10.00
DVD/CD player	per unit	200	1.50
Vacuum cleaner	per unit	150	1.00
Scotch whisky	per bottle	50	0.15
Coffee	per kg	15	0.15
Biscuits	per tin	3	0.05
Beer	per can	1	0.01

Source: International Shipping Carrier of World Trade, Maritime International Secretariat Services Ltd, London, 2007, pp. 2–6.

---

[4] Review of Maritime Transport 2007, UNCTAD, New York and Geneva, 2007, pp. 98–99.

16.5.1   Types of Ocean Cargo

Bulk

Cargo that is loaded and carried in bulk, without mark or count, in a loose unpackaged form, having homogenous characteristics is termed as bulk cargo. To be loaded on a containership, bulk cargo is put in containers first. It could also be stowed in bulk instead of being loaded into containers. Examples of such cargo are coal, iron ore, fertilizers, grains, oil, etc.

Break-bulk   It refers to packaged cargo that is loaded and unloaded on a piece-by-piece basis, i.e., by number or count. This can be containerized or prepared in groups of packages covered by shrink wrap. Examples are coffee, rubber, steel, etc.

Neo-bulk   Certain types of cargo that are often moved by specialized vessels, e.g., auto, and logs are termed as neo-bulk.

Containerized

It refers to the cargo loaded at a facility away from the pier or at a warehouse into a metal container usually 20 to 40 feet long, 8 feet high, and 8 feet wide. The container is then delivered to a pier and loaded onto a 'containership' for transportation. Some cargo cannot be containerized, e.g., automobiles, live animals, bulk products, etc.

.The physical form of cargo and the way it is shipped is shown in Exhibit 16.3. Both dry and bulk commodities can be shipped in unit loads, break bulk, and as bulk cargo.

16.5.2   Types of Commercial Vessels

As international managers are expected to handle international shipping operations too, various types of vessels used in international trade have been briefly elucidated. To explain in simple terms, a ship is made up of two main parts, i.e., hull and machinery. The hull is the shell, including the superstructure. Most often the hull is divided into two sections, i.e., holds or tanks, especially in larger vessels. The machinery includes

	Exhibit 16.3 Physical form and the way of shipping		
The way of shipping/ physical form	**General cargo**		**Bulk cargo**
	Unit load	**Break bulk**	
Dry cargoes	e.g., bagged rice in whole load	e.g., machinery parts in crates and boxes	e.g., loose grain in holds
Liquid cargoes	e.g., whole load of oil in drums	e.g., part loads of wine in cases	e.g., crude oil in tank vessels

Source: 'Use of Maritime Transport', in *Economic and Social Commission for Asia and the Pacific*, vol. 1, United Nations, p. 50.

Exhibit 16.4   Measurement units used to express vessel capacity

Dead weight tons   Dead weight tons (dwt) refers to the maximum weight of cargo a vessel can carry, which is also known as 'tonnage'. The dead weight tonnage of a ship includes both the bunker (the fuel carried on board the vessel for travel) and the stores (supplies carried on board needed to function). dwt is measured by using the weight of the difference in water displacement when the ship is empty and when it is fully loaded to its maximum.

Gross registered tonnage (GRT)   This represents the total volume of a vessel's carrying capacity, measured as the space available below the deck expressed in hundreds of cubic feet. It means one gross registered ton (GRT) equals to a volume of 100 cubic feet (2.82 m^3).

Net registered tonnage (NRT)   This represents the volume of cargo a vessel can carry. It is arrived by subtracting the volume of space that would not hold the cargo such as engine room, the crew space, etc., from the GRT.

Displacement tonnage   It refers to the total volume of the ship, when fully loaded. It is measured by the weight of the volume of water displaced by the fully loaded vessel.

Light tonnage   It refers to the total weight of the ship, when empty. It is measured by using the weight of the water displaced by the empty vessel.

---

engines, auxiliary equipment, serving electrical installations.[5] The cost of operation of vessel is influenced by the type of machinery which interests a shipper.

The classification of ships on the basis of size is generally based on their capacity expressed in tonnage. A variety of ways customarily used to express tonnage in the shipping industry often makes it difficult to comprehend. A brief description of various types of tonnage used to describe vessel capacity is given in Exhibit 16.4.

On the basis of registry groupings

The review of maritime transport prepared by UNCTAD categorizes vessels into five groups that cover 20 principal types of vessel categories. The changes in various categories of vessels over the years, as shown in Fig. 16.9 reveals increasing share in container vessels. The composition of present world fleet (2007) by vessel types comprise oil tankers (37%), dry bulk carriers (35%), container ships (12%), general cargo carriers (10%), and other vessels (6%).

Oil tankers   Vessels that carry oil. Crude oil tankers are further classified into the following categories on the basis of dead weight ton[6] (dwt):

ULCC (Ultra-large crude carriers)	above 300,000 dwt
VLCC (Very large crude carriers)	150,000–299,999 dwt
Suezmax	100,000–149,999 dwt
Aframax	50,000–99,999 dwt

---

[5] Branch, A.E., *Elements of Shipping*, London: Chapman & Hall Ltd, 1981, p. 3.
[6] *Review of Maritime Transport* 2007, United Nations Conference of Trade and Development, New York and Geneva, 2007, pp. 23–28.

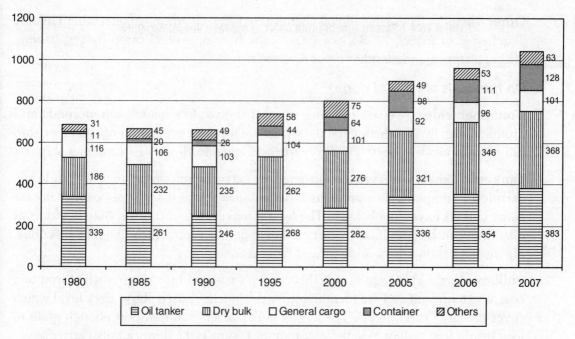

Fig. 16.9 World fleet (by principal vessel types) (millions of dwt)

Source: Review of Maritime Transport 2007, United Nations Conference of Trade and Development, New York and Geneva, 2007, pp. 23–26.

Bulk carriers It includes ore and bulk carriers and also ore/bulk/oil carriers. Vessels carrying dry bulk cargo are known as dry bulk carriers which may further be classified as

Cape size Ships above 80,000 dwt and too wide to pass through the Panama Canal and hence through the Cape of Good Hope from Pacific to Atlantic, and vice versa. These ships mainly carry iron ore, coal, and to a lesser extent grain, and have limited gears restricting them to the largest well-equipped ports only.

Panamax Ships of 50,000–79,999 dwt, and maximum beam of 32.2 mtr, the largest that can pass through Panama Canal, mainly carrying grain and coal and have limited gears, restricting them to the largest well-equipped ports.

Handymax Ships of 35,000–49,999 dwt, mostly with gears making them independent of shore facilities, are included in this category.

Handysize Handysize ships are of 20,000–34,999 dwt, mostly with gears (Cranes or Derricks) making them independent of shore facilities.

General cargo vessel These include vessels designed to carry refrigerated cargo, specialized cargo, Ro-Ro cargo, general cargo (single and multi-deck), general cargo/passengers.

Container ships These are fully cellular vessels that carry container cargo.

Other vessels   These include oil chemical tankers, chemical tankers, other tankers, liquefied gas carriers, Ro-Ro, passenger, tank barges, general cargo barges, fishing, offshore supply, and all other types of vessels.

On the basis of type of cargo

Container ships   Vessels carrying most of the world's manufactured goods and products, usually on scheduled liner services. The latest generation of container ship can carry equivalent of 10,000 heavy trucks. Figure 16.10 shows a container ship.

Tankers   Tankers are vessels designed to carry liquid cargo, such as crude oil, chemicals, and petroleum products in large tanks. More than 70 per cent of ocean-going tankers have double hulls. The largest tankers can carry over 300, 000 tons of oil. They can be modified to carry other types of cargo, such as grain or coffee. Figure 16.11 shows the world's largest oil-tanker ship.

Bulk carriers   These are vessels that carry a variety of bulk cargo, such as iron ore, coal, and food-stuff and are identifiable by the hatches raised above deck level which cover the large cargo holds. The largest bulk carriers can transport enough grain to feed nearly four million people for a month. Figure 16.12 shows a bulk carrier.

Neo-bulk carriers   These are vessels designed to carry specific types of cargo.

Combination carriers   They are vessels that carry passengers and cargo, oil and dry bulk, or containers and bulk cargo. Other combinations are also possible.

Other vessels   These include other specialist vessels, such as car carriers, gas carriers, heavy lift vessels, salvage tugs, ice breakers, research vessels, and ships for off-shore drilling. It also includes general cargo vessels and large number of small vessels.

Fig. 16.10   Container ship

Fig. 16.11   Tanker ship (world's largest oil tanker *Knock Nevis*)

Fig. 16.12   Bulk carrier

Fig. 16.13   Roll-on/roll-off (Ro-Ro) vessel loading cars for exports

General cargo vessels

Roll-on and roll-off (Ro/Ro) vessels   Vessels that allow rolling cargo such as tractors and cars to be driven aboard the vessel (Fig. 16.13).

LASH (lighter aboard ship) vessels   Vessels that can carry very large containers, such as barges. It enables cargo to be loaded on barges in shallow waters and then loaded on board a vessel.

Barges   Unmanned vessels generally used for oversized cargo and towed by a tugboat.

On the basis of decks

Ships may be classified on the basis of number of decks[7] as follows:

Single deck vessel   Such vessels have one continuous deck as depicted in Fig. 16.14. Easy access with one hatch for each hold means economic loading and discharging. Many single deck vessels have very large hatches, and some are known as 'self-trimmers' because of provisions for the cargo to flow into all corners of the hold. This reduces loading costs and time spent in ports.

The most suitable cargoes for single deck vessels are heavy bulk cargoes, such as coal, grain, and iron ore. However, these vessels also carry light cargoes, such as timber, which can be stowed on deck as well as below. Single decked vessels are

---

[7] Cufley, C.F.H., *Ocean Freights and Chartering*, London: Crosby Lockwood Staples, 1970, pp. 232–38; *Use of Maritime Transport*, Volume I, Economic and Social Commission for Asia and the Pacific, United Nations, p. 73.

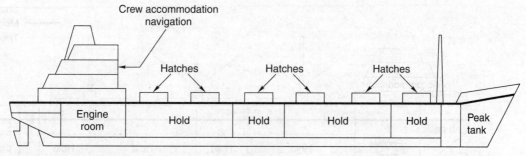

Fig. 16.14   The single deck vessel (gearless bulk carrier)

Source: Use of Maritime Transport, Volume I, Economic and Social Commission for Asia and the Pacific, United Nations, p. 73.

not suitable for general cargoes, since there are few means of separating cargo tiers and lots.

The tween deck vessel   It has an additional deck ('tween decks') below the main deck as depicted in Fig. 16.15, all running the full length of the ship. A vessel with tween decks is suitable for general cargo, because the cargo space is divided into separate tiers, and the decks eliminate risks of cargo damage by preventing too much weight to be placed on the cargo at the bottom.

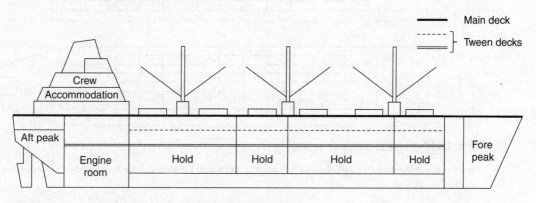

Fig. 16.15   The tween deck vessel (with cargo gear)

Source: Use of Maritime Transport, Volume I, Economic and Social Commission for Asia and the Pacific, United Nations, p. 74.

Shelter deck vessels   Shelter deck vessels (Fig. 16.16) have an additional deck above the main deck—a shelter deck. The advantage of the shelter deck is that it provides more under-deck space for carrying light cargoes. There are two types of shelter deck vessels, the closed and the open. The difference relates to the measurement of the ship. For new tonnage the difference has been abolished through changes in the measurement rules.

Specialized cargo vessels   In addition to traditional single deck, also called full scantling ships, and tween–and shelter deckers, there exists a multitude of specialized

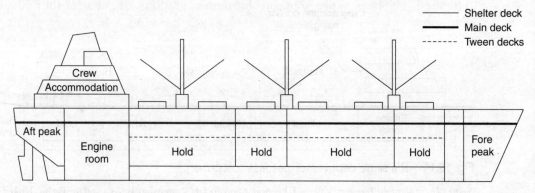

Fig. 16.16 The shelter deck vessel

Source: Use of Maritime Transport, Volume I, Economic and Social Commission for Asia and the Pacific, United Nations, p. 74.

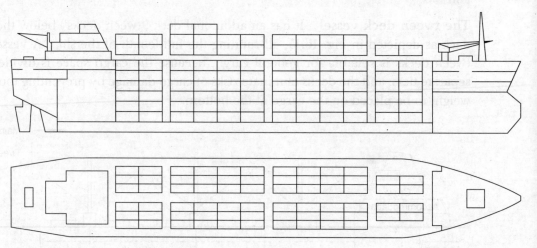

Fig. 16.17 Typical container vessel

Source: Use of Maritime Transport, Volume I, Economic and Social Commission for Asia and the Pacific, United Nations, p. 76.

cargo carrying vessels. These include gas carriers, wood carriers, refrigerated ships, oil tankers, container ships, and roll-on/roll-off vessels.

Container vessel For shipping containerized cargo as in case of multi-modal transportation, a container vessel (Fig. 16.17) is used, which is designed to load, stack, and unload containers.

16.6 ALTERNATES FOR OCEAN SHIPMENT

A firm has specific requirements for ocean transport of cargo. The size, type, unit value, and frequency of shipment often determine alternative forms of ocean transport to be used. The basic types of ocean shipping operations, i.e., charter shipping, liners, and multi-modal transport may be summarized as under:

16.6.1   Charter Shipping

For shipment of bulk cargo, such as grain, coal, ores, fertilisers, and oil, which are to be carried in complete ship-loads, charter shipping is often used. It is also known as trump shipping. The charter vessel does not have any fixed itinerary or fixed sailing schedule. These can be hired or engaged to ship the firm's cargo on charter basis as per the terms and conditions of the Charter Party. The contract made between the charterer and ship-owner is known as charter party that contains details of the ship, routes, methods of cargo handling, port of call, etc. A shipper may pay charter rates either on the basis of amount of cargo shipped or fixed prices. The chartering services are generally offered in auction markets. The rates are negotiated with the help of brokers or charter agents to get the lowest market price.

Forms of chartering

Various forms of chartering the ships for carriage of bulk cargoes follow:

Voyage charter   Contract of carriage in which a vessel is hired for transport of a specified cargo from one port to another port is termed as voyage charter. The ship owner pays for all the operating costs of the ship, while payment for port and cargo-handling charges are the subject of agreement between the parties. Freight is generally paid per unit of cargo (per ton) based on an agreed quantity or as a lump sum, irrespective of the quantity loaded. Terms and conditions are set down in a document, which is called a Charter Party. The ship is said to be on 'voyage charter'.

Time charter   Time charter refers to hiring of a ship from a ship owner for a period of time, whereby the ship owner places the ship with crew and equipment at disposal of the charterer, in exchange of hire money. Subject to restrictions in the contract, the charterer decides on the type and quantity of cargo to be carried and ports of loading and discharging and is responsible for supplying ships with bunkers and for payment of cargo handling operations, port charges, pilotage, towage, and ship's agency. The technical operation and navigation of the ship remain the responsibility of the ship owner. The ship is said to be on 'time charter'.

Bare boat charter (demise charter or charter by demise)   In a bare boat charter, the hiring or leasing of a ship is for a period of time during which the ship owner provides only the ship, while the charterer provides the crew along with all stores and bunkers and pays for all operating costs. The ship is said to be on 'bare boat' or 'demise' charter.

Back-to-back charter   This involves a contract between a charterer and a sub-charterer, whose terms and conditions are identical to the contract (charter) between charterer and ship owner. Identical terms mean any money for which the charterer may be liable to the sub-charterer and which is recoverable from the ship owner.

Trip time charter   A charterer hires the vessel for a single voyage or a round trip on terms and conditions similar to that of time charter.

Contract of affreightment   A contract of affreightment is a long-time agreement to carry a certain amount of cargo between two ports. The choice of vessel and timing will usually be at the ship owner's discretion. Alternatively, the contract may specify a certain amount of shipping that must be completed within a specific time period.

Contract terms used in vessel chartering

Various alternative arrangements for loading and unloading of cargo between the vessel owner and the charterer used in Charter Party are as follows:

Gross terms   As per gross terms, the ship owner is responsible for the cost of loading, stowing, trimming, and unloading of the vessel.

Net terms   The ship owner is not responsible for cost of loading and discharge. Typically, net terms are used in voyage charter parties, as the ship owner has no control over loading and discharging. There are suitable clauses for laytime and demurrage to allow for delays at the loading and discharging ports. The specific terms used for net terms are as follows:

Free in and out (FIO)   It confers the responsibility to the charterer or shipper to arrange the stevedores and to load/discharge the cargo on the charterer's own account, i.e., free of expense to the ship owner, who is still accountable for the port charges.

Free in and out stowed and trimmed (FIOST)   This is similar to FIO, but here, the charterer is also responsible for bearing the expenses of stowing and trimming, i.e., free to ship-owner.

Shared responsibilities   The charterer and the ship owner both have shared responsibilities in the following terms:

Free in liner out (FILO)   The ship owner is not responsible for the cost of loading but is responsible for the cost of unloading.

Liner in free out (LIFO)   The ship owner is responsible for cost of loading but not for vessel unloading.

Laytime   In addition, the charterer's responsibility in terms of agreed timeframe known as 'laytime' is included in the charter party. This can be expressed in days, hours, tons per day, etc. The charterer has to pay 'demurrage' to the ship-owner by way of financial compensation for delays for exceeding allowed laytime. However, accomplishing loading and/or discharge in less than the agreed time is often rewarded financially by the ship-owner by a payment called 'dispatch'. Usually dispatch is paid at half the demurrage rate.

As a matter of shipping trade practices, certain terms are used for accounting laytime in a charter party. Sundays and holidays are generally excluded for calculation of 'laycan' in most countries where Sunday is a weekly public holiday. However, in case of Middle-East and some other Islamic countries where Friday is a holiday, it is excluded for computing 'laycan'. The terms used in charter party for such exclusions are as under.

Other terms

SHEX   :   Sundays and holidays excluded
SHINC :   Sundays and holidays included
FHEX   :   Fridays and holidays excluded
FHINC :   Fridays and holidays included

The other terms used in charter party are

- *As fast as the vessel can (FAC)*   Maximum rate at which a vessel can load/unload
- *Notice of readiness (NOR)*   Formal advice that the vessel is ready for loading/ unloading.
- *Running days*   Days that run consecutively after each other
- *Weather permitting*   Inclement weather is excluded from laytime
- *Weather working day (WWD)*   A day or part of a day when weather does not prevent loading/unloading

Terms of sales as agreed between the buyer and the seller as per INCOTERMS 2000, as discussed in Chapter 18 also influence the charter party terms regarding vessel loading and unloading negotiated between the ship owner and the charterer.

- Free along Side (FAS) requires the seller to place the goods alongside the vessel whereas Free on Board (FOB) requires the seller to load them. When the vessel is chartered by the buyer, the seller generally prefers FAS as s/he is often unwilling to become involved in vessel loading. Whereas a buyer who is not very familiar with the port of loading may ask the seller to arrange loading by requesting FOB. Besides, sellers may prefer to arrange vessel loading by them if they control or own their own loading facility at the port of shipment.
- In cases where the seller charters the vessel and goods are sold on the basis of 'Delivered Ex Quay' (DEQ) and 'Delivered Ex Ship' (DES), the seller is responsible for unloading in DEQ contracts whereas s/he is not responsible for unloading in DES contracts. As sellers have little familiarity with the port of discharge, they generally prefer DES and the buyer has to take care of and bear the expenses of unloading operations.

16.6.2   Liner Shipping

Regular scheduled vessel services between two ports are termed as liner shipping. Generally, liner shipping is used for cargo with higher unit value and manufacture and semi-manufacture goods. The shipping lines offer speedier shipping services, i.e., services useful for goods that are prone to market fluctuations due to changes in fashion, designs, season, technology, etc.

In liner shipping, for determining responsibilities of shipper and ship owner regarding cargo loading and discharge, Liner Terms are used. Under Liner Terms, shippers have no responsibility to the ship other than to have cargo delivered to the terminal, ready for loading prior to cut-off date and the consignees are responsible for collecting their arrived cargo in a timely manner.

The major differences between charter and liner shipping are given in Exhibit 16.5.

'Liner' or 'shipping' conferences

When two or more shipping companies collaborate to operate vessels in the same trade lanes, legally agree not to compete on price, and charge the same freight for the same type of cargo and the same voyage, it is referred to as 'liner' or 'shipping

Exhibit 16.5 Charter vs liner shipping	
Charter shipping	**Liner shipping**
Single deck gearless vessels are used	Tween or shelter deck vessels with cargo gears are used
As used for moving bulk cargo, vessels with larger size, generally 75,000 dwt or more are engaged	As liner ships sail more frequently, smaller ships are engaged
Speed of operation is not of much significance.	Speed and early delivery are crucial to liner operators for providing them a competitive edge
Carries bulk homogeneous or single low value cargo	Carries large variety of manufactured and semi-finished goods
A charter vessel is engaged by a single shipper at a time	A liner ship provides service to large number of shippers
Generally cargo is shipped in bulk as loose	Cargo is packed in parcels, packages, cases, rolls, etc.
Non-scheduled service	Operates regularly on a fixed schedule
Vessels are hired through ship brokers or agents	Cargo booking is done through freight forwarders
Market forces determine the freight rates	Liner vessels have pre-determined tariff structure
Rates fluctuate frequently	Rates are generally stable
'Charter party' used as the document of transport contract	'Bills of Lading' used as document of transport contract
No cartel or association so as to ensure cargo availability	Liner vessels generally operate as conferences or cartels so as to eliminate competition and ensure cargo availability

Source: Joshi, Rakesh Mohan, *International Marketing*, Oxford University Press, New Delhi, 2005, p. 452.

conference'. Thus, under a 'conference', the members agree to a set of tariffs, conference terms and conditions of carriage, the number and type of ships, each member will contribute, and the timetable for sailing. Besides, setting the freight rates, the shipping conferences also adopt a wide number of policies, such as allocation of customers, loyalty contracts, open pricing contracts, etc. A secretariat, often run by one of the members, coordinates the activities.

Cost calculations for liner shipping

For liner shipping, the cost of freight is calculated from the commodity-based published price list of shipping companies. These lists indicate the cost of pure freight, also known as 'base rate' and any applicable surcharges, i.e., 'accessorial charges'. The base rate is often commodity-specific, calculated on a billing unit known as a revenue term. Revenue terms are calculated by comparing a shipment's size (measurement terms) vs its gross shipping weight. Various methods used for determining the total number of revenue terms in a given shipment are as follows:

Metric ton (MT)   A unit of weight equivalent to 2205 pounds or 1000 kilograms.

Short ton (ST)   A unit of weight equivalent to 2000 pounds or 907 kilograms, generally used in the US. Also known as *net ton.*

Long ton (LT)   A unit of weight equivalent to 2240 pounds or 1016 kilograms, used in the UK and a number of other countries too. Also known as *gross* or *imperial ton.*

Measurement ton   A unit of volume used in transportation by sea, generally equal to 40 cubic feet or 1.13 cubic meters. Also known as *shipping ton.*

Freight ton   A unit of volume for freight that weighs one ton, varying with the type of freight measured, as 40 cubic feet of oak timber or 20 bushels of wheat.

In addition to the base rate as mentioned above, some other surcharges that reflect extra costs over which the carrier has little direct control are also to be paid. The major surcharges include

- Bunker Adjustment Factor (BAF): It reflects the cost of fuel (called bunkers). It is handled separately, as fuel is subject to frequent price fluctuations.
- Currency Adjustment Factor (CAF): It reflects changes in the exchange rate of the currency in which the freight costs are billed. It is handled separately because exchange rates fluctuate more often than freight costs do.
- Port Congestion Surcharge: It reflects additional expenses that ship lines incur when calling at congested ports.
- Terminal Handling Charge (THC): It covers vessel-loading and unloading and cartage within the port area. It is handled separately as such costs are port specific.
- Container Positioning: It is an additional fee for the use of the carrier's container, imposed for destinations with little return cargo or high risk of loss or damage to the container.

- Arbitrary: It is an additional fee that shipping lines charge for serving markets outside the hinterlands of their normal ports of call. For instance, an Irish arbitrary is often applied to shipments made through hub ports in the UK.

16.6.3 'Multi-modal' or 'Inter-modal' Transportation

International 'multi-modal' or 'inter-modal' transport means transport of goods by at least two different modes of transport, such as rail, road, sea, or air on the basis of a multi-modal transport contract, from a place in a country at which the goods are taken in charge by the multimodal transport operator (MTO) to a place designated for delivery situated in different countries. Multi-modal transportation has revolutionized the carriage of goods in international trade. It covers the door-to-door movement of goods under the responsibility of a single transport operator. Multi-modal Transportation of Goods Act, 1993, and Amendment Act, 2000 provide a regulatory framework for use of containers and multi-modal transportation of goods in India.

MTO means any person who on his/her own behalf or through another person acting on their behalf concludes a multimodal transport contract and who acts as a principal and not as an agent or on behalf of the consumer or of the carriers participating in the multimodal transport operations and who assumes responsibility for the performance of the contract.

Multi-modal transportation of goods developed with the container revolution initiated in the late 1950s by Malcom McLean and his trucking operations. Containerization accounts for over 50 per cent of the world merchandize trade and is expected to grow up further. Informational and technological progress has contributed to rapid growth of container traffic facilitating transnational movement of highly perishable goods. The Asian region has emerged as a major hub with around 48.1 per cent share of world container traffic,[8] followed by Europe (21.8%), North America (16.6%), and others (13.5%). Major benefits offered by transportation through containers include

- Substantial reduction in risk of damage to the goods during transport due to pilferage or mishandling
- Cargo arrival in good condition at final destination creating a positive impact on the buyer's perception
- No cargo damage due to mishandling during trans-shipments

World's top containership companies as shown in Fig. 16.18, reveals that APM-Maersk, with 17.05 per cent share, is the largest container ship company in the world[9] followed by Mediterranean Shipping Company with 10.81 per cent share, CMA CGM Group with 7.83 per cent, and Evergreen Line with 5.47 percent in Twenty-Feet

---

[8] *Containerization—Global and Indian Scenario*, Centrum, New Delhi, 2006, pp. 2–6.
[9] AXS Marine, 1 March 2008.

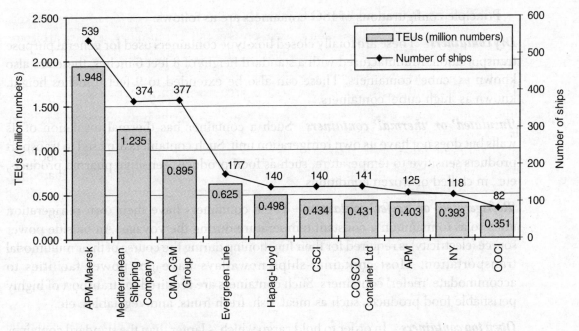

Fig. 16.18 World's top 10 container ship companies

*As on 1 March 2008.
Source: AXS Marine, 1 March 2008.

Equivalent Units (TEUs). APM-Maersk also owns the highest number of 539 containerships in the world, followed by CMA CGM Group (377 containerships), Mediterranean Shipping Company (374 containerships), Evergreen Line (177 containerships), and COSCO Container Ltd (141 containerships).

Types of containers

Containerization has been the most significant development in transportation of goods that has made 'multi' or 'inter'-modal transport of cargo possible. Containers may be classified into two main categories:

ISO containers   Since these containers conform to the specification of International Organization for Standardization (ISO), Geneva, these are also referred as 'standard' or 'inter-modal' containers. ISO containers are manufactured in standard sizes as follows:

• Width: 8 feet
• Heights: 8 feet 6 inches and 9 feet 6 inches
• Lengths: 20 feet and 40 feet

Besides, some less common lengths of standard containers include 24, 28, 44, 45, 46, 48, 53, and 56 feet.

Principle configurations of ISO containers are as follows:

Dry containers   These are totally closed box-type containers used for general purpose transportation. Manufactured with a standard height of 8 feet 6 inches, these are also known as 'cube' containers. These can also be extended to 9 feet 6 inches height, known as 'high cube' containers.

'Insulated' or 'thermal' containers   Such a container has thermal insulation of its walls but does not have its own refrigeration unit. Such containers are used to transport products sensitive to temperature, such as food products, sensitive pharma products, etc., in chilled or frozen conditions.

'Refrigerated' or 'reefer' containers   These containers have their own refrigeration units so as to maintain a constant temperature during the voyage. An outside power source (electricity) is required for their functioning during the course of their multimodal transportation. Most container-ships nowadays have got power facilities to accommodate 'reefer' containers. Such containers are required for transport of highly perishable food products, such as meat, fish, fresh fruits, and vegetables, etc.

Open top containers   In order to hold cargo which is larger than the standard container size of 8 feet, open top containers are required. These containers are designed to hold cargo too large to fit through the doors of a regular container. Therefore, the cargo needs to be loaded in open top containers from the top and then covered with a tarpaulin. Since another container cannot be stacked above an open top container, these containers are always stacked at the top of the stack either above or under the deck.

Liquid bulk container   Such containers are designed in the shape of a cylindrical tank mounted within a rectangular steel framework to transport liquid cargo. They have the same standard dimension as other inter-modal containers and can also be stacked with standard containers.

Dry bulk container   In order to save packaging space in drums or bags, such containers are designed to hold dry bulk cargo, such as food grains or polymer pallets which may have the same dimensions as standard containers.

Flat racks and platforms   To transport heavy machinery, open-sided containers are used that have no side walls but may have end bulkheads than can be folded down when the rack is empty. Nowadays, flat rack containers, which are collapsible, are also available.

Swap bodies

In most of Europe, 'swap bodies' are used, which have many characteristics of inter-modal containers but are not the standard ISO containers. A strong bottom and a minimal upper body constitute their major characteristics. These can also have an open top that allows them to be transferred from road to rail mode. Swap bodies cannot be stacked and can only be bottom-lifted. They also have bottom fittings so they can be locked onto either a road chassis or a rail car.

FCL vs LCL containers

A shipper has option either to use an entire container, known as full container load (FCL) or partial space in a container, known as less than container load (LCL) of a liner operator. The major advantages of FCL over LCL container are as follows:

- The freight cost of FCL is more economical than LCL
- As the FCL has the common origin and destination there is no loss of time once the FCL is loaded and sealed
- FCL provided ease of handling as the final destination is one
- Much lower chances of mishandling and pilferage of cargo in FCL as handling is only at the time of loading at origin
- As there is no transit handling, FCL facilitates in avoiding transit damages
- Effective utilization of container both in weight as well volume terms
- Easy tracking of FCL cargo

However, certain limitations associated with FCL cargo are as follows:

- FCL is cost-effective only when the cargo is more than 75 per cent of load availability
- Since container is to be stuffed and sealed at factory in presence of a local excise official, firm's responsibility becomes much higher
- The utilization of the FCL container by weight and volume must be to the maximum for attaining the freight efficiencies.

16.7 INTERNATIONAL ORGANIZATIONS ASSOCIATED WITH INTERNATIONAL MARITIME TRANSPORTATION

Shipping is highly regulated at the global level by a number of organizations as discussed here. International shipping has a framework of global regulations on matters, such as construction standards, navigational rules, and crew qualifications; these are common to all ships in international trade. When a ship sails from Mumbai to Rotterdam or Singapore to New York, the same rule applies during the voyage.

16.7.1 International Maritime Organization

It is a specialized agency of the United Nations responsible to develop and maintain a comprehensive regulatory framework for shipping which includes maritime security and safety, environmental concerns, legal matters, technical cooperation, and the efficiency of shipping. Presently, it has 168 member states. The convention establishing the International Maritime Organization (IMO) was adopted in Geneva in 1948 and the IMO members first met in 1959. IMO keeps legislation up-to-date and ensures that it is ratified as many countries as possible. Presently, many conventions apply to more than 98 per cent of the world merchant shipping tonnage. The IMO also considers proposals to integrate appropriate cargo security procedures based on or compatible with the standards of various conventions. The three key IMO conventions include

- International Convention for the Safety of Life at Sea (SOLAS)
- The Standards of Training, Certification, and Watch-keeping Convention (STCW)
- The International Convention for the Prevention of Pollution from Ships (MARPOL)

The International Ship and Port Facility Security (ISPS) Code was introduced in 2004 as a fall out of 11 September 2001 in the US when the need to tighten up security for all modes of transport, which can be potential threat to the national security, was realized. The ISPS code provides for the international framework through which ship and port facilities can cooperate to detect and deter acts which threaten security in the maritime transport sector. The code has been implemented with effect from 1 July 2004 with respect to all contracting parties, including India. IMO regulations are enforced on a global basis and nations have power to detain foreign ships that do not conform to international rules.

16.7.2 International Labour Organization

Standards of employment and working conditions for seafarers are established by the International Labour Organization (ILO). It is also adopted by the Maritime Labour Convention (MLC) to provide a level playing field on a global basis with regard to seafarers' employment standards.

16.7.3 World Customs Organizations

In June 2005, the World Customs Organization (WCO) unanimously adopted the Framework of Standards to Secure and Facilitate Global Trade (SAFE Framework) which provides broad outlines and overarching principles concerning security and facilitating global supply chain, based on two main 'pillars': customs-to-customs cooperation and customs-to-business partnership. Its four core elements are as follows:

- Harmonizing advance electronic cargo information requirements concerning inbound, outbound, and transit shipments
- Developing and implementing a common risk management approach
- Using non-intrusive detection equipment to conduct inspection of high-risk containers and cargo
- Defining benefits for businesses that meet minimal supply-chain security standards and best practices

16.7.4   United Nations Conference on Trade and Development (UNCTAD)

As a part of its mandate, UNCTAD monitors development in the field of transport security and disseminates information in form of various reports and its annual 'Review of Maritime Transport'. There are a number of international conventions affecting the commercial and technical activities of maritime transport. A brief overview of such conventions under the auspices of UNCTAD is shown in Exhibit 16.6.

16.7.5   International Organization for Standardization

In order to enhance supply chain security, consistent with ISPS code, and the WCO Framework of Standards, International Organization for Standardization (ISO) has developed certain procedures and standards. Although ISO standards are voluntary, they are developed in response to market demand based on consensus of interested parties. Besides, the ISO standards for containers, as discussed earlier, are also used worldwide in multimodal transportation.

	Exhibit 16.6	Major conventions on maritime transport[a]
Title of convention	**Date of entry into force or conditions for entry into force**	**Contracting states**
United Nations Convention on a Code of Conduct for Liner Conferences, 1974	Entered into force 6 October 1983	81 countries (including Bangladesh, Belgium China, Chile, Denmark, Egypt, Ethiopia Finland, France, Germany, India, Jamaica, Kenya, Mauritius, Norway, Portugal, Russian Federation, Saudi Arabia, Spain, Sweden, UK, Venezuela)
United Nations Convention on the Carriage of Goods by Sea, 1978 (Hamburg Rules)	Entered into force 1 November 1992	33 countries (including Austria, Egypt, Hungary, Jordan, Kenya, Romania, Tanzania, Tunisia)
International Convention on Maritime Liens and Mortgages, 1993	Entered into force 5 September 2004	12 countries (including Ecuador, Russian Federation, Peru, Spain, Tunisia, Ukraine)
United Nations Convention on International Multimodal Transport of Goods, 1980	Not yet in force—requires 30 contracting parties	11 countries (including Chile, Georgia, Lebanon, Mexico, Morocco, Senegal, Zambia)
United Nations Convention on Conditions for Registration of Ships, 1986	Not yet in force—requires 40 contracting parties with at least 25 per cent of the world's tonnage	14 countries (including Bulgaria, Egypt, Georgia, Hungary, Iraq, Mexico, Oman)

[a] As on 30 September 2007.

Source: Review of Maritime Transport 2007, United Nations Conference of Trade and Development, New York and Geneva, 2007, p. 112.

16.8   INSTITUTIONAL FRAMEWORK FOR MARITIME TRANSPORT IN INDIA

India has a long coastline of about 7517 km. About 95 per cent by volume and 70 per cent by value of India's merchandise trade is carried out through maritime transport. India's maritime transport sector comprises ports, shipping, shipbuilding, ship-repair, and inland water transport systems. India has 12 major ports and 187 non-major ports. India is among the top 20 merchant fleets in the world with 8.42 million gross tonnage (GT) and 13.92 dead weight tons (dwt) under the Indian flag.[10]

16.8.1   Ministry of Shipping

Although the nomenclature of the Ministry has changed several times over the years similar to as in other government departments, but the function, by and large, remains the monitoring and development of maritime transport infrastructure in the country. Presently, the Department of Shipping under the Ministry of Shipping, Road Transport, and Highways is responsible for formulating policies and programmes for development of shipbuilding, ship-repair, major ports, and inland water transport.

16.8.2   National Shipping Board

To advise the Government of India on matters related to shipping and its development, the National Shipping Board is a permanent statutory body established in 1959 under section 4 of the Merchant Shipping Act, 1958. The board comprises six members of parliament, five representatives from central government, three representatives each of ship-owners and seamen, and five representatives of other interest and is re-constituted after every two years.

16.8.3   Directorate General of Shipping

It is a statutory organization established in 1949 under the Ministry of Shipping, Road Transport, and Highways. Its basic functions include administration of the Indian Merchant Shipping Act, 1958 on all matters related to shipping policy and legislation, implementation of various international conventions relating to the safety, prevention of pollution and other mandatory regulations of the International Maritime Organizations, promotion of maritime education and training, examination and certification, supervision of subordinate offices, etc.

16.8.4   The Shipping Corporation of India Ltd

The Shipping Corporation of India Ltd (SCI) was formed on 2 October 1961 by the amalgamation of Eastern Shipping Corporation Ltd (ESC) and Western Shipping Corporation of India Ltd (WSC) with a paid up capital of Rs 235 million. The highly

---

[10] As on 31 December 2006; Annual Report 2006–07, Department of Shipping, Ministry of Shipping, Road Transport and Highways, Government of India, 2007, pp. 4–13.

diversified fleet of SCI includes bulk carriers, crude and product tankers, combination carrier, general cargo vessels, cellular container vessels, LPG/ammonia carriers, phosphoric acid/chemical carriers, offshore supply vessels, and passenger-cum-cargo vessels.

16.8.5   Container Corporation of India

Container Corporation (CONCOR) of India was set up in 1988 with the objective of developing multi-modal logistics support for India's international and domestic containerized cargo and trade. The task was to provide customers with the advantages of direct interaction and door to door services while capitalizing on the Indian Railway network. Though rail is the mainstay of CONCOR's containerized freight transportation plan, road services are also provided according to market demand and operational exigencies. CONCOR also operates container terminals across the country to cater to the needs of trade. The major services offered by CONCOR are as follows:

- Transit warehousing for import and export cargo
- Bonded warehousing, which enables importers to store cargo and ask for partial releases, thereby deferring duty payment
- Less than Container Load (LCL) consolidation, and reworking of LCL cargo at nominated hub
- Air cargo clearance using bonded trucking

This chapter brings out the concept of operations management and its expansion across the world that includes sourcing of inputs, production of goods and services, transportation and managing the supply chain on global scale. Various strategic options for transnational operations and selecting the optimal strategy have also been examined. A business enterprise has to strike a balance between global integration and local responsiveness while managing its global operations.

The concept of supply chain which comprehensively covers a range of activities from procurement of inputs, through operations to making goods and services available to the ultimate customer, has become crucial to achieve business competitiveness. The principal objective of any supply chain system remains that the goods reach to final customer in correct quantity, at desired location, at right time, in usable condition and in most cost-efficient manner. All these logistics objectives are interrelated to each other and may be achieved by a firm's integrated supply chain management strategy. The global expansion of business has necessitated global development and management of supply chain too.

Since maritime transport is the oldest and the most cost-effective means of transport used in international trade, it is governed by a large number of shipping practices derived by the customs of trade. Depending upon the size, type, and nature of trade operations, a firm may either opt for charter or liner shipping. Containerization and 'multi-modal' transport facilitates cargo exports from inland locations using more than one means of transport. International shipping industry often uses a framework of global regulations on matters such as construction standards for ships, navigational rules, crew qualifications, etc. Various international and national organizations associated with maritime transport have briefly been discussed.

SUMMARY

Operations management refers to transformation process from inputs such as materials, machines, labour, and capital into outputs which should have a greater economic value than those of inputs. Gobalizing forces, such as reduction in trade barriers, wage differentials, and growing opportunities in emerging economies have led to globalization of business operations. Relocation of business process to a low cost location is termed as off-shoring, which could either be captive or outsourcing.

Strategic options available for transnational operations may include globally concentrated operations, home market operations, product specialization for a global or regional market, and transnational and vertical integrations. A global firm has to strike a balance between global integration and local responsiveness.

Supply chain management refers to integrating and managing business processes across the supply chain which includes three major subsystems: supply, transformation, and distribution. Major constituents of supply chain include transportation, warehousing, inventory, packaging and unitization, and information and communication technology. Outsourcing of more sophisticated logistics and supply chain services, especially on a global scale, defined as Third Party Logistics (3PL) has grown rapidly during the recent years.

Transportation is an important part of international logistics comprising various modes, such as air, road, rail, and ocean. Various types of ocean cargo include bulk, break bulk, neo bulk, and containerized. An exporter may use either a charter or a liner vessel for international shipments. Various forms of chartering include voyage charter, time charter, bare boat charter, back-to-back charter, trip time charter or contract of affreightment. Containerization has facilitated multi-modal transportation of goods facilitating cargo handling and transport besides enabling door-to-door delivery of goods in international markets.

International organizations associated with international maritime transportation include International Maritime Organization (IMO), International Labour Organization (ILO), World Customs Organizations (WCO), United Nations Conference on Trade and Development (UNCTAD), and International Organization for Standardization (ISO). Institutional framework associated with promotion of maritime transport in India include Ministry of Shipping, National Shipping Board, Directorate General of Shipping, The Shipping Corporation of India Ltd (SCI), and Container Corporation (CONCOR) of India.

KEY TERMS

Back-to-back charter Contract between a charterer and a sub-charterer, whose terms and conditions are identical to the contract (charter) between the charterer and the ship-owner.

Bare boat (demise) charter Hiring of a ship for a period of time during which ship owner provides only the ship whereas the charterer has to provide the crew together with all stores and bunkers and pays for all operating costs.

Barges Unmanned vessels generally used for oversized cargo and towed by a tugboat.

Break bulk Packaged cargo that is loaded and unloaded on a piece-by-piece basis, i.e., by number or count.

Bulk cargo Cargo with homogeneous characteristics in loose, unpackaged form without mark or count, loaded and carried in bulk.

Bulk carriers   Vessels carrying a variety of bulk cargo, such as iron ore, coal and food-stuffs and are identifiable by the hatches raised above deck level which cover the large cargo holds.

Captive off-shoring   Relocating business processes to a low cost location and delivering from a shared service centre owned by the company itself.

Charter shipping   A ship that does not have any fixed itinerary or sailing schedule and can be engaged to ship the firm's cargo from one port to another port.

Combination carriers   Vessels carrying passengers and cargo, oil and dry bulk, or containers and bulk cargo.

Container   Transport equipment, strong enough for repeated use, to facilitate handling and carriage of goods by one or more modes of transport.

Container ships   Vessels carrying manufactured goods and products, usually on scheduled liner services.

Contract of affreightment   A long-time agreement to carry a certain amount of cargo between two ports.

Dead weight tons (dwt)   The maximum weight of the cargo a vessel can carry, also known as tonnage, including both bunker and the stores.

Displacement tonnage   Weight of the ship, when fully loaded measured by the weight of the volume of water displaced by the fully loaded vessel.

Free in and out (FIO)   The charterer has to arrange the stevedores and to load/discharge the cargo on his/her own account.

Free in and out stowed and trimmed (FIOST)   Similar to FIO, but charterer is also responsible and bears the expenses of stowing and trimming.

Free in liner out (FILO)   Ship owner is not responsible for the cost of loading but is responsible for cost of unloading.

Full container load (FCL)   Use of an entire container.

Global integration   Coordination of activities across the country to build efficient operations network and take optimal advantage of internalized synergy at similarities across the operational locations.

Global sourcing   Procurement of inputs for production of goods and delivery of services globally from the most optimal sources.

Gross registered tonnage (GRT)   The total volume of a vessel's carrying capacity, measured as the space available below the deck expressed in hundreds of the cubic feet.

Gross terms   The ship owner is responsible for the cost of loading, stowing, trimming, and unloading of the vessel.

ISO containers   Containers conform to the specification of International Organization for Standardization (ISO).

LASH (lighter aboard ship) vessels   Vessels carrying very large containers, such as barges. It enables cargo to be loaded on barges in shallow waters and then loaded on board a vessel.

Less than container (LCL) load   Use of partial space in a container.

Light tonnage   The total weight of the ship, when empty is measured by using the weight of the water displaced by the empty vessel.

Liner in free out (LIFO)   Ship owner is responsible for cost of loading but not for vessel unloading.

Liner shipping   Regular scheduled vessel services between two ports.

Local responsiveness   Response by a firm to specific needs within various host countries.

Materials management   Procurement of inputs, such as raw materials and components for processing or value-addition by the firm.

Near-shoring   Relocation of business process to a country within the same geographical region.

Neo-bulk   Certain types of cargo that are often moved by specialized vessels, viz. auto, logs, etc.

Neo-bulk carriers   Vessels carrying specific types of cargo.

Net registered tonnage (NRT)   The volume of cargo a vessel can carry arrived by subtracting the volume of space that would not hold the cargo from the gross registered tonnage (GRT)

Net terms   The ship owner is not responsible for cost of loading and discharge.

Off-shoring   Relocation of business processes to a low-cost location by shifting the tasks overseas.

Operations The process which transforms inputs, such as materials, machines, labour, capital, and management, into output (i.e., goods and services).

Roll-on-roll-off (Ro/Ro) vessels Vessels that allow rolling cargo, such as tractors, cars to be driven aboard the vessel.

Tankers Vessels carrying liquid cargo, such as crude oil, chemicals, and petroleum products in large tanks.

Third party off-shoring/outsourcing Relocation of business processes from within the client country to an outside vendor operating at low cost location.

Time charter Hiring of a ship for a time period whereby the ship owner places the ship with crew and equipment at the disposal of the charterer.

Trip time charter A charterer hires the vessel for single voyage or a round trip on terms and conditions similar to that of time-charter.

Voyage charter Contract of carriage in which a vessel is hired for transport of a specified cargo from one port to another port

CONCEPT REVIEW QUESTIONS

1. Explaining the concept of operations management, elaborate upon the reasons that led to globalization of operations.

2. Critically evaluate the strategic options available with a firm for transnational operations.

3. Briefly explain the concept of global supply chain management.

4. Write short notes on
   (a) Off-shoring
   (b) Global sourcing

   (c) Contract of affreigtment
   (d) International Maritime Organization (IMO)

5. Differentiate between the following:
   (a) Charter vs liner shipping
   (b) Voyage vs time charter
   (c) FIO vs FIOST
   (d) FILO vs LIFO
   (e) LCL vs FCL container

CRITICAL THINKING QUESTIONS

1. Select a firm operating globally and find out its operations across the countries. Find out the reasons for globalization of its operations. Critically evaluate the strategy used for its transnational operations based on the concepts studied in the chapter.

2. Identify a few companies providing 3PL services located near your place and compare the services provided and costs involved.

PROJECT ASSIGNMENTS

1. Visit an Inland Container Depot (ICD) or terminal and find out various activities carried out. Meet and discuss various issues and problems associated with international cargo shipment using containers.

2. Visit a sea-port and explore various types of vessels used for cargo shipment.

3. Visit an international trading company and find out various forms of ship chartering used by it and try to find out the reasons for the same.

17 International Human Resource Management

LEARNING OBJECTIVES

> To explain the concept of international human resource management
> To elucidate various types of international organizational structures
> To discuss strategic orientations and practices for international human resource management
> To elaborate upon the management of various human resource activities

17.1 INTRODUCTION

The practice of organizing and managing people in order to carry out pre-determined tasks to achieve certain goals and objectives has prevailed in some form or the other since the dawn of human civilization. Harnessing human potential has historically been the key to wealth and power for leaders—from tribal heads to the merchant class to kings and emperors. Little has changed since in the concept of achieving basic objectives and goals through people management. What has changed indeed is the multiplicity and complexity of tasks involved to achieve the goals and objectives of mammoth organizations having transnational reach, spread over enormous physical distances, and cultural diversity. This complexity has led to the evolution of novel systems, tools, and techniques in managing 'people'.

In simple terms, human resource management (HRM) refers to the processes and practices involved in managing people so as to achieve organizational goals. It involves a wide range of activities right from identifying the manpower requirements, identifying the most appropriate sources, attracting the best talent available from the most cost-effective places, nurturing and enhancing their skills to suit the organizational needs, motivating them through an effective system of compensation to perform optimally, and continuously monitoring their performance with suitable reward-rebuke mechanism. The application of these principles and practices to manage 'people' in more than one country is termed as international human resource management (IHRM). Features specific to IHRM include multiculturalism, geographical dispersion, relocation of expatriates, diverse regulatory environment for taxation, and labour laws.

Managing human resources efficiently on the global basis is increasingly becoming crucial to a firm's success. For optimal performance of an international company, it is extremely important to attract the most competent personnel, deploy them most efficiently, and provide them a working environment where they perform to the best of their efficiency. Globalization of business operations has significantly contributed to the rapid growth of an international workforce with diverse skills and experiences. The advent of information and communication technology (ICT) has enabled off-shoring of tasks to numerous low-cost but distant locations where face-to-face contact becomes less essential.

The access to skilled manpower at comparatively lower costs is highly significant in choosing a location for business operations and determining competitiveness. Labour markets widely differ, both in terms of availability of workforce and the costs involved. Countries with low wages are often preferred locations for labour-intensive production. Availability of highly skilled professionals with world class competence at a fraction of cost compared to developed countries make India the most favoured destination for locating knowledge-intensive business processes and sourcing professionals.

A conceptual understanding of IHRM for global business facilitates international managers to appreciate and make decisions related to personnel associated with its global operations. This chapter elucidates the concept of human resource management and brings out the impact of globalization. Various types of international organizational structures have also been elaborated. Strategic orientations and practices reflecting a company's basic philosophy and tactics used for coordinating its IHRM activities for employees have also been elucidated. This chapter also explicates various human resource activities, such as staffing, expatriate management, training and development, performance management, and compensation and benefits in the context of global business.

17.1.1 Globalization and HRM

It may sound bizarre to most readers in the Eastern world, especially India, but the fact remains that in nineteenth century America, the phrase 'seeing an elephant' implied encountering an exotic phenomenon, an unequal experience, an adventure of a lifetime, or a particularly dangerous situation. Some contemporary management thinkers view 'globalization' as a phenomenon similar to encountering an elephant and emphasize organizational preparedness to face emerging challenges.[1] The rapid globalization of business has resulted in new challenges for cross-country management of human resources, which may briefly be summarized as follows:

- Managing human resources globally is gaining increasing significance as a crucial determinant to a firm's success or failure in international business.

---

[1] Mark, E., J. Mendenhall, Stewart Black, Robert J. Jensen, and Hal B. Reverse, 'Seeing the Elephant: Human Resource Management Challenges in the Age of Globalization', in *Readings and Cases in International Human Resource Management,* 4th ed., Oxon: Routledge, 2007, pp. 19–34.

- The significance of trans-national experience for top management jobs in global corporations is growing.
- 'Off-shoring' of business operations to low-cost locations has augmented the complexity of staffing, performance, monitoring, and differential compensations, especially when employees are located far from corporate headquarters.
- Most HRM text-books are based on research on human resource practices followed in the West which may not be very relevant in other countries due to differences in socio-cultural and regulatory environments; MNEs are increasingly under pressure to effectively manage their human resources located beyond the Western world.

17.2 CONCEPT OF INTERNATIONAL HUMAN RESOURCE MANAGEMENT

Human resources refer to the people an organization employs to carry out its various tasks and activities in exchange of wages, salaries, and other non-monetary rewards. Human resource management refers to all those activities undertaken by an organization to utilize its human resources effectively. It includes activities, such as staffing, training and development, expatriate management, performance management, compensation, fulfilment of regulatory obligations, such as labour relations, human welfare and safety, etc., and industrial relations. HRM is generally considered a staff function, where the HR department assists the line managers in other functional divisions, such as marketing and operations, which are directly responsible for accomplishing organizational goals.

Increasingly, the term 'human capital management' is also being used which refers to acquiring, developing, and managing human skills, expertise, and knowledge within the organization. 'Strategic human resource management' refers to HRM issues, functions, policies, and practices that result from the strategic activities of MNEs and that impact on international concerns and goals of these enterprises.[2]

International HRM comprises identifying diverse requirements of various subsidiaries, and developing and sustaining human resource capabilities to achieve organizational goals. Thus, adaptation of all HRM functions to international settings is known as IHRM. Managing human resources in the international context is much more complex compared to domestically as it encompasses increased functional activities, both in number and magnitude.

A model developed by Morgan, as shown in Fig. 17.1, provides useful insight into HRM in the international context.[3]

[2] Schuler, H, P.J. Dowling, and H. De Cieri, 'An Integrative Framework of Strategic International Human Resource Management', *International Journal of Management,* vol. 4, 1993, p. 720.

[3] Adopted from Morgan, P.V., 'International Human Resource Management: Fact or Fiction?' *Personnel Administration,* vol. 31, no. 9, 1986, p. 44.

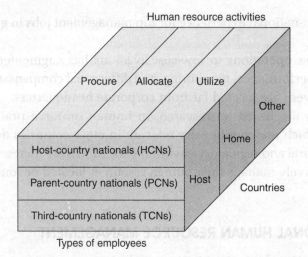

Fig. 17.1   A model of international human resource management

- Employees of an international firm may be classified into three broad categories as follows:
  - Host country nationals (HCNs)
  - Parent country nationals (PCNs)
  - Third country nationals (TCNs)
- HRM activities may be broadly grouped into three major categories, i.e., procure, allocate, and utilize.
- Countries involved in HRM may also be grouped into the following three categories.
  - *Host countries*   Countries where the subsidiary of an MNE are located
  - *Home countries*   Country where an MNE is headquartered
  - *Other countries*   Countries other than home or host nations where inputs are sourced or products or services marketed

IHRM may be defined as an interplay among three dimensions, i.e., human resource activities, types of employees, and countries of operations.

17.2.1   Domestic vs International HRM

Managing human resource activities in the international context requires adaptation of human resource practices in the trans-national context under diverse regulatory frameworks and cross-cultural management. It enlarges the scope of HRM activities and makes it much more complex, as explicated below.

Increased functional activities   In order to manage human resources across countries, the functional activities of human resource departments increase multi-fold. These activities include managing expatriation, cross-country relocation, international taxation, trans-national labour legislation, etc.

Functional heterogeneity   Since an MNE operates in diverse business environments with wide variations in government policies, culture, and regulatory environments, it has to carry out a variety of HRM functions, such as recruitment and selection, performance evaluation, managing compensation, and training and development, with considerable heterogeneity. Satisfying various stakeholders, such as the employers, business partners, and the host country governments with effective human resource management in cross-country settings is indeed a challenging task.

Increased involvement in employees' personal lives   Managing expatriates involves relocating their entire families across countries: this is an important factor in ensuring employees' satisfaction as satisfied employees are crucial to effective output. Relocating includes preparing not only the employees but their entire families, including spouse and children, to develop an understanding and appreciation for cross-cultural environment and equip them for potential cultural shock. Further, issues such as education of children, meaningful engagement/employment for the spouse, accommodation, and transport become highly significant for employees, not only in the capacity to influence the decision to take up an overseas assignment but also in determining the employees' level of satisfaction and job performance.

Enhanced risks   Since human resource activities involve relocation of employees and their families across countries, which requires substantially higher costs in terms of their travel, training, and relocation expenses, the consequences of under-performance of expatriates or their premature return from international assignments is much higher compared to domestic assignment. Therefore, an MNE has to develop and implement its international HRM strategies effectively so as to minimize such risks. Besides, the risks of employees' and their families' safety in terms of health and life increases multi-fold in trans-national assignments due to changes in climatic conditions, epidemic, war, terrorism, and incidence of riots and robbery.

Increased influence of external environment   Like all other activities in international business, managing human resources is also influenced by external environment. The diversity of cultural, regulatory, financial, and political environments requires considerable adaptations in a firm's HRM strategy. International managers have to take into account the cultural differences in values, expectations, behaviours, negotiation, and communication styles of international workforce while designing organizations and recruiting, selecting, training, motivating, compensating, evaluating, and controlling of employees.

17.3   INTERNATIONAL ORGANIZATIONAL STRUCTURES

As a firm expands its business internationally, it has to undergo structural changes so as to meet the changing demands of the international business environment. Designing the organizational structure is the first step in controlling and managing an organization. Decisions regarding the numbers, characteristics, and assignment of personnel are often based on the firm's resources and capabilities, current and potential market conditions, and the local work environment. Principal types of organizational structures as discussed below reflect an evolutionary pattern of organizational structure along the process of internationalization.

17.3.1   Expodocuments against acceptancert Department

Most business firms internationalize through exporting to foreign countries, as discussed in Chapter 11. Exports are often looked after by a company's marketing or sales department in the initial stages when the volume of exports sales is low. However, with increase in exports turnover, an independent exports department is often setup and separated from domestic marketing, as shown in Fig. 17.2.

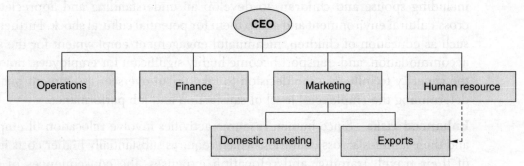

Fig. 17.2   Exports department

Exports activities are controlled by a company's home-based office through a designated head of export department, i.e. Vice President, Director, or Manager (Exports). The role of the HR department is primarily confined to planning and recruiting staff for exports, training and development, and compensation. Sometimes, some HR activities, such as recruiting foreign sales or agency personnel are carried out by the exports or marketing department with or without consultation with the HR department.

17.3.2   International division structure

As the foreign operations of a company grow, businesses often realize the overseas growth opportunities and an independent international division is created which handles all of a company's international operations (Fig. 17.3). The head of international division, who directly reports to the chief executive officer, coordinates and monitors all foreign activities.

The in-charge of subsidiaries reports to the head of the international division. Some parallel but less formal reporting also takes place directly to various functional heads at the corporate headquarters. The corporate human resource department coordinates and implements staffing, expatriate management, and training and development at the corporate level for international assignments. Further, it also interacts with the HR divisions of individual subsidiaries.

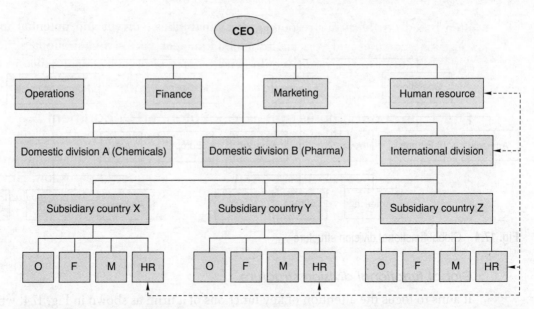

Fig. 17.3   International division structure

O—Operations; F—Finance; M—Marketing; HR—Human Resources.

The international structure ensures the attention of the top management towards developing a holistic and unified approach to international operations. Such a structure facilitates cross-product and cross-geographic co-ordination, and reduces resource duplication. Although an international structure provides much greater autonomy in decision-making, it is often used during the early stages of internationalization with relatively low ratio of foreign to domestic sales, and limited foreign product and geographic diversity.

17.3.3   Global Organizational Structures

Rise in a company's overseas operations necessitates integration of its activities across the world and building up a worldwide organizational structure. While conceptualizing organizational structure, the internationalizing firm often has to resolve the following conflicting issues:

- Extent or type of control exerted by the parent company headquarters over subsidiaries
- Extent of autonomy in making key decisions to be provided by the parent company headquarters to subsidiaries (centralization vs decentralization)

It leads to re-organization and amalgamation of hitherto fragmented organizational interests into a globally integrated organizational structure which may either be based on functional, geographic, or product divisions. Depending upon the firm strategy and demands of the external business environment, it may further be graduated to a global matrix or trans-national network structure.

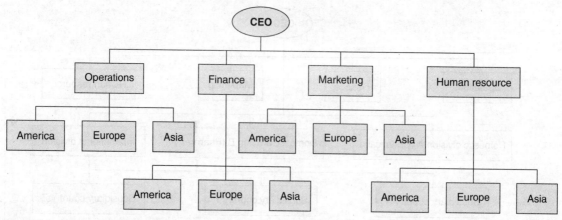

Fig. 17.4 Global functional division structure

Global functional division structure

It aims to focus the attention of key functions of a firm, as shown in Fig. 17.4, wherein each functional department or division is responsible for its activities around the world. For instance, the operations department controls and monitors all production and operational activities; similarly, marketing, finance, and human resource divisions co-ordinate and control their respective activities across the world. Such an organizational structure takes advantage of the expertise of each functional division and facilitates centralized control. MNEs with narrow and integrated product lines, such as Caterpillar, usually adopt the functional organizational structure. Such organizational structures were also adopted by automobile MNEs but have now been replaced by geographic and product structures during recent years due to their global expansion.

The major advantages of global functional division structure include

- Greater emphasis on functional expertise
- Relatively lean managerial staff
- High level of centralized control
- Higher international orientation of all functional managers

The disadvantages of such divisional structure include

- Difficulty in cross-functional coordination
- Challenge in managing multiple product lines due to separation of operations and marketing in different departments
- Since only the chief executive officer is responsible for profits, such a structure is favoured only when centralized coordination and control of various activities is required.

Global product structure

Under global product structure, the corporate product division, as depicted in Fig. 17.5, is given worldwide responsibility for the product growth. The heads of product divisions

Fig. 17.5 Global product structure

do receive internal functional support associated with the product from all other divisions, such as operations, finance, marketing, and human resources. They also enjoy considerable autonomy with authority to take important decisions and operate as profit centres.

The global product structure is effective in managing diversified product lines. Such a structure is extremely effective in carrying out product modifications so as to meet rapidly changing customer needs in diverse markets. It enables close coordination between the technological and marketing aspects of various markets in view of the differences in product life cycles in these markets, for instance, in case of consumer electronics, such as TV, music players, etc.

However, creating exclusive product divisions tends to replicate various functional activities and multiplicity of staff. Besides, little attention is paid to worldwide market demand and strategy. Lack of cooperation among various product lines may also result into sales loss. Product managers often pursue currently attractive markets neglecting those with better long-term potential.

Global geographic structure

Under the global geographic structure, a firm's global operations are organized on the basis of geographic regions, as depicted in Fig. 17.6. It is generally used by companies with mature businesses and narrow product lines. It allows the independent heads of various geographical subsidiaries to focus on the local market requirements, monitor environmental changes, and respond quickly and effectively.

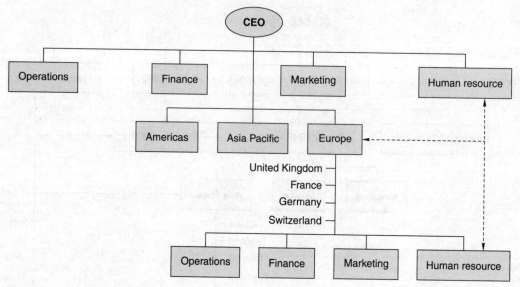

Fig. 17.6 Global geographic structure

The corporate headquarter is responsible for transferring excess resources from one country to another, as and when required. The corporate human resource division also coordinates and provides synergy to achieve company's overall strategic goals between various subsidiaries based in different countries. Such structure is effective when the product lines are not too diverse and resources can be shared. Under such organizational structure, subsidiaries in each country are deeply embedded with nationalistic biases that prohibit them from cooperating among each other.

Global matrix structure

It is an integrated organizational structure, which super-imposes on each other more than one dimension. The global matrix structure might consist of product divisions intersecting with various geographical areas or functional divisions (Fig. 17.7). Unlike functional, geographical, or product division structures, the matrix structure shares joint control over firm's various functional activities.

Such an integrated organizational structure facilitates greater interaction and flow of information throughout the organization. Since the matrix structure has an in-built concept of interaction between intersecting perspectives, it tends to balance the MNE's prospectives, taking cross-functional aspects into consideration. It facilitates ease of technology transfer to foreign operations and of new products to different markets leading to higher economies of scale and better foreign sales performance. Matrix structure is used successfully by a large number of MNEs, such as Royal Dutch/Shell, Dow Chemical, etc.

In an effort to bring together divergent perspectives within the organization, the matrix structure may also lead to conflicting situations. It inhibits a firm's ability to

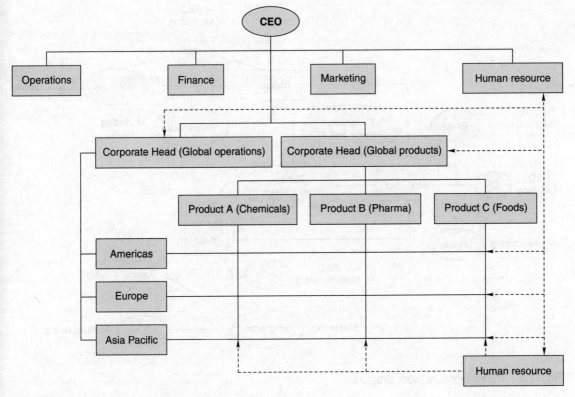

Fig. 17.7 Global matrix structure

respond quickly to environmental changes in case an effective conflict resolution mechanism is not in place. Since the structure requires most managers to report to two or multiple bosses, Fayol's basic principle of unity of command is violated and conflicting directives from multiple authorities may compel employees to compromise with sub-optimal alternatives so as to avoid conflict which may not be the most appropriate strategy for an organization as a whole.

Transnational network structure

Such a globally integrated structure represents the ultimate form of an earth-spanning organization, which eliminates the meaning of two or three matrix dimensions. It encompasses elements of function, product, and geographic designs while relying upon a network arrangement to link worldwide subsidiaries (Fig. 17.8). This form of organization is not defined by its formal structure but by how its processes are linked with each other, which may be characterized by an overall integrated system of various inter-related sub-systems. The trans-national network structure is designed around 'nodes', which are the units responsible for coordinating with product, functional and geographic aspects of an MNE. Thus, trans-national network structures build-up multi-dimensional organizations which are fully networked.

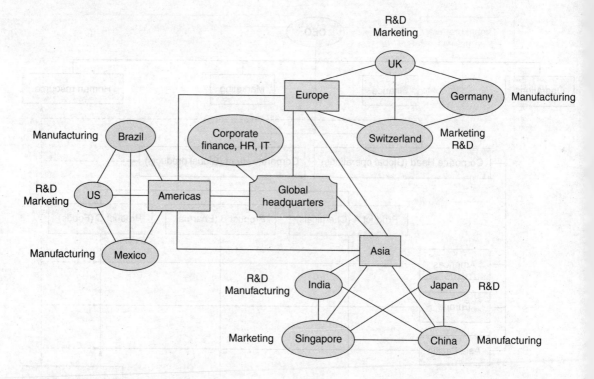

Fig. 17.8   Transnational network structure

The conceptual framework of a trans-national network structure primarily consists of three components:

Disperse sub-units   These are subsidiaries located anywhere in the world where they can benefit the organization either to take advantage of low-factor costs or provide information on new technologies or market trends

Specialized operations   These are the activities carried out by sub-units focussing upon particular product lines, research areas, and marketing areas design to tap specialized expertise or other resources in the company's worldwide subsidiaries.

Inter-dependent relationships   It is used to share information and resources throughout the dispersed and specialized subsidiaries.

Organizational structure of N.V. Philips which operates in more than 50 countries with diverse range of product lines provides a good illustration of a trans-national network structure.

17.3.4   Evolution of Global Organizational Structures

Organizational structures often exhibit evolutionary patterns, as shown in Fig. 17.9, depending upon their strategic globalization.[4] The historical evolution of organizational

[4] White, Roderick E., Toomas, A. Poynter, 'Organizing for Worldwide Advantage' *Business Quarterly* (Summer 1989), pp. 84–89; Daft, Richard L. 1995, *Organization Theory and Design*, MN/St. Paul: West.

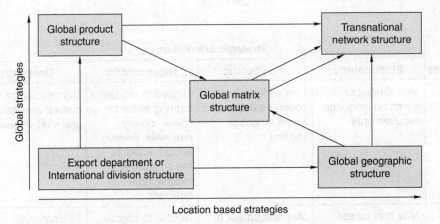

Fig. 17.9 Evolution of global organizational structures

patterns indicates that in the early phase of internationalization, most firms separate their exports departments from domestic marketing or have separate international divisions. Companies with emphasis on global business strategies move towards global product structures whereas those with emphasis on location base strategies move towards global geographic structures. Subsequently, a large number of companies graduate to a matrix or trans-national network structure due to dual demands of local adaptations pressures and globalization. In practice, most companies hardly adopt either pure matrix or trans-national structures; rather they opt for hybrid structures incorporating both.

17.4 STRATEGIC ORIENTATIONS AND PRACTICES FOR IHRM

The basic tactics and philosophy of a firm for coordinating its IHRM activities, reflected in its orientation, may be categorized into four basic approaches: ethnocentric, polycentric, regiocentric, and geocentric as elaborated in Exhibit 17.1.

	Exhibit 17.1 Strategic orientations and practices for IHRM			
	Strategic orientation			
IHRM practices	**Ethnocentric**	**Polycentric**	**Regiocentric**	**Geocentric**
Planning, recruitment, and selection	Home country nationals are developed and appointed at key positions across the world; host country nationals employed for lower positions only	Host country nationals employed at key positions in their own country	Managers are developed and deployed for key positions anywhere in the region but not across the region	Based on qualifications, skills, and experience, best personnel are developed and deployed for key positions anywhere in the world within an MNE

Contd

Exhibit 17.1 Contd

IHRM practices	Strategic orientation			
	Ethnocentric	**Polycentric**	**Regiocentric**	**Geocentric**
Training for cross-cultural adaptations	Very limited or none; no language requirements	Limited for parent country nationals. Some language training	Limited to moderate training levels for home country nationals; English is often used as the language of international business	Continuous for cultural adaptation and multi-lingualism
Effect of international assignments on employees' career growth	May hurt career	May hurt career of parent country nationals; host country nationals' advancement often limited to their own country	Neutral to slightly positive career implications; international assignments of longer duration	International assignments required for career advancement
Evaluation and control	Home standards applied worldwide to evaluate employees' performance	Independent performance standards determined locally for host countries	Determined regionally	Globally integrated performance standards
Compensation	High in headquarters; low in subsidiaries	Wide variation; can be high or low rewards for subsidiary performance	Rewards for contribution to regional objectives	Rewards to international and local executives for reaching local and worldwide objectives based goals of global corporations
Communication; information flow	High volume of orders, commands, advice to subsidiaries	Little to and from headquarters; little among subsidiaries	Little to and from corporate headquarters, but may be high to and from regional headquarters and among countries	Horizontal network relations

Source: Adapted from Heena, D.A. and H.V. Perlmutter. *Multinational Organization Development,* Reading, MA: Addison Wesley, 1979; Ghadar, Fariborz, 'International Strategy from the Perspective of People and Culture: The North American Context', *Research in Global Business Management,* 1, 1990, pp. 179–205.

17.4.1 Ethnocentric IHRM Orientation

Under the ethnocentric approach, the company tends to follow the parent company's home country HRM practices for its employees across the world. Key managerial and technical personnel are recruited from the parent country nationals (PCNs).

Locals are employed only for supporting or lower level jobs with limited opportunities to grow.

Generally such an approach is adopted in the early stages of a firm's internationalization in the circumstances when the types of personnel required with the specific skill-base are not available outside the home country. Besides, employing PCNs is believed to facilitate better co-ordination and control over subsidiaries. Parent country standards are often used for evaluation and promotion with little adaptation. Japanese companies have historically followed such practices.

17.4.2 Polycentric IHRM Orientation

Under the polycentric approach, different HR strategies are adopted for different countries depending upon the need. Host country nationals (HCNs) are often employed in foreign subsidiaries whereas the headquarters are generally managed by the PCNs. HCNs have higher opportunities for career advancement. Besides, performance evaluation measures and compensation also vary considerably from subsidiary to subsidiary.

17.4.3 Regiocentric IHRM Orientation

It reflects a region-specific approach to HRM where most HR strategies are adopted regionally. Depending upon the nature of business and marketing strategy, employees are transferred within a region rather than across the region. For instance, an MNE may have several subsidiaries within Asia-Pacific but its international staff may be transferred within the region. This facilitates creating strong communication networks between the managers, especially the expatriates, within the regions. This approach is also considered to be a federal approach unlike polycentric approach, albeit on a larger scale, and managers view little opportunities for career growth beyond the region. Regiocentric approach is often employed as the interim approach for those organizations who desire to graduate from ethnocentric to geocentric approach.

17.4.4 Geocentric IHRM Orientation

Under this approach, the HR policies and practices of the firm are globally integrated leading to development of a real global corporation. The best talented personnel are posted throughout the MNE irrespective of their nationalities. This does away with the nationalistic bias of federal organizations under polycentric approach and prepares a team of global managers who can be given higher responsibilities of trans-national assignments. It often leads to reduction in the autonomy of subsidiaries in recruiting managerial personnel. An MNE needs a longer lead time and more centralized control of human resource process to implement a geocentric approach.

17.5 MANAGING INTERNATIONAL HUMAN RESOURCE ACTIVITIES

Major international human resource activities, such as staffing, recruitment and selection, expatriate management, training and development, performance management, compensation, and regulatory framework are elucidated below. HRM policies and activities aim at achieving an organization's strategic goals by way of developing employee competence and motivating them to perform accordingly.

17.5.1 Staffing

Staffing refers to the process of determining the organization's current and future human resource requirements to meet the organizational goals and taking appropriate steps so as to fulfil those requirements. The process involves identifying the human resource requirement of an organization, and recruitment, selection, and placement of human resources.

Human resource planning refers to the process of forecasting supply and demand for the organization and the action plan to meet its human resource requirements. It is the decision-making process as to what positions a firm has to fill and how to fill them and places optimally the human resource systems in the organization. The process by which an organization estimates its future human resource needs is termed as 'human resource forecasting'.

International companies need to assess their human resource requirements, assess availability of right type of manpower, decide upon the form and type of international assignments, evaluate pros and cons of alternative sources of personnel for international staffing, and select an appropriate approach for international staffing.

Manpower availability

Availability of desired manpower affects a firm's decision to hire locals or expatriates. MNEs often hire locals for lower level jobs except for some countries such as in the Middle East which import people even for labour and other low-paid jobs. However, for most skilled and professional assignments, quality of educational system, availability of scientists and engineers, and quality of management schools play an important role in a firm's decisions to hire locals or expatriates.

Globally, India ranks third in quality of management schools[5] with a score of 6.0 on a 7 point scale, as shown in Fig. 17.10, after France (6.2), and Switzerland (6.0), and followed by the UK (5.9), the US (5.8), and Singapore (5.7). Australia ranks at 17th place with 5.4, Germany at 28th place with 5.0, Japan at 59th place with 4.2, Brazil at 64th place with 4.1, and China at 92nd place with 3.4. India also ranks at fourth place in availability of scientists and engineers after Israel, Japan, and Finland whereas France ranks at fifth, Germany at 11th, Singapore at 15th, the US at 13th, the UK at

---

[5] The Global Competitiveness Report 2006–07, World Economic Forum, Geneva, Palgrave Macmillan, p. 542.

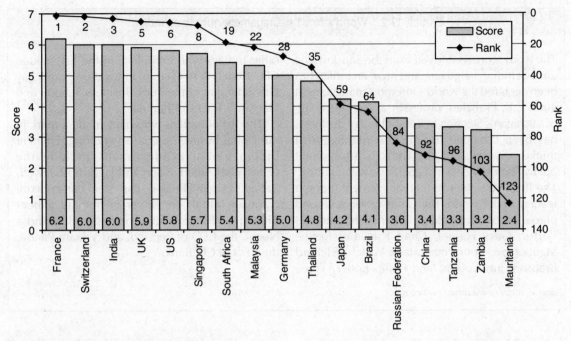

Fig. 17.10 Quality of management schools*

* India's score of 6.0 is the same as Switzerland that has been ranked at the second place.

Note: 1—limited or of poor quality; 7—among the best in the world.

Source: Based on The Global Competitiveness Report 2006–07, World Economic Forum, Geneva, Palgrave Macmillan, p. 468.

22nd, and China at 86th place. Besides, India is also home to world class professionals (Exhibit 17.2).

With the baby-boomer population in the US reaching retirement and average age increasing in most Western countries, global corporations are looking at India for the right talent. India is the topmost on the list of preferred destinations for countries facing an internal talent crunch situation. IBM has its largest non-US workforce of over 70,000 in India. Further, most multinationals strategically intend to increase their skilled workforce in India.

Forms of international assignments

Based on organizational goals and objectives, various forms of international assignments may be classified as follows.

Filling up job positions Trans-national companies often fill up job positions through expatriates when host country nationals with required skill-base are not available. Foreign postings are often required for filling up key positions or technical positions even at a middle or lower level. Besides, international assignments are strategically needed in order to maintain better co-ordination and higher level of control over foreign operations through international transfers.

Exhibit 17.2   World's No. 1 management guru is an Indian

The word 'guru' is derived from the Sanskrit, the ancient Indian language. And now, an Indian has been declared the world's foremost management guru. C.K. Prahalad, professor at the University of Michigan's Stephen M Ross School of Business, has been crowned the greatest management thinker alive in 2007, by Thinkers 50, brought out by Suntop Media in association with Skillsoft. The list names the top 50 management thought leaders in the world. Bill Gates ranks at second place, followed by Alan Greenspan, Michael Porter, Gary Hamel, Chan Kim and Renee Mauborgne, Tom Peters, Jack Welch, Richard Branson, Jim Collins, and Philip Kotler. Three

other Indians who find place in the list include CEO Coach Ram Charan, Innovation guru Vijay Govindarajan of the Tuck Business School, and Harvard's Rakesh Khurana.

The list of Indians who have made a mark in the global business arena is very long. Eminent Indian global academicians include the economists Amartya Sen and Jagdish Bhagwati; Kellogg's Dean Dipak C. Jain; steel baron Laxmi Narayan Mittal; conceiver of hotmail Sabeer Bhatia; and professional managers like Indra Nooyi, the CEO of Pepsico, and Vikram Pandit, the CEO of Citi Bank.

Source: http://www.thinkers50.com.

Management development   Foreign assignments facilitate development of managers and prepare them to take up higher responsibilities at the international level.

Organizational development   Increasing use of expatriates to fill up key positions facilitates development of a team of global managers with strong communication networks at the international level.

Types of international assignments

Depending upon the purpose of assignments and nature of tasks, MNEs often transfer their employees internationally. Based on the duration of stay, international assignments may be classified as

Short-term (up to three months)   Assignments related to small project work, machinery or plant repairing, or an interim arrangement till a suitable permanent arrangement is made

Extended (up to one year)   Involving similar activities as for short-term assignments for a relatively longer duration

Long-term (one to five years)   Also referred to as 'traditional expatriate assignment', involve a well-defined role in foreign operations. Assignments, such as production or marketing manager or a managing director of a subsidiary

Within the above categories of international assignments, there may be non-standard assignments as well:

Commuter assignments   Special arrangements where a person travels from one country to another for work. For instance, a professor residing in New Delhi travels to

Washington or Singapore once in a fortnight or a month to take classes and teach a course.

Rotational assignments   An arrangement where the employees travel from home country to a foreign country either on rotational basis or with breaks in-between. For instance, an institute runs a long-duration management programme in a foreign country and professors travel to take different courses related to their areas of competence on rotational basis. Besides, such rotational assignments are used in certain areas of international project management, such as oil-rigs.

Contractual assignments   When a specialized skill is vital to managing a project or is required for a short duration, contractual assignments are often preferred over permanent assignments as they offer little long-term liability on part of the organization. Such assignments are common in teaching, research and development, and project management.

Virtual assignments   It refers to assigning international responsibilities to home base managers for organizing foreign activities. Such virtual assignments are often used either due to cost reasons or scarcity of mobile employees willing to accept long-term foreign assignments.

Sources of Human Resources for International Staffing

Multinational companies can source human resources from the following major sources.

Local citizens or HCNs   Local employees hired by an MNE of the host country are known as HCNs. A large number of MNEs engage host country citizens for middle and lower level jobs.

Pros

- Conversant with the host country business environment
- Familiarity with host country culture and language
- Often less expensive compared to PCNs
- Increases morale of HCNs due to greater prospects of career growth
- Longer duration of stay in the MNE by HCNs leads to continuity of management and improvements

Cons

- MNEs often fear lack of effective control and coordination over subsidiaries by appointing HCNs at key positions
- HCNs may have difficulty in communication with headquarters
- HCNs have limited career opportunities outside the subsidiary
- Hiring HCNs may lead an MNE to become federation of national units rather than a truly global organization

Expatriates   Employees who temporarily reside and work outside their home country are commonly known as 'expatriates' or 'expats'. Expatriates are often used as agents of direct control, socialization, networking, and gathering business intelligence. Expatriates may be either PCNs or third country nationals (TCNs) as discussed below.

Parent country nationals (PCNs)   Employees who are citizens of the country where the MNE is headquartered are known as PCNs or home country nationals. Historically, MNEs filled up key positions in their foreign affiliates with PCNs.

Pros

- Familiarity with parent company's objectives, strategies, policies and practices
- Facilitates higher level of organizational control and coordination
- Availability of highly talented managers with special skills and experiences
- Promising managers from parent headquarters are deputed for international assignments

Cons

- Employing PCNs is often more expensive compared to HCNs or TCNs
- Difficulty in adapting to foreign country environment in terms of foreign languages and socio-economic and cultural issues
- Appointing PCNs at key positions by MNEs is often perceived by HCNs as blocking their career growth opportunities within the organization
- Tendency of PCNs to impose the headquarters style on its subsidiaries often overlooking the local needs
- Differences in compensation packages between PCNs and HCNs is often perceived as discriminatory by HCNs

Third country nationals (TCNs)   Employees who are citizens of countries other than the country in which they are assigned to work or the country where the MNE is headquartered, are often referred to as TCNs. In countries with lower level of skill base, such as African and Latin America, MNEs often employ TCNs from countries with cost-effective availability of skilled manpower and professionals from countries such as India rather than from their home country where the workforce is relatively more expensive.

Pros

- It is easier to find TCNs as global managers with high level of skills and competence
- Cost of employing TCNs is generally lower compared to PCNs
- Trans-national relocation of personnel creates opportunities for career advancement and motivates employees
- Cross-country transfers contribute to build up a truly global work-force leading to a global corporation

Cons

- Reluctance and resentment by host country government towards hiring TCNs

- Diplomatic sensitivity of host country in employing personnel from certain nationalities
- Some TCNs may be reluctant to return home after a foreign assignment

Inpatriates   As opposed to expatriates, employees assigned to work in the MNE's home country who are citizens of either a host country of firm's operation or a third country are termed as 'inpatriates'. In order to meet international competition, MNEs increasingly make use of inpatriates. This facilitates MNEs to develop their global core competencies.

MNEs often use a mix of personnel based on the company need, its HR strategy, and availability of right type of employable workforce. For instance, Microsoft employs Indian citizens (HCNs) for its Indian operations, often sends US citizens to its Japanese operations (PCNs), and sends British citizens to its Middle East operations (TCNs).

Off-shoring

Off-shoring refers to transferring jobs to foreign countries which were previously carried out domestically. The breakthroughs in information and communication technology have made it possible to off-shore various service activities too. The human resource department has the prime responsibility to identify low cost, high quality personnel abroad and equip them with company information to carry out their assigned tasks efficiently. Besides, an effective supervisory and management structure is also to be put in place so as to carry out screening, provide necessary trainings, and monitor their performance. The motivation level of employees located at vast geographical distances is also to be maintained by way of conducive working conditions, compensation, and benefits so as to get maximum output and curb attrition.

International Staffing Approaches

Since an MNE has to operate under cross-country business environment, its strategic approaches to international staffing may be categorized into four broad categories, as elucidated in Exhibit 17.1 such as ethnocentric, polycentric, regiocentric, and geocentric.

17.5.2 Recruitment and Selection

'Recruitment' refers to the process by which an organization attracts the most competent people to apply for its job openings whereas 'selection' refers to the process by which organizations fill their vacant positions. The process of recruitment and selection varies widely among countries. For instance, extensive formal testing and screening techniques are often employed in Asian countries where people are highly test-oriented and comfortable with formal tests. Testing is often discouraged in the US due to its negative impact on equal employment opportunities and affirmative action efforts. Europeans test considerably more than Americans but not as much as Asians. Rigorous staffing practices such as formal testing are used even less in Canada where equal employment and human rights legislation is even more restrictive compared to the US.

Characteristics of global managers

Traditionally, managers used to specialize not only in their functional area but also in the geographic region of their operations so as to effectively respond to its specific business demand. However, during recent years, rapid rise in globalization of businesses has led to the emergence of a new breed of global managers with multi-lingual and multi-cultural skills and trans-national experience. The common traits of global managers are summarized here.

Global mindset To pursue global business strategies of a firm, its managers need to understand the interdependence of rapidly changing business environment on firm's activities. The global mindset is characterized by identifying similarities across countries and adapting business strategies to local conditions. It calls for managers to 'think globally, but act locally'.

Strategic vision and long-term perspective Global managers should have a strategic vision and be persistent to pursue the long-term goals of the organization.

Ability to work in diverse cultures International managers are often required to work with people with diverse cultural backgrounds. Therefore, they should be able to develop a quick understanding of different cultures and deliver results under multi-cultural environments.

Willingness to relocate for international assignments Depending upon the requirements of an MNE, international mangers should be willing to relocate across countries for taking up the challenges of new assignments.

Ability to manage change and transition International managers often come across novel business situations in different countries which require innovative solutions. Therefore, the ability to manage organizational change and transition is key to the success of international managers.

Selection criteria for international assignments

An MNE needs to decide upon the factors to select personnel for international assignments. Depending upon the company's experience of its international operations and culture, a firm may choose one or more factors from those discussed below and adopt a model by assigning them appropriate weights.

Technical and managerial competence Most companies place high priority on technical and managerial skills to determine suitability of potential managers for international assignments. Academic background, job experience, skills acquired, and past performance of the employees within the company and their previous jobs often serve as useful measures to assess their competence for international assignments.

Ability to perform under cross-cultural environments Managers selected for international assignments should have the ability to operate under diverse cultural environments and work with various stakeholders, such as fellow-employees, customers, and government officials. Sensitivity to foreign cultures and respect towards their value systems, customs, traditions, religions, besides emotional maturity and empathy are some of the key attributes required to successfully perform under cross-cultural situations.

Family attitude towards international assignments   Support of family members, especially the spouse, is crucial for optimal performance of an employee at job. This becomes extremely important for taking up an international assignment and performing overseas. The willingness of family varies significantly across their apprehensions regarding housing, safety, children's education, spouse's career prospects, and also the fear of the unknown. Most studies suggest that adjustment of the spouse is highly co-related to the adjustment and the performance of an expatriate.

As discussed earlier in Chapter 7, most western cultures separate work from employees' private lives and therefore western MNEs are often reluctant to include the spouse either formally or informally in the expatriate's selection process. In certain countries, such as Australia, MNEs fear inclusion of spouse in the formal selection process could evoke issues related to individual civil liberties. Suitability of potential expatriate's family for an overseas assignment may be appraised through 'adaptability screening' which evaluates how well the family is likely to stand up to the rigours and the stress of overseas life.

Regulatory framework in host countries   For international postings, it is essential to get work-permits for the selected candidates. MNEs need to look into the restrictions imposed by host countries on citizens of certain nationalities. Host country restrictions on relocation of families and freedom to take up any job by the spouse also restrict employees' decision to accept a foreign assignment. For instance, free mobility among nationals in the European Union speeds up the relocation process for citizens of member countries within the European Union. Certain Middle Eastern countries do not issue a work permit to single women.

Language   Working knowledge of foreign languages, especially those of the host country, offers an added advantage while selecting managers for international assignments. It facilitates communication of expatriates with the locals in a foreign country.

17.5.3 Managing Expatriates

People working out of their home countries, also known as expatriates, form an integral part of a firm's international staffing strategy, especially for higher management positions. Beside identifying and recruiting the right personnel with desired skills for international assignments, it is also extremely important to provide them with a conducive environment to get their optimum output.

Expatriates also contribute significantly to international remittances. Worldwide remittances are estimated to have exceeded US$318 billion in 2007, of which

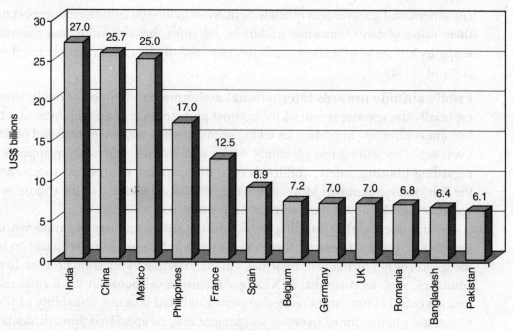

Fig. 17.11 Top remittance recipient countries (2007)

Source: Migration and Remittances Factbook 2008, The World Bank, Washington DC, 2008, pp. 1–43.

developing countries received US$240 million. India had been the largest receiver of foreign remittance in absolute terms with US$27 billion, as shown in Fig. 17.11, followed by China (US$25.7 billion), Mexico (US$25.0 billion), Philippines (US$17.0 billion), France (US$12.5 billion), Spain (US$8.9 billion), Belgium (US$7.2 billion), Germany (US$7.0 Billion), UK (US$7.0 billion), Romania (US$6.8 billion), Bangladesh (US$6.4 billion), and Pakistan (US$6.1 billion) in 2007.

However, due to the massive size of Indian and Chinese economies, the share of remittances in GDP was only 2.8 and 0.9 per cent respectively in 2006. The US has been the top remittance sending country with US$42.2 billions, followed by Saudi Arabia (US$15.6 billion), Switzerland (US$13.8 billion), Germany (US$12.3 billion), and the Russian Federation (US$11.4 billion) whereas the remittance sent by Japan, China, and India in 2006 were US$3.5 billion, US$3.0 billion, and US$1.6 billion, respectively.[6]

The principal concepts in managing personnel for foreign assignments, i.e., expatriate failure, expatriate adjustment process, and repatriation are discussed in the ensuing sections.

Expatriate Failure

Premature return of an expatriate before completion of a foreign assignment is termed as expatriate failure. Expatriate failure represents faulty selection process, often

---

[6] *Migration and Remittances Factbook 2008*, The World Bank, Washington DC, 2008, pp. 1–43.

compounded by ineffective expatriate management policy. Major reasons for contributing to expatriate failure include

- Inability to adjust in alien cultures
- Career apprehensions on repatriation
- Relocation anxieties
- High costs of living and income gaps
- Problems related to lifestyle adjustments, such as uncomfortable living conditions
- Family problems, such as spouse dissatisfaction, children's education, and safety concerns
- Health and medical concerns
- Adaptation problems to different management styles

Such failures have considerable implications on MNEs, both in terms of direct and indirect costs. Direct costs include airfare of employees and their families, relocation expenses, salaries, and training costs. Besides, there are considerable indirect costs involved, although difficult to quantify, both for the employer and the employee. Since many expatriate positions are required to interact with local government officials, customers and other stakeholders, expatriate failure results in difficulty in dealing with host-government officials, productivity losses, and often a demoralizing effect on the local staff. Moreover, failure to perform and adjust in an overseas assignment leads to loss of self-esteem, self-confidence, and one's reputation among colleagues which may also hamper the employee's future performance.

Expatriate adjustment process

Expatriates and their families often find it difficult to adjust to a foreign environment. The series of phases expatriates undergo while adjusting to a foreign culture is termed as expatriate adjustment process. As there are considerable psychological upheavals in the adjustment process in a foreign culture, it is also referred to as 'culture shock cycle'. 'Culture shock' refers to the pronounced reactions to psychological disorientation that is experienced in varying degrees when spending an extended period of time in a new foreign environment.[7] Although the duration and extent of culture shock may vary from individual to individual, depending upon the nature of assignment and environmental differences. The expatriate adjustment process may broadly be categorized under the following four heads, as depicted in Fig. 17.12.

Initial euphoria   In the initial stage of foreign assignments, also referred to as the 'honeymoon' or 'tourist' phase, expatriates often experience upswing in their mood and a great deal of excitement in the new culture. International travellers who visit foreign countries for a shorter duration have a luxury of experiencing the new cultural excitement and remain only in the euphoric stage.

---

[7] Kohls, Robert L., *Survival Kit for Overseas Living*, Yarmouth, ME: Intercultural Press, 1979, pp. 62–68.

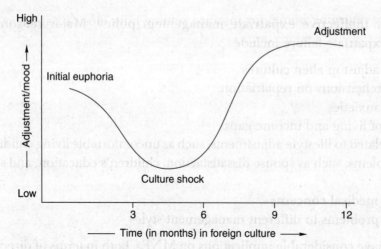

Fig. 17.12 Adjustment process to alien cultures

Cultural shock With the passage of time, the novelties of foreign assignment tend to dwindle, and the realities of every-day life in the foreign country become increasingly challenging. Homesickness sets in; expatriates often enter into a phase of disillusionment with heightened irritation, hostility, and mood downswing. This leads to disruption in the established patterns of the expatriate's behaviour. This phase is the most critical in determining an expatriate's success in a foreign assignment.

Adjustment If the cultural shock phase is handled carefully and successfully, the expatriate enters into the next phase of coping with the new environment, known as 'adjustment' phase. After the crisis of cultural shock is over, the expatriate begins to develop a more positive attitude towards the new culture, and begins to lead a more satisfying and rewarding life.

Re-entry Once an expatriate stays with family in a foreign environment over an extended period, she/he gets adjusted to the culture and faces a 'reverse cultural shock' on return. She/he may suffer from maladjustment which may adversely affect her/his performance level and job satisfaction. She/he needs to be supported by the company so as to minimize its detrimental impact.

Repatriation

The process of returning home by an expatriate after completion of foreign assignment is known as 'repatriation'. The ability to attract potential expatriates also depends considerably on a firm's effective managing of the repatriation process.[8] The repatriation process may be divided as follows:

Preparation It refers to planning for future posting and gathering all information about the new assignments. Companies generally provide a check-list of tasks to be

---

[8] Dowling, Peter, J., and Denise E. Welch, *International Human Resource Management: Managing People in a Multinational Context*, 4th ed., New Delhi: Thomson Learning, 1999, pp. 160–62.

completed before returning home, for instance settling bills, closing bank-accounts, and other tasks associated with relocation of the expatriate's family.

Physical relocation   The actual movement of expatriates and their families along with their household belongings to the next place of posting, usually the home country, is referred to as physical relocation. Comprehensive HR policies to assist in relocation considerably reduce the hassles, disruptions, and associated apprehensions, not only for expatriates but also for their families.

Transition   Once the expatriate returns to his/her home country after completion of an overseas assignment, provisional arrangements are to be made for accommodation and other household tasks, including opening or reviving bank accounts, getting insurance and driving licence, etc.

Re-adjustment   It is the coping phase where expatriates face reverse cultural shock on their returning home. Loss of career-growth and direction, fear of loss of income, status, and autonomy are some of the other problems associated with re-entry into the home organization.

17.5.4 Training and Development

'Training' refers to the process by which employees acquire skills, knowledge, and abilities to perform both their current and future assignments in the organization. Training aims at altering behaviour, attitude, knowledge, and skills of personnel so as to increase the performance of employees.

The need for imparting pre-departure training to spouse and children, besides the employee, is increasingly recognized by MNEs. Pre-departure training is aimed at smooth transition of expatriates and their families to a foreign location. It includes

Cultural sensitization programmes   Expatriates and their families need to be sensitized on cultural issues at the place of work so as to facilitate their smooth transition to an alien culture (Fig. 17.13). It also helps expatriates deal with other employees in the host country location and manage effectively. The type and extent of such training varies, depending upon the country of assignment, duration of stay required, nature of posting, and the training provider.

Preliminary visit   Sending employees on a preliminary trip to the host country for orientation often provides a useful insight into their suitability and interest in the overseas assignment. Such pre-departure visits constitute a useful component of pre-departure training along with culture sensitization programmes. It also facilitates during the initial adjustment process of expatriates and helps in reducing the costs associated with expatriate failure.

Language training   Although English is generally accepted as the language of global business, it is always desirable for international managers to develop linguistic abilities in the foreign languages of the host country. Ability to understand and speak local

Fig. 17.13 An ongoing cultural sensitization session for global managers

languages enhances expatriates' effectiveness to deal with local personnel and their ability to negotiate. However, the degree of fluency of foreign language required also depends on the level and nature of the foreign assignment and the need for interaction with local stakeholders, such as clients, government officials, and other host country nationals. Moreover, language skills on the country of operation also help the expatriates and their family members develop social contacts with local communities and evolve their own social support networks.

MNEs from non-English speaking countries tend to use the language of the parent country for intra-firm communications. With the geographical dispersion of its activities, often a common corporate language is evolved which facilitates standardization of information and reporting systems. As a result, fluency in corporate language also becomes a pre-requisite for effective performance at an overseas assignment. Therefore, pre-departure training should include developing expatriates' proficiency both in the host country and corporate languages.

Practical training To assist expatriates and their families relocate overseas, the corporate HRM division often provides information on practical aspects for adaptation to the new environment. It includes brief working information on the host-country, such as its historical background and geography, economic and legal environments, social and cultural etiquettes, political environment, and the relationship between the two countries and religious beliefs and their impact on daily life and current affairs.

Some MNEs also employ a relocation specialist to provide practical assistance to its expatriates such as in finding accommodation and schools for children, etc.

Skill development is a lifetime process that enhances one's job performance. Management development programmes (MDPs) are long-term efforts aimed at training and developing the managers to harness their fullest potential at job. Type and duration of MDPs vary, depending upon the nature of job, hierarchy level, career and organizational goals.

17.5.5 Performance Management

'Performance management' is a comprehensive term that refers to the process that enables a firm to evaluate the performance of its personnel against pre-defined parameters for their consistent improvements so as to achieve organizational goals. The system used to formally assess and measure employees' work performance is termed as performance appraisal. Evaluation of an employee's performance is required for assessing employee's contribution to achieve organizational goals, facilitate administrative decisions related to compensation, promotion or transfer, etc. Determination of the evaluation criteria, the choice of the evaluators, and the delivery of timely and culturally sensitive feedback constitute the principal challenges related to the performance evaluation of expatriates.

In the international context, performance appraisal becomes more complex due to possible conflict between the objectives of an MNE's headquarters and subsidiaries, non-comparability of information between the subsidiaries, the volatility of international markets, and differences in levels of market maturity. Therefore, international HR managers need to reconcile the differences between the need for universal appraisal standards and the specific objectives of the local subsidiaries, and to recognize that more time may be needed to achieve results in markets, which enjoy little supporting infrastructure from the parent company.[9]

MNEs need to evolve systematic processes for evaluation of employees from different countries who work in different environments. Developing consistent performance evaluation methods often conflicts with the diverse cultural factors of the host countries. For instance, it may be appropriate in a country with low-context culture like the US to precisely point out an employee's shortcomings directly whereas public criticism in high-context cultures, such as China, Japan, and to some extent, India may prove counterproductive; in such cultures the opportunity to save one's face is extremely important. Praise is often given in groups in appraisal process in Japan, whereas it is given individually in the US. Besides, the Western system of performance appraisal, especially in the US, emphasizes merit, fairness, and short-term orientation whereas in Eastern cultures perceived loyalty to the superior or the employer, ability to function in groups, attitude, seniority, etc., carry considerable weightage.

The criteria for assessing employees' effectiveness in a foreign subsidiary may be totally different compared to home country. For instance, for long-term success of a firm in emerging markets like China and India, projecting a positive company image,

[9] Schuler, R.S., J.R. Fulkerson, and P.J. Dowling, 'Strategic Performance Measurement and Management in Multinational Corporation', *Human Resource Management*, 30(3), 1991, pp. 365–92.

developing relationship with suppliers and the local government authorities is much more important compared to growth in profitability and market share during the review period.

As indicated in Exhibit 17.1 an MNE applies home standards worldwide to evaluate employees' performance under the ethnocentric approach, whereas under the polycentric approach, performance evaluation varies from country to country. Global corporations often monitor employees' performance based on the firm's global objectives and goals.

17.5.6 Compensation

Compensation refers to the financial remuneration that employees receive in exchange of their services rendered to the organization. It includes wages, salaries, pay rise, and other monetary issues. A good compensation system should be designed within the regulatory framework of the country of operation of an MNE and should be able to attract and retain the best available talent. Besides, it should be equitable among employees and motivate them to achieve high levels of performance.

Wages only become meaningful in relation to price, i.e., what can be bought with the money earned. The relationship between wages and prices at different places becomes clearer by comparing global standard products like the Big Mac burger, bread, or rice, as shown in Table 17.1. On a global average, 35 minutes of work buys a Big Mac, 22 minutes a kilo of bread, and 16 minutes a kilo of rice. However, the duration of time required to work to buy one Big Mac or a kilo of bread or rice varies significantly across places. It takes just 5 minutes of work to buy a kilo of bread in London whereas it takes 16 minutes in New York and Tokyo, 22 minutes in Delhi,

Table 17.1   Time (in minutes) required to work for buying

Place	One Big Mac	One kg of bread	One kg of rice
Jakarta	86	47	36
Mexico City	82	53	22
Mumbai	70	14	32
Bangkok	67	49	22
Delhi	59	22	36
Beijing	44	42	29
Shanghai	38	35	23
Moscow	25	12	12
Dubai	25	11	12
Singapore	22	26	10
Paris	21	16	13
Brussels	20	12	12
London	16	5	5
Sydney	14	15	5
New York	13	16	8
Tokyo	10	16	12

Source: UBS Prices and Earnings, UBS AG, Wealth Management Research, Zurich, 2006.

49 minutes in Bangkok, and 53 minutes in Mexico City. Therefore, buying power needs to be taken into consideration while determining wages for employees in different countries.

Culture also plays a significant role in determining compensation. In most Western companies, the compensation is determined by the nature of job and individual performance whereas in Japan, compensation is based on the traditional *Oyabun-Kobun*, or parent-child relationship, in which pay and promotions are determined almost entirely by seniority.

Key components of international compensation systems

Base salary   Generally, an expatriate's base salary is in the same range for a similar position in the home country but in the international context, it often serves as a benchmark for other compensation elements. The base salary may be paid either in home country currency or the local currency.

Foreign service premium   To accept a foreign assignment, an extra pay is often offered to expatriates as an inducement, known as foreign service premium. Such extra premium is paid to compensate the expatriate for living in an unfamiliar country isolated from friends and family.

Allowances   It refers to the payments made to expatriates for extra costs required to be incurred for residing overseas. Various types of allowances that form part of expatriate compensation package are discussed below.

Hardship allowance   It is paid when an expatriate is posted in a difficult location that has grossly deficient level of basic amenities, such as healthcare, schools, transport, and safety compared to the expatriate's home country. Quality of life index, as given in Fig. 17.14, provides a useful tool to carry out comparison between various international locations. Zurich ranked as the world's top city in terms of quality of life with a score of 108.1 in 2007, followed by Germany, and Vancouver whereas Baghdad ranked at the last.

Cost of living allowance   Cost of living allowance (COLA) is paid based on the differences in the price of food, transport, clothes, household goods, entertainment, etc., between expatriate's home country and place of overseas posting. Since it is difficult to precisely determine the COLA, MNEs may make use of information provided by specialist organizations. Companies often make use of secondary information from the UN, World Bank, IMF, or private publications, such as UBS, Mercer, or EIU surveys. Cost of living computed on the basis of a weighted shopping basket of Western European consumer habits containing 122 goods and services, including rent, considering an index of 100 for New York reveals that London is the most expensive place in the world[10] with an index of 120.2 as shown in Fig. 17.15,

---

[10] UBS Survey, 2008.

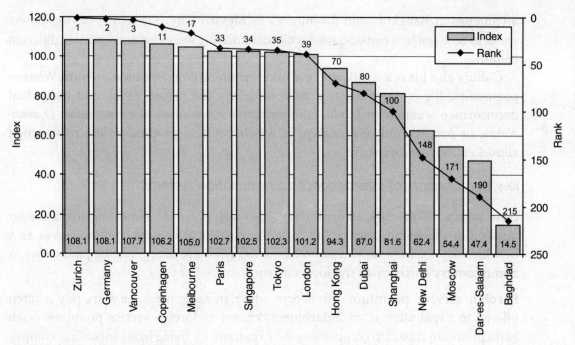

Fig. 17.14 Quality of life index (2007)

Source: 'Worldwide Quality of Living Survey', Mercer, 2007.

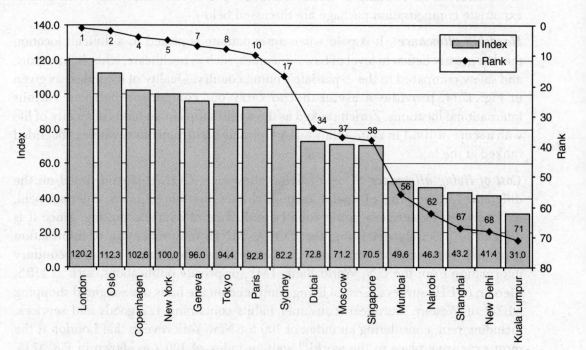

Fig. 17.15 Cost of living index (2008)

Source: UBS Survey, 2008.

followed by Oslo (112.3) whereas Copenhagen has index value of 102.6, Geneva 96.0, Tokyo 94.4, Paris 92.8, Sydney 82.2, Dubai 72.8, Moscow 71.2, Singapore 70.5, Mumbai 49.6, Nairobi 46.3, Shanghai 43.2, New Delhi 41.4, and Kuala Lumpur 31.0.

Housing allowance   Expatriates are often provided company accommodation or housing allowances to maintain their living standard at home country level.

Home leave allowances   MNEs often provide paid leave and travel costs to expatriates and their families so as to enable them to visit their home country usually once in a year as a part of their compensation package.

Education allowances   Allowances for education of expatriates' children is often an integral part of expatriate's compensation package so as to ensure that their children receive the same level of education as in the home country. It may include enrolment fee, tuition fee, fee for language classes, costs of books and stationary, transport, etc.

Relocation allowances   MNEs often provide travel costs of expatriates and their families and cost of transporting household belongings overseas. Transit accommodation in a company guest house or a hotel overseas is often provided till final housing arrangements are made and the arrival of household goods. It may also include some perquisites, such as car, club membership, domestic help, etc.

Assistance for tax equalization   Tax equalization refers to an adjustment to expatriate pay to reflect tax rate in the home country. Expatriates face two potential sources of income tax liabilities, both from host and home country. Although most countries exempt their citizens on foreign income, it is also taxed in some countries, such as the US, subject to certain exemptions.

Expatriates may have to pay income tax to both host and home country governments, unless there is a reciprocal tax treaty between the two. Generally MNEs pay expatriate's income tax in the host country when a reciprocal tax treaty is not in force. Sometimes international firms also make up the difference when the income tax rate in host country is higher which may otherwise reduce expatriate's take home pay.

Other benefits   Benefits are usually monetary in nature, such as insurance, pensions, medical and educational benefits and are monitored closely with compensation management. Such benefits may also include vacations and special leaves, provisions for emergency leaves, and free air fare for the home country for expatriates and their family in case of emergency. Most firms ensure that expatriates receive the same level of benefits abroad as in their home country. Sometimes it can be much costlier for the firms as such benefits may not be tax deductible for the firm out of the country unlike in the home country.

Strategic approaches to international compensation

An MNE may follow either home-, or host-country-based compensation systems or a hybrid of the two, as summarized in Exhibit 17.3.

	Exhibit 17.3 Expatriate compensation systems		
	Home-based	**Host-based**	**Hybrid**
Features	▪ Consistent treatment of expatriates of same nationality ▪ Link with home-country structure/economy ▪ Different pay levels for different nationalities ▪ No relationship to local employee	▪ Equity with local nationals ▪ All nationalities paid the same ▪ Simple administration ▪ Variation in 'value' by localities ▪ No link to home-country structure/economy	▪ All nationalities paid equitably ▪ Some link to home-country structure/economy ▪ No relationship to local employees
Applicable conditions	▪ Temporary international assignment (2–5 years) ▪ Expatriates will ultimately be repatriated to their country of origin ▪ The number of different nationalities in any one host location is relatively low ▪ International staff predominate in higher-level host location jobs	▪ International assignments are of indefinite duration ▪ Expatriates tend to be assigned to high-pay countries and will ultimately be repatriated to their country of origin ▪ The number of different nationalities in any one host location is relatively high ▪ Host-country local staff predominate in higher-level host location jobs	
Advantages	▪ Expatriates neither gain or lose financially ▪ Facilitates mobility ▪ Eases repatriation	▪ All employees operate on equivalent pay ▪ System is easy to administer ▪ All employees, including expatriates, are paid the same ▪ Most suitable for international assignments of indefinite duration	▪ Expatriate from all nationalities are paid equitably ▪ Assists transfers and development of an international management cadre
Disadvantages	▪ Expensive ▪ No link to local pay structure ▪ Expatriates of the same seniority from different origins are paid differently ▪ Administration can be complex	▪ Complicates re-entry ▪ Most applicable when salary and living standards improve, thereby becoming expensive ▪ Unprotected fluctuations in the exchange rate puts company and employee at additional risk ▪ Certain host-country benefits are not applicable to expatriates ▪ Difficult to transfer to lower-paying location	▪ Complicated administration ▪ Sometimes difficult to communicate ▪ No link to local pay structure

Source: Milkovish, G.T. and J.M. Newman, *Compensation*, Chicago: Irwin/McGraw-Hill, 1999.

Home-country-based compensation system   Under this system, expatriate's base salary is linked to the salary structure of the home country. For instance, salary of an Indian manager posted to the US would be based on the Indian rather than the US level.

It is also known as 'balance sheet approach', which aims at maintaining the home country living standard for expatriates and their families, besides providing some financial inducements to work overseas. It is designed to equalize the purchasing power of expatriates at comparable position levels at the host and the home country and to provide incentives to offset qualitative differences between the job locations.

Host-country-based compensation system   Expatriate's base salary is linked to the pay structure in the host country. However, other allowances and benefits are linked to the home country salary structure.

It is also known as the 'going rate approach', under which the base salary of an expatriate is linked to the prevailing salary structures in the host country. It is based on information obtained through compensation surveys of locals (HCNs), expatriates of same nationality, or expatriates of all nationalities. However, the basic pay and benefits may be supplemented by additional payments in low-pay countries.

Hybrid compensation system   It combines the features of both the home- and host-country-based compensation approaches to create a global workforce. It is based on the principle that all expatriates regardless of their country of origin belong to one nationality.

17.6   REGULATORY FRAMEWORK AND INDUSTRIAL RELATIONS

Regulatory framework to manage human resources varies substantially across countries. MNEs are required to adhere to various legislative provisions under the labour laws; compensation and benefit laws; and individual rights laws related to civil rights, immigration, discrimination, and sexual harassment at workplace in countries of their operations which often have considerable differences.

Participation of workers in a company's management, often termed as 'co-determination', began in German coal and steel industries in 1951 giving workers and shareholders representatives each 50 per cent of directorship. The differences are usually resolved mutually both by labour and shareholders representative. Over the years, the phenomenon of co-determination has also become prevalent in other European countries. Terms like 'workers participation' and 'industrial democracy' have become increasingly popular in several other countries, including the US and India to denote increased participation of workers in decision making.

The process through which management and workers identify and determine the job relationship at the workplace is termed as 'labour relationship'. Often the labour relationship is communicated orally, but it may also be informed of written contract mutually negotiated and agreed upon between the management and labour unions.

A 'union' refers to an organization that represents the workers and has the legal authority to negotiate with the employer and administers the labour contract.

An impasse in reaching upon a mutually agreeable settlement between management and labour unions leads to conflict. As a result, a trade union may call for a strike or management may declare a lock-out. Strike refers to a collective refusal to work, aimed at pressurizing the management to accede to union's demands. On the other hand, company management may prevent the workers from entering company premises, a step known as a 'lock-out'. Other strategic options used by labour unions include slow-downs, boycotts, sit-ins, pen-down, or tool-down, etc. Trade unions considerably restrain the strategic options by multinationals in a variety of ways including

- Employing casual or contractual workers and lay-off policies
- Number of personnel employed
- Wage level and negotiability
- Integrating global employment policies

In Europe, especially in northern European countries, collective bargaining either at national or regional basis between an employers' association and an umbrella organization of unions often establishes conditions for the entire industry whereas the negotiations in Japan are on the company level. Trade unions in India and Europe often identify with political ideologies and are politically motivated whereas in the US, emphasis is laid on improving the overall quality of workers' lives. In emerging economies, such as China, India, and South Asia, unions are less prevalent, labour is less powerful, and workers are often compelled to accept work conditions set by management.

Industrial conflicts have to be handled differently in different countries. For instance, strikes and lock-outs in Japan are very rare, it is prohibited in the US and Germany during the period when a labour contract is in effect whereas labour unions are relatively more powerful in the UK and strikes are more prevalent compared to the US. In most countries labour relations are regulated by the government. Therefore, a polycentric approach wherein the HR strategy varies from country to country is more effective and is often adopted in managing labour relations in various subsidiaries across the countries.

This chapter highlights the basic concepts of human resource management in an international context. The basic objective of HRM is to identify, recruit, and retain the best available personnel and consistently motivate them to perform to the best of their abilities so as to achieve the organizational goals. Alternatives available for designing the organizational structures have also been discussed. Various forms and types of international assignments and strategic approaches to HR functions in global context have been elucidated. Special emphasis has been laid on managing expatriates and related concepts, such as culture-shock cycle, expatriate failure, and repatriation. Strategic options available to an international firm for managing its human resources include ethnocentric, polycentric, regiocentric, and geocentric approaches. Principal HR activities in international context have also been discussed.

SUMMARY

Consequent to rapid globalization, managing human resources efficiently has increasingly become crucial to a firm's success in its global business operations. Human resource management refers to all those activities undertaken by a firm to utilize its human resources effectively. Major HRM activities include staffing, managing expatriates, training and development, performance management, compensation, regulatory framework, and industrial relations. Adaptation of HRM functions to international settings is termed as international human resource management. International HRM has also been explained as interplay among three dimensions, i.e., HR activities, types of employees, and countries of operations. The basic differences between domestic and international HRM include increased functional activities, function heterogeneity, increased involvement in employees' personal life, enhanced risks, and increased influence of external environment.

Various types of international organizational structures discussed in this chapter include the export department, international division structure, global organizational structures, i.e., global functional, product, or geographic structure or global matrix and trans-national network structures.

Strategic orientations and practices for IHRM adopted by an international firm include ethnocentric, polycentric, regiocentric, and geocentric approaches. Sources of human resources include host country nationals (HCNs), expatriates who may either be parent country nationals (PCNs), or third country nationals (TCNs) and inpatriates. MNEs have to manage expatriates' cultural shocks on foreign assignments so as to reduce the incidence of expatriate failure.

Selection criteria for international assignments include technical and managerial competence, ability to perform under cross-cultural environment, family attitude towards international assignments, regulatory framework in host countries, and language abilities. Pre-departure training for foreign assignments includes cultural sensitization programmes, preliminary visits, and language and practical training.

Financial remuneration received by the employees in exchange of services rendered to the organization is termed as compensation. Key component of international compensation system include base salary, foreign service premium, and various allowances, such as hardship, cost of living, housing, home leave, and education and relocation allowances besides various benefits, such as insurance, pension, medical, etc. International compensation system may either be home- or host-country-based or a hybrid of the two. Since regulatory framework related to workplace and labour issues differs significantly among countries, the MNEs often adopt a polycentric approach to effectively manage industrial relations.

KEY TERMS

Compensation The financial remuneration that employees receive in exchange of their services rendered to the organization which includes wages, salaries, pay rise, and other monetary issues.

Culture shock Pronounced reaction to psychological disorientation experienced by expatriates.

Expatriate failure Premature return of an expatriate before completion of foreign assignment.

Expatriates Employees who temporarily reside and work outside their home country.

Host country nationals (HCNs) Local employees of the host country hired by an MNE.

Human resource management (HRM) All activities undertaken by an organization to utilize its human resources effectively. It includes staffing, training and development, performance management, compensation, and fulfilling regulatory obligations.

Impatriates Employees, who are foreign citizens, assigned to work in the MNE's home country.

International human resource management (IHRM) Adaptation of all the HRM functions to international settings.

Parent country nationals (PCNs) Employees who are citizens of the country where the MNE is headquartered.

Performance management The process that enables a firm to evaluate the performance of its personnel against pre-defined parameters and consistently improve it so as to achieve the organizational goals.

Recruitment The process by which an organization attracts the most competent people to apply for its job openings.

Repatriation The process of returning home by expatriates after completion of their foreign assignments.

Third country nationals (TCNs) Employees who are citizens of countries other than the country in which they are assigned to work or the country where the MNE is headquartered.

Training The process by which employees acquire skills, knowledge and abilities to perform both their current and future assignments in the organization.

Union An organization that represents the workers and has the legal authority to negotiate with the employer and administers the labour contract.

CONCEPT REVIEW QUESTIONS

1. Explaining the concept of international human resource management, identify the distinguishing features between domestic and international HRM.

2. Elucidate various types of international organizational structures.

3. Evaluate pros and cons of employing host country nationals (HCNs), parent country nationals (PCNs), and third country nationals (TCNs).

4. Briefly discuss the expatriate adjustment process.

5. Describe the key components of an international compensation system.

CRITICAL THINKING QUESTIONS

1. Find out the organizational structures of multinationals, one each from Japan, the US, India, and China. Identify the similarities and differences and make your observations on their strategic perspectives.

2. Identify one company each with a different strategic orientation for human resource management, i.e., ethnocentric, polycentric, regiocentric, and geocentric. Critically evaluate their various HR strategies.

3. Explore various Internet sites providing information about expatriates and carry out a critical comparison.

PROJECT ASSIGNMENTS

1. Meet five professionals who have been overseas on a long-duration assignment and find out their experiences. Identify the differences in their experiences and evaluate your findings on the basis of cultural adjustment process learnt in the chapter.

2. Find out the types and forms of pre-departure trainings provided by three MNEs of different origin. Carry out a critical comparison to arrive at similarities and differences.

18

International Trade Procedures and Documentation

LEARNING OBJECTIVES

> To outline the framework of international trade transactions
> To elucidate the export-import procedures
> To explain incoterms
> To explicate the significance of documentation in international trade transactions
> To discuss commercial and regulatory documents used in international trade

18.1 INTRODUCTION

Over a period of time, international trade transactions evolved a customary and regulatory framework so as to facilitate the smooth flow of cargo from the exporter to the importer and ensure receipt of payment from the importer. In order to carry out cross-country trade, international managers are required to follow a certain set of procedures and deal with a wide range of documents. The exporter needs to comply with rules, regulations, and trade customs of both the exporting and importing countries. Besides, the exporter on one hand has to assure herself/himself of receiving timely payment, while on the other, the importer has to ensure that she/he timely receives the imported cargo in good condition. Further, the cargo is exposed to a number of risks factors, such as damage, fire, loss, and maritime damage due to perils of voyage.

The international trade transaction chain consists of a number of entities that form an integral part of the entire system. It includes a number of government regulatory agencies in both exporting and importing countries, such as government agencies under the ministry of trade, commerce, or industry like the Directorate General of Foreign Trade (DGFT) in India, inspection agencies, insurance companies, customs and central excise, banking institutions, clearing and forwarding (C&F) agents, shipping companies or airlines, carriers for inland transportation, etc.

As exporters and importers are located in two different countries and are governed by different legislative frameworks, the modus operandi of international trade transactions becomes not only crucial but also highly complex. Therefore, international managers have to make themselves fully aware of various legislations governing international trade in the exporting as well as the importing country. The detailed implications of these legislations have already been discussed in detail in previous chapters.

To carry out an international trade transaction, one has to follow various international commercial practices and laws, such as the Carriage of Goods by Sea Act, 1924, Uniform Customs and Practices for Documentary Credit (UCPDC), 1993; International Commercial Terms (INCOTERMS), 2000; etc., and any amendment thereof from time to time. In case of India, the relevant laws/acts include Insurance Act, 1938; Central Excise Act, 1944; Customs Act, 1962; Marine Insurance Act, 1963; The Export (Quality Control and Inspection) Act 1963; Foreign Trade (Development and Regulation) Act, 1992; Foreign Exchange Management Act, 1999; Central Excise Rules, 2001; *Export-Import Policy and Handbook of Procedures* and amendments thereof brought out from time to time by the DGFT; etc.

An illustrative export transaction framework is depicted in Fig. 18.1 in simplified form so as to make the readers appreciate the process. For entering into international markets, an exporter has to identify an importer and strike a deal with him/her. The export contract should explicitly indicate the description of goods, price of each item, net and gross shipping weights, the terms of delivery, the terms of payment, insurance and shipping costs, currency of sales, the port of loading, port of discharge, and estimated shipping date and validity period of the contract.

In an export transaction, the documents are generally routed through banking institutions in the exporter's and importer's country so as to substitute the risk of

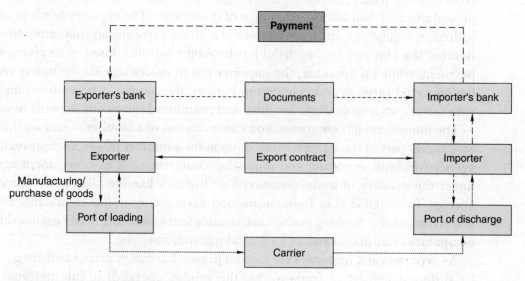

Fig. 18.1   Export transaction framework

Source: Joshi, Rakesh Mohan, *International Marketing,* New Delhi: Oxford University Press, 2005, p. 605.

non-payment by the importer and non-receipt of goods from the exporter. As soon as the export contract is finalized and the payment terms are decided, the exporter initiates action for procurement or manufacturing of goods.

As the documentary requirements and procedure for export transaction is considerably complex, the exporter generally avails services of clearing and forwarding agents at the ports who specialize in these operations. Depending upon the terms of export contract, the export cargo is delivered to the carrier against the receipt of Bills of Lading. The ocean Bills of Lading serve as a receipt of cargo by the shipping company, the contract of transport (or carriage), and a negotiable 'document of title'. Therefore, the goods can be claimed at destination only by the lawful holder of Bills of Lading. As a part of international commercial practices, the Bills of Lading is handed over to the importer by the importer's bank only after payment is made; or in case of usance documents, when the importer makes a commitment to make the payment on a future date. This process ensures receipt of payment to the exporter on one hand and receipt of cargo to the importer on the other. Therefore, international managers have to develop a thorough understanding of export procedures and documentation practices in international trade.

Considerable time is required to export or import merchandise as the complexity of processes involved such as obtaining all the documents, inland transport, customs clearance and inspections, and port and terminal handling procedures, vary across countries. It takes only five days to export and three days for import from Singapore, six and five days from the US, seven days each from Germany, nine and 12 days from Australia, 10 days each from UAE, 10 and 11 days from Japan, 13 days each from the UK, 14 and 19 days from Brazil, 17 and 20 days from India, 18 and 14 days from Malaysia, and 20 and 17 days from Italy for exports and imports respectively as shown in Fig. 18.2. On the other hand, it takes 102 days to export and 101 days for import from Iraq, 36 days each from Russian Federation, 30 and 35 days from South Africa, 24 and 31 days from Tanzania, and 21 and 24 days for exports and imports, respectively, from China. The time taken to effect an export shipment is crucial as each additional day that an export product is delayed is reported to reduce a country's exports by more than 1 per cent. For time-sensitive agricultural products, reducing delays by 10 per cent increases country's exports by more than 30 per cent.[1]

To effect export or import, various costs are incurred for obtaining documents, administrative fees for customs clearance and technical control, terminal handling charges, and inland transport. A cross-country comparison indicates that the cost incurred in exports is the lowest at US$450 per container in Malaysia whereas the cost to import is the lowest at US$439 in Singapore, as shown in Fig. 18.3. In Chad, the per container cost incurred to export and import is US$5,367 and US$6,020,

---

[1] Djankov, Simeon, Caroline Freund, and Cong Pham, 'Trading on Time', Policy Research Working Paper 3909, World Bank, Washington DC, 2007, pp. 2–23.

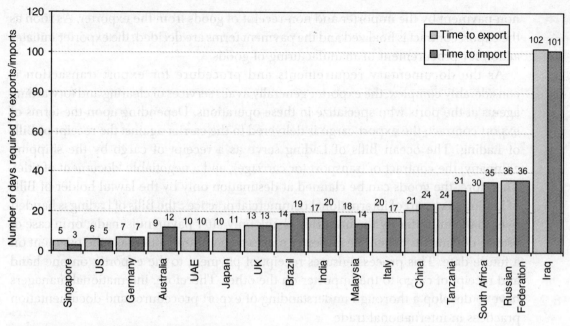

Fig. 18.2   Time required for international trade

Source: 'Trading Across Borders', in *Doing Business 2009*, The International Bank for Reconstruction and Development/World Bank, Washington DC.

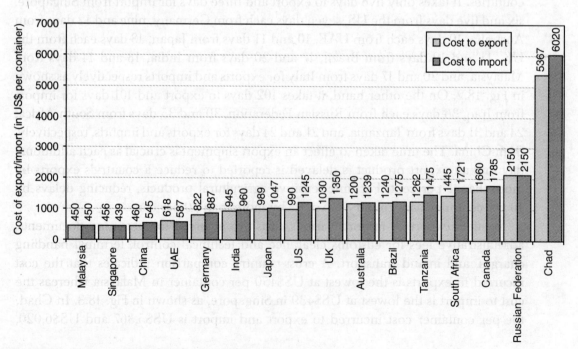

Fig. 18.3   Cost incurred in an international trade transaction

Source: 'Trading across Borders', *Doing Business*, The International Bank for Reconstruction and Development/World Bank, Washington, DC, 2009.

respectively, which is the highest. Interestingly, the cost incurred in exports and imports in India is comparatively lower than many developed countries, including Japan, the US, the UK, and Australia.

Therefore, a thorough understanding of the procedures and documentation involved facilitate decision-making while handling an international transaction. This chapter discusses in detail the step-by-step procedure for executing an export order. The set of international commercial terms, widely known as INCOTERMS, have also been elucidated. Besides, the important regulatory and auxiliary documents, such as commercial invoice, packing list, transport documents, such as Bills of Lading, airways bill, combined transport documents, certificate of origin, inspection and insurance certificates, Bills of Exchange, Shipping Bill, Bill of Entry, mate's receipt, exchange control declaration forms, etc., have also been discussed. Readers may also refer to the sample copies of each of the documents used in international trade transactions given in the CD-ROM accompanying the author's book on International Marketing.[2]

18.2 EXPORT–IMPORT PROCEDURES

The execution of an export order involves a complex procedure wherein the exporter has to come across a number of regulatory and trade agencies. The export procedure involves compliance with the exporting country's legal framework, concluding an export deal, arranging export finance, procuring or manufacturing goods, appointing C&F agent, arranging cargo insurance, booking shipping space, sending documents and goods to C&F agent, customs clearance and port procedures for cargo shipment, submitting documents to bank, and receiving payment from the importer and export incentives from the government or agencies thereof. The flowchart given in Fig. 18.4 summarizes the procedure adopted for exports in order to facilitate readers' understanding.

18.2.1 Compliance with Legal Framework

Each country has its own legal framework for export–import transactions which need to be complied by those entering into international trade. In the process of executing an export order, an exporter needs to interact with the exporting country's principal agency governing international trade, i.e., generally, the ministry of commerce and trade or its body, for example, the DGFT in India, customs and central excise authorities, central bank (e.g., Reserve Bank of India), banks, port trust authorities, insurance company, shipping company or airline, freight forwarders, chambers of commerce, inspection agencies, Export Promotion Council or authority, etc.

[2] Joshi, Rakesh Mohan, *International Marketing*, New Delhi: Oxford University Press, 2005, Annexed CD-ROM.

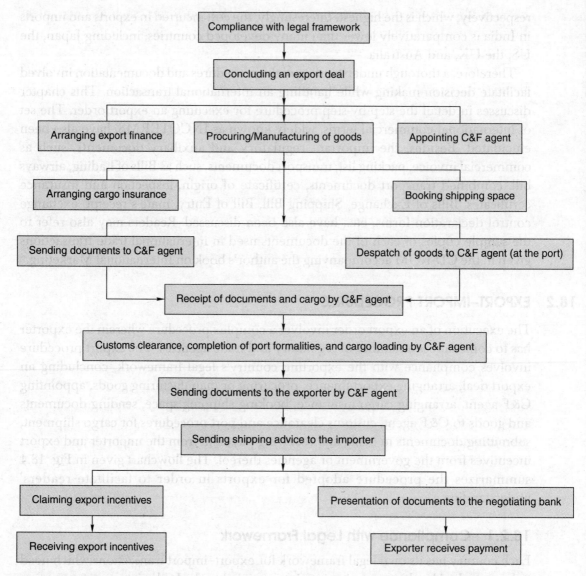

Fig. 18.4   Export procedure flowchart

Source: Joshi, Rakesh Mohan, *International Marketing*, New Delhi: Oxford University Press, 2005, p. 626.

Obtaining import export code number

It is mandatory for every exporter to hold a valid Import-Export Code (IEC) Number for exporting or importing goods from India or into India without which Indian customs would not permit the export-import transaction. The IEC number is required on any other documents prescribed under the Foreign Trade (Development and Regulation) Act, 1992 or the Customs Act, 1962. The IEC number can be obtained from the Regional Authority (RA) under DGFT. This number needs to be mentioned in various international trade documents, including shipping bill or bill of entry as the case may be. It is also required for foreign exchange declaration forms, such as Guaranteed Remittance (GR) forms, to be submitted to the negotiating bank.

In its efforts to simplify the export-import procedures, the Government of India has dispensed with the requirement of obtaining the RBI Code Number from Reserve Bank of India since 1997.

Registration with sales tax and central excise authorities

Goods which are shipped out of the country are generally eligible for exemption from the states' sales tax, central sales tax, and central excise duties. Therefore, Indian exporters are required to get themselves registered with the sales tax authority of the state under the Sales Tax Act varying from state to state.

Both manufacturer and merchant exporters have the option either to deposit the central excise duty at the time of taking goods out of the factory and avail its refund later or take out the goods under a bond to the central excise authority without paying duty. Once the central excise authorities receive the proof of shipment, including Bills of Lading, Shipping Bill and ARE1/ARE2 Form, exporters running bond account is credited.

Registration with export promotion organization

For obtaining benefits under the foreign trade policy, an exporter is required to get registered with an appropriate export promotion organization relating to his or her main line of exports. The application for registration needs to accompany by self-certified copy of IEC Number, issued by the Regional Authority. Besides, Export Promotion Councils, the registration authorities include Marine Products Export Development Authority (MPEDA), Agricultural and Processed Food Products Export Development Authority (APEDA), Commodity Boards, such as Tea Board, Coffee Board, Spices Board, Jute Commissioner, Khadi and Village Industry Commission (KVIC), Development Commissioners of Special Economic Zones (SEZs), and Federation of Indian Export Organisation (FIEO). The Export House or Trading Houses need to get themselves registered with FIEO. Export Promotion Agencies issue a Registration-Cum-Membership Certificate (RCMC) which is valid for five years. Exporters are required to submit regular export returns to the registration agency.

18.2.2   Concluding an Export Deal

While concluding an export deal an exporter should negotiate the terms of the deal in detail, including the price, the product description, packaging, port of shipment, and delivery and payment terms. The process of concluding an export deal is summarized in Fig. 18.5. It is recommended that exporters conclude and comply with the written contract rather than relying on verbal agreements so as to avoid future disputes. However, a substantial amount of exports from India, especially in case of gems and jewellery, garments, handicrafts, handloom, etc., are carried out without written contracts.

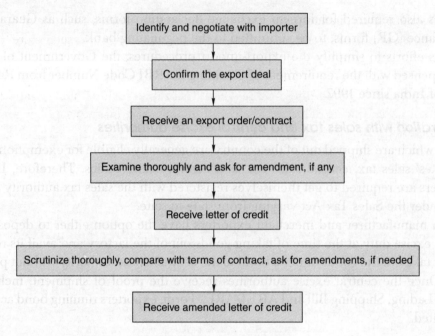

Fig. 18.5 Flowchart for concluding an export deal

Source: Joshi, Rakesh Mohan, *International Marketing,* New Delhi: Oxford University Press, 2005, p. 628.

In case there is no written contract, considerable communication between exporter and importer does take place by way of e-mail, fax, telex, letters, proforma invoice, Letter of Credit, commercial invoice, etc. Under such situations, a 'constructed contract' comes into existence. Thus, under a 'constructed contract', the existence of the contract can be inferred from relevant documents, such as e-mail, fax, telex, proforma invoice, Letter of Credit, commercial invoice, etc. However, in such cases an exporter is required to preserve all these documents carefully.

Depending upon the export product and the importing country, the export contracts may differ, but an exporter should take care of the following aspects:

- Details of contracting party
- Description of products, including quality specifications
- Quantity
- Unit price and total value of the contract
- Packaging
- Marking and labelling
- Inspection requirements for quality, quantity, and packaging as per the inspection agency
- Shipment details, such as the choice of carrier, place of delivery, date of shipment/delivery, port of shipment, trans-shipment, etc.

- Payment terms, including currency, credit period, if any, and mode of payment, such as Letter of Credit (including type of Letter of Credit, such as revocable, irrevocable, confirmed, unconfirmed, etc.)
- Insurance requirement and risk liabilities
- Documentary requirement for payment realization include number and type of invoices, certificate of inspection, certificate of origin, insurance policy, transport document, Bill of Exchange, etc.
- Last date of negotiating documents with bank
- Force *Majeure,* in case of non-performance of contract
- Arbitration
- Jurisdiction

Once an exporter receives an export order as above, she/he should examine it carefully to ensure that it serves her/his capability and interest to execute the export deal. The exporter should also scrutinize it carefully to see if it meets commercial and legal provisions of both the countries of export and import. In case an exporter finds it difficult to fulfil the contractual obligations, such as the quality specifications, delivery schedule, mode of payment, availability of the inspection agency, etc., she/he should ask for an amendment from the importer.

Although export contracts are concluded between two private firms and the government does not interfere in such contracts, these contracts should nevertheless abide by the legislative provisions of both the exporting and importing countries.

Generally, an exporter prepares a proforma invoice mentioning details of the description of goods, number and kind of packaging, marks and container numbers, quantity, rate, amount, etc., as per the contract. The importer returns the signed copy of the proforma invoice, which becomes part of an export contract. The exporter should also examine the Letter of Credit for any discrepancy and ask for amendment, if needed.

18.2.3 Arranging Export Finance

The exporters may avail packing credit facility from commercial banks, generally at concessional rates, for manufacturing, purchasing, and packaging of goods. Export credit is extended to exporters to meet their working capital requirements. Pre-shipment credit is generally provided for the following activities:

- Packing credit or shipping loan in local currency, e.g., in Rupees in India
- Packing credit advance in foreign currencies
- Advances against export incentives
- Import financing for opening Letter of Credit for the importing goods needed as input for manufacture of export goods
- Export credit, normally given on collateral security through a third party guarantee or mortgage of immovable property

The procedure followed for disbursement of export credit is discussed here:

- The exporter has to submit an evidence of export, such as an irrevocable Letter of Credit issued by a reputed international bank or confirmed order placed by a foreign buyer.
- The bank calculates the amount of packing credit to be granted which generally does not exceed FOB value of the goods.
- Generally, banks fix 10 to 25 per cent as margin (i.e., exporters' contribution) and release the funds debiting to the packing credit amount and credit to the exporters' account.
- The exporter would be required to send the goods through approved transport and forwarding agency.
- Besides, exporters are also required to take adequate insurance while warehousing and transport of goods.

The details of export credit are discussed in Chapter 15.

18.2.4 Procuring or Manufacturing of Goods

After receiving the confirmed export order, the exporting firm should make preparations for the procurement or production of goods (Fig. 18.6), as the case may be, for merchant or manufacturing exporter respectively. Different companies have their own internal communication systems which generally involve sending a 'delivery note' in duplicate to the factory for manufacture and dispatch of goods to the given port of shipment. The delivery note should mention in clear terms the description of goods, the quantity, quality specifications, packaging and labelling requirements, the date by which the

Fig.18.6   Procuring or manufacturing of goods for exports

Source: Joshi, Rakesh Mohan, *International Marketing*, New Delhi: Oxford University Press, 2005, p. 630.

goods should be manufactured, and the details of formalities, such as pre-shipment inspection and central excise clearance. In case of merchant exporters, similar activities follow in case of procurement of goods instead of their production.

18.2.5 Pre-shipment Inspection

At the time of exports before clearing the shipment, customs authorities require submission of an inspection certificate in compliance with the rules and regulations of the exporting country under force regarding compulsory quality control and pre-shipment inspection. Under the Export Quality Control and Inspection Act, 1963, about 1000 commodities, including the major groups of fisheries, food and agriculture, organic and inorganic chemicals, light engineering, jute products, etc., are subject to compulsory pre-shipment inspection. Inspection of export goods may be carried out in one or more of the following manners:

- In-process quality control
- Self-certification
- Consignment-wise quality control

The pre-shipment inspection should be completed before the consignment is sealed by the excise authorities. The exporter has to apply to the nominated export inspection agency for conducting the pre-shipment and quality control inspection for the export consignment and obtain an inspection or quality certificate conforming to the prescribed specifications. This inspection certificate would be required for customs clearance of cargo before shipment.

18.2.6 Central Excise Clearance on Goods for Exports

The exports are free from the incidence of indirect taxes as per internationally accepted practice. Therefore, all goods exported from India are exempt from payment of central excise duties. The act also provides rebate on excise duty levied both on inputs used for manufacture of export products and the final export production under the 'Export Rebate/Exemption Scheme' of Rule 18 of Central Excise (No. 2) Rules, 2001 under the Central Excise Act, 1944. Soon after manufacturing the goods, for getting the central excise clearance, the exporter has to adopt any one of the following options available:

Option 1: Export of goods under claim for excise duty rebate

Under this procedure, the exporter first makes payment on the excise duty and subsequently gets refund (rule 18). Complete refund of excise duty paid on raw materials used for exports and excisable finished goods for exports is allowed except for exports to Nepal and Bhutan. However, in case the exporter has availed the benefits under the Duty Drawback Scheme or the Central Value Added Tax Credit (CENVAT) on excisable inputs, she/he is not eligible for refund of the excise duty paid.

The exporter has an option to get the goods examined and sealed by central excise authorities at his/her own premises before removal of goods for exports so that the goods are not examined at the port/airport by the customs authorities. The exporter prepares six copies of ARE1/ARE2 forms and submits them to superintendent of central excise having jurisdiction over the premises of the exporter. The superintendent may depute an inspector of central excise or may in person carry out inspection and sealing of export cargo. The central excise authorities put their seal on the cargo after its examination and their satisfaction.

Option II: Export of goods under bond

Exporters are allowed to remove excisable goods for exports or inputs for export production from the place of manufacture or warehouse without payment of excise duty under rule 19 using the following procedure:

(i) Examination of goods at the place of dispatch The exporter submits four copies of ARE-1 to the jurisdictional central excise authority. However, the exporter has an option to submit the fifth copy of ARE-1 for availing any export facility for her/his record. On the basis of information furnished, the concerned central excise authority identifies and examines the goods in accordance with rules and regulations laid down in the export import policy and other related regulations in force. After conforming to these requirements, the goods are allowed to be sealed and an endorsement is made on all the copies of ARE-1 form that the goods have been examined, sealed, and are permitted for exports.

The original and duplicate copies of ARE-1 form are given to the exporter, the triplicate is sent to the central excise (bond) authority and the quadruplicate copy is kept for the purpose of central excise records. At the time of shipment, the exporter encloses the original and duplicate copy of the ARE-1 form with the Shipping Bill to the customs at the port of loading. Customs authorities verify the examination report and the seal on the goods and permits goods for loading on board the carrier. Subsequently, an endorsement is made on the original and duplicate copy of ARE-1 by the customs. The original endorsed copy is handed over to the exporter and the duplicate is sent to the concerned central excise authorities. The exporter submits the original copy endorsed by customs to the concerned central excise authorities as a proof of exports and gets his/her obligation under Legal Undertaking (LUT) or Bond discharged.

(ii) Removal of goods under self certification An exporter can move the goods from the factory or warehouse under self-certification in the ARE-1 form. The original and duplicate copies are sent along with the goods while the third and fourth copies are sent to the concerned central excise authorities within 24 hours of removal of goods for verification and record. The endorsement is made by the customs on ARE-1 and export is allowed. The exporter submits the original and duplicate to the customs as a proof of exports and discharges his/her obligation under LUT or bond.

(iii) Examination of goods at the place of export This is similar to the procedure discussed in the preceding section but in this case, the physical examination of goods is carried out by the customs authorities as per the information furnished in the ARE-1 form. Subsequently, goods are allowed to be exported and the exporters' obligation under LUT/bond is discharged.

However, the following conditions need to be observed for central excise clearance:

- The central excise duty leviable on the goods should not exceed the bond amount
- The goods meant for exports must be exported within a period of six months after clearance. However, the period can be extended by the competent central excise authority in special cases.
- Proof of export of goods is mandatory for getting LUT or bond discharged.

(iv) Removal of excisable inputs for export production The central excise rules provide facility for procurement of excisable goods without payment of excise duty to be used as input in export production. To avail this facility the manufacturer exporter is required to register under rule 9 of Central Excise (No. 2) Rule, 2001. The manufacturer exporter has to furnish details of input-output ratio and the rate of excise duty levied on such excisable goods. After verification and countersigning by the competent central excise authority, the exporter may avail benefit of removing the goods used as inputs for production without payment of duty. The goods are exported under this case using ARE-2 formalities which are similar to ARE-1.

As a rule, central excise authorities are required to settle all claims within three months from the date of acceptance. For any delay beyond three months, the exporter becomes eligible for getting interest.

18.2.7 Packaging, Marking, and Labelling of Goods

Proper packaging of export cargo facilitates in minimizing transit and delivery costs and losses. Besides, the insurance companies also insist upon adequate packaging for settling the claims. After packaging, marking of the packages is done so as to facilitate identification of goods during handling, transportation, and delivery. Labelling contains detailed instructions and is carried out by affixing labels on the packs or by stencils.

18.2.8 Appointment of Clearing and Forwarding Agents

Clearing and forwarding (C&F) agents or freight forwarders are essential links in international trade operations. They carry out a number of functions, including the following:

- Advising exporters on choice of shipping routes
- Reservation of shipping space
- Inland transportation at port
- Packing
- Studying provisions of L/C or contract and taking necessary action accordingly

- Warehousing insurance
- Complying with port, shipping, and customs formalities
- Arranging overseas transport service
- Rendering assistance in filing claims
- Monitoring movements of goods to the importer
- General advisory services

The export department of the company prepares detailed instructions regarding shipment of consignment and sends the following documents to the C&F agent:

- Original export order/export contract
- Original letter of credit
- Commercial invoice
- GR forms (original and duplicate) indicating the IEC number
- Certificate of origin
- Inspection/quality control certificate
- Purchase memo (in case of merchant exporters)
- Railway receipt/truck/lorry receipt
- Consular/customs invoice (if required)
- ARE-1/ARE-2 forms
- Declaration form (in triplicate) by the exporter that the value, specifications, quality, and description of goods mentioned in the shipping bill are in accordance with the export contract and statement made in shipping bill are true.

18.2.9 Arranging Cargo Insurance

The marine insurance cover is arranged by the export department soon after receiving the documents and obtaining insurance policy in duplicate. The liability to take the insurance cover is determined by the conditions of the export contract. In case of FOB and CFR contracts, the importer has to obtain the insurance cover once the cargo is loaded 'on board' the vessel. In case of CIF contacts, the insurance is to be arranged by the exporter but the policy is to be endorsed in favour of the importer. The nature of risk coverage and insurable value is also specified in the export contract. Other procedural formalities such as arranging ECGC cover, certificate of origin, consular invoice etc., are completed at this stage.

18.2.10 Booking Shipping Space

While obtaining the excise clearance and pre-shipment inspection by the manufacturing office, the export department gets the shipping space reserved in the vessel by sending shipping instructions either through the C&F agent or through freight broker who works on behalf of the shipping company. Once the space is reserved, the shipping company issues shipping order as a proof of space reservation.

18.2.11   Dispatch of Goods to Port

On receiving information on reservation of shipping space, the production department makes arrangements for transport of goods to the port of shipment, either by road and obtaining lorry/truck receipt or by rail and obtaining railway receipt. The goods are generally consigned to the port town in the name of the C&F agent. Indian Railways allots wagons on priority basis for transportation of export cargo to the port of shipment for which the following document are required to be submitted:

- Forwarding note (a railway document)
- Shipping order (proof of booking shipping space)
- Receipt of wagon registration fee

After the loading of goods is completed in the allotted wagons, the railway department issues railway receipt (RR). At this stage, the manufacturing office prepares a 'Dispatch Advice' and sends it to the export department along with the following documents:

- Railway receipt/lorry/truck receipt
- ARE-1/2 form
- Inspection certificate

18.2.12   Port Procedures and Customs Clearance

At the port town, procedure for the customs clearance and other port formalities are relatively complex which need not only the knowledge of export procedures but also the ability to get the shipment speedily with least hassles. Therefore, exporters generally avail the services of C&F agents. The activities related to port procedures and customs clearance for exports from India are summarized for ease of understanding in Fig. 18.7.

After receiving the documents, the C&F agent takes delivery of the consignment from the road transportation company or the railway station. The cargo is stored in C&F agent's warehouse till shipment. Soon after receiving the cargo, the C&F agent initiates action to obtain customs clearance and seek permission of port authorities for bringing the cargo to the shipment shed.

Customs departments in all countries are entrusted with control of export-import of goods in compliance to the law of the land. The basic objectives of customs control are

- To ensure that goods exported out of the country or imported in to the country comply with various regulations related to export-import
- To ensure authenticity of value of goods in the export-import trade and check under-invoicing or over-invoicing.
- To accurately assess and collect the customs duty, wherever applicable
- To compile the data

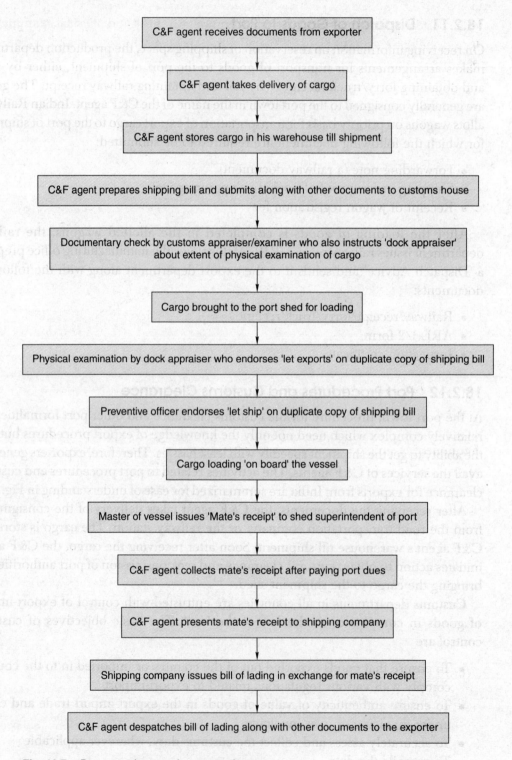

C&F agent receives documents from exporter

C&F agent takes delivery of cargo

C&F agent stores cargo in his warehouse till shipment

C&F agent prepares shipping bill and submits along with other documents to customs house

Documentary check by customs appraiser/examiner who also instructs 'dock appraiser' about extent of physical examination of cargo

Cargo brought to the port shed for loading

Physical examination by dock appraiser who endorses 'let exports' on duplicate copy of shipping bill

Preventive officer endorses 'let ship' on duplicate copy of shipping bill

Cargo loading 'on board' the vessel

Master of vessel issues 'Mate's receipt' to shed superintendent of port

C&F agent collects mate's receipt after paying port dues

C&F agent presents mate's receipt to shipping company

Shipping company issues bill of lading in exchange for mate's receipt

C&F agent despatches bill of lading along with other documents to the exporter

Fig. 18.7 Port procedures and customs clearance

Source: Joshi, Rakesh Mohan, *International Marketing,* New Delhi: Oxford University Press, 2005, p. 637.

The customs department makes both documentary check and physical examination of goods before clearance. The C&F agent prepares the shipping bill and submits the following documents to the customs house for their clearance:

- Shipping bill (4–5 copies)
- Export order/contract
- Letter of credit (original), where applicable
- Commercial invoice (one each for Shipping Bill)
- GR form (original and duplicate)
- Inspection certificate (original)
- ARE-1/ARE-2 form (original and duplicate)
- Packing list, if required
- Any other document needed by the customs

These documents are examined by the customs appraiser for

- Compliances with the rules, regulations, and other procedural requirements for exports
- Declaration of value and quantity in the shipping bill vis-à-vis export order or letter of credit

After value appraisal and examination of documents, the customs appraiser/examiner makes an endorsement on the duplicate copy of the shipping bill and gives direction to the dock appraiser to the extent of physical inspection required to be made at the docks. Except for the original shipping bill, original GR form and a copy of commercial invoice, all documents are returned to the C&F agent.

The C&F agent submits the Port Trust Copy of the shipping bill to the shed superintendent of port trust and obtains order for carting the cargo in the transit shed for physical examination by the dock appraiser. In case of shed cargo, separate dock challan is prepared, while in case of ship loading over-side, no separate dock challan is needed and the dock charges are mentioned in the shipping bill itself. For having the physical examination carried out by the dock appraiser, the following documents need to be submitted:

- Shipping bill (duplicate, triplicate, and export promotion copies)
- Commercial invoice
- Packing list
- Inspection certificate (original)
- ARE-1/ARE-2 form
- GR form (duplicate)

After conducting the physical examination, the dock appraiser endorses 'Let Export' on the duplicate copy of the shipping bill and hands it over to the forwarding agent along with all other documents. The forwarding agent then presents these documents to the preventive officer of the customs department who supervises loading of cargo on vessel, examines and checks content, weight, etc., and makes an endorsement 'Let Ship' on the duplicate copy of shipping bill. This endorsement authorizes the shipping company to accept the cargo in the vessel for shipment.

On completion of loading 'on board', the master of the vessel issues 'mate's receipt' to the shed superintendent of the port. The C&F agent takes delivery of the mate's receipt after payment of port charges to the port authorities. The mate's receipt is presented to the preventive officer, who makes certification that shipments has taken place on all the copies of the shipping bill, original and duplicate copies of ARE-1/ARE-2 form, and all other copies which need post-shipment endorsement from the customs. The mate's receipt is presented to the shipping company, which in turn issues bills of lading (two or three negotiable in original and about 10 non-negotiable copies) in its exchange.

The bills of lading is prepared in strict accordance to the mate's receipt. The exporter has to ensure that the bills of lading is 'clean on board' since 'claused' or 'dirty' Bills of lading are generally not acceptable to the importer unless otherwise specifically stipulated in the letter of credit.

18.2.13 Dispatch of Documents to the Exporter

Soon after obtaining the bills of lading from the shipping company, the C&F agent sends the following documents to the exporter:

- Full set of 'clean on board' bills of lading
- Copies of commercial invoice attested by customs
- Duty drawback copy of shipping bill
- Original export order/export contract
- Original letter of credit
- Copies of consular invoice/customs invoice, if any
- ARE-1/ARE-2 forms
- GR form (duplicate)

18.2.14 Sending Shipment Advice

Soon after the shipment, the exporter sends a shipment advice to the importer intimating the importer about the date of shipment, name of the vessel, and it's expected time of arrival (ETA) at the port of discharge. The shipment advice is accompanied by commercial invoice, packing list (if any), and a non-negotiable copy of bills of lading so as to enable the importer to take delivery of the shipment.

18.2.15 Presentation of Documents at the Negotiating Bank

Soon after the shipment, the exporter has to present the documents to the negotiating bank as under:

- Bill of exchange (first and second of original)

- Commercial invoice (two or more copies as required)
- Full set of 'clean on board' bills of lading (all negotiable and non-negotiable as required)
- GR form (Duplicate)
- Export order/contract
- Letter of credit (Original)
- Packing list
- Marine insurance policy (two copies)
- Consular and/or customs invoice, if required
- Bank certificate (in the prescribed form)

The negotiating banks thoroughly scrutinize all the documents strictly as per the terms of the letter of credit. The bank sends a set of documents to the issuing (importer's) bank by two consecutive airmails so as to ensure delivery of documents to the importer's bank and subsequently, subject to fulfilment of importer's payment obligations as already agreed upon, the importer's bank hands over these documents to the importer to enable him/her to take delivery of the cargo at destination. The set of documents sent by the negotiating bank to the issuing bank includes:

- Bill of exchange
- Commercial invoice
- Negotiable bills of lading
- Insurance policy
- Customs/consular invoice, if any
- Packing list (if any)
- Inspection/quality control certificate
- Certificate of origin

The payment is made by the negotiating bank on receipt of these documents. Once the payment is received from the importer's bank, the duplicate copy of the GR form is directly transmitted by the negotiating bank to the Exchange Control Department of the RBI. The exporter is returned the original copy of bank certificate along with attested copies of commercial invoice. The authorized dealer forwards the duplicate copy of the bank certificate to the jurisdictional DGFT office.

18.2.16 Claiming Export Incentives

Soon after the shipment, the exporter files claims for getting export incentives as follows.

Claiming excise rebate

After the shipment, the exporter or his/her C&F agent files claim with the Maritime Commissioner of Central Excise in the port town or jurisdictional central excise authorities for getting refund of the excise duty paid or getting credit in the Personal

Ledger Account (PLA) and getting discharge of bond liabilities. The duplicate copy ARE-1/ARE-2 certified by customs and a non-negotiable copy of bill of lading or shipping bill are the only documents required for the purpose.

Receiving duty drawback

The exporter has to file duty drawback claim with the drawback department of customs by submitting drawback claim proforma, bank or customs certified copy of commercial invoice, and non-negotiable copy of bills of lading. After examining the exporter's claim, the duty drawback claim amount is sent to the exporter's bank under her/his intimation.

18.3 TERMS OF DELIVERY IN INTERNATIONAL TRADE TRANSACTIONS

In an international transaction, a set of trade terms is often used to describe the rights and responsibilities of the buyer and the seller with regard to sale and transport of goods. Uniform rules for interpretation of international commercial terms (incoterms) defining the costs, risks, and obligations of buyers and sellers in international transactions have been developed by the International Chamber of Commerce (ICC) in Paris. These incoterms were first published in 1936 and have subsequently been revised to account for changing modes of transport and document delivery. Incoterms 2000 is the current version in force. Although it is difficult to cover all possible legal and transportation issues in an international transaction, incoterms provide a sort of contractual shorthand among various parties. Incoterms 2000 facilitate the contracting parties

(i) To complete sale of goods
(ii) To indicate each contracting party's costs, risks, and obligations, with regard to delivery of the goods as follows:
- When is the delivery completed?
- How does a party ensure that the other party has met that standard of conduct?
- Which party must comply with requisite licenses and government-imposed formalities?
- What are the mode and terms of carriage?
- What are the delivery terms and what is required as proof of delivery?
- When is the risk of loss transferred from the seller to the buyer?
- How will transport costs be divided between the parties?
- What notices are the parties required to give to each other regarding the transport and transfer of the goods?
(iii) To establish basic terms of transport and delivery in a short format

Various categories of incoterms used for departure, shipment, and main carriage unpaid and paid and delivery terms vis-à-vis their applicability to the mode of transport are given in Exhibit 18.1.

	Exhibit 18.1 Incoterms 2000 and its applicability	
Category	**Applicable for sea transport only**	**Applicable for all modes of transport (including water)**
E terms: Departure terms		EXW (Ex works)
F terms: Shipment terms, main carriage unpaid	FAS (Free alongside ship) FOB (Free on board)	FCA (Free carrier)
C terms: Shipment terms, main carriage paid	CFR (Cost and freight) CIF (Cost, insurance, and freight)	CPT (Carriage paid to) CIP (Carriage and insurance paid to)
D terms: Delivery terms	DES (Delivered ex ship) DEQ (Delivered ex quay)	DAF (Delivered at frontier) DDU (Delivered duty unpaid) DDP (Delivered duty paid)

Source: Based on Joshi, Rakesh Mohan, *International Marketing*, New Delhi: Oxford University Press, 2005, p. 383.

Incoterms 2000 include a set of 13 terms as under:

EXW (Ex works) *named place*   Any mode of transport is used; the seller makes goods available to buyer at the seller's premises or other location, not cleared for export and not loaded on a vehicle. The buyer bears all risks and costs involved in taking the goods from the seller's premises and thereafter.

FCA (Free carrier) *named place*   Any mode of transport used; seller delivers goods, cleared for export, to the carrier named by the buyer at the specified place. If delivery occurs at the seller's premises, the seller is responsible for loading; if delivery occurs elsewhere, the seller must load the conveyance but is not responsible for unloading.

FAS (Free alongside ship) *named port of shipment*   Maritime and inland waterway only; the seller delivers when the goods are placed alongside the vessel at the named port of shipment. The seller also clears the goods for export.

FOB (Free on board) *named port of shipment*   Maritime and inland waterway only; the seller delivers when the goods pass the ship's rail at the named port. The seller clears the goods for export.

CFR (Cost and freight) *named port of destination*   Maritime and inland waterway only; the seller delivers when the goods pass the ship's rail at the port of export. The seller pays cost and freight for bringing the goods to the foreign port and clears the goods for export.

CIF (Cost, insurance, and freight) *named port of destination*   Maritime and inland waterway only; the seller delivers when the goods pass the ship's rail at the port of export. The seller pays cost and freight for bringing the goods to the foreign port, obtains insurance against the buyer's risk of loss or damage, and clears the goods for export.

CIP (Carriage and insurance paid to) *named place of destination* Any mode of transport; the seller delivers the goods to a carrier it nominates but also pays the cost of bringing the goods to the named destination. The seller also obtains insurance against the buyer's risk of loss or damage during carriage and clears the goods for export.

CPT (Carriage paid to) *named place of destination* Any mode of transport; the seller delivers goods to the carrier it nominates and pays costs of bringing goods to the named destination. The seller also clears the goods for export.

DAF (Delivered at frontier) *named place* Any mode of transport to a land frontier; the seller delivers when goods are placed at the buyer's disposal on the 'arriving means of transport' (not unloaded), cleared for export but not cleared for import before the customs border of the destination country.

DES (Delivered ex ship) *named port of destination* Maritime and inland waterway only; the seller delivers when goods are at the buyer's disposal on board the ship not cleared for import. The buyer pays discharging costs.

DEQ (Delivered quay) *named port of destination* Maritime and inland waterway only; the seller delivers when the goods are placed at the buyer's disposal, not cleared for import, on the dock (quay) at the named port of destination. The seller pays discharging costs, but the buyer pays for import clearance.

DDU (Delivered duty unpaid) *named place of destination* Any mode of transport; the seller delivers the goods to the buyer not cleared for import and not unloaded from the arriving means of transport at the named destination, but the buyer is responsible for all import clearance formalities and costs.

DDP (Delivered duty paid) *named place of destination* Any mode of transport; the seller delivers goods to the buyer, cleared for import (including import licence, duties, and taxes) but not unloaded from the means of transport.

The rights and obligations of buyers and sellers indicating their responsibility in an international sales transaction have been indicated in Fig. 18.8. Ex-works (EXW) involves lowest obligation while the DDP involves highest obligation for a seller. However, one has to decide upon the delivery terms in view of prevailing trade practices and competitive structure of the market.

The price quotation under various incoterms should include the expenses as mentioned. For instance, Mayank International, a Jaipur-based export firm, has to make price quotations for 1000 pieces of greeting cards made from hand-made paper. The firm decides to offer a unit price of US$5 per piece that works out to a total price

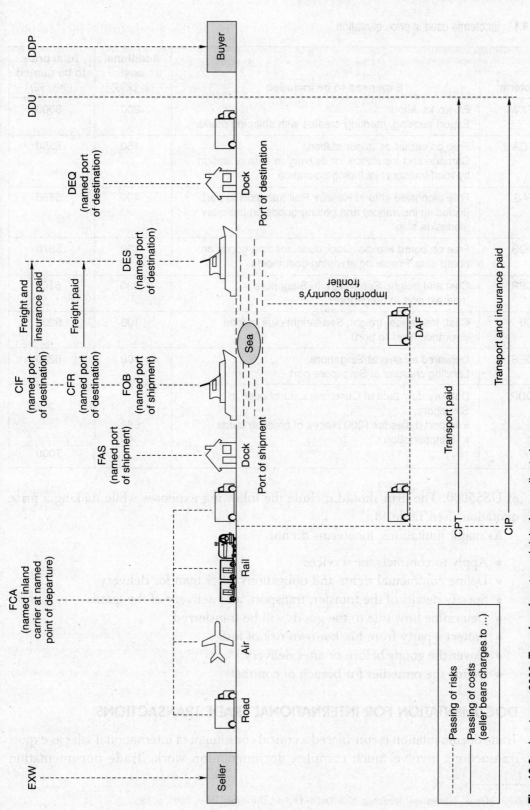

Fig. 18.8 Incoterms 2000: Transfer of costs and risks from seller to buyer

- - - - - Passing of risks
——— Passing of costs (seller bears charges to ...)

* Export clearance is taken by the seller under all terms except EXW and import clearance is taken by the buyer except under DDP.

Table 18.1   Incoterms used in price quotation

Incoterm	Expenses to be included	Additional cost (in US$)	Total price to be quoted (in US$)
EXW	Ex-works Jaipur Export packing, marking creates with shipping marks	200	5000
FCA	Free on carrier at Jaipur station. Carriage and insurance for delivery to railway station by road transport including insurance	150	5350
FAS	Free alongside ship at Kandla. Rail transport to port (including insurance) and getting goods on the quay alongside ship	400	5750
FOB	Free on board Kandla. Dock dues, loading goods on board ship. Preparing shipping documents	120	5870
CFR	Cost and freight. Sea freight to Singapore (nearest port to Singapore)	330	6100
CIF	Cost, insurance, freight. Sea freight plus marine insurance (port to port)	100	6200
DES	Delivered ex ship at Singapore. Landing charges at Singapore port	80	6280
DDP	Delivery duty paid at Customer's warehouse in Singapore. ■ Import duties for 1000 pieces of greeting cards ■ Transportation	680 40	7000

of US$5000. The firm should include the following expenses while making a price quotation[3] (see Table 18.1).

As major limitations, incoterms do not

- Apply to contracts for services
- Define contractual rights and obligations other than for delivery
- Specify details of the transfer, transport, and delivery of the goods
- Determine how title to the goods will be transferred
- Protect a party from his/her own risk of loss
- Cover the goods before or after delivery
- Define the remedies for breach of contract

18.4   DOCUMENTATION FOR INTERNATIONAL TRADE TRANSACTIONS

Trade documentation is considered a critical constituent of international sales as export transactions involve much complex documentation work. Trade documentation

---

[3] Joshi, Rakesh Mohan, *International Marketing*, New Delhi: Oxford University Press, 2005, p. 386.

facilitates international transactions, protecting interests of exporters and importers located in two different countries governed by different statutory and legislative frameworks. The successful execution of an export order ensuring physical delivery of goods and remittance of sale proceeds is as important as procurement of an export order and sourcing or production of goods for exports. An export manager should carry out the documentation meticulously so as to avoid problems related to smooth flow of goods and getting remittances from overseas importers.

Certain documents are essential in international trade as a matter of 'customs of international trade' and conventions governing international commercial practices. Besides, some documents are required to fulfil the statutory requirements of both exporting and importing countries, such as the export import trade control, foreign exchange regulations, pre-shipment inspections, central excise and customs requirements, etc. In an international trade transaction, a number of trade intermediaries and government authorities are inevitably involved[4], such as government agencies monitoring international trade, e.g., DGFT, export promotion councils, export inspection agencies, shipping companies, freight forwarders, insurance companies, banks, port trust, central excise, custom authorities, etc., which have their own documentary requirements. Strict compliance with procedural formalities and fulfilling documentary requirements need meticulous planning and desired skills for successful consummation of an export order.

Consequences of poorly completed documentation

Poor documentation may result in a number of problems in executing an export order which may lead to additional costs to the exporter. These costs[5] may be of three types:

- The cost of interest charges incurred by exporters as a result of delays in receiving payment
- The cost of putting the problem right, such as telephone bills, courier charges for sending replacement documents, bank charges for amending documents, such as letter of credit and, possibly, loss of credit insurance cover
- Perhaps the most serious, but also the most difficult to quantify, is the cost to the relationship between the exporter and the customer. More often than not, a new customer will be so upset by poor documentation and the problems that it causes that she/he will be reluctant to do further business with such an exporter.

The number of documents required for exports and imports vary considerably across countries. Merely two documents are required each for exports and imports from France, as shown in Fig. 18.9, whereas three and four from Canada, four documents

---

[4] 'Standardized Pre-shipment Export Documentation', Export Facilitation Committee of India, Ministry of Commerce, Government of India, New Delhi, 1990, pp. 1–42.

[5] *ITC Training Handbook of Export Documentation*, UNCTAD/GATT, International Trade Centre, Geneva, 1994, pp. 2–23.

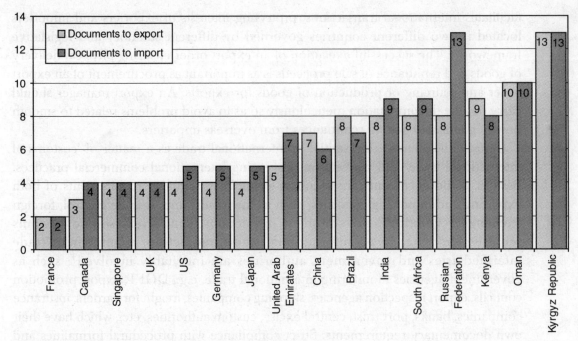

Fig. 18.9 Number of documents required for exports and imports

Source: 'Trading Across Borders', *Doing Business*, The International Bank for Reconstruction and Development/World Bank, Washington DC, 2009.

each from Singapore and the UK, four and five each from the US, Germany and Japan, five and seven from UAE, seven and six from China, eight and seven from Brazil, eight and nine documents each for exports and imports, respectively, from India and South Africa. However, 13 documents each for exports and imports are required from Kyrgyz Republic, 10 each from Oman, nine and eight from Kenya, and eight and 13 documents each for exports and imports, respectively, from Russian Federation.

Adaptation of Aligned Documentation System in India

Prior to 1990, the form of documents and related formalities which had been developed by different government agencies and authorities in India were aimed to suit their own individual requirements with little regard to inter-relationship of different documents and their effects on total documentation burden in an export transaction. For instance, quotations and invoices made by various exporters used to differ widely. Even the regulatory documents used by different government departments had little synergy. Moreover, all these documents were to be prepared individually and separately, which were highly prone to errors and discrepancies. As a result, export documentation in India became extremely complicated and overlapping in nature.

The aligned documentation system (ADS) is a methodology of creating information on a set of standard forms printed on a paper of same size in such a way that items of identical specification occupy the same position on each form. The basic objectives of ADS are

(a) To simplify and prioritize information required by various commercial interests and government agencies and align it in a standardized format.
(b) To achieve economy of time and effort involved in the prevailing methodology of export documentation

The commercial documents under ADS are prepared on a uniform and standard A4 size paper (210 mm × 297 mm) while the regulatory documents are prepared on full-scale paper (34.5 cm × 21.5 cm). All the documents were aligned to one another in such a way that common items of information are given in the same relative slots in each of the documents included in the system. Based on the UN layout key, the ADS provides an effective alternative to repetitive, dilatory, and unproductive methods of preparation of export documents. The ADS documentation system in India was implemented in 1990–91.

For the purpose of the understanding of an export manager, these documents may be divided into two main categories, i.e., commercial and regulatory documents. An overview of pre-shipment export documents is summarized in Fig. 18.10.

18.4.1 Commercial Documents

Commercial documents are defined as those documents which, by customs of trade, are required to be prepared and used by exporters and importers in discharge of their respective legal and other incidental responsibilities under the sales contract. These are required for effecting physical transfer of goods and their title from exporter to the importer and realization of export sale proceeds. These documents have to be prepared strictly as per the terms of the letter of credit, which has been discussed separately in Chapter 15. It should also be kept in mind while carrying out documentation work that banks deal in documents and not the goods.[6] Therefore, the documents have to be prepared meticulously with due diligence. The principal commercial documents are discussed below.

Commercial invoice

Commercial invoice is the key document for an export transaction and must be prepared by the exporter. Since it is the basic export document, it should provide information as comprehensive as possible. Besides, the information provided should be mentioned clearly and accurately so as to make it understandable to a person with limited knowledge of the language used.

A commercial invoice contains information on the exporter's detail, the consignee's detail, as country of origin of goods, country of final destination, terms of delivery and

---

[6] Uniform Customs and Practices for Documentary Credit, International Chamber of Commerce (ICC Publication No. 600).

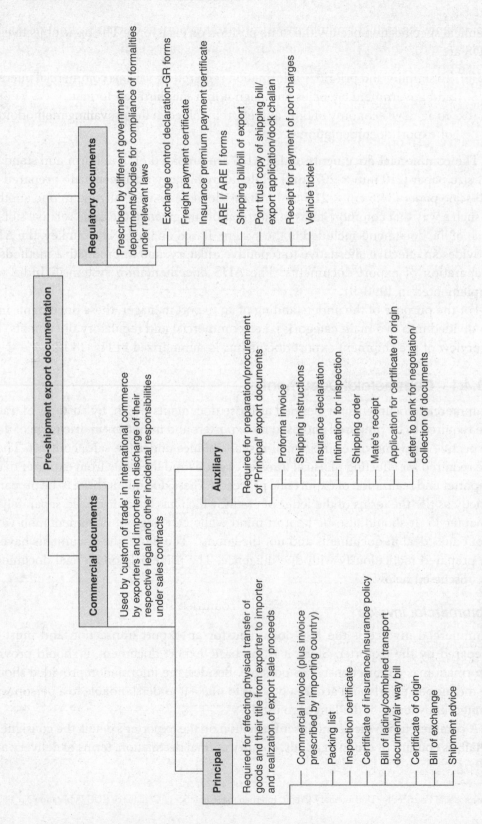

Principal

Required for effecting physical transfer of goods and their title from exporter to importer and realization of export sale proceeds

- Commercial invoice (plus invoice prescribed by importing country)
- Packing list
- Inspection certificate
- Certificate of insurance/insurance policy
- Bill of lading/combined transport document/air way bill
- Certificate of origin
- Bill of exchange
- Shipment advice

Auxiliary

Required for preparation/procurement of 'Principal' export documents

- Proforma invoice
- Shipping instructions
- Insurance declaration
- Intimation for inspection
- Shipping order
- Mate's receipt
- Application for certificate of origin
- Letter to bank for negotiation/collection of documents

Commercial documents

Used by 'custom of trade' in international commerce by exporters and importers in discharge of their respective legal and other incidental responsibilities under sales contracts

Pre-shipment export documentation

Regulatory documents

Prescribed by different government departments/bodies for compliance of formalities under relevant laws

- Exchange control declaration-GR forms
- Freight payment certificate
- Insurance premium payment certificate
- ARE I/ ARE II forms
- Shipping bill/bill of export
- Port trust copy of shipping bill/export application/dock challan
- Receipt for payment of port charges
- Vehicle ticket

Fig. 18.10   Framework of international trade documentation

payment, vessel/flight number, port of loading, port of discharge, final destination, marks and numbers, number and kind of packaging, detailed description of goods, quantity and rate, and total amount payable. As a customary trade practice, soon after striking an export deal, the exporter prepares a proforma invoice and sends it to the importer. Once the importer accepts and countersigns the proforma invoice, it becomes a part of an export contract. A proforma invoice also facilitates the importer to arrange finances and open the letter of credit.

Commercial invoice serves three main functions.

(a) As a *document of content* A commercial invoice provides

Identification of the shipment by recording leading identification marks and numbers given on the package being shipped. Every shipment must provide marks in the form of words. Besides, every shipment must have numbers to indicate the total number of packs or any other unit of account

Detailed description of goods so as to correspond with the description given in the letter of credit or contract as the case may be

Description of quantity in the commercial invoice must tally the requirement of letter of credit/contract. The quantity described should neither be less nor more than the contracted quantity. The exporter should take care while finalizing the export deed that part shipments are not prohibited. The exporter should ship and mention only the contracted quantity unless specifically permitted.

(b) As a *seller's bill* It should indicate the net price (net of commission or discount), unless otherwise required under the contract. Generally, the detailed break-up of price is also required to be given in the invoice as per the contractual requirement.

(c) As a *packing list* Since the description of goods and quantity thereof is given in detail, the commercial invoice can also serve as a packing list especially when the packaging is simple or in a standard pack.

Some importing countries may need specific commercial invoices as follows.

Legalized invoice Some of the importing countries, such as Mexico, require legalized invoice wherein the commercial invoice is to be certified by the local chamber of commerce of the exporting country to verify that the invoice and declaration in the invoice are correct.

Consular invoice A specific invoice verified by the counsel of the importing country. Some of the countries in the Middle East require the invoice to be verified by the commercial section of their embassy in exporting country (i.e., in India) that the facts mentioned in the invoice are correct. The certification or legalization is being done by way of stamp or seal for payment of processing fee. The process may take about a week's time. However, the consular invoice is a form of non-tariff barrier.

Customs invoice   Some countries, such as the US and Canada require customs invoice to be prepared in the prescribed format primarily for their actions related to anti-dumping. The customs invoice may vary in format but contains similar information as in the commercial invoice and packing list. The customs invoice is self-certified by the exporter. However, certain countries need completed customs invoice from the importers rather than exporters for customs clearance.

Certain importing countries require that commercial invoice and packing list to be prepared or translated to the language of the importing country, e.g., in Italian for shipment to Italy, in French to France, and in Spanish to Mexico and Venezuela.

Packing list

Packing list provides details of how the goods are packed, the contents of different boxes, cartons, or bales, and details of the weights and measurements of each package in the consignment. Packing list is used by the carrier while deciding on the loading of the consignment. Besides, this is an essential document for the customs authorities. It also helps the importer to check inventory of the merchandise received.

When the consignment is small or consists of one simple product in a standard pack, the packing information is generally incorporated in the commercial invoice. However, as a general trade rule, it is better to provide financial and packing information separately in invoice and packing list, respectively.

Transport documents

All the documents that evidence shipment of goods, such as bills of lading (in ocean transport), combine or multimodal transport document (in multimodal transport), way bill or consignment note (for rail, road, air or sea transport), and receipt (in postal or courier delivery) are collectively known as transport documents.

Ocean (marine) bills of lading (B/L)   It is a transport document issued by the shipping company to the shipper for accepting the goods for carriage of merchandise. This document has got unique significance in shipping—it is the *document of title*, which means that the legitimate holder of the document is entitled to claim ownership of the goods covered therein. Therefore, it would be impossible for the importer to obtain possession of the cargo unless she/he surrenders a signed original bills of lading to the shipping company at destination. Thus, bills of lading serves the following three purposes:

- A receipt of cargo by the shipping company
- The contract of carriage (or transport)
- A document of title

A document of title means that lawful holder of bills of lading has the right to claim goods from the carrier at destination. The bills of lading becomes a 'negotiable' document, through endorsing it, in which case the goods specified in it can be transferred from one party to another. The negotiability is created in bills of lading by mentioning 'to order' bills of lading. An exporter should insist upon 'to order' bills of lading in which case any cargo would be released on presentation of an original of 'to order' bills of lading. However, the 'consignee-named' bills of lading is prepared in the name of specific party which cannot be negotiated (transferred). The consignee named B/L should be accepted by an exporter only in case she/he is confident of receiving timely payment as in case of either advance payment or an irrevocable letter of credit.

If the B/L includes a trans-shipment clause, the carrier has the right to trans-ship even if the letter of credit prohibits trans-shipment. Besides, the B/L should not indicate that the cargo is loaded or has been loaded on the deck, unless otherwise stipulated in the L/C. Modern cellular vessels may carry one-third of the containers on deck. If there is a provision in the B/L that the cargo may be carried on the deck, then the loading on the dock is acceptable even if L/C stipulates otherwise, provided that B/L does not specifically mention that cargo is or will be loaded on the deck.

There can be several variants of B/L:

On board or shipped bills of lading   It indicates that the goods have been placed 'on board' the carrier.

Received for shipment bills of lading   It indicates that goods have been received by the shipping company pending shipment and cargo is under custody of the carrier. In case of shipment on FAS terms, a 'received for shipment' bills of lading is required while for FOB shipment 'on board ship' bills of lading is required.

Clean bills of lading   It is one that does not contain any adverse remark on the quality or condition of package of the cargo received. In fact all importers insist upon a clean bills of lading.

Dirty (claused) bills of lading   In case, shipping company places remarks about damage of cargo or its packaging on the bills of lading, it becomes dirty or claused bills of lading. Generally, claused bills of lading is not accepted by most importers unless otherwise explicitly stipulated in the export contract.

Stale bills of lading   This refers to a bills of lading presented after the vessel has sailed and the goods have arrived at the port of discharge before the bills of Lading could reach the buyer. This may lead to delay in customs clearance of goods, payment of warehousing charges, and the risk of loss or damage to the cargo at destination. However, the issuing bank may issue the importer a guarantee for delivery of goods and a bond, both of which need to be countersigned by the issuing bank for getting the goods clearance through customs in absence of the bills of lading. However, the importer is required to surrender the properly endorsed bills of lading upon its receipt or replace it in case of its loss.

Through bills of lading   This is issued when cargo is to be moved from one carrier to another; it is a form of combined transport document wherein the first carrier acts as the principal carrier and is responsible for the total voyage and is liable in the event of any loss or damage to the cargo.

Trans-shipment bills of lading It is also issued when trans-shipment of cargo is required but the first carrier issuing the bills of lading acts as an agent in subsequent stages of voyage. Therefore, the first carrier cannot be held liable for any loss or damage in the subsequent stages of transport by the holder of trans-shipment bills of lading. Importers generally prefer a through bills of lading. However, from the exporter's point of view, they should insist that presentation of trans-shipment Bills of Lading is not prohibited at the time of finalizing the export contracts.

House (or freight forwarders') bills of lading It is issued by the freight forwarder, consolidator, or non-vessel carrier (NVC). Under the Carriage of Goods by Sea Act, 1971, it is a non-negotiable document and not subject to The Hague Rules relating to bills of lading where the non-negotiable documents provide evidence that they relate to contracts of carriage of goods by sea.

Short forms bills of lading It has got all the attributes of bills of lading except that it does not contain all the conditions of contract of affreightment. Unless specifically prohibited, banks accept short forms bills of lading.

Charter party bills of lading Issued by the carrier or its agent in case of charter shipping, the charter party bills of lading is not accepted for L/C negotiation unless otherwise authorized in the letter of credit.

The bills of lading may be marked 'freight paid' or 'freight to pay'. If the freight is pre-paid by the exporter, the bills of lading is marked or stamped as 'freight paid' while in case the freight has not been paid, 'freight to pay' or 'freight collect' is marked on the bills of lading. Bills of lading is issued by the shipping company in exchange for mate's receipt. Therefore, the shipping company ensures that all the clauses appearing on the mate's receipt are reproduced on the bills of lading prior to signing and issuing it.

Airway bill (AWB) It is also known as air consignment note or airway bill of lading. The airway bill is a receipt of goods and an evidence of contract of carriage but unlike ocean bills of lading, it is not a document of title and therefore, it is non-negotiable. The goods are consigned directly to the named consignee and are delivered to the consignee (i.e., the importer) without any further formality once the customs clearance is obtained at the destination. Therefore, it is risky to consign the goods directly to the importer unless the exporter has ensured receiving the payment of goods. Alternatively, the exporter may insist upon a provision in the letter of credit to consign the goods to a third party like the issuing bank or arrange for receiving the payment on cash on documents (COD) basis.

The International Air Transport Association (IATA) Airways Bill is issued in a set of 12 copies, three of which are originals having the same validity and commercial significance as under:

Original 1 (green)   For the issuing carrier which is to be signed by the consigner or its agent

Original 2 (pink)   For the consignee, accompanies the goods through the destination, is signed by the carrier or its agent

Original 3 (blue)   For the shipper, is signed by the carrier and is handed over to the consigner or its agent after goods have been accepted by the carrier. In the cases wherein the L/C requires full set original documents to be submitted, the bank requirement is satisfied by presenting the original three, i.e., the shipper's copy.

It is generally impossible to trace the consignment and get it cleared through customs without an airway bill or its reference number. In case the airway bill indicates trans-shipment clause, the trans-shipment will or may take place even if it is not allowed under the Letter of Credit. The split shipment mentioned in the airway bill means a part of shipment would enter the importing country at different times.

Combined or multimodal transport document (CTD/MTD)   With the container shipments becoming increasingly popular, the combined or multimodal transport document (CTD/MTD) is increasingly being used. The CTD covers movement of cargo from the place of containerization to that of destination using multimodal transport. While making shipments from inland container depots (ICD), the exporters can stuff the goods in the containers, and get them examined and sealed by the customs authorities for dispatch to gateway ports in customs-sealed containers. In such cases when goods are exported from ICD and the letter of credit does not require a marine B/L, the CTD is subject to be drawn as per the Foreign Exchange Dealers Association of India (FEDAI) rules is accepted by the authorized dealers.

In situations where the letter of credit does not allow acceptance of CTD or specifically requires ocean bills of lading, the authorized dealers may accept the CTD drawn as per the FEDAI regulations with undertaking from the combined transport operator (CTO) that the CTD would be replaced by the ocean bills of lading soon after the cargo is loaded on board the vessel. However, only after submission of the ocean bills of lading are the documents negotiated by the authorized dealer.

Certificate of origin

This document is used to establish evidence of origin of goods into the importing country. It includes the details of the goods covered and the country where the goods are grown, produced, or manufactured. The manufactured goods must have substantial value addition in the exporting country. Operations like packaging, splitting, assembling, or sorting may not be sufficient for qualifying the country of origin. It is also needed for deciding whether the import from the country of origin is partially or completely prohibited. The certificate of origin is required for deciding the liability and rate of import duty in the importing country. Besides, it is also used for granting preferential duty treatment to goods originating from the importing country, for example, in case of Generalized System of Preferences (GSP) certificate.

The certificate of origin is of two types:

Preferential certificate of origin   The preferential certificate of origin is required by countries offering tariff concessions to imports from certain countries. Such preferential certificates of origin are required for exports among members of various regional trading agreements as discussed in detail in Chapter 6. For exports from India, various types of preferential certificate of origin include

Generalized System of Preferences (GSP) Certificate   It is a non-contractual instrument by which developed countries unilaterally and on the basis of non-reciprocity extend tariff concessions to developing countries. The countries extending preferences under their GSP scheme include the US, Japan, Hungary Belarus, European Union, Norway, Switzerland, Bulgaria, Slovakia, Canada, Russia, Poland, Czech Republic, and New Zealand.

GSP schemes of these countries specify the sectors/products and tariff lines under which these benefits are available, besides the conditions and the procedures governing the benefits. These schemes are renewed and modified from time to time. Normally the Customs of GSP-offering countries require information in a prescribed GSP form.

Global System of Trade Preference (GSTP) Certificate   In the GSTP, trade concessions are exchanged among developing countries, who have signed the agreement. Presently, there are 46 member countries of GSTP and India has exchanged tariff concessions with 12 countries on a limited number of products. The Export Inspection Council (EIC) is the sole agency authorized to issue a certificate of origin under the GSTP.

Exports to SAPTA/SAFTA countries   The preferential certificate of origin for exports to SAPTA/SAFTA countries that include India, Pakistan, Nepal, Bhutan, Bangladesh, Sri Lanka, and Maldives.

Exports to Asian Pacific Countries under Bangkok Agreement   The Bangkok agreement is a preferential trading arrangement designed to liberalize and expand trade in goods progressively in the Economic and Social Commission for Asia and Pacific (ESCAP) region through such measures as the relaxation of tariff and non tariff barriers and use of other negotiating techniques.

Exports to Sri Lanka under Free Trade Agreement   A Free Trade Agreement (FTA) between India and Sri Lanka was signed on 20 December 1998. The agreement was operationalized in March 2000 following notification of the required customs tariff concessions by the Government of Sri Lanka and India in February and March 2000, respectively. Export Inspection Council is the sole agency to issue the certificate of origin under India, Sri Lanka Free Trade Area (ISLFTA).

Non-preferential certificate of origin   It merely evidences the origin of goods from a particular country and does not bestow any tariff benefit for exports to the importing nations. Generally, such a certificate of origin is issued by the local Chamber of Commerce. An exporter has to make an application to the local Chamber of Commerce in the prescribed format for getting certificate of origin.

It is a significant document for deciding the importability and tariff in a number of importing countries. Therefore, the exporter should complete the certificate of origin carefully and accurately as per rules of the importing country.

Inspection certificate

Under the Export (Quality Control and Inspection) Act 1963, it is mandatory to obtain an export inspection certificate for a number of products by the notified agency. The agencies entrusted with compulsory pre-shipment quality inspection include Export Inspection Agency (EIA), Bureau of Indian Standards (BIS), Agricultural Marketing Advisor (Agmark), Central Drugs Standard Control Organisation (CDSCO), Tea Board, Coffee Board, etc.

Generally, importers insist upon inspection to be carried out by a private agency (viz. SGS, Geochem, etc.) nominated by him/her so as to ensure the quality of merchandise as per the export contract. The exporter has to submit the intimation for inspection in a prescribed format and the inspection certificate is issued by the inspecting agency for payment of a fee.

Insurance policy/certificate

Since the carrier and other intermediaries, such as C&F agents, port authorities, warehousing operators, etc., have got only limited liability during the process of cargo movement from exporter to importer, they cannot be held responsible in the event of loss under the situation beyond their control such as man-made accidents, natural calamities (acts of god), etc. Therefore, in order to provide protection to the cargo-owner, an insurance cover is necessary to be taken while the cargo is in transit from consignor to consignee.

The risk to be covered under a cargo insurance policy is governed by the international practice to write policies on standard forms devised by the Institute of London Underwriters. Usually the insurance policy uses Institute Cargo Clauses, Institute War Clauses, and Institute Strike Clauses. A policy with Institutional Cargo Clauses 'A' plus Institute War Clauses and Institute Strike Clauses provides maximum insurance cover while a policy with Institutional Cargo Clause 'C' provides minimum cover for various types of risks related to international trade. In view of various factors, such as nature of cargo, mode of transport, port condition, etc., one has to select the most appropriate cargo insurance policy.

Usually regular exporters obtain an open cover or open insurance policy with the insurance company. As and when the shipments are made, the exporter gives a marine insurance declaration to insurance company which later issues the insurance certificate. Thus, insurance certificate is a negotiable instrument and saves time for the regular exporters in taking the insurance policy. Many a times, the export contract requires submission of insurance certificate instead of the policy.

Mate's receipt

On receipt of cargo on board, the master of the vessel issues mate's receipt for every shipment taken on board. Port authorities collect the mate's receipt from the master or chief officer of the vessel. Any 'claused' mate's receipt is not accepted by the port authorities unless authorized by the shipper. The shipper or her agent has to collect the mate's receipt from the port authorities after payment of all port dues. After receiving the mate's receipt, the shipper or the agent prepares the bills of lading as per the mate's receipt on blank forms supplied by the shipping company and presents 2/3 originals and some non-negotiable copies along with original mate's receipt to the shipping company for signature of the authorized officer of the shipping company. Mate's receipt is merely a receipt of goods shipped. It is not a document of title. It is an important document because the shipping company issues the bills of lading in exchange of the mate's receipt. Therefore, the exporter must collect mate's receipt soon after its receipt from the shed superintendent so as to avoid any problem and delay in getting the bills of lading.

Bill of exchange (draft)

It is an unconditional order in writing prepared and signed by the exporter and addressed to the importer requiring the importer to pay on demand (sight bill of exchange) or at a future date (usance bill of exchange) a certain sum of money (contract value) to the exporter or his/her nominee (or endorsee). The maker of the bill (i.e., the exporter) is known as the 'drawer' while the person receiving the bill (i.e., the importer) is called 'drawee'. Sight drafts (or bills of exchange) are used when payment is received by D/P (documents against payment) while the Usance drafts are used in D/A (documents against acceptance). In case of usance bills of exchange, the drafts are drawn for 30 to 180 days and are negotiable instruments which can be bought and sold.

The bill of exchange is invariably prepared in two original copies; each bears reference of the other and both of which are equally valid. The two originals are sent by different airmails and the one which reaches earlier is used for exchanging the title documents and the sale amount. Once an original bill of exchange has been honoured, the other becomes redundant. The exporter should ensure before sending the bill of exchange that the details mentioned therein tally with the other documents; the amount is invariably mentioned in words and it is signed in the same way a cheque is signed by the authorized representative of the exporting firm.

As the bill of exchange does not provide security to the exporter on its own, therefore as matter of customary practice it is used in international trade in conjunction with a letter of credit. The L/C provides the guarantee that a bill of exchange would be honoured.

Shipment advice

Soon after the shipment has taken place, the shipment advice is sent to the importer informing him/her of the details of the shipment. The shipment advice indicates details of vessel or flight number, port of discharge and destination, export order or export contract number, description of cargo, quantity, etc. This gives advance information to the importer about details of shipment so as to enable him/her to make arrangements to take delivery of the goods at destination. Generally, importers insist upon sending the copy of shipping advice by fax followed by the first airmail. A non-negotiable copy of bills of lading, commercial invoice, customs invoice (if any), and packing list are also to be attached with the shipping advice.

18.4.2 Regulatory Documents

Regulatory documents are those which are required to fulfil the statutory requirements of both importing and exporting countries. These documents are related to various government authorities, such as the relevant departments or their principal agencies controlling foreign trade, for example, Directorate General of Foreign Trade in India, the central bank (Reserve Bank of India), export promotion councils, export inspection agencies, banks, customs and central excise authorities, etc.

Exchange control declaration forms

Under the Foreign Exchange Management (Export of Goods and Services) Regulations, 2003, for every export taking place out of India, the exporter has to submit an exchange control declaration form in the prescribed format. Exports to Nepal and Bhutan are exempted from such declaration. The basic objective of such declaration forms is to ensure realization of export proceeds by the exporter as per the provisions of the Foreign Exchange Management Act (FEMA), 1999.

Various types of forms used for foreign exchange declaration are as under:

GR form   For all type of physical exports including software exports in physical form, such as using magnetic tapes or paper media (to be filled in duplicate)

SDF form   For all such exports where the customs have the facility for electronic data interchange (EDI) processing of shipping bill and to be attached in duplicate with the shipping bill

PP form   For all exports by post (in duplicate)

SOFTEX   For software exports in non-physical form, such as data transmission through satellite link

The declaration forms should explicitly contain the following details:

- Analysis of full export value of goods shipped including the FOB value, freight, insurance, etc.

- Clear indication whether the exports is on 'outright sale basis' or 'consignment basis'
- Name and address of the dealer through which export proceeds have been realized or would be realized
- Details of commission or discount due to foreign agent or buyer

As per FEMA, all the documents relating to export of goods from India should be submitted to the authorized dealer in foreign exchange within 21 days and the amount representing the full export value must be realized within six months from the date of shipment.

GR forms have to be submitted to the customs authorities in duplicate at the port of shipment. Customs authorities verify the declared value and record their assessed value. The original copy of GR form is directly sent by the customs to the RBI. At the time of actual shipment, the customs make their endorsement certifying the quantity passed for shipment and return to the exporter. The exporter is required to submit the customs certified copy of GR form to the authorized dealer. Once the export proceeds are received, the authorized dealer makes his/her endorsement and sends it to RBI.

Shipping bill/bill of export

Shipping bill is the main document required by the customs authorities. The export cargo is allowed to be carted on port sheds and docks only after the shipping bill has been stamped by the customs authorities. The shipping bill mentions the description of goods, marks, numbers, quantity, FOB value, name of the vessel or flight number, port of loading, port of discharge, country of destination, etc. In case of shipment by sea/air/ICD, the document is known as shipping bill, while in case of shipment by land, the document is known as bill of exports. Under section 50 of Customs Act, 1962, the shipping bill is to be submitted to customs for seeking their permission. The main types of shipping bills are

- Shipping bill for dutiable goods
- Shipping bill for duty-free goods
- Shipping bill for goods claiming for duty drawback

The exporter is required to submit the appropriate shipping bills for customs clearance depending upon the nature of goods.

Bill of entry

After unloading, the imported cargo is transferred to the custody of authorized agency, such as Port Trust Authority or Airport Authority or any other customs approved warehouse prior to its customs examination, duty payment, and handing over to the importer. For getting customs clearance on the imported cargo, bill of entry is required to be submitted in four copies by an importer or his/her agent to customs. The format of bill of entry has been standardized by the Central Board of Excise and Customs (CBEC). There are three types of bills of entry:

Bill of entry for home consumption (white)   It is used to get goods cleared in one lot by the importer.

Bill of Entry for warehousing (yellow)   Using 'into bond' bill of entry, an importer can get the goods shifted to a warehouse and get them cleared in small lots. It is especially useful when the importer has shortage of warehousing space or she/he is unable to pay the import duty at one go.

Ex-bond bill of entry (green)   For removing goods from the warehouse, an importer has to use ex-bond Bill of Entry.

While importing by post, there is no bill of entry. The foreign post office prepares a way bill for assessment of import duty.

ATA carnet

In order to facilitate temporary import of duty-free goods for short duration, such as exhibitions, trade fairs, shows, etc., and ease of its movement, the ICC, Paris, has evolved an international system of a document called the ATA carnet (Exhibit 18.2). All designated chambers in each country are authorized to issue or endorse a carnet. Thus, there is a chain of national chambers governed and controlled by ICC, Paris, which is authorized to issue such carnets or endorse the carnets of other designated national chambers issued for temporary importation of exhibits into their own country.

Exhibit 18.2   ATA carnets

The ATA carnet is an international customs document that permits duty-free and tax-free temporary import of goods during its validity period. The initials ATA are an acronym of the French and English words 'Admission Temporaire/Temporary Admission'. ATA carnets cover

- Commercial samples
- Professional equipment
- Goods for presentation or use at trade fairs, shows, exhibitions at the like

The ATA carnet services are available to business and sales executives, exhibitors at trade fairs and travelling professionals, and large and small companies. Federation of Indian Chambers of Commerce and Industry (FICCI) is the sole National Guarantor Chamber in India for issuing and endorsing foreign carnets for a fee of Rs 15,000. Virtually all goods can be included on carnet except for disposable items or consumable goods, including food.

FICCI also endorses all ATA carnets issued by other notified chambers in the ATA countries. The ATA carnet is for facilitation of temporary duty-free import/export of goods in about 60 countries.

Documents for central excise clearance

Invoice   The goods are to be delivered against a document known as invoice under Rule 11 of Central Excise (No. 2) Rules, 2001. It is issued by manufacturer in a set of three copies. The original copy is for the buyer, the duplicate is for the transporter, and the triplicate for the assessee. Transportation of goods without invoice is violation of rules.

Personal ledger account (PLA)   When the goods are removed after payment of duty, the personal ledger account is required to be maintained by the exporter. The estimated amount of excise duty to be paid by the exporter is deposited to the nationalized bank or treasury. The amount deposited in the bank is shown as credit in the PLA on the basis of the proof of deposit. At the time of removal of consignment, the amount of duty actually levied is shown as debit entry. An equivalent amount is again re-credited after the proof of export is received. Thus debit and credit entries are continuously maintained in the personal ledger account. However, in case of exports against bond or LUT (legal undertaking) where the duty is not actually paid, the exporters are not required to maintain personal ledger account.

ARE-1 (application for removal of excisable goods-1)   This document is in the form of an application to the jurisdictional central excise superintendent made by the exporter while removal of the goods. It mentions separately all the details of the consignment, such as value of the consignment and the amount of duty involved. An exporter has to submit the ARE-1, 24 hours in advance from the time of removal of the goods, in four copies. Once the goods are handed over to the carrier, the ARE-1 form is endorsed by the Customs, and it becomes the proof of exports.

ARE-2 (application for removal of excisable goods-2)   This document is used for refund of excise duty paid on the finished goods as well as the production inputs used in the manufacture of final products. Since the refund of central excise duty on the finished products is obtained against the ARE-1 formalities, the ARE-2 is a consolidated application for removal of goods for exports under claim for rebate of duty paid on excisable material used in the manufacture and packaging of such goods and removal of excise dutiable goods for export under rebate claim on the finished stage or under bond without payment of excise duty. However, due to the cumbersome procedure involved, ARE-2 formalities have not gained popularity among exporters.

CT-1   This document is used for procurement of excisable goods without payment of excise duty for exports. It mentions details, such as description of goods, quantity, value and the excise duty payable on goods to be removed duty-free on the basis of information furnished by the exporter. CT-1 form is issued by the designated central excise authority with which the manufacturer exporter or merchant exporter executes the legal undertaking (LUT) or bond, respectively.

Black list certificate

Countries that have strained political relations or are at war require the Black List Certificate as evidence that

- The origin of goods is not from a particular country
- The parties involved, such as the manufacturer, bank, insurance company, shipping line, etc. are not blacklisted
- The ship or aircraft would not call at ports of such country unless forced to do so

It is required to be furnished only by the exporter only when specifically asked for by the importer for exports to certain countries.

Health/veterinary/sanitary certificate

The importer or the importing county's customs department sometimes requires a certificate for export of foodstuff, livestock, marine products, hides and skins, etc., from health, veterinary, or sanitary authorities. This is done so as to ensure that imported cargo is not contaminated by any disease or health hazard.

This chapter brings out the significance of procedure and documentation involved in international trade transaction in view of the different regulatory frameworks of the buyer and the seller. In order to assure the exporter about the receipt of payment and to the importer of the transfer of the title of the goods, banking channels are commonly involved in international trade transactions for routing the payments.

The detailed procedure for export-import transaction has been explained in a simplistic way with the help of flowcharts so as to facilitate readers' understanding about the complex process. Significance of export documentation in view of much greater risk and number of intermediate trade and regulatory entities involved has also been discussed. This chapter explains in detail various export documents, a copy of each one of the documents may be obtained from the CD-ROM annexed with the author's book *International Marketing*.

SUMMARY

Trade procedures and documentation have become highly significant in international trade transactions, since the exporter and importer are located in two different countries and are governed by different regulatory frameworks. This chapter delineates the export-import procedures and documentation in view of the much greater risk and a number of intermediate trade and regulatory entities involved. Although the time required, and the cost incurred in an international trade transaction vary among countries, this chapter attempts to provide a broad outline of international trade procedures and documentation involved.

The execution of an export order involves a complex procedure and interaction with a number of regulatory and trade agencies. It also involves compliance with legal framework, such as obtaining Import Export Code (IEC) number, registration with sales tax and central excise authorities and Export Promotion Councils, concluding an export deal, arranging export finance, procuring or manufacturing of goods, pre-shipment inspection, central excise clearance, packaging, marking and labelling, booking shipping space, appointing clearing and forwarding agent, dispatch of goods to the port, arranging cargo insurance, port procedures and customs clearance, sending shipment advice, presentation of documents at the negotiating banks, and claiming export incentives.

The set of trade terms, often used to describe the rights and responsibilities of the buyer and the seller with regard to the sales and transport of goods, referred to as international commercial terms or incoterms. EXW involves the least liability of the seller wherein the merchandise is delivered at the seller's place without even getting export clearance whereas DDP involves the highest liability of the seller as the merchandise is delivered after getting import clearance at the buyer's place.

Documents used in an international trade transaction may either be commercial or regulatory. Those documents which are required by the customs of trade in discharge of legal and other incidental responsibility under the sales contract are known as commercial documents whereas regulatory documents are required to fulfil the statutory requirements of both importing and exporting countries. The major commercial documents include commercial invoice, packing list, transport documents such as bills of lading (B/L), airway bill (AWB), combined or multimodal transport document (CTD/MTD); certificate of origin, inspection certificate, insurance policy/certificate, mate's receipt, bill of exchange (draft), shipment advice, various exchange control declaration forms, shipping bill/bill of export, bill of entry, and documents for central excise clearance are the principal regulatory documents used in international trade.

Marine bills of lading which is not only a receipt of cargo and a contract of affreightment by the carrier but also a document of title, is unique. Therefore, the legitimate holder of the Bills of Lading can claim the title of the goods at the destination. Moreover, it is impossible for an importer to claim the cargo without valid documents. In order to eliminate the risk of exporter and importer, the documents are routed through banking channels.

Aligned documentation system (ADS), a methodology of creating information on a set of standard forms printed on a paper of same size in such a way that items of identical specification occupy the same position on each form, has also been explained.

KEY TERMS

Affreightment A contract for the carriage of goods by sea for shipment expressed in charter party or bills of lading.

Airway bill It is also known as air consignment Note issued by the carrier as an evidence of contract of carriage.

Aligned documentation system (ADS) A methodology of creating information on a set of standard forms printed on a paper of same size in such a way that the items of identical specification occupy the same position on each form.

Bill of entry A document needed for customs clearance of imported cargo.

Bill of exchange An unconditional order in writing prepared and signed by the exporter, addressed to the importer requiring the importer to pay a certain sum of money to the exporter or his/her nominee.

Bills of lading A transport document issued by the shipping company to the shipper for accepting the goods for carriage.

Clean bills of lading A bill of lading which does not have super-imposed claused expressly declaring a defective condition of packaging of goods.

Clearing and forwarding (C&F) agent An essential link in international trade operations who carries out a number of functions including cargo handling, documentation, and customs clearance for shipment.

Combined/multimodal transport document (CTD/MTD)   Used in place of bills of lading in case of multi-modal transportation of cargo.

Commercial documents   Those documents which are required to be prepared by customs of trade and used by exporters and importers in discharge of their respective legal and other incidental responsibilities under the sales contract.

Consignor   The party sending the consignment, i.e., shipper.

Consignee   The party to whom goods are to be delivered.

Consul   Commercial representative of a country residing officially in a foreign country who is primarily responsible for facilitating commercial transactions.

Counsular invoice   An invoice verified by the counsel of the importing country.

Customs invoice   An invoice to be prepared in the prescribed format provided by the importing country.

Dirty (claused) bills of lading   A bill of lading stating damage of cargo or its packaging.

Drawee   The party to whom a draft is addressed and who is expected to honour it.

Drawer   The party who issues a draft, generally the beneficiary of the credit.

Drawing   The presentation of documents under a credit.

Endorsement   Signing of a document, i.e., draft, insurance document, or bill of lading, usually on the reverse to transfer title to another party. Generally, the documents are endorsed in blank so as to permit in future the holder to gain title.

Export documentation software   Software which facilitates preparation of export documents.

Generalized system of preferences (GSP)   A non-contractual instrument by which developed countries unilateral and on the basis of non-reciprocity extend tariff concessions to developing countries.

Globalized system of trade preference (GSTP)   A preferential tariff system in which the member developing countries exchange tariff concessions among themselves.

Import export code (IEC) number   Number issued by regional licensing authority needed for completing export documentation.

Indemnity   Compensation for loss/damage or injury.

Legalised invoice   A variant of commercial invoice, certified by the local chamber of commerce of the exporting country so as to confirm the accuracy of furnished information.

Mate's receipt   A cargo receipt issued by the master of the vessel for every shipment taken on board.

Port of discharge   Seaport/airport at which the exported goods are to be unloaded.

Port of loading   Seaport/airport at which the goods are loaded.

Shipping bill/bill of export   The principal document required by customs authority mentioning details of shipment for exports.

Stale bills of lading   In banking practices, a Bills of Lading presented after the cargo has arrived at the port of discharge.

Transport documents   All the documents that evidence shipment of goods, such as Bills of Lading, combined transport document, waybill, consignment note, etc.

Waybill   A receipt of goods and evidence of the contract of carriage but not a document of title.

CONCEPT REVIEW QUESTIONS

1. Explain the significance of procedures and documentation in international trade transactions.

2. Briefly explain the steps involved in executing an export order.

3. Delineating the significance of international commercial terms, explicate the costs and risks to buyers and sellers involved under various incoterms in an international trade transaction.

4. Elucidate various types of certificates of origin used in export transactions.

5. Write short notes on

   (a) Consequences of poorly documentation for export transaction

   (b) Aligned documentation system (ADS)

   (c) Types of commercial invoices

   (d) Bills of lading (B/L)

   (e) ATA carnet

PRACTICE EXERCISES

1. Explore the Internet and prepare a list of documents required for exports from the US, China, India, and Singapore. Critically evaluate the similarity and differences in export documentation needed.

2. Take out a print out of marine bills of lading, airway bill, and combined transport document (CTD) from CD ROM annexed with the author's *International Marketing* and identify the differences between the above three transport documents. Critically evaluate legal implications for each.

PROJECT ASSIGNMENTS

1. Contact an exporting firm located in your city and find out the step-by-step procedure followed for executing an export order and present it in the form of a flow-chart. Compare the procedure followed with the flowchart given in Fig. 18.4.

2. Meet the local customs authority in your vicinity at any of the two customs check points: sea port, air cargo complex, or land customs stations. Find out the customs documents used for exports and imports and identify the similarities and differences in customs documents for different modes of transport.

19

Global E-business

LEARNING OBJECTIVES

> ➤ To elucidate the conceptual framework of e-business
> ➤ To examine e-business technology and environment
> ➤ To explain various e-business models and strategic options
> ➤ To discuss global e-marketing and e-services
> ➤ To explicate electronic processing of international trade documents
> ➤ To evaluate policy framework for global e-business

19.1 INTRODUCTION

The breakthroughs in information and communication technology (ICT), especially the advent of the Internet and the World Wide Web, have significantly changed the way people communicate and manage their daily lives across the world. The Internet is becoming increasingly integrated with day-to-day activities both in developed and developing economies. It has revolutionized relationships within and between organizations and individuals. In markets where there are many more mobile phones in hands than personal computers on desks, including most of the developing world, wireless devices are becoming delivery mechanisms for Internet services.

The use of ICT is gaining significance as a strategic tool to increase productivity, reduce costs, enable mass customization, and encourage greater customer participation. The advent of the Internet and web-based technology has brought down the distinctions between traditional marketplaces and the global electronic marketspace. The name of the game is strategic positioning—the ability of a company to determine emerging opportunities and utilize the necessary human capital skills (such as intellectual resources) to make the most of these opportunities through an e-business strategy that is simple, workable, and practicable within the context of a global information milieu and new economic environment.[1]

---

[1] Andam, Zorayda Ruth, *E-commerce and E-business*, e-ASEAN Task Force, UNDP-APDIP, May 2003, p. 5.

Companies are progressively integrating ICT in their traditional ways of doing businesses and moving towards e-business to achieve competitiveness. Businesses that fail to recognize the rapidly growing competitive strengths of rivals as a result of technological integration are likely to vanish, as illustrated in Exhibit 19.1.

In view of the growing significance of digital technology, especially as a tool to achieve and sustain competitiveness, a thorough conceptual understanding of e-business becomes crucial to managing global business effectively. This chapter brings out the significance of integration of ICT to business processes in achieving competitiveness. The conceptual framework that facilitates readers to understand e-enabled business systems vis-à-vis traditional marketing systems has been examined. The prerequisites for e-business transactions, e-enabled transformation in business processes, and the major challenges involved have been elucidated. The chapter also explains the principal technological arenas of e-business, such as electronic data interchange (EDI), Internet,

---

Exhibit 19.1   Sinking of *Encyclopaedia Britannica* and rising of Wikipedia

The world's first and the most famous encyclopaedia since 1768, *Encyclopaedia Britannica*, synonymous with erudition and wealth of knowledge, was the most accessible brand name in the publishing world. The reputation of brand Britannica was built over two centuries and its sales peaked at all-time high of US$650 million in 1990.

In 1990, Microsoft bought the rights to an encyclopaedia by Funk & Wagnalls, a third-rate product with hardly any brand recognition. Microsoft produced its multi-media version, renamed it Encarta and released in the form of a CD-ROM in 1993. The marginal cost to produce a copy of *Encarta* was US$1.5 and it was distributed free with new PCs. On the other hand, the marginal reproduction cost of *Encylopedia Britannica* was about US$250 per copy plus a sales commission of about US$500 to US$600 for each copy sold. It was sold at a market price of US$1500 to US$2200, depending upon the quality of binding.

Initially, Britannica grossly undermined the product strength of Encarta, considering it a frivolous toy that was no match to Britannica's own profile of a scholastic classic. However, contrary to Britannica's market analysis, the sales of the mighty brand plummeted miserably. Compared to 117,000 in 1990, only 55,000 hard copies were sold in 1994, which later declined to 20,000. In order to arrest the steep decline in sale, Britannica brought out a text-only CD-ROM version. Since its sales force received huge commissions on sales of the printed copies, it vehemently protested the CD-ROM version. To appease its sales force, Britannica decided to offer the CD-ROM as a gift with the printed version. Moreover, the price of the stand-alone CD-ROM was kept a whopping US$1000.

In 2001, a web-based multilingual free content encyclopaedia, Wikipedia was launched, which presently contains more than 10 million articles in about 250 languages and has over 75,000 active contributors. Availability of exhaustive content for free and ease of use made it rapidly popular among Internet users across the world with over 684 million visitors yearly by 2008. Thus, the rapid integration of technology in the publishing industry has seriously threatened the two-century-old unrivalled brand of encyclopaedia, leaving several lessons to learn, for others too.

Source: 'Encyclopaedia Britannica Changes to Survive', *BBC News*, 17 December 1997; http://www.microsoft.com/uk/encarta; 'Will Wikipedia Mean the End of Traditional Encyclopaedias?' *The Wall Street Journal*, 12 September 2006.

extranet, and intranet. Further, this chapter elaborates various e-business models and alternative strategies. Global e-marketing and e-services have been separately discussed at length. Use of digital technology in trade documentation, which considerably contributes to efficiency and increases process transparency, has also been elucidated.

19.2   CONCEPTUAL FRAMEWORK OF E-BUSINESS

Prefixing 'e' to any word implies an 'electronic' involvement or integration of ICT. Examples of such terms include e-business, e-shopping, e-learning, e-governance, e-logistics, etc. Thus, in simple terms, e-business refers to integration of ICT with business processes. Although the extent and scope of such integration and applications varies widely, it contributes to enhanced efficiency in managing businesses. Moreover, competitive pressures have compelled most businesses to go online. Major reasons for companies making online presence include

- Expand global market reach
- Creating world-wide virtual presence
- Improving business visibility
- Increasing responsiveness to customers and business partners
- Reduction in business cost
- Nurturing and strengthening relationships with customers and business partners

ICT is employed to collect information at the point of sales and to transmit it instantaneously from the retailer to the manufacturer. Electronic linking of the entire supply-chain has contributed not only to speedy flow of information but also to boost the overall efficiency of business processes. The World Wide Web has transformed the entire world into a virtual local market. It has transformed the markets from 'physical marketplace' to 'virtual marketspace' leading to basic alteration in the consumer-decision process. The way of offering services across geographical boundaries has also been revolutionized by ICT.

Unlike the traditional marketing approach, which is based on customer segmentation, e-marketing enables a company to target an individual customer, i.e., a 'segment size of one'. By integrating technology, business enterprises may adopt a company-led approach to target individual customers and adopt a marketing strategy customized to the segment of even one customer. Michael Dell, founder of Dell Computers, was among the first to adopt innovative business processes that integrated digital technology with marketing, as illustrated in Exhibit 19.2. These processes have made Dell Computers the largest seller of PCs in the US.

Integration of information technology also allows businesses to estimate lifetime value of customer (LVC) that may be used to facilitate business decision making. LVC refers to the estimate of potential profit a company is likely to derive from a customer during his or her lifetime. It is arrived at by subtracting lifetime costs such as costs of customer acquisition, operating expenses, customer service, etc. from the

---

Exhibit 19.2 Dell's e-business strategy

Michael Dell began to assemble computers in 1983 in his college dormitory as a student at the University of Texas at Austin with a capital of US$100. As his business grew, he pioneered the direct sales of computers through the telephone. In 1996, Dell started selling computers over the Internet through its own website.

Leading computer manufacturers, such as IBM and Compaq, had built extensive worldwide distribution networks and relied heavily on resellers for sales of their products. Dell's decision to sell directly to customers through its new e-business model could have alienated market intermedi-

aries. However, Dell effectively overcame the resellers' threat by mass customization of its computers for each of its customers. This resulted in much higher customer satisfaction on one hand and cost savings by elimination of middlemen on the other.

As a result, Dell had become the largest seller of personal computers in the US in 1999, overtaking Compaq. It ranked as the 25th largest company in the Fortune 500 list in 2006, however slipped to 34th place in 2008 list with a revenue of US$61.13 billion and US$2.95 billion in 2007.

Source: 'Dell Changed the Industry with Direct Sales', *The Statesman*, 3 May 2004; 'The Company File: Dynamic Dell' *BBC News*, 20 August 1998; *Fortune 500*, 2006 and 2008 issues.

---

lifetime earnings of a customer. For instance, if the total costs of maintaining a customer exceeds his/her lifetime value, the company needs to take a decision either to drop the customer or charge higher prices.

The major factors contributing to the growth of e-business may be summarized as

- Advent of the Internet and world-wide web offers cost-effective alternative to proprietary and value-added networks
- Cost savings through integrating business processes with network-based technology
- Growing use of the Internet as marketing channel
- Opportunities to enhance supply-chain efficiency and cost-effectiveness
- Improved customer service in the form of round-the-clock online access to the company contributes to enhancing relationship with its customers

However, e-business has also threatened a number of traditionally well-established industries and businesspersons especially

Travel agents Airlines and railways across the world are selling tickets online, some are even offering discounts to direct customers and cutting commissions to travel agents.

Wholesalers Traditional wholesalers hardly add value to the exchange processes.

Insurance agents Although most insurance companies are reluctant to alienate their existing massive agent structure, they are simultaneously making attractive online offers for direct insurance.

Business applications of digital technology have given rise to an era of information asymmetry where customers are much better informed, information is controlled by customers, and customers also initiate market exchanges. Moreover, since integration of ICT with business operations provides a level playing field, it enables small and medium enterprises (SMEs) to compete with large and capital-based businesses. The basic concepts of e-commerce, e-business, and m-commerce are discussed below.

19.2.1 E-commerce

Commerce is a basic economic activity involving trading or the buying and selling of goods. An electronic transaction primarily involves three stages, i.e, searching and deciding upon products to be bought, ordering and making payments, and delivery of products bought. E-commerce involves exchanges among customers, business partners, and vendors. Thus, in simple terms, e-commerce refers to buying and selling of goods or services through a computer-mediated network. It includes all forms of business transactions in which the transacting parties interact electronically over digital networks rather than by physical exchanges or physical contact.

A conceptual framework of e-commerce, as shown in Fig. 19.1, reveals that it involves electronic exchange of information or 'digital content' between two or more parties, i.e., the business enterprise and the buyer or the supplier. In order to operationalize an e-commerce system, the seller is required to produce the content, and its digitization (i.e., conversion of the content into digital format), storage of digital content, and linking to electronic network and electronic payment system and electronic delivery for information goods or arranging for physical manufacturing and delivery for physical goods. Electronic payment system (EPS) refers to a system of financial exchange

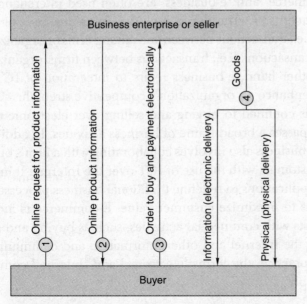

Fig. 19.1 Conceptual framework of e-commerce

between buyers and sellers in the online environment that is facilitated by a digital financial instrument (such as encrypted credit card numbers, electronic checks, or digital cash) backed by a bank, an intermediary, or by legal tender. On the other hand, the buyer also has to link to an electronic network, search and locate content on network, retrieve information from network, display information, place a purchase order, and link to an electronic payment system.

In an e-commerce system, several disparate technologies are required to make an 'any information-anywhere' system operational. These include

Content production Word processors, video cameras, music synthesizers, and editing software

Digitization Dictation software, digital cameras, scanners, etc.

Storage Floppy diskettes, CD-ROMs, tapes, memory sticks or pen drives, hard disk drives

Network communications Electricity cables, telephone cables, dedicated lines, mobile phones, etc.

Network connections Personal computers, modem or broadband connections, televisions and set-top boxes

Information search and retrieval mechanisms Search engines and directories

Display devices TV, PC monitor, mobile phones,[2] etc.

19.2.2 E-business

Although the terms 'e-commerce' and 'e-business' are often used interchangeably, these are two distinct concepts. E-commerce includes inter-business or inter-organizational transactions (i.e., transactions between and among firms or organizations) and business to customers transactions (i.e., transactions between firms/organizations and individuals). On the other hand, e-business refers to integration of ICT with business processes so as to enhance an organization's competitive strength.

The term 'e-commerce' is confined to buying and selling over electronic media, whereas 'e-business' encompasses a broad frame of business activities. In addition to online buying and selling, e-business also involves collaborating with a firm's business partners and servicing its customers with the use of ICT over the Internet. It includes both front and back-office applications to redefine traditional business processes with the help of technology so as to maximize customer value. E-commerce is indeed a subset of e-business that deals with commercial activities, such as buying and selling of goods and services using the Internet and other information and communication technologies. However, in practice, the terms 'electronic' and 'Internet' commerce are often used interchangeably.

---

[2] Chen, Stephen, *Strategic Management of E-business,* Singapore: John Wiley & Sons, Ltd, 2004, pp. 3–6.

E-business refers to the performance of business activities, such as designing products, managing supply-chain, operations, marketing, and offering services to various stakeholders through extensive use of electronic technology. Thus, e-business leads to transformation of an organization's business processes so as to deliver additional customer value through application of technology and processes. E-business usually enhances three primary processes:

Production processes, which include procurement, ordering and replenishment of stocks; processing of payments; electronic links with suppliers; and production-control processes, among others

Customer-focussed processes, which include promotional and marketing efforts, selling over the Internet, processing of customers' purchase orders and payments, and customer support, among others

Internal management processes, which include employee services, training, internal information-sharing, video-conferencing, and recruiting. Electronic applications enhance information flow between production and sales forces and improve their productivity. Workgroup communications and electronic publishing of internal business information are likewise made more efficient.[3]

Hence, e-business may be defined as the process of carrying out business activities using electronic technologies. It includes the use of technology for online buying and selling and to forge and foster linkages with various stakeholders, such as customers, suppliers, government, and other business partners. E-business integrates traditional business practices and information systems with the world-wide reach of the web and connects its various stakeholders.

Thus, e-business is a much broader concept which involves the use of *extranets,* the Internet links between the business suppliers and purchasers and *intranets,* the Internet links within a business. It also includes the strategic adaptations of business practices integrating the use of technology. It comprises of generating business needs, providing sales support and integrating business partners; linking various aspects of business operations to distributors and suppliers through extranets, and carrying out communications within the organization control through intranets.

Traditionally a marketing system, as depicted in Fig. 19.2, consists of basic 4Ps of marketing, i.e., product, price, place, and promotion. The traditional marketing strategy requires dividing the heterogeneous universe of customers into homogeneous sub-groups, known as market segmentation, who would respond more or less similarly to a given marketing strategy. A business enterprise generally adopts a uniform strategy for a given market segment. Thus, advertising, promotion, product, and the marketing channel remain the same for all the customers in a given market segment. Distribution channels are often elaborate and market intermediaries play a crucial role in sales transactions.

[3] Kalakota, Ravi and Andrew B. Whinston, *Electronic Commerce: A Manager's Guide,* Addison Wesley, Boston, 1997, pp. 2–32.

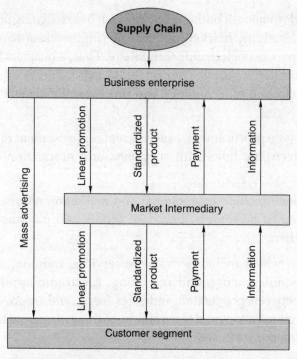

Fig. 19.2 Traditional marketing system

E-business system facilitates business enterprises to leverage upon ICT to achieve competitiveness. In an e-business-based marketing system (Fig. 19.3), firms can target an individual customer and adopt customized marketing strategies targeting a

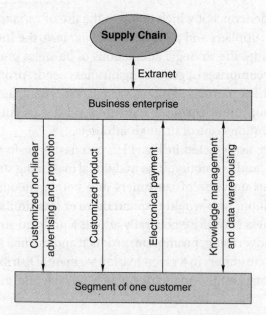

Fig. 19.3 The e-business-based marketing system

single-customer segment. Instead of discrete flow of information under the traditional marketing system, the e-business system facilitates a business enterprise to have elaborate knowledge management and database management systems which can be used to design individualized market promotion and customized products. Contrary to the traditional marketing system which often has several intermediaries for making its products available to the end customers, electronic business systems are either direct or have shorter channels of distribution, often dominated by facilitators. In an e-enabled system the payments flow from end customers to the seller directly takes place electronically unlike through market intermediaries in a traditional system. Moreover, e-based business systems greatly contribute to speed and efficiency of business operations, adding to effective customer relationship management (CRM).

19.2.3   M-business

Although conduct of business transactions through computers has greatly facilitated business activities, the use of wireless technology, relieves all the stakeholders in the business from the constraints of time and place, greatly enhancing convenience and accessibility. m-business is defined as the conduct of business activities through use of wireless technology, such as mobile phones, personal digital assistant (PDA), and telematics. M-business facilitates interaction among business stakeholders with the World Wide Web, irrespective of location-specific context. It also enables business communication through mobile devices and text applications such as SMS, using e-mail, and through the web.

To illustrate, mobile banking alerts keep its customers alerted when the event, the customer has subscribed to, get triggered. Customers can subscribe for receiving SMS alerts for a number of transactions, such as when an amount is credited, an amount over a specified amount gets debited or credited, balance falls below or goes above a specified limit, or when a cheque bounces. Under the alert facility, customers get alerts only when the events they have subscribed to occurs, unlike the request facility where the customer requests for information as and when desired.

M-commerce finds enormous applications in various businesses, especially the following:

Financial services   Mobile banking and stock investments carried out over wireless devices

Retail   Placing orders and making payments over wireless devices for retail purchase

Telecommunication   Single wireless device for getting account status, changing services, and making payment

Information services   Delivery of news, stocks reports, sports figures, such as cricket or football scores, entertainment, such as jokes, ring-tones, astrological predictions, etc.

Global System for Mobile (GSM) communications accounts for 85 per cent of world's mobile connections. The first GSM network was launched in 1991. By the

Table 19.1 World's top mobile markets

	Subscriber connections (Million)	Market penetration (%)	YoY growth (%)
China	524	39.3	18.3
US	254	86.9	9.5
India	237	21.0	59.7
Russian Federation	168	120.7	11.2
Brazil	117	62.6	16.0
Japan	100	78.5	5.9

Source: Global Mobile Market Q 4 2007, GSM Association, Atlanta, 2008.

end of 2007, the number of subscribers' connections crossed 3 billion marks with more than 700 mobile operators across 218 countries and territories of the world adding new mobile connections at the rate of 15 per second or 1.3 million per day.[4] Nearly 7 billion text messages are sent every day and over 64 percent of mobile users are from emerging markets.

India has emerged as the highest growing market[5] with 59.7 per cent growth over the previous year (Table 19.1) followed by China (18.3%), Brazil (16%), Russian Federation (11.2%), the US (9.5%), and Japan (5.9%). However, China has the largest number of mobile subscriber connections in the world (524 million), followed by the US (254 million), India (237 million), Russian Federation (168 million), Brazil (117 million) and Japan (100 million), whereas the market penetration rate was the highest at 120.7 per cent in Russian Federation, followed by the US (86.9%), Japan (78.5%), Brazil (62.6%), China (39.3%), and India (21%).

Japan is the global leader in m-commerce. It is believed that the wireless m-commerce may surpass the wired e-commerce for digital commercial transactions, as the content delivery over wireless devices become faster, scaleable, and more secure.

19.3 PREREQUISITES FOR EFFECTIVE E-BUSINESS TRANSACTIONS

In order to make e-business function effectively, a number of inter-related factors and prerequisites involved in the transaction loop[6] need to be put in place. The scope of e-commerce goes far beyond hosting a website for buying and selling of goods over the Internet. The principal players in an e-commerce transaction and the corresponding requisites are summarized below:

Business enterprise or seller

- A corporate website with e-commerce capabilities so as to conduct secured transactions

---

[4] '3 Billion GSM Connections on the Mobile Planet', GSM Association, Press Release, Atlanta, 2008.
[5] *Global Mobile Market Q 4 2007*, GSM Association, Atlanta, 2008.
[6] Based on Andam, Zorayda Ruth, 'E-commerce and E-business', e-ASEAN Task Force, UNDP-APDIP, May 2003, pp. 16–18.

- A corporate Intranet so that orders are processed promptly and efficiently
- Workforce with IT proficiency so as to manage and sustain the e-commerce system

Transaction partners

- Financial institutions offering online transaction services, such as processing payments over credit cards and electronic funds transfer
- Logistics service providers linked electronically and providing efficient physical movement of cargo
- Authentication authority that serves as a trusted third party to ensure the integrity and security of transactions

Consumers (in business to consumer transactions) should

- Form a critical mass of the population with access to the Internet and disposable income enabling widespread use of credit cards
- Possess a mindset for purchasing goods over the Internet rather than by physically inspecting items

Companies/businesses (in business to business transactions)

- Should together form a critical mass of companies (especially within supply chains) with Internet access and the capability to place and take orders over the Internet.

Government needs to establish

- A legal framework governing e-commerce transactions (including electronic documents, signatures, and the like)
- Legal institutions that would enforce the legal framework (laws and regulations) and protect consumers and businesses from fraud, among others.

Companies should have

- A robust and reliable internet infrastructure
- A pricing structure that doesn't discourage consumers from spending time on and buying goods over the Internet

19.4 E-ENABLED BUSINESS PROCESS TRANSFORMATIONS AND CHALLENGES

Integration of digital technology into the business processes has considerably transformed the traditional ways of doing business. Some of the changes brought about by e-business are summarized below:

Physical marketplace to virtual marketspace   The Internet has transformed the traditional ways of buying and selling of goods at physical marketplaces into virtual marketspace enabling almost unlimited movements beyond physical borders.

Physical products to digital products   Breakthroughs in ICT have made possible to sell and buy some products online. For instance, computer software, music, movies, video games, drawings, designs, research papers, reports, and even books can be accessed, evaluated, bought, and downloaded over the net.

Mass production of standardized products to mass customization   Consequent to industrial revolution in the eighteenth century, the large-scale production of standardized products was used as the most significant tool to achieve scale economies and competitiveness. Advent of electronic technology and Internet facilitated real-time interaction and information-sharing between the businesses and their various stakeholders, especially the customers and suppliers that made it possible to integrate manufacturing systems to produce customized products for different customers.

Fixed pricing to dynamic pricing   E-business models offer flexibility in price determination in several ways, such as buyer-determined customized pricing, dynamic pricing by way of online auctions, unlike the traditional fixed-pricing approach.

Mass marketing techniques to customized marketing   Traditional marketing heavily relied upon mass marketing techniques with some adaptations for different market segments. Advent of ICT has facilitated businesses to gather information about individual customers' tastes and preferences, their buying behaviour and customized marketing strategy to cater to each of the customers.

Hierarchical organizations to network organizations   The traditional 'hierarchical organizational structures' are transforming into 'network organizational structures' so as to take benefit of emerging e-business opportunities and meet the potential challenges.

However, businesses going online face several challenges, including

- As most businesses are making their online presence, the market competition has grown multi-fold from local to global level.
- Online buying and selling of goods often results in elimination of market intermediaries; the process is frequently referred to as 'disintermediation', and leads to channel conflict.
- Increase in availability of information online on the public domain augments the chances of its copying by the competitors who make its use for their own benefits.
- Since the Internet can be accessed from across the world, there is no single binding legal framework.
- Most businesses and customers often fear breach of security in terms of both the theft and misuse of classified and personal information over the Internet.
- A large segment of customers is resistant to carrying out business transactions over the Internet.
- Viability of carrying out business transactions differs across firms, depending upon their nature of business and resource availability.

19.5   E-BUSINESS TECHNOLOGY AND ENVIRONMENT

In the initial phases of development of e-commerce, proprietary networks were often used under an EDI framework. The advent of the Internet, which interlinks millions of networks across the world and offers a much wider platform for business transactions at a global scale, has largely replaced the earlier EDI systems. Intranets provide platforms for communications within organizations whereas extranet links a business organization with its various stakeholders.

19.5.1   Electronic Data Interchange

Electronic data interchange (EDI) was the first approach used for information-sharing and business transactions; it began in the 1970s and predates the Internet. It refers to the exchange of information through computers between organizations in a standard, computer-processable, and universally accepted format using proprietary networks (Fig. 19.4).

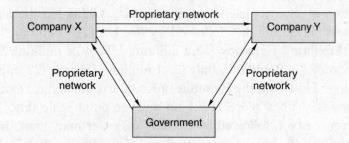

Fig. 19.4   Electronic data interchange

EDI had generally been used to eliminate paperwork in supply chain management and getting regulatory clearances from government authorities. Major components required to send and receive EDI messages include

- EDI standards
- EDI software
- Third-party networks for communication

The United Nations defined a set of rules in 1987 for electronic data interchange for Administration, Commerce and Transport, known as UN/EDIFACT. EDI has been the dominant technology used by large business firms, such as Wal-Mart, Ford, Suzuki, General Motors, etc., to exchange information with its business partners, especially for managing supply chains. Besides, it also facilitated information-sharing within different departments of a firm.

19.5.2   Internet

The advent of the Internet has facilitated almost-instantaneous worldwide communication and has metamorphosed traditional communication processes. The Internet refers to a 'network of networks' or 'interconnected computer networks' comprising millions of small domestic, business, academic, and government networks linked by copper-wires, optical fibre cables, or wireless connections. Internet or *Inter*connected *Net*work began as a sponsored project to link computing systems by the US government. The ability to transmit information packets between widely dispersed computer networks was perceived as a means of lowering the computing costs. The original project in 1969 was called ARPANET, the grand-parent of today's Internet. The National Science Foundation incorporated the ARPANET into its own network, the NSFNET, by the 1980s, which became the core of the US Internet, until its privatization and ultimate retirement in 1995. The US Federal Networking Council unanimously passed a resolution defining the term 'Internet' on 24 October 1995.

The World Wide Web or the web is relatively a new addition to the Internet. It is the universe of network-accessible information. The www uses the Internet as a backbone to send information from servers or repositories of file information, to browsers, or to software designed to display the files. It also facilitates the transfer of hypermedia-based files, allowing links to other pages, places, or applications.

There is wide variation in Internet users among countries. China has the highest number of Internet users[7] (221 million), followed by the US (216 million), Japan (87.5 million), India (60 million), Germany (53.2 million), UK (40.4 million), South Korea (34.9 million), France (34.9 million), Italy (33.1 million), Canada (22 million), and Malaysia[8] (15 million). However, the Republic of Korea has the highest extent of Internet use for businesses[9] with a score of 6.1 on a seven-point scale (Fig. 19.5), whereas the UK has a score of 6.1, followed by Sweden (5.7), Germany (5.6), the US (5.5), Japan (5.4), Australia (5.2), Singapore (5.0), Brazil (5.0), Thailand (4.7), India (4.6), Russian Federation (4.1), United Arab Emirates (4.1), South Africa (4.0), China (3.5), Tanzania (3.2), Vietnam (2.8), and Chad (1.9).

The level of Internet penetration also varies widely among countries. Norway has the highest level of penetration rate[10] of 88 per cent of the population, followed by the Netherlands (87.8%), Iceland (85.4%), New Zealand (77.7%), and Sweden (77.3%), whereas the US has 71.7 per cent, Japan 68.7 per cent, UK 66.4 per cent, Canada 65.9 per cent, France 54.7 per cent, and Singapore 53.2 per cent of penetration rate. The level of penetration in India is quite low, merely 5.3 per cent, despite India's ranking fourth in terms of total number of Internet users. Such wide variation in these two parameters is due to considerable differences in Internet users among the urban and rural population.

English is the highest used language on the web[11] with 30.1 per cent of total users, followed by Chinese (14.7%), Spanish (9.0%), Japanese (6.9%), French (5.1%), German

---

[7] 'China Tops US for Internet Population Lead', *PC World*, 25 April 2008.

[8] Based on data from International Telecommunication Union, December 2007.

[9] The Global Competitiveness Report 2006–07, World Economic Forum, Geneva, p. 519.

[10] International Telecommunication Union, December 2007.

[11] International Telecommunication Union, November 2007.

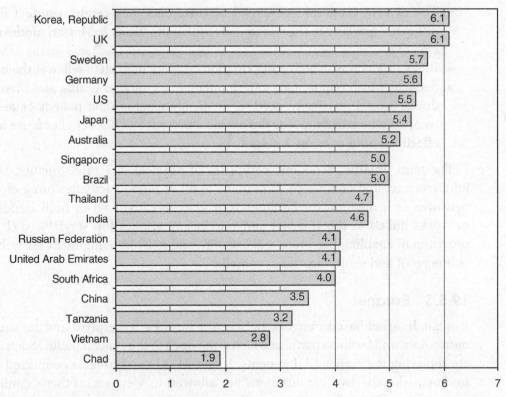

Fig. 19.5 Extent of business Internet use

Note: 1—lowest; 7—highest.
Source: The Global Competitiveness Report 2006–07, World Economic Forum, Geneva, p. 519.

(4.9%), Portuguese (4.0%), Arabic (3.7%), Korean (2.7%), and Italian (2.6%) whereas other languages account for 16.3 per cent.

Internet can be accessed round the clock from all over the world. Besides, it is easy to use and it involves extremely low transaction costs. The two-way communication over the Internet facilitates businesses to instantaneously customize marketing mix and integrate business processes. Internet has made mass customization possible for different users so as to create individualized web pages, products, and services. The customized web page not only offers the preferred layout of the customer, but also provides the company with the useful information about its customers in terms of their individual interests. This allows a firm to work out a proactive customized business strategy to suit the needs of individual customers and make customized market promotions and product offerings.

Although it provides a good medium for electronic transactions, not everything can be sold effectively over the Internet:

- As far as 'high-touch' products, such as clothes, jewellery, and fashion goods are concerned, customers like to touch, feel, or experience first-hand the product before making a buying decision.

- The diverse geographical spread of customers may render product delivery difficult, especially in the countryside where the 'Brick & Mortar' model is more effective.
- Bulky products with high transportation costs are difficult to sell over the Internet.
- Services which require face-to-face interactions, such as healthcare, wherein the doctor would physically need to medically examine the patient or aesthetics wherein a beautician needs the physical presence of his/her clients are also not effectively sold over the Internet.

The term 'Internet economy' comprises of physical ICT infrastructure, business infrastructure, and commerce. It pertains to all economic activities using electronic networks as a medium for commerce or activities involved in both building the networks linked to the Internet and purchasing application services, such as the provision of enabling hardware and software and network equipment for web-based online retail and shopping malls—e-malls.

19.5.3 Extranet

It is an Internet-based network between a business enterprise and its suppliers, distributors, and business partners which is not open to the general public. Such systems are replacing the earlier EDI systems. It consists of two intranets connected via the Internet, whereby two organizations are allowed to view each other's confidential information. Generally, only a small portion of information, required to conduct business, is made available through the extranet to its business partners. Interestingly, such business to business networks have existed since long before the present-day Internet.

19.5.4 Intranet

It refers to an internal private network used to link various divisions of a business around the world into a unified communication network using the same types of software, hardware, and connections as the Internet. It uses Internet standards for electronic communication within the organization, separating these websites from the rest of the world by firewalls and other security measures.

In technical terms, there is hardly any difference between the Internet, the extranet, and the intranet. Since intranet and extranet can be viewed by specific groups, these also form subsets of Internet.

19.5.5 E-readiness

E-readiness is a measure of the quality of a country's ICT infrastructure and the ability of its consumers, businesses, and government to use it to their benefit. It provides a broad framework to assess the world's largest economies on their abilities to absorb the technology and use it for economic and social benefits. It also provides an overview of the world's most prominent investment locations for online operations.

The Economist Intelligence Unit annually publishes e-readiness ranking for the world's 70 largest economies based on nearly 100 separate quantitative and qualitative criteria to assess countries' technology infrastructure, their general business environment, the degree to which e-business is adopted by consumers and companies, social, cultural and legal environments and government policy and vision.

The US ranks the highest in terms of its e-readiness[12] in 2008, as depicted in Fig. 19.6, with an overall score of 8.95 on a 10-point scale, followed by Hong Kong (8.91), Sweden (8.85), Australia (8.83), Denmark (8.83), Singapore (8.74), and the UK (8.68), whereas Germany has a score of 8.39, Japan 8.08, South Africa 5.95, Brazil 5.65, Thailand 5.22, India 4.96, China 4.85, Russia 4.42, and Iran 3.18. The Economist Intelligence Unit finds India a shining example of an emerging market[13] for its famed IT-enabled services sector that contributes significantly to its economy. Besides, India's success story has been replicated throughout the region. This has transformed Asia into an emblem of borderless economy.

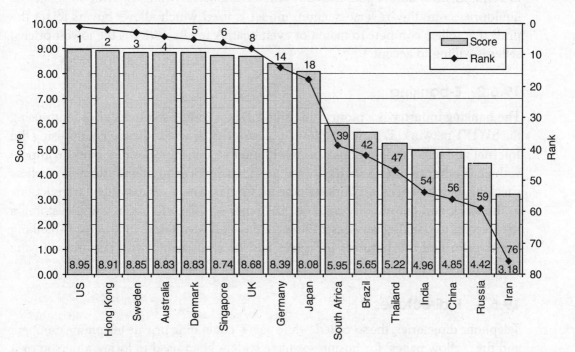

Fig. 19.6   E-readiness ranking (2008)

Note: 1—world's least e-ready country; 10—world's most e-ready country.
Source: 'E-readiness Ranking, 2008: Maintaining Momentum', The Economic Intelligence Unit, p. 5.

---

[12] 'E-readiness Ranking, 2008: Maintaining Momentum', The Economic Intelligence Unit, p. 5.
[13] 'The 2004 E-readiness Rankings', Economist Intelligence Unit, 2004, p. 14.

19.6   E-BUSINESS APPLICATIONS

Integration of ICT finds wide applications in a range of business activities, including the following.

19.6.1   E-auctions

In traditional auctions, buyers and sellers gather at an agreed place, often the auction house, at a pre-determined time. Bids are usually placed over and above the reserved price set by the seller until the biding stops at a higher offer rate and the final bidder makes claims to the goods. Using a similar approach, electronic auction sites allow Internet users either to sell or bid for the products offered.

Auction sites generally serve as a forum of buying and selling and charge a commission on sales made. Sellers may post an item they wish to sell along with a minimum price and the deadline to close the auction. Moreover, some site also allows addition of conditions of sales and product photographs. On the other hand, bidders may explore the site to check its availability and place a bid, usually in designated increments. eBay allows people to buy and sell almost anything. In some sites, such as liquidprice.com, the 'reverse-auction' model is used which allows buyers to set the price that sellers compete to match or even beat. A reverse price is the lowest price a seller is willing to accept.

19.6.2   E-banking

The banking industry is a pioneer in using EDI for intra-bank transfer of funds using the SWIFT network. E-banking allows its customers to access their accounts using the Internet and make online transactions with no extra charge. Besides, banks compete with each other to offer a variety of value-added services to their customers, such as checking their balances, account statements, fund transfers, bill payment, transactions in the stock and commodity markets, customer service, etc. As a result, customers have access to banking services 24 hours a day and seven days in a week. E-banking has transformed the business processes and its relationship with customers in the banking industry.

19.6.3   E-directories

Telephone directories, the so-called 'white pages' containing private telephone numbers and the 'yellow pages' for businesses have widely been used to locate a person or a company. Conversion of traditional directories from paper to electronic form and integrating them with the Internet has facilitated their online access round the clock from any part of the world. Besides, a large number of online directories allow users to update their entries any time they wish, irrespective of their geographical locations. Thus the information which could earlier be updated only at the time of printing a new or revised directory has become dynamic in nature. Moreover, electronic directories are often user-friendly. Users may online access detailed information upon entering the desired fields. For instance, one can get the name and complete address of a person or a company by entering only the telephone number.

19.6.4   E-manufacturing

Integration of technology has facilitated sharing real-time information with a firm's customers and trading partners, leading to the use of such information for making collaborative production decisions. As a result, businesses are increasingly adopting e-manufacturing using real-time information on customer needs and preferences and productive capacity across the entire supply-chain so as to speedily deliver customized products directly to the customers rather than huge volumes of mass production to fulfil anticipated demands.

An automated manufacturing system integrated through computer technology is known as computer integrated manufacturing (CIM). With globalization of markets and production and with the advent of the Internet, CIM has evolved into a web-centric collaborative venture, termed as e-manufacturing. E-manufacturing involves Computer-Added Designs (CAD), robots, automated guided vehicles, Computer Numerical Control (CNC) machines, Automated Storage and Retrieval Systems (ASRS), and Flexible Manufacturing Systems (FMS).

19.6.5   E-business Research

The uses of electronic surveys for business research have increased tremendously in the last decade. Due to variation in the extent of availability of personal computers and Internet penetration, mass electronic surveys are possible only in a few developed countries while stratified sampling for select market segments can even be carried out in developing countries. With the intensification of cyber cafes in India and other emerging economies, the Internet has the reach of far greater population than that captured in most multilateral surveys and publications. Hence, business and institutional surveys are gaining popularity even in the developing countries. Although electronic surveys are cost-effective and quick, the sample surveyed may not be representative of the population and may lead to faulty inferences. Therefore, due care is to be taken while selecting samples for electronic surveys.

19.6.6   E-governance

Governments across the world are using the Internet to augment their communication systems with their citizens. Government websites often provide a wealth of information which is extensively used by various stakeholders, such as foreign and multilateral agencies, officials, researchers, and most importantly by their own citizens. In addition to information provided, governments across the world are evolving new systems to integrate technology for providing value-added services. Integration of technology with a system of governance has made it possible to make online queries, file complaints, make applications for various statutory approvals, receive approvals online, and track online interactions. E-governance has significantly contributed to transparency and efficiency in public administration.

19.7 E-BUSINESS MODELS

Basic process-flow and linking together of diverse business functions is termed as a 'business model'. Principal e-business models (Fig. 19.7) can basically be categorized, as follows:

19.7.1 Business to Business (B-to-B)

It involves intra-firm transactions using an electronic network. Business to business (B-to-B or B2B) transactions account for about 80 per cent of total electronic transactions and are predicted to move faster compared to the B-to-C segment. B-to-B e-business comprises two primary components:

E-infrastructure

It is the architect of B-to-B, which primarily consists of

- Logistics—Transportation, warehousing, and distribution (i.e., Procter and Gamble)
- Application service providers—Deployment, hosting, and management of packaged software from a central facility (i.e., Oracle)
- Outsourcing of functions in the process of e-commerce, such as web-hosting, security, and customer-care solutions (i.e., outsourcing providers, such as eShare, NetSales, etc.)
- Auction solutions software for the operation and maintenance of real-time auctions over the Internet (i.e., Moai Technologies and OpenSite Technologies)
- Content management software for the facilitation of website content management and delivery (i.e., Interwoven and ProcureNet)

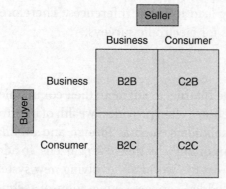

Fig. 19.7 Types of e-businesses

- Web-based commerce enablers (i.e., Commerce One, a browser-based, XML-enabled purchasing automation software)[14]

E-markets

It includes web portals where buyers and sellers interact with each other and conduct transactions. For instance, Hewlett Packard (HP), IBM, Cisco, etc.

Major areas of B2B applications include supplier management (especially purchase-order processing), inventory management (i.e., managing order-ship-bill cycles), distribution management (especially in the transmission of shipping documents), channel management (i.e., information dissemination on changes in operational conditions), and payment management (i.e., electronic payment systems or EPS).

Benefits of B2B E-business

Reduction in transaction costs   Conduct of B2B e-business reduces costs in the following areas:

- Cost reduction in search for alternatives, as buyers need not go through multiple market intermediaries as in the traditional supply chain, to search for information about supplier's products and prices. Besides, the Internet is a more efficient channel in terms of effort, time, and money spent compared to its traditional counterparts.
- Cost of processing transactions (invoices, purchase orders, and payment schemes), as B2B allows for the automation of transaction processes and therefore, the quick implementation of the same compared to other channels (such as, the telephone and fax). Efficiency in trading processes and transactions is also enhanced by way of processing sales through online auctions.

Disintermediation   The process of eliminating the middlemen from the exchange processes is known as 'disintermediation'. The B2B transactions enable suppliers to interact and transact directly with buyers, thereby eliminating intermediaries and distributors (Fig. 19.8). Most middlemen who survived merely on knowledge about the requirements of buyers and sellers and hardly added value to the exchange processes face extinction in a variety of industries, such as insurance, real estate, travel agencies, stock brokerages, etc.

Fig. 19.8   Process of disintermediation

---

[14] 'E-commerce/Internet: B2B: 2B or Not 2B?', *Goldman Sachs Investment Research*, vol. 1.1, 16 November 1999, pp. 68–71.

Transparency in pricing   Collective participation of multiple buyers and sellers in a single e-market reveals market price information and transaction processing to all the participants. This not only increases transparency in prices but also pulls down the prices.

Economies of scale and network effect   B2B e-marketing brings together a large number of buyers and sellers who provide demand side economies of scale and network effects. Each additional incremental participant in the e-market creates value for all participants in the demand side. More participants form a critical mass, which is crucial to attract more users to an e-market.

19.7.2   Business to Consumers

Business to consumers (B-to-C or B2C) is the second largest and the earliest form of e-business, the origin of which can be traced to e-tailing or online retailing. B2C e-commerce is often used for purchasing products and information, mainly personal finances and investments, with the use of online banking and investment tools. Business transactions between companies and consumers involve customers gathering information, purchasing physical goods (i.e., tangibles, such as books or consumer products) or information goods (goods of electronic material or digitized content, such as software, or e-books), and for information goods, receiving products over an electronic network.[15]

The Internet has greatly facilitated the proliferation of B2C e-commerce during the recent years. It is estimated that the major items purchased[16] online include books (58%), music (50%), software (44%), air tickets (29%), PC peripherals (28%), clothing (26%), videos (24%), hotel reservations (20%), toys (20%), flowers (17%), and consumer electronics (12%). However, e-marketing transactions are less popular in product categories that need to be physically touched and examined by the buyers, such as clothes, furniture, etc. Consumers buying online tend to be relatively younger, better-educated, and generally affluent. B2C e-marketing leads to an exchange process initiated and controlled by customers. Until customers invite marketers to participate in their exchange processes, marketers have to wait. Moreover, the rules of marketing engagement are also determined by the end customers.

The world's most favoured online retailers (Table 19.2) include Amazon.com, eBay.com, Wal-Mart.com, BestBuy.com, JCPenney.com, Target.com, Google.com, Overstock.com, Kohls.com, and Sears.com. The sales of Amazon.com grew at a very rapid rate compared to other e-retailers, with its stellar 93 per cent annual growth rate. Its virtual marketing channel made it 'the earth's biggest book store' in July 1995. Since then it has expanded into broad range of product lines. Dell computer sells personal computers directly through the Internet to its global customers on a

---

[15] Based on Lallana, Quimbo, C. Andam, Ravi Kalakota, and Andrew B. Whinston, *Electronic Commerce: A Manager's Guide*, US: Addison Wesley Longman, Inc., 1997, pp. 19–20.

[16] Kotler, Philip, *Market Management*, 11th ed., New Delhi: Prentice Hall, 2002, p. 40.

Table 19.2   Top 10 most favourite online retailers

Rank	Retailers	Headquarters	Main product
1.	Amazon.com	Seattle	Books
2.	eBay.com	San Jose, California	Auction
3.	Wal-Mart.com	Bentonville, Arkansas	General merchandise
4.	BestBuy.com	Richfield, Minnesota	Electronics
5.	JCPenney.com	Plano, Texas	Apparel
6.	Target.com	Minneapolis	General merchandise
7.	Google.com	Mountain View, California	Information
8.	Overstock.com	Salt Lake City	General merchandise
9.	Kohls.com	Menomonee Falls, Wisconsin	Apparel
10.	Sears.com	Hoffman Estates, III, Chicago	General merchandise

Source: The Online Retailers Stores.org, October 2008.

'build to order' basis rather than a 'build to forecast' basis. However, the firm has very efficient supply chain management so as to ship PCs on local or regional basis.

19.7.3   Consumers to Business

In a complete reversal of traditional business models, consumers to business (C-to-B or C2B) e-business allows individuals, especially professionals, such as lawyers and accountants, to offer their services to businesses as well as sites that allow individuals to offer their services or products to businesses. Under C2B transactions, 'reverse auctions' are often involved, where customers, rather than the seller, initiate market transactions. It includes tendering by the buyers, inviting suppliers to put forward their bids.

19.7.4   Consumers to Consumers

It involves horizontal interaction between consumers, who generally share their experiences with the product by way of chat rooms. Consumers to consumers (C-to-C or C2C) e-commerce takes place through

- Auctions facilitated at a portal, such as eBay, which allows online real-time bidding. eBay's pioneered online person-to-person trading by developing a web-based community wherein the buyers and sellers transact personal items (Fig. 19.9). eBay permits sellers to list items for sale, buyers to bid on the items of their interest, and all eBay users to browse through listed items on easy to use online services. Items generally transacted under eBay include apparel and accessories, books and magazines, computers and peripherals, fitness and sports, jewellery and watches, music and instruments, stamps, coins and hobbies, consumer electronics, mobiles and accessories, movies and videos, etc.
- Peer-to-peer systems, such as the Napster Model, a protocol of sharing files between users used by chat forums, and other file exchanges
- Classified ads at portal sites, such as e-class, click India, e-classifieds, classified-e-ads, etc.

Fig. 19.9 eBay: The world's largest and most popular C2C portal

19.7.5 Business to Government/Government to Business

Application of e-business between government agencies with businesses may be categorized under government to business (G2B) or business to government (B2G) e-business. It is often used for public procurement, regulatory procedures and approvals, and other government-related operations using ICT tools. A number of countries have introduced Electronic Trade Document System (ETDS) for export-import transactions, as explained later in this chapter, which facilitates online submission of applications to various government agencies for regulatory approvals, electronic payments, and receiving online approvals and clearances. It greatly adds to transparency in government processes and curbs irregularities and corrupt practices, leading to reduced transaction costs.

19.7.6 Citizens to Government/Government to Citizens

Governments often use ICT to enhance interaction with their citizens under citizens to government (C2G) or government to citizens (G2C) models. These are generally used to disseminate to its citizens a variety of government information such as general rules and regulations directly concerned with the citizens and other information of public departments. Generally each ministry, government departments and agencies thereof do have separate portals that not only host relevant information but also provide interactive platforms. These portals also enable citizens to submit their queries for specific information or lodge complaints or make suggestions online that facilitate two-way interactions between the governments and their citizens.

19.8   ALTERNATIVE E-BUSINESS STRATEGIES

Depending upon the integration of Internet technologies with the firm's business strategies, a firm may opt any of the following alternatives.

19.8.1   Brick and Mortar

The phrase 'brick and mortar' refers to tangible physical assets, such as a manufacturing unit or building, or a storage facility. This is the traditional business model wherein websites are used only as a company brochure. 'Brick and mortar' firms generate their total revenue from traditional means of sale whereas the website is only used to provide information. However, such brick and mortar firms, consequent to a favourable market feedback, often develop as 'brick and click' companies.

19.8.2   Pure Click

Under this model, the entire marketing transactions are carried out online with little physical presence. Such firms are also known as 'dotcoms' or 'pure-plays'. Such 'pure-click' firms include search engines, commercial sites, Internet Service Providers (ISPs), transaction sites, content sites, and enabler sites. Engines, such as Google, Yahoo, Sify, and AltaVista, primarily started as search engines, now also provide a variety of services such as free mails, weather reports, news, entertainment, etc. The commercial sites of pure click companies, such as amazon.com and indiatimes.com, sells books and other products. eBay provides platform for auction for a commission on transaction conducted on the sites. In the late 1990s, pure click firms achieved a very high level of market capitalization and were considered a major threat to traditional marketing business. However, the hype of dotcoms was short-lived and bust in 2000.

19.8.3   Brick and Click

Under this model, a firm conducts marketing activities and transactions, both online and offline. Firms using 'brick and click' model need to be cautious that their online sales do not cannibalize existing sales through traditional marketing channels. Such firms also emphasize reduction of channel conflicts between their own channel intermediaries and online sales. Firms such as Avon, Compaq, etc. evolved models so that their e-marketing activities became complimentary, rather than competitive, to the traditional marketing model. In January 2000, Walmart.com was founded as a subsidiary of Wal-Mart stores, which provides easy access to more than 1 million products available online. It combines technology and world-class retailing aimed at gaining customers and offers a wide assortment of products round the clock.

19.9 GLOBAL E-MARKETING

Conduct of marketing transactions, such as buying, selling, distributing or delivering goods or services using electronic methods is termed as e-marketing. It includes use of electronic data and its applications for conceptualization, planning, pricing, and distribution and promotion of goods and services so as to create exchanges to satisfy customer needs. Global e-marketing involves marketing transactions through electronic methods across the world.

Earlier, EDI used proprietary-dedicated networks to transmit highly structured machine-readable data. However, the Internet has facilitated creating an electronic marketspace as depicted in Fig. 19.10 where buyers and sellers can exchange information through e-mail, video, voice, and image, in a cost-effective manner.

Although Internet-based e-marketing networks are highly cost-effective, the transactions are less secure as these are open networks. B2B e-commerce adds to the efficiency of marketing transactions. It facilitates greater access to information to the buyers about the sellers worldwide. As the prices have become more transparent through the Internet, it has increased price pressures on undifferentiated commodities. At the same time, it provides greater information on highly differentiated brands.

The traditional approach to marketing calls for market segmentation, i.e., dividing the customers into sub-groups, who would respond similarly to a given marketing strategy, and target a group of customers with a uniform marketing strategy. 'Personalization' implies market targeting to the extreme by using a unique marketing mix for each customer. The term 'customization' refers to manufacturing systems and is a 'company-led approach' and focuses on developing production systems so as to provide unique products to individual customers, whereas 'personalization' is more appropriate for e-commerce as it incorporates both the customer-led and company-led approaches to target a customer segment size of one. Thus, digital technology is

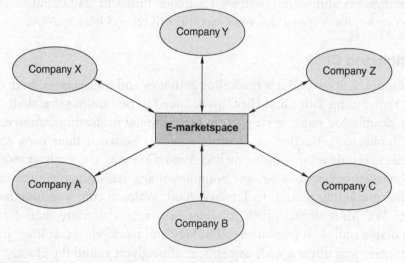

Fig. 19.10 Internet-based virtual e-marketspace

increasingly harnessed to create and offer a highly personalized marketing mix and to develop an effective and sustainable customer relationship management (CRM).

19.9.1   Impact of ICT on Consumer Purchase Decision Process

E-marketing has also transformed the marketing process from a physical marketplace to a virtual marketspace, which has considerably altered consumer's buying behaviour. Integrating ICT applications with marketing has led to considerable changes in the consumer's purchasing-decision process,[17] briefly summarized below.

Problem recognition

Conventional marketing communications stimulate market demand via conventional media, i.e., advertisements in print media, radio, or television. Communication strategy on the Internet should be user-specific rather than a mass-communication approach as used in traditional media. Thus, the communication strategy has undergone a fundamental change with an increased focus on the customized communication approach targeting individual customers.

Information search

In traditional marketing systems, customers gather information through either internal or external sources, including peer group discussions, company brochures, etc. The availability of market information varies widely between the firms and the customers. However, in the virtual marketspace, customers can scan information on the Internet and make comparisons to suit their individual requirements. The intermediary function performed by Internet sites is mainly related to providing information and exchange. For instance, airlines, railways, tour operators, etc., provide online booking that bypasses traditional market intermediaries, such as travel agents. Internet websites also provide links with other websites that help customers gather more information.

Evaluation of alternatives

In a traditional marketplace, the evaluation of alternatives is greatly influenced by one's peer groups, family members, friends, and publicity through word of mouth whereas in an electronic marketspace, the virtual community has taken up the role of traditional reference groups. Various discussion groups and consumer forums share with each other their experiences over the net.

Purchase decision

The decision to select a seller for a purchase is traditionally based on the previous experience of the buyer with the seller, his/her proximity, range of products offered, and the price charged. However, in the electronic marketspace, sellers often attract

---

[17] Butler, P. and J. Peppard, 'Consumer Purchasing on the Internet: Process and Prospects', *European Management Journal*, vol. 16, no. 5, 1998, pp. 600–10.

buyers by way of creating interesting websites, offering competitive prices, and superior purchasing experience so as to induce purchase decisions. In Internet transactions, the payment is usually through credit cards but delivery mechanisms differ, depending upon the product type. It may be in the form of either online delivery or physical delivery. For instance, software, music, design, etc., may be delivered online whereas physical goods have to be delivered physically.

Post-purchase behaviour

In traditional markets, a firm should respond to customer complaints and enquiries through the marketing channels. However, in an electronic marketspace, the emphasis is on information and communication technologies, such as continuous updating of websites, and on satisfying customer needs. A firm should endeavour to offer value to its customers through its websites by promptly responding to their queries and providing latest information to encourage new purchases.

19.9.2   E-business Communication

To communicate with various stakeholders, businesses traditionally used various methods of 'linear' communication such as print media (i.e., newspapers, magazines, journals, etc.), electronic media (i.e., television and radio), telephone, direct sales, etc. The advent of the Internet and the World Wide Web has fostered a 'hypermedia' environment making it possible to deliver targeted messages to specific audiences. This environment allows 'non-linear' communication using hyperlinks with search and retrieval processes to collect information.[18] Hypermedia advantage may be measured by various method (Exhibit 19.3), such as hit count, page view, click through, unique visitors, reach, etc.

Today, the Internet is extensively used by businesses to communicate with their external and internal audiences. External audiences include stockholders, customers, the general public, etc., whereas both suppliers and employees constitute a firm's internal audiences. Suppliers and employees often use the intranet for communicating within the organization. Unlike the linear communication that follows a scripted flow, hypermedia communication over the Internet allows a free flow and exchange of information.

19.9.3   Emergence of Reverse Marketing

Earlier, the information flow between the companies and the customers was generally a one-way process. The information was market controlled, customers were ill informed, and the exchanges were market initiated.[19] The industrial era was known

---

[18] Hoffman, Donna L. and Thomas P. Novak, 'Marketing in Hypermedia Computer-Mediated Environments: Conceptual Foundations', *Journal of Marketing*, vol. 60, July 1996, pp. 50–68.

[19] Sawhney, Mohanbir and Philip Kotler, 'Marketing in the Age of Information Democracy', *Kellogg on Marketing*, (ed.) Iacobucci, Dawn, New York: John Wiley & Sons, p. 401.

	Exhibit 19.3	Measurement of hypermedia advertising
Measurement method	**Definition**	**Comments**
Hit count	Measures the number of times a page is requested but not necessarily seen or displayed at the user's browser	Provides information on actual hits, but there could be multiple hits counted for every click of the mouse or page refresh. Records activity regardless of the viewer's location, such as workplaces, homes, schools, or other countries. Provides no information on users.
Page view	Tracks the number of individual pages sent to web viewers	Gives no indication of how many users receive or view pages and no profile data on users.
Click-through	Tracks the number of times an online ad is clicked on	Gives no information about the customers. Customers who click through may dump a page before it loads.
Unique visitors	Allow tracking by the IP address of the viewer	Many people use the same IP address to access a site.
Reach	Measures sampled group's visits (if 25% of sample has visited site, reach obtained 25%)	Requires the use of panels or surveys. This can pair information on the individual's background with individual behaviour. These panels may be narrow in scope and not account for all web surfers, such as those at work or from other countries,
New measures	Include linking individuals by demographic data, loyalty, site behaviour, and other measures	May allow online, constant measures of who visits a site and how long they stay at a site.

Source: 'Media Audience Measurement', FastInfo.org, http://www.fastinfo.org/measurement/pages/index.cgi/audiencemeasurement, 22 September 1999; Vonder Haar, Steven, 'Web Metrics: Go Figure', *Business 2.0,* June 1999, pp. 46–47.

as the era of information asymmetry. With breakthroughs in information and communication technology, information has become affordable and universal. The ease of access and availability of information about a firm's products and those of its competitors to the customers have greatly increased around the world. This has resulted in a shift of power from manufacturers to customers. This has led to not only customer-oriented marketing but also to customer-initiated marketing. The use of the Internet has empowered buyers significantly. Today, the buyers can[20]

- Get information about the manufactures of the products and brands around the world
- Carry out comparison of product features, quality, prices, etc., from a variety of sources

[20] Sawhney, Mohanbir and Philip Kotler, 'Marketing in the Age of Information Democracy', *Kellogg on Marketing*, (ed.) Iacobucci, Dawn, New York: John Wiley & Sons, p. 401.

- Initiate requests for advertising and information from the manufacturers
- Design market-offerings
- Hire buying agents and invite market offers from multiple sellers
- Buy ancillary products and services from a specialized third party

Earlier, the marketers used to initiate the marketing activities, but the breakthroughs in ICT have metamorphosed the marketing system, enabling customers to initiate marketing activities. The phenomenon is termed as *reverse marketing* wherein the customers initiate the exchanges and gather the required information.[21] The customers can now initiate and carry out the following activities:

Reverse promotion

A customer may search for product information and solicit promotion from the marketers or through the intermediaries. These intermediaries relay customer requests to the marketers without divulging personal information and block unwanted offers.

Reverse advertising

Traditionally, firms used to push advertisements to the customers, generally as a mass communication tool. ICT has now enabled customers to request for more information from manufacturers and click on the advertisements they are interested in. Thus, advertising becomes customer-initiated as it can be pulled by customers.

Reverse pricing

Buyers can place their offer for bidding and set the prices. A number of e-marketing firms, such as indiatimes.com, allow the customers to set their own price. Buyers can specify the price and model options. A variety of branded consumer durables are also available for auction on such sites.

Reverse product design

The e-marketing firms enable customers to customize the products of their own choice. HMV's HamaraCD.com enables customers to customize their own CD with their own titles.

Reverse segmentation

Traditionally the marketing firms used customer purchase history to create customized offer. However, under e-marketing customers can self-select and co-customize offers with marketers.

---

[21] Sawhney, Mohanbir and Philip Kotler, 'Marketing in the Age of Information Democracy', *Kellogg on Marketing*, (ed.) Iacobucci, Dawn, New York: John Wiley & Sons, pp. 386–408.

19.10 GLOBAL E-SERVICES

The ICT has revolutionized the ways services are offered breaking the geographical boundaries. With digitization, the Internet, and high-speed data networks as the driving forces, all kinds of knowledge-related work can now be done almost anywhere in the world. Corporate downsizing in the US and Europe is also helping create more high-skilled jobs in developing countries. This covers a wide range of professions, such as life sciences, legal services, art and design, management, business operations, computing, architecture, sales, and office support.

The Indian BPO business began with basic data entry and transcription of medical records. Gradually it moved up the ladder to rules-set based processing where agents made judgements based on rules set by the customer, for instance, upgrading travellers from economy to business class. Further up the ladder, offshore IT-enabled services (ITeS) included trouble-shooting by BPO agents, such as the discretion to enhance credit card limits. Direct customer interaction requires BPO workers to handle more elaborate transactions with a client's customers. Collecting delinquent payment from credit-card customers or sorting out computer snags.

Companies are increasingly offshoring knowledge intensive activities such as engineering drawings and design, marketing, research, legal services, etc. which transforms the role of traditional Business Process Outsourcing (BPO) vendor to a Knowledge Process Outsourcing (KPO) vendor. Over recent years, the scope of IT-enabled services has expanded considerably to include the increasingly complex processes involving rule-based decision-making and even research services requiring informed individual judgement. The rapid expansion in scope of BPOs has been accompanied by an equally rapid adoption across a range of vertical industries. The various ITeS may be categorized as

Finance and accounting (F&A) services   These include activities, such as general accounting, transaction management (accounts receivables and payables management), corporate finance (i.e., treasury and risk management, and tax management); compliance management and statutory reporting, etc.

Customer interaction services   These include all forms of IT-enabled customer contact; inbound or outbound, voice or non-voice based support used to provide customer services, sales and marketing, technical support and help desk services.

Human resource administration services   These include payroll and benefit administration, travel and expense processing, talent acquisition and talent management services, employee communication design, and administration.

Other-vertical specific and niche services   These include innovation of the underlying business processes being outsourced, improved competitive positioning, managing customer expectations, elevation of the strategic role of the retained organization, optimal resource allocation, support for globalization of businesses, and technology support and access.

With abundance of professional manpower at much lower cost compared to developed economies, India has emerged as the most preferred location for expert knowledge service. GE's former CEO, Jack Welch brought out a 70:70:70 vision, which means GE would outsource 70 percent of its work, 70 percent of that will be off-shored and 70 percent of the off-shored tasks will be done from India.

India witnessed the world's highest growth of 37.5 per cent—from US$8.5 billion in 2000 to US$41.7 billion—in 2005 among the top 30 major exporters of ICT-enabled services, as depicted in Fig. 19.11. The US was the top exporter of IT-enabled services during 2005 with an export of US$184.7 billion followed by UK (US$132.8 billion), Germany (US$73.8 billion), Japan (US$52.5 billion), and France (US$42.0 billion), whereas Canada exported for US$28 billion, Switzerland for US$28.7 billion, Singapore for 27 billion, and China for US$26.6 billion.

Banking, financial services, and insurance (BFSI) remained the largest vertical markets for Indian IT exports in 2006–07, accounting for 40.4 per cent of such exports, followed by high technology and telecom (19.1%) manufacturing (15%), retail (8%), media, publishing, and entertainment (3.3%), construction and utilities (3.5%), healthcare (2.5%), airlines and transportation and others (4.7%). The US is the largest market for India's IT BPO exports, accounting for 61.4 per cent of total market share[22]

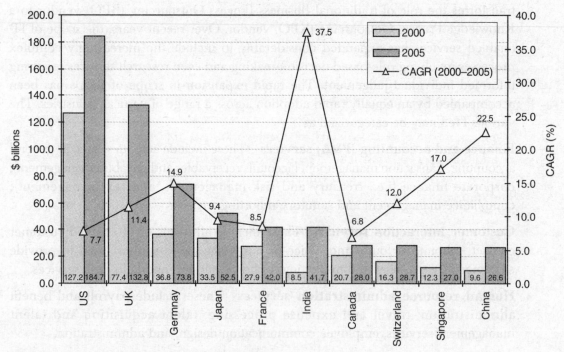

Fig. 19.11 Major exporters of ICT-enabled services

Source: The National Association of Software and Services Companies (NASSCOM).

---

[22] The National Association of Software and Services Companies (NASSCOM).

in 2006–07, followed by the UK (17.8%), Continental Europe (12.3%), Asia Pacific (6.4%), and the rest of the world (2.1%).

19.11 ELECTRONIC PROCESSING OF INTERNATIONAL TRADE DOCUMENTS

Traditionally, exporters and importers were required to prepare multiple copies of trade documents on paper and physically deliver them to various government agencies for processing and clearances, as depicted in Fig. 19.12. Such a system was not only tedious but also involved delays ranging from a few hours to several days, lack of transparency, and widespread unethical corrupt practices among government officials. Besides, enormous paper-work led to additional business costs for both the government and the traders.

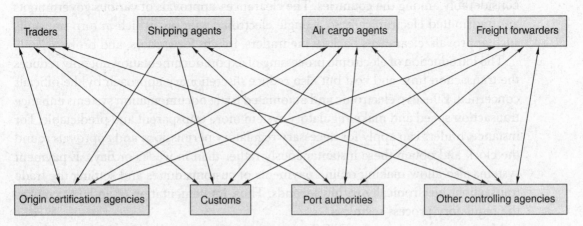

Fig. 19.12 Traditional system of trade documents flow

Rapid growth of international trade volume tends to reduce considerably the speed of traditional paper-based document processing systems, besides enhancing the chances of error. Such systems are also vulnerable to corruption, besides lack of transparency and unpredictability.

19.11.1 Electronic Trade Documentation System

The manual ways of trade documentation and its processing are being transformed into paperless means by way of introduction of the electronic data interchange (EDI) trade system. Besides, trade procedures are also being streamlined and automated so that a single form could be used for all trade documentation requirements. An ideal single electronic window system should provide a single point of data entry to achieve a number of completed transactions with the multiple government agencies. The conceptual framework of single electronic window for trade facilitation, as depicted in Fig. 19.13 reveals that the traders, freight forwarders, and brokers may send their documents to a single electronic window, which carries out the sorting of the documents and in turn transmits them electronically to various government agencies, such

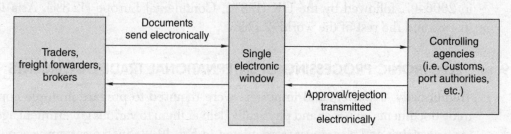

Fig. 19.13   Conceptual framework of single electronic window for trade facilitation

as Customs, port authorities, certification agencies, etc. However, the extent of implementation of the Electronic Trade Documentation System (ETDS) varies considerably among the countries. The clearances/approvals of various governments are transmitted electronically to a single electronic window, which in turn transmits such approvals/clearances back to the traders, freight forwarders, and brokers.

The introduction of electronic processing of export documentation not only reduces the transaction time and cost but also reduce discretionary approach by the officials concerned. Effective electronic and automated trade documentation systems enhance transaction speed and make regulatory system more transparent and predictable. For instance, traders can apply for necessary regulatory permissions and approvals round the clock and obtain these instantaneously rather than in weeks or days. E-payment systems also allow making online payments of customs duties and settling the trade transactions electronically within seconds. Thus, implementation of an ETDS makes the regulatory process seamless.

Major concerns about the ETDS relate to security aspects and legal framework and need to be tackled both at national and multilateral level.

19.11.2   Singapore's Electronic Trade Documentation System

Given its geographical size constraint, the government of Singapore recognized that the key to providing opportunities for its economy and attaining competitiveness lay in enhancing operational efficiency of all economic activities by way of integrating them with information technology. To this end, it established the Committee on National Computerization (CNC) in 1979. Consequently, under this computerization project, several government agencies were brought under computerization and exemplary systems for electronic trade documentation established.

TradeNet

Since 1989, the TradeNet system has been operational in Singapore. It is an EDI system that allows computer-to-computer exchange of inter-company business documents in an established format between connected members of the Singapore trading community (Fig. 19.14). It links multiple parties involved in international trade transactions, including 35 government institutions, to a single point of transaction for

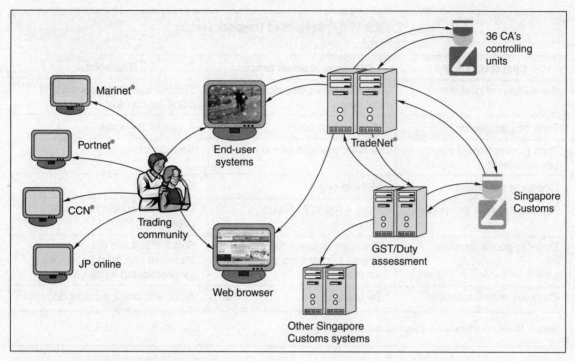

Fig. 19.14   Singapore's TradeNet system

most trade documentation tasks. It is an electronic trade clearance system that allows customs brokers, traders, ports, banks, customs, and other government agencies to exchange structured trade messages and information electronically. It integrates import, export, and transhipment documentation processing procedures, resulting in a reduction in cost and turnaround time for the preparation, submission, and processing of trade and shipping documents. The benefits of the TradeNet system are summarized in Exhibit 19.4.

TradeXchange

The TradeXchange is the world's first nation-wide electronic trade documentation system that offers a single point of data entry to achieve a number of completed transactions with the government. It's a multi-agency initiative launched in October 2007 that processes 100 per cent of all trade declarations and integrates the requirements of all 35 controlling units in Singapore.

In addition to TradeNet, which connects users to government agencies, TradeXchange also provides seamless inter-connectivity among commercial and regulatory systems for the Singapore trade and logistics community. Moreover, it offers a single electronic window for integrated workflow, submission, and enquiries to seaports, airports, maritime authorities, customs, and controlling agencies. It also provides connectivity to commercial and regulatory systems in other countries. Besides, a number of value-added service providers also offer application services to the trade

	Exhibit 19.4 Benefits of TradeNet system	
Characteristics	**Previous manual process**	**TradeNet**
Submission of documents	Via expensive dispatch clerks/ couriers	Electronically from comforts of office (or home)
Time of submission	Within office hours	Available 24 hours
Trips per controlling agency per document	At least two trips or more	No trips required
Copies of document	Multiple copies	Single copy
Turnaround time for approval	From 4 hrs to 2–7 days	Within two minutes (general goods handling)
Dutiable goods handling	Separate documents sent to different controlling agencies for processing	Same electronic document routed to controlling agencies for processing
Customs duties collection	By cheque	Automatic bank account deduction

Source: Based on information from CrimsonLogic, Singapore.

and logistics community in areas, such as trade document preparation, supply chain management, logistics and freight management, trade finance, and insurance.

The earlier TradeNet facilitated business to government transactions only and users had to access disparate, stand-alone systems to perform trade transaction (Fig. 19.14). The currently introduced TradeXchange system, as shown in Fig. 19.15, offers a neutral and secure IT platform that enables information exchange between commercial entities and government, through a comprehensive suite of trade services summarized as follows:

Shipping line linkages   The shipping line linkages facilitate sending and receiving relevant messages to and from shipping lines. Messages include vessel schedule, cargo booking, draft bills of lading, and track and trace status (i.e., loaded on vessel, carrier release, container out gate, etc.).

Overseas highway customs   They enable sending data for customs clearance via the Pan Asia e-commerce Alliance (PAA) network to Malaysia, Taiwan, Korea, Macau, Shanghai, Hong Kong, Philippines, and Thailand besides direct customs clearance connection to Australia, Canada, etc.

Title registry   End users and providers of value added services can leverage on electronic title registry to facilitate secured registration and transfer of title of the goods and to allow secured access to the title record as needed in the entire export-import process.

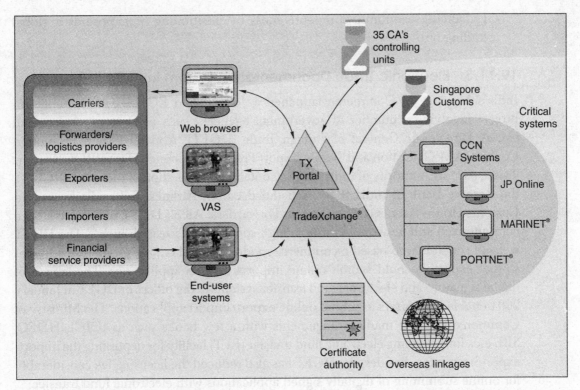

Fig. 19.15 Singapore's TradeXchange

Source: Trade Xchange, Singapore.

Overseas highway manifest   Global linkages facilitate sending advanced manifest data electronically to other countries, such as the US (Automated Manifest System, AMS), Canada (Advance Commercial Information, ACI), Australia (Integrated Cargo System, ICS), etc.

Integrated multimodal solution   Integrated Multi-Modal Solution (IMS) interface with Cargo Community Network (CCN) and Port Net provides sea/air schedule and tracking modules to critical system services.

TradeXchange was developed as a public-private partnership (PPP) project with CrimsonLogic Pte Ltd., which is also responsible for its operations and maintenance. Exporters and importers can deposit extract and transmit information to trade exchange through value added service solutions. TradeXchange system has greatly facilitated Singapore's trade processes in a number of ways including

- Providing single interface for users
- Improving trade documentation process by way of business process re-engineering
- Simplifying permit declaration requirement
- Reducing errors from repeated data entry

- Enhancing economic competitiveness by positioning Singapore as a global trading hub

19.11.3   Electronic Trade Documentation System in India

India's Ministry of Commerce launched a coordinated EC/EDI implementation project involving a number of government agencies, such as Customs and central excise, Directorate General of Foreign Trade (DGFT), Apparel Export Promotion Council (AEPC), Cotton and Textile Export Promotion Council (TEXPROCIL), Port Trusts, Airport Authority of India (AAI), Container Corporation of India (CONCOR), the Reserve Bank of India (RBI), scheduled banks, Airlines, Indian Railways and Customs House Agents (CHA)/Freight Forwarders. All 33 DGFT offices have been computerized and networked through high speed VSATs/leased lines.[23] The DGFT website contains web-based e-commerce modules for all export promotion schemes so that exporters could submit online imports/exports applications. The launch of digital signature and electronic fund transfer systems in the offices of DGFT in January 2004 enabled exporters to submit online export/import applications. The Ministry of Commerce has also made arrangements with a few banks such as ICICI, HDFC, SBI, etc., for providing electronic fund transfer (EFT) facility for depositing the import-export license fee. Besides, the DGFT has also reduced the licensing fee considerably for online submitting of digitally signed applications with electronic fund transfer.

For electronic filing and processing of documents, the Indian Customs and Central Excise Electronic Commerce/Electronic data interchange (EC/EDI) gateway has been created, popularly known as ICEGATE. The ICEGATE runs on a software programme that offers a variety of technological options with regard to communication and messaging standards. The software also ensures efficient management of all incoming and outgoing messages/documents. It offers the facility of filing shipping bills, bill of entry, and related electronic messages between the customs, port authority, and traders through communication facilities like the communication protocols commonly used on the Internet. This facility ensures smooth flow of data between customs authorities and various regulatory agencies.

All electronic documents/messages handled by the ICEGATE are processed at the Customs' end by the Indian Customs EDI system (ICES), which is running in 23 Customs locations, handling nearly 75 per cent of India's international trade in terms of import and export consignments. The electronic processing of documents by EDI has three systems components, which are:

Indian customs EDI system (ICES)   ICES has to automatically receive and processes all incoming messages at all its 23 operational locations. It generates all outgoing messages automatically at the appropriate stage of the clearance process.

---

[23] Arun Jaitely launches digital signature and electronic fund transfer facility—major EDI initiatives to boost exports, press release, Ministry of Commerce, 28 January 2004.

Message exchange servers (MES)   These are computers installed in the custom houses alongside the ICES computers and act as intermediate stations, which hold incoming and outgoing messages.

ICEGATE and ICENET (Indian Customs and Central Excise Gateway, and Indian Customs and Central Excise Network)   ICENET is a network of all ICES at 23 locations, Central Board of Excise and Customs (CBEC), Directorate of Valuation, National Informatics Centre (NIC), and Directorate General of Revenue Intelligence (DGRI).

The entire network of the three systems ICES, MES, and ICEGATE/ICENET have been divided into five service areas as depicted in Fig. 19.16.

The ICES performs the following functions:

- Internal automation of the custom house for a comprehensive, paperless, fully automated customs clearance system
- Online, real-time electronic interface with the trade, transport, and regulatory agencies concerned with customs clearance of import and export cargo.

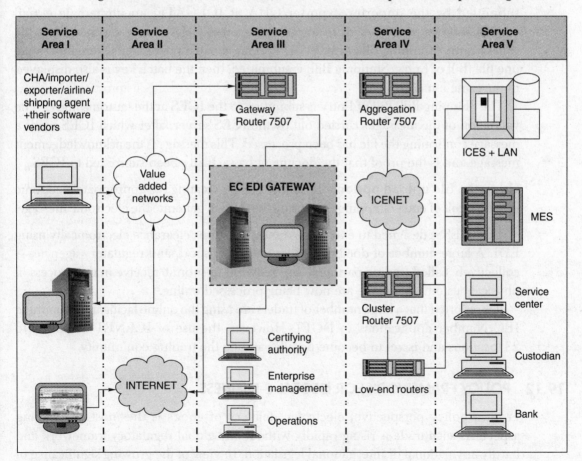

Fig. 19.16   Framework for electronic processing of trade documents in India

The exporter may use any of the following options for submitting data (shipping bill/bill of entry) to the custom house.

Using SMTP option While filing on simple mail transfer protocol (SMTP), the security aspects are taken care of by using digital signature certificate. The following steps have to be taken:

- Create the appropriate electronic message (bill of entry/shipping bill) by using the Remote EDI System (RES) or local application to generate the electronic message
- Installation of SMTP client by using Netscape Messenger, which is the default SMTP client used by the CHA/importer/exporter for sending and receiving e-mails on ICEGATE
- Configure the SMTP client
- Receiving electronic messages on ICEGATE

The importer/exporter/CHA receives e-mails from ICEGATE on an e-mail address established at the time of membership registration. Upon receipt of the documents submitted by the importer/exporter/CHA at ICEGATE, an immediate e-mail confirmation message is sent to importer/exporter/CHA stating receipt of the file (Bill of Entry/Shipping Bill) at ICEGATE. If it is a batch processing where more than one file (Bill of Entry/Shipping Bill) is submitted, then the batch key is also displayed in the same e-mail.

The Shipping Bill/Bill of Entry is submitted to the ICES at the customs house. The validation of the messages carried out by the ICES server, after which ICES sends a message confirming the file has been processed. This message is the acknowledgement message and is the proof that the document has actually been submitted to ICES.

Using the file upload option It can be used by creating the appropriate electronic message (bill of entry/shipping bill), using the RES to generate the electronic message.

The ICES is designed to exchange/transact customs clearance electronically using EDI. A large number of documents that trade, transport, and regulatory agencies—collectively called trading partners—are required to submit/receive in the process of physical customs clearance are now being processed online.

It is reported that a large number of traders are using the online facility for submitting IEC Number applications to DGFT. However, the use of ICENET is limited to 23 locations and is yet to become popular among the trading community.

19.12 POLICY FRAMEWORK FOR GLOBAL E-BUSINESS

From a policy perspective, electronic delivery of goods is the most challenging aspect. As such trade is rising rapidly without any global regulatory framework and hardly any national or international legislation. In view of the growing significance of e-business in international trade, the Second Ministerial Declaration of the WTO at

Geneva adopted a declaration on global electronic commerce on 20 May 1998, which directed the WTO General Council to establish a comprehensive work programme to examine all trade-related issues arising from electronic commerce. The work programme includes issues like characterization of electronic transmission as goods or services or something else, market access involving the method of application of customs duties to electronic transmission, classification of digitized products under the existing Harmonized System (HS) of trade classification, rules of origin, standardization; development dimensions involving the effect on revenue and fiscal positions of developing countries in future, etc. The 1998 declaration also included a so-called moratorium stating that 'members will continue their current practice of not imposing customs tariffs on electronic transmissions'.

The penetration of B2C e-business is of high significance for developing countries as the ban on customs duty is applicable to digitized products which mostly fall in this category. Traditional trade transactions of digital products through a carrier media in the form of diskettes, tapes, CDs etc. were subjected to customs duties in the importing countries. However, the breakthroughs in ICT have made it possible to transmit these products through electronic networks, which are not subject to customs duties.

With rapid growth in international trade of digital products, such as printed matter, software, music and other media, films and video games, most developing countries are becoming net importers of digitized products. The revenue implications of e-commerce have made both developed and developing countries equally concerned, although they differ in terms of the type of tax which can be addressed to stop erosion of revenue. Consumption taxes are important sources of revenue for developed countries; therefore OECD countries decided to impose VAT at a 1998 conference in Ottawa, whereas developing countries are more dependent on customs duties and moratorium on customs duties on digitized products has caused significant losses.

Since e-commerce differs from normal trade in goods, the trade policy requirement also differs for transactions involving digital transmission. Therefore, a specific trade policy is required for international trade electronically.

The technological breakthroughs are likely to transform a large portion of present day 'non e-trade' into 'e-trade' in the near future both in B2B and B2C segments. Besides, increase in FDI and growth in inter-corporate transfers could increase the scope of B2B form of e-commerce for developing countries as well. In view of the rapidly growing significance of e-commerce, the national commitments under GATS agreement would also be required to be reviewed.[24]

This chapter elucidates the conceptual framework of e-business and related technologies. Various applications of e-business have also been elaborated. Besides, various e-business models and alternative strategic options are discussed. This chapter

---

[24] Economic Survey 2007–08, Ministry of Finance, Government of India, New Delhi, pp. 152–53.

also brings out e-enabled business process transformation and global e-marketing and e-services. The process changes brought out by digital technology in international trade documentation system have also been explicated. The policy framework and related concerns in implementing e-enabled business processes have also been examined.

SUMMARY

Rapid economic globalization and advances in information and communication technology (ICT) has made e-business an essential component of a firm's business strategy. The term 'e-commerce' is confined to buying and selling of goods over electronic media, whereas, 'e-business' encompasses a broad framework of business activities. In addition to traditional commercial activities of buying and selling, it also involves collaborating with business partners and servicing customers. Conduct of business activities through use of wireless technology, such as mobile phones, personal digital assistant, and telematics is termed as e-business.

Major changes brought out by integration of digital technology to business processes include physical marketplace to virtual marketspace, physical products to digital products, mass production of standardized products to mass customization, fixed pricing to dynamic pricing, mass-marketing techniques to customized marketing, and hierarchal organizations to network organizations.

The former system of exchange of information between the organizations through computers using proprietary networks, known as electronic data interchange (EDI), has now been widely replaced by the Internet. The network between business enterprises and its suppliers, distributors, and supplier partners which is not open to public is known as extranet whereas intranet refers to the internal network within an organization across geographical boundaries.

The major types of e-business models include business to business (B to B), business to consumers (B to C), consumers to business (C to B), and consumers to consumers (C to C) besides, electronic exchanges between business firms and citizens with the government, such as G to B or B to G and G to C or C to G. Alternative e-business strategies include brick and mortar, pure click, and brick and click.

Conduct of marketing transactions, such as buying, selling, and distributing or delivering goods or services using electronic methods is termed as e-marketing. Use of electronic methods for marketing transactions across the world is termed as global e-marketing. E-marketing has transformed the marketing process from 'physical marketplace' to 'virtual marketspace' that has changed considerably the process of consumers' purchasing decision. E-marketing has also given rise to 'reverse marketing' wherein marketing activities are initiated by the customers rather than marketing firms. The ICT has revolutionized the ways services are offered across geographical boundaries.

Electronic processing of trade documents not only reduces cost, saves time, and increases systems efficiency, it also considerably reduces the discretionary approach by government officials and increases efficiency. An electronic trade documentation system which facilitates documents submission and obtaining trade clearances from multiple government authorities through a single electronic window is fast replacing traditional paper documentation systems across the world. There exists hardly any global regulatory framework for conduct of electronic transactions across borders and limited national or international legislation on e-business, that too with wide variations.

KEY TERMS

Brick and click Conduct of commercial activities and transactions both online and offline.

Brick and mortar Conduct of business activities through tangible physical assets, such as manufacturing unit or building, or a storage facility.

Business to business (B2B) e-commerce Intrafirm transactions using an electronic network.

Disintermediation A process that enables suppliers to interact and transact directly with buyers, thereby eliminating intermediaries and distributors.

E-business Performance of business activities, such as designing products, managing supply-chain, operations, marketing and offering services to various stakeholders using electronic technologies.

E-commerce Buying and selling of goods or services through computer mediated networks.

Electronic data interchange (EDI) The exchange of information between organizations through computers using proprietary networks.

Electronic payment system (EPS) A system of financial exchange between buyers and sellers in the online environment that is facilitated by a digital financial instrument.

E-readiness Measures a country's e-business environment indicating how amenable a market is to Internet-based opportunities.

E-tailing Retailing through the Internet.

Extranet An Internet-based network between a business enterprise and its suppliers, distributors, and business partners, which is not open to the general public.

Global e-marketing Conduct of marketing transactions such as buying, selling, distributing, or delivering goods or services using electronic methods.

Intranet An internal private network used to link various divisions of a business around the world into a unified communication network.

Lifetime value of a customer (LVC) The estimate of potential profit a company is likely to derive out of a customer during her/his lifetime.

M-business Conduct of business activities through use of wireless technology such as mobile phones, personal digital assistant (PDA), or telematics.

One to one (1:1) marketing Marketing targeted at the individual customer, i.e., 'segment size of one'.

Personalization Market targeting to the extreme by using a unique marketing mix for each customer.

Pure click Entire commercial transactions are carried out online with little physical presence.

Reverse marketing Marketing system wherein the customer initiates the exchanges and pulls the required information.

CONCEPT REVIEW QUESTIONS

1. Explain the significance of integrating information and communication technology (ICT) with business processes.

2. Elucidate the conceptual framework of e-business; identify the significant changes it has brought to business processes.

3. Describe the prerequisites for conducting effective e-business transactions.

4. Describe the impact of ICT on consumers' purchase decision process.

5. Write short notes on
   (a) Electronic data interchange (EDI)
   (b) Internet
   (c) Extranet and intranet

CRITICAL THINKING QUESTIONS

1. Explore the Internet and find out three companies each employing the following business models:
   (a) Business to business (B2B)
   (b) Business to consumers (B2C)
   (c) Consumer to business (C2B)
   (d) Consumer to consumer (C2C)

2. Find out the salient features of regulatory framework for e-business transactions in your country and compare it with any two other countries that have relatively higher level of online business transactions.

PROJECT ASSIGNMENTS

1. Select a firm in your country operating internationally with use of e-enabled business processes. Find out its constraints and strengths and its impact on the company's business competitiveness.

2. Visit a nearby company involved in international trade and study the extent of electronic processing of trade documents. Compare it with Singapore's TradeXchange System. Find out the pros and cons of the electronic trade documentation system vis-à-vis traditional paper documentation system.

20 Ethics and Social Responsibility

LEARNING OBJECTIVES

> To delineate the significance of ethical practices in business
> To explain the concept of ethics
> To elucidate unethical business practices
> To explicate corporate social responsibility

20.1 INTRODUCTION

The degradation of moral and ethical values across the world, the proliferation of corruption in all walks of life, and the lack of responsibility and accountability in bureaucrats, politicians, and even businesses towards their stakeholders have led to unethical practices to achieve selfish objectives. Corrupt and unethical business practices by MNEs contribute to corporate frauds at global scale, while a wide range of unscrupulous business practices, such as piracy, counterfeiting, tax evasion, bribery, grey marketing, money laundering, smuggling, and mega-scams in the stock markets leave millions of stakeholders cheated. The lack of social responsibility in businesses has not only tarnished the corporate image of some mega-corporations, but has also led to huge losses, bringing them to the verge of collapse. Unethical business practices not only violate the fundamental righteousness of stakeholders, i.e., customers, stockholders, suppliers, government, and society at large, but also hamper a firm's long-term sustainability and even survival. Therefore, it is in the larger interest of businesses to carry out their activities ethically and in a socially responsible manner, not for the sake of charity but for their own survival and sustainability in the long run.

Although, in the present era, business ethics and corporate social responsibility (CSR) are often touted as 'Western' concepts, India has had a long and illuminating tradition that has espoused and expounded the idea of ethical business. The ancient Indian texts, both scriptural and non-scriptural, such as Manu's *Manavdharmasastra* (treatise on human duty), Kautilya's *Arthashastra* (treatise on economics), Shukra's

Nitisara (essence of policy), the two epics—Vedvyasa's *Mahabharata* and Valmiki's *Ramayana*—and Chanakya's *niti* (policy) and Vidur's *niti* (policy) have all discussed extensively ethical considerations at all levels of trade and business dealings, including between trading nations. The ancient Indian tradition encompasses three broad principles: dharma or duty, the spirit of sacrifice and sharing, and integrity and moral scrupulousness.[1]

This chapter delineates the concept of ethics and its business implications. A wide range of unethical business practices, such as corruption, bribery, smuggling, money laundering, *hawala*, tax havens, unethical marketing practices, grey marketing, counterfeiting and piracy, transfer pricing, dumping, and unethical practices in marketing communications have been explicated. During recent years, there has been a growing awareness and realization among corporates to carry out their businesses in a socially responsible manner. The chapter also elucidates the concept of CSR and related initiatives. In addition to the lucid explanation of theoretical concepts with the help of conceptual diagrams, empirical analysis and cross-country comparisons have also been given.

20.2 ETHICS

The study of moral conduct and its evaluation is termed 'ethics'. Ethics refer to the study of what is 'right' or 'good' for human beings. Ethics are a society's concept of fairness and justice whereas 'morality' refers to individual virtues. The study and determination of what is right and good in business settings is termed as 'business ethics'. Something that is legal need not necessarily be ethical. In fact, unethical business practices are often employed to circumvent the law. For instance, import of an item may be legal but sometimes unethical, for example, sub-standard products, such as contaminated steel or other toxic materials. The hefty margins on medicines by multinational pharma companies and the use of regulatory framework as a strategic tool both within a country and at multilateral level has often been employed for a corporation's own wealth creation (Exhibit 20.1), leaving millions of poor and needy in developing and developed countries alike at the mercy of the Almighty.

Unlike a legal framework, which has a set of rules and a judicial mechanism, ethics hardly have structured norms and universal standards. The code of ethics too varies considerably from country to country. Therefore, the study of ethics becomes extremely significant for international business as different beliefs about what is right can lead to ethical relativism, resulting in different groups differently perceiving what is good. International managers are expected to appreciate ethical differences across the countries and respond accordingly.

---

[1] Singh, Karan, *Business Ethics and Corporate Social Responsibility*, (ed.) Sahni, S.K., Foundation for Peace and Sustainable Development, New Delhi, 2006, pp. xi–xii.

Exhibit 20.1   Drug pricing and human life

Access to basic healthcare and medicines is the fundamental right of every human being on this earth. Countries with low income are home to most diseases and people lack both awareness and affordability to the required medicines. An estimated 1.1 billion people remain in extreme poverty, on less than US$1 a day, mainly concentrated in South Asia (39.2%), Sub-Saharan Africa (29.3%), and East Asia and the Pacific (23.7%). The issue of supplying HIV/AIDS medicines to developing countries has been a matter of serious concern for development agencies and various social groups across the globe. Sub-Saharan Africa has an alarming level of HIV prevalence in 7.7 per cent of its population against the world average of 1.1 per cent. The HIV situation is worst in countries like Swaziland where 38.8% of population is affected, Botswana (37.3%), Lesotho (28.9%), Zimbabwe (24.6%), Namibia (21.3%), and South Africa (21%).

The prohibitively high cost of treatment worsens the condition, as it is hardly affordable by the majority of the target consumers. Moreover, in the absence of free-market competition, consumers have to pay higher prices. Multinational corporations have traditionally priced their brands, astonishingly, at much higher levels and there have been vast price variations across the countries. For instance, the price of diclofenac sodium is 193 times higher in the US as compared to the same in India. A strip of 10 tablets of 500 mg each of ciprofloxacin HCl, a widely used antibiotic, costs about Rs 29 in India whereas it costs the US consumer about Rs 2353. The price differential between the two countries is about 81 times.

The wide price variations are often attributed to regulatory practices such as the patent regime, where an inventor is awarded monopoly of the said product for a given period. This prevents new market entrants, and in near monopolistic market conditions consumers are forced to pay sky-high prices. Under the WTO's TRIPS agreement, member countries are required to give exclusive rights of manufacturing to the patent owner for 20 years. TRIPS prescribes universal minimum protection to intellectual property, such as trademarks, copyrights, geographical indications, patents, industrial designs, plant varieties, topography of integrated circuits, and trade secrets. It is often argued that such product patents are necessary for recovery of investment made on research and development and to motivate firms to invest on innovation. However, there are serious concerns about 'evergreening' of patents over the same drug. It is not uncommon that multinational firms get several patents on a single medicine because a patent protects the invention and not the medicine. Apart from the new molecule (active medical ingredient), they get patents for formulations, isomers, polymorphs, combinations, new delivery devices, new uses, manufacturing processes, etc. By patenting these features at different points of time, MNEs effectively tend to extend the monopoly beyond the 20 years of the first patent.

To illustrate, till 2000, the antiretroviral (ARV) drugs used to treat AIDS were priced between US$12,000–13,000 annually per person around the world. The international prices of drugs used for HIV treatment fell drastically to US$800 in September 2000 when Cipla introduced generic versions of ARV drugs. Besides, three more Indian pharma companies—the Delhi-based Ranbaxy Laboratories, the Hyderabad-based Matrix Laboratories, and the Bangalore-based Hetero—further pushed down the prices. The fall in drug prices have prompted governments of Brazil, South Africa, China, and India to announce free HIV/AIDS treatment to anyone in need. Presently, such ARV drugs are sold by a few Indian companies to some NGOs for as little as US$240 annually per person to treat millions of poor patients.

Multinational pharma companies lobby with their full might against such generic drugs on the ground of investments made in R&D. The sharp price cut from about US$12000 to US$800 per

Contd

Exhibit 20.1 Contd

person's annual dose (i.e., 93% reduction) for ARV drugs in less than four months revealed the exorbitant margins earned by the MNEs. A number of social activist groups have been vociferous in their concern about life-saving drugs. However, the enormity of the profit margins of transnational firms and the oligopolistic price structure make the consumer the ultimate loser.

Source: Joshi, Rakesh Mohan, 'Cost Determines Price: Just a Myth', *Gulf Log,* October–December 2007, Dubai, pp. 16–17; Joshi, Rakesh Mohan, 'Drug Pricing in International Markets' in *International Marketing,* Delhi: Oxford University Press, 2005, pp. 404–05.

During recent years, the ethical behaviour of international firms has become a major issue of debate across the world. The growing scepticism about the social benefits of international firms has led to increased resistance by nationalistic movements, environmentalists, opposition parties, and NGOs worldwide. This has put tremendous pressure on multinational firms to be ethical and socially responsible in their international business operations.

A cross-country comparison of the ethical behaviour of business enterprises reveals the highest ethical behaviour in the world among Swedish firms, with a score of 6.6 (Fig. 20.1) on a seven-point scale, followed by Finland (6.6), Denmark (6.5),

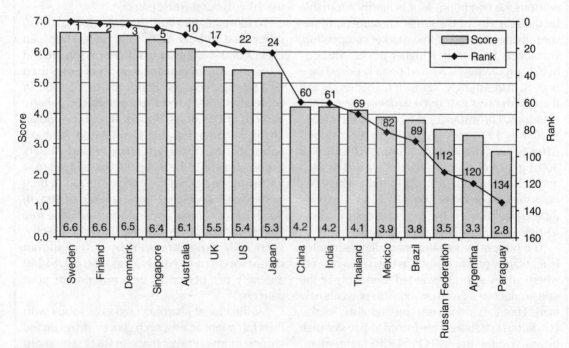

Fig. 20.1 Ethical behaviour of firms

Note: 1—among the world's worst; 7—among best in the world.

Source: The Global Competitiveness Report 2008–09, World Economic Forum, Geneva: Palgrave Macmillan, 2008, p. 378.

Singapore (6.4), Australia (6.1), the UK (5.5), the US (5.4), Japan (5.3), China (4.2), India (4.2), Thailand (4.1), Mexico (3.9), Brazil (3.8), and the Russian Federation (3.5). Argentina (3.3) and Paraguay ranked last[2] with a score of 2.8.

The United Nations (UN) Global Compact provides a voluntary framework for cross-cultural ethical practices for businesses, as indicated in Exhibit 20.2, based on four broad areas of ethical concern: human rights, labour standards, environment, and anti-corruption. The UN Global Compact is not a regulatory instrument, but relies on public accountability and the self-interest of companies to further its aims without enforcing or measuring business actions.

20.3 UNETHICAL BUSINESS PRACTICES

Businesses resort to a wide range of unethical practices, such as corruption and bribery, financial misappropriations, circumventing law enforcement, evading taxes and duties, dumping, making exaggerated and even false claims, exploiting customers, flouting basic norms of civil decency, and even manufacturing and distributing pirated and fake products. Such business practices are detrimental not only to customers but also to the civil society at large.

20.3.1 Corruption

The word corruption is derived from the Latin verb *corruptus*, which means 'to break'. It literally means a broken object similar to a corrupt electronic file. It refers to a form of behaviour that departs from ethics, morality, tradition, law, and civic virtue. There is hardly any universally accepted definition and the perception of corruption also varies from culture to culture. However, corruption broadly includes fraud, bribery, extortion, nepotism, sectarianism, embezzlement, racketeering, and conflict of interests.

Transparency International, the global civil society organization that leads the fight against corruption, defines[3] corruption as the 'abuse of entrusted power for private gain'. It includes not only financial gains but also non-financial favours. The acquisition of massive wealth by corrupt means from the states by the senior officials is termed as 'grand corruption'. It represents embezzlement and misappropriation of public assets.

Corruption remains a major cost to international business. The misuse of public offices for private gains in businesses is historical. German economic historian, Jacob van Klaveren, asserts that the origin of corruption in business began with the East India Companies. Since the days of establishing the East India Companies in the 1600s, Europeans evolved ways and means of misusing entrusted power for their personal gains. Warren Hastings, the first Governor General of India, accumulated £200,000 in India and transferred it to England in the eighteenth century. During the

[2] The Global Competitiveness Report 2008–09, World Economic Forum, Geneva: Palgrave Macmillan, 2008, p. 378.
[3] Global Corruption Report 2007, Transparency International, UK: Cambridge University Press, 2007, p. 296.

Exhibit 20.2   UN global compact: Ten principles

Human rights
Businesses should
Principle 1: Support and respect the protection of internationally proclaimed human rights
Principle 2: Make sure that they are not complicit in human rights abuses

Labour standards
Businesses should uphold
Principle 3: The freedom of association and the effective recognition of the right to collective bargaining
Principle 4: The elimination of all forms of forced and compulsory labour
Principle 5: The effective abolition of child labour

Principle 6: The elimination of discrimination in respect of employment and occupation

Environment
Businesses should
Principle 7: Support a precautionary approach to environmental challenges
Principle 8: Undertake initiatives to promote greater environmental responsibility
Principle 9: Encourage the development and diffusion of environment-friendly technologies

Anti-corruption
Principle 10: Businesses should work against corruption in all its forms, including extortion and bribery.

Source: UN Global Compact.

---

same period, Robert Clive, a civil servant with the East India Company transferred £280,000.

Edmund Burke, the eighteenth century statesman, argued that Clive ought to be removed from office. At the same time, Lord North, who served as Britain's prime minister from 1770 to 1782, contended that Hastings's £200,000 was not an excessive sum. Moreover, a large number of other, nominally salaried and low-ranking employees of the company, such as writers (similar to present-day clerks), cadets, ship captains and ship husbands, who handled charters, too found opportunities to acquire wealth for themselves. The East India Company employees were also engaged in smuggling goods to Europe and dealt in opium with China. The office of ship commander was bought and sold, typically for £2,000 to £5,000, but sometimes for up to £10,000 and once even for double that sum.

By the nineteenth century, business corruption was so much a fact of life that it became a prominent theme for European novelists. Among them were Honore de Balzac in *The Human Comedy*; Charles Dickens, *Little Dorrit*; William Makepeace Thackeray, *The Newcomers*; Anthony Trollope, *The Way We Live Now*; Gustav Freytag, *Soll und Haben*, Alexandre Dumas, *Black Tulip*; and Emile Zola, L'Argent.[4]

Since then, not much has changed and corrupt business practices remain a key concern for a firm's stakeholders. Although it is difficult to assess the magnitude of corruption objectively, the Corruption Perception Index brought out by Transparency

---

[4] Kindlegerger, Charles, 'Corruption, Crime, Chicanery: Business through the Ages', *New York Times*, 16 December 2002; Phata, V. Arvind, Bhagat S. Ravi, and Roger J. Kashlak, 'Ethics and Social Responsibility for International Firms', *International Management: Managing in a Diverse and Dynamic Global Environment*, New Delhi: Tata McGraw-Hill, 2006, pp. 511–12.

International serves as a useful tool to quantitatively assess the degree to which corruption is perceived to exist among public officials and politicians. Interestingly, the world's poorest countries are also the most corrupt as indicated in the Corruption Perception Index, 2008 (Fig. 20.2) on a scale of 0–10. Somalia (1.0), Myanmar (1.3), Venezuela (1.9), Kenya (2.1), Russia (2.1), Pakistan (2.5), Indonesia (2.6), Egypt (2.8), and Tanzania (3.0) are among the most corrupt countries of the world, whereas Denmark, Sweden, and New Zealand (9.3), Singapore (9.2), Finland and Switzerland (9.0) rank among the highly clean countries.

Somalia and Myanmar are the two most corrupt states in the world, yet Myanmar's Junta regime is often attributed to force resettlements, whereas Somalia is wrecked by extreme poverty, lawlessness, and urban violence.

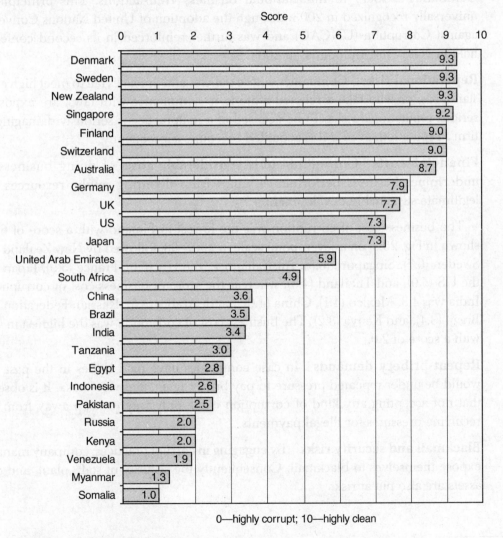

0—highly corrupt; 10—highly clean

Fig. 20.2 Corruption Perception Index, 2008

Source: Transparency International, UK.

Detrimental effects of corrupt practices on business

Corruption involves misuse of power and position that has a detrimental impact on the poor and the disadvantaged. Corrupt business practices are also detrimental to business enterprises[5] in numerous ways:

Legal risks Obvious legal risks are often involved in corrupt practices, regardless of their form in the countries where they occur. Moreover, corrupt business practices overseas are increasingly becoming illegal even in a firm's home country. For instance, under the US Foreign and Corrupt Practices Act of 1977, it is even illegal to bribe foreign officials. This principle gained legal standing within the whole of Organization for Economic Co-operation and Development (OECD) under the Council on Combating Bribery in International Business Transactions. This principle was universally recognized in 2003, through the adoption of United Nations Convention against Corruption (UNCAC) and was further reinforced in its second conference held in Nusa Dua, Indonesia, in 2008.

Reputational risks Companies whose policies and practices fail to meet high ethical standards, or who take a relaxed attitude to compliance with laws, are exposed to serious reputational risks. To be accused of a malpractice is seriously damaging to a firm's reputation, even if it is acquitted by courts subsequently.

Financial costs Corruption adds considerable costs of doing business and undermines business performance, apart from diverting public resources from legitimate sustainable development.

The business cost of corruption was the lowest in Finland with a score of 6.8, as shown in Fig. 20.3, on a seven-point scale in 2007–08, followed by New Zealand (6.8), Sweden (6.7), Singapore (6.5), Australia (6.4), the UK (6.0), France (5.9), Japan (5.1), the US (5.0), and Thailand (4.5), whereas the score of business cost of corruption in India was 4.3, Mexico (4.1), China (4.0), Saudi Arabia (3.5), Russian Federation (3.5), Brazil (3.4), and Kenya (3.2). The business cost of corruption was the highest in Chad with a score of 2.0.

Repeat bribery demands In case companies have paid bribes in the past, they would be under repeated pressure to pay bribes again, and vice-versa. It is observed that not accepting any kind of corruption is the only way to keep away from such recurring pressures for illegal payments.

Blackmail and security risks By engaging in corrupt practices, company managers expose themselves to blackmail. Consequently the security of staff, plant, and other assets are also put at risk.

---

[5] 'Business against Corruption: A Framework for Action', UN Global Compact, International Business Leader Forum and Transparency International, 2005, pp. 3–7.

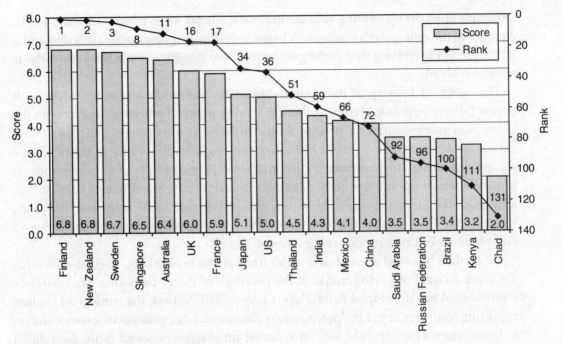

Fig. 20.3 Business costs of corruption

Note: 1—significant adverse impact; 7—no adverse impact.
Source: The Global Competitiveness Report 2007–08, World Economic Forum, Geneva: Palgrave Macmillan, 2008, p. 395.

Risk of getting cheated There is a saying, 'The one who cheats will be cheated against.' If a company engages in or tolerates corrupt practices, this fact will soon be widely known, both internally and externally. Unethical behaviour erodes staff loyalty to the company and it can be difficult for the staff to see why high standards should be applied within the company when they do not apply in the company's external relations. Internal trust and confidence are in turn eroded.

Undermines businesses' vested interest in sustainable development Corruption undermines the development of social-economical environment by diverting resources from their proper use. It has devastating impact on the poor and unprivileged, undermining the very fabric of society. Corruption results in lost opportunities to extend markets and supply chains, distorts competition, and creates gross inefficiency in both the public and private sector, adversely affecting long-term sustainability of business.

20.3.2 Bribe

Bribe may be defined as any voluntary offering of an object of some value, such as money, gifts, privilege, etc., with an objective to influence the action of the receiver who is generally a government official or a person with power. It refers to an offer or receipt of any gift, loan, fee, reward, or other advantage to or from any person as an inducement to do something that is dishonest, illegal, or a breach of trust, in the conduct of the enterprise's business. A bribe becomes extortion[6] when this demand is accompanied by threats that endanger the personal integrity or the life of the private actors involved.

The scope of bribery in international business transactions is much wider as it covers bribery in public sectors, bribery involving political parties as well as both the active and passive sides of private sector bribery. It also covers solicitation and extortions of bribes. Payment of bribe has become a business tool as revealed in a survey carried out by Transparency International[7]; about 43 per cent of respondents from companies operating internationally believed that their companies failed to win a contract or gain new business because a competitor paid bribe in the last five years, whereas one-third of the respondents believed that they lost their business due to non-payment of bribe in the last 12 months.

Given their financial strength and widespread global networking, international firms are often accused of paying bribes in the countries of their operations. Transparency International has developed Bribe Payers Index (BPI) to rank the world's 30 leading exporting countries as per the propensity of firms with headquarters in those countries to bribe when operating abroad.[8] It is based on the responses of more than 8,000 business executives from companies in 125 countries. As shown in Fig. 20.4, a higher score reveals a lower propensity of companies from a country to offer bribes or undocumented extra payments when doing business abroad. On a 10-point scale of 1 (bribes are common) to 10 (bribes never occur), Switzerland ranks first at 7.81, followed by Sweden (7.62), Australia (7.59), Austria (7.50), and Canada (7.46), whereas India is at the bottom with a score of 4.62, preceded by China (4.94), Russia (5.16), Turkey (5.23), and Taiwan (5.41). As all countries fall short of the perfect score of 10, there is considerable propensity for companies of all nationalities to bribe when operating abroad.

International companies often circumvent anti-bribery legislations by using intermediaries, such as commercial agents or joint venture partners, to pay bribe on their behalf. This is despite the fact that OECD Convention on Combating Bribery of Foreign Public Officials in International Business prohibits bribes paid 'directly' or 'indirectly' and national laws, such as Foreign Corrupt Practices Act (FCPA) of the US have successfully prosecuted companies paying bribe via middlemen.

Bribery in export-import transactions

In international trade, a firm is often required to make certain irregular payments that vary widely across countries. Although such irregular payments are unethical, they

---

[6] The OECD Guidelines for Multinational Enterprises, Paris, 2000; *OECD Observer*, June 2003, pp. 1–7.

[7] John, Bray, 'International Business Attitudes to Corruption', Global Corruption Report 2007, Transparency International, Cambridge University Press, UK, 2007, pp. 335–37.

[8] Mark, Diane, *Bribe Payers Index (BPI) 2006*, Global Corruption Report 2007, Transparency International, Cambridge University Press, UK, 2007, pp. 331–34.

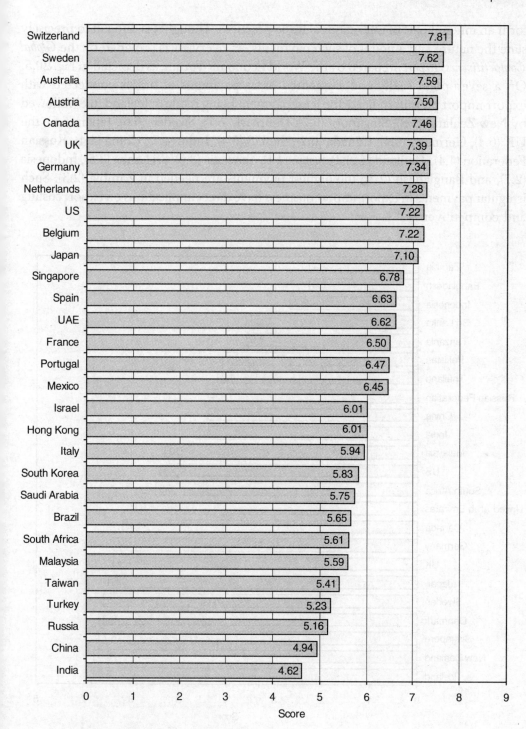

Fig. 20.4   Bribe payers index 2006

Note: 0—bribes are common; 10—bribes never occur.

Source: Global Corruption Report 2007, Transparency International, UK: Cambridge University Press, 2007, pp. 331–34.

form an integral part of international trade practices. Though it is difficult to precisely state the nature and amount of such payments, an overview is provided by the *Global Competitiveness Report* prepared by the World Economic Forum, as depicted in Fig. 20.5. On a seven-point scale, undocumented extra payments of bribes connected with export-import permits indicate the least payment being made in Iceland (6.8) followed by New Zealand (6.8), Singapore (6.7), Denmark (6.7), Sweden (6.6), Japan (6.5), the UK (6.4), Germany (6.4), Canada (6.2), the US (5.4), India (4.7), China (4.4), Russian Federation (4.4), Thailand (4.2), Pakistan (4.1), Tanzania (3.6), Sri Lanka (3.5), Indonesia (2.7), and Bangladesh (2.3); the highest payments are needed in Zambia (2.3). Such irregular payments in export-import business have direct implications on export costing and competitiveness.

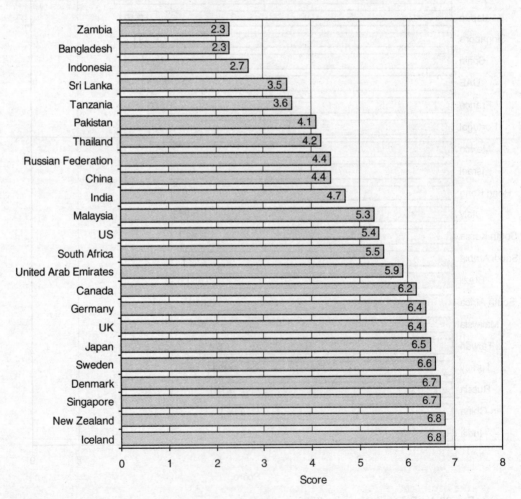

Fig. 20.5 Irregular payments in exports and imports

Note: 1—common; 7—never occur.
Source: The Global Competitiveness Report 2006–07, World Economic Forum, Geneva, p. 425.

Fighting corruption

To fight corruption and implement its tenth principle, as shown in Exhibit 20.2, the UN Global Compact suggests the following three elements to its participants:

Internal   Introduce anti-corruption policies and programmes within the organization and business operations.

External   Report on the work against corruption in the annual communication on progress and share experiences and best practices through the submission of examples and case stories.

Collective   Join forces with industry peers and with other stakeholders.

To curb bribery in international business operations, transnational companies need to develop activities, such as training programmes, disciplinary procedures, proper remuneration of agents, introduction of adequate control systems, accounting and auditing practices, and how to deal with non-discrimination against employees reporting incidents of corruption, as shown in Exhibit 20.3.

A new chapter on combating bribery was also added during the 2000 review of the OECD Guidelines for Multinational Enterprises (Exhibit 20.9), which states 'enterprises should not, directly or indirectly, offer, promise, give, or demand a bribe or other undue advantage to obtain or retain business or other improper advantage'.

20.3.3   Smuggling

Smuggling refers to the surreptitious trade across the borders aimed at circumventing enforcement of regulatory prohibitions and restrictions and evading payment of legitimate customs duties. Smuggling may have both financial and non-financial motives. Smuggling implies either ill-formulated national policies or their ineffective implementation or a combination of the two. Products with higher prohibition and restrictions, such as liquor, cigarettes, drugs, and arms and ammunitions are generally appealing to smugglers. Due to restrictive immigration laws, organized gangs smuggle millions of illegal immigrants into US and Europe with the promise of lucrative jobs.

The incentive to smuggle generally increases with the rise in customs duties and other restrictions, and vice-versa. To illustrate, smuggling flourished as a full-fledged industry in most developing countries a few decades back when the customs duties and other import restrictions were very high. As a result, a few markets in India, such as Palika Bazar in Delhi, *Chor* Bazar (Thief Market) in Mumbai, Moreh Market in Imphal, etc., became famous (or infamous) for smuggled goods. Hefty margins in smuggling became so lucrative, implying lavish lifestyles, that smuggling even became the preferred theme for Bollywood movies. As import restrictions were eased and duties declined, the incentive to smuggle also diminished considerably.

Smuggling has a detrimental effect on national trade policies and their implementation. Besides, the competition from smuggled goods severely hampers fair market

Exhibit 20.3 Implementation process for anti-bribery policy

Step	I	II	III	IV	V	VI
Action	Decide to adopt a 'no bribes policy'	Plan implementation	Develop anti-bribery programme	Implement programme	Monitor	Evaluate the performance
Primary responsibility	Owner of the company/board/CEO	Appointed senior manager/project team	Appointed senior managers/heads of departments	Appointed senior manager/line managers/support functions/business partners	Ethics/compliance officer/internal and external auditors	Owner of company/board/CEO/audit committee
Process	▪ Obtain commitment to no-bribes policy 'from the top' ▪ Decide to implement an anti-bribery programme ▪ Appoint senior manager/cross-functional project team	▪ Define specific company risks/review current practices ▪ Review all legal requirements ▪ Decide extent of any public disclosure ▪ Develop and write anti-bribery programme ▪ Test/get commitment from senior management/selected employees	▪ Integrate no-bribes policy into organizational structure and assign responsibilities ▪ Review ability of service functions to support new programme ▪ Develop detailed implementation plan to include: □ HR polices □ Communications □ Training Programmes ▪ Set up complaints function ▪ Prepare for incidents	▪ Communicate anti-bribery programme: internal/external ▪ Run training courses for employees and business partners ▪ Ensure capabilities are in place and specialist functions up to speed: internal audit, finance, legal department ▪ Deal with incidents	▪ Regular reviews of the system ▪ Capture knowledge from incident ▪ Use external assurance providers ▪ Review use of complaints channels ▪ Review role of project team	▪ Receive feedback from monitoring ▪ Evaluate effectiveness of programme ▪ Develop improvements to programme ▪ Report to management ▪ Board review and sign-off on programme ▪ Publish programme process and results (optional)
Time span	*One month*	*Three to six months*	*Three to six months*	*One year*	*Continuous*	*At least annually*

Source: Transparency International.

competition by legitimate importers. Counterfeit and pirated goods also find their way into the distribution channels of smuggled goods, tarnishing manufacturers' image.

20.3.4   Hawala

Long before the introduction of the Western banking system, *hawala,* also referred to as *hundi,* an alternative or parallel remittance system, was developed in India. Informal funds transfer (IFT) systems were used in earlier times for trade financing. Such systems were evolved to avoid the dangers of travelling with physical monetary assets, such as gold, silver, and other forms of payment, on routes beset with robbers and bandits. A similar system known as *chop, chit,* or 'flying money' is indigenous to China. Other local systems of fund transfer were widely used in Asia under different names: *fei-ch'ien* (China), *padala* (Philippines), *hundi* (India), *hui kuan* (Hong Kong), and *phei kwan* (Thailand). Nowadays, these systems are often referred to as 'underground banking'; this term is not always correct because the system often operates in the open with complete legitimacy and the services are often heavily and effectively advertised.

The hawala system refers to an informal channel for transferring funds from one location to another through service providers, known as *hawaladars,* regardless of the nature of the transactions and the countries involved. Hawala is currently used as a major remittance system around the world. It is primarily used by the members of expatriates' communities that migrated to Europe, the Persian Gulf region, and North America to send remittances to their relatives in the Indian subcontinent, East Asia, Africa, Eastern Europe, and elsewhere. These emigrant workers have reinvigorated the system's role and importance.

It is the trust and extensive use of personal connections such as family relationships and the regional affiliations that distinguishes hawala from other remittance systems. Unlike traditional banking or even the *chop,* hawala makes minimal (often no) use of any sort of negotiable instrument. Transfer of money takes place based on communications among the members of a network of hawaladars, or hawala dealers. In hawala parlance, *peti* is often used to denote an amount of 1,00,000 or a lakh and *khoka,* 10 million or a crore. Hawala works by transferring money without actually moving it.[9]

The term 'white hawala' is used for legitimate transactions, especially remittances; whereas 'black hawala' refers to illegitimate transactions, specifically hawala money laundering. Although, hawala transactions are illegal under the Indian and Pakistani law they are not illegal in many other jurisdictions.

Hawala transaction process

In a typical hawala transaction, a customer, often an expatriate, remits cash (1) to a hawala service provider (HY), known as hawaladar, in currency of his/her workplace

---

[9] 'The Hawala Alternative Remittance System and Its Role in Money Laundering', *Interpol General Secretariat,* Lyon, January 2000.

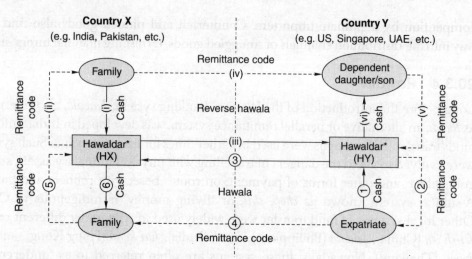

Fig. 20.6 Hawala transaction process

* Hawala service provider.

(country Y), as shown in Fig. 20.6. In return, the hawaladar offers a remittance code (2) to its customer. The service provider instructs (3) his/her correspondent (HX) to deliver an equivalent amount in the local currency to a designated beneficiary. The customer transmits (4) the remittance code to the beneficiary, often a member from the expatriate family who disclose the remittance code (5) to the corresponding hawaladar (HX) in his/her home country (X) to receive the cash (6). In a hawaala transaction, HY has a liability to HX, and the deal may be settled by various means, either financial or goods and services. Their positions can also be transferred to other intermediaries, who can assume and consolidate the initial positions and settle at wholesale or multilateral levels. The transaction need not necessarily be financed by the service provider (HY) charging a commission, rather it may be based even on the exchange rate spread.

The settlement of liability between the two service providers created by the initial transaction can also be carried out through 'reverse hawala' or import of goods. The reverse hawala transaction is often used for investment purposes or to cover educational, medical, or travel expenses from a developing country. Stringent foreign exchange regulations, especially from developing countries, compel the citizens of developing countries to evolve alternate ways to transfer money abroad for tuition fees, travel, and medical expenses of dependent children or relatives. Such families in developing countries (X) remit cash (i) in local currency to a home-based hawaladar (HX), who in turn provides the customer with a remittance code (ii). The home based hawaladar (HX) instructs (iii) his correspondent hawaladar (HY) in a foreign country Y to deliver the equivalent amount in foreign currency to the designated beneficiary. The customer passes on this remittance code (iv) to the beneficiary, for example, dependent daughter, son, or relative, who on disclosure of the remittance code (v) receives the cash (vi) abroad (country Y) from a corresponding hawaladar (HY). A reverse hawala transaction may also involve other hawaladars and may be tied to several different transactions for making settlements. Thus, a hawala transaction is both simple and complex at the same time.

The hawala system is attractive since it is swifter, more reliable, more convenient, and less bureaucratic than the formal financial sector. Hawala transactions are often attractive to expatriates, especially for those with low-paying jobs, as these do not require opening up of a bank account for carrying out the transaction and offer a better exchange rate.[10] Hawaldars charge fees or sometimes use the exchange rate spread to generate income. The fees charged by hawaladars on the transfer of funds are much lower than those charged by banks and other remitting companies, mainly due to minimal overhead expenses and the absence of regulatory costs to the hawaladars, who often operate other small businesses. To encourage foreign exchange transfers through their system, hawaladars sometimes exempt expatriates from paying fees. In contrast, they generally charge a higher fee to those who use the system to avoid exchange and capital or administrative controls. These higher fees often cover all the expenses of the hawaladars.

Hawala transactions are not reflected in official statistics, neither in the remittance of the recipient country's foreign assets, nor in the remitting country's liabilities, unlike funds transferred through the formal sector. As a consequence, value changes hands, but broad money remains unaltered. Hawala transactions cannot be reliably quantified because records are virtually inaccessible, especially for statistical or balance of payments purposes.

As long as there are strong reasons, such as cost effectiveness, convenience, and reliability, for people to prefer hawala over the formal banking system, any sort of regulatory measures are likely to be ineffective in reducing its attractiveness. Rather it would continue not only to exist but also expand.

20.3.5 Money Laundering

Money laundering is a serious, highly sophisticated, and global criminal activity. It refers to conversion or 'laundering' of money obtained through illegal means so as to make it appear to originate from a legal source. It involves disguising financial assets so that they can be used without detection of the illegal activity involved in their generation. Money laundering is often used worldwide to transform monetary proceeds derived from illegal means or criminal activities into funds with apparently legal sources. Illegal arms sales, smuggling, and the activities of organized crime can generate huge amounts of proceeds. Embezzlement, insider trading, bribery, and computer fraud schemes can also produce large profits and create the incentive to legitimize the ill-gotten gains through money laundering.

---

[10] 'The Hawala Alternative Remittance System and Its Role in Money Laundering', *Interpol General Secretariat*, Lyon, January, 2000.

'Dirty' money

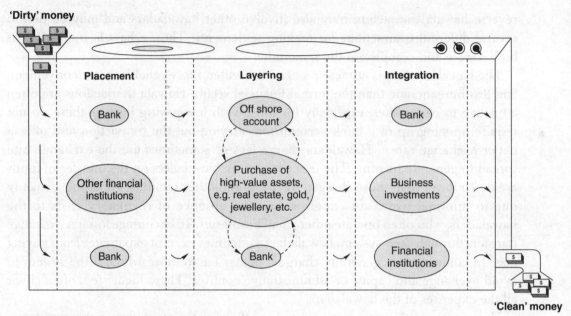

Fig. 20.7 The money laundering process

Money laundering process

The process of money laundering, as depicted in Fig. 20.7, has the three independent stages as discussed below.

Placement It refers to the physical disposal of bulk cash proceeds derived from illegal activity. It aims at removing the cash from the location of acquisition so as to avoid detection by the authorities and to then transform it into other asset forms; for example, travellers' cheques, postal orders, etc. The launderer inserts the illegal or 'dirty' money into a legitimate financial institution. It is the riskiest stage of the laundering process because large amounts of cash are pretty conspicuous and banks are required to report high-value transactions.

Layering It refers to the separation of illicit proceeds from their source by creating complex layers of financial transactions. Layering aims at making the original 'dirty' money as hard to trace as possible. It involves various financial transactions, such as several bank to bank transfers, electronic transfers between different accounts in different names in different countries, making deposits and withdrawals to continually vary the amount of money in the accounts, changing the currency, and purchasing high-value items, such as real estate, precious stones, gold, jewellery, etc., so as to change the form of money.

Integration It refers to the re-injection of the laundered proceeds back into the economy in such a way that the money re-enters the financial system as normal business funds. Commonly used methods under this stage include

- Establishing anonymous companies in countries where right to secrecy is guaranteed. This also enables money launderers to grant themselves loans out of laundered money in the course of a future legal transaction. In addition to increase their profits, launderers also claim tax relief on loan repayments and charge themselves interest on loan.

- Sending of false export-import invoices by overvaluing goods allows the launderer to move money from one company and country to another, with the invoices serving to verify the origin of the money placed with financial institutions.
- Transferring money through electronic funds transfer (EFT) to a legitimate bank from a bank owned by the launderers, as 'off the shelf banks' are easily purchased in many countries.

It becomes extremely difficult to distinguish between the legal and illegal wealth at this stage. Exploiting banking loopholes by opening 'nested' accounts, employing shell companies, and trade-based laundering represents the most common forms of money laundering in the US, as delineated in Exhibit 20.4. These are fake companies that exist for no other reason than to launder money. They take in dirty money as "payment" for supposed goods or services but actually provide no goods or services; they simply create the appearance of legitimate transactions through fake invoices and balance sheets.

Exhibit 20.4   Money laundering in the US: Three most-used methods

'Nested' accounts: *Exploiting banking loopholes*

Step 1: Foreign banks open correspondent accounts at US banks. Then they solicit other foreign banks to use these accounts.

Step 2: These accounts then provide third parties (usually second-tier or even shell banks) indirect access to the US financial system.

Step 3: These second-tier foreign banks, in turn, solicit individuals as customers. A large number of individuals thus acquire signatory authority over a single account in a banking entity.

Step 4: Illicit money is, thus, injected into a common pool with a large number of simultaneous transactions.

Shell companies: *The old-fashioned way*

Step 1: Shell companies having no physical presence are used as holding companies or fronts by anonymous individuals.

Step 2: Intermediaries, called nominee incorporation services (NIS), establish shell companies and set up bank accounts on their behalf in the US.

Step 3: NIS could be located anywhere in the world. By hiring an NIS, a company's real owners can mask their real identities.

Step 4: Launderers use NIS to set up shell companies and then use company accounts with US banks to funnel illicit funds.

The black market peso exchange: *Trade-based laundering*

Step 1: In Colombia, importers need permits to exchange pesos for dollars. Black market currency brokers are big facilitators.

Step 2: Brokers keep illicit funds (from drug deals) in the US, buying money orders via individuals or putting cash via foreign banks.

Step 3: The money is then used to make fictional payments to exports by Colombian businessmen to the US.

Step 4: The dollars are then converted into pesos in Colombia and go to drug traffickers, who use the cash to fund the next deal.

Source: Based on Pocha, Jegangir S. and Uttara Choudhury, 'For Love of Money', *Business World,* June 2007, pp. 28–31.

Curbing money laundering

The aggregate size of the money laundering industry in the world is estimated to be 2 to 5 per cent of the world gross domestic product. The increasing technological sophistication and transfer of funds have given rise to ease of financial transactions and also increased the need to establish institutional and operational mechanisms to curb money-laundering activities.

Since criminal proceeds can enter into mainstream financial system, banks and financial institutions are often vulnerable to money laundering activities. Therefore, financial institutes need to exercise constant vigil in opening of new accounts, use large cash transactions, and identify suspicious transactions. Financial institutes often emphasize upon knowing their customers and employees as the basic principle to steer clear of the money laundering track.

In order to detect money laundering activities, financial institutions are required to be vigilant[11] over the following transactions:

- Customers depositing cash through a large number of cash deposit slips into the same account or customers having numerous accounts into which large cash deposits are made. Each deposit is such that the amount thereof is not significant but the aggregate of all credits is sizeable, also known as 'smurfing'
- A substantial increase in turnover in a dormant account
- Receipt or payment of large sums of cash, which have no obvious purpose or relationship to the account holder and/or his/her business
- Reluctance to provide normal information when opening an account or providing minimal or fictitious information
- Depositing high-value third-party cheques endorsed in favour of the customer or other transactions on behalf of non-account holders
- Large cash withdrawals from a previously dormant or inactive account or from an account that has received an unexpected large credit from abroad
- Sudden unjustified increase in cash deposits of an individual

Basel principles   A set of principles, known as Basel principles, to address the dangers posed by money launderers, as evolved at a meeting of the Committee on Banking Regulations and Supervisory Practices of the G10 in December 1998, at Basel in Switzerland. The principles deal with preventing the use of banking system for the purpose of money laundering. The Basel principles set out an effective guideline for what banks and financial institutions should do to cope with money laundering. The Basle principles suggest policies and procedures to curb money laundering as discussed below.

Customer identification   It emphasizes the adage 'know your customer' (KYC), which requires that financial institutions should make reasonable efforts to determine the

---

[11] Ganesh, S., 'Money Laundering', Reserve Bank of India.

customers' true identity and must introduce effective procedures for verifying the bonafides of new customers.

Compliance with law   The bank should observe the laws and regulations pertaining to financial transactions as enacted in different statutes. It should not offer services or provide active assistance in case of transactions supposed to be associated with money laundering activity.

Co-operation with law and enforcement authority   The bank should fully co-operate with the national law enforcement authority to the extent permitted by specific local regulations concerning customer confidentiality.

Adherence to the statement   Banks need to adopt policies consistent with the statement of principles and ensure that all staff members are not only informed but also trained to implement specific procedures for customer identification and retaining the internal records of transactions.

Financial action task force   In order to combat money laundering and financing of terrorists, and to facilitate the development and promotion of policy both at the national and international levels, the Financial Action Task Force (FATF) was established as an inter-government body in 1989 by the G7 Summit held in Paris. It monitors members' progress in implementing anti-money laundering measures, reviews money laundering and terrorist financing techniques and counter-measures, and promotes the adoption and implementation of appropriate measures globally. The FATF focuses on the following three principal areas:

- Setting standards for national anti-money laundering and countering terrorist financing programmes
- Evaluating the degree to which countries have implemented measures that meet those standards
- Identifying and studying money laundering and terrorist financing methods and trends

The FATF reviews its mission every five years; however, in 2004, its mandate was extended for eight years till 2012.

20.3.6 Tax Havens

In simple terms, a country that either levies taxes at a very low rate or levies no taxes at all may be termed 'tax haven'. To assign a country the tax-haven status, the Organization for Economic Co-operation and Development (OECD) considers four criteria:

- Insignificant or non-existent tax levels
- Absence of transparency in tax matters
- Absence of fiscal data exchange with other countries
- Attractiveness for straw companies with fictitious activities

---

Exhibit 20.5   Tax havens

Anguilla	Dominica	US Virgin Islands	Saint Kitts and Nevis
Antigua and Barbuda	Gibraltar	Jersey	Saint Lucia
Dutch Antilles	Grenada	Liberia	San Marino
Aruba	Guernsey	Maldives	Saint Vincent and
The Bahamas	Cayman Islands	Malta	the Grenadines
Bahrain	Cook Islands	Montserrat	Seychelles
Barbados	Isle of Man	Nauru	Tonga
Belize	Marshall Islands	Niue	Turks and Caicos
Bermuda	Mauritius	Panama	Vanuatu
Cyprus	British Virgin Islands	Samoa	

On the basis of the above criteria, OECD accords the tax-haven status to 41 countries, out of which 38 countries (Exhibit 20.5) have made commitments to ensure transparency and exchange of data. However, the three countries termed as 'non-cooperative' include Andorra, Liechtenstein, and Monaco.[12]

Tax havens are often used for unethical business practices (Exhibit 20.6), in the following ways:

- Businesses often form offshore subsidiaries for the purpose of re-invoicing. Such subsidiaries are formed with the explicit purpose of showing high profits without the performance of any economic activity in the books of accounts of the MNEs in tax havens, rather than in countries with high tax jurisdiction.
- Holding assets in tax havens, such as an investment portfolio, trading companies, or physical assets so as to evade taxes on transfer of ownership

Modus operandi of routing money to tax havens

Money is generally routed through tax havens to create wealth, though unethical, by several ways such as round tripping and treaty shopping as explained below.

Round tripping   Such transactions are aimed at converting unaccounted or black money into legitimate wealth.

- A foreign company transfers funds to a tax haven such as Mauritius. For instance, an Indian company X inflates its exports while the importer pays, e.g., US$20 and the book shows an outflow of US$60. The difference of US$40 is routed overseas through hawala channels.
- The money is transferred to Mauritius by setting up a Global Business Company (GBC-1), a conduit of company X.

---

[12] '41 Countries Are Tax Havens According to OECD Criteria', *The Economic Times*, 27 February 2008.

Exhibit 20.6   Tax havens: Conduit of unethical global business practices

Tax havens have emerged as lucrative destinations for unethical global businesses activities. For instance, 1 Cathedral Square and similar buildings in the Mauritian capital 'Port Louis' have become a must-visit destination for global financial investors. 'Global Business Companies' (GBC-1), with no office, no staff, and not even a name plate, daily transact millions of dollars of businesses. Most GBC-1 companies exist only in the files of the management company that provides them all services after they help them to start operations. These management companies provide staff, secretaries, chartered accountants, and 'nominee directors' to the GBC-1, the last being a pre-requisite for setting up such a company. These directors lend their names as they are 'supposedly' participating in board meetings of hundreds of companies. The board meetings are held telephonically with only the Mauritian directors present. In effect, all investment decisions are taken by individuals who are not residents in Mauritius.

Setting up these companies in Mauritius is fairly easy. All it needs is one shareholder and one director. It costs about US$7,000 to set up such a company and US$5,000 a year to maintain it. The real ownership of the GBC-1 is known only to the management company (MC) that helps its set up. The management companies are not in a position to verify the source of funds as the money comes through the banking system, which maintains confidentiality.

The companies are not allowed to hold immovable property, cannot invest in securities listed on the stock exchange of Mauritius, and cannot transact with the residents either, unless authorized to do so. They can open and maintain a bank account in foreign currency only. Since such companies are set up for one purpose alone, these are not required to pay tax on capital gains and interest income under the Mauritian Law. These companies are a conduit for routing investments from all over the world.

Source: Based on 'Inside India's Favourite Tax Haven', *Business World,* December 2006, pp. 36–44; 'Tax Haven Crackdown', *Sunday Times,* 9 March 2008.

- The GBC-1 then buys equity in company X, and the money routed through the hawala channel is returned to company X.

Treaty shopping   It aims at reducing total tax incidence on capital gains made in countries with high tax incidence. Though the ethical issues about treaty shopping may be debated upon, treaty shopping is certainly not illegal.

- Instead of directly investing in the stock markets in countries with high incidence of capital gains taxes (for example, India), an investor based in a third country sets up a GBC-1 in Mauritius.
- A management company (MC) facilitates setting up the GBC-1 and provides all administrative support. The GBC-1 invests in the Indian stock market through this foreign institutional investor's (FII) sub-account, which costs US$20,000 to set up and US$70,000 a year to maintain. If US$10 million invested sells to US$15 million and the proceeds are repatriated to Mauritius, the GBC-1 makes a gain of US$5 million and pays no taxes.

- An FII investing into India would have to pay a 10 per cent short-term capital gains tax on gains made on listed companies (US$500,000) and 40 per cent on unlisted companies (US$2 million). But due to the Double Tax Avoidance Treaty (DTAT), the GBC-1 need not pay any tax in India. The money is sent back to the parent company.

Investors all over the world choose the best jurisdiction to invest through. It is often used to maximize one's returns in a legitimate way by structuring international investment. For instance, a number of Indian companies, including the Mahindra Group, are investing in China through Mauritius as the investment treaty between India and China is less favourable compared to the one between Mauritius and China.[13]

20.3.7 Unethical Marketing Practices

The axiom 'everything is fair in love and war' is often endorsed by marketers since marketing is also considered to be a strategic war fought against competitors, though in a civilized manner. Companies often resort to several business tactics, even if these violate basic ethics, to establish the edge of their products and services over competitors. Therefore, businesses often adopt means and ways, both fair and unfair, to entice customers and establish their supremacy in the marketplace. Companies barely hesitate to make exaggerated and sometimes even false claims about their products and uses to win fierce marketing rivalries.

Multinational companies are frequently accused of adopting unethical business practices to achieve and retain their competitive edge. Nestle has long been accused of promoting its infant foods in low-income countries by projecting it as the key to infant health and grossly undermining the importance of breastfeeding. The situation worsened, especially in low-income countries with poor quality of potable water and widespread illiteracy among expectant and nursing mothers. The company adopted aggressive strategies to convince mothers about the benefits of its infant formulae that would make their babies healthy and chubby. This has been in violation of globally accepted norms that the infant should mainly be breastfed in its initial few months. The World Health Organization (WHO) estimates that over 1.5 million infants die every year around the world because they are not breastfed. In countries where water in unsafe, a bottle-fed child is up to 25 times more likely to die as a result of diarrhoea than a breastfed child. Despite this, companies manufacturing baby foods continue to market their products in ways that grossly undermine breastfeeding.

Soft drink companies are often accused of selling sub-standard drinks with high levels of pesticide content, polluting groundwater and soil around bottling plants, causing severe water shortages in communities, and distributing toxic waste as fertilizer to farmers. In 2003, Delhi based Centre for Science and Environment (CSE), released

---

[13] 'Inside India's Favourite Tax Haven', *Business World*, December 2006, pp. 36–48.

a report revealing that soft drinks sold in India contained unacceptable levels of pesticides and other harmful chemicals. In response, the soft drink lobby led by Pepsi and Coke sought to completely discredit the report, accusing the role of the clandestine hand of European lobbies in maligning the US multinationals.

Three years later, another CSE investigation, which was even more widespread and scientifically rigorous, made the shocking revelation that average pesticide residues in all brands of PepsiCo were 25 times and in Coca-Cola 22 times higher than the norms set by the Bureau of Indian Standards (BIS). Moreover, the concentration of Lindane, a confirmed cancer-causing chemical, was found 54 times the standards set by BIS, adding to consumers' nightmare.

In March 2006, the news of an Indian consumer court fining Pepsi Rs 1,00,000 for a condom was found in its bottle,[14] aggravated consumers' concerns. The incident revealed the lackadaisical attitude of multinationals in developing countries. Such irresponsible behaviour of mega-corporations may be largely attributed to the fact that in developing countries like India they remain largely unpunished unlike in the US, where the corporate entities are often imposed huge penalties, as shown in Table 20.1. The strong nexus of unethical practices between corporates, bureaucrats, and politicians adds to the woes of consumers in low-income countries. Besides, the complicated judiciary system in such countries takes several years to arrive at the final outcome. Moreover, the maximum penalty of a fine ranges from Rs 1,00,000 to Rs 7,00,000, which is too meagre to be of any consequence to the mighty global corporations.

Table 20.1 Transnational culprits and charges

The culprit	The charges	The action
Citibank	Various consumer civil charges	Fined a massive US$6.71 billion over a decade
Adelphia	Wire fraud and financial fraud	Had to forfeit 95 per cent of its assets worth US$1.5 billion
Philip Morris	Various civil law suits	Fined US$1.25 billion by the European Union
Merck	Three Vioxx killer drug cases lost	Ordered to pay US$298 million as damages
Merill Lynch	Stock market fraud	Paid US$2000 million to SEC in 2002; US$1.68 million in 2005
Pfizer	Neurontin killer drug marketing	Was fined US$450 million in criminal and civil charges
Samsung Electronics	Fixing prices in the chip market	Fined US$300 million by the US Federal Department of Justice.

Source: 'Thanda Matlab Toilet Cleaner', *Business Economy*, New Delhi, 11–24 August 2006, pp. 71–75.

[14] 'Condom in Bottle Costs Pepsi Rs 1 Lakh', *The Times of India*, 26 April 2006.

20.3.8 Grey Marketing

Grey marketing refers to import or export of goods and their distribution through unauthorized channels. International brands with high price differentials and low cost of arbitrage constitute typical grey market goods. The arbitrage costs of grey market goods include transportation, customs tariffs, taxes, and, in a few cases, costs towards product modification, generally changing the language of instructions. If the transportation costs are relatively lower than price differences between two markets, grey marketing channels often become attractive.

In grey markets, legitimate products are also distributed through unauthorized channels. These grey marketing channels can also facilitate distribution of counterfeit products, both knowingly and unknowingly. Since grey market distributors have no way to distinguish between the genuine and fake products, sudden influxes of counterfeit products also takes place through unauthorized distributors.

Types of grey marketing channels

Alternate channels of grey marketing, as depicted in Fig. 20.8, include parallel importing, re-importing, and lateral re-importing, as discussed below.

Parallel importing   This type of grey marketing takes place when a product is sold at a higher price to the authorized importer in the overseas market than the price at which the product is available in the home market. This makes parallel importing directly through unauthorized marketing channels attractive as compared to buying from authorized importer or market intermediatory.

Re-importing   Re-importing becomes an attractive means of grey marketing when a product is priced lower in overseas market as compared to its pricing in the home market.

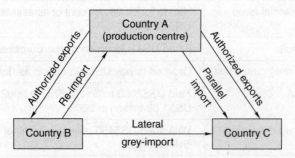

Price in country B (P_B) < price in country A (P_A) < price in country C (P_C)

Fig. 20.8   Types of grey marketing channels

Source: Assmus and Weiss, 'How to Address the Grey Market Threat Using Price Coordination' in Doole, I. and R. Llowe (eds), *International Marketing Strategy Contemporary Reading,* Thomson Business Press; Doole, Isobel and Robin Lawe in *International Marketing and Strategy: Analysis, Development and Implementation,* London: Routledge, 1994.

Lateral re-importing   Products are sold from one export market to another through parallel importing when the price differences exist in different markets, which make such grey marketing channels attractive.

The difference between prices of automobiles in the US and Canada is substantial. As Canadian prices are relatively cheaper and there is hardly any customs tariff between the two countries, the Canadian distributors often engage in selling to the US market, for which they are not authorized by the companies.

Grey marketing channels adversely affect the established distribution channels of the firm. Products are sold through grey marketing channels at prices lower than that of legitimate importers and distributors. Therefore, firms need to carefully control the prices of similar products sold through multiple markets. A firm has to adapt reactive and pro-active strategies to combat grey marketing activities. Reactive strategies include strategic confrontation, participation, price cutting, supply interference, promotion of grey market product limitations, collaboration and acquisition, whereas pro-active strategies include product or service differentiation and availability, strategic pricing, dealer development, marketing information systems, long-term image reinforcement, establishing legal precedence, and lobbying.[15]

20.3.9   Counterfeiting

Counterfeiting means imitating something with the intent to deceive or defraud. Counterfeiting accounts for 5 to 7 per cent of world trade, worth an estimated US$600 billion a year. It has grown by over 10,000 per cent in the past two decades. A wide range of products such as consumer goods, currency, and documents are counterfeited internationally. Customers find it difficult to differentiate between a genuine and a counterfeit product. The wider the price difference between branded and generic products, the more lucrative becomes the business of counterfeit products.

Counterfeiting, one of the fastest growing economic crimes of modern times, presents companies, governments, and individuals with a unique set of problems and poses a serious threat to global health and safety. It is also one of the most significant threats to free market systems. Counterfeiting not only steals the value of intellectual capital, but also stifles innovation and robs customers of the quality they expect from a brand.[16] It devalues corporate reputations, hinders investment, funds terrorism, and costs hundreds of thousands of people their livelihood every year. What was once a cottage industry has now become a highly sophisticated network of organized crime with the capacity to threaten the very fabric of national economies. Counterfeiters are often hardened criminals, exploiting consumers, businesses both large and small, inventors and artists and children labouring in sweatshops, especially in third world countries.

---

[15] S. Tamer Causgil and Ed Sikora, 'How Multinationals Can Counter Grey Market Imports', *Columbia Journal of World Business* 23 (Winter 1988), pp. 75–85.

[16] 'Managing the Risks of Counterfeiting in the Information Technology Industry' KPMG 2005.

Exhibit 20.7   Driving factors for counterfeit and pirate activities

Supply drivers	Demand drivers
Market characteristics High unit profitability Large potential market size Genuine brand power	**Product characteristics** Low prices Acceptable perceived quality Ability to conceal status
Production, distribution, and technology Moderate need for investments Moderate technology requirements Unproblematic distribution and sales High ability to conceal operation Easy to deceive the consumers	**Consumer characteristics** No health concerns No safety concerns Personal budget constraint Low regard for IPR
Institutional characteristics Low risk of discovery Legal and regulatory framework Weak enforcement Penalties	**Institutional characteristics** Low risk of discovery and prosecution Weak or no penalties Availability and ease of acquisition Socio-economic factors

Source: The Economic Impact of Counterfeiting and Piracy, OECD, 2007, pp. 10–15.

Counterfeit and pirate activities are driven by a separate but related set of both supply-and demand-side drivers, as shown in Exhibit 20.7. Supply-side drivers include market opportunities, associated technological and distribution challenges, and the risks involved. The demand for such products is driven by product characteristics, individual consumer characteristics, and the institutional environment in which the consumer operates.

The markets for counterfeit and pirated products are distinctly segmented into two inter-related sub-markets as follows.

Primary markets   Consumers demand genuine goods, but the counterfeiters sell their products deceptively to customers, portraying their products as legitimate items and competing with genuine products. For instance, markets for fake medicines, food products, luxury goods, etc.

Secondary markets   Consumers are willing to purchase counterfeit products, generally at a low price, knowing well the product is not legitimate. For instance, markets for pirated CDs, software, etc.

Free trade zones and free ports are often used by counterfeiters to carry out the following three types of illegal operations:

- 'Merchants' import shipments of counterfeit goods into the warehouses in FTZs and then re-export them to other destinations. Thus, FTZs become 'distribution points' in the supply chain of counterfeit goods in addition to being used to 'sanitize' shipments and documents so as to disguise their original point of manufacturer or departure.

- Counterfeiters import unfinished goods and then 'further manufacture' them in the FTZs by adding counterfeit trademarks, or repackaging or re-labelling the goods, and then export these 'finished' counterfeit goods to other countries.
- FTZs are also used for complete manufacturing of counterfeit goods.[17]

Although counterfeiting is serious business across the world, its size varies considerably across countries. The Aggregated Trade-Related Index of Counterfeiting (ATRIC) provides an objective means to assign a unique number to every economy known as a source of counterfeit and pirated products, reflecting the intensity, scope, and durability of counterfeiting activities in the economy.[18] The Aggregated Trade-Related Index of counterfeiting was the highest in China at 3.000 (Fig. 20.9) in 2006, followed by Hong Kong (2.957), Korea (2.580), South Africa (2.539), Russia (2.328), Pakistan (2.116), UAE (2.087), Singapore (1.966), Thailand (1.257), Italy (0.791), India (0.765), Germany (0.320), the US (0.234), France (0.091), Japan (0.005), and Brazil (0.001).

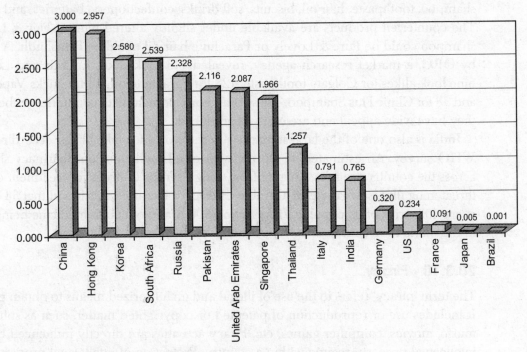

Fig. 20.9 Aggregated Trade-Related Index of Counterfeiting (ATRIC)

Source: Economic Impact of Counterfeiting and Piracy, OECD, 2007, pp. 133–36.

---

[17] 'The International Anti-Counterfeiting Directory 2008: Protecting the World against the Plague of Counterfeiting', ICC Counterfeiting Intelligence Bureau, London, p. 7.
[18] 'Economic Impact of Counterfeiting and Piracy', OECD, 2007, pp. 133–36.

In terms of the overall quantity seized by the EU customs in 2006, China remained the main source of counterfeit goods, accounting for 79 per cent of all articles seized, followed by 5 per cent from UAE, 1 per cent each from India, Algeria, Hong Kong, Egypt, Turkey, and Iran, and 10 per cent from other countries. In US too, China accounted for 81 per cent of the total IPR seizures by customs, followed by Hong Kong 5 per cent, Taiwan 3 per cent, Pakistan 1 per cent, Egypt 1 per cent, and others 9 per cent.[19]

The levels of counterfeit products vary across countries. It is estimated that China is the world's largest source and market for counterfeit goods,[20] causing great losses to consumers and original producers. Counterfeits and look-alikes are common in most industries: pharmaceuticals, cosmetics, software, computer peripherals, auto components, audio and video cassettes, food, soft drinks, liquor, watches, clothing, and even currency.

The market for counterfeit products in India was estimated at around Rs 150 trillion.[21] While the problem of fakes is witnessed across the country, counterfeiting is particularly rampant in the states of Delhi, Punjab, Haryana, and Uttar Pradesh. The other industries hard-hit by counterfeit products include all major brands of soap, shampoo, toothpaste, hair oil, biscuits, soft drinks, confectionery, batteries, and so on. The counterfeit products are available under slightly altered names: Fair & Lovely shampoo could be Pure & Lovely or Parachute hair oil could be Parashudh. A study by ORG, a market research agency, revealed 113 look-alikes for Fair and Lovely, nine look-alikes for Colgate toothpaste, 128 for Parachute oil, 44 for Vicks VapoRub, and 38 for Clinic Plus Shampoo. These brands are popular with counterfeiters because they have wide appeal and are easily reproduced.

India is also one of the largest markets in the world for fake drugs, according to a WHO survey. An estimated 15–20 per cent of all medicines on pharmacy shelves across the country are fake, ranging from cough syrups to drugs for treatment of life-threatening illnesses. Procter & Gamble (P&G), for example, has found that 54 out of every 100 strips of its popular Vicks Action 500 brand of cough medicine being sold in the market are counterfeits.[22]

20.3.10 Piracy

The term 'piracy' refers to the use of illegal and unauthorized means to obtain goods. It includes use or reproduction of patented or copyrighted matter, such as software, music, movies, computer games, etc. Piracy activities are directly influenced by the intellectual property regime within a country. Protection of intellectual property and

[19] 'The International Anti-Counterfeiting Directory 2008: Protecting the World against the Plague of Counterfeiting', ICC Counterfeiting Intelligence Bureau, London, pp. 30–36.
[20] *Asia Pulse*, 24 June 2005.
[21] 'The Rs 15,000 Crore Fake Market', *Outlook Business*, 5 July 2006.
[22] 'Indian Industry: Laws on Counterfeiting Are Ineffective', *EIU Business—New Analysis*, 28 February 2005.

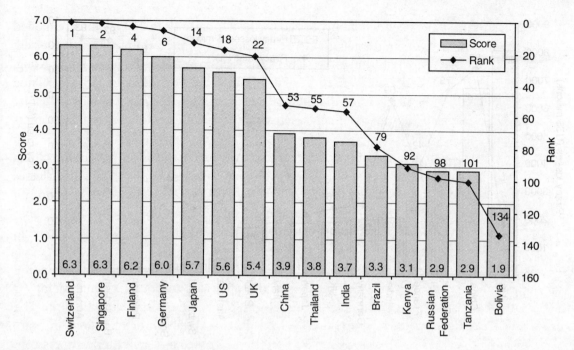

Fig. 20.10   Intellectual property protection

Note: 1—weak and not enforced; 7—strong and enforced.
Source: The Global Competitiveness Report 2008–09, World Economic Forum, Geneva: Palgrave Macmillan, 2008, p. 365.

its enforcement has been reported to be the strongest in Switzerland with a score of 6.3 (Fig. 20.10) on a seven-point scale, whereas Singapore ranked at 2nd place with a score of 6.3, Denmark and Finland at 3rd and 4th, respectively (6.2), Germany and France at 6th and 7th, respectively (6.0), Japan at 14th (5.7), the US at 18th (5.6), the UK at 22nd (5.4), China at 53rd (3.9), and Thailand at 55th (3.8). India ranked at 57th with a score of 3.7, followed by Brazil at 79th (3.3), Kenya at 92nd (3.1), Russian Federation at 98th (2.9), Tanzania at 101st (2.9). Bolivia has the weakest intellectual property protection[23] with a score of 1.9 and a rank of 134.

Software piracy has been a matter of grave concern as the global software piracy has led to about US\$48 billion losses on total package PC software with a global piracy rate of 38 per cent. The US had the highest piracy losses of US\$8040 million in 2007 with a piracy rate of 20 per cent, followed by China at US\$6664 million (82%), Russia US\$4123 million (73%), France US\$2601 million (42%), India US\$2025 million (69%), Germany US\$1937 million (27%), the UK US\$1837 million (26%), Japan US\$1791 million (23%), Italy US\$1779 million (49%), and Brazil US\$1617 million (59%), as depicted in Fig. 20.11. The highest rate of software piracy in 2007 was reported in Armenia at 93 per cent, followed by Bangladesh, Azerbaijan, and Moldova (92%

---

[23] The Global Competitiveness Report 2008–09, World Economic Forum, Geneva: Palgrave Macmillan, 2008, p. 365.

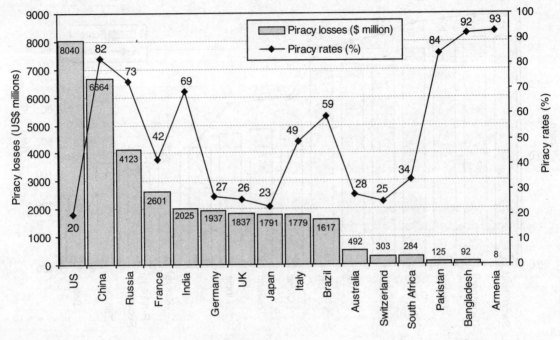

Fig. 20.11   Cross-country comparison of software piracy

* Data for the year 2007.

Source: The Fifth Annual BSA and IDC Global Software Piracy Study, May 2008.

each), Zimbabwe (91%), and Sri Lanka (90%). Worldwide, for every two dollars' worth of software purchased legitimately, one dollar's worth is obtained illegally. In countries with 75 per cent piracy or higher, for every one dollar spent on PC hardware, less than seven cents were spent on legitimate software.[24]

20.3.11   Transfer Pricing

With globalization, corporates are making use of differential rates of transfer pricing to optimize their profitability in low-tax regimes at the expense of high-tax regimes. Globally, about 60 per cent transactions take place among associated firms. Transfer pricing refers to the price between related parties in an international transaction (Fig. 20.12).

The purpose of transfer price apparently seems simple allocation of profits among the subsidiaries and the parent company, but the differences in the taxation patterns in various countries make it a complex phenomenon. Transfer prices come under scrutiny of taxation authorities when they are different from the arm's length price, as discussed later to unrelated parties. Transfer pricing involves several stakeholders, such as parent company, foreign subsidiary or joint venture or any other strategic

24 'The Fifth Annual BSA and IDC Global Software Piracy Study', May 2008.

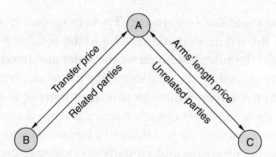

Fig. 20.12   Concept of transfer pricing

alliance, strategic alliance partners, home country and overseas mangers, home country governments, and host country government. International transactions based on intra-company transfer pricing involve conflicting interests of various stakeholders.

Types of transfer pricing

Market-based transfer pricing   Also referred to as arm's length pricing, here the sales transactions occur between two unrelated (arm's length) parties. Arm's length pricing is preferred by taxation authorities. Transfer pricing comes under the scrutiny of tax authorities when it is different from the arm's length price to unrelated firms.

Non-market pricing   Pricing policies that deviate from the market-based arm's length pricing are known as non-marketing-based pricing.

Pricing at direct manufacturing costs   It refers to the intra-firm transactions that take place at the manufacturing costs.

Thus, apparently, the simple concept of transfer pricing is often used to circumvent law[25] with the following objectives:

- Maximizing of overall after-tax profits
- Reducing the incident of customs duty payments
- Circumventing the quota restrictions (in value terms) on imports
- Reducing exchange exposure and circumventing exchange controls restrictions on profit repatriation so that the transfer firm's affiliates to the parent can be maximized
- Operations improving the apparent (i.e., reported) financial position of an affiliate with 'window dressing' so as to enhance its credit ratings

A number of transnational corporations have re-invoicing centres at low-tax countries (tax havens) such as Jamaica, Cayman Islands, Bahamas, Mauritius, etc., to coordinate transfer pricing around the world. These re-invoicing centres are often used to carry out intra-corporate transactions between two affiliates of the same parent

---

[25] Apte, P.G., *International Financial Management*, New Delhi: Tata McGraw Hill, 2007, p. 547.

company or between the parent and the affiliate companies. These re-invoicing centres take the title of the goods sold by the selling unit and resell it to the receiving units. The prices charged to the buyer and the prices received by the seller are determined so as to achieve the transfer pricing objectives. In such cases, the actual shipments of goods take place from the seller to the buyer, while the two-stage transfer is shown only in documentation. Thus, the basic objective of such transfer pricing is to siphon profits away from a high-tax parent company or its affiliate to low-tax affiliates and portion funds in locations with strong currencies and virtually no exchange controls.

Countries use transfer pricing laws to stop shifting of income from their jurisdiction by ensuring that the price at which related parties transact is at fair market value or arm's length price. In India, the detailed law on transfer pricing was introduced by Finance Act, 2001. The transfer pricing law encompasses all multinational companies (MNCs) that transfer goods and services across borders. The law often requires corporates to submit details of their own transactions with those of related parties along with comparable data of similar transactions by others to justify their transfer pricing to tax authorities.

20.3.12 Dumping

Dumping is considered an 'unfair' trade practice under the WTO regime. Despite dumping being an unfair business practice, it makes sound economic sense as a profit maximization strategy. Therefore, it is frequently used as an integral part of international business strategy. Anti-dumping duties can be levied on imports of certain products under the Agreement on Anti-Dumping Practices.

A product is considered to be dumped if its export price is less than either its cost of production or the selling price in the exporting country. For dumping to occur, the following conditions need to be satisfied:

- The industry must be imperfectly competitive so that the firm acts as a price setter rather than price taker.
- Markets must be so segmented to make it difficult for the domestic buyers to purchase goods easily intended for overseas markets.

Besides, for taking anti-dumping action, there should be genuine 'material' injury to the competing domestic industry. The government in the importing country needs to assess the extent of dumping and estimate the injury cost to prove dumping.

Forms of dumping

Dumping may be sporadic, predatory, or persistent, based on its objectives, as discussed here.

Sporadic dumping It refers to the practice of occasionally selling excess goods or surplus stock at lower prices in overseas markets as compared to the domestic price or the cost price. In sporadic dumping, the basic objective of a firm is to liquidate the excessive inventories without initiating a price war by reducing the price in the home market. This form of dumping is the least detrimental.

Predatory dumping The strategic objective of such intermittent dumping by way of predatory pricing is to force competitors to leave the market, thus enabling the predator to raise the price in the long run.[26] This form of dumping is highly detrimental. The practice of predation is more common where the predator firm operates in numerous markets or where the potential competitors, who are the ultimate victims of predatory prices, and their national governments do not have sufficient information to prove occurrence of predation. The regulatory framework regarding predatory pricing varies widely among countries. Anti-dumping actions against such dumping practices are often justified. European countries have long been accused of dumping agricultural products with huge farm subsidies and Japan of dumping consumer electronics.

Persistent dumping It involves a consistent tendency of a firm to sell the goods at lower prices in foreign markets as compared to the prices in domestic markets. Firms generally sell the product using marginal costing approach at lower prices in foreign markets. Since this form of dumping is most common, it is highly detrimental to the competing firms. The Chinese consumer goods industry is accused of persistent dumping internationally, primarily with an objective to utilize their large-scale production capacities.

20.3.13 Unethical Marketing Communications

Advertising has become a socialization agent within present-day culture, since it is omnipresent, convincing, and the target audience is generally separated from the traditional sources of social influence. As the younger generation spends increasingly more time with TV and other means of mass communications, advertising serves as a powerful tool to transmit social values. Youngsters often attempt to imitate social roles, status, fashions, and value systems as to what is 'right' or 'wrong' from what is shown in ads. For instance, ads have taught us that only a soft drink is required to quench one's thirst or *thanda matlab* (cold means) *Coca-Cola*, which may be far from reality. Marketing communications have given rise to novel social phenomena and even social celebrations, such as Valentine's Day, Mother's Day, Father's Day, Friendship Day, etc.

In their quest to win over customers, advertisers often exploit customers' emotions. Moreover, the diverse socio-cultural norms in different parts of the world make it difficult to draw a line between modernity, fashion, and vulgarity. To seek customers' attention seems to be the foremost advertising mantra. Most fashion companies have mastered this art even if it flouts the basic decency of a civil society. Benetton's

[26] OECD, Predatory Pricing, Organization for Economic Cooperation and Development, Paris, 1989.

memorable ad with a beautifully directed art photograph of a priest and a nun in a passionate kiss created enormous furore in the early 1990s. Another ad with a picture of a black woman nursing a white baby appeared in 77 countries; while not used in the US and the UK, the ad won awards in France and Italy. Calvin Klein, America's best-known designer, used print ads for its underwear (bulging briefs) and Obsession perfume depicting nude black and white twosomes, threesomes, and even moresomes.[27] Over the last few decades, ads have become progressively more interesting, striking, sexy, disturbing, and shocking.

Regulatory framework for ethical marketing communications

Since 1937, when the first ICC Code on Advertising Practices was issued, the International Chamber of Commerce (ICC) has been the major rule-setter in the field of international marketing and advertising. The present consolidated ICC Code on Advertising and Marketing Communication Practices aims at promoting high standards of ethics in marketing through business self-regulations. It also offers national governments principles of sound business for their consideration while elaborating initiatives related to marketing and consumer protection. The basic objectives[28] of the Code are

- To demonstrate responsibility and good practices in advertising and marketing communication across the world
- To enhance overall pubic confidence in marketing communication
- To respect privacy and consumer preferences
- To ensure special responsibility as regards marketing communication and children/young people
- To safeguard the freedom of expression of those engaged in marketing communication
- To provide practical and flexible solutions
- To minimize the need for detailed governmental and/or inter-governmental legislation or regulations

The Advertising Standards Council of India (ASCI), a voluntary organization, brings out a code for self-regulation in advertising so as to bring in fair advertising practices in the best interest of the ultimate customers, which applies to advertisers, advertising agencies, and media. The basic objectives of the Code are[29]

- To ensure the truthfulness and honesty of representations and claims made by advertisements and to safeguard against misleading advertisements

---

[27] Marconi, Joe; *Shock Marketing: Advertising, Influence and Family Values*, New Delhi: Vikas Publishing House, 2000, pp. 126–32.
[28] 'Advertising and Marketing Communication Practice: Consolidated ICC Code', International Chamber of Commerce, Paris, 2006, pp. 5–11.
[29] The Advertising Standards Council of India.

- To ensure that advertisements are not offensive to the generally accepted standards of public decency
- To safeguard against the indiscriminate use of advertising for the promotion of products that are regarded as hazardous to society or to individuals and is unacceptable to society at large
- To ensue that advertisements observe fairness in competition so that the consumers are informed on choices in the marketplace and the principles of generally accepted competitive behaviours in business are served

The ASCI regularly decides upon the complaints contravening the code and suggests its modifications and withdrawal, if required. For instance, Hindustan Unilever's ad claiming 'Moo snack' as an alternate to milk was discontinued since it undermines the benefits of natural fresh milk.[30]

20.4 CORPORATE SOCIAL RESPONSIBILITY

Just as all human beings have a personal responsibility to each other and the world around similarly businesses, whether large or small, private or public, have responsibility to their stakeholders, such as customers, shareholders, employees, suppliers, and society in general. Businesses have obligations to be good citizens and contribute to the communities in which they operate. The four faces of corporate citizenship[31] of a business enterprise include

Economic responsibility

- Being profitable
- Maximizing sales
- Minimizing costs
- Making sound strategic decisions
- Being attentive to dividend policy

Legal responsibility

- Obeying all laws and adhering to all regulations
- Fulfilling all contractual obligations
- Honouring warranties and guarantees

Ethical responsibility

- Avoiding questionable practices
- Responding to the spirit as well as the letter of law
- Assuming that the law only provides bottom-line of ethical behaviour
- Operating above the minimum required

---

[30] Consumer Complaint Council (CCC) Decisions, The Advertising Standard Council of India, October 2007–December 2007, pp. 1–10.
[31] Based on Archie B. Carroll, 'The Four Faces of Corporate Citizenship', *Business and Society Review* 100, no. 1, 1989, pp. 1–7.

- Doing what is right, fair, and just
- Asserting ethical leadership

Philanthropic responsibility

- Being a good corporate citizen
- Making corporate contributions
- Providing programmes supporting community, for example, education, health and human services, culture, arts, and civic duties
- Providing for community development and betterment on a voluntary basis

Corporate social responsibility (CSR) refers to the commitment of business enterprise to work with employees, their families, the local communities, and society at large so as to improve their quality of life and contribute to sustainable economic and social development. It is the process of assuming responsibility by a business enterprise across its entire supply chain for the social, ecological, and economic consequences of the company's activities, report on these consequences, and constructively engage with stakeholders. Major initiatives undertaken[32] by businesses to promote CSR include

- Introducing measures to improve employees' health and well-being
- Providing internship and work experience
- Donating to community causes and charity
- Promoting cultural diversity and equality in the work place
- Allowing flexible working to accommodate family-friendly work practices
- Improving waste management and energy efficiency
- Participating in community activities
- Adapting socially responsible products and services
- Helping other businesses to improve performance
- Sourcing local or ethical products and services

Charity for charity's sake is considered passé. In today's business environment, corporate social responsibility makes sound business sense. CSR facilitates the firms to fulfil their roles as socially responsible citizens while promoting their own business interests. Small companies traditionally have fewer stakeholders to satisfy, with greatest concern regarding their customers, and their own ability to satisfy the demand for products effectively. Well-managed CSR actually supports business objectives, especially among large companies, where improved compliance, reputation, and relationships tend to increase shareholders' value and profitability. Major driving factors[33] for CSR include

- Ease of recruitment and retention of staffs by adopting socially responsible policies

---

[32] Adapted from 'Corporate Social Responsibility: A Necessity Not a Choice', International Business Report, Grant Thornton International, 2008, pp. 1–20.

[33] 'Corporate Social Responsibility: A Necessity Not a Choice', International Business Report, Grant Thornton International, 2008, pp. 1–20.

Exhibit 20.8   MNEs strive to boost their CSR image

Vodafone Ranked the world's most responsible major company by monitoring group Account Ability, Vodafone is excelling with socially useful yet profitable services. Since inception of its money-transfer-by-text service in Kenya, where many phone owners don't have bank accounts, it has attracted 5,00,000 users.

Henkel The German household-goods firm tops in its class worldwide on the Dow Jones Sustainability World Index. Henkel's CSR programme allows employees paid time-offs for volunteering, a move many believe helps staff recruitment and retention.

HSBC In recent years, HSBC has been a leader in environmental initiatives. But a cornerstone of the bank's community work beginning in the 1870s has been education. It currently donates computers and books to schools and funds financial literacy classes.

Wal-Mart While often criticized by labour activists, the retailer pledges zero net-waste by 2025. Wal-Mart encourages recyclable and bio-degradable packaging and uses its formidable clout to coax suppliers into making small boxes, thereby cutting transport and materials costs.

Honda The automaker is improving fuel efficiency and safety features in vehicles, has provided road-safety seminars to over 4,00,000 people in Japan, and recently distributed 3,00,000 safe-driving manuals in China.

BP A leader in green-tech, the petroleum giant's Alternative Energy Unit runs solar projects in Malaysia and Germany and wind farms in Holland. It also has ambitious programmes to develop hydrogen power and advanced bio-fuels.

Sony Winner of a European Commission Sustainable Energy Award in February, Sony has just rolled out a national consumer electronics recycling programme in the US. The number of electronics drop-off sites, 75 in 2007, is likely to double within a year.

Procter and Gamble In three-and-a-half years, P&G's not-for-profit safe drinking water project delivered 70 million sachets of PUR, a power to purify even the foulest water. P&G estimates that PUR has averted 29 million days of diarrhoea, saving more than 3800 lives.

Source: 'Social Capitalists. Firms the World Over Want to Boost Their CSR Image', *Time*, 1 October 2007, p. 41.

- Need to control costs by encouraging ethical business behaviour
- Positive public attitude and building brand
- Tax relief
- Building investor relations
- 'Saving the planet' and 'government pressures'

Moreover, businesses operating ethically and in a socially responsible manner have a greater chance of sustainability and success. Firms are increasingly associating CSR as a strategic tool for their operations in global markets. MNEs are increasingly taking numerous proactive measures, as shown in Exhibit 20.8, to boost their CSR image.

Based on how businesses act, how much governments demand, and how well civil society holds, a UK-based NGO, AccountAbility ranks countries in terms of CSR. Sweden ranks the highest (Fig. 20.13) with a score of 81.5 on a 100 point scale in 2007, followed by Denmark at 2nd place (81.0), the UK at 5th place (75.8), Germany at

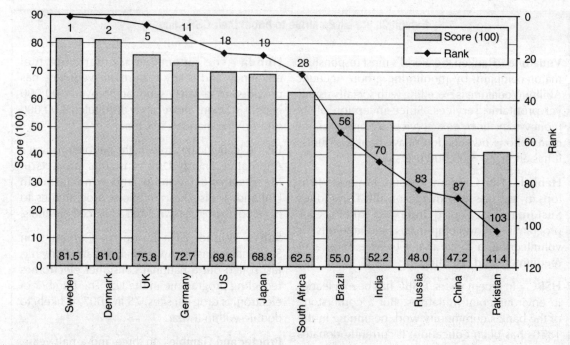

Fig. 20.13 Cross-country comparison of corporate social responsibility

Source: Account Ability and Fundacao Dom Cabral; 'Global Business: Special Report—Corporate Social Responsibility', *Time*, 1 October 2007.

11th (72.7), the US at 18th (69.6), and Japan at 19th (68.8), whereas South Africa ranked at 28th with a score of 62.5, Brazil at 56th (55.0), India at 70th (52.2), Russia at 83rd (48.0), and China at 87th (47.2) place. Pakistan with a score of 41.4 ranked at 103rd place.

20.4.1 Multilateral CSR Initiatives

Major initiative taken by multilateral agencies, such as OECD guidelines for multinational enterprises, Global Reporting Initiative (GRI), and ISO 26000 are discussed below.

OECD Guidelines for Multinational Enterprises

The OECD guidelines for multinational enterprises present the world's foremost corporate responsibility instrument and are becoming an important international benchmark for corporate responsibility. The guidelines aim to promote MNEs' positive contributions to economic, environmental, and social progress. These contain voluntary principles and standards for the conduct of responsible business (Exhibit 20.9) in areas such as human rights, disclosure of information, anti-corruption, taxation, labour relations, environment, and consumer protection. These express the shared values of the 37 countries (30 OECD and 7 non-member countries) that have adhered to the guidelines.

Exhibit 20.9   The OECD guidelines for multinational enterprises: Major recommendations

1. *Concepts and principles* Sets out the principles that underlie the guidelines, such as their voluntary character, their application worldwide, and the fact that they reflect good practices for all enterprises

2. *General policies* Contains the first specific recommendations, including provisions on human rights, sustainable development, supply chain responsibility, and local capacity building, and more generally calls on enterprises to take full account of established policies in the countries in which they operate

3. *Disclosure* Recommends disclosure on all material matters regarding the enterprise, such as its performance and ownership and encourages communication in areas where reporting standards are still emerging, such as social, environmental, and risk reporting

4. *Employment and industrial relations* Addresses major aspects of corporate behaviour in this area, including child labour and forced labour, non-discrimination, and the right to bonafide employee representation and constructive negotiations

5. *Environment* Encourages enterprises to raise their performance in protecting the environment, including performance with respect to health and safety impacts. It includes recommendations concerning environmental management systems and the desirability of precaution where there are threats of serious damage to the environment

6. *Combating bribery* Covers both public and private bribery and addresses passive and active corruption

7. *Consumer interests* Recommends that enterprises, when dealing with consumers, act in accordance with fair business, marketing, and advertising practices, respect consumer privacy, and take all reasonable steps to ensure the safety and quality of goods or services provided

8. *Science and technology* Aims to promote the diffusion by multinational enterprises of the fruits of research and development activities among the countries where they operate, thereby contributing to the innovative capacities of the host countries

9. *Competition* Emphasizes the importance of an open and competitive business climate

10. *Taxation* Calls on enterprises to respect both the letter and spirit of tax laws and to co-operate with tax authorities

Source: Organization for Economic Cooperation and Development.

Although, these guidelines are not a substitute for, nor do they override, the applicable law, they represent standards of behaviour to supplement applicable law. Since all companies domiciled within OECD countries are covered by the guidelines, they are not really voluntary. However, some of the problems associated with the guidelines include[34]

- These are non-binding.
- These fail to empower affected communities.
- The enforcement mechanisms, National Contact Points (NCPs), address allegations of non-compliance through consensual, non-adversarial means and by issuing unenforceable recommendations.

---

[34] Picciotto, Sol, 'Corporate Social Responsibility for International Business', *The Development Dimension of FDI: Policy and Rule-Making Perspectives*, United Nations, New York and Geneva, 2003, pp. 175–85.

- Procedures for filing complaints are opaque and vary significantly from country to country.
- NCPs are often staffed by inexperienced personnel who have the dual role of NCP and helping the private sector to attract investment and commercial opportunities.

Although many business codes of conduct are now endorsed and publicly available, the guidelines are the only multi-laterally endorsed and comprehensive code that governments are committed to promote.

Global reporting initiative: sustainability reporting framework

Global Reporting Initiative (GRI) has pioneered the development of the world's most widely used sustainability reporting framework. It sets out the principles and indicators that organizations can use to measure and report their economic, environmental, and social performance (Table 20.2). In order to ensure the highest degree of technical quality, credibility, and relevance, the reporting framework is developed and continuously improved through a consensus-seeking process with participants drawn

Table 20.2 Framework for sustainability reporting

Section	Dimension	Aspects
Economic	Economic	Economic performance Market presence Indirect economic impacts
Environmental	Environmental	Materials Energy Emission, effluents, and waste Products and services Compliance Transport
Social	Labour practices and decent work	Employment Labour/management relations Occupational health and safety Training and education Diversity and equal opportunity
	Human rights	Investment and procurement practices Non-discrimination Child labour
	Society	Community Corruption Public policy
	Product responsibility	Customer health and safety Marketing communications Customer privacy

Source: The GRI's Sustainability Report July 2004–June 2007, Global Reporting Initiative, Amsterdam, 2007, pp. 35–39.

globally from business, civil society, labour, and professional institutions. Sustainability reports based on the GRI framework can be used to benchmark organizational performance with respect to laws, norms, codes, performance standards, and voluntary initiatives; demonstrate organizational commitment to sustainable development; and compare organizational performance over time. GRI promotes and develops this standardized approach of reporting to stimulate demand for sustainability information, which benefits reporting organizations and those who use the report information.

ISO 26000: Social responsibility guidelines

The International Organization for Standardization (ISO) has launched development of standards to address social responsibility in a broad area, to be published in 2010 as ISO 26000, and be voluntary to use. It encompasses issues relating to the environment, human rights, labour practices, organizational governance, fair business practices, community involvement and social development, and consumer issues. The standards would provide harmonized and globally relevant guidance on international consensus among expert representatives of the main stakeholder groups so as to encourage the implementation of best practices in social responsibility worldwide.

This chapter brings out the rapid degradation of moral and ethical values, giving rise to unscrupulous business practices. This has led to growing dissatisfaction, distrust, and a feeling of being cheated by business enterprises, more so if these are multinationals. The cross-country comparisons of wide-spread unethical practices in international business facilitate readers' appreciation and understanding. Carrying out business in ethical and socially responsible manner has become crucial not only for the sake of mere charity but for the long-term sustainability and survival of firms too.

SUMMARY

In order to attain long-term sustainability and success in business, adoption of ethical and socially responsible business practices becomes a fundamental condition. Moral values and principles that judge human actions as right or wrong are termed as 'ethics'. The United Nations' Global Compact provides a voluntary framework of cross-cultural ethical business practices comprising of human rights, labour standards, environment, and anti-corruption laws.

The 'abuse of entrusted power for private gain' is termed as 'corruption'. Corrupt business practices are detrimental due to increased legal, reputational, security, and cheating risks, besides increased financial costs and repeated demands for bribery. Bribe, any voluntary offering with an objective to influence the receiver's action, has a much wider scope in international transactions and its magnitude varies widely across countries.

The conversion of money obtained through illegal means to make it appear to originate from a legal source, known as 'money laundering', is a serious, highly sophisticated, and criminal global activity. Although informal ways of funds transfer, such as hawala are swifter, reliable, more convenient, and less bureaucratic compared to formal systems even today, these not only pose serious threats to formal banking system but are also used frequently for illegitimate, even criminal, activities on a global scale. Regulatory prohibitions and the high incidence of customs duties are often circumvented through smuggling.

'Grey marketing' refers to the import and export of goods through unauthorized channels, and it facilitates distribution of counterfeit and pirated products. Counterfeiting, imitation with the intent to defraud, has evolved as a highly sophisticated network of organized crimes that has the capacity to threaten the very fabric of national economies and even endanger human safety and security. Pricing between related parties, known as transfer pricing is often abused to circumvent exchange controls, repatriate profits, evade taxes, and maximize corporate profits. Businesses often resort to 'dumping' internationally, selling below the cost of production or at a lower price than domestic price, as a strategic tool.

In their quest to win over customers, companies frequently make exaggerated claims about their products and services and many a time even cross all the limits of basic social decency while advertising. Carrying out business in a socially responsible manner, known as corporate social responsibility (CSR), has become crucial to success, long-term sustainability, and even survival. Multilateral CSR initiatives include OECD guidelines for multinational enterprises, Global Reporting Initiative (GRI), and ISO 26000.

KEY TERMS

Bribe Any voluntary offering of an object of some value, such as money, gift, privilege, etc., with an objective to influence the action of the receiver.

Corporate social responsibility Carrying out business activities in a socially responsible manner.

Corruption Abuse of entrusted power for private gains.

Counterfeiting Imitating something with the intent to deceive or defraud.

Dumping Selling of a product or commodity below the cost of production or at a lower price in overseas markets as compared to the price in the domestic market.

Ethics Study of moral conduct and its evaluation as to what is right or wrong.

Extortion Demand of bribe accompanied by threats that endanger the personal integrity or the life of the persons involved.

Grey marketing Import or export of goods and distributing them through unauthorized channel.

Hawala An informal fund transfer system from one location to another through service providers, known as hawaladars, which originated in India much before the Western banking system, but now being used across the world.

Integration The re-injection of the laundered money back into the economy in such a way that the money re-enter the financial system as normal business funds.

Layering The separation of illicit proceeds from their source by creating complex layers of financial transactions.

Money laundering Conversion of money obtained from illegal means so as to make it appear to originate from a legal source.

Placement The physical disposal of bulk cash proceeds derived from illegal activity.

Round tripping Financial transactions aimed at converting unaccounted or black money into legitimate wealth.

Smuggling Surreptitious trade across borders aimed at circumventing enforcement of regulatory prohibitions and restrictions and evading payment of legitimate customs duties.

Tax haven A country that levies taxes either at a very low rate or no taxes at all.

Transfer pricing Pricing of any international transactions between related parties.

Treaty shopping Financial transactions aimed at reducing total tax incidence on capital gains made in countries with high tax incidence.

CONCEPT REVIEW QUESTIONS

1. Explain the significance of ethical practices in business transactions.
2. Examine briefly the unethical practices adopted in international business.
3. Describe the reasons why businesses should not engage in corrupt practices.
4. Explaining the concept of money laundering, briefly examine various measures taken by

financial institutions at multilateral and national level to curb it.
5. Write short notes on
   (a) Smuggling
   (b) Grey marketing
   (c) Dumping
   (d) ISO 26000

PRACTICE EXERCISES

1. Carry out a comparative analysis of the tax structure of your country and any three countries classified by OECD as tax havens. Critically evaluate attractiveness of tax havens for companies operating in your country. Illustrate with a few examples where some companies have made use of lax regulations in select tax havens.

2. Collect copies of print or TV ads that have either offended basic social norms or made exaggerated claims difficult to be empirically justify. Find out if any complaints were made by consumer organizations and the decisions taken by enforcing authorities.

PROJECT ASSIGNMENTS

1. Explore the magnitude of counterfeit and pirated goods in your country. Also attempt to assess its category or industry-wise breakup. Find out the major distribution centres of such goods in your country.

2. Try to locate a hawala service provider (hawaldar) in your vicinity. Find out the terms of money transfer and compare it with the

formal banking system. Critically evaluate the pros and cons of the system.

3. Contact a firm in your vicinity and find out the CSR measures taken. Critically evaluate such measures about their positive contribution to the civil society and its impact on the firm's business.

CASE STUDY

Multinational's Lackadaisical Attitude led to World's Worst Industrial Disaster

The world's worst industrial accident[1] occurred in the early hours of 3 December, 1984 in the Indian city of Bhopal. It killed an estimated more than 20,000 people and left over 120,000 survivors chronically ill due to their exposure to a highly toxic gas, methyl isocyanate (MIC). On the fateful

---

[1] Condie, Steve, 'How a Dream Turned into a Nightmare', *BBC News*, 4 December 2004.

morning, MIC accidentally leaked from Union Carbide's plant in Bhopal, which claimed to be making a miracle pesticide with reportedly 'the best safety measures in the country'. The reality is that MIC is a highly volatile gas which must be stored at zero degrees centigrade. Yet the refrigeration unit in the factory had been shut down to cut costs as per directions from Union Carbide headquarters in Danbury, US. Any escaping MIC should have entered a caustic-soda scrubber to be neutralized. But the scrubber was not operating on the night of the disaster. Escaping toxic gases were supposed to go the flare tower, where a pilot flame would burn off the gas. The pilot flame was off and the pipeline to the flare tower disconnected. Water sprayers designed to take care of leaks in the atmosphere did not have sufficient pressure to reach the required height.[2] The toxic legacy of the disaster continues till today with tens of thousands of survivors suffering from chronic illnesses, the persistent presence of poisons in soil, water, and breast milk, and the alarming rise in cancers and congenital problems among children born to exposed people. The accident occurred due to lack of adequate safety measures and non-functioning of safety equipment designed to stop the escape of the gas or turn off gas-flow. However, Union Carbide tried to blame the accident on a human error and escape compensation.

The mega-corporation underplayed the hazardous health effects of the leaked poisonous gas and fought its best to avoid or minimize compensation. Moreover, Union Carbide even refused to release its research on the health impacts of the gas, which could have helped develop more effective treatment.

In 1985, the Union Carbide Corporation (UCC) and its chairman, Warren Anderson, were charged with manslaughter, grievous assault, and other serious offences. In addition to denying any responsibility, UCC adopted multiple strategies for corporate survival:

- It fought for the legal case to be heard in India, were any compensation was likely to be far lower than in the US.
- It delayed the legal case at each stage in its progress through the courts
- It divested itself of products that could be targeted by a consumer boycott campaigning (i.e., Eveready-TM batteries, anti-freeze-TM automotive products, Gladwrap-TM plastic food wrap and pesticides, including carbaryl and aldicarb, sold as Sevin and Temik), which had been made at the Bhopal plant.
- It took on debts of over US$6 billion to put off potential corporate raiders.
- The company argued that the subsidiary was independent in spite of the fact that 51 per cent of Union Carbide India Limited (UCIL) was owned by UCC, and the plant fully designed by UCC.
- Finally, in 1989, it persuaded the Indian government to settle without consultation with the victims.

Moreover, not even a single company, industry organization, or government body publicly argued for the closer of Union Carbide and the stripping of its assets to pay full compensation to those affected. Union Carbide continued to claim even the full impact of MIC on health as 'trade secrets', which it had accumulated over 60 years of research, including research on human 'volunteers'. Withholding of such information and propagation of miss-information considerably impeded healthcare efforts.

The Government of India appointed itself the sole representative of the Bhopal victims which originally filed a claim in 1985 for US$3.3 billion from UCC in the US. However, the UCC succeeded in having the case shifted back to India where any compensation was likely to be lower compared to the US. The outcome of the protracted legal battle was disastrous for the gas victims as the

[2] Morehouse, Ward and M. Arun Subramaniam, 'The Bhopal Tragedy: What Really Happened and What It Means for American Workers and Communities at Risks', *Council on International Public Affairs*, New York, 1986; Dinham, Barbara and Sarangi Satinath, 'The Bhopal Gas Tragedy 1984 to The Evasion of Corporate Responsibility', *Environment and Urbanization*, vol. 14, no. 1, April 2002, pp. 89–99.

Indian government and UCC reached a settlement for US$470 million. In August 1999, the UCC announced merger with multinational petrochemical major, Dow Chemicals. Dow proposed to invest US$1 billion in India in 2007. Till May 2008, Indian Law Ministry was still examining the case to fix up a legal liability on Dow Chemicals[3] while survivors waited to seek[4] 'concrete action'.

Questions

1. Identify the reasons that led to the world's worst industrial disaster in the Indian city of Bhopal.

2. Union Carbide fought for shifting the legal case to India as any compensation decided by Indian courts was anticipated to be much lower compared to that in the US courts, and because of the extraordinarily long and tedious legal process in India. The company succeeded which ultimately added to the woes and sufferings of the gas victims. Critically evaluate the ethical aspects of the accident.

3. Union Carbides' approach to adopt multiple strategies to renounce its due responsibility of the disaster reveals the multinational's well-thought of strategy to avoid compensation on one hand and maintain its corporate image globally on the other. In view of the above, assess the significance of ethical business practices and earnestness of businesses to adhere to the concept of corporate social responsibility.

[3] 'Dow May Have to Clean Up Bhopal Site', *Economic Times*, New Delhi, 13 May 2008.
[4] 'Bhopal Gas Tragedy Survivors Seek "Concrete Action"', *The Times of India*, New Delhi, 28 March 2006.

Index